The History of the JOINT CHIEFS OF STAFF in World War II

THE WAR AGAINST JAPAN

By Grace Person Hayes

NAVAL INSTITUTE PRESS
ANNAPOLIS, MARYLAND

Copyright © 1982 by the United States Naval Institute
Annapolis, Maryland

All rights reserved for copyrighted material.
No copyright is claimed for material in the public domain.

Library of Congress Cataloging in Publication Data

Hayes, Grace P.
  The history of the Joint Chiefs of Staff in World War II.

  Bibliography: p.
  Includes index.
   1. World War, 1939-1945--United States.
2. United States. Joint Chiefs of Staff--History.
3. World War, 1939-1945--Pacific Ocean. 4. World
War, 1939-1945--East Asia. 5. World War, 1939-
1945--Japan. 6. United States--History, Military
--20th century. I. Title.
D769.1.H39   940.53'73   81-14107
ISBN 0-87021-269-9   AACR2

Printed in the United States of America

WITHDRAWN
NDSU

The History of the
JOINT CHIEFS OF STAFF
in World War II

AUTHORITY

    This volume is a portion of the history of the wartime activities of the Joint Chiefs of Staff, prepared by the Historical Section of their organization pursuant to their directive. It is published with the understanding that the work is a product of the best minds which could be made available for the task but that the Joint Chiefs of Staff have not passed upon it for either accuracy or substance.

                                          Edwin H.J. Carns
                                          Colonel, USA
                                          Secretary, Joint Chiefs of Staff

CONTENTS

Foreword	xiii
Preface, 1982	xv
Preface, 1953	xvii
Abbreviations	xxi

PART I Pearl Harbor Through Trident

I Introduction	4
The Orange Plans	4
Rainbow No. 5 and Collaboration with the British	8
American-British Cooperation in the Far East	13
Reduction of the Pacific Fleet	15
Reenforcement of the Philippines	16
Support for China	19
The Last Days	22
Summation	23
II Adjusting for War in the Pacific	26
Emergency Measures	26
Meeting the Emergency in Hawaii	26
Modification of ABC-1	30
Reenforcements for the Southwest Pacific	31
The Arcadia Conference	36
Agreement on Grand Strategy	36
Disposition of Reenforcements	42
Establishment of the ABDA Command	44
Strengthening the South and Southwest Pacific	53
End of Arcadia	59
III Developments in the Far East, January-February 1942	61
Inauguration of Unified Command	61
ABDA and Its Problems	64
The China Theater. Burma and Malaya.	71
The End of ABDACOM	81
IV Reorganization of Strategic Commands in the Pacific	88
Spheres of Responsibility	88
Evacuation of General MacArthur from the Philippines	91
Over-all Command Organization	93
Establishment of the Pacific Areas	96
V Maintaining the Defensive in the Pacific, February-May 1942	104
Allocating Resources	104
The Pacific vs. Bolero	114

CONTENTS

V Maintaining the Defensive in the Pacific, February–May 1942--Continued
    Forces for the Southwest Pacific . . . 121
    The Battle of the Coral Sea . . . 127
    Assistance to Russia . . . 130

VI Development of Plans for an Offensive in the Pacific . . . 136
    A Pattern for the Pacific . . . 136
    An Operation in the Solomons . . . 140
    Abandonment of Sledgehammer, July 1942 . . . 149

VII Problems of Distribution and Deployment . . . 154
    Attempt to Define a Strategic Policy . . . 154
    Problems of the Defense of Australia . . . 164

VIII Supporting the Guadalcanal Campaign . . . 168
    Conflicting Views of the Strategic Importance of the Pacific . . . 168
    Attempts to Strengthen the Forces in the South Pacific, July–August 1942 . . . 171
    The Theater Commanders' Views of the Situation, August 1942 . . . 177
    Additional Aircraft for the Pacific, September–October 1942 . . . 181
    The Shipping Problem . . . 188

IX China-Burma-India, 1942 . . . 198
    Supply and Support . . . 198
        Fighting in Burma, February–May 1942 . . . 200
        Supply and Transportation . . . 202
        Air Support for India . . . 205
        China's Bid for Representation in Washington . . . 207
        The 3,500-Ton Program . . . 210
        The "Three Demands" . . . 214
        The British and the Tenth Air Force . . . 217
        The End of the "Three Demands" . . . 219

X China-Burma-India, 1942: Strategic Developments . . . 225

XI Strategic Discussions in Late 1942: Background for Casablanca . . . 250
    The Basic Strategic Concept, November–December 1942 . . . 250
    On from Guadalcanal . . . 264
    The North Pacific Area . . . 272
    China-Burma-India . . . 276

XII The Casablanca Conference . . . 278
    General Discussion . . . 278
    The Pacific Theater . . . 283
    Conduct of the War in 1943 . . . 288
    Anakim . . . 291
    Pacific Strategy . . . 299
    Report to President and Prime Minister . . . 301

XIII Operations in the South and Southwest Pacific, January–March 1943 . . . 304
    Interpretation of the Casablanca Decisions . . . 304

XIII	Operations in the South and Southwest Pacific, January–March 1943—Continued	
	Washington Planning	307
	The Pacific Military Conference	312
	The New Directive for the South-Southwest Pacific	328
XIV	Post-Casablanca Problems: China and Burma	335
	Arnold, Dill, and Somervell at New Delhi and Chungking	336
	Air Power in China	342
	Shipping Shortages Again	348
	Review of the Strategic Situation	350
	Shipping for Anakim	352
	The British Position	356
	Clarification of Casablanca Decisions	358
XV	Preparation for Trident	363
	General Plans	363
	Operations Against Japan	367
	Conference Tactics	374
	Operations in Burma	376
	Use of the Papers	378
	The Stilwell-Chennault Problem	379
XVI	Trident	386
	Opening Discussions	386
	The Fate of Anakim	392
	Strategic Plan for the Defeat of Japan	401
	Conclusions Reached at Trident	403

PART II The Advance to Victory

XVII	Strategic Planning for the Pacific Theater in the Summer of 1943: Quadrant	413
	Operations in the North Pacific Area	414
	Opening up the Central Pacific	415
	Operations in the Pacific, 1943–1944	427
XVIII	China-Burma-India in the Summer of 1943: Quadrant	434
	Chiang Kai-shek and the Trident Decisions	434
	Building up the Airlift	436
	Southeast Asia Command	437
	The Campaign in Burma	446
	Discussion at Quadrant	448
	Amphibious Operations	455
	Strategic Plan for the Defeat of Japan	458
	Practicability of the Decisions	470
	Air Plan for the Defeat of Japan	470
	Conclusion	471
XIX	The Fall of 1943: Quadrant-Sextant	472
	Employment of British Naval Forces	472
	Plans for the Gilberts and Marshalls	476
	Joint Command in the Pacific	479
	The North Pacific Area	482
	Pushing Ahead in the Solomons and New Guinea	487
	Specific Operations for 1944	488
	Long Range Planning for the Defeat of Japan	492

CONTENTS

XX The Far East and the Sextant Conference	508
China-Burma-India	508
Southeast Asia Command	508
Stilwell Crisis - October 1943	511
Interpreting the Quadrant Decisions	512
Operations in SEAC: Buccaneer	518
Sextant	520
Eureka - The Meetings at Teheran	531
Cairo Again	534
Final Report	542
XXI Months of Critical Decision, January-May 1944	543
Moving on in the Pacific	543
Shipping	560
Problems of Command	563
Redeployment of the South Pacific Forces	566
XXII SEAC and Burma in Early 1944	569
Strategic Discussions	569
A New Directive for SEAC	579
Transport Aircraft	582
XXIII China's Role in the Pacific Campaign	588
Future Plans for China	588
The Twentieth Air Force	590
Allocating Hump Tonnage	596
PAC-AID	601
XXIV Luzon or Formosa	603
XXV The Octagon Conference	625
A New Strategic Concept for the War Against Japan	627
British Participation in the Pacific	630
Operations in Burma	638
Logistics Problems	642
Conclusion of Octagon	643
XXVI The Recall of General Stilwell	645
XXVII Planning, from Octagon to Argonaut	653
British Air Assistance in the Pacific	654
Operations for the Defeat of Japan	655
Air Forces for the Pacific	659
Operations in Southeast Asia	661
XXVIII Russian Participation in the War Against Japan	668
XXIX The Argonaut Conference	677
Southeast Asia	678
The War in the Pacific	680
Preparations for the Yalta Conference	681
The Discussions at Yalta	682
XXX Argonaut to Terminal	686
Reorganization of Commands in the Pacific	686
The Future of the Southwest Pacific Area	695

CONTENTS

XXX	Argonaut to Terminal--Continued	
	Olympic	701
	Priorities and Redeployment	707
	Future Operations in Southeast Asia Command	710
	General Wedemeyer's Plans for China	711
XXXI	Terminal - The Potsdam Conference	713
	The Japanese Situation	713
	Participation of Other Nations	716
	Directive for Supreme Commander, Southeast Asia	717
	Meetings with the Soviets at Potsdam	720
XXXII	Victory	722
	Notes	731
	Bibliographic Essay	899
	Index	911

FOREWORD

The story of the Joint Chiefs of Staff in World War II is an inspiring and significant one, deserving a primary place in the military annals of the United States. In recognition of the importance of that story the Joint Chiefs directed that an official history be written "for the record." Although a utilitarian purpose has always shaped the aims of the undertaking, the authors hope that the history will serve as a memorial of the wartime endeavors, problems, and accomplishments of the American military leadership.

The record of the Joint Chiefs of Staff does exist, but in a mass of papers, minutes, memoranda, and reports immense in volume and intricate in detail. While specific data as to JCS actions may be found with relative ease, the broader relationships, causes, and consequences are beyond immediate comprehension. They become apparent only after the searching study and constructive reasoning of the historian have produced a useful synthesis. Thus the JCS History is the practical means by which the wartime experience can be effectively applied. Its value for instructional purposes, for the orientation of officers newly assigned to the JCS organization, and as a source of background information for staff studies will be readily recognized.

The primary function of the Joint Chiefs of Staff in World War II was to provide the strategic direction for American forces in both the European and the Pacific areas. This is the first of two volumes relating their discussions and decisions in respect to the strategy of the war against Japan. The problems of the war against Germany and Italy will be covered in subsequent portions of the JCS History.

The author, Lt. Grace Person Hayes, USN, has been with the JCS Historical Section since October 1946, having served the previous year in the Office of Naval History as assistant to Dr. Robert G. Albion, Historian for Naval Administration. Mrs. Hayes, a native of Ware, Massachusetts, received a B.A. from Wellesley College and an A.M. in archaeology from Columbia University. She had completed the residence credits for the doctorate there when she entered the Navy in 1943.

Thos. G. Dobyns
Colonel, USA
Executive, Historical Section
Joint Chiefs of Staff

Washington, D.C.
July 1953

PREFACE, 1982

Very little of the enormous body of literature about World War II that is now available had appeared in print when I reported to the Joint Chiefs of Staff historical section in October 1946. The war was still vivid in everyone's mind, and in all the services war historians were at work. It was a time for sharing information and trying out interpretations on one another. Many of the books the service historians were writing then have long since been published. However, this book, completed in 1953, was classified as secret, and even I did not see it again until, at my request, it was declassified in 1971, after the Pentagon Papers had revealed secrets of a later war. I am happy that the Naval Institute Press is publishing it, and I hope that the work will be helpful to those who had no access to it heretofore.

The JCS historical section had been established for almost a year when I joined it. By that time the section included a navy captain, an army air forces colonel, an army lieutenant colonel, a navy commander, a part-time senior civilian, and five junior civilians who worked as research assistants and kept the office going. As the junior officer and the only woman in uniform, I didn't fit neatly into the group.

I was assigned, on the basis of my branch of service, to assist Captain Tracy Kittredge, USNR, who was charged with writing the history of the war against Japan. Captain Kittredge has served with Admiral Harold Stark, Commander, Naval Forces, Europe, and he was deeply involved in writing a history of that organization. Since he continued with the project--although strictly speaking it was not part of the basic plan--full responsibility for writing about the war in the Pacific gradually devolved upon me.

The history project--to be completed in two or three years, I was told--had been divided into sections to fit the experience of those working on them: the two major theaters of war, administrative history, and separate projects focussing on military government and psychological warfare. Of these sections, only the administrative history and the account of the war against Japan--treated in this book--have been completed.

The original Joint Chiefs of Staff had agreed that a history of the organization and its part in the war should be written for future direction and with no thought of publication. Beyond that they said virtually nothing about its content or its purpose, and there was no provision for guidance or review in the Joint Staff. As far as I know neither they nor their successors ever officially discussed it again.

This is not to say that there was no guidance at all. The successive directors of the historical section made policy decisions, and they and the senior members of the section met occasionally with the directors of the army and navy historical projects. But I don't recall that anything was ever changed as a result of those meetings.

Those of us in the historical section reviewed each other's work as units were completed, and my colleagues' comments were always helpful. So too were the discussions I had with the historians of other services who were studying various aspects of the war against Japan. As the original preface and the notes indicate, I had a chance to talk with some of the participants, and Admiral King read and commented on many of the chapters.

This is a history of the involvement of the Joint Chiefs of Staff in the war against Japan. It is not a history of that war. The reader may want to seek information elsewhere about the results of the decisions and directives issued by the Joint Chiefs and to follow contemporary operational developments in other histories. Nor is this book a thoroughly analytical history. The war was still too close, the records too numerous, and time too short to do more than unravel the threads and recount what was done. And of course this history was not written for publication.

The notes that follow the text give some idea of the vast amount of material that was consulted in the process of writing the manuscript. The thousands of documents that had been generated in the Joint Chiefs organization and in the offices of the Chiefs and their service staffs were still in their various records offices when this was being written, under the care of people who had been there when they were written. There is no substitute for the custodian of records who was around when documents were written and who organized the files. I was fortunate in having several such people to help me. Thanks to them I doubt that I missed anything pertinent to this story, with the exception of documents on the atomic bomb and the breaking of codes. (However, information on the latter was available at the time, much of it being disclosed during the Pearl Harbor hearings that were in progress.)

The original manuscript, printed at the Pentagon in two volumes and in fifty classified copies, has received only minor editorial changes of mine. Omitted from this edition are the few maps that had been copied from contemporary documents and that reproduced too poorly to warrant inclusion.

The reader will note one significant addition. An extensive bibliographic note written by Dr. Dean Allard explains where the sources in my notes may be found and discusses important relevant publications that have appeared since this was written.

Grace Person Hayes

PREFACE, 1953

In December 1941 the top level military and political leaders of the United States and the United Kingdom reaffirmed a principle set almost a year before that if the two nations found themselves at war simultaneously with Germany and with Japan the Axis in Europe should have precedence and its defeat should be the first objective. The rapid spread of the Japanese over wide areas of the Pacific, however, created a series of emergencies that made it necessary first to attempt to establish and hold a line of defense in that area. It was months before forces could be sent to the European Theater in strength sufficient for major action against Germany. This volume tells the story of the strategic discussions and decisions of the Joint Chiefs of Staff in the period of emergency action in the Pacific, of the first offensive moves against Japan, and of planning for the first steps in the long offensive drive to victory. The second volume will tell of the strategic decisions that finally accomplished the defeat of Japan.

Although the major operations of the war against Japan took place in the Pacific area, forces of the United Nations faced the same enemy in the area of China, Burma, and India as well. Whereas the Pacific was a theater of U.S. responsibility under the Combined Chiefs of Staff, in China-Burma-India the U.S. Chiefs shared responsibilities and problems with the Chinese and the British. In addition many matters were handled directly by President Roosevelt with Generalissimo Chiang Kai-shek or with Prime Minister Churchill. The situation in that area developed independently of the situation in the Pacific and the Joint Chiefs of Staff played a very different part in each. Since few aspects of the two were related it had been necessary to treat them almost entirely as separate facets of the war against the Japanese.

This history describes not only the strategic decisions of the Joint Chiefs of Staff concerning the war with Japan but the evolution of those decisions through the JCS committee structure. It attempts to give a complete account of the thinking and the planning that developed as the war progressed, in detail proportionate to their contemporary significance rather than to their contribution to the final outcome. Thus, for example, joint and combined discussions of plans for operations in Burma had been presented at considerable length because they occupied a large amount of the chiefs' time, although most of the plans were wholly or partially abortive and action in the area contributed little toward the defeat of Japan.

Since this is one portion of a larger project designed to cover all the wartime activities of the Joint Chiefs of Staff there has been no attempt to include an account either of the JCS organization or of JCS activities that had no direct bearing on the war against Japan. Background material has been used to orient the reader chronologically with military operations and to make JCS decisions and attitudes more readily understandable. More detailed accounts of other JCS problems will be found in other portions of the JCS History.

The chief sources of material for this study are the voluminous records of the Joint Chiefs of Staff. In addition wide use has been made of several collections of records both of the Army and of the Navy. This has been particularly necessary for the early period of the war when many matters were settled directly by General Marshall and Admiral King outside the formal structure of the JCS. When feasible, military participants in the events herein described have been consulted on specific problems not adequately documented by the written records.

The author has been most fortunate in the interest shown in the JCS History and in this section in particular by Fleet Admiral Ernest J. King, USN, Fleet Admiral King read drafts of almost all the chapters with great care and thoroughness. His many comments on specific points and his several conversations with the author have been inspiring and extremely useful.

Admiral Harold R. Stark, USN, read the second and third chapters and provided the author with many helpful comments and much new information. Admiral Thomas C. Hart, USN, read the portion relating to his return from the Pacific. Vice Admiral Vincent R. Murphy, USN, read the sections concerning the development of plans for an offensive in the Solomons and made many constructive suggestions. Vice Admiral F.S. Low, USN, read some of the same material and contributed several additional details. Various problems of planning were discussed by the author with Major General W.E. Todd, USAF. Rear Admiral Milton E. Miles, USN, contributed helpful information about Naval Group, China. Colonel E.H. McDaniel, USA, who participated in much of the planning, read most of the manuscript and made many pertinent remarks and recommendations.

The preparation of a complete and accurate history has been assisted considerably by other historians who were working with the same or similar problems. Especially to be mentioned are the members of the JCS Historical Section, who have generously discussed problems and read and commented on various drafts. They have done much to insure adequate explanation of less obvious developments and to keep the focus as sharply as possible on the level of the Joint Chiefs of Staff, offering constructive criticism whenever asked. The style and form of the history have profited greatly from the untiring efforts of the Section's several editors.

Several members of the Office of the Chief of Military History, Department of the Army, have been of great assistance to the author, many of them having worked with the same material from a different point of view. Dr. Louis Morton read the entire manuscript of Volume I with great care and made many valuable suggestions for improvement. The problems of China-Burma-India were discussed at length with Mr. Charles Romanus and Mr. Riley Sunderland, who illuminated many dark corners and directed the author to much new material. Mr. Ray Cline, Mr. Edwin M. Snell, and Mr. Maurice Matloff all have discussed top level strategic problems. Dr. John Miller, Mr. Robert R. Smith, and Mr. Samuel Milner have generously provided answers to specific questions concerning Pacific operations.

Finally the author acknowledges with deep appreciation the constant encouragement and unwavering support of the successive Executives of the Historical Section, Rear Admiral C.J. Moore, USN, Colonel Max Johnson, USA, Colonel C.H. Donnelly, USA, and Colonel T.G. Dobyns, USA, and of the Section's Consultant, Dr. Richard A. Newhall.

Washington, D.C.
July 1953

Grace P. Hayes
Lieutenant, USN

ABBREVIATIONS

A	Army (used in combination)
AAF	Army Air Forces
ABC	American British-Conversations
ABDA	American, British, Dutch, Australian
ABDACOM	American, British, Dutch, Australian Commander
acct	account
ACNB	Australian Commonwealth Naval Board
ACofS	Assistant Chief of Staff
actg	acting
ADB	American, Dutch, British
adee	addressee
adm	administrative; administration
Adm	Admiral
AGO	Adjutant General, Office of the
Alusna	U.S. Naval Attaché
amb	ambassador
ann	annex
ANZAC	Australian-New Zealand Army Corps
app	appendix
ASN	Assistant Secretary of the Navy
asst	assistant
Asst Sec	Assistant Secretary
ASW	Assistant Secretary of War
ATC	Air Transport Command
atchd	attached
Aust	Australia; Australian
AVG	American Volunteer Group
BAD	British Admiralty Delegation
BCOS	British Chiefs of Staff
bd	board
BEW	Board of Economic Warfare
BJSM	British Joint Staff Mission
bk	book
br	branch
Brig Gen	Brigadier General
Brit	British
bur	bureau
C	Confidential
CAdC	Combined Administrative Committee
Capt	Captain
CBI	China-Burma-India

ABBREVIATIONS

cc	carbon copy
CCS	Combined Chiefs of Staff
CD	Compilation of Decisions
Cdr	Commander
CDS	China Defense Supplies, Inc.
cf	compare
ch	chapter
chm	chairman
chmen	chairmen
CIC	Combined Intelligence Committee
CinC	Commander in Chief
CinCPac	Commander in Chief, Pacific
CinCPOA	Commander in Chief, Pacific Ocean Areas
CinCSWPA	Commander in Chief, Southwest Pacific Area
circ	circulating; circulated
CISC	Combined Intelligence Subcommittee
CMAB	Combined Munitions Assignments Board
CMTC	Combined Military Transportation Committee
cmte	committee
CNAC	Chinese National Aviation Corporation
CNO	Chief of Naval Operations
CofS	Chief of Staff
Col	Colonel
CominCh	Commander in Chief, U.S. Fleet
Comm	Commission
conf	conference
conv	conversation
CPRB	Combined Production and Resources Board
CPS	Combined Staff Planners
CSAB	Combined Shipping Adjustment Board
CTF	Commander Task Force
DA	Department of the Army
DCofS	Deputy Chief of Staff
Dep	Deputy
dept	department
desp	despatch
D/F	Disposition Form
dft	draft
dg	downgraded
dir	directive, director
dist	district, distribution
doc	document
dtd	dated
Emb	Embassy
encl	enclosure
Ens	Ensign
env	envelope
exec	executive
FAdm	Fleet Admiral
FCB	Federal Communications Board

ABBREVIATIONS

FCC	Federal Communications Committee
ff	following page
fig	figure
Flt	Fleet
FM	Field Marshal
fn	footnote
fwd; fwded	forward; forwarded
Gen	General, General of the Army
govt	government
GS	General Staff
hist	history, historical
HMG	His Majesty's Government
HMSO	His Majesty's Stationery Office
hrgs	hearings
ibid	in the same place
incl	inclusive, including, inclosing
info	information
interv	interview
J	Joint (used in combination)
JAdC	Joint Administrative Committee
Jap	Japan; Japanese
JB	Joint Board
JCS	Joint Chiefs of Staff
JCS HS	Joint Chiefs of Staff Historical Section
JIC	Joint Intelligence Committee
JLC	Joint Logistics Committee
JMTC	Joint Military Transportation Committee
JPC	Joint Planning Committee (of the Joint Board)
JPS	Joint Staff Planners
JPWC	Joint Psychological Warfare Committee (1942)
JS	Joint Staff
JSSC	Joint Strategic Survey Committee
jt	joint
JUSSC	Joint U.S. Strategic Committee
JWPC	Joint War Plans Committee
LPS	Lord Privy Seal
LRPG	Long Range Penetration Group
Lt	Lieutenant
Lt Cdr	Lieutenant Commander
Lt Col	Lieutenant Colonel
Lt Gen	Lieutenant General
ltr	letter
MA	Military Attaché
MAB	Munitions Assignments Board (Washington)
MAB(L)	Munitions Assignments Board (London)
MAC(A)	Munitions Assignments Committee (Air)
MAC(G)	Munitions Assignments Committee (Ground)
Maj	Major
Maj Gen	Major General
memo	memorandum

ABBREVIATIONS

mil	military
mns	minutes
MRP	Military Representative of the Associated Pacific Powers
MS or ms	manuscript
MS	Most Secret (British)
msg	message
mtg	meeting
N	Navy (used in combination)
NA	Naval Attaché
nat	national
ND	Navy Department
nd	no date
NEI	Netherlands East Indies
no.	number
NR&L	Naval Records & Library
NZ	New Zealand
O	Office, order, or officer (used in combination)
OEW	Office of Economic Warfare
ONH	Office of Naval History
OPD	Operations Division, WDGS
orig	original
OSS	Office of Strategic Services
OWI	Office of War Information
p. (pp.)	page (pages)
par	paragraph
plen	plenary
plng	planning
PM	The Prime Minister
P&O	Plans and Operations Division, GSUSA
POA	Pacific Ocean Areas
Pres	The President
pt	part
PWC	Pacific War Council
R	Restricted
RAAF	Royal Australian Air Force
RAdm	Rear Admiral
RAF	Royal Air Force
RBCOS	Representatives, British Chiefs of Staff
rec	record
ref	reference
rev	revised
RN	Royal Navy
RNZAF	Royal New Zealand Air Force
rpt	report
S	Secret
SACO	Sino-American Cooperation Organization
SC	Security Control
SC SWPA	Supreme Commander, Southwest Pacific Area
SEAC	Southeast Asia Command

sec	section
SecNav	Secretary of the Navy
SecState	Secretary of State
sect	secretariat
SecWar	Secretary of War
secy	secretary
sen	senior
sess	session
sgd	signed
sig	signature
sp	special
SS	Secret Security; Sealed Secret
Stat(s)	Statute(s)
State Dept	State Department
subcmte	subcommittee
subj	subject
supp	supplement
suppl	supplemental
SWPA	Southwest Pacific Area
tp	telephone
Tri	Tripartite
TS	Top Secret
U	Unclassified
UK	United Kingdom of Great Britain and Northern Ireland
uniden	unidentified
UNK	Classification unknown
US	United States of America
USA	United States Army
USec	Under Secretary
USMC	United States Marine Corps
USN	United States Navy
USSR	Union of Soviet Socialist Republics
vol	volume
VAdm	Vice Admiral
w/	with
WD	War Department
WDGS	War Department General Staff
WDSS	War Department Special Staff
WH	White House
w/o	without
WPB	War Production Board
WPD	War Plans Division, WDGS or OCNO
WSA	War Shipping Administration

PART I

PEARL HARBOR THROUGH TRIDENT

Chapter 1

INTRODUCTION

After the beginning of the twentieth century, when the United States had annexed the Philippines, the Open Door Policy toward China had been established, and U.S. ties with the western Pacific were growing stronger, the possibility grew of a serious conflict of U.S. interests with those of Japan, whose desires for expansion were steadily increasing. There were several periods of tension between the two nations in the first decade or so of the century, but during World War I Japan fought at the side of the Allies and seemed as sympathetic as any with the various movements for permanent peace. In the division of German possessions that followed the war Japan received a mandate over the Pacific islands north of the equator, the Carolines, Marshalls, Marianas, and Palau. It was not long before there were indications that fortifications were being placed upon them. Soon, too, Japanese eyes turned toward the mainland of China and the southwestern region of the Pacific, so rich in the vital materials the Japanese islands could not supply. As armed forces from Japan put Japanese plans for expansion into action in the thirties, primarily at the expense of China, the United States became aware that U.S. interests were in serious jeopardy and took steps to attempt to curb Japanese aggression before it should produce world-wide conflict. Diplomacy was unavailing, however, and at the end of 1941 the United States and Japan were at war.

The diplomatic developments and the Japanese actions that led to war are discussed in other sections of the History of the Joint Chiefs of Staff and will not be related here.[1] Nor will the account of the increasing involvement of U.S. production and U.S. naval forces on the side of Great Britain in its stand against the European Axis be discussed. Rather an attempt will be made to survey the development in the years before hostilities began of strategic thinking as to how a war with Japan should be fought.

THE ORANGE PLANS

In November 1904 the Joint Army and Navy Board, established the year before, approved for planning purposes a series of color designations for various nations of the world.[2] To Japan was assigned the code color Orange. In the succeeding years Army and Navy planners, separately and jointly, drafted a series of Orange plans outlining the strategy by which, if necessary, Japan was to be defeated.

The Navy took the lead in strategic planning for a war with Japan, for it was evident that it would be the U.S. Fleet that would have to defend U.S. interests in the Far East or fight its way back across the Pacific if the Philippines should fall to Japanese attack. Class after class at the Naval War College at Newport, R.I., studied the strategy for defeating Japan as a major problem. Thus many of the top ranking naval officers of World War II, among them Admiral Ernest J. King, who as Commander in Chief, U.S. Fleet, and Chief of Naval Operations guided the over-all strategy during the war, had fought the war on the game board at Newport and had firm ideas as to how Japan should be defeated. Within the Navy Department and subordinate naval commands Orange war plans were continually being studied. Planning by the Army, meanwhile, centered around its primary responsibility, local defense of the Philippine Islands and in particular of Manila Bay. Although the Army planners never undertook the detailed study of strategic problems in the Pacific that their naval colleagues did, both services worked together in the period between the wars to develop a series of top level joint Orange plans. For the most part these were hypothetical plans based upon forces which did not exist, but the pattern of advance against Japan which evolved through them was essentially that which was followed in World War II.

The first of the joint Orange plans, submitted by the Joint Planning Committee (JPC) to the Joint Board (JB) in March 1924, characterized a possible war with Japan as

> An offensive war, primarily naval, directed toward the isolation and harassment of Japan, through control of her vital sea communications and through offensive sea and air operations against her naval forces and economic life; followed, if necessary, by such further action as may be required to win the war.[3]

The first objective was to be the establishment of U.S. sea power in the western Pacific in strength superior to that of Japan. Success would probably require holding or retaking Manila Bay, occupying and controlling all harbors in the islands mandated to Japan, and perhaps taking over territory as well. Japan had agreed at the Washington Naval Conference in 1922 that fortifications on the mandated islands would not be increased or new bases established, and it was assumed that the islands would not be a serious threat to U.S. operations. The war was expected to be long and preceded by a period of mobilization. At least 50,000 troops were to be ready for transfer from the west coast of the United States to Oahu on D Day plus ten and prepared to leave the Hawaiian Islands for Manila Bay four days later. This was more than a third of the current total strength of the U.S. Army.[4]

The drafters of this first Orange plan were insistent that all forces should be under the immediate command of an officer of their respective services, but that it was essential to have a single over-all commander with a joint staff to control each phase of the operations. Through the period of isolation and harassment this would be the Commander in Chief, U.S. Fleet; the President would designate the commander for any subsequent operations. When the Joint Board viewed the plan, there was objection to the provision for unified command, and before approving the paper the board insisted upon substitution of the principle of mutual cooperation between the services.[5] Late in 1928 the Secretaries of War and the Navy approved a detailed revision of the joint Orange war plan which did provide initially for unified command under the Navy, in accordance with the principle of paramount interest.[6] The strategic concept was approximately the same as the earlier one, with the added point that large army forces might be employed in major land operations in the western Pacific. The plan was a little more realistic than the earlier version, for it allowed more time for a smaller number of troops to be ready to leave the west coast of the United States and provided for the establishment of secure lines of communication before the troops were moved to the western Pacific.

During the twenties, when these plans were written, U.S. forces were small indeed. The universal urge for peace that followed World War I and found international expression in agreements on disarmament had fostered within the United States a widespread support for isolationism and a reluctance to maintain armed forces. In the economic depression of the thirties Congress reflected the public reluctance to spend money for anything related to war. Between 1923 and 1935 the total strength of the Army ranged between 131,000 and 141,000 men. The Navy, traditional first line of defense, received somewhat better support from Congress, but it was maintained below the limits of international agreements and many obsolescent naval vessels were not to be replaced.[7]

While U.S. strength declined Japanese strength increased. In 1922 the United States, Great Britain, Japan, France, and Italy had agreed to limit construction of new naval vessels and to scrap some already built. These agreements were extended at London in 1930. It was principally U.S. ships that were sacrificed and Japan's navy grew proportionately closer in size to that of the United States. In 1931 Japan began its program of aggression, moving troops into Manchuria, thereby violating the Paris Peace Pact of 1928 and the Nine Power Treaty of 1922 which had guaranteed the sovereignty, territorial integrity, and independence of China. The League of Nations succeeded in stopping the fighting but could not force the Japanese to withdraw their troops. In February 1933 the small nations in the League Assembly passed a resolution condemning Japan and asking for restoration of Manchuria to Chinese sovereignty. Japan responded by walking out of the League. This was only a month after Adolph Hitler had been made Germany's Chancellor of State and set about building up his power much as Benito Mussolini had been doing for eleven years in Italy.

The increasing military strength of the Axis nations in Europe did not have an immediate effect upon military planning in the United States. In 1934, however, the Army, recognizing the impracticability of its existing Mobilization Plan, revised it to bring it nearer to reality. The joint Orange plan was revised accordingly, and a slower schedule was set for the embarkation of forces for the western Pacific. At the same time it was provided that U.S. forces in the early stages of the war would eject the Japanese from their bases in the Marshall and Caroline Islands and establish advanced U.S. bases there to protect the line of communications to the western Pacific.[8] In 1936, after considerable protest from the local commanders in the Philippines, the Joint Board finally accepted the fact that the small garrisons there could not hold the islands against strong Japanese attack and reduced the missions of forces in the Philippines from holding the Manila Bay area to holding the entrance to Manila Bay. The Asiatic Fleet was assigned the task for furthering the advance of the military and naval forces from the United States, particularly by attacking Japanese commerce and diverting the Japanese Fleet.[9]

By 1937, the year when Japan started undeclared war with China, realization had grown in Washington that U.S. forces in the Philippines could not hold long enough against a serious Japanese attempt to take the islands for the U.S. Fleet to reach the area. Increasing the defenses there was out of the question, for appropriations were still low and other demands had priority on limited resources. In these circumstances some officers, particularly in the Army, began to feel that the United States should no longer plan to push westward across the Pacific, fighting an offensive war with Japan, but should concentrate on maintaining a defense in the eastern Pacific and seek by economic pressure to accomplish Japan's collapse. Late in 1937 the Joint Board directed the Joint Planning Committee to prepare a new Orange plan that would provide for holding an initial "position of readiness" on the general line Alaska-Oahu-Panama and offer practicable alternative courses of subsequent action.[10] Army members of the committee disagreed strongly with naval members, who insisted that the war should be fought offensively and the westward advance retained. The new plan was finally drawn on a revised and conservative concept:

> The defeat of Orange through military and economic pressure, made progressively more severe until the national objective is attained. The initial operations will be primarily naval in character, coupled with measures designed to insure the security of Continental United States, Alaska, Oahu, and Panama.[11]

Command of the sea was to be extended westward as rapidly as secure lines of communication could be built up, and the enemy's armed forces and sea communications were to be attacked in order to increase military and economic pressure against Japan. An organized force of about 750,000 men was to be made available by the Army, but there was no indication of where they would be sent.

By the end of 1938 war clouds were looming large on the eastern horizon. For three years Germany and Italy had been challenging the other nations of the world with one act of aggression after another. In 1935 Hitler repudiated the Versailles Treaty and Mussolini's troops invaded Ethiopia. The following year German soldiers marched into the Rhineland, the Rome-Berlin Axis was formed, and Germany and Japan signed the Anti-Comintern Pact. The year 1938 saw German occupation of Austria in March, followed by annexation of the Sudeten area of Czechoslovakia in September, abetted by the appeasement policy of France and Great Britain. Despite the optimistic belief of Mr. Neville Chamberlain, Britain's Prime Minister, that he had achieved "peace in our time," it was soon evident that Hitler's aims did not end with the Sudetenland.

In November 1938 the Joint Board faced the fact that U.S. interests and policies were in conflict with those of Germany and Italy as well as with those of Japan and recognized the possibility that war might come with all three at the same time. Accordingly the Joint Planning Committee was put to work on studies of joint action to be taken "in the event of (a) violation of the Monroe Doctrine by one or more of the Fascist powers, and (b) a simultaneous attempt to expand Japanese influence in the Philippines."[12] The resultant study was a thoughtful analysis of the situation, estimate of the likelihood of war, and discussion of the strategy which the United States might follow under various circumstances.[13]

The members of the JPC concluded that Japanese aggression against the Philippines was more likely than German or Italian penetration into the Western Hemisphere. Should the European powers violate the Monroe Doctrine in the Atlantic at the same time that Japan moved against the Philippines, "there can be no doubt," the planners insisted, "that the vital interests of the United States would require offensive measures in the Atlantic against Germany and Italy" and the maintenance of a strong defensive in the eastern Pacific. Germany and Italy could well take action seriously threatening the security of the Caribbean area and the Panama Canal, which must be kept open for the free passage of naval vessels from one area to the other. Faced with a defensive attitude by the United States, however, the Japanese were expected to restrict their operations to the far western Pacific. This concept of the Atlantic first was to be affirmed and reaffirmed in subsequent planning and made the basic strategic principle when war came.

The joint planners agreed that the primary objective of a war with Japan alone should be, as in the Orange plans, establishment in the western Pacific of U.S. naval power superior to that of Japan. Since the Philippines and Guam were not expected to hold, it would be necessary to fight back across the Pacific, using one of four routes long since defined in naval studies: (a) via the

Aleutians; (b) directly from Pearl Harbor and Midway to northern Luzon; (c) step by step from Hawaii via the Marshalls, Carolines, and possibly Marianas, Yap, and Pelews; (d) via Samoa and New Guinea to the southern Philippines. The planners predicted a combination of (b) and (c). There was no thought that it might be necessary to start the offensive from bases as far back as Australia and New Caledonia. There was expectation, however, that an advanced base would have to be set up in the Philippines or on the China coast and perhaps an expeditionary force put into China to cut off all supplies from Japan.

From this study was developed a series of hypothetical situations in which the United States would be at war with one or more enemies and with varying allies and objectives. During the next two years corresponding plans, the Rainbow series, were written as events appeared to validate one or another of the sets of assumptions. Only the last of the group, Rainbow No. 5, need be discussed here, for it was the one under which the war was begun.[14]

RAINBOW NO. 5 AND COLLABORATION WITH THE BRITISH

War between Germany and Great Britain and France started in September 1939, and from the beginning there was never any doubt as to where U.S. sympathies lay. The United States had become increasingly involved in support of Great Britain, particularly after the fall of France left the British alone in their fight against the Axis. Restricted always by a strong strain of isolationism within the country, the administration repeatedly sought ways in which to lend material assistance to the British, first on a cash-and-carry basis, then by the destroyer-bases exchange, finally at the beginning of 1941 under the unique system of lend-lease. The U.S. public was deeply hopeful that this "aid short of war" would guarantee no "shooting war" for the United States. By 1940, however, military leaders saw the likelihood that the country might be forced to fight at the side of the British, and they bent their efforts to preparing for such an eventuality. During the summer of 1940 Congress passed the Two Ocean Navy Bill, authorized procurement of thousands of planes and tons of army equipment, and passed the Selective Service Act to provide more men to use the arms in defense of the nation.

Since 1940 was an election year, any strategic planning for active participation in the war had to be done in the greatest secrecy. Instigated by Admiral Harold R. Stark, Chief of Naval Operations, realistic appraisals of the situation were made in Washington, and a series of staff conferences, primarily on technical problems, were held between U.S. and British officers. The following year, between 29 January and 27 March, conversations in Washington yielded a blueprint for combined military action should the United States became actively belligerent.

In preparation for the American-British Conversations (ABC), the Joint Board in December 1940 adopted a study of the "National Defense Policy of the United States," which was developed from an earlier one prepared by Admiral Stark and his advisors.[15] The paper predicted that if the United States were at war simultaneously with Germany, Italy, and Japan, it would have four alternatives: (a) concentrating on the defense of the Western Hemisphere and aiding Great Britain in order to permit the British to send reenforcements to the Far East, meanwhile reserving U.S. strength for a major effort at some time in the future; (b) preparing for a full offensive against Japan with British and Dutch assistance, while maintaining a defensive position toward Germany; (c) expending the greatest possible effort simultaneously against both Germany and Japan; (d) preparing for an eventual major offensive in the Atlantic while maintaining a defensive in the Pacific. The Joint Board agreed that the United States should follow the first course as long as it stayed out of war. If war came, however, it should adopt the fourth. This was the recommendation the U.S. representatives made at ABC. The British were in agreement, and the final report, ABC-1, incorporated "Germany first" as a fundamental principle.[16]

ABC-1 was an agreement on combined action "should the United States be compelled to resort to war," reached by military staff officers, subject to confirmation by the U.S. Chief of Naval Operations (Admiral Stark), the Army Chief of Staff (General George C. Marshall), the British Chiefs of Staff, and the governments of the two nations. The instructions to the U.S. representatives at the conversations were approved not only by the Joint Board but by the President as well. The chiefs and President Franklin D. Roosevelt were constantly informed of the progress of the discussions. Inasmuch as all subsequent planning was based on ABC-1, there can be no doubt that Mr. Roosevelt unofficially approved it, although he withheld official approval with the explanation that the British Government had not yet accepted the paper. It is highly probable that he was in fact reluctant to give official sanction to a plan drawn on the supposition that the United States was going to be forced to fight, for large sections of the American public were stoutly opposed to any action that could possibly be interpreted as likely to embroil the nation in the "foreign war" and were not sufficiently informed in the late spring of 1941 to realize that war was probably inevitable.

ABC-1 included general provisions for collaboration in warfare and for combined action against the Axis Powers. Since Germany was considered the predominant member and the European area the decisive one, most of the measures listed as "offensive policies" were aimed at Germany. But the list included also the use of raids and minor offensives wherever possible and the "application of economic pressure by naval, land, and air forces and all other means, including the control of commodities at their source by diplomatic and financial measures," which applied to Japan as well as to the Axis in Europe.

British interests in the Far East were and long had been considerably greater than those of the United States. But Great

Britain was engaged in a struggle with the Axis in Europe and could ill spare for the Far East the forces which could guarantee defense of British possessions against Japanese aggression. With Japan already occupying northern Indo-China and threatening Burma and Malaya the British were deeply concerned about the security of their colonial possessions. They sought agreement from the United States to increase U.S. strength in the Far East and to accept some of the responsibility for defense of the area. However, Americans were opposed to risking the loss of U.S. forces in defense of the British Empire, and they considered it wiser to concentrate U.S. strength in the Atlantic and leave the defense of the Far East, except for the Philippines, to the British and to the Dutch, whose interests there were also strong. A firm statement on the subject was incorporated in ABC-1:

> ...The United States does not intend to add to its present Military strength in the Far East but will employ the United States Pacific Fleet offensively in the manner best calculated to weaken Japanese economic power, and to support the defense of the Malay barrier by diverting Japanese strength away from Malaysia. The United States intends so to augment its forces in the Atlantic and Mediterranean areas that the British Commonwealth will be in a position to release the necessary forces for the Far East.

This was part of a continuing difference of opinion between the United States and Great Britain as to the importance of the Far East Area and the desirable strategic policy. The British placed first priority on the defense of Singapore. Both before and during the ABC meetings they tried to persuade American representatives to agree to send the Pacific Fleet to be based there. Loss of Singapore, the British Chiefs felt, "would be a disaster of the first magnitude, second only to the loss of the British Isles." They said, "If Singapore were in serious danger of capture, and the United States still withheld their aid, we should be prepared to send a Fleet to the Far East, even if to do so would compromise or sacrifice our position in the Mediterranean."[17] The U.S. Navy, however, wished to avoid being drawn into a major war in the Far East. U.S. naval leaders doubted the adequacy of Singapore as a base for the Pacific Fleet, and while they recognized that its loss would be a tremendous blow to British prestige, they questioned the strategic significance of its fall. They believed that the defense of the Far East should be built on the whole area of the southwestern Pacific instead of the single objective of Singapore.[18] The U.S. view that American forces should be deployed primarily in the Atlantic prevailed. It was finally agreed in ABC-1 that as soon as the situation in the Pacific permitted a U.S. force of three battleships, one aircraft carrier, four cruisers, thirteen destroyers, and twelve patrol type seaplanes could be transferred to Gibraltar to relieve the British Force "H" for transfer to the Indian Ocean or the Far East Area. Allowance was made for the possibility that the strategic situation in the Atlantic might dictate a different decision, but there was no mention that U.S. forces in the Pacific might be unable to spare the ships for transfer.

For purposes of command ABC-1 divided the world into strategic areas and assigned to one nation or the other "strategic direction of all forces of the Associated Powers [the United States, British Commonwealth, their associates or allies] normally operating" in each. Under U.S. responsibility was the Atlantic Ocean Area west of Longitude 30° West and north of Latitude 25° South and the Pacific Ocean Area north of Latitude 30° North and west of Longitude 140° East, north of the equator and east of Longitude 140° East, and south of the equator and east of Longitude 180°. In addition U.S. naval forces were to support the British south of the equator as far west as Longitude 155° East, which is still east of the coast of Australia. In the Far East Area, which included the sea areas west of the Pacific Ocean Area beyond Australia-New Zealand, the command system was to be mutual coordination rather than unified control. Naval forces in that region, however, except for those engaged in defending the Philippines, were to be under the strategic direction of the British naval Commander in Chief, China Station.

General tasks were assigned to the forces in each of the several areas of war. For land and air forces in the Pacific they were mainly defensive. Naval forces, however, were to:

(a) Support the forces of the Associated Powers in the Far East Area by diverting enemy strength away from the Malay Barrier through the denial and capture of positions in the Marshalls, and through raids on enemy sea communications and positions.

(b) Destroy Axis sea communications by capturing or destroying vessels trading directly or indirectly with the enemy.

(c) Protect the sea communications of the Associated Powers within the Pacific Area.

(d) Support British naval forces in the area south of the equator, as far west as Longitude 155° East.

(e) Protect the territory of the Associated Powers within the Pacific Area, and prevent the extension of enemy Military power into the Western Hemisphere, by destroying hostile expeditions and by supporting land and air forces in denying the enemy the use of land positions in that Hemisphere.

(f) Prepare to capture and establish control over the Caroline and Marshall Island area.

Four tasks were assigned to the combined naval forces in the Far East Area and the area of Australia and New Zealand:

(a) Raid Japanese sea communications and destroy Axis forces.

(b) Support the land and air forces in the defense of the territories of the Associated Powers.

(c) Destroy Axis sea communications by capturing or destroying vessels trading directly or indirectly with the enemy.

(d) Protect sea communications of the Associated Powers by escorting, covering, and patrolling, and by destroying enemy raiding forces.

Land and air forces were to:

(a) Defend Hong Kong, the Philippines, the Netherlands East Indies and such other territories and islands as it may be decided from time to time to occupy as bases.
(b) Hold Malaya, Singapore, and Java against Japanese attack.
(c) Support the naval forces.

These were the general tasks and the general objectives for the combined forces of the United States and Great Britain when and if war came. In order to make them workable there had to be more detailed plans for national forces, for the separate services, and for the subordinate commands. In Washington the first step was preparation of the final of the series of joint Rainbow plans, Rainbow No. 5.[19] Much of ABC-1 was incorporated verbatim in Rainbow No. 5, which differed from ABC-1 primarily in that it was a national rather than a combined agreement and consequently included details of troop deployments and mobilization planning which would have been inappropriate in ABC-1. Rainbow No. 5 provided that 23,000 troops would embark at Seattle for Alaska on M Day plus ten or possibly sooner, and 23,000 at San Francisco for Hawaii at about the same time. How this figure had been determined and what the troops were to do the plan did not say. Otherwise the only significant change in the portions of the plan pertaining to war against Japan was extension of the tasks assigned to U.S. naval forces in the Pacific and the Far East to provide more specifically for defense of U.S. territory--the islands of Midway, Johnston, Palmyra, Samoa, and Guam, and the coastal frontiers of the United States and the Philippines.

The joint plan Rainbow No. 5 was a "strategic" rather than an "operating" plan. There remained to be drafted operating plans for the separate services and the various commands as well as plans for specific operations to accomplish the tasks therein assigned. Many were not completed when war came.

It was impossible to know what specific operations would prove most essential until the United States was actually at war and to plan with any degree of exactness the means that would be required for the total war effort. Thus production planning to accomplish the objectives of Rainbow No. 5 had to be in kinds of things, military organizations and equipment, and in maximum figures. By 1941 Congressional appropriations for defense had allowed considerable expansion of both Army and Navy, and both were being rapidly built up but without direct relation to specific strategic plans for war. In July 1941 President Roosevelt directed the two services to prepare a study of "the over-all production requirements required to defeat our potential enemies." The result was a union of separate studies by the Army and the Navy rather than a carefully balanced program between the two. Civilian production requirements were

not related to military needs at all. But at least the study forced
military thinkers to concentrate on long-range production planning
and to realize the enormity of the task of procuring the means for
achieving victory.[20]

There would have to be constant revision of plans for procurement
of men and material just as there would for strategic plans. Rainbow No. 5 may be said merely to have pointed the general direction
the war was to take and the objectives to be achieved. It offered
no blueprint for the defeat of Japan or of Germany. Specific operations would have to be determined later by the action of the enemy
and availability of forces.

AMERICAN-BRITISH COOPERATION IN THE FAR EAST

Rainbow No. 5 set the pattern for unilateral planning by the
United States for the Pacific Theater, but the Far East was an area
in which British, Dutch, and U.S. forces would all be operating.
Consequently, in an attempt to achieve maximum effectiveness of the
local forces, after completion of ABC-1 the U.S. and British Chiefs
of Staff directed their commanders in the Far East to get together
with the Dutch and "prepare plans for the conduct of military operations...on the basis of [the] report of Washington conversations."[21]
Previous staff conversations had been held by the British and Dutch,
with American representatives present, in November 1940 and February
1941, and by the Americans and Dutch in January 1941.[22] None of
them was, or indeed was intended to be, decisive. The April conference was not much more successful, and the final report (ADB-1)
fell far short of the practical operating plan for which U.S. and
British Chiefs of Staff had hoped.[23]

Unlike Rainbow No. 5, ADB-1 bore little relation to ABC-1 and
seems to have been drafted with the combined report only vaguely in
mind. After positing the defensive initially against Japan ADB-1
mentioned the two "most important interests in the Far East":
security of sea communications and security of Singapore. The second of these was contrary to the views of the U.S. Chiefs of Staff,
as has already been related, and certain to meet with objection.
There followed a survey of the situation and the courses Japan
might follow which would either directly involve the territory of
one of the ADB powers or place them at a distinct military disadvantage. Some steps the Japanese might take, the group in Singapore felt, would warrant military counteraction, and they agreed
that they should advise their respective governments to take collective action against Japan under certain circumstances: if Japanese forces should commit a direct act of war against the territory
or mandated territory of any of the ADB powers; if Japanese forces
moved into Portuguese Timor, New Caledonia, the Loyalty Islands, or
any part of Thailand west of 100° East or south of 10° North; or if
Japanese ships threatened the Philippines, the Kra Isthmus, or the
east coast of Malaya. This recommendation was one of those which
the U.S. Chiefs of Staff rejected when the report reached them, on
the grounds that this was a political measure beyond the scope of

their authority. Although they disapproved such a statement in a military paper, however, they were apparently in agreement with it in principle. In two joint memoranda to the President in the tense days of November 1941, while urging that no steps be taken that might lead the Japanese to start a war, they recommended that only the conditions proposed in ADB-1 be considered provocation for military action against Japan.[24]

There was much in ADB-1 which Admiral Stark and General Marshall did not like. They disapproved the new "Eastern Theater" it devised, comprising all the sea areas of the Far East, where the British naval Commander in Chief, China Station, was to have strategic control of all naval forces. This included virtually all the U.S. Asiatic Fleet, which was to be "released" and sent to Singapore as the situation in the Philippines developed. The U.S. Chiefs of Staff objected to the plan that British and Dutch forces would be assigned mainly to escort and convoy duty while U.S. ships fought the enemy. They also objected to the recommendation that guerrilla forces in China and subversive activities in Japan be supported by the United States and Great Britain and steps be taken at once to organize them. This the chiefs characterized as a "political measure," and they hesitated to run the risk that Congress might discover that U.S. funds were being spent in ways which Japan might easily find cause for war. For these and other reasons Admiral Stark and General Marshall informed the British Chiefs of Staff in July 1941 that they could not approve ADB-1, for it was too much at variance with ABC-1 and it was contrary to some of their fundamental convictions.[25]

In August President Roosevelt and Prime Minister Winston Churchill and their military staffs met at Argentia, Newfoundland, to discuss some of their mutual problems and in particular ways in which the United States could assist the British war effort. The military staffs found time during the meetings to discuss the U.S. objections to ADB-1.[26] As a result the British prepared a revised draft of the paper. That, too, failed to satisfy the American Chiefs, however, and both were discarded. The commanders in the Far East were directed to prepare joint operating plans based on ABC-1 but only a start had been made before war came.[27]

For the most part the military discussions at Argentia were concerned with technical problems of supplying the British with munitions of war. The U.S. Chiefs were not authorized to discuss war plans, and the President was studiously avoiding any agreement that pledged the United States to belligerency. However, the British Chiefs of Staff did present for consideration a "General Strategy Review," summarizing their views of the situation, primarily in respect to the war against Germany.[28] It included one statement concerning the area of the Pacific and the Far East:

> The security of our communications with Australia, New Zealand and India, and the safe passage from Malaya and Dutch East Indies of commodities essential both to ourselves and the United States, are vital to the successful continuance of our

war effort. If these are to be achieved we must be certain of holding a secure base at Singapore. Our defences there have been strengthened in recent months, and we are making constant efforts to provide the requisite forces. The difficulty, of course, is to strike a balance between the essential needs of the theatres in which we are fighting, without neglecting the theatres where war may develop at any moment.

The members of the Joint Board were displeased with many aspects of this "Review," chiefly because it appeared to be at variance with the agreements in ABC-1. It was clear from the statement quoted above that there was still a difference of opinion as to the strategic significance of Singapore and the whole Far East Area. Thus in a formal comment, sent to the British Chiefs of Staff on 25 September 1941, the U.S. position was stated:

While the security of the base at Singapore is important, it ought to be accepted that the strategy of the Far East Area should be considered as a whole. It seems unlikely that Singapore could be held, were the major portion of the Dutch East Indies and the Philippines to fall to the Japanese. Furthermore, offensive operations by the Chinese Nationalist armies and air forces might have an important influence on the effectiveness of a Japanese attack on the Malay Barrier. For this reason, the Joint Board considers that British military authorities, in allocating military materials which may be made available to them by the United States, might well take into consideration the diversion of appropriate amounts of these materials for use by the Dutch and Chinese military forces.[29]

There was no resolution of this difference.

REDUCTION OF THE PACIFIC FLEET

The tempo of the war in Europe had increased considerably while ABC-1 and its derivatives were being developed. In April and May German forces overwhelmed Yugoslavia, Greece, and Crete in rapid succession. On 22 June they turned to bigger game and invaded Russia. In Africa General Erwin Rommel held the advantage over British forces who had been greatly weakened by a vain attempt to save Crete. U.S. Marines had landed in Greenland in April. The following month President Roosevelt proclaimed a state of unlimited national emergency. When the Germans threatened the security of the Iberian Peninsula, he directed the Secretaries of War and the Navy to prepare plans for a joint expeditionary force to occupy the Azores. This project was suspended, however, and plans for occupation of Iceland instead were undertaken in mid-June. Meanwhile materials of war were beginning to flow from the United States to the nations fighting the Axis. In March Congress had passed the Lend-Lease Act, giving the President authority to extend material aid to "the government of any country whose defense the President deems vital to the defense of the United States."[30] While more and more shipments of the much needed equipment headed across the Atlantic, however, additional protection from German U-boats became a necessity. The only source of more ships for the Atlantic Fleet was the Pacific.

In 1940, at the insistence of the President and the Secretary of State, decision had been made to base the U.S. Fleet at Pearl Harbor rather than on the west coast of the United States, on the theory that it would have a deterrent effect on Japanese plans for further aggression in the Pacific.[31] In the spring of 1941, however, the risk of Japanese reaction seemed a lesser one than the threat of German U-boats to shipping in the Atlantic, and it was decided to move some of the Pacific vessels to the other ocean.[32] At the same time the British were to initiate some of the transfers from the Mediterranean to the Far East scheduled under ABC-1. The plan was temporarily halted after Japan and Russia signed a treaty of nonaggression on 13 April, but it was soon resumed at the President's direction. In June, however, Admiral Stark put himself on record in a memorandum to Secretary of the Navy Frank Knox as opposed to further reductions in naval strength in the Pacific in view of the increasingly tense relations with Japan and the inability of the British, following the reverses at Crete, to send important naval reenforcements to the Far East.[33] The transfers were subsequently suspended.

REENFORCEMENT OF THE PHILIPPINES

As tension in the Pacific increased in 1941 plans had been developing for enlarging land and air defenses of the Philippines. Since 1936, when passage of the Tydings-McDuffie Act assured independence for the islands in ten years, General Douglas MacArthur had been Field Marshal of the Philippine Army and military advisor to the Philippine Commonwealth. He had prepared a long-range plan for developing what he considered an adequate force for Philippine defense, but the Japanese threat to the islands became serious before much progress could be made toward putting his plan into effect. In 1940 General MacArthur and President Manuel Quezon added their voices to those of U.S. officers stationed in the islands, seeking reenforcements for the small U.S. defenses.[34] President Quezon's requests for approximately $52,000,000 to build up his defenses were received with sympathy in Washington, but it was not until April 1941 that President Roosevelt finally approved a plan to allocate funds for the purpose from sugar excise taxes and currency devaluation.[35] War had begun before the necessary legislation was passed by Congress.[36] By that time other action had been taken.

On 12 July 1941 Admiral Stark presented to the Joint Board a recommendation from his War Plans Director, Rear Admiral R.K. Turner. Alarmed over the German attack on Russia and the corollary lessening of restraining Russian influence on Japanese forces in northeast Asia, Admiral Turner proposed that "action be taken to lay mines and nets and to alert and deploy the Army and Navy forces now stationed in the Philippines."[37] General Marshall was afraid such action would require a Presidential proclamation calling the Philippine Army to active duty in the service of the United States and might well be interpreted by the Japanese as an aggressive act and provoke military action.[38] It was decided, however, that this might be avoided if there were no undue publicity and the forces were activated ostensibly for training.[39] Two weeks later the President approved a recommendation from the Secretary of War for mobilization of the Philippine forces and allocation of approximately $10,000,000 from the President's Emergency Fund to defray the cost.[40] The armed forces were nationalized by military order for the duration of the emergency. General MacArthur was ordered to command them and U.S. forces in the Philippine Islands, with the title, Commanding General, United States Army Forces, Far East.[41]

Some progress was made toward sending reenforcements to the Philippines during the last months of 1941. In July, even before General MacArthur received his orders, air officers in the War Department proposed to allocate to the Far East four heavy bombardment groups (272 aircraft plus 68 reserve) and two pursuit groups (130 planes).[42] Part of a regiment of antiaircraft troops and some reserve supplies sailed for the Philippines on 26 August inaugurating a program of reenforcements designed to achieve defense against strong Japanese attack. It was felt in the War Department that although the Philippines could not be defended against a maximum Japanese effort without jeopardizing the policy of defeating Germany first, considerable reenforcement of the defenses might deter the Japanese from attempting further conquests in the southwest Pacific. Men, planes, and equipment were despatched to the Philippines periodically in the remaining months of 1941. Unfortunately, however, the program was not to be completed until February or March 1942.[43]

In mid-November 1941 the Joint Board approved a recommendation from General MacArthur that the Philippine Coastal Frontier be changed from Luzon and the land and sea areas required for its defense to include "all the land and sea areas necessary for the defense of the Philippine Archipelago." In a revision of Rainbow No. 5 three more tasks were assigned to the Army Ground and Air Forces in the Far East:

> *b.* Support the Navy in raiding Japanese sea communications and destroying Axis forces.
> *c.* Conduct air raids against Japanese forces and installations within tactical operating radius of available bases.
> *d.* Cooperate with the Associated Powers in the defense of the territories of these Powers in accordance with approved policies and agreements.[44]

With British agreement Luzon was added to Malaya, Singapore, and Java in ABC-1 as points to be held against Japanese attack. Forces in the Philippine area and Australia and New Zealand were given the additional task of conducting air raids against Japanese forces and bases.[45]

Admiral Thomas C. Hart in Manila had already decided that it might be well to alter the existing war plan which called for deploying the fleet southward in the event of war and to operate from Manila, assuming that the stronger Army forces could hold Manila Bay and defend it from aerial bombardment. Reasoning that Manila's location was strategically better for fleet operations than the Malay Barrier and that the U.S. Fleet would be more effective operating with other U.S. forces than in loose cooperation with Dutch and British, he recommended the revision to Admiral Stark and set about preparing to act accordingly.[46] Admiral Stark, however, was not impressed with the idea. He pointed out: the inadequacies of air and antiaircraft defenses in the Philippines; the danger that the Japanese might cut off the route for eventual retirement southward; the impossibility of operating submarines and naval aircraft effectively if their tenders were lost in the Philippines; the defenseless condition of the logistic supply line; and the value of combining the strength of cruisers and destroyers with the British Far Eastern Fleet. It was almost a month before Admiral Stark's reply reached Admiral Hart, who then abandoned his plans and proceeded to arrange to send major fleet units south. In the first days of December Rear Admiral William A. Glassford departed with the major surface ships, constituted as Task Force 5.[47]

In October the British announced that Admiral Tom Phillips, RN, was to become Commander in Chief, Eastern Fleet, to replace the Commander in Chief, China Station.[48] Certain British vessels were sent to the new command from the Mediterranean, among them two new ships, *Repulse* and *Prince of Wales*. The British Chiefs began to think seriously of basing a force of capital ships north of the Malay Barrier or even in the Philippines and of drawing up a strategic operating plan for the area, based on ABC-1.[49] The U.S. Chiefs were interested in both ideas, and when Admiral Phillips arrived in the Far East at the beginning of December, he went almost at once to Manila to confer with Admiral Hart.

From the conferences between the two naval commanders came agreements that promised much toward achieving effective coordinated defense of the Far East Area. It was agreed that the British battle fleet would be based in Singapore as a striking force to defend the Dutch East Indies and the Malay Barrier, while a cruiser striking force was to be based on East Borneo-Soerabaya-Darwin and provide convoy protection in the Dutch East Indies-Philippine area. Only minimum forces would be maintained in the Australia-New Zealand area and the Indian Ocean for escort of convoys. It was recommended that Manila Bay be prepared for the British battle fleet to use as an advanced base. Strategic control of British and U.S. forces was to be left to their respective commanders and mutual cooperation was to be the rule.[50]

By the time the report of the Phillips-Hart conversations

reached Washington war had begun. Admiral Stark approved the agreements,[51] but events moved too fast for them to become operative. Two days later the Japanese sank *Repulse* and *Prince of Wales* and Admiral Phillips was lost. With the Japanese spreading rapidly through the Far East there was no time for developing combined plans. It is in any case doubtful that detailed arrangements for combined action could have been carried out or would have appreciably altered the course of events.[52]

SUPPORT FOR CHINA

While the U.S. and British military chiefs had been talking about what they would do if compelled to fight Japan, China since 1937 had been at war, albeit undeclared war, with the same nation. Provided it did not surrender, China would stand on the side of the United States and Great Britain against Japan. The part it would play in such a circumstance was strongly affected by political considerations, particularly by President Roosevelt's determination that China should be treated as a Great Power. Despite this factor China did not figure in combined military plans for war with Japan except as an area where eventually it might be strategically desirable to build an advanced base and as a nation whose troops should be supported because they were resisting the Japanese. There were no staff discussions between Americans, British, and Chinese; Chinese representatives were not invited to participate in the various staff discussions in the Far East. Thus there were no plans for using the forces of China in cooperation with those of the United States and Great Britain and no agreements on the assistance China could be expected to give. China, with its vast land areas already overrun by Japanese,[53] its lines of communication with the outside world cut to the narrow, inefficient, corruption-ridden Burma Road, its miserably equipped armies falling back before the advancing enemy, its customs and procedures so strange to western minds, just did not fit into the pattern of primarily naval and economic warfare the United States and Britain planned to wage against Japan.

Although China was not an active participant in strategic planning, there was not the least doubt that the United States would support China in its resistance to Japan. Stories of the sufferings of the Chinese people and exaggerated accounts of the exploits of the Chinese armies had increased the natural sympathy of the U.S. public. During the first years of the hostilities between China and Japan the United States had loaned money to China through the Export-Import Bank. In 1940 China began to seek arms and economic aid through Mr. T.V. Soong, Harvard-educated Foreign Minister. His first overtures brought little result. In November a more specific appeal was made, when Major General P.T. Mow of the Chinese Air Force and Colonel Claire L. Chennault, a retired U.S. Army pilot who was working for the Chinese Air Force, arrived in Washington in search of planes and men to fly them in China. Their request was approved by President Roosevelt, but finding planes was a difficult problem, for the British were taking all they could and the United States was trying to build up its own air forces. Finally the British agreed to let the Chinese have 100 P-40B's. The first shipment left New York for China in February 1941. It was June before the first group of pilots had been recruited and sent on its way, to be formed upon arrival in China into the American Volunteer Group (AVG), a unit of the Chinese forces.[54]

Passage of the Lend-Lease Act in March 1941 opened the way for expansion of material aid to China. At the end of the month Mr. Soong submitted China's bid for assistance, including an air force of 1,000 planes, technical advisors, arms and equipment for the equivalent of thirty army divisions, a narrow gauge railway to run between Yunnan and Burma, and improvement of the Burma Road.[55] The list had apparently been drawn with the idea of procuring for China the latest in modern equipment whether or not it could be used under the conditions prevailing there. There was no consideration of the availability of material in the United States or of the problem of transportation to China. Some items were listed in great detail; other categories were vague and impossible to work with. Few were the things which could be supplied to the Chinese without cutting into U.S. requirements or into production allocated to the British. To speed procurement of China's needed supplies the President assigned an administrative assistant, Mr. Lauchlin Currie, who had recently been to China to investigate conditions.

The aircraft problem was a particularly difficult one. In May 1941 the Joint Aircraft Committee, confronted with the necessity of refusing China's requests or changing production schedules, sought from the Joint Board a recommendation of policy.[56] The Joint Planning Committee took up the problem together with a "Short Term Aircraft Program for China" which Mr. Currie had developed from the original larger requests.[57] The committee reminded the Joint Board of the importance of taking advantage of China's ability to assist the United States and Great Britain in their program of economic pressure against Japan by cutting the lines of communication between the interior of China and the coast and by threatening Japanese shipping along the China coast to southeast Asia. There were not in China at the time trained pilots to fly the planes needed for strong attacks on Japanese forces or adequate fields from which to operate them. Consequently the committee recommended that initially only as many planes should be sent to China as could be organized into a force capable of harassing Japanese lines of communication and helping to defend the Burma Road. As a general policy the committee proposed:

> (1) That the United States and Great Britain, subject to United States and British requirements, furnish material aid to China by providing aircraft of pursuit, bombardment, and training types, together with accessories, spares, armament and ammunition, in quantities sufficient for effective action against Japanese military and naval forces operating in China and in neighboring countries and waters.

(2) That the United States provide a cadre of American instructor pilots in China aided by such technical personnel and equipment as may be necessary to the accomplishment of the training of Chinese personnel as flight and maintenance crews. This instructor cadre will render advisory assistance in the maintenance and employment of all training and combat aircraft, and equipment pertaining thereto, which has been made available to China by the United States Government.[58]

The JPC report served also as the vehicle for another recommendation, which seems to have been made simultaneously by several people. Reports from U.S. observers in China of inefficiency and graft in the Chinese army and the lack of realism in the first lend-lease requests made it seem desirable to send to China a U.S. military group that could assist the Chinese in determining and procuring their lend-lease requirements, oversee the distribution of lend-lease material to insure that it was being properly used, and keep an eye on the interests of U.S. military personnel in China. The project had been discussed with approval in the War Department and was incorporated in the JPC report in the form of a recommendation.

That to aid China in the proper utilization of the large amount of material resources being furnished by the United States, the United States send a military mission to China to act in an advisory capacity.

The Joint Board approved all the committee's recommendations on 12 July 1941.[59] Subsequently they were approved also by the Secretaries of War and the Navy and by the President.[60] At the end of August Brigadier General John Magruder was assigned to head the mission[61] and was given five tasks approved by the Joint Board:

a. To advise and assist the Chinese Government in all phases of procurement, transportation and utilization of military materials, equipment and munitions requisite to the prosecution of its military effort.

b. To advise and assist the Chinese Government in the training of Chinese personnel in the use and maintenance of materials, equipment and munitions.

c. To assist the Chinese Government in obtaining prompt and coordinated administrative action by United States authorities necessary to insure the orderly flow of materials and munitions from the Lend-Lease agencies to the Chinese military forces.

d. To explore the vital port, road and railroad facilities with a view to the establishment and maintenance of an adequate line of military communications. Japan is at present in virtual possession of the entire coast of China and has blocked off ingress to China and the Chinese armies except through Burma and Russia.

e. To assist the personnel of other United States Government departments in carrying out their respective duties in furtherance of the objectives of the Lend Lease Act as pertains to China.[62]

General Magruder's duties, it will be noted, were all concerned with advice and assistance and with lend-lease. Neither in his original orders nor in later communications was he told what to do in the event the United States should go to war with Japan. Nor was he instructed to discuss with the Chinese any plans for military cooperation. No one had yet decided what would happen to the AVG if war came to the United States or what part China was to play in the over-all strategy for the defeat of Japan.

THE LAST DAYS

As military preparations were being made for a war that seemed inevitable Secretary of State Cordell Hull since February 1941 had been engaged in conversations with the Japanese Ambassador, Admiral Kichisaburo Nomura, in an attempt to reach an agreement that would guarantee the integrity of China and of southeast Asia.[63] The effort was futile, however, for the demands of the Japanese were irreconcilable with the policies of the United States, and as the conversations continued through the summer and the fall of 1941 their chief result was to postpone action that seemed ever more certain to come. Hope of some alternative remained, however, and again and again the Chief of Naval Operations and Chief of Staff of the Army urged the President to avoid anything that might provoke Japanese attack before the defenses of the Philippines should have been built up and the armed forces of the United States strengthened.[64] Economic pressures in the form of embargoes on exports, including, in July, petroleum, and freezing of Japanese assets in the United States were no more effective than diplomatic negotiations. In November a special representative, Saburo Kurusu, was sent from Tokyo to Washington and the last Japanese proposal for settlement of the differences was made. In the words of Mr. Hull:

> The plan thus offered called for the supplying by the United States to Japan of as much oil as Japan might require, for suspension of freezing measures, for discontinuance by the United States of aid to China, and for withdrawal of moral and material support from the recognized Chinese Government. It contained a provision that Japan would shift her armed forces from southern Indochina to northern Indochina, but placed no limit on the number of armed forces which Japan might send into Indochina and made no provision for withdrawal of those forces until after either the restoration of peace between Japan and China or the establishment of an "equitable" peace in the Pacific area. While there were stipulations against further extension of Japan's armed force into southeastern Asia and the southern Pacific (except Indochina), there were no provisions which would have prevented continued or fresh Japanese aggressive activities

in any of the regions of Asia lying to the north of Indochina--for example, China and the Soviet Union. The proposal contained no provisions pledging Japan to abandon aggression and to revert to peaceful courses.[65]

After discussions among military and civilian officials in Washington Mr. Hull insisted that before the United States would agree to resuming commercial relations with Japan the Japanese must agree to withdraw their forces from China and stop their policy of aggression in the Far East. This was an impasse with little prospect of resolution. Japanese warships were already steaming toward Pearl Harbor.

While these diplomatic discussions were being held with Japan, U.S. aid to Britain had become more and more open and involved U.S. forces nearer and nearer to active warfare. Something of what was being done in relation both to Japan and to Germany was published in the press, and the hurried attempts to rearm and to mobilize an army by selective service were directly affecting large segments of the American people. There was fear of war and in some quarters expectation of it, but there were few indeed who expected Japan to strike before Germany. Thus when war came there was nation-wide surprise, at the enemy, the objective, and the horror of the attack without warning.

SUMMATION

In December 1941 the United States was speeding preparation of its military forces for war, should war be forced upon it. The Army had already reached a strength of 1,500,000 men, the Navy and Marine Corps, 400,000.[66] The weapons of war were being turned out in large number to equip the U.S. forces and to support the resistance of Great Britain, Russia, and China. U.S. ground and air forces had been sent to Iceland, and U.S. Navy ships were escorting convoys in the Atlantic. On the distant islands of the Pacific Ocean small groups of Americans were scattered as defenders of U.S. territory. With the possible exception of Hawaii none of these outposts had sufficient strength to resist a determined attack, although reenforcements were on the way to the Philippines even as the enemy struck. There had been hope that the Japanese would wait until the defenses there were stronger, but it is probable that the completed reenforcement program would not have provided enough to hold the islands against the invasion that came. It is also doubtful that the Pacific Fleet, even with the elements that were lost at Pearl Harbor, could have maintained a line of support to the Philippine defenders.

Exactly how a war with Japan would be fought could not be determined in advance, for under U.S. policy it was the enemy who would strike the first blow. Although U.S. intelligence did ascertain approximately when the blow was coming, it did not establish where, and so no one could predict the circumstances under which the United States would have to start the long road to the defeat of Japan.

Certain prewar decisions did set the general pattern the war would follow. There was the agreement for cooperation with the British to concentrate first on the defeat of Germany and maintain the defensive in the Pacific. That, however, did not anticipate that the Japanese would strike such a blow that U.S. public opinion would be unified behind a desire to hit back hard and fast.

Years of discussions of the best route across the Pacific had evolved a concept of a step-by-step advance due west to a position from which Japan could be brought to its knees by economic pressure, blockade, and air attacks. The specific points to be taken could not be determined until relative strengths and positions were known, but the general conception was of an advance through the Marshalls and Carolines to the Philippines. In Rainbow No. 5 U.S. naval forces were assigned the task of initiating this program. When war came, however, direct progress along the route through the central Pacific was complicated by the Japanese infiltration in strength into the Dutch East Indies, the Bismarck Archipelago, and the Solomon Islands, and especially by the establishment in the Pacific Theater of two equal commands, the Southwest Pacific Area (SWPA) under General Douglas MacArthur and the Pacific Ocean Areas (POA) under Admiral Chester Nimitz. There were two converging thrusts to the western Pacific rather than a single direct one. Progress on both was speeded up as amphibious techniques were perfected and the potentialities of carrier task forces, long range bombing, and other new weapons of warfare, largely undeveloped in the prewar years, were realized. Still it was a long road to victory in the Pacific.

Besides the British in the fight against Japan there were the Dutch in the Netherlands East Indies and the Chinese. But there were only general prewar agreements for cooperation with the British and the Dutch during the initial defensive period. U.S. and British strategists still disagreed as to whether the defense of the Far East should be based on Singapore or on the whole southwestern Pacific area. There were no plans at all for partnership with China in the fight against Japan. The United States was sending lend-lease material there and a military mission had been sent to provide advice and technical assistance. Current planning included equipping thirty ground divisions; but there were already strong indications that the Chinese Government was in no hurry to do so, preferring to build a big air force that could defeat Japan without protracted ground fighting. How Chinese forces could coordinate action with those of the United States and Great Britain or whether any attempts toward coordination would be made was unknown.

During the last weeks of November U.S. military intelligence disclosed that Japan was preparing for further action. Movements of Japanese forces in the far Pacific appeared to foreshadow attacks on some point in southeast Asia, the Dutch East Indies, or possibly the Philippines. Instead, on 7 December 1941 Japanese bombers attacked the U.S. Fleet in its base at Pearl Harbor.

Japan held the advantage, and for the first long months of war the United States and its allies would have to struggle to try to hold the defensive line somewhere while Japan determined the course of war in the Pacific.

Chapter II

ADJUSTING FOR WAR IN THE PACIFIC

EMERGENCY MEASURES

Meeting the Emergency in Hawaii

    For several days following the Japanese attack on Pearl Harbor on 7 December 1941, information concerning the forces making the raid was contradictory and incomplete. No one in Washington could feel certain that Japan might not next attempt to land a force in the Hawaiian Islands, or launch attacks on the West Coast, Alaska, or the Panama Canal. At the same time, word came constantly of new advances by Japanese forces at other points in the Pacific and Far East. Within the first week of hostilities in the Pacific the enemy virtually eliminated U.S. air power in the Philippines; with undisputed superiority in the air, Japanese planes attacked the islands and Japanese troops landed on Luzon; Guam was occupied; the British garrison withdrew from the mainland to the island of Hong Kong in the face of Japanese attack; landings were made in Malaya, and the British ships *Repulse* and *Prince of Wales* were sunk by torpedo planes as they tried to attack the Japanese naval escort; Thailand surrendered to the Japanese; and air attacks were made on points in Burma, the Netherlands East Indies, and numerous islands throughout the Pacific. As December passed, the strength and wide extent of the Japanese onslaught and the comparative weakness of the forces of the Associated Powers, in the air, and on the sea, became increasingly apparent.
    In the Atlantic there was no comparable crisis. Merchant ship sinkings in November 1941 had been the lowest since March of the previous year. On the Eastern Front, the Russians had retaken Rostov and were in the process of driving the Germans back from the outskirts of Moscow. In Africa, the situation was relatively quiet. General Sir Claude Auchinleck's drive to relieve Tobruk was not to be initiated until January. Lend-Lease and the policy of "aid short of war" had been under way for some months, and U.S. vessels were escorting convoys in the North Atlantic. Declarations of war between the United States and Germany and between the United States and Italy on 11 December were hardly more than a formality and altered the situation only to the extent that hostilities had now officially and openly begun.

ADJUSTING FOR WAR IN THE PACIFIC

In the first days of the war Army and Navy planners reviewed their pre-war studies of German and Japanese capabilities and attempted to estimate the course the enemy might follow and the moves the United States could make in the immediate future. A study completed by the Army War Plans Division on 12 December 1941 illustrates how the situation looked at the time.[1] The Japanese, the Army planners thought, were capable of doing one or more of five things:

1. Continue operations against Philippines and Malay.
2. Attack or contain Hawaiian Islands.
3. Secure a base in the Aleutians.
4. Possibly an air attack against Panama Canal.
5. Raid shipping and possibly important exposed military objectives on West Coast.

The United States was currently limited to defensive action in the Pacific and could:

1. Resist Japanese attacks against the Philippines with present forces. Reinforcement of these forces to the extent necessary to insure the defense of the Philippines is not possible.
2. Reinforce Hawaii and make determined defense of that outpost. The naval situation in the Pacific is such that a successful defense of Hawaii cannot be absolutely assured.
3. Defend Alaska, the West Coast of Continental United States, and Panama Canal. Prevent hostile lodgement in Central and South America north of the 10° South Latitude.[2]

In the Atlantic and Mediterranean the planners predicted:
1. Greatly increased air activity over [the] North Atlantic....
2. German occupation of Northwest and West Africa and air and submarine operations therefrom over the South Atlantic....
3. The operations in 1 and 2 may be followed by an all-out attack on England.
4. A German attack against the Middle East, with a view to cleaving the British Empire and joining hands with Japan, is possible but less likely than the other operations indicated....

The United States in this area could:

1. Defend the Continental United States, the Panama Canal, and our outlying bases in the Atlantic and Carribean.
2. Prevent hostile lodgement in Central and South America, north of 10° South Latitude.
3. Immediate and drastic curtailment of our aid to associated powers will be necessary to insure the above.

For some months prior to December 1941, military leaders in both the United States and Great Britain had been developing plans for a possible war in which they would be fighting both Germany and Japan. Neither ABC-1 nor Rainbow No. 5,[3] the current war plans for such an eventuality, had counted on the initiation of hostilities by a major blow to the Pacific Fleet, executed simultaneously with strong offensives throughout the Pacific area. It had been agreed in ABC-1 that the Atlantic and European area was the decisive theater, that the initial primary effort would be made there, and that the strategy elsewhere would be defensive. Although this order of priority remained the accepted basic strategic principle, the crises in the Pacific in December 1941 forced the U.S. Chiefs of Staff immediately to turn their attention to attempting to bolster up the U.S. position in that area.

The Joint Board, as the only top level military organization available for coordinating the efforts of the Army and the Navy, met frequently during the first weeks of the war. In addition, the Army Chief of Staff, General George C. Marshall, and the Chief of Naval Operations, Admiral Harold R. Stark, were constantly in touch, as were their respective planners. The official minutes of the Joint Board meetings give a fair idea of the numerous problems that developed as both Army and Navy attempted to put their own war plans into operation and to distribute their own resources, inadequate in most essential items, where they were most vitally needed. In many cases action was taken individually, and it was frequently at the Joint Board meetings that each service was informed what the other was doing.

The first step in repairing the damage was to try to remedy the situation in Hawaii, especially the weakened condition of the Pacific Fleet,[4] while expecting at any time that the Japanese would follow up the success they had achieved on 7 December with a full-scale attack. It had been provided in ABC-1 that, when the United States became actively engaged in the war, certain units of the Pacific Fleet would be transferred to the Atlantic to relieve the British Force "H" at Gibraltar, which would then be sent to the Indian Ocean or the Far East.[5] This represented a compromise with the British, who, after the fall of France, were unwilling to send a major naval force away from the Atlantic and urged the United States to send its fleet to the Far East to be based on Singapore. Subsequent developments during 1941 had involved the United States more closely in the war in the Atlantic, and it had become necessary to initiate movements of ships from the Pacific during that spring with the transfer of three battleships, one carrier, four cruisers, and seventeen destroyers from the Pacific Fleet.[6] The British later decided to add considerably to their naval forces in the Far East, and the process was under way when the Japanese struck. Immediately after the attack on 7 December, the Navy Department assessed the damage and decided to order back to the Pacific approximately the same force which had earlier been removed--three battleships, one carrier, nine destroyers, thirty-six patrol bombers, and twelve old submarines.[7]

Strengthening of the fleet alone was not sufficient. The large losses in planes, equipment, and personnel and the damage to shore installations in Hawaii weakened the islands as a defense post between Japan and the west coast of the United States itself. How to find reenforcements for Hawaii and deliver them there before the Japanese could attack again was the chief topic of discussion at the first war meetings of the Joint Board. Although all members were anxious that the Hawaiian Islands be made secure, they differed as to the measures which could be taken immediately. The Navy members, concerned about protection of the fleet, were particularly anxious over the inadequacies of Hawaiian defenses. Major units of the fleet were being kept at sea temporarily for protection. The Army was faced with a shortage of equipment, particularly of vital antiaircraft equipment, and the necessity of distributing it not only to Hawaii but also to Army installations on the west coast of the United States and the Panama Canal, at either of which points the Army particularly feared the enemy might strike next. The Army members insisted on the importance of these other responsibilities[8] and could not agree with Admiral Stark, who "expressed his opinion that all available antiaircraft artillery should be diverted to Hawaii even at the risk of taking a chance on leaving some installations in the United States unprotected."[9] Nor were they prepared to support enthusiastically a Navy plan sponsored by Admiral Turner for dispersion of a large air force on bases throughout the Hawaiian Islands. They did, however, recommend immediately strengthening defenses of Oahu with all possible measures short of jeopardizing the security of the Panama Canal and the Continental United States.[10]

Both services proceeded to make plans for shipping reenforcements to Hawaii. But their efforts were not coordinated, and lack of understanding of each other's problems led to hard feelings and further complicated the situation.[11] Despite delays, however, planes, men, and equipment did begin to move toward Hawaii.[12]

The physical defenses of Hawaii were not the only weakness the Joint Board undertook to remedy in December 1941. The surprise attack indicated dramatically the difficulties inherent in coordinate responsibility for defense of the whole Hawaiian area. It likewise made President Roosevelt and his advisors determined that there be no uncertainty as to responsibility for protection of the Panama Canal.

The question of establishing unified command in certain coastal frontier areas in accordance with the principle defined in "Joint Action of the Army and the Navy, 1935"[13] had been under consideration for some time preceding the outbreak of war. But the Army and Navy members of the Joint Planning Committee, who were discussing it for Hawaii, Panama, and the Caribbean, had not reached agreement. They disagreed on the areas in which unified command might apply, on the conditions under which one service or the other should exercise it, and, indeed, on the effectiveness of unified command as opposed to mutual cooperation. Their differences remained unresolved on 7 December.[14]

On 12 December 1941, at a meeting with representatives of the Army,[15] the President decided that a unified command under the Army should be established for defense of the Panama Canal. Admiral

Stark called a meeting of the Joint Board for consideration of the measure the following day. Although some of the Navy members were reluctant to accept Army command of operating naval forces, they had no alternative since the President had already given approval. Indeed, it was recorded that, "Regardless of personal feelings of either Army or Navy, some of the members of the Board were in agreement with the view that unless unified control was affected [sic] by joint agreement between the Army and the Navy, the establishment of a department of National Defense, appointed by the Administration, might be considered a certainty."[16]

Concurrently with plans for Panama, arrangements were made for unity of command in Hawaii under the Commander in Chief, Pacific Fleet, after Admiral Stark submitted a draft directive based on Army proposals.[17] Directives for both were approved by the Joint Board on 17 December, and the new commands were established immediately.[18]

Modification of ABC-1

The combined American-British agreement, ABC-1, and the Army-Navy war plan, Rainbow No. 5, were ordered placed in effect by both Army and Navy as soon as hostilities began. Almost at once the Navy command in Washington decided that, although ships were to be ordered from the Atlantic to replace those lost at Pearl Harbor, the Pacific Fleet even so augmented would not be able to carry out all the tasks with which it was charged. Consequently, the Commander in Chief, Pacific Fleet, was ordered by despatch to modify the tasks assigned by the Navy's version of the war plan.[19] Admiral Stark reported this decision to the Joint Board, whose Army members apparently accepted the Navy's verdict as to the capabilities of its fleet.[20] About ten days later, after the Navy War Plans Division had studied the situation more carefully, this decision was communicated to the British Chiefs of Staff by the Chief of Naval Operations and the Chief of Staff, U.S. Army. They reported that it had been decided that the fleet could not

    (a) Support the forces of the Associated Powers in the Far East area by diverting enemy strength from the Malay Barrier through the denial and capture of positions in the Marshalls;

    (b) Support British naval forces in the area south of the equator, as far west as longitude 155 degrees East;

    (c) Prepare to capture and establish control over the Caroline and Marshall area.

The fleet would now operate under the following tasks:

    (a) Protect the sea communications of the Associated Powers by escorting, covering, and patrolling as required by circumstances, and by destroying enemy raiding forces;

    (b) Support the army in the defense of the Hawaiian Coastal Frontier...;

    (c) Defend Samoa, Midway, Johnston Island and Palmyra Island...;

    (d) Defend Wake...;
    (e) Raid enemy sea communications and positions;
    (f) Destroy Axis sea communications by capturing or destroying vessels trading directly or indirectly with the enemy;
    (g) Protect the territory of the Associated Powers in the Pacific area east of 180th Meridian, and prevent the extension of enemy military power into the Western Hemisphere by destroying hostile expeditions and by supporting land and air forces in denying the enemy the use of land positions in that hemisphere;
    (h) Cover the operations of the naval coastal frontier forces and the Canadian local defense forces;
    (i) Establish fleet control zones, defining their limits from time to time as circumstances require;
    (j) Route shipping of Associated Powers within the fleet control zones.[21]

When the British at ABC-1 had urged projection of the U.S. Fleet to the western Pacific to aid in the defense of Singapore, the U.S. representatives had argued that, by operating against Japanese bases and lines of communication in the central Pacific, the Pacific Fleet would divert enemy forces from the Malay Barrier. Maintenance of the fleet in that area would insure its availability for transfer, in an emergency, to the Atlantic, where the United States would be making its principal effort. Further, capture of the Carolines and Marshalls would be a first step westward in an operation that would culminate in recapture of the Philippines and initiation of an all-out offensive against the Japanese. Now, temporarily, any attempt at an organized offensive was to be postponed.

Reenforcements for the Southwest Pacific

In the years between the wars it had been generally accepted (although Army and Navy opinion was by no means unanimous on the subject) that it would probably prove impossible to hold the Philippines indefinitely against a sustained and powerful Japanese attack. Neither men nor funds were available to add considerably to the island defenses. It was hoped that those forces in the Philippines could hold out until relief could be brought by the fleet across the Pacific. Nevertheless, it was recognized that it would probably be necessary to fight back across the Pacific from the Hawaiian Islands, via the Carolines, Marshalls, and Truk, eventually to retake the Philippines.

With both men and funds more plentiful in the summer of 1941, it was decided by the Army that Philippine defenses could be strengthened sufficiently to make it reasonably certain that they could withstand a strong Japanese attack, although in view of the prior demands of the European Theater it was impractical to attempt to strengthen the islands sufficiently to withstand a maximum Japanese effort. A program for considerable reenforcement with men, planes, and equipment was initiated immediately, but it was not scheduled for completion until at least February or March 1942.[22] Consequently, during the prolonged negotiations with the Japanese in the fall of 1941, the U.S. Chiefs repeatedly urged the President to avoid any political moves which might precipitate Japanese action before the projected reenforcement had been completed.

Despite U.S. efforts, however, the project was still incomplete when, on 8 December, the Japanese commenced an attack in force upon the islands of the Philippines. They immediately achieved overwhelming superiority in the air by destroying on the ground half of the U.S. heavy bomber force and a third of the fighter strength and by damaging many of the other seventeen B-17's, fifteen P-35's, and fifty P-40's.[23] Two days later Japanese troops landed on northern Luzon and the battle of the Philippines was on.[24]

In Washington the problem of getting reenforcements to the Philippines was one of the major ones facing the military leaders in the days after the Pearl Harbor attack. A convoy with equipment and troops for the Philippines was already in the South Pacific when the war broke. Uncertain what might develop the Navy immediately ordered it to put into Suva in the Fijis and to await further orders.[25] On 9 December the Joint Board considered what disposition should be made of these ships and their cargo. With the fleet reduced and air forces decimated, it appeared no longer possible to get shipping through to the Philippines. Navy members, led by Admiral Turner, suggested that the planes and ammunition be sent back to Hawaii where they would help alleviate the critical situation, and that consideration be given to sending personnel and equipment to Port Darwin, the Netherlands East Indies, or Samoa, the latter an important base for guarding the line of communications to Australia. Further consideration of these suggestions was postponed, and it was agreed that the convoy and its contents (with the exception of one artillery regiment which was to be returned to the United States) should be ordered back to Hawaii to help meet the emergency there.[26]

The President, however, supported by the Secretary of War and undoubtedly influenced by public demands for assistance to the Philippine defenders, felt strongly that every attempt should be made to deliver reenforcements to the Far East, lest it appear that the United States had abandoned the area. Consequently, the Joint Board reconsidered its decision the day after it was made. The members weighed the comparative risk involved in proceeding to Australia as against returning to Hawaii, the possibility of getting some of the supplies through to the Philippines, the use to which they might be put in Australia or the Dutch East Indies, the immediate needs of Hawaii, and the possibility of supplying Hawaii with defense materials from the United States. Army members followed the President's lead in recommending that the convoy proceed to Australia, believing that the needs of Hawaii could be adequately supplied from the United States and hopeful that at least the planes could somehow be delivered to the Philippines. Ultimately, it was decided to order the convoy to Brisbane, whence its movements were to be directed in accordance with the situation obtaining at the time of its arrival.[27] Brigadier General Julian F. Barnes, as Senior Officer in the convoy, was then designated Commander, U.S. Troops in Australia, given unlimited credit from the Treasury, and ordered to make every effort to deliver the planes in his cargo to the Philippines.[28]

Despite the increasing hopelessness of the situation in the Philippines, it was then determined in the War Department, with the support of the President, "to make every effort to reenforce the United States Army forces in the Far East,...and to make endeavor to provide these forces with additional munitions and supplies." There was opposition to this decision, particularly among naval leaders who, feeling that the weakened fleet could not rush to the aid of the Philippines without running unwarranted risks since Japan already exercised almost complete control over both sea and air around the islands, thought that effort should be concentrated rather on trying to defend a position farther south where the prospects of success would be brighter. There were, however, several reasons for not deserting the Philippines. Although, isolated as they were, the Philippines could not be of great immediate strategic importance, the staunch resistance of their defenders could contain, and was containing, considerable numbers of Japanese troops. Already, rumors had begun to spread in the islands that the United States was going to make no attempt to break the Japanese blockade. It was feared that if such reports were widely believed the Filipino resistance might collapse. At the same time, in the United States itself, public opinion was growing for rushing support to the island defenders. And from the theater General MacArthur continually urged that every attempt be made to assist him and his forces.[29]

In mid-December the Army set about trying in one way or another to deliver reenforcements to the Philippines. To expedite transfer of supplies arriving in Australia orders were issued on 17 December to Major General George H. Brett, then arriving in China from the Middle East, to assume command of a service of supply in Australia with the "primary immediate mission" of forwarding "vitally needed equipment to the Philippines as rapidly as possible."[30]

In the meantime, the Commander in Chief, Asiatic Fleet, in accordance with the Navy's plan not to retain the fleet in the Philippines where it could not be supported, had ordered Admiral Glassford to retire southward from Manila with the major surface vessels, constituted as Task Force 5. Admiral Glassford proceeded to Soerabaya, where he remained with his combat vessels, and sent his auxiliaries on to Port Darwin. To him the Chief of Naval Operations issued orders to assist the Army in transporting equipment by air when practicable and in transferring the ships of the convoy soon to arrive in Australia from Brisbane to Port Darwin. Task Force 5 and the remainder of the Asiatic Fleet, when it was considered advisable for the latter to leave Manila, would be based on Port Darwin.

To assure cooperation between the Army and the Navy in the effort to deliver reenforcements to the Philippines the Joint Planning

Committee made recommendations for a joint agreement which was approved by the Joint Board on 21 December.[31] It outlined the following policy: As much material as possible was to be procured directly in the southwest Pacific area. Further reenforcements, including smaller aircraft, were to be shipped from U.S. ports to Brisbane, whence they would be forwarded overland and/or by ship to Port Darwin. From there they would be transported to Luzon, by air, by suitably escorted fast ships, or by any available small vessels, to proceed independently to any port that might be accessible.

To assure coordination of Army and Navy efforts orders were issued to General Brett and Admiral Glassford to

(a) Cooperate...in the protection of Army reenforcements, and Army and Navy logistic material required by the U.S. Army and Navy Forces in the Philippines.
(b) Cooperate with United States Army authorities (United States Naval authorities), and with Australian authorities, in the establishment and protection of a joint Army and Navy base in Port Darwin, and in the defense of northwest Australia.
(c) As soon as practicable a conference should be held between Major General Brett and Admiral Hart's representatives for the purpose of agreeing upon common action.[32]

Although safe delivery of cargo vessels was problematical, it was hoped that at least some planes could reach the islands. The route from Australia to the Philippines was hazardous, for enemy forces were already in position to attack from the air. Early in December development was begun of a route from Natal to Cairo to Basra to Karachi to Rangoon and Singapore. But it was too late to use that for delivery of planes to the Philippines.

The Japanese attack in the Philippines moved more swiftly than U.S. attempts to deliver reenforcements to check it. On Christmas Day, Major General Lewis H. Brereton, with the last of the heavy bombers on Luzon (the rest had preceded him) which could no longer be maintained in the Philippines, left for Soerabaya and ultimately Darwin.[33] The surviving planes offered valiant opposition to the Japanese but with negligible effect on the disproportionate forces. In a series of rapid moves the Japanese made landings in force on Luzon and Mindanao and, halted only briefly by courageous but ineffectual U.S. resistance, moved rapidly ahead. By 24 December General MacArthur decided to give up the attempt to hold Manila, declare it an open city, and withdraw his forces to Bataan and Corregidor.[34]

Before the joint plans for coordinating efforts to deliver supplies to the Philippines could be carried out, it was realized in Washington that the islands could not be supported. On 1 January General MacArthur estimated that without support his garrison could hold out for three months at most. He further stressed the critical nature of the situation by saying:

...I wish to reemphasize my firm belief that loss of the Philippines will be followed by the fall of the NEI [Netherlands

East Indies] and Singapore. Even if this were not true, the yielding of the Philippines by default and without a major effort would mark the end of white prestige and influence in the east. In view of the Filipinos effort the United States must move strongly to their support and promptly or withdraw in shame from the Orient....[35]

In reply, General Marshall could only say that Washington was trying to devise some way of halting the Japanese advance and order General MacArthur to defend his position as long as possible since "every day of time you gain is vital to the concentration of the overwhelming power necessary for our purpose." With the limited means available and the demands of other theaters of war, it was impossible immediately to assemble a powerful naval force to attack Japanese lines of communication and to advance to the Philippines as General MacArthur continually urged. The only hope was to try to achieve air supremacy in the near future and to build up a powerful force to oppose the enemy advance.[36] U.S. military authorities fully realized that, despite the hopelessness of the situation in the Far East, for the sake of morale both at home and in the area, as long as the forces in the Philippines and in the East Indies area could hold out an attempt must be made to support them. Although it was realized that most of the area would probably be lost, for psychological as well as strategical reasons attempts to assist the defenders continued.

At the instigation of the President at the end of December, the Army War Plans Division undertook a new study of the possibility of conducting successful operations for relief of the Philippines.[37] The resulting paper, dated 3 January, initialed without comment by the Army Chief of Staff and the Secretary of War, contained a careful analysis of the strategic importance of the Philippines and the effect their loss would have on the whole Far East Area. After a survey of the operations involved in re-establishing a position there, and the forces available for their execution in contrast to those required, the conclusions were entirely negative:

    a. That the forces required for the relief of the Philippines cannot be placed in the Far East area within the time available.

    b. That allocation to the Far East area of forces necessary to regain control of the Philippines would necessitate an entirely unjustifiable diversion of forces from the principal theater - the Atlantic.

    c. That the greatest effort in the Far East area which can be sustained on strategic grounds is that contemplated by the Chiefs of Staff in their directive ABC-4/3 (hold Malay Barrier, Burma and Australia, projecting operations to the northward to provide maximum defense in depth).

Consequently, it was recommended that operations for the relief of the Philippines should not be undertaken.[38] Although its policy appears never officially to have had the approval of the President, in effect it was followed. Available forces were inadequate to do otherwise.

By this time arrangements for a unified command in the Far East (ABDACOM) were practically complete. Although the Philippines were nominally included in it, they played no part in its operation. Sporadic attempts were made by the Commander, ABDA Naval Forces, to deliver supplies by submarine and other available craft to the defenders of Bataan, but although the morale value of the small shipments that arrived was high their military value was doubtful, and the submarines were considered of more vital importance for operations against enemy convoys. Bombing attacks on Japanese targets in the Philippines by U.S. planes based in the Dutch East Indies were largely psychological gain. With no immediate hope of relieving the Philippines, military leaders in Washington directed their efforts toward attempting to build up a powerful force in Australia and the south Pacific, to oppose the enemy advance as far north as possible, and ultimately to undertake an all-out offensive for his defeat.

THE ARCADIA CONFERENCE

Agreement on Grand Strategy

In late December 1941 Prime Minister Churchill and the British Chiefs of Staff arrived in Washington for a series of discussions with their opposite numbers in the United States, to draw up plans for cooperating in prosecution of the war against Germany and Japan.[39] The United States was represented at this conference, known as Arcadia, by the chiefs of the military services: Admiral Harold R. Stark, USN, Chief of Naval Operations; Admiral Ernest J. King, USN, who had been appointed Commander in Chief, U.S. Fleet, on 20 December 1941; General George C. Marshall, USA, Commanding General of the Field Forces and Chief of Staff, U.S. Army; and Lieutenant General Henry H. Arnold, Chief of Air Forces and Deputy Chief of Staff; U.S. Army. Various staff officers of the Army, Navy, and Marine Corps also attended some of the meetings.[40]

The British Chiefs of Staff took advantage of the ocean voyage from London to discuss the views they would present and to prepare papers on some of the projects they were planning to support at the Washington conference. The problem that loomed largest in their minds was what effect the shocking blow struck by the Japanese would have on U.S. military thinking, whether their new allies would feel it desirable to change the established strategic concept and turn full attention to the Pacific rather than concentrating first on the defeat of Germany. In British minds there was no question where the initial effort should be made. Still, the British Chiefs were not unmindful of the advantage held by the Japanese and the threat they were to British territory, particularly to Singapore. Australia and New Zealand also seemed in danger, but to those in the British Isles the peril appeared of smaller proportions. There was concern lest the dominions "down under" demand too much assistance or play upon U.S. sympathies to such an extent that considerable forces would be taken from the European Theater.[41]

While en route to Washington the British Chiefs of Staff sent ahead to the U.S. Chiefs a list of the points on which they hoped to reach agreement.[42] It was a general program:

   (i) Fundamental basis of joint strategy.
   (ii) Interpretation of (i) into terms of immediate Military measures, including re-distribution of forces.
   (iii) Allocation of Joint Forces to harmonize with (i).
   (iv) Long term programme based on (i), including forces to be raised and equipped required for victory.
   (v) Set up joint machinery for implementing (ii), (iii) and (iv).

In response to this the Joint Board prepared for the President its tentative views on the subjects proposed by the British and the broad strategic decisions it felt should be made at the approaching conference.[43]

In developing this review the Navy planners had drafted a brief estimate of the military situation as they saw it at the time.[44] They pointed out that Japan enjoyed a considerable air and naval superiority in the western Pacific which it might use in continued raids on the Hawaiian Islands and on naval detachments and outlying bases (Samoa, Palmyra, Wake, and Midway, in particular). Japan was "heavily" threatening sea communications between the United States and Australasia, and there was even "a distinct possibility" that it might undertake devastating raids on Alaska, the West Coast, and the Panama Canal. The United States still retained most of its fast naval striking forces and submarines, although its defensive strength had been reduced by the Japanese attack to a "dangerously low level." Without many more naval vessels and troops for the Pacific Islands, U.S. sea communications could not enjoy even a reasonable degree of security.

In the Far East the major Japanese attack was against the Malay Peninsula and Burma. At this time enemy troops had landed only in Borneo of the Netherlands East Indies, and the Navy planners thought that the Japanese might intend only to contain the Philippines, postponing complete control and expansion into other areas until success had been attained in southeast Asia. Although with control of all of Malaysia the Japanese were expected to be able to attack communications lines in the Indian Ocean to Australia, India, and the Middle East, the planners did not think that the enemy could "operate in superior strength in both the Pacific Ocean and the Indian Ocean unless the United States and the British Commonwealth sustain further important losses."

As for the Middle East the Navy planners ventured little in the way of predictions. Germany might be unable because of reverses in Russia to undertake an offensive through Turkey. The British might take Benghazi; they probably could not take Tripoli; and if the Germans reenforced French North Africa, the British could not push through it. They must, however, together with Russia, hold Iran, Iraq, the Caucasus, and Syria.

In the Atlantic area the Navy planners feared that the Germans would invade Spain, Portugal, and French North and West Africa, since Germany had not achieved full success in Russia. Removal of naval forces to the Pacific and Indian Ocean might afford an opportunity for Germany and Italy to concentrate strong surface forces. In any case they were expected to increase the use of surface raiders and submarines.

In view of the disastrous blow the Japanese struck at Pearl Harbor, the strong public demand for retaliation it aroused, the potential ability of the Japanese with superior air and sea power to spread their attacks even to the west coast of the United States as well as throughout the Pacific and Far East Areas, and the obvious necessity of rushing reenforcements to the threatened areas, it would not have been surprising if the U.S. Chiefs had decided that efforts should be focused on defeating Japan first and Germany second. But if the U.S. Chiefs gave a change of strategy serious thought in the busy post-Pearl Harbor days, the record does not indicate it. They remained convinced that the decisive theater was Europe and the first enemy to be defeated had to be Germany.[45] This, then, was the root of the Joint Board's statement on the first point the British proposed to discuss.

Realizing that the Associated Powers were not yet in a position to undertake a sustained offensive, the Joint Board prescribed initially the maintenance of the strategic defensive in all areas while local offensives were conducted in appropriate theaters. Ultimately would come an all-out offensive against Germany and its European allies and against Japan. Air forces would have to be built up first, for an air offensive was expected to "precede any other form of decisive offensive action." In support of the common purpose, essential lines of communication would have to be maintained.

In proposing interpretations of the basic strategy into immediate military measures, the Joint Board paper recommended action to be taken by each of the Associated Powers (Russia, China, the British Commonwealth, and the United States). Most of the measures were concerned with the war against Japan, where a crisis existed. They were based on the following circumstances: Russia was containing large portions of the German army; the British Commonwealth was attacking Germans in the Middle East and by air in Germany; the United States lacked only antiaircraft equipment for home defense; China needed military material; and China's safety and the defense of air and sea communications required defense of the Singapore-Philippine-Dutch East Indies area. Under these conditions Russia, alone in direct contact with the Germans in Europe, was to continue its offensive operations. China could do little else than continue its defense, assist in the defense of Burma, and provide bases for air operations against Japan itself. The United States was charged with increasing production and strengthening continental defenses and the defenses of the whole Western Hemisphere. Great Britain and the United States were to cooperate in maintaining air and sea communications and to supply the other powers with such land and air equipment as was possible. Each was not only to build up the defenses of its own possessions but also to assist in defending the whole area by rushing reenforcements to Singapore, the Dutch East Indies, and Burma, and to the Philippines, Dutch East Indies, and Australia, respectively, "to further the security of China and [the] Southwest Pacific." Thus, the U.S. effort which, up to this time, had been directed toward endeavoring to deliver supplies to the Philippines would henceforth be concerned with supplying the whole area of the Far East.

In addition to recommending general measures to be taken by each of the Associated Powers, the Joint Board report proposed tasks to be pursued immediately in each theater of operations. Again the emphasis was on strengthening the Pacific and the Far East. In the Atlantic and Middle East it was proposed to continue current operations and to support Russia and Britain with supplies and ultimately with air power. More specific were the tasks for the Pacific Area:

1. Operate the Pacific Fleet and coastal frontier forces in the Central Pacific, for the protection of sea communications, and in offensive raids for the reduction of Japanese naval strength.
2. *Hawaii* - Build up air and troop strength as rapidly as possible not only in Oahu but in at least three other large islands of the group so that we may have a defended area rather than a single defended position.
3. *Wake and Midway* - Continue to support.
4. *Palmyra, Christmas and Johnston* - Support and build up.
5. *Samoa* - Reenforce.
6. Prepare amphibious and expeditionary forces for overseas efforts.
7. Induce Chile to protect shipping along her coasts.

And for the Far East Area:

1. Support the defense of the Philippines, the Netherlands East Indies, Australia, and New Zealand, building up bases as necessary.
2. Endeavor to obtain Russian assistance in the Far East in any way practicable and with particular reference to the early establishment in Siberia of air forces for operations against Japan.
3. British hold India, and if possible Burma, and Malaya.
4. Dutch hold the Netherlands East Indies.
5. British protect communications from the Cape of Good Hope and the Middle East to India, Malaysia and Australia.
6. Increase support to China.

This was certainly idealistic, for with the Japanese holding the advantage in virtually the entire Pacific and Far East Areas, the U.S. Chiefs could do little but hope that somehow defenses would hold and somewhere reenforcements would be found and rushed to the vital areas.

The third point on the British list of basic problems was the allocation of forces. On this the Joint Board agreed that until military action was more clearly defined U.S. forces should be used to reenforce the Philippine Islands and the Dutch East Indies while available forces of the British Commonwealth went to Singapore, the Dutch East Indies, and Burma.

The Joint Board dismissed the question of a long-term armaments program with a recommendation for joint discussion of necessary adjustments in the prewar Victory Program.[46] Pending such discussion industrial efforts should be accelerated.

The British Chiefs of Staff had reported that they were discussing at some length the joint machinery to be set up to implement the conference decisions. Apparently the Joint Board's discussion of the matter was brief, for it simply proposed the creation of a Supreme War Council (otherwise undefined) with a Military Joint Planning Committee and a Joint Supply Committee to "propose the plans and take the actions necessary to implement approved recommendations."

The President approved the Joint Board paper on 21 December 1941. At that White House meeting it was further decided that the United States should establish a base on Australia, secure the line of communications across the Pacific to it, and, if possible, strengthen the Asiatic Fleet to patrol the whole area of the Southwest Pacific.[47] This was a significant departure from prewar plans which had not anticipated Japanese invasion of such large areas of the Pacific. The use of Australia as a base would result not only in a strategic concept oriented northward from there instead of from bases closer to the United States but would draw large amounts of U.S. resources both for its building up and for the defense of the long route to it across the Pacific.

The Prime Minister and the British Chiefs of Staff arrived in Washington on 22 December. Mr. Roosevelt and Mr. Churchill met that evening with some of their political advisors,[48] and the following day they held the first session with the combined United States-British military staffs.[49] This was an informal meeting. The two heads of state apparently did most of the talking, reporting to the group the topics they had considered the preceding evening. It was a miscellaneous list, including: a declaration of their joint "intentions"; an agreement to send a small number of American bombers to England and troops to Ireland and Iceland; a decision that U.S. troops would not be sent to the Near East; the air route across Africa; an agreement that the British would hold Singapore; a build-up of U.S. forces in Australia for offensives to the north; air operations from China against Japan; the likelihood that Russia would not attack Japan; the importance of Dakar; bases in Ireland; increases of production; the situation in North Africa and the possibility of a U.S. landing there; the President's insistence that American troops must fight somewhere soon; Norway; Brazil; the decentralization of aircraft plants; immediate needs of the United States; a possible German move to the southeast; and the defense of India and Burma. There seems to have been little or no general discussion of these matters at this first plenary meeting. Some of them required no further consideration. Others were political problems. Most of the rest were discussed at greater length in the military conference which started the following day.

The official minutes of the first Arcadia meeting record that there were "informal discussions" of the points that had come up at the White House the night before.[50] Although the minutes are divided topically, there was no formal agenda, and most of the topics were simply discussed briefly with no decision. This was the case with a general review of the situation in the Pacific area and a few remarks on the use of Chinese air bases for the bombardment of Japan. Consideration of Russia's potential participation in the war against Japan was indefinitely postponed when "it was stated" by an unidentified member of the group that if Russia took on another adversary it might jeopardize its efforts against Germany.[51] The only other item directly concerned with the war against Japan was the introduction by the British Chiefs of Staff of a memorandum predicting that there was little likelihood of a Japanese attack in force on the west coast of the United States.[52] This was set aside for further consideration and was not discussed again.

One important paper was introduced and partially revised at this first meeting of the combined military staffs. It was a review of over-all strategy for the defeat of Germany and Japan, prepared by the British Chiefs of Staff.[53] The U.S. Chiefs delayed their approval of the paper for a week, but with a few amendments which they suggested it was finally approved on 31 December 1941. This paper, ABC-4/CS1, was to serve during the year ahead as the authoritative statement of how the war was to be fought and how available resources were to be divided.[54]

The first three paragraphs were a definition of the basic strategic concept:

> 1. At the A[merican]-B[ritish] Staff conversations in February, 1941, it was agreed that Germany was the predominant member of the Axis Powers, and consequently the Atlantic and European area was considered to be the decisive theatre.
>
> 2. Much has happened since February last, but notwithstanding the entry of Japan into the War, our view remains that Germany is still the prime enemy and her defeat is the key to victory. Once Germany is defeated, the collapse of Italy and the defeat of Japan must follow.[55]
>
> 3. In our considered opinion, therefore, it should be a cardinal principle of A-B strategy that only the minimum of force necessary for the safeguarding of vital interests in other theatres should be diverted from operations against Germany.

The implications of this statement were then defined. It would involve the achievement of the victory program of armaments, including defense of essential areas of production in the United States, the United Kingdom, and Russia. Vital lines of communication, both sea and air, would have to be maintained, by well-balanced dispositions of naval and air forces and by holding and capturing unspecified essential bases. Germany was to be attacked in three ways: by closing and tightening the ring (defined as a line Archangel-Black Sea-Anatolia-the northern seaboard of the Mediterranean-the western seaboard of

Europe) around Germany; by wearing down Germany's resistance through bombing, blockade, subversive activities, and propaganda; and by offensives against Germany, probably not in 1942, but perhaps in 1943, by returning to the continent across the Mediterranean, from Turkey into the Balkans, or directly in Western Europe.

In the meantime, in the war against Japan, activity was to be directed toward "Maintaining only such positions in the Eastern theatre as will safeguard vital interests...and denying to Japan access to raw materials vital to her continuous war effort while we are concentrating on the defeat of Germany." This restricted objective was considerably extended by a definition of the meaning of "safeguarding vital interests": First, it would be necessary to maintain the security of Australia, New Zealand, and India and to support the Chinese war effort. How this was to be done was not suggested. In the second place, "points of vantage from which an offensive against Japan can eventually be developed must be secured." Presumably this did not mean that new positions should be seized, for the immediate objective was to be to hold Hawaii, Alaska, Singapore, the East Indies Barrier, the Philippines, Rangoon, the route to China, and the maritime provinces of Siberia.

There was no attempt in ABC-4/CS1 to estimate what this program would entail. It was, in fact, specifically stated that the minimum forces that would be required to hold the positions in the Pacific would have to be "a matter of mutual discussion." Nor was there consideration of whether available resources were sufficient to support the general program outlined. American and British staffs had agreed in broad terms without analyzing the implications of the agreement to reach a common understanding. The distribution of resources to the various projects and the procedure for attaining the objectives outlined were to require numerous papers and lengthy discussions in the year ahead.

Disposition of Reenforcements

As the combined military staffs met for the second time on Christmas Day of 1941, the situation in the Far East had assumed an extremely critical aspect. Guam had been occupied on 11 December, Wake Island on the twenty-second. In the Philippines, General MacArthur was starting to withdraw his troops to Bataan, and Admiral Hart was preparing to depart with his command for Soerabaya. General Brereton and his remaining bombers were leaving for Soerabaya and Darwin. The British had lost two major ships, *Repulse* and *Prince of Wales*, two days after war started. In Malaya, British troops were retreating before the Japanese advance; U.S. Military Intelligence was predicting air attacks on Singapore in two weeks and siege within a month.[56] British forces in Hong Kong were surrendering on that very Christmas Day. The first Japanese troops had landed in Borneo on the twenty-second. Thailand had ceased resistance, and the Japanese were attacking Burma. Throughout the area, the prescribed Allied "strategic defensive" had more the proportions of a "strategic withdrawal." It was apparent that something would have to be done soon.

Mr. Roosevelt had met with some of the British representatives the night before, and in the course of discussion the President had stated that it seemed unlikely that land and air reenforcements then en route to the Philippines via Australia could reach their destination. He recommended that they "should be utilized in whatever manner might best serve the joint cause in the Far East." Together with the Prime Minister, he requested that the combined staffs meet the next day to see what should be done.[57]

The U.S. Chiefs of Staff were not enthusiastic about combined discussion of the allocation of resources in the Far East, particularly as long as the Philippines were still in U.S. possession.[58] General Marshall expressed his view that it was more important to establish some sort of unified command in the southwestern Pacific area than to attempt to settle details of allocations of resources. The British Chiefs did not agree with him, however, and urged that the disposition of forces should be settled first. They were concerned lest too much of the total available resources be diverted to the Pacific. Ultimately it was agreed that the Joint (i.e., combined) Planning Committee[59] should be directed to prepare a study of what ought to be done with the reenforcements arriving in the Southwest Pacific.

On the premise that "Until such time as the wider problem of the unified control of all available forces in the Southwest Pacific Area is solved, the aim must be to reinforce the Philippine Islands, Malaya, and the Netherlands East Indies, to the maximum extent, and to make the best possible arrangements for ensuring the safe arrival and the most effective intervention of these reinforcements," the planners were directed to present recommendations for the disposition of reenforcements expected to be available in the area on 15 January and 1 February 1942. They were to consider three alternative assumptions: "(1) The Philippines and Singapore both hold, (2) Singapore and the Netherlands East Indies hold, but the Philippines do not," and "(3) Neither Singapore nor the Philippines hold."[60] The report was finished on 28 December 1941, but approval was delayed until 31 December, when the Chiefs of Staff had reached agreement on unified command in the area.[61]

The planners recognized that the strength of forces currently in the Southwest Pacific theater was insufficient to maintain the defensive position the basic strategic concept prescribed for the area. Consequently, immediate reenforcements for defense would have to be provided and operations so conducted as to defend the area and prepare to undertake an offensive at the appropriate time. In furtherance of this concept they proposed a general strategic policy:

 a. To hold the Malay Barrier, defined as the line Malay Peninsula, Sumatra, Java, North Australia, as the basic defensive position of the Far East Area, and to operate air and sea forces in as great depth as possible forward of the Barrier in order to oppose the Japanese southward advance.

 b. To hold Burma and Australia as essential supporting positions for the Far East Area, and Burma as essential to the support of China and to the defense of India.

  c. To reestablish communications with Luzon and to support the Philippines' Garrison.
  d. To maintain communications to Burma and Australia, and to and within the Far East Area.
  e. To obtain in the Far East Area and Australasia all possible supplies to relieve shipping requirements.

This policy did not differ essentially in respect to the areas considered vital from the early statement approved by the Joint Board before the Arcadia Conference opened.[62] It did differ, however, in that there was no division of responsibility between the United States and the United Kingdom.

Annexing lists of the American, British, Dutch, and Australian forces already in the Far East or scheduled for arrival there, the Joint Planning Committee recommended their deployment in the three alternative circumstances:

  (a) Under the assumption that the Philippines and Singapore both hold, the total reinforcements available up to 1st February, 1942,...should go forward as now arranged, subject to the direction of the commander to whom they are assigned.

  (b) Under the assumption that Singapore and the Netherlands East Indies hold, but the Philippines do not, the total U.S. reinforcements available up to 1st February, 1942, should be employed in furtherance of the defense of key points on the Malay Barrier, and for protection of the vital lines of communication from the east. In the absence of unity of command, detailed dispositions of these reinforcements must be left to the senior, U.S. Army commander, in collaboration with the senior British, Dutch, and Australian commanders. Under this assumption the planned disposition of British reinforcements remains unchanged.

  (c) Under the assumption that neither Singapore nor the Philippines hold, the total reinforcements available up to 1st February, 1942, be used for the defense of the remainder of the Malay Barrier, Burma, and Australia, U.S. reinforcements being used to the eastward, and British reinforcements to the westward.

By the time the combined chiefs approved this report, it had become a certainty that a unified command would be set up in the area of the southwestern Pacific. Until that should become effective, however, at the suggestion of Admiral Sir Dudley Pound the chiefs agreed to send to the local British and U.S. commanders the statement of general strategic policy as a guide for distribution of the forces which arrived in their theaters.[63]

Establishment of the ABDA Command

  Before the Arcadia Conference opened, American, Dutch, and British representatives had met at Singapore on 18 December, at the suggestion of President Roosevelt, to "report operational plans as they see the situation in the Southern zone."[64] The U.S. Army representative, Lieutenant Colonel Francis G. Brink, Military

Observer in Singapore, was instructed to present the views of Genneral MacArthur, although General MacArthur's insistence on the vital importance of the Philippines to the Allied defensive structure in the Philippines and his call for offensive operations to take advantage of the over-extension of the enemy's lines were not entirely in consonance with military opinion in Washington. There a more practical view was taken of the discrepancy between available resources and demands upon them.

The Singapore Conference met on two days and drew up an agreement which outlined the important military objectives in the area, recommending that steps be taken toward their accomplishment. The final report was not received in Washington until 3 February,[65] but preliminary despatches from Colonel Brink and Mr. Duff Cooper, who had served as chairman, arrived during the Arcadia Conference.[66]

Although Colonel Brink had presented General MacArthur's views of the strategic importance of the Philippines in the final agreement, the traditional British conception of the supreme importance of Singapore had predominated. Singapore's importance, however, was predicated on its position in the defense of the whole Far East Area, rather than on the purely British view of its essential value to the defense of the British Empire.

> The importance of Singapore to the war in the Far East and to the World War could not be exaggerated. Its loss would probably be followed by that of the N.E.I., would confer on the enemy not only the power to isolate Australia and New Zealand from the west, to separate the British Far Eastern Fleet and the American Asiatic Fleet, but would also put at his disposal vast oil supplies and practically all the rubber supplies of the world. Hardly less serious would be the loss of the N.E.I. which would isolate Singapore and deprive the Allies of a naval base of vital importance. The Philippines are also of first rate importance as an advanced and flanking base for offensive action against Japanese lines of communications.

The Japanese attack at this time was still confined principally to Malaya and the Philippines, and it was hoped by the Singapore Conference that stubborn defense of these could hold the enemy away from other points. With only limited forces available in the area the conference agreed on a limited objective: "*a*. To keep the enemy as far north in Malaya as possible and hold him in the Philippines," and "*b*. To prevent the enemy acquiring territory and particularly airdromes which will threaten the arrival of reinforcements." Dispositions of Allied land, sea, and air forces were proposed, lines of communications which must be kept open were outlined, and specific operations to be initiated immediately, largely concerned with delivering reenforcements to vital areas, were proposed. In addition, a list of minimum reenforcements of men and equipment required in Malaya were included.

Subsequently, the U.S. and Dutch naval commanders in the Far East agreed on separate spheres of operations such as the British and Dutch had planned prior to the outbreak of war. Each nation was to retain strategic control of its own forces in its own area, but it was agreed that under certain unspecified conditions forces of one might be placed under operational control of the other.[67]

Colonel Brink drew an important conclusion from the discussions at Singapore. In a preliminary report he said he felt "an immediate need for one supreme head over a combined allied staff for detailed coordination of USA, British, Australian, and Dutch measures for movements to their designated locations, institution and maintenance of air and sea lines of communication and the strategic direction of all operations in [the] Pacific area." He urged that such a unified command be set up both to meet the immediate defensive situation and to make plans for and conduct the offensive operations that would subsequently be undertaken in the area.[68]

Colonel Brink's despatch was brought to the attention of the Assistant Chief of Staff, Army War Plans Division, with a memorandum by Major Elmer J. Rogers, Jr., recommending that establishment of a unified command for the Far East was absolutely essential, and that the matter should be brought up for discussion at the Arcadia Conference.[69]

At the meeting of the American and British staffs on 25 December, in the course of the discussion of what should be done with reenforcements arriving in the Southwest Pacific, General Marshall, who had undoubtedly read the reports and comments on the conference at Singapore, made the following significant remarks:

> ...As a result of what I saw in France and from following our own experience, I feel very strongly that the most important consideration is the question of unity of command. The matters being settled here are mere details which will continuously reoccur unless settled in a broader way. With differences between groups and between services, the situation is impossible unless we operate on a frank and direct basis. I am convinced that there must be one man in command of the entire theater--air, ground, and ships. We can not manage by cooperation. ...If we make a plan for unified command now, it will solve nine-tenths of our troubles.
>
> There are difficulties in arriving at a single command, but they are much less than the hazards that must be faced if we do not achieve this. We never think alike--there are the opinions of those on this side of the table and of the people on the other side; but as for myself, I am willing to go the limit to accomplish this. We must decide on a line of action here and not expect it to be done out there. I favor one man being in control, but operating under a controlled directive from here. We had to come to this in the first World War, but it was not until 1918 that it was accomplished and much valuable time, blood, and treasure had been needlessly sacrificed....[70]

Although General Marshall emphasized that he did not propose placing portions of national forces under commanders of other nationalities and recommended suitable limitations on the commander's power, his proposal was not greeted with a great burst of enthusiasm from either side. The U.S. naval representatives were in favor of a unified command, but there was some hesitation in the group lest national interests be inadequately safeguarded. The official minutes record only one comment on General Marshall's remarks, that of Air Chief Marshal Sir Charles Portal, who expressed the opinion that once the allocation of forces was decided in Washington, operations in the theater would move smoothly. The question of allocations was given priority, and the Joint Planning Committee was directed to study that problem while the question of a unified command was set aside.[71]

The U.S. Chiefs apparently discussed the subject with the President, for on the following day, at a meeting at the White House attended by the Prime Minister, both military staffs, the Secretaries of War and Navy, and Mr. Harry Hopkins, the President inquired whether anything had been done about a unified command, expressing himself as in favor of the idea. Mr. Churchill was initially opposed, feeling particularly that it was impracticable, since there was no continuous line of battle in the Far East such as had existed in France in World War I and "that in some cases the troops are separated by a thousand miles." The Secretary of the Navy, on the other hand, expressed the opinion that this scattered condition was a good argument in favor of a single over-all command.[72]

Following this meeting both the President and General Marshall separately went to work on the Prime Minister, trying to convince him of the advisability of the proposal.[73] Even when persuaded of the merit of the scheme for ground and air forces, the Prime Minister was reluctant to agree to the necessity for including naval forces under a unified command, fearing that their mobility might not be adequately exploited. However, the efforts of the President and General Marshall were ultimately successful.[74]

By 27 December both the Prime Minister and his staff were willing to accept the principle of a unified command, but they hesitated over the question of who should exercise it. Initially they all favored appointment of an American officer. Although they were somewhat concerned that it might make the United States too Pacific-minded, they thought such an appointment would result in the United States sending substantial additional naval forces to the area, which the British were not in a position to do, and which they had consistently and vainly urged of the United States in prewar planning. Moreover, they believed that public opinion both in the United States and in Australia would be better satisfied with an American commander, and that, in the event of an unhappy outcome, the blame would not rest so squarely on the British command. The Prime Minister expressed some surprise when the Americans took the opposite position, and the President and General Marshall proposed that General Sir Archibald Wavell be appointed to the new command.[75]

The Americans felt that the British had a greater interest in the area, and they were probably no more anxious than the British to have the blame in case of failure fall on one of their commanders.

Moreover, the only U.S. officer whom they considered qualified by rank and experience, General MacArthur, was tied up in the Philippines, and the U.S. Chiefs did not think it advisable to attempt to remove him. On the other hand, they maintained that General Wavell's previous command experience and acquaintance with the area made him eminently suitable. The Prime Minister finally accepted the U.S. recommendation and persuaded his staff to agree also. Accordingly, preliminary notification of his appointment was sent to General Wavell, then Commander in Chief, India, while the details of the new organization were still being decided.[76]

Although the principle of a unified command was accepted, there was no immediate haste to establish it. The chiefs were already at work on a project for an expedition to Northwest Africa; they were preparing the combined agreement on grand strategy; and they were concerned as well with numerous problems of supply and operation in both the Atlantic and the Pacific Theaters. It was still necessary for General Marshall to urge them on to develop the project.

Following his original proposal for a unified command at the meeting on 25 December 1941, General Marshall directed Brigadier General Dwight D. Eisenhower, then in the Army War Plans Division, to draw up a draft directive for the new commander.[77] General Marshall presented the report at the combined meeting two days later.[78] After some discussion in which the British Chiefs showed themselves still not entirely convinced of the advisability of such a scheme, the directive was given to the Joint Planning Committee for development. Before the committee's revision was presented, a new problem arose.

Having been persuaded that there should indeed be a unified command in the Far East, on 28 and 29 December Mr. Churchill, with the approval of Mr. Roosevelt and the U.S. Chiefs, reported the proposal to the Lord Privy Seal for approval by the British Cabinet and submission of the plan to the Australian and New Zealand Governments.[79] The details of the new command had not yet been worked out, but it had been agreed that the control would be exercised from Washington and London. Consequently the Prime Minister included in his second telegram a statement that the new commander "would receive his orders from an appropriate joint body, who will be responsible to me as Minister of Defence and to [the] President of the United States, who is also Commander-in-Chief of all United States forces." In the words of Mr. Hopkins, this statement "kicked up a hell of a row."[80]

The British Cabinet immediately inquired as to the composition of this "joint body." The British Chiefs of Staff persuaded the Prime Minister to delay his reply until they had expressed their views, and the question was raised immediately at the combined meeting on 29 December.[81]

The British staff had prepared a proposal for control machinery which provided for the following: The British assumed that the chief problems requiring decisions would be reenforcements, policy changes, and changes in the Supreme Commander's directive. In order to avoid the complications which would evolve from the necessity of including

Dutch, Australian, and New Zealand representatives on a controlling body, the British recommended that no new organization should be established. The Supreme Commander would submit his proposal by despatch to the Chiefs of Staff Committees in London and in Washington. The London Committee would notify the Washington Committee whether or not it would be sending any opinion, would consult the Dutch and Australians, and would ultimately submit its opinion to Washington. The U.S. Chiefs and British representatives would meet in Washington and would in turn submit their recommendations to the President and the Prime Minister and the British Minister of Defence for approval. When this was received, orders would be despatched from Washington to the Supreme Commander.[82]

Admiral King, in the meantime, had been asked by the President for his advice on the matter. He had hurriedly proposed establishment of a Southwestern Pacific Council, consisting of one American, one British, one Dutch, and one Anzac representative, to advise the President and a deputy of the Prime Minister in Washington. But Admiral King was willing to accept the British proposal.[83]

General Marshall was in favor of establishing the command first and worrying later about machinery for controlling it. However, he accepted the opinion of the others that the machinery was part of the command, and the proposal of the British was sent to the President and the Prime Minister for approval.

The following day the President returned an alternate scheme which provided for the establishment of a special body in Washington, consisting of three Americans, three British, and one each Australian, New Zealand, and Dutch representative. This group would receive all direct communications from ABDA and pass the word along to London.[84] The London Committee would submit its opinions to Washington, following receipt of which the Washington Committee would submit recommendations to the President and the Prime Minister. Then the Prime Minister, having consulted the Australian, New Zealand, and Dutch Governments, would report his opinions to the President. When the two of them agreed, orders would be sent to the Supreme Commander.

The combined staffs reconsidered the question but remained convinced that no additional body should be set up. They opposed any possible political domination of strategic decisions and believed that the U.S. Chiefs and representatives of the British Chiefs in Washington would be best equipped to consider ABDA problems in relation to other theaters. Moreover, they saw the disadvantages of trying to direct the war through a large and unwieldy committee. The combined chiefs further agreed that the Dutch and representatives of the Dominions should be consulted only in London, where machinery for consultation with the Dominions already existed, and that the sending back and forth of communications should be minimized by the original duplication of messages from the Supreme Commander to London and Washington. Consequently, with minor changes in phraseology and an explanation of their action, they returned essentially their original proposal to the President.

This time it was accepted.[85] Subsequently the "joint body" was formalized in the organization of the Combined Chiefs of Staff (CCS) in Washington, and the Pacific War Council in London acted as a consultative body there.[86]

This discussion had taken only two days. During that time the Joint Planning Committee had prepared a revised draft of a directive for the new commander.

The draft submitted by General Marshall on 27 December had been intended principally as a basis for discussion and as such had been designed to show "whether a directive could be drawn which would leave the Supreme Commander with enough power to destroy national interests or to exploit one theater without due consideration to another."[87] As a result, close limitation had been placed on the commander's authority. At the meeting of the combined staffs at which General Marshall's draft was discussed, both Admiral Stark and Admiral King had expressed themselves as favoring inclusion of the restrictions in order to assure approval by the governments involved. They felt that the limitations could be modified if they proved excessive. The British Chiefs had approved the draft in general but considered the limitation too great. All had agreed, however, to refer it to the Joint Planning Committee as a basis for development of a realistic directive.

The planners, apparently in a single meeting on 29 December 1941, in the light of the agreements on grand strategy and on the disposition of reenforcements in the southwest Pacific which had already been drafted, produced a revised draft directive which the combined staff planners considered on the following day.[88] With very few alterations they approved it on 31 December and submitted it to the President and Prime Minister.[89] Some revisions were made subsequently at the request of the Dutch Government, and the revised final directive was approved on 10 January 1942.[90]

The directive provided for a unified command over a strategic area including Burma, Malaya, the Netherlands East Indies, the Philippines, and all the sea areas therein contained, as far south as Australia, to be known as the ABDA Area for the national forces (American, British, Dutch, Australian) fighting there.[91]

The decision to include Burma within the area had been the result of some discussion. Before completion of the arrangements for ABDA, the President had insisted that Chiang Kai-shek, who had from the first been clamoring for a part in the formulation of over-all strategy for the war, should be informed of the plan in progress for the Southwest Pacific prior to its publication. Subsequently it was decided to create for Chiang Kai-shek a Chinese theater, including China and such parts of Indo-China and Thailand as became accessible but, because of British opposition, excluding Burma despite its importance as the supply route to China.[92] Burma had recently been transferred from the British Far East Command to the Indian Command, at that time exercised by General Wavell.[93] But now the British and American Chiefs decided that Burma would be better defended as part of ABDA than as part of the Indian Command,

and Burma was included in the draft directive which the combined staffs approved on 31 December 1941. The Chiefs of Staff Committee in London and General Wavell, however, were opposed to removing British Burma from the British Indian Command.[94] Consequently their opinions were considered at length in a full meeting at the White House. On this occasion the President and the Prime Minister stressed the political angle that transferring Burma to the combined command would at least give the appearance of attempting to assist Chiang Kai-shek. General Marshall further introduced the more practical point that "if Burma were excluded from the ABDA area it might appear logical to the Chinese mind that it should be included in the Chinese area, and control of operations be given to Chiang Kai-shek," a possibility most unattractive to the British in particular. Ultimately it was agreed to adhere to the original plan of including Burma in ABDA, a decision that was never approved by General Wavell, who felt that Burma's defense could be more readily handled from India.[95]

The planners' draft provided that all the ABDA governments should be represented on the staff of the Supreme Commander but it included no description of the organization of that staff. To guard against a preponderance of officers of one nationality, at the suggestion of the U.S. Chiefs the combined chiefs added a provision for a Deputy Supreme Commander and, if required, commanders of the combined naval and air forces, to be appointed by the ABDA governments. It had already been decided that Lieutenant General George H. Brett, USA, should be appointed Deputy and Admiral Thomas C. Hart, USN, Commander of the Combined Naval Forces. Air Marshal Sir Richard Peirse, RAF, was subsequently named Commander of the Air Forces and Lieutenant General H. ter Poorten, RNEI Army, Commander of Land Forces.[96]

The directive contained a statement of strategic concept similar to that incorporated in the planners' study on the disposition of reenforcements in the southwest Pacific. When the chiefs approved it, the statement read:

> to maintain initially the strategic defensive. The ABDA Governments intend to provide immediate reinforcements for defense. As additional forces become available, it will become possible to take the offensive and ultimately to conduct an all-out offensive against Japan. The first essential is to gain general air superiority at the earliest possible moment, through the employment of concentrated air power. The piecemeal employment of air forces should be minimized. Although your operations in the near future must be primarily for defense, they should be so conducted as to further preparations for that offensive.[97]

To the draft they had received from the Joint Planning Committee, the chiefs had added the statements, proposed by the U.S. Army representatives, that attainment of air superiority was the first essential and that the air forces in the area must be properly employed. It had already become painfully obvious that without superiority in the air the ABDA powers were very greatly handicapped. Since the air forces immediately available were limited, the U.S. Chiefs were anxious that they be concentrated where their operations could be most effective and not weakened by scattering them in small groups throughout the area.[98]

Between 31 December, when the chiefs approved it, and 2 January, when the ABDACOM directive received the approval of the President and the Prime Minister, the statement of strategic concept was revised to read more strongly:

> not only in the immediate future to maintain as many key positions as possible, but to take the offensive at the earliest opportunity and ultimately to conduct an all-out offensive against Japan. The first essential is to gain general air superiority at the earliest possible moment, through the employment of concentrated air power.... Your operations should be so conducted as to further preparations for the offensive.[99]

Who altered the statement and why it was done are not known. It seems plausible, however, to assume that the intention was to avoid the appearance of having established the new command solely for maintaining the defensive indefinitely and to emphasize that a major organized offensive was contempleted for the earliest possible moment.[100]

The same statement of general strategic policy which had been sent to the theater commanders[101] was repeated in this directive for the ABDA commander. Thus, despite the positive strategic concept, immediate measures would be largely defensive and necessarily so: to hold the Malay Barrier; to hold Burma and Australia, operating as far north in the area as possible; to re-establish communications with Luzon and support the Philippine garrison; and to maintain communications to and within the area.[102]

The duties and authority of the Supreme Commander, as well as the limitations on them, were clearly outlined in his directive. He was assigned command "of all armed forces, afloat, ashore and in the air" then present in the area or in Australia and allocated to it. The scope of his authority was summarized in the statement: "In general, your instructions and orders will be limited to those necessary for effective coordination of forces in the execution of your mission." Specifically, his duties were to "coordinate in the ABDA Area the strategic operations of all armed forces of the ABDA Governments; assign them strategic missions and objectives; where desirable, arrange for the formation of task forces, whether national or international, for the execution of specific operations; and appoint any officer, irrespective of seniority or nationality, to command such task forces." His control was to be exercised through the subordinate commanders. In administrative matters he was limited to suggestions for coordination of facilities, required reports, and broad allocations of materials and such personnel reenforcements as might be sent to the area.[103] "Except in the case of urgent necessity" the Supreme Commander could not alter the basic tactical organization of the national forces under him or subdivide them. To the subordinate commanders was reserved the right of appeal to their respective governments in the event that they considered their national interests would be jeopardized by compliance with the orders of the Supreme Commander. The Supreme Commander in turn was protected by an agreement that none of the governments concerned would reduce its forces in the area without first notifying him of the intention. All the ABDA governments pledged support "jointly and severally... in the execution of the duties and responsibilities as herein defined, and in the exercise of the authority herein delegated and limited."[104]

With the chiefs' previous agreement on machinery for control of the ABDA Command from Washington included as an annex, the directive was sent to the President and the Prime Minister and to the Dutch and Dominion Governments for approval. Australia and New Zealand, although they felt they should have been party to the discussions, accepted the terms of the directive. The Dutch were upset that they had not been consulted earlier in the proceedings and were offended that none of the three most important functions of the new commands had been given to a Dutch officer who would be more intimately acquainted with the war area than the Americans or the British. In addition, pressure was put upon the U.S. War and State Departments by the Dutch representatives in Washington in an attempt to achieve Dutch representation on the controlling body in Washington. The combined American-British staffs realized, however, that the Dominions would also clamor for the same arrangement, and the result would be an unwieldy committee. Consequently, they tried to satisfy the Dutch by agreeing to amendments offered by the U.S. Chiefs which specified that the Netherlands Government in London would be consulted before the British Government's opinions on ABDA problems were sent to the Combined Committee in Washington. They also assured the Dutch that when technical information or advice was required, their representatives in Washington would be called in for consultation.[105] The directive was approved in final form on 10 January 1942, and orders were sent to General Wavell.

Formal agreement on a unified command in ABDA was one of the significant achievements of the Arcadia Conference. Handling of the numerous problems involved in its establishment and operation forced the newly formed Combined Chiefs of Staff organization at the start of its career to make decisions and establish procedures and precedents for the years of war still ahead.

Strengthening the South and Southwest Pacific

After the combined meeting of 31 December 1941, the British military staff and the Prime Minister went to Canada for talks with Dominion leaders, and the Arcadia Conference did not reconvene until 10 January.[106] On that occasion final approval was given to the directive for the Supreme Commander of the ABDA Area, progress on planning for Super-Gymnast (the plan for occupation of northwest Africa) was discussed and the British introduced a paper outlining a proposed organization for continuing collaboration between the American and British Chiefs after the close of Arcadia.

On the following day Admiral Stark introduced a discussion of the critical military situation in the ABDA Area where the Japanese were advancing in Malaya on the west, in the Philippines on the east, and down into the Netherlands East Indies, with only slight resistance from the totally inadequate defending forces.[107] The U.S. Chiefs of Staff had been considering the matter carefully, and they were of the opinion that it was of the greatest importance to subordinate everything else to an attempt to deliver reenforcements immediately to the area. They had decided that delivery of the reenforcements then allocated for the area must be accelerated in order for them to arrive in time to be of use. Although there were critical shortages of many vital items, notably of aircraft, in the United States and Great Britain, in the case of troops, as General Marshall pointed out, the problem was not so much providing men for the Far East as finding unallocated shipping to transport them and their equipment. At the same time considerable numbers of troops and supplies and the shipping to deliver them had been committed to Iceland and northern Ireland and to building up for Super-Gymnast, for which the immediate urgency did not seem so great. Therefore, the U.S. Chiefs inquired as to the possibility of diverting some ships from the North Atlantic temporarily to deliver reenforcements to the Far East.

The British, whose main interest in the Far East centered on Singapore, believed that that bastion could hold out, provided reenforcements already en route arrived before the Japanese advanced too near. They were anxious that British troops in Iceland and Ireland be replaced by Americans as had been agreed and pointed out that this was the first step in a relay of troops to the United Kingdom-Middle East-Far East. Moreover, they were eager that planning for Super-Gymnast proceed as rapidly as possible. Consequently, they were reluctant to agree to any considerable cut in shipments to the North Atlantic and urged that all ways of finding additional shipping for the Pacific be explored before it was decided to cut back on other projects.

The American and British Chiefs finally agreed to ask the British and American shipping experts who were at hand for a recommendation of where shipping might be found to expedite the move of reenforcements to the ABDA Area and the effect its diversion to that use might have on other projects then under way.[108]

A meeting of the shipping experts was called immediately. By the following afternoon the U.S. planners had incorporated their recommendations in a plan for the consideration of the chiefs.[109] With the net result of delaying despatch of troops to Iceland and northern Ireland by about one month, it provided for 21,800 troops, mainly air and supporting units, to sail from New York for the Far East on 20 January and an additional 23,300 British troops at a later date. In addition, 393 planes of various types, $4\frac{1}{2}$ million gallons of gasoline, and 228,000 cargo tons would be shipped to the Far

East. Concern was expressed by the British lest the shipping of planes might interfere with planned reenforcements for the Middle East, but they were assured that this would not be the case.

Accomplishment of the proposed program would necessitate cutting down shipments of lend-lease supplies to Russia by as much as 30 per cent. Since the President had repeatedly insisted that every effort should be made to assist the Russians to the greatest possible extent and to carry through on agreed programs of lend-lease with that country, any question of cutting back on supplies for Russia was beyond the scope of the military staffs for final decision. So, although the chiefs agreed to approve the program presented by the shipping experts, they referred it to the President and the Prime Minister for a ruling on the political problem involved.[110]

At a meeting with the chiefs the same afternoon, the President and the Prime Minister approved the program for diversion of shipping from the North Atlantic, including the delay that would result in execution of Super-Gymnast. At the same time they emphasized their feeling that "it was highly important that there be no indication of reductions in the shipments to Russia," and Mr. Hopkins stated his belief that additional ships could be found to keep supplies flowing there and to the Middle East.[111]

Orders to rearrange shipping schedules were immediately issued by General Marshall.

With firm establishment of a policy of rushing reenforcements to the Southwest Pacific, the problem of assuring the security of the line of communications between the United States and the Far East became of even greater importance. In August 1941 it had become apparent that the direct route for delivery of aircraft in particular to the Philippines, via Hawaii, Midway, and Wake, was too exposed and too vulnerable to attack from the Japanese mandated islands. Consequently, a study had been made in the War Department of an alternate route farther to the south, and the Navy developed plans for island bases both for airfields and for fueling depots. Work had been undertaken on bases on Palmyra, Christmas, Canton, Samoa, Fiji, and New Caledonia but had not progressed very far when the war broke.[112]

Local defense responsibility for these islands had been divided between the Army and the Navy, but the over-all defense was, in accordance with ABC-1 and Rainbow No. 5, the responsibility of the Pacific Fleet. That fleet, in addition to defending U.S. Territory east of 180°, had been assigned the task of supporting British naval forces south of the equator, as far as Longitude 155° East. Thus, in effect, it was charged with defense of the whole line of communications from Hawaii to Australia. Following the attack on Pearl Harbor, however, the Chief of Naval Operations immediately decided that the fleet's sphere of operation would have to be confined to the Pacific, east of Longitude 180°, where it was still charged with defense of the Navy's most important bases on Samoa, Midway, Johnston, and Palmyra.[113]

Soon after Admiral King assumed the position of Commander in

Chief, U.S. Fleet (CominCh), in late December 1941, he sent a despatch to the Commander in Chief, Pacific Fleet (CinCPac), stating clearly what he considered the most important immediate objective in the Pacific.

> Consider tasks assigned you summarize into two primary tasks: in order of priority first, covering and holding line Hawaii-Midway and maintaining its communication with West Coast, second, and only in small degree less important, maintenance of communication West Coast-Australia, chiefly by covering, securing, and holding line Hawaii-Samoa which should be extended to include Fiji at earliest practicable date...[114]

Defense of the whole line of bases between the United States and Australia became a subject for consideration at the Arcadia Conference after urgent requests for assistance had been received in London from the New Zealand Government. On the recommendation of the British Chiefs of Staff, the Joint Planning Committee was directed to study the problem.[115]

The committee members found difficulty in reaching agreement on the scope of U.S. naval action in the Pacific and on the priority to be accorded to the reenforcement of critical islands. The British members were anxious that the United States agree to use its Pacific Fleet to protect convoys right up to the shores of Australia, and they urged that the United States send Army garrisons to New Caledonia and Fiji, giving these islands priority on the reenforcements projected for American Samoa. The U.S. planners, supported by Admiral King, upheld the principle of ABC-1, that each nation should be responsible for defense of territory within its own sphere of strategic responsibility. Convoy protection in that area was the responsibility of the Australia-New Zealand naval force, and the U.S. Navy did not wish to become deeply involved there. In regard to New Caledonia and Fiji, although the United States was building an airfield of some importance on New Caledonia and was receiving New Caledonia's total output of nickel, which would be the principal objective of a Japanese attack, the U.S. planners considered that defense of the islands themselves should be the concern of Australia and New Zealand, in whose sphere they lay. Although the U.S. planners recognized the importance of securing the whole line of communications, spreading out U.S. forces over these additional islands, they felt, would render the defenses inadequate at all points. The British members pointed out, however, that the Dominions lacked facilities of their own for adequate defense of those islands (Australia, in particular, having four divisions overseas), and that provision of troops from Great Britain would be wholly impracticable.[116]

The paper finally submitted to the chiefs by the Joint Planning Committee[117] assigned responsibility for the defense of New Caledonia in principle to Australia. However, since the Australians were unable to assume the entire responsibility, it was recommended that the United States furnish troops temporarily for defense of

New Caledonia "even if this has to be at the expense, initially, of
the ABDA area." The chiefs were not in agreement, however, with the
planners' recommendation that the needs of New Caledonia should be
met at the expense of ABDA. General Arnold did not consider New
Caledonia even as vital as Samoa since loss of Samoa would mean
cutting of the air route for heavy bombers from the United States.
Admiral King pointed out, however, that loss of New Caledonia would
mean the necessity of routing all reenforcements south of New
Zealand as well as loss of the nickel mines on the island. It was
finally agreed that the United States should supply forces temporarily for the defense of New Caledonia but not until the emergency
in ABDA had been met.[118]

The chiefs also agreed that the shipping experts, already at work
on the problem of diverting shipping from the North Atlantic to
carry urgently needed reenforcements to the ABDA Area, should investigate the possibility of finding additional shipping to carry
reenforcements to New Caledonia without interfering with the ABDA
program. They further proposed that the practicability of arming
the Free French in New Caledonia be discussed with the Australians.
It was agreed that as an added precaution arrangements should be
made with the Free French for demolition of the valuable nickel
mines and facilities in the event of Japanese invasion.

In addition to aiding Australia in New Caledonia, it was proposed
by the Joint Planning Committee, and approved by the chiefs, that
the United States should assist New Zealand in its responsibility
for providing extra forces for the Fijis, and that the United States
should assume full responsibility for local defense of its own
island bases, Palmyra, Christmas, Canton, and American Samoa, and
of Bora Bora in the Society Islands, where establishment of an
additional base was already projected.[119]

In the last analysis, however, shore garrisons would not alone
be able to hold off a powerful Japanese attack. Of greatest importance for defense of the island bases and for ensuring safe delivery of convoys to Australia was adequate naval protection.

The Australian Government, on receipt of information that a unified command was to be set up in the ABDA Area, expressed concern
lest this involve the concentration within that area of all available naval forces, leaving the north and northeast approaches to
Australia without adequate naval protection. Although the British
Chiefs of Staff were aware that the ABDA arrangements contemplated
no substantial change in the disposition of naval forces, they were
anxious that the United States assume responsibility not only for
convoy protection right up to the shores of Australia but for naval
defense of New Caledonia and Fiji and the other islands along the
air and sea route as well. They had not been pleased with the U.S.
Navy's decision to relinquish the task of assisting British naval
forces as far as Longitude 155° East.[120]

Although the U.S. Navy would have preferred that Australian and
New Zealand naval forces assume responsibility for the area included
in the triangle Australia-New Zealand-Fiji, which was, by ABC-1

agreement, under the strategic direction of the British Naval Commander in Chief, China, the Dominions considered themselves unable to do so. Consequently, while plans for ABDA were being developed and the disposition of reenforcements in the Southwest Pacific was being studied, Admiral King directed the Navy War Plans Division to investigate the problem of naval defense of this area.[121]

The investigation was made by Admiral Turner in connection with the study which, as a member of the Joint Planning Committee, he was making of the problem of defense of the island route from the United States to Australia. In his report to Admiral King, Admiral Turner pointed out the inadequacy for defense of the line of communications of the sea and air forces then present in the area. He recommended that the ANZAC Area established in ABC-1[122] be extended on the north and east to include Fiji and New Caledonia.[123] Within this area Australia and New Zealand would be responsible for sea and air patrols. The Pacific Fleet would furnish escorts for troop convoys to a point where ANZAC forces would take over. Initially, the United States would provide planes urgently needed for operations from Fiji and New Caledonia, and the Pacific Fleet would support the defense of the islands.

Admiral King modified these proposals by recommending that operations in the ANZAC Area should be under command of a U.S. admiral but implemented primarily by ANZAC forces with token assistance from U.S. units. The United States would furnish all practicable aid in the way of ships and planes, etc., to be manned by ANZAC forces. The forces in the ANZAC Area would be assigned the tasks of securing and holding key points and attacking enemy points adjacent to the area, escorting shipping, and operating in correlation with U.S. forces in the Pacific and Southwest Pacific.

On 8 January Admiral King submitted a further modification to the British First Sea Lord, Admiral Pound. He proposed that the ANZAC Area be designated an adjunct of the Pacific Ocean Area and the combined naval forces therein an adjunct of the U.S. Pacific Fleet, with a U.S. flag officer in command, directly responsible to CinCPac.[124] Under the strategic direction of CinCPac, the ANZAC naval forces would cover the eastern and northeastern approaches to the area, escort convoys within the area limits, support the defense of the islands therein, and operate in correlation with the naval forces of ABDA and the Pacific area.

This proposal was referred by the CCS to the Australian Government, who, although much concerned about the critical situation facing them, delayed reply for almost two weeks.[125] By this time, the ABDA Command was in operation and the Japanese had approaches as close as New Britain and New Guinea. The Australians agreed to the proposal for institution of an ANZAC Area with a U.S. naval officer in command. But they assumed that the Commander in Chief, Pacific Fleet, was responsible for escort of convoys direct to Australia, that additional cruisers and destroyers would be furnished from the Pacific Fleet for covering convoys to ABDA, and that the U.S. officer in command in the ANZAC Area would be responsible also for Australia's coastal shipping.[126]

Admiral King took exception to these assumptions, particularly pointing out that the protection of shipping west of Australia to and from the ABDA Area would not be a concern either of the ANZAC Commander or of the Commander in Chief, Pacific Fleet, and that he had never intended that the Pacific Fleet should escort convoys all the way to Australia. However, he accepted two proposals of the British Chiefs of Staff which were presented by Admiral Sir Charles Little at the first meeting of the newly organized Combined Chiefs of Staff on 23 January 1942. These were that the U.S. Commander of ANZAC have headquarters ashore at Melbourne, where he would be in close touch with the Australian Commonwealth Naval Board (ACNB) on the question of convoys, and that the provision of convoys from Australia to the ABDA Area be settled by joint discussions among the British Commander in Chief, Eastern Fleet (in the Indian Ocean), and the naval commanders in ABDA and ANZAC, through all of whose territory such convoys would pass.[127]

After further consultation between Admiral King and Admiral Little a directive was drawn up and, with the approval of the Combined Chiefs of Staff, was put into operation on 30 January. Command of the ANZAC naval forces was assigned to Rear Admiral H.F. Leary, USN.[128]

The ANZAC agreement provided for establishment of a naval area approximately as originally proposed.[129] The ANZAC naval force was to be composed of ships to be furnished by the United States, Australia, and New Zealand. It would be under the strategic direction of the Commander in Chief, U.S. Fleet, "through one or more U.S. Flag Officers assisted by one or more Flag Officers named by Australia and/or New Zealand," and not under the Commander in Chief, Pacific Fleet. Australian seagoing vessels not included under the ANZAC Command were to be assigned to ABDA, and smaller vessels of both Dominions would be responsible for local defense. To the ANZAC force were given the tasks originally proposed by Admiral King but so stated that the limitations of its responsibilities vis-a-vis other naval forces were more clearly outlined. Its duties were:

> *first* cover Eastern and Northeastern approaches to Australia and New Zealand by destroying enemy forces, *second* protect shipping including coastwise shipping and safeguard convoys in ANZAC Area by escort patrol and/or covering operations, *third* support defence of islands in ANZAC Area with emphasis on key points and attack adjacent enemy island key points, *fourth* correlate operations with forces in ABDA area and with United States Pacific Fleet as well as with local defence forces of Australia and New Zealand.

Events were to render the ANZAC Command of short duration.

End of Arcadia

On 14 January 1942 the Arcadia Conference was terminated. The British Prime Minister and Chiefs of Staff returned to London, leaving behind them a staff who, together with the American Chiefs, continued combined discussions throughout the war years in the organization of the Combined Chiefs of Staff. Shortly thereafter, in the process of adjusting to the demands of coalition warfare, the U.S. Joint Board gave way to the Joint Chiefs of Staff (JCS), comprised initially of the U.S. Army Chief of Staff, the Chief of the Army Air Forces, the Commander in Chief, U.S. Fleet, and the Chief of Naval Operations.[130] These officers were also to serve as U.S. representatives on the Combined Chiefs of Staff.

Establishment of a United States-British military organization to which representatives of other nations were supposed to be available for consultation on specific issues did not satisfy the desires of some of the nations who wished to be represented directly on the body that was to determine how the war was to be fought. Especially was this true of the Australians who, both in official communications and in the press, demanded that "they be adequately represented in whatever council controls the high strategy in the Pacific."[131] Their feelings were only partially soothed by the establishment in London at the end of January of a Pacific War Council (PWC), composed of political representatives of Great Britain, Australia, New Zealand, the Dutch East Indies, and later China. The council's function was "to review the broad fundamental policies to be followed in the war against Japan throughout the Pacific area" and to transmit the official view of the members to the CCS in Washington. In practice the recommendations received were considered by the CCS but did not necessarily influence their decision.[132]

Chapter III

DEVELOPMENTS IN THE FAR EAST, JANUARY-FEBRUARY 1942

INAUGURATION OF UNIFIED COMMAND

General Wavell arrived at Batavia on 10 January and immediately held conferences with those who had been appointed as his principal subordinate commanders: Lieutenant General G.H. Brett, U.S. Army Air Forces, Deputy Supreme Commander and Intendant General; Admiral T.C. Hart, U.S. Navy, Chief of Naval Staff and Commander of Allied Naval Forces (ABDAFLOAT); Lieutenant General H. ter Poorten, RNEI Army, Commander of Allied Land Forces; and Lieutenant General Sir Henry Pownall, Chief of Staff. Until the arrival of Air Marshal Sir Richard Peirse, RAF, on 28 January, Major General L.H. Brereton, USA, acted as Commander of Allied Air Forces (ABDAIR), as well as, initially, commander of all U.S. Army forces in ABDA and Australia.[1] Despite some opposition from the naval commanders, it was determined by the Supreme Commander that ABDA Headquarters should be established inland at Lembang, north of Bandoeng in Java.[2]

Thereafter the ABDA staff met at least once a day for discussion. Its effectiveness as a unified body was hampered by the differing strategic concepts of its members and by their preoccupation with their respective governments' territory and their own national forces, most of which remained under their direct command. None of them was trained in the practice of international military cooperation, and there was little time to adjust their differences or even to attempt development of a coordinated plan of operations. Consequently, they operated primarily in accordance with their own national interests.

On 14 January 1942, in a despatch to the British and U.S. Chiefs of Staff, General Wavell reported his intention of taking over command of ABDA as of 1200 G.C.T., 15 January.[3] He proposed to exclude the Philippines temporarily from his command since he did not consider himself sufficiently well informed of the situation there. Since Mr. Churchill had already left Washington Mr. Roosevelt took the initiative and, by despatch, approved General Wavell's proposed action immediately.[4] Almost at once, a modification to the approval was sent, for General Marshall pointed out to the President that it was essential for the future defense of the Philippines that they be included in ABDA.[5] General MacArthur had already been informed that, although the new command would have little effect on his isolated campaign or the size of his forces, he was to be nominally under

General Wavell.[6] Subsequently, official approval sent to General Wavell by the Combined Chiefs clarified the policy in regard to the Philippines:

> ...The Philippines will be included in your command from the start. The U.S. Air Forces now assembling in the ABDA area were initially dispatched to Australia from the Philippines and from the United States with the sole mission of supporting the Philippine garrison. The Combined Chiefs of Staff realize that comprehensive operations looking toward the immediate relief of the Philippines are not feasible at present. However an important reason for the establishment of unity of command in the ABDA area was the realization that uncoordinated Allied effort in the region could neither save the Philippines nor block the Japanese advances that threaten the security of the Malay Barrier. If the Philippines should be excluded even temporarily from your command the bases of the ABDA agreement would be destroyed...[7]

The impossibility of achieving the relief of the Philippines was but one of the unpromising conditions under which ABDA was established. When General Wavell took over his widely scattered command, it was already too late to stop the flood of Japanese invaders penetrating from several directions. In his official report, written after ABDA had ceased to exist, he described the situation as follows:

> Hong Kong had fallen.
> The U.S. garrison in the Philippine Islands was besieged on the Bataan Peninsula and Corregidor Island.
> Minahasa in the Celebes was in enemy hands as was North Borneo and Tarakan and there were indications of hostile advances southward from these places.
> In Malaya 3rd Indian Corps after constant fighting and retreating for five weeks could be counted on for little further effort. The enemy had approached close to Johore and the possibility of getting in reinforcements through Singapore was already open to some doubt.
> Burma had not yet seriously been attacked by land forces.
> In many parts of the outer N.E.I. islands, air raids indicated further imminent enemy advances.[8]

In the month and ten days of ABDA's existence under General Wavell, the Japanese advance progressed according to a prearranged pattern, hindered only slightly by the small forces which opposed it. In November 1941 the Japanese Army and Navy had drawn up detailed joint plans for seizing control of the Southwest Pacific in a series of operations following the pattern: air attack, landing, consolidation, air attack from new base, landing, consolidation. It was planned to move in from two directions, capturing the Philippines, Borneo, Celebes, Moluccas, and Timor on the one hand and Malaya and Sumatra on the other, then to attack Java, the heart of the Netherlands East Indies.[9] This the Japanese proceeded to do.

To oppose the well-organized Japanese advance, General Wavell had initially a land force consisting of approximately three divisions in Malaya, the equivalent of three in the Philippines, and two in Java, plus small garrisons of Dutch troops elsewhere in the Netherlands East Indies, contrasted with some twenty-six Japanese divisions. His naval forces comprised one heavy cruiser, eight light cruisers, two sloops, twenty-three destroyers, and thirty-six submarines, in contrast to a Japanese force of approximately three battleships, twenty-eight cruisers, seven aircraft carriers, seventy-one destroyers, four seaplane carriers, and thirty-four submarines. There were less than 250 aircraft in Burma and Malaya, 4 fighter and 6 bomber squadrons in the Netherlands East Indies, opposed to approximately 1,300 Japanese aircraft.[10] Strongly outmatched in strength on land, sea, and air, and with his limited forces unified on paper rather than in the concepts of their commanders, General Wavell could hope to do little but try to hold as much as possible of his territory while awaiting the arrival of reenforcements that never came.

ABDACOM's directive had outlined for him the general strategic policy of holding the Malay Barrier and behind it Burma and Australia, while operating in as great depth as possible forward of the barrier to oppose the enemy advance. The details of the strategy by which he would attempt to accomplish his objective were his responsibility. With a motley and wholly inadequate assortment of land, sea, and air forces of four nationalities dispersed throughout the area, it was hardly to be expected that General Wavell would at once develop an effective theater-wide operating plan. There is in fact little evidence that he attempted to do so.

From reports of the ABDA operations it is apparent that General Wavell concentrated his attention on Malaya, adhering to the well-established British conception of the vital importance of Singapore. Actually, it was only in Malaya and in Burma that sufficient land troops were concentrated to attempt to resist the Japanese.[11] Elsewhere in the area, garrisons were small, scattered, and totally inadequate to oppose the enemy. With no hope of reenforcing them sufficiently to hold their positions, General Wavell left their operations largely to the local commanders and concentrated on attempting a land defense of Malaya. Pursuance of this policy resulted in the continuing employment of British and Dutch naval forces in escorting troop convoys to Singapore and the concentration of fighter aircraft and bombers in and around the Malay Peninsula. To both of these conditions the American subcommanders, in particular Admiral Hart and General Brereton, were opposed. They felt strongly that both naval surface craft and bombers should be concentrated in the Macassar Straits and the Molucca Sea for combined attacks upon the Japanese lines of communication and the Japanese invasion forces that were flowing into that area by sea, at the same time that Japanese land forces were advancing rapidly in Malaya. U.S. forces alone were insufficient to inflict major damage, although they attacked wherever possible. The submarines especially were constantly in operation, but they were greatly hampered by their crews' inexperience with war operation and by defective torpedoes. The outnumbered air forces of ABDA were expended with small total effect, and it was not until the naval base at Singapore had been abandoned that Dutch and British ships were released for striking operations. By then the Japanese were within bombing range of Australia and firmly entrenched through the area. It is in any case doubtful that full cooperation with the American desire to concentrate attacks on the enemy lines of communication would have done more than delay temporarily the ultimate occupation by the Japanese of most of the Southwest Pacific.[12]

ABDA AND ITS PROBLEMS

As the first attempt at a combined operational command, ABDA and its problems received considerable attention from the Combined Chiefs of Staff, more detailed attention than commands established later in the war when distinctions between matters for high level decision and matters for theater or unilateral national settlement were more clearly drawn. In general, however, problems such as over-all policy, reenforcements, and relationships with other areas and other commands came for decision to the CCS. Problems of theater strategy and tactics and of internal administration General Wavell endeavored, not always with unqualified success, to handle within his command.[13] The chiefs were kept informed of the progress of operations through General Wavell's direct report as well as through communications from the national commanders in the ABDA Area. The chiefs in turn consulted General Wavell before making final decisions on problems relating to ABDA which came to their attention from sources outside the ABDA Command.

In addition to the immediate problems within his own area, the ABDA commander was faced with problems resulting from the tendency of Australians to concentrate their attention on the defense needs of their own continent and to overlook their dependence for security upon the successful defense of the Netherlands East Indies.

The relation of Australia to the ABDA Area was from the first somewhat uncertain. Although the Australians were included in the agreement, they were not consulted during its formulation but, like the Dutch, were presented with a virtual *fait accompli*. There had been some discussion at Arcadia as to whether or not the whole Australian Continent should be included in ABDA. The British had recommended against it, feeling that it would create an area too large for practical operation, and their recommendation was adopted. With four divisions already overseas in the Middle East, however, the Australians felt themselves inadequately defended in the face of the growing threat of a sustained Japanese attack. Consequently, although nominally a party to ABDA, Australia was inclined to think first of defending its own land and of insuring that the forces assigned to ABDA did not cut too deeply into those Australia considered essential for its immediate protection. Australia's views of what was essential did not always coincide with those of the ABDA commanders.

DEVELOPMENTS IN THE FAR EAST, JANUARY-FEBRUARY 1942

Since early in December both the U.S. Army and the U.S. Navy had been increasingly interested in Port Darwin on the northwest coast of Australia. The Army had instituted a service of supply with headquarters there in order to control the delivery of reenforcements to the Philippines. Naval forces retiring from the Philippines had intended to use Darwin as a base. The auxiliaries were sent there, but the combat ships stopped in Soerabaya and remained there as long as the ABDA Area, and they, survived. General Brett and Admiral Glassford had been ordered by agreement of the Joint Board in December to cooperate in developing Port Darwin as a base for transfers of supplies to the Philippines and to other points in the southwest Pacific.[14] Work had begun before the Arcadia Conference met.

Although General Wavell was assigned command of all armed forces "located in Australian territory when such forces have been allotted by the respective governments for services in or in support of the ABDA Area," his orders did not indicate clearly whether Port Darwin was intended to be included in his area.[15] Consequently, on 10 January, before actually assuming command, he requested clarification.[16]

The Arcadia Conference was still in session, and the British and American Chiefs readily agreed that Darwin was vital to the defense of ABDA because of its importance for control of the Timor Sea and as an essential base for supplying the ABDA Area. For a final decision, however, they referred the matter to the Australian Government.[17]

The Australians were by this time deeply concerned over the situation in the area north of their continent, where the Japanese were attacking as close as Rabaul. Reply on the question of Darwin was delayed for some two weeks, during which time the Australian Government was apparently considering seriously the whole problem of continental security. Ultimately the Australians approved assigning responsibility to ABDA for defense of Darwin and a portion of the northwest coast of Australia which they considered essential to that defense. The British Chiefs of Staff recommended acceptance of this arrangement. With the informal approval of the U.S. Chiefs, General Wavell, who had by then assumed command in ABDA, was informed of the extension of the southern limit of his area to include the mainland of Australia north of a line from Onslow to the southeast corner of the Gulf of Carpentaria.[18]

During this same period, the Combined Chiefs gave serious consideration to the practicability of including even more of northern Australia under the ABDA Command. On 20 January the Japanese had attacked Rabaul from the air. Two days later they made landings at two points in New Ireland. On the twenty-third, the same day on which the Australians submitted their comments on the ANZAC and Port Darwin questions, the Australian Government sent to the Government of Great Britain an urgent message, reporting their deep concern over the military situation in Malaya and New Guinea.

Word had reached Australia that some of the Australian Imperial Forces in Malaya had been cut off with no hope of relief, that the campaign there was poorly organized, and that the British Defense Committee was contemplating abandoning Malaya and Singapore. Nearer at hand the enemy was threatening the security of Port Moresby, the only base for control of the Torres Strait, chief supply route from the east to Darwin, the Netherlands East Indies, and Malaya, and was approaching within bombing range of northern Australia. The War Cabinet was well aware of the necessity for strong fighter protection in the event of Japanese attack and of the inadequate equipment of the Royal Australian Air Force (RAAF). Consequently, they requested from the British an immediate allotment of 250 fighters and transfer to the RAAF for use at Port Moresby of a squadron of the U.S. P-40's being assembled at Townsville for ABDA.[19]

When the Australian request was brought to the attention of the Combined Chiefs of Staff via the President, General Marshall pointed out that with serious shortages of aircraft in all theaters it would not be possible to send to ABDA or to Australia any beyond those already allotted for the next two months. Consequently, if Australia was to be assisted in this regard, it must be at the expense of ABDA. General Arnold suggested that the necessity of diverting planes from General Wavell might be obviated by adding the northeast peninsula of Australia to his command, making him responsible for furnishing fighter protection from his own forces. It was pointed out, however, that by the terms of his directive General Wavell could already base planes outside ABDA limits if he saw fit, and if he considered it essential for defense of ABDA, he could send them to northeast Australia. The chiefs finally decided to submit the matter to General Wavell for his opinion as to whether they should divert some of his undelivered planes to Australia or make him responsible for defense of the northeast approaches to that continent.[20]

In reply, General Wavell stated his view that inclusion of the northeast approaches to Australia under his command would create too large an area to cover with his limited facilities. He had recently refused a direct request from the Australians for a squadron for Port Moresby because he considered that his limited forces were more urgently needed elsewhere in his command. While reserving for himself the right included in his directive to allocate forces within his command, he expressed his conviction that the division of forces between ABDA and Australia, as among all other strategic areas, was a function of higher authority.[21] The CCS had recently emphasized this in response to continued direct requests from the Dutch for supplies for their forces within the ABDA Area. They had agreed that once supplies were sent to ABDA it was the responsibility of ABDACOM to allocate them within the area in accordance with strategic necessities.[22]

Following receipt of General Wavell's comments on the question of diverting planes to Australia, the Combined Chiefs reconsidered the matter. They agreed to accept a suggestion made by General Marshall that, since the northeast approaches to Australia were so vital to security of the lines of communication to ABDA, one group of the U.S. fighters then in Australia en route to ABDA should be diverted to the RAAF.[23] Up to this time there had been no complete accounting of the forces under General Wavell's command. In order to clarify the situation, the chiefs instructed the Combined Staff Planners (CPS) to prepare at once a statement of all the land, sea, and air forces allocated to the ABDA and ANZAC Areas.[24]

The temporary diversion of fighter craft to Australia did not satisfy the requests of that government for air protection. On 5 February 1942, the British Chiefs of Staff presented a paper to the Combined Chiefs of Staff, reporting that they could arrange to provide 134 of the additional fighters requested by Australia and New Zealand, and proposing that the United States consider sending 199 more.[25] The U.S. Chiefs pointed out that U.S. production was far behind demands for planes and that almost half of it was allocated to the British, who also were getting planes from their own production. Allocation of additional planes to Australia could be accomplished only at the expense of other areas where they were urgently needed, and the chiefs were opposed to cutting back elsewhere. Consequently, they could send no additional fighters to Australia. In accordance with a suggestion which General Arnold presented for the U.S. Chiefs, the Combined Staff Planners were directed to prepare a comprehensive review of aircraft production and requirements in all areas before any additional allocations to Australia or New Zealand were made.[26]

This was only one of four requests for planes for the Southwest Pacific that were submitted to the chiefs in the first week of February by the various nations involved in the area. In each case the requests could be met only by readjusting previous allotments. At the British suggestions that such *ad hoc* decisions could not be continued, the Combined Staff Planners were given still another assignment--to prepare an over-all study of the strategic deployment of aircraft in the war against Japan. Their several reports will be discussed later.[27]

The decision of the chiefs to divert for use at Port Moresby a squadron of fighters that had been assigned to ABDA was accepted by General Wavell, but the predominant concern of the Australians with their local defense caused some alarm among the ABDA commanders. On 31 January General Brett complained to the Army Chief of Staff that the Australian Government, concentrating on its own coastline, seemed insufficiently aware of the importance to the defense of Australia of the security of all of the Netherlands East Indies and particularly of the air ferry route by which fighters were delivered from Darwin via Timor to Java. General Brett requested that pressure be brought to bear on the Australians to furnish forces for the defense of the vital airfield at Koepang in Dutch Timor, or, should this prove fruitless, that U.S. forces en route to New Caledonia be diverted to Timor since there were not sufficient troops available to ABDACom to secure the field.[28]

The island of Timor, owned jointly by the Dutch and the

Portuguese, had been a source of political difficulties for some months. In the fall of 1941 the Japanese and Portuguese Governments had signed an agreement which permitted the Japanese use of Dilly in Portuguese Timor as a commercial air base site. This act was greeted with some alarm by the Associated Powers. In November Brigadier General Sherman Miles, Acting Assistant Chief of Staff, G-2, drafted a memorandum for the Chief of Staff, drawing attention to the psychological victory the Japanese thus gained by penetrating the Malay Barrier even to so slight an extent. Pointing out that in the event of war occupation of Timor by the "Democracies" would be clearly indicated in order to protect the air route, and that such a move would be welcomed by the Portuguese there, he recommended that the Dutch or the Australians initiate negotiations with the Portuguese for purchase of the island.[29] This proposal was discussed informally with the Army and Navy War Plans Divisions, and it was generally agreed that nothing should be done until the tense situation then existing throughout the Far East was cleared up.[30]

Later in the fall inconclusive negotiations were conducted by the British and Dutch with the Portuguese Government, seeking an agreement that in the event of war Australian and Dutch troops should be sent to the aid of the Portuguese garrison on Timor. When Japanese attack threatened the island, on 15 December, a mixed Dutch and Australian detachment was landed at Dilly without authorization. Objections from both the local government and the Lisbon Government were met with the information that the troops would remain until the Portuguese replaced them with their own forces.

As the situation became more tense and attack on Timor appeared more imminent,[31] the British, after consultation with the Australians and Dutch held discussions in Lisbon which resulted in an agreement that the Allied troops would be removed as soon as Portuguese troops then en route from Portuguese East Africa should arrive, and that in the event of an attack on Portuguese Timor Allied assistance should be invited. It was arranged that a Portuguese officer should proceed to ABDA headquarters for direct consultation with General Wavell. By approval of the CCS, General Wavell was informed of the preceding discussions and was instructed to attempt to achieve an agreement that assistance would in fact be summoned before actual attack on Timor began.[32] Because of language difficulties and the Portuguese representative's lack of familiarity with the situation, conversations at ABDA headquarters had not proceeded very far when Timor was actually attacked and the discussions consequently suspended.[33]

In the meantime General Brett's request for reenforcements for Koepang from Australia or from U.S. forces intended for New Caledonia had been under consideration by the Combined Chiefs of Staff. The second alternative was turned down by the United States, since the forces headed for New Caledonia were vitally needed there and would not in any case arrive in time to be of assistance in Timor.[34] However, the U.S. Joint Chiefs recommended to the CCS that "the necessity for immediately providing a force to insure the continued use of Koepang as an air field on the ferry route from Darwin to Java should again be urged upon the Australian and Dutch governments."[35]

Before the Combined Chiefs could take action, however, word was received from General Brett that arrangements had finally been made by General Wavell with the Australians to send U.S. and Australian troop reenforcements from Darwin to Koepang.[36] It was not possible to despatch this convoy from Darwin until 15 February. Following receipt at ABDACOM headquarters of information that a Japanese attack on Timor was imminent, the convoy was turned back the day after its departure. The Japanese air attack began in force on the seventeenth, and initial landings were made on the twentieth.[37]

With loss of Timor went the only possibility of delivering fighters to Java by air. A subsequent attempt to ferry planes by carrier proved unsuccessful.[38]

In this period of the ABDA Command, when air and ground forces were sadly inadequate and attempts were being made to deliver reenforcements to the area, naval forces also were considerably outnumbered by the Japanese.[39] The majority of the British vessels in the Far East were in the Indian Ocean or engaged in escorting convoys to and from Singapore, where they were assisted by most of the Dutch surface vessels. There remained for offensive operations in the southwestern Pacific principally the ships of the U.S. Asiatic Fleet, which, following departure from Manila, had been based at Soerabaya in Java. There was little hope of reenforcements. Those vessels not already assigned to convoy duty under Admiral Hart were employed to oppose the Japanese wherever possible. Despite an occasional success such as the sinking of four transports off Balikpapan on 23-24 January, they had little effect on the major Japanese plan of advance.

On 19 January the British Chiefs of Staff suggested to the CCS that there were not enough cruisers in ABDA to protect convoys northeast of Java-Sumatra to Malaya and the Netherlands East Indies. It was doubtful that Admiral Hart, who was concentrating U.S. ships in defense of the Macassar Strait area, could spare enough for this purpose. The British were contemplating removing some of their cruisers and their destroyers to the Indian Ocean and could not furnish any more. Consequently, they suggested that the United States endeavor to send additional cruisers to ABDA.[40]

The British request raised the question of the proper functions of British naval forces in the Far East Area. In 1941 attempts to reach agreement on American-Dutch-British cooperation in the Far East had been unsuccessful largely because no one wished to provide sufficient naval forces to make possible any strategic operational planning. The British insisted that their fleet should be employed in protecting shipping in the Indian Ocean and escorting convoys to Singapore while Americans refused to project the U.S. Fleet into that area of the Pacific.[41] At his eleventh hour meeting with Admiral Hart at Manila, Admiral Tom Phillips had agreed to assign some of his forces to offensive operations in defense of the Malay Barrier and to retain a minimum on convoy duty in the Indian Ocean.[42] But Admiral Phillips and the two ships were lost before the new plan could be put into operation, and the majority of the British forces were deployed in the Indian Ocean, convoying or supporting the defense of Singapore, which loomed in British eyes next in importance to holding the British Isles themselves.[43] The Dutch at the same time were reluctant to deploy their limited number of vessels otherwise than in directly defending their own territory and in assisting British convoying to Singapore. Consequently, Admiral Hart's attempts to formulate plans for strong naval resistance to the Japanese landings and operations in the Macassar Strait and Molucca Sea, which he considered the essential function of ABDA naval forces, were considerably hampered.

The U.S. Chiefs were not informed what naval forces the British had assigned to the ABDA Area. They pointed this out in their reply to the British request for reenforcements from the United States. They further remarked that inasmuch as the ABDA naval forces were supposed to be furnished by the four participating countries it would be well to wait until the ANZAC Area was established and the number of ships the Australians could provide for ABDA was determined, and until the British had furnished information on the ships they themselves were contributing.[44]

The discussion was continued by the Combined Chiefs until arrangements for ANZAC were completed at the end of January, when it was found possible to reenforce ABDA with some Australian vessels.[45]

Allocation of the Australian vessels to ABDA did not, however, reconcile the differences between the commander of the combined naval forces, Admiral Hart, and the commanders of the national components of his command. The Dutch in particular, who considered their interests in ABDA predominant, were deeply disappointed that the fleet was not placed under Dutch command. They felt strongly that the total naval effort should be deployed for defensive action in support of the Netherlands East Indies. They disapproved Admiral Hart's strategy and thought that the Dutch commanders had more thorough knowledge of the area that was not being adequately utilized.[46] Their attitude, coupled with British reluctance to deploy their ships from the Indian Ocean and otherwise than on convoy duty and with lack of support from General Wavell, rendered Admiral Hart's attempts at coordinated naval operations extremely difficult.

Toward the end of January General Wavell reported to the Prime Minister the general unpleasantness of the situation and the dissatisfaction of the Dutch naval command with Admiral Hart. General Wavell interpreted certain remarks by Admiral Hart in regard to his age as meaning that he would not object to being relieved, and General Wavell recommended that Admiral Hart be replaced by the Dutch Vice Admiral Conrad Helfrich or some younger American, provided there was a promise of considerable naval reenforcements.[47] The Prime Minister forwarded this recommendation to the President, who consulted with Admirals King and Stark, both of whom were averse to relieving Admiral Hart. Despite Admiral Hart's reply on inquiry that he did not consider himself unfit to continue,[48] however, it was finally decided by the President to turn over the command to the Dutch. In view of the attitudes of General Wavell and the Dutch, the fact that no further U.S. naval forces were to be sent to ABDA, and the expectation that the Dutch would give more willing support to a Dutch commander, there seemed to be little or no alternative. Consequently, ComInCh recommended to Admiral Hart that he request detachment because of ill health.[49]

Admiral Hart's request for relief was formally presented to the Combined Chiefs of Staff on 7 February. With the approval of the chiefs, the President, and the Prime Minister, the Secretary of the Navy ordered him home four days later.[50]

Relief of Admiral Hart left the United States unrepresented among the commanders of combined operating forces. The U.S. Chiefs of Staff believed that this situation would be unacceptable to the American people, and consequently they urged that the combined ABDA air forces be placed under General Brett, leaving his post as Deputy Supreme Commander temporarily vacant. Despite a recommendation from the President to the Prime Minister, and subsequently from the latter to General Wavell, this was not accomplished.[51] By the time Admiral Helfrich took over the naval command, however, ABDA's days were limited.

THE CHINA THEATER. BURMA AND MALAYA

While the Japanese were advancing by sea and air through the islands of the Southwest Pacific, on the western flank of the ABDA Area Japanese land forces pushed down through Malaya and, crossing the border into Burma, drove easily before them the British Imperial forces they encountered. Burma had been included under the ABDA Command against the advice of General Wavell, who felt that its defense could be better handled from India, and against recommendations of some U.S. officers that it would more logically be coupled with China, whose sole land route for supplies since the Japanese controlled the East China ports lay through Burma, via the Burma Road from Lashio in Burma to Kunming in China. The considerable interest of the Chinese in Burma complicated General Wavell's problems of defending the area. In order to understand the situation that existed in regard to Burma during the period of the ABDA Command, it is desirable to consider the relations among China, the United States, and Great Britain during December 1941 and January 1942.

When the United States found itself at war with Japan on 7 December 1941, there were no plans for coordinating U.S. efforts, in the event of such an occurrence, with those of China, where undeclared war with Japan had been in progress since 1937. Strategically China was thought of as a base from which ultimately operations would be conducted against Japanese shipping and against the Japanese home islands. It was also thought of as a source of manpower, largely undeveloped, but potentially important. For strategic reasons China's retention in the war was considered important, but above that it was a firm national policy to render support to China. Public sympathy for China was great and continually intensified by many outspoken friends of that nation in the United States as well as by the exaggerated accounts of Chinese military accomplishments which found their way to the public press. In May 1941 President Roosevelt had declared the defense of China to be vital to the defense of the United States, thus making China eligible for lend-lease aid. The President was insistent, and in order to understand subsequent developments it is important to remember this basic attitude, that China should be treated as a Great Power, as nearly as possible on a par with the United States and Great Britain. That meant that the Generalissimo was to be treated with dignity and to as great an extent as possible on equal terms.

Informed military officers in Washington were aware that China's armies were overrated and the reports of their exploits exaggerated, if not false. Nevertheless it was the conviction of those in the highest Army positions that potentially the Chinese armies could be as effective as those of any other nation, provided that the men were properly equipped, trained, and led. Under those conditions they could be called upon for effective action on the mainland in coordination with the final offensive of U.S. forces from the east. This conviction was shared by the Joint Chiefs of Staff and the President and was the primary motivation for the mission of Lieutenant General Joseph W. Stilwell.

With these views of the importance of China and the potential value of the Chinese armies the British did not agree. They accepted rather the opinion, not unknown in U.S. military circles, that the Chinese soldier had never proved himself capable of effective action and that it was useless to waste more than a minimum of effort on China. As Prime Minister Churchill put it, "If I can epitomize in one word the lesson I learned in the United States [at the Arcadia Conference], it was 'China.'"[52] He found himself differing strongly with the American estimate of the contribution the Chinese could make to the total war effort and unable to accept the American views. Later he reported the terms he gave the President "...I said I would of course always be helpful and polite to the Chinese, whom I admired and liked as a race and pitied for their endless misgovernment, but that he must not expect me to adopt what I felt was a wholly unreal standard of values."[53] By mutual consent negotiations with the Generalissimo were carried out throughout the war period through Mr. Roosevelt. The opposing attitudes of the two nations remained unchanged and influenced in later months the attempts to reach combined agreements on strategy in the whole area of the Far East.[54]

The Japanese attack on Pearl Harbor was scarcely over when Generalissimo Chiang Kai-shek summoned the American and Soviet Ambassadors at Chungking and announced the readiness of his government "to collaborate...on any concerted military plan which may be adopted against Japan and the other members of the Axis." He recommended that the United States, the Soviet Union, Great Britain, Canada, China, Australia, New Zealand, and the Netherlands conclude a military alliance at the earliest opportunity.[55] Within a few days he repeated his views to Brigadier General John Magruder and to the military representatives of Great Britain and Russia, specifically recommending:

   1. The United States should propose a comprehensive plan for joint war activities for America, Britain, China, Netherlands East Indies and Russia.
   2. Immediately and before Russia participates in the war, the United States should take the leadership in initiating a comprehensive plan for the action of the United States, Britain, Netherlands East Indies and China in the west Pacific.
   3. The locale for joint working out of details of the ABCD Plan should be Chungking.
   4. There should result a military pact among the ABCDR for mutual assistance.[56]

General Magruder relayed reports of his conversations with the Generalissimo to Washington where plans were already in hand for the visit of Prime Minister Churchill and the British Chiefs of Staff late in the month.[57] As a preliminary to these discussions, the President, as has already been mentioned, suggested that talks be held in Singapore, Chungking, and Moscow, to consider combined strategy in the several areas of war and to submit recommendations to Washington. On 22-23 December 1941 a combined conference was held at Chungking, where the United States was represented by Major General George H. Brett; Great Britain by General Sir Archibald Wavell, Commander in Chief, India; China by General Ho Ying-chin, Minister of War, and by Generalissimo Chiang Kai-shek.[58]

The Generalissimo was eager to discuss over-all strategy for the defeat of Japan and repeatedly insisted that a combined body must be set up in Washington to direct political and military action for the defeat of the Axis Powers. In the course of the meetings he "distributed a scheme for associated action of the Powers," comprising a general plan for the defeat of Japan within the year 1942, to be followed by a combined effort to destroy Germany and Italy.[59] As a result of the conference a military council of representatives of the United States, China, and Great Britain was formed in Chungking to operate under directives from the Supreme War Council which it was assumed would be set up in Washington. Subcommittees were appointed to investigate specific problems. In addition, a general strategic plan for military operations was approved, largely at the insistence of General Brett. It was agreed that it was of primary importance to secure Rangoon and Burma, continue furnishing supplies to China, maintain Chinese resistance to the Japanese, and prepare "as soon as resources permit to pass to an offensive against Japan."[60]

Despite the eagerness of the Generalissimo to discuss grand strategy, the major part of the discussion at the Chungking conference centered around more immediate problems and particularly those connected with the defense of Burma, where Japanese air raids had already begun.[61] Both the British, whose Crown Colony it was, and the Chinese, whose only land route for supplies was over the Burma Road, were concerned over the security of Burma. The eagerness of the Chinese to assist in the defense of Burma was not matched, however, by British eagerness to accept Chinese assistance. The fundamental, long-standing, Chinese distrust of the British colonial policy in Asia had been aggravated by the temporary closing of the Burma Road by the British in 1939. The British for their part were fearful of an "Asia for the Asiatics" movement and hesitated to build up the strength or prestige of the Chinese lest they foster ideas of independence among the British colonials. Moreover, there had long been a dispute over the northern boundary between Burma and China, and the British suspected the Chinese of entertaining hopes of annexing part of Burma or at least establishing a Chinese zone of influence in that country. Consequently, cooperation between the British and the Chinese in Burma was extremely difficult.

Early in December the Chinese had stated their desire to send troops to assist in the defense of Burma. At the meetings at Chungking they offered to send at once two Chinese armies (the equivalent of two Japanese divisions) to the area. But General Wavell, who shared the general belief that the Japanese were overextended and thought it undesirable that part of the British Empire should be defended by foreign troops,[62] turned down the offer on the grounds that it would be too difficult to arrange a separate line of communications and a separate front for the Chinese troops, and that in any case he was expecting reenforcements from India which should be adequate.

Although the British did not want Chinese troops in Burma, they were very anxious to have assistance from the Chinese in the way of supplies. A considerable amount of lend-lease material en route to China from the United States had accumulated in Rangoon with no immediate prospect of transportation across the Burma Road to China. Confronted by the possibility of a Japanese invasion of Burma in the near future, the British were eager to take over some of the material for their own use, and they appealed to the United States to bring pressure on China to transfer it to them.[63] After discussion of the problem in the War Department, with Mr. Lauchlin Currie, Special Assistant to the President, and the British, a despatch was sent from the Secretary of War to General Magruder, assigning him responsibility for handling the problem, underlining the principle that "in any event this property should be used to resist Japanese aggression."[64] At the combined conference at Chungking the British presented their case to the Generalissimo and secured his agreement to consider a list of specific items in which they were particularly interested.

While the matter was still unsettled, the *Tulsa*, carrying lend-lease cargo from the United States, had arrived at Rangoon where the Burmese authorities, at the request of the U.S. representative, had impounded its cargo, pending redistribution of the material among Burma's defenders. A highly colored version of this incident which reached Chungking after the meetings had ended considerably enraged the Generalissimo. At the request of the British, General Magruder went around and mollified Chiang, who, however, warned "that if the British do anything to interfere with Chinese affairs in the future there will be a great crisis."[65]

Reports of the Chungking conference and of the *Tulsa* incident reached Washington as plans were being formulated for establishment of unified command in the ABDA Area. There was no consideration of including China in ABDA, but both from a political and from a military standpoint it seemed desirable to inform the Generalissimo of the ABDA plan before public announcement was made and to arrange for some way of coordinating the American, British, and Chinese war effort in China.[66] Accordingly, the Army War Plans Division prepared a draft message to Chiang Kai-shek announcing the decision to set up ABDACOM and proposing that he assume such a unified command of all forces in the China Theater. During discussion of the draft with the Secretary of War, the Army Chief of Staff, Mr. Harry Hopkins, and representatives of the Navy and the Marine Corps, Colonel W.G. Wyman, who had prepared it, urged that, although the British would probably object, the dependence of China on Burma as a route for supplies and the close physical relation of Burma, Thailand, Indo-China, and China made it imperative that Burma should be included in the proposed China Theater. Ultimately, the draft as approved by this group for submission to the Combined Chiefs of Staff defined the area to be under Chiang's command as including China, "northeast Burma and such portion of Thailand and Indo China as may become accessible to troops of the Associated Powers."[67]

As was expected, the British objected to putting any part of Burma under Chinese control, and the chiefs removed "northeast Burma" from the draft before sending the paper on to the President and the Prime Minister for approval.[68] Subsequently, despite Burma's geographical position, and over the objections of General Wavell, the ABDA commander, it was decided to include Burma in the ABDA Command. With the approval of the President and the Prime Minister, Chiang Kai-shek was informed as follows:

> 1. In order to insure immediate coordination and cooperation in our common effort against the enemy, there is being established a Supreme Commander for all British, Dutch, and American forces in the Southwest Pacific theater.
> 2. The advisability of a similar command of activities of the Associated Powers in the Chinese theater appears evident. This theater we suggest should initially include such portion of Thailand and Indo-China as may become accessible to troops of the Associated Powers. In agreement with the representatives of the British and Dutch Governments, I [the President] desire to suggest that you should undertake to exercise such command over

all forces of the Associated Powers which are now, or may in the future be operating in the Chinese theater.

 3. It is our thought that, in order to make such command effective, a joint planning staff should at once be organized consisting of representatives of the British, Dutch, American, and Chinese governments. If you consider it practicable, and Russia agrees, a Russian representative might be included. This staff should function under your supreme command.

 4. The commander of the Southwest Pacific theater and the commander of the British forces in India would be directed to maintain the closest liaison with your headquarters. A mutual exchange of liaison officers between the three headquarters would be desirable.

 5. Such arrangements would enable your counsel and influence to be given effect in the formulation of the general strategy for the conduct of the war in all theaters. Your views in this matter will be greatly appreciated by me.[69]

This was hardly the full partnership in controlling strategy which Chiang Kai-shek desired. There was no indication what military action was to be taken in the Chinese Theater or what forces other than Chinese would actually be under the Generalissimo's supreme command. He was given little that he did not already have as commander of his own military forces. However, on paper the command sounded impressive, and it was hoped that it would satisfy Chiang that he was to have a part in the combined war effort.[70]

By this time decision had been reached in the War Department that it would be highly desirable to send a high-ranking U.S. Army officer to China, with ample powers and funds, to represent the United States on the joint planning staff which had been proposed to Chiang and to head up all American military and lend-lease affairs there.[71] As a candidate for the post, Lieutenant General Hugh A. Drum was called to Washington on 1 January 1942. Explanation of the reason for his summons came as a surprise to General Drum, who remembered a promise made by the President that he would be put in command of U.S. field forces in the event of war.[72] His surprise was increased when he discovered, on interviewing various officials of the War Department and such outsiders as Secretary of the Navy Knox and Mr. Lauchlin Currie, that there was no agreement among them as to what the objective of the United States in China was to be and what part U.S. Army activities in China were to play in the total effort for the defeat of Japan. At one extreme was General Drum's own view, which was substantially that voiced by Secretary of War Henry L. Stimson and the staff assembled for General Drum in the War Department, that forces in China should be built up to strength sufficient to undertake a decisive offensive to defeat Japan. At the other extreme was the view of General Marshall and the Army War Plans Division that only sufficient forces should be accumulated to keep China in the war and eventually to conduct air raids against Japan from Chinese bases.[73] The latter view was ultimately to prevail.

While General Drum was trying to reconcile the various concepts of the potential role of the U.S. Army in China, the Army War Plans Division was formulating a statement of the mission he would be expected to perform. Initially intended to clarify the American general's relationship to the British forces in the area,[74] the provisions of the statement were broadened to include closer relations with the Generalissimo after a request came from Chiang, via Mr. T.V. Soong, Chinese Minister for Foreign Affairs, to the Assistant Secretary of War, for an American officer above the rank of brigadier general to serve as Chief of Staff for the joint staff to be set up in Chungking.[75]

After discussion with U.S. Navy planners, the Army War Plans Division presented the results of its study to the Joint Planning Committee (forerunner of Combined Staff Planners) of the Arcadia Conference on 9 January 1942.[76] The War Department, it was stated, reregarded it "as of profound importance that such steps as may be practicable and are consistent with other commitments be promptly taken" to halt the apparent progressive weakening of China's war effort. The almost complete isolation of China made effective assistance difficult. In order to improve the military situation it would be necessary to achieve closer liaison with the Generalissimo, increased security for Rangoon and the Burma Road, improvement in the control and maintenance of the road, increase in base facilities and technical services, a resultant increase in Chinese combatant strength, and closer liaison between China and ABDACOM. To accomplish these objectives the War Department was considering sending a U.S. military representative (General Drum) to Chungking. Subject to the approval of the Generalissimo, he would supervise and control lend-lease; command all U.S. forces in China and, under General Wavell, all U.S. and Chinese forces in Burma; represent the U.S. Army on any international war council in China; and control and maintain the Burma Road in China. In addition to a military representative, the War Department planned to despatch greater aviation strength to the South China-Burma area and arrange for auxiliary bases and technical troops in that area. It was considered possible that several Chinese divisions might be quickly equipped for effective combat service under the command of the U.S. representative. It would be necessary to secure British agreement and cooperation for the use and construction of bases, airfields, and staging areas in India and Burma, for control and maintenance by the U.S. representative of the Burma Road from Rangoon to Chungking, for command by him, under control of the ABDA commander, of American and Chinese forces in the Burma region, and from him to serve as liaison between General Wavell and Chiang Kai-shek.[77]

The Joint Planning Committee agreed with the emphasis placed on the Burma Road as the best route by which to speed aid to China. It made certain changes in the paper, however, notably revising the functions of the proposed U.S. representative in China to read:

(1) Supervise and control all U.S. Defense Aid affairs for China.

(2) Under the Generalissimo, to command all U.S. Forces in China, and such Chinese forces as may be assigned. To command any U.S. or Chinese forces in Burma which have been alloted [sic] by their respective governments for service under him, operating these forces in collaboration with the Supreme Commander of the ABDA Area.

(3) Represent the U.S. Government on any international War Council in China.

(4) Control and maintain the Burma Road, in China.[78]

The points on which agreement of the British was sought remained the same, except that the U.S. representative would exercise command of forces in Burma *in cooperation* with the Supreme Commander of ABDA rather than under his control.

Granting to an American officer command of any forces in Burma or control over communications via the Burma Road within the Burma limits was not an attractive thought to the British Chiefs of Staff. It would be, they agreed among themselves, "quite unsound and unworkable to have a divided command in Burma."[79] Consequently, at the combined meeting they proposed certain amendments which limited very considerably the authority of the U.S. representative. Instead of exercising control of the Burma section of the road, he would be

> authorised to make every effort to increase the capacity of the Burma Route, throughout its length from Rangoon to Chungking. To do this he will probably be given complete executive control of the China Section of the Route. On the British Section control will still be exercised by the British authorities, both military and civil. To achieve the general aim these British authorities will be instructed to carry out every possible improvement to the Route in accordance with the requirements of the U.S. Representative and will accept such American technicians and equipment as may be necessary for the improvement of facilities in the Port of Rangoon and along the Route itself.

He might construct and/or use airfields in Burma only by arrangements with British commanders there. Should any of the forces under his command in China be employed in Burma, they would be under the Supreme Commander of the ABDA Area while so engaged.

These changes caused considerable discussion between the U.S. and British Chiefs. The British finally secured agreement, and the amendments were incorporated in the paper as approved on 10 January 1942.[80]

The position the Combined Chiefs of Staff thus established was indeed a complicated one and fraught with political implications. It would involve dealings on both military and political terms with the Chinese and with the British. There was no promise of large-scale military operations and no indication that the U.S. forces which the U.S. representative would command would ever reach proportions large enough to take decisive action. The original Army War Plans Division paper had been prepared without the knowledge of General Drum, and it did not represent his views of what the

U.S. objectives in the China Theater should be. Consequently, when he saw it, in memoranda to the Secretary of War and the Chief of Staff, U.S. Army, he expressed his dislike for the paper and his concern over the apparent uncertainty in the War Department with respect to China.[81] His dissatisfaction with the minor role in the war against Japan which the agreement appeared to assign to China and to the U.S. military representative made an adverse impression on Mr. Stimson, who decided that General Drum was unsuitable for the job. Consequently, General Joseph W. Stilwell, then in Washington preparing for command of Gymnast, was selected in his stead.[82]

While plans for General Stilwell's mission were being developed, difficulties arose between the ABDA Command and the China Theater over the defense of Burma. In December a squadron of the American Volunteer Group had been sent from China to Rangoon to oppose the Japanese attack on Burma. It was its achievements against the Japanese air attacks there that established the reputation of the Flying Tigers, as the group was called. When General Wavell took command of ABDA, he was informed by the Combined Chiefs of Staff that since the AVG was a Chinese unit, operating in support of China, it might be withdrawn from Burma to China upon request of Chiang Kai-shek. Orders had been issued to induct the AVG into the U.S. Army, but in that status it would still be assigned to the support of China and could still be withdrawn from Burma at the desire of the Generalissimo.[83]

Operating almost continuously against the enemy, the P-40's and the personnel of the AVG in Burma suffered considerable attrition both from combat action and from excessive wear. Consequently, with the approval of Chiang, late in January Colonel Claire L. Chennault sent word to the British Command in Burma that he would have to withdraw these units to China. The British, who had no planes with which to replace the AVG immediately and too few in Burma to operate without them, reported in alarm to the British Chiefs of Staff, who relayed the matter to the Combined Chiefs in Washington. The Prime Minister also brought the matter to the attention of the President. As a result the War Department directed General Magruder in Chungking to point out to the Generalissimo that these forces were indispensable to the defense of Rangoon, the only port for entry of supplies for China, and to persuade him to delay their withdrawal until British reenforcements could arrive to relieve them. General Magruder succeeded, and General Wavell was informed that the planes would remain.[84]

Meanwhile the Combined Chiefs of Staff had become involved in the question of using Chinese troops in Burma. As has been recounted above, at the Chungking conference in December General Wavell turned down the offer of two armies, and only parts of two Chinese divisions were sent into Burma. As the Japanese moved into southern Burma and the defending troops withdrew before them, the Generalissimo, in a telegram delivered by Mr. Soong to the Secretary of War, expressed his view that "China alone would take on the responsibility of holding Northern Burma for the British, but even up to the present the British do not wish Chinese armies to enter Burma and cooperate in its defense. This obstinate attitude on the part of the British is as incomprehensible as it is regrettable."[85] At the instance of the U.S. Army members, the matter was brought to the attention of the Combined Chiefs of Staff with the recommendation that "regardless of possible political disadvantages or later administrative difficulties," in the interests of stopping the Japanese every effort should be made at once to utilize to the utmost the available forces of Chiang Kai-shek. It was pointed out that Chinese forces could both strengthen the defenses of Burma and attract Japanese forces away from the vicinity of Singapore, where the defenders had already withdrawn to the island. It was urged that permission be sought from London to enlist Chinese help.[86]

At the suggestion of the British, Chiang's complaint was reported to General Wavell with the recommendation that "nothing should stand in the way of the acceptance of any Chinese forces which might be of assistance" and with a request for General Wavell's comments.[87] General Wavell in reply carefully outlined his negotiations with the Chinese. As soon as the unexpectedly quick advance of the Japanese had indicated danger to Burma, he reported, he had authorized the General Officer Commanding in Burma to accept any further Chinese assistance. As a result an agreement had just been reached with the Generalissimo to move the Chinese Fifth Army into Burma, and the outlook for smoother relations appeared hopeful.[88]

By the end of January 1942 details of the mission and authority of the U.S. Army Representative in China had been settled in conversation and correspondence between the Secretary of War and Mr. Soong in Washington. Mr. Soong had agreed to the following functions:

> To supervise and control all United States defense-aid affairs for China.
> Under the Generalissimo to command all United States forces in China and such Chinese forces as may be assigned to him.
> To represent the United States Government on any International War Council in China and act as the Chief of Staff for the Generalissimo.
> To improve, maintain and control the Burma Road in China.[89]

On 2 February 1942 General Stilwell was instructed to proceed to Chungking, "for service in the Chinese Theater, under the Supreme Command of Generalissimo Chiang Kai-shek," to "act as the United States Army Representative in China, carrying out the instructions of the Secretary of War." His mission was to be: "[1] to increase the effectiveness of United States assistance to the Chinese Government for the prosecution of the war and [2] to assist in improving the combat efficiency of the Chinese Army." He was authorized to accept any appropriate staff and/or command position that the Generalissimo might tender him, and he was directed to follow the provisions of the combined agreement of 10 January and Mr. Soong's letter (quoted above) as far as possible.[90]

The mission to which General Stilwell was assigned was indeed a complicated one. As U.S. Army Representative he was under the Secretary of War. As supervisor and controller of lend-lease he was under the President. As Chief of Staff of the Generalissimo's Joint Staff he was under the Generalissimo and at the same time the representative of the U.S. Government. A further complication resulted from the fact that major strategic problems in the theater and its relation to the whole war against Japan were the concern of the Combined Chiefs of Staff.[91] Thus General Stilwell was confronted with a combination of political and military functions in an area whose part in the campaign to defeat Japan had not yet been determined. In attempting to evaluate his accomplishments and failures, it is essential to bear in mind the complexity of his position and to remember that his directive was explicitly to increase the effectiveness of U.S. aid and to assist in improving the combat efficiency of the Chinese Army.

By the time General Stilwell's orders were issued, the Japanese had made great advances in both Burma and Malaya. Despite the initial optimism of the local commanders and of the British Government, the enemy proceeded rapidly southward in the Malay Peninsula at high cost to the defending troops. The concentration of effort under ABDACom to deliver supplies and reenforcements had little effect on the situation. On 31 January the defending commander, Lieutenant General A.E. Percival, withdrew his forces into the island of Singapore. Five days later it became necessary to close the naval base, thus removing any possibility of delivering reenforcements by sea. The enemy landed on the island on 8 February, and a week later the garrison surrendered.

Meanwhile, the British Imperial troops in Burma withdrew before the Japanese, crossing the Salween River on 31 January. Thereafter the retreat continued until, by 22 February, they had crossed the Sittang, bringing the invaders within close range of Rangoon and spelling the doom of the defense of Lower Burma.

THE END OF ABDACOM

The loss of Singapore, although a severe blow to ABDACOM and to the British Empire, was only one aspect of a totally unfavorable situation in ABDA in the second week of February 1942, as the enemy moved in on Java from two directions. Throughout January and the first half of February the Japanese, with amazing rapidity, had overrun or strongly attacked by air a large part of the territory under General Wavell's command. Despite individual valiant efforts and occasional small successes at sea and ashore, the combined disadvantages of insufficient equipment and forces, particularly air forces, and inadequate preparation for organized resistance resulted in a series of reverses that culminated in the fall of Singapore on on 15 February 1942. By that date the troops in Burma had been driven across the Salween River, to pause very temporarily on the west bank of the Bilin River before continuing their retreat.

There was no hope of maintaining an effective defense of Burma. Throughout the Netherlands East Indies, the Japanese had followed up systematic and thorough air attacks on major air bases and ports with landings aimed to secure them. They had invaded Borneo and Celebes, occupying various points around the coasts, establishing air and sea bases, and seeking oil. Similarly, landings had been made in New Ireland and New Britain, and air attacks on points in Halmahera. Repeated air raids on Timor had emphasized the need for reenforcing its defenses. But the convoy which started out from Darwin for Timor on 15 February was turned back the following day on the basis of intelligence received at ABDA of an imminent enemy attack on Timor, and the convoy subsequently suffered heavy attack from the air. In the so-called Eastern Archipelago--Bali, Lombok, Soembawa, etc.--extensive air raids, beginning the last week in January, indicated that Japanese attempts to effect landings in that area were imminent. Since 17 January various points in Sumatra had undergone air attacks, and on 13 February landings were initiated in South Sumatra (Palembang) where limited forces could hope to offer only brief resistance. Air attacks on Java had not begun until 3 February. By 15 February, although activity there waned temporarily while Japanese landings on Sumatra proceeded, it was apparent that in Java, too, seaborne attack might soon be expected.[92]

The U.S. Pacific Fleet, meanwhile, had carried out its first offensive operation of the war. On 1 February two task forces under command of Vice Admiral William F. Halsey, Jr., conducted raids on Japanese-held islands in the southern Marshall and the northern Gilbert Islands, inflicting considerable bomb and bombardment damage on enemy installations, while suffering little damage in return.[93] These raids were important for their effect on morale, both of those participating in their first direct attack on enemy and of the U.S. public, who, unaware how much damage had been done at Pearl Harbor and hearing nothing but bad news from the Pacific, had been clamoring for some action by the U.S. Fleet. These and subsequent naval raids carried out in February and March helped to limit the extent of Japanese conquest in the Pacific. Their effect on the enemy advance in the ABDA Area was negligible.

General Wavell's reports during much of this period were optimistic.[94] However, two days before the fall of Singapore, he sent a despatch to the Combined Chiefs of Staff, describing the situation then existing and warning that a drastic change of plans might prove necessary. It had for some time been apparent that the enemy's ultimate aim was to capture Java. Unable to defend the whole area, General Wavell had determined to concentrate on trying to defend what he considered the most essential objectives: Singapore, air bases in South and Central Sumatra, the naval base at Soerabaya in Java, and the airfield at Koepang in Timor.[95] It now appeared doubtful that any of these points could long be held. General Wavell felt that for moral and political reasons he must do his utmost to reenforce and to hold Sumatra. However, it seemed unlikely that the Australian 6th Division would arrive from the Middle East in time to be effective there, and his own forces were far from sufficient. Without Sumatra, he warned the chiefs, he could not hope to hold Java.[96]

Two days later the Japanese captured the airfield at Palembang in South Sumatra, where most of the available troops of the island had been concentrated. After a conference with the Dutch Governor General, Admiral Helfrich, and General ter Poorten, General Wavell again reported to the CCS. The Governor General was most insistent that Java be defended to the utmost despite the fact that it was by then apparent that Sumatra could not be held with the forces available and despite ABDACOM's view that Java could not be held without Sumatra.[97]

The following day General Wavell elaborated on the situation in a personal telegram to the Prime Minister and to Field Marshal Sir John Dill in Washington. He recounted the totally inadequate forces, land, sea, and air, which remained to him and he predicted that Java would be invaded before the end of the month. Although loss of Java would mean loss of Soerabaya, the only remaining naval base on the China Seas, and of an air base for operations in the whole area north of Java, as General Wavell pointed out it would not be fatal to the total effort in the Far East as would be the loss of Burma or of Australia. Since he did not think that the Australian Corps due to arrive in Java toward the end of the month would arrive in time to be of much help to the defense of Java,[98] he recommended that at least one division of it be diverted to Burma. Furthermore, he urged that immediate steps be taken to build up a heavy bomber force in Burma for operations against the Japanese line of communications and eventually against Japan itself.[99]

At their meeting of 17 February, the Combined Chiefs of Staff discussed this series of despatches and the situation in the ABDA areas as General Wavell had reported it. They agreed with his conclusion that further reenforcement of Java would be futile and that it would be wise to send at least one Australian division to Burma. This, however, could not be decided independently of Australia and of the Pacific War Council, which had recently been set up in London. The British pointed out further that with the probable loss of Java as well as Sumatra, Burma would be cut off entirely from the rest of ABDA and that it could be more effectively controlled from India. The U.S. Chiefs, and Admiral King in particular, had begun to consider plans for dividing strategic responsibility between the British and the Americans in the war against Japan, and they readily accepted the proposal that Burma be transferred to British control from India.[100] Since he had never approved of the original decision to include Burma in his command, General Wavell was quick to agree that it should now revert to complete control of India. By a despatch from the CCS on 21 February Burma was removed from the ABDA Command.[101]

Diversion of the Australian troops to Burma, however, was not so easily achieved. The Australian Government refused to authorize their use elsewhere than in Australia, insisting that the risks involved in committing them in Burma were too great and that they were needed for defense of Australia. Mr. Churchill solicited help from Mr. Roosevelt, who appealed to Prime Minister John Curtin that the United States already had planned to send a large force to Australia, and that the security of Burma was vital to the defense of the whole area, including Australia. Nevertheless the Australian Government remained firm in its decision and the Australian troops were not available.[102]

On 18 February the Pacific War Council in London submitted to the Combined Chiefs of Staff its comments on ABDACOM's series of despatches. The council stressed the importance of defending Java to the utmost, leaving it to the discretion of General Wavell to augment his forces there with prospective naval reenforcements (where these were to come from was not clear) and with U.S. planes assembled in Australia. The council urged the U.S. Joint Chiefs of Staff to consider the possibility of sending more ships, particularly submarines, to ABDA and to investigate the question of attacking the mainland of Japan with carrier-based planes. The council recommended that troops en route to Java from the Middle East should be used to augment the defenses of Burma, Ceylon, and Australia, with one British division going to Burma and Ceylon, one Australian division to Burma, and two other Australian divisions directly to Australia.[103]

The Combined Chiefs of Staff were concerned that a copy of the resolutions of the Pacific War Council had been sent directly to ABDACOM. They interpreted it as "usurping the functions of the Combined Chiefs of Staff in that they [the council] were exercising control over military strategy." However, at a meeting attended by Dutch and New Zealand military representatives, they approved a despatch which incorporated most of the council's proposals. After approval by the President and the Prime Minister, it was sent to ABDACOM.

Despite the several reports from General Wavell and statements by the Dutch that Java could not be held without considerable reenforcements, the chiefs were anxious that there be no appearance of deserting the Dutch in the East Indies. Consequently, their orders to General Wavell were that "Java should be defended with the utmost resolution by all combatant troops at present in the Island for whom arms are available.[104] Every day gained is of importance. There should be no withdrawal of troops or air forces of any nationality and no surrender." To assist his defense, General Wavell, at his discretion, might employ the aircraft being assembled in Australia and whatever naval forces were available. There could be no further reenforcements. All the land troops scheduled for transfer to Java from the west were to be diverted to Burma, Australia, and Ceylon.[105]

The following day General Wavell reported losses in his fighter force so heavy that instead of holding out for a maximum of two weeks, as he had predicted two days previously, it could hope to be effective for a few days at most. With only an irregular Dutch division and an assortment of British, Australian, and American troops for land defense, and with a naval force that could not possibly cover both ends of the island, General Wavell was faced with what appeared to be final preparations by the Japanese for an invasion of Java. A naval attack on a Japanese convoy assembled at Bali had done considerable damage but had failed to deter the threat of invasion. Consequently, General Wavell requested immediate decisions as to the destination of the Australian divisions en route to Java and the corps headquarters that had already arrived, as to whether Dutch shipping should be held for the eventual evacuation of personnel, and as to the policy regarding ABDA Headquarters.[106]

The CCS replied immediately to only the third of General Wavell's questions, and their answer to that one was only tentative until they should have decided the future of the ABDA Area. The U.S. Chiefs had agreed prior to their meeting with the other military representatives that ABDA Headquarters should be broken up, recommending "that Wavell be instructed to evacuate the British personnel contingent to India, and the United States and Australian contingents to Australia. And, that he adjust the matter of the Dutch with those officials direct."[107] The British Chiefs of Staff had recommended from London that the headquarters be moved to Fremantle. The Combined Chiefs agreed not to break up the headquarters immediately but to order it withdrawn and to leave the problem of its future location to General Wavell. Their orders were brief: "Your own headquarters will be withdrawn in such a manner, at such time and to such a place within or without the ABDA Area as you may decide, but its timely withdrawal is important.... When you withdraw report to whom you have transferred Command of Java."[108] Subsequently, with the approval of the President and the Prime Minister, they announced the following policy for personnel in Java:

> All men of fighting units for whom there are arms must continue to fight without thought of evacuation, but air forces which can more usefully operate in battle from bases outside Java and all air personnel for whom there are no aircraft and such troops particularly technicians as cannot contribute to defence of Java, should be withdrawn. With respect to personnel who cannot contribute to defence, general policy should be to withdraw U.S. and Australian personnel to Australia.[109]

On the same day orders were sent to General Brett from the War Department to proceed to Australia, when released by General Wavell, to assume command of U.S. forces there.[110] On the following day, the President made his decision to order General MacArthur out of the Philippines.

After a conference with Governor General Van Mook, who had recently returned from a visit to the United States, General Wavell returned to the CCS a recommendation that instead of ABDA Headquarters being withdrawn, the command be dissolved. He pointed out that the transfer of Burma to India left virtually only Java to be defended, and that that defense could be best conducted by the local Dutch command. He recommended further that the Philippines should revert to American control and northwest Australia to Australian command. In carrying this out General Wavell planned to disperse his command on the twenty-fifth, moving most of Headquarters to Colombo and leaving the remaining forces under Dutch command.[111]

At the same time Governor General Van Mook sent a despatch to General Marshall in a somewhat different tenor. He pointed out that abandonment of the ABDA Area would irreparably damage the white man's prestige in Asia, lower morale in Java, and throw away the opportunity to hold the island, giving Japan a chance to strike elsewhere while it consolidated a strong position in the East Indies. He urged that reenforcements to Java continue.[112]

Despite recommendations from the British Chiefs of Staff in London that the whole southwest Pacific area be partitioned between the British and the Americans, the CCS were reluctant to break up the ABDA Command lest such a move be interpreted as abandoning the Dutch. Consequently, they ordered General Wavell to dissolve his own headquarters and transfer the command of the ABDA Area to the Dutch, making it clear to them that the supply of reenforcements already allotted to the area would continue.[113] Although they were not prepared to decide on future arrangements in the area, the chiefs visualized ABDA's gradual disappearance. The Dutch would nominally exercise the command, including over-all command of the Philippines, and the program of reenforcements would continue, but in time some other system would be devised for the area. What that system would be was already under discussion.[114]

General Wavell turned over the command to the Dutch on 25 February 1942. The Dutch Governor General, General Wavell, and the Combined Chiefs of Staff all favored an immediate public announcement of the change in command. They felt that the word would get out anyway, and that to prevent general interpretation of the move as indicating total defeat of the United Nations and abandonment of the Far East, a carefully phrased communique should be issued, explaining the action and stressing continuing support of the Dutch. The Prime Minister, however, refused to approve it. He thought that the wrong interpretation would be put on any announcement that was released and that it would add unnecessarily to the dangers of General Wavell's journey to India.[115]

On receipt of the Prime Minister's opinion, the President reversed his original approval. However, the news of General Wavell's departure soon leaked. After considerable discussion a press announcement was finally issued on 2 March:

> 1. After the loss of Malaya and the entry of the Japanese into Sumatra, which separated Burma from the Netherlands East Indies, it was decided that command of land, sea and air forces of the United Nations in the Netherlands East Indies should pass to the Dutch, who are continuing to receive all available assistance from the United Nations.

2. With the approval of His Majesty the King, General Wavell is resuming his appointment as Commander-in-Chief, India, which now includes responsibility for operations in Burma, and close cooperation with China.

3. There is no change in the present arrangements for the general coordination of strategic policy in the war against Japan.[116]

This was the end of the first attempt at unified command in the Pacific. ABDA had existed in a period of crisis and uncertainty, when the JCS and CCS organizations were just being developed and when they were confronted with numerous problems for whose solution there was no precedent. ABDA and its detailed problems occupied the chiefs' attention to an extent that commands established later in the war did not, but those commands would profit from this first experience. While ABDA had not succeeded in holding against the determined Japanese advance, by the time of its dissolution that advance had slowed to a considerable extent and ABDA's successors in the Pacific could stabilize a line of defense and shortly take the first steps of the offensive that finally led to the defeat of Japan.

Chapter IV

REORGANIZATION OF STRATEGIC COMMANDS IN THE PACIFIC

SPHERES OF RESPONSIBILITY

Establishment of the ABDA Command during the Arcadia Conference was essentially an emergency measure designed to coordinate the efforts of the participating nations to stem the tide of Japanese aggression. Outside ABDA's borders lay the great areas of the Pacific Ocean, the major portion of Australia, all of New Zealand, the huge mass of China, and following the transfer in February, Burma with the only line of communications to China. The U.S. Pacific Fleet was responsible for defense of most of the Pacific Ocean area, Australia and New Zealand defended their own shores, China was charged with its own defense, and Burma came under the Commander in Chief, India. If there was to be a large-scale coordinated effort against the Japanese and a systematic attempt to defeat them, some other command organization was clearly called for.

The progress of the enemy in the first months of war was rapidly dividing the area in two, splitting off Australia and the Pacific Ocean from the continent of Asia. Thus it was natural that thinking in Washington and in London should develop along the lines of a basic division of command units between the same two areas. This concept seems to have been generally accepted for some time before it was officially defined.[1] It was not until the fall of Singapore on 15 February 1942 that earnest discussions of the future command setup for the war against Japan began.

In the evening of 15 February President Roosevelt and Mr. Harry Hopkins had a long talk, reviewing the current situation and the immediate demands upon the United Nations. Afterward Mr. Hopkins drew up a list of priorities for United Nations action, headed by the recommendation that the United States take primary responsibility for reenforcing the Netherlands East Indies, Australia, and New Zealand, sending men, munitions, and material to the area by 31 March. The United States also should continue primary responsibility for military aid to China "in terms of materiel." The British, on the other hand, would take primary responsibility for reenforcing Burma and defending Rangoon. Each would furnish supplementary aid in the other areas as available.[2]

A few days later Mr. Roosevelt incorporated similar ideas in a message to Prime Minister Churchill expressing sympathy over the loss of Singapore. He spoke of two flanks, "the right based on Australia and New Zealand and the left in Burma, India and China," and he recommended that the United States take immediate responsibility for reenforcement of the right, with Australia as the main base, and the British take immediate responsibility for reenforcement of Burma and India. The United States would continue to move supplies, mainly aircraft, through into China. This, he realized, would mean reconsidering the ABDA Command and shifting personnel.[3]

The question of reorganization had been introduced into the CCS discussions by Admiral Ernest J. King the day before the President's message was sent.[4] Prompted by the threat of Japanese attack on the line of communications between Hawaii and Australia and the imminent splitting of ABDA into two areas by the loss of Sumatra, Admiral King proposed that immediate consideration be given to the question of establishing an integrated theater, India-Burma-China, which would be primarily a British concern, and enlarging the ABDA area, possibly eventually to include all of ANZAC, or vice versa. If this was not considered desirable, perhaps the remainder of ANZAC after modification of ABDA should be absorbed into the Pacific Fleet area. In any event, Admiral King pointed out, the primary interest in the ANZAC Area was American and closely related to the activity of the Pacific Fleet. Might it not be well to make this "a U.S. sphere of activity"? At least it was essential to take immediate steps to develop strong defenses on the route from America to Australia and to interest the Australian Government to concern itself more with the protection of this line of communications and less with its own defenses.

There is no indication that Admiral King's suggestions were discussed at any length at this meeting, but in the next few days similar proposals were made in various quarters. The Joint U.S. Strategic Committee (JUSSC), for example, in a report on "The Strategic Situation in the Japanese Theater of War," recommended that, since loss of the Malay Barrier would divide the Pacific Theater in two, defense of Burma and India, which the committee considered the more important area to the United Nations, strategically and politically, should be made a responsibility of the British, whose economic and political interests there predominated.[5] A minority report presented by one unidentified member of the committee recommended that defense of Australia and New Zealand should also be a British responsibility.[6] The Joint Staff Planners (JPS) offered their suggestions in an informal paper, recommending that Northwest Australia and British New Guinea be detached from ABDA to Australia and an "Australian Command" be established, under the principle of unity of command. The ANZAC naval area would continue unchanged. Command in ABDA would be given over to the Dutch, and General Wavell would be transferred to India.[7] No action was taken on either of these suggestions.

On 23 February the Combined Chiefs of Staff considered a report from the British Chiefs of Staff in London adopting the President's principle of strategic responsibility.[8] The British recommended establishment of a United States area, comprising the Pacific Ocean including Australia and New Zealand, and a British area, the Indian Ocean, with the dividing line from Singapore through the Java Sea, Flores Sea, and Bandar Sea as far as 129° East, thence due south to Australia. Local governments within the areas would be responsible for their local defense, but the power exercising strategic control would furnish necessary additional military forces. This power would also be "responsible for military policy within that area but in accordance with the general policy agreed between London and Washington for the conduct of the war as a whole."[9] The CCS took up this proposal together with the question of transferring General Wavell and breaking up the ABDA Area. They decided, however, that a simultaneous removal of General Wavell and transfer even of northwest Australia from the ABDA Area "might be construed as abandoning the Dutch in difficult circumstances." So they postponed consideration of subdivision of ABDA and "instructed the Combined Staff Planners to recommend a line of demarcation between the Pacific and Indian Ocean predicated on the assumption that Java fell to the Japanese."

The planners' report was prepared by Admiral Turner of the Navy War Plans Division.[10] It disagreed with the British line of division which would have placed all of the Malay Barrier as far east as Timor in the British Indian Ocean Area, creating a situation in which islands within range of planes based on Australia and vital to its defense would not be under control of the power responsible for Australia's protection.[11] Admiral Turner pointed out that the passes of the Malay Barrier would have to be closely guarded by submarines, and there were only two attached to the British Eastern Fleet. Furthermore he thought that those submarines and aircraft operations designed to execute "the strategy of attrition and economic pressure," to contain as much of the enemy forces as possible within the ABDA Area, and to support American forces in the Philippines would best be conducted from bases on Australia.[12] Consequently Admiral Turner recommended that the ABDA Area not be subdivided but be enlarged to the south to include all of Australia and on the other sides be modified to conform more closely to the requisites of a defensive strategy. This meant running the western boundary down the east coast of Asia to Singapore, along the east coast of Sumatra, and then southward to Australia, placing all of the Netherlands East Indies except Sumatra east of the dividing line. On the north and east Admiral Turner proposed to move the ABDA boundaries 10° closer to the Philippines. He recommended deferring consideration of the future of the ANZAC Area.

The CCS limited discussion to the line of division between U.S. and British spheres of responsibility and ultimately accepted the line Admiral Turner proposed, but more precisely defined.[13] They deferred consideration of the other boundaries in the Pacific and of the system of command there. The U.S. planners, however, had begun to develop new command schemes for the Pacific, and other events were precipitating a solution to the problem.

EVACUATION OF GENERAL MACARTHUR FROM THE PHILIPPINES

Despite determined American efforts to get supplies through to the Philippines by plane, submarine, and small surface craft, it became increasingly apparent during the first two months of 1942 that only a miracle could deliver reenforcements and equipment to the beleaguered forces on Bataan in sufficient strength to furnish hope of holding any position on the peninsula. It appeared almost certain that within a short time the defenders would be forced to seek refuge in the fortress of Corregidor.

As the prospect worsened it seemed wise to consider evacuating certain key personnel from Bataan to a position where they could be of greater benefit to the total war effort. The desirability of removing President Manuel Quezon had already been discussed at the end of December, but at the time General MacArthur had recommended against it, suggesting that "Quezon's departure would undoubtedly be followed by the collapse of the will to fight on the part of the Filipinos...."[14] On 2 February, however, the situation was such that General MacArthur inquired from General Marshall whether, in the event of the loss of Bataan, it would be possible to provide means of escape for President Quezon and other government officials.[15] President Roosevelt and his military advisors approved the plan to evacuate key personnel, whoever and whenever General MacArthur should decide, and it was arranged with the Navy that a submarine should be available for transportation.[16] They also began to consider the advisability of evacuating General MacArthur himself from the islands rather than leaving him to the inevitably hopeless stand on Corregidor.

In the days that followed the situation grew worse. President Quezon, embittered by the lack of visible evidence that the United States was sincerely trying to aid the Philippines, and with no hope of driving the invaders from Philippine soil, finally proposed to President Roosevelt that the U.S. Government immediately grant independence to his country and that both the United States and Japan agree to remove their troops and respect the islands' neutrality.[17]

General MacArthur forwarded this message born of desperation to Washington together with a strong statement of his own estimate of the military situation:

> You must be prepared at any time to figure on the complete destruction of this command. You must determine whether the (mission?)...of delay would be better furthered by the temporizing plan of Quezon or by my continued battle effort. The temper of the Filipinos is one of almost violent resentment against the United States. Every one of them expected help and when it has not been forthcoming they believe they have been betrayed in favor of others.... In spite of my great prestige with them, I have had the utmost difficulty during the last few days in keeping them in line. If help does not arrive shortly nothing, in my opinion, can prevent their utter collapse and their complete absorption by the enemy.

Shocked by these messages, Secretary of War Stimson and General Marshall hastened to the White House to discuss them with President Roosevelt and then spent most of the day, aided by Mr. Sumner Welles, Admiral King, and Admiral Stark, drafting appropriate replies.[18] The results of their efforts were strong and dramatic as the situation required. In the reply he sent to President Quezon, Mr. Roosevelt stressed the contrast between the historic attitudes of the United States toward the Philippines and the actions of the Japanese toward those nations which came under their sway. Was it any "longer possible for any reasonable person to rely upon [a] Japanese offer or promise"? He pledged the support of American troops to the end, closing his message with the assurance that

> Whatever happens to the present American garrison we shall not relax our efforts until the forces which we are now marshaling outside the Philippine Islands return to the Philippines and drive the last remnant of the invaders from your soil.

To General MacArthur President Roosevelt gave permission, should he consider it necessary, to arrange for capitulation of the Filipino forces. For U.S. forces, however, the policy was firm and clear:

> American forces will continue to keep our flag flying in the Philippines so long as there remains any possibility of resistance.... The duty and the necessity of resisting Japanese aggression to the last transcends in importance any other obligation now facing us in the Philippines.
> ...It is mandatory that there be established once and for all in the minds of all peoples complete evidence that the American determination and indomitable will to win carries on down to the last unit.
> ...I particularly request that you proceed rapidly to the organization of your forces and your defenses so as to make your resistance as effective as circumstances will permit and as prolonged as humanly possible.[19]

Despite the apparent uncertainty with which he had forwarded President Quezon's proposal, General MacArthur's reply to President Roosevelt's directive was emphatic in disclaiming any intention of surrendering the Filipino elements of his command.[20] He assured Mr. Roosevelt, "My plans consist in fighting my present battle position in Bataan to destruction and then holding Corregidor in a similar manner." But events moved rapidly, and he was not to be left much longer to direct the defense of the Philippines.

On 16 February 1942 plans were set in motion to evacuate President Quezon to Mindanao, and with the increasing urgency of the situation in the southern portion of ABDA the President and the military leaders in Washington began to discuss more seriously the advisability of moving General MacArthur himself, at least as far as Mindanao.[21] As General Marshall reported it to General MacArthur their consideration dwelt on: (1) the basic importance of continuing the defense of Bataan and Corregidor; (2) the problem of continuing resistance in the southern islands of the Philippines; (3) the effects of the departure of President Quezon; (4) the effect continuing American resistance would have on the future of the Philippines; (5) the greater range of personal influence General MacArthur could exert if removed to Mindanao.[22] In addition, one of the strongest factors in the final decision was the enormous reputation which General MacArthur had acquired and the boost in morale which his arrival would give to the worried peoples of Australia and New Zealand.

On 22 February, in conference with General Marshall, Admiral King, and Mr. Hopkins, President Roosevelt made the decision, and orders were sent at once to General MacArthur to leave Fort Mills and proceed via Mindanao to Australia to take command of all U.S. troops there.[23] General MacArthur was also told that the President intended to persuade the British and Australian Governments to accept him as commander of the reconstituted ABDA Area. He did not leave at once, replying that he would delay his departure until what he considered the proper psychological moment, lest the Filipino people feel that they were being deserted.[24] By 17 March, when he reached Australia, plans for reorganizing the commands in the Pacific were practically complete.

OVER-ALL COMMAND ORGANIZATION

Two days after the Combined Chiefs of Staff had reached agreement on a dividing line between the Pacific Ocean and the Indian Ocean, Prime Minister Churchill sent Mr. Roosevelt a message requesting that the United States send two additional divisions to Australia and New Zealand and furnish emergency shipping to transport more troops from the United Kingdom to the Middle East.[25] After a series of meetings with U.S. and British military leaders the President agreed to the request in an official reply prepared by the Combined Staff Planners. At the same time he sent a second, personal message, which he seems to have drafted himself after talking with General Marshall, expressing to the Prime Minister his view that the existing organization of operational commands, particularly in the southwestern Pacific, required simplification.[26]

The President proposed that the world be divided into three general areas: (1) A Pacific Area, including "the Pacific Ocean and all of the land areas touching thereon, such as China, Australia, New Zealand, etc." Local operations there would be under local command, but over-all command would be vested in a single American officer with the JCS exercising strategic control, advised by a council including representatives of Australia, New Zealand, the Netherlands East Indies, and China. Mr. Roosevelt thought the Pacific Council should be moved to Washington, possibly retaining a duplicate council in London which would consider political problems. (2) A Middle Area, "extending from Singapore to and including India and the Indian Ocean, Persian Gulf, Red Sea, Libya and the Mediterranean." There the British would have responsibility for operations and major decisions, and the United States would allocate to the area as much equipment as possible. (3) A European and Atlantic Area which would be a combined U.S.-British responsibility. The CCS would not only control the third area but also coordinate and define grand strategy in all areas, their "authority...reinforced by the fact that they hold the strings on distribution of war materials."[27]

President Roosevelt discussed his views thoroughly with General Marshall before passing them on to the Prime Minister, and General Marshall acted as spokesman for the President to the Joint Chiefs of Staff. He presented them with a formal, comprehensive statement of the suggestions that had been made to the Prime Minister, specifically outlining the plans for division of the world into three areas of strategic responsibility. The paper also included a statement, drafted at the President's request, of the relation of the Joint and the Combined Chiefs of Staff to these strategic commands:

> (b) In any area for which either the United Kingdom or the United States is hereinafter assigned separate strategic responsibility, the Joint Chiefs of Staff of the government concerned shall exercise jurisdiction over all matters of minor strategy and all operations.
>
> (c) Each government will be responsible (within any area over which it exercises separate strategic direction) for arranging necessary coordination and cooperation with other United Powers whose territory or operational forces may be involved therein, and will, by agreement with such other governments, set up necessary control machinery.
>
> (d) The Combined Chiefs of Staff will exercise direct supervision over both grand and minor strategy in areas of joint responsibility and are charged with arranging necessary cooperation and coordination in such areas with other United Powers whose territory or operational forces may be involved therein.[28]

The JCS and the CCS, to whom General Marshall's paper was subsequently presented, discussed it initially as a matter for information. At a later meeting the British representatives agreed to send it to London for comment.[29] But, although the Prime Minister accepted the division of the world into three areas and indirectly approved the principle of strategic control incorporated in the directives to the Pacific commanders, the paper in which they were formally presented to the CCS never received official approval from London.[30]

Mr. Churchill did not respond to Mr. Roosevelt's message for over a week, during which the JCS had proceeded to approve directives to the new Pacific commanders. When he did reply, he postponed comment on the proposed Atlantic Area, but he reported that he and the British Chiefs of Staff saw "great merits in [the] simplification resulting from American control over [the] Pacific sphere and British control over [the] Indian sphere, and indeed there is no other way."[31] He approved the President's proposal for a single American commander in chief over all allied forces in the Pacific under the U.S. Chiefs of Staff. However, he had one reservation. He thought that the U.S. and British navies from Alaska to Capetown should work "to a common strategy," under a single command, that is, under the

Combined Chiefs of Staff, who in turn would be directly under himself and President Roosevelt.

Mr. Churchill approved the idea of giving the U.S. Chiefs executive control of the Pacific Area, but he thought that on larger issues advice would have to be sought from a second Pacific War Council in Washington. Mr. Roosevelt also had suggested two councils, one in Washington to give advice on operational matters and one in London to advise on political questions. This separation of jurisdiction is a feature of the U.S. Government, but it is not true of the British, and the Prime Minister rejected it on the grounds that the two matters are interwoven at the top and cannot be separated. In his view the Pacific Council in London should discuss the whole state of war against Japan and send their views to Washington where responsibility for war in the Pacific was vested. The Council in Washington would in turn send its views to London where lay the executive control of the Indian theater.

Mr. Churchill had forwarded the President's proposals to the Governments of Australia and New Zealand, and he sent their comments to Washington a few days after despatching his own.[32] Both of the Dominions approved the principle of areas of strategic responsibility, although not entirely in agreement with the suggested boundaries between them.[33] But they had consistently argued for representation on the body that determined strategy in the Pacific and had been dissatisfied with the Pacific War Council in London. They now renewed their pleas and announced that they desired

> to establish in Washington a Staff comprising a Naval and Army and an Air Force Officer who would act as the technical advisers to the Australian Government Representative on the Pacific War Council and who for the purpose of Anzac strategy should be associated with the American Chiefs of Staff as the joint body for advice to the Pacific War Council on the larger issue.[34]

The U.S. Joint Chiefs of Staff were strongly opposed to this arrangement, fearful as ever of political control over military strategy.[35] They thought, too, that if it were necessary to have approval of Australian, New Zealand, Free French, Chinese and Dutch representatives and their governments before instituting a military operation, the whole process would be unwieldy and too slow. As General Marshall pointed out, the other nations held a power of veto in that theoretically they could at any time withdraw their forces from any operation of which they disapproved. Of course, General Marshall added, "the geography of the Southwest Pacific, coupled with enemy aggressiveness, made actual withdrawal of forces a practical impossibility." The chiefs were agreed that operations of the Pacific Council should be "political and of a nature to let off steam but not such as would in any way affect the United States in its military decisions."[36]

The Joint Chiefs of Staff incorporated their views on the Pacific War Council and their plans for subdivision of the Pacific Theater in a memorandum to the President intended to be sent to the Prime

Minister[37] as a reply to the original proposals from the Dominions. This was the last officially recorded action of the Joint and Combined Chiefs of Staff in respect to the Pacific War Council. The final decision was made on a higher level.[38]

Dr. H.V. Evatt arrived in Washington from Australia on 30 March 1942, announcing to the press that it was his mission to secure establishment of a Pacific Council in Washington on which Australia would be represented. Ten days later it was announced from the White House that a Pacific War Council, on the ministerial level, was being set up in Washington, a "consultative" body which "would discuss broad questions relating to the war effort." Its first meeting was held on 1 April.[39] This body, composed as it was of representatives of many different national views, however, still did not entirely satisfy the Australians, who soon learned that the most effective way of achieving desired ends was to establish "relationships with the President, who of course indirectly influences decisions down the line."[40]

ESTABLISHMENT OF THE PACIFIC AREAS

While areas of strategic responsibility and establishment of a second Pacific War Council were being considered on the top level, the Joint Chiefs of Staff had proceeded with plans for subdivision of the Pacific Theater into two commands. Despite the President's suggestion to the Prime Minister that there be a single commander over the whole theater, the Joint Chiefs' discussion from the beginning was concerned with separate commands directly under the JCS. The desirability of single direction for operations against Japan in the Pacific is so obvious that it must be assumed that the U.S. Chiefs did not agree on how such an arrangement could be set up. The obvious choice for the position, obvious because of his popularity, was General MacArthur, to whose direction the Navy would never have given the fleet. Apparently there was no naval commander acceptable as senior to General MacArthur, and so the solution was to establish two commands under the Joint Chiefs of Staff.

Discussion of the future organization of the ABDA Area had repeatedly been postponed by the Combined Chiefs of Staff, but the problem was not unrecognized. On 2 March 1942 Admiral King suggested to the JCS that the islands of Fiji, Samoa, and New Caledonia be included with ANZAC as bases for future offensive action.[41] He visualized ANZAC (revised) and ABDA as two subdivisions of a single command and proposed to divide the remainder of the Pacific into three large units that could be controlled with available troops, a South, a Central, and a Northern Pacific Area, separated at the equator and at 40° North. This scheme was more detailed than any that had yet come up for discussion by the Joint Chiefs of Staff, and Admiral King explained it at considerable length, but there was no decision.

Three days later the Combined Chiefs of Staff took the first step toward breaking up the ABDA Area. The extremely weak condition of that command and the virtually unrestricted advance of the Japanese had impressed upon the Australian and New Zealand Governments the vulnerability of their positions and led them to formulate joint plans for creation of a new strategic command, primarily for defense of their own territory but also as a base for an ultimate offensive against the Japanese. The first step was for the Australian Government to request, in accordance with agreed procedure, that that part of northern Australia still under ABDA revert to Australian command, reserving to the Dutch the right to operate aircraft from bases in the area as desired.[42] Apparently the Dutch representatives in London agreed with the Australian premise that their commander in Java had more than enough to handle with his own local defense problems, for the Pacific War Council approved the request, and it was sent via the British Chiefs of Staff to the CCS on 5 March. The U.S. Chiefs approved it informally, and the U.S. member of the Combined Secretariat reported the decision to the Dutch on the following day.[43]

During the preceding week Lieutenant General George H. Brett had sent summaries of the discussions of the Dominion Governments to Washington, urging immediate action to reorganize the strategic areas. He was assured by General Marshall that thinking in Washington was much the same as that in Australia, although official discussion of what was to follow ABDA was thought to be premature. General Marshall also implied that the War Department would approve an official suggestion, already recommended in the Australian press, that General MacArthur be assigned a new unified command in the southwestern Pacific, an interesting comment in view of General Marshall's earlier statement to General MacArthur that the President intended to persuade the British and Australian Governments to accept him for such a post.[44]

The official views of the Australian and New Zealand Governments on command in the Pacific were relayed to the CCS by the British Chiefs and the Prime Minister on 7 March.[45] The Dominion Governments proposed that the existent ANZAC Area be expanded to include Australia, New Zealand, and the neighboring islands, the area to the north including Timor, Ambon, and all of New Guinea, and as much sea area to the west as should be determined. An American officer would be made Supreme Commander (General Brett was recommended because of his familiarity with the area), with a subordinate naval commander and separate Army and air commanders in Australia and New Zealand. Representatives of the two Dominions would sit on the CCS, where strategical control would be vested. An ANZAC Council, comprising representatives of the United States, the United Kingdom, Australia, and New Zealand, would be created above the CCS, to determine and direct the total effort in the Pacific.

Inasmuch as the Combined Chiefs of Staff had agreed four days before that this area would be in the U.S. sphere of strategic responsibility, the Australian proposal was turned over to the U.S. Joint Chiefs of Staff.[46] Admiral King at once objected to the organization. It would, he said, "cut across the whole system of command and operations of the United States Pacific Fleet." In his view a more logical arrangement would be to place Australia and New Zealand in separate commands, for Australia and the approaches to it through New Guinea and through the Dutch East Indies formed a strategic entity while New Zealand belonged more logically with the islands of the line of communications from America.[47] This principle was adopted by the naval planners, who immediately prepared a paper commenting on the Australian proposals.[48] The planners proposed establishing a new "Australian Area" which, except for the exclusion of the Philippine Islands, had approximately the same boundaries as the enlarged ABDA Area, suggested earlier by Admiral Turner, with the eastern line between the Solomon Islands and the New Hebrides. East of the "Australian Area" the Navy's plan subdivided the "Pacific Ocean Area" into a Southeast Pacific Sub-Area, east of 110° West and south of 15° North, a South Pacific Sub-Area, and a North Pacific Sub-Area, divided at the equator. The Commander in Chief, U.S. Pacific Fleet, would assign an officer to command the South Pacific Area, presumably a naval officer, although the paper did not say so, and would himself command forces in the North Pacific. Operational control of both the Australian Area and the Pacific Ocean Area would be vested in the Joint Chiefs of Staff, who would consult as necessary with the military representatives in Washington of Australia and New Zealand. It was recommended that the Pacific War Council be moved from London to Washington. Its function and status there were not defined except that, jointly with the President, it would appoint a U.S. officer Commander in Chief of the Australian Area, placing all United Nations forces there under his command.

The Army War Plans Division also prepared a paper "to implement instructions issued by the President...and in response to the proposals of [the] New Zealand and Australian Governments." The Army planners adopted the arrangement recommended by the Dominions, including within a single strategic area all the major land masses of the south and southwest Pacific. It was proposed to establish a Southwest Pacific Area comprising "all land and sea areas in the Pacific for which the United States is made responsible, Southwest of the line Philippines, Samoa (both inclusive), thence south along the meridian of 170°W." The region to the northeast would be designated the North Pacific Area, under command of a U.S. naval officer. The participating governments would select a Supreme Commander for the Southwest Pacific Area, perferably an American, and General MacArthur must certainly have been tacitly understood to be the Army's choice. Military representatives of the other governments would sit with the Joint Chiefs of Staff for all combined questions relating to the area.[49]

The JCS discussed the two proposals on 9 March 1942.[50] Admiral King spoke at some length in support of the Navy's view, pointing out that he thought it was essential to get the Australians interested in defense of the approaches to Australia instead of concentrating solely on continental defense. He argued again that the two Dominions did not logically constitute a single strategic area, and he foreshadowed subsequent difficulties by stating a further reason for the line the Navy recommended, "to give freedom of action to the Naval Commander as it would not be possible for a supreme commander in Australia to control contemplated offensive operations toward the northwest. This control must be exercised from Washington."[51]

General Marshall apparently saw the wisdom of yielding on this point, for he did not argue for the Army's proposal. He did urge, however, that the Philippine Islands be included in the Southwest Pacific Area for "psychological reasons." On this Admiral King yielded, explaining that they had not been included in the Navy's plan because he thought the Southwest Pacific Area "did not have the means to extend itself northwest and westward from Australia." With this modification the JCS accepted the Navy's scheme for subdividing the Pacific. Preliminary notification was sent to the other nations concerned and to the local commanders.[52]

There remained the question of commanders to discuss, and most important of the commander in the Southwest Pacific Area. Despite the fact that General MacArthur had already been ordered to Australia and virtually promised command of the combined forces there, the minutes of the Joint Chiefs give no indication that his name was mentioned as a possible commander. Admiral King, who knew of these orders, proposed at this meeting that the commander be selected from the U.S. Army Ground or Air Forces and suggested that General Brett be directed to prepare to be Deputy Supreme Commander. General MacArthur arrived in Australia on 17 March. At the suggestion of President Roosevelt, Prime Minister Curtin at once nominated General MacArthur "Supreme Commander of all Allied Forces in the Southwestern Pacific." Although the establishment of this command was still not approved beyond the Joint Chiefs of Staff, preliminary notification was sent to General MacArthur on 18 March, ordering him to relinquish direct command of all forces and initiate arrangements for setting up the projected over-all organization.[53]

The following day the Navy War Plans Division completed drafts of directives for the commanders of the two areas. The planners had reverted to Admiral King's original proposal to subdivide the Pacific Ocean Area in three instead of two sections. They had also decided to go ahead with directives for both commanders although there was no such urgency in the Pacific Ocean Areas as in the Southwest Pacific Area where the Japanese were well entrenched and General MacArthur was waiting to take over a new command.[54] On 19 March Admiral Turner presented drafts to Admiral King, recommending that they be sent to the War Department and that both be enacted at the same time. The following day Admiral King forwarded the drafts to General Marshall, urging that the two chiefs decide on specific directives even though final agreement had not yet been reached by the various governments on political matters. He did not send the drafts to the JCS, he explained, "because, the proposals involved being on such a high level, I believe that you and I must solve them between ourselves, in order to save the time that might be lost through possibly prolonged discussions of the Planning Staff."[55]

General Marshall passed the draft directives to his planners, who undoubtedly discussed them with their naval colleagues, although the record does not specifically indicate any collaboration. The Army decided that they were satisfactory. At the JCS meeting of 30 March it was agreed to submit the directives to the President for approval.[56] If there was any objection to them on the part of General Marshall or any prolonged discussion, either at the JCS meeting or previously, the records give no sign. Mr. Roosevelt approved them on 31 March 1942.[57]

Except for the tasks assigned and one distinction in command authority, both of which will be discussed later, the provisions of the two directives were the same. They were developed from the original directive to the Supreme Commander of the ABDA Area and retained some of the conditions of that directive. There was a basic difference, however, in that whereas ABDA had been a unified command over the forces of four nations, each of which theoretically had an equal responsibility and equal representation, these were subdivisions of a larger theater for which the United States was to have strategic responsibility. This distinction was emphasized immediately when the British Chiefs of Staff insisted that the initial statement of the directives should read

> By agreement among the governments of Australia, New Zealand, the United Kingdom, the Netherlands, and the United States, the Pacific Theater...is designated an area of United States strategic responsibility.

rather than

> By agreement, etc., the Pacific Ocean Area (or the Southwest Pacific Area) has been constituted...

The United States was thus clearly responsible for subdivision of the larger area.[58]

The authority of ABDACOM had been limited rather stringently on the theory that it was easier to reduce than to add. The authority of the Supreme Commander, Southwest Pacific Area, and the Commander in Chief, Pacific Ocean Area (CinCPOA),[59] was not so strictly defined.[60] There survived from the ABDA directive specifically the restriction on responsibility for internal administration of the forces within the command, designed to prevent the over-all commander from becoming too deeply involved with any one force to the exclusion of the others. He might "coordinate the creation and development of administrative facilities," but the respective forces were responsible for their function. As in ABDA the orders of the Supreme Commander were to be considered by his subordinates "as emanating from their respective governments." Each was to have representation on the Commander's staff, but there was no provision for a balanced combined staff such as the ABDA Command had been intended to be. The United States was to be responsible for operations. The voices of the other Powers would be heard on higher levels in Washington. Finally, as in ABDA, the Supreme Commander was to control the issue of all communiques concerning the forces under his command.

The position of the new commanders in relation to higher military authority was clearly defined. Each was to receive his orders from the head of his own branch of service, i.e., Admiral King for the Pacific Ocean Area and General Marshall for the Southwest Pacific Area, who for this purpose would be acting as executive for the Joint Chiefs of Staff. To that body was assigned jurisdiction over all matters pertaining to operational strategy. Its decisions in turn were subject to agreements on grand strategical policy and related factors made by the Combined Chiefs of Staff. Either the Joint or the Combined Chiefs of Staff, whichever was appropriate, would coordinate operations of specific forces with those of the local forces when the former chanced to operate outside their own boundaries. There was no attempt to state the relationship between the chiefs and higher political authority.

In defining the relation of the commanders to their subordinate forces the two directives differed. Both men were designated as commanders "of all armed forces which the governments concerned have assigned, or may assign" to their areas; but the Supreme Commander, Southwest Pacific Area, was declared ineligible "to command directly any national force," while the Commander in Chief, Pacific Ocean Area, was to "exercise direct command of the combined armed forces in the NORTH and CENTRAL PACIFIC Areas." He would also exercise directly the command of forces in the South Pacific through a commander he would appoint. This distinction was included for the same reason that the two were given different titles. The "Supreme Commander" was to have under him sizable Australian forces as well as British and Dutch. As had been the case with General Wavell, General MacArthur was to be denied special categories for any of the forces under him in order to assure equivalent attention to all and to avoid complications involved in direct command of the forces of another nation.[61] With the intention of assuring equitable employment of naval and air forces as well as ground troops the naval planners had also carefully drawn the tasks assigned to General MacArthur so as to outline the proper functions of the other two branches.[62] The forces in the Pacific Ocean Area, on the other hand, would be largely U.S. Navy and Marine Corps, and the operations would be supported by the Pacific Fleet. In the vast expanse of the Pacific, where mobility and speed were vital, it was logical that the Commander in Chief should have direct command of the forces which were to execute the widely separated operations.

Each of the commanders was assigned tasks "in consonance with the basic strategic policy of the governments concerned," although no policy was defined.[63] The Supreme Commander, Southwest Pacific Area, was directed to:

>   *a*. Hold the key military regions of Australia as bases for

future offensive action against Japan, and in order to check the Japanese conquest of the SOUTHWEST PACIFIC AREA.

    b. Check the enemy advance toward Australia and its essential lines of communication by the destruction of enemy combatant, troop, and supply ships, aircraft, and bases in Eastern Malaysia and the New Guinea - Bismarck - Solomon Islands Region.

    c. Exert economic pressure on the enemy by destroying vessels transporting raw materials from the recently conquered territories to Japan.

    d. Maintain our position in the Philippine Islands.

    e. Protect land, sea, and air communications within the SOUTHWEST PACIFIC Area, and its close approaches.

    f. Route shipping in the SOUTHWEST PACIFIC Area.

    g. Support the operations of friendly forces in the PACIFIC OCEAN Area and in the INDIAN Theater.

    h. Prepare to take the offensive.

The Commander in Chief, Pacific Ocean Area, was directed to:

    a. Hold the island positions between the United States and the SOUTHWEST PACIFIC Area necessary for the security of the line of communications between those regions; and for supporting naval, air, and amphibious operations against Japanese forces.

    b. Support the operations of the forces in the SOUTHWEST PACIFIC Area.

    c. Contain Japanese forces within the PACIFIC Theater.

    d. Support the defense of the continent of North America.

    e. Protect the essential sea and air communications.

    f. Prepare for the execution of major amphibious offensives against positions held by Japan, the initial offensives to be launched from the SOUTH PACIFIC Area and SOUTHWEST PACIFIC Area.

Land defense of New Zealand was made a responsibility of the New Zealand Chiefs of Staff, subject to strategic decisions of the Commander in Chief, Pacific Ocean Area.

In the absence of records of the discussions that preceded approval of these directives or any extensive contemporary comment one can only speculate as to the significance of the difference between task "h" of the first and task "f" of the second. Apparently the Navy planners had worded the directives as they did with the intention that when the major offensives came they would be under naval command. The traditional Navy view of war against Japan in any case was that the major offensive would be across the Central Pacific rather than through the East Indies. But any large amphibious operations, in whatever area, should, naval planners thought, be under naval command. That the Army did not interpret Admiral Chester Nimitz's directive in the same way is evident in later discussions. Thus, when planning began for operations in the Solomons-New Britain-New Guinea area, Admiral King argued that although these islands lay within the Southwest Pacific Area, Admiral Nimitz should have strategic control, for these offensives were what the planners had visualized when they included task "f" in Admiral Nimitz's directive. In order to assign responsibility for the Guadalcanal campaign to the Commander, South Pacific, however, it was necessary to change the area boundary so that the island would not be in the Southwest Pacific Area.[64] A year later, when Admiral King proposed that the Joint Chiefs of Staff delegate to CinCPOA responsibility for coordinating timing of offensive operations in the whole Pacific Theater, the Army members of the Joint Staff Planners objected that such an arrangement would actually make General MacArthur subordinate to Admiral Nimitz. The Navy planners, however, insisted that Admiral Nimitz's task "f" must have been so worded in order that he would be responsible for coordinating major overseas operations with fleet operations throughout the Pacific.[65] It was probably to allow for just such flexibility that the original directives contained no further explanation of which offensive operations each man was to command.[66]

The two directives met with the immediate approval of the President.[67] With the change in the initial statement of agreement, they were also approved by the British and the representatives of the Netherlands Government.[68] The Governments of Australia and New Zealand expressed their dissatisfaction with the subdivision which placed them in different commands, but reluctantly they agreed to accept it "because of the necessity of an immediate decision."[69] They were concerned, however, that the proposed directives contained no guarantees that their forces might not be moved arbitrarily from their own areas, nor assurance that the local commanders might communicate freely with their own governments or appeal any order of the Supreme Commander which they found unacceptable, conditions that had been clearly stipulated in the ABDA directive. Their objections were met by a statement the chiefs had prepared for the President to answer the Australian Government's earlier objections to his proposal for division of strategic responsibility:

> Proposals of the U.S. Chiefs of Staff...made to the President as U.S. Commander in Chief are subject to review by him from the standpoint of higher political considerations and to reference by him to the Pacific War Council in Washington when necessary. The interests of the nations whose forces or whose land possessions may be involved in these military operations are further safeguarded by the power each nation retains to refuse the use of its forces for any project which it considers inadvisable.[70]

This statement was subsequently added to the text of the directives.[71]

Following receipt of official approval from the Australian and New Zealand Governments, orders were sent to General MacArthur to assume command of the Southwest Pacific Area as soon as practicable.[72] He took over officially on 18 April 1942. On 8 May 1942 Admiral Nimitz assumed command of the Pacific Ocean Areas including temporarily direct command of the South Pacific Area. It was not until 21 May that Vice Admiral Robert L. Ghormley arrived to become Commander, South Pacific Area and South Pacific Forces.[73]

Chapter V

MAINTAINING THE DEFENSIVE IN THE PACIFIC, FEBRUARY-MAY 1942

ALLOCATING RESOURCES

    Reorganization of the strategic commands in the Pacific areas was but one of numerous problems confronting the U.S. and British Chiefs of Staff in the first half of 1942. It was a time of shortages and of many conflicting demands. Shipping in particular was scarce, and every time a strategic decision was made something had to be cut back in order that the necessary forces might reach the chosen destination at the proper time. Aircraft, too, were in insufficient supply, and there was a difference of opinion between the services as to what project should have priority on available planes. Because of the scarcity of the means of war and because the machinery of the joint committees was just evolving, the Joint and Combined Chiefs of Staff concerned themselves as they never did later with a handful of planes or a couple of ships. During the first half of 1942 General Marshall's plan for the invasion of the European Continent was accepted in principle both by the Joint Chiefs of Staff and the President in Washington and by the British Chiefs of Staff and the Prime Minister in London. It was soon apparent, however, that others in the United States held different ideas of the degree to which all efforts should be concentrated on preparation for the operation and that the British were convinced that it could not be done on anywhere near the time schedule for which General Marshall hoped. In the war against Japan there was no hope for offensive action until June, for the enemy still held the initiative and U.S. strength was being built up slowly in the areas still held by friendly forces. There could be no major offensive in any theater of war until U.S. production had turned out the means to undertake it.

    The Arcadia agreement on grand strategy, it will be recalled, had included the statement that "only the minimum of force necessary for the safeguarding of vital interests in other theatres should be diverted from operations against Germany."[1] There had been no attempt to define "the minimum of force," and before the conference was over developments in the Pacific had clearly shown that the term could not be interpreted to mean that only a small amount of the available resources would be needed to hold against Japan and all else could be assigned at once to the war against Germany. It had proved necessary to attempt to salvage the situation in the Southwest Pacific by diverting there large amounts of shipping originally allocated to major projects in the Atlantic Area. This rearrangement had resulted in postponing the transfer of troops to Iceland and northern Ireland and in delaying the projected date for executing Gymnast, the British plan for occupation of Northwest Africa, on which combined planning had already begun. Subsequent developments had necessitated further increases for the Pacific and further modification of the original scheme for Gymnast until it became apparent that sufficient shipping was not available. At length the British planners recommended that, since planning for Gymnast had in fact become "an academic study," it should be treated as such and "no forces, material, or shipping, should be held in readiness for the operation."[2]

Another factor that complicated the basic strategy of preparing for an offensive first against Germany and maintaining the defensive elsewhere was the growing possibility that the Russians might not be able to prevent the Germans from breaking through the Caucasus and attempting to join the Japanese thrusting up from the Indian Ocean. Such a union of Axis forces would remove from British control the oil of the Middle East and would probably result in the collapse of Russia, since the supply route from the south would no longer be in Allied hands. Although British interests in the region predominated, Americans had interests there also, and the potential strategical consequences of an Axis linkage rendered it essential that the needs of the Middle East be given careful consideration.[3]

The rapid advance of the Japanese in the early months of the war resulted in an attempt to relieve the situation by emergency transfers of U.S. men and equipment to the Pacific Theater. With no agreement as to what constituted the essential minimum that would be diverted from the war against Germany and no established program of operations for which to concentrate resources, there were differences of opinion among military leaders throughout most of 1942 as to how much should go to the Pacific, and frequently distribution of the limited resources of the United States was determined by *ad hoc* decision.

The most serious shortage throughout the world in 1942 was in shipping. Whenever the Chiefs of Staff contemplated sending reenforcements to an area, it was necessary to investigate carefully the sources from which transportation could be secured and to weigh the anticipated gains from one project against the curtailment that would be necessary in another. So drastic was the situation that the Combined Chiefs of Staff even gave serious consideration to the possibility that it might become necessary to make a choice between holding the Middle East or the Far East, if it proved impossible to find ships to deliver adequate forces to both.[4] Losses from submarines and other causes were maintaining such a rate that it appeared doubtful that the net gain from new construction by the end of 1942 would be sufficient to do much toward alleviating the situation.[5]

Demands upon the limited resources of the United States were many and urgent as more of everything was needed in all the theaters of war. For planes in particular demands were heavy. Before the United States entered the war, the estimated production of all types of aircraft had been allocated, under the lend-lease policy of aid short of war, among the nations fighting the Axis. Thus much of the production vitally needed by a United States at war, with the air force in the process of expansion and large numbers of aircraft required for training as well as for equipping newly formed squadrons and fulfilling commitments overseas, was already promised to other nations. In addition Great Britain, scheduled to receive, in addition to its own manufactures, almost half of the total U.S. plane production in 1942, more than the United States of most types, had numerous new demands on its supply which the prewar allocations would not satisfy. From Russia, from the British Dominions, from South America, and from every American commander in the field came requests for more equipment.

It was aircraft for which the cries were loudest. With planes in such short supply and the joint and combined staff systems not yet completely organized the addition or subtraction of a very few planes from a given project was a matter for determination by the chiefs themselves. In the first week of February four requests for additional planes for the Southwest Pacific were received by the CCS. Two of these came from the British Chiefs of Staff. The previous week they had been approached by Australia and New Zealand, requesting fighter planes for local defense. Considering themselves able to meet only part of the request the British Chiefs asked the United States to allocate 199 P-40's to the Dominions in addition to 80 which the CCS had previously diverted from ABDA assignments to the defense of northeast Australia.[6] Meanwhile the British Staff Planners, concerned with the inability of New Zealand to furnish bombers and reconnaissance planes both for its own needs and for those of Fiji, for whose defenses New Zealand had been made responsible,[7] recommended to the Combined Staff Planners that the United States supply Fiji with bombers and New Zealand provide personnel to operate them.[8]

It was apparent that the unchecked approach of the Japanese was rendering Fiji's position increasingly vulnerable and that Australia and New Zealand were by no means secure from Japanese attack. But a War Department study of allocation figures for estimated U.S. plane production in 1942 indicated that the United States could not make additional commitments to meet these two requests without cutting into previous assignments for other critical needs.[9] Since the British were scheduled to receive an unknown quantity of planes from their own production as well as the major share of U.S. production, the Joint Staff Planners recommended that the system of allocations and commitments be reviewed. They also proposed that the British furnish sixteen medium bombers for New Zealand from February allocations, make every effort to provide New Zealand with thirty-six fighters, and as soon as practicable supply aircraft for at least four medium bomber reconnaissance squadrons. The proposals were turned down by the British planners, who did not feel that their previous commitments would allow any such diversions. The CPS finally compromised by recommending that New Zealand furnish light bombers to Fiji where the need for them was most urgent and that sufficient planes be given to the naval commander of the ANZAC Area to enable him to assume responsibility for reconnaissance in the area.[10]

The Combined Chiefs of Staff made no immediate decision on either request. Following the recommendation of the U.S. members they referred the whole question of plane allocations to the CPS with instructions to prepare, in collaboration with the Munitions Assignments Board (MAB), "A review of the aircraft production of the United Nations and the requirements of the various theatres of war."[11]

In the meantime the Joint U.S. Strategic Committee, alarmed at the threat of the Japanese forces moving into the Solomon Islands and the Bismarck Archipelago to New Caledonia, Fiji, New Guinea, and potentially Australia and New Zealand, recommended to the CPS that a force of heavy bombers be established immediately in northeastern Australia and New Guinea. The U.S. planners suggested that twelve U.S. heavy bombers be sent temporarily from Hawaii to the threatened area, to be replaced in Hawaii from a group of planes which had been produced for the British in January and were still available in the United States.[12] The British planners agreed to this diversion, but they pointed out that it would mean cutting down on the Royal Air Force's vital Coastal Command and that the planes would have to be replaced as soon as possible.[13] The bombers were sent to the area almost immediately and attached to the Pacific Fleet to avoid being placed under command of the Royal Australian Air Force, since a complete U.S. air organization had not yet been set up in Australia.[14] A report on the matter was finally presented by the Combined Staff Planners to the Combined Chiefs of Staff, who gave official approval to the plan on 3 March 1942, some three weeks after it had been executed.[15]

The fourth request that reached the CCS was for seventy-two fighters for the Netherlands East Indies. It was submitted by the Munitions Assignments Board. The board had ascertained that there was reasonable expectation that seventy-two more planes than estimated would be produced in the United States in February, and it had given the Dutch, who were clamoring for aid, provisional promise of thirty-six. The Combined Chiefs of Staff were somewhat unhappy that the board should have initiated such action, particularly since there were constant unfulfilled demands for planes from the Russians and from South America, in addition to the short supply in the United Kingdom and the United States. But in view of the board's prior commitment the CCS approved assignment of the planes to ABDA for Dutch use rather than directly to the Dutch.[16]

While these questions were still being considered, the British Chiefs of Staff, feeling that *ad hoc* assignments could not be long continued, urged formulation of "a broad strategic plan for the

conduct of the whole war against Japan" and tentatively outlined
their ideas of the air forces required in the Pacific for defense of
naval and air bases and for long range bomber offensives and reconnaissance.[17] The CCS agreed that a thorough study of the matter
should be made and directed the Combined Staff Planners to examine
the strategic situation in the Pacific and prepare a plan covering
all forces, which would include:

(a) The roles to be played by the Eastern and Pacific fleets,
the broad distribution of naval forces and the naval bases which
must consequently be held and developed.

(b) The air forces required to defend essential naval and air
bases, for the control of sea areas, and for building up the air
offensive.

(c) The land forces required to hold base areas in the first
defensive stage and the organization of amphibious striking
forces for the assumption of the air offensive.

The problem was referred to the Joint U.S. Strategic Committee,
which was already at work on an over-all study of the strategic deployment of U.S. forces.[18]

The JUSSC agreed first upon a revised statement of the basic
strategic concept for conduct of the war against two major enemies.
Reiterating the broad objective of "decisve defeat of (1) Germany
and her European Allies, (2) Japan," they emphasized the importance
of maintaining initially the strategic defensive in all theaters,
concurrently accelerating and expanding production. This involved
maintaining lines of communication and holding potential base areas
in the Pacific, stabilizing the theaters of actual operations, i.e.,
the Pacific and Middle East, and supporting the Russians and Chinese,
who were in direct contact with the enemy, while concentrating on
blockade, propaganda, and economic and diplomatic measures to wear
down enemy resistance. When superiority of forces had been attained, presumably in 1943, the United Nations could seize the
initiative, first against Germany, and undertake offensive action
according to a plan of their own devising.[19]

The members of the JUSSC found themselves unable to agree on the
interpretation of this concept in respect to the war against Japan.
Specifically they differed as to the amount of effort that could be
expended in the Pacific and the forces that would have to be sent
there while the major offensive was being undertaken against Germany and its allies in Europe. Consequently two reports were submitted.[20]

Support of Russia had been made a national policy, and the committee agreed that support should include not only supplies but an
offensive from Great Britain, initially from the air, of sufficient
magnitude to divert a large amount of German strength from the Russian front.[21] This, the minority (one member) thought, should be
undertaken in effective strength in 1942. It was agreed, however,
that planning for an offensive against Germany would have to be
reconciled with the situation in the Pacific, where the Japanese

held the superior position, both economically and strategically. Under the agreed strategy the United Nations could hope to do little more throughout that area than attempt to keep the positions they held and when possible make raids upon the enemy. The imminent Japanese occupation of the Malay Barrier would further complicate the situation by dividing the Pacific Theater into two regions: Burma-China-India and Australia-Anzac-Mid Pacific. Of these the former was more important, the committee reasoned, because: Burma was the gateway to China and India; China was containing large numbers of Japanese land and air forces; China was an important base area for future offensives against Japan; India was the key to the defense against a possible German-Japanese union in the Middle East, essential to security of the sea route to Russia via the Persian Gulf and to Egypt via the Red Sea, and an essential unit in the British economic and political system. Since British interests were paramount in India and Burma, it was agreed that that region should be a British responsibility. The minority maintained further that defense of Australia and New Zealand as well should be primarily a British responsibility.

The basic disagreement among the committee members had to do with the force to be allocated to defend the line of communications between the United States and the Southwest Pacific. The members agreed that the principal offensive effort for the time being would include only attacks by naval and air forces against Japanese shipping and outlying bases. The majority, however, advocated developing and securing major bases in Hawaii and Australia and a chain of air bases between them to give depth to the line of defense. This meant short and long range aircraft under a single command, the short range planes for local defense, the long range bombers in a mobile force based primarily in Hawaii and Australia, operating closely with carrier aircraft. The minority believed that such a program would jeopardize the immediate offensive against Germany, and he recommended that only the forces already committed to the Pacific should be sent there. He advocated a defensive effort concentrated on making secure only the major base areas of Hawaii and the mid-Pacific Islands and went so far as to say,

> it must be accepted that we are unable to establish a system of bases and forces, so disposed as to give depth to the defense of the line between Hawaii and Australia. We may be forced to relinquish our line of communications with Australia, if the Japanese attack elements of that line in force.[22]

Far from reconciling the differences among the members of their working committee the Joint Staff Planners apparently disagreed even more radically. From the fact that they met four times to discuss the report it may be concluded that there was wide difference of opinion, although the official minutes contain only a brief summary of the ultimate conclusions.[23] Admiral Turner, displeased with the indecisiveness and the controversial nature of the JUSSC paper and with what he considered overemphasis on air units and underemphasis on the strategic importance of the Middle Pacific islands to the defense of Australia and New Zealand, advocated scrapping the whole thing and making a new study on the basis of forces available, "presenting for immediate decision a picture of what we might be actually able to do, and thus avoid trying to settle the problem on more or less theoretical, and probably controversial, grounds."[24] The Army, however, was opposed to cancelling entirely the work the JUSSC had already done.[25] Ultimately, the Joint Staff Planners directed the committee to condense and combine the original reports, reconsider the problem of world-wide strategic deployment of U.S. forces, and estimate the major combat units and shipping that would be required in 1942 to "(1) (a) secure the Southwest Pacific Area, including Australia, or (b) secure the Eastern Pacific" and to undertake "(2) offensive action in the European theatre which will result in material diversion of German forces from the Russian front." Further, they were to recommend general courses of action and specific assignments for U.S. forces in 1942. Their study was to be based on three assumptions:

    a. Territorial integrity of North and South America and safety of coastal communications are vital, and are the responsibility of the United States.
    b. Increased safety of Atlantic Sea Communications is essential, and is a joint charge of the United States and the United Kingdom.
    c. Continuing an active Russian front against Germany is the surest means of absorbing German military energy, thus contributing to the security of India in the Middle East. Maintaining this front is essential to the defeat of Germany within a reasonable time.[26]

On the day this directive was given to the Joint U.S. Strategic Committee (24 February 1942) the outlook in the Southwest Pacific was far from promising. General Wavell, who had been ordered the day before to turn over command in ABDA to the Dutch, was preparing to depart for Ceylon, and the Joint Chiefs of Staff were just beginning to discuss reorganizing the command areas in the Pacific. The Japanese had already overrun most of ABDA and were threatening invasion of Java, the last major island and the heart of the Netherlands East Indies. It seemed probable that the enemy would consolidate his position in the islands of the East Indies and continue his operations in Burma, where he had already gained a foothold. Whether he would then move to attack Australia and/or New Zealand as the local governments feared, but the Combined Chiefs of Staff considered unlikely, whether he would branch out to the southeast and attack U.S. island bases, endeavoring to sever the line of communications between the United States and Australia, whether he would push on into the Indian Ocean and through Burma into India, or whether he would be satisfied with the territory he had already gained, no one could be certain. Against this background, the JUSSC undertook to study the deployment of forces of the United Nations.

    The committee concluded that whether it was decided to secure the entire area of the Southwest Pacific or only the Eastern Pacific would have little effect on the numbers of forces available for the European Theater.[27] In any case there would not be enough immediately available for a major offensive. There would, however, be enough to assist the British effectively in such an offensive in the fall of 1942, and of course the forces could be progressively increased. The committee's report included as an annex a plan for an invasion of Western Europe to be undertaken in 1942 and estimates of the forces required as compared with those actually available for such an operation. In view of the agreement on an initial offensive against Germany the committee recommended that "if the forces of the United Kingdom and the United States are to be successful in diverting German strength from the attack on Russia this year, an offensive must be initiated this summer of sufficient mass and intensity to be effective against Germany."

Again there was disagreement among the members of the Joint U.S. Strategic Committee as to how much of the resources of the United Nations would be required in the Pacific. Although one of the tasks recommended by the committee was to "secure the major base areas of Hawaii, the Mid-Pacific Islands, Australia and New Zealand and their sea and air communications with the United States,"[28] there were three views as to what this program would entail. The committee's report recommended that 202,508 ground troops of the Army, Navy, and Marine Corps be stationed in Hawaii, Australia, and on the islands between, and that the following air forces be assigned to the Pacific Theater:

	Heavy Bombers	Medium Bombers	Light Bombers	Pursuit
Hawaii	70		13	240
Christmas				25
Fiji		26		55
Tongatabu				25
Efate				25
New Caledonia		31		80
Australia	70	57	57	240

The bombers in Hawaii and Australia were to be employed as a mobile force to defend the islands between. Some of the committee members thought these assignments would not be enough; others thought they were too large. Since the group was unable to reach agreement, the members drafted alternative final recommendations incorporating the three points of view.[29]

The day before the Joint Staff Planners received this paper Mr. Churchill wrote to President Roosevelt, expressing great concern over the situation in the Middle East, where it appeared that the Germans might break through in the Caucasus.[30] When the war against Japan began, some of the forces of Australia and New Zealand that had been stationed in the Middle East had been sent to help meet the emergency in India and the Far East. Now the Dominions were clamoring for the return home of their troops still remaining in the

Middle East. To satisfy their demands for home defense without withdrawing these forces at a critical time the Prime Minister requested that the United States provide an additional division each to Australia and New Zealand. He also asked for a loan of U.S. shipping to carry approximately 40,000 British troops from the United Kingdom to the Indian Ocean and the Middle East, in addition to those British shipping could carry. Finally he requested information on the disposition and the operational plans of the U.S. Air Forces, recommended building up a large "Commando" force for attack on the Japanese flank, and urged increased naval protection for the ANZAC Area.

The President conferred with both U.S. and British military leaders, and the reply he sent to the Prime Minister was prepared by the Combined Staff Planners.[31] It was agreed that two U.S. Army divisions in addition to the 41st, already scheduled for departure for Australia, could be sent to the area in the next two months, provided the Australian and New Zealand divisions remained in the Middle East and provided some twenty-five cargo ships assigned to transport lend-lease material to the Red Sea and China were withdrawn. It was also determined after consultation with the Combined Military Transportation Committee (CMTC) that U.S. shipping could be furnished to move two British divisions from the United Kingdom to the Middle East and India in April and May.[32] This second movement would mean, however, that Gymnast could not be undertaken, that only the troops which these ships could carry could be moved from the United States to Great Britain, that no direct moves to Iceland could be made, that eleven cargo ships would have to be withdrawn from sailings to Burma and the Red Sea, and that American contributions to an air offensive or to land operations in Europe in 1942 would have to be curtailed. Such was the shipping shortage in early 1942.

This new commitment of troops and shipping altered the availabilities between the time the Joint U.S. Strategic Committee finished its report and the time the Joint Staff Planners discussed it. Consequently the planners directed the committee to prepare an estimate of the effect the President's decision would have on their study.[33]

In discussing the paper the JPS found themselves unable to reach agreement on any of the alternative recommendations their subcommittee offered, for apparently their views followed the same different lines. They finally redrafted the alternatives and submitted them together with the amended estimates to the Joint Chiefs of Staff in JCS 23, requesting an immediate decision.[34] The planners outlined three opinions of the relative urgencies of the situation in the two major theaters of war: (1) that, despite Russia's need of help in Europe, reenforcement of the Pacific should have priority, for the whole situation in that area would soon collapse without immediate support in greater strength than was allocated in this report; (2) that the basic objectives of the war effort would be most effective if the original concept was strictly adhered to and only the minimum of forces (as listed in this study) was assigned to maintaining the defensive in other areas while preparing for an early offensive against Germany; (3) that everything should be concentrated for an immediate offensive in Europe and no further increase be made in the Pacific. The first of these was certainly the view of the Navy members and particularly of Admiral Turner; the second represented the opinion of the Army War Plans Division and the Army Air Force members; it seems likely that the third was included primarily to balance the first and was not considered by anyone to be practicable.[35] Because of their difference, the Joint Staff Planners reported themselves

> unanimous in recommending that the Joint Chiefs of Staff at once decide on a clear course of action, and execute this decision with the utmost vigor. They suggest that the Chiefs of Staff may find a suitable course of action in one of the following:

> POSSIBLE COURSES OF ACTION

> (A) Ensure the security of the military position in the Pacific Theater by strong reinforcements, considerably stronger than those estimated by the Joint U.S. Strategic Committee, which would be at the expense of executing a vigorous offensive against Germany with United States Forces. Contain Japanese forces in the southern portion of the Pacific Theater; inflict attrition; and exert economic pressure by the destruction of vessels carrying strategic and war materials between the Empire and the Southwest Pacific Area. Transfer to the United Kingdom forces available after the security of the Pacific is ensured.

> (B) While Russia is still an effective ally, concentrate the mass of our forces for a vigorous offensive, initially from bases in England, with the objective of defeating Germany. Until Germany has been defeated, accept the possibility that the Southwest Pacific may be lost.

> (C) Provide the additional forces in the South Pacific Area considered by the Joint Strategic Committee as the minimum required for the defensive position and simultaneously begin to build up in the United Kingdom forces intended for offense at the earliest practicable time. This course of action contemplates that the British would provide the bulk of the forces for any offensive undertaken in 1942 from the United Kingdom.[36]

When the paper (JCS 23) was brought up for discussion at the JCS meeting on 16 March 1942, the situation in the Middle East was critical. Despite a strong stand the Russians had found it necessary to retreat to the Kerch Peninsula and were preparing to make a desperate fight for Sevastopol. It seemed highly possible that should the Crimea fall to the Germans they could continue on to take Rostov and penetrate into the Caucasus. To strengthen the defenses of the Middle East Area the British were requesting additional air forces from the United States.

Well aware of the potential consequences of the much feared linkage of German and Japanese forces through the Middle East, the Joint Chiefs of Staff were willing to agree to send men to that area provided the British, whose supply was greater, furnished planes for them to operate. But the chiefs felt strongly that pressure on the Russians could be effectively relieved only by opening an offensive against the Germans from the west. At their meeting of 16 March the JCS made no commitment in respect to the JUSSC's recommendation for an invasion of Western Europe in 1942, but they did reiterate the long-established concept that gave priority to the offensive in the European Theater. Although they did not accept verbatim any of the planners' alternatives, their decision was clear:

it was preferable;
    (a) To begin to build up in the United Kingdom forces intended for offense at the earliest practicable time.
    (b) To provide forces in the South Pacific Area in accordance with current commitments.[37]

THE PACIFIC VS. BOLERO

The Joint Chiefs' decision of 16 March that forces should be built up in the United Kingdom for an offensive at the earliest practicable time gave no indication of when the chiefs considered that time might be. The report of the Joint U.S. Strategic Committee included a plan for an invasion of Western Europe to assist the Russians in 1942, stressing the necessity for a firm, clearly defined military objective toward which to plan. The committee even suggested, "If the British are not willing to implement this concept adopted at Arcadia by launching an offensive in the European Theater this year, the agreed strategic concept should be re-evaluated, and the possibility of concentrating U.S. offensive effort in the Pacific Area considered."[38] However, the Joint Chiefs of Staff did not immediately commit themselves.

A week after the JCS decision Sir John Dill produced a British plan for an invasion of Europe. Prepared before Arcadia but not previously officially presented to the U.S. Chiefs, the plan called for an operation to be undertaken on the continent in 1943.[39] Confronted thus with two plans for a continental invasion, the Joint Chiefs recommended, and the Combined Chiefs directed, that the CPS study the two and attempt to reconcile them, estimating the possibilities of success for such an operation in 1942 and in 1943.[40]

The Army War Plans Division in the meantime had been preparing for General Marshall a study of its own which was completed before the CPS could get to work on a report. The study proposed an invasion of Western Europe in April 1943. Should the Russian situation become desperate, or the German position considerably weakened, the Army planners recommended a limited emergency operation to be undertaken in the fall of 1942, primarily with British troops, since no large U.S. force could be transported to the United Kingdom by that time. In order that the efforts of the United States and the United Kingdom could be concentrated on a specific objective as soon as possible, it was strongly recommended that *some* decision be made at once. The Navy and the President agreed that it was essential that a specific plan be adopted in order that some approved operation could be undertaken as soon as possible. They approved the proposal of the Army planners, and General Marshall was sent to London at the beginning of April to present it to the British Chiefs of Staff.[41]

General Marshall arrived in England to find the British greatly concerned over a Japanese naval force of considerable strength which had penetrated into the Bay of Bengal and attacked Colombo (5 April) and Trincomalee (9 April) in Ceylon, sunk a carrier, two cruisers, and several merchant ships, and inflicted considerable damage on shore installations.[42] The appearance of this force so close to the shores of India greatly alarmed the British, who had always dreaded the possibility of the Japanese gaining control of the Indian Ocean and had consistently deployed their Eastern Fleet with the purpose of preventing such an eventuality.

The anxiety of the British was reflected in their reaction to General Marshall's proposals. While favorably inclined to the operation on the continent in 1943, and at least temporarily willing to accept the limited operation in 1942, the British insisted on discussing at length the immediate requirements for defense of the Indian Ocean. They stressed the probability that, were the enemy to control that area, the United Nations would be unable to support their forces in the Middle East, oil supplies from Abadan would be lost, the southern supply route to Russia would be cut, and Turkey would probably fall easy prey to the Axis. To prevent such a turn of events the British requested that the United States send battleships, carriers, cruisers, and destroyers to reenforce the Eastern Fleet and despatch additional air forces to the Indian Theater.[43] Their suggestions were sent directly from the Prime Minister to the President, as well as being relayed by General Marshall to the War Department and the Joint Chiefs of Staff.[44]

However, U.S. naval leaders were opposed to combining vessels of the two nations in the Indian Ocean under British command. They had never approved the British scheme of concentrating on the defensive in that area, and they felt that the U.S. Navy's job was to engage the enemy wherever possible in the U.S. Navy's own area of strategic responsibility--the Pacific. Such operations, they felt, would also serve to divert Japanese attention from the Indian Ocean. Moreover it was suspected that part of the Japanese purpose in carrying out raids in the Bay of Bengal was to induce the United States and the United Kingdom to increase their forces in the Indian Ocean at the expense of the Atlantic and Pacific Theaters. Consequently the President and the U.S. Chiefs informed the British that they would continue to attempt to ease the situation in the Indian Ocean by engaging Japanese forces in the Pacific and to replace British forces in the Atlantic for transfer to the Eastern Fleet, but they could provide neither ships nor additional aircraft directly for the Indian

Ocean. They proposed, however, to deliver to India some British planes on hand in the United States, either to build up the 10th Air Force or to be operated by British crews in India. A few days later the crisis was considerably reduced by the reappearance of the Japanese striking force in home waters.[45]

General Marshall returned to Washington with the agreement of the British to invasion plans for 1942 (Sledgehammer) and 1943 (Roundup). Despite the decision that all effort was to be concentrated primarily on the build-up of forces in the European Theater (Bolero), there remained considerable disagreement in Washington as to how much would have to be diverted from that project in order to maintain the security of the South Pacific. Army and Navy planners held variant ideas as to what the military program in the Pacific should be and how it was to be accomplished. The Army took the view that the agreed basic strategic concept called for concentrating all effort on the defeat of Germany, and only the minimum of men and equipment should be sent to the Pacific to hold basic positions in that area until such time as it became possible to divert attention from Europe to the Pacific and concentrate on the defeat of Japan. The Navy, however, felt that a passive defense could not be maintained in the Pacific. Navy planners thought that opportunities for limited tactical offensives against the enemy should be seized and forces built up, not only to defend the area in U.N. possession but to initiate the advance through enemy territory on the long road to Japan. The Navy stressed particularly the importance of providing an adequate defense for the island chain that connected Hawaii and Australia, both to insure the continuing security of communications by sea and air between the two points and to serve as a protection for operations into enemy territory to the north and northwest. The amount of effort that must be provided to accomplish U.S. aims in the Pacific became such an issue between the Army and the Navy in 1942 that the Joint Chiefs of Staff finally referred the matter to the President for a decision.

As the Japanese moved into New Guinea and spread down into the Solomons the Navy had become increasingly concerned that only small air forces, primarily fighters, had been assigned to the individual islands between Australia and Hawaii while small bomber forces were to be concentrated at the ends of the island chain. Delivery of the allocated planes was not scheduled for completion until late in 1942. With the division of command between the Southwest Pacific and the Pacific Ocean Areas (including the South Pacific Area) it seemed less practical to rely for defense of the South Pacific islands and for air support of naval operations in the Pacific on mobile air forces assigned to another command.

At the end of March Admiral Turner reported to Admiral King that, contrary to a CCS agreement of 10 March 1942 that aircraft allocated to the Dutch prior to the loss of the East Indies should be sent to Australia, it appeared that the planes were to be taken over by the Army Air Forces for use in the United Kingdom and the Middle East. Admiral Turner predicted that if the Air Forces carried out their apparent intention of sending no more air units to the Pacific until fall, it would be "*impossible* to hold our position in the Pacific."[46] At Admiral Turner's suggestion Admiral King recommended to General Marshall that a move be made to remedy the situation in the South Pacific Area by assigning there at least one heavy bomber group. He urged that the despatch of units already allocated to the area should be speeded up, even given priority over movements to Europe, the Indian Ocean, and the Middle East. But the Army's reply was not made until after General Marshall's departure for London with the invasion plans that were designed to absorb all available forces. Then Admiral King was informed that the Army's plans for the South Pacific would continue according to schedule. A heavy bombardment group for the area, they agreed, was undoubtedly "desirable," but in the Army view it was not "essential."[47]

While this matter was under consideration, President Roosevelt requested information from the Joint Chiefs of Staff as to the adequacy of the defenses of Fiji and New Caledonia.[48] The Navy planners, in drafting a reply, considered the whole system of islands, Samoa, the Fijis, Tongatabu, New Caledonia, and Efate. They urged that the air defense there provided be increased to be sufficient, when concentrated at any spot in the group, to meet any moderate Japanese attack. The total the Navy planners recommended must certainly have been more than they hoped to get: two groups of heavy bombers, two groups of medium bombers, one group of dive bombers, three and a half groups of pursuit planes, four squadrons of patrol bombers, four squadrons of scout observation, and two groups of observation planes. In addition they proposed that the second island of the Fijis, previously left undefended in order to concentrate on defense of the other, be garrisoned.

The Army planners, supported by General Arnold and Major General Joseph T. McNarney, while inclined to agree that the air defense provided was by itself inadequate, felt that the demands for planes elsewhere were such that the risk of insufficient defense in the South Pacific must be accepted. They considered land defenses adequate as already set up, and they believed that the planes already provided for should be based in Hawaii and Australia as a mobile force which could be flown to the islands in case of attack. Admiral Turner pointed out that equipment and maintenance facilities on the islands were inadequate to operate the planes should such an emergency deployment be necessary. But General Arnold considered this a good reason for not increasing the allocation of planes to a greater number than the islands were already equipped to accommodate.[49]

Since the chiefs were unable to reconcile their differences in their meeting of 6 April, they agreed to send a memorandum to the President, merely listing the existing defense forces in Fiji and New Caledonia, without comment as to their adequacy. They also directed the Joint Staff Planners to study the problem to determine:

(1) The number of bombers of all types required to provide an

adequate mobile defense for the Island bases along the lines of communication between Hawaii and Australia, considering:
  (a) The time required for concentration;
  (b) Landing fields and operating facilities available.
(2) The minimum necessary pursuit, anti-aircraft and local ground protection and facilities required to provide for rapid concentration and effective operation.[50]

The Army and Navy members of the special subcommittee[51] to which the problem was referred by the JPS were unable to reach complete agreement. After studying the air, ground, and naval forces that had been allocated to the South and Southwest Pacific Areas in JCS 23, as well as the circumstances that had altered since that document was drawn up, they did agree that the time had come for an amphibious Marine division assigned to Hawaii in JCS 23 to be replaced by an Army division. This and another amphibious division assigned to Samoa they designated mobile, available for advance operations when required. They agreed that naval forces in both the Pacific and the Indian Ocean were inadequate although they could recommend nothing to improve the situation. But they were unable to reconcile their divergent views as to what was needed for an adequate air defense of the South Pacific islands.

Recommendations made by the Army and Navy members for allocation of Army planes to the South Pacific islands compared with each other and with JCS 23 and the War Department's existing plans for immediate deployment as follows:

Type	JCS 23	"A" (Army)	"B" (Navy)	W.D. Plans
Bombers (H)			35	
Bombers (M)	57	26	109	26
Bombers (L)		13	13	
Pursuit	210	155	210	130

The differing estimates of the subcommittee members were supported by their respective service colleagues on the Joint Staff Planners. After some indecisive discussion, the planners forwarded the subcommittee's alternative recommendations, together with a memorandum outlining the conflicting views of the Army and the Navy, to the Joint Chiefs of Staff for decision.[52]

By this time the Navy planners were working on long range plans that contemplated use of the South Pacific islands as bases for offensives designed to regain control of the areas occupied by the Japanese, as well as to support the Pacific Fleet's interim program of striking against the enemy wherever he could be reached. In order to provide adequate cover for naval operations and to defend the islands in the absence of the fleet, the Navy felt that it was essential to station bombers as well as fighters at each of the island bases. Aware that the enemy held the initiative in the area, the Navy planners conjectured that his next move would be an attack on the islands in the South Pacific Area rather than on the mainland of Australia. By gaining control of these islands the Japanese would not only reenforce the flank of the area already occupied but effectively intercept the vital line of communications from Hawaii to Australia. The Navy planners were insistent that not only was the mobile bomber force provided in Hawaii and Australia inadequate to perform essential operations from its home bases but it could not be concentrated at any point in the islands in time to prevent an enemy attack.

The Army planners were uninformed as to the extent of the U.S. naval operations contemplated in that area, and as to the support which would be afforded to the islands by the fleet. They felt that the island chain lacked sufficient depth of defense (although they had only reluctantly agreed to earlier attempts by the Navy to remedy the situation by garrisoning Bora Bora, Efate, and Tongatabu), and they thought that bombardment forces would be better protected if they were based on the flanks of the line of communications they were to defend. Arrangements were being made with General MacArthur to furnish air support at least for New Caledonia until one medium bomber squadron could be set up there.[53] Although the planners realized that bombers based in Australia or Hawaii probably could not be sent to any point in the island chain in time to prevent a raiding attack, they believed that the planes could be effective in opposing a reasonably strong landing. In principle, the general Army attitude was opposition to any significant increase of strength in the Pacific Area until adequate provision had been assured for the Bolero effort and there would clearly be no delay in initiation of an offensive in Europe.[54]

This difference of opinion between the two services was further complicated by receipt by the Joint Chiefs of Staff of a memorandum from the President's naval aide (Captain J.L. McCrea, USN), informing them that the President at the Pacific War Council meeting of 29 April 1942 had expressed "his desire that the total number of planes assigned to the U.S. Army in Australia be raised to one thousand," and "to have in Australia 100,000 troops in addition to the personnel of air forces required to maintain the plane program." What prompted such a remark or whether what the President said was correctly interpreted by Captain McCrea is not clear. In any event the memorandum caused considerable concern in the War Department.[55] General Marshall, who had only recently returned from persuading the British Chiefs in London that the forces available could be sufficient for a cross-Channel invasion in 1942, immediately expressed his views in a memorandum to the President. He pointed out that such a deployment as the President advocated would reduce from two and a half to one and a half divisions the number of troops that could be in England to participate in an emergency operation by 15 September. In addition the longer turn-around of shipping required to carry the troops to the Pacific would so limit those arriving in the United Kingdom in time for the major offensive planned for April 1943 as virtually to cancel that project.[56]

At the JCS meeting of 4 May the whole question was discussed.

Admiral King had prepared a memorandum, in which he expressed agreement with the Army that there should be no undue delay in preparations for Bolero. But he did not agree that forces in the Pacific, where the United States had full strategic responsibility, should be kept at a bare minimum. With the Japanese free to strike in any direction in the Pacific, and already known from intelligence sources to be massing forces in the Mandates and in home waters for new offensive operations, Admiral King felt that U.S. forces in the South Pacific were not sufficient to maintain the positions currently held. In his opinion the problem of holding in the Pacific was as important as and more urgent than the mounting of Bolero. He felt strongly that the United States "must not permit diversion of our forces to any proposed operation in any other theater to the extent that we find ourselves unable to fulfill our obligation to implement our basic strategic plan in the Pacific theater, which is to hold what we have against any attack that the Japanese are capable of launching against us."[57]

After considerable discussion, the chiefs still were unable to reconcile their differences. General Marshall continued to insist that any increase in the South Pacific "would preclude the possibility of the Bolero operation." Admiral King still maintained that the defenses in the South Pacific islands would have to be strengthened in order to withstand the anticipated strong Japanese offensive. Consequently the JCS agreed that the divergent views should be submitted to the President for a clear decision.[58] Accordingly General Marshall, in a memorandum outlining his views and those of Admiral King, requested a formal directive from the President as Commander in Chief as to "whether or not we are now to decide that no further commitments will be made in U.S. air and ground forces where such commitments will reduce the strength of our concentration in England or postpone the time when we can undertake active operations there."[59]

The President's reply was firm: "I do not want 'Bolero' slowed down." He had not, he said, directed an increase to 1,000 planes and 100,000 ground troops in Australia but had merely inquired if it could be done. He was convinced that it was inadvisable. All he thought should be sent to the South Pacific was "a sufficient number of heavy and medium bombers and pursuit planes in order to maintain the present objective there at the maximum."[60] Just what would constitute "a sufficient number" had, of course, been the issue between the two services. However, both the Army and the Navy accepted the President's Bolero statement as approval of the Army recommendation. In a second memorandum of the same date Mr. Roosevelt indicated more clearly that he did not favor increasing strength in the Pacific.[61]

The Navy continued to be dissatisfied with the allotment of aircraft to the South Pacific islands, as the Army proceeded to carry out previous plans for partial completion of aircraft distribution in the Pacific by 31 August 1942 and final disposition according to the Army's proposal some time in 1943.[62]

FORCES FOR THE SOUTHWEST PACIFIC

While the Joint Chiefs of Staff in Washington were disagreeing on the question of air forces for the islands of the South Pacific, loud and persistent demands were being raised by the Australian Government and by the new Supreme Commander, Southwest Pacific Area, General MacArthur, for more forces for the Southwest Pacific. The Australians had from the beginning of hostilities in the Pacific considered themselves neglected by the British and had not hesitated to say so. They had repeatedly endeavored to solicit more support from the United States. Apprehensive over the close approach of the Japanese and the threat to the security of the Australian mainland, Dr. H.V. Evatt, the Australian Minister of State for External Affairs, had even suggested to General Marshall in March that the United States should stop all shipments to Russia, the Middle East, and other areas and send everything available immediately to Australia. Washington and London, however, were inclined to consider the possibility of Japanese attack on Australia less serious.[63]

Relations between the British and the Australian Government had become more and more strained during the early months of the war, and the Australians had turned increasingly toward the United States for assistance. The British had been considerably upset by the persistent refusal of the Australians to permit the Australian divisions which were en route from the Middle East to Java to be diverted to Burma rather than returned to Australia when further defense of Java became impossible. Eventually the matter was straightened out by an appeal from the President to Prime Minister John Curtin. The hard feelings this event engendered were further aggravated when Prime Minister Churchill, in the middle of March, appointed Mr. R.G. Casey, then Australian Minister in Washington, to a place in the British War Cabinet as Minister of State for the Middle East. Mr. Curtin's objections to this move and the differences between the two governments were widely aired in the U.S. press, much to the embarrassment of President Roosevelt and the U.S. Government.[64]

General MacArthur arrived in Australia from the Philippines in mid-March, announcing that he would at once set to work to develop a strong offensive to drive the Japanese back out of the conquered territory. Such statements, repeated frequently by General MacArthur and members of his staff and given wide circulation in the world press, considerably raised the morale of the local population and led the U.S. public as well as the Australians to believe that under his command the strategy of defend-and-retreat was to be abandoned and an all-out offensive initiated at once.[65] When his directive as Supreme Commander, Southwest Pacific Area, was issued at the beginning of April, General MacArthur found himself charged with the general task: "Prepare to take the offensive." His staff went to work at once on plans for initiating offensive operations. Official requests to Washington began to place more emphasis on building up forces to attack enemy positions rather than merely on developing local defenses for Australia. Both from the Australian

Chiefs of Staff and from General MacArthur's staff came estimates of forces required for defense and for preparation for the offensive to come.[66]

The U.S. Chiefs of Staff had no plans for operations such as General MacArthur's staff proceeded to visualize. Such long-range plans as had been developed in Washington, mostly in the Navy Department, did not contemplate large-scale offensives under General MacArthur's command or, indeed, in the Southwest Pacific Area.[67] Moreover, the demands of other theaters precluded allocating to that area equipment or forces sufficient for an extensive program.

In the first week of April the Combined Chiefs of Staff made two decisions which actually resulted in reducing the number of aircraft to be delivered to Australia. Following the virtual collapse of resistance in the Netherlands East Indies the CCS had agreed that approximately 500 aircraft on order for the Dutch should be sent to Australia as they became available, to be manned by Dutch, Australian, or American pilots, whoever were available at the time.[68] Toward the end of March the Dutch found themselves unable to furnish crews for thirty-four bombers and thirty-six fighters already completed for their account and they informed the Munitions Assignments Board through the Netherlands Purchasing Commission that they wished to turn the planes over to the disposition of the United States.[69] The Munitions Assignments Committee (Air) (MAC(A)) recommended to the MAB, who passed it along to the JCS, that nineteen of the bombers on hand should be sent to Australia to support the Royal Australian Air Force, implying that the remainder of the Dutch aircraft should be retained for the U.S. Army Air Forces.[70]

This suggestion immediately caused great anxiety in both the Navy Department and the Australian delegation in Washington. Admiral Turner predicted to Admiral King that unless more air units were sent immediately to the Pacific it would be impossible to hold basic positions.[71] Dr. Evatt wrote General Marshall, expressing his great concern over the possibility that the original CCS decision might not be carried out.[72]

At the CCS meeting on 31 March the British members supported the Australians and urged that deliveries of aircraft to Australia be continued. Admiral King indicated "that he knew of no change of view on the part of the Combined Chiefs of Staff with regard to the necessity for the continued flow of these aircraft to the Australian area." However, General Marshall pointed out that there were insufficient training facilities for Dutch and Australian pilots in Australia and limited facilities for maintenance of operational craft. Rear Admiral J.H. Towers suggested that the remaining Dutch plane contracts be cancelled and the aircraft upon completion be allocated by the CCS. It was finally agreed that the planes already available should be sent on to Australia, and the JCS should reconsider the whole question.[73]

The Netherlands Mission subsequently indicated its desire for eighteen B-25's and eighteen P-40's of its order for the Netherlands Air Force in Australia in addition to a number of training planes for use in the United States, the remainder of the planes on order to be at the disposal of the United States but to be replaced when needed by the Dutch. Since the Pacific had been made an area of U.S. responsibility and the planes were currently assigned to the Pacific, the Joint Chiefs of Staff recommended that the problem of reallocation should be handled by them even though some of the planes might not (and, in fact, did not) go to that theater. The British considered this proposal somewhat irregular, for it had been established that all aircraft should be in a pool for allocation by the Combined Chiefs of Staff. They were apparently afraid that the U.S. Chiefs would assign all the planes to their own use, overlooking the demands of other forces and other theaters. But the Combined Chiefs finally decided that the U.S. Chiefs should act as agents of the CCS and take over the Dutch planes as they were produced, making arrangements for their eventual replacement. The allocation of the Dutch aircraft to the Pacific Theater would be considered in the over-all picture of allocations to all theaters of war. The MAB then took over the arrangements with the Dutch and reassigned the planes as they became available.[74]

The British Chiefs of Staff, in the meantime, had become more alarmed over the critical shortage of fighter planes in the Middle East, whose security was at that time being threatened both by the German offensive in Russia and by the Japanese naval raid in the Bay of Bengal. So they sought and obtained the approval of the U.S. Chiefs to retain in the Middle East eighty Kittyhawks which had recently been promised to Australia, under pressure, through the London Munitions Assignments Board (MAB(L)).[75]

These two decisions not only resulted in cutting back the aircraft allocated to the Australian area, but they brought out clearly the need for a new assignment of the aircraft resources of the United Nations. Study of this problem, undertaken at the direction of the Combined Chiefs of Staff on 7 April, ultimately produced the so-called Arnold-Slessor-Towers Agreement, which determined the number of planes to be allocated to the British from U.S. production through April 1943 and the air forces to be sent by the United States to British and combined theaters of war. The study did not, however, cover the question of the assignment of aircraft to U.S. areas in the Pacific.[76]

Throughout April Dr. Evatt continued to press the demands of his government and to agitate in Washington for more attention for the Southwest Pacific and more forces and equipment for Australia. He made his desires well known to military leaders in Washington, and as the representative of the Australian Government he endeavored to plead his case before the Pacific War Council. But his comments to Prime Minister Curtin indicate where the power of decision lay:

> At the Pacific Council any attempt to introduce detailed consideration of equipment problems is inadmissible because it causes a complete confusion, with China, United Kingdom, Australia, New Zealand, Canada and Netherlands East Indies all

taking up somewhat differing attitudes. The competition between the theatres is so great that only the service authorities can resolve it. Political and governmental action is best directed towards establishing relationships with the President, who of course indirectly influences decisions down the line.[77]

Dr. Evatt's talk in the council was not without effect. At the meeting of 21 April he raised the question of aircraft allocated to Australia, indicating that he understood that the amount to be sent had not been settled and that General MacArthur was not informed as to how much of an air force was to be in his command.[78] Actually this information had already been sent to General MacArthur in the series of despatches concerning the establishment of his new command in Australia.[79] When the President referred Dr. Evatt's query to the War Department he was told of this, and Dr. Evatt was furnished with a summary of both air and ground forces to be assigned to General MacArthur's command.[80]

Dr. Evatt relayed the War Department's letter to Prime Minister Curtin in Australia, who in turn called in General MacArthur to discuss it. General MacArthur's view of the forces to be at his disposal was clear from Mr. Curtin's reply: "He points out that the only item of his directive with which he can comply, either now or in the immediate future, is to route shipping in the South West Pacific Area.... Far from being able to take offensive action... the forces will not...be sufficient to ensure an adequate defense of Australia as the main base."[81]

In his message to Dr. Evatt, Mr. Curtin related in detail General MacArthur's view of the situation confronting him and the measures General MacArthur felt should be taken in order to enable him to carry out his mission. The Australian Prime Minister summarized the recommendations in a series of instructions for his representative in Washington:

(4) You should support the earlier possible provision of (1) [equipment required for bringing to fighting efficiency the land and air forces that Australia can raise] and seek a statement of United States naval, land and air forces together with equipment for them which it is proposed to send to Australia within the next three, six and twelve months.

(5) You should seek allotment of a greater tonnage of shipping to provide as early as possible the forces and equipment allotted and to build up strength for offensive action.

(6) You should support allotment of an aircraft carrier to... naval forces of the Southwest Pacific area.

(7) You should support temporary diversion of British Armoured Division and an Infantry Division to Australia pending the return of the whole A.I.F.

(8) You should seek an appreciation from Combined Chiefs of Staff on total war position in order that the Government and the Commander in Chief may be aware of their conclusions and inten-

tions relating to Pacific production and general strategic basis governing allotment forces and equipment to various theatres and shipping for their services overseas.

Dr. Evatt accordingly sent Mr. Hopkins, for the President, copies of the messages exchanged with Prime Minister Curtin, together with a letter strongly supporting General MacArthur's views. Dr. Evatt proposed that the rate of delivery of aircraft to the Southwest Pacific be accelerated by sending planes without respect to monthly allocations. He suggested that "the President, as Commander-in-Chief, [could] insist upon accelerating decisions on all MacArthur's requisition." Further, pointing out that since the strategy was already agreed there remained only the problem of assessing what was required to carry it out, Dr. Evatt recommended that any disagreement in the matter of assessment should "reasonably be resolved in favour of the Commander on the spot."[82]

On the same day the President received a message from Mr. Churchill which summarized a telegram he had received from the Prime Minister of Australia.[83] Mr. Curtin reported that General MacArthur had asked him to request Mr. Churchill to divert two British divisions temporarily to Australia instead of to India. General MacArthur was also said to have asked for a British aircraft carrier and an additional allocation of shipping between Australia and the United States. Disturbed by these irregular requests the British Prime Minister inquired whether they had been approved in Washington. This strong plea to the highest political level both in Washington and in London gave the impression that General MacArthur was endeavoring to accomplish his ends by circumventing the established channels. It caused considerable distress in Washington and did not help the strained relations between the Governments of Great Britain and Australia. General Marshall immediately originated a despatch to General MacArthur pointing out that

> ...It is realized that you are not concerned in the nature of communications passing between the 2 Prime Ministers but where these take form of definite request for reinforcements for Southwest Pacific area they create confusion unless originated by you as Supreme Commander and transmitted directly to the U.S. War Department which acts as Executive for U.S. Joint Chiefs of Staff in controlling that area.... It is requested that all communications to which you are a party and which relate to strategy and major reinforcements be addressed only to the War Department.[84]

The President also started to prepare his comments,[85] but before they were formulated in a despatch a reply came from General MacArthur to General Marshall's charges.[86] General MacArthur expressed embarrassment at apparently having been accused of a breach of frankness. He stated that he knew nothing of the message between the Prime Ministers and explained that Mr. Curtin frequently called him in to ask his opinion on the general situation, and on specific matters. He gave his views freely, "but with no idea that it was

for other purpose than his [Mr. Curtin's] own personal information."
He insisted that he had tried to follow established channels scrupulously, had made observations on military matters, and had submitted requests to General Marshall alone. He could not accept responsibility, he felt "for any heresay [sic] observation no matter from however high a source which may without my knowledge be connected with my name." However, he felt that he must continue to discuss the situation freely with the Australian Prime Minister in order to accomplish his assigned task. Finally, he pointed out that "the complete absorption of the Australian government is to attain security.... They are fearful that the forces now here are insufficient for the purpose and professional military opinion cannot fail to support that view."

Following receipt of General MacArthur's defense, the President's comments, prepared with General Marshall's approval, were only a mild reproof.

> ...I want you to know that I fully appreciate the difficulties of your position. They are the same kind of difficulties which I am having with the Russians, British, Canadians, Mexicans, Indians, Persians and others at different points of the compass. Not one of them is wholly satisfied but I am at least succeeding in keeping all of them reasonably satisfied and have so far avoided any real rows. I am especially trying to avoid any future public controversies between Mr. Churchill and Mr. Curtin.

After suggesting that General MacArthur endeavor to censor the loose newspaper talk about forces and operations which was coming from Australia, the President commented:

> I see no reason why you should not continue discussion of military matters with the Australian Prime Minister, but I hope you will try to have him treat them as confidential matters and not use them for public messages or for appeals to Churchill and me.[87]

President Roosevelt also asked General MacArthur for his "personal guess" as to whether the Japanese would continue operations against India and Ceylon and whether an all-out attack would be launched against Australia or New Zealand. It was in response to this that General MacArthur submitted his estimate of the situation on 8 May.[88]

General MacArthur pointed out first that the collapse of resistance in the Philippines and the fall of Burma would release at least two enemy divisions and all the Japanese air force in the Philippines for other operations. He thought it would be strategically unsound for the Japanese to attempt large-scale operations against India until they had gained added security by continuing their southward move in the Pacific. Consequently he recommended that adequate security be provided for Australia and the Pacific Area to maintain a frontal defense and a threat to the enemy's flank, to be followed "at the earliest possible moment by offensive action or by at least a sufficiently dangerous initial threat of offensive action to affect the enemy's plans and dispositions." In fact he urged that a second front be opened in the Pacific Theater, where it would assist the Russians, protect Australia and India, and "have the enthusiastic psychological support of the entire American nation." The first step would be to increase the defenses of his area with two carriers, 500-1,000 front line planes, and three Army divisions. With the Bolero program just getting underway there was no likelihood that the agreed strategy would be reversed.

THE BATTLE OF THE CORAL SEA

On 9 April 1942 those troops on the Bataan Peninsula who had not been able to withdraw to Corregidor surrendered. The American public had hardly gotten used to this depressing news when, ten days later, word came that the city of Tokyo had been bombed. This token raid by Army B-25's, taking off for the first time from the carrier *Hornet*, was originally proposed by Captain F.S. Low, Operations Officer on Admiral King's staff. At Admiral King's direction he and Captain D.B. Duncan, USN, presented the idea to General Arnold, and preparations began.[89] It was not intended as a strategic move but rather designed to have a positive effect upon morale in the United States and an adverse effect upon Japanese spirits. It was also hoped that as a result of it the Japanese would hold in the islands for defense some of the forces which might otherwise be assigned to combat the United Nations efforts at closer range. Morale in the United States did indeed receive a tremendous boost from the announcement that U.S. Army planes "from Shangri-la" had actually dropped bombs on the enemy capital, but this seems to have been the only sizable profit from this dramatic episode. Japanese popular morale suffered no equivalent setback, for the attack coincided unfortunately with the conclusion of an air raid drill and the damage done was largely concealed from the Japanese public. All of the attacking bombers and some of the personnel were lost. Generalissimo Chiang Kai-shek, on whose airfields it was intended that the planes should land, was unhappy because he was not fully apprised of the plan in advance. The Japanese followed it shortly with attacks in China which gave them possession of the airfields for which the planes had headed. Finally, the operation involved in the North Pacific a task force including two carriers, which were still not available when the opportunity offered a month later to foil an enemy seaborne attack on Port Moresby in New Guinea.[90]

Ever since February intelligence reports had indicated that the Japanese were gathering considerable forces in the mandated islands of the Pacific and were consolidating positions in the Solomons and northern New Guinea.[91] By the middle of April it was known from intercepted communications that the enemy would launch a seaborne and possibly a land attack on Port Moresby during the first week in May. Preparations were made to meet the advancing force.[92]

A few days before the beleaguered troops on Corregidor finally gave up, a combination of two naval task forces, built around the carriers *Lexington* and *Yorktown* and under the over-all command of Rear Admiral F.J. Fletcher, proceeded into the Coral Sea to meet the enemy. On 4 May a preliminary air attack was made on a small Japanese invasion force in Tulagi harbor. The main Japanese naval force was not discovered by U.S. search planes until 7 May, at almost the same time that Japanese planes discovered the U.S. force. On that and the following day planes of both nations carried out air attacks on each other's ships, but the naval forces never were close enough to exchange fire. As a result of the action the United States lost 1 carrier (*Lexington*), 1 tanker, 1 destroyer, 66 planes, and 543 personnel, while the Japanese lost 1 carrier, 1 destroyer, 4 landing barges, 80 aircraft, and about 900 personnel. The enemy withdrew to Rabaul and postponed the attempt to occupy Port Moresby until July. By that time, however, the greater losses at Midway had forced abandonment of the project and had reversed the tide in the Pacific.[93]

The extent of the damage the Japanese had suffered in the Coral Sea battle was not immediately known in Washington, and early estimates placed it higher than it actually was. Still it was known that while the United States now had only two carriers in the Pacific besides the damaged *Yorktown*, the enemy had at least one and possibly two carriers in the South Pacific and six or eight in home waters. Consistently during the preceding months the Japanese had capitalized on superior air strength, both in planes and in strategically placed bases from which to operate. The temporary reversal in the Coral Sea by no means upset their advantage in air power and in strategic position nor removed the threat to the poorly defended islands of the South Pacific. Consequently, immediately after the battle of the Coral Sea CinCPac made a new plea to CominCh for more planes for the Pacific areas, to build up both a defensive and an offensive air force.[94]

It had been ascertained at this time that the Japanese were organizing carriers, battleships, and destroyers into a task force in their home waters in preparation for a campaign to be launched in May or June. Where, or precisely when, the attack would come was still not known. But despite their failure in their first attempt to capture Port Moresby, Admiral King felt that the Japanese would revamp their forces in the South Pacific and, with or without the larger task force, would either make another try at Port Moresby or shift their efforts to an attack on New Caledonia or the Fijis.[95] Admiral King had never been convinced that the Army's scheme of defending the islands with bombers based on Hawaii and Australia would actually work, or that the ground crews, equipment, and planes located on some of the chain of islands were adequate. Consequently he took up Admiral Nimitz's plea and recommended to the Army Chief of Staff

> that steps should be taken at once
>   (a) not only to make ready for the basing of aircraft in New Caledonia, Efate, Fiji and Samoa, but that
>   (b) the maximum practicable basing of aircraft, land-based, (from Australia, perhaps Hawaii) on these islands should be set

up as of about May 25th, even as a "trial run" of arrangements and basing.[96]

Following the CCS meeting on 12 May, Admiral King, General Marshall, General Arnold, and Admiral Towers discussed Admiral King's recommendation, which had been sent in a memorandum to General Marshall that morning. Admiral King apparently impressed the others with his conception of the seriousness of the situation, for although they were unwilling to order additional planes to the area, they agreed tentatively that the Army would divert to Fiji and New Caledonia some of the planes then en route to Australia. These would form provisional squadrons for immediate strengthening of the island defenses. It was feared that curtailment of the allotment of planes to Australia would stir up a protest from General MacArthur. However, General Marshall and General Arnold agreed that the move should be made as a temporary measure, to strengthen the South Pacific Area until such time as the next move of the Japanese became known. The Air Forces went to work on the project, and the Army ordered an antiaircraft regiment from Hawaii to Fiji to protect the planes on the island bases.[97]

Before much progress could be made on this program, however, Pacific Fleet Intelligence learned that the enemy's plan was not to strike at Port Moresby but to seize and occupy Midway and points in the Aleutians, starting from bases in Japan and Saipan about 20 May. Consequently, again at Admiral King's recommendation, plans were changed, and the bombardment units scheduled for delivery from Hawaii to New Caledonia were halted at Hawaii and ordered to prepare for combat operations from there.[98] In the North Pacific Area Rear Admiral Robert A. Theobald was put in command of a number of U.S. naval vessels organized as Task Force 8 and given charge of the defense of the Aleutians and Alaska, with Brigadier General W.O. Butler in command of air elements. A few air reenforcements, including some B-17's, were sent to the area.[99]

Thus in the middle of May the Japanese, recouping their forces in the South Pacific before launching a new attack on New Guinea and embarking a considerable force from home waters for campaigns in the Central and North Pacific Areas, remained a constant threat to the security of U.S. positions. As U.S. forces prepared to repulse the anticipated attack a message came from General MacArthur. "Lack of sea power in the Pacific," he said, "is and has been the fatal weakness in our positions since the beginning of the war. Every disaster in that theatre is due fundamentally to this fact and they will continue and increase until a sufficient force is concentrated to challenge the Japanese Navy." Since intercepted messages had revealed the enemy's plans, he recommended that the Indian and Atlantic Oceans be stripped temporarily of naval forces in order to concentrate sufficient force to overwhelm the enemy. Were any other course followed, General MacArthur predicted, "the United States itself will face a series of such disasters and a crisis of such proportions as had never been faced in the long years of her existence."[100] In the absence of General Marshall, who had gone to the West Coast to inspect defenses, Admiral King replied to General MacArthur, reassuring him that the Joint Chiefs of Staff shared his anxiety and that steps were being taken to meet the emergency.[101]

These temporary precautions to meet a specific attack were all very well, but the Navy remained unconvinced that the basic defenses in the Pacific were adequate. On the same day Admiral King replied to General MacArthur he sent General Marshall a memorandum he wished to bring before the Combined Chiefs of Staff immediately.[102] In it he pointed out that the prior intelligence of the enemy's movements gained through intercepted communications was the only advantage the United States held in the Pacific Theater. Were this source of information lost, Admiral King predicted, disaster would result. The position of the United Nations in the area would be rendered untenable, and the Japanese would be in a position to make serious raids on the United States and to carry out operations in the Indian Ocean. He did not go so far as to recommend shifting the major effort to the Pacific, but he did recommend that, to forestall catastrophe, the movement of air forces to the Pacific should be given priority "even over Bolero" until the air strength had been built up to that which the Navy had recommended in JCS 48. He also proposed to transfer a considerable naval force from the Atlantic[103] and to move the British Eastern Fleet (which had been based in Indian and African ports since the Japanese raids in April) to Colombo. All of these movements were to be completed by 1 July 1942.

General Marshall did not return from his West Coast inspection trip until 27 May. When he replied to Admiral King it was to say that he favored the naval movements, but, with considerable restraint, he was "not in complete accord" with the proposals in regard to aircraft.[104] The schedule for delivery of planes had already been speeded up by the War Department, and dispositions within the Pacific Theater had been rearranged in response to earlier Navy requests. But these moves would still fall far short of the program advocated by the Navy. Again General Marshall made it clear that he did not propose to interfere in any way with the buildup for Bolero. The subject was temporarily dropped, but it was clear that the defense requirements of the Pacific Theater still remained very much at issue.

ASSISTANCE TO RUSSIA

In addition to the problems of the Pacific Theater and of China-Burma-India, an important but less controversial problem in 1942 was the role of Russia in the strategic program for the war against Japan. During most of the year there was considerable speculation in Washington and in London as to whether or not Russia would become involved in the war with Japan. Intelligence sources early in the year indicated that the Japanese feared a Russian attack and were seeking assurance that Russia would adhere to their mutual non-aggression pact.[105] It had seemed wise to some, in December 1941, to attempt to persuade the Russians to initiate hostilities with Japan, both for the purpose of diverting Japanese forces from the Southwest Pacific and to make bases in Siberia available for attacks against the Japanese mainland. From the Pacific came recommendation from both General MacArthur and General Wavell that if Russia was not actually to join the war, the Soviets should be urged to keep the Japanese apprehensive over the possibility that they might do so.[106] When the President asked for an opinion of the Chiefs of Staff in December, General Marshall and others in the War Department were inclined to believe that an immediate attack by Russia on Japan would be advantageous. However, Admiral Stark, feeling strongly the loss of a large part of the Pacific Fleet at Pearl Harbor, recommended against such a move, pointing out that the United States would be unable to assist Russia in such an eventuality.[107] The Russians themselves soon made it clear that they would not initiate hostilities until success had been assured in their war with Germany and that a Soviet war with Japan would result only at the instigation of the Japanese.

That the Japanese, having carried out their initial program of conquest in the Southwest Pacific, might take advantage of the Russian difficulties on the western front remained, however, an ominous possibility. In March 1942 the Russians fell back into the Kerch Peninsula, and despite successes in the winter campaigns near Leningrad and Moscow, they were threatened with new German gains in the anticipated spring offensive. Against this background President Roosevelt sent a memorandum to Admiral Stark and General Marshall recommending that the "United Staffs" consider what action should be taken by the United States and Great Britain in the event of Russian involvement in the war with Japan. He proposed that the problem be studied

> from all angles, such as an offensive by the United Nations, starting from the southern area, thus compelling Japan to send more forces there; second, from the point of view of the use of Chinese territory by Russia and the United States to conduct various kinds of offensives against Japan; third, from the point of view of opening up the Aleutian Islands route to Kamchatka and Siberia; the latter would also include, during the Summer months, the possibility of sending supplies to the Russian forces by an even more northerly route--past Wrangel Island to the Arctic coast of Siberia and thence South.[108]

Even a cursory study of the question clearly indicated the necessity for more cooperation and more information as to Russian plans and forces than had previously been forthcoming. In December 1941 and again in January 1942, U.S. Army planners had considered the advisability of attempting to ferry planes to Russia and down into China via Alaska and Siberia as well as the possibility of using bases in Siberia for air operations against the Japanese islands. But efforts to secure information from the Russians in regard to air bases in the area north and west of Vladivostok had produced no results.[109]

After discarding as impractical the suggestion that an attempt be made to obtain desired information about Russian installations indirectly by some such device as establishing a commercial airline to Siberia, the Joint Staff Planners agreed that the only satisfactory way to find out what was considered essential was through military staff conversations. They set aside a paper prepared for them by the Joint U.S. Strategic Committee recommending possible ways of assisting the Russians, directly and indirectly, and directed Admiral Turner to draft a two-page report for the Joint Chiefs of Staff, advising that no specific recommendations could be made until complete information was obtained from the Russians.[110] Admiral Turner's paper, which was forwarded to the JCS, pointed out that without such knowledge the United Nations could help the Soviets only by occupying Japanese forces with operations already projected in the Southwest Pacific. He recommended that

> the Joint U.S. Chiefs of Staff...request the President to initiate steps on the political level looking toward a more complete military collaboration between the United States and the U.S.S.R. If agreement can be reached, United States officers could then be sent to Siberia on an inspection trip, and staff conversations undertaken after they return. The problems of cooperation could be examined during the conversations, and realistic plans developed.[111]

The JCS approved the planners' report. On 30 March 1942 they sent a memorandum to the President, embodying their recommendations. Although he had himself initiated the study of the question, the President returned the chiefs' memorandum without comment and appears to have taken no direct action.[112] Subsequent negotiations by Ambassador William H. Standley and General Arnold with Soviet representatives yielded little information about Siberian installations.[113]

When Mr. V.M. Molotov was in Washington in the spring of 1942, the President took the occasion of a conversation with him on 1 June to raise the question of organizing a civilian air service for postal connections and air travel from Washington to Nome, to be continued on by either American or Soviet planes to some such point as Petropavlovsk, at the end of the Trans-Siberian railway. He also suggested the possibility of ferrying military planes from Nome to Siberia. Mr. Molotov acknowledged that these questions were already under consideration but not yet decided. It was apparently as a result of this that Ambassador Maxim Litvinov informed Mr. Harry Hopkins about a week later that the Soviet Government had agreed to the scheme of flying bombers to Russia by that route. But it was still some time before the technicalities of establishing such a system had been ironed out and the project could be put into operation.[114]

Early in June intelligence from Chinese sources contained the report that the Russians had been informed by the Japanese that "no ships could pass without permission [of the] Japanese Navy through area 32 to 40 degrees north latitude and 123 to 147 degrees east longitude." This was interpreted by the source of information as indicating Japanese preparation for an attack on Russia.[115]

At the same time it was known in Washington that the enemy was preparing for operations both at Midway and in the Aleutians. Extensive preparations were made to meet the assault on Midway, and the limited forces in Alaska were alerted for attack. The northern campaign began with an air raid on Dutch Harbor on 3 June. That day and the next raiding attacks by Japanese planes on U.S. installations were countered with attacks by AAF planes on the enemy naval task force. But the latter suffered virtually no damage, and on 6 and 7 June Japanese troops were landed on both Kiska and Attu.[116] Their presence was not discovered, however, until four days later.

The existence of Japanese forces in the Aleutians caused considerable concern in Washington, in particular in the Navy Department, not only because of the threat to Western Hemisphere security but because of the possibility that establishment of these bases was part of Japanese preparations for an attack on Siberia. This interpretation was further supported by evidence that the Japanese were moving considerable air forces to Paramushiru. The bombing of Tokyo, from an as yet unrevealed base, had made the enemy more than ever aware of the danger of operations from bases in both China and Siberia. These factors, coupled with the fact that the time was ripe for a new German offensive in Russia, indicated to the Navy War Planners that the Japanese might well be planning to attack St. Lawrence Island and Nome in order to cut communications from Alaska across the Bering Sea, preliminary to an attack on Siberia. Consequently in a paper prepared by Rear Admiral C.M. Cooke and forwarded by Admiral King to the Joint Chiefs of Staff the recommendation was made that not only should the defenses of Alaska be improved but ways of assisting the Russians in the event of Japanese attack should be explored and an attempt made to conduct military staff conversations with the Soviets.[117]

Admiral King independently secured the President's permission to initiate such discussions. But the problem of how to persuade the Russians to participate remained. It had already become apparent, as it was subsequently to be so often illustrated, that the Soviet representatives in Washington were not empowered to make decisions without first consulting Moscow. General Arnold had had little success in trying to negotiate with the Soviet Air Representative in Washington. Consequently General Marshall proposed, in order to expedite arrangements, that they request the President to ask Russian Ambassador Litvinov to ask Mr. Stalin to authorize U.S.-Soviet military staff conversations.[118]

In a message dated 17 June Mr. Roosevelt informed Mr. Stalin that the U.S. Chiefs expected a Japanese attack on Siberia. The President requested an exchange of detailed information relative to installations in Alaska and Siberia, both for military and for ferrying purposes, and proposed the initiation of staff conversations.[119] When no reply had been received by 23 June, the President sent a second message, stressing the advantage of delivering aircraft through Siberia and Alaska and proposing that a U.S. plane be allowed to make a survey of this route in order to expedite its development as a speedier delivery route to Russia. Mr. Roosevelt made no mention of the military use to which Siberian bases could be put, and it may perhaps be surmised that Washington believed the Russian delay in answering was due to a desire to have no part in assisting operations against Japan.[120]

No reply to the President's message was forthcoming until 2 July, when Ambassador Standley in Moscow received a note from Mr. Molotov, which was further clarified by conversation with Mr. Stalin on the same day. It appears from the ambassador's reports that the Russians avoided discussion of the possibility of a Japanese attack on Siberia and that the conversation, like the official message, concerned solely the air route from Alaska across Siberia. Mr. Stalin announced that work was already progressing on airfields for that purpose. He felt that the aircraft might be flown in by Soviet pilots, who could also make the suggested survey flight, accompanied by American representatives. He was agreeable to a meeting of military representatives "for the purpose of exchanging information so far as this will be necessary." But despite the fact that President Roosevelt had suggested conversations in both Moscow and Washington and the fact that the United States had no air experts in Moscow, Mr. Stalin insisted that the meetings should be held in the Russian capital. He would not agree that conversations in Washington as well would be necessary "since it was clear that it was only a question of the number of planes that could be delivered per month."[121]

At the end of July orders were issued to Major General Follett Bradley, USA, Colonel Joseph A. Michela, USA, and Captain J.H. Duncan, USN, to conduct conversations with Soviet representatives in Moscow. Although the Russians had agreed only to discussions of the trans-Siberian ferry route, the U.S. representatives were authorized to discuss and arrange cooperative action against Japan in the event the question should be raised. Arrangements for a survey flight from Alaska were immediately undertaken.[122]

The Joint Staff Planners meanwhile had been restudying the possible means of assisting the Russians in the event of a Soviet war with Japan. At the same time that Admiral Cooke had recommended staff discussions to the JCS, he had persuaded the JPS to appoint a special subcommittee to "analyze the courses of action open to the United States in the event Japan initiates a campaign against Russia, in Siberia and the Maritime Provinces."[123]

After studying the situation, the committee concluded that conditions had not changed appreciably since the Joint U.S. Strategic Committee prepared its paper on 20 March 1942. Information about Siberian bases had still not been obtained, and the JUSSC paper, while advocating the buildup of air forces in Siberia prior to Japanese attack, had recommended that the whole question be restudied after details of the installations had been learned. It had been further recommended that operations as planned elsewhere in the Pacific be continued in the meantime, Russia be supported with munitions, and the maximum effort be concentrated toward the defeat of Germany.

So the special committee resubmitted the JUSSC paper to the Joint Staff Planners, who in turn agreed to forward it to the Joint Chiefs of Staff, recommending that no action be taken until machinery for U.S.-Soviet collaboration had been established.[124] Inasmuch as the Russians did not declare war on Japan until three years later and never allowed U.S. forces to operate from Siberian bases, U.S. assistance to Russia in the Pacific continued to be that of so occupying the attention of the Japanese that they could not take on the additional risk of war with Russia.

Chapter VI

DEVELOPMENT OF PLANS FOR AN OFFENSIVE IN THE PACIFIC

A PATTERN FOR THE PACIFIC

In July 1942 decisions were made that sent U.S. forces into the first major offensive operations in both of the primary theaters of war. The first operation, in the South-Southwest Pacific, was dictated by the strategic situation, the threatening position of Japanese forces, and the anxiety, particularly among naval strategists, to improve the strategic position of the United States. The second operation, in North Africa, resulted from the basic decision to concentrate first on the defeat of Germany and the political pressure to get U.S. troops into action against Germany in 1942.

The joint prewar plan, Rainbow No. 5, did not outline a program for the ultimate all-out offensive aimed at the decisive defeat of Japan. It did provide for limited tactical offensives against shipping and bases in the Central Pacific, to weaken Japanese economic power and divert Japanese forces away from the Malay Barrier, where the main defense was to be made. The Pacific Fleet was to "prepare to capture and establish control over the Caroline and Marshall Island area" and, in the Navy's version of Rainbow No. 5, "to establish an advanced fleet base in Truk." These were but the first steps of what it was understood would eventually develop into an advance across the Pacific to the Philippines and Formosa from which the Japanese could be brought to surrender by naval blockade and air bombardment and possibly invasion of the islands of Japan. This was the pattern of the Orange plans and of the numerous studies made by naval planners in the years between the wars. There were variations in the objectives to be taken along the way, but even those who argued the advantages of one route over another recognized that the conditions under which war was fought would possibly determine the course it would take.[1]

The immediate reaction of Admiral Harold R. Stark, Chief of Naval Operations, and his staff when word came of the disastrous attack on the fleet in Pearl Harbor was that naval activities in the Pacific would have to be limited to something less than those prescribed in Rainbow No. 5 and the potentialities of the remaining forces would have to be reconsidered. Consequently the Pacific Fleet was restricted to defensive operations east of the 180° meridian. This limitation was eased somewhat by Admiral Ernest J. King when he became Commander in Chief, U.S. Fleet, at the end of December. He instructed the Commander in Chief, Pacific Fleet, to extend his responsibility for the security of the line of communications between Hawaii and Samoa to include Fiji "at the earliest practicable date." In the months that followed a series of despatches went from Admiral King to Admiral Nimitz, recommending raiding operations and limited offensives wherever possible in order to defend the vital areas of Hawaii and Australasia and the line of communications between and to divert Japanese attention from reenforcements headed for points in those regions.[2]

In order to wage naval warfare with inferior naval forces it was essential to have superior intelligence of the disposition of the enemy's fleet. In the spring of 1942 this meant securing control of the Solomon Islands before the Japanese became too deeply entrenched there. It meant particularly capturing the naval base at Tulagi, both to improve the position of U.S. forces by obtaining a post from which the enemy's movements could be more closely watched and to deny to the Japanese the similar advantage of an advance base close to the line of communications from the United States to Australia. As early as 12 February Admiral King reminded Admiral Nimitz of the need for "a strong and comprehensive offensive to be launched soon against exposed enemy naval forces and the positions he is now establishing in the Bismarcks and the Solomons."[3] With all the equipment of war in short supply and an extreme military crisis rapidly developing in the ABDA Area initiation of a major operation to seize and occupy enemy positions in the Pacific was out of the question. But raiding attacks were possible, and while forces were being built up planners in the Navy Department and on the CinCPac staff at Pearl Harbor developed outlines of strategic plans for the long series of operations that would ultimately lead to victory in the Pacific.

There was general agreement that before there could be an offensive there would have to be a period of primarily defensive action, when defenses would be strengthened and forces accumulated. To Army planners in Washington this meant establishing a line and holding it with the minimum of forces, risking the loss of additional territory if increasing its defenses would mean cutting available resources for the war against Germany. Naval planners insisted that every opportunity to strike at the enemy should be seized and that a consistent effort should be made to improve the strategic position of the United Nations in the Pacific Theater until such time as the all-out offensive could be undertaken. It was a question of timing and of how much should be allocated to the war against Japan, and upon it feelings ran strong.

The first step toward moving to an offensive in the Pacific was recommended to the Joint Chiefs of Staff by the Navy War Plans Division through Admiral King on 5 February 1942, when the Japanese had moved into New Britain and the Solomon Islands and task forces of the Pacific Fleet under Admiral William F. Halsey had made their first raids on the Marshalls and Gilberts and other Japanese-held islands in the vicinity. In a paper prepared some two weeks before, the Navy proposed that an advance base be established at Funafuti in the Ellice Islands "to provide: (a) An outpost coverage of Fiji-Samoa. (b) A linkage post toward the Solomon Islands. (c) Support for future offensive operations in the Southwest Pacific."[4] Although the Army War Plans Division immediately went on record to the Chief of Staff as opposed to the occupation of additional islands in the Pacific as an unnecessary diversion of Army resources, there was no immediate joint action on the study.[5]

Some two weeks later Admiral King proposed to the Combined Chiefs of Staff that the U.S. Joint Staff Planners at once make a study of defense of the vital route to Australia and the means for occupation of essential positions on it.[6] The following day he recommended to the Chief of Naval Operations (Admiral Stark) and the Army Chief of Staff that Army garrisons be established as soon as possible on two additional islands: Efate in the New Hebrides and Tongatabu in the Tonga Island group. These would then form part of "a system of groups of islands, whose air contingents will provide mutual support, and which would offer security for the operations of our naval forces and sea communications."[7]

It was suspected in the War Department that this naval plan was intended as a first step in initiation of a major offensive in the Pacific, to which the Army was not willing to agree. Consequently, General Marshall requested information on the subject.[8] He was anxious, he said, to do anything reasonable to make offensive action by the fleet possible, but he felt that the limitations of shipping and the demands of other theaters for ground and air power were such as "definitely to limit for some time to come the extent to which we can provide for a further expansion in the Pacific-Australia theatre."

Admiral King's reply included a summary of current Navy strategic thinking. It was concentrated, he said, on three primary objectives in the Pacific Theater: to hold the Hawaiian Islands, to support Australasia, and to advance northwest into Japanese-held territories from bases in the New Hebrides. The garrisoning of Efate and Tongatabu was intended as a preparatory move in

> the general scheme or concept of operations...not only to protect the line of communications with Australia, but, in so doing, set up "strong points" from which a step-by-step general advance can be made through the New Hebrides, Solomons, and the Bismarck Archapelago [sic]. It is to be expected that such a step-by-step general advance will draw Japanese forces to oppose it, thus relieving pressure in other parts of the Pacific - and that the operation will of itself be good cover for the communications with Australia.

The plan was to use amphibious troops (Marines) to capture positions, then to relieve them with garrison troops (Army), repeating the process as the advance to the northwest continued. What he expected to be done when this program was completed, Admiral King did not disclose.[9] General Marshall apparently did not object to this explanation. President Roosevelt also was informed of the Navy's over-all plan and approved it. The more specific project for garrisoning Efate and Tongatabu received joint approval, and work began on their fortification.[10]

The Japanese continued their advance to the south and east throughout March and April 1942, taking Java to complete their conquest of the Netherlands East Indies, consolidating their position through the New Guinea-New Britain area, and occupying new points down into the Solomons. On 9 April Bataan surrendered and U.S. troops withdrew to Corregidor to continue their hopeless resistance for another month. Forces of the Pacific Fleet and U.S. bombers based in the South Pacific islands made raiding attacks on enemy strongholds; the enemy in turn attacked United Nations bases in the islands and in Australia. Although U.S. forces were being built up in the area, they were not yet ready to undertake operations designed to capture enemy bases.[11]

By the middle of April the Navy War Plans Division had drawn the outline of a campaign which visualized an advance against the Japanese in four successive stages:

> (a) *First Stage*, in which we are now engaged, envisages building up forces and positions in the Pacific Theater and particularly in the South Pacific and Southwest Pacific for the purpose of holding these areas, and in preparation for launching an ultimate offensive against the Japanese; and for supporting the fleet forces operating there. During this stage the amphibious forces necessary to carry on this offensive will be assembled in the areas and trained;...available air, amphibious and naval forces will take minor offensive action against enemy advanced positions and against exposed enemy naval forces for purposes of attrition....
> (b) The *Second Stage* as now envisaged involves a combined offensive by United States, New Zealand and Australian amphibious naval and air forces through the Solomons and New Guinea to capture the Bismarck Archipelago and the Admiralty Islands. Heavy attrition attacks would then be undertaken against the enemy forces and positions in the Caroline and Marshall Islands.
> (c) The *Third Stage* involves seizure of the Caroline and Marshall Islands and the establishment there of Fleet and air advanced bases.
> (d) The *Fourth Stage* involves an advance into the Netherlands East Indies or, alternatively, into the Philippines whichever offers the more promising and enduring results.[12]

In anticipation of undertaking at least limited offensives Admiral King had sought and received from the British "blanket authority for U.S. forces to occupy any of the Pacific Islands under British or Dominion jurisdiction as may be required."[13]

In this outline plan the long-established program of advance through the Central Pacific which was to open with operations in the Carolines and Marshalls remained unchallenged, but it was to be delayed while steps were taken to secure the islands of the Southwest Pacific. There is no record of opposition to this pattern within the Navy Department, and the Army planners, who seem to have had only a general idea of what their colleagues were contemplating, were more concerned over the timing of projected operations than the objectives.[14]

AN OPERATION IN THE SOLOMONS

It was in June 1942 that the first prospect of successfully undertaking an attack in force on enemy-held territory arose. There were then in Australia two U.S. Army divisions in addition to one and one-half combat-trained Australian divisions. The Americal Division under Major General Alexander M. Patch was in New Caledonia, the 37th Division was en route to Fiji, most of the First Marine Division was in New Zealand, and a Marine raider battalion and a Marine regiment were in Samoa, ready for action. Morale had been somewhat raised by the surprise attack on Tokyo, and the enemy advance on Port Moresby had been blocked in the battle of the Coral Sea. Both in the Pacific and in Washington serious consideration was being given to the possibility of using the available troops in some offensive action.

The Japanese in the meantime had completed the conquest of the Netherlands East Indies and extended their operations into New Guinea and the Solomons. As they consolidated their conquered territory and built airfields and naval bases in the New Guinea-New Britain-Solomons area, their threat to the security of the northeast coast of Australia and the vital line of communications from the United States grew ever greater. It was already estimated that they had as many as two brigades on New Britain, two companies on New Ireland, one battalion in the Admiralties, a regiment in the Solomons (Tulagi), and a small garrison on Bougainville.[15] It was clear that the sooner an attack was made on some strategic point the more effective it would be in stopping the Japanese before they could dig in too securely in their advance position.

Planning for a limited operation in the Pacific Theater was given an additional impetus during the first week of June 1942. As has already been recounted,[16] in mid-May intercepted enemy communications revealed that the Japanese were preparing for an attack in force on Midway and the Aleutians. Fortunately forewarned, the United States was ready to meet the enemy forces as they approached Midway Island. Repeated attacks by land- and carrier-based planes of the Army, Navy, and Marine Corps and submarines of the Pacific Fleet on 3-6 June divested the enemy of four carriers and a heavy cruiser at the price of one carrier (*Yorktown*) and one destroyer (*Hammann*) of the Pacific Fleet. In separate action the Japanese occupied Attu and Kiska, two islands well out on the Aleutian chain. The battle of Midway marked the turning point of the war in the Pacific. The Japanese cancelled their plans to occupy strategic points in New Caledonia, Fiji, and Samoa. The attacks on Midway and the Aleutians were the last major operations they initiated.[17]

Even before the important events at Midway Admiral Nimitz had alerted the Amphibious Forces, Pacific Fleet, for possible operations to recapture outlying bases. He had also proposed to General MacArthur that the First Marine Raider Battalion at Tutuila, Samoa, be used, with naval support from the Southwest Pacific, in a landing attack on Tulagi or some other vital Japanese base in General MacArthur's territory.[18] This suggestion met with the approval of Admiral King, but General MacArthur, himself already contemplating operations in the New Guinea-New Britain region, misconstrued the proposal for a raiding attack as a project for establishing permanent occupation and turned it down on the basis that available forces were not adequate to achieve success.[19]

With enemy naval and naval air forces materially weakened by their disastrous attempt to capture Midway U.S. authorities looked with renewed interest at the prospect of striking back. General MacArthur at once reported to General Marshall the plans his staff had been developing for limited offensives within his area of command. Provided already with three Army divisions (U.S. 32nd and 41st and Australian 7th) which could be used to support a landing force, General MacArthur recommended that he be furnished with a division trained for amphibious operations and a naval task force, including two carriers. Thus equipped General MacArthur was confident that he could move into New Britain and New Ireland and "retake that important area, forcing the enemy back 700 miles to his base at Truk with manifold strategic advantages both defensive and offensive with further potential exploitation immediately possible."[20]

General MacArthur's proposal was well received in the War Department, and much discussion followed within both the War and the Navy Departments, where plans for an operation in the Solomons had been developing independently for some time. There was joint discussion also between members of the two services on three levels--the working members of the two Plans Divisions, the heads of the divisions, and finally the Army Chief of Staff and the Commander in Chief, U.S. Fleet. On the lowest echelon agreement was fairly easily reached on approximately what General MacArthur proposed. However, the next higher echelon was divided in its views, and it became necessary for the two chiefs to iron out the major problems. There is no evidence that the matter was formally raised within the JCS organization until after the initial directive had been issued to the commanders in the field.[21]

While plans for an operation in the Southwest Pacific were being discussed the attention of the Joint Chiefs of Staff, and particularly of General Marshall, was considerably occupied during the middle of June by the presence in Washington of Prime Minister Churchill and his military staff. They had become alarmed at the emphasis the American Chiefs of Staff appeared to be placing on a possible cross-Channel operation in 1942, and they had crossed the ocean for an informal conference to determine how matters stood. The situation in Africa was rapidly deteriorating as General Rommel advanced toward the British stronghold of Tobruk. The British Chiefs were not eager to commit to a possible, but doubtful, operation on the European continent in the fall of 1942 (Sledgehammer) forces which might be desperately needed in Egypt. At the same time they felt that some form of invasion of northern Africa might be extremely helpful to the beleaguered forces in the east. Moreover British planners had not succeeded in developing what they considered an acceptable plan for Sledgehammer. A detailed account of the discussions in Washington in June will be found in another section of the History of the Joint Chiefs of Staff.[22] Suffice it to say that the conversations resulted in a reaffirmation of the decision to build up forces in the United Kingdom for a landing on the continent of Europe in 1943 (Bolero-Roundup) and to examine more thoroughly the possibilities of Sledgehammer in 1942. It was also agreed that alternate plans would be developed for possible operations in North Africa, Norway, and the Iberian Peninsula. Although the main subject for discussion was the war against Germany, there was general approval that in the Pacific Theater "gnawing" or "step-by-step" amphibious operations should be launched as soon as possible, probably about the first of August, to attempt to take advantage of the victory at Midway.[23]

The Plans Divisions of the Army and the Army Air Forces had taken General MacArthur's proposal and outlined an operation under his command for seizure of objectives in the New Britain-New Guinea area. With the occupation of Rabaul and its vicinity as the ultimate objective this limited offensive was to be preceded and supported by intensive air bombardment of enemy points in the Solomons and New Guinea, designed to assure air supremacy for the American forces and to eliminate the enemy's potentiality for air attack on the occupying force. Air planners were of the opinion that the bases available and being developed in Australia and the vicinity of Port Moresby in New Guinea would be insufficient for air operations on the scale required for this neutralizing process and for support of the landing force. Consequently they proposed seizing and utilizing bases already built by the Japanese at Lae, Salamaua, and other points in the Madang-Lae-Buna Bay area. Since the impassable terrain of New Guinea made a land invasion from the Port Moresby area impractical, and a seaborne invasion was ruled out by the enemy air capabilities in the region, it was proposed that paratroops be employed for securing these vital bases. Even these bases would be too far from the ultimate objective for fighter operation, and fighter support would have to be furnished by carrier-based planes. After air bombardment had neutralized the surrounding area, the War Department planners proposed, the Marine amphibious division would seize and occupy Rabaul, to be relieved by Army garrison forces already available in Australia. Once Rabaul was secured, it was expected that the neutralized enemy bases in the Solomons area would be cut off and could easily be brought under allied control. Completion of the campaign would place the whole area in the hands of General MacArthur and open the way for land-based air attacks on the enemy stronghold at Truk and extension of the offensive to other objectives.[24]

Although the representatives of the Army and Navy Plans Divisions[25] were in agreement on such an operation with a naval task force commander under over-all command of General MacArthur, opposition was encountered from Rear Admiral Charles M. Cooke, Jr., head of the Navy War Plans Division, who was supported by Admiral King. Not only were they averse to placing naval forces under General MacArthur, who they felt did not know how to handle naval and amphibious forces, but they disapproved the strategic concept of the proposed operation. It appeared certain that by 1 August, the preliminary target date, the enemy would have considerably strengthened his positions in the Solomon Islands. The objecting naval authorities were not convinced that air bombardment alone could eliminate the serious threat of newly developed Japanese airfields both to U.S. advance bases in the South Pacific and to the operation against Rabaul. A naval task force moving directly up from the south between New Guinea and the Solomon Islands to participate in the attack would pass for a considerable distance through a relatively narrow channel within range of any land-based air forces that had not been wiped out. Having already lost two carriers the Navy was reluctant to expose those remaining to the hazards of such an operation.[26] Consequently they favored initially occupying the islands of Tulagi and Bougainville and other enemy strong points in the Solomons area before attempting an attack on Rabaul. Thus pressure would be put on the Japanese and a step-by-step advance would proceed until such time as sufficient force was available to launch a full-scale, continuous offensive.[27]

In the matter of command naval leaders emphasized the fact that the Navy and the Marine Corps would play the major role in the initial attack wherever it came. Army-Navy cooperation at Midway and in the Aleutians had been far from perfect, and the Navy feared a wasteful, if not disastrous, repetition unless the action of the Army, the Navy, and the Marine Corps was coordinated under the Commander in Chief, Pacific Fleet. They were unwilling to entrust the command to General MacArthur.[28]

Although the differences between the Army and the Navy had not yet been settled, on 23 and 24 June 1942 Admiral King sent preliminary notice to Admiral Nimitz that operations for the seizure of Tulagi were being planned, outlining the forces that would be available, and directing him to commence preparations within his command. There was no mention of securing the entire New Britain-New Guinea area.[29]

Neither in the Pacific, however, nor in Washington could the Navy organize the operation independently, for not only was it necessary to assure the cooperation of forces assigned to the Southwest Pacific Area but the objectives involved lay within the area assigned to the control of General MacArthur. On 25 June Admiral King sent General Marshall a draft directive, reminding him that it was urgent that the United States take the initiative in the Pacific before the Japanese could seize it themselves.[30] The draft, prepared in the Navy War Plans Division and intended for issuance by the Joint Chiefs of Staff, provided "that forces be assembled and organized for commencing offensive operations about 1 August with the immediate objective of seizing and occupying Santa Cruz Island and positions in the Solomon Islands, with the ultimate objective of occupying eastern New Guinea and

New Britain." The seizure and initial occupation of the islands were to be conducted by a task force under the Commander in Chief, Pacific Fleet, and the permanent occupation of islands captured was to be under the Supreme Commander, Southwest Pacific Area.

General Marshall had received a message from General MacArthur the day before, virtually reducing the points of disagreement to the sole question of command.[31] The Navy's idea that taking Rabaul at once would involve too great a risk, General MacArthur said, showed a misconception of what he proposed to do. What he actually contemplated was not that but "a progressive movement" with initial action in the Solomons and on the northern coast of New Guinea "in order to protect the naval surface forces involved and to secure airfields from which essential support can be given to the forces participating in the final phase of the operation." He emphasized the necessity that all ground operations in that area should be under his direction. "To bring in land forces from other areas with a view to their operation under Naval direction exercised from distant points can result in nothing but complete confusion and such a lack of coordination as would probably jeopardize the success of the movement." Moreover, he added, the very purpose for establishing the Southwest Pacific Area was to obtain unity of command, and the Commander in Chief alone was in a position and had requisite staff to direct any campaign in the area.

This new statement from General MacArthur virtually eliminated the area of disagreement on strategic grounds, and General Marshall accepted the Navy's strategic plan. Like General MacArthur he thought command of the operation should be vested in the Army. Commenting to Admiral King on the great difficulty of coordinating land, sea, and air action in such an operation he remarked that "a complication of almost unsurmountable command difficulties" would be added by the fact that naval vessels and naval commands operated largely under radio silence. General Marshall thought he realized the Navy's concern for the hazards to which naval vessels would be exposed, "especially if under Army direction." Still he thought this problem could be controlled by the Joint Chiefs of Staff by defining the general manner in which naval forces would be used and the waters in which they should operate. This campaign would have fixed objectives, he argued, and the action could be controlled to a degree not practicable in the Midway battle.[32]

Capped as it was by the objection to radio silence General Marshall's argument was not a strong one. He overlooked the fact that naval forces normally monitored radio broadcasts even while originating none and when practicable employed methods of visual communication (e.g., blinker, semaphore, flag hoist). Once battle was joined, of course, radio silence was dropped. General Marshall also seems not to have realized that radio communications between Army forces would be equally damaging to the project in the period when the Navy would not have employed radio. It was perfectly true, and it was the strong point in the argument, that the locality in which operations were contemplated was within the command area of the Southwest

Pacific. On the other hand initial landings in the Solomons and preliminary occupation would be executed primarily by forces of the Navy and Marine Corps, started from bases in the South Pacific. Yet General Marshall realized that the limited naval and Marine forces would have to be augmented later by Army troops. He thought the project ought to be under Army command.

Admiral King remained convinced that the only way to assure success for the operation would be to set it up under the control of the Commander in Chief, Pacific Fleet.[33] He pointed out to General Marshall that just such an operation had been contemplated when the JCS listed among the tasks of CinCPOA, "Prepare for the execution of amphibious offensives to be launched from the SOUTH PACIFIC AREA and the SOUTHWEST PACIFIC AREA." The assault would be executed mainly by forces mounted in the South Pacific Area, and it ought to be fully integrated into the whole picture in the Pacific Theater. Permanent occupation after the landings had been made should be, in the view of Admiral King, under the direction of the Supreme Commander, Southwest Pacific Area. In the initial phases of the operation, however, he foresaw little contribution from the existing bases in the Southwest Pacific. As far as he was concerned Army over-all command was out of the question, and he insisted,

> the primary consideration is the immediate initiation of these operations. I think it is important that this be done even if no support of Army forces in the Southwest Pacific is made available.

The implication in the last sentence disturbed General Marshall, who asked to see Admiral King to discuss the subject.[34] The latter then proposed that, instead to setting up the whole operation under CinCPac they assign to Vice Admiral Robert L. Ghormley, Commander, South Pacific Area and South Pacific Force, command for the seizure of Tulagi, under the direction of CinCPac, and after that operation turn over control to General MacArthur for the remainder of the campaign against New Britain and New Guinea. A command of that type was approximately what naval planners had had in mind when they set up the position Admiral Ghormley then occupied, and his assigned tasks had included, "Prepare to launch a major amphibious offensive against positions held by Japan."[35] Admiral King's suggestion was apparently still under consideration when he offered another proposal, that command of the entire operation be given to Admiral Ghormley directly under the JCS rather than under Admiral Nimitz, thereby presumably eliminating objections from both services.[36]

General Marshall had immediately referred the first proposal to General MacArthur for comment, and the reply was emphatic.

> The entire operation in the Solomons-New Guinea-New Britain-New Ireland area should be considered as a whole in which successful accomplishment of the offensive will depend upon complete coordination of the land, sea and air components. A change in command during the course of tactical operations in which it is

impossible to predict the enemy's reaction and consequent trend of combat would invite confusion and loss of coordination.

There was no question but that an over-all naval command would be unwelcome to General MacArthur, for before learning of the "transfer" proposal he had warned General Marshall dramatically:

> It is quite evident...that the Navy contemplates assuming general command control of all operations in the Pacific theatre, the role of the Army being subsidiary and consisting largely of placing its forces at the disposal and under the command of Navy or Marine officers. By using Army troops to garrison the islands of the Pacific under Navy command the Navy retains Marine forces always available giving them inherently an army of their own and serving as the real bases for their plans by virtue of having the most readily available unit for offensive action. This Navy plan came under my observation accidentally as far back as ten years ago when I was Chief of Staff and senior member of the Joint Board. The whole plan envisioned the complete absorption of the national defense function by the Navy, the Army being relegated merely to base training garrisoning and supply purposes. I cannot tell you how completely destructive this would be to the morale of the Army both air and ground units. It is of course unnecessary to point out the deleterious far reaching effect of such a program.[37]

Despite General MacArthur's objections General Marshall informed Admiral King on 1 July 1942 that he favored the first suggestion of vesting control in CinCPac until after the occupation of Tulagi, then transferring it to the Supreme Commander, Southwest Pacific Area. Accordingly he submitted a draft directive for an operation in three phases, "with the ultimate objective of seizure and occupation of the New Britain-New Ireland-New Guinea area:"

Task One. Seizure and occupation of Santa Cruz Islands and Tulagi.
Task Two. Seizure and occupation of Lae, Salamaua, and Northeast coast of New Guinea.
Task Three. Seizure and occupation of Rabaul and adjacent positions in the New Guinea-New Ireland area.[38]

Admiral King suggested again that the operation be conducted directly under the Joint Chiefs of Staff, "whose authority cannot properly be questioned by either principal - General McArthur [sic] on the one hand or Admiral Nimitz on the other."[39] This arrangement was not approved by General Marshall, however, and the directive was issued with the first task assigned to a commander to be designated by the Commander in Chief, Pacific Fleet, and the other two placed under the direction of the Supreme Commander, Southwest Pacific Area.[40] Admiral Nimitz was directed to name Admiral Ghormley Task Force Commander "at least for Task One." Tactical command of the amphibious forces was in each case to remain with the task force commander.

At the suggestion of Admiral King there was no attempt to set target dates for more than the first task. That was assigned the planning date of 1 August in order that preparations for the seizure of Tulagi and vicinity might get under way at once. It was agreed that the dates for the second task, including also seizure and occupation of the Solomon Islands, and the third task should be decided later in the month of July.

To the Joint Chiefs of Staff was reserved responsibility for determining "the composition of the forces to be used, the timing of the tasks, and the passage of command." In general terms the directive listed the elements which would participate: ground, air, and naval forces currently under General MacArthur's command; at least two aircraft carriers with cruisers and destroyers; the South Pacific Amphibious Force, Marine air squadrons, and Army occupational forces to garrison Tulagi. Other garrisons were to be provided from Australia. The Joint Chiefs of Staff could withdraw attached naval units upon completion of any phase if the aircraft carriers were unduly jeopardized or an emergency in some other areas of the Pacific dictated withdrawal.

In order to assure that the permanent garrison for Tulagi should come from the South Pacific Area rather than the Southwest and further to justify the transfer of command after completion of the first task, General Marshall suggested, and it was agreed, that the boundary between the two areas should be moved westward to 159° East Longitude, thus including most of the Solomons in the South Pacific Area.

The directive which was to set the stage for the first limited offensive action in the Pacific Theater was issued by the Joint Chiefs of Staff on 2 July 1942.[41] On the same day agreement was reached on two other matters that were closely related: establishment of the position of Commanding General, Army Forces, South Pacific Area, and creation of two mobile air forces in the Pacific Theater. Ever since it had been decided that Vice Admiral R.L. Ghormley would be Commander, South Pacific Area, and Rear Admiral J.S. McCain would be Commander, Air Forces, South Pacific, the Army had been discussing the advisability of setting up a commander of all Army forces in the same area. Lieutenant General D.C. Emmons in Hawaii particularly urged that it be done. When a definite proposal was finally sent to Admiral King at the end of June, he approved it, and Major General Millard F. Harmon was appointed to the position.[42] The concept of a mobile air force in the Pacific Theater had been discussed also for a long time, with the Army advocating one bomber force at either end of the line of communications to Australia and the Navy insisting that bombers should be stationed on the islands in between. When the Army planners finally offered a concrete proposal that a portion of the Hawaiian Air Force be designated a Pacific Mobile Air Force "earmarked for use anywhere in the Pacific if and when directed by the Chief of Staff," Admiral King approved it but recommended modification. At his suggestion it was agreed:

that there be created two mobile air forces in the Pacific Theater, each comprising at least one heavy bombardment group, to be available to support operations anywhere in the Pacific Theater, as may be directed by the United States Chiefs of Staff. These... will...comprise:
- (1) a Hawaiian mobile air force, from units duly assigned to the Hawaiian department, which will normally base and operate in Hawaii;
- (2) an Australian mobile air force, from units duly assigned to the South West Pacific Area, which will normally base and operate in Australia.[43]

Admiral King went at once to San Francisco to keep a prearranged appointment with Admiral Nimitz for discussion of the current situation. General Marshall, obviously relieved that the problems had been resolved, explained to General MacArthur the reasons for reducing his area and providing for possible withdrawal of naval forces during the operation.[44] At the same time General Marshall advised, "I wish you to make every conceivable effort to promote a complete accord throughout this affair. There will be difficulties and irritations inevitably but the end in view demands a determination to suppress these manifestations."

Upon receiving the directive General MacArthur and Admiral Ghormley met to discuss preparations for the campaign. They were unhappy that they had been directed to prepare only for the first task, and they agreed that once begun the entire project should be carried to completion. After considering the forces available to them, the program of operations, and the strength and position of the enemy in the area, they expressed the opinion that, with new Japanese airfields building at Kavieng, Rabaul, Lae, Salamaua, Buka, and Guadalcanal, it was highly doubtful that the fields and planes available to U.S. forces would be sufficient to achieve air superiority and maintain adequate air coverage during all three tasks. Moreover, although adequate ground troops were available, transport shipping was not. Their discussions led Admiral Ghormley and General MacArthur to the conclusion that "the successful accomplishment of the operation is open to the gravest doubts." Consequently they recommended to the Joint Chiefs of Staff that airfield construction in New Guinea be accelerated, forces in the South and Southwest Pacific Areas be further developed, and infiltration into the New Hebrides and Santa Cruz, which had already begun on a small scale, be continued, and that the proposed offensive operation be deferred until all three tasks could be carried out without pause.[45]

Comment in the Navy Department on the joint despatch from General MacArthur and Admiral Ghromley was decidedly unfavorable. Admiral Cooke pointed out to Admiral King that although only a short time earlier General MacArthur had asked for an amphibious division and two carriers and proposed to go straight through to Rabaul, "now, confronted with the concrete aspects of the problem, MacArthur (as well as Ghromley) state that considerable additional air and transportation must be furnished."[46] This, Admiral Cooke acknowledged, was true in respect to tasks two and three, and in order to insure success the Army would have to provide more planes, more shipping, and more antiaircraft. He felt strongly that it was essential to develop supporting positions in the Santa Cruz Islands without delay and to halt the Japanese program of developments on Tulagi by an attack in force as soon as possible, before the enemy installations there could constitute a really serious threat to the security of all the advance bases within range. This vital objective could not be accomplished without the full support of General Marshall and unless the responsible commander was thoroughly convinced of probable success.

Admiral King agreed with Admiral Cooke that it was imperative to proceed with the seizure of Tulagi. He sent General Marshall a memorandum in the same tenor, which Admiral Cooke prepared for him. Included with it was a draft reply to the theater commanders.[47] It was this memorandum which introduced at the JCS meeting of 10 July 1942 the first recorded formal discussion by that body of the projected operations in the Southwest Pacific.[48] It was at once evident that the Army was prepared to agree with the Navy in the matter. The Army representatives came equipped with figures showing additional aircraft and transports which could be available for the operation. General Marshall endorsed the sentiments of Admiral King, expressing his view that the enemy's haste to occupy territory in the Solomons indicated that he had already guessed the plans in progress. With General Marshall's approval General MacArthur and Admiral Ghormley were informed that the Joint Chiefs of Staff did "not desire to countermand operations already underway for the execution of Task One." Both the Army and the Navy were making arrangements to supply additional support. Although it was recognized "that other demands to meet the world situation may prevent the assembly of forces and equipment in the Southwest Pacific for immediate execution of Tasks Two and Three, it is desired that local efforts in preparation for these tasks be vigorously pushed, including detailed operational planning."[49] Actually at this very moment there was a possibility that the major U.S. effort might be transferred to the Pacific.

ABANDONMENT OF SLEDGEHAMMER, JULY 1942

From the time it was decided that forces should be built up in the United Kingdom for a possible limited operation on the European continent in 1942 (Sledgehammer) and in any event for a larger operation (Roundup) in April 1943, planning for these had been underway in Washington and London. Despite British skepticism of the practicability of undertaking cross-Channel operations that fall, the objectives had been reaffirmed during the visit of Prime Minister Churchill and his staff to Washington in June. The buildup (Bolero) and planning for Sledgehammer had continued, and study was begun of possible alternative operations in North Africa, Norway, and the Iberian Peninsula.

Throughout June and early July the situation in the Middle East became increasingly unfavorable. At the same time the Russian defenders of Sevastopol were finally surrendering to the Germans (1 July), General Rommel in Egypt had forced the British back to make their stand at El Alamein. Sinkings by submarines in the Atlantic had risen considerably in May and June and showed evidence of continuing at a comparable rate during July. Faced with these unpleasant prospects the British War Cabinet in London decided that the conditions requisite for successfully launching Sledgehammer in a few months were unlikely to exist. As long as the assembling of material and the training of forces for this operation continued, the British felt, effort was being wasted and preparations for the more important Roundup were being curtailed. Consequently the British War Cabinet recommended that, while continuing training for Roundup, the Americans undertake an operation in North Africa and the British consider the possibilities of landings in Norway. The views of the British War Cabinet were sent via the British representatives in Washington to the Combined Chiefs of Staff. At the same time Mr. Churchill wrote in the same vein to President Roosevelt.[50]

The British communication reached Washington just at the time the JCS were reaffirming to the Pacific theater commanders their conviction that, even though available forces were inadequate for executing the entire three-part operation, it was essential that the first phase be undertaken as soon as possible. The British suggestion that an operation in North Africa be substituted for Sledgehammer, for which men and equipment sorely needed in the Pacific had been building up in the United Kingdom, met with approximately the reaction that might have been, and at least by Sir John Dill was, expected.[51]

The Joint Chiefs of Staff had never strongly favored Gymnast, the North African operation for which some planning had been done earlier in the year, and they had argued firmly against it during the visit of the Prime Minister in June as strategically unnecessary and an ineffectual waste of resources. They earnestly felt that all effort should be concentrated in preparation for a cross-Channel attack but realized that it could not be successful without full support of the British. Incensed by the new turn of events, General Marshall recommended at the JCS meeting of 10 July that if the British were unwilling to go along with the plans for the European Theater, the United States should turn its attention to the Pacific and take decisive action against Japan.[52] There were definite advantages to such a strategy, as he pointed out:

> this would tend to concentrate rather than to scatter U.S. forces;...it would be highly popular throughout the U.S., particularly on the West Coast;...the Pacific War Council, the Chinese, and the personnel of the Pacific Fleet would all be in hearty accord; and..., second only to Bolero, it would be the operation which would have the greatest effect towards relieving the pressure on Russia.

The threat of a change of basic strategy and transfer of the major effort to the Pacific Theater was one that was to recur at intervals until the date for landings in France was firmly established. In later instances the threat was suggested at JCS meetings as a last argument to use against the British if they proved otherwise unwilling to accept U.S. ideas, and with the strategic situation already developing in favor of the United Nations it was highly unlikely that if called to make good on the threat the U.S. Chiefs would have shown much enthusiasm for carrying it out. In this instance, however, the strong reaction of General Marshall to the apparent confounding of the program for which he had been working and in which he earnestly believed indicated that he was serious in his proposal that the United States give up temporarily on the European Theater, even if it meant adopting what he considered a side issue, and turn to the war against Japan in which the United States might be able to achieve victory without British help and where the United States was about to launch its first offensive. Admiral King agreed with him, although his recorded remarks were less strong. The two chiefs stated their views forcefully in a joint memorandum to the President, recommending that he urge the Prime Minister to agree to go through with Bolero and attempt no other operation:

> If the United States is to engage in any other operation than forceful, unswerving adherence to full Bolero plans, we are definitely of the opinion that we should turn to the Pacific and strike decisively against Japan; in other words assume a defensive attitude against Germany, except for air operations; and use all available means in the Pacific. Such action would not only be definite and decisive against one of our principal enemies, but would bring concrete aid to the Russians in case Japan attacks them.[53]

In a second memorandum General Marshall explained to President Roosevelt that his object was "again to force the British into acceptance of a concentrated effort against Germany, and if this proves impossible, to turn immediately to the Pacific with strong forces and drive for a decision against Japan."[54]

How the British would have reacted if confronted with this ultimatum must remain a matter for conjecture, for the President did not allow the chiefs to present it to them. From Hyde Park, where he received the chiefs' memorandum, he requested an immediate "detailed comprehensive outline of the plans, including estimated time and over-all totals of ships, planes, and ground forces," involved in transferring to the Pacific, as well as the effect of such an operation on the Atlantic, the Russian, and the Middle East fronts, in all of which the situation was critical.[55]

Inasmuch as no one had foreseen any possibility of such a change of strategy there was no complete detailed plan in Washington for major offensives in the Pacific. However, a hasty survey was made and a paper drawn up outlining in general terms immediate adjustments that would be made and reassignments of men and material.

It was proposed that an advance would be made from the South and the Southwest Pacific along the Truk-Guam-Saipan line and/or through the Malay Barrier and Borneo to the Philippines. The study predicted that the reversal of strategy would have an adverse effect on United Nations effort on the Russian-European front, but it would affect the Russian-Asiatic front favorably should the Japanese attack the Soviets. Except for eliminating the threat to India it would have little immediate effect on the situation in the Middle East.[56]

President Roosevelt soon made it known that he was not in favor of transferring the major effort to the Pacific. Cryptically he referred to the proposal as "something of a red herring," and he went so far as to suggest that "the record should be altered so that it would not appear in later years that we had proposed what amounted to the abandonment of the British." His views on the matter were based primarily on two considerations: first, the continuing crises in the Atlantic, the Middle East, and Russia. With both the British and the Russians hard pressed, the President did not wish to add to the situation a switch of U.S. interests away from that theater and away from coordinated action to a strictly American campaign. His sympathies were with the Prime Minister, who had just survived a Vote of Censure in the House of Commons, and with the Russians, who, he was keenly aware, were still alone in their struggle against the Germans on the continent of Europe and to whom he had promised every effort to open a second front in 1942. He felt strongly that nothing should be done that might result in Russian capitulation or in British disaffection. In the second place he firmly believed that it was absolutely essential that U.S. troops in considerable numbers fight the Germans somewhere in 1942. He decided to send General Marshall, Admiral King, and Mr. Harry Hopkins to London at once to settle the matter for once and for all.[57]

The group departed for London with written instructions from the President to reach agreement on definite plans for the balance of 1942 and tentative plans for 1943.[58] In so doing they were to consider certain factors:

> 3. (a) The common aim of the United Nations must be the defeat of the Axis Powers. There cannot be a compromise on this point.
> 　　(b) We should concentrate our efforts and avoid dispersion.
> 　　(c) Absolute coordinated use of British and American forces is essential.
> 　　(d) All available U.S. and British forces should be brought into action as quickly as they can be profitably used.
> 　　(e) It is of the highest importance that U.S. ground troops be brought into action against the enemy in 1942.
> 　4. British and American materiel promised to Russia must be carried out in good faith.

They were to push Sledgehammer strongly, for the President considered it "of such grave importance that every reason calls for the accomplishment of it." If agreement should prove impossible they were to examine the world situation for some other place for U.S. troops to fight in 1942 and report to him. He warned, however, that the security of the Middle East must be assured. As for the Pacific:

> I am opposed to an American all-out effort in the Pacific against Japan with the view to her defeat as quickly as possible. It is of the utmost importance that we appreciate that defeat of Japan does not defeat Germany and that American concentration against Japan this year or in 1943 increases the chance of complete German domination of Europe and Africa. On the other hand, it is obvious that defeat of Germany, or the holding of Germany in 1942 or in 1943 means probable, eventual defeat of Germany in the European and African theatres and in the Near East. Defeat of Germany means the defeat of Japan, probably without firing a shot or losing a life.[59]

In London the U.S. representatives met with stubborn resistance to proceeding with plans for Sledgehammer. When it became apparent that agreement could not be achieved, they consulted President Roosevelt, and a compromise was reached which laid the foundations for Torch, the invasion of North Africa.[60]

The war against Japan and the requirements of the Pacific Theater played a relatively small part in the combined discussions. The final agreement, however, did provide that certain air forces and shipping committed to Bolero would be reassigned to the support of offensive operations in the Pacific. As will be discussed later, the intent behind this provision is not clear.[61] As the outcome of the fighting on Guadalcanal hung in the balance in the months ahead, the destination of these aircraft was to become a point of contention.

Chapter VII

PROBLEMS OF DISTRIBUTION AND DEPLOYMENT

By the end of July 1942 the Joint Chiefs of Staff were committed to a limited offensive operation in the South Pacific and to combined planning for a landing in North Africa in the fall of the year. The huge requirements of these two projects were part of the many demands upon the limited resources of the United Nations. Chief among the others came from the Middle East, where General Sir Harold R. Alexander was strengthening his forces, and from proponents of the buildup of a great air force in the United Kingdom for full scale bombing of objectives on the European continent. Although President Roosevelt had made it clear that the North Africa project, Torch, was to be the major action for 1942,[1] there was no firm decision as to how resources should be divided among the various projects. Shortages, particularly of shipping and aircraft, were still serious. Distribution of what was available continued to be complicated by differing interpretations of where it was most needed.

The story of the second half of 1942 in the war against Japan is one of continuing crisis in the Solomons and continual conflict between the needs of that area and those of other interests of the United Nations. Since the allocation of aircraft was the greatest problem, it is necessary to look back to the spring of 1942 and discuss the attempt that had been made to reach combined agreement on how the forces of Great Britain and the United States should be deployed.

ATTEMPT TO DEFINE A STRATEGIC POLICY

The broad terms of the agreed policy of concentrating first on the defeat of Germany while maintaining a strategic defensive against Japan were not sufficient to enable the chiefs and their committees to make all the decisions arising from the complications of global war. In the first months after the Arcadia Conference, each problem required a study of availabilities and a search for resources. There had been attempts to establish allocations of forces for the remainder of 1942, but there was no firm assignment upon which the services could make their plans.[2]

By April 1942 repeated requests from agencies faced with the problems of planning details for waging a war that was world-wide had impressed the Combined Chiefs of Staff with the need for a consistent guide for allocation of forces, production of munitions and ships, and expansion of the armed services. Consequently on 7 April they accepted a suggestion made by Sir John Dill that the Combined Staff Planners should be directed to prepare an over-all general appreciation leading up to an agreed strategic policy for the United Nations. The study was particularly to cover "major deployment of forces and courses of action for 1942, and intentions for 1943."[3] At the same time Admiral King urged upon his colleagues the need for a thorough study of the aircraft resources of the United Nations, those available and those in prospect. His views were seconded by General Arnold, who emphasized the lack of available information on the current strength of the air forces of the United Nations, proposed expansions, current and proposed production, and air missions in various theaters. Aircraft production was being allocated in accordance with the so-called "Arnold-Portal Agreement," based on the prewar lend-lease formula that the United States would furnish the equipment and Great Britain would supply the manpower.[4] Its assignments were rapidly growing out of date, and the CCS recognized the advisability of replacing it. Accordingly they directed General Arnold, Admiral Towers, and Air Marshal D.C.S. Evill to investigate the aircraft situation.[5] Both studies were begun at once.

The CPS appointed a subcommittee and directed it to consider a paper on basic strategy recently prepared by the British Joint Planners, taking

> into consideration whether or not, under what conditions, and with what strength of forces, offensive operations may be undertaken in Western Europe in 1942 and the spring of 1943. Show in tabular form, by areas, a recommended deployment of forces as of June 30 and December 31, 1942, and March 31, 1943.[6]

The group went to work, but a month later they had not finished a report, because the U.S. and the British members were unable to agree on the basis to be used for listing air strengths. The Royal Air Force member was "not free to participate in planning not based on the so called 'Arnold-Portal Agreement.'" The U.S. members, however, were unwilling to use that exclusively, for they considered it misleading. They recalled that in earlier instances its use had resulted in assigning the same planes to the RAF and to the USAF. Moreover they thought its allocations to the British were excessive.[7] Since the Arnold-Portal Agreement was being revised, the U.S. representatives suggested to the Joint Staff Planners that they agree with the British either to wait until the Arnold-Evill-Towers report was completed or to authorize alternate reports, one based on the old Arnold-Portal Agreement, the other on production allocation figures recommended by General Arnold and Admiral Towers.[8] The British members of the Combined Staff Planners were of the opinion that "the strategic deployment of air forces could be made based on the practicability of shipping and maintenance, without the necessity for determining the nation which would be responsible for operating them." However, the U.S. members succeeded in obtaining a decision that, because of the importance of the deployment study, it should not be submitted until all possible material, including the aircraft report, was available, in order to make it a complete study of land, sea, and air forces.[9]

It was still another month before the study on aircraft allocations (known as the Arnold-Slessor-Towers Agreement, since Air Vice Marshal Slessor had taken Air Marshal Evill's place on the committee) was completed.[10] Then instead of presenting it to the CPS and the CCS for discussion before final acceptance, Air Vice Marshal Slessor independently presented it directly to the President and the Prime Minister, who approved it. Thus, when the CCS and the JCS received it for comment, it had already been accepted by their chiefs, and the military chiefs were committed to its terms.[11]

The Arnold-Slessor-Towers Agreement opened with a definition of the policy of the United States and Great Britain in regard to the use of air power:

> powerful United States Air Forces must be created and maintained and...every appropriate aircraft built in the United States should be manned and fought by American crews, subject to the following conditions:
> (a) That our combined aim shall be to create and bring into decisive action as quickly as possible fully trained United States and British Air Forces adequate for the defeat of our enemies, and that the combined aircraft production, trained man-power and shipping available to the United States and British Commonwealth should be used in creating and employing those air forces to that end.
> (b) that the revision of previously agreed allocations of aircraft to Great Britain shall be made so as to avoid weakening the combined strength in any theatre.

Annexed to the report was a statement of the number of aircraft to be allocated to Great Britain from U.S. production and a summary, projected through 1 April 1943, of U.S. air forces to be assigned to areas for British and combined strategic responsibility. Since this was a combined study it made no allocations to the United States from U.S. production and no assignments of planes to areas under U.S. control. The agreement stipulated, however, that the United States should provide for the requirements of British Dominions lying within areas of U.S. strategic responsibility.[12] Assignments of aircraft to the Dominions had previously been a British or a combined responsibility. Attempting to provide adequately for the Dominion needs in accordance with the Arnold-Slessor-Towers Agreement was to cause the U.S. Chiefs considerable difficulty.[13]

As soon as the Combined Staff Planners tried to apply the Arnold-Slessor-Towers report to their study they encountered difficulties. They found themselves with a report that made no specific mention of the Pacific Theater, and that, furthermore, provided for allocating specific numbers of aircraft to the British regardless of the number actually produced in the United States. Moreover, there had been no long range figures available previously in regard to aircraft to be allocated to the British Dominions, and now, instead of providing them, the Arnold-Slessor-Towers Agreement made the assignments a U.S. responsibility. Far from assisting the preparation of the aircraft section of the deployment study, the new agreement had added further complications.[14]

On 24 June 1942, two and a half months after receiving its directive, the special subcommittee finally submitted its report, entitled, "Strategic Policy and Deployment of United States and British Forces," to the CPS, who forwarded it with some minor changes to the Combined Chiefs of Staff on 7 July as C.C.S. 91.[15] The report contained first a summary of the situation, at sea, in the Japanese Theater, and in the German Theater. Japan, it was noted, had already gained territory that would eventually make the nation economically self-sufficient. Japan still retained the initiative, and it might undertake any of the following:

> (a) Seizure of Ceylon, which would control the Bay of Bengal and harass our sea communications with the Red Sea and Persian Gulf.
> (b) Seizure of Bengal, which would cut off access to China, except through Russia, Assam, or Tibet.
> (c) An attack on Australia or the island positions between Australia and Hawaii.
> (d) Seizure of Eastern Siberia.
> (e) Reinforcement and extention of footholds gained in the Aleutians.

The strategy of the United States and Great Britain in facing the problems of war against the two major enemies was based on two fundamental considerations:

> (a) Securing the main areas of war industry and the essential intervening sea and air communications, and securing the lines of communication to the fighting forces of the United Nations.
> (b) Expanding our fighting forces and taking offensive action against the enemy in a decisive theater, while providing the other United Nations with the munitions and military support needed to keep them effectively fighting the Axis Powers.

Consideration of the foregoing situation led the planners to recommend that the basic strategic concept be reaffirmed, that an offensive with maximum forces be undertaken against Germany at the earliest practicable date, while "minimum adequate forces" maintained a strategic defensive in all other theaters. The courses of action recommended in implementation of this concept were revised by the Combined Staff Planners in view of the fact that by the time the planners received the paper the directive for a limited offensive in the South Pacific had already been issued. The order in which the items were listed was rearranged also to indicate the relation of each to the fundamental objectives. The following courses of action were recommended to the CCS:

Strategic Offensive.

(a) Initiate a major combined offensive against Germany in the European theater. Plans to be flexible so as to meet the situation if Russia should crack.[16]

(b) Wear down and undermine German resistance by increasing bomber offensive, blockade, raids, subversive activities and propaganda.

Strategic Defensive.

(c) Secure essential land, sea and air communications of the United Nations, particular emphasis being placed on an increasing anti U-boat offensive.

(d) Secure the Middle East.

(e) Secure Ceylon and stop the Japanese penetration towards India and the Indian Ocean.

(f) Secure Australia, New Zealand, Hawaii and Alaska.

(g) While the above strategic defensive roles are being carried out, employ amphibious forces in the Pacific theater on limited offensive operations. At the same time inflict attrition and exert economic pressure on Japan.

(h) Without prejudice to (a) above, prepare to reoccupy Burma in order to reopen land communications with China.

Munitions of War.

(i) Accomplish the maximum acceleration of balanced production for war, which requires the security of the main areas of industry and of the indispensable sources of raw materials.

(j) Continue the flow of essential munitions to Russia and to other United Nations engaged in fighting the enemy.

Included with the report as annexes were recommended deployments of forces to the various theaters of war to implement the basic strategic concept and to support the proposed courses of action. The deployments were "based on the availability of units," and on reasonable expectations of being able to ship them "to the areas concerned."[17] It was recognized that as long as the Axis forces held the initiative changes might have to be made to meet new enemy offensives. Likewise, new developments in the strategy of the United Nations would have far-reaching effects, since it would be necessary to rearrange shipping schedules in order to deliver requisite forces to the areas where they were to be used.[18]

After examining the figures presented by the CPS, the Operations Division of the War Department (OPD) pointed out that there appeared to be some considerable increases in numbers of ground forces deployed in the various theaters over the numbers approved in JCS 23 and the later paper for the Pacific, JCS 48.[19] When CCS 91 came up for discussion before the JCS, General Marshall presented OPD's recommendation that the figures be reviewed to determine whether the troops in some of the theaters might be cut down, thereby releasing shipping for Bolero.[20]

Admiral King had already brought to the attention of the Joint Chiefs of Staff the difficulties the CPS had experienced in preparing a complete study on the deployment of forces of the United Nations as of 1 April 1943 when the only aircraft figures available for the British Dominions were the numbers of planes that had been committed to them, although not yet delivered, by 24 June 1942. The planners had used these figures, and recommended that the Combined Munitions Assignments Board (CMAB) be directed to provide for maintenance of the Dominions' air forces at these strengths from the Dominions' own aircraft production, and that the planes for such expansion as the JCS should determine in accordance with the Arnold-Slessor-Towers Agreement should come from combined aircraft production. Admiral King insisted that, in order that the interests of the United States and the Dominions might be adequately protected, the strategic requirements of the Dominions would have to be ascertained. The U.S. Chiefs were not informed as to what provisions the British had already made for supplying their Dominions with aircraft. Consequently Admiral King appended a list of questions for presentation to the Combined Chiefs of Staff concerning the size and sources of air forces already in the Dominions, the Dominions' own views of their needs, and the views of the British as to their strategic requirements.[21]

The Combined Chiefs of Staff accepted the planners' basic paper (CCS 91) as a guide for the production authorities, but the U.S. Joint Staff Planners were put to work, at the direction of the U.S. Chiefs, on the points the Army's Operations Division had raised in regard to the annexes. The British agreed to furnish the information requested by Admiral King, and the CCS deferred consideration of the deployment of aircraft until the question of the Dominions had been settled.[22]

Investigation of the demands of Australia for aircraft disclosed that the Australian Government was planning an air force of approximately seventy squadrons. The Australian representatives in Washington claimed that there were several hundred pilots in Australia who lacked planes to fly. It was manifestly impossible at the current rate of plane production in the summer of 1942 both to supply the Australians with planes for some seventy squadrons and to continue to build up sizable U.S. air units in Australia. Consequently the suggestion was made that planes should be sent to the RAAF, rather than to the U.S. air forces stationed in Australia, and that it might even be advisable to equip the RAAF pilots with U.S. planes and return the U.S. pilots from the Southwest Pacific to the United States for reassignment to other theaters. When General Marshall forwarded this suggestion to General MacArthur he was informed that the Australian plan had been designed to utilize planes primarily for coastal defense from British allocations. Although the existence of "several hundred" available pilots in Australia was an exaggeration, the project was proceeding according to schedule. General MacArthur insisted that it should be carried out, but not at the expense of U.S. air forces. The latter he described as "pitiably inadequate to support the eventual offensive based upon Australia." General MacArthur strongly opposed withdrawal of any American units from the Pacific, "for it [might] be accepted as a fact that the cessation of American effort in the Pacific and the consequent continued and increasing ascendancy of Japan [would] be followed by the collapse of China and an immediate attack by Japan upon Russia in Siberia."[23]

The Joint U.S. Strategic Committee, meanwhile, had undertaken to investigate the question of furnishing aircraft for the Dominions, and on 28 July came up with a report to the JPS. They suggested three alternative ways of solving the problem:

> (a) Provide for the Dominions at the expense of planned U.S. air strength.
>
> (b) Provide only a very moderate number of U.S. aircraft to Australia and New Zealand, and:
>> (1) Permit Australian and New Zealand squadrons to decrease in strength through wastage except as offset by Australian production, U.S. and British present allocations.
>>
>> (2) Allow Canada to use her production and such aircraft as can be obtained from British sources to maintain Canadian squadrons.
>
> (c) Readjust the Arnold-Slessor-Towers agreement by re-writing paragraph 7, [24] together with those relevant portions of the annexes in order to provide aircraft to properly meet Dominion requirements either by:
>> (1) Diverting aircraft from American allocations to Britain, or,
>>
>> (2) Reduction of U.S. commitments contained therein.[24]

Solution (a), JUSSC agreed, was unacceptable because it was contrary to the U.S. policy that U.S. aircraft should be manned by U.S. crews, it would necessitate cutting expansion of U.S. air units, and it would reduce the air forces in defensive areas below the minimum required by CCS 91. Solution (b), the committee pointed out, was untenable politically. It would give the Dominions grounds for complaining that the United Kingdom had failed to look out for their interests and, at the same time, that the United States was failing to fulfill its agreements. There was a definite maximum of U.S. aircraft production that could be allocated to other countries. The JUSSC thought the Arnold-Slessor-Towers Agreement was unfair in its assignments, for it did not take into consideration the requirements of the Dominions from U.S. production as well as the requirements of the United Kingdom. Consequently the committee recommended that the agreement be modified, to insure that the greater part of Dominion production of aircraft would go to the Dominions themselves and that additional planes would be provided by reducing the number of aircraft of various types allocated from U.S. production to Great Britain. The committee's report included a summary of existing commitments for the Dominions, according to CPS 28/3 (i.e., CCS 91), and recommendations based on study of the actual requirements of the Dominions. Thus for Australia JUSSC recommended assignment of thirty-three squadrons, an increase from twenty-eight provided in CPS 28/3, and for New Zealand they recommended thirteen and one-half, an increase from ten. The allocations made to the British in the Arnold-Slessor-Towers Agreement were to be modified accordingly.[25]

The British Chiefs of Staff, meanwhile, had been studying the problem, particularly with a view to replying to the questions the U.S. Chiefs had presented to them. It appears that they were also acquainted with the study being made by the JUSSC. They called the attention of the U.S. Chiefs to CCS 57/2, the paper concerning worldwide spheres of responsibility which had established the policy that the U.S. responsibility for Australia and New Zealand included "provision of essential assistance for security of Australia and New Zealand." It was on this that the Arnold-Slessor-Towers provision for the Dominions had been based, the British pointed out. Since defense of these Dominions was the strategic responsibility of the United States, the British preferred to express no opinion as to their requirements. They cautioned, however,

> that agreed strategy demands that United Nations forces in the Pacific and North America must for the time being be limited to the minimum requirements for defense of vital positions, and that limitations of shipping are such that those forces should be built up in the most economical manner making the fullest use of locally raised and trained personnel and maintenance facilities.

The British Chiefs agreed that the requirements of the Dominions should be established and that necessary allocations to meet those requirements should be made. CCS 91 had not established the first, but it had made clear that expansion of the Dominion air forces could be made only at the expense of British air forces in the active theaters of war. In this connection the British pointed out the presence in Australia of air personnel without planes and of U.S. air units that were badly needed in other theaters. The Dominions' production was designed to fill the requirements of the Royal Air Force rather than their own needs. Allocations to the Dominions which the British had previously made had ceased with the enactment of the Arnold-Slessor-Towers Agreement, which terminated British responsibility. If the United States did not make further allocations of aircraft to meet the requirements of the Dominions, the requirements would not be met, or they would be met by "making further inroads on the allocations on which the R.A.F. is relying to build up its strengths in active theatres of war where it is now engaged with the enemy." The British Chiefs of Staff insisted that it had not occurred to them when they approved the Arnold-Slessor-Towers Agreement that the allocations of aircraft to the Dominions that lay within the U.S. spheres of responsibility would be met by reducing the allocations the British had accepted for themselves. Those figures had already been reduced from the earlier Arnold-Portal Agreement, with the understanding that the difference was to be used to meet Dominion requirements. The British insisted they could accept no further reductions without seriously affecting the air strengths required in active theaters of war.[26]

These two papers were given to the Air member of the Joint Staff Planners, Colonel O.A. Anderson, for study and comment.[27] He decided that the Arnold-Slessor-Towers Agreement should not be changed since it had presumably been arrived at after a careful evaluation of minimum requirements for the British in active theaters. Moreover, it had been approved by the President and the Prime Minister, and the Combined Chiefs of Staff were morally obligated to stand by its terms. He did not favor increasing the number of aircraft already allocated to the Dominions, for he thought they were sufficient to satisfy the political requisite of maintaining air forces there. They had not all been delivered as yet, and he recommended that the numbers provided in CCS 91 be accepted as the objective for the Dominions for 1 April 1943. Subsequent modification might be desirable as operations developed.[28]

The JPS discussed the problem and the various papers which had been presented on it at some length, but the official minutes give no indication to what extent there may or may not have been disagreement. Eventually the planners turned the whole thing over to Colonel Anderson and Commander C.R. Brown, USN, to prepare a report, including a strategic appreciation of the air requirements of the U.S. areas of strategic responsibility and the sources from which the Dominion requires could be filled.[29]

The report thus prepared was passed along by the Joint Staff Planners to the Joint Chiefs of Staff as a study of the two papers, CCS 91 and CCS 92. Adjustments had been made in the deployment figures for ground forces to satisfy the objections of the Army Operations Division. In regard to aircraft the opinion of Colonel Anderson and of the British had prevailed over the suggestion of the JUSSC, and it was agreed that any augmentation of air forces in the Dominions would come not from British but from U.S. aircraft resources. Revised figures on deployment of air forces were attached, setting those for Australia at thirty squadrons and those for New Zealand at ten, but altering the types of squadrons to be assigned. It was recommended that the figures on aircraft deployment be accepted by the JCS as a basis for allocation by the CMAB and for submission to the CCS for approval.[30]

At the JCS meeting on 11 August the new paper was presented. By this time the Guadalcanal operation, which had just been ordered when the original papers were drafted, was under way, and decision had been made to undertake Torch. Delivery of aircraft committed to the Dominions had been held up awaiting the policy decision that had been hanging fire, and the local authorities were anxious for a decision. The Joint Chiefs agreed to accept the recommendations as an initial allocation but recommended that General Arnold, Air Marshal Evill, Admiral Towers, and the Air representatives of the Dominions confer on a program for further expansion of the Dominion air forces.[31] The JCS forwarded their recommendations and the deployment figures of the JPS to the CCS, who in turn set General Arnold, Air Marshal Evill, Admiral Towers, and the Dominion Air representatives to work examining the Dominions' requirements.³² From their study came the decision that with certain amendments the recommendations the Joint Chiefs had submitted in the form of revised annexes to CCS 91 were acceptable. It would be impossible, the group agreed, to provide more than thirty squadrons of planes to the RAAF or more than ten to the RNZAF and at the same time supply the American units in the area with the aircraft that had been committed to them. In order fully to utilize available manpower in the Dominions, the Air experts offered the same solution that had been suggested before, i.e., that aircraft be withdrawn from the U.S. units in the areas and given to Dominion pilots and the U.S. units be transferred to other theaters. This idea, which was referred to the theater commanders and local governments by despatch, was attractive to the Australian and New Zealand military representatives in Washington but not at all acceptable to the Australian Government, nor to General MacArthur and Major General M.F. Harmon. From both of the latter came strong pleas that no such cut be made in the U.S. Air Forces organization in their respective areas and that both forces be continued as strong as possible.³³ The views from the theater were adopted, with some regret, at least on the part of the British. The scheme of transferring aircraft from U.S. units was abandoned entirely in regard to Australia, but decision as to the practicability of such a procedure in New Zealand was left for further study. At the same time investigation was to be made of the feasibility of forming additional squadrons in the Southwest Pacific, using NEI pilots and Australian ground crews.³⁴

On 21 August, more than four months after the CPS had been directed to prepare a study, the Combined Chiefs of Staff finally agreed to accept the revised annexes of CCS 91 as a basis

   (1) For strategic planning....
   (2) For calculating the production requirements for ground and naval forces for 1942.
   (3) For the assignment of weapons, munitions, and aircraft to the ground, naval, and air forces (other than Canadian air forces [which would be the subject of a separate report]) to April 1, 1943.

They agreed, however, that this was not to be a final agreed deployment but subject to change caused by requirements for Torch and other strategic developments.³⁵

Thus, in general terms, the Combined Chiefs of Staff had reached agreement on the strategic deployment of ground, naval, and air forces among the several theaters of war as of 1 April 1943. But this was not, nor was it intended to be, the final word on the subject. The first of April 1943 was more than seven months away. Before that time, there were many problems to be solved.

PROBLEMS OF THE DEFENSE OF AUSTRALIA

The question of supplying the British Dominions with aircraft which had developed with the study of the deployment of United Nations forces was but one of the Combined Chiefs' problems related to the land "down under." The necessity of defending Australia and New Zealand against Japanese encroachment was vastly complicated by political considerations with which the chiefs were inevitably involved.

In April 1942 defense of the Southwest Pacific Area, including Australia, had been made a U.S. responsibility, and Australian military and naval forces had been placed under U.S. strategic command. Australian troops were fighting under General MacArthur in New Guinea; Australian air and naval forces were participating in the operations in both the South and the Southwest Pacific Areas. The Solomons-New Guinea campaign was looked upon by U.S. strategists as a contribution to the defense of Australia since it was keeping Japanese forces occupied in other areas. Australians, however, were naturally worried lest the enemy land on their very shores, and they continued to insist on stronger local defense forces and to urge that more naval and air forces be sent to the area, not only to defend Australia but to drive the Japanese back as far as the Mandates. With other more immediate demands on United Nations resources it was necessarily the comparative strategic need that determined how many of Australia's requests could be granted.

The problems of the defense of Australia were complicated by the political necessity of preserving its good will and the assistance which it alone could furnish, with troops, materiel, and bases. Considerable friction had already developed between the Australian and British Governments over the use of Australian troops in the Middle East and the representation of Dominion Governments on the body that was to direct the strategy against Japan. Australian representatives were sometimes called in to CCS meetings for consultation, and they sat on the Pacific War Councils in Washington and London and on the committee known as the Military Representatives of the Associated Pacific Powers (MRP), which met sporadically in Washington beginning in May 1942.[36] But when the Australian Government wanted fast action Prime Minister Curtin communicated directly with Prime Minister Churchill or President Roosevelt.

At the end of August, when General MacArthur was predicting to General Marshall that unless strong forces were concentrated in the Pacific an extremely serious crisis would develop, Mr. Curtin reported to Mr. Churchill and Mr. Roosevelt his views of the situation and his recommendations to meet the urgent needs of the Southwest Pacific Area.[37] Like General MacArthur he recommended that a large naval concentration be built up in the Pacific, strong enough to defeat the Japanese and drive them from the southern Pacific. When his suggestion that units of the British Eastern Fleet be transferred from the Indian Ocean to the Pacific was met with a refusal from London, Mr. Curtin urged that at least enough land and air strength for local defense of Australia be provided. President

Roosevelt turned over his copies of these exchanges to the CCS for preparation of a reply that would emphasize the Japanese shipping situation and the Japanese tonnage that had been sunk in the first nine months of the war in the Pacific. Accordingly the CPS, who produced the paper, pointed out that, with U.S. naval attacks on Japanese shipping increasing, the enemy's capacity for mounting operations was likely to be continually decreasing. Moreover the current operations in the Solomons were actually strengthening the Southwest Pacific and the vital communications link and so contributing to Australia's security. Mr. Curtin was told that under the existing circumstances no ground or air forces could be promised beyond commitments already made and that in the U.S. view the forces then in Australia, when fully equipped, would be sufficient to insure defense against invasion.[38]

The Australian Government accepted this decision but remained unconvinced. Toward the end of October, when forces in the Solomons area were tensely awaiting a Japanese attack, Mr. Curtin cabled Mr. Churchill and Mr. Roosevelt, outlining the results of a study by the Australian War Council of the manpower situation in Australia. The council had concluded that a manpower deficiency of 22,000 existed and that the best way to improve the situation would be to return the 9th Australian Division, which was still in the Middle East. In April, and again in July, the Australian Government had agreed to a British request that return of these troops be postponed; but it was proving impossible to reenforce the division or adequately to maintain it from Australia. The Australian Government felt that the division had contributed its share to the campaigns in the Middle East and that it should be allowed to return home.[39]

The request from Prime Minister Curtin came at just the time that the British Eighth Army, commanded by General Sir Bernard L. Montgomery, was starting its offensive west from Egypt against the Germans at El Alamein. It was also less than three weeks before D Day for Torch and a time of extreme tension in the Solomons area. All of these projects had been putting great strain on the limited resources, particuarly of shipping, of the United Nations, and it would certainly have been difficult to find sufficient tonnage to bring the Australian division back from the Middle East and replace it there with a British or a U.S. division. Militarily there was considered to be little likelihood that the Japanese would attempt to invade Australia.[40] The Joint Staff Planners, who were directed to prepare the President's draft reply to this request, were of the opinion that the demands of the Australian Advisory War Council for adequate defense forces could be satisfied by promising to send additional U.S. troops to Australia on condition that the 9th Division remain in the Middle East. This could be easily arranged, for the 25th U.S. Infantry Division was at that time in Hawaii, loaded for movement to the South Pacific. It could be sent to Australia instead, take over the facilities of troops that had been moved into New Guinea, and receive necessary additional training in defense technique. Consequently Mr. Curtin was told that a U.S. division would be transferred to Australia, subject to diversion to some other locality in the Pacific should necessity develop.[41]

The campaign in Egypt met with great success, and the Germans fled west from El Alamein at a rapid pace. While the British were pursuing them, in mid-November, Mr. Curtin expressed his dissatisfaction with the substitution proposal. Pointing out the contributions Australian troops had already made outside their home territory, and outlining the agreements the British had made to return the 9th Division from the Middle East, the Australian Prime Minister reported that, now that the crises in the Middle East appeared to be under control, the Australian Government expected its troops to be sent home.[42]

President Roosevelt was of the opinion that nothing should be done that might interrupt the steady progress of the British drive in Africa and that Mr. Curtin should be persuaded of the major benefit Australia would reap from the opening of the communications route through the Mediterranean. Mr. Roosevelt was interested, however, in having the division returned to Australia and reconstituted for use in New Guinea or elsewhere. He turned the Prime Minister's request over to the Combined Chiefs of Staff for decision as to the advisability of returning the 9th Division after completion of the African campaign.[43]

Since the 9th Division had suffered many casualties and could no longer be maintained to standard from Australia, its value to the Middle East Command was diminishing. But it was wholly impractical to cut back on shipping in all other theaters in order to carry out the non-essential transfer of so large a force. So, on recommendation of the Combined Chiefs of Staff, the President informed Mr. Curtin that he was prepared to urge that the division be returned to Australia as soon as practicable, the exact time to be dependent upon first, final and decisive victory over General Rommel's forces, and second, availability of shipping. Inasmuch as cargo shipping in particular was in short supply, however, the movement would include personnel only, and the division's equipment would have to remain in the Middle East. Mr. Roosevelt also reassured Mr. Curtin that Australian defenses would be adequate, for the U.S. 25th Division would shortly leave Hawaii for Australia and would be there long before the 9th Australian Division could leave the Middle East.[44]

Even before President Roosevelt sent his answer to Prime Minister Curtin, there came a request from the Prime Minister of New Zealand to Prime Minister Churchill that the New Zealand division which had been in the Middle East for three years also be allowed to return home. This request was obviously made for political reasons and not for military necessity, but the decision could not be made entirely on political considerations. So the President, at Mr. Churchill's suggestion, consulted the Combined Chiefs of Staff as to the military implications of complying with the New Zealand request.[45] After consultation with the Combined Military Transportation

Committee, the Combined Staff Planners submitted their conclusions. They found, first, that there were no military arguments whatsoever which would justify the movement of the 9th Australian Division and the 2nd New Zealand Division from the Middle East; second, that although it would be possible to find personnel shipping by cutting back on other projects, the shipping required to carry the troops to the Dominions would not be available for any other urgent troop movements for about three months.[46]

The members of the CCS were in full agreement with the conclusions of their planners, but before passing them along to the heads of state they called in the Australian and New Zealand military representatives in Washington. Although these officers presented their countries' views as to the necessity of having their troops returned, however, the CCS insisted that such a movement would actually weaken the military situation and that political considerations must not be allowed to affect the military outlook. They even strengthened the conclusions of the Joint Staff Planners by pointing out that "every military argument is against the move.... Such a move would involve a definite reduction of the impact upon the enemy in 1943, and a major diversion of shipping resources which are urgently required for other troop movements."[47]

Political considerations eventually prevailed. As has already been discussed, relations between the British and the Australian Government had been somewhat strained since the beginning of the war, and a major bone of contention had been the desires of the British to transfer Australian troops from the Middle East to Burma in February.[48] In view of this situation and the subsequent interchanges between the two governments which had resulted in agreement by the Australians to postpone the return, Mr. Churchill apparently felt that he must now agree to send the 9th Division home.[49] In any event the British independently made arrangements for the movement. They informed the Joint Chiefs of Staff in mid-December that the decision had been made and that all Australian troops remaining in the Middle East would be returned to Australia in early 1943.[50]

Chapter VIII

SUPPORTING THE GUADALCANAL CAMPAIGN

CONFLICTING VIEWS OF THE STRATEGIC IMPORTANCE OF THE PACIFIC

Both in Washington and in the South and Southwest Pacific Areas in July 1942 staffs were working on details of plans for the three-part operation which the Joint Chiefs of Staff had determined to undertake in the Solomons-New Guinea-New Britain area.[1] Intelligence reports that the Japanese were fortifying Guadalcanal had led the Pacific commanders to the conclusion that that island should be the major objective of Task One. Efforts to estimate the timing and scope of the operations to follow the first step were hindered by uncertainty as to what U.S. forces would be available for the area. The chiefs had considered it essential to proceed with Task One, in order to dislodge the Japanese and stop the enemy's southward advance, even though they could not predict when forces could be in the area to continue on to the ultimate capture of Rabaul. As the Joint Chiefs of Staff directed the local commanders to proceed with preparations for landings in the Solomons they informed them that additional shipborne aircraft and surface forces would be provided by the Commander in Chief, Pacific Fleet, and that the Army planned "to increase [the] rate of flow of replacement aircraft and...take all followup measures possible in support of the seizure and firm occupation of the Tulagi area." General MacArthur and Admiral Ghormley were to itemize the additional forces they considered "absolutely essential to the execution of Task One."[2] Except for these agreements in principle the JCS made no detailed decisions as to how much the forces already available in the Pacific might have to be augmented in order to support the first operation and follow up the landings on Guadalcanal and Tulagi. They could hardly have foreseen the long campaign that developed as the Japanese fought to maintain their hold on Guadalcanal, but the failure to decide ahead of time to what extent the operation would be supported with additional troops and equipment was the cause of continuing disagreement throughout the fall of 1942 and carried on into 1943.

Whenever the problem of sending more men or equipment to the South Pacific was discussed among the Joint Chiefs of Staff consideration had to be given to the effect such reenforcement would have on projects in other theaters of war, North Africa, the Middle East, the China-Burma-India theater, the buildup of a bombing force in the

SUPPORTING THE GUADALCANAL CAMPAIGN

United Kingdom, and the numerous other areas where there was never quite enough. Requests from the South Pacific for additional forces, and especially for aircraft, encountered different reactions from the several chiefs as they evaluated differently the relative urgency of those demands and the numerous others upon the resources of the United Nations.

As would be expected, the principal support for the demands from the Pacific came from the Navy Department and its chief spokesman, Admiral King. During the period between the wars naval officers, among them Admiral King, had made a continuing study of the strategy of a war with Japan and had developed opinions that amounted to doctrine as to how such a war should be fought. From the beginning of hostilities Admiral King had been impressed with the demonstrated capabilities and strength of the Japanese, and he continually insisted that the seriousness of the situation in the Pacific should not be understimated. He had immediately directed the Pacific Fleet to defend the line of communications from Hawaii to the Southwest Pacific and consistently urged that a strong series of island bases be built up, each equipped with fighter and bomber forces for defense against Japanese attack. Until such time as a major effort could be made to defeat Japan, Admiral King insisted, U.S. forces should not only defend what territory they had but should constantly seize every opportunity to improve their strategic position and put the greatest possible pressure on the Japanese. The Guadalcanal operation was conceived as a means of following up the advantage gained at Midway and also as an operation that was strategically essential to check the advance of the Japanese toward the vital line of communications and to place U.S. forces in an advantageous position to observe enemy movements. Admiral King and his staff feared the consequences not only of failure on Guadalcanal but of a victory that was not followed by maintenance of sufficient force in the area to hold it and to prevent the Japanese from striking at some other objective. Admiral King believed in the basic concept that had been settled upon even before the war began, i.e., that Germany was to be defeated first. He, like General Marshall, accepted the President's decision that U.S. troops had to be fighting Germans somewhere in 1942 and that North Africa was to be the spot. While supporting these, however, he did not for a moment forget the constant threat in the Pacific and he repeatedly urged that everything possible should be sent to that area. When requirements of the South Pacific conflicted with allocations to the war against Germany, he maintained that the item in question should go to the former where action was already joined and the need was immediate rather than to Europe where strength was being built up for operations which could be postponed without serious strategic consequences.

General Marshall's views were somewhat different. Since the early spring of 1942 he had been striving for an agreement with the British to return at the earliest possible moment to the continent of Europe and at least gain a toehold from which the all-out offensive to defeat Germany might ultimately be launched.

When Torch became the order of the day he and his planners concentrated on preparations for that operation. Unlike Admiral King he had not devoted a major part of his time and thinking in prewar years to the strategy of war with Japan. When war came his thinking concentrated rather on holding a defensive position in the Pacific than on constantly trying to improve it and planning for ultimate offensive action on a large scale. As emergencies arose he sent Army forces to meet them, but he and his staff did not continuously consider how forces in the Pacific could be utilized prior to the defeat of Germany. General Marshall had realized the threat of the advancing Japanese to the security of U.S. positions in the South and Southwest Pacific, and he had heartily endorsed General MacArthur's plan to attack. However, he did not visualize sending additional forces in any considerable quantity to support the operation. Estimates prepared in the War Department as to what constituted the "essential minimum" that should go to the Pacific were inevitably lower than those produced by the Navy. When demands from the two major theaters of war conflicted, unless General Marshall was convinced of an immediate need in the Pacific and was assured that forces already available were being adequately used, he disapproved taking anything from the war against Germany.

General Arnold was more extreme in his views than General Marshall. His main interest was in building up a strong air force in the United Kingdom and, as soon as possible, launching a tremendous air offensive against Germany to knock it out of the war, by air bombardment alone if possible and at least by preparing the way for land invasion to follow. In his view there was no question but that the Pacific was a secondary theater and only the minimum should be sent to it. General Arnold did not share Admiral King's view of the urgency of maintaining constant pressure on the Japanese and holding the optimum strategic position. He considered the Navy's scheme of basing aircraft on a series of islands between Hawaii and Australia wasteful of planes and a failure to appreciate the strategic mobility of aircraft. His views, supported by the Army planners, had prevailed in the spring of 1942 over recommendations from the Navy for a considerable increase in the number of planes allocated to the Pacific, and in July mobile air forces had been set up in Hawaii and Australia instead of the smaller forces the Navy wanted on the islands between. General Arnold had not participated directly in the negotiations that resulted in the decision to attack in the Solomons and his views of the strategic necessity for such an operation are not recorded. However he clearly considered that there were enough aircraft assigned to the area to support the operation if only they were effectively used. He did not think that more were needed or indeed that more could be maintained, and he was firmly opposed to cutting back on the European Theater, and particularly on the buildup in the United Kingdom, in order to send more planes to the Pacific.[3]

Admiral William D. Leahy, who as Chief of Staff to the Commander in Chief had joined the JCS in July 1942, had no part in the directive that launched the attack on Guadalcanal. He participated little in the recorded discussions of what should be sent to the South Pacific, but in general his views were similar to those of Admiral King, that everything possible should go to that area.[4]

These various opinions clashed repeatedly during the months in which the struggle for Guadalcanal continued. As had been the case in the development of the directive for the three-phase operation in the Solomons-New Guinea-New Britain area, most of the negotiations for support of the operation were carried on through direct correspondence between General Marshall and Admiral King, and only occasionally were the problems raised within the formal organization of the Joint Chiefs of Staff.

ATTEMPTS TO STRENGTHEN THE FORCES IN THE SOUTH PACIFIC, JULY-AUGUST 1942

As preparations for the execution of Task One[5] in the South Pacific proceeded it became obvious both to the local commanders and to naval planners in Washington that, without more forces than were currently in the area, successful completion of the operation in the Solomons was doubtful.[6] The Navy was prepared to increase naval forces in the South Pacific as much as possible and felt that the Army too should make every possible effort to strengthen its forces in the South and the Southwest Pacific. From the middle of July on there was a continuing discussion between the two services, and more particularly between the two chiefs (with General Arnold a frequent participant), as to what should go to the Pacific and when.

About two weeks after the Solomons directive was issued, when General Marshall, Admiral King, and Mr. Hopkins were preparing to depart for London to attempt to straighten out with the British the question of an offensive in the European Theater in 1942, Admiral King sent an urgent memorandum to General Marshall, outlining his views on the situation in the South Pacific. The admiral felt strongly that the enemy would never permit his bases in the Solomons to be captured without offering strong resistance and making a concerted attempt to recapture them. Intelligence sources already indicated that ground, sea, and air forces were being assembled in considerable numbers in the region of the major Japanese base at Rabaul. It was highly likely that the enemy would use these to resist the attack in the Solomons. Admiral King pointed out to General Marshall that forces would have to be provided to relieve the Marines once the island objectives had been seized and to consolidate and defend the newly-won position. The JCS directive for the Solomons operation stated that Army occupational forces already in the South Pacific area would be used as garrison forces in the Solomon Islands, and the Army had already signified its intention not to send any more forces except aircraft to the area. But Admiral King considered that the provisions which had been made were not enough. Admiral Ghormley had reported that he had enough forces to take his objectives but would need garrison troops and antiaircraft regiments. General MacArthur had said simply that he needed as much air strength as possible, and he had offered nothing to help in the South Pacific Area. Admiral King, therefore, urged that the Chiefs of Staff consider, before their departure for London the following day, the possibility of providing additional antiaircraft regiments for defense of the captured territory. He also recommended that General MacArthur be directed to prepare to send garrison troops to the Solomons area as needed.[7]

General Marshall's answer was that since units from the United States could not arrive in time for the operation, provision would be made to alert antiaircraft regiments stationed at Bora Bora and Tongatabu for movement into the newly occupied positions. At Admiral King's insistence that Bora Bora and Tongatabu themselves not be left unprotected, the Army arranged to order the 76th CA(AA) from the Western Defense Command to the South Pacific as a partial replacement. General Marshall considered it unnecessary to order garrison troops from General MacArthur's command, since the directive called for garrison troops for the Solomons from the South Pacific Area. Moreover, it had been explained to General MacArthur that the boundary between the South and Southwest Pacific Areas was being moved to 159° East at General Marshall's suggestion, in order to insure against the use of General MacArthur's troops for garrison duty in the South Pacific Area.[8]

While Admiral King and General Marshall were in London word came to Washington from Admiral Nimitz that he considered this scheme of depleting Bora Bora and Tongatabu to garrison the Solomons unsatisfactory. CinCPOA emphasized the inevitability that enemy effort to recover any territory captured by U.S. forces would result in losses of U.S. troops, aircraft, and probably ships. "Unless these losses...are made good by a steady flow of replacements from the United States," he said, "not only will we be unable to proceed with Tasks Two and Three of this campaign, but we may be unable even to hold what we have taken."[9]

In the absence of the two service chiefs the next in command, Vice Admiral Russell Willson and Lieutenant General Joseph T. McNarney, exchanged comments on these despatches. Admiral Willson asked for two more antiaircraft regiments besides the one already promised. Again the reply was: The Army considered that its arrangements were adequate. Reenforcements for the Solomons should be moved forward as needed from New Caledonia and replaced by forces from Bora Bora and Tongatabu. No more antiaircraft forces could be sent to the South Pacific without inadvisably depleting the forces of the Western Defense Command. And no further air reenforcements could be made available for the area without cutting into commitments for the European Theater.[10]

Thus it was already obvious that the Army did not share the Navy's view of the urgency of strengthening the South Pacific forces. But Admiral King returned from London with hope of getting at least air reenforcements to the Pacific.

173 SUPPORTING THE GUADALCANAL CAMPAIGN

The agreement (CCS 94) General Marshall and Admiral King finally secured at their meetings with the British Chiefs of Staff contained one important provision for the Pacific Theater. Recognizing that cancellation of Sledgehammer in 1942, and possibly also of Roundup in 1943, would make available a considerable amount of equipment which had been scheduled for delivery to the United Kingdom under the Bolero program, General Marshall had insisted on inclusion in CCS 94 of the stipulation

> That over and above the U.S. forces required from Bolero for operations in North and North West Africa, the following readjustment of present U.S. commitments to Bolero will be made for the purpose of furthering offensive operations in the Pacific:
> (1) Withdrawal of the following air forces:
>   3 groups heavy bombers
>   2 groups medium bombers
>   2 groups light bombers
>   2 groups fighter planes
>   2 groups observation planes
>   4 groups transport planes
> (2) Probably shipping to move one infantry or Marine division from U.S. West Coast to South West Pacific.[11]

This provision had not been included in the written instructions the three Americans received from the President, but a rough list Mr. Roosevelt had given to General Marshall as a guide for the discussions included in connection with the abandonment of Sledgehammer the item:

> Take all planes now headed from U.S. to England & reroute them to (a) Middle East & Egypt (majority) (b) S.W. Pacific (minority).[12]

The official records of the London meetings do not mention this matter. The only documentary evidence of the basis on which General Marshall presented it to the British is a statement made by General A.C. Wedemeyer some two months later that General Marshall told the British that since they had abandoned the Bolero-Sledgehammer concept he did not feel justified in continuing to take risks in the Pacific.[13] Whatever he may have said at the meeting General Marshall did not himself interpret the statement in CCS 94 literally, and upon his return to Washington he explained to General Eisenhower:

> I regarded the list of withdrawals for the Pacific as one which gave us liberty of action though not necessarily to be carried out in full, and no dates were mentioned.... I am quite certain that an additional heavy bomber group must go into the Pacific in August. Additional withdrawals will depend on the development of the situation there.[14]

Whether General Marshall discussed his interpretation of the statement with Admiral King at the time is not clear. In any case

Admiral King interpreted the provision at its face value. The chiefs had hardly returned to Washington when he sent a memorandum to General Marshall referring to it. On the last day of July CinCPac had sent a despatch to Washington, pointing out that there was no reserve of bombers in Hawaii that he considered adequate to follow up Task One in the South Pacific and furnish defenses for the newly occupied areas, or to support the Hawaiian area while the main part of the fleet was deployed to the south. Admiral King requested that, "in the light of recent decisions reached in London to reenforce with air the Pacific Ocean Areas," General Marshall and his staff review their decision of a few days previous that "Army commitments in other areas will not permit further air reenforcements for the South Pacific."[15]

It was the intention in the War Department to inform Admiral King that there would be no change in regard to ground reenforcements for the South Pacific Area, and that, although the details of the London agreement were under consideration, there were no air units presently available for the Pacific Ocean Areas and no date could be predicted when there might be.[16] But before the War Department replied to the memorandum the operations in the South Pacific had begun and no answer was sent to Admiral King.

On 7 August elements of the First Marine Division landed in the Solomons, taking the islands of Tulagi, Gavutu, and Tanambogo, and making favorable progress with virtually no opposition toward their primary objectives on the larger island of Guadalcanal. On the night of 8-9 August the forces in the Solomons suffered a heavy blow in a surprise attack on naval forces patrolling south of Savo Island. The loss of four cruisers in this disastrous encounter and the planned withdrawal of the U.S. naval transport and carrier forces from the area even before all supplies had been unloaded left the Marines on Guadalcanal without naval support, as Japanese resistance on the island stiffened and the long difficult campaign began.

Meanwhile on the western flank of the South Pacific Area the Japanese were becoming increasingly active. Intelligence reports reaching Washington in July and August had indicated that the Japanese were not only hastening to build up an airfield on Guadalcanal and at other points in the Solomons but also massing strength on the northeast coast of New Guinea. Japanese troops had landed at Buna and Gona in July and rapidly spread into the interior of the island, up to Kokoda, where they started the long, hard climb across the Owen Stanley Mountains toward Port Moresby, the most important base under General MacArthur's control in the Southwest Pacific Area.

In order to support the Solomons operation, it was essential that every effort be made in the Southwest Pacific Area to hold the Japanese there and to divert as much Japanese strength as possible to that area. In view of General MacArthur's lack of enthusiasm for the directive, the Navy doubted that he appreciated the fact that it was essential that he do everything possible to maintain and improve his position in New Guinea and to support the operations in the South Pacific. Reports of the activities of General MacArthur's forces gave little indication of his plans for holding the Japanese in check in New Guinea until such time as Task Two, which he was scheduled to command, could be undertaken and the Japanese bases at Lae and Salamaua could be attacked in force. Consequently at the end of July Admiral King sent a memorandum to General Marshall, expressing his dissatisfaction with the use of air power and limited ground forces north of the Owen Stanley Mountains in New Guinea. These appeared to be the only measures being employed to restrain the Japanese there. Admiral King did not believe that these measures would suffice to prevent the Japanese from penetrating to Port Moresby, and he suggested that General Marshall inquire by despatch into General MacArthur's views of the situation and his plans for holding the Japanese in New Guinea.[17]

General MacArthur sent a prompt reply to General Marshall's query summarizing the information available to him about Japanese forces at various points in the Southwest Pacific Area and optimistically outlining his plans preventing further Japanese advances in New Guinea. He proposed to move forces from Australia to New Guinea if transports could be made available. He would land troops at Port Moresby and at Milne Bay and work along the north coast and through the Owen Stanley Mountains to secure control of the Wau-Kokoda line and the region bordering on the Japanese base at Buna. He anticipated that by the time that was accomplished the amphibious troops of the First Marine Division, having been relieved from Guadalcanal, would be available for his use in a five step operation with the ultimate objective the capture of Rabaul. His operations under Tasks Two and Three, he made clear, would require carrier task forces and the land-based bombers of the South Pacific Area. But it was apparently his assumption that he could carry out a rapid step-by-step advance direct to Rabaul.[18]

Unfortunately for the execution of General MacArthur's plans, the enemy defenders proved more stubborn than had been anticipated, and while the Marines were held pinned down on Guadalcanal, General MacArthur's forces made slow progress in New Guinea. It was many months before it became possible to proceed with Tasks Two and Three. While the Solomons campaign continued, the Navy was not prepared to provide the naval forces General MacArthur requested and certainly had none of the desired task forces which could be spared from the Pacific Ocean Areas to be sent to the Southwest Pacific, despite the strategic importance of maintaining pressure on the Japanese in the SWPA.

Just as the Solomons operation was getting under way, a despatch was received from Admiral Ghormley, Commander, South Pacific Force, containing the estimate of the Commanding General, Army Forces, South Pacific, as requested in the operational directive, of additional ground and air forces required "in connection with Guadalcanal-Tulagi operation, relief of marine and naval forces, [and] responsibilities in relation to succeeding phases two and three subsequent thereto."[19]

In order adequately to fulfill obligations in the South Pacific Area, the Commanding General recommended the following increases:

a. GROUND
   2 Infantry Divisions plus 2 Infantry Regiments
   3 Regiments C.A. (A.A.)
   2 Battalions C.A. (A.A.) auto weapons
   1 Regiment C.A. (H.D.) plus 1 Bn. (Less 1 Btry)
   2 Bns F.A. (105 MM How.)
b. AIR
   6 Fighter squadrons (3 equipped with P-38)
   2 Bomb squadrons, heavy (To be permanently based at Fantan and Poppy for use as needed anywhere in this area)
   1 Bomb squadron, medium
   3 Bomb squadrons, dive

After studying the recommendations of General Harmon and Admiral Ghormley, as well as the plans of General MacArthur, Admiral King reported to General Marshall that the requests for air reenforcements were approximately what he himself estimated. The figures for ground forces seemed excessive at first glance. But Admiral King pointed out, they were intended to provide both for completing Task One and for continuing on to Task Two as planned by General MacArthur, and they were the studied conclusions of the commanders in the field. Admiral King accepted the recommendations of Admiral Ghormley and General Harmon, and he recognized only one limitation on the Army's ability to fill the requests:

> It is realized that the shipping situation in the Pacific precludes the immediate dispatch of all forces requested, yet it would appear prudent to commence assembly and planning for first, the Air reinforcements and second, Ground reinforcements in strengths required to execute plans for the immediate future.[20]

But it was months before the estimated requirements of the local commanders were finally met.

On 13 August Admiral King reminded General Marshall that he had not yet had an answer to his requests for more air reenforcements made immediately after their return from London. The Commander in Chief, Pacific Fleet, was finding it necessary to move all possible air strengths from Hawaii to the South Pacific. Consequently, Admiral King urged that the Army take immediate action to send reenforcements to the Pacific. It was still another week before General Marshall answered. He reported that forty-four fighter planes were soon to leave for the South Pacific. No bombers were scheduled directly for the South Pacific Area, but twenty-nine B-17's, fifty-two B-25's, and nine B-26's were en route as replacements to Australia. General Harmon had been authorized to divert for his own use any of the bombers passing through his area that he felt desirable. For the other end of the line, the Army intended to send one heavy bombardment group from those scheduled for Bolero to Hawaii about 10 September.[21]

These arrangements did not fill the requirements estimated by the local commanders. On the same day Admiral King tried again to secure for the South Pacific the air reenforcements and the troops for which shipping had been set aside in the London agreement. Again he stressed the need of garrison troops to relieve the Marines in the Solomons and to consolidate forces in preparation for Task Two.[22] This time General Marshall decided that, if shipping could be provided, more ground troops could be sent to the South Pacific. After consulting the Services of Supply and the Operations Division he reported that, if the Navy could provide shipping for approximately 13,000 men, the 43rd Division, about 20,000 troops, could be moved from the West Coast to the South Pacific Area in September and early October. Tentatively, the Navy agreed to supply shipping.[23]

THE THEATER COMMANDERS' VIEW OF THE SITUATION, AUGUST 1942

After the first tense days of action in the Solomons there had been a breathing spell of about two weeks, during which the Marines on Guadalcanal organized their defenses on the perimeter of Henderson Field, which had been taken in the first days of the campaign.[24] The U.S. aircraft carriers of the South Pacific Force were being operated well to the southward for concealment, and, almost nightly, groups of enemy cruisers and destroyers bombarded the island with little opposition. In the Rabaul area the Japanese were building up forces, preparing to attempt to land reenforcements on Guadalcanal.

Although subsequent developments could not be predicted, the lack of opposition to the Guadalcanal landings encouraged General Marshall to feel that completion of the capture of Guadalcanal would not be too long deleyed. Moreover General MacArthur's despatch of 2 August indicated that he considered early initiation of that part of Task Two which included seizure of Lae and Salamaua a possibility. Consequently General Marshall proposed to Admiral King that the theater commanders be asked for their views as to when Task Two might be mounted in order that when it became necessary the Joint Chiefs of Staff could make a decision as to what action should follow completion of Task One. Upon the admiral's approval the chiefs requested Admiral Nimitz, General MacArthur, and Admiral Ghormley for their opinions as to (1) the forces to be used for mounting a limited Task Two at an early date, (2) the estimated target date upon which it could be launched, and (3) the time passage of command of the joint forces, as provided for in the 2 July directive, should be executed. In addition, Admiral Ghormley was asked for an estimate of the time required to consolidate the positions occupied under Task One and for his plans for relieving the Marines; General MacArthur was asked what progress he anticipated making in his area before the forces he would require for Task Two could be released from the South Pacific.[25]

Admiral Ghormley reported two days later that no further advance could be made until the positions then held were firmly established and the South Pacific was reenforced with air and ground troops. It was even doubtful whether the positions already taken could be held. His cautious statements were borneced out by the events that followed, both in his area and in the Southwest Pacific.[26]

By 21 August Japanese destroyer transports had landed some 900 men on Guadalcanal. On that day this force engaged the U.S. Marines on the island, and after approximately sixteen hours of stubborn, hard fighting, the Japanese troops were virtually eliminated. But, in the meantime, a Japanese naval force had started from Rabaul and headed for Guadalcanal, escorting transports which carried approximately 1,500 more Japanese troops. Their progress was observed, and a naval force from the South Pacific was sent to meet them. In the battle that ensued on 24-25 August, the so-called Battle of the Eastern Solomons, the Japanese lost a carrier, an old destroyer, and a transport and caused considerable damage to the U.S. carrier *Enterprise*. Temporarily the enemy abandoned the attempt to land forces on Guadalcanal.

Meanwhile, in New Guinea, the Japanese had been strengthening their forces on the Kokoda trail south of Buna and pushing on across the formidable Owen Stanley Mountains. On 25 August a Japanese force was landed on the north shore of Milne Bay, and the Japanese instituted a naval patrol there which successfully cut off supply to the Australian garrison on the other side of the bay. The enemy held on to their position until 5 September, when they were finally driven out. Allied shipping into Milne Bay was resumed on 6 September. With the Japanese holding the advantage in New Guinea, General MacArthur's project for gaining control of the northeast coast was seriously retarded.

The request of the Joint Chiefs for comments on the undertaking of Task Two found General MacArthur considerably less optimistic as to the capabilities of his own forces than when he had presented his plans on 2 August. Faced with an enemy of growing strength in the Southwest Pacific Area, with no immediate prospect of getting additional forces from the South Pacific, and with no indication that more help was coming from the United States, the general painted a dim picture of the whole Pacific Theater. In the last two months, he said, there had been a drastic change in the Pacific situation.

> Warned by his defeats in the Solomons the enemy has definitely abandoned any present intent of striking in Siberia, has slackened his efforts in China, is thinning his forces in the Pacified [sic] occupied zones and is moving the center of gravity of his forces in this general direction. His main battle front is now definitely in South and South West Pacific areas. His potential - air, sea and land - is increasing and his relative strength is rapidly growing greater than the allied potential in these areas.... It is no longer a question here of preparing a projected offensive.

General MacArthur begged that the President and the Joint Chiefs of Staff review the situation.

> Unless additional Naval forces, either American or British, are concentrated in the Pacific and unless steps are taken to match the heavy air and ground forces the enemy is assembling to launch, I predict the development within a reasonable period of time of a situation similar to those which produced the disasters that have successively overwhelmed our forces in the Pacific since the beginning of the war.[27]

General MacArthur's views were closely mirrored in messages Prime Minister Curtin of Australia sent at approximately the same time to Prime Minister Churchill and President Roosevelt, also expressing alarm and urging more naval and air support and a concerted effort to drive the enemy from the area.[28]

General Marshall sent a sympathetic reply to General MacArthur, telling him that the Pacific was not being forgotten and recommending that he cooperate closely with Admirals Nimitz and Ghormley to achieve the most effective use of naval and air forces already at hand. Then General Marshall turned over the MacArthur report to the Joint Chiefs of Staff.[29]

Admiral Ghormley sent a similar report from the South Pacific to Admiral King at about the same time. "My considered opinion," he said, "is that at this time the retention of this area is more vital to the prosecution of the war in the Pacific than any other commitment." It was apparent that the Japanese were contemplating an all-out offensive against Guadalcanal, and Admiral Ghormley predicted that he could not hold the area without strong naval and air forces.[30]

In view of the increased Japanese activity in the South Pacific, the Joint Chiefs agreed, at their meeting of 1 September, to turn over both of these messages to the Joint Staff Planners, directing them to review the situation in the Pacific and recommend action.[31]

A subcommittee of the JPS went to work on the messages but found themselves unable to reach agreement. On 8 September Major R.W. Davis reported to Lieutenant Colonel R.L. Vittrup, JPS Secretary, the recommendations of the Army members of the subcommittee. These, it was stated, had the informal concurrence of two of the members of the JPS, Major General A.C. Wedemeyer and Colonel O.A. Anderson. The Army members concluded that the pessimistic views of the local commanders were somewhat exaggerated, and that, if full advantage were taken of the mobility of air forces, those already available in the theater

> should be sufficient to ensure consolidation of present positions. The movement of additional forces...to the South and Southwest Pacific Areas at this time, would constitute further diversions from the theater in which our principal effort has been directed by the President. Extensions of present positions which cannot be accomplished by those forces already available in, or committed to, the subject areas, must await the implementation of plans for operations in the theater of our principal effort.

Consequently, the Army members recommended that the requests for additional air forces be disapproved; that planned reenforcements of aircraft and personnel be expedited; that no additional ground forces be provided; and that the JCS clarify, for the benefit of the local commanders, the strategic policy for the Pacific.[32]

About a week later, Admiral Cooke submitted a separate report as Navy member of the JPS. He disagreed with the Army thesis that everything must be subordinated to preparations for operations in the European Theater. In his opinion

> conduct of such military and naval operations and the provision of such supporting measures as are necessary to defeat Germany... should be undertaken only after the necessary steps have been taken to assure the safety of the Western Hemisphere, and the lines of communications from the United States to Hawaii, to Australia and New Zealand, and to Alaska.

Admiral Cooke pointed out that, while arrangements had been made to send the ground reenforcements which the local commanders had requested to the South Pacific by the middle of October,[33] no such provision had been made in regard to air reenforcements. He reiterated the view that adequate fighter forces must be provided for defense of the South Pacific islands. Bombers, he agreed, were mobile, but the mobility of fighters from island bases was limited. He proposed a despatch to be sent in answer to General MacArthur's plea, reassuring him that the Pacific was not forgotten and that some additional forces were to be sent there, and recommending close cooperation and coordination with Admiral Ghormley.[34]

The discussion of the two papers in the JPS meeting of 16 September brought out some interesting points in the planners' views of the agreed strategy. The members of the committee agreed that the security of Australia, the line of communications thereto, and the Western Hemisphere was the first order of priority for the United States. But they were not in agreement as to the means of accomplishing these objectives. General Wedemeyer made it clear that he was not entirely in sympathy with the planned operation in the European Theater, which he characterized as in effect providing for a strategic defensive in that area. He thought that the currently planned operations should be investigated to determine whether their ultimate requirements could be filled, while still providing effectively for the security of Australia, the line of communications, and the Western Hemisphere. He felt that the British were following a basic strategy designed to maintain the integrity of the British Empire, not to provide for the defeat of the enemy. General Wedemeyer expressed his opinion that, if necessary, forces would have to be diverted from other projects in order to save the situation in the Pacific and the resultant situation in the Western Hemisphere.

Colonel Anderson, representing the Air Forces, pointed out

that, while he agreed with the basic Pacific strategy, he was unwilling to accept the Navy's views on the use of air power.

He stated that he believed that General Arnold was in favor of supporting the Solomons and any other active operation with land based aircraft to the operating capacity of available bases, and local logistical support, but that he is strongly opposed to immobilizing the striking power of the air arm by fixed assignment to outlying island bases of major components of the air arm.

When Captain C.R. Brown, USN, pointed out that there was little depth to the line of communications in the Pacific, and that shifting planes to any great extent along it would certainly leave the line denuded, Colonel Anderson insisted that it was not militarily sound to strengthen all the individual points. Rear Admiral R.L. Conolly, on the other hand, stressed the Navy view that, even at the expense of Bolero, the bases supporting the Solomons area must be filled to the saturation point with aircraft in order to achieve success. Colonel Anderson indicated that the Air Forces would not countenance cutting down on Bolero, which would mean reducing air operations from the United Kingdom. It was the Air Forces view, he said, that the air offensive was actually complementary to Torch in that it, too, was opposing the Germans.

Since it was apparent that no agreement was to be reached at that meeting the Joint Staff Planners decided that the subcommittee should reconsider the situation in the South and Southwest Pacific and make recommendations as to how to rectify the existing situation and preclude the recurrence of a similar one. Their study was to be made "in the light of more objective planning to secure Australia, the line of communications thereto, and the Western Hemisphere," and to contain charts and tables indicating the facilities and forces in the area.[35]

This report was never produced, for at the next JPS meeting (23 September) the committee agreed to recommend cancellation of the study in view of provisions which had been made for sending some reenforcements to the area. The 43rd Division had been ordered to the Pacific, to arrive in October and November.[36] Some additional air forces had been allotted to the area by the War Department,[37] and General Arnold was in the Pacific, checking on the defense situation. Consequently, the JPS recommended to the JCS that the paper be removed from the agenda. Admiral King, however, objected to such action since he felt that the question of reenforcements for the Pacific was still of great importance. The directive for the report remained on the agenda, although inactive, until 1 December 1942. In the meantime the question of air forces for the South Pacific received considerable consideration.[38]

ADDITIONAL AIRCRAFT FOR THE PACIFIC, SEPTEMBER-OCTOBER 1942

In the third week of August, as the Japanese were preparing for their first strong counterblow on Guadalcanal and naval forces were squaring off for the Battle of the Eastern Solomons, the Combined Chiefs of Staff reached agreement on CCS 91, which included figures on the deployment of ground, naval, and air forces among the various theaters of war as of 1 April 1943.[39] With shipping in extremely short supply and production far behind demands there still remained a basic question of the priority in which forces scheduled for arrival by 1 April should be delivered to the widely scattered areas. And there remained unsettled the question of disposal of the air groups which General Marshall had insisted in London should be removed from commitments to Bolero and made subject to U.S. control.

The annexes to CCS 91 as finally accepted showed the fifteen air groups still in the United Kingdom, with a note that, when final decision was made as to where they were to be deployed in the Pacific, a separate report would be submitted. Mention has already been made of Admiral King's vain attempt to secure some of the air units for the Pacific soon after his return from London, as well as of the recurrent demands from the theater commanders for air reenforcements. It was clear in the middle of August that the Army and Navy held different views as to how many aircraft were needed in the Pacific and how they should be distributed in order best to provide defense for the lines of communication to the Southwest Pacific and support for the Marines on Guadalcanal. A study of the distribution of aircraft in the Pacific Theater was clearly called for. Consequently on 20 August the JPS directed the Joint U.S. Strategic Committee to incorporate the anticipated transfer of fifteen air groups into a preliminary study they had prepared, and to produce a report on the "Detailed deployment of aircraft in the Pacific Theater."[40]

The JUSSC succeeded in about a week in drafting charts which indicated: (1) the recommended deployment of the fifteen air groups among the four areas of the Pacific and (2) a detailed breakdown by Pacific areas and types of planes of all aircraft allocated to the Pacific in CCS 91 and in CCS 94. However, although they could agree on the disposition of the planes once they were sent to the Pacific, the Army and Navy members of the JUSSC disagreed on when they should go.[41]

Commitments in CCS 91 of planes for the United Kingdom, Torch, and the Middle East, including the fifteen groups that were to be diverted elsewhere, totalled sixty-nine groups. It was the view of the Army members of the committee that Torch, the Middle East, and the United Kingdom should be provided with planes first, a total of fifty-four groups; only after the commitments that had been made to those regions were delivered should the fifteen groups (less one that had already been diverted to Hawaii) be sent. The Navy members, on the other hand, gave first priority to Torch and to the Middle East (a total of twenty groups). But they believed that the fifteen groups to be removed from Bolero should be sent to the South and the Southwest Pacific, in that order, before the remaining groups were sent to the United Kingdom. This was approximately the same order of priority the Combined Chiefs of Staff had approved for shipping: (1) Torch, Middle East, Pacific Ocean, Russia via southern route; (2) U.S. Army Air Forces to the United Kingdom and China; (3) Relief of Iceland; (4) Bolero; (5) India and China.[42] The Navy's proposed order of procedure at the existing rate of aircraft production would mean a delay of from one to three months in the arrival of air units in the United Kingdom.

The naval planners were confronted with a critical situation in the Solomons, for the final outcome of the Marines' struggle on Guadalcanal was by no means certain. Progress had been slowed down all through August by a lack of air support. Although Henderson Field had been secured early in the campaign it was not immediately usable, and when some fighters and bombers were finally put in there operations were still handicapped by limited supplies of gasoline and equipment. The naval planners believed that with strong air support in the area final victory on Guadalcanal could be more speedily achieved and they could be assured of hanging on to the territory thus taken from the enemy. They viewed the current situation as a very real crisis and one in which planes could be more immediately utilized than if they were allocated to potential operations in the European Theater.

Army planners, on the other hand, thought that the fifteen air groups in question would be of more real value in the United Kingdom than in the South Pacific. Their information was that General Harmon already had more medium bomber groups there than facilities for operating them effectively. Army G-2 estimated that as of 1 April 1943 the Japanese would have only about 4,000 combat planes, some of which would be in Japan, Manchuria, and other areas where they were not in contact with United Nations forces, whereas CCS 91 provided for approximately 5,000 U.S. land and carrier-based aircraft in the Pacific by the same date. In pointing to this apparent advantage the Army planners ignored the question of the inferior quality of many of the U.S. planes already in the Pacific, the fact that only a fraction of the 5,000 planes had as yet been delivered, and the difficulties of attempting so to dispose the planes as to anticipate enemy attacks and maintain a strategic position throughout the Pacific as well as to support the operations in the Solomons. They argued broadly that "we should be clever enough to accomplish a defensive mission with an over-all superiority of 1,000 planes."[43]

The differing views of the Army and Navy members of the JUSSC were supported by their respective colleagues among the JPS. So again, in early September, the Joint Chiefs of Staff were presented with a split report concerning the deployment of air forces.[44]

Two days before the indecisive report from the Joint Staff Planners was forwarded to the Joint Chiefs of Staff, Admiral King again strongly outlined to General Marshall the gravity of the situation in the Tulagi-Guadalcanal area and the strategic necessity of preventing the enemy from retaking it and building it up for operations against the line of communications to Australia. Presenting again a summary of the estimates of requisite forces which had been received from Admiral Ghormley and General Harmon a month before,

Admiral King once more expressed his opinion, and the "opinion of all the responsible Field Commanders both Army and Navy," that reenforcements of Army aircraft for the area were still entirely inadequate. He had, he said, frequently sacrificed the Pacific in order to send more to the Eastern Atlantic. He did not think that the diversion of U.S. equipment to U.S. needs could "be justifiably challenged because of so-called commitments." He considered that it was "imperative that sufficient Army aircraft be moved to the South Pacific Area immediately to the extent found necessary, regardless of interference with 'commitments' for the Eastern Atlantic."[45]

General Arnold and his staff drafted a firm reply for General Marshall to send to Admiral King, indicating clearly that they were in agreement with the views of their Army colleagues on the JPS. Again they insisted that the air reenforcements Admiral King proposed, particularly fighter reenforcements, could not be supplied immediately to the South Pacific unless they were taken away from commitments approved by the Combined Chiefs of Staff. As of 2 September, the memorandum stated, there were available under Admiral Nimitz's control the following aircraft:[46]

	On Hand	En Route or Being Prepared	Total
Heavy Bombers	75	44	119
Medium Bombers	24	11	35
Light Bombers	7	0	7
Fighters	270	202	472

It was the opinion of General Arnold that short-range aircraft could not reach the area in time to assist in current operations, and full utilization of the aircraft already available to the Guadalcanal Area should make it possible for some time to come to meet the requirements for operations of the intensity then being experienced. Admiral Ghormley, realizing the superiority of most Japanese fighter planes to the U.S. types assigned to his area, had requested more P-38's. But General Arnold considered that P-40's, despite their inferior altitude and maneuverability, were adequate for the Pacific and that all available P-38's should be reserved for Torch. Withdrawal of some from that operation would, he said, "impose a drastic change, if not the abandonment of Torch. This should be considered by the U.S. Chiefs of Staff and the President...before going to the Combined Chiefs of Staff."[47]

At the JCS meeting which followed this exchange the chiefs had at hand for discussion the split report from the Joint Staff Planners that had developed from their study of the distribution of the fifteen air groups earmarked in CCS 94 for the Pacific. The discussion that developed at the JCS meeting brought to light the differing interpretations the various members had as to just what had been agreed to in London.

Admiral Willson, in Admiral King's absence from the meeting,[48] supported the recommendations of the Navy planners for priority of delivery of the air groups. He insisted that Admiral King had understood that the CCS had agreed in London that the fifteen groups from Bolero were to be committed definitely to operations in the Pacific. It was at this point that General Marshall explained that at the time the stipulation "had been recorded only as an agreement for the transfer of planes from one jurisdiction to another." Although he was not entirely convinced that the Middle East should be given such a high priority as the Joint Staff Planners recommended, General Marshall felt that "Once commitments to Torch and possibly the Middle East had been fulfilled, [priority of allocations] should be made in accordance with strategic necessity as the planes became available." As for what that priority would be, General Marshall made it clear that he sided with the Army planners. He believed that the "losses to the Germans in planes and production, plus the effect of diverting large numbers of German planes from the eastern front, make Europe the area in which the operation of U.S. planes gives the greatest return for the investment of forces."[49]

Admiral Cooke went so far at this meeting as to suggest that additional aircraft, particularly fighters, were so urgently needed in the Solomons that it might even be necessary to cut into commitments to Torch and the Middle East to provide them. But the Army and Air Forces members considered the needs of the South Pacific far less drastic than that. General Arnold, in an attempt to reenforce his own expressed views as to the relative importance of the European Theater, before the next JCS meeting circulated a paper in which he quoted Generals Eisenhower, Spaatz, and Patton on the importance of air offensives from the United Kingdom. Preparations for Torch were under way, and General Eisenhower was quoted as saying, "Any sign of failure at this stage and a delay of reinforcements to arrive might be seized upon by the Axis as a reason for coming into Spain and if Spain should then enter the war, the results would be most serious." General Arnold recommended that Torch should be recognized as the beginning of the offensive against Germany and that it should be accepted as a "basic principle" that operations both in the Middle East and from the United Kingdom were complementary to Torch. In particular was this true of air operations against the continent, since they would force the Germans to divert aircraft that could otherwise be used against the North African forces. Consequently General Arnold recommended "that no diversion of air forces be made to other areas except those necessary to secure our essential positions elsewhere, until the needs for Torch, the Middle East and the United Kingdom are met."[50] What he considered the "essential positions" to be, General Arnold did not explain.

In the meantime Admiral King had not allowed his correspondence with General Arnold to end with the latter's insistence that Admiral King's requests for aircraft for the South Pacific could not be filled "without reduction from commitments approved by the Combined Chiefs of Staff." Admiral King immediately pointed out to General Arnold that in CCS 94 the CCS had specifically agreed that fifteen air groups would be withdrawn from Bolero "for the purposes of furthering offensive operations in the Pacific."[51]

In reply, General Arnold repeated the strategic concept that had been accepted by the Combined Chiefs of Staff in CCS 91:

> To conduct the strategic offensive with maximum forces in the Atlantic-Western European Theater at the earliest practicable date, and to maintain the strategic defensive in other theaters, with appropriate forces.

In furtherance of this concept, he pointed out, the President had directed execution of Torch, and the President, the Prime Minister, and the Combined Chiefs of Staff had given it the highest priority. In General Arnold's opinion, the air offensive against the Continent was an absolute essential to the success of Torch, because it would involve German planes which could otherwise be sent to North Africa. He insisted that any diversion of aircraft from Torch, or from the supporting air operations from the United Kingdom, was in contradiction of the agreed strategic concept, would seriously jeopardize the success of the North Africa operation, and should be given most careful consideration by the Combined Chiefs of Staff.[52]

Admiral King presented these two memoranda to the Joint Chiefs of Staff for discussion, together with a plea he had received from Admiral Nimitz that sufficient troops and land-based aircraft be made available to the Commander in Chief, Southwest Pacific Area, to furnish adequate support and obviate the need of risking aircraft in the operations in New Guinea under Task Two.[53]

At the JCS meeting on 15 September Admiral King was present to support his own position, and he and General Arnold argued the matter at some length. Admiral King was willing to give first priority to Torch and to the Middle East, but he was opposed to placing the Pacific Theater last on the order of priority. The Middle East was fairly well stabilized, and Torch had not yet been launched. It was essential, he felt, that air forces in the Pacific be strengthened to the limit of operational facilities in the area. General Arnold admitted that he was not sure just how many planes were needed in the South and the Southwest Pacific. He thought that there were already as many planes as the facilities could accommodate but that they were not distributed as effectively as possible. Admiral Leahy temporarily halted the argument by suggesting that, inasmuch as the planes in question were not yet actually available and General Arnold was about to make a visit to the Pacific, the subject be deferred until his return.[54]

General Arnold was absent during the period of the last two September meetings of the Joint Chiefs of Staff. At the first meeting after his return Admiral Leahy again brought up for discussion the question of the deployment of air forces in the Pacific Theater. Again General Arnold and Admiral King disagreed.

From his investigations of airfields in the South Pacific, General Arnold had confirmed his previous opinion that there was already in the area the maximum number of planes that could be operated from the available fields. The only advance operating bases, Guadalcanal and Espiritu Santo, and their supporting bases at Efate and New Caledonia, could accommodate no more than a fixed number of planes, and General Arnold believed that with the planes en route and in reserve the maximum had been reached. He recommended that the location of bases and the distribution of planes to those bases should be restudied in order to get the most effective use of the available aircraft.

Admiral King pointed out that more airfields were in the process of construction and insisted that the number of planes in the Pacific Theater should at all times be kept at the saturation point. In view of anticipated Japanese counterattacks the South Pacific needed at once all the planes that could be maintained there. Again he called attention to the commitment in CCS 94 of fifteen air groups "for furthering offensive operations in the Pacific." Admiral Leahy supported him in the view that if planes were needed in the South Pacific they should be sent there rather than to the United Kingdom where the need was not so immediately urgent.

Again General Marshall pointed out that "the main purpose of inserting into C.C.S. 94 the statement that fifteen groups would be withdrawn from the United Kingdom due to cessation of Bolero was to completely eliminate combined discussions regarding the use of planes." And again General Arnold insisted that the air offensive from the United Kingdom was intended to support Torch, and that reserves must be built up in England "to back up Torch." The front line bases of the South Pacific, he said, could be reenforced from bases in the rear, which in turn could be replenished from Hawaii. There were three squadrons in Hawaii that, in an emergency, could be moved to the South Pacific Area within forty-eight hours. However, Rear Admiral J.S. McCain, who had recently returned from duty as Commander, Aircraft, South Pacific Force, and was present at the JCS meeting, volunteered the information that in practice the system advocated by General Arnold was unsatisfactory inasmuch as the replacements arrived ahead of their maintenance crews and spare parts and so could not be serviced at the advanced bases.

It was clear that no decision could be reached through further discussion by the Joint Chiefs of Staff on the basis of the information at hand. So Admiral Leahy recommended referring the problem to the Joint Staff Planners. The Joint Chiefs directed the planners to consult with General Arnold and Admiral McCain and study the distribution of aircraft in the South Pacific Area and the number that would be required to reach the saturation point at all facilities, leaving the larger question of planes for the whole Pacific area for later consideration.[55]

After obtaining the opinions of General Arnold and Admiral McCain as to the capacities of the various islands of the South Pacific, the subcommittee presented a partial report which was informally accepted by the Joint Chiefs of Staff for immediate implementation.[56] This was followed about a week later by a final report, incorporating the recommended air strengths listed earlier as well as the figures General Arnold and Admiral McCain had given the committee. The figures the JCS accepted were lower than the recommendations of either man. They provided for increases of thirty heavy bombers, thirty-two medium bombers, thirty-four fighters, fourteen Navy patrol bombers, three Navy scout bombers, twenty-four Navy scout observation planes, and twelve Navy torpedo bombers. The chiefs agreed that, although the planes were approved as they were listed, distributed among specific island bases, the agreement was to be understood actually to be on the total number of planes for the South Pacific Area. Final decision as to where they should be based within the area was a responsibility of the area commander.[57] In accordance with this principle a directive was sent to CinCPac, informing him that air organizations assigned to his areas were subject to deployment and redistribution within the area at his discretion, without prior authority of the War or Navy Department.[58]

Although this solution did not provide as many aircraft for the South Pacific as the theater commanders and the Navy planners in Washington had estimated necessary, it did represent an increase over previous commitments. It did not, however, answer the question that had been the original source of controversy, i.e., the distribution of the fifteen air groups set aside from Bolero commitments. But this was no longer so important. By this time informal commitments had taken care of three of these groups. The other twelve still were not actually available. The October crisis in the Solomons had just passed, and the JCS had reached a compromise agreement on additional aircraft for the South Pacific.[59]

At the preceding JCS meeting the question of policy in regard to the deployment of air forces had come up in the course of discussion of the provision of five hundred additional aircraft by 1 April 1944 for the antisubmarine campaign in the Atlantic. The JCS had agreed at that time that it was not feasible to plan deployments of forces that far in the future. They had accepted General Marshall's recommendation "that except for the air forces already committed to theaters in accordance with agreed combined or joint operations, all U.S. air resources should be considered as a strategic reserve."[60] Now the chiefs agreed that this policy should be applied to the twelve Bolero groups which had not yet been allocated and they should be considered part of the strategic reserve.[61] Subsequently the JPS assigned to the JUSSC responsibility for maintaining a continuing study of the aircraft requirements of the several theaters of U.S. strategic responsibility and the commitments of U.S. operated aircraft to other theaters.[62]

THE SHIPPING PROBLEM

The third week of September found the issue on Guadalcanal still unsettled. The previous week the enemy had launched a fierce attack with naval and aerial support, which, when finally halted, had cost the Marines who participated casualties of twenty per cent. Several actions involving smaller numbers of troops had occurred in the preceding weeks, as the Marines encountered portions of the forces the Japanese had been steadily building up on the island. Although some U.S. reenforcements were being landed, ultimate success for the Marines on Guadalcanal was by no means assured.

In New Guinea at this time General MacArthur was preparing plans for a limited counteroffensive to regain the crest of the Owen Stanley Mountains from the Japanese who had made considerable progress on the long, hard Kokoda trail toward Port Moresby. General MacArthur's offensive to clear the enemy from all of Papua got under way on 26 September, when the Australian 7th Division began the advance back north across the Kokoda trail.

With the Japanese resisting stubbornly on Guadalcanal and well entrenched on New Guinea, there seemed little immediate prospect of moving on to Tasks Two and Three of the original joint directive for operations in the Solomons-New Britain-New Guinea area. Consequently on 21 September Admiral King suggested to the Joint Chiefs of Staff that the directive be reviewed in order to determine what changes should be made in regard to the succeeding tasks.[63] The matter was turned over by the Joint Staff Planners to a subcommittee for a report.

The difficulties of trying to achieve final victory on Guadalcanal and to maintain pressure on the enemy in the South Pacific with only limited forces of men and equipment continued to loom large. Hampered by the shortage of materiel, particularly of aircraft, by the shortage of shipping for transport both to the South Pacific and within the theater, and by the conflicting evaluations of the urgencies of the various theaters of war, the Joint Chiefs of Staff continued unable to satisfy the demands of the local commanders in the South Pacific.[64]

As October began intelligence reports indicated quite clearly that the enemy was massing land, air, and naval strength in the Rabaul area, with the intention of launching an all-out attack on either New Guinea or the Solomons, or both.[65] Consequently Admiral King again pressed the question of reenforcements for the South and Southwest Pacific. In a memorandum to Admiral Leahy and General Marshall he pointed out the necessity of concentrating support in the South and Southwest Pacific as soon as possible in order to counter the enemy's next move. Admiral King recommended that instructions be given to the JPS "to revise the current directive for operations in the NEW GUINEA-SOLOMONS ISLANDS AREA and to determine the *additional* forces and logistic support that must be moved to this area to meet this situation."[66] This matter, too, was referred to the Joint Staff Planners for study. Despite the urgency of Admiral King's recommendation other matters claimed the planners' attention. The Guadalcanal campaign dragged on, and it was several months before the planners produced any reply.[67] However, the needs of the Pacific were not being forgotten.

October was a critical month in the Solomons, with the Japanese continuing to land reenforcements on Guadalcanal, usually accompanying the land operations with naval bombardment of Henderson Field. On 11 October a U.S. naval force, sent from Espiritu Santo to try to halt this Japanese process, encountered a Japanese naval force and succeeded in executing the classic naval maneuver of "crossing the T." After losing a heavy cruiser and a destroyer the Japanese retired, having sunk one U.S. destroyer in the action.

This setback was only temporary, however, and there was every indication that the Japanese were preparing to make a large-scale attempt to drive the Americans from Guadalcanal and to regain full control of the Solomons area. On 18 October Admiral William F. Halsey, USN, relieved Admiral Ghormley as Commander, South Pacific Force, and found himself with a far from promising situation.[68]

Naval bombardment of Henderson Field went on continually in such force that virtually all the planes on the island were put out of commission. Despite some reenforcements from Espiritu Santo there were not enough planes available to maintain an adequate air force on Guadalcanal. Operation of those at hand was sharply curtailed by a critical shortage of fuel.[69] After General Harmon, Commanding General, South Pacific Force, urged that he be sent another infantry division, the War Department in mid-October alerted the 25th Division at Hawaii for transfer to the South Pacific. But its actual departure would not begin until mid-November.[70] Naval surface units were limited and inferior in number to the Japanese as a result of the repeated naval activity since the first landings of 7 August. As the forces squared off in the last week of October only one U.S. carrier, *Hornet*, was in the area, and *Enterprise* was speeding to the South Pacific after a rushed repair job at Pearl Harbor.[71]

On the night of 23-24 October the Japanese launched a full-scale offensive on Guadalcanal, supporting their attack with naval gunfire. Weakened by the incessant attack, the Marine line on the vital Lunga Ridge broke on the night of 25 October, and the Japanese advanced to the edge of Henderson Field, whence they were ultimately driven back by a desperate counterattack. At this critical point the two naval forces encountered each other off the Santa Cruz Islands. The battle that ensued was not decisive, and the U.S. forces finally retired to Espiritu Santo, having lost *Hornet* and the destroyer *Porter*. The Japanese withdrew to the north with some damage but no ships sunk. Ashore activity slackened, as the enemy withdrew inland after the vain attempt to take the airfield.

In New Guinea during October the 7th Division advanced slowly over the Kokoda trail. By 10 October it had made contact with the Japanese, who, having abandoned their project for attacking Port Moresby, were returning to their northern bases. During this period the bombers of the Southwest Pacific Area raided Japanese positions in northern New Guinea, Rabaul, and other objectives in that region. But their activity was restricted by Japanese air raids on Port Moresby, which led General MacArthur to keep most of his heavy bombers based in northern Australia, thereby considerably reducing the range of their effectiveness.

In Washington it appeared that little progress was being made toward driving the Japanese out of New Guinea and that little support was being given in that area to the hard-pressed forces in the Solomons. As it became apparent that the enemy was massing forces in the ports of Bougainville and the Shortland Islands Navy planners brought to General Marshall's attention the overwhelming naval strength of the Japanese in comparison to U.S. naval forces in the area. With the enemy poised for further action in the Solomons it seemed highly desirable that all possible support for the area be given by the forces in the Southwest Pacific. Consequently General Marshall pointed out the critical situation to General MacArthur and inquired into the possibility of increasing bomber activity from New Guinea against the Japanese naval forces by risking the basing of heavy bombers at Port Moresby, rather than in North Australia, and operating medium bombers from Milne Bay despite the resultant weakening of support for ground operations in New Guinea. General Marshall also inquired whether anything could be done to expedite the operations to seize Japanese airfields on the northeast coast of New Guinea.[72]

General MacArthur's reply was prompt and made it apparent that the implications of the messages from Washington had not been appreciated. He had, he said, made every effort to support the operations in the Solomons and had received thanks from the South Pacific Command for his activity. Most of his bombing had been done in the Rabaul area because the planes flying there could carry a full bomb load instead of having to take extra gas tanks as was required to reach the Solomons. Moreover, two heavy bomber squadrons were now being based at Port Moresby, and a new airstrip to accommodate B-17's and B-26's was being rushed to completion at Milne Bay. Although complicated by a shortage of shipping, operations to capture the north coast of New Guinea were "in full swing."

But again, General MacArthur painted a dark picture of the future in the South and Southwest Pacific Areas.

> If we are defeated in the Solomons, as we must be unless the Navy accepts successfully the challenge of the enemy surface fleet, the entire Southwest Pacific will be in gravest danger.... I urge that the entire resources of the United States be diverted temporarily to meet the critical situation; that shipping be made...available from any source; that one corps be dispatched immediately; that all available heavy bombers be ferried here at once; that urgent action be taken to increase the air strength at least to the full complement allotted for this area; that immediate action be taken to prepare bases for Naval operations on the East coast of Australia, that the British Eastern fleet be moved to the West Coast of Australia.[73]

It was obviously impossible to comply with all of General MacArthur's suggestions without postponing or cancelling the operation in Northwest Africa. The Joint Chiefs of Staff and the President were much concerned at this time about the situation in the Solomons, and they were giving serious consideration to what measures could be taken to reenforce the area. The War Department had, in fact, just ordered transfer of the 25th Division from Hawaii to the South Pacific. But they did not view the situation with sufficient alarm to warrant reversing the whole agreed world strategy. On at least the last of General MacArthur's recommendations, however, action was taken.

Ever since the beginning of the war and, indeed, in prewar planning, there had been a difference of opinion between the Americans and the British as to the proper role of the British Eastern Fleet. The British clung to the belief that the Eastern Fleet should remain in the Indian Ocean, in a defensive position, to forestall Japanese penetration through to the Middle East. The Americans, on the other hand, believed that it should be used to as great an extent as possible to support action in the Pacific Ocean. When plans for the initial landings in the Solomons were being drawn up, an attempt was made to obtain agreement to British naval support in the Pacific for the operation. The British, however, did not feel they could afford to risk their limited forces away from the Indian Ocean while the Japanese were still capable of going there, and the U.S. chiefs were informed by Admiral Sir Andrew Cunningham that the Eastern Fleet would be available for use only against Nicobar, Sumatra, and the Andamans, and not so far from the Indian Ocean as the Malay Barrier, where it could perhaps have served an important diversional purpose.[74] At the end of August Prime Minister Curtin of Australia had approached Prime Minister Churchill on the subject of transferring part of the Eastern Fleet to the Pacific Ocean in order to concentrate a superior naval force there and inflict a decisive defeat on the enemy. But Mr. Churchill replied that the time was not considered opportune for transferring British naval forces from the Indian Ocean.[75] Following General MacArthur's recommendation in October another attempt was made to secure some assistance from the British and to shift the Eastern Fleet from its purely defensive role. But again the British Admiralty announced that they could see no practicable help which could be given by the Eastern Fleet to the operations in the South and Southwest Pacific.[76]

By this time preparations for Torch were nearing completion. Since mid-September it had been settled that D Day was to be 8 November, and while the forces of the South Pacific were tensely awaiting a Japanese attack in late October and hoping for reenforcements from the United States, the convoy which was to sail from Norfolk direct to North Africa was preparing to depart from Hampton Roads. At the same time the British in Egypt were starting their drive to the west against the Germans at El Alamein. Torch had held first priority on U.S. resources, including shipping, consistently during the fall. Now that the action in North Africa was about to begin it was highly impractical to suppose that any of the forces assigned to it could be diverted to the South Pacific. Those in Washington who were informed of the serious situation in the Solomons viewed it with deep concern, but the assistance they could hope to rush to the area was extremely limited.

President Roosevelt had been pressing since Arcadia for U.S. forces to be brought into action in the European Theater in 1942. It was he who had made the final decision that Torch was to be executed, and he had insisted upon the concentration of all possible efforts on preparation for it. At the same time he had been keeping a close eye on developments in the Pacific, and he had been anxious that the Solomons and New Guinea be brought under control in order that pressure might be brought to bear on more vital Japanese positions beyond.[77] He was probably also aware of the difficulties involved in reaching agreement on reenforcements for the Pacific.[78]

As the situation in the Guadalcanal area in October became more and more critical Mr. Roosevelt sent an urgent message to the Chiefs of Staff:

FOR LEAHY, KING, MARSHALL AND ARNOLD only.

> My anxiety about the Southwest Pacific is to make sure that every possible weapon gets into that area to hold Guadalcanal, and that having held it in this crisis that munitions and planes and crews are on the way to take advantage of our success. We will soon find ourselves engaged on two active fronts and we must have adequate air support in both places even though it means delay in our other commitments, particularly to England. Our long range plans could be set back for months if we fail to throw our full strength in our immediate and impending conflicts. I wish therefore, you would canvass over the week-end every possible temporary diversion of munitions which you will require for our active fronts and let me know what they are. Please also review the number and use of all combat planes in the continental United States.[79]

It is not clear whether the President expected a complete report on the munitions headed for Torch as well as for the Pacific, nor whether he expected to be told what effect the operations in progress in the Pacific as well as the operation in prospect in North Africa would have on long range commitments to other areas. In any event the chiefs and their staffs set to work on this large weekend order as land action on Guadalcanal commenced. By Monday both the Army and the Navy had drafted memoranda in reply, in both cases almost entirely concerned with the South Pacific, where the outcome was at that very moment hanging in the balance.

General Marshall outlined for the President the ground and air forces in the South and Southwest Pacific Areas and the estimated forces of the Japanese opposing them. He pointed out that the United Nations appeared to have a superiority in both but that their effectiveness was dependent upon the ability to transport them to and maintain them in the combat areas where they were needed. Both for the South and Southwest Pacific, he said, additional logistical support, especially in shipping, seemed urgently necessary. It was estimated that the Army and Navy shipping in the Pacific would be short by twenty-five ships per month for the next three months. This could be made up only "by discontinuing troop movement to the U.K.; discontinuing the Persian Corridor project; freezing troop movement to the Middle East (14,000 air, air maintenance and S.O.S. troops) and India (3000 - Air - Signal and Medical Troops); withholding the proposed transfer of 5 ships per month to the Russian flag for West Coast Lend-Lease shipments." Approximately nineteen ships could be furnished from these projects. The rest would have to come from lend-lease commitments. The second limiting factor on action in the South Pacific was the shortage of ammunition. Without cutting into lend-lease commitments to Russia and Great Britain or training requirements in the United States and in Defense Commands, no additional units in the South Pacific could be adequately supplied before 1 July 1943. As for the number of combat aircraft in the continental United States, General Marshall told the President that it represented "the bare minimum to provide a basis for tactical training and for a minimum of security.... *The only practicable source from which combat aircraft* could be diverted to the South Pacific from the U.S. is from the heavy bombardment units now in or en route to England....to carry out diversionary or supporting missions for Torch." Finally, General Marshall said, all possible efforts were being made to concentrate air support in the South Pacific. Without additional shipping no further Army reenforcements could be delivered there. He concluded with the recommendation "that there should be a further unification of command in the entire Pacific theater, certainly in the South and Southwest Pacific."[80]

Admiral King submitted a separate memorandum which listed by types the naval vessels being diverted to the South Pacific from other areas and the naval combat planes in the continental United States, allocated to the South Pacific and various other projects. He, too, stressed the urgent need of additional shipping for the Pacific, stating that in order to move supplies and equipment to the South Pacific and to maintain it twenty ships (7,000 DWT) would have to be withdrawn from other employment.[81]

Whether or not the President ever saw these memoranda he certainly discussed their portent at least with Admiral Leahy, and probably with the other Chiefs of Staff as well,[82] for he took immediate action to improve the shipping situation in the Pacific. On the afternoon of the day the reports were submitted, Admiral Leahy asked Brigadier General John R. Deane, Secretary of the Joint Chiefs of Staff, to prepare for his signature a letter to Mr. Lewis Douglas, Deputy Administrator of the War Shipping Administration (WSA), informing him that

> The President desires that you provide without delay twenty additional ships (of not less than 7000 tons) for use in the Southwest Pacific not at the expense of Russia or the new expedition.[83]

Vice Admiral Emory S. Land, WSA Administrator, and Mr. Douglas at once had a report prepared for the President on the problems of shipping availabilities. They pointed out that although certain economies were being followed and some new construction was being completed there still would not be sufficient tonnage available to meet shipping requirements in the remaining months of 1942. The Army and Navy had suddenly demanded forty-nine more ships for the whole Pacific area in November than they had had in October, only three of which the WSA could provide. In addition, the British had announced a shortage of fifteen ships in the Red Sea. It was a simple fact that there just were not enough ships "to sustain two major military operations simultaneously in widely separated theaters of war, unless, on the American side, tonnage is removed from (a) some of our other military and naval services..., (b) the vital importation of bauxite, and (c) minor miscellaneous services; and, on the British side, from such services as the Red Sea...; India; the Persian Gulf; the U.K. import program." Again the WSA regretted that there had not yet been prepared "a statement of the overall military demands...for shipping carefully related to the major strategy of the war." It was not the WSA's function to determine which military projects could be cut back, and Admiral Land and Mr. Douglas presented the problem to the President for determination.[84]

Mr. Douglas reported to Admiral Leahy that, in response to the President's request, twenty ships were to be allocated to the Southwest Pacific, beginning immediately. This would not satisfy all the demands of the Southwest Pacific since it would still make the total number of ships available in November only thirty-nine, whereas the requests for that area of the Pacific were for fifty-four. So Mr. Douglas asked that, if more than thirty-nine were actually required, the JCS indicate what military services should be cut back to provide them.[85] The whole problem was turned over by Admiral Leahy to the Joint Staff Planners for recommendation.[86]

On 5 November 1942 the JPS produced a report on the matter.[87] There was no question of transferring vessels from the Atlantic in time to be of assistance in the Pacific. So the JPS recommended that the shipping available be reallocated to provide six additional vessels for the South and Southwest Pacific from assignments to Hawaii, Alaska, and the Canal Zone. They also proposed reducing sailings from the Pacific Coast to the Red Sea-India-Australia by fifty per cent, or six vessels. By the assignment of cargo priorities for loading in accordance with a list designated by the planners further reductions could be effected in the requirements of the Pacific. Should any additional vessels become available on the Pacific Coast they were to be allocated equally to Army and Navy use. Since it was still probable that the demands of the Pacific would not have been fully met, recommendation was made that a minimum of thirty of the estimated forty-five vessels to become available as new construction on the Pacific Coast in December be allocated between the Army and the Navy. The planners' recommendations were informally approved by the members of the JCS and the information forwarded to Mr. Douglas.[88]

This did not settle the problem. From Mr. Douglas came a strong protest to the proposal to take away six vessels from the Red Sea. This, he said, must necessarily affect combined strategy, for the WSA had been informed by the CCS in August 1942 that the Middle East had the second highest military shipping priority. He presumed, therefore, that the matter was being submitted to the CCS. For his part, he was informing the Combined Shipping Adjustment Board (CSAB) of this development.[89]

The CSAB, of which Admiral Land, WSA Administrator, was the American member, sent a prompt letter referring the question to the Combined Chiefs of Staff. The board pointed out that the six vessels were part of the standard allocation for the area. Important military cargoes had already been assigned to them, and were, in fact, already on the West Coast. The Red Sea-Indian Ocean area had suffered considerably from the requirements of the North African operation, and the CSAB thought that any further diversion of shipping should be made only after full consideration of the repercussions on both the Red Sea-Indian Ocean area and the North African operations.[90]

Admiral Leahy answered Mr. Douglas by informing him that the JCS in making their recommendations had weighed the conflicting demands of the various theaters for shipping before proposing cutting down on the Red Sea-India assignments. "Their decision to make the diversion [could] be taken as an indication that the needs of the South and Southwest Pacific had not received adequate consideration by the War Shipping Administration in their original allocations, or in pressing the United States position before the C.S.A.B."

Actually the Joint Chiefs of Staff were aware of the inadvisability of taking six ships away from British assignments without some combined study. Consequently, at the next JCS meeting they agreed to refer the matter to the Combined Military Transportation Committee (CMTC) for recommendations as a matter of urgency, for a month had passed since the question of additional shipping for the Southwest Pacific had first arisen.[91] The whole problem was settled even before the CMTC could meet. It was already mid-November, and more shipping had become available than the WSA had anticipated. On the day after the problem was turned over to the CMTC, Mr. Douglas informed Admiral Leahy that the WSA had found it possible, without taking away the British assignments, to allocate to both the Army and the Navy for the Pacific for November actually more vessels than the reallocations requested by the Joint Chiefs of Staff provided. Consequently the problem of shipping for the South Pacific was considered temporarily settled.[92] By this time the campaign on Guadalcanal was oriented at last toward U.S. victory.

By the beginning of November a sizable U.S. force with both Marine and Army elements had been assembled on Guadalcanal under command of Major General A.A. Vandegrift, USMC. This force, including six infantry regiments and part of a seventh, the equivalent of two artillery regiments, and a large number of special units, was making considerable progress toward wiping out the Japanese on the island.

The enemy, after abandoning the attempt to land reenforcements on Guadalcanal in late October, had begun again to assemble a large force in the Buin-Faisi area for a full-scale attempt to overwhelm the island. The attack was launched on 11 November with heavy raids by land-based planes on U.S. transports unloading supplies at Guadalcanal. A series of actions, partly naval and partly air, between 11 and 15 November brought large losses to both sides. Most vital was the attack by Marine land-based aircraft and naval aircraft from the *Enterprise* on twelve Japanese transports, which resulted in the destruction of eight and the beaching of the other four. Although U.S. losses in these engagements were extremely heavy the Japanese were driven off and abandoned all efforts to recapture the island.[93]

The action of 11-15 November, known as the Battle of Guadalcanal, marked the turning point in the campaign to wrest the island from Japanese control. A last enemy attempt to deliver supplies by sea to their troops on Guadalcanal was repulsed on 30 November, again at considerable cost to the naval force involved. Land action and air attacks continued until 8 February 1943, but from the end of November the eventual outcome was no longer in doubt. There was no longer an urgent need of reenforcements to insure success for Task One. Still there remained the problem of holding the positions in the Solomons and moving on to Rabaul. Only the first step of the long campaign to defeat the Japanese had been taken.

Chapter IX

CHINA-BURMA-INDIA, 1942

SUPPLY AND SUPPORT

In 1942 China, Burma, and India constituted an area of strategic potentiality but not an area for which the Joint and the Combined Chiefs of Staff contemplated large-scale, decisive military operations in the immediate future. In their studies of strategic policy, China-Burma-India (CBI) appeared regularly among the areas to be defended. However, the U.S. Chiefs in particular anticipated that, in the final phases of the war against Japan, China, because of its geographical position, would prove to be of great strategic importance. Their ideas of what was to be done in Burma and India were based on that assumption.

China had long figured prominently in the Navy's prewar plans as a base for operations in the late stages of a war with Japan. Army, Navy, and joint plans in the first year of war continued to point toward an eventual advance across the Pacific and the establishment of naval and air bases in China from which to attack the Japanese islands. Early in 1942 Admiral King sent Commander Milton E. Miles to China to explore the possibility of establishing liaison with the Chinese and assuring that China's ports would be opened to U.S. naval vessels when the progress of war rendered their availability desirable, although the time for their use might be several years away. During that same period the air force commanded by Brigadier General Claire L. Chennault undertook limited air attacks on enemy bases from airfields in China, and General Chennault and the air officers on Lieutenant General Joseph W. Stilwell's staff were preparing, albeit with different views, for eventual air operations against the Japanese home islands. It was a fundamental policy of the United States, and to a lesser extent of Great Britain, in 1942 to keep China actively belligerent, in order that it might contain as many Japanese troops as possible and that the Allies might retain access to China's air bases and more easily gain control of the left flank of the Pacific for the final attack on Japan. Maintenance of the security of Burma and India was an important factor in this program, for, with the Chinese ports all in Japanese hands, equipment for China's armies and for U.S. forces in China could be supplied from outside only through Burma or, after that country fell, by air from India. In addition, Burma and India had considerable strategic importance in their own right, for they lay on the route through which it was feared the Germans and the Japanese might move to connect their forces as well as on the flank of the sea routes to Russia via the Persian Gulf and to Egypt via the Red Sea.

The story of China-Burma-India from the viewpoint of the Joint Chiefs of Staff, however, is not alone a story of military strategy. To a greater extent than those of any other area the military problems of CBI were closely bound in with political considerations and developments, and the decisions and actions of the Joint Chiefs of Staff were strongly affected by events above them on the political level as well as below them on the military level in the theater. In order to relate intelligibly the part played by the Joint Chiefs, it is necessary to discuss in some detail matters that were initially far removed from their purview.

Burma and India were, of course, parts of the British Empire; consequently, the British were vitally concerned with their preservation. British interest in China, however, was by no means as deep. The British and Chinese were, in fact, mutually antipathetic. The reasons for their feelings were various, but, stated briefly, the Chinese resented Britain's influence on Chinese economy and thoroughly disliked its colonial policy, while the British constantly feared that Chinese actions and influence would inspire an "Asia for the Asiatics" movement which would cost them their colonies. The tenuous relations between the Chinese and the British were constantly being inflamed by misunderstandings or by actions on one side which were offensive to the other. One of General Stilwell's most difficult tasks was to try to achieve cooperation between the two.

After the collapse of ABDA, Burma and India were included in the area for which the British assumed strategic responsibility under the Combined Chiefs of Staff. The British could take independent action there (just as the United States could in the Pacific), but when American and Chinese forces or interests were concerned the action was subject to CCS approval. During the Arcadia meetings China had been set up as the China Theater under supreme command of Generalissimo Chiang Kai-shek. China was not represented on the Combined Chiefs of Staff, however, and that body did not directly control military strategy within the China Theater. Liaison between the Generalissimo and the CCS was normally through the President, or, occasionally, through General Stilwell and General Marshall. Although China and Burma and India were thus in different systems of command, because of their geographical proximity strategic problems frequently involved all three and, as has been pointed out, China was dependent upon the other two for delivery of supplies. Consequently it is convenient to discuss the three together as "China-Burma-India." It should be borne in mind that in this history the term is used to refer to the geographical area and not to the U.S. Army's China-Burma-India Theater, established in 1942 to consolidate administration of all U.S. Army forces in the area under General Stilwell.

Among the duties of General Stilwell, administration of the Army's CBI Theater was a relatively simple one. In order to understand the development in the area in 1942, it is desirable to review the position in which General Stilwell was placed. Illustrative of that is a story that has been told about one of General Stilwell's staff. Trying to explain the chain of command to a newcomer one day, the officer remarked that it could not be shown on the ordinary sort of organization chart. "But I'm working now," he said, "on a three-dimensional organization chart with a wire framework and five shades of colored ribbon, which ought to indicate at least the simpler relationships."[1]

If the lines downward from General Stilwell on the organization chart were confusing, the lines upward were no less so. He was, in the first place, U.S. Army Representative in China, assigned a twofold mission: "[1] to increase the effectiveness of United States assistance to the Chinese Government for the prosecution of the war, and [2] to assist in improving the combat efficiency of the Chinese Army." In executing this mission he performed several functions which frequently overlapped and not infrequently conflicted. First, he served as controller and supervisor of all lend-lease affairs for China. In this capacity he was under the President. Second, he was commander of all U.S. Army forces in China, Burma, and India and such Chinese forces as were assigned to him. In this capacity he was subject to the orders of the Generalissimo, Supreme Commander of the China Theater. He was also responsible, for administration of U.S. Army forces, to the Chief of Staff, U.S. Army. Third, General Stilwell was supposed to represent the U.S. Government on the International War Council at Chungking if one were set up. Finally, he was Chief of Staff for the Generalissimo's Joint Staff of American, British, and Chinese representatives. In addition to these several immediate chiefs, General Stilwell was subject to indirect control by the CCS, who were responsible for the over-all strategy of the war and who approved and provided forces for combined operations in the theater. Confusing as these relationships may seem on paper, they were even more so in operation, for, as the succeeding pages will show, the various figures involved held different views of what military action should be taken in CBI and of what the functions and the mission of General Stilwell were intended to be.

Fighting in Burma, February-May 1942

"Our object," the British Chiefs of Staff had informed General Sir Archibald P. Wavell as he prepared to turn over command of ABDA to the Dutch and head for India, "is to maintain a front in Burma, with the particular object of keeping open a supply route to China, preferably through Rangoon, but failing that through Assam."[2] When General Stilwell arrived in New Delhi on 25 February, the prospects of being able to accomplish this objective looked dubious as the British, unable to hold a line in Burma, retreated before the advancing Japanese.

The agreement reached by Secretary of War Stimson and Mr. T.V. Soong, Chinese Minister for Foreign Affairs, included the provision that General Stilwell was "under the Generalissimo to command all United States forces in China and such Chinese forces as may be assigned to him."[3] The Generalissimo had explained to Mr. Soong what he considered this to imply:

> I agree with the United States Government that it will be best for the Chief of Staff [of the Joint Staff, i.e., Stilwell] to have executive power for the coordination of American, British and Chinese military factors, especially in the Burma theater, which will amount to direct command of forces of the three nations. However, the designation of such an officer will have to be the Chief of Staff of the Generalissimo's headquarters in the China Theater.[4]

When General Stilwell arrived in Chungking he found, as he had hoped, that the Generalissimo was prepared to put him in command of the Chinese troops in Burma.[5] Indeed, Chiang went beyond this. He sent a cable to Mr. Roosevelt pointing out that the Chinese would probably outnumber the British troops remaining in Burma, that it was essential that there be a supreme command of all British and Chinese troops in Burma, and that General Stilwell was just the man for the position. He urged the President to make such a recommendation to Mr. Churchill.[6]

Mr. Roosevelt had just offered Mr. Churchill some unsolicited suggestions about the future status of India, a subject on which the two men did not by any means agree,[7] and he appears to have hesitated to offer more advice in regard to another British possession, at least until more effort had been made to work out an arrangement on the spot. He recommended to Chiang that General Stilwell be given a chance to try to develop some workable command arrangement and suggested that possibly the problem might be solved by leaving the British in control in southern Burma and putting Chiang and General Stilwell in command in north Burma.[8] The latter proposal, however, did not meet with the approval of the Prime Minister when it was subsequently made to him. If General Stilwell was to be in Burma, the Prime Minister felt that there should be unified command in that area under General Sir Harold Alexander, commander of British forces.[9]

By the time Mr. Churchill's views were known General Stilwell had gone to Burma to take command of the Chinese forces. He soon succeeded in arranging for ccooperation with General Alexander and informed Washington that the matter of unified command need not affect the conduct of operations.[10]

During his first weeks in the CBI Theater General Stilwell was hopeful that a favorable defensive position could be held in Burma until such time as manpower, equipment, and efficient organization were available for effective offensive action. He found himself hindered in his attempts to establish a clear definition of his own status of command and to achieve workable and effective arrangements with British and Chinese by the absence of American troops who would give visible evidence of American concern for the outcome in the theater. Consequently, he strongly urged that the United States strengthen his position by sending an American division at least as far as India, if not actually to participate in the fighting in Burma.[11] His request was refused, however, for in the broader picture as seen in Washington the crisis in the Pacific islands and the embryo plans for an offensive in the European Theater loomed larger and commanded priority on the limited resources of American men, equipment, and particularly shipping.[12] Similarly, the British Chiefs of Staff, anxious though they were that India be held and Burma, too, if possible, found that the demands of other projects limited the number of troops that could be sent to Burma and India.

All the complications of command in Burma only further confused a military situation that from the beginning had been badly muddled. With Rangoon lost, the British planned to defend a line east to west across Burma, posting their forces in the Irrawaddy Valley at Prome and the Chinese Fifth Army in the Upper Sittang Valley at Toungoo. But the Japanese broke this line with comparatively little difficulty and drove into upper Burma. By 26 April they had occupied Lashio, and British, Chinese, and Americans were seeking a way out. Ultimately, General Stilwell himself led a mixed group, on foot most of the way, over the mountains to Imphal in the Assam region of India. The remnants of the British forces headed for India also, as did part of the Chinese troops. The rest of the Chinese retreated into the Southern Shan States and on into China. The Allies had been badly defeated in Burma.[13]

Supply and Transportation

The program of lend-lease for China was set up in the spring of 1941 with China Defense Supplies, Inc. (CDS), representing Chinese interests in Washington. Later in the year a project was arranged by Mr. T.V. Soong as Chinese representative on CDS to obtain supplies via lend-lease to re-equip completely by 1942 thirty Chinese ground divisions to form a spearhead for a drive to get the Japanese out of China.[14] This thirty-division plan continued to be the basis for the allocation of war materials under lend-lease to China and a major charge upon General Stilwell was to see that the plan was put into operation and lend-lease materials were actually assigned to it.[15] Unfortunately, allocation of material in the United States was only the beginning. As more and more goods were set aside for China, the problem of actual delivery became more and more complicated.

Even before the Burma Road was lost Mr. Soong brought to the President's attention the need for some substitute delivery route and suggested that an air route from Sadiya in northern Assam to Kunming or Suifu in China might be substituted. To operate such a transport system he recommended that sixty-five more C-53's be allocated to China for use as transports.[16] American pilots of the China National Aviation Corporation (CNAC) had surveyed the possibilities of an air route over the Hump as early as November 1941. During the Burma campaign this non-military Chinese-

American company flew over 10,000 refugees out of Burma into India. Despite a high rate of efficiency, however, the CNAC lacked the planes and personnel to carry all the supplies headed for China. The Chinese Air Force was not capable of handling such a project, and it was apparent that if there were to be an air supply route the U.S. Army Air Forces would have to undertake it.[17]

When the ABDA Command was broken up, Major General Lewis H. Brereton, at his own request, was ordered to India, where he assumed command of the newly organized Tenth Air Force on 5 March.[18] To him was assigned the mission, under direction of General Stilwell, of conducting offensive air operations in the China Theater, "with the ultimate aim of operating against Japanese lines of communications through the China Seas and of direct attack against Japan."[19] Even before he took over command of the Tenth Air Force, the task of delivering supplies by air to China was added to his combat mission. By the end of March General Naiden, then Chief of Staff to Brigadier General Earl L. Brereton, had drafted plans for two transport commands: the trans-India, between Karachi and Dinjan, and the Assam-Burma-China from Dinjan to Myitkyina to Loiwing, and in time to Kunming and Chungking. These two commands were eventually merged into the India-China Ferry Command and their routes were changed as some of the original bases proved impractical. Inadequate airfields, inexperience, and limited equipment, coupled with Japanese occupation of Myitkyina, retarded development of the system. It was many months before really large amounts were being delivered to China by air.[20]

Upon the small trickle of supplies across the Hump in 1942, the lend-lease program, while a major claimant, was not the only one. Conflicting with the long range project for equipping thirty ground divisions with lend-lease material for combat use in China. Burma, and Indo-China were the demands of General Chennault's American Volunteer Group and later the 14th Air Force. The considerable accomplishments of the AVG and the spectacular claims of its commander captured the imagination of the Generalissimo and inspired him considerably with confidence that air power alone could defeat the Japanese. Since this was not the view of General Stilwell, apportionment of the Hump tonnage between air and ground forces became a major source of controversy in the months ahead.

Still another claimant on the supplies carried over the Hump, albeit a smaller one, was the U.S. Navy's project known as Friendship (later SACO--Sino-American Cooperative Organization) which was set up, independent of General Stilwell, by a directive issued by the Chief of Naval Operations on 11 March 1942. Although this project, under Commander Milton E. Miles, USN, was not initially sponsored by the Joint Chiefs of Staff, problems relating to its support occasionally came to their attention. In addition to the task mentioned above[21] of arranging for eventual utilization of Chinese ports, Commander Miles was charged with three basic missions: organizing a Chinese naval guerrilla mine warfare unit, organizing a weather information network, and establishing a radio intelligence unit. Some of the supplies for the projects could be procured locally or delivered secretly by U.S. submarine, but, like all other military projects in China, Friendship was largely dependent upon the Hump for support.[22]

By February 1942 transportation facilities between the United States and China were totally inadequate for the volume of material that the Chinese were receiving in the United States under the thirty-division program.[23] The port of Rangoon was closed to incoming shipping even before the Burma Road was actually cut by the Japanese. Hope of Rangoon's being reopened was fading fast, and Mr. Soong, through the Assistant Secretary of War, Mr. John J. McCloy, urged that the CCS take steps to build up a depot and an adequate transportation route in India to connect, probably by air, with China.[24]

Mr. Soong was finally informed that the War Department considered that arrangements for transportation in India were within General Stilwell's authority.[25] Before this word was delivered, however, the Chinese representative approached Mr. McCloy with another transportation problem. There were, he said, approximately thirty thousand tons of vital supplies for China already accumulated at Newport News. More were arriving daily, but the Maritime Commission had scheduled only one ship to transport this material to China during the month of February. Thus, he complained,

> We find ourselves in a vicious circle. Owing to our lack of ships (we were also without a ship from December 8th until mid-January), Government officials are refusing to allocate or are stopping shipment of important materials to us. The Maritime Commission, hearing that we are not getting such allocations, further delays giving us ships.

So he called on Mr. McCloy to advise the Maritime Commission of the "policy of all-out aid to China now!"[26] But shipping was short in all theaters of war, and delivery of any large amount of supplies to China, even if they reached India, was uncertain. Rather than accumulate a stockpile of unused material in India, it seemed advisable to arranging shipping for other projects at the expense of the China Theater. By the same token, the Combined Chiefs of Staff agreed in March that the Munitions Assignments Board (MAB) should allocate to China only such munitions as could be delivered.[27]

Mr. Soong did not get more ships in February. Three weeks later he made another plea for more than the three or possibly four ships that had been scheduled for China during the month of March. This time he pointed out the various projects that were under way for improving transportation between India and China and expressed the view that the ships scheduled for China could not carry enough to occupy fully the facilities in prospect. The routes he mentioned (an Indian road through Imphal and Tamu to Kalewa, estimated capacity 1,000 tons the first six months; a road from Ledo to Myitkyina to be built within three or four months; and the air route from Sadiya to the Burma Road or into China, estimated to carry 7,500 tons per month), however, were not yet ready to carry supplies to China, and materials continued to accumulate at Newport News.[28]

Air Support for India

China was not the only country in the Far East with a transportation problem. India, also receiving lend-lease from the United States and serving as a base for British activities in Burma as well as a base for aircraft flying to China, was not without its difficulties of supply and transportation. American supply experts who went to the CBI Theater to investigate the matter of transportation were struck both by the inadequacy of the roads and railroads in the area and by the inefficiency with which they were operated.[29] Early in the campaign in Burma the troops fighting there became dependent largely on air transport from India for their maintenance. When the nucleus of the Tenth Air Force, eight heavy bombers, arrived in India just after the collapse of ABDACOM, they were pressed into service immediately to carry supplies for ground troops and gasoline for air forces, and to evacuate refugees from the fighting in Burma. In late February the British put in a bid for more air transports from U.S. production to be sent at once to India to assist in supporting the Burma forces. But transport planes, like everything else, were scarce, and General Arnold carefully explained that the United States could do no more than proceed with plans to increase the number of planes flying between Takoradi and Calcutta from the current 38 to 144 and to send 100 transports to India to deliver supplies to China. It seemed unwise to divert transport planes from other projects to India, and General Arnold recommended instead that the British use U.S. facilities in the area where possible.[30]

By April it appeared that the Japanese might overrun Burma and continue on to invade India. General Wavell, considering his air force inadequate for such an eventuality, wrote to Mr. Louis Johnson of the State Department, then the President's personal representative to India, requesting 40 transport aircraft, 80 reconnaissance aircraft, 120 medium bombers, and 120 fighters. This letter arrived in due time, via the White House, at the CCS meeting of 7 April. There, however, it got no results, for transports were still very scarce articles. The U.S. Chiefs were ready to agree with Sir John Dill's view that the requests should more properly have been sent to London, and Dill volunteered to send the letter there.[31]

It was at just this time that units of the Japanese fleet entered the Bay of Bengal and attacked Colombo and Trincomalee Reports reached Washington that General Wavell appeared to have his eyes on the aircraft consigned to China under lend-lease, thinking to put them to his own use in India, and it became necessary for the War Department to assure General Stilwell and, through him, the Generalissimo, that no one had authority to divert Chinese lend-lease planes without the permission of Chiang himself.[32] Meanwhile, General Marshall, in London trying to get the agreement of the British Chiefs of Staff to Bolero, found them more concerned with the Japanese threat to India than with the possibilities of an operation on the continent of Europe in 1942. Before much progress had been made in the Bolero discussions, General Marshall forwarded to Washington the British requests for naval and air support in the Indian Ocean-Bay of Bengal region. The Joint Chiefs followed Admiral King in his view that the crisis in the Indian Ocean was abating and that it would be unwise to commit U.S. naval forces to this British area when they could be used more profitably in the Pacific. To ease General Marshall's way a bit in London, however, and to assist in the eastern crisis, the chiefs agreed to try to help with air support.[33] Orders proposed by General Marshall in London were sent to General Stilwell, informing him that temporarily the Tenth Air Force would "be employed in conformity with British direction in [the] Indian Ocean Bay of Bengal region in [the] general area from Ceylon northward." In an attempt to reassure General Stilwell and the Generalissimo, word was included that the AVG would have first priority on fighter planes arriving in India until the AVG's operational strength and attrition losses were filled. Any planes in excess would go to the Tenth Air Force.[34]

This action only succeeded in angering the Generalissimo, who was informed of it by General Bissell. (General Stilwell was busy in Burma.). Chiang wanted to know at once the date on which the AVG would be brought to full strength in aircraft and personnel, specifically, when, how many, and what type, planes would be diverted to the Tenth Air Force, and what the President was going to do about a request he had made for 300 planes for the defense of Burma. The Generalissimo made it clear that he would not consent to the diversion of Chinese aircraft to the defense of India, even though General Bissell tried to explain that unless India was defended and the line of communications kept open to China little or nothing from the United States could actually reach China.[35] General Stilwell also opposed the idea of employing the Tenth Air Force otherwise than in support of the Burma campaign.[36] However, although orders were sent to General Brereton that no planes actually consigned to China were to be diverted to the Tenth Air Force, until late in May General Brereton had orders that his planes were to execute missions for the British in the Indian Ocean region. By late May, Burma was lost. Fear of Japanese naval penetration into the Indian Ocean had subsided. When two messages came from Chiang Kai-shek outlining a serious Japanese threat to the air bases in eastern China and predicting that, "unless effective steps are taken immediately, [the] situation will grow worse and worse until it will be too late," General Brereton's instructions were rescinded and the deployment of the Tenth Air Force within the CBI area was placed entirely at the discretion of General Stilwell.[37]

Meanwhile, General Wavell's request for more transport planes for the India-Burma theater had landed back before the Combined Chiefs of Staff. Unable to find forty transports to spare among its own aircraft stocks, the British Air Ministry had made an urgent plea to the Munitions Assignments Committee (Air) in Washington for forty C-47's to be assigned immediately to the Burma theater. But all such planes on hand or soon to be were already assigned to high priority projects in other theaters. The CCS "Directive for Assignment of Munitions" under which the MAB was trying to operate placed India-Burma-Ceylon in Priority "A" together with the Middle East, Australia, New Zealand, and the Pacific Islands, and, for aircraft, the United Kingdom. There was no indication of the relative strategical priority of the various projects, and the MAB was not in a position to decide that itself. The board's request for a statement of strategical policy was endorsed by the representatives of the British Chiefs of Staff who recommended that "40 C-47's or equivalent be sent to India within the next four weeks either - (i) as additions to the U.S. ferry organization in that theatre; or (ii) as British assignments."[38]

The U.S. Chiefs of Staff, led by General Arnold, stuck to their view that there were already enough transports scheduled for the CBI Theater and enough separate commands controlling them. Although various figures were mentioned in the course of the discussions, it appears that a total of about seventy-five more planes had already been committed to the China National Aviation Corporation, the Tenth Air Force, and the 1st Ferry Group under General Stilwell's control. Despite strong urging from Sir John Dill the U.S. Chiefs refused to agree to cut further into insufficient stocks of U.S. transport planes and continued to recommend that the British try to make more use of the facilities available in India, in particular of the planes (five!) under General Brereton, who still had instructions to operate under British control.[39]

China's Bid for Representation in Washington

Chiang Kai-shek's rather blunt demand for information on the supply and employment of aircraft in the China Theater[40] is indicative of his reactions as, repeatedly, matters in which China was involved were decided in Washington with no consultation either with him or his representatives.[41] Since December Chiang had been urging that China be given a place on the body controlling grand strategy, the Supreme War Council, if one were set up, or the CCS. Like the Australians and the New Zealanders, he considered the Pacific War Council[42] an inadequate substitute. However, although President Roosevelt appeared to treat China as one of the great powers, Americans and British agreed that, since they were to furnish the major portion of the materials and, with the Russians, to do the major part of the fighting in the war against the Axis, they should make the major decisions of policy and strategy, accepting the advice of their allies but not granting them full participation in top level councils. Whether this system was in fact fair to the less powerful members of the United Nations is not for discussion here. In any event, it rendered the committee system considerably less complicated and presumably more efficient than it would have become had each committee included representatives of China, Australia, Canada, and the various other nations participating in the war.

Understandably, however, it seemed to Chiang Kai-shek that, without direct Chinese participation in the planning groups, his country's interests were not receiving adequate consideration.[43]

So it was that in March 1942 Chiang sent to Washington a military mission headed by General Hsiung Shih-Fei. In April, when he arrived with a letter of introduction to the President, the Generalissimo through Mr. Soong took occasion to outline the instances in which the United States had failed to live up to his expectations in the matter of shipping and supplies and to offer his complaint about the top level management of the war:

> The President had accorded generous recognition of China as one of the four principal powers fighting the Axis. But in the matter of supplies, Russia is protected by protocol. The U.S. and Britain are on the Munitions Assignment Board, but they are interested parties, legitimately anxious to build up their own armies....When China's requirements are considered, frequently she is not even consulted. When consultations are made, Chinese representatives appear for a hearing, and a verdict is arrived at without their knowing the basis for the decision. Again, these decisions are frequently adversely changed without consultation or even explanation.
>
> ...The Generalissimo feels himself entirely out of touch with the main decisions of strategy, which profoundly affect China's future. Whether an offensive will start from Australia, whether it is considered feasible to hold Burma, what steps are taken to protect the Indian Ocean route, what air forces will be sent to India, Burma and China, on all these vital questions his role is that of an occasional listener. Also, be it remembered it is from these decisions of strategy that stems the question of allocations of munitions.

Therefore Chiang made two requests: (1) That the Anglo-American joint staff be enlarged to include China; (2) That China be represented on the sub-committees for ground and air of the Munitions Assignments Board.[44]

To Mr. Soong, in a message that also reached the President, the Generalissimo more bluntly stated his strong feelings in the matter:

> If in the future the Anglo-American joint staff is not enlarged to include China, and China is kept out of the Munitions Assignments Board, then China would be just a pawn in the game. Gandhi told me when I visited India: "They will never voluntarily treat us Indians as equals; why, they do not even admit your country to their staff talks." If we are thus treated during the stress of war, what becomes our position at the peace conference? You must insist that we have our own stand, as we have our own independent position to uphold.[45]

On the day these messages arrived in Washington the President attempted to answer Chiang's earlier requests made to General Bissell about specific plans for the AVG, still an independent group in China, and the Tenth Air Force. His message to Chiang plainly stated that no airplanes consigned to the AVG in China would be delivered to the Tenth Air Force. Those being sent were from British and American allocations and bore no relation to previous commitments to China. A total of 456 planes had been allocated for operations in China, of which 67 had reached Karachi and 126 were en route, 54 were about to leave the United States, and 209 would depart in the future, including 91 in April. It was a clear bid to reassure the Generalissimo that China's interests were not being neglected in regard to aircraft.[46]

Chiang's requests for membership in the CCS organization met with no such favorable response. On 26 May a new organization, the Military Representatives of the Associated Pacific Powers,[47] met for the first time in Washington. This group, assembled largely to try to appease the various nations demanding participation in war planning, met occasionally during the next two years to discuss with the Joint Chiefs of Staff the current situation in the war against Japan. At the first meeting General Hsiung made an urgent plea for the full participation the Generalissimo sought and for greater attention to the war against Japan, with particular emphasis on the support of China. He recommended immediate establishment of a Supreme War Council similar to that of World War I to "serve as the supreme machinery for the direction of the war,...not...merely an advisory body."[48]

General Hsiung's remarks were circulated to the Combined Chiefs of Staff and to the British Chiefs in London. All were agreed that a council such as the Chinese advocated would be undesirable and unworkable and that the United States and Great Britain should continue to make the decisions, hearing China's case through the military mission and the Pacific War Council, and running no risk of the great powers being forced by a majority of lesser powers to a decision contrary to the interests of the United States and Great Britain. The British pointed out further that the Supreme War Council of 1917 had been by no means an ideal organization, it had operated only on the Western Front, and final decisions on strategy and deployment had still rested with the various governments. Moreover, Japan had never been included in its membership. In World War II Russia was actually bearing the brunt of the fighting and it had shown no desire for cooperation in military planning. So the Combined Secretariat was put to work drafting a reply to General Hsiung,[49] pointing out delicately that the situations were not the same and that, "rather than attempt to extend the formal machinery which exists today, the Combined Chiefs of Staff will seek to improve co-ordination of effort through close but less formal personal contacts within that machinery."[50] This reply did not satisfy General Hsiung, who responded at once with a plea that, while close cooperation would be very desirable, neither he nor the Generalissimo felt that anything less than full participation and full knowledge of how decisions were made would suffice.[51] Nor did it satisfy Chiang, who repeatedly thereafter made futile bids for membership on the CCS and even as late as July 1945 vainly requested participation in CCS deliberations.[52]

The 3,500-Ton Program

The problem of delivery of lend-lease material to China had become increasingly difficult as March 1942 moved into April. The estimated date for completion of the Ledo-Myitkyina Road had been put off until the most optimistic guess was November. Through traffic on the Imphal-Kalewa route was not expected before October.[53] The Japanese were advancing rapidly into upper Burma, and now that the Burma Road was in Japanese hands it was becoming more and more doubtful that a ground route to China would materialize. The one hope lay in air transport over the Hump, where regular operations had begun, however haltingly, in April.[54]

All this time material for China had been accumulating, both at Newport News and in India, awaiting transportation that did not arrive. General Stilwell finally recommended that, rather than amassing great quantities in idleness, until more shipping facilities were clearly foreseen contracts for China in the United States and Canada be restricted to items the U.S. forces could use in the event they could not be delivered to China.[55]

In addition to some 45,000 tons in India, some 1,800 carloads of munitions, an estimated 54,000 tons, had piled up at Newport News by April awaiting shipment to China. Included in the stockpile were numerous items, e.g., railroad equipment and copper, which could have been readily utilized in U.S. production for its own war effort. The War Department was anxious that the port be cleared and that some of the material be put to useful work elsewhere. Consequently, the MAB strongly recommended reduction of the Chinese lend-lease program.[56] This was, however, a step firmly opposed by the Chinese, who would not agree to cutting back on their large lend-lease orders and who contended that the delivery problem was, or could be, considerably less difficult than it appeared. Views which General Stilwell had submitted in regard to China's lend-lease needs and the transportation situation differed from those which Chiang and his representatives were offering in Washington. To remedy this situation General Marshall suggested to General Stilwell that he and the Generalissimo get together and send joint lend-lease cables, the first of which would indicate precisely what tonnage could be carried from India to China over existing or developing routes, what level of stocks should be maintained in India, and what priority should be followed for shipments to India in the next three months.[57]

General Stilwell was still in Burma when General Marshall's suggestion arrived. However, Brigadier General John Magruder, who had remained temporarily on General Stilwell's staff, replied to General Marshall, stating his view, in terms similar to those used several times by General Stilwell, that some restrictions should be put on the lend-lease program for China. What was needed, General Magruder said, was a clear-cut statement by our government to the Chinese government of our objectives in affording Lend-Lease aid. It should be expressed unmistakably that Lend-Lease aid to China involved mutual assistance between the United States and China for the purpose of winning this war and not the building up of war material in China or India unrelated to a specific military need and practical employment. It should also be made clear that Lend-Lease aid is no part of a program of post war reconstruction.

It was further recommended that, having made clear to Chiang the terms under which lend-lease aid was to be given, the United States should reach agreement with the Generalissimo on a limited organization of forces that could be equipped and restrict the Chinese lend-lease program to equipment for those forces. As for the accumulation of supplies beyond shipping means, it was "obvious that our government should insist upon its release. This irrational retention of needed material can only be viewed as Chinese political coercion for national and not allied ends."[58]

It was not so simple in Washington to get agreement to any such tough lend-lease policy toward China. Lend-lease policies toward other nations, particularly toward Russia, set no precedent for conditional agreements. Whether or not there was suspicion in Washington, as apparently there was conviction in General Stilwell's mind, that the Chinese were intentionally ordering materials and storing them up, not for the current conflict, not to fight Japan, but for future use in strengthening the postwar position of the Kuomintang, is difficult to ascertain. If there was any strong feeling that the materials were to be used to fight the Communists in China, there would have been little sympathy for it, because at that time the United States was cooperating as thoroughly as possible with Communist Russia and, in addition, the view that the Chinese Communists were not real Communists but just "agrarian reformers" was widely held. Moreover, Mr. T.V. Soong, spokesman for China Defense Supplies, had a highly placed, sympathetic friend in Mr. Harry Hopkins who, in addition to his influential position in the White House, had been the first Administrator of Lend-Lease and knew its system. From the military point of view, because of China's potential use as a base for operations against the Japanese home islands and for containing Japanese troops it was considered important that the Chinese be kept in the war against Japan. To achieve this it seemed to be necessary to go more than halfway with Chiang Kai-shek, for it was strongly feared that he might give up and negotiate with the Japanese. Besides it seemed undesirable to bring pressure to bear on Chiang in May 1942 when the United States was not in a position to follow through with prompt and effective military assistance.

The suggestion that the MAB was advocating cutting back on allocations to China because of the bottleneck at Newport News brought forth protests from the Chinese. On 8 May a personal representative of Mr. Soong approached the Chairman of the Munitions Assignments Committee (Ground) (MAC(G)) (Brigadier General H.S. Aurand) with an emergency air transportation program for China, stating that it was a result of a White House conference and that he, the representative, believed Mr. Soong considered the requirements an ultimatum. This program was based on the assumption that 7,500 long tons per month could be carried into China over the air route, a figure considerably above General Arnold's maximum contemporary estimate of 1,200 tons. The MAC(G) looked over the requirements and tentatively cleared items totaling somewhere between those two figures. They passed the matter up to the MAB for a decision on the maximum tonnage to be used as a basis for assignments, requesting authority to negotiate a program with the Chinese for the months May to October and to recommend assignments for May and June.[59] The MAB had figures from OPD to the effect that, with Sadiya as a base, the air route could carry from 4,118 to 6,270 tons per month, but only 1,200 if the route had to go farther west.[60] In June 4,247 tons would be required to maintain the AVG, a figure that would be reduced monthly to 2,647 tons in October.[61] Mindful that the AVG could not be neglected, the MAB authorized the Ground Committee to make assignments for May and June on the basis of 3,500 tons a month exclusive of airplane fuel. They inserted in the directive a new principle, aimed to relieve congestion in India and to give to General Stilwell the authority to see that materials under the program were used where needed. The board "directed that shipments be made to the War Department representative in India, earmarked for China."[62]

The War Department sent word to General Stilwell and Major General R.A. Wheeler, head of the Services of Supply in India, that future shipments of lend-lease materials for China would be sent to SOS India and General Stilwell would decide the place and date of transfer and delivery of title to China. If he felt that the situation warranted some other assignment of the material, he was to submit recommendations to the War Department for consideration by the MAB. This procedure was instituted with the knowledge of Mr. Soong, who, however, failed to inform the Generalissimo of the new set-up, thereby causing considerable subsequent misunderstanding as will be discussed below.[63]

Settling on a future program and establishing a new system for transfer of jurisdiction of lend-lease goods for China did not improve the congested situation at Newport News. In mid-May the War Department moved to reclaim some of the material most urgently needed by the United States and to attempt to clear the port. This action was inevitably displeasing to the Chinese, and Mr. McCloy took pains to explain to Mr. Soong that "the matter of replacing this material will be a matter of my personal concern when the prospect of transportation is improved."[64]

Although the Generalissimo said later that he had instructed Mr. Soong to release materials that could not be shipped from the United States, the seizure of munitions by the War Department and the change in lend-lease jurisdictional policy, of which Chiang was not informed, were hardly calculated to increase good will between the United States and China. These developments were particularly unwelcome, coming as they did just as the Japanese were completing their conquest of Burma, moving Madame Chiang to report that the morale of the Chinese army and the people was "never lower during five years of war."[65] The establishment of a fixed 3,500-ton monthly allotment, however, was accepted quite happily. Unfortunately, the figure of 3,500 tons plus aviation gasoline had been arrived at without thorough investigation of the air transport situation in India and China and before the air route had been given adequate trial. More unfortunately, while the members of the Munitions Assignments Board considered 3,500 tons a figure for tentative planning, at least for the months of July to October, the Chinese considered it a firm commitment. Almost at once difficulties arose.

By the end of May only disappointingly small amounts of cargo had actually been delivered to China by air. The Generalissimo decided that the failure to carry more resulted from the inadequacies of the two-motored transports being used on the Hump route. So he cabled Mr. Roosevelt that he understood that the United States was going to be producing fifteen four-motored DC-4's (same as C-54) per month by June, and he requested that all of these planes and more of the same type be allocated to the India-China air route. His request was refused, however, for the fact was that only two C-54's had been produced for the Army, one in March and one in May. Two were scheduled for June, three for July, and four each for the next three months. There were none yet available to send to India.[66]

The War Department was not disposed to make too great an effort to send more transports to the India-China route, for word was being received from that theater that no more planes could be accommodated. No sooner had General Stilwell been told of the 3,500-ton emergency air transport program than a message arrived in Washington from General Brereton, indicating uncertainty as to what effect the approaching monsoons would have on the air project, and estimating the tonnage that could actually be carried into China by air in the next few months. The figures were pitifully low: June, 128; July 264; August, September, October, 400 each. Airfields were not yet developed and radio equipment was inadequate. General Brereton reported that it would be 15 July before more planes could be used to good advantage, and then all he hoped to take care of was seventeen more.[67] Close behind this came messages from Generals Stilwell and Wheeler (SOS), outlining the physical difficulties of operating the Hump supply route and pointing out that it would be a grave error to build up Chinese hopes for delivery of all material being allocated under the Emergency Air Transport Program. General Wheeler predicted that "practically none" could be transported during the monsoon season, and General Stilwell estimated 5 to 10 per cent in addition to supplies for the AVG and a small medium bombardment unit in China.[68]

At the next MAC(G) meeting, on 22 June 1942, the three cables from the theater were given serious consideration. Seven thousand tons of ground equipment had already been transferred to the Chinese on the May and June programs. Since there seemed little likelihood that these could be delivered at their ultimate destination, the chairman proposed that no assignments be made for July. This recommendation was sent to the MAB, with General Handy of OPD dissenting. He argued that General Stilwell was currently holding important discussions with Chiang Kai-shek in regard to training Chinese troops in India, the military situation in China was very serious, and under the circumstances a breach of agreement with the Chinese would seriously compromise General Stilwell's position.[69] It is interesting to note that, even before the MAC(G) met, Mr. Soong had word that the MAB was considering cutting the July program down to 400 tons, a possibility which he protested to both Mr. McCloy, on the eighteenth, and Mr. Hopkins, on the twentieth, recommending rather an increase of the carrying capacity of the airlift.[70] Similarly, the day after the MAC(G) proposal for no allocation for July reached the MAB and was referred by them to a special committee for consideration, Mr. Soong was protesting to Mr. Hopkins against a program that would send nothing at all to China in July.[71] Ultimately, the MAB submitted the matter to the Combined Chiefs of Staff for a solution. Before it was brought up before that committee, a crisis had arisen in United States-Chinese relations.

The "Three Demands"

While Prime Minister Churchill and his military staff conferred with their U.S. opposite numbers in Washington in June 1942, the military situation of the British forces in the Middle East rapidly deteriorated. General Rommel defeated the British in a great tank battle and pushed on through Libya to take Tobruk. There was seemingly nothing to prevent his sweeping on across Egypt and participating in the much-dreaded move of German forces to link with Japanese forces moving in from the opposite direction. This sudden disaster in Libya deeply jarred the British and considerably affected U.S. efforts to secure a firm commitment to Sledgehammer for 1942. The U.S. Chiefs began at once to investigate ways in which they could assist to ease the situation in the Middle East, and, specifically, to look for ground and air forces they could send to help the British.

Within the days immediately following receipt of word of the fall of Tobruk, three different air units originally earmarked for operations in the China-Burma-India Theater were diverted to the Middle East. The first of these was a task force of twenty-three B-24's, the Halverson Detachment (HALPRO), which had started for China as a special American unit to conduct bombing operations against Japanese objectives from bases in China. This detachment had been detained in Egypt earlier in the month for a special operation against the Ploesti oil fields. Now it was to remain indefinitely, with little prospect of its ever continuing on to its destination in China.[72]

The second group of planes thrown into the effort was part of the still only partially developed Tenth Air Force. Assigned as it was to operations in China, Burma, and India, with the primary mission of supporting China, the Tenth Air Force was actually defending one end of the area through which a junction of German and

Japanese forces might be made and helping to secure the line of communications to India. With the German successes in the Middle East, the security of the communications route and of the potential linkage area was threatened at the opposite end. It appears that the transfer of the Tenth Air Force to Egypt was defended as a temporary movement to another part of the same strategic area, where it would continue to perform the same defensive function from differently located bases.[73] However justifiable the action, diplomatically it was badly handled. With no prior consultation with the Chinese, General Brereton was ordered to proceed immediately to the Middle East to assist General Sir C.J.E. Auchinleck temporarily and to take with him such heavy bombers as were available and such personnel and transport planes as would be required for proper functioning of his command.[74] Early the following morning word of a third step was sent to General Stilwell. Thirty-three A-29 Lockheed-Hudsons had been earmarked for China under lend-lease in January 1942. For one reason and another their departure from the United States had been held up and they were just starting out at the end of June. Since their ferry route led through Khartoum it was decided, again without consulting the Chinese, that they, too, would be held in Egypt and become a part of General Brereton's Middle East air force.[75]

It fell to General Stilwell to inform Generalissimo Chiang Kaishek of the last two of these diversions. The Generalissimo's reaction, as should have been expected, was most unfavorable. General Stilwell reported back to Washington the gist of a tense and caustic conversation with the Generalissimo and Madame Chiang, illustrating clearly that failure to inform him before the decisions were made was a diplomatic blunder.

> ...Chiang Kai-shek believes the President is sincere and feels these orders were given without his knowledge or consent. Feels that Allies do not regard China as part of...allied war theater. China had done her best for five years. Questions whether allies are doing their best for China. If crisis exists in Libya, a crisis also exists in China. He had assurances that Tenth Air Force was to operate in China and expected notification before any part of it was taken away. Now it appears that Allies have no interest in China Theater, and he wants an answer, yes or no, to the question "do the Allies want the China Theater maintained?" Madame then added that pro-Japanese activity here was pronounced and the question was whether or not the United States wanted China to make peace. Both Chiang Kai-shek and Madame were bitter about this matter, and they were not mincing words when they asked for an unequivocal answer to the question as to whether or not the Allies were interested in maintaining the China War Theater.

Chiang insisted, and General Stilwell agreed, on sending Brigadier General W.R. Gruber, General Stilwell's Chief of Staff, at once to Washington to present the detailed picture of the situation in the theater.[76]

When General Stilwell's cabled report reached Washington, the President at once despatched a message prepared in the War Department to the Generalissimo. No attempt was made to explain why Chiang had not been consulted; however, the suddenness of the crisis and the relation between the Middle and the Far East were stressed. "The urgency of the situation," it was explained, "demanded that any and all means immediately available be despatched to preserve our lines of communication to the China Theater." In answer to the Generalissimo's blunt question, the President assured him that "the United States and our allies do regard China as a vital part of our common war effort and depend upon the maintenance of the China theatre as an urgent necessity for the defeat of our enemies."[77]

It appears that the diversion of the Tenth Air Force was for the Generalissimo a "last straw." Throughout the first six months of the war his repeated attempts to gain acceptance as a full partner in over-all planning through membership on the CCS and its subsidiary committees had been consistently rebuffed. Requests for more shipping for the China Theater had been refused. Some of the material his representatives in the United States had gathered together had been taken back by the U.S. Army when transportation to move it to China was not forthcoming. The British had made a mess in Burma and had definitely worsened already touchy British-Chinese relations by their handling of Chiang's offer to send Chinese troops to assist in that campaign. The three Chinese armies that finally went to Burma had been badly defeated, and General Stilwell had not hestitated to point out to Chiang their inadequacies. The air transport route that had been promised as a more effective means than the lost Burma Road for the delivery of supplies into China had scarcely begun to operate and that on only a very limited and disappointing scale. Yet the United States would not agree to send more transport planes to China. On top of all these disappointments, the diversion of the heavy bombers and some of the transports of the Tenth Air Force was more than Chiang cared to take. The President's reassuring words had a hollow sound.

On 29 June the Generalissimo handed to General Stilwell a memorandum listing three measures which he considered the minimum of assistance he should receive from the United States. These "Three Demands" were: (1) Three American divisions in India by September to help retake Burma; (2) 500 effective combat planes available to China continuously starting in August;[78] (3) 5,000 tons monthly delivered to China by air beginning in August. General Stilwell pointed out to Chiang that the shipping shortage would prevent sending a ground force to India, that gas and munitions available in China would keep the planes already available in operation only six months, and that existing fields were "totally inadequate to handle the transport planes necessary to deliver five thousand tons a month." He refused to recommend to the U.S. Government that Chiang's demands be granted, taking the position that it was not within his province to support any ultimatum to his government and that he was not subject to Chiang's orders in matters of lend-lease, but directly under the President. However, Chiang only became enraged at General Stilwell and persisted in his demands, proffering liquidation of the China Theater as the alternative to their acceptance.[79]

This ultimatum from Chungking went without formal answer for several months; however, within a few days Mr. Lauchlin Currie, presidental advisor, was on his way to China to try to straighten out the situation.[80]

It was at this stage, at the beginning of July 1942, that the Munitions Assignments Board requested a decision from the Combined Chiefs of Staff as to whether or not 3,500 tons of munitions should be allocated to China for the month of July. The Ground Committee's recommendation against any assignment to China for July, together with the dissent of the OPD member, had been referred by the MAB to a special committee. The U.S. members of that group, while aware that it was impossible to deliver the material to China immediately, recognized the political importance of not cutting back on commitments to China when relations were critical, and they followed the dissenting line.[81] However, the British member supported the recommendation for a cut on the grounds that, in addition to the unlikelihood of delivery to China, "many of the supplies scheduled previously for delivery to China from July production were critical items of British type which, particularly on account of losses recently sustained in the Middle East, could not be spared from British service."[82]

The JCS recommended to the British representatives on the CCS that, because of the negotiations being conducted with Chiang and the uncertainty of the situation, 3,500 tons of ground munitions must be allocated to China. This recommendation was answered by insistence from the British that, if 3,500 tons were to be sent, their representatives on the Combined Munitions Assignments Board must approve the items to be included. The JCS felt that something else could easily be substituted for the materials the British did not want sent to China (1,500 Bren guns and 10,000,000 rounds of .303 ammunition). So, although the prospects of much of the allocated material reaching China soon were very slight, the 3,500-ton program was continued for another month.[83] Subsequently it was extended beyond that.

The British and the Tenth Air Force

As has already been pointed out, the British view of China-Burma-India, conditioned as it was by Britain's political interests in the area, was very different from that of the United States. Britain was concerned with maintaining the Empire and retaking those portions of it that had already fallen to the Japanese. It was not in the British interest to support a strong China, lest it point the way for Britain's colonies to agitate for independence. With Burma and Malaya lost, the chief British objective in the area was to defend India and recapture lost territory for its own sake, not as a road into China. The potential strategic importance of China also seemed less vital than it did to American military planners, for the war against Japan was being fought primarily by the United States and in any case it was not supposed to reach a crescendo until Germany had fallen.

The British viewpoint was clearly shown by an attempt they made in the summer of 1942 to get control of the U.S. Tenth Air Force, which, it will be remembered, had been assigned the primary mission of supporting China. On 3 July, just after Chiang's Three Demands had arrived in Washington, when it appeared possible that China might give up its struggle against the Japanese, Air Marshal Evill sent General Arnold a letter recommending that agreed directives be sent to the American and British commanders in India, elucidating the terms of the newly completed Arnold-Slessor-Towers Agreement on aircraft assignments. That document provided that: "American air combat units assigned to theatres of British strategic responsibility will be organized in homogeneous American formations. They will be under the strategic control of the appropriate British Commander-in-Chief." Consequently, the British air marshal suggested a directive which would place the Tenth Air Force under the strategic control of the Air Officer Commander-in-Chief, India, and assign it primarily to the defense of India and Ceylon. However, the Tenth Air Force would "also be employed whenever possible in offensive operations in Burma and to give all possible support to China." Since the reductions in allocations to the British under the Arnold-Slessor-Towers Agreement would necessitate reductions in assignments to the RAF, including the RAF detachments in India, the British felt that compensating aircraft should be sent from the United States to reenforce the Tenth Air Force.[84]

One can well imagine the reactions of the Joint Chiefs of Staff to this proposal, received at a time when the Generalissimo was demanding 500 combat planes, three American divisions, and an air transport system many times expanded. Their feelings were increased by word that Air Marshal Sir R.E.C. Peirse in India had complained about the transfer of the major part of the Tenth Air Force to the Middle East, a move which had been made because of urgent requests from the British. Pointing out that the British had been responsible for this transfer, the JCS informed Air Marshal Evill that, "due to prior commitments of the Tenth Air Force to the support of China, it would be unwise at this time to remove it from the direct control of General Stilwell. Such a move would have a very serious effect on Chinese morale...." The JCS felt confident that Generals Wavell and Stilwell could cooperate in use of the aircraft to ward off any attack on India or Ceylon or to support operations in Burma.[85]

The British were not satisfied, however, and later in July Air Marshal Evill again recommended to General Arnold that identical instructions to cooperate with each other be sent to Generals Wavell and Stilwell, including the statement that "the role of the 10th Air Force will include collaboration with the British in offensive operations in Burma to relieve pressure on China. In the event of a threat to India, the 10th Air Force will co-operate to defeat that threat." Since such a directive would restrict General Stilwell's freedom to decide where in China, Burma, and India his forces would most satisfactorily serve to carry out his principal mission of support of China, the Joint Chiefs of Staff stuck by their original decision and again turned down the British proposal.[86]

Once again in September the British recommended that General Stilwell be instructed to place himself at General Wavell's disposal in order that the Tenth Air Force might be used to provide adequate support for the operations then contemplated by the British in Burma during the approaching winter.[87] Again they were turned down, this time with the implication that, if the British would permit Chinese participation in the Burma operation, which they had refused, the Tenth Air Force would certainly furnish air support.[88]

The End of the "Three Demands"

By July 1942 it was apparent, even in Washington, that relations between General Stilwell and Generalissimo Chiang Kai-shek were far from harmonious. In May Madame Chiang informed General Marshall that the Generalissimo had entire confidence in General Stilwell, blaming the debacle in Burma not on him but on British staff inefficiency or negligence.[89] In July, however, when General Stilwell refused to agree to support Chiang's Three Demands on the grounds that his duties did not extend to procurement, Chiang took offense. Subsequently Madame Chiang tried without success to persuade General Stilwell to transmit a recommendation of the 500-plane program to Washington. When the Generalissimo tried to get two transport planes for his own use from those assigned to China under lend-lease, General Stilwell took advantage of the occasion to outline his conception of his own position:

    1. I am U.S. Government representative on any war council held in China. This means that I must present and maintain the policy of the United States of America as it is communicated to me and that in any such council no other status I may hold is effective.

    2. I am in command of American forces in China, Burma, and India and therefore have responsibility beyond the limit of China war theatre.

. . . .

    3. I am charged with the supervision and control of lend-lease materials and am to decide the place and time that title passes. After title passes, Generalissimo controls disposition of the materials. I was given this responsibility to ensure that American Lend-Lease equipment would be employed solely for the effective prosecution of the war and in such matters I act as the representative of the President who can under the law recall Lend-Lease materials any time prior to delivery.

    4. I am the Chief of Staff of the Generalissimo's Joint Staff which functions when forces of the Allies carry on operations in the China war theatre in conjunction with the Chinese Army.

. . . .

> 5. And intrinsically I have my basic status as an officer of the U.S. Army sworn to uphold the interests of the U.S.A.
> 6. Within above limitations my only objective is the effective prosecution of the war, our common cause.[90]

Clearly the Generalissimo had not been informed of all the agreements his representative, Mr. Soong, had made in Washington, in particular the directive of the MAB that lend-lease consignments for China were to be sent to General Stilwell in India for transfer by him to the Chinese at the time and place he might designate, for Chiang had a different view of General Stilwell's position. He considered that as his Chief of Staff General Stilwell was subject to his orders. At once Chiang sent a message to Mr. Soong to pass on the President, indignantly stating his own views.

> I have always held in high esteem both the status and the duties assigned to General Stilwell. I have refrained from issuing orders to him in my capacity of Supreme Commander in the Chinese theatre of war. However, General Stilwell has maintained throughout that he is the representative of the President of the United States and has acted accordingly. I refrained from questioning this frame of mind and took no action....
> His attitude is since clarified by the memorandum in which he takes the position that the Supreme Commander in the Chinese Theatre of War must beg of him Lend-Lease supplies already delivered to China.
> What kind of situation does this create?
> ...I hold that the Chief of Staff of the Supreme Commander of the China theatre in the performance of the duties of his office within the scope of that theatre must obey orders of the Supreme Commander....
> For several months I have refrained from asking for war supplies from General Stilwell. The reason is simple; I did not want to run the risk of refusal by my own Chief of Staff.
> ...in view of the attitude adopted and the psychology revealed by General Stilwell I am compelled to request the United States Government to reconsider and clarify the duties of the Chief of Staff in the China theatre of war.[91]

The President's reply to this hot outburst supported General Stilwell's stand and attempted to outline clearly his actual status, as Chief of Staff to Chiang and Commander of American forces in China, and as U.S. representative on any war council and superintendent and controller of lend-lease aid to China. Upholding General Stilwell, the message pointed out that only for the first of these was he subject to Chiang's orders as Supreme Commander. In the second capacity he was responsible only to the United States Government. "If you find this method does not work," said the President, "we could separate the functions by limiting General Stilwell's authority to one function or the other, sending another General to undertake one of the functions, but not both."[92]

Unfortunately, instead of sending his answer directly to Chiang via General Stilwell, the President replied through Mr. Soong, through whom he had received the Generalissimo's complaint. Before transmitting the message, Mr. Soong talked with the President and subsequently sent not the reply that had been drafted in the War Department but a revised version that gave quite a different picture of General Stilwell's functions in China. He later told the Assistant Secretary of War that he had reported to the Generalissimo:

> ...General Stilwell has three functions. First, he is a member of the International Council acting as a representative of the President. Inasmuch as the International Council to date has scarcely functioned, this position has very little significance. If and when it becomes of great importance and if there is any embarrassment by reason of General Stilwell's acting as a member of it, we can cross that bridge when we come to it, but it obviously can be no source of embarrassment at the present time. Secondly, General Stilwell is a director of the Lend-Lease Administration in China. This does give rise to some embarrassment, apparently, and the President has suggested that this embarrassment could be largely if not entirely avoided if the determinations of what should be shipped to China could be worked out here in Washington. I could represent your views fully to the authorities here. Thirdly, General Stilwell also occupies the position of Chief of Staff to the Generalissimo and Commander-in-Chief of the American Forces in that area. These functions are well defined and need no further comment.[93]

Ignoring, as it did, General Stilwell's real functions in respect to lend-lease and command of American forces in China, Burma, and India to which Mr. Soong had agreed, this report created the total impression that the President was supporting the Generalissimo against his own representative. When Mr. Soong's action became known in Washington, steps were taken at once to remedy the situation.[94] Fortunately Mr. Lauchlin Currie was then in Chungking and was able to straighten things out with the Generalissimo, discovering in the process that Mr. Soong had never completely explained to Chiang the original agreement made in Washington on General Stilwell's role in China.[95] Despite this clear indication that Mr. Soong was not reporting to the Generalissimo the whole truth of what he was agreeing to in Washington, his views and recommendations continued to be accepted by the White House and no attempt was made to remove him.

At the end of August Mr. Currie, having smoothed things over temporarily between Chiang and General Stilwell, returned from Chungking and presented a full report of his impressions and views of what should be done in the China Theater. He had finally succeeded in explaining to the Generalissimo what General Stilwell's status was supposed to be and the basis for the strategic decision that Germany must be defeated first. As a result of the discussions Chiang had agreed to modify his demands. He no longer insisted on 500 combat aircraft as an immediate objective but set that number as a goal for attainment as soon as possible. Instead of three American divisions in India he now urged only that some American troops be sent there, perhaps one division. As for the 5,000-ton air transport program, that, too, he was willing to set as a goal rather than demanding it by August. On this point, however, Mr. Currie sided with the Generalissimo. He felt the project was not getting support in Washington and that many more planes than were actually in the area could be readily accommodated. He argued that it would take only eighty planes on 24-hour day operations to carry in 4,800 tons per month, which made the Generalissimo's figure of 5,000 tons far from unreasonable. Mr. Currie strongly urged compliance with the Generalissimo's modified demands, but he did not advocate exacting some conditions in return.

The chief difficulty Mr. Currie reported from his observations of the CBI Theater was the unfortunate combination of personalities handling Chinese-American relations. He recommended three individuals for replacement. First of these was Mr. T.V. Soong. Reciting several specific instances in which one side or the other had been misinformed, he stated that "Mr. Soong neither reflects accurately to us the attitudes of the Generalissimo nor interprets and explains our attitudes to him." The second was the American Ambassador, Mr. Clarence E. Gauss, whom Mr. Currie considered worse than valueless, since he was thoroughly disliked by the whole Chinese Government. Third candidate for replacement was General Stilwell. Mr. Currie pointed out that there had from the beginning been a basic misunderstanding between General Stilwell and Chiang as to the function of a chief of staff. General Stilwell, Mr. Currie reported, considered that it was actually a position of military command, while Chiang looked on it as merely the job of advisor to him. The relations of the two men were further complicated by the mutual admiration of General Chennault and Chiang Kai-shek and the position of General Chennault under General Bissell. Temperamentally General Stilwell and Chiang were quite different and they clashed frequently. So Mr. Currie recommended that General Stilwell be recalled.[96]

After his return to Washington, Mr. Currie stressed his opinion of General Stilwell's unsuitability for his position to both the President and General Marshall. Mr. Roosevelt was inclined to agree that General Stilwell had better be removed from China;[97] after General Marshall had discussed his own views with Secretary Stimson, General Marshall was convinced that General Stilwell should remain. The decision was based primarily on the fact that the agreed military objective in the theater was taking Burma, a project General Marshall believed neither British nor Chinese could manage alone and for which neither would agree to command by the other. General Marshall felt that an American officer well qualified as a troop leader was required for the job, and he considered no one better fitted than General Stilwell. On this, as on subsequent occasions, General Marshall persuaded the President to agree to retaining General Stilwell.[98] Thus, the line was clearly drawn in the matter between General Marshall and Mr. Currie, the President's two advisors on this question. As General Stilwell went down in the estimation of the White House group, General Chennault came up, and the two factions would conflict for many months to come.[99]

In the meantime, while Mr. Currie was still in China, OPD had studied General Gruber's report and recommended to General Marshall that, since the current program for the Asiatic Theater was all OPD considered warranted, the Generalissimo's Three Demands be considered only as a basis for discussion and that that discussion await the return of Mr. Currie.[100] After Mr. Currie brought back word of the modification of the Three Demands, OPD drafted a message for the President to send to Chiang, informing him of what the United States would do for China and incorporating some of the conditions General Stilwell and General Gruber had recommended. These included provision for active development of the long-delayed thirty-division plan and reorganization of his army with General Stilwell as advisor.[101] To these conditions Mr. Currie objected, and the draft was modified to omit them by the time it was sent General Stilwell for comment on 25 September.[102] General Stilwell, who had never been told whether or not the Generalissimo's Three Demands had previously been answered, recommended that the Chinese be queried on the progress of the thirty-division project and that the limitation of air transport be pointed out to them, making it clear that only through effort on the ground could Rangoon be reopened and an adequate supply route be established. Chinese action on the thirty-division plan "would be the best evidence to honest intentions and the best proof to the United States that it would be wise to continue shipments." General Stilwell also recommended that the organization of the Chinese Air Force not be specifically prescribed, as it was in the draft he had received.[103]

The President's reply to the Three Demands of late June, as it was finally received at General Stilwell's headquarters on 12 October for delivery to the Generalissimo, outlined a joint program designed to achieve "maximum combat effectiveness" from the joint U.S.-Chinese forces. First, the Tenth Air Force would continue to operate in support of the China Theater, built up to a strength of fifteen squadrons. At least 160 fighters, 48 medium bombers, 31 heavy bombers, and 13 photo reconnaissance planes, a total of 242 planes, were to be in the theater by 31 October. These, together with 218 planes scheduled for the Chinese Air Force,[104] came closer to the 500 planes Chiang had asked for. Second, in order to use to best advantage the lend-lease planes the United States had been sending to China, the Chinese Air Force should organize them into appropriate squadrons, under operational control of General Chennault. Third, beginning in October, subject to achievement of production objectives, two lend-lease and four U.S. Air Forces transport planes would be sent each month until a total of one hundred transports on the Hump project was reached. Although it was not specifically stated, this number of planes could be expected to deliver the Generalissimo's figure of 5,000 tons per month. Thus, although not within the time limitation which Chiang had set, two of his Three

Demands were being met. As for troops, however, it was carefully explained that it would be impracticable to try to send any U.S. divisions to the theater. Still, American support was promised, including lend-lease, for the training project at Ramgarh. By this time the practicability of a campaign to retake Burma was under discussion in Washington. This fact was reported to Chiang, and occasion was taken to inquire about the progress being made with the forces being organized at Yunnan for that operation as a basis for a practical reappraisal of lend-lease requirements. It was pointed out that, "due to the limitations of supply by air, there appears to be little justification for accumulating in India our vitally needed combat equipment beyond the needs of say 45,000 Chinese troops at Ramgarh and the available capacity of our Air Freight Route to China." The equipping of the thirty divisions would be completed after reopening of the Burma Road.[105]

Chiang Kai-shek received this word with some satisfaction. However, he continued to urge increasing the number of transports to 100 by 1 January and 150 by 1 March, and he suggested establishment of two new air routes from India to China to increase the air capacity. Both of these proposals were turned down in Washington.[106]

Chapter X

CHINA-BURMA-INDIA, 1942: STRATEGIC DEVELOPMENTS

    Against the background of friction over matters of supply and support in 1942, a strategic program for the CBI Theater was gradually being developed. For the first half of the year the Joint and Combined Chiefs of Staff attempted no precise definitions of strategic objectives in that area. Their discussions and their formal papers repeatedly included general statements about the necessity or the desirability of defending China, Burma, and India and of preventing the junction of German forces with Japanese through the Middle East; but they contained no plans for future campaigns to defeat the Japanese in that theater and to drive them out of the territory they had already overrun. China was looked on as a base for future operations, primarily air operations, against Japan, but these would have to await the availability of bombers and solution of the problems of maintenance, and they would probably not be undertaken until Germany had been defeated in Europe and the slow advance across the Pacific had brought the tide of battle to the shores of China. Beyond the task of improving, maintaining, and controlling the Burma Road in China General Stilwell went to the theater with no directive for specific operations.
    As in the Pacific area, so on the mainland of Asia it was the Japanese who made the initial decision as to where the war would be fought. They chose, rather than continuing their advance into the vastness of China where for some time preceding Pearl Harbor the situation had been maintained in a state of virtual equilibrium, to move into Burma after Indo-China, Thailand, and Malaya were safely under Japanese control. Conquest of this physically formidable country would not only cut off the only remaining ground supply route into China from the outside, but also safeguard the flank of the newly won Japanese territory in the Southwest Pacific and place Japanese forces in a position to push on into India or, if it should prove expedient, into southern China. The British in Burma, unprepared, untrained, outmaneuvered, although, initially at least, not outnumbered,[1] accepted a defensive role and, despite eleventh hour assistance from the Chinese, finally withdrew as many as possible of their men into India. At the same time the Chinese armies which had arrived late in the campaign were badly beaten also and their remnants withdrew into China, northern Burma, and India.

In Washington the defeat in Burma was accepted as another in the string of disasters and disappointments which the war had brought, and no plans were made to try immediately to regain military control. Loss of the Burma Road complicated the supply problem for China and the logical project to be undertaken next appeared to be an offensive that would ultimately restore the road to control of the United Nations.[2] However, while an operation by British or Chinese forces designed to recapture Burma was considered highly desirable, the louder demands of the other theaters of war on limited American resources in the spring of 1942 militated against even long range planning for a campaign with American forces in Burma.

In the theater the vanquished commanders set about planning for a return to the region whence they had just been driven. Even before General Stilwell emerged from the jungle he had begun to make plans for a campaign to drive the Japanese out of northern Burma. Similarly, the British under General Wavell had begun to outline an amphibious operation in southern Burma designed ultimately to recapture their colony and buttress the defenses of India on the east. At the same time a faction in China, led by General Chennault, began to argue that the best idea would be to check Burma off as lost and concentrate on building up air power in China for an immediate air offensive against the Japanese. In the second half of 1942 the Combined Chiefs of Staff were to be brought into the discussion.

At the end of April the final outcome in the Burma campaign was still not decided, but it had become evident that the best that could be hoped for was to be able to hold a strategic position in upper Burma. Although the Burma Road and its mouth at Rangoon had been lost, General Stilwell was hopeful that ground communications to China could be reopened from India and that Burma could ultimately be regained by an offensive from bases in Assam and northern Burma and concentrated effort on the road from Ledo across upper Burma on which work had been started by the British. General Stilwell had found the performance of the British military forces in Burma most disheartening. However, despite the corruption and inefficiency of the officers of the Chinese armies and the poor showing which they had made, General Stilwell had faith in the potential value of the Chinese soldier as a fighting man. Since it was apparent that he could count on no American troops for a campaign in Burma, and an all-out effort by the British seemed unlikely, General Stilwell proposed to use Chinese troops, those already scheduled for reequipment and retraining under the thirty-division plan and a second large group (100,000 men) that he would train under American officers in northern India. There he could use Chinese lend-lease equipment which had already arrived or which would be sent from the United States but could not be carried farther. Transportation facilities were not adequate to move large quantities of motorized equipment and heavy field pieces from India to China, but men could be marched from China to India if no other means of transportation was available.[3]

General Stilwell's training project met with approval in Washington where the War Department saw in it a way of easing their problems with lend-lease for China as well as a method of acquiring sizable forces for operations in the CBI Theater without having to send American divisions to that distant and unattractive region.[4] Chiang Kai-shek agreed in general to the plan. However, he doubted the possibility of setting it up within a reasonable length of time, and he hedged his agreement around with stipulations that half of the commanders of regiments and above should be Chinese instead of all being American as General Stilwell proposed and that under no circumstances should the Chinese soldiers be used for operations in India.[5] The latter point bothered the British also. Although they were eager to have as many troops as possible on hand in India in the event of a Japanese attack, they were fearful of having Chinese troops there in large numbers should the ever-lurking "Asia for the Asiatics" movement develop into an active military move for the independence of India. Chiang Kai-shek had shown too much interest in the Congress Party of India, a major source of irritation to the British. Moreover, it seemed politically undesirable to have a highly developed Chinese force in India when there was no immediate prospect of equipping Indian forces in the same fashion. The prospect of sending well-trained Chinese forces into Burma, where Chinese interests were already large, was scarcely more attractive.[6] In order to get full British agreement on the project, General Marshall had to bring pressure to bear on the British Chiefs of Staff.[7] However, arrangements were made by the fall of 1942, and General Stilwell's training project was set up under his command at Ramgarh in northern India, where the initial group of refugees from the Burma campaign was eventually augmented by 66,000 more Chinese soldiers flown in over the Hump.[8]

Shortly after General Stilwell's emergence from Burma he met with General Wavell and General Brereton at New Delhi to discuss future plans for the theater. He found General Wavell primarily interested in the possibility of a Japanese invasion of India and less enthusiastic than the two Americans about renewing military activity in Burma. Although the three generals reached no firm decisions at this time, General Stilwell and General Brereton did agree on plans for use of the Tenth Air Force, recently released by General Marshall from operations under British direction. In fulfilling the Tenth's basic mission of supporting the China Theater, they agreed, first priority should be given to air operations in Burma to protect the air transport line over the Hump. As soon as possible most of the fighters and one medium bomber squadron should be sent to China, where the American Volunteer Group was soon to be incorporated into the Tenth Air Force.[9]

Following the New Delhi meetings General Stilwell submitted a summary of his own strategic views to the War Department, again asking for American troops. "My belief in [the] strategic importance of China is so strong," he said, "that I feel certain a serious mistake is being made in not sending American Combat Units into this Theater to regain Burma, clear Thailand, and then from China force entry into the triangle Hanoi-Hainan-Canton from which control can be disputed of major enemy air lanes from Japan and Manchuria and enemy sea lanes in the South China sea." He felt that such action by American troops would raise Chinese morale and interest in continuing the war and help him in his efforts to organize Chinese forces for offensive action. Consequently he recommended that one or more American divisions be transferred to India "without delay."[10]

General Stilwell's plea was received with some sympathy in Washington, particularly since a report came in at the same time from Madame Chiang that Chinese morale had reached the lowest point in five years.[11] There was no dispute over the strategic objectives General Stilwell advocated. In response to his request for troops, however, sympathy was all General Stilwell received, for General Marshall and his staff did not consider the China Theater of sufficient strategic importance to warrant diverting from other projects the shipping necessary to transport large numbers of American troops to India and maintain them there.[12]

About a month later Chiang Kai-shek thrust his Three Demands upon General Stilwell. Probably not the least startling to Washington planners was the requirement of three American divisions in India by September to assist the Chinese in restoring the line of communications through Burma to China. However, when General Gruber arrived in Washington late in July to report on the situation in the CBI Theater, it was apparent that on this point he and General Stilwell were in agreement with the Generalissimo, at least to the extent that they felt that American troops, eventually to the strength of three divisions, should be sent to India. In his report to General Marshall, General Gruber explained that the Generalissimo's program required an American corps to cooperate with the Chinese to reopen the line of communications through Burma. General Gruber recommended that the corps be set as an objective and that at least one division be definitely scheduled for India, giving as reasons:

> China is potentially the best avenue of approach to Japan; there are *great* prospects of success and successes may become politically necessary; it will serve to galvanize the Chinese forces and British forces in India; it will insure the success of the India Training Plan; it will be possible to obtain at least twice an equivalent force of Chinese for offensive operations against Burma; it will force the British to undertake the Burma operation.

Although he understood that the British Joint Plans Section had recommended to the British War Office that a campaign to retake Burma be launched in September, after the monsoon, he doubted that the operation would actually be executed, for the British had appeared only halfhearted in their efforts to defend Burma earlier in the year and it was not vital to their interests to reoccupy it. General Gruber felt that the British attitude was that Burma was not essential to the defense of India and a strong China was not in accordance with British policy for Asia. He believed that the presence of American soldiers in the theater might spur both Chinese and British to more serious efforts and force the British to go through with their Burma campaign.[13]

General Gruber's pleas for troops and more equipment for the CBI Theater, like earlier ones from General Stilwell, were turned down. The first limited offensive in the Pacific was just getting under way with the landings on Tulagi and Guadalcanal, but the combined decision had long been made that an all-out effort in the Pacific must await the defeat of Germany, and the Joint Chiefs of Staff had no detailed plans for major operations against Japan. Although it was not yet beyond the realm of possibility that the basic strategy might be reversed, particularly if Russia collapsed,[14] that contingency was considered unlikely. If the larger area of the Pacific was to remain largely undeveloped, there was no compelling reason for increasing effort in the CBI Theater. Moreover, the old question of shipping capacity was still a controlling factor. Consequently, no American troops were scheduled for India.

Despite General Gruber's failure to accomplish much toward getting material support, his reports, coupled with those from General Stilwell, and the Generalissimo's strongly worded Three Demands with their ominous hint of a separate peace were not going unheeded by the JCS. Since mid-July the Combined Staff Planners had been working on an estimate of forces that would be required by the United Nations as of 1 April 1944, an estimate intended to serve as a basis for determining the required production of munitions.[15] Included among the six basic assumptions of their preliminary hypothesis as to what the strategic situation would be in all the theaters of war in the spring of 1944 was the general statement that "operations from India against Burma will be restricted to strategic defensive operations."[16] This CPS strategic hypothesis (CCS 97) was discussed by the Joint Chiefs of Staff in the atmosphere of disillusion and disappointment that followed the return of Admiral King and General Marshall from the meetings in London in July 1942 where almost all hope for execution of Roundup was lost and the substitution of Torch became a virtual certainty. The London decisions had so altered the outlook for 1944 that the JCS, and subsequently their British colleagues on the CCS, agreed that CCS 97 should go back to the planners for revision.[17] The new version (CCS 97/1) hastily prepared and dated 1 August, included eleven instead of six basic assumptions. There was no basic change in regard to the CBI Theater, for there had been no decisions about it in London, but the previous statement was expanded to read, "Operations from India against Burma to be restricted to such strategic defensive operations as are necessary to defend India and to encourage Chinese resistance." This wording survived an unsuccessful attempt by the British to make considerable revision in the paper by playing down the Pacific and building up the situation in the European Theater beyond what the Joint Chiefs of Staff considered had been agreed.[18]

Although most of the British suggestions were rejected when the JCS discussed the only slightly altered paper (CCS 97/2) on 11 August, Navy members expressed strong views that it put insufficient emphasis on the war against Japan. The Solomons operation had by that time been launched, and there could be no question of reducing the scope of commitments to the Pacific without inviting disaster. Word of a projected campaign to reopen the Burma Road had come both from the London discussions and from General Stilwell and General Gruber, together with numerous reports of low morale in China and threats from Chiang Kai-shek to make a negotiated peace. It was Admiral Leahy who pointed out the strategic relationship between the CBI Theater and the new limited offensives in the Pacific. "Any prospective operations which would not soon provide for aid to China would, in his opinion lead to the collapse of that country's resistance and thence to a very possible U.S. defeat in the Pacific. He therefore considered it essential that a specific commitment be made to open the Burma Road and that other means of aiding China should be adopted."[19] Thus it was at Admiral Leahy's suggestion that, although little else in the paper was altered, point No. 6 of the "Strategic Hypothesis" was changed to read, "Operations from India against Burma have been restricted to such strategic defensive operations as are necessary to defend India, to open the Burma Road, and otherwise to encourage Chinese resistance."[20]

The clear indication of JCS views given at this meeting apparently encouraged the Army OPD, then engaged in studying General Gruber's report, to propose acceptance of one of his recommendations, namely, that the Chief of Staff, U.S. Army, present a paper to the Combined Chiefs of Staff, "requesting their consideration of the necessity for the retaking of Burma after the monsoon season." Perhaps by presenting the matter formally to the CCS, General Marshall could force the British into action and thereby partially satisfy the unhappy Generalissimo without sending Americans to fight in CBI.[21] At the meetings with the British Chiefs during the Prime Minister's visit to Washington in June, the Joint Chiefs had learned of British interest in reopening the Burma Road by a land campaign from Assam and amphibious operations to retake Rangoon.[22] General Marshall and Admiral King had been told in more detail of British plans for a Burma operation (by then known as Anakim) when they were in London in July.[23] However, it was not a combined project, and the British apparently did not bring it up for combined discussion. Now, in mid-August, there was no clear indication of whether they intended to go through with it in the fall.

OPD's recommendation received ready support from General Marshall. Aside from strategical advantages to be gained, for many reasons it seemed logical at this time to undertake to recapture control of Burma. Morale in China was reported to be very low. The strong feelings of the Generalissimo had been demonstrated by his blunt demands for tangible evidence of U.S. interest in the Chinese cause and by his subsequent conflict with General Stilwell over that officer's position in the CBI Theater. Chiang's demands could hardly be fully satisfied, however, for limited resources and the stronger claims of other theaters of war militated against appreciable increases in commitments to the CBI Theater. Loss of the Burma Road meant that even if materials of war were set aside for the Chinese they could not be delivered by land. The substitute transport system by air over the Hump had to date proved disappointing. Airfields were inadequate, transport planes were few in number, the monsoon was introducing new and serious problems, and the loss of Burma placed the route in danger of disastrous attack. Whether air transport could be built up in time to a size sufficient to keep the Chinese in the war was questionable, and it was impractical to suppose that under existing conditions a military operation of considerable size in China itself could be supported.

Burma and the security of the Burma Road had long played an important role in U.S. thinking in regard to China. First lend-lease allotments had gone toward upkeep and improvement of the Road and for material to build a parallel railway from Burma to China. General Stilwell's orders had directed him to improve and maintain the Burma Road in China. Although there had been no official agreement on grand strategy since the fall of Burma, for production purposes the CCS in July accepted a study of strategic policy for 1942 and 1943 which included the objective, "without prejudice to... [the major combined offensive against Germany] prepare to reoccupy Burma in order to reopen land communications with China."[24] While this was not a commitment, it indicated a disposition toward renewing military action in Burma. Regaining control of that country and its ground route to China would increase many times the rate at which supplies could flow across the Chinese border and should immediately raise Chinese spirits and help safeguard the positions of U.S. forces in the Pacific by encouraging China to remain in the war against Japan. To be sure no American soldiers could be assigned to do the fighting in Burma; but perhaps the Chinese soldiers General Stilwell was planning to train at Ramgarh and the large numbers of troops under British command in India could carry out a successful campaign.

These and similar thoughts must have passed through the minds of the Army planners. They were probably recognized, if not defined, by General Marshall and the other chiefs. However, the memorandum that was drafted in OPD for General Marshall's signature and that he presented to the Combined Chiefs of Staff on 25 August based its recommendations for a Burma campaign primarily on strategic grounds. Pointing out that Japan was currently employing a quarter of its combat divisions and independent brigades in China and Burma, the memorandum warned that if these were released by the collapse of China they could be used to advantage by the Japanese in India, Australia, or possibly Siberia. In order to insure that the Chinese would continue to contain as many Japanese divisions, General Marshall recommended that the Combined Chiefs of Staff consider the problem of retaking Burma after the monsoon, with the objective of reopening the Burma Road.[25]

The other members of the Joint Chiefs of Staff readily agreed to General Marshall's proposal. General Arnold remarked that reopening of the Burma Road might possibly reduce pressure on the United States to convert medium bombers to transports in order to increase the capacity of the air route into China. Admiral King, aware of the difficulties of cooperation between British and Chinese, recommended that the supreme commander of the Burma operation should be a U.S. officer.[26] At the recommendation of the Joint Chiefs of Staff the Combined Chiefs of Staff referred the matter to the Combined Staff Planners to consider together with a study by the Combined Intelligence Committee which concluded that without economic or military assistance organized resistance in China might well cease, and that if Chiang Kai-shek were eliminated the Communists would probably continue to fight Japan, but the other Chinese armies would be more likely to give in.[27]

By this time Mr. Launchlin Currie had returned from his trip to China, bringing with him a proposed plan of operations which had been developed by General Stilwell and conditionally approved by Generalissimo Chiang Kai-shek and which became known in Washington as the "Generalissimo's Plan."[28] Mr. Roosevelt passed a copy to Admiral Leahy, who in turn, with the approval of the Combined Chiefs of Staff, gave it to the Combined Staff Planners.[29] Based on the assumption that the Chinese would push the project for reorganization and reequipment of thirty divisions and would prepare at once for the threatened Japanese invasion of Yunnan, the Generalissimo's Plan called for: first, a triple thrust from Assam into Burma, via Kalewa, Tamu, and Ukhrul-Homalin, using one American division ("an absolute necessity"), three British divisions,[30] and the Chinese who were to be trained at Ramgarh; second, a thrust by four Chinese Army Corps (12 divisions) south from Yunnan Province through Lashio, to Mandalay and west to Bhamo and Katha, where they would join the forces moving in from Assam; third, a holding attack by at least three Chinese Army Corps (9 divisions) south from the Yunnan-Indo-China border through Laokai toward Hanoi and Haiphong, supplemented by a Chinese offensive toward Canton; fourth, an offensive from Australia on New Guinea, Timor, and New Britain; fifth, an "all-out" naval offensive against Japanese sea communications in the West and Southwest Pacific. As the British-American-Chinese armies moved south through Burma they would swing toward the east, with Americans and Chinese pushing on into Thailand and Indo-China and British continuing south to Rangoon to reoccupy their own territory. Although the Chinese forces would require extensive training and reorganization and it would take considerable time to transport an American division to the area, even if it were sent from Australia as suggested, operations were scheduled to get under way between 15 November and 1 December 1942, in order to avoid bogging down during the monsoon season the following spring. The Generalissimo recommended that the supreme commander of this five-part operation be General MacArthur.[31]

Included with the Generalissimo's Plan, although not strictly a part of it, were papers prepared by American officers in the theater: two by General Chennault ("Air Force units required to support offensive operations in Burma and maintain defensive operations in central, eastern and northern China," and "Notes on Strategic Possibilities of a Small American Air Force in China"), one by Major General R.A. Wheeler, Commanding General, Services of Supply ("Monthly Shipping Tonnage Required from United States to Supply One Triangular Division in India"), one by Lieutenant Colonel E.H. Alexander, Assistant Air Officer ("Monthly Tonnage Requirements of Supplies to support 500 Airplane Air Force"), and one by General Bissell, Aviation Officer ("Resume of Aviation Situation in China Burma India Theater").

In his first paper, General Chennault assumed that the Chinese Air Force would continue responsible, as it had been under the AVG agreement, for all operations north of the Yangtze except the defense of Chungking. American air units would be responsible for the rest. General Chennault estimated that to support the contemplated ground operation in Burma, to continue defensive operations in central and eastern China, and to supply the Chinese Air Force would require a total of 530 combat planes in China plus replacements. To maintain a force of 500 planes, according to Colonel Alexander's study which also accompanied the Generalissimo's Plan, would require 14,606.9 tons per month, a fantastic figure at a time when tonnage being delivered over the Hump was still being measured in three figures.

General Chennault's other paper ("Notes on Strategic Possibilities of a Small American Air Force in China") made no mention of a ground campaign in Burma but gave instead the author's views of how much he could accomplish with a small air force, adequately supported. He pointed out that, although the Japanese controlled all the coast line of China as well as all of Indo-China and Thailand, with the exception of a narrow area along the Yangtze River, their occupation lacked depth and they did not have an efficient aircraft warning service. Thus their installations and their shipping were subject to surprise attacks. Their bases and their coastwise shipping were well within range of medium bombers operating from the numerous airfields in unoccupied China. General Chennault's own air forces, he said, had not only been able to bomb Japanese objectives repeatedly with astonishing success and little opposition, but also had inspired the Chinese people and armies to continue their resistance.[32] It was his belief that the Japanese air force could be destroyed or rendered incapable of supporting Japanese ground forces in China, and, in fact, that by cooperative action between a small, efficient air force and Chinese armies Japan could be defeated more quickly in China than anywhere else in the world. In this paper General Chennault did not say how big he thought the air force must be nor outline specific objectives for an air offensive. In a similar statement to General Stilwell at about the same time, however, he predicted that with 500 bombers and fighters and 100 transports, delivered over a period of five months, plus full authority, he could destroy much of the war material flowing through and around Formosa to the southern Pacific islands, inspire Chinese ground forces to action in occupied China, neutralize the Japanese air efforts in Burma and Indo-China; relieve the Japanese threat to India, safeguard the air transport line to China, and supply a successful offensive.[33]

General Bissell's paper on the aviation situation in the CBI Theater painted quite a different picture. Japanese bombers, he pointed out, could reach any landing field in unoccupied China, could concentrate at any point and had easy access to supply by sea. Wherever Japan wished to fight on the ground, it could maintain air control. The opposing Chinese Air Force consisted of fewer than 50 fighters and 50 bombers--"antiquated, worn-out, totally without spare parts, and totally unsuitable for combat operations against the Japanese military aircraft." China had a considerable number of reasonably good airfields, a heterogeneous supply of gasoline and bombs, and a unique warning net that could not, however, distinguish friendly and unfriendly aircraft. General Bissell was very pessimistic about the air transport service from India on which were dependent both the Chinese ground and air forces and the American air forces in China. Current plans called for operating seventy-two P-40's and eleven B-25's plus a few B-24's in China in addition to any operations by the Chinese Air Force. These would exhaust the supply of 100-octane gasoline in 5.9 months, 1000-pound bombs in 8, and 250-pound bombs in 4.7 months. "Unless some means can be found greatly to augment the tonnage delivered by air freight service," said General Bissell, "it is obvious that protracted air operations by any substantial air force from China will be impossible." His more practical approach to the question of air in China prevailed in Washington, and if serious consideration was given to General Chennault's paper there is no indication of it in the study by the Combined Staff Planners.

The CPS did, however, pay considerable heed to British ideas of what should be done in the CBI Theater. Shortly after the collapse of the Burma campaign the British had prepared an "Appreciation of the Problem of Reopening the Burma Road in the Autumn of 1942,"[34] a plan for an operation to be executed primarily by British forces in a British area of strategic responsibility. Although it was recognized that Chinese forces attacking from Yunnan could be very useful, the likelihood of the Chinese undertaking offensive operations was discounted and it was recommended that on security grounds it would probably be advisable to keep them in ignorance of British intentions concerning Rangoon. Rangoon was to be the first major objective in the British plan, for although the Japanese had already proved able to support two divisions overland from Thailand it was considered that their main line of communications for their forces in Burma was bound to be by sea through Rangoon. Moreover, the British felt that only a limited operation in upper Burma could be supplied over the poor roads that then existed, and, unless the Japanese line of communications was cut, the enemy could support larger forces than the British in that area.

According to the British study, the "most suitable plan" would be developed in three phases:

Phase I.

   (a) A sea-borne advance down the coast to Akyab and the establishment of air forces.

   (b) A diversionary advance into Upper Burma via Imphal, combined, if possible, with a Chinese offensive directed on Lungling.

   (c) A heavy and sustained air offensive directed primarily against the Rangoon and Mandalay areas and Japanese communications.

   (d) Attack by submarines, minelayers and light naval forces on Japanese sea communications with Rangoon.

These operations could be executed with reasonably small resources and considerable chance of success. The combined moves would set the stage for

Phase II.

   (a) Direct assault on Rangoon from the Gulf of Martaban and capture of the Rangoon-Pegu-Sittang area; or

   (b) The further establishment of air forces step by step down the coast of Burma to Bassein, followed by an assault on Rangoon and capture of the Rangoon-Pegu-Sittang area.

The choice between these alternatives was dependent upon the size of Allied naval forces in the Bay of Bengal. When Rangoon was in British hands and British forces had moved to the Pegu-Sittang area to cut Japanese land communications from Thailand, the operation would enter

Phase III.

   Advance on Mandalay from north and south; mopping up and consolidation.

The feasibility of the whole operation depended on preventing the Japanese from building up the strength of their defending air forces. As for timing it was considered unlikely that sufficient forces would be at hand to reopen the Burma Road between October 1942 and May 1943. However, in the winter of 1943 Akyab could probably be secured and possibly a limited land offensive from India into upper Burma could be undertaken. These would be first steps on the way and should serve to encourage the Chinese, improve morale in India, and keep the Japanese extended.

This British plan had not been officially submitted to the Combined Chiefs of Staff, but the British members of the Combined Staff Planners certainly introduced it into the discussions of the Generalissimo's Plan. The CPS report followed closely the conclusions of the British paper. The planners agreed that recapture of Burma and reopening of the Burma Road were important measures which should be taken to help sustain Chinese resistance. However, they decided that the Generalissimo's Plan was strategically unsound, for "the forces and resources necessary to launch an offensive on this scale are not available in the near future." The inadequacy of communications into northern Burma would limit the force that could be supported there to an estimated two divisions, insufficient for the operations contemplated. The CPS pointed out that for air support for this force it would be necessary to secure the airfields in the coastal strip of south Burma by a seaborne attack on Akyab, Rangoon, and Moulmein. For this operation there would probably not be sufficient landing craft or supporting naval forces in the area before April 1943. Consequently the operation to retake Burma could not be launched before April, when it would actually have to be postponed again because of the monsoon. That made October 1943 the earliest date on which large-scale operations could be begun. As for participation by the Chinese the CPS concluded that that was unlikely to be effective for some time, for they thought it doubtful that enough material could be provided to train and equip all the forces Chiang was promising. The planners noted that an estimated "600 [additional] transport aircraft would be required to supply the United States Air forces necessary to support the Chinese forces." It was hardly likely that so many would be provided. Nor was it likely that shipping and escorts would be available to move an American division to India.

The CPS reported to the CCS that, although the full-scale offensive could not be undertaken until October 1943, the British would have "appropriate forces and sufficient resources to launch a limited land offensive by December, 1942, as a first phase in their operations to recapture Burma and to bolstering Chinese morale." As had the British paper, so did the CPS report recommend that "for reasons of security" the Chinese not be told of British plans. They proposed that Chiang be let down gently with the information

> (a) That the British and the United States are firmly determined to recapture Burma and to re-open the Burma Road as soon as the necessary forces and resources are available.
> (b) The forces necessary to implement this plan cannot be available in the immediate future in view of the existing shortage of supplies and equipment.
> (c) That the Generalissimo's plan has contributed many well supported suggestions which will be most helpful in determining appropriate lines of action when the available means make such operations in the Burma area feasible.[35]

On 18 September the CCS approved recommendations of the JCS (originally drafted by OPD) which neither accepted nor rejected the CPS report. The Combined Staff Planners were directed to estimate air, ground, and naval forces required to recapture Burma and reopen the Burma Road before the next monsoon season and the effect such an operation would have on other operations current or projected. The

Combined Chiefs of Staff authorized the Joint Chiefs to direct General Stilwell to inform Chiang that the CPS were studying possible action to retake Burma, and the Combined Chiefs agreed that the Joint Chiefs should draft a message from the President to Chiang along the same lines. Sir John Dill reported that General Wavell was in fact preparing a limited operation to capture Akyab during the winter 1942-1943, and the CCS agreed that the possibility of coordinating this action with U.S. operations in the southwest Pacific should be investigated.[36] Thus the CPS went to work on a detailed study of practical possibilities of offensive action in Burma, this time provided with copies both of the British "Appreciation" and with General Stilwell's own differently worded version of the Generalissimo's Plan.[37]

While the CPS study was being prepared, General Wavell and his planners in India were developing details of their contemplated operation in southwest Burma, and their thoughts not unnaturally ran to the desirability of assistance from the U.S. Tenth Air Force. Despite two previous vain attempts to achieve some sort of control of it, General Wavell tried again, this time serving notice on the British Chiefs of Staff that, if it was intended that he have American help, he must have a definite arrangement placing all U.S. air forces in India at his disposal. The chiefs directed Sir John Dill to ask the U.S. Joint Chiefs to have General Stilwell put himself at General Wavell's disposal in Delhi to plan support by the Tenth Air Force for the action in Burma during the coming winter.[38] Sir John Dill passed the word along to General Marshall with little enthusiasm[39] and received a strongly negative reply. Since the greatest contribution being made to Chinese morale was the activity of the Tenth Air Force, withdrawal of it from General Stilwell's command would not only create a strategical situation unfavorable for him but would also undoubtedly enrage the Generalissimo. General Marshall further put himself on record as opposed to the British insistence on secrecy concerning the project for Burma, taking the stand that it was a subject of vital importance to the Chinese and that Chinese participation in the Burma Campaign was most desirable. Moreover, he pointed out that if the Tenth Air Force were put under British command the necessity of explaining the reason for diverting it from its mission of supporting China would undoubtedly disclose the Burma plans to the Chinese. Again, as he had before, General Marshall stated his belief that satisfactory arrangements could be worked out by the local commanders.[40]

Combined discussions in Washington obviously had not convinced the British of the desirability of combined operations on a large scale in Burma, but they had convinced General Marshall and his top planners not only that a campaign to recapture Burma and reopen the Burma Road must be undertaken, but also that such a campaign should be a cooperative effort of Chinese and British ground forces with American participation, primarily in the air.[41] In the theater General Stilwell's attempts to achieve an agreement with British and Chinese commanders on a three-way operation met with considerable opposition, not least of which resulted from the fact that neither was willing to accept command by the other. It appeared to him that both were willing, if not anxious, to make no major move and wait for the Americans to do it.

General Stilwell reported in early September that General Wavell had no enthusiasm for anything but a purely British operation, and General Stilwell doubted that the British were sincere in their talk even of that.[42] His attempts to increase the size of his training project for Chinese soldiers at Ramgarh were so thoroughly blocked in Delhi that General Marshall had to bring the matter up with the British Chiefs through Sir John Dill in order to settle it.[43] As for the Chinese General Stilwell felt that if the Generalissimo were convinced of British cooperation in a Burma campaign he would furnish twenty divisions. As it stood, however, Chiang was still delaying on the long promised thirty division project, apparently at least half convinced that an increased air force and air transport system might render ground operations in Burma unnecessary. While agreeing in principle to the three-way plan for a campaign to retake Burma, he was making little effort to prepare his troops to participate there or elsewhere. Consequently, General Stilwell urged that the British be forced into action and that pressure be put on Chiang to make definite commitments in return for the material assistance he sought from the United States.

The long delayed reply to the Generalissimo's three blunt demands of the preceding June provided a convenient vehicle to present these matters to him with some force as well as to include the President's announcement of planning in Washington for a campaign in Burma. So it was that the message as sent not only stated what the United States was planning to send to China but also mentioned specific items on which Chinese action was expected. Chiang was informed that, although shipping shortages and the demands of other theaters made it impracticable to send U.S. divisions to the CBI Theater, U.S. planners were developing the plan that he and General Stilwell had tentatively agreed on, and it was firmly stated that "Burma must be recaptured in order to establish a practical supply route to China."[44]

In October and November General Stilwell gradually made progress toward getting local British and Chinese cooperation with his project. After discussion with the British he took over responsibility for construction of the road from Ledo to the Hukawng Valley.[45] The Ramgarh training program was increasingly promising, and arrangements were finally made to set up the thirty division plan.[46] The Chinese General Staff agreed that thirty divisions would be assigned to the project, reduced to twenty, and those brought up to full strength. This was the force that trained at Yunnan under American instructors and became known as the Yunnan or the "Y" Force. From both British and Chinese, however, General Stilwell encountered difficulties in the matter of which should command a combined military operation in Burma. In the midst of discouragingly slow negotiations, Mr. T.V. Soong appeared in Chungking, and he succeeded in straightening out some of the differences between Chiang and General Stilwell over command.[47] By December it appeared that the operation would be begun with the British commanding in the south, General Stilwell commanding the Ramgarh forces in the northwest, and the Generalissimo himself commanding the Chinese forces from Yunnan. Who would take over when the three forces merged was left for future decision.[48]

In the meantime a subcommittee of the Combined Staff Planners had been working on the "estimate of the air, ground, and naval forces necessary to recapture Burma and reopen the Burma Road at the earliest possible date and prior to the next monsoon season, [including] ...the effects of such an operation on other operations current or projected." By 30 October the study had been completed, approved by the CPS with slight modification, and a six-page summary of the bulky study (seventy-five pages) submitted to the Combined Chiefs of Staff.[49]

The CPS conclusions bore a strong resemblance, even in wording, to those of the earlier British "Appreciation," but the plan of campaign provided also for General Stilwell's dual advance by Chinese troops from Assam and Yunnan into Burma. However, the CPS pointed out that overland supply routes were limited, and consequently the operation should be mainly amphibious. In order to be completed before the monsoon, action would have to be begun by 1 February 1943. The plan, like the British plan, was outlined in three phases:

(a) *Phase I:*

An amphibious attack on the Akyab area, and establishment of air forces there.

An advance into Upper Burma from Assam, combined with an offensive from Yunnan directed on Lashio.

A heavy and sustained air offensive directed primarily against the Rangoon and Mandalay areas and Japanese communications with Rangoon.

(b) *Phase II:*

Direct assault on Rangoon from the Gulf of Martaban and capture of the Rangoon-Pegu-Sittang area; or, the further establishment of air forces step by step down the coast of Burma to Bassein, followed by an assault on Rangoon and capture of the Rangoon-Pegu-Sittang area; or, landings on the beaches from Moulmein to Amherst, advance overland on Rangoon, at the same time blocking routes from Thailand.

The choice of plan in Phase II to be left to the Commander in Chief of the theater [not designated].

(c) *Phase III:*

Advance on Mandalay from north and south; mopping and consolidation.

It was estimated that this campaign would require use of six Chinese divisions from Yunnan and ten infantry divisions, one armored division, and one parachute brigade from India. Including attrition replacements for one month, it would require 510 fighter planes, 544 bombers, 35 reconnaissance planes, and 100 transports. To support the operation, it was recommended that the Eastern Fleet should include not less than six battleships, four carriers, four heavy cruisers, twelve light cruisers, twenty-four destroyers, and twenty submarines, as well as assault shipping and landing craft to lift two infantry divisions and one armored brigade. Such a force would prove extremely useful in any extension of operations to Malaya and Sumatra, objectives which were certainly in the minds of the British although no mention of them was made in this paper. When the advantages and the disadvantages of the Burma operation were weighed, it appeared that the former predominated. However, from their study of the forces required, the CPS concluded that the necessary means could not be assembled before the next monsoon season. The supply of landing craft and troops trained in amphibious operations would be particularly short. Consequently, the planners concluded that it would not be practicable to undertake the operation before the fall of 1943.

At the CCS meeting on 6 November the Joint Chiefs of Staff recommended that this study be returned to the Combined Staff Planners for further consideration of the logistical problems involved, a question that had been more fully treated in the longer paper which the Joint Chiefs did not see. They also inquired what *could* be done toward the recapture of Burma before the next monsoon season and proposed that the paper be revised in the light of the situation on 15 December. At the suggestion of Sir John Dill it was directed that the revision be correlated with current and projected operations in the Southwest Pacific, the Middle East, and the Mediterranean, especially in regard to timing, logistics, and availability of resources. In addition, the planners were to take into consideration General Wavell's plans for operations in southern Burma. The resultant paper was not completed until mid-January. By then the limited British offensive toward Akyab had already begun and the Combined Chiefs of Staff, meeting at Casablanca, had developed a program for Burma without it.[50]

In December Colonel Thomas S. Timberman, who had been sent out to the CBI Theater to discuss the views of the War Department with General Stilwell, returned to Washington to report on the situation as he found it. By this time it had been accepted that the large scheme for retaking Burma could not be undertaken in the spring of 1943 and the planning at General Stilwell's headquarters was concentrated on a limited offensive using available forces with the objective of opening up northern Burma and building up ground supply routes into that region sufficient to support the forces which would be advancing from Assam and China. The plan was for a British corps to attack from Assam via Imphal to the Chindwin River, while two divisions of Chinese troops from Ramgarh advanced from Ledo through the Hukawng Valley toward Bhamo, and six Chinese divisions under Chiang's personal command drove from Yunnan toward Bhamo. The immediate objective was to take and hold a line from Akyab to

Myitkyina. As the forces advanced, supporting roads would be built. These would be developed into a land route from Ledo through northern Burma to China to tie into the Burma Road.[51] A project to reopen a ground supply line seemed certain of support from the Chinese and might encourage the British to proceed with a supporting campaign to cross the Chindwin. The fighting would be done by British and Chinese soldiers, but the road construction was a project for Americans, and General Stilwell's plans called for over 60,000 tons of engineering equipment and 6,000 engineering troops.[52]

Up to this time General Stilwell had received comparatively little material assistance from the United States. When he asked for American troops he was refused with words of encouragement. Chiang's requests for large numbers of men, planes, and equipment similarly had had little effect on established programs for the theater. The reply was always that the program of supply would be carried out as it had been scheduled, and that shipping shortages and the demands of other areas of war prevented any increase in what had been promised earlier. The resultant scarcity of visible evidence of U.S. military interest in the CBI Theater had sorely disappointed General Stilwell and caused considerable difficulty in his attempts to get British and Chinese support for his project in Burma. Early in November General Stilwell submitted a list of items essential for his project, similar to that brought back by Colonel Timberman. He was told that only a fraction, virtually nothing more than was already scheduled, would be provided.[53] His strong reaction to the noncommittal response to his request and Colonel Timberman's support of his plea caused the War Department and General Marshall to reconsider the matter.[54]

On 7 December 1942 General Marshall presented the matter of the Joint Chiefs of Staff. After outlining the progress General Stilwell had made toward preparing for a limited operation in Burma, General Marshall pointed out that if it were successful in opening up a supply route into China greater amounts of gasoline, bombs, and maintenance equipment could be transported for the air force which was already accomplishing great things in China and which promised more to come. The emphasis of his remarks, and apparently of the whole consideration of the problem in Washington at the time, was not on the feasibility of a supply route from Ledo to China but on the availability of men and equipment to execute the plan for north Burma. General Marshall told the JCS of the things General Stilwell needed: 63,000 cargo tons of equipment and 5,000-6,000 men, most of them to be shipped during January 1943. The troop lift, General Marshall felt, must come from Army and Navy shipping; but he considered the projected operation of such importance that cargo shipping should be taken from lend-lease or similar commitments. Consequently he had drafted a memorandum to be sent to the President, presenting the situation and recommending that he direct the War Shipping Administration to increase allotment of shipping to the Army to 40,000 tons in January and 23,000 tons in February.[55]

In discussing the matter at the next JCS meeting General Marshall suggested that the troops in question might have to come from reenforcements planned for the Southwest and South Pacific whose gear had already departed for those areas. He emphasized the dependence of the operation on the availability of shipping, a factor that would be affected by whether or not it was decided to attempt to occupy Sardinia in the spring. The British at this time appeared to favor such a move following completion of the North African campaign, and there was some sympathy for it in Washington. However, on this occasion Vice Admiral Russell Willson spoke out strongly, saying that "operations in Burma appeared to him to be an immediate matter, not to be deferred because of proposed operations in Sardinia." All the naval representatives present appear to have supported a Burma operation in principle although they were not well informed as to what would be entailed. At Admiral King's suggestion, it was decided to send the memorandum about the shipping to the President for his views and to refer General Marshall's paper to the Joint Staff Planners for a study of its implications and to the recently established Joint Strategic Survey Committee (JSSC) for comment and recommendations as to the advisability of undertaking the operation.[56]

Approval of the project for the CBI Theater and recommendation that the requisite shipping arrangements be made came through from both of these committees in time for discussion at the JCS meeting of 15 December 1942. General Marshall and Lt. General Brehon Somervell were able to report that the necessary shipping, both cargo and personnel, had already been provided. When Admiral King suggested that it might be necessary to obtain British concurrence for the operation in Burma, General Marshall said he would rather expedite provision of General Stilwell's forces first and then seek British assistance and concurrence.[57]

Meanwhile another crisis had arisen which in General Stilwell's view threatened to jeopardize all the progress he had made toward getting the British and the Chinese to cooperate on a campaign in Burma. On 1 December the air transport service over the Hump from India to China was transferred to the Army Air Transport Command (ATC) with the anticipation that direct control from Washington would render the operations more efficient and insure more effective support.[58] A week later ATC informed General Stilwell that twelve C-87's that had been scheduled to be available in the theater on 15 December would be delayed from one to four months. General Stilwell immediately complained loudly to General Marshall:

> ...If the meager means promised this theater cannot be depended upon to arrive the Chinese cannot be expected to continue with present plans.... The important aspect of the case is not the gain or loss of a few planes but that the US has once more fallen down on a promise of aid.... Either the War Department is or is not interested in having the Chinese continue this fight. If not, it would be better to close out here....We

have set up an offensive and with pitifully scanty means the Chinese are ready to throw in a respectable force to make it go. The British have all along been lukewarm in their cooperation. ...The obvious way to help this situation is to get tough with the British, who have a million and a half men on the rolls in India, and to send at once to this theater a substantial air reinforcement, both combat and transport planes, drawn from anywhere, even though the need elsewhere appears great. Up to now other theaters have been favored at the expense of this one. For once this one should be favored at the expense of some other.... I recommend as strongly as it can be stated that a material increase be made at once in our help to China, that two groups of fighters, one group of medium bombers and fifty additional transport planes be sent to India immediately, and that the Chinese 3500 ton program be raised to 10,000 monthly beginning now....[59]

General Stilwell's agitation may well have strengthened General Marshall's view that his efforts should be supported. General Marshall took steps to see that the C-87's were put back on schedule,[60] and action was taken at once to provide the other items General Stilwell had requested.[61]

Although General Stilwell was given some material support, his attempts to secure cooperation from the British in India were not supported by a firm American-British agreement at the top level as to what action was to be taken in Burma. In the theater, General Stilwell's concept of military action in Burma was opposed by some of the officers on both the American and the British staffs. Differing views of the Burma situation were being brought forcibly to the Joint Chiefs' attention even as they were deciding to assist his plan with men and equipment. While General Stilwell was carrying on serious discussions with General Wavell, trying to overcome his reluctance to agree to try to advance British troops very far into Burma lest they reach a spot where they could not be supported when the monsoon began, a considerable uproar was caused in Washington by a report submitted to the Navy Department by a Marine Corps officer who had been stationed in China as naval attaché. In his report, Lieutenant Colonel James M. McHugh strongly criticized General Stilwell and five of his subordinates for their lack of comprehension of air strategy and their plans for a ground campaign to recapture Burma, even going so far as to recommend that the "war in the Chinese Theater would be materially aided by removing Stilwell and Bissell." With his report he enclosed a plan that had been drawn up by General Chennault for Mr. Wendell Willkie when he visited Chungking in October 1942. Colonel McHugh had left China in November, stopping en route to the United States to talk with General Wavell, with whom he discussed his views of the impracticability of the Burma campaign and the preferability of General Chennault's suggestions. He also reported having discussed with Chiang Kai-shek the desirability of replacing General Stilwell with General Chennault in the China Theater.

Colonel McHugh's report was sent by the Navy to the War Department early in December. The insubordination implied in it and the difficulties which it appeared he might have put in General Stilwell's path by his conversations with General Wavell were, in General Marshall's view, inexcusable, particularly during time of war. Consequently General Marshall presented the matter formally to the Joint Chiefs of Staff, stating that

> Colonel McHugh's action has caused irreparable harm to the war effort proposed by the U.S. Chiefs of Staff in the China and India Theaters, having also in mind the effect on the situation in the Southwest Pacific.... Condoning Colonel McHugh's conversations with General Wavell would involve a complete renunciation of our confidence in General Stilwell. But what is even more important it would, in effect, place all theater commanders under the Joint Chiefs of Staff on an extremely fragile basis.

Disciplining Colonel McHugh was not within the province of the JCS, but a repetition of such action could perhaps be prevented. General Marshall recommended that the President be requested to issue a military order placing all military and naval attachés under control of the theater commander. Admiral Leahy expressed considerable doubt that the President would be willing to issue such an order since attachés were basically officials of the Department of State. However, with substitution of "instructions" for "military order," the Joint Chiefs agreed to forward General Marshall's recommendation to the President. Mr. Roosevelt, however, did not approve such blanket action, agreeing rather to take action in individual cases when necessary.[62] How much effect Colonel McHugh's opinions had on British and Chinese commanders is not known.

General Chennault's plan, which Colonel McHugh had so strongly supported, was a remarkable one but not entirely new. A similar program, although not with such specific detail, had come to the attention of the Joint Board while it was setting up the first schedules for aircraft deliveries to China in the spring of 1941.[63] General Chennault claimed that, if given full authority, he could bring about the defeat of Japan with an air force composed of 105 fighters of modern design, 30 medium bombers, 12 heavy bombers, 30 two-motored transports, increased later by 17 two-motored and 20 four-motored transports, plus 30 per cent replacements in fighters and 20 per cent in bombers. General Chennault based his claim on confidence in his standing with the Chinese and in his ability to force the Japanese to fight him where he chose. He would first defeat the Japanese air force in China, then render their shipping within range of air bases in China ineffective, then, with the 12 heavy bombers, reduce the industrial potential of the mainland of Japan itself.[64]

It does not appear that the Chennault plan was submitted directly to the War Department at this time. Although OPD did discuss it, they seem not to have been concerned primarily with the feasibility of the operation as outlined but rather with the relationship of air operations from China to General Stilwell's campaign in upper Burma. This is as would be expected, for General Chennault was, after all, under General Stilwell's command and normally only plans that came via the chain of command would be studied. Colonel Timberman had, in fact, reported that General Stilwell himself did not envisage operations by a million-man American army in Burma and China but that he concurred in General Chennault's plan for air operations.[65] Certainly, however, General Stilwell did not approve it as an alternative to a ground campaign in Burma. Without making a commitment as to whether General Chennault could actually accomplish what he promised with a limited air force, OPD pointed out that General Stilwell's campaign was designed to open a supply route into China and to protect more adequately the existing air transport route, both of which factors would increase the practicability of maintaining air forces for offensives from China bases. This view was adopted by General Marshall as he urged support with men and equipment for General Stilwell's campaign.[66]

Although General Marshall and most of the War Department were standing firmly behind General Stilwell at the end of 1942, Colonel McHugh was by no means alone in his antagonism to him. From numerous others, adverse reports had been coming into Washington, a large proportion of them directly to the White House, to the President or to Mr. Hopkins, who had become a supporter of General Chennault. The details of the Stilwell-Chennault disagreement are not part of the history of the Joint Chiefs of Staff. Nevertheless, certain aspects of it should be brought to the reader's attention. By integration of his American Volunteer Group into the U.S. Army, General Chennault had been placed under General Bissell, with whom he had a long history of disagreement. He chafed under the restrictions and the formal procedures the new arrangement entailed. Nor was he happy over the prospect of employing his planes in support of the proposed campaign in Burma, limiting their independent operations in China where targets were plentiful. With no clear understanding of the tremendous logistical problem involved, he had developed a dramatic plan for defeating Japan with air power alone and sold it to the Generalissimo, to whose imagination it appealed as an easy way to victory. Thus, although apparently willing to participate in the campaign in northern Burma, Chiang found numerous excuses for delaying and numerous reasons for not agreeing to essential details.

In addition to the Stilwell-Chennault differences, of course, there were obvious difficulties in the Stilwell-Chiang relations. These were by no means entirely the result of General Stilwell's undiplomatic personality. In large part his impossibly complicated mission and the lack of firm support and clear direction from Washington were responsible for the difficulties he had encountered in trying to cooperate with Chiang Kai-shek. In Washington by the end of 1942 the unpleasantness was strongly felt, and a difference of opinion had begun to develop between the War Department and the

White House, as General Marshall continued to support General Stilwell despite opposition.

At the end of December President Roosevelt, apparently convinced that General Chennault's capabilities were not being realized, suggested that he be given a task force of 100 planes, independent of General Stilwell's command, to operate against the Japanese north of the Yangtze River on and near the seacoast.[67] General Marshall rejected the idea because of its impracticability. If the planes already under General Chennault's command (seventy-six fighters and twelve medium bombers) were withdrawn north of the Yangtze, the Chinese operations from Yunnan into Burma which General Chennault was supposed to be supporting would be jeopardized. On the other hand, if 100 more planes were to be sent to the theater General Marshall felt that they should go to General Stilwell, who had requested additional air support for the Burma campaign. In any event the size of the air force that could be maintained was limited by the capacity of the Hump traffic to supply it.[68]

It appears from the records that General Marshall had not shown General Arnold his answer to the President's memorandum, although he may have asked for suggestions as to what the reply should be. In any event two days later General Arnold sent a memorandum on the same subject to General Marshall, stating his belief that,

> because of [Chennault's]...demonstrated accomplishments, his background of experience in China, and his peculiar knowledge of enemy air tactics and technique,...he would, if his present force was augmented by the addition of 1 Bomb Squadron (M) and if he was allowed freedom of action to strike targets of opportunity, be able with this small force to cause the Japanese a vast amount of shipping and air attrition as well as a considerable disruption of vitally important coast-wise shipping.

General Arnold recognized that at present General Chennault must operate in support of the limited objective offensive in Burma, and consequently he proposed no immediate action. However, he recommended

> that the principle of the establishment of a separate air force in China with an assigned mission, be accepted and that as soon as the supply problem can be overcome, action be initiated to establish a separate air force in China, commanded by General Chennault, composed of 1 Fighter Group and 2 Bomb Squadrons (M), with the assigned mission of operating north and south of the Yangtze River and on or near the Chinese seacoast against the Japanese.[69]

General Marshall, however, had already sent his comments on the suggestion to Admiral Leahy and the problem of an independent air force in China was left for later discussion.[70]

It is clear that General Marshall stood squarely behind General Stilwell and his proposed campaign in northern Burma. There was no such enthusiasm, however, from the British and the Chinese. To

General Stilwell, trying to reach agreement on important aspects of the operation, it appeared that both General Wavell and the Generalissimo were delaying unnecessarily. General Stilwell had little patience with their arguments, feeling strongly the importance of retaking Burma and reopening ground communications with China.[71]

General Wavell was apparently reluctant to agree to an operation unless success was assured. His great fear was that his troops might get so far into Burma that they could not be supplied during the rainy season. Corollary to this was a dread of malaria. Consequently he hesitated to commit himself to moving even as far as the Chindwin River. In their initial stages the advances by the Chinese from Ledo and Yunnan would have little effect on the British move toward the Chindwin. Although he considered both undertakings impractical, he thought that the concentration of troops in Yunnan was useful for defensive purposes and that the opening of a ground route into China would have great advantages. He was very dubious, however, as to whether the logistic arrangements for these operations were adequate.[72]

The difficulties of trying to get cooperation from the British were minor compared with the difficulties of trying to get cooperation from the Chinese. Late in December, just as the problem of who was to command the Yunnan force, which had been a stumbling block, appeared settled, the Generalissimo insisted that he would not move his troops into Burma without naval support in the Bay of Bengal.[73] He reported to the President that the Prime Minister had assured the members of the Pacific War Council in the spring that before the end of the next monsoon season eight battleships, three aircraft carriers, and various other vessels would be in the Indian Ocean to support the Burma campaign. Now Vice-Admiral Sir J.F. Somerville, Commander of the Eastern Fleet, had announced that there would be no such force. Moreover, General Wavell originally had promised seven divisions for operations in Burma. Now this had been reduced to three. So Chiang informed the President that unless the British carried out their part of the undertaking it would be impossible for him to do his.[74]

It appeared in Washington that the Generalissimo was confusing the operation in northern Burma before the rains in 1942 with the full-scale Anakim. No one could recall any such promise of naval support and it hardly seemed essential for the success of the campaign in northern Burma.[75] However, General Marshall at least felt that every effort should be made to get the support of the Chinese for the project. In a non-committal reply to Chiang's message on 2 January 1943, the President stressed the importance of Chinese help and agreed to "take up with the highest allied authorities at the earliest possible date the matter of opening the Burma Road without any avoidable delay.[76] Although they were scheduled to meet with the British at Casablanca in about ten days, General Marshall circulated to Admirals Leahy and King and General Arnold a proposed message from the President to the Prime Minister which the Joint Chiefs of Staff then submitted to Mr. Roosevelt at a meeting at the White House on 7 January 1943. General Marshall recommended, and the draft message to Mr. Churchill urged, that something be done to insure that the Chinese would cooperate fully in the approaching operations. Presented with a summary of the Generalissimo's message to the President, the Prime Minister was asked to suggest assurances that could be given to Chiang in order to gain his complete support.[77]

Before anything could come of this message, the Generalissimo replied to the President's communication to him of 2 January. Clearly he had no enthusiasm for the north Burma campaign. The Japanese, he pointed out, had always fought tenaciously, and it was reasonable to assume that their resistance would be even stronger when a hard blow such as the proposed advance into Burma was struck. He feared that the Japanese could reenforce themselves by sea and could concentrate more strength in northern Burma than the Chinese and the Indian forces could support over their weak lines of supply. The only way to avoid a fiasco in northern Burma was to cut off the supply lines into south Burma by sea and to land troops in the rear of the enemy in that region. Moreover, a successful campaign would require more troops from India than General Wavell was proposing to use. "For these reasons," said Chiang,

> I regretfully conclude that if the Navy is unable to control the Burma seas, it will be better to wait a few months longer, or even until the Monsoon season ends next autumn, than to run the risks involved in the suggested North Burma campaign. Keenly as China desires the reopening of her land communications, ready as I am to do anything in my power to bring the day nearer, I cannot forget that another failure in Burma would be a disaster for China so grave that the results cannot now be predicted....

This would not mean, however, that no preparatory measures should be taken. On the contrary, he considered that an early air offensive, presumably along the lines that General Chennault advocated, was feasible and would directly prepare for the ultimate general offensive. He concluded by urging that the British be induced to set a definite date by which they would have enough troops on hand for a Burma campaign and by promising that when the Allies were ready his armies would be prepared to go.[78]

Thus, with a flourish, the Generalissimo made it clear that he was not going to move until the British fulfilled what he considered their part of the bargain, that he wanted a full-scale campaign to recapture all of Burma or no ground campaign at all, and that he would be satisfied to wait as long as necessary, in the meantime letting General Chennault try to defeat the Japanese with air forces. His message drew a hurried and worried reply from the President:

> In my message to you of January 2, I told you that I would definitely take up with the highest Allied authorities at the earliest possible date the matter of opening the Burma Road without avoidable delay. Confidentially and for your personal

information only, I expect to confer shortly with the Prime Minister in person. I urge you to delay final decision in the matter until you hear from me further. I hope to send you word in about a week.[79]

It was obvious that a major problem to be settled at the approaching meetings at Casablanca would be what was to be done in the CBI Theater.

Chapter XI

STRATEGIC DISCUSSIONS IN LATE 1942: BACKGROUND FOR CASABLANCA

THE BASIC STRATEGIC CONCEPT, NOVEMBER-DECEMBER 1942

The second of the full-scale conferences of President Roosevelt and Prime Minister Churchill with the British and American Chiefs of Staff convened at Casablanca in North Africa in January 1943. The discussions at those meetings were largely a development from discussions that had been held and papers that had been written in Washington and in London during the several months preceding. Hence it is desirable to consider some of the activities of the Joint and the Combined Chiefs of Staff during the last months of 1942 as preparation for the developments at Casablanca.

American and British forces landed on the shores of North Africa on 8 November 1942 to commence the first combined offensive against the Germans. American troops had already been fighting it out with the Japanese on Guadalcanal for three months, and before November was out the balance swung for the last time in the long campaign toward American victory. Thus, as 1942 drew to a close, American troops had come to grips with their enemies in both of the major theaters of war.

What was to come next? Did the undertakings in North Africa, which the JCS had not really wanted, commit the United Nations to a strategic program that would be centered around the Mediterranean? Was the next step to be attack on southern Europe? Or could the Americans return now to their preferred plan for invasion across the English Channel? And, in the Pacific, was the three-part operation in the Solomons-New Guinea-New Britain area to be considered complete in itself? Or was it a step to further advances against Japan? To what extent would the wherewithal be supplied to Pacific forces in order that they might continue to strike at the Japanese and take advantage of every opportunity to prevent the enemy from regaining the initiative? When requests from the European Theater conflicted with requests from the Pacific, were they always to be decided in favor of the former? In short, now that war materials were rapidly becoming available in sizable amounts what was to be done with them? Where could they best be used? These and other similar questions confronted the Joint Chiefs of Staff and their British counterparts during the last months of 1942.

251 STRATEGIC DISCUSSIONS: BACKGROUND FOR CASABLANCA

The very broad "basic strategic concept" upon which Americans and British had agreed at Arcadia[1] had proved inadequate for solving the numerous detailed problems which prosecution of a war against two widely separated enemies had entailed. To be sure the fundamental principle, "Defeat Germany first!" had not been abandoned, but its practicability had been seriously questioned. When the Joint and the Combined Chiefs of Staff attempted to decide just what the implications of this principle were and what strategy had best be employed to implement it, they discovered numerous areas of indecision and conflict.

As the problems of waging war came up for consideration, several papers were developed which included or implied some modification of the narrow terms of the Arcadia concept. One of these, presented for discussion in July 1942, was CCS 91, "Strategic Policy and Deployment of United States and British Forces."[2] In an attempt to make practical estimates as far ahead as 1 April 1943, the planners had restated the basic strategic concept as follows:

> To conduct the strategic offensive with maximum forces in the Atlantic-Western Theater at the earliest practicable date, and to maintain the strategic defensive in other theaters, with appropriate forces.

Without specifically endorsing this statement, the Combined Chiefs of Staff had accepted CCS 91 as a guide for production authorities.

The need for a firm basis on which to make longer-range decisions in the very tangible field of production requirements led the CCS to direct the Combined Staff Planners to prepare tables similar to those in CCS 91, projecting the deployment of forces to 1 April 1944.[3] Preparation of estimates almost two years in advance necessarily demanded some serious consideration of the direction in which the military situation would by then have developed. At the beginning of July 1942 this was sheer speculation, for Bolero-Sledgehammer-Roundup were the basis for planning in the war against Germany, and orders had just gone out to prepare for the limited offensive in the Solomons. The condition of American and British forces and the operations currently set up gave little definite indication of what might develop by 1944.

At the CPS meeting of 13 July the British members presented a paper outlining their conception of a strategic hypothesis for April 1944 as a basis for the study the planners were to make.[4] Assuming that Russia would remain actively belligerent, they sketched a general situation, still limited by shortages of cargo shipping, in which a landing on the Continent had been made in early summer 1943 and offensives from India against Burma or China and offensives in the Pacific were so confined as not to take shipping away from the Atlantic.

The Joint Staff Planners went to work on the British paper, agreeing after some discussion that for practical purposes a single, broad hypothesis should be presented to the CPS.

Subsequently, it might prove desirable to offer an alternative.[5] They drafted a strategic hypothesis which was slightly modified by the CPS and submitted to the Combined Chiefs of Staff on 24 July 1942.[6] When the CCS took it up for discussion six days later, Torch had become a virtual certainty. The British Chiefs of Staff, General Marshall, and Admiral King had agreed in London the preceding week that commitment to Torch would probably render a cross-Channel operation "impracticable of successful execution in 1943," and further had agreed to withdrawal of fifteen air groups and some shipping from Bolero commitments.[7] These decisions had changed the strategic outlook for April 1944 considerably. Consequently the CCS accepted the U.S. Chiefs' proposal that the CPS be directed to review their paper in the light of the new developments.[8]

Although both U.S. and British members of the CPS worked on the revision, the paper they produced did not entirely agree with the views of the British Chiefs of Staff which Sir John Dill presented at the CCS meeting of 6 August. The British gave more emphasis to operations in and from North Africa and foresaw less support for operations in the Pacific. Where the CPS paper visualized "an augmentation of forces in the Pacific by a readjustment of present United States commitments to the European Theater in order to further offensive operations against Japan," the British Chiefs predicted that "so far as operations against Germany have allowed, augmentation of forces in the Pacific have [sic] been carried out to secure our positions there and to further offensive operations." Faced with these divergencies the Combined Chiefs of Staff recommitted the matter to the Combined Staff Planners for another revision.[9]

At the next CPS meeting Admiral Cooke immediately took exception to the British statement about the Pacific. He said that he "certainly could not agree..., since C.C.S. 94 laid down without qualification that forces in the Pacific should be augmented between now and April 1943." They had been directed to follow the provisions of CCS 94 and they must do so.

Air Commodore S.C. Strafford pointed out that apparently the British Chiefs of Staff and the U.S. planners interpreted CCS 94 differently. If that paper was ambiguous, certainly the strategic hypothesis on which they were now working should be explicit.

Colonel O.A. Anderson raised another point, expressing opinion that the hypothesis was not sufficiently definite as to whether the offensive was to be taken in the East or the West. Surely this basic point should be clearly stated.

The planners then went over their original draft, paragraph by paragraph. They emerged from the discussion with only two relatively minor changes: Where the earlier version had said, "We have opened or are in the process of opening the Mediterranean," the new one said, "We have opened the Mediterranean to the extent that shipping can be moved between Gibraltar and Suez"; and "North Africa is in our hands and intensified operations are being conducted therefrom" had been substituted for "A lodgement in North Africa has been made and intensified operations are being conducted therefrom." The statements in regard to the Pacific stood.[10]

The Joint Chiefs of Staff had been ready to accept the planners' strategic hypothesis practically as written before the British Chiefs' comments were received, but they now took exception to points which had not been altered in the revised version. Again the situation had changed, for the Solomons operation had been launched, the South Pacific naval forces had suffered the staggering loss of four cruisers at Savo Island, and attempts on the part of Admiral King to obtain more equipment for the Pacific to support the Guadalcanal campaign had already disclosed fundamental differences of opinion between Army and Navy as to how much would have to be sent to that area and what the real implications of CCS 94 were. Admiral King characterized the planners' hypothesis as "visionary" and "weak with respect to future U.S. commitments in the Pacific." Admiral Leahy took somewhat the same view and insisted that "it must be realized that our forces now operating in the Southwest Pacific must and will be successfully maintained." Moreover, he advocated a specific commitment to open the Burma Road and otherwise provide tangible aid to China. General Marshall, on the other hand, considered the hypothesis adequate for its purpose. However, giving voice to the dissatisfaction of the Joint Chiefs of Staff with the turn strategy of the war against Germany had taken and to the divergent opinions of the chiefs as to what was to be done in the Pacific, he pointed out that "actually the big issues to be decided were whether the major U.S. effort was to be made in the Pacific as against Europe and the Middle East...."[11] Again, after considerable discussion at the Joint Chiefs' meeting, the paper emerged with only slight changes, in this case largely grammatical. With two minor amendments, it was approved by the Combined Chiefs of Staff on 13 August.[12]

The final paper, CCS 97/3, was a prediction rather than a commitment and its terms were sufficiently general to allow considerable developments of which it took no direct notice. Nevertheless, in the course of its preparation, as has been shown, it was discussed in some detail by the chiefs themselves. Consequently, rather than being classed as a paper with CCS approval, it may be considered a compromise of the views of the various men who approved it as to how much progress might be made in the next two years. It is interesting to note that no military operations that were not actually in progress or agreed were considered. In the European Theater it was conjectured that landings on the Continent would still be in prospect but not executed, and the general term "intensified operations" was used in respect to what was to be done after North Africa was secured. As for the war against Japan the estimate was no more committal:

> Operations from India against Burma have been restricted to such operations as are necessary to defend India, to open the Burma Road, and otherwise to encourage Chinese resistance....
>
> An augmentation of forces in the Pacific by a readjustment of United States commitments to the European Theater has been made in order to further offensive operations against Japan.

Despite the broad generalities of these statements, they represented a considerable development from the minimum diversion of force the Arcadia agreement had allowed for the war against Japan. It was, indeed, not beyond the realm of possibility to interpret these statements to support a switch to an all-out offensive in the Pacific should conditions warrant it. Such a contingency was in fact being considered by the Joint Chiefs of Staff at this same time.

Early in August the JUSSC completed a lengthy study on the subject, "Strategic Policy of the United Nations and the United States on the Collapse of Russia," on which it had been working since the end of May.[13] With the approval of the Joint Staff Planners the conclusions of the report were forwarded to the Joint Chiefs of Staff.[14]

The members of JUSSC had gone at their problem from many angles. First, they had attempted to determine the relative fighting strengths of the Axis and the Allied Nations by investigating political, economic, and psychological factors, intelligence, manpower, and the status of ground, naval, and air forces. Then they had examined the capabilities of the enemy on the one hand and, on the other, the suitable, feasible, and acceptable courses of action for the United Nations and the United States. Weighing the last two items against each other, they arrived at the decision that in the event that Russia collapsed the basic strategy should be reversed and the strategic defensive should be adopted in the European Theater while the strategic offensive was undertaken in the Pacific.

The paper presented to the Joint Chiefs of Staff contained only the decision and a list of measures to be taken by the United States and the United Kingdom to implement it. General Arnold expressed misgivings that providing personnel, material, and equipment for the defense of the British Isles *after* providing necessary means for offensive operations against Japan as the paper stipulated would leave England to defend itself alone; but the other JCS members were favorably impressed with the report.[15] Admiral King assured General Arnold that there was a saturation point in the war against Japan and there would be plenty left to help Great Britain. This General Marshall seconded, with the comment that the complete study did in fact provide for helping England. There were no other exceptions taken to the paper, and the chiefs decided to send it to the JPS for comment as to whether the conclusions would be affected by successful completion of Torch.[16]

After restudying the paper, the planners added to the measures required to implement the change in strategy the task of defending any additional territory in Africa and Asia in the possession of the United Nations. They also charged the British more firmly with assisting in the offensive operations against Japan.[17] The JCS agreed with General Wedemeyer's suggestion that it would be inadvisable to refer the revised paper to the CPS lest the British be led to believe that U.S. efforts were not being directed wholeheartedly toward the initial defeat of Germany. Collapse of Russia in any event did not appear to be imminent. Consequently, the recommendations were accepted and the paper was set aside for possible future use.[18]

Discussions of these and numerous other papers by the Americans and British on combined committees as well as the chiefs themselves had by November made it apparent that the two groups had different conceptions as to what strategy should be developed in the succeeding months, particularly in the war against Germany. The wide divergencies of thought were brought clearly to the attention of the U.S. planners when Sir John Dill, on 7 November 1942, unofficially presented Admiral Leahy, General Marshall, and Admiral King with copies of a paper entitled, "American-British Strategy." This document was a short version of a study on the subject which the British Chiefs of Staff had been preparing but which did not yet have official approval of the British Government.[19] Despite the formal way in which they acquired the British paper, both Army and Navy planners went to work at once preparing comments on it.[20] They immediately discovered that the British views were far from identical with their own.

It was apparent that the British anticipated fundamental strategic discussions with their American colleagues and suspected deep uncertainties in American minds, for their paper started with the question, "Germany or Japan first?" and their answer was emphatically, "Germany." They returned, moreover, to the Arcadia concept—"It is essential...to maintain the present strategy and to direct all efforts to the early and decisive defeat of Germany, diverting from that object only the minimum of forces necessary for the safeguarding of interests in the East, until we are in a position to turn, after the defeat of Germany, to a full-scale offensive against Japan." They argued that Germany's fighting power was already waning but if allowed breathing space it might become unbeatable. Japan, however, could not expand its fighting strength to any great degree. More U.S. forces could be deployed against Germany with a given amount of shipping than against Japan, and the Germans were sinking shipping constantly. Finally, Russia was a more important factor in the war against Germany than China was in the war against Japan, and Russia, after Germany's defeat, might be of great assistance in fighting Japan.

Although the British recognized that invasion of Europe against an unbroken Germany army would be the move most helpful to Russia, they stated bluntly that "sufficient experience has already been gained...to show that it will not be tactically possible to establish and maintain a large Allied army on the Continent until German military power has been broken." Consequently they advocated conducting heavy air bombardment and various supplementary operations and standing by to take advantage of any break in German morale. They thought the main amphibious action in 1943 should be in the Mediterranean with the object of reopening the

Mediterranean Sea route. In the Pacific the strategical position of the United Nations would not be advanced, for the British believed:

> Offensive action should be taken finally to check the Japanese threat to allied bases and communications. Such offensive action will contain Japanese forces and so prevent her liquidating China or successfully attacking the Western Coast of America, Russia, India, Australia or New Zealand.
>
> With the object of keeping China in the war offensive action should be undertaken in Burma with a view to the ultimate reopening of the Burma Road as soon as the necessary forces can be provided.

Although the Joint Chiefs of Staff took no action on this British paper, both the Army and the Navy planners prepared comments on it for their chiefs.[21] OPD's remarks were in the form of a memorandum,[22] while the Navy's were marginal notes, but the gist was the same. Bluntly OPD stated: "Until the results of the Torch Operation become apparent and until we have more information concerning Russia and future combat effectiveness, we cannot establish a priority in which Germany and Japan can be defeated." Further, "The fact is, we are confronted by an aggressive enemy in the Far East as well as in Europe.... It will be disastrous to place all the emphasis on reinforcing the United Kingdom and Europe while attempting the impossible, the maintaining of a static defense in the Pacific." Between them the Army and Navy planners took exception to almost every point in the British paper, especially disagreeing with the statement that a large-scale invasion of Europe against existing German forces was not practicable.

OPD outlined its own views as to the desirable combined strategical plan for victory in a second paper prepared on the same day.[23] The recommendations turned upon the question of whether or not the British would agree to cross the Channel before German power had collapsed. If so, there should be an all-out offensive in Europe; if not, a major offensive against Japan. Landings in southern Europe were not an acceptable alternative, for distance and logistics difficulties rendered them impracticable and even if successful they would not put Allied forces in a position to bring strength to bear effectively on Germany. So OPD felt that the main effort should be directed toward an assault on Germany itself and the strategic defensive should be maintained against Japan through a series of "limited-objectives offensives." If Russia collapsed and the British refused to participate in a cross-Channel operation while German strength was unbroken, this strategy should be reversed and the United States should turn to the offensive in the Pacific.

Neither the British paper nor the OPD memorandum became topics of formal discussion before the Joint Chiefs of Staff, but the chiefs must certainly have been aware of the differing viewpoints which were presented in them. At least one of the chiefs was more sympathetic with the British views than with those of OPD. On 16 November, General Arnold, apparently mistrusting the developments that might follow Torch, well aware of the differing views of himself and Admiral King as to what was to be done and what was to be sent to the Pacific, and unhappy about the aircraft that had already been diverted from the strategic bombing force in the United Kingdom, presented a memorandum to the JCS, to open the discussion of strategic policy for 1943 by outlining his own views in the matter.[24] He pointed out that the Allied successes in North Africa, combined with two indecisive campaigns in Russia and aerial bombardment from the United Kingdom, had considerably weakened the German position and presented an opportunity which might not again exist. Temporarily the United Nations had the initiative in North Africa. The only way they could maintain it under existing conditions was by intensive bombing both from the United Kingdom and from the newly acquired African bases. In six months, General Arnold predicted, a minimum force of 2,225 heavy and medium bombers using U.S. precision methods could so weaken German military strength that a successful offensive would be made possible. His recommendations gave evidence of his lack of sympathy with the demands from the Pacific:

1. That the Joint U.S. Chiefs of Staff follow consistently the strategic principle that the main effort of the United States be directed toward the defeat of Germany while maintaining such offensive operations against Japan as are consistent with the above undertaking.

2. That the air offensive against the European Axis be pressed to the limit of our capacity; and that aircraft be assigned so as to have a minimum of 2,225 United States heavy and medium bombers operational from United Kingdom bases alone by January 1, 1944.

3. That the air requirements of other theaters be filled by mobile air forces rather than by large numbers of fixed static units.

General Arnold's paper came up at the JCS meeting on 17 November 1942. At his suggestion and without discussion, it was referred to the Joint Strategic Survey Committee (JSSC) for study.[25]

Although the minutes do not record that the other members of the JCS presented their own views on this occasion, it is apparent that they did not share those which General Arnold had expressed. Admiral Leahy arrived at the meeting armed with recommendations that first, no action be taken on General Arnold's first point since no change was considered necessary in the agreed basic strategy then being followed; second, the agreement made four meetings earlier that all U.S. air resources be considered a strategic reserve was preferable to the commitment General Arnold suggested of a certain number of planes for a particular theater; and third, General Arnold's third point was unacceptable because it was subject to misinterpretation.[26] Colonel L.J. Lincoln of OPD also had prepared a paper which it may be assumed General Marshall had with him. This recommended considering: first, the limitations the weather would impose on any bombing offensive and hence the possibility that the mission could not be accomplished in the six-month period that General Arnold predicted; second, the fact that the British were lukewarm on the subject of a cross-Channel operation before Germany collapsed and hence it might be preferable to concentrate on Japan rather than to proceed with plans for a follow-up to air bombardment which the British did not support; and third, the capabilities and logistic limitations of North Africa.[27] Discussion of these points was obviated by the decision to have the JSSC study the problem.

The lack of a clear-cut strategic concept was being strongly felt during this period by both the Joint and the Combined Staff Planners. It was General Wedemeyer in particular who urged on his colleagues the need to obtain something definite on which to base their plans. At the JPS meeting on 18 November, when a paper on "Deployment of U.S. Air Forces as of April 1, 1944" (JCS 93-revised) came up for discussion, at General Wedemeyer's suggestion it was decided to appoint a subcommittee "to determine the global strategy of the United Nations for 1943 based on the assumptions: (1) That the 'Torch' objectives would be successfully accomplished, and (2) That no radical changes in accepted strategy would be injected in other areas."[28] Similarly, the Combined Staff Planners, attempting to reach agreement on a combined estimate of "Strategic Deployment of U.S. and British Forces as of April 1, 1944," arrived at the conclusion "that a high priority should be given to obtaining a combined agreement to a basic strategic concept which would bring up to date and replace W.W.I, and that revised tables should be prepared as early as possible on such a basis."[29] Again, the CPS, having been directed to recommend action subsequent to Torch,[30] found themselves unable to reconcile the views of the various members. They agreed that before they could recommend any future action in the Mediterranean area "the global strategic concept of the United Nations should be reviewed...in order that policies recommended for the Mediterranean may be in consonance with such over-all strategic concept."[31] The members of the Joint U.S. Strategic Committee put it more strongly. Their attempts to produce a study on objectives of war production ran into such difficulties that they included in their report the statement:

> The lack of an overall strategic plan upon which to base production planning is deplored. Production programs are now geared to the equipment and employment of forces for which no general strategic plan has been enunciated.... It is vital that broad strategic plans be developed which will determine objectives, troops strength, shipping, and advanced bases necessary. Until such plans are developed and promulgated, our production planning is on an unsound basis.[32]

The Joint Strategic Survey Committee studied both the Arnold memorandum on "Strategic Policy for 1943" and the directive it had received at the same JCS meeting to submit recommendations as to strategic possibilities following completion of Torch and operations in the Middle East.[33] On 11 December 1942 the committee produced its first paper. It was presented as JCS 167,[34] entitled, "Basic Strategic Concept for 1943." The recommendations were nothing if not general, but they did firmly support certain basic principles. In the first place, in an attempt to clarify the strategic concept in regard to the Pacific Theater, the JSSC recommended restating it thus:

> At the earliest practicable date, to conduct a strategic offensive in the Atlantic-Western European theater directly against Germany, employing the maximum forces consistent with insuring, by such offensive-defensive operations as are necessary, the security of our communications and positions in the Pacific and Burma, and the maintenance of the strategic defensive in other theaters.

To support this the JSSC advocated wearing down German strength by an integrated air offensive from bases in the United Kingdom and North Africa against German production and resources "on the largest possible scale." The major effort would go into building up forces in the United Kingdom, including transfers from North Africa, to launch a decisive offensive against Germany in 1943, after its resistance had been worn down by the air operations. Russia would be supported and the Middle East assisted with the eventual aim of bringing Turkey into the war. As for the Pacific, it was the usual broad statement:

> Maintain our communications and positions in the Pacific by conducting such offensive-defensive operations as are necessary to secure Australia, New Zealand, Hawaii, Alaska, and the approaches and lines of communications thereto.

Recommendations for the Far East took note of the approval given to operations in Burma:

> Conduct limited offensive operations in Burma with a view to reopening the supply routes to China, thereby encouraging China, and supplying her with munitions to continue her war effort and maintain, available to us, bases essential for eventual offensive operations against Japan proper.

The Joint Chiefs of Staff discussed this report in closed session at their meeting of 15 December. Only four copies were made of the minutes, all of which went to the members of the Joint Strategic Survey Committee.[35] Apparently Major General George E. Stratemeyer, who was representing General Arnold at this meeting, opened the discussion with a statement which has not been preserved. Admiral Leahy took exception to his remarks and to many points in the JSSC study.[36] He considered it inadvisable to direct the strategy as a whole against Germany. Germany was currently, to be sure, the principal concern, but he was not certain that it was the "primary enemy." Nor was he convinced that making the primary effort against Germany was "acceptable strategy."[37]

Admiral King was prepared to accept Germany as the primary enemy in Europe, but he was concerned by the offhand manner in which the Pacific situation was laid aside. He voiced the mistrust of the British that was certainly often felt though seldom recorded when he said that he did not understand why it was assumed that the British would continue to assist the United States after the defeat of Germany. He cautioned further that they would interpret all phraseology literally to fortify their own arguments. Instead of the term "offensive/defensive" in JCS 167, he recommended "offensive." He felt there should be constant pressure applied against Japan in order not to postpone the end of the war indefinitely. The admiral urged that a fixed percentage of the war effort be agreed for the Pacific, suggesting that the appropriate proportion would be 25 to 30 per cent. In regard to strategy he wondered whether the Japanese were not actually fighting a delaying action in the Solomons in order to consolidate their positions in the Netherlands East Indies and the Philippines. The only way to upset such a scheme would be to provide enough forces for the Pacific to insure steady advance. Personally, he favored flanking operations toward the Philippines rather than a series of frontal attacks. The Burma campaign also he considered vital, for not only would it provide a way to deliver equipment to the Chinese, but ultimately it would produce bases for an assault against Japan itself.

General Marshall agreed with Admiral King that continuous offensive operations in the Pacific were necessary in order to make progress; but the major part of General Marshall's remarks concerned the war against Germany. He showed little patience with operations based on North Africa, indicating that he felt landings in Sardinia or Sicily were just what the Germans themselves would recommend. Instead he thought strong forces should be built up in the British Isles as fast as possible and a move made into the Brest salient of France in the spring of 1943.

After this meeting the JSSC revised its paper and presented a new version on December 20.[38] The committee had added a statement to the list of factors considered in arriving at its recommendations:

> That until such time as major offensive operations can be undertaken against Japan, we must prevent her from consolidating and exploiting her conquests by rendering all practicable support to China and by inflicting irreplaceable losses on Japanese naval, shipping, and air resources.

The committee now proposed quite firmly a land offensive against Germany in 1943, removing the qualification that the air offensive must first have reduced Germany's defensive capabilities. For the war against Japan, operations in Burma were no longer classified as "limited" and a new objective was set for the Pacific:

> Conduct such offensive and defensive operations as are necessary to secure Alaska, Hawaii, New Zealand, Australia and our lines of communications thereto, and to maintain the initiative in the Solomon-Bismarck-East New Guinea Area with a view to controlling that area and involving Japan in costly counter operations.

The JSSC had not altered its statement of the over-all strategic concept except to change "offensive-defensive" to "offensive and defensive." However, at the JCS meeting of 22 December 1942 when the revised version was discussed, Admiral King presented a new statement which was accepted by the other members. It read:

> Conduct a strategic offensive in the Atlantic-Western European theater directly against Germany, employing the maximum forces consistent with maintaining the accepted strategic concept in other theaters. Continue offensive and defensive operations in the Pacific and in Burma to break the Japanese hold on positions which threaten the security of our communications and positions. Maintain the strategic defensive in other theaters.

The JCS also accepted Admiral King's specification that antisubmarine warfare must be intensified to improve the critical shipping situation and his spelling out in the objective for the Pacific that the Solomon-Bismarck-East New Guinea area was to be controlled "as a base for further offensive operations."[39]

The Joint Chiefs of Staff further changed the JSSC paper by adding a paragraph indicating that the strategic concept as therein stated was subject to alteration as the situation changed. In this form they presented the paper to the CCS.[40] By this time preparations for the second full dress combined conference, to be held at Casablanca, were well advanced, and this report, CCS 135, provided a vehicle for exchanging views with the British in preparation for the combined discussions.

The British Chiefs of Staff responded to CCS 135 with two papers, the first (published as CCS 135/1) containing their comments on the American document and the second (CCS 135/2) expounding their own views as to the basic strategic concept for 1943.[41] Consideration of the JCS paper had led the British Chiefs to conclude that, while on most points they were agreed, the main point of difference was that they advocated following up Torch vigorously while building up as large a Bolero as possible, and the Americans were in favor of making Roundup the main effort and adopting a holding policy in the Mediterranean except for air operations. The British Chiefs then proceeded to investigate these two possible courses of action, in regard to the war against Japan noting only that if the JCS program were followed all available landing craft would be needed in the United Kingdom and hence Anakim could not be done in 1943, whereas under the British program Anakim could probably be done in the winter of 1943. They arrived at the conclusion that Torch should be exploited with a view to knocking out Italy, bringing Turkey into action, and giving Germany no respite; that bombing of Germany should be increased; supply of Russia should be continued, and Bolero should be built up as much as possible in order that about twenty-one divisions might be at hand in August or September 1943 to reenter the Continent, provided there was good chance of success.

The second British paper was essentially a fuller exposition of the one that had come into the hands of the JCS in November. It contained the same estimate that the Japanese war effort was incapable of much expansion and that, with limited pressure on it, Japan could never become unbeatable. The conclusions at the end were essentially the same, with the war against Japan dismissed in two statements:

> Limited offensive operations in the Pacific on a scale sufficient only to contain the bulk of Japanese Forces in that area.

and

> Operations to reopen the Burma Road to be undertaken as soon as resources permit.[42]

Hastily, the JSSC studied these two papers in order to prepare a report in time for the JCS meeting of 5 January. The JSSC members agreed that there was indeed an important difference between American and British views in regard to Torch, but they believed that there was a more fundamental difference in the two concepts of the relation of the war in the Pacific to the war as a whole. Quoting the few brief remarks the British made about the Pacific, the JSSC recommended that the United States stick to the United States concept. They commented on some of the obvious inconsistencies in the papers, and they concluded that making the major effort in the Mediterranean would also render Anakim impossible just as concentrating on Roundup would. In conclusion, they recommended that the papers be referred to the Joint Staff Planners for examination of the accuracy of the basic data and to the Joint Strategic Survey Committee for further study and more detailed comment, and that the JCS adhere to their approved basic strategic concept for 1943.[43]

The Joint Chiefs of Staff were inclined to accept the JSSC's views, although it appears that General Marshall, at least, realized that the British proposals might be adopted in the end. He expressed concern in particular about what invasion of Sardinia (Brimstone) would entail, for United States and British estimates on such an operation differed. It was evident to him that the British were firmly opposed to an invasion of France and although the JSSC felt almost equally strongly about the invasion of Sardinia,[44] he thought it would be desirable to try to reconcile the difference of opinion in regard to Brimstone. Admiral King reverted to the perennial argument that constant pressure had to be maintained on the Japanese to prevent them from consolidating their conquests. Again he recommended that serious consideration be given to establishing a fixed percentage of the over-all war effort to be directed against Japan. Upon inquiry from General Marshall as to how such a percentage could be determined, he admitted that an exact analysis of individual arms was probably impossible. However, he thought a reasonable over-all analysis could be made. He estimated that probably less than 15 per cent of the total naval effort was currently directed against Japan. Admiral Willson agreed that, unless pressure was maintained against Japan, that enemy might force a showdown in the Pacific.

All this discussion led Admiral Leahy to state that "it was desirable for the United Nations to say specifically what should be done; i.e., what operations should be undertaken and what means are needed to accomplish them," a conclusion that in retrospect seems elementary. The absence of such a statement in 1942 had made the task of those on the planning levels difficult and in some instances well-nigh impossible. However, it should be remembered that in the early months of the war the United Nations were not in a position to take the offensive on any large scale and could only estimate when they might be able to do so. There were so many problems to be settled, both on the combined and on the joint level, that it seemed easier to put off resolution of the basic difference of opinion between Americans and British as to what strategy should be employed for defeating Germany and how the war against Japan fitted into the picture and to deal with problems of strategy individually as they arose. Moreover, there had been no full combined meeting for discussion of these matters since Arcadia. The approaching conference at Casablanca was clearly the turning point, for the resources were at hand, or soon would be, for some major effort, and the North African operation in the European Theater as well as the long Guadalcanal campaign and the first moves in New Guinea in the Pacific were well advanced. Some agreements in regard to future strategy would have to be made. The repeated requests from "working levels" made it obvious that the more specific and the firmer those agreements were the easier would be future decisions in numerous subsidiary matters.

The JCS were not prepared to accept the views of the British Chiefs of Staff without considerable study. So they referred the two British papers to the Joint Staff Planners for detailed examination as to the accuracy of the data from which the conclusions had been drawn and to the Joint Strategic Survey Committee for further study and comment. In addition, at General Marshall's suggestion, they directed the JSSC to investigate the attrition in shipping which would result from Brimstone and the possibility of some alternative operation in Cyprus or the Near East area.[45]

The JUSSC prepared comments that were distributed as a JPS paper but did not acquire the status of a JCS paper. The committee's conclusions in regard to the Pacific were fundamentally the same as those of the JSSC: Japan's capabilities were underestimated, and Anakim could not be undertaken in 1943 if either Roundup or Brimstone were mounted.[46] The JSSC, after more deliberation on the matter, stated the positions of the two Allies as follows:

The British advocate a policy of putting the main effort into following up Torch vigorously with air and amphibious operations in the Mediterranean, accompanied by as large a "Bolero" buildup as possible; while the U.S. Chiefs of Staff favor putting their main effort into an integrated air offensive against Germany from the U.K. and North Africa, accompanied by as large a "Bolero" buildup as possible for a land offensive against Germany in 1943.

After developing their views they suggested points the U.S. Chiefs should raise with the British in support of their position, recommending first of all, however, that they obtain British acceptance of the American concept for the Pacific.[47]

Armed with these papers and with a paragraph-by-paragraph comparison of them, the Joint Chiefs of Staff set off to meet their British colleagues at Casablanca.[48] It was clear that considerable discussion would take place before the two positions could be reconciled.

ON FROM GUADALCANAL

While the Combined Chiefs of Staff attempted to define their views of over-all strategy in the closing months of 1942, on the joint level also there was disagreement as to what course was to be followed in the Pacific Theater. Task One of the operation in the South and Southwest Pacific Areas had not yet been completed when the combined American and British staffs met at Casablanca. Tasks Two and Three were still to be undertaken. Although they were included in the original directive and there had been considerable discussion in Washington as well as in the theater as to the steps to be taken to implement them, there was no decision as to who should command or when the operations under Task Two should begin.

Mention has already been made of two memoranda Admiral King sent to the other members of the JCS in September 1942 recommending that the 2 July directive be reviewed by the Joint Staff Planners to determine what changes had been made necessary by the strong resistance of the Japanese on Guadalcanal and the slow progress that had been made in New Guinea.[49] The planners considered these memoranda in connection with a study of the deployment of aircraft in the South and Southwest Pacific and never did try to revise the directive. However, the question of what to do after completion of Task One was receiving consideration in other quarters.

As has been related, one of the major issues in the June discussions between General Marshall and Admiral King was who should exercise command in the Solomons-New Guinea-New Britain campaign. With some reluctance General Marshall had agreed that Task One would be executed under strategic direction of the Commander, South Pacific Area, while Tasks Two and Three would be controlled by the Supreme Commander, Southwest Pacific Area. By October the widely divergent views of the Army and the Navy as to how the Guadalcanal campaign should be supported and how available forces, particularly air forces, should be employed and the reports of friction and lack of coordination which reached Washington had strengthened the conviction of General Marshall and his planners that General MacArthur must command the forces involved in the two subsequent tasks. More than that, the Army planners were impressed with the desirability of shifting boundaries and jurisdictions in the Pacific in order to establish a truly unified command, preferably under an Army officer, at least in the South and Southwest Pacific and if possible in the whole Pacific area.

After General Arnold returned from an inspection trip to the Pacific he presented the problem to General Marshall in a memorandum that outlined his views in blunt fashion. He was convinced, he said, that the forces in the South and Southwest Pacific Areas could be properly employed only under a single commander with authority over the entire Pacific Theater. Moreover, only an Army officer could be expected to produce proper results. His reasons for this were two:

    a. That the Navy has not demonstrated its ability to properly conduct air operations, particularly land-based air operations.

    b. That Naval planning and operations to date have demonstrated a definite lack of appreciation of the logistic factor, and as a consequence operations to date have lacked continuity by reason of the shortage of essential supplies and installations to support military operations.

General Arnold realized that the Navy would object strongly to such a proposition and that it would therefore probably be necessary to achieve unified command by Presidential decree. However, it was to his mind essential that ground, naval, and air forces be under unified operational control, and he suggested three officers whom he thought capable of exercising such command: General MacArthur, Lieutenant General Joseph T. McNarney, and Lieutenant General Leslie J. McNair.[50]

General Marshall turned General Arnold's memorandum over to his planners in OPD, where it struck a responsive chord. Brigadier General St. Clair Streett, Chief of the Theater Group, remarked that it expressed a "Utopian view," but that it apparently represented General Marshall's opinions in the matter. He thought the idea of a single commander for the Pacific could be made palatable to the Navy, but the problem was to select a commander.[51] General Wedemeyer agreed that unified command was a necessity and felt that the commander must come "from that service which will exercise the strongest influence in the consummation of our plans for the entire area." This to him indicated an air officer, and he suggested General Arnold himself.[52]

After further consideration General Streett enlarged on his own views. He concluded that the chief obstacles to "a sane military" solution of the Pacific command problem were the political implications revolving around General MacArthur. Consequently he suggested removing General MacArthur and making him Ambassador to Russia, replacing him with Lieutenant General Robert L. Eichelberger, and combining the South and Southwest Pacific under Admiral Nimitz or General McNarney, depending on whether air or Navy was considered to have the dominant role.[53] No action was taken on his suggestion. General Marshall included in a report to the President at the end of October the recommendation that there should be further unification of command in the Pacific, at least in the South and Southwest Pacific Areas,[54] but the question did not come formally to JCS attention at this time.

By late November 1942 the tide seemed to have turned in the fighting on Guadalcanal. Sufficient U.S. Army troops had arrived there to make it feasible for the JCS to order the weary 1st Marine Division to be relieved at once and proceed to Australia for rehabilitation, thereafter to be available to General MacArthur for amphibious operations. To fill the gap this left in the South Pacific Area, the 25th Army Division, already on its way from Hawaii, was ordered to Noumea.[55]

On the first day of December 1942 General Marshall sent Admiral King a memorandum enclosing the draft of a directive for completing the next phases of the campaign. The tasks were stated in general terms: "Seizure and occupation of the remainder of the Solomon Islands, northeast coast of New Guinea, New Britain and New Ireland." Task forces for the operations were to come jointly from the South and Southwest Pacific Areas with the approval of the Joint Chiefs of Staff. Naval and amphibious operations would be under direct command of a naval officer, but, as in the original directive of 2 July, the Commander in Chief, Southwest Pacific Area (CinCSWPA), was charged with strategic direction of the campaign.[56]

Admiral Cooke, Admiral King's Assistant Chief of Staff (Plans), favored accepting General Marshall's proposal, but Admiral King did not concur.[57] The day before General Marshall's memorandum was written Admiral King had expressed to Admiral Nimitz his uneasiness at the prospect of trying to gain control of the whole Solomons-Rabaul area by a series of "frontal attacks" of the type then consuming so much time and effort on Guadalcanal. Such a program he felt would keep U.S. forces bogged down for years to come. Admiral King suggested that both the 1st and the 2nd Marine Divisions could now be relieved by Army garrison troops and the 2nd Division could be employed for a "flanking operation" against one of the enemy's supporting bases northwest of Guadalcanal, thereby rendering that position untenable for the Japanese. He requested that Admiral Nimitz comment on such a procedure, assuming, first, that the next move would be under the Commander, South Pacific, and second, that it would be under the Commander, Southwest Pacific.[58]

Admiral Nimitz had not counted on the transfer of the 1st Division to the Southwest Pacific, and he estimated that both the 1st and the 2nd Divisions would be required for the next operation he planned, seizure of Buin, the enemy airfield nearest to Guadalcanal. Until the Japanese had given up entirely all attempts to drive U.S. forces from Guadalcanal and until a secure air and naval base had been established there, in Admiral Nimitz's view Task One could not be considered completed. Additional land, sea, and air forces would have to be made available before further moves could be made. Admiral Nimitz urged that Task Two of the original directive be revised to provide that the Commander, South Pacific, would continue to command the forces that carried out the succeeding operations in the Solomons Sea area, giving as his reason, "I estimate that the bulk of the Pacific Fleet will continue to be required and I consider that any change of command of these forces which Halsey has welded into a working organization would be most unwise."[59]

Admiral Nimitz expanded these views in a letter Admiral King received some two weeks later and circulated to General Marshall and Admiral Leahy.[60] Again Admiral Nimitz stressed his contention that Task One would not be completed until the area of Tulagi was secure and developed as a useful base of operations. Since the forces in the area were not sufficient for immediate initiation of Task Two, he urged that U.S. strength be built up until it became large enough to attack the Japanese bases, while every opportunity was being seized to cut down the enemy's power. Equality of air forces appeared to have been reached and superiority was within grasp, but Admiral Nimitz did not foresee superiority in naval forces until late in the spring of 1943. There was no certainty at all in his mind as to when amphibious forces would be sufficient for advancing further.[61]

Admiral Nimitz recognized that there was a temptation to bypass one or more of the intervening Japanese positions and make Rabaul the next objective, but for several reasons he considered such a procedure unwise. In the first place, the Japanese had a string of bases outside New Guinea--Kavieng, Rabaul, Buka, Kieta, Buin, and Basmata--which were in fact mutually supporting. Loss of one of them would not cause the rest to collapse. Second, northeast New Guinea lacked land communications and would not be a highly desirable base of operations since its real communications, by sea, were flanked by enemy bases. A similar situation would exist in respect to any base that might be taken, for the enemy's bypassed positions would unavoidably flank it. Finally, Admiral Nimitz did not foresee sufficient preponderance of strength in the area to make it possible to establish and hold a base with one or more enemy positions behind it or to attack two or more Japanese strongholds simultaneously. With what forces he estimated would be available, he concluded that the problem narrowed down to whether the next objective should be Buin (300 miles from Guadalcanal) or some intervening position such as Munda, New

Georgia (180 miles from Guadalcanal), where the Japanese were building an airfield. Again he urged that the existing command organization be maintained and that the prospective advance up the Solomons be under the control of the Commander, South Pacific.

General Marshall commented on this letter at some length. He outlined the forces, both United States and Japanese, available in the South and Southwest Pacific Areas according to Army estimates, omitting Navy and Marine land-based aircraft for which OPD had no figures. In so doing, he pointed out, "Admiral Nimitz's omission of the forces available in the Southwest Pacific and our lack of data available here in the War Department as a matter of routine information, is, to my mind, the most compelling argument against the continuance of divided command for future operations in the Solomons-Bismarck Archipelago."

The Japanese, General Marshall continued, were operating on interior lines, with their forces disposed in the form of an inverted "V" with the point on Rabaul. Each end of the "V" was opposed by a strong force, but the headquarters of those forces, on New Guinea with General MacArthur and in Hawaii with Admiral Nimitz, were separated by thousands of miles. He felt that the Japanese advantages of position and direction could be offset by combinations of flanking and frontal actions, but that unified direction of the forces attacking both sides of the "V" was essential for success. General Marshall agreed with Admiral Nimitz that the command set-up of the South Pacific Force should be maintained for tactical command, but in view of the fact that all future action in the campaign would come within the boundaries of the Southwest Pacific Area, he proposed that unified strategic command be vested in the Commander in Chief of that area. He included a proposed radio to be sent to the local commanders informing them that at a time to be announced by the Joint Chiefs of Staff strategic direction of the operations of the South Pacific Force would pass to the CinCSWPA, for continuing operations against the enemy in conjunction with the forces of the Southwest Pacific.[62]

A few days after he had sent his comments on the Nimitz letter, General Marshall answered another memorandum from Admiral King. Admiral King had recommended that certain Marine Corps units, totalling some 17,000 men, assigned to garrison duty in the areas of Samoa and Hawaii be relieved by Army troops in order to advance the date on which the 3rd Marine Division could be organized and ready for offensive operations in the South Pacific.[63] Again it was the shortage of shipping that was used to decide the matter. The Army did not see how the troop lift and cargo shipping to transfer 17,000 men could possibly be found. Moreover, the needs of Torch for air support were such that there was little possibility of committing the necessary men and planes to the Pacific to relieve the Marine air units on Samoa and Hawaii. Finally, General Marshall pointed out, if his suggestions recently advanced were followed, designation of what forces would be assigned to the task forces involved in offensive operations and what would be assigned to defense of the line of communications would be joint responsibility of the Commander in Chief, Southwest Pacific, and the Commander in Chief, Pacific Fleet. Conceivably they might arrange to relieve the marine garrisons with Army troops.[64]

At about the same time Admiral King raised again the question of more aircraft for the South Pacific Area. Submitting to the JCS extracts from some letters he had received from various naval commanders in the Pacific requesting additional air strength, he recommended that, in view of the fact that Task Two would soon be undertaken, the entire question of the supply of aircraft to the South and Southwest Pacific Areas be re-examined.[65] This problem was passed along by the chiefs to the Joint Staff Planners to consider together with Admiral King's two earlier recommendations for restudy of the 2 July directive.[66]

On 6 January the subcommittee that had been set up to study the matter turned in its report to the Joint Staff Planners, who did not, however, get around to discussing it until 13 January, after the chiefs had gone to the meetings at Casablanca. The report had been restricted to the air aspects of the situation, listing the deficiencies and surpluses of Army and Navy aircraft in the South and Southwest Pacific as of 1 January and 28 February 1943 in relation to commitments. Despite the fact that the number of planes listed as available as of 28 February was in several cases lower than the number requested by the theater commanders, the subcommittee concluded, without explaining why, that it was sufficient to continue the offensive operations contemplated by Task Two.[67] At the JPS meeting at which the report was discussed, Brigadier General O.A. Anderson, who had not been on the committee, explained that when planes were not sufficiently plentiful to meet the requirements of all theaters the shortage had to be divided among them all and consequently the requests from the Pacific would not be met. Furthermore, he pointed out, the figures in the report allowed attrition of 20 per cent whereas the actual attrition rate was considerably lower and the total number of planes would be proportionately increased.[68] In the absence of the Joint Chiefs, who were by then at Casablanca, the report was referred to the Joint Deputy Chiefs of Staff, who noted it and took no action.[69]

In the meantime, Admiral King had delayed formal answer to General Marshall's suggestion that command of the South and Southwest Pacific forces be transferred to General MacArthur for initiation of Tasks Two and Three. However, the matter was being discussed in the Navy's War Plans Division and a draft of a proposed reply was submitted informally by the Navy planners to General Handy, head of Army's OPD, for comment.[70] The paper expressed doubt that the time had come to turn over the Solomon Islands campaign to General MacArthur's direction. It professed sympathy with General Marshall's desire to attain unified command but stressed the necessity of operating the Pacific Fleet with complete strategic flexibility. Consequently it proposed that the

Southwest Pacific Area be made a part of the Pacific Ocean Area and General MacArthur be given strategic direction of Task Two under Admiral Nimitz. In commenting, General Handy pointed out that General Marshall had recommended merely unified strategic command in the South and Southwest Pacific Areas under General MacArthur. The question of unified command in the entire Pacific Theater was a more comprehensive problem with political, international, and organizational implications. Realizing that feeling in the Army was strong against over-all naval command in the Pacific and that General MacArthur's position would be difficult to reconcile, General Handy urged that the designation of a single commander for the operations already under way not be delayed by attempts to settle the larger question of over-all Pacific command.[71]

Despite the comments from General Handy, the Navy planners continued to feel that unified command should be set up as soon as possible in the whole Pacific Area under CinCPOA.[72] On 6 January, Admiral King made clear his reluctance to agree to put naval forces under strategic control of the Army, at least in the Pacific. He wrote to General Marshall and pointed out that the original directive of 2 July 1942 had not anticipated that the entire Pacific Fleet would be required in the South Pacific-Solomons area for such extended periods as had proved necessary. There seemed every likelihood that this necessity would continue. Admiral Nimitz's basic directive as Commander in Chief, Pacific Ocean Areas, charged him with responsibility for the security of the entire Pacific position as well as of the West Coast of the United States. As Admiral King saw it, it was impossible to divorce from Admiral Nimitz's responsibilities his means for meeting Japanese threats to the security of his area wherever threats might come by taking away from him control over the Pacific Fleet. General MacArthur had already started operations under Task Two in his area. His actions and Admiral Halsey's in the South Pacific Area had proved to be mutually supporting, and Admiral King felt that the system of separated, coordinated command could be continued until joint efforts were directed against Rabaul itself. Then, he proposed, Admiral Nimitz's command should be extended to include the Southwest Pacific Ocean Area, thus giving him the responsibility of carrying out Navy tasks there as elsewhere, a necessity that had been recognized in the Battle of the Coral Sea. If the forces involved in the action against Rabaul remained under Admiral Nimitz's control so that he could move them to meet any sudden enemy attack at any point, then General MacArthur might feasibly be given strategic direction of the Rabaul operation. They might solve the problem, Admiral King suggested, by considering moving the boundaries of the areas. This, however, would "be psychologically undesirable, and not consistent in general with the radius of operation of forces now assigned to the Southwest Pacific Area."[73]

General Marshall's reply followed the same lines as the unofficial reply General Handy had made. He agreed that there ought to be a single commander of the entire Pacific, charged with all defensive and offensive operations and controlling all forces in the theater. However, he did not believe that merely extending Admiral Nimitz's current command to include the Southwest Pacific Area would solve the problem. Careful consideration would have to be given to international and organizational implications, and the commander would have to be selected as an individual and not because of any specific military or naval qualifications. However, the immediate problem of a single command for the operations in the South and Southwest Pacific could be readily resolved. He did not think that mutual coordination would be satisfactory, for already the operations were in fact a joint effort directed against Rabaul. Seizing upon Admiral King's suggestion that it would be feasible to give General MacArthur strategic direction of operations, provided that naval forces remained under Admiral Nimitz's general control, he proposed:

1. Give to General MacArthur, at once, strategic direction of all forces involved in the operations in the Solomons Island [sic] New Guinea, Bismarck Archipelago area, with the objective Rabaul.
2. Retention by CINCPAC of sufficient general control of all elements of the Pacific Fleet involved in this action to permit him to make a quick shift of Naval units to meet any emergency which may arise in other Pacific areas.
3. COMSOPAC to exercise direct command of naval forces involved in the Rabaul action.

Strategic movement of air forces to meet emergency conditions elsewhere can be controlled by the Joint Chiefs of Staff, as was satisfactory in the battle of Midway.[74]

Setting aside for the present the question of single command, Admiral King recommended in return that General MacArthur be instructed to submit his plan for carrying out Tasks Two and Three. A request from the Joint Chiefs of Staff to that effect was despatched the same day.[75]

So, at the time of Casablanca, the directive of 2 July with its three-part plan to capture Rabaul remained the only specific directive for offensive operations in the Pacific. Both General Marshall and Admiral King felt that plans should be made for proceeding after completion of the Guadalcanal campaign, but they were not agreed as to who was to command. General Marshall held to terms of the original directive which provided for transfer of strategic command to General MacArthur for Tasks Two and Three. He was strongly supported by the air planners, who felt as strongly that the Navy did not understand the capabilities of land-based aircraft and consequently did not utilize them most effectively as the naval planners did that the Army did not understand the uses of naval forces and were totally incapable of directing their actions. The mistakes and friction that had occurred thus far in the war in the Pacific had convinced both that they did not want to operate under over-all command of the other service. And yet both were convinced that unified command was desirable if not imperative.

General MacArthur's position added further complications. He had already become a political figure by virtue of having been discussed in the press as a possible Republican candidate for the Presidency. The publicity that attended his removal from the Philippines to set up a command in Australia had rendered transfer from that post practically impossible. In addition, the necessity of providing for the defense of the British dominions involved him further in an international situation from which he could not be readily removed. However desirable might be a single command for the entire Pacific, it was certainly not a matter that would be easily settled.

THE NORTH PACIFIC AREA

While the greater part of the U.S. forces in the Pacific was concentrated in the Central, South, and Southwest Pacific Areas in the closing months of 1942, the Joint Chiefs of Staff could not ignore the third of the Pacific Ocean Areas under Admiral Nimitz's command, i.e., the North Pacific Area. The Aleutian Islands, stretching in a great arc from Alaska south and west toward the Kamchatkan Peninsula and the islands of Japan, appear a natural route for invasion of Japan from the United States or vice versa. Actually, the constantly inclement weather and the rugged terrain of the islands as well as their long distance from mainland ports rendered the route uninviting to both nations. Not certain of each other's intentions, each felt it necessary to be prepared for attack by the other from that direction. In addition, the United States foresaw the value of bases in the Aleutians, should the Japanese attack Russia and U.S. bombers be permitted to use Siberian bases for striking against Japan.

It will be recalled that the Japanese had bombed the U.S. base at Dutch Harbor and landed troops on the islands of Kiska and Attu at the same time that they had tried to capture Midway. Their presence in the Aleutians was viewed with some alarm, for it was feared that the move might be preliminary to an attack on Siberia or that further attacks on U.S. positions in Alaska might be planned. Consequently, negotiations were begun with the Russians for staff conversations with a view to planning combined action in the event of war between Russia and Japan, and serious consideration was given to the possibility of ejecting the Japanese from the Aleutians as soon as possible.[76]

With all the other, stronger demands on U.S. forces in 1942, and with no certainty of the strength of the Japanese on Kiska and Attu or the reenforcements Japan would be prepared to rush to the area, an immediate, direct attack on the enemy-held islands was deemed impracticable. Consequently it was first decided to build up U.S. positions within striking range. Although local army and naval commanders disagreed as to what positions should be occupied and what forces would be required to occupy and defend them, at the end of July the Joint Chiefs of Staff directed the naval Commander, Alaskan Sector, and the Army Commanding General, Western Defense Command, to make a joint reconnaissance of Tanaga and Adak Islands and report the major equipment that would be required to establish advanced air bases on them.[77] Occupation of Adak began in August; plans for a base on Tanaga were made, but the project was abandoned in December.[78]

The desirability of attacking Kiska directly was discussed between the Army and Navy and within the two planning sections during the fall of 1942. With Admiral Nimitz and General DeWitt, Commanding General, Western Defense Command, urging that Kiska be taken as soon as possible, General Marshall and Admiral King finally agreed on 23 November that, subject to availability of means, a target date of 15 May 1943 should be set for the operation.[79] They decided, however, that prior to that Amchitka Island should be occupied and an airfield built there, in a position where it would completely dominate Kiska. A JCS directive was issued to Admiral Nimitz on 18 December 1942, to occupy Amchitka at the earliest possible date, provided reconnaissance showed that a satisfactory airfield could be constructed there in a reasonable length of time. This operation was to be preliminary to an attack on Kiska, but on the recommendation of General Marshall no target date was given, for General Marshall felt that limited facilities in other areas where larger scale operations were scheduled rendered planning firmly for the Kiska operation impractical.[80]

In the meantime the Joint Staff Planners had been investigating the potentialities of the North Pacific Area as a route to Japan itself. War between Russia and Japan remained a constant possibility and it seemed advisable to be prepared to move in to assist Russia should such a situation develop. On 21 September Admiral King brought the matter to the attention of the Joint Chiefs of Staff, recommending "an *intensive* study of the potentialities of a campaign against Japan via Alaska, the Aleutians, and the Bering Strait into the Kamchatkan Peninsula via northeast Siberia." Although it would probably not be immediately practicable, the admiral felt that the United States should be more ready than it then was "with ways and means not only to aid Russia but to exploit the availability of Russian territory to strike at Japan proper - which will have to be done chiefly by air from air bases within air striking distance."[81]

Admiral King's memorandum was turned over to the Joint Staff Planners for study.[82] They finally forwarded a report to the Joint Chiefs on 30 December 1942.[83] It was a lengthy study, with several annexes and appendices. Assuming that Russia had become an active ally in the Pacific, it surveyed several routes by which the war might be carried across from Alaska to Siberia and focused from there on the Japanese islands, investigating also the logistical problems involved and the estimated forces required. The gist of the conclusions was that there was not a great deal that could be done operationally at the present time. There was not sufficient information to proceed with operational planning; no amphibious operations against Japan proper on the outbreak of war with Russia was practicable; operations in force on the mainland of Asia could not be undertaken before adequate sea supply lines and interior land supply routes in Siberia were established; if Russia could provide logistical support, a taken force of one heavy bomber group could be sent to Siberia at the outbreak of hostilities; and PT boats could be operated from Petropavlovsk or Bering Sea ports. However the planners offered specific recommendations:

(a) That the Army be directed to
  (1) Train one reinforced Army division equipped for Arctic climates to be held for dispatch on short notice;
  (2) Prepare a plan to augment the existing Siberian Air Ferry Service facilities.
(b) That the Army and Navy be directed to prepare joint plans for the development of port facilities at Port Teller and Petropavlovsk.
(c) That plans for the efficient operation of U.S. air force units in Siberia be initiated.
(d) That a directive be issued to the Commanders in Chief, Pacific Areas, and the Commanding General, Western Defense Command, to prepare joint plans to
  (1) recapture Kiska as soon as feasible;
  (2) establish air bases on the island of Amchitka and on either Shemya or Agattu;
  (3) reinforce the Russian forces in the Kamchatka Peninsula.
  (4) capture and occupy Paramushiro and Shimushu.
(e) That efforts be continued to secure from the Russian Government information as to
  (1) the strength and disposition of Russian military and naval forces;
  (2) military and naval logistical support;
  (3) transportation and communication facilities; and
  (4) existing airfields.
(f) That a joint mission be sent to Siberia to conduct a survey of the areas concerned.
(g) That Russia be invited to state what aid they are likely to require from the United States in the event of hostilities between Russia and Japan.

With only brief discussion the Joint Chiefs of Staff approved the JPS recommendations.[84] Action was in fact already being taken on the last three points. Late in December Major General Follett Bradley had returned from Moscow, where he had been representing the United States in staff conversations. A summary of his report, presented to the JCS by General Marshall,[85] had been the subject of considerable discussion at the last meeting in December.[86]

General Bradley had reported that at last the Alaska-Siberia air ferry route had been established and planes could be delivered to Russia that way. In October Stalin had given him permission to make a survey of air bases in Siberian areas,[87] a survey which promised to yield information as to what facilities could be used by U.S. air forces should Russia go to war with Japan. General Bradley, however, had not availed himself of the opportunity, preferring to discuss the matter first in Washington. He felt that no survey should be made until the United States was prepared to make definite commitments as to what forces would be furnished to that area. Such a survey would be essential before final plans were made to use Siberian bases, but General Bradley was certain that Stalin would not permit any U.S. forces in the area prior to the outbreak of hostilities with Japan. This the Russians did not seek, for they wished to concentrate on the defeat of Germany, and they would not enter into any agreement with the United States for cooperative action against Japan.

In forwarding General Bradley's report to the JCS, General Marshall proposed that the Commanding General, Army Air Forces, be directed to plan for the allocation and logistic support of three heavy bomber groups (105 planes) in Siberia, and that the Joint Chiefs of Staff recommend to the President that he inform Stalin that the three groups could be provided and propose that General Bradley make the authorized survey of Siberian bases. The Joint Chiefs approved General Marshall's recommendations and the draft of a radio he had submitted for the President to send to Stalin. Its terms were clear:

> In the event that Japan should attack Russia in the Far East, I am prepared to assist you in that theater with an American Air Force of approximately 100 four-engined bombardment airplanes as early as practicable, provided that certain items of supply and equipment are furnished by Soviet authorities and that suitable operation facilities are prepared in advance. Supply of our units must be entirely by air transport, hence it will be necessary for Soviet Government to furnish such items as bombs, fuel, lubricants, transportation, shelter, heat, and other minor items to be determined.
>
> Although we have no positive information that Japan will attack Russia, it does appear to be an eventual probability. Therefore, in order that we may be prepared for this contingency, I propose that the survey of air force facilities in the Far East, authorized by you to General Bradley on October 6, be made now, and that the discussions initiated on November 11 on your authority between General Bradley and General Korolenko be continued.
>
> ...General Bradley...will be empowered to explore for the United States every phase of combined Russo-American operations

in the Far East Theater and, based upon his survey, to recommend the composition and strength of our air forces which will be allocated to assist you should the necessity arise. He will also determine the extent of advance preparations practicable and necessary to ensure effective participation of our units promptly on initiation hostilities....[88]

Whether intentionally or not, Stalin misinterpreted the message. He would be delighted, he said, to receive 100 planes, but the Russians did not need them in the Far East, for they were not at war there. They could be very useful, however, on the Soviet-German front.[89] He persisted in this view even after a second message from Mr. Roosevelt, in which the President explained that the planes that were being offered would be obtained by rearranging air units in other areas of the Pacific in order to shift three groups to Siberia but were not then available.[90] Furthermore, Stalin flatly turned down the suggestion that General Bradley be permitted to make the agreed survey of Siberian bases with the blunt statement: "It would seem obvious that Russian military objects can be inspected only by Russian inspectors, just as American military objects can be inspected only by American inspectors. In this respect must be no misunderstanding." He also expressed great skepticism of the purpose of a proposed visit of General Marshall to Moscow, indicating no interest in having him come.[91] Although the Army OPD drafted a blunt reply, it was not sent,[92] the Bradley survey and General Marshall's visit were called off, and the Joint Chiefs remained uncertain of whether any bases in Siberia would be made available to U.S. planes in the event that Russia and Japan went to war.

CHINA-BURMA-INDIA

Operations in the Pacific Ocean Areas were, of course, primarily a responsibility of the U.S. Joint Chiefs of Staff, and their details were not expected to be a topic of discussion at the Casablanca conference. China-Burma-India, on the other hand, was partially under British strategic responsibility, and what was to be done in that area in 1943 was certain to be a matter of major interest when the two staffs met.

The Combined Staff Planners, it will be recalled, had been directed in October 1942 to restudy the plan for the retaking of Burma which they had submitted as CCS 104/3, and

(a) To report what limited operations in Burma could be undertaken before the next monsoon season.

(b) To revise their plan for the retaking of Burma (C.C.S. 104/3) in the light of the whole strategic situation as of December 15, 1942.

(c) In so doing to correlate it with current and projected operations in the Southwest Pacific, the Middle East, and the Mediterranean, with particular reference to the timing of such operations, the logistics involved and the availability of resources.[93]

After deciding that, since limited operations were already in preparation in the theater, point (b) would be discussed separately at a later date, the subcommittee presented a report on the other two points to the CPS in mid-December.[94] This proved unsatisfactory, especially in respect to air requirements.[95] It was not until 14 January 1943, after two more attempts, that the CPS finally approved the report.[96]

The paper, circulated as CCS 104/4 concluded that, if some additional air forces were made available, the maximum that could be undertaken would be: (a) advance down the Arakan coast to capture Akyab (already under way); (b) advance as soon as practicable from Assam via Imphal to the Chindwin Valley; (c) advance by the Ramgarh forces as soon as practicable from Ledo via the Hukawng Valley to form a bridgehead in northern Burma and prepare to establish contact with (d) advance by Chinese forces from Yunnan via the Burma Road.

CCS 104/4 was discussed in Washington by the Joint Deputy Chiefs of Staff, who recommended that action be deferred. It was not presented at Casablanca,[97] however, for by the time the paper was completed the conference was already in session and the U.S. Chiefs devoted their efforts to seeking a commitment to the full-scale operation in north Burma and the larger campaign to retake the whole area and reopen the prewar ground route to China.

Chapter XII

THE CASABLANCA CONFERENCE

GENERAL DISCUSSION

At 1030 on 14 January 1943 the British and American Chiefs of Staff met together at Casablanca for their first full meeting since the Arcadia Conference, more than a year before. The following day they joined the President and the Prime Minister for one of three plenary sessions held during the ten days of the conference. Only General Marshall, Admiral King, and General Arnold represented the United States, for Admiral Leahy had been taken sick en route to Casablanca and remained behind. The chiefs had brought with them only three planners, Admiral Cooke, General Wedemeyer, and General Somervell, a most unfortunate circumstance, for the three simply could not handle adequately the volume of work they were called upon to do and were no match for the British staff, who not only came armed with a large volume of prepared papers but outnumbered the U.S. planners many times over.[1]

The desirability of a meeting of the President, the Prime Minister, and their military advisors had been under discussion since November 1943,[2] for there were many matters that required settlement on the top level. A week before the conference the British Chiefs of Staff sent to Washington a proposed agenda headed by five questions, the settlement of which they suggested should be the objective of the discussions:

(1) Anglo-American World-wide strategy.
(2) European (including Mediterranean) Strategy
(3) Pacific Strategy
(4) Indian Ocean (including Burma) strategy.
(5) Major Operations for 1943 (These will be governed by decisions reached on (1) above.)
    (i) Mediterranean
    (ii) Continental
    (iii) Pacific
    (iv) Indian Ocean

Subsidiary to these was a long list of matters requiring combined consideration. Most of these were specific operations and technical matters such as oil and shipping. Included on the list was only one project that involved uniquely the war against Japan. That was stated as "Indian Ocean (A) Anakim (B) Command in Burma."[3] General Marshall remedied this situation by suggesting twelve additional topics for discussion, six of which were concerned with the war against Japan: Pacific Operations, Southwest Pacific Operations, Assistance to Siberia in event of attacks by the Japanese, Assistance to China, "Ravenous" (i.e., north Burma campaign),[4] and Employment of Chinese troops in Burma.[5] Since Admiral King added two more topics, both related to the war against Germany, the tasks ahead were numerous indeed.

At a preliminary meeting of General Marshall, Admiral King, and General Arnold with their immediate staffs on the afternoon of 13 January 1943, the Joint Chiefs considered how they should meet the British and direct the discussion in the approaching conference. The main problem on the American minds was the need for a firm agreement on world-wide strategy and a plan for accomplishing the defeat of Germany and Japan, an agreement of which the want had been strongly felt by so many subordinate committees, particularly those concerned with production and allocation. The Joint Chiefs feared that the British would try to divert the discussion at once from broad considerations to specific operations, and especially to Brimstone, the plan for invasion of Sardinia for which the U.S. Chiefs had little appetite. Although they were well aware that decision would have to be reached on the next operation to be undertaken against Germany and that they might be forced to agree to something in the Mediterranean area, the U.S. Chiefs were anxious that the broader problems be settled first. Admiral King therefore suggested that initially they should discuss the most vital matters:

1. Man Power
2. Munitions and Equipment
3. Man Power vs. Munitions and Equipment
4. That part of the total effort that should be directed against Germany and against Japan.

There was general approval of this suggestion and general agreement that the U.S. Chiefs should stand by the views expressed in their recent paper on basic strategy. Beyond this there were no detailed conclusions as to what should be discussed or how it should be presented.[6]

The first meeting of the military staffs at Casablanca (numbered as the 55th CCS meeting) was devoted largely to presentation by the British of their views in very broad terms.[7] General Marshall, as the senior U.S. member, opened the discussion by raising at once the question that was Admiral King's greatest concern, the fundamental problem of the allocation of resources between the two major theaters of war. Surely this was a basic and inclusive topic, and it seemed calculated to keep the discussion away from specific operations until more general matters had been settled. General Marshall suggested acceptance of a working concept of 70 per cent of resources to the Atlantic Theater and 30 per cent to the Pacific. Admiral King picked up the discussion, stating as he had to the Joint Chiefs ten days before that he estimated that currently only 15 per cent of available resources was being allotted to the war against Japan, including the Indian Ocean and Burma. This was to his mind not enough, and he urged that, before the discussion was turned to specific operations, the Combined Chiefs of Staff settle on a general proportion between the two theaters. No such settlement was made.

General Sir Alan Brooke took over the conversation for the British, suggesting that in attempting to fix on a proportionate division they first "weigh up the enemy situation as both the U.S. and British Chiefs of Staff saw it." Thereupon he delivered a long statement on the situation in the European Theater that took the discussion far afield. Although he thought an assault on southern Europe held more promise than a landing in the north, he ventured to suggest that the internal situation in Germany was so precarious that final victory might be possible before the end of 1943. Even though operations were undertaken in the Mediterranean area, he felt, preparations should and could be made for landings on the north coast of France if German forces weakened notably.

Speaking of Burma Sir Alan reported that the limited operation designed to capture Akyab was under way. Before complete conquest of Burma could be achieved, however, naval supremacy would have to be attained in the Bay of Bengal. Admiral of the Fleet Sir Dudley Pound bore him out in his doubts that it could be attained, reporting that the *Illustrious*, the only carrier attached to the Eastern Fleet, would probably be needed in the future in the Mediterranean.

The discussion turned next to general problems: to the submarine menace, to air operations, to Ravenous and to further operations in the Mediterranean. There was no further discussion of the allocation of resources between theaters.

The Combined Chiefs of Staff met again on the afternoon of the fourteenth. Again the discussion was largely in general terms.[8] At Sir Alan Brooke's request Admiral King outlined JCS views of the situation in the Pacific. After summarizing the events of the past year, he turned to the question of where to go when the Rabaul campaign was finished. Since the JCS had not yet agreed on this, Admiral King expressed primarily his own views, mapping in broad terms the future strategy for the Pacific Theater. His ideas at this stage of the war closely followed the concept developed in the preceding years of war games at Newport and of successive plans named Orange. The advance, said Admiral King, should aim for the Philippines rather than farther south into the complexities of the Netherlands East Indies. And the route to be followed to the Philippines should go into the Marshall Islands, then to Truk and the Marianas. As he was to do many times Admiral King stressed the Marianas as "the key of the situation because of their location on the Japanese line of communications." Thus in January 1943 Admiral King described for the CCS the line of advance through the Central Pacific to the Philippines that was in fact to be the primary strategic pattern for the war against Japan. His views on the significance of the Philippines would later change but the Central

Pacific approach was in fact to be the dominant feature of Pacific strategy.

Admiral King next raised again the matter of proportionate division of resources. Urging the necessity of preventing the Japanese from consolidating their gains he pointed out that the estimated 15 per cent of the total war effort currently being applied against Japan was enough only to hold the line, not to maintain pressure on the enemy. Admiral King was supported by General Marshall, who reiterated Admiral King's concept that the only way to defeat the Japanese was to retain the initiative and force them to fight.

The U.S. Chiefs' insistence that more effort should go to the war against Japan and that pressure should be maintained in the Pacific did not impress their British colleagues favorably. They held to the idea of establishing a line in the Pacific and defending it against any Japanese attempt to break through it. Sir Alan Brooke expressed fear that "if operations were too extended it would inevitably lead to an all-out war against Japan" for which sufficient resources could not be available at the same time a major effort was being made against Germany. Air Chief Marshal Sir Charles Portal then suggested that it might be determined what it was the Japanese had to be prevented from doing and what forces would be required to prevent it. Then the Combined Chiefs would know what forces remained for use elsewhere in the world.

Obviously, the British still took a different view of the material needs of the American theater of responsibility, the Pacific. Perhaps, although during the morning session they had reported that there would not be sufficient naval forces available in the Eastern Fleet to support Ravenous, they could be persuaded of the necessity of greater support for their own theater, Burma-India. Admiral King pointed out that the 30 per cent the U.S. Joint Chiefs of Staff had mentioned would include material for operations in Burma. Unless some attempt such as Ravenous were made to assist Chiang Kai-shek, Admiral King remarked, the Chinese might give up entirely. Sir Alan Brooke, however, doubted the value of the objective of Ravenous. It would open a route that actually could support only an estimated two divisions and deliver little or nothing to the air forces operating in China. Still, Ravenous would not cut across the main effort against Germany the way the large-scale Anakim would, and it might be worth a try. Admiral King pointed out that Ravenous would also secure territory that would protect the air supply route over the Hump. Both General Marshall and General Arnold remarked on how much General Chennault had already accomplished with a very small air force and how much more could be done with only a slight increase.

It was apparent that the British looked upon the war against Japan as a secondary matter and that they were reluctant to agree to devoting more than a minimum of resources to fighting the Japanese, whether in the Pacific or in Burma. Their lack of enthusiasm was trying to all the U.S. Chiefs, and particularly to Admiral King, who finally asked bluntly "on whom would fall the principal burden of beating Japan once Germany had been knocked out." This question must frequently have been discussed in Washington, for the British had given little concrete evidence that they would make any considerable contribution to the defeat of Japan and had in fact refused to support the Solomons-New Guinea operations with their Eastern Fleet. When so confronted, Sir Alan Brooke hastened to say that "once Germany was defeated, practically all the British naval forces would be released for the war against Japan." Moreover, forces were already forming in India to recapture Burma and Malaya. He just did not think it wise to launch a full-scale campaign like Anakim until they were quite prepared. Sir Charles Portal backed him up with a statement that India had already been asked to furnish airfields for twice as many air forces as would be based there before the defeat of Germany. He was sure that the British would turn all their resources against Japan as soon as Germany was eliminated. The question was dropped, but the British Chiefs of Staff apparently reported it to the Prime Minister, for early in the discussion at the plenary session of 18 January Mr. Churchill "stated that he wished it made clear that if and when Hitler breaks down, all of the British resources and effort will be turned toward the defeat of Japan."[9]

After some further development of the respective views of the representatives of the two nations, in which Sir Dudley Pound gave his opinion that "the correct strategy was to establish a line where we had better air facilities than the Japanese and then to allow them to wear out their air force by attacking us on that line," the Combined Chiefs of Staff finally agreed to put the Combined Staff Planners to work on what Sir Charles Portal had suggested, determining what situation should be established in the Pacific and Burma in 1943 and what forces would be needed to establish it.

After this first day of general discussion, the Combined Chiefs of Staff turned to specific problems, and in particular to future operations in the European Theater. At the first meeting with the President and the Prime Minister the following afternoon General Eisenhower reported on the situation in North Africa, and the plenary discussion centered around the war against Germany. There was no presentation, as there had been at Arcadia, of matters in which the two chiefs of state were particularly interested or matters on which they had already reached agreement. Between plenary sessions the Combined Chiefs worked at various problems, and at the succeeding meetings with their chiefs they reported on the progress they had made. Several times, too, the U.S. Joint Chiefs of Staff met separately to prepare for the next meeting with their British colleagues. Since many of the matters considered at Casablanca did not pertain to the war against Japan, they are not related in the succeeding portions of this chapter. Discussion of them will be found in other sections of the History of the Joint Chiefs of Staff.

THE PACIFIC THEATER

The JCS efforts to concentrate the discussions at Casablanca on an over-all plan for the conduct of the war had run into difficulties almost at once. In respect to the European Theater, British interests obviously lay in what was to be done next and not in a long range plan for the defeat of Germany. The British Chiefs of Staff had not changed their view, expressed in the pre-Casablanca interchanges on the question of a strategic concept, that a landing should be made in northern France in 1943 only in the event that Germany already showed definite signs of collapse. Early in the conference the U.S. Chiefs resigned themselves to this and concentrated on the problem of which operation in the Mediterranean area would be most desirable. But disagreement over what was to be done about the war against Japan was more basic than this. Upon what forces were to be sent to the Pacific depended the strategy of both of the major theaters of war.

As had been related, the British Chiefs' view of the war against Japan had come out clearly in the discussions of the first day of the Casablanca Conference. They stood by the letter of the Arcadia agreement that only the minimum should be diverted from the theater of primary interest. They believed that a line should be established in the Pacific to be defended against all Japanese efforts to cross it. Until Germany was defeated, Allied forces would not advance beyond that line in the opposite direction. The U.S. Chiefs of Staff, on the other hand, insisted that constant pressure must be maintained on the Japanese in order to prevent their regaining the initiative and to put Allied forces in the best possible strategic position ("position of readiness") for the ultimate all-out drive to defeat Japan. Whether forces were to be made available for a gradual advance across the Pacific or whether only the excess was to be allotted to the Pacific after liberal provision had been made for the war against Germany was indeed a question which affected all future strategy in both areas. Before the Joint Chiefs of Staff would agree to the next operation in the war against Germany, they insisted that the matter of the strategic concept for the Pacific in 1943 must be settled.[10]

Unfortunately the Joint Chiefs had not arrived at Casablanca armed with a paper setting forth their views as to just what should be done in the war against Japan. As has been pointed out, they had not yet agreed among themselves what was to be done after completion of the Guadalcanal campaign. Following the decision at the afternoon conference of the CCS on 15 January that the CPS should "report, on the basis that Germany is the primary enemy, what situation...we wish to establish in the Eastern Theater (i.e., the Pacific and Burma) in 1943, and what forces will be necessary to establish that situation," the U.S. Joint Staff Planners went to work on the problem. They found their colleagues on the British Staff more easily convinced than their chiefs that adequate means had to be provided to handle the Pacific situation. They did not agree, however, with U.S. views of what was to be done in Burma, their own theater of strategic responsibility.

The U.S. Joint Staff Planners did not resolve their differences with the British planners, but circulated their study as CCS 153, with two enclosures, "A", concerning the Pacific theater, and "B", the Burma theater.[11] "A" was based on four assumptions:

> that the ultimate objective of the basic global strategy is to bring the war to a successful conclusion at the earliest practicable date,
>
> that in gaining this objective efforts must be made toward the destruction of the economic and military power of all our adversaries at a rate exceeding their power of replacement,
>
> that Germany is recognized as the primary, or most powerful and pressing enemy,
>
> and that the major portion of the forces of the United Nations are to be directed against Germany insofar as it is consistent with the overall objective of bringing the war to an early conclusion at the earliest possible date.

Tentative assumptions were also made that Russia and Japan would not be at war and that the Chinese would continue belligerent if supported by the United States and Great Britain. These statements constituted what was in effect a new concept, for within these terms the ultimate objective of achieving victory as soon as possible *might* be attained by giving priority to action against Japan over action against Germany. It was just such an eventuality that the British Chiefs consistently opposed.

Having set these assumptions, the Joint Staff Planners discussed the situation which should be created in the eastern theater. Accomplishment of the over-all objective, they believed, required "that the Japanese be kept under continual pressure sufficient in power and extent to absorb the disposable Japanese military effort." In order to defend the long line of island bases occupied by the United Nations, the initiative must be maintained by offensive action against objectives of sufficient importance to the Japanese to cause counteraction. Thus the Japanese would be prevented from consolidating their positions and initiating offensive action at their own volition. The major portion of the U.S. Fleet had to be deployed in the Pacific and sufficient ground and air forces and shipping had to be available to undertake continuing limited offensives against Japanese positions. Specifically, the following actions were visualized for 1943:

> (a) Seizure and consolidation of United Nations forces in the Solomon Islands, Eastern New Guinea up to Lae Salamaua peninsula, New Britain-New Ireland (Rabaul) area.
>
> (b) Seizure and occupation of Kiska-Agattu (Western Aleutians).

(c) Seizure and occupation of Gilbert Islands, Marshall Islands, Caroline Islands, up to and including Truk. It is planned that these operations will be undertaken subsequent to Rabaul.

(d) Extension of occupation of New Guinea up to approximately the Dutch border. This will be an extension of the Truk campaign for the second part.

Enclosure "B", with which the British planners did not agree, presented the U.S. planners' view of what was to be done in Burma:

> Limited operations during present favorable weather conditions such as to permit improvement of communications from India to China, to be followed by more extended operations towards the end of the year with the objective of re-establishing the communications along the Burma Road. The objective of this campaign is to strengthen forces in China with the view to keeping China in the war, keeping pressure on the Japanese in this area, and to the establishment and operation of air strength on Japanese shipping in Chinese and Indo-China ports as well as on the flank of Japanese sea communications along the China coast.

Depending on the Japanese strength, these operations would require increases in force in the Pacific-Burma area of approximately 250,000 troops, 500 airplanes, the major portions of new U.S. fleet construction except for destroyers and escorts for the Atlantic, and 1,250,000 tons of shipping for the British Eastern Fleet.

The U.S. Joint Chiefs of Staff anticipated objections from the British to this program and they got them. Initially they took the form of a paper prepared by the British Joint Planning Staff commenting on CCS 153.[12] Its first point changed the emphasis of the basic assumptions by rewording them in a single paragraph:

> The Combined Planners assume that the ultimate objective of the basic global strategy is to bring the war to a successful conclusion at the earliest practicable date. The quickest way of achieving this will be to concentrate on defeating Germany first and then to concentrate our combined resources against Japan. Meanwhile such pressure must be maintained in [sic] Japan as will prevent her from damaging interests vital to the Allies, and will hinder her from consolidating her conquests.

Nothing was to be done in the eastern theater without providing that the earliest possible defeat of Germany would not be prejudiced thereby. As for operations, only completion of the Solomons-New Guinea-New Britain project, plus limited operations before the monsoon of 1943 in Burma to capture Akyab, establish a bridgehead in the Chindwin Valley, and construct the road from Ledo to Myitkyina and Lungling were considered "certainly required." The British recognized that further operations might prove necessary in order to retain the initiative, and they recommended that detailed plans be made for the other projects the U.S. planners had mentioned, including the campaign to reopen the Burma Road. However, "a decision whether or not to launch these further operations should be taken by the Combined Chiefs of Staff later in the year." The paper ended with a definite restriction:

> It is certain that the provision of the naval and amphibious forces required for simultaneous Truk and Anakim operations cannot but react adversely on the early defeat of Germany. It may be possible to carry out one of these operations without such a violation of our agreed strategy. The decision as to the right course of action should be taken later in the light of the development of the war.

These comments could hardly fail to incense the U.S. Chiefs of Staff, who felt in the first place that the question of Pacific strategy was not a matter for combined discussion since the Pacific was not a combined theater. Moreover, they were disappointed at the British refusal to plan for an invasion of the Continent in 1943 and their insistence on concentrating in the Mediterranean area. Admiral King probably spoke for the rest at a JCS meeting on the morning of 18 January when he expressed resentment at the British insistence that nothing must interfere with the defeat of Germany first. "The British have always been opposed to our Pacific proposals," he said. "Nevertheless, in spite of our Pacific operations we can bring against Germany either in Sicily or on the Brest Peninsula everything that the British are willing to do." He had already gotten the Prime Minister's agreement to Anakim, and he urged that emphasis be put on carrying that out. Admiral Cooke suggested that if the British insisted on having a say in what was to be done in the Pacific they be pinned down as to what forces they were going to contribute toward the defeat of Japan. No one objected to Admiral King's recommendation that the Joint Chiefs of Staff stand on the paper their planners had submitted.[13]

The feelings of the U.S. Chiefs carried over into the combined meeting later that morning.[14] When Sir Alan Brooke mentioned that the U.S. plans did not provide specifically that Germany must be defeated before the campaign to defeat Japan was undertaken, General Marshall expressed the United States views with some vigor:

> in his opinion, the British Chiefs of Staff wished to be certain that we keep the enemy engaged in the Mediterranean and that at the same time [we] maintain a sufficient force in the United Kingdom to take advantage of a crack in the German strength either from the withdrawal of their forces in France or because of lowered morale. He inferred that the British Chiefs of Staff would prefer to maintain such a force in the United Kingdom dormant and awaiting an opportunity rather than have it utilized in a sustained attack elsewhere. The United States Chiefs of Staff know that they can use these forces offensively in the Pacific Theater.

...the number of troops used in the Pacific would not have much effect on the build-up of forces in the United Kingdom. The conflict arises chiefly in the use of landing craft and shipping. He said that to a large measure the shipping used in the Pacific is already committed and, therefore, could not be made available for a build-up of forces in the United Kingdom and the necessity of maintaining them. These forces [in the Pacific] are at the end of a long line of communications and the question arises as to whether we should let them remain there precariously or do something to improve their situation.

In reply Sir Alan Brooke insisted again on the British view that it was better to concentrate first on defeating Germany and that attempting to defeat Japan first would result in losing the war. The British Chiefs of Staff felt that an all-out effort should be made in the Mediterranean "so as to draw the maximum number of German ground and air forces from the Russian front." Unless constant pressure was maintained on Germany it could recover and prolong the war. General Marshall said that this was not the point. The U.S. Chiefs did not propose doing nothing in the Mediterranean or in France. They had no idea of not concentrating first on defeating Germany. They did feel, however, that the war should be ended as soon as possible and that this could not be accomplished if the Pacific Theater were entirely neglected and the Japanese allowed to consolidate their gains and unnecessarily strengthen their positions. He "was opposed to immobilizing a large force in the United Kingdom, awaiting an uncertain prospect, when they might be better engaged in offensive operations" elsewhere. "His primary concern with the operations in the Pacific was to insure that our positions would be so strengthened as to provide us with the means for necessary operations rather than to continue conducting them on a 'shoe string.'"

To this Sir Alan Brooke insisted that "the British Chiefs of Staff certainly did not want to keep forces tied up in Europe doing nothing.... His point was that we should direct our resources to the defeat of Germany first." That was why the British Joint Planning Staff had agreed to the U.S. strategy in the Pacific "provided always that its application does not prejudice the earliest possible defeat of Germany." This remark aroused Admiral King, who "pointed out that this expression might be read as meaning that *anything* which was done in the Pacific interfered with the earliest possible defeat of Germany and that the Pacific theatre should therefore remain totally inactive." Sir Charles Portal entered the discussion to insist that that was not the understanding of the British Chiefs of Staff. Perhaps they had misunderstood and thought the point at issue was whether the main effort should be in the Pacific or in the United Kingdom. They felt that the Mediterranean offered better prospects of getting at Germany in the immediate future than northern France, and so they were advocating amphibious operations in the Mediterranean. This was another sore point with General Marshall, who remarked that he was "most anxious not to become committed to interminable operations in the Mediterranean." He had always wanted the main effort against Germany to be in northern France and he still did.

Admiral King then went over the U.S. position again. He said that "the real point at issue was to determine the balance between the effort to be put against Germany and against Japan." The United States did not intend to plan for anything beyond gaining positions in readiness for the final offensive against Japan. Details of the operations were not a matter for combined decision. In any event the operations contemplated in the Pacific would have no effect on what could be done in the Mediterranean or from the United Kingdom. To emphasize this General Marshall pointed out that lack of resources in the Pacific had already jeopardized the whole concept of defeating Germany first by making it necessary to divert forces, such as heavy bombers, to the Pacific in order to avert disaster. It was most uneconomical to live from hand-to-mouth as had been necessary in the past.

The British Chiefs seemed a bit reassured that the United States was not trying to transfer the major effort to the war against Japan. Turning to the specific projects the United States paper had listed, they recommended that it would be sufficient to stop at Rabaul and Anakim and not go on to Truk, for that would be too great a drain on available resources. In reply to this they were told that the operations outlined were intended to be continuous and to use the same forces repeatedly. Surely these troops would not be allowed to remain idle for months if Rabaul were taken in May and Anakim could not be launched until November. The British Chiefs, however, were not convinced that Anakim would not interfere with operations in the European Theater, and they insisted that, although preparations for it should proceed, the commitment should not be so firm that it would not be postponed if a favorable opportunity opened up to defeat Germany in 1943.

This discussion could hardly be characterized as conclusive. Nevertheless, the meeting adjourned temporarily at this point, and when it was reconvened a note had been drafted, presumably by the Secretaries, "setting out tentative agreements which appeared to have been reached in the preceding discussion." The chiefs set General Sir Hastings Ismay and General John E. Hull to work redrafting it and decided to discuss it further at the next meeting.[15] It was this document that formed the basis for the oral report made to the President and the Prime Minister at the plenary session that evening.

CONDUCT OF THE WAR IN 1943

The report Sir Alan Brooke made to the chiefs of state on 18 January 1943 summarized the decisions the Combined Chiefs of Staff had thus far reached in respect to all the theaters of war. Although most of the problems the chiefs had been considering were not directly concerned with the war against Japan, in order to present a fuller picture of the business of the conference it is desirable to quote the entire summary as recorded in the minutes of the plenary session:

1. A statement that the measures to be taken to combat the submarine menace are a first charge on the resources of the United Nations and provide security for all of our operations.

2. A statement that we shall concentrate on the defeat of Germany first which will be followed by the defeat of Japan.

3. Our efforts in defeating Germany will be concerned first with efforts to force them to withdraw ground and air forces from the Russian front. This will be accomplished by operations from North Africa by which Southern Europe, the Dodecanese Islands, Greece, Crete, Sardinia, and Sicily will all be threatened, thus forcing Germany to deploy her forces to meet each threat. The actual operation decided upon is the capture of Sicily.

At the same time, we shall go on with preparing forces and assembling landing craft in England for a thrust across the Channel in the event that the German strength in France decreases, either through withdrawal of her troops or because of an internal collapse.

4. Operations in the Pacific are to be continued to include the capture of Rabaul and Eastern New Guinea while plans are to be prepared to extend the operations to the Marshall Islands and the capture of Truk if the situation permits.

5. Plans and preparations to undertake Operation Anakim late in 1943 are to be instituted at once with the understanding that the United States will assist to make up deficiencies in landing craft and naval vessels needed for this operation. The operation is to be planned for December of 1943 with the view to capturing Burma and opening the Burma road prior to the monsoon season of 1944.

6. The maximum combined air offensive will be conducted against Germany from the United Kingdom. By this and every other available means, attempts will be made to undermine Germany's morale.

7. Every effort will be made, political and otherwise, to induce Turkey to enter the war in order that we may establish air bases there for operations against Rumania.

8. Operation Ravenous will be undertaken for the purpose of establishing bridgeheads over the Chindwin River, and also to prepare roads and airfields in northern Burma which will facilitate the mounting of Operation Anakim toward the end of the year. In this connection, Operation Cannibal is now being undertaken with a view to securing air bases in the Akyab area.

It was following this report that the Prime Minister "stated that he wished it made clear that if and when Hitler breaks down, all of the British resources and effort will be turned toward the defeat of Japan.... If it were thought well for the effect on the people of the United States of America, the British Government would enter into a treaty or convention with the U.S. Government to this effect." Mr. Roosevelt did not consider such a treaty necessary, but he did recommend that an agreement be sought from Russia that they would concentrate on the defeat of Japan after Germany had been defeated. Nothing further was done about it at Casablanca.

The President and Prime Minister took no exception to the outline of CCS decisions as thus presented to them. They talked at length about various aspects of the action planned against Germany for the coming year. In respect to the war against Japan they agreed that the air force in China should be increased; but they did not discuss Pacific strategy. At the CCS meeting the following day the Combined Chiefs gave formal approval to the paper from which Sir Alan Brooke's report had been drawn.[16]

Thus, on 19 January, the Combined Chiefs of Staff had reached agreement on how the war was to be conducted in 1943. Examination of the document they had approved, CCS 155/1, however, shows that it was far from being a concrete working plan. Provisions for the Pacific and Far East were stated in the most general terms:

> 5. In order to ensure that the operations and preparations [in the European Theater] are not prejudiced by the necessity to divert forces to retrieve an adverse situation elsewhere, adequate forces shall be allocated to the Pacific and Far Eastern Theatres.
> 6. *OPERATIONS IN THE PACIFIC AND FAR EAST*.
>   (a) Operations in these theatres shall continue with the forces allocated, with the object of maintaining pressure on Japan, retaining the initiative and attaining a position of readiness for the full scale offensive against Japan by the United Nations as soon as Germany is defeated.
>   (b) These operations must be kept within such limits as will not, in the opinion of the Combined Chiefs of Staff, jeopardize the capacity of the United Nations to take advantage of any favorable opportunity that may present itself for the decisive defeat of Germany in 1943.
>   (c) Subject to the above reservation, plans and preparations shall be made for:-
>   (i) The recapture of Burma (Anakim) beginning of 1943.
>   (ii) Operations, after the capture of Rabaul, against the Marshalls and Carolines if time and resources allow without prejudice to Anakim.[17]

Although the general air of the minutes of the plenary session at which these decisions were discussed indicates satisfaction, and Admiral King went so far as to say that "he was well pleased with" the document as it was, he included the reservation "that he personally would like to have had it expanded to present a complete concept for concluding the war." It is difficult to see that, particularly from the United States viewpoint, these agreements settled much in respect to the war against Japan. To be sure they were an advance over the "minimum essential" that had been granted to the Pacific at the Arcadia Conference a year before, and they did recognize the desirability of conducting some offensive operations instead of maintaining a "strategic defensive" on an established line. In respect to the war against Germany it was decided that Sicily should be invaded and certain operations and preparations should be developed in the United Kingdom. But the divergent views of the British and the Americans about what was to be done in the Pacific were concealed in generalities which promised scope for different interpretations as the war progressed. What, for example, were "adequate forces" for the Pacific and the Far East? Presumably these were the "forces allocated" of paragraph 6 (a), but how were they to be allocated? On their actual strength would greatly depend what position of readiness could be attained while Germany was still undefeated. Moreover, contrary to the expressed desires of the U.S. Chiefs, operations in the Pacific were to be subject to CCS scrutiny, for the CCS were to set the "limits" and to decide whether or not operations would "jeopardize the capacity of the United Nations to take advantage of any favorable opportunity that may present itself for the decisive defeat of Germany in 1943." Plans and preparations were to be made for advances beyond Rabaul, but execution of such plans was subject to the requirements of Anakim. This was a far cry indeed from the recommendation with which General Marshall had opened the Casablanca discussions, i.e., that 30 per cent of the total war effort be allocated to the war against Japan.

CCS 155/1 was a statement of concept rather than a detailed working plan. That it was intended as a starting point is shown by the companion document which the Combined Staff at Casablanca produced at the same time.[18] With a view to finishing the work of the conference they reviewed the agenda that had been prepared before the meetings and suggested to the Combined Chiefs of Staff what should be done to complete it. Since most of the problems had been decided in general terms in CCS 155/1, the staff recommended that the various operations mentioned in that document be examined to determine what resources each would require, how they would be made available, and, where practicable, target dates. This meant that for the war against Japan the British were to draft a paper on Anakim and the Americans another on operations in the Pacific. The rest of the conference was occupied with discussions of the various papers that were thus produced.

ANAKIM

One of the most pressing problems confronting the Combined Chiefs of Staff at Casablanca was what was to be done in Burma. As has been related [19] the limited operation in northern Burma which General Stilwell had developed had the support of the U.S. Joint Chiefs of Staff. However, his attempts to prepare to launch it before the monsoon of 1943 had run into difficulties when Field Marshal Wavell proved reluctant to participate without guarantee of success and Chiang Kai-shek threatened to refuse altogether unless the British provided naval forces of a strength they declared impossible. Just before leaving Washington the President had strongly urged the Generalissimo not to refuse to cooperate, promising to discuss the matter with the Prime Minister at the approaching conference.

The views of their theater commanders were reflected in the views of both the U.S. and the British Chiefs of Staff. General Marshall in particular had been convinced of the desirability of attempting to open a ground route into China through northern Burma; and the other members of the JCS had gone along with him to find shipping and equipment to send to General Stilwell. The British Chiefs, however, listened to Field Marshal Wavell, to whom it seemed unwise to undertake the operation without sufficient men and equipment to assure success.[20] Moreover, they were inclined to look upon the proposed plan less from the point of view of aiding Chinese morale and more from the point of view of its practicability. Their estimates of the time it would take to open a road through northern Burma and the limited capacity of such a road made them highly skeptical of the value of even attempting it. Still, the British Chiefs might have been more eager to support the proposed campaign had they not viewed with disfavor any operation which offered a possibility of diverting material from the war against Germany. They were not opposed to doing *something* in Burma. In fact, they were prepared to agree to a plan to retake the whole country; but they were extremely reluctant to commit themselves to anything until after Germany had been defeated.

The Joint Chiefs of Staff arrived at Casablanca interested, in the first place, in getting British agreement to undertake the limited operation in northern Burma (Ravenous), at least the initial stages of it, by 1 March 1943. They were also deeply interested in getting a commitment for 1943 to the full-scale operation to retake all of Burma (Anakim) which had already been approved in principle but not scheduled. As has been seen, the British had decided before the Casablanca meetings that if Roundup were executed in 1943 Anakim could not be. The U.S. Joint Strategic Survey Committee had gone farther, estimating that either Roundup or Brimstone in 1943 would render Anakim impracticable. The Joint Chiefs of Staff, however, did not adopt this JSSC view. At first they argued for both Ravenous and Anakim, but when the British showed extreme reluctance to commit themselves to Ravenous and had strong doubts about Anakim, the Americans concentrated on the larger operation.

The question of Burma came up for discussion at Casablanca on several occasions. The discussions were not organized, and it appears that the United States side presented no paper.[21] Most of the talking was done by General Marshall and Admiral King, who were particularly interested in the projects. Few of their points were new and there was considerable repetition and reiteration.

The JCS, and Admiral King in particular, thought that the British Eastern Fleet was accomplishing little or nothing, based as it was at Kilindini in eastern Africa. Yet they did not urge on the British their opinion that it could be of assistance to the operations in Burma by protecting the shipping route to Calcutta. Nor did they try to persuade the British to provide the naval forces and the ground divisions which Chiang wanted, in order to secure the cooperation of the Chinese. Instead, the U.S. Chiefs based their arguments on the strategic importance of undertaking a campaign in Burma.

General Marshall and Admiral King repeatedly offered two main lines of argument. The first of these was that Ravenous and Anakim would divert some of the Japanese forces that were exerting pressure on operations already under way in the South and Southwest Pacific, thereby decreasing the amount of shipping that would have to be sent to those areas. After stressing this point several times, General Marshall finally underlined the importance of thus attacking the Japanese on their flank and dispersing their strength: "unless Operation Anakim could be undertaken, he felt that a situation might arise in the Pacific at any time that would necessitate the United States regretfully withdrawing from the commitments in the European theater....He said that he [was]...desirous of undertaking the Burma operation in order to reduce our hazards in the Pacific and thus undertake the campaign against Germany."[22]

This, however, was not the only strategic importance of Ravenous and Anakim. Just as in the European Theater the U.S. Chiefs had stressed the importance of supplying the Russians with the wherewithal to fight the German ground troops, so, said Admiral King, "the key to our successful attack on the Japanese homeland is the geographical position and the manpower of China."[23] China must be kept in the war in order that its bases would be available for attacks on Japan. The proposed operations in Burma would eventually reopen a ground route into China and almost at once secure the existing air transport route, thereby increasing the flow of supplies both to the Chinese armies and to the air forces already operating in China to the limit of their resources. The need of supplying and of increasing those air forces was a matter on which President Roosevelt felt strongly, and at Casablanca he recommended that General Chennault's air force should be doubled as soon as possible.[24]

The arguments of the U.S. Chiefs of Staff were not unacceptable to the British. Although no minutes of their meetings among themselves are available for this study, it is apparent from the combined records that they too felt it was probably strategically desirable to undertake operations in Burma. However, they remained unconvinced that sufficient landing craft and naval forces could be available even by the fall of 1943 to undertake Anakim. Their own landing-craft resources were divided into two main forces, one for operations on the Continent, the other for operations farther afield, for which Burma shared its claims with other theaters, notably the Mediterranean, which was the pet project of the British Chiefs. Since they would not cut into the first force lest it be needed for an invasion of Europe, the number of landing craft available for Burma was dependent upon the other operations in progress at the time. The craft lying idle in the United Kingdom while they were needed in the Pacific were a bone of contention between United States and British planners.

By 17 January the Joint Chiefs of Staff had become seriously tried with their British colleagues over their reluctance to agree to operations in Burma. The attempt of the Combined Staff Planners to reach agreement on the conduct of the war in the Pacific in 1943 was bogged down over this question. At the JCS meeting on the morning of the seventeenth, Admiral Cooke reported the status of the planners' discussions. It was his understanding that the British were proposing that nothing be done in Burma until November 1944, a suggestion that he strongly opposed. Admiral Cooke contended that in the ten months before November 1943, when the operation would be mounted, sufficient landing craft and larger naval forces would have become available. It was Admiral King who now took a firm stand that Anakim must be included in the broad Pacific plan for 1943. Emphasizing that the geographical position and manpower of China were the key to the defeat of Japan, he characterized the British proposal to do nothing in Burma until the end of 1944 as "fantastic." As an additional compelling reason he mentioned the difficulties the JCS had encountered in their attempts to obtain cooperation from Russia, greatly diminishing their hopes of being able to use air bases in Russia for operations against the Japanese. Admiral King proposed to ask Admiral Pound to move the Eastern Fleet to Ceylon whence it could operate in the Bay of Bengal. In return he would arrange that six U.S. submarines cover the northern end of the Straits of Malacca. He suggested that the JCS take up the Pacific situation at the CCS meeting that morning and insist that Ravenous be carried out and Anakim be initiated not later than 1 November 1943.[25]

Admiral King's views were supported by General Marshall and by General Wedemeyer of the planners, and the Joint Chiefs of Staff presented them strongly to the British that morning. Still the British expressed doubt that naval cover and landing craft could be assembled in time, following the invasion of Sicily which had by that time been agreed upon.[26] That evening, however, Admiral King talked with Mr. Churchill and secured his commitment to undertake Anakim in 1943. The Prime Minister also appeared agreeable to Ravenous, subject to Chinese cooperation.[27]

At this stage in the discussions the British Joint Planning Staff incorporated the British position in a paper which was circulated as CCS 154.[28] Starting with the statement, "The reconquest of Burma should be undertaken as soon as resources within the existing strategic priorities permit," the paper stressed the importance of the Burma Road as the only trans-Burma route by which China could receive substantial supplies and presented Anakim as the operation which should be undertaken in Burma. The British took a dim view of the ground route across northern Burma from Ledo via Shingbwiyang and Myitkyina to Lungling. They discussed it as an alternative route by which supplies might reach China, but they pointed out that according to latest reports the all-weather route on which construction had started would probably not reach Shingbwiyang until the winter of 1943-1944. A dry-weather track might, however, be pushed through as far as Myitkyina after the monsoon of 1943. Protection of the road during construction would be difficult, for no more than one brigade group (or two Chinese divisions) could be maintained on it, while the Japanese could readily supply their forces around Myitkyina. With little immediate prospect that this road would be effective or that the old Burma Road would be opened up, the British strongly recommended that the air transport route to China be maintained.

It was the reconquest of all Burma that must be undertaken. Preliminary to a campaign to accomplish this, Field Marshal Wavell had already initiated an operation (Cannibal) to recapture Akyab. In addition, Ravenous would be begun in February, probably without Chinese cooperation, when the British IV Corps would move to establish a bridgehead in the Chindwin Valley whence pressure could be exerted on Mandalay when an attack was made by sea on Rangoon. Both of these operations should be completed before the monsoon in May 1943. They were not designed to open any alternative ground route into China; they were preliminary to the full-scale reconquest of Burma. At the earliest that could not be accomplished before the winter of 1943-1944. It involved: recapture of Rangoon, capture of the Moulmein area to block overland reenforcements from Thailand, concurrent pressure from the forces in the Chindwin Valley and if possible the Chinese forces from Yunnan, and the defeat of the Japanese in the Rangoon-Mandalay area. The monsoon situation limited the period of possible activity from 1 November 1943 to 30 April 1944. At the latest the attack must be begun by early December if the whole operation was to be completed. If only the Rangoon-Moulmein area was to be taken action could be postponed until the end of January. The requisite army forces would be available in India by October and the air forces by November 1943. Provided there were no other amphibious operations under way in the European or Mediterranean Theaters, the necessary capital ships and carriers might be found, although considerable help would be required from American light naval forces. As the British had always maintained, it was assault shipping and landing craft that were the bottleneck. They estimated as follows:

(i) If NO major amphibious operations are carried out elsewhere in 1943, the assault shipping and landing craft could be found by the British by 1st October 1943.

(ii) If Operation Brimstone [invasion of Sardinia] is carried out not later than the end of June 1943, and no other

amphibious operation takes place, the assault shipping and
landing craft could be found by the British by 1st December
1943 in Indian waters. This would permit of an assault on
Rangoon about 30th December 1943.

(iii) If Husky [invasion of Sicily] is carried out after
June 1943 - or any other operation, such as the Dodecanese,
in addition to Brimstone - it will not be possible to provide
the assault shipping and landing craft for Anakim from British
sources until about February 1944.

(iv) If Operation Anakim is carried out with British assault shipping and landing craft at any time during the winter
1943/44, it would seriously curtail the British share of any
cross-channel operations in the early spring of 1944.

In short the British were ready to agree to Anakim in principle,
but they made it clear that what was done in Burma would affect
what they would do in the war against Germany and vice versa. It
was a question of which theater was to be given priority. Obviously the British were not going to cut down in Europe in order
to move in Burma.

With an oral commitment by the Prime Minister to Anakim for the
fall of 1943 and the British Planners' presentation of the practicability of that operation, the U.S. Joint Chiefs of Staff hastened to pin down an agreement that Anakim would actually go
through. At the CCS meeting of 18 January Admiral Cooke reported,
without giving figures, that the U.S. Planners had estimated the
number of landing craft that would be required for Anakim and
figured that these could be made available from U.S. production
over and above existing allocations by November 1943. This, however, did not win the British over to enthusiastic support of the
operation and Lord Louis Mountbatten offered the remark that the
British could not man any more landing craft than those for which
they had already asked. Then Admiral King came to the rescue by
promising that some landing craft, complete with crews, could be
shipped from the Southwest Pacific to Burma, probably by November. As for naval coverage, "he did not see why necessary naval
coverage could not be assembled, either by having the United States
relieve the British from naval missions elsewhere so that they
could furnish the Burma coverage, or by supplying the deficiency
from the United States naval units to participate in the Burma
operation. This put a different light on the situation. If the
United States would help out with the two short items, the British
would agree to Anakim.[29]

There were still variable factors in the situation, however.
It had not yet been definitely decided just what was to be done
in the war against Germany, and of course no one could predict
what the developments in that theater in the next ten months
would be. The British insisted that Anakim not be considered so
firm a commitment that it could not be abandoned if an opportunity
to defeat Germany by invading the Continent should develop in
1943. Consequently, the Combined Chiefs of Staff left a loop-

hole by postponing final decision on Anakim to a later date. At the 18 January meeting, they:

    (a) Agreed that all plans and necessary preparations should be made for the purpose of mounting Anakim in 1943.
    (b) Agreed that the actual mounting of Operation Anakim would be determined by the Combined Chiefs of Staff in the summer of 1943 (preferably no later than July) in the light of the situation then existing.
    (c) Took note that if Anakim is mounted in 1943, the United States will assist in making up deficiencies in the necessary landing craft and naval forces by diversion from the Pacific Theater, and in merchant shipping, if necessary.[30]

Three days later they approved a provisional schedule of forces for Anakim which the British Joint Planning Staff had drawn up and set 15 November 1943 as the provisional date for the assault.[31]
    It was, of course, the British program that was thus approved. Although it was hoped that the Chinese would cooperate and would move from Yunnan to exert pressure on Mandalay, Chiang's forces were not included as an essential element in the operations. The British commitment actually to execute Anakim might help to persuade the Chinese not to withdraw from the war with Japan, but in any event further steps were taken at Casablanca to furnish Chiang with more tangible evidence of CCS interest in his theater.
    Mention has already been made of the President's interest in increasing the strength of the air force in China. From the minutes of the conference it appears that he was more concerned about that than about the reconquest of Burma. In several instances when Burma was under discussion, Mr. Roosevelt's recorded remarks indicate clearly that his main interest was to get more planes into China and that it was for that purpose primarily that he thought the Burma Road should be reopened. Thus in a meeting with the Joint Chiefs of Staff on 15 January he remarked "that for psychological reasons he thought it would be advisable to double General Chennault's force in China and also to bomb Japan proper."[32] On the following day he recommended sending more transport planes to insure the supply of a larger air force in China.[33] Again, at the second plenary session on 18 January, he expressed his view that 200 to 250 planes should be sent to China.[34] When the final CCS report came up for discussion by the President and the Prime Minister at the third plenary session five days later, Mr. Roosevelt stated his views plainly.

    He was disturbed to find that this section contained no reference to operations in or from China. Operations in Burma, though desirable, would not have the direct effect upon the Chinese which was necessary to sustain and increase their war effort. Similarly, an island-to-island advance across the Pacific would take too long to reduce the Japanese power. Some other method of striking at Japan must be found. The

> opportunity was presented by Japan's shipping situation....
> The most effective weapon against shipping was the submarine,
> and the U.S. submarines were achieving notable results. There
> was another method of striking at the Japanese shipping, and
> that was by attacking the routes running close to the Asiatic
> shore from Korea down to Siam. This could be done by aircraft
> operating from China. He thought that 200 aircraft should be
> operating in China by April. They could spend most of their
> time in attacks on shipping, but occasionally they could make
> a special raid on Japan. There seemed to be two methods of
> achieving this object: either the planes could be based and
> maintained in China or else they could be based in India,
> moving to China each time for a mission, returning to their
> bases in India on completion....[35]

General Arnold's view was not unlike that of the President. He felt that the only intelligent move was immediately to strengthen General Chennault's air force and get about the bombing of Japan.[36] However, he was more aware of the practical difficulties of maintaining a larger air force than was already under General Chennault's command in China. He had given somewhat quiet support to the Ravenous-Anakim discussions, and although he doubted that the Burma Road would actually be reopened, he realized that restoring it to usefulness would greatly assist the supply problem. The logistic difficulties of increasing General Chennault's force loomed larger in General Marshall's view. Still he appreciated what General Chennault had already accomplished with a small air force in China and he used as one of his arguments for Ravenous the greater results that could be expected if General Chennault had as many as fifty bombers at his disposal. To Admiral King also, the prospect of more planes in China was attractive, because he was anxious to coordinate action from bases in China into the over-all strategy for the defeat of Japan. The British participated little in the discussions of more planes for China. It was, after all, an American problem. However, the Prime Minister endorsed the President's proposal that additional planes be provided.[37] Consequently, in its final form the report to the two chiefs of state contained the statement of principle, albeit no definite allocation commitment:

> In order to support the Chinese war effort, to provide means
> for intensifying attacks on Japanese shipping, and to strike
> at Japan herself when opportunity offers, it is intended to
> improve air transportation into China by supplying additional
> transport aircraft, and to build up the U.S. Air Forces now
> operating in China to the maximum extent that logistical
> limitations and other important claims will permit. We hope
> that more sustained operations with increased Air Forces may
> begin in the spring, and we regard this development as of
> great importance in the general scheme.[38]

PACIFIC STRATEGY

On the next to the last day of the Casablanca Conference the discussion finally came to the question of the conduct of the war in the Pacific in 1943. The paper on the subject written by Admiral King and presented by the Joint Chiefs of Staff was not a study of requirements and availabilities.[39] The figures for these probably were not available at Casablanca, and in any case the detailed planning for the program in the Pacific was not considered a matter for combined discussion, in spite of the fact that the availability of means was dependent on combined allocations. The Joint Chiefs instead outlined their concept of what could and should be done in the Pacific in the following year.

The chiefs introduced their discussion with a statement of the long range method by which they intended to defeat Japan. It was to be "by measures which greatly resemble those which would be effective against the British Isles - blockade (attack on ships and shipping), bombing (attack on forces, defenses, industries, and morale), and assault (attack via the sea)." The last of these might not prove necessary. The first was inherent in all offensive operations. It was the U.S. purpose to work in 1943 toward the second, positions from which Japan could be attacked by land-based aircraft. It is on this point alone that the official minutes record discussion in connection with the paper. Apparently Sir Charles Portal inquired what bases were contemplated for these bombing operations since none were specifically mentioned in the paper. General Arnold's reply indicates that the program that was actually followed, using island bases for the B-29's (still not in operational use), had not yet been developed. General Arnold mentioned only bases in the Nanchang area of China and in the Maritime Provinces as including Japanese targets within the radius of action of the new very long range bombers.[40]

This then was the method by which Japan would be defeated. In 1943 the Joint Chiefs estimated that the Allied effort could in general:

  (a) Keep Japan from further expansion, and from consolidating and exploiting her current holdings.
  (b) Maintain the vital Midway-Hawaii line (key to the Pacific).
  (c) Secure the line of communications to Australia and New Zealand.
  (d) Block enemy approaches to Australia (1) from the Northward via Rabaul (2) from the Northwestward via the Malay barrier.
  (e) Attain positions which menace enemy line of communication with the Dutch East Indies, the Philippines, and the South China Sea.
  (f) Open the line of communications with China via Burma - in order to make use of Chinese geographical position (as to attack enemy line of communication in Formosa Straits and along the coast of China, perhaps to bomb Japan).

(g) Make ready to support Russia in case of war with Japan.

(h) Continue and intensify attrition of enemy strength by land, air, and sea (including submarine) action.

Specifically the paper listed Japan's potentialities for offensive action during 1943 and balanced them, point for point, with corresponding feasible objectives for the Allies during 1943. First, Japan might attack the Maritime Provinces and Russia and conversely the United States might attack Japan via the Maritime Provinces. But this was dependent upon a condition of war between Russia and Japan. Second, Japan could attack Alaska via the Aleutians, or the United States might reverse the process and attack Japan by the reverse of the same route. But this had already proved an unprofitable area for both. Third, Japan might attack the vital Midway-Hawaii line. Japan had tried this, and might try again, but it would probably again be unsuccessful. For the United States, however, an advance from Midway toward the Truk-Guam line via Wake and the northwest Marshall Islands would be most useful, for it would retain the initiative, help prevent the Japanese move, and draw off enemy forces from the Rabaul area. Fourth, Japan might attack the Hawaii-Samoa-Fiji-New Caledonia line, cover for the line of communications to Australia and New Zealand. This had been rendered unprofitable by the Solomons campaign, except via the Gilbert and Ellice Islands toward Samoa. The Allies might forestall this move by reversing the route and advancing on the Samoa-Jaluit line via the Gilbert and Ellice Islands, thus making the line of communications secure and again drawing off forces from Rabaul. Fifth, Japan might attack Australia and New Zealand via the Bismarck Archipelago and/or the Solomons. This was actually currently in question. Assuming that Rabaul was taken by the Allies, further Japanese advance would be impossible and the Allies could themselves advance from the Rabaul area on the Truk-Guam line. Perhaps this should be undertaken. Sixth, Japanese might attack Australia via the Malay Barrier, but this would serve only to prevent the Allies from advancing from northwest Australia. Conversely the Allies might move into the Dutch East Indies via the Malay Barrier, thus heading off the enemy and involving his forces and employing Allied forces available in Australia. Finally, the Japanese might attack India or China. Except for the fact that they were already well extended, this was considered perfectly feasible. As for the Allies, they were already planning on Anakim in November. Here the Joint Chiefs emphasized their views: "...Anakim is of such importance in respect of its objective (bringing Chinese manpower and geographic position to bear on Japanese forces and positions) as to merit that priority which may be found indispensable to mount it."

Having thus surveyed the potential moves of the enemy and their own feasible moves in the same areas, without, however, attempting to estimate specifically their capacity in respect to forces to carry out any or all of these moves, the Joint Chiefs of Staff announced their intentions, following completion of the operations already under way in the South Pacific: To make the Aleutians as secure as possible; to advance from Midway toward the Truk-Guam line as practicable; to advance along the Samoa-Jaluit line; not to advance from Rabaul unless forces were in hand to carry through to the Truk-Guam line and follow it up; to advance on the Malay Barrier on a limited scale; and to particpate in Anakim. These listings were probably intentionally general in order not to rouse opposition from the British and to leave opportunity for exploiting whatever potentialities developed. There was no attempt to include a timetable for the initiation of the various actions, nor any indication of whether they would be undertaken simultaneously or in sequence.

When Admiral King explained the paper to the Combined Chiefs of Staff on 22 January, they accepted it, apparently without dissension,[41] and the projects intended to be undertaken in the Pacific in 1943 were included in the final report of the conference to the President and the Prime Minister. If all the operations were to be carried through, it was an ambitious program, but it was subject to the restriction that had been made in CCS 155/1, that operations in the Pacific must not jeopardize the capacity of the United Nations to defeat Germany in 1943, should opportunity offer.

REPORT TO PRESIDENT AND PRIME MINISTER

Having discussed most of the problems listed on their agenda, the Combined Chiefs of Staff submitted to the President and the Prime Minister a summary of the decisions they had reached.[42] This was for the most part an extension of the points made in CCS 155/1, more specific as to timing in some instances, and more detailed as to requirements. The section concerning the Pacific and the Far East proposed for 1943 those operations which the JCS had listed in CCS 168, adding the target date for Anakim on which decision had been reached, 15 November 1943. As has been noted, the chiefs of state found little fault with the document. At the President's insistence, however, a statement was included of the policy to be followed toward China, with emphasis on increase of the air forces assigned there.

The conference closed on a note of satisfaction and a sense of accomplishment. To be sure a considerable amount had been accomplished, or appeared to have been. At least the Combined Chiefs of Staff were now agreed that the next objective in the war against Germany was to be the capture of Sicily. They had not, however, determined what would follow that. Bolero would be continued, but when and where the forces to be assembled under that program would be used no one knew. As for the war against Japan, it seemed that the British were going to support Anakim for the fall of 1943, provided, of course, that nothing in the European Theater conflicted. And it appeared that the British were now convinced that something more than holding a line had to be done in the Pacific Theater. What was to be provided in order to do that "something more" was another, and an undecided, matter. Also undecided were the relation and relative priority between Anakim and operations in the Pacific, a significant lack in this period of shortages and conflicting demands.

The Casablanca discussions had not followed the line nor produced the results the Joint Chiefs of Staff had hoped they would. They had achieved no blueprint for the defeat of either of the major opponents. As the Joint Chiefs had expected, they had found the British interested in deciding what was to be done in 1943, but not anxious to formulate a program for 1944, 1945, or however long it might take to defeat Germany and Japan. The British were more than half-convinced that Germany would be defeated in 1943, perhaps by air bombardment, perhaps by an emergency landing in northern France at the first sure sign of German collapse, perhaps by the Russians, who were carrying the brunt of the fighting on the ground. Consequently, they were eager to reach agreement on a specific operation in the Mediterranean to follow Torch, and such an agreement was necessary, of course; but they did not consider it essential to plot a continuous strategic program that would terminate with the defeat of Germany. Much less were they concerned about spelling out the steps that would lead to the defeat of Japan. The historian with access to only one side of the records, who views the British case only as it was presented in combined meetings, is handicapped, and the temptation is great to consider the better known side as the correct one. In this instance the failure to reach a decision on the strategic program for more than a twelve-month period, with details even of that program left for decision later in the year, was a serious one. It was a failure to solve one of the most basic difficulties, a difficulty which had been pointed out repeatedly, to the U.S. Chiefs at least, by their subordinate committees, who had found it next to impossible to develop programs for production, deployments, allocations, and even operational plans, lacking as they were a meaningful statement as to what was to be done and consequently what would be needed where and when. Yet there was considerable virtue in the British theory of preparing to seize opportunities as they arose. There was also considerable virtue in their opinion that Germany would be better attacked from the Mediterranean than across the Channel into northern France. At Casablanca the British Chiefs were not prepared to commit themselves firmly to a cross-Channel operation. Nor were the U.S. Chiefs prepared to commit themselves firmly to a continuing campaign in and around the Mediterranean region. Reconciliation of the two views was perhaps impossible at this time, and consequently a long range program could not have been achieved. However, these are matters for discussion elsewhere in the History of the Joint Chiefs of Staff. Suffice it to say that, as succeeding chapters will show, the "decisions" reached at Casablanca were for the most part in such broad terms that in the months that followed they lent themselves readily to different interpretations in the two capitals and soon proved that the satisfaction evident in the closing meetings of the Casablanca Conference was sadly misplaced.

Chapter XIII

OPERATIONS IN THE SOUTH AND SOUTHWEST PACIFIC, JANUARY-MARCH 1943

INTERPRETATION OF THE CASABLANCA DECISIONS

Although since July 1942 General MacArthur and Admiral Nimitz had had a directive for operations which were to culminate in the seizure of Rabaul, the moves to be made after completion of the Guadalcanal campaign and the designation of the commander for these actions remained unsettled when the Joint Chiefs of Staff returned from the conference at Casablanca. Consequently, as in the following weeks they attempted to implement the decisions that had just been reached they found it necessary to devote considerable time and effort to determining what should next be done in the Pacific, the U.S. theater of strategic responsibility.

During 1942 there had been considerable discussion of the strategy to be followed in defeating Japan, but there had been no joint decision on a long range strategic plan. In August the Joint U.S. Strategic Committee, at its own suggestion, had set to work on a very detailed study of a strategic plan for the defeat of Japan.[1] At the end of the year it was still uncompleted.[2] By that time the Joint Strategic Survey Committee had submitted its paper on the "Basic Strategic Concept for 1943," which, in revised form, was approved by the Joint Chiefs of Staff on 22 December.[3] Apparently the JUSSC felt that this paper, with its statement of strategic policy and its very general outline of operations to be undertaken in all areas, filled part of the need for a plan for the defeat of Japan as well as the requirements of a second directive the committee had received in November from the Combined Staff Planners "to evolve a broad strategic concept involving the employment of the combined forces of the United Nations for the defeat of their enemies." In any event the committee recommended to the Joint Staff Planners on 4 January 1943 that both the directives be cancelled and the JUSSC be directed instead to prepare a campaign plan for the defeat of Japan.[4]

The new study would be based on seven assumptions: (a) That initially most of the U.S., British, and Free French ground and air forces would be in the European Theater. (b) That most of the British naval forces would be in the European Theater, but enough would be available to control the Indian Ocean. (c) That most of the U.S. naval forces would be in the Pacific, with enough for escort and antisubmarine operations in the Atlantic. (d) That Japan would invade Siberia at a time advantageous to it and disadvantageous to Russia. (e) That Russia would stay in the war and would oppose a Japanese invasion of Siberia. (f) That only planning for coordination of effort with Russia against Japan would be possible until war existed between the two. (g) That China would remain in the war against Japan. There was no indication of how the study would be organized, but clearly it was intended to recommend a series of specific operations to be undertaken all the way from the Solomons to Tokyo.

The JUSSC's proposed directive did not find ready acceptance among the Joint Staff Planners to whom it was presented about a week before the Casablanca Conference. The Joint Chiefs of Staff had just reached agreement among themselves on a strategic concept, but it had not been accepted by the British Chiefs, nor had there been any attempt to translate its broad generalizations into a concrete program of world-wide action. The Army members of the JPS felt that, before any component plan was formulated, a strategical plan for the whole war should first be prepared. Moreover, they were doubtful that the Russians would actually enter the war against Japan.[5] The Navy members, however, did not think it necessary to wait until a plan for the defeat of Germany was developed before preparing one for the defeat of Japan. The planners were unable to reach agreement at their meeting of 6 January, and they put off decision until the next meeting to give the Army members a chance to propose a substitute directive.[6]

A week later Colonel Ray T. Maddocks suggested to the planners that the directive be approved and the JUSSC be further directed to prepare, either concurrently or after completion of the first study, an over-all strategic plan for implementing the basic strategic concept for 1943.[7] Rear Admiral B.H. Bieri pointed out that the Combined Chiefs of Staff at Casablanca were even then working on plans for future action against Germany, but in the Pacific the United States was practically on its own. Although the Army and Navy had agreed on certain operations against Japan, it was essential that further decisions be reached soon. The JPS finally accepted Colonel Maddocks's suggestion and the JUSSC went to work on the study.[8]

The result, which the committee presented on 15 February,[9] was very different from what the planners had envisaged. The Casablanca Conference decisions were by that time available and the committee members had devoted a good part of their effort to analyzing the implications of the new agreements, trying to ascertain their real meaning. In addition the committee had narrowed its subject down to prospective operations in the Solomons-New Guinea area in 1943 rather than attempting the larger plan for the defeat of Japan. Although the JPS did not approve the paper and no action was taken on it, it is worth discussing as an indication of the practicability of the decisions reached on the top level at Casablanca.

The JUSSC arrived at the conclusion that the following had been decided at Casablanca in regard to the war against Japan:

(a) *With the forces now available in the Pacific, or enroute thereto, or earmarked for duty therein,* the following operations are "intended":
  (1) "Make the Aleutians as secure as may be."
  (2) Advance along the line Samoa-Jaluit.
  (3) Advance on the Malay Barrier (as Timor) on a limited scale.
  (4) Capture Rabaul. (*There is some question whether or not this should be undertaken if it is so delayed as to interfere with Anakim*).
(b) *When necessary forces are available without prejudice to Anakim or the basic requirement that Germany is the principal enemy*, the following operations can be undertaken:
  (1) Advance toward Truk-Guam.
(c) Operations in support of China, as follows:
  (1) Cannibal and Ravenous operations.
  (2) Operations in China:
    a. Improving air transportation and
    b. Building up U.S. Air Forces in order to intensify air operations
  (3) Reconquest of Burma and reopening of the Burma Road.

Of these three, the first two may be undertaken if without prejudice to the basic requirement that Germany is the principal enemy. The third depends upon a Combined Chiefs of Staff decision to be made in July, 1943.

Having studied the Casablanca decisions and the situation in the South and Southwest Pacific, the JUSSC proceeded to relate the one to the other. It was apparent that the Japanese defenses of Rabaul were exceedingly strong[10] and the U.S. forces available in the area insufficient to attack and seize the major Japanese base directly. The United States could, however, advance in New Guinea, establish airfields on unoccupied islands within range of Rabaul, and seize strategically placed Japanese-held positions preliminary to assault on the final objective. Specifically, the committee recommended developing airfields on Kiriwina Island, a location which, as will be discussed below, the local theater commanders had been considering since mid-December, and on some island in the southern Solomons area (Santa Isabel, Russell Islands, etc.) which could be occupied without much opposition. In addition, airfields would be available in New Guinea when Lae and Salamaua were taken. As soon as amphibious troops were at hand, either Munda or Rekata Bay should be seized from the enemy. Thence U.S. forces should advance to southern Bougainville and to the Shortland Island-Fauro Island-Choiseul Bay area. With those positions secure and a favorable state of progress in New Guinea, operations preliminary to the recapture of Rabaul itself could be begun. Currently, however, the committee estimated tha only enough forces were in the area to develop Kiriwina and a site in the southern Solomons and to continue operations already in progress in New Guinea.

In presenting the results of its study the committee stressed the importance the Joint Chiefs of Staff had placed on Anakim in the Casablanca discussions. The committee's examination had disclosed that the Rabaul operation would necessarily be so delayed as to prejudice Anakim, but the projects on Kiriwina and in the southern Solomons could be carried out without interfering with that operation. Whether or not Munda or Rekata Bay could be captured within the time limit allowed was not certain, but in all likelihood no moves could be made beyond that without conflicting with the requirements of Anakim. In order to release the landing craft and naval support which were to be contributed from the South and Southwest Pacific, all amphibious operations there would have to be completed by 15 July 1943. Since it was not clear in the Casablanca agreements whether the Rabaul operation was to be allowed to interfere with Anakim, the JUSSC pointed out the need for decision on this, recommending "that no major amphibious operations be undertaken which will interfere with Anakim." The committee further recommended that those of the projects it had outlined which would not conflict be carried out and that opportunities be exploited to destroy the Japanese Fleet.

As has been mentioned above, the Joint Staff Planners were not particularly pleased with the paper their subcommittee presented. Only Admiral Bieri's comments at the meeting of 24 February 1943 are recorded, but his views were probably not unlike those of his Army and Navy colleagues. He thought that the reason that the committee had concerned itself more with analyzing what was decided at Casablanca than with a plan for operations after the defeat of Germany was probably because its directive had not been well worded. Consequently he proposed that this report simply be noted and the committee be given a new directive. This time the committee should be expected to investigate all possible plans for the defeat of Japan and not to confine its study to any particular one or part of one. If there was any difference of opinion among the JPS it was not recorded. The paper was put aside, and the JUSSC was sent back to work on "a broad strategic plan for the defeat of Japan, based on attaining the strategic objectives established by the strategic concept of the Combined Chiefs of Staff as stated in C.C.S. 155/1."[11] The new study was presented two months later.

WASHINGTON PLANNING

Although the JUSSC's paper of mid-February did not receive wide distribution and was not officially approved, it is illustrative of the uncertainty in Washington after Casablanca as to what steps were next to be taken in the South and the Southwest Pacific. To be sure, the capture of Rabaul had been confirmed at Casablanca as an objective for 1943. However, three important problems connected with it remained to be settled by the JCS, whose responsibility the theater was: (1) what intermediate objectives must be taken before Rabaul itself could be seized; (2) who would command the next operations; (3) what significance had Rabaul in the whole program for the defeat of Japan.

It will be recalled that the JCS directive of 2 July 1942 had set up two further tasks for the South and the Southwest Pacific Areas after completion of the Guadalcanal operation: (1) Seizure and occupation of the remainder of the Solomon Islands, of Lae, Salamaua, and the northeast coast of New Guinea; (2) Seizure and occupation of Rabaul and adjacent positions in the New Guinea-New Ireland area.[12] Despite the fact that the same directive stated quite plainly that strategic control of these tasks was to be under the Supreme Commander, Southwest Pacific Area, Admiral King had considered it inadvisable to transfer command from the Commander, South Pacific Area (Vice Admiral William F. Halsey), to General MacArthur, and General Marshall and Admiral King had been unable to reach agreement after numerous exchanges of memoranda. Finally, on 8 January, Admiral King recommended that an attempt be made to find out just what was involved in the command of the next two tasks by asking General MacArthur how he planned to carry them out.[13] Consequently, on 8 January 1943 General MacArthur was asked to report his plans in detail to the Joint Chiefs of Staff, first consulting with Admirals Nimitz and Halsey if possible.[14]

General MacArthur's reply arrived in Washington after the Joint Chiefs of Staff[15] had returned from Casablanca. His general plan, he said, had not changed since 8 July when he and Admiral Ghormley had submitted their comments on the 2 July directive. At that time the two commanders had divided the second and third tasks into five phases: (1) Capture of Lae and Salamaua and the airfield at Gasmata (on this phase General MacArthur had already embarked); (2) Occupation of Cape Gloucester and Talasea on New Britain and Madang on New Guinea; (3) Capture of Lorengau (on Manus Island) and Buka Island; (4) Capture of Kavieng; (5) Capture of Rabaul.[16] He was still disposed to follow that plan, said General MacArthur, based as it was on "the fundamental necessity for the progressive advance of airfields in order to provide land based air protection for naval movements, both tactical and logistical, and to bring heavy and medium bombers in force with fighter coverage over the objective." It would now be necessary to capture additional Japanese bases at Munda, Buin, Tonolei, Kieta, Buka, Finschhafen, and perhaps others. For none of these, however, was General MacArthur ready, because neither ground nor air forces were available in sufficient quantity to undertake the offensive.[17]

General MacArthur's reply did not satisfy Admiral King's desire to find out how General MacArthur would proceed if command were turned over to him. Characterizing his statement as a *"concept"* rather than a *"plan,"* Admiral King remarked to General Marshall, "It does not give us any concrete idea of what he intends to do or how he expects to do it or what the command set-up is to be." General MacArthur appeared to be proceeding with that part of Task Two that involved New Guinea but not coordinating his program with what Admiral Halsey could or should do in the Solomons. Unless the Joint Chiefs of Staff could get more definite plans from General MacArthur, Admiral King recommended that they "should call on Admiral Nimitz (Admiral Halsey) for his plans for going ahead in the Solomons *in support of* what General McArthur [sic] plans to do in phase 2."[18]

Some of the plans on which Admiral Halsey and Admiral Nimitz were working were already known in Washington, at least in the Navy Department, for CominCh had been apprised of them, both through direct reports to him and through information copies of despatches exchanged by the local commanders. In December 1942, when victory on Guadalcanal at last seemed assured, Admiral Nimitz had urged caution in proceeding farther in the South Pacific Area before additional forces had been made available. Guadalcanal, he felt, should be secured and built up as a strong base before the next move was attempted. As for what that move should be, he was undecided between Buin, on the southeast end of Bougainville, three hundred miles from Guadalcanal, and some intermediate point such as Munda, New Georgia, where the Japanese were beginning to construct an airfield. Which of those objectives was selected would depend on when sufficient forces became available, how firmly dug in the Japanese were, and whether or not Admiral Nimitz's recommendation was accepted that the existing command arrangement under the Commander, South Pacific Area, be continued.[19]

A few days after this Admiral King had learned that Admiral Halsey was considering the desirability of building an air base on one of the islands between New Guinea and the Solomons and south of New Britain, where it would be particularly useful in the support of naval operations. Admiral Halsey suggested to General MacArthur, in a despatch which went to CominCh for information, that Woodlark Island appeared to offer particularly good strategic possibilities, and he asked General MacArthur to furnish him any topographical information he happened to have available about the island.[20] The following day Admiral King recommended to Admiral Halsey that he consider Kiriwina and others of the Trobriand Islands in his survey, but Washington heard nothing more on the subject immediately.[21]

The Navy War Plans Division during this period had been exploring the possibilities of undertaking new projects in the Pacific. Completion of the Rabaul campaign was desirable, but wresting control of Guadalcanal alone from the enemy should serve to halt the threat of Japanese attack on the vital communication line, and capturing all of the Solomons-New Britain-New Guinea region seemed to promise to advance U.S. forces but little on the road to Japan itself. The extended campaign on Guadalcanal had slowed down that advance considerably, and the

Navy planners thought it was time to consider seriously getting started on the campaign across the Central Pacific. The enemy's apparent decision at last to give up Guadalcanal might well indicate that he was preparing to strike somewhere else, and it was desirable that he not be allowed to seize the initiative.

By the time fighting finally ceased on Guadalcanal, at the beginning of February, the Navy War Plans Division was making plans in accordance with the Casablanca decisions to branch out first into the Gilbert and the Ellice Islands, east and northeast of the Solomons, where operations would serve both to advance U.S. forces strategically and to divert Japanese forces from the Solomons.[22] The enemy had been developing bases in the Gilberts since 9-10 December 1941 when the first Japanese units landed on Tarawa and Makin.[23] Dislodging them would be a considerable undertaking. In the Ellices, on the other hand, American forces had already arrived, with the transfer of a small garrison from Samoa to Funafuti on 10 October 1942. Development of bases in the Ellice group and seizure of advance positions in the Gilberts from the Japanese would put U.S. forces in position to push on into the Marshalls and the Carolines.

On 9 February 1943 Admiral King asked Admiral Nimitz and Admiral Halsey for comment on operations in the Gilbert and the Ellice Islands designed to secure the line of communications to the Southwest Pacific and to divert Japanese air and shipping from the Solomons preparatory to continuing the campaign there.[24] Admiral Halsey, however, thought that he was busy enough without taking on this new project. Consequently he pointed out to Admiral King that the Japanese were rapidly consolidating their positions in New Georgia and he considered it necessary to attack them there as soon as possible. The enemy was also building up strength in the Russell Islands, between Guadalcanal and New Georgia, and Admiral Halsey was planning to occupy positions there about 21 February in order to strengthen the Guadalcanal-Tulagi area and provide an advance base for further offensive operations. The Gilbert-Ellice project, he felt, would divert considerable forces that could ill be spared and involve costly delay in the Solomons. Consequently he recommended that it not be undertaken and all possible pressure be continued in the Solomons area.[25] Admiral Halsey's views were supported by Admiral Nimitz, who informed Admiral King that, until the existing balance of power in the Pacific was upset by further destruction of Japanese naval and air power and increase of American, he believed that seizure of the Gilberts and Ellices was not advisable.[26]

To Admiral King the Pacific commanders seemed to be missing the point. It was quite necessary, he thought, to attack in the Central Pacific as well as in the Southwest Pacific in sufficient strength and at such a time that the two areas could support each other. At least an attempt should be made "to whipsaw [the] enemy rather than enable him to concentrate in [the] Solomons or attack on Jaluit-Gilbert-Samoa line or on Midway-Pearl line." So

Admiral King instructed Admiral Nimitz to consider the desirability of moving simultaneously up through the Solomons and the Ellices and Gilberts and to report his plans for the next four months.[27]

Admiral Halsey insisted that he recognized the desirability of operations that would confuse the enemy and give mutual support. However, he pointed out, a strike at the Gilberts and Ellices would be a frontal attack, it would not advance U.S. forces toward any critical objective, and support of the islands seized would be a constant tactical and logistical drain unless the advance were continued in that direction. Rabaul, on the other hand, was a vital point in the Japanese system and a strong offensive against it was the surest way of pinning down the Japanese fleet in that area. He planned to press on to Rabaul as soon as possible, occupying the Russells on 21 February and getting troops into New Georgia by infiltration or otherwise at the earliest possible moment.[28]

By this time word had been received from General MacArthur that he would like to send representatives to Washington to explain the details of his suggestions for Tasks Two and Three and to give his strategic conceptions of the steps to take to penetrate the Japanese area and cut off Japanese positions in the south.[29] A conference of the theater staffs with the Washington planners seemed a good idea, and a joint despatch was sent to General MacArthur, Admiral Nimitz, and Admiral Halsey, inviting them to send officers to Washington for a meeting to determine what course was to be followed in the Pacific.[30]

For over a month now no direct attempt had been made by Admiral King and General Marshall to settle the question of who was going to exercise command in Tasks Two and Three. With the conference in prospect, however, Admiral King made another effort to secure naval control of the remainder of the Solomons operations. On 18 February 1943 he suggested to General Marshall that the Joint Chiefs of Staff

> would do well to clarify the military situation as to the South-Southwest Pacific by modifying the boundaries between the South Pacific and Southwest Pacific areas as follows:
> "From the Equator at 154° East south to 8° South thence southeasterly to point 13° South 160° East thence South."[31]

The 2 July directive, it will be recalled, had moved the boundary to 159° East south from the equator in order that Tulagi and Guadalcanal would be included in the South Pacific Area. The modification Admiral King now proposed would extend the South Pacific Area to include all of the Solomon Islands. Admiral Halsey's right to control the successive operations up through the islands would then be virtually undebatable. But Admiral King's attempt was not successful. General Marshall continued to insist that the directive of 2 July had specified the command arrangement for the entire operation. The plans to be discussed at the approaching conference were based on that directive and General Marshall thought it inadvisable to modify the area boundaries before the conference convened.[32] Admiral King went to the west coast at this point to confer with Admiral Nimitz and the matter of command was temporarily dropped.[33]

THE PACIFIC MILITARY CONFERENCE

The Pacific Military Conference convened in Washington on 12 March 1943 at 1030, when Admiral King, speaking for the Joint Chiefs of Staff, welcomed the representatives from the Southwest, the South, and the Central Pacific Areas. The first meeting was attended by fifty-three officers (Army, Navy, and Marine Corps), including the members of the Joint Strategic Survey Committee and the Joint Staff Planners as well as the Officers from the Pacific. The attendance at the succeeding meetings was considerably smaller, but, except for the JSSC, who attended no others, the same groups were represented at all.[34]

After Admiral King had briefed the theater groups on the organization and functions and current plans and decisions of the JCS, General McNarney spoke for General Marshall, recommending the program that the conference should follow. Then the group got down to work, with Admiral King inviting Major General R.K. Sutherland, Chief of Staff to Supreme Commander, Southwest Pacific Area, to present the plan he had brought with him.[35]

General Sutherland proceeded to read a strategic plan, bearing the code name "Elkton," which outlined a program carrying out in five steps Tasks Two and Three of the directive of 2 July 1942. The plan was based on the concept of advance on two general axes: along the northeast coast of New Guinea to New Britain on the west and through the Solomons on the east. The two would culminate in the capture of Rabaul and adjacent positions. Since only the sea and land areas south of the line Buna-Guadalcanal were currently under United Nations control, it was necessary to plan operations to capture all the rest of the area. This the planners of the Southwest Pacific Area proposed to accomplish in five stages:

(1) Seizure of operating airdromes in the HUON PENINSULA area to provide necessary direct land-based air support for subsequent operations along the line of NEW BRITAIN.

(2) Seizure of operating airdromes in NEW GEORGIA to provide necessary direct land-based air support for subsequent operations along the line SOLOMONS-NEW IRELAND.

(3) Seizure of operating airdromes in NEW BRITAIN on the west and BOUGAINVILLE ISLAND on the east, to provide direct land-based air support for subsequent operations against KAVIENG and RABAUL.

(4) The capture of KAVIENG and the isolation of RABAUL by air and naval action. (The capture of KAVIENG may be delayed until after Step (5) if the situation justifies.)

(5) The capture of RABAUL after necessary reduction of enemy strength by combined attack to eliminate the center of enemy resistance.

The order in which the tasks were listed was not intended necessarily to indicate the timing, for favorable conditions were to be exploited and advantage was to be taken of momentum achieved on either axis. In the more detailed analyses of the several tasks, however, it was made clear that the order in which they were listed was considered the most desirable order in which to carry them out. Attempting to advance initially on both axes simultaneously was not considered practicable. In this connection the planners pointed out that New Georgia lay between Guadalcanal and the enemy bases in southeastern Bougainville, the Buin-Faisi area. Consequently, New Georgia must be captured before Bougainville. However, as long as the enemy had a line of supporting airfields at Kavieng, Rabaul, Buka, and Buin-Faisi, the planners thought it improbable that an amphibious assault on New Georgia could be successful. Therefore, these enemy airfields must first be neutralized. Since this process could be carried out only from bases in the Vitiaz Strait area, positions there must be captured before the seizure of New Georgia was attempted.

For each of the tasks the "scheme of maneuver" was discussed in general terms and the forces that would be required for the operations were estimated. It was assumed that the enemy would offer determined resistance to all the attacks and that, consequently, ground forces assigned to each operation would be permanently committed there and not available for subsequent actions. As a result of this it was estimated that a total of ten divisions would be required in the South Pacific Area and a total of twelve and two-thirds in the Southwest Pacific Area. Air forces, on the other hand, would be constantly available, and the requirements were set at fifteen and thirty groups, respectively. Designation of naval forces was left to the Joint Chiefs of Staff. Although the study was presented by the Southwest Pacific group alone, the representatives from the South Pacific Area approved the forces which it would provide for them.[36]

Accompanying the Elkton Plan were charts of the operations, a G-2 estimate of the enemy's strength and reinforcement rate, and a summary of the Allied situation in the South and Southwest Pacific Areas. No attempt was made to calculate the amount of time each step would take or to plot a time-table for initiation of the successive operations. Timing was to be decided by the Supreme Commander, Southwest Pacific Area.[37]

Since this was the first information that had been received in Washington as to just what forces the Supreme Commander, Southwest Pacific Area, judged essential for the completion of the Rabaul campaign, no estimates had been prepared in advance to show how much of the required force could be provided. Nor were there any tables showing planned deployments to the Pacific in 1943. Consequently, at the recommendation of Rear Admiral C.M. Cooke, Jr., who, as senior member of the Joint Staff Planners, acted as chairman of the conference, the second meeting, held on the same afternoon, was adjourned until the War Department should produce some definite figures on the numbers of ground troops and aircraft it was prepared to commit to the South and the Southwest Pacific Areas.[38]

The following day the War Department circulated tables showing the forces contemplated for deployment to the Pacific in 1943.[39] They proved to be most disappointing to the officers from the Pacific commands, for they fell far short of the requirements of the Elkton Plan. In respect to ground troops, by the end of the third quarter of 1943 it was planned that a total of twenty-seven divisions, U.S. Army, U.S. Marine Corps, and Australian, would be in the Pacific. No more would be available until the following year. Two divisions were to be in the Central Pacific Area, eight in the South Pacific Area, and seventeen, including eleven Australian divisions, in the Southwest Pacific Area. Since six of the Australian divisions were earmarked for defense or seriously deficient in equipment, the Southwest Pacific would have approximately two divisions less than the twelve and two-thirds estimated necessary, while the South Pacific would be short two of the necessary ten. In respect to aircraft the situation was worse. The figures had been prepared in accordance with the Army Air Forces interpretation of the world-wide distribution of forces required to implement the agreements made at Casablanca and not in relation to the requirements of Elkton. Whereas Elkton called for a total of 30 groups or 1,964 U.S. planes (plus 569 in depot overhaul) for the Southwest Pacific, the War Department proposed to provide a total of 18 groups or 982 planes (just half) by the end of 1943.[40] For the South Pacific Area there were to be $7\frac{1}{4}$ groups or 367 planes instead of the recommended 25 groups. This figure represented a reduction of eighty-four fighters by the end of the year below the number present or en route on 8 March 1943, and although in most other types there were to be increases, there would be a total reduction of thirty-seven aircraft. The reductions in the Central Pacific Area were more significant. Only two observation planes were to be added there. All other types were to be reduced, so that from 10 March 1943 to 30 June 1943 the total number of aircraft would have shrunk from 336 to 232.[41]

It was the decrease in aircraft assignments to the Central Pacific Area that became the first point of argument at the conference meeting of 13 March. A reduction had been suggested by the Joint Strategic Survey Committee a few weeks earlier in a study on personnel and deployment in the Western Hemisphere. The JSSC had decided, and the Joint Chiefs of Staff had approved its report, that the threat to the security of the Hawaiian

Islands had decreased and consequently some decrease in the garrison maintained there might be practicable.[42] This conclusion did not agree, however, with the conclusion reached at CinCPac headquarters, as Rear Admiral Raymond A. Spruance, Chief of Staff and Deputy Commander in Chief, Pacific Fleet, hastened to point out.[43] There it was considered that the threat of enemy attack on the Hawaiian Islands had increased considerably since the Japanese Fleet was no longer pinned down at Guadalcanal. Brigadier General O.A. Anderson, Army Air Forces member of the Joint Staff Planners, hastened to defend the JSSC estimate and the War Department figures, suggesting that in order to attack Hawaii the Japanese would have to use carriers, of which they had already lost so many that it appeared doubtful that they would care to risk any more in such an action. Captain Forrest P. Sherman, also from the Pacific Fleet staff, then introduced another aspect of the problem by pointing out that while the War Department's figures showed a decrease of one heavy bomber group in the Central Pacific they allowed an increase of only two bombers in the South Pacific. For some time aircraft allocated to the Central Pacific had been considered available to assist in the South Pacific. Consequently any decrease in the former was in effect a decrease in the latter also. General Anderson replied by suggesting that the system might be worked in the opposite direction, with the aircraft of the South Pacific considered available for the Central Pacific if necessary. He was still a strong advocate of the principle the Air Forces had supported all through 1942, that large air forces should not be concentrated in a single area in the Pacific, but mobile forces should be used to the maximum to cover a large field. He felt that a calculated risk must be taken in Hawaii and that the Army air forces assigned to the Central Pacific Area, plus naval aircraft also there, were sufficient for the purpose.

At this point the discussion went back to the Elkton Plan as Brigadier General A.C. Wedemeyer of the JPS reminded the group that the CCS at Casablanca had committed themselves to the capture of Rabaul. "Now either sufficient means should be furnished to do this while maintaining the security of the Hawaiians, or a change of directive must be sought." The representatives from the Southwest Pacific Area, General Sutherland, Chief of Staff, and Lieutenant General G.C. Kenney, Commanding General of the Allied Air Forces in the Southwest Pacific, were clearly discouraged about the possibility of accomplishing much of anything with the forces they were to receive. They were insistent that the Elkton requirements represented the absolutely essential minimum. After some prodding from Admiral Cooke, General Sutherland finally said that he thought the first step could be accomplished, but General Kenney pointed out that it would have to be postponed until the extra planes allocated for September arrived and by that time the Japanese strength would have so increased as to decrease the chances for success. As for the South Pacific

Area, Captain M.R. Browning, Chief of Staff to the Commander, South Pacific, said that operations there would certainly be limited to an attempt at Step Two, for which preparation had already begun. But Lieutenant General M.F. Harmon, Commanding General, Army Forces, South Pacific, expressed his view that even Step Two would be hazardous with the forces allotted. Unless Step Three could also be accomplished the carrying out of Step Two would be "very delicate."

Despite the obvious dissatisfaction and discouragement of the representatives of the Pacific commands, the Washington planners held out little hope for a considerable increase in the forces to be made available to them. General Anderson stated clearly that the allocation figures had been calculated on the basis of priorities set up by the Combined Chiefs of Staff. He explained that the decisions of the Casablanca Conference had given high priority for aircraft to North Africa and the United Kingdom, thereby affecting allocations to all other areas. As a matter of fact aircraft were being sent to the United Kingdom in excess of the number that ground crews could be shipped over to maintain. Shipping shortages in the Pacific restricted even more the number of planes that could be supported there. Admiral Cooke's remarks were somewhat different from General Anderson's and a little more hopeful. He reminded the group that it had been agreed at Casablanca that the pressure on the Japanese should be intensified and that adequate forces must be provided to maintain the initiative and to undertake certain operations, notably Elkton and Anakim subject to the limitation that Germany was to be defeated first. Shipping and aircraft were the two items in shortest supply and they still had to be allotted where they would do the most good. The scheduled allocations were in implementation of the decisions at Casablanca and it was up to the conference to determine what could be done and when.

Since the requirements listed in Elkton and the allocations proposed by the War Department had been drawn up independently of each other, the meeting finally came to the obvious conclusion that some attempt should be made to bring the two together. A subcommittee was appointed and directed to "re-explore the various aspects of the Elkton Plan with a view to determining any readjustment of forces available and needed that might affect a change in the estimate of forces required for the execution of the plan." In the meantime the Joint Staff Planners were to report to the Joint Chiefs of Staff that either additional forces would have to be provided or a modified directive must be issued.

The following day General Sutherland and General Harmon circulated a memorandum to the Joint Staff Planners:

> The Southwest Pacific and South Pacific groups have conferred further with regard to the means required to execute the directive of the Joint Chiefs of Staff, taking into consideration the naval means whose allocation has just been

made known. It is the opinion of the two groups that the estimate of forces required as shown in the ELKTON PLAN, cannot be reduced.[44]

With this as a beginning, Admiral Cooke proceeded at the fourth meeting of the conference, held on 15 March, to attempt to evolve a statement of the situation that would make clear to the Joint Chiefs of Staff the difference between the air forces required and the air forces allotted.

Admiral Cooke's approach to the problem was one that would inevitably aggravate the latent differences of view between the Army Air Forces and the Navy as to what was to be done with available air power. Between the meetings he had apparently been discussing the matter with Admiral King and others, for his earlier attitude of reluctant acceptance of the Air Forces deployment figures had become one of complete disagreement with the basis on which the figures were developed. Initially he expressed his desire to make it a matter of record that the deployment of air forces in the United Kingdom and North Africa had been given primary consideration when air allocations to the Southwest Pacific were being made. Although such a procedure might have been consistent with the policy, established long before Casablanca, that only the minimum of forces was to be diverted from the war against Germany, at that conference other decisions had been made which appeared to him to modify that policy somewhat. Notable among these was the statement contained in paragraph 5 of CCS 155/1:

> In order to ensure that these operations and preparations are not prejudiced by the necessity to divert forces to retrieve an adverse situation elsewhere, adequate forces shall be allocated to the Pacific and Far Eastern Theaters.

Admiral Cooke stated at the fourth meeting that "certain definite allocations to meet certain objectives were made on the basis of results of the Anfa Conferences and...he desired to explore these allocations for purposes of clarification." The intention that became apparent from the subsequent discussion, however, was to show that "adequate forces" were not being provided to the war against Japan by the War Department's allocations.

Virtually ignoring the representatives from the Pacific Commands, Admiral Cooke presented his case in a series of pointed questions directed at his colleague on the Joint Staff Planners, General Anderson of the Army Air Forces. Since this was one of the few instances in which the differing views of the two groups were recorded at some length in the official minutes, it will be informative to summarize the questions and the answers they received.

Question 1: "Do you consider the efforts achieved by the Air Forces now in the United Kingdom an effective contribution to the war effort?"

General Wedemeyer immediately protested that "questions along these lines are irrelevant," a view in which he was seconded by General Anderson. The question went unanswered.

Question 2: "In the statement of air forces allotted to the Southwest Pacific, are these the aircraft which remain available after allotting the aircraft to meet objectives in North Africa and those of United Kingdom based aircraft?"

General Anderson avoided a direct answer by replying "that there had been made a tentative deployment of air forces designed to carry out the intent of the agreements reached at the Anfa Conferences."

Question 3: "What is the intent of the Anfa Conference?"

General Anderson referred Admiral Cooke to CCS 155/1, paragraph 4; which read:

The main lines of offensive action will be:
In the Mediterranean:
(a) The occupation of Sicily with the object of:
   (1) Making the Mediterranean line of communications more secure.
   (2) Diverting German pressure from the Russian front.
   (3) Intensifying the pressure on Italy.
(b) To create a situation in which Turkey can be enlisted as an active ally.
In the U.K.:
(c) The heaviest possible bomber offensive against the German war effort.
(d) Such limited offensive operations as may be practicable with the amphibious forces available.
(e) The assembly of the strongest possible force (subject to (a) and (b) above and paragraph 6 [operations in the Pacific and Far East] below) in constant readiness to reenter the Continent as soon as German resistance is weakened to the required extent.[4][5]

Question 4: "What is your understanding of the purpose of the air offensive from the United Kingdom?"

The answer was simply, "to soften the enemy, thereby contributing toward his defeat in 1943, if possible."

Question 5: "Are the current operations now doing this?"

Again General Wedemeyer protested that the questions were irrelevant and a waste of time since no one present was empowered to make any final decision in such matters. Admiral Cooke, however, was insistent that he wanted the questions answered, and if there was objection to answering them, he wanted that in the record. General Anderson at this juncture quoted paragraph 4 of CCS 155/1, although it did not answer question 5.

Question 6: "In the allocations of aircraft to the South Pacific was the number decided to be available after deployments were made to other areas, including North Africa and the United Kingdom?"

Again General Anderson referred to paragraph 4 of CCS 155/1.

Question 7: "If forces now allocated to the South West Pacific were diverted to the United Kingdom would the war effort be increased thereby?"

Admiral Cooke also inquired whether General Anderson had estimated the number of aircraft that would be required for operations in the South and Southwest Pacific. To this General Anderson replied that he had not since that was a function of the area commanders. He had given to the Pacific "the aircraft which remained available after aircraft had been otherwise allotted in accordance with the Army Air Forces' interpretation of the set-up agreed to at the Anfa Conference." He then read paragraph 5 of CCS 155/1, which has been quoted above.[46]

Question 8: "In your estimation are the forces allotted to the South and South West Pacific adequate?"

General Anderson refused to make any statement on this, insisting that it was not his function to make estimates and that the commanders of the areas concerned had presented their requirements. He gave the same sort of answer to

Question 9: "What is your estimate of the numbers of airplanes required for operations in North Africa and from the United Kingdom?"

His organization, said General Anderson, was concerned only with the availability and commitments of aircraft. He then asked whether or not the requirements for the South and Southwest Pacific were known to Admiral Cooke and General Wedemeyer when they attended the Casablanca Conference. Admiral Cooke said he was just going to discuss that.

Question 10: "When the 1943 Air Construction Program[47] was estimated by the Army Air Forces was this based on the needs of the theaters?"

General Anderson: "Yes."

Question 11: "At that time what was your estimate of the needs of the South and South West Pacific Areas?"

When General Anderson said that he did not recall exactly what the figures were, Admiral Cooke proceeded to quote:

South Pacific:
   192 Heavy Bombers
   144 Medium Bombers
   576 Light Bombers
  1119 Fighters (Day)
    48 Fighters (Night)

South West Pacific:
   240 Heavy Bombers
   192 Medium Bombers
   192 Light Bombers
   600 Fighters[48]

He noted also that a total of 2,232 heavy and medium bombers were to be provided for use in the United Kingdom. There followed an exchange of remarks between Admiral Cooke and General Anderson from which it appeared that the allocations made by the Army Air Forces were based on CCS 155/1 in respect to the United Kingdom and on various other JCS papers in respect to the Pacific. They had the approval of the Deputy Chief of Staff and the tentative concurrence of the Chief of Staff, but as yet joint agreement had not been reached on allocations of Army-Navy aircraft.

At this stage General Wedemeyer took over the direction of the discussion by asking Admiral Cooke whether the Navy had made a careful study of the various types of landing craft and of transport and cargo vessels needed for Elkton. In reply Admiral Cooke offered some Navy figures on possible increase in assignments of these vessels, provisional on return of the craft from other operations.

All this discussion had obviously not convinced General Anderson that any substantial change could be made in the numbers of aircraft allocated in the paper already introduced. He suggested that the Joint Chiefs of Staff be informed what could be done in the South and Southwest Pacific with the forces that could be made available. To this General Wedemeyer took exception, preferring "to see first how nearly the Chiefs of Staff could make available the forces required. If sufficient forces finally appeared unavailable, he considered it appropriate then to request the Chiefs of Staff to modify their directive." He asked General Anderson to provide figures on the number of planes presently deployed in the United Kingdom and North Africa.

Up to this point the visitors from the Pacific had sat silently by, listening to the heated discussion among the Washington planners. While the latter were considering which figures should be presented to the JCS, General Harmon from the South Pacific spoke up. Since receipt of the Army Air Forces deployment figures the conference had also been given figures prepared by the Navy showing deployment of its forces in the three Pacific areas.[49] To the Central and the South Pacific the Navy was prepared to send a considerable number of shore-based planes by the end of 1943--a total of 381 to the Central Pacific and 1,062 to the South Pacific. To the Southwest Pacific, however, only 72 naval reconnaissance planes would be sent by the end of the year. General Harmon now volunteered that, if the Army air forces were increased from 72 to 96 heavy bombers (the Navy was providing none of that type), from 150 to 200 fighters plus 100 reserve in the area, and from ¼ to 1 group of troop carriers, the allotment of planes to the South Pacific would be adequate, provided the Southwest Pacific had strength enough to meet its part of the joint operation and to provide diversion and support for actions in the South Pacific. (In preparing requirements for Army planes, it seemed that the availability of naval aircraft had not always been considered.) The officers from the Southwest Pacific gave no evidence that they anticipated having the requisite strength.

The meeting ended on a more amiable tone than had been in evidence during most of it. Admiral Cooke and General Wedemeyer agreed that, on behalf of the JPS, they would give the JCS a summary of the situation "with a view to requesting that the Chiefs of Staff either find ways to augment the forces now allocated to the Pacific areas or modify their current directive regarding operations to be carried out in these areas."[50]

Hastily Admiral Cooke and General Wedemeyer drafted a paper[51] in time for the Joint Chiefs of Staff to discuss it as the first item at their meeting the following afternoon. In it they summarized very briefly the developments to date, appending the figures on deployments which had been provided by the War and Navy Departments. Pointing out the discrepancies between the forces required by the Elkton Plan and the forces promised by the War Department, they recapitulated the views of the representatives of the Army Air Forces as disclosed at the conference meeting on 15 March, thereby indicating that General Wedemeyer was in sympathy with Admiral Cooke:

    (a) The decisions taken at the Anfa Conference require that the heaviest possible bomber offensive should be made against the GERMAN war effort.

    (b) This directive prevents the allocation of additional aircraft to the SOUTH PACIFIC and SOUTHWEST PACIFIC.

    (c) The War Department is not in a position to determine the Air Forces required for offensive operations in the SOUTH and SOUTHWEST PACIFIC, and could not, therefore, specify the "adequate forces to be allocated to the PACIFIC and FAR EASTERN THEATERS", but that the demands of the heaviest possible bomber offensive against GERMANY were, according to the interpretation of the War Department overriding as to forces required in the PACIFIC THEATER.

After discussing the availability of naval forces, the Joint Staff Planners stated their impressions of the situation. They were of the opinion that the Joint Chiefs of Staff intended that adequate forces should be provided to the Pacific and Far Eastern Theaters to maintain pressure on Japan and retain the initiative, but not to the extent of jeopardizing the capacity of the United Nations to take advantage of an opportunity to defeat Germany in 1943. The planners also felt that unless the Japanese Fleet and other enemy forces were pinned down in the Pacific it would not be practicable to undertake Anakim in 1943.

In specific relation to the proposed operations in the South and Southwest Pacific, the planners realized that shipping shortages would prevent fulfilling all the requirements of the Elkton Plan, yet they considered that available shipping would permit a substantial increase over the War Department's allocations without jeopardizing the offensive capabilities of the United Nations against Germany. Unless something was done, the 2 July directive could not be carried out. Until the Joint Chiefs of Staff made a decision as to what forces would be deployed in the South and the Southwest Pacific Areas, the planners did not consider that they or the area representatives could prepare directives or make plans. Informing the Joint Chiefs that the Commander, South Pacific, had already made preparations to seize Munda, New Georgia, in April, the Joint Staff Planners recommended that an early decision be made as to future operations in the South and Southwest Pacific.

Without having time themselves to study the JPS paper, the Joint Chiefs of Staff discussed it with them at a meeting attended also by the representatives from the Pacific.[52] Admiral Cooke, explaining briefly the contents of the paper, noted that "the senior Army and Navy Joint Staff Planners," i.e., himself and General Wedemeyer, disagreed with the allocations which the War Department had made on the basis of its interpretation of the Anfa agreements. Since the planners were not agreed as to the intent of these agreements, he requested the JCS to give their interpretation and to make a firm decision as to the forces to be allocated to the Pacific Theater in 1943. General Wedemeyer pointed out that the Army and Navy had almost reached agreement on deployments, only to find that the resources that appeared to be available for the Pacific were not sufficient in the estimation of the theater representatives. But the JPS were not authorized to allocate additional air forces nor to change the directive the theater commanders were endeavoring to execute.

Upon Admiral Leahy's suggestion that a new plan was therefore required, Admiral Cooke explained at greater length the significance of the difference of interpretation. One of the Anfa agreements called for the heaviest possible bomber offensive against Germany; another called for continuing operations in the Pacific and Far East in order to maintain pressure on Japan, retain the initiative, and attain a position of readiness for a full scale offensive against Japan after Germany was defeated. In his view these conflicted, and he asked for the interpretation of the Joint Chiefs, a basis for allocation of aircraft for 1943.

The discussion that followed is a good illustration of the dangers of generalization, for it appeared that the chiefs themselves were not sure what the agreements really meant. Admiral King suggested that the phrase in CCS 155/1, "the heaviest possible bomber offensive against the German war effort," not be taken too literally. He noted that Admiral Sir Dudley Pound had recently said that another statement in the same document, "the defeat of the U-boat must remain a first charge on the resources of the United Nations," should not be taken too literally, for other operations must go on concurrently. Neither of the statements should be interpreted as according priority so high that nothing would be left for other operations. Admiral King thought that probably the Joint Chiefs of Staff should give their interpretation of the decisions, perhaps reviewing them with the CCS. General Marshall's assumption that by "interpretation" Admiral King meant "translation of broad statements into terms of actual units" went undisputed.

Again Admiral Cooke, reminding the JCS that the air forces could be increased if the chiefs so desired, stated that a decision must be reached "as to what forces are required to carry out a continuous offensive and retain the initiative to a degree which will not jeopardize the opportunity of realizing on favorable circumstances on the Continent." Here Admiral King offered his view that the statement in CCS 155 that Anakim would be mounted in 1943 and certain operations would be carried out "after the capture of Rabaul" implied that Rabaul was to be taken in 1943, "a fact which [had]...considerable bearing on the interpretation of the problem now under discussion."

General Marshall stated that, as a practical matter, there were certain means already in the areas and others to be added. First it must be decided how the forces already available could be used, and then investigation could be made of what additional forces would be required. General Handy suggested that the Joint Staff Planners should provide recommendations, but they would need a definite interpretation of how many aircraft were to be sent to the United Kingdom. The whole strategy of the war would be changed if the groups Elkton called for were sent to the Pacific.

Admiral King now brought up the question of shipping. That available in the Pacific should be regarded as a firm commitment, he felt, on the basis of which the planners could decide the forces that could be moved. He recommended that the Joint Chiefs of Staff be informed of the most that could be done with the shipping available during the next three months. Again General Wedemeyer said the Joint Staff Planners should be able to produce some alternative plans if additional planes could be furnished.

Although the discussion had by now been going on for some time, no interpretation of the Anfa agreements had yet been arrived at. The differences of opinion on that subject within the JCS group were brought out into the open in the ensuing discussion. Major General G.E. Stratemeyer, representing General Arnold, led into the subject. He

> desired that it be noted that the primary aim of the United Nations is first the defeat of Germany and then the defeat of Japan. He said that every heavy and medium bomber which is taken from the United Kingdom allotments cuts down just that much on the bomber offensive against Germany. Any reduction of this bomber offensive is, in his opinion, contrary to the intent of the Anfa Agreements.
>
> Admiral King inquired of General Stratemeyer how he interpreted the Anfa agreements with regard to Pacific operations.
>
> General Stratemeyer said that, in his opinion, slight increases were to be made in the Pacific which would not affect operations against the Continent. He suggested that the Pacific representatives, once having been notified definitely of what they can get, then state what they can do.

Admiral King said that neither theater should be considered by itself, but as part of the whole. The only fixed thing at present is the amount of shipping available, and this must be considered the determining factor in deciding what forces can be shipped and maintained.

Here was the same argument that had been carried on all during the fall of 1942, whether it was more important to supply to the utmost the specific operations already under way in the Pacific or to send all possible planes to the United Kingdom to build up for potential operations against Germany. This difference Admiral Cooke recapitulated, insisting that if only the planes now allocated were sent to the Pacific and none were diverted from elsewhere no progress would have been made at the conference. General Marshall put in some support for General Stratemeyer, contending that if the bombing operations from the United Kingdom could be conducted with twice as many planes, losses would be less and morale would be higher. This, however, Admiral King pointed out, applied equally well to operations in the Pacific.

Admiral Leahy, who had been silent most of the time, now indicated that his sympathies were closer to those of Admiral King than those of General Stratemeyer. Whether Germany was bombed or not he felt that U.S. forces in Africa and the South Pacific must be adequately protected, for if these troops were neglected the Joint Chiefs could not face the people of the United States.

Ultimately, the JCS decided that the JPS should submit a report indicating:

(a) What forces over and above those now allocated to the Pacific can be sent to Pacific Theaters by full utilization of all shipping now available or to become available in the next several months in the Pacific Ocean.

(b) Where the additional forces, particularly the air forces involved, are to be obtained and what the implications of any other forces from other theaters would be.

(c) Concrete alternate proposals to the Joint Chiefs of Staff based on the studies directed in (a) and (b) above.

Two days later, on 18 March, the Joint Staff Planners submitted their report.[53] Their study of shipping availabilities had shown that an estimated 127,722 troop spaces and 87 cargo sailings would probably be available between 1 April and 30 September 1943. Since the planners had been unable to agree on the best way to utilize these resources they submitted two possible plans. Plan I was based on the War Department's interpretation of the operations contemplated in the Casablanca agreement (CCS 155/1). It provided for the movement of one division to the South Pacific, two divisions to the Southwest Pacific, "and a moderate increase in Air Force units to both areas" including the necessary supporting troops. This meant approximately 45,000 ground troops, 17,000 air forces, and 44,700 supporting and service. Plan II decreased the first of these by one division, leaving 30,000 ground forces, and increased the air forces to the full extent of the available shipping, 32,000 men. In addition Plan II would require three ship sailings in excess of the estimated eighty-seven, whereas Plan I stayed within the estimated figure. The reductions of aircraft assigned to the United Kingdom that would result from the increases in the Pacific were tabulated for each plan and for a variant of Plan I which would provide more aircraft than Plan I allotted to the Pacific. For Plan II the increase would be larger, but the Navy considered the consequent decrease in the United Kingdom entirely warranted and not sufficiently large to be of serious consequence.

The Army view of the alternatives were spelled out at greater length. Plan I, the Army felt, was in consonance with the Anfa concept, i.e., concentration of the maximum possible air and ground forces in the European and Mediterranean Theaters until Germany was defeated, at the same time providing forces for the Pacific adequate to prevent development of an adverse situation which would require retrieving by a diversion from the main effort against Germany. Since Plan II would provide forces to the Pacific more than adequate to fulfill the Anfa concept, the Army considered the plan's provisions inconsistent with United Nations global strategy for 1943. Moreover, they pointed out, Plan II would result in an inconclusive diversion from the United Kingdom, for the theater representatives had already said that the forces it would provide were not sufficient to conduct the Rabaul operation in 1943. In an enclosure to the paper, entitled "Army Views," the requirements for "proper execution of the bomber offensive directed by C.C.S. 155/1" were discussed at some length, with the conclusion that Plan II would cause "an unwarranted weakening at a critical time of the major bomber effort in 1943." Besides recommending approval of Plan I and consequent modification of the 2 July directive, the enclosure concluded with the recommendation:

> That the bomber offensive from the U.K. be implemented to a minimum strength of 1,200 heavy day bombers and appropriate supporting air forces in the shortest possible time, with subsequent rapid expansion by a firm plan.

This radical, and somewhat irrelevant, proposal was not included in the recommendations made by the Joint Staff Planners at the end of the paper. The planners simply proposed that the JCS made a decision as to the allocation that should be made and then issue a new directive to the Pacific commanders.

The Joint Chiefs of Staff, still including General Stratemeyer in General Arnold's place, met with the Joint Staff Planners on 19 March to discuss the paper, which bore the number JCS 238/1.[54] Admiral Cooke explained the alternate proposals the planners were presenting, pointing out that the question of allocation had proved so important that they had decided to request a resolution of it before attempting to prepare the alternate operational plans for which they had been asked.[55] The discussion centered around the controversial matter of plane assignments, but if it became heated the minutes give no indication of it. Both Admiral Cooke and General Wedemeyer assured the chiefs that the commanders in the Pacific area, if forced to make a choice, would prefer air forces rather than ground, however much they might need ground troops. In the course of the meeting General Marshall offered an explanation, not generally given, of why the Army Air Forces wanted such large numbers of bombers in the United Kingdom. It was, he explained, because when large numbers of planes (200 to 300) were sent over in one mission actual losses in numbers were no greater than when smaller missions were sent. This resulted in smaller percentage losses, greater impact on the enemy, and consequent raising of morale. General Marshall, however, joined with his Navy colleagues, and the Joint Chiefs gave official approval to Plan II as presented in JCS 238/1.[56] Having further agreed to inform the Pacific theater commanders and the members of the Pacific Conference of their decision, the Joint Chiefs of Staff directed the latter to explore the possibilities of offensive operations that could be undertaken in 1943 with the forces allotted and to be prepared to present their views to the chiefs, not, however, committing their respective commanders by so doing.

The deliberations of the theater representatives have not been preserved. However the following day General Sutherland, Admiral Spruance, and Captain Browning responded to the Joint Chiefs' directive with a brief statement:

> It is the opinion of the conferees of the Pacific Conference that with the means allotted on the schedule specified in the JCS memorandum of March 20, 1943, the forces of the two areas, during 1943, can execute task two of the JCS Directive of July 2, 1942, to include Madang, the Southeast portion of Bougainville Island, and can extend this line forward to include Cape Gloucester, Kiriwina Island and Woodlark Island.[57]

With this at hand, the Joint Chiefs of Staff, General Arnold again among them, met with the theater representatives for amplification of the theater views.[58]

General Sutherland acted as spokesman for the group. The completion of these objectives would, he explained, achieve control of a line of communications between the Netherlands East Indies and New Britain, leaving for the Japanese only the route south from Truk. It would also "facilitate prospective operations," provide take-off points for further operations in the South Pacific, prepare the way for a converging attack on Rabaul from both areas, provide bases from which medium bombers could operate with fighter coverage against Rabaul, and, in general, move up covering land-based planes to support further advances against that ultimate objective.

One of the major modifications of Elkton which the new concept offered was the establishment of air bases on Kiriwina and

Woodlark Islands. Although the feasibility of occupying at least one of those islands had been considered earlier, they had been left out of the version of Elkton which was presented at the conference, for that plan called for sufficient heavy bombers to provide support from greater distances. Woodlark and Kiriwina were suggested again by the Joint War Plans Committee and seized upon by the theater representatives as feasible objectives.[59] As General Sutherland explained, it was felt that essential support would best be furnished by medium bombers based on the two islands. Moreover, Woodlark at least was within medium bomber range of Buin on southern Bougainville and Faisi, just below, and could probably render those areas untenable for the Japanese. An additional advantage, one which appealed to representatives from both areas, was that Woodlark would provide a convenient stepping stone for the interchange of air units between the South and the Southwest Pacific Areas. Occupation of Kiriwina and Woodlark would come first, initiated simultaneously some time in April.

Another important change from Elkton was omission of occupation of New Georgia as the next objective in the Solomons area. With bases on Woodlark and Kiriwina as well as at Lae and Salamaua and possibly at Cape Gloucester, it was felt that sufficient air support could be provided so that New Georgia could be bypassed and Bougainville next occupied, thereby advancing U.S. forces that much closer toward Rabaul. Should it prove desirable, however, New Georgia would be occupied first.

The sequence of the operations after Kiriwina and Woodlark became a topic of considerable discussion. General Sutherland expressed the opinion that occupation of the points in New Guinea should precede any operations by the South Pacific forces, for there would not be sufficient means for simultaneous attacks on both the Solomons and New Guinea. "He felt that the Huon Peninsula should first be secured and the Bougainville operations deferred until Lae and Salamaua were taken." On further questioning he suggested that operations in the Solomons might be put off until after the capture of Cape Gloucester on New Britain. The theater representatives were disposed to accept this time sequence, but to Admiral King it seemed questionable. While they awaited securing of the Huon Peninsula naval forces in the South Pacific Area would be immobilized, and he suggested that they should be in use elsewhere, for instance against the Gilberts and Marshalls.

Although the theater representatives recognized Admiral King's point that the naval forces should not be held to the South Pacific Area during this period, they were not in favor of moving immediately against the Gilberts and Marshalls. Admiral Spruance advocated moving part of the fleet back to the Hawaiian area, since the Japanese plans were not known, and putting another part to work clearing the Japanese from the Aleutians. If there was to be an attack on the Gilberts and Marshalls, he felt that at least two or three Japanese positions should be taken. Operations there would be unprofitable unless they could be continuous. Captain Browning took a less serious view than Admiral King of the freedom the Japanese Fleet would enjoy while the U.S. forces in the South Pacific were idle. He pointed out that the South Pacific Area was closest to the Japanese shipping lanes and that U.S. naval forces there were nearest to the area the Japanese considered vital. To be sure, unless the Japanese Fleet entered the area the U.S. Fleet would be relatively immobilized. Yet Captain Browning considered that, unless naval action elsewhere would materially aid the South Pacific, operations against Rabaul offered the most promising method of containing the Japanese Fleet. Of course, as General Sutherland pointed out, the time sequence was not hard and fast and the situation that developed in the area might well indicate that modification would be desirable. Certainly no final decision could be made at this meeting, and although it was apparent that Admiral King favored action in the Solomons as soon as possible, he did not pursue the matter further.

After a rather long discussion the Joint Chiefs of Staff went into closed session, of which no minutes were kept. They emerged having agreed to approve in principle the concept of operations which the theater representatives offered and to direct the Joint Staff Planners to prepare a directive that would provide for its implementation.

Following this decision in respect to the Southwest Pacific, Admiral King brought to the attention of General Marshall the desirability of action in the northern area of the same ocean. Pointing out that the Japanese were known to be establishing an airfield on Attu Island, he warned that if it were completed and the enemy built supporting fields on Shemya and Agattu eventual recapture of the areas would be much more difficult. Since the JCS had just decided to defer extensive operations in the Solomons, Admiral King felt that they had additional reason and sufficient forces for proceeding to attack Attu, and he submitted a draft directive for General Marshall's approval.[60] Concurrence was received the same day, 22 March 1943, and the directive was issued for the operation ultimately launched on 11 May.[61]

THE NEW DIRECTIVE FOR THE SOUTH-SOUTHWEST PACIFIC

The final agreement of the Pacific Military Conference had completely overlooked the knottiest problem of them all--who was to exercise over-all command of the operations. The subject had in fact been entirely omitted from the discussion, at least from that part which is recorded, but it had by no means been forgotten.

While the Joint Chiefs of Staff were awaiting the comments of the theater representatives as to what operations could be undertaken in the South and the Southwest Pacific Areas with the forces to be available, Admiral King, on the recommendation of Admiral

Cooke, sent to General Marshall a draft of a proposed new directive for the theater commanders. It provided in general terms for seizure and occupation of the Solomons and seizure and occupation of Salamaua, Lae, and Markham Valley positions in New Guinea, with the ultimate objective seizure and occupation of the New Britain-New Ireland-Admiralty Island area. The Solomons would be placed temporarily in the South Pacific Area and operations in the two areas would be coordinated by the JCS.[62] Nothing came of this proposal, for the Joint Chiefs' approval in principle of the concept of operations presented to them on 21 March altered the situation, and Army and Navy planners set to work anew to attempt to draft a directive for General MacArthur and Admiral Nimitz.

The initiative came first from Admiral Cooke, who submitted a draft to General Wedemeyer of Army OPD on 22 March.[63] Admiral Cooke proposed to cancel the directive of 2 July, substituting another that would follow closely the limited concept. He set as immediate objectives the two operations which it had been agreed should be undertaken at once, i.e., occupation and establishment of airfields on Kiriwina and Woodlark Islands. These, it was explained, would provide ready air communications between the South and the Southwest Pacific Areas and support for operations to seize and occupy: (a) Lae, Salamaua, Finschhafen, Madang, and the western portion of New Britain; (b) the Solomons. Forces in both areas would then be in a position to converge on Rabaul. The operations were designed to inflict losses on the Japanese, deny the areas to them, and make the areas available instead to U.S. forces for further operations against the enemy.

As has already been related, the problem of command for the next moves in the South and Southwest Pacific Areas had long been unresolved. Admiral Cooke now proposed that the Solomon Islands be temporarily assigned to the Commander, South Pacific, for the operations outlined in this directive. Specific phases of the operations would be coordinated between the two areas by mutual cooperation, the two commanders keeping each other advised as to their plans and progress by frequent exchanges of visits of their staff officers. In addition, air efforts against the New Britain-New Ireland area were to be coordinated under the supervision of the Commander, Southwest Pacific, while coordination of naval operations in the Coral Sea-Solomons area would be under general supervision of the Commander, South Pacific. The latter would also furnish naval support as needed and practicable.

Admiral Cooke and General Handy apparently discussed this draft the same day it was sent and determined their area of disagreement, for Admiral Cooke immediately submitted a revised version in which only the details of coordination were changed. Mutual cooperation was still to be the rule, and the Solomons were to be under the Commander, South Pacific, but the Commander, Southwest Pacific, was to make recommendations to the JCS in respect to coordination, initiation, and sequence of operations.

He was to be responsible for coordination of all air operations between the two areas instead of being limited to those in the New Britain-New Ireland area.⁶⁴

In presenting this revised draft to General Handy, Admiral Cooke pointed out certain problems that remained unsolved. Despite the provision that General MacArthur would be responsible for coordination of air operations in the two areas, when fleet units were brought into the South and Southwest Pacific Areas the naval commander would have to have shore-based air supporting units under his command. Placing shore-based air in the South Pacific Area completely under General MacArthur's control would break up the unity of command indispensable to naval operations. Furthermore, it was not possible to disassociate amphibious operations in the Solomon Islands from the Pacific Area. "If the sine qua non is to be a unity of command, that must be under the Commander in Chief of the Pacific Area,--and by 'Pacific Area' I mean the strategic whole not separated by artificial lines." Should an emergency elsewhere necessitate withdrawing fleet forces from the Solomons during the operations, CinCPac would have to evaluate their need there against the new threat. In Admiral Cooke's estimation, only if CinCPac were responsible for both could he make the proper evaluation.

In a separate memorandum to General Handy, Admiral Cooke listed seven factors which led him to the conclusion that, if there was to be unified command, as the War Department urged, it was "up to the War Department to take the steps necessary to set it up as a unified Naval Command." The list is a good summary of the arguments advanced frequently by naval spokesmen:

(a) The July 2nd Directive stated that necessary land based air support would be attached by MacArthur to Ghormley's command for TASK ONE. This was never carried out or suggested by either MacArthur or the War Dept.

(b) After receiving July 2nd Directive MacArthur stated that it could not be started nor carried out. Later, after 10 July Despatch he did not agree nor acquiesce.

(c) When Plan was produced and brought to Washington both the Plan and the representatives stated flatly that no effective operations could be carried out without the minimum addition of six divisions and 1,000 new planes.

(d) It was upon Navy urging in opposition to War Dept that the present accretions and allocations have been determined.

(e) In urging reinforcements to the SOUTHWEST Pacific the Navy had taken the position that it is necessary to our Naval position in the PACIFIC as a whole.

(f) When commands were set up in England for operations in FRANCE and for the invasion of AFRICA with subsequent Mediterranean operations in view, the Navy recognized that this was an Army matter and accorded unified command to the Army upon its own initiative. The problem for the immediate, as well as the more distant future, is an Army problem.

(g) In the PACIFIC the battles of the CORAL SEA, of DUTCH HARBOR, of MIDWAY, the dozen Naval battles in the SOLOMON ISLANDS-SANTA CRUZ AREA would appear to give conclusive demonstration that the PACIFIC is one strategic problem,--is and will continue to be a Naval problem as a whole.[65]

On 24 March Admiral Cooke presented General Handy with still another draft directive, superseding all those previously offered.[66] This one, he explained, was in line with two provisions of the original directives establishing the Pacific Ocean Area: "Support the operations of the forces in the SOUTHWEST PACIFIC AREA"; and "Prepare for the execution of major amphibious offensives against positions held by Japan, the initial offensives to be launched from the SOUTH PACIFIC Area and SOUTHWEST PACIFIC Area." In his opinion the fleet and supporting air forces would have to remain under the control of CinCPOA, if he was to carry out the other tasks in his directive, i.e., holding island positions between the United States and the Southwest Pacific Area, containing Japanese forces, supporting North American defense, and protecting essential air and sea communications. Either there must be unity of command under Admiral Nimitz or the tasks must be divided between him (or specifically between his representative, the Commander, South Pacific) and General MacArthur. The latter arrangement was what Admiral Cooke's draft of 24 March provided. The two local commanders were to make recommendations to the Joint Chiefs of Staff who would then determine the time of the various operations. In the theater, when forces from both areas operated jointly, the Supreme Commander, Southwest Pacific, was to coordinate the air operations, except for those in direct support of naval surface operations. When naval surface and subsurface forces from both operated jointly, they were to be coordinated by the Commander, South Pacific. The other alternative Admiral Cooke offered, unity of command under Admiral Nimitz, was spelled out in still another draft prepared by the Navy planners.[67]

While Admiral Cooke was submitting his numerous drafts, the Army planners had not been ignoring them. There had undoubtedly been oral discussion, and the Army officers had also prepared some drafts of their own which their Navy colleagues may well have seen, although available records do not indicate that they were sent from General Handy to Admiral Cooke. On 25 March, however, General Handy made a move to clarify the issues by presenting three alternative directives, the first providing for unified command under the Supreme Commander, Southwest Pacific, the second, unified command under the Commander in Chief, Pacific Areas, and the third, mutual coordination.[68] The first of these had been developed by the Army planners. The second and third were a modification of the Navy's drafts. In wording and arrangement the three varied, but each provided for accomplishment of the same immediate tasks and for achievement of the same ultimate objective, for all were based on the concept the Joint Chiefs of Staff had just approved in principle.

It was the first arrangement, unified command under the Supreme Commander, Southwest Pacific Area, that appealed particularly to the Army, for it had consistently advocated carrying out the letter of the 2 July directive that provided for transfer of command to General MacArthur for Tasks Two and Three. After receiving some comments on the first alternative,[69] the Army planners rewrote it on the skeleton provided by the Navy's draft directive to establish unified command under CinCPOA, and General Marshall submitted it to the Joint Chiefs of Staff.[70]

It read as follows:

1. The Joint Chiefs of Staff directive communicated in COMINCH despatch 022100 of July 1942 is cancelled and the following directive is substituted therefor.

2. Command.
   a. The operations outlined in this directive will be conducted under the direction of the Supreme Commander, Southwest Pacific Area.
   b. Operations in the Solomons Islands will be under the direct command of the Commander, SOPAC Area, operating under general directives of the Supreme Commander, Southwest Pacific Area.
   c. Naval units of the Pacific Fleet assigned as task forces engaged in these operations will remain under the control of the Commander in Chief, Pacific.

3. Forces. Additional forces will be allocated to the Southwest Pacific and South Pacific Areas as indicated in Joint Chiefs of Staff dispatch 232357.

4. Tasks.
   a. Establish air fields on Kiriwina and Woodlark Islands.
   b. Seize Lae Salamaua Finschaven Madang Area and occupy Western New Britain.
   c. Seize and occupy Solomon Islands to include the southern portion of Bougainville.

5. Purposes. To inflict losses on Japanese forces, to deny these areas to Japan, to contain Japanese forces in the Pacific Theater by maintaining the initiative, and to prepare for ultimate seizure of Bismarck Archipelago.

6. Plans. Supreme Commander, Southwest Pacific Area, will submit general plans including sequence and timing of major offensive operations to the Joint Chiefs of Staff.

Brigadier General J.R. Deane, the JCS Secretary, passed this proposed directive informally to Admiral Leahy and Admiral King for comment. Their remarks were of such a nature that discussion seemed desirable and a special JCS meeting was called for 1100 on Sunday, 28 March.[71]

Both of the admirals, in memoranda commenting on General Marshall's draft, expressed dissatisfaction with paragraph 2 c. Admiral Leahy's sole suggestion removed control of Pacific Fleet units from Admiral Nimitz, stating, "Units of the Pacific Fleet necessary to the accomplishment of the directive will be assigned by the Commander in Chief of the Pacific Fleet."[72] Admiral King's comments were more extensive. He proposed substituting for paragraph 2 c, "Forces assigned the PACIFIC OCEAN AREAS and used as Task Forces engaged in these operations will remain under the control of the Commander in Chief, Pacific Ocean Areas, except for those forces specifically assigned to the direct command of the Supreme Commander, Southwest Pacific Area." He based his suggestion on his view that all forces, ground, air, naval surface and subsurface, were required for mutual support in maintaining the security of the Pacific Ocean Areas. Consequently, all elements of the forces used in the Solomons operations should remain available to meet situations anywhere in the Pacific Ocean areas. Separating the operations in the Solomons from operations elsewhere in the Pacific Ocean areas, while it might achieve unified control in that area, would result in divided control within the Pacific Ocean areas as between the Central and North Pacific on the one hand and the South Pacific on the other. If there was to be unified control, he urged, it should be in accordance with the Navy planners' draft directive which vested it in CinCPOA. He included a copy of that draft as well as one of those providing for mutual coordination, but he made no attempt to argue the superior merits of either arrangement. He did, however, attempt to insure that the operations in the Solomons would not be forced to await completion of the operations in New Guinea by recommending inclusion in paragraph 6 of General Marshall's draft of the statement: "The Joint Chiefs of Staff do not desire the timing of Task 4 c. be delayed to follow the completion of Tasks 4 a. and 4 b."[73]

At the special meeting of the Joint Chiefs[74] the discussion centered upon paragraph 2 c and the question of command, but no consideration was given to the possibility of assigning over-all command to anyone but General MacArthur. General Marshall explained that the troublesome paragraph had been worded as it was in order to overcome the usual Navy objection to placing a large naval force under the control of an Army officer. It was a problem of attempting to achieve coordination of the ground and air operations without embarrassing fleet movements. It seemed to the group that the statement thus made might easily lead to differences of opinion between General MacArthur and Admiral Nimitz and that it must be so put that the operations would be adequately provided for and yet CinCPOA could call on necessary units, not just ships, but ground and air as well, to meet a threat elsewhere to the security of his large command. After considerable discussion, Admiral King finally proposed saying, "Units of Pacific Ocean Areas other than those assigned by the Joint Chiefs of Staff to task forces, will remain under command of the Commander in Chief, Pacific Ocean Areas (CINCPAC)." This pleased everyone, for it removed from both of the local commanders responsibility for deciding which forces were essential to the operation and it left the way open for the remainder of the Pacific Fleet to participate or not as the situation demanded. Inclusion of that statement in the directive led to addition by General Marshall of the composition of task forces as an item on which the Supreme Commander, Southwest Pacific Area, should make recommendations. And it also led Admiral King to suggest rewording paragraph 3 to read, "Forces will be allocated for these operations as determined by the Joint Chiefs of Staff."

With these changes, but without Admiral King's suggestion for paragraph 6, which the other chiefs considered unnecessary, the revised directive was sent to the theater commanders.[75] Thus, despite the long discussion that had been carried on between Admiral King and General Marshall as to who should command Tasks Two and Three, and the strong stand the Navy planners had taken against vesting control in General MacArthur, the provision of the original 2 July directive was amicably adopted, with the guarantee that fleet units would be available to Admiral Nimitz.[76]

Chapter XIV

POST-CASABLANCA PROBLEMS: CHINA AND BURMA

Strategic planning for the Pacific Theater was only one of the numerous problems that confronted the Joint Chiefs of Staff in the months following the conference at Casablanca. The necessity to curtail plans for the Pacific Theater because of the demands of Sickle (the bombing program from the United Kingdom) had involved an interservice conflict within the JCS organization. During the same period, however, other problems, developing in attempts to implement the Casablanca decisions, had revealed the existence of basic differences between the American and the British Chiefs of Staff, as well as shortages of items essential to the several projects.

It will be recalled that at Casablanca it had been decided that the next operation in the European Theater was to be invasion of the island of Sicily, the operation that was to be called by the code name "Husky." As an action against Germany, Husky would have priority on the resources of the United Nations, after completion of Torch. At the same time, the Combined Chiefs of Staff agreed to support and develop several other projects of strategic importance, among them the heaviest possible bomber offensive against the German war effort (Sickle), continuation of the Bolero build-up, support of Free French in Tunisia, encouragement of Turkey to become an active ally, recapture of Burma (Anakim), continuation of offensive operations in the Pacific, and, as a first charge, defeat of the U-boat in the Atlantic.[1]

The U.S. Chiefs had returned to Washington at the end of January with a sense of accomplishment and had set about trying to implement the decisions they had just made. Almost at once they ran into difficulties. Their troubles rose from two basic causes: inaccurate and incomplete estimations of available resources, especially of shipping, in comparison with the demands being placed upon them, and lack of precise statements of the meaning and import of the agreements and decisions being made. These circumstances soon resulted in conflicts, conflicts among the various projects as their requirements impinged on one another's needs, and conflicts between American and British Chiefs of Staff as their interpretations and understandings of the Casabalnca agreements varied. Most of the problems of the period were definitely concerned with the war against Germany and are discussed elsewhere in the History of the Joint Chiefs of Staff.[2] This chapter will consider only those matters which directly affected the progress of the war against Japan.

ARNOLD, DILL, AND SOMERVELL AT NEW DELHI AND CHUNGKING

After considerable talk and some pressure by the U.S. Chiefs, Anakim, the project for retaking all of Burma, had finally been approved by the Combined Chiefs of Staff at Casablanca. Specifically, it was agreed "that all plans and necessary preparations should be made for the purpose of mounting Anakim in 1943,"[3] and 15 November 1943 was settled upon "as the provisional date for the Anakim assault." Although a "provisional schedule of forces," dependent upon the situation in the late summer, was approved, the way was left open for cancellation of the whole project by the stipulation that the Combined Chiefs of Staff would "confirm in July 1943 the decision to undertake or to postpone Operation Anakim."[4] As plans were developed during the succeeding weeks, Anakim's material needs soon conflicted with the needs of other strategic undertakings and the prospects of launching it on schedule grew dimmer.

Immediately after the conclusion of the Casablanca Conference, General Arnold and Sir John Dill headed east for India and China to confer, as representatives both of the CCS and of the President and Prime Minister, with Field Marshal Sir Archibald P. Wavell and Generalissimo Chiang Kai-shek. The purpose of their trip was to explain the Casablanca decisions and to ascertain what the local commanders could do in the way of a campaign to recapture Burma and what reenforcements they would need.[5] In addition, General Arnold and Lieutenant General Brehon Somervell, who was also in the party, were to investigate the situation in respect to aviation, both air transport and combat operations. The President at Casablanca had emphasized that reconquest of Burma was not to be an end in itself, but that the objective for the theater was to build up as much air strength as possible in China in order to attack Japanese shipping and to bomb Japan. So it was that in both New Delhi and Chungking General Arnold stated plainly that the main purpose of the proposed action was to deliver supplies to General Chennault and thus expedite direct attack from China on Japanese shipping and bases.[6]

Before the formal discussion with Field Marshal Wavell began, General Arnold was given a copy of the plan prepared by the local planning staff for a campaign to recapture western Burma.[7] To his considerable disappointment he discovered that it "expressed all the difficulties but did not give any indication of how Burma could actually be reconquered." In view of the decision at Casablanca to give Anakim priority, he felt that there was more likelihood than the paper assumed that the requisite resources would be available.[8] At the first meeting with Field Marshal Wavell on 1 February General Arnold presented his views, recommending that "it was for the [theater] J.P.S. to prepare a paper stating what was needed to take Burma in one cold season. It would then be for the Combined Chiefs of Staff to see if the resources could be made available."[9] Field Marshal Wavell was prepared to agree that a more extensive plan was required, but he, too, pointed out difficulties, mainly of climate and geography, which the mere addition of resources could not overcome. In brief outline he sketched the plan to retake all of Burma in one winter, by Chinese troops advancing from Yunnan and Ledo to converge at Mandalay with British troops advancing from the Chindwin River. The group at New Delhi discussed at considerable length the desirability of controlling the southern shore of Burma, capturing Rangoon or at least rendering it useless to the Japanese. It was finally concluded that the theater joint planners should

> examine the requirements necessary to take Burma in one season, their outline plan being as originally proposed by the British Joint Planning Staff for Upper Burma; while for Lower Burma the plan would be:-
> (a) A landing at Taungup with an offensive overland employing about one division, with the object of containing and using up enemy forces;
> (b) The capture of Bassein by assault from the Arakan coast with the primary object of taking the airfields in that area and the secondary object of containing and using up enemy forces;
> (c) A direct assault on Rangoon by an advance up the river, landing small parties or parachutists on the banks to deal with the defenses.

Field Marshal Wavell, Sir John Dill, and General Arnold were joined at their meetings the following day (2 February) by Lieutenant General J.W. Stilwell and by Lieutenant General Brehon Somervell, head of the Army's Services of Supply, who had accompanied them from Casablanca, with the main objective of investigating the air transport situation over the Hump. Brigadier General Albert C. Wedemeyer of Army OPD, who was also visiting the theater, attended three of the four subsequent meetings of the group. Various high ranking officers attached to the theater were also occasionally in attendance. The discussions covered a wide range of local problems connected with the project to recapture Burma and afforded the visitors from Washington an opportunity to become acquainted with the local commanders and their methods of operation.

At the second meeting of the group, general agreement on objectives for immediate action in the brief period remaining before the onset of the monsoon was reached with little discussion. The following would be undertaken:

> (a) From Yunnan--limited offensive operations with a view to gaining positions for an offensive after the monsoon.[10]
> (b) From Ledo--limited offensive operations to cover the road construction which is to be pushed as far as possible in the direction of Mogaung.[11]

(c) From the Imphal area--an advance to the Chindwin between Tamu, Kalewa and Kalemyo with raids by the land forces east of the Chindwin, with a view to the establishment of bridgeheads.

(d) From Tiddim in the Lushai Hills--control of the Chin Hills.[12]

(e) On the Arakan Coast--the capture of Akyab and, if possible, Ramree Island.

The ill-fated attempt by the British to seize Akyab by an overland assault (Cannibal)[13] was already under way, and despite an unpromising start there was still hope for ultimate success. Assuming that these preliminary operations would have been successfully executed before the onset of the monsoon, the joint planners drew up an outline plan for the recapture of Burma in one season, starting in the fall of 1943 when the monsoon subsided. The group meeting with Field Marshal Dill gave careful consideration to this plan and its implications and agreed on the outline of the campaign:

(a) An offensive from Yunnan on the Mandalay area by about 11 Chinese divisions to which about 5 additional Chinese divisions from east Yunnan might possibly be added as a reserve....

(b) An advance from Ledo on the Mandalay area by the Chinese Corps now training at Ramgarh.

(c) An advance from the Tamu-Kalewa area on the Mandalay area by British forces of approximately 3 divisions.

(d) The following series of assaults by British forces on the Arakan Coast:

(1) At Kyaukpyu (Ramree Island) if not already taken, and at Sandoway and Gwa, with the object of capturing airfields.

(2) At Taungup, to open the way for an offensive overland to Prome and the Rangoon Road, employing about one division, with the object of containing and using up enemy forces.

(3) On the coast opposite Bassein, to open the way for an overland advance to capture Bassein, with the primary object of capturing the airfields in that area; and the secondary object of containing and using up enemy forces by an advance overland towards Henzada and then Rangoon.

(e) A direct assault on Rangoon by an advance up the river, landing commando parties or parachutists to deal with the defenses.[14]

In order to execute these operations successfully, reenforcements of men, ships, and planes would be required. It would be particularly necessary to reenforce the British Eastern Fleet in order that it might supply the support which the group at New Delhi considered essential to success and on which the Generalissimo insisted. Unfortunately, although Admiral Sir F.J. Somerville, Commander of the Eastern Fleet, was not there to speak for himself, the British officers present believed that the prospects were slim for large-scale reenforcements of naval vessels or for prolonged deployment of the fleet in its current condition in the Bay of Bengal.

The outlook on shipping, however, seemed more favorable. The British shipping expert, Major General S.W. Kirby, on hand for discussion of that problem, estimated that the program before them would require about 150,000 tons a month from the United States and 50,000 tons a month from the United Kingdom, in addition to existing allotments, for a period of six months. General Somervell's reaction to this estimate indicated that he at least considered that Anakim had been given firm approval at Casablanca and that its requirements would be accorded high priority. Optimistically he commented "that he did not think this figure looked too formidable. He said that as soon as he got back he would try to arrange for the shipping that was necessary to carry the American consignments to be made available, the object being to get the last consignments in by August or September."[15]

Leaving details of the plan to be worked out on the planning levels, General Arnold and Sir John Dill went on to Chungking to discuss the Chinese view of the operation.

The discussions in the Chinese capital were of a somewhat different nature from those at New Delhi, for the Generalissimo's interests lay less in the campaign in Burma and more in the development of air power in China. At this first meeting with General Arnold, on 6 February, Chiang presented a list of "points with relation to operations in China":

(a) Very important that a separate Air Task Force under Gen. Chennault be formed in China. That Task Force to be under Generalissimo's direct control. No other organization would work. Chennault only air man who understood Chinese.

(b) He has reorganized Chinese Air Force and had put it under Chennault's control.

(c) He wanted a firm commitment for 500 planes for the operations in China prior to November, 1943.

(d) The Chinese Air Force must be built up.

(e) The tonnage from India into China must be built up far beyond its present capacity.

(f) There must be a firm commitment of strength for naval forces to be used in Burma operations.[16]

Only the last two points had direct bearing on the campaign in Burma. The first four had far-reaching implications and will be discussed in a separate section of this chapter.

General Arnold was not in a position to promise to supply all of the Generalissimo's requests. He did, however, tell Chiang that both the U.S. and the British navies were going to give "full support" to the Burma operations. At a meeting later in the day Sir John Dill spoke of naval support as a requisite for any conquest of Burma. The Generalissimo accepted the assurances of British assistance and expressed gratification that adequate naval forces would be provided. In respect to transport over the Hump, General Arnold reported that a request had already been made to Washington to augment the 62 planes operating over the Hump to 137 by 31 March 1943. Thirteen of these would be assigned to General Stilwell's headquarters. The remaining 124 would have an estimated capacity of 4,000 tons monthly, whereas the maximum that had been achieved up to that time was 1,700 tons. The Generalissimo made no particular comment then nor at a larger meeting that evening when General Bissell told in more detail the plans for development of the Hump route. The following morning, however, Chiang announced that he could not successfully prosecute the war without a minimum of 500 planes operating in China by November and a monthly delivery of 10,000 tons, a figure which General Arnold could not promise for any given time, for 4,000 tons at that moment seemed optimistic. He could only attempt to satisfy the Generalissimo with the assurance that every effort would be made to increase the Hump capacity as rapidly as possible and point out that facilities and personnel in China did not then suffice to accommodate and maintain 500 planes.

In the meantime, plans for the operations in Burma had also been under discussion. At the first meeting he attended, Sir John Dill outlined for the Generalissimo the project that had been approved at New Delhi. With only general reference to British plans for direct attack on Rangoon, for the British were still unwilling to disclose their plans to the Chinese, Sir John stressed the importance of attacks by ground forces from the north, coordinated with whatever type of assault on Rangoon might prove feasible. Again General Arnold introduced the point "that the purpose was to prepare the way through Burma to make it possible to hit Japan more effectively." In answer to a direct question the Generalissimo stated that he would give the President a letter assuring that the Chinese would do their part in the coming operation. When he found, however, that he was not to be guaranteed satisfaction for any of his requests, his assurance was less definite. At the final meeting he still said that "he was quite ready to play his part," but he insisted that 4,000 tons monthly was not enough. "Unless the air cargo capacity of 10,000 tons a month can be met by the end of November and...the air forces in China--United States and Chinese--have 500 planes for operations by November, he...[could not] give any assurance of success of the campaign." He did not, however, refuse to participate if his requests were not granted, and, questioned by General Stilwell, Chiang stated: "China has been fighting for six years. It will continue to fight. China is ready to carry out its part, but equipment and supplies are necessary to give a smashing blow." The British and American representatives closed the conference by signifying their understanding that the Chinese would participate in the Burma campaign. They then returned to Calcutta to complete arrangements there.

On 9 February the group met again with Field Marshal Wavell, joined this time by General Ho Ying-chin, Colonel T.T. Chen, and Mr. Soong.[17] This time the discussion was largely among the local commanders, comparing information as to the potential strength of the Japanese in Burma and planning the moves each force would make in the full scale campaign. At the conclusion of the meeting, Field Marshall Wavell "summed up by saying that all were in agreement, and it remained only for all to press on with the greatest possible energy their preparations to start the battle immediately after the monsoon."

Field Marshall Wavell at once reported the conclusions of the meetings in India in a despatch to the British Chiefs of Staff. This was forwarded to the Joint Chiefs of Staff by the British Staff Mission in Washington.[18] Upon General Arnold's return the minutes of all the meetings were circulated to the CCS, who were thus acquainted with the decisions and with the major points of disagreement which had arisen. It remained for the British to investigate the detailed requirements of the outline operational plan Field Marshal Wavell was to develop and to determine what they could supply and what would be required from the United States. Then, in accordance with the agreement at Casablanca, the CCS would make the final decision as to when Anakim should be mounted.[19]

Thus in mid-February it appeared from the formal records that the way was prepared for development of detailed plans for the limited operations in Burma in the spring and for the full scale Anakim in the fall. But there were two large areas of uncertainty that are obvious in retrospect and were not wholly unrecognized at the time. One was cooperation by the Chinese, which Chiang himself had indicated was dependent on the provision of adequate supplies. At least one of the participants in the discussions reported to Washington his doubts that the Chinese would actually pull their weight in the projected campaign. This was General Wedemeyer, who, in a radio message commenting on the conferences, informed General Marshall that if the British did accomplish the objectives outlined for the period before the monsoon "the Chinese will only half heartedly collaborate if at all."[20] Despite Sir John Dill's remark to the Combined Chiefs of Staff on 19 February that the participation of the Chinese in the Burma operation "should be regarded in the nature of a bonus and it would at least pin down Japanese forces,"[21] their participation had a definite place in the agreed plan. General Wedemeyer also touched on the other area of doubt, namely British lack of enthusiasm for the plan, by recommending that the British be stimulated to increased activity in order that Akyab could be taken before the monsoon. A similar misgiving may be read in General Arnold's later published account of his discussions at New Delhi, where the inadequacies of the plan with which he was presented and the inertia of the British officers impressed him in particularly striking fashion.[22] By the time

General Arnold returned to Washington the prospects for success in the British attempt to capture Akyab were fading rapidly and the likelihood of full British support in the fall if the limited spring offensives failed seemed questionable. By then, too, the demands of other projects that had been approved at Casablanca had begun to prove greater than the available resources of the United Nations and the possibility of providing in full for the requirements of Anakim was growing increasingly doubtful.

AIR POWER IN CHINA

While the conferences held in Chungking on 6 and 7 February 1943 served to advance preparations for combined operations in China-Burma-India, they were also of great significance in the development of U.S. relations with China. By demonstrating clearly that General Chennault had the enthusiastic support of the White House, the discussions increased his prestige with the Chinese while lessening that of General Stilwell, for the policies and the programs the two men supported were not without conflict.

When Mr. Lauchlin Currie returned from his special mission to China in August 1942,[23] recommending that General Stilwell be relieved and more support be given to General Chennault, it will be remembered, General Marshall advised against it, for he was convinced that General Stilwell was doing a good job and should remain.[24] In December clamors for more planes in China had grown louder and Mr. Roosevelt had suggested consideration of giving "our 'prima donna' Chennault" one hundred planes to operate north of the Yangtze, independent of General Stilwell's command.[25] General Marshall, however, had expressed the view "that the time was not right to establish a separate air force in China; that as soon as adequate lines of communication, including the land route, were established from India to China, the entire U.S. Air Force in the Asiatic Theater should be based in China."[26] His view prevailed and no change was made.

When General Arnold went to Chungking he carried a letter from the President to the Generalissimo which, while containing no mention of General Stilwell's project of reorganizing thirty Chinese Army divisions in Yunnan, made it clear that the President was ready to support General Chennault's program.

> This note will be given to you by Lieutenant General Henry H. Arnold, U.S. Army, Commander of our Air Forces. I am sending him to you because I am determined to increase General Chennault's Air Force in order that you may carry the offensive to the Japanese at once. General Arnold will work out the ways and means with you and General Chennault.[27]

This was certain to be pleasing to the Generalissimo, in whose esteem General Chennault held a high place, and who felt that it was entirely possible that the Japanese could be defeated by air power alone, without the need of strong ground forces.

How pleasing the President's words were to Chiang is apparent from the minutes of the meetings in Chungking. The Generalissimo was prepared to ask for more planes and more independence for General Chennault, and, as has already been mentioned, he did both at his first conference with General Arnold. Since his arrival in China General Arnold had been studying the air situation and had decided to take steps to increase the number of planes in operation there.[28] Consequently he was able to tell Chiang that he had asked for 137 cargo planes for the Hump by the end of March, but that their operation would depend on completion of airfields at both ends of the route, that a heavy bombardment group of 35 planes was already on the way to China, and that plans were being made to form a Chinese fighter group and a light bombardment group to operate with the U.S. air forces in China. General Chennault had at that time approximately 75 fighters; 13 medium bombers and 35 heavies would soon arrive; the Chinese fighter group would have 80 planes; the light bombardment group, 57: a total of 260 planes in China. Because of logistic difficulties the heavy bombers operating from China bases would have to sustain themselves. As General Bissell pointed out, of the projected 4,000-ton Hump delivery, 2,250 tons were designated for the Chinese Army and 1,750 for the China Air Task Force, which actually required 1,950 to operate the planes already assigned to it. As fast as facilities for maintenance and operation were available, the number of planes would be increased, but there was no certainty that 500 could be supported at any time in the immediate future. As for the independent air force for General Chennault, although General Arnold himself approved the principle[29] and he knew the President was interested in the possibility, the project had been vetoed just before the Casablanca Conference and he could not promise it to Chiang.

These answers did not satisfy the Generalissimo, who remained unimpressed with the logistical problems involved in operating a large air force in China. As has already been pointed out,[30] General Chennault had a tendency to overlook the problems of supporting the air force with which he proposed to defeat Japan, and it was to General Chennault that Chiang listened on matters of air operations. The depth of his feeling was brought out at a meeting alone with General Arnold on the morning of 7 February. This time his requests were more in the nature of demands. He could not successfully prosecute war without three things:
    (a) Independent air force under Chennault.
    (b) 10,000 tons of cargo a month over India-China Transport route.
    (c) A minimum of 500 planes operating in China by November.

Of these things the first was most important as without it others would be of no avail. There were too many objections being raised toward meeting these points. He wanted the President to know--Chinese troops had fought long and hard and were about out of resources.

General Arnold patiently explained again that it was impossible to promise any of these things. Good and sufficient reasons made it impracticable to attempt to put so many planes in China before they could be effectively operated. But the Generalissimo remained insistent that in order to ensure success against Japan his requests must be met by November 1943.[31]

Although General Arnold went to Chungking as a representative of the President, he could not grant or refuse the Generalissimo's requests, both because he lacked authority and because he was aware of the many other demands on available resources. He could merely attempt to persuade Chiang of the impracticability of the things for which he asked. Unconvinced, and strongly impressed with the importance of his own problems, the Generalissimo presented his requests directly to the President in a letter carried back to Washington by General Arnold.

    1.) General Chennault should not only receive increased air strength; his authority should also be enhanced by conferring on him an independent air force command. His present subordination to the Tenth Air Force in India is inherently unworkable. The air units in China ought to be a separate air force, under his leadership. Here is one man of genius in the Far East, whose talents should be given full play, both for more effective offensive operations against the enemy, and because General Chennault is the one American airman who enjoys the confidence of the Chinese air force and the entire Chinese army. Only with him is it possible to work with the necessary unquestioning cooperation.

    2.) There are now in all only 62 transport planes carrying freight between India and China, and the total of freight carried was 1,700 tons in January. General Arnold promises to have 137 planes in service by the end of March, so that beginning April 1, tonnage carried will be 4,000 tons monthly.

By November this year, when the Burma campaign is to begin, the minimum Chinese requirements for the Army and Air Force will be 10,000 tons monthly, as against the Burma Road's capacity of 17,000 tons. There are any number of reasons that may be given why it will be impossible to gradually build up to such a tonnage by air into China. You and I have all heard in the past tales of the impossibility of flying during the monsoon; of the Japanese threat to the air transport route; and how twin-engine transports are supposed to be unable to make the grade. Yet surely the United States, with its great industrial power, its air production, and its bold ingenuity, will be able to meet this challenge, which must be met if China's minimum requirements are to be satisfied....

    3.) I requested long ago that the Chinese air force should be increased to a combat strength of 500 planes. Despite the mounting production of aircraft by the United Nations, very little has yet been done. General Arnold assures me that airplanes are there, but asserts that the difficulty lies in bringing into China gasoline, spare parts and other material necessary to maintain this strength. If out of the total of 10,000 tons monthly, 5,000 tons are allocated to the air force, I am assured by competent authorities that the air force I ask for will be fully ready to bear its part in carrying forward the task assigned to China.[32]

Immediately upon General Arnold's return to Washington the decision was made, upon the President's insistence, to establish a separate air force under General Chennault as a unit under General Stilwell's command.[33] Thus the China Air Task Force became the Fourteenth Air Force.

As for the other two requests from the Generalissimo, the War Department and the President approved both the plans General Arnold had proposed: building up the Chinese Air Force and placing 137 cargo planes on the India-China route by the end of March. On the basis of these decisions General Marshall submitted to the President a draft reply to Chiang's letter.[34] No sooner was the draft turned in than the President discovered that the bombers projected for the theater could not carry on one trip sufficient gas and munitions for four bombing missions as he had understood. So Admiral Leahy returned the draft to the War Department with the word that the President "now wants the number of cargo planes increased by 30 to a total of 167 and he wants the increase to begin without delay."[35] On the surface this seemed like a reasonable arrangement, and General Marshall informed the President that he could find the necessary planes and make them available at once. However, he carefully pointed out that this rearrangement would cut further into the supply of aircraft for Husky, which was already short over a hundred planes, and would further delay availability of planes for Lieutenant General J.L. DeWitt in the Aleutians and General MacArthur in the Southwest Pacific. Moreover, he said, the planes alone would not increase the tonnage, for there was already a shortage of flight crews and ground personnel to maintain them. Consequently they would be grounded much of the time.[36]

General Marshall's explanation was accepted, and in the message the President finally sent to the Generalissimo on 6 March[37] he promised only 137 planes, but by 15 March rather than 1 April. The number would be increased as rapidly as possible, with an objective of 10,000 tons monthly delivery. Chiang was assured that General Chennault's air force would be built up to 500 planes as rapidly as facilities became available. At the same time the message cautioned the Generalissimo that air transport alone could not supply the Chinese armies, the Chinese Air Force, and the U.S. Fourteenth Air Force with sufficient material to defeat the Japanese. Consequently he was urged to support the campaign to open the land route through Burma.

During the month of March considerable criticism of General Stilwell and appeals for more support for General Chennault were received in the White House.[38] The President was not unaffected by these influences. He took advantage of a message from General Stilwell, commenting on the conferences with General Arnold and Sir John Dill, to urge General Marshall to ensure that General Chennault and air operations in China received adequate attention. General Stilwell had recommended again that the Generalissimo be talked to "in sterner tones," and that "for everything we do *for* him, we should exact a commitment *from* him."[39] This the President characterized as "the wrong approach," pointing out that Chiang was "the Chief Executive as well as the Commander-in-Chief, and one cannot speak sternly to a man like that or exact commitments from him the way we might do from the Sultan of Morocco."[40] The President also expressed concern over General Stilwell's failure in his message to mention air action in China in 1943. He felt that it was essential for General Chennault to get his full share of the supplies going to China and to have complete control over his own operations and tactics. Mr. Roosevelt was "hopeful of the Burma operation," he said, but he wanted full realization of the strategic importance of General Chennault's air operations, both by General Stilwell and by the staff in Washington.

It is important to note that, although the President was in effect expressing distrust of the methods General Stilwell advocated for dealing with the Chinese and misgivings as to General Stilwell's appreciation of the value of General Chennault's operations, Mr. Roosevelt was not recommending, as he had in the fall, that General Stilwell might well be brought out of the theater. He was, however, giving strong support to the program of General Chennault.

It apparently seemed to General Marshall that the President was not fully informed on the long range program of the War Department for the China Theater, for he carefully explained it in his reply. General Stilwell, he pointed out, was fully cognizant of the air effort planned ultimately to take place from China bases against Japanese objectives. Supply was already a tremendous problem, but a larger one was ground protection for the fields in China and for the air transport route. General Marshall feared Japanese attacks on the ground when the air offensive really got under way, and it was necessary to prepare troops to meet such an emergency and protect the air bases. Realizing that the resistance must be made by the Chinese Army, General Stilwell was concentrating on trying to prepare and equip Chinese troops. In order to increase the air effort from China and secure the airfields there, it was necessary to recapture Burma and its ground supply line. This General Stilwell had been trying to do in the face of opposition and indifference. He had incurred the displeasure of the Generalissimo by his blunt presentation of the situation, but General Marshall was squarely behind him and urged that "conditions must be created in China and a land route established to make an all-out effort continuous and effective."[41]

General Marshall relayed the gist of the President's remarks to General Stilwell a week and a half later, cautioning him to "see that everything is done to begin Chennault's operations, particularly the heavy bombers, the moment it is practicable to do so; also that Chennault is given wide latitude in staging a demonstration of what he has maintained he can do."[42] General Marshall also reported (apparently in conversation since it does not appear in the President's memorandum) that the President stipulated that General Chennault should receive of the tonnage flown into China "on basis of 1,500 tons of a total of 4,000" per month.[43] Up to this time 4,000 tons per month had not yet been achieved, and it would be several months before General Chennault would receive 1,500. But the paper division of tonnage had become an issue both in the theater and in Washington, and pressure was being put on the President's advisor, Mr. Harry Hopkins, to obtain for General Chennault's air force final, absolute, and unchallengeable priority over the ground force for Hump tonnage.[44] Mr. Roosevelt apparently decided to settle the matter.

Differences between General Stilwell and General Chennault were becoming more pronounced by the end of March, and Mr. Hopkins was also being urged by interested persons to suggest to the President that he call General Chennault to Washington for consultation in hopes of clearing up the aviation problems.[45] On 10 April Chiang Kai-shek officially recommended to Mr. Roosevelt that he summon General Chennault to Washington to present to the President and to General Arnold the plan which General Chennault had discussed with the Generalissimo.[46]

Chiang's request, as General Marshall hastened to point out to the President, created an "embarrassing situation." Ignoring General Stilwell while summoning General Chennault would virtually necessitate General Stilwell's relief and General Chennault's appointment to both ground and air command, a situation which General Marshall characterized as a "grave mistake." He informed Mr. Roosevelt that the War Department was already making arrangements to call General Stilwell to Washington and that Field Marshal Wavell, Air Marshal Sir R.E.C. Peirse, and Admiral Somerville had been called to London from India to discuss the prospects for Anakim. Consequently he suggested that Generals Stilwell, Chennault, and Bissell all be called to Washington to discuss the situation in a conference similar to the recent Pacific Military Conference.[47] With the President's approval, orders were issued to the first two to return and discuss the situation with Washington headquarters.[48]

Thus in late April all of the top American and British field commanders in CBI were headed for their respective national capitals to discuss with their Chiefs of Staff the situation they left behind. To Washington then came the two generals whose views on what should be done were so incompatible. Their arrival in Washington confronted the Joint and the Combined Chiefs of Staff with the necessity of trying to decide whether they would accord priority on the trickle of supplies going to China to the build-up of the Chinese ground forces or whether they would devote the major effort to developing air strength in China. How the decision was made will be related in later pages.

SHIPPING SHORTAGES AGAIN

As detailed plans for Anakim and for Husky were being developed the Combined Chiefs of Staff found themselves confronted with the same problem that had complicated all strategic planning during 1942, i.e., the shortage of shipping. Estimated requirements for Husky proved inadequate as D Day approached, and it became increasingly apparent that Husky's needs, particularly in shipping, would cut into available resources for at least some of the other projects then in prospect. Attempts to secure additional shipping by cutting down allocations to other operations were met with opposition from one or another quarter whose interests were threatened with curtailment. Especially did resistance come from General Arnold, who firmly supported the Sickle project of bombing Germany, and from Admiral King, who stated plainly that "he would... stand firm as long as any effort was made to try to hamstring his operations in the Pacific."[49] However, when it became essential to ensure that the requisite number of troops would reach North Africa in time to be trained before D Day in June, the Combined Chiefs of Staff agreed on 5 March to divert to Husky some of the troop shipping assigned to Bolero and to the Indian Ocean.[50]

The problem of finding troop shipping for Husky was symptomatic of a deeper problem of supplying shipping for all the various undertakings upon which the Combined Chiefs had agreed at Casablanca. Recognizing the necessity of reviewing the availability of shipping in the light of agreed strategic decisions, at the end of February the CCS directed the Combined Staff Planners to investigate the matter and recommend priorities for the use of available shipping for military movements.[51] Before the planners could produce a report, however, the British Chiefs of Staff presented a "Review of the Availability of United Nations Shipping," a study of their own capabilities for providing dry cargo shipping to the various projects for which they had responsibility.[52] The British concluded that, without additional American assistance, they could not: provide fourteen sailings in April and possibly the same number in May and June to build up material in the Middle East for the early stages of Husky; provide twenty-five sailings per month in April, May, and June, and 19 in July and August to build up material in India for Anakim; provide any cargo shipping for Bolero; adequately assist Turkey. They based their conclusions on the following order of strategic priority:

> (a) It has always been agreed that the security, which of course includes the maintenance of the economy and productive capacity of the United Kingdom at the minimum necessary level is a first charge on the resources of the United Nations. There can be no question, therefore, of finding any of the shipping required for military purposes at the expense of

tonnage which has been earmarked for meeting the minimum import program....

(b) Husky must have priority over all military operations except, of course, the maintenance of Torch, which is in effect the prelude to Husky.

(c) Buildup of 8th Air Force.

(d) It was agreed at Anfa...that one of our objectives in the Mediterranean was to create a situation in which Turkey could be enlisted as an active ally.... In the opinion of the British Chiefs of Staff, the attainment of this objective would have more beneficial effects upon our immediate strategy than Anakim or Bolero (apart from the buildup of the 8th Air Force).

(e) Anakim.

(f) Bolero.

The U.S. Chiefs immediately questioned the statement about the British import program, contending that while it was an agreed "first charge" there was no established "minimum necessary level." The Combined Chiefs decided to refer the British report to the Combined Staff Planners and to direct the Combined Military Transportation Committee to study the implications of providing U.S. or British shipping to take care of what the British estimated themselves unable to supply for Husky and for Anakim.[53]

As the committee studied the problem during the following week they found themselves uncertain as to just how much additional tonnage the British needed and what it had previously been agreed the United States would furnish them.[54] But the chief obstacle to providing for shipping deficits was the large program of imports the British deemed essential and the Americans considered excessive. The committee's reports (British and Americans submitted separate reports of the implications of making up the deficits from their own resources) did not resolve the problem.[55] Nor did they or the subsequent CCS discussion produce a clear decision of how shipping deficits would be made up. However, from the Combined Chiefs' discussion came a decision of considerable importance in the war against Japan.[56]

As the chiefs took up the CMTC reports they were informed that the problem was about to be taken out of their hands, for the President was going to appoint a combined board, under the chairmanship of Mr. Harry Hopkins, to study the shipping situation. The chiefs agreed that if such a board was to be set up they should furnish it with broad strategic guidance in the form of a priority for military operations. Sir John Dill, who first proposed the idea, suggested that the order of priority might be (1) Husky, (2) Sickle, (3) South Pacific, (4) Anakim, (5) Bolero. Upon the reminder of Lieutenant General G.N. Macready that any priority list would have to include "Aid to Russia," Admiral Leahy proposed (1) Husky, (2) South Pacific, (3) Anakim, (4) Bolero, (5) Lend-Lease Supplies. But Sir John Dill objected, stating that Sickle should not be included with Bolero but should be placed before the South Pacific since it was part of the main effort against Germany. Admiral King took exception to this, however, and it was finally agreed to bracket Sickle and South Pacific together as item (2), thereby leaving unresolved the conflict between the two which had been a problem for many months. The first four items were then approved as an order of priority to be followed in the allocation of dry cargo shipping. The last item was replaced by the statement "that concurrently shipping should be provided for minimum essential fixed charges for the United Kingdom, Russia and other areas now being supplied from United Nations' resources."

This discussion took place on 19 March 1943, a month after General Arnold's return from China-Burma-India and on the same day the Joint Chiefs of Staff approved Plan II for the South-Southwest Pacific. Thus even as plans for them were being made it was apparent that the Pacific operations would continue to conflict with Sickle and that Anakim and Bolero stood a good chance of receiving an inadequate supply of shipping. The shipping shortage was still to control strategic decisions.

REVIEW OF THE STRATEGIC SITUATION

Toward the end of March the Joint Strategic Survey Committee, concerned over the obstacle which the shipping shortage was proving to be to implementation of the decisions of the Casablanca Conference and over the growing evidence that British and Americans were interpreting those decision differently, submitted a significant report to the Joint Chiefs of Staff. After carefully studying the developments since Casablanca, on its own initiative the committee reported that it had arrived at the conclusion that "the overall strategic situation, or more exactly the capabilities of the Allies to control that situation," had "considerably deteriorated."[57]

In two papers, of which the second[58] was an extension of the first, the JSSC discussed its conclusion. The committee listed the following as indications or explanations of the the deterioration:

(a) Over-estimates of available shipping.
(b) Unexpected difficulties and delay in eliminating the Axis from North Africa.
(c) Increased requirements for Husky.
(d) Resurgence of the German offensive against Russia.
(e) Recent and prospective increase in shipping losses.
(f) Under-estimate of forces required for Rabaul campaign.
(g) Uncertainty as to post Rabaul operations.
(h) Slow progress in Cannibal and Ravenous operations.
(i) Delay in build up of Sickle [bombing offensive from the U.K.].

POST-CASABLANCA PROBLEMS: CHINA AND BURMA

All of these developments indicated to the committee that the Casablanca Conference had overestimated prospective resources and underestimated the demands being placed upon them.

The committee felt that the difficulties being encountered in interpreting the Casablanca decisions resulted from their form and wording, specifically the attempt "to establish the relative priority of the prospective strategic undertakings for 1943, while of necessity expressing them in general terms." To obviate a recurrence of this situation the JSSC recommended that subsequent documents recognize two types of strategy--strategic commitments and strategic undertakings. The first of these would include such continuing items as maintaining shipping, maintaining forces committed to certain areas, supporting the British economy, and supporting Russia and China. After the size of these commitments had been estimated and established, the Combined Chiefs of Staff could determine the strategic undertakings in which remaining resources could best be employed.

At Casablanca, the JSSC pointed out, resources had been committed to seven strategic undertakings: Anakim, Bolero (modified), Elkton, Husky, Post-Elkton, Sickle, and gaining Turkey as an ally. By this time Elkton had already been curtailed; yet it still infringed on Sickle. The committee predicted that additional air requirements for antisubmarine warfare would probably infringe further on the bombing program in the United Kingdom. Requests had been received for air and naval increases for Husky well beyond original estimates. Bolero had been recognized as impracticable of attainment because of its low priority. Anakim seemed to be getting into the same category. The British appeared to be particularly interested in Turkey's prospective position. With all these alterations in the concept of Casablanca, the JSSC recommended, the decisions of that conference should be re-examined. The committee proposed to the Joint Chiefs of Staff that the basis for such a re-examination be:

    (a) Make the firmest possible estimate of Strategic commitments, with provision for keeping such estimates up to date.

    (b) Estimate conservatively the resources remaining over and above Strategic commitments, and then apportion such resources on a realistic basis among the agreed Strategic Undertakings.

The JCS were sympathetic with the views of the JSSC, although General Somervell, who was present at the meeting at which the first paper was discussed, expressed the view that sufficient shipping could be found to supply all the commitments made at Casablanca. After some discussion, the chiefs decided to submit the gist of the report to the CCS.[59] On recommendation of Admiral King,[60] however, they subsequently reconsidered and on 30 March directed the Joint Strategic Survey Committee to "provide a clarification of the Casablanca decisions for guidance of the Joint Chiefs of Staff's actions and those of the Army, Army Air Forces, and the Navy."[61] Before this report was completed, Anakim and its importance in relation to other projects had come squarely before the Joint Chiefs of Staff.

SHIPPING FOR ANAKIM

Almost a year had elapsed since the first British-American agreement had been reached on Bolero, the plan to stockpile supplies and assemble forces in the United Kingdom for ultimate invasion of the European Continent.[62] During that year the original scope of the project had been cut into repeatedly, to meet emergencies in the Pacific and to provide forces for other operations against Germany, notably Torch, the invasion of North Africa. Now, in the spring of 1943, the other Casablanca commitments threatened again to reduce considerably the actual deliveries to Bolero. On 30 March President Roosevelt, always an advocate of action against Germany, raised with General Marshall the question of the prospects for Bolero. The extent of the discussion is not recorded, but in the course of it the President expressed his view that it was "more important to built up Bolero even at the expense of Anakim."[63]

In retrospect, this relative emphasis on the part of the President does not seem surprising, for not only was he intent on defeating Germany first but his support of General Chennault's air program in the preceding weeks, almost to the point of repudiating General Stilwell, leads one to think that his interest in a ground campaign in Burma was of a secondary nature. Indeed, General Marshall, reporting the President's remark to General Handy in a memorandum, seems not to have been surprised by it. However, he felt that it required refutation, for he himself was impressed with the importance of the ground campaign and of General Stilwell's project of reforming the Chinese armies. Consequently he explained to the President the relation of the action in Burma to the air operations in China, indicating his fear that the Japanese might move in to attack the transport airfields, especially if General Chennault's bombing efforts proved effective. However, General Marshall, without committing himself to abandonment of Anakim, said that he would look into the matter of some modification of the plan, along the lines of passive resistance, and he asked General Handy to have a study prepared at once.[64]

The paper which the Operations Division promptly produced surveyed the implications of two situations: first, abandonment of Anakim; second, execution of the operation.[65] In the first case, it was concluded, adoption by the United Nations of a passive resistance would offer great opportunities to the Japanese. They might minimize their activities in Burma, thereby releasing forces for action in the Pacific, perhaps even to conduct operations against the mainland of Australia; or they might seize the opportunity to neutralize Allied air operations by launching effective offensives against installations in Burma and China, and to bomb Calcutta and other eastern Indian cities. If Japanese activities in the South and Southwest Pacific increased, OPD predicted, more Allied shipping and larger Allied forces than had been contemplated at Casablanca would probably be diverted to the area, reducing the scale of operations in other theaters, particularly of Bolero, since the other projects had been given a higher priority. A Japanese landing in Australia, it was pointed out, would have serious political repercussions, as would reduction of the effectiveness of air operations in China-Burma-India. The latter might even result in the overthrow of the Generalissimo's government.

If Anakim were carried out, on the other hand, it would serve to implement the agreed Pacific strategy, creating pressure on the Japanese in Burma, protecting air installations in Asia, opening a land route to China, and providing tangible evidence of support for China. OPD suggested a possible modification in general terms of the full scale Anakim, with the object to occupy only northern Burma in order to "protect the UN airfields in ASSAM, INDIA, and YUNNAN; force the Japanese on the defensive in this area; and permit the construction of a new land route (*LEDO-MYITKYINA-BHAMO-LASHIO*) into China. This route, in conjunction with the air ferry route could handle approximately 30,000 tons of supplies per month." OPD cautioned, however, that it would probably be undesirable to tell the Chinese that any modification of Anakim was contemplated. Its success in any form depended on the wholehearted cooperation of the British and Chinese. In this connection it was noted that the current successful Akyab campaign indicated clearly that the British were not wholeheartedly supporting operations in Burma. OPD made no attempt to estimate the capacity of the United Nations to carry out the modified operation, but the paper concluded with the recommendation that offensive operations in the area be undertaken to the limit of current capabilities, to include at least the minimum objective suggested.

Following a discussion of Anakim at a meeting of the Joint Chiefs of Staff and the President on 2 April, General Marshall submitted to Admiral Leahy and Admiral King for comment a revised draft of a memorandum for the President incorporating most of the points in the OPD paper.[66] He outlined OPD's suggested modification of Anakim, but refused to commit himself as to its pros and cons and did not recommend its adoption. Apparently the President had requested information on the shipping situation, for General Marshall discussed that at some length. The British, he said, had committed to Anakim the equivalent of one cargo ship per month and sufficient personnel ships to lift 7,000 men monthly. They had requested 113 U.S. sailings to the Indian theater during the period April-August 1943, but General Somervell considered that 90 would be enough. If Anakim were cancelled or modified and the 90 ships made available for Bolero and not for British imports, the shipping people estimated that during the remainder of 1943 the initial equipment and maintenance of 215,000 troops could be transported to the United Kingdom. If the British troop ships committed to Anakim were diverted to the North Atlantic, an additional 10,000 men per month could be moved to the United Kingdom. All in all, before the end of 1943 the effective strength in the United Kingdom would be materially increased.

Admiral Leahy concurred with General Marshall's memorandum.[67] But Admiral King expressed the opinion that it should include a positive recommendation. His own was "to stick to these plans until we have determining reason for changing them." He felt that the Combined Chiefs should continue to allocate shipping and prepare to implement Anakim, recognizing, however, that some modification of the current plan might prove necessary.[68] Together with these comments General Marshall sent the memorandum to the President.[69]

Within the next few days the Prime Minister sent an important message to the President, relating his views of the strategy to be followed in the European Theater, and including only one statement in regard to the war against Japan: "Now that 'Anakim' has receded owing to the shipping shortage, Mediterranean operations gain more prominence."[70] Despite the President's earlier championing of Bolero "even at the expense of Anakim," he informed the Joint Chiefs at a special White House meeting that he did not agree with the Prime Minister that Anakim had receded, and he did not think that the United States had taken any steps that would create that impression.[71] However, the prospects *were* jeopardized by the shortage of shipping, and the President doubted that all of Burma could be taken. He told the chiefs that he was anxious to strike at Japan proper and preferred to conduct only a limited ground offensive in northern Burma to secure the line of communications to China and then defend it against Japanese interference. Although he gave the campaign to recapture all of Burma only a 40 per cent chance of success, the President suggested that preparations continue until about 1 July and then the situation be reviewed and a decision be made as to whether to continue.

The Joint Chiefs of Staff felt more strongly than the President that Anakim should be carried out, and General Marshall, General Arnold, and Admiral King all mustered arguments in support of the full campaign.[72] Admiral King brought up the British viewpoint on strategy in Burma, pointing out that the British Chiefs of Staff said that all of Burma would have to be captured in order to make the route to China secure. They were sponsoring an amphibious attack against Rangoon in order to cut the Japanese line of communications, on the theory that if it were not cut the Japanese could reenforce more quickly than the British in Burma and constitute a constant threat against the British southern flank. The last point was reiterated by General Marshall, who also pointed out that the roads and railroads in Burma ran north from Rangoon following the direction of the mountain ranges, whereas the British and Chinese lines ran perpendicular to them, across extremely difficult terrain. When the President suggested that the British desire to recapture all of Burma might be influenced by their ambition to win back every one of their colonies, General Marshall hastened to say that, "on the contrary, the British had been reluctant at Casablanca to undertake Anakim and that the United States Chiefs of Staff had really 'booted' them into it." From his conversations with Field Marshall Wavell, General Arnold had gained the impression that Field Marshal Wavell, too, was opposed to any operations in Burma "even favoring an operation to retake Sumatra." Admiral King pointed out in this connection the reluctance of the British to undertake naval operations in the area and to operate light naval forces in the Bay of Bengal, despite the fact, which General Arnold mentioned, that the Generalissimo was insistent on naval support and the Combined Chiefs were committed to it.

During the course of the discussion General Arnold stressed the necessity of proceeding with plans to open the Burma Road, a course of action to which he felt the Combined Chiefs had committed themselves with the Generalissimo. Chiang was insistent that his Yunnan troops he supported by ground offensives from the west, and he must not be "let down." It was imperative that there be enough troops in Burma to open the northern Burma Road and to support air operations. When Mr. Roosevelt remarked that even if the Burma operations were successful in the next winter, it would be autumn before the road would be ready for traffic, General Arnold replied that that would be true of the old Burma Road but "it was possible to open a new Burma Road almost as soon" as control was gained of northern Burma. At this point General Marshall drew attention to the increased Japanese activity in northern Burma, where the enemy was already threatening General Wheeler's forces building the new road. The Japanese were also threatening the security of the air transport route, and General Marshall believed that unless some offensive action were taken against them the line of communications to China would be lost.

The status of Anakim was, in fact, an important problem, for decision had not yet been made as to whether the United States could supply twenty-two cargo ships which the build-up required in April and which the British could not provide. The President finally turned the discussion to shipping, stating that he had already decided that the ships should go, but he was still skeptical of trying to retake all of Burma. He inquired whether the cargoes would be wasted if the operation were not undertaken and was assured that they would not. Mr. Hopkins, who had apparently been investigating the shipping situation, then said that Anakim could be undertaken in full provided an immediate decision was given to send 22 cargo ships during the month of April and provided that all of the rest of the ships necessary could go through the Mediterranean. He said if it was necessary for the ships to be sent around the Cape of Good Hope there were not sufficient ships available to undertake Anakim and still meet our other commitments.

Since April was already begun, Mr. Hopkins suggested that a committee be formed to determine that night from what projects the twenty-two ships should be taken, with instructions not to take any from Africa, the Southwest Pacific, Sickle, Russia, or the Aleutians.[73] Before the close of the meeting the President appointed a committee composed of Rear Admiral E.S. Land, Mr. Lewis Douglas, General Somervell, and Rear Admiral W.W. Smith. They were instructed to report to him not later than the following day, and the President promised that if they were unable to reach agreement he "would arbitrarily determine the sources from which the 22 ships were to be made available."

The ships were selected and made available to the British. But their availability did not serve to ensure execution of Anakim in 1943.[74]

THE BRITISH POSITION

The apparent weakening of British support for the Anakim operation was cause for considerable concern in Washington in the first weeks of April 1943. On 12 April, Rear Admiral C.M. Cooke, Admiral King's Assistant Chief of Staff (Plans), in an attempt to obtain clarification of the British position, introduced a paper for the JCS to submit to the CCS. Admiral King and Generals Marshall and Arnold had already given it tentative approval.[75] Initially the paper quoted the decisions reached at Casablanca in respect to operations against Japan. Then it pointed out that, if success was to be achieved in the objective agreed on in CCS 155/1, namely, to "attain (or maintain) a position of readiness for the full scale offensive against JAPAN by the United Nations as soon as GERMANY is defeated," effective measures must be taken during the next dry season to improve the flow of supplies into China.

It was bluntly stated that the progress of Ravenous (the Akyab operation) had been disappointing and that the U.S. Chiefs were anxious to get on with the preparation of Anakim. Therefore, they requested that the British Chiefs of Staff have a report made "of the present status of operations, plans for Anakim, and preparation for Anakim," and that a report be furnished to the Combined Chiefs of Staff once a month until final decision on timing of the operation was made in July. U.S. contributions to preparations for Anakim were related in general terms and the assumption was included "that the preparations by the Field Commander and the UNITED KINGDOM are also being pushed."

The week before this General Arnold had submitted a paper,[76] also with the intention that it be sent to the CCS, in which he recommended that the JCS approve the transfer of one heavy bomber group and one medium bomber group from the Ninth Air Force in the Mediterranean to the Tenth Air Force in China-Burma-India after completion of the Husky operation. He also recommended that the Joint Chiefs of Staff propose that certain British-type aircraft essential to the operation be made available for Anakim from British resources. These papers were taken up together by the JCS on 13 April.[77]

The Joint Chiefs of Staff readily agreed to General Arnold's recommendation. In regard to the other matter, General Marshall informed the group that Field Marshal Wavell, Air Marshal Peirse, and Admiral Somerville had been called from India to London to discuss possible modification of Anakim. He thought it quite possible that the President would approve a modification, and he questioned whether under those circumstances it was wise to press the British to continue their Anakim preparations. His query was settled, however, by Admiral King's reminder that whether or not the operation was modified the material would be needed eventually in the Burma Theater. The chiefs decided to delete from the paper the assumption that the British were also pushing preparations for Anakim. They then approved both papers and submitted them to the Combined Chiefs of Staff.[78]

On the same day General Marshall received an indication, in the form of a letter from General Macready, of how the papers were likely to be received by the British Chiefs. The British general reported that he had informed the British Chiefs of Staff in London that the United States was going to provide twenty ships to take the place of those the British were unable to spare for Anakim. At the same time he had asked the British Chiefs to give him a statement in regard to the status of Anakim. To General Marshall he paraphrased their reply:

> We are delaying taking a final decision on Anakim or on possible alternatives to it until the arrival of Wavell, who has been instructed to return to London as soon as possible with Air Marshal Peirse and Admiral Somerville. It is clear, however, from preliminary examination that Anakim depends not only on the provision of sufficient cargo shipping, but also on other factors, the chief of which are the availability of air bases, assault shipping and enough landing craft with crews to lift nine Assault Brigade Groups.
>
> You should, therefore, inform the U.S. Chiefs of Staff that we are deferring the decision here on Anakim or on possible alternatives, pending Wavell's arrival. In the meantime, as stated in cables which have passed between the President and Prime Minister, it seems unlikely that Anakim can be mounted as planned. At the same time, owing to the time and space problem if we are to launch Anakim or a modified form of it

in the winter of 1943/44, it is essential that these twenty ships should be accepted. You should, therefore, accept the ships, but on the clear understanding that we are not as yet committed in any way to mounting Anakim or any alternative operation.[79]

The British representatives made approximately the same statement at the CCS meeting to which the two JCS papers were presented. Both papers were set aside until a reply to the proposals contained in them could be received from the British Chiefs in London.[80] No direct response was received, however, for in both capitals conferences were about to begin with the commanders called in from CBI; and the CCS, at the suggestion of the U.S. members, were soon to have the opportunity of meeting with all of the CBI theater commanders in Washington.[81] In the meantime the differing views of U.S. and British Chiefs as to the implications of all the Casablanca decisions, not only in respect to Anakim, had become a matter of serious discussion.

CLARIFICATION OF CASABLANCA DECISIONS

The Joint Strategic Survey Committee, it will be remembered, had been directed by the Joint Chiefs of Staff on 30 March to "provide a clarification of the Casablanca decisions for guidance of the Joint Chiefs of Staff's actions and those of the Army, Army Air Forces, and the Navy." On 9 April the committee submitted the clarification in the form of a restatement of the agreed strategic concept.[82]

The committee's paper began with a clearer statement than had yet been made of the "over-all strategy of the war."

    (a) In cooperation with Russia and the lesser allies, to force an unconditional surrender of the Axis in Europe.
    (b) Simultaneously, in cooperation with the other Pacific Powers, to maintain and extend unremitting pressure against Japan.
    (c) Thereafter, in cooperation with the other Pacific Powers and if possible with Russia, to combine the full resources of the United States and Great Britain to force the unconditional surrender of Japan.

Two important points appeared here for the first time in a statement of an over-all strategic concept for World War II. One was the assumption that the full resources of Great Britain as well as of the United States would be turned against Japan after the defeat of Germany. The other was the term, "unconditional surrender," which had first been used publicly by the President at the Casablanca Conference. In this statement, as on the public occasion, there was no precise definition of what the term was intended to mean.

The JSSC's statement is particularly striking because of the emphasis placed upon maintaining and extending pressure against

Japan. Although this seemed to offer wider scope for operations in the Pacific, the JSSC later explained that that had not been its intention.[83] Indeed in a later section of this same paper the implications were explained in wording similar to paragraphs 6 (a) and (b) of the Casablanca paper, CCS 155/1. It was provided that resources would be allocated to the war against Japan

> adequate to ensure that operations in Europe are not prejudiced by the necessity to divert forces therefrom, in order to relieve an adverse situation arising from operations against Japan; the extent of such operations, however, to be kept within limits which will not, in the opinion of the Combined Chiefs of Staff, jeopardize the ability of the United Nations to take advantage of a favorable opportunity to defeat Germany decisively in 1943.

Following the recommendations it had made in its earlier paper the Joint Strategic Survey Committee divided the demands upon the resources of the United Nations into strategic commitments and strategic undertakings, with the provision that allocations to each would be subject to revision from time to time. The strategic commitments were subdivided into two priority groups, the first consisting of

> (a) Maintain the security, and war-making capacity of the Western Hemisphere and British Isles.
> (b) Support and maintain our forces in all areas to which committed.
> (c) Keep enemy submarine effort under increasingly effective control.

The second included

> (d) Meet requirements of Russian protocol to greatest extent possible without prohibitive cost in shipping.
> (e) Sustain China by the greatest volume of supplies that can be got into China, without prohibitive cost in transport.
> (f) Other firm commitments, approved from time to time, for political or military reasons as essential to the conduct of the war.

Finally, priority as among specific operations in the Pacific was left to the decision of the Joint Chiefs of Staff. Priority for major operations in the European Theater and the Far East was assigned in order in accordance with the decision the Combined Chiefs of Staff had made on 19 March in respect to the allocation of dry cargo shipping: Torch, Husky, Sickle, Anakim, Bolero. Except for the general statement as to the allocation of resources, there was no attempt to gear the operations in the Pacific into this list of relative priorities.

There is no indication in the minutes of the JCS meeting on 13 April when this paper was presented that they discussed it at any length. They neither approved nor disapproved its contents, merely "took note" of it. At the suggestion of Admiral King they agreed to furnish a copy of it to the Combined Chiefs of Staff for their information, and the paper was republished as CCS 199.[84]

The reaction of the British Chiefs of Staff was entirely unfavorable. Admiral Sir Percy Noble, presenting their views to the CCS on 23 April, said

> ...The first point which they did not understand was why clarification of the Casablanca decisions was required. The precise wording of C.C.S. 155/1 was discussed, he was informed, with meticulous care by the Combined Chiefs of Staff at Casablanca and unanimously approved. Thereafter it was also approved by the President and Prime Minister. The British Chiefs of Staff realize naturally that shades of meaning in English might be differently expressed by the Americans than by the British but even so, it was not understood why the new document was required unless it was desired to introduce some change in our approved strategy. In the British view, C.C.S. 155/1, was quite clear. It was felt that if in the United States' opinion it was not clear, it would be better for proposals to be put up for the amendment or interpretation of that paper, paragraph by paragraph, with relation to the existing text, rather than that a completely fresh paper should be produced which could hardly fail to have shades of meaning different from those of the original paper. Naturally, the British would need time to consider more carefully any such proposed amendments, and they felt that these would have to be agreed between the Combined Chiefs of Staff and referred to the President and Prime Minister for approval.[85]

With this statement Admiral Noble submitted a paper of comments on CCS 199.[86]

The objection of the British to the JSSC study was "that C.C.S. 199 by implication would seem to give pride of place to war in the Far East, whereas the clear decision at Casablanca was that the decisive defeat of Germany must come first." They did not feel that the existing situation in the Pacific was such that it was likely soon to become so adverse as to have to be retrieved at the expense of operations against Germany nor that there was danger of the United Nations losing the initiative there. Consequently they could not agree that any "extension" of the pressure against Japan at the expense of the war against Germany was justifiable. They expressed uncertainty as to how it was intended that allocations should be modified in accordance with the changing situation and who would have the right to make such modifications. And they expressed dissatisfaction with the suggested priority among specific operations, feeling that "whereas perhaps as regards the Pacific it is not binding enough, as regards the other theatres it is perhaps rather too binding." It was too early, they thought, to say that Anakim should follow Sickle. They pointed out that there was no reference to operations to

POST-CASABLANCA PROBLEMS: CHINA AND BURMA

follow Husky. The position of Bolero in relation to commitments in the Pacific they thought required further investigation. Finally, in view of the differences they observed between CCS 155/1 and CCS 199 they recommended that CCS 155/1 continue to be accepted and that careful consideration be given before any amendments were made to it.

At the request of the Joint Chiefs of Staff, the Joint Strategic Survey Committee studied the British paper and commented on it, pointing out that the British Chiefs of Staff had interpreted CCS 199 "as an attempt to reopen the Casablanca Conference and to rewrite its decisions," while in fact it was "an attempt to bring up to date in one short paper for the use of the Joint Chiefs of Staff and U.S. Services the current accepted strategic concept with particular reference to furnishing an adequate basis for allocation of resources."[87] Paragraph by paragraph the JSSC discussed CCS 199, indicating the agreed CCS paper or decision from which each had been taken. They commented similarly upon the British paper, noting particularly the dissatisfaction with the listing of relative priorities. To the Joint Chiefs of Staff the Joint Strategic Survey Committee recommended that the purpose of CCS 199 be carefully explained to the British and an attempt be made to reach agreement upon a similar statement. Should that prove impossible the committee proposed that it still be retained to furnish guidance to the JCS and to the U.S. Army, Army Air Forces, and Navy.

The Joint Chiefs decided to pass along to the British Chiefs of Staff the JSSC's statement as to the intention behind CCS 199.[88] At the next combined meeting they took care to explain that no alteration of CCS 155/1 had been intended and that CCS 199 had been prepared for the convenience of the U.S. Chiefs and passed to the British representatives purely for information. Although the latter accepted this explanation, they made it plain that they could not agree to the interpretation in the document. As Admiral King pointed out, "there was a difference of opinion between the U.S. Chiefs of Staff and the British on the adequacy of forces for the Pacific. This difference of opinion would always remain."[89]

Lest there be future misunderstanding of the status of the paper, the situation was carefully spelled out in the conclusions of the meeting:

THE COMBINED CHIEFS OF STAFF:
   a. Took note that C.C.S. 199 had been put forward by the United States Chiefs of Staff for the information only of the British Chiefs of Staff as a brief interpretation of what they understood by the decisions of the Casablanca Conference.
   b. Agreed that C.C.S. 199 was not intended as a directive and that the decisions set forth in C.C.S. 155/1 continue to be in full force and effect.

  c. Took note of the views expressed by the British Chiefs of Staff in C.C.S. 199/1 and those expressed by the United States Chiefs of Staff in C.C.S. 199/2.

  d. Agreed that it was not likely that any major differences of interpretation of the terms of C.C.S. 155/1 would arise, but that should they arise each specific case should be settled at the time by the Combined Chiefs of Staff.

There the episode ended, but the subject of an over-all strategic concept was not closed. Plans for another full scale conference the next month were already being matured and it was partly because of this that the Joint Chiefs of Staff did not pursue their differences further.[90] Despite the complacent tenor of the decision quoted above, the problems did exist and many of them were to be brought out into the open at Trident the following month.

Chapter XV

PREPARATION FOR TRIDENT

GENERAL PLANS

As April 1943 drew to a close, the United Nations forces in Tunisia were rapidly accomplishing final victory, and preparations were being made to move on across the Mediterranean Sea and capture the island of Sicily. There were some major problems still unsettled in connection with the Sicily operation, and no decision had been made as to what the next move in the war against Germany was to be. In the Far East the attempt by the British to capture Akyab on the south coast of Burma had resulted in failure. Not much more had been accomplished in the other operations which were scheduled for launching before the onset of the monsoon season. It was becoming increasingly doubtful whether Anakim (recapture of Burma) could be carried out as tentatively scheduled for the fall of 1943. During the months following the conference at Casablanca, as has been pointed out in the preceding chapter, many divergencies of view between British and American Chiefs of Staff had become apparent, both in details and indeed in the strategic concept for prosecution of the world-wide war. Clearly it was time for another meeting of the heads of state and their military staffs. Although no specific date had been set, by the last week of April U.S. planners were busily preparing for the next conference.

As Admiral King remarked later, "the Joint Chiefs of Staff found at Casablanca that every time they brought up a subject, the British had a paper ready."[1] The experiences of the U.S. Chiefs on that occasion and subsequent difficulties with varying interpretations had convinced the American staff that such a thing must not happen again, and planning for the next conference was begun before the date of meeting had been determined. On 24 April 1943 the old working committee of the Joint Staff Planners (JPS), the Joint U.S. Strategic Committee (JUSSC), went out of existence, superseded by the Joint War Plans Committee (JWPC). This group, comprising thirteen members (many of whom had been on the JUSSC), plus a secretariat of two, plunged immediately into the task of preparing studies on the major issues the next combined conference would be expected to face.[2] Less than a week later the President and Prime Minister agreed that the conference, to be known as Trident, would convene in Washington on 12 May 1943.[3] In the brief time between the new working group's organization and the opening of Trident, the JWPC produced a remarkable series of thirty-one different studies and reports intended to prepare the Joint Chiefs of Staff to meet with their British opposite numbers. During the same period the Joint Strategic Survey Committee was also busy turning out studies designed to provide the JCS with a basic line of arguments and with a plan for presentation of their views to best advantage.

The first task upon which the Joint War Plans Committee embarked was preparation of an agenda for the next conference, still assuming that it would not be held until mid-summer. Complying with an informal directive from the Joint Staff Planners, the JWPC submitted its proposals on 24 April, the day on which the committee first functioned officially. Two days later, with a few minor changes, the paper was passed on to the Joint Chiefs as JCS 272.[4]

The JWPC had obviously attempted to profit from the experience of the U.S. staff at Casablanca, which on several occasions had found itself with no predetermined position on important problems and no guarantee of support from the President. The committee urged in the first place that an agenda be agreed upon and that the Joint Chiefs issue directives to insure that the necessary studies and data were available and approved by the chiefs and, when appropriate, *by the President also*, before the next conference opened. It was recommended that the Joint Strategic Survey Committee be directed to prepare at once a realistic basic study of current British policy and strategy in relation to that of the United States. For the agenda itself, the committee recommended first a discussion of strategy under three headings: global strategy, strategy against the European Axis, and strategy against Japan both in Asia and in the Pacific. Then would follow discussion of supporting policies in respect to: arming, equipping, and employing United Nations forces, economic support of Allied nations and occupied countries, and use of United Nations shipping. Finally would come supporting data--shipping; ground, air, and naval forces; and enemy strength and capabilities.

The Joint Chiefs of Staff apparently had had no part in directing preparation of JCS 272.[5] However, when it came before them for discussion on 27 April they gave it a warm reception. Readily agreeing with the principle involved, they gave tentative approval to the proposed agenda, noting that a firm one would be considered after the JSSC had completed the study of current British policy and strategy. In the meantime, they instructed the Joint Staff Planners to initiate studies in accordance with their proposals.[6]

The JWPC had hardly completed a general plan of studies[7] based on the supposition that the conference would be held in mid-summer when it was announced that the meetings would be held in May.[8] The outline of studies was modified accordingly to provide for a total of ten, the first to be a global estimate of the situation in 1943 and 1944. Six of the others were concerned with the war against Germany and two with the war against Japan. The tenth was to integrate the conclusions of the first with all of the subsequent papers. By 3 May, when this revised outline was approved by the Joint Staff Planners, the Joint War Plans Committee was already at work.[9]

The Joint Strategic Survey Committee had by this time completed its study of the relationship between British and United States policy and strategy.[10] The committee had concluded that the different evaluations the two nations put upon the importance of the Mediterranean and upon the threat in the Pacific was indicative of the difference in their interpretations of the objective of defeating Germany first. This, the report implied rather than specifically stated, was because the United States was anxious to bring the war in both theaters to a conclusion by military action as rapidly as possible and therefore was eager to undertake those operations that would most hasten victory, while the British viewed all potential operations with an eye to the effect their accomplishment would have on the postwar position of Great Britain. Fundamentally, the committee suggested, the divergencies sprang from such causes as the respective geographical situations of the two nations and the contrast in territorial structures and bases of power. To the British, restoration of control of the Mediterranean and improvement of their prewar position there were objectives of national policy. The length of time before Japan was defeated was of relatively little concern, for, however it was accomplished, they expected Japan's defeat to result automatically in restoration of the British imperial position in the Far East. The United States, on the other hand, advocated direct attack on the European Continent as the quickest way to defeat Germany and at the same time felt that long delay in initiating decisive action against Japan would be disastrous.

The Joint Strategic Survey Committee did not point up what seems obvious in retrospect, viz., that the United States, despite the separation within the government of responsibility for political and military matters, would do well to consider more carefully the postwar significance of military action. The paper rather cautioned the U.S. Chiefs to remember that the British did consider postwar problems in the actions they proposed, and recommended that British proposals be examined to ascertain to what extent they would further the prosecution of the war or absorb available means to the detriment of the operations the United States considered important: the air offensive from the United Kingdom, the build-up of forces for a cross-Channel invasion (Bolero), and operations in the Pacific.

In an enclosure to the paper, the JSSC presented, item by item, what it estimated to be the British position in respect to its earlier survey of the strategic situation.[11] The committee emphasized again the British desire to minimize the war against Japan and added a word of caution:

> They may be counted upon to perform the letter of their commitments in this connection, but they are traditionally expert at meeting the letter while avoiding the spirit of commitments, and such action in regard to British support of the war against Japan should always be kept in mind as a possibility.

This was not the only attempt made before Trident to define the British viewpoint in preparation for meeting their points in discussion. It was, however, the first given very wide circulation. At the JCS meeting of 4 May the paper was greeted with approval. The chiefs decided to send it to the Joint Staff Planners as a guide, but, on the suggestion of General McNarney, also to return it to the Joint Strategic Survey Committee for recommendation of an alternative to the anticipated British proposal to extend operations in the Mediterranean.[12]

The Joint War Plans Committee had by this time completed a first basic paper, its "Global Estimate of the Situation."[13] After investigating the current situation and capabilities of Germany, Japan, and the United Nations at some length, the JWPC estimated that in 1943 the European Axis would intensify the war of attrition against United Nations shipping and resume the offensive against Russia as soon as practicable, while assuming the defensive on all other fronts and holding the Tunisian bridgehead as long as possible. Much the same thing could be expected if Russia was still in the war the following year, but if Russia had been defeated the European Axis would probably try to gain control of the Mediterranean and the Persian Gulf. As for Japan, if Russia's defeat was clearly imminent in 1943 it was estimated that Japan would attack Siberia. Otherwise Japan would

> remain on the strategic defensive, exploit and consolidate her gains, intensify the war of attrition against shipping, and undertake limited offensive operations in the AUSTRALIA-NEW GUINEA-SOLOMONS area, CHINA, and BURMA, and vigorously counter UNITED STATES offensive action in the WESTERN ALEUTIANS.

Approximately the same prospect was visualized for 1944.

On the basis of these estimates the planners recommended that the United Nations continue their main effort against the European Axis in 1943-44, concentrating on the U-boat menace, the invasion of Sicily (Husky), a bomber offensive from the United Kingdom (Sickle), limited operations in the Mediterranean area, air attacks against Italy, and furnishing supplies to Russia while building up for a full scale assault on the Continent as early as possible in 1944 unless disintegration of Germany made landings feasible before that. In respect to the Pacific, in terms very similar to those in the Casablanca agreements,

> The UNITED NATIONS [should] conduct limited offensive operations in order to maintain pressure on Japan, retain the initiative, and attain or retain positions of readiness for a full-scale offensive against JAPAN and in order to keep CHINA in the war.

Naval forces should be increased to a maximum and air and ground forces provided to make optimum use of the growing naval strength.

If Russia went down, the planners recommended, the basic concept of the United Nations should be reviewed and, depending on their capabilities, they should either reverse the agreed strategy and launch all-out offensives against Japan while holding Germany, or, if Germany were sufficiently weakened, continue operations calculated to bring about its defeat. In either case the air offensive from the United Kingdom should be continued, and supplies and air support "to the greatest extent practicable" should be furnished China to assure its continued participation in the war.

By the time this general study was approved by the Joint Staff Planners, the Joint War Plans Committee had completed two studies concerned with operations against Japan. One of these "set forth proposed operations in the Pacific and Far East in 1943-44, and... [discussed] alternatives to Anakim."[14] The other defined the strategy on which the first was based and bore the title, "A Strategic Plan for the Defeat of Japan."[15]

OPERATIONS AGAINST JAPAN

Work on a long range plan that would result in the defeat of Japan had been undertaken by the JUSSC in August of the preceding year, but by February 1943 no satisfactory results had yet been produced. On the twenty-fourth of that month the Joint Staff Planners directed the committee to continue the study, basing it on the strategic concept approved at Casablanca in CCS 155/1.[16] The basic report and some of the numerous projected annexes had been completed at the end of April when the JUSSC ceased to exist, and the paper was submitted in incomplete form to the JPS in expectation that it might be of assistance to the JSSC in its study of over-all strategy.[17] By that time, however, the planners were all busy with preparations for the next meetings with the British, and the paper, JPS 67/4, was neither accepted nor rejected. However, parts of it were used extensively in the development of the JWPC's study. Assuming that Japan would in general remain on the defensive, that it intended to invade Siberia before Germany was defeated, and that China would remain active in the war, the JUSSC considered certain facts pertinent. In the first place, achieving the unconditional surrender of Japan might require actual invasion of the Japanese homeland.

On the other hand, if the United Nations gained undisputed control of the seas or carried out a sustained air offensive against the islands of Japan, the Japanese might surrender, obviating the necessity of invasion. China was to be used as the base for the ultimate air attacks, and, since the necessary forces and airfields there could not be adequately supplied by the Burma Road supplemented by air transport, an additional route to China would have to be opened up. This would best be effected by sea, through a port on the east coast, preferably Hong Kong, long in Japanese possession. The paper concluded that the best route from the United States to Hong Kong would lie across the Central Pacific and through the Celebes, Sulu, and South China Seas, while from the United Kingdom it would lie through the Strait of Malacca and the South China Sea.

These "pertinent facts" in reality constituted a strategic concept, and most of them were incorporated in the JWPC's "Strategic Plan for the Defeat of Japan" (JWPC 15).[18] The JWPC, however, did not suggest that a sustained air offensive alone might bring Japan to surrender. They also put more emphasis on the possibility of effecting that surrender through gaining control of the seas, which was offered as an alternative objective to invasion of the home islands. Advances to Hong Kong through both the Central and the Southwest Pacific were suggested as possibilities, without decision as to which would be best.[19]

The JWPC did not offer a detailed plan for operations leading up to the defeat of Japan since specific objectives could not yet be determined. But it followed the lead of the JUSSC and sketched a general plan in five broad phases, employing forces of the United States, the United Kingdom, and China, and such others as were available in the various areas. In general the United States was to operate in the Pacific and the British in areas of Southeast Asia where it would contribute to the total effort but not become involved in U.S. operations. Phase I was to see the United Kingdom, assisted by the United States and China, recapture Burma and reopen the Burma Road, while a line of communications to the Celebes Sea was opened by an advance of U.S. forces westward from Pearl Harbor. In Phase II, U.S. forces would recapture the Philippines, while forces of the United Kingdom conducted an offensive in southeast Asia to gain control of Indo-China, opened the southern entrance to the South China Sea, and operated to divert enemy forces from the Pacific. At the same time the Chinese would be preparing forces for land operations to capture Hong Kong, and, after the United States, in Phase III, had secured control of the northern part of the South China Sea, American forces would assist the Chinese in retaking Hong Kong. In Phase IV, the three nations, with the Chinese primarily involved, would combine efforts to seize suitable air bases in China from which to bomb the Japanese islands. In Phase V, the other two nations would assist the United States to conduct an intensive air offensive against

Japan preparatory to the ultimate invasion. To these the JWPC added a sixth phase, the invasion itself, for which the United States would take the lead.

In furtherance of this long-term, general plan for Japan's defeat, the second paper, submitted to the Joint Staff Planners by the Joint War Plans Committee on the same day,[20] recommended specific operations to be undertaken in the Pacific and the Far East in 1943-1944. The study concluded that in the Asiatic theater either Anakim, the plan for recapture of all of Burma, or Modified Anakim, the plan for opening up a route across northern Burma and making preliminary advances from the west, would satisfy the contention of the United States that it was of vital importance to open land supply routes to China. However, the report recognized the obstacles in the form of conflict between British reluctance to undertake any serious moves in the theater and Chinese insistence on operations on a grand scale, including a direct attack on Rangoon and a naval demonstration in the Indian Ocean. The JWPC had serious doubts about the competence of the command of either the British or the Chinese in the area and thought that both would be more effective if an American division were present. There was doubt, too, as to the feasibility of Anakim in its original form involving direct assault on Rangoon and completion of the operations in one season. Despite its uncertainty, the committee concluded that both Anakim and Modified Anakim were "feasible and acceptable courses of action." The committee recommended proceeding with caution in order to secure the support of the British and Chinese:

> A determined insistence on Anakim, coupled with a threat to discontinue large shipments of Lend-Lease material now being furnished to the Indian Army, on the grounds that it is not being put to effective use, may induce the British to actively support a Modified Anakim. Chinese suspicions and reluctance must then be overcome, insofar as it is possible, by every practicable means. In this connection it is considered of utmost importance that the U.S. avoid accepting the onus of having suggested any modification of Anakim, since this position would seriously weaken our influence with the Chinese.

As a second course of action in the Asiatic theater, the Joint War Plans Committee discussed air operations in China, of which the feasibility was limited by the amount of supplies that could be delivered to China by air transport. It was pointed out that, in addition to opening a land route, completion of Anakim or Modified Anakim would result in rapid expansion of the air route, for more facilities would be available at the western terminus and operating conditions would be more favorable when the enemy no longer held northern Burma. Current plans were to expand the capacity of the air route to reach 10,000 tons monthly by the end of 1943.[21] If ground support forces were cut almost in half and local sources of supply were exploited, Major General Claire L. Chennault estimated that a force of 455 planes could be operated in China on a monthly delivery of 7,128 tons. Such a force, it was believed,[22] could cause costly attrition of the Japanese Air Force, "permit sustained and damaging attacks against Japanese shipping on the YANGSTE [sic] RIVER, along the CHINA coast and out to sea to include all the islands of FORMOSA and HAINAN and the sea lane between JAPAN and SHANGHAI," permit attacks on Japanese industrial targets in China and Formosa and limited bombing of the mainland of Japan itself, as well as preparing for the eventual large-scale offensive against the islands. The JWPC cautioned, however, that the scale of air offensives in China should be gauged to probable Japanese reaction, lest a large-scale land offensive in China be precipitated.

Finally, in the Asiatic theater, the JWPC recommended that, after the recapture of Burma, British Commonwealth forces initiate action to open the Strait of Malacca. This would include operations from the Rangoon area down the Kra Peninsula toward Singapore and into Sumatra.

In the Pacific Theater, subsequent to the operations already outlined in the Joint Chiefs' directive of 28 March 1943 to the theater commanders the JWPC contemplated capture of the Bismarck Archipelago, including the occupation or neutralization of Rabaul and the control of New Ireland and the Admiralty Islands, thereby projecting air and naval power into the Central Pacific Area. The committee did not venture to estimate what enemy resistance to these moves might be, but, since the Supreme Commander, Southwest Pacific Area, had stated that the forces available to him were not sufficient to carry on into the Bismarck Archipelago, feasibility of the operation was made subject to the allocation of necessary forces.

Just what was meant by "control of NEW IRELAND and the ADMIRALTY ISLANDS" is not entirely clear. One must conclude, however, that air supremacy in the area must have been intended, for the next operation recommended for the Pacific Theater was the capture and occupation of Manus Island, the largest of the Admiralties. Establishment of airfields on Manus, it was pointed out, would project land-based air operations into the Central Pacific, support the fleet in the area, and assist ground operations on the north coast of New Guinea. The JWPC believed that if sufficient forces to take the New Britain-New Ireland area were available enough could be released thereafter to make the seizure of Manus feasible.

The third course of action recommended for the Pacific Theater was capture and occupation of the Marshall Islands, an operation separate from the other two, which would extend control of the sea two thousand miles westward into the Central Pacific. Inasmuch as availability of estimated requirements was dependent upon the completion of other operations, and since the necessary number of cruisers (8 CA's, 8 CL's) could not be available until about 1 April 1944, it was concluded that operations in the Marshalls would be delayed until about that time.

Finally, the committee rejected any amphibious operations in the North Pacific west of the Aleutians after the capture of Attu until such time as the Russians became involved in the war against Japan and conditions were favorable for operations to support them in the area of the Kamchatka Peninsula.

These then were the operations proposed for 1943-1944: Anakim, or at least a modification of it, air operations in China, operations to open the Strait of Malacca, completion of the tasks already assigned in the South and Southwest Pacific, capture of the Bismarck Archipelago and of Manus Island, and seizure of the Marshall Islands. Initiation of some would be dependent upon completion of others, but some, as, for instance, Anakim and the Solomons-New Guinea action, would be under way concurrently. JWPC concluded its discussion by urging that all operations be coordinated by the Joint or the Combined Chiefs of Staff "in order that each operation not be considered as an independent operation, but as a part of a larger picture."

Before this paper was presented to the JCS, the plan was somewhat modified in accordance with a broader study on the "Conduct of the War in 1943-1944," which the Joint Staff Planners submitted to the chiefs on 7 May 1943 as JCS 290.[23] In the original plan of studies this report was to have tied together the conclusions of the various theater programs outlined in the other papers. Instead, it proved to be the basis on which some of the others were written.

JCS 290 was more of a drawing together of conclusions from earlier studies than a new contribution. Like several papers that had preceded it, it contained a statement of the over-all objective and a formulation of the strategic concept for achieving it. The objective was in line with the JSSC's analysis in its comparison of U.S. and British policy and strategy, viz., "to bring the war against GERMANY, JAPAN, and ITALY to a successful conclusion at the earliest possible date." The strategic concept was similar to that outlined a month earlier by the JSSC in its study of the Casablanca decisions,[24] differing chiefly in the last sentence, which had, however, appeared in JWPC's own "Global Estimate":

 a. In cooperation with RUSSIA and other Allies to force an unconditional surrender of the AXIS in EUROPE.

 b. Simultaneously, in cooperation with other PACIFIC Powers concerned, to maintain and extend unremitting pressure against JAPAN with the purpose of continually reducing her military power and attaining positions from which her ultimate unconditional surrender can be forced.

 c. Upon the defeat of the AXIS in EUROPE, in cooperation with other PACIFIC Powers and, if possible with RUSSIA, to direct the full resources of the UNITED STATES and GREAT BRITAIN to force the unconditional surrender of JAPAN. If, however, conditions develop which indicate that the war as a whole can be brought more quickly to a successful conclusion by the earlier mounting of a major offensive against JAPAN, the strategical concept set forth herein may be reversed.

JCS 290 outlined policy for the Pacific in 1943-1944 in general terms less restricted than those used in the "Global Estimate":

> Conduct operations to maintain lines of communication in the PACIFIC, particularly to AUSTRALIA; to maintain pressure on JAPAN, retain the initiative, force attrition, contain the Japanese Fleet in the PACIFIC, and attain or retain positions of readiness for a full scale offensive against JAPAN; and to keep CHINA in the war.

Specifically, the paper listed five military objectives for the war against Japan in 1943-44:

(1) Ejection of the Japanese from the ALEUTIANS.
(2) Seizure of the MARSHALL and CAROLINE ISLANDS.
(3) Seizure of the SOLOMONS, the BISMARCK ARCHIPELAGO, and Japanese held NEW GUINEA.
(4) Seizure of BURMA.
(5) Conduct of air operations in and from CHINA.

There is no mention of why the Caroline Islands were included as practicable objectives for 1944 when the JWPC study of two days before had gone only as far as the Marshalls. Perhaps it was in order to avoid the risk of being restricted should opportunity to go farther present itself. In any event it is important to note that here was the start of the Central Pacific advance, the program that had been favored in the prewar Orange plans for moving directly across the Pacific to retake the Philippines. This was to be the decisive axis, and the operations projected by JCS 290 for the South-Southwest Pacific were primarily to support the Central Pacific program, to secure the flank, and to finish up action that had already been started. From this point on it was a case of adopting step by step the development of the advance through the Central Pacific.

On 8 May 1943, the Joint Chiefs of Staff discussed and approved ten papers which the JSSC, the JPS, and the JWPC had developed in preparation for Trident.[25] Several of these were concerned with the procedure to be followed at the approaching conference; the rest were studies of specific problems related to the strategy of the war. The "Strategic Plan for the Defeat of Japan" (JCS 287) was among them, but "Operations in the Pacific and Far East in 1943-44" was not, being in the process of revision to conform with JCS 290. The minutes of the JCS meeting record only briefly the discussion that took place, giving no indication in most cases that the chiefs raised any but minor objections to the reports before approving them. Two of the remarks that were recorded had to do with the war against Japan. Both were made by General

Marshall and both related to the same point, i.e., that there was not sufficient emphasis on air operations from bases in China.[26] As a result of General Marshall's comment, the list of military objectives for 1943-1944 included in the JWPC's "Conduct of the War in 1943-1944" was rearranged so that the two items concerned with the Far East came first. Similarly, a revision was made of the "Strategic Plan for the Defeat of Japan," stressing the importance of the air offensive from China and the operations required in preparation for it. At the same time, with no explanation, and with no modification of the provisions of the plan, the statement was removed that the plan being presented provided for achieving the defeat of Japan either by invasion of the home islands or by gaining control of the seas.[27]

The Joint War Plans Committee submitted its revised draft of "Operations in the Pacific and Far East in 1943-44" to the Joint Chiefs as JCS 304 on 12 May 1943.[28] By this time a separate paper had been prepared on Anakim and consequently JCS 304 concentrated on future operations in the Pacific Theater. It was pointed out that a target date had been set for only one of the tasks included in the JCS directive of 28 March 1943. That was the occupation of Kiriwina and Woodlark Islands, to be undertaken on 15 June 1943. Since enemy reaction to this first move was unknown, no close estimate could be made of when all the operations under the directive would be completed, but it was recognized that it might well be in 1944. It was estimated, in fact, that, with the forces available and the time that would be required for preparation, capture of the Bismarck Archipelago could not be completed before 1 April 1944. The entire program was planned on the basis of four more amphibious divisions as well as other additional ground, air, and naval forces.

JCS 304 discussed at some length the operations that would follow the seizure of the Bismarck Archipelago. It was pointed out that the advance would proceed in two areas. First was that of Halmahera-Celebes, to be preceded by capturing New Guinea, extending operations along the north coast and seizing the Vogelkop region. Should this for some reason (the paper suggested none) not be done, it was recommended that other "offensive-defensive" operations be undertaken in the area of Timor-Celebes-Ceram, recognizing, however, that these would probably be limited to air action.

The second area in which operations would be launched was, of course, the Central Pacific. As in the earlier paper, operations in the Marshalls were scheduled to include neutralizing or occupying all the major atolls in the group, as well as Wake Island. Six months after action began in the Marshalls, it was estimated, forces could move on to the Carolines, first capturing Ponape and Truk and establishing air and garrison forces there, then neutralizing and establishing forces in the western Carolines, finally setting up a main fleet operating base on Truk. These operations would take several months and would result in wresting control of the Central Pacific from the Japanese, placing U.S. forces in position to continue westward across the Pacific or even to threaten the Japanese home islands directly. In the meantime, it was suggested, carrier-based attacks on Japan could be inaugurated as a means of rendering support to whatever form of Anakim was in progress.

It was not recommended that all of these operations necessarily be carried out, and JCS 304 set no order for their execution. Instead it stated that, before completion of the operations already scheduled by JCS directive, decision would have to be made as to whether to launch the campaign in the Bismarck Archipelago or attack the Marshall Islands. Then the Joint Chiefs of Staff would have to decide the relative value of further operations in New Guinea and in the Carolines. Thus, the way was left open for a turn away from the Southwest Pacific and a single advance westward through the Central Pacific Area. Already it was becoming questionable whether Rabaul would finally be captured.

By 12 May, when JCS 304 was completed, the Joint Chiefs of Staff were busy with last-minute preparations for the conference with the British and with problems which would come up for discussion at the first meetings. Pacific operations were not high on the list of priorities and, consequently, although JCS 304 was put on the Joint Chiefs' agenda, it was not actually discussed until the Combined Chiefs had decided what was next to be done in the war against Germany and what the fate of Anakim was to be.

CONFERENCE TACTICS

While the Joint War Plans Committee was working on its series of studies, the Joint Strategic Survey Committee had been analyzing the basic views of the U.S. Chiefs and working on several papers concerned with the tactics that should be followed at the conference in order best to present U.S. views to the British Chiefs of Staff. One of its most important papers, produced in time for consideration by the Joint Chiefs of Staff at their 8 May meeting, developed as a result of the receipt in Washington from the British Chiefs of Staff of a suggested agenda for the Trident Conference.[29]

The British had suggested two main topics for discussion: first, post-Husky strategy in 1943 against the Axis in Europe, including further action in the Mediterranean and Sickle and Bolero in the United Kingdom, and, second, action against Japan in both the Pacific and the Indian Ocean Theaters. There would, of course, they acknowledged, be contingent problems such as shipping to discuss. In addition, it might be "convenient to consider in general terms without going into any details Anglo-American machinery required for defeating Japan." With this British proposal as a starting point, and following the directive of the JCS at their 4 May meeting to restudy JCS 283 "with a view to submitting an alternative line of action to the anticipated proposal of the British of expanding operations in the Mediterranean,"[30] the JSSC recommended a "line of action" for the Joint Chiefs of Staff to follow at the approaching conference.

Consistently, since the beginning of the war, the U.S. Joint Chiefs of Staff had argued that the way to defeat Germany was to cross the Channel from England and fight Germany on the continent of Europe. There had been differences among the chiefs as to the timing of such an operation and as to the extent to which air bombardment of Germany and German-occupied territory from bases in the United Kingdom could weaken the enemy and facilitate the invasion when it came. But it had been with reluctance that the chiefs had postponed the date of the Continental landings, put troops into North Africa, and agreed to move across the Mediterranean into Sicily. Now that there were Allied troops in that area the U.S. Chiefs were less reluctant to use them again in the same region. But they clearly considered operations in the Mediterranean a diversion from the main line of approach to the final objective of defeating Germany.

The paper prepared by the Joint Strategic Survey Committee took full cognizance of this basic position and of the apparent British desire to attack objectives in the eastern Mediterranean area, and it made no attempt to point out any advantages in Mediterranean operations. Arguments against them were put as strongly as possible, with the blunt recommendation that "we should state that such a commitment is contrary to sound strategy and should firmly maintain that the United States will not become so committed." The paper went so far as to say:

> Should the British insist on operations to the east of Sicily, the United States should inform them (1) that they will have to rely entirely on British resources, and (2) that to the extent such employment of resources detracts from the effectiveness of operations directly against Germany, the United States may be forced to increase its commitments in the Pacific.

What the United States wanted, according to the JSSC, was the air offensive against Germany in 1943, to be followed by invasion of the Continent in 1944. If it seemed advisable to use the forces in the western Mediterranean rather than leaving them idle, occupation of Sardinia was less objectionable than other operations in the area.

While not questioning the long-established strategy of defeating Germany first, the JSSC reminded the Joint Chiefs of Staff of the importance of the war against Japan, insisting that it should be emphasized early in the conference that strategy against Germany and strategy against Japan were closely interrelated and the other theaters of war should not be forgotten when operations in the European Theater were under discussion. The committee did not overlook the tactical value of an intimation during the conference that if the British insisted on a course of action in Europe which the United States considered unsound, the United States might be forced to pay increased attention to the Pacific. As for Anakim, on which differences seemed certain to arise, the JSSC felt that the operation should be done. If, however, the British refused to support it, or for some other reason Anakim proved impossible and no acceptable substitute was offered, it was recommended that the United States "expand and intensify its operations in the Pacific, in order to counteract the advantage which Japan gains by Allied failure adequately to support China."

This, then, was the line of action the Joint Strategic Survey Committee recommended. The committee submitted it to the chiefs with the opinion that "what is of greatest immediate importance is an agreed line of action definitely approved by the President, to be followed by the United States representatives at the conference." The Joint Chiefs of Staff apparently agreed entirely with the contents of the paper and with its significance, for they decided on 8 May to present it, with only one minor amendment that had no bearing on the war against Japan, to the President for his approval.[31] Whether or not he approved it is not known.

OPERATIONS IN BURMA

The last papers concerning the war against Japan which the Joint War Plans Committee completed had to do with the operation on which there was sure to be considerable discussion since it fell within a British sphere of responsibility. That, of course, was Anakim. On 10 May 1943 the committee submitted two papers on the subject[32] directly to the Joint Chiefs of Staff. The first, circulated as JCS 297, was a restudy of the Anakim plan as developed at New Delhi. The other, JCS 303, was a revised plan for recapturing Burma.

There was not much optimism in the conclusions of JCS 297, which read:

    a. That if the NEW DELHI tactical concept is adhered to, there is no reasonable chance of success.
    b. That with tactical modification of the NEW DELHI plan, there is a reasonable chance of success.

The "tactical modification" recommended was abandonment of the attempt to attack Rangoon directly by sea and substitution of a landing at Bassein, west of there, followed by overland attack, via Henzada, on Rangoon, a move which was expected to take the Japanese by surprise. "Tactical modification" of the original Anakim was not the only requisite, however. There must be also the will to succeed. The failure of the pre-monsoon operations the British had undertaken in the spring just ending, both of the attack on Akyab and of advances from Imphal and into the

Chin Hills, boded no good for the attempt to recapture all of Burma the following fall and winter. Consequently, the JWPC recommended that there would have to "be a marked improvement in leadership, [and] calibre of troops, and that the major proportion of the amphibious troops [would have to] be British."

Anakim could not, of course, be executed unless shipping was made available to supply it. Of the 113 sailings, or 733,500 long tons of shipping, which the British had requested from the United States for the theater,[33] the committee found that all but approximately 100,000 tons could be provided. Without indicating its source of information, the JWPC stated that that shortage could be met one month later than the required date.[34] Additional air forces, both U.S. and British, would be needed, and the committee recommended that they be provided even at the expense of operations in the European-African area. It was recognized that the British had a difficult problem in providing the necessary personnel and equipment for the operation. Nevertheless, the committee was of the opinion that the problem could be overcome "by early and decisive action." In short, the Joint War Plans Committee expressed its belief "that if the deficiencies in forces and equipment...are made up, BURMA may be recaptured in the dry season of 1943-44, provided there is the necessary determination."[35]

Whether that determination would be forthcoming was another matter. It was well realized that the American and British Chiefs of Staff put different values on the recapture of Burma. This had been made clear at Casablanca, where much discussion had been required in order to obtain agreement to attempt Anakim in the fall of 1943. Indications of a subsequent weakening in British enthusiasm for the operation were borne out by a report from the Secretary of the British Joint Staff Mission to the Secretary of the Joint Chiefs of Staff on 5 May 1943 that "the British Chiefs of Staff have strong arguments for exploiting Husky and for showing that Anakim in 1943 cannot be advocated either on strategic or operational grounds. They will, however, have alternatives to Anakim to propose."[36] Thus it was that despite the JWPC's own warning in JWPC 9/1 that the United States should "avoid accepting the onus of having suggested any modification of Anakim, since this position would seriously weaken our influence with the Chinese," the committee felt it desirable to have at hand a suggestion for a modified Anakim and presented it to the Joint Chief of Staff in JCS 303.

The alternative which the Joint War Plans Committee offered was based first of all on the premise that the minimum objectives acceptable in respect to Burma were "to maintain pressure on JAPAN, to retain the initiative in the area, and to maintain and improve the flow of supplies and munitions to CHINA in order to insure her continuance in the war." Assuming that the full scale Anakim could not be accomplished in 1943-1944 and that only those forces would be available which were already in the area or could be moved there and equipped and trained in time, the committee examined four possible plans. The one on which the committee settled as the most acceptable and the most feasible was divided in two phases: Phase I, to be initiated in November 1943, would consist of an advance into upper Burma, the British proceeding toward Pakokku and Mandalay while the Chinese moved from Ledo to Myitkyina and from Yunnan to join both the other groups. At the same time Akyab and Ramree Island in the south would be captured. On 1 December Phase II would be launched with simultaneous amphibious assaults on Sandoway and Gwa to capture airfields and on the coast opposite Bassein in order to prepare to advance overland to capture Bassein and nearby airfields. Included in Phase II also was the securing of the Bassein River to provide logistic support from the sea. Throughout both phases an air offensive would be conducted in Burma and naval operations in the Pacific to divert the Japanese Fleet from the area. Completion of the operations would put United Nations forces in position to capture Rangoon and to open up the Irrawaddy River in the next dry season.

These rather hastily prepared papers were accepted by the Joint Chiefs of Staff, without much detailed discussion, on 12 May, the morning of the first day of the Trident meetings. Recognizing the value of having something to offer the British when the subject of Anakim arose, the chiefs agreed to present them with JCS 303 "as soon as it had been indicated by the British that the present Anakim plan is not feasible."[37] At the last minute, on the strength of a rumor that Admiral Leahy had heard to the effect that the capture of Sumatra was being considered, the Joint Chiefs put the JPS to work on a study of such an operation.[38] The plan was ready three days later, but it was never introduced.[39]

USE OF THE PAPERS

By 10 May 1943 the Joint Chiefs of Staff had received from their two main working groups, the Joint War Plans Committee, via the Joint Staff Planners, and the Joint Strategic Survey Committee, a large number of papers covering a wide variety of subjects. Ten of them[40] had come up for discussion two days before, and several others were ready for consideration on the tenth. The JSSC had even drafted some opening remarks for Admiral Leahy to deliver at the first combined meeting.[41] There would be still more papers completed before the Trident Conference officially opened. The Joint Chiefs of Staff had approved almost all of the recommendations that appeared in the numerous studies, and they had readily endorsed the "line of action" which the JSSC recommended they adopt in the combined discussions. But this large body of papers, even though reflecting the views of the Joint Chiefs of Staff, would be of little immediate help unless it was decided in advance what use should be made of them.

General McNarney reminded the Joint Chiefs of the advisability of determining what was to be done with the papers by stating at the meeting of 10 May that "he believed the Joint Chiefs of Staff should definitely accept certain papers and submit them as proposals to the British at the proper time during the coming Conference."[42] The chiefs apparently had not given this problem much thought, for Admiral Leahy was the only one who had a suggestion to make. He recommended that they insist on: "(a) cross-channel operations; (b) Anakim or an acceptable substitute." Without much discussion they agreed to propose to the British "at the propitious time" four plans suggested by General McNarney:

(a) invasion of the European Continent from the United Kingdom in 1943-44; (b) a specific plan for operations in the Mediterranean area; (c) a modified Anakim; (d) a long range plan for the defeat of Japan.

The Joint Staff Planners incorporated the chiefs' decision in a "Memorandum for Information" which they presented to the Joint Chiefs on 12 May, the morning of the first of the Trident meetings.[43] Including with the four General McNarney had listed a fifth already prepared, entitled "Defensive Garrison Required and Forces Available for Transfer to other Areas or for Limited Offensives in the Mediterranean, 1943-44," the JPS recommended that the Joint Chiefs of Staff study the papers carefully "with a view to approving them for presentation to the British Chiefs of Staff as representing U.S. views." The planners included also a list of sixteen other papers, including those discussed in the preceding pages, which they thought "should be of assistance... in discussion of the subjects covered." The brief minutes of the Joint Chiefs' meeting of 12 May do not indicate whether or not the chiefs discussed the best way to introduce these papers. Only in respect to Anakim did they decide, reminded by Admiral King that Burma was an area of British responsibility, to let the British bring up the subject first.[44] Presumably they would present the others as opportunity offered.

THE STILWELL-CHENNAULT PROBLEM

While the joint committees were working on papers for the Joint Chiefs of Staff to use in their combined discussions at Trident, another problem that would eventually come up at the Trident meetings was under discussion in the War Department. This was the controversy between General Stilwell and General Chennault.

Coincident with the arrival of the two generals in Washington at the end of April, there came a letter from the Generalissimo to the President expressing Chiang's views of what should be done for China. As reported by Mr. T.V. Soong to Mr. Harry Hopkins on 29 April, the Generalissimo's sentiments were clearly sympathetic with those of General Chennault:

after careful consideration he [Chiang] has concluded all resources must be concentrated in the immediate future on launching an air offensive in China. Specifically, after weighing the various claims, he now desires that the entire air transport tonnage during the months of May, June and July be devoted to carrying into China gasoline and aviation supplies, in order to build up the required reserves for decisive offensive action. It is the Generalissimo's view that since initiation of the air effort has both most urgent and presently feasible and since the ground effort had been deferred until next Autumn military logic demands the requested alteration in schedules.

...The question is not whether the ground effort is to be finally sacrificed to the air effort, but whether ground supplies or air supplies are to be carried into China in the months just ahead.... The capacity of the air transport line into China is planned to expand very rapidly, and as this expansion occurs, all needed ground supplies may also be carried into China in ample time to be on hand when called for. Indeed, the Generalissimo believes that the air offensive will not only have great strategic results, in and of itself, but also, and perhaps more importantly, will serve as a direct preparation for the ground effort by weakening the enemy air strength and attacking his main line of communication to the southward.

The Generalissimo also wishes me to transmit to you his personal assurance that in the event the enemy attempts to interrupt the air offensive by a ground advance on the air bases, the advance can be halted by the existing Chinese forces.[45]

To present his views more effectively in Washington, as has already been related, the Generalissimo had asked the President to call General Chennault home, since the Generalissimo's views were identical with those of the Commanding General, Fourteenth Air Force. General Chennault's ideas were already known in the War Department, where they had been presented some months earlier but not approved.[46] Upon his arrival at the end of April he offered in greater detail his plan for the use of an air force in China.[47]

General Chennault's plan emphasized the importance to Japan of maintaining control of the shipping lanes along the coast of China in order to keep open its supply line to Indo-China, Thailand, Malaya, and Burma. From Japan's concentration on lines of supply and communication, General Chennault concluded that it did not desire to fight in China, particularly in the air. Indeed, he pointed out, most of Japan's current air operations in China were for training purposes. Moreover, he believed that the Japanese were not prepared to fight there, having far-flung areas to defend, all the way from Alaska through Manchuria, north and central China, along the China coast and the islands to Indo-China, Thailand, Malaya, and Burma, as well as through the Netherlands East Indies, the Philippines, and the islands of the Southwest Pacific. With its military effort spread so far and so thin, General Chennault considered that Japan was "fully prepared to fight only on her Empire frontiers such as Burma, the southwest Pacific and Manchuria."

If Japan preferred not to fight in the air over China, General Chennault felt that "every effort should be exerted to make her fight there." Japanese supply lines, shipping, coastal ports, and inland resources in China were all within range of U.S. air units based on fields in China, and General Chennault was anxious to attack them. He recognized the possibility that the Japanese might react to intensive air operations by moving to occupy central China where U.S. airfields were located. But he discounted the seriousness of such a threat, pointing out that the Japanese had made several vain attempts to occupy those areas and a successful attempt would require considerable increases in shipping and air power, with corresponding decreases elsewhere.

In order to carry out "consistent offensive air operations against the Japanese forces in China," General Chennault stated that he would require two fighter groups of three squadrons each, one medium bomber group, one heavy bomber group, and one reconnaissance squadron, with 25 per cent reserve of fighters and fighter pilots training in India and 20 per cent reserves for the bomber and reconnaissance planes and crews there also. In addition the Chinese Air Force would need two groups of fighters and one of medium bombers. Most of the U.S. groups were already in China or at least in India and so it was largely supplies, including planes, which General Chennault would need.

With this relatively small collection of aircraft General Chennault proposed to execute a program in three continuous phases. First, one American fighter group and one medium bomber group would move into the Kweilin-Hengyang area to initiate operations against Japanese airdromes at Canton, Hong Kong, Hankow, Nanchang, and Hainan; Japanese shipping at Canton, Hong Kong, Kwanchowwan, Hainan, the Formosa Channel, and on the Yangtze; and Japanese supply bases and industries in the same general area. When air supremacy had been gained, one heavy bomber group would move in to exploit it, extending operations against shipping along the China coast and to the islands of Formosa and Hainan and the sea lane from Japan to Shanghai, attacking industrial targets north to Shan Kai Kwan and east to Nanking, Shanghai, and Formosa. Meanwhile, the airfield area would be pushed eastward to include Suichwan, Kienow, Yushan, Lishui, and Chuchow. Finally in the third phase, operations would be further extended to attack shipping from the coast of Korea to Camranh Bay and industrial targets in Japan proper north as far as Tokyo. The speed with which this ambitious plan could be carried out would necessarily depend on the delivery of supplies on schedule and prompt arrival of reserve personnel and replacement equipment as well as on the coordination of offensive operations in the Southwest Pacific and Burma with the effort in China. It was suggested, however, that the first phase could be carried out between 1 July and 31 August, the second between 1 September and 31 October, and the final one could begin on about 10 November.

Could this project be supplied? General Chennault thought so, carefully pointing out that to date not even 40 per cent of the estimated required tonnage had been delivered. His project would have to be given priority on the Hump deliveries, however, or it could not succeed. Initially, he would need 4,790 tons per month. Ultimately, this would have to be increased to 7,129.[48]

Seriously conflicting with General Chennault's ideas and with the views of Chiang Kai-shek were the views of General Stilwell. He had no such detailed plan of operations to offer on his arrival in Washington as did General Chennault. His immediate plan for operations was represented by Anakim, which had been submitted long before. Basic to his position was the directive he had been given in the beginning, that is, to increase the combat effectiveness of the Chinese army. He was working toward that objective through the training program at Ramgarh, the plan to train thirty divisions in Yunnan, and a second thirty-division plan the Generalissimo had approved but which had not yet gotten under way. General Stilwell considered it essential to build a strong army in China in order to seize and to hold vital bases from which to launch the final offensive against Japan as well as to participate in the campaign to recapture Burma. He contended that China could not hold out economically for another year, that Yunnan must be held, and that a force must be built to hold it. The supplies carried across the Hump by air should, he felt, be devoted to the greatest possible extent to building up the ground forces for these purposes. As long as supplies were limited the air force should receive only enough to make its support for the Burma operation and its defensive operations in China effective. He feared lest heavy air attacks such as General Chennault advocated lead the Japanese to retaliate by attacking Kunming and other areas of Free China, and he insisted that the Chinese army should be bolstered up in order to resist such an eventuality. For operations within China General Stilwell had no strategic plan. China was under the Generalissimo's supreme command, and in any case the time was not ripe for large-scale military operations. If, as General Stilwell understood, the China coast was to be the objective of the advance across the Pacific, he felt that operations within China should be tied in with operations in the Southwest Pacific. His experiences with Chiang and his difficulties in trying to get commitments from the Chinese led him to insist that American aid should not be given until the Chinese had given something in return. General Stilwell's attitude was summed up in a memorandum to General Marshall on the first of May:

> It is vital that the British and Chinese be held to their commitments for Anakim. It is vital that the present training program be uninterrupted. It is vital that the President show

enough confidence in his representative in China to prevent further intrigue aimed at splitting the American organization and effort. It is vital that the C in C [sic] be brought to understand that concessions only bring more demands, and that insistence on the wholehearted fulfillment of commitments is the only way to avoid delay, obstruction and failure.[49]

Meanwhile, on 30 April 1943 General Stilwell and General Chennault met with General Marshall and other top Army officers to present their impressions of the current situation in China. This was the first of a series of meetings and conferences in which the two men argued in much the same manner their views of what should be done in China and more specifically what should be included in the still small trickle of supplies across the Hump.

General Stilwell's picture of the current situation in China was gloomy and pessimistic. He spoke in some detail of widespread and serious corruption in the Chinese army, of its deficiencies in men and equipment, of the small amount it had actually accomplished in contrast with its published achievements, and of his difficulties in getting cooperation from the high officials of the Chinese Government and the army.[50] He described the Generalissimo as "a very slick political manipulator...crafty and shrewd." As far as General Stilwell could see, the only plan that Chiang had was "to finish the war with a big stock pile of ammunition and weapons and an air force."

In respect to India and the British military forces there, General Stilwell was hardly more complimentary. Pointing out that although there were six divisions in India during the campaign of the previous year in Burma Field Marshal Wavell had sent in only 200 reenforcements, General Stilwell hinted at a long range British policy of keeping China weak. Already there was talk of postponing Anakim and only the Americans seemed to want to do anything toward retaking Burma.

In contrast to the unpleasant facts presented by General Stilwell, General Chennault's report centered around the potentialities of an air force, adequately supplied, in China. Taking a dim view of the existing program which kept his aircraft employed largely in defensive operations, he outlined, in brief and conservatively, some of the operations he believed could be done if 4,000 to 7,000 tons of supplies a month could be delivered. He did not place the blame for his not already receiving that amount entirely on General Stilwell but spoke particularly of the inadequacies of the airfields in India, predicting that it would be four to six months before they could all be operative. General Chennault, without specifically saying so, indicated that continuing the existing ratio of three to eight of the tonnage delivered to China for the air forces and five to eight for all other purposes, which General Stilwell approved, was not sufficient for the program General Chennault hoped to carry out in China. It would compel his forces to concentrate almost entirely on defensive operations. Although he said that General Stilwell was "a far better authority" than he as to whether the Chinese could hold the air bases in east China in the face of a strong Japanese attack, and, although General Stilwell predicted that they could not as then constituted, General Chennault reported without comment that the Generalissimo had told him that he believed his army could.

In the few days before the Trident meetings began, General Stilwell and General Chennault had an opportunity to present their views to the President and to the Joint Chiefs of Staff, the latter at a meeting which Mr. Soong was also invited to attend.[51] As would be expected, Mr. Soong supported the views of Chiang Kai-shek and General Chennault. The JCS were particularly interested in the condition of the airfields in India and the time it would take to complete those still under construction in order to increase the tonnage going over the Hump. Although the question "Should all available tonnage [over the Hump] be utilized to support the air force, or should part of it be used to support ground forces?" was clearly stated to the group by General Stilwell, the decision was not a responsibility of the Joint Chiefs of Staff and the discussion ended with the remark of Mr. Soong that "the build-up of air strength or ground strength is a matter which had given the Generalissimo much concern. His decision had been to utilize available tonnage for building up the air force."

The conversations of Generals Stilwell and Chennault with the President are known only from the officers' own reports.[52] It was soon apparent that Mr. Roosevelt's sympathies lay with General Chennault and the Generalissimo. For some time supporters of the plan to defeat Japan in China by air alone had been influencing the President through Mr. Hopkins.[53] Since Mr. Roosevelt was insistent that Chiang Kai-shek, as head of the state, must be supported, he was not to be persuaded readily to promote the course his War Department advisors recommended[54] at the expense of the course the Generalissimo urged. He had, of course, just received a report from Chiang that Chinese morale was low and only an increased air program could raise it. General Stilwell's case was apparently not assisted by his undramatic presentation, and it is not surprising that General Marshall reported to General Stilwell as early as 3 May that he had "talked to the President yesterday morning regarding China matters and found him completely set against any delay in Chennault's program." Despite General Marshall's own explanation to Mr. Roosevelt of the importance of preparing the Chinese force in Yunnan in order to support the air operations by preventing Japanese advances on the ground, and his indication "that the Generalissimo's desire to divert all tonnage away from this Force would be fatal to his purpose as well as to ours," the president insisted that "politically he must support Chiang Kai-shek and that in the state of Chinese morale the air program was therefore of great importance." Anakim, too, he felt should be subordinated to the air operations. He was, in fact, in favor only of a modified operation in north Burma, not at Rangoon.⁵⁵

Whether the President had made his final decision at this time is not clear from the record. It was not until almost two weeks later, in any event, that it was reported to Mr. Soong, who passed it along to the Generalissimo:

(1) Starting July 1, 1943, the first 4,700 tons of supplies per month flown into China over the India-China route shall be for General Chennault's air force; after this priority is fully satisfied, the next 2,000 tons per month shall be for all other purposes, including ground forces; thereafter the next 300 tons per month shall also be for the air force.

(2) President has ordered that starting September 1, the original goal of 10,000 tons per month shall be reached and even stepped up.

(3) I asked the President for all the tonnage for the remainder of May and June 1943 on both Air Transport Command and CNAC planes for air force supplies for the Fourteenth Air Force. The President replied that certain small exceptions might be needed for ground forces and asked me to work out this problem with the Deputy Chief of Staff of the United States Army.⁵⁶

This allocation of tonnage would result in postponement of the Yunnan project and consequently have a strong effect on what was to be done in Burma, particularly on what Chinese forces could be used there. Thus it was necessarily to be an important factor in the decisions to be made at the Trident Conference.

Chapter XVI

TRIDENT

OPENING DISCUSSIONS

The Trident Conference started off as Casablanca had before it with a meeting of the Chiefs of Staff of the two nations with the President and the Prime Minister. This time it was held at the White House at 1430 on 12 May 1943.[1] General McNarney was present in place of General Arnold. Mr. Hopkins also attended all the meetings with the heads of state.

The discussion at the first meeting was confined almost entirely to remarks by the President and the Prime Minister, general statements of those things which they considered more important and which they hoped the Combined Chiefs of Staff would be able to settle during the meetings ahead. Mr. Churchill at once removed any doubts as to what the chief interest of the British staff would be by stating that the first objective was operations in the Mediterranean to get Italy out of the war by the best means possible. He believed that knocking Italy out would have various advantages which he enumerated, including, by elimination of the Italian Fleet, the release of "a considerable British squadron of battleships and aircraft carriers" for the war against Japan. It would also be, in his opinion, the best way in 1943 to take the weight off Russia. Relieving the strain on Russia was the Prime Minister's second objective. The third was "to apply to the greatest possible extent our vast Armies, Air forces, and munitions to the enemy." Fourth came Bolero, Sledgehammer, and Roundup, the three plans related to the invasion of Europe, although Mr. Churchill's comments on these lacked the earnest emphasis that the U.S. Chiefs placed upon them. He insisted that His Majesty's Government was anxious to invade the continent of Europe as soon as possible, but he stated plainly that invasion was dependent upon a plan "offering reasonable prospects of success." His fifth objective was aid to China, with which he included the whole question of the war against Japan. Without specifically saying so he made it evident that he had serious doubts of the practicability of Anakim. At later meetings he was to speak eloquently of his dislike for fighting in jungles, but on this occasion he only hinted at his distaste for the Anakim operation and at his interest to see that possible substitutes were explored, noting for example an attack on Sumatra or Penang, where, as in Torch, he felt that sea power could play its full part. The fleet required for such operations would, he promised, be available from the Mediterranean after elimination of Italy. In addition to deciding on aid to China he felt that the chiefs should study a long-term plan for the defeat of Japan. Once that had been agreed, operations could be planned to fit into it.

Mr. Roosevelt spoke at greater length of over-all problems. He dwelt upon the effectiveness of attrition as a weapon and the desirability of using available manpower rather than allowing it to remain idle. He remarked that he had "always shrunk from the thought of putting large armies into Italy" and recommended that the cost of occupying all or part of that country be weighed against the cost of achieving the same results by air attacks from Sicily. As for the invasion of the Continent, he insisted that Sledgehammer or Roundup must be decided upon definitely for the spring of 1944.

The President said practically nothing about extending operations in the Pacific, but he stressed the importance of sinking Japanese shipping as a means of attrition. This led him to the desirability of attacking shipping from air bases in China. Questioning the value of Anakim on the grounds that it would not be immediately effective for keeping China in the war, he urged that the Generalissimo, head of both the army and the state, should have what he wanted, namely, a strong air force. The President said nothing of the plans of General Stilwell, but he asserted with confidence

> that air in China would accomplish three objectives: it would be able to harass Japanese troops South of Hankow or those advancing from the South against Chungking; it could harass Japanese attacks against Chunking from the North; and it could stop Japanese attacks against Chungking which might be made up the Yangtze.

Moreover, he felt, it could be built up to strike against Japanese shipping and against Japan itself. He emphasized to the Combined Chiefs that they "must bear in mind the political fact that China is in danger of collapse." The Generalissimo and his country must be supported. As an important element in accomplishing that support the airfields in Assam must be built up.

After this very general introduction by the heads of state, the Combined Chiefs of Staff went to work. Their first meeting, held the next morning, 13 May 1943, was devoted to a general presentation by both sides of their views on the problems before them. Admiral Leahy started off by reading a memorandum which had been prepared for him by the Joint Strategic Survey Committee, summing up the views of the U.S. Chiefs, stressing two points: that all problems were inextricably interrelated and consequently should be viewed in the light of the whole situation, and that all proposed operations should be judged primarily on the basis of their contribution to defeating one enemy or the other in the shortest possible time.² The U.S. interpretation of the global strategic concept was restated in the terms the Joint Strategic Survey Committee had used in its clarification of the Casablanca decisions:³

> a. In cooperation with Russia and the lesser Allies, to force an unconditional surrender of the Axis in Europe.
> b. Simultaneously, in cooperation with our Allies, to maintain and extend unremitting pressure against Japan in the Pacific and from China.
> c. Thereafter, in cooperation with the other Pacific Powers and if possible with Russia, to combine the full resources of the United States and Great Britain to force the unconditional surrender of Japan.

Only two specific operations were mentioned, the two which the U.S. Chiefs considered the most essential for decision at the Trident Conference. These were the cross-Channel invasion of Europe and an early opening of communications with China in order to keep China in the war and achieve victory over Japan. With the exception of the cross-Channel operations, none of the points in the U.S. Chiefs' paper had been mentioned by the President the day before. Especially notable is the absence from the paper of any mention of the air transport route or air operations in China.

The British made no effort to comment on what Admiral Leahy had read, asking for time to consider the paper, but Sir Alan Brooke countered the prepared American statement by reading one containing the views of the British Chiefs of Staff.⁴ It made essentially the same points that Mr. Churchill had made the day before. It was not, as was the American, a summary of basic concepts. It was rather a discussion of what the British advocated doing during the next year and a half. Assuming that the assault on the Continent would be undertaken in 1944, they were insistent that Anglo-American forces must not stand idle during the period between the capture of Sicily and the cross-Channel attack. In the British view the most effective way in which the forces could be used was to eliminate Italy from the war, probably by amphibious operations against Italy itself or against the Italian islands, backed up by "operations in other parts of the Mediterranean." As for the war against Japan, the British candidly stated that "it is necessary to say straight away that we are of the opinion that the full [Anakim] operation should not be attempted in the winter of 1943-44." They offered four reasons:

> (a) The magnitude of the assault and the scope of the operations to which it would be the prelude, are such that we do not feel able to undertake them at a critical period in the war with Germany, on whom we cannot afford to relax the pressure.

(b) We are very doubtful of the feasibility of the operation at the present time. For any reasonable prospect of success it would demand a sufficiency of forces specially trained and equipped, and backed up by ample reserves of men and material. These conditions cannot be fulfilled in the coming winter.

(c) Until long-term plans for the ultimate defeat of Japan have been decided upon, it cannot be assumed that the re-conquest of Burma, however desirable the political effect, especially on China and India, is indispensable from the military point of view.

(d) Operation Anakim, even if successful in 1943-44, would not be likely to reopen the Burma Road until the middle of 1945.

The British professed to be unwilling to do nothing in the Far East Area, however, and promised alternative suggestions for action there. They also recommended a close examination of the method by which Japan was to be defeated (although no such recommendation was made in respect to Germany) in order that the commanders in chief in the Indian Ocean area could fit their planning into the whole frame. The final point in the paper was that the eternal problem of shipping should be examined in detail and settled during the conference ahead.

The reluctance of the British to concentrate on preparation for Roundup, their remarks during the discussion at the meeting of 13 May that the cross-Channel invasion might not even be possible until 1945, and their evident desire to extend operations in the Mediterranean area caused the U.S. Chiefs of Staff considerable distress. They met the next morning before the CCS meeting to discuss the points to be taken up with the British, and their displeasure with the British attitude is clearly recorded.[5] After a lengthy discussion Admiral King is reported to have said that he "felt if no firm commitment could be agreed upon regarding Roundup, we ought to convert our forces into the Pacific." Admiral Leahy was inclined to agree but questioned whether they were prepared to tell the British what they would do with the forces once they got them out there. General Marshall pointed out that the troops actually were not needed for the Pacific, but he agreed that, if Roundup was not to be done, landing craft, shipping, and air forces should go to the Pacific. This was a device for the "last resort," however, for the JCS were anxious to get agreement to Roundup and to have their views of strategy against Germany accepted by the British. In order to gain a tactical advantage by getting their ideas before the British first, Admiral Cooke recommended that this was the desirable time to introduce the JPS paper on "Conduct of the War in 1943-44," which had been converted into CCS 219.[6] His suggestion was immediately supported by Admiral King; slight uncertainty on the part of Admiral Leahy and of General Marshall as to whether that was the best time to present the paper was overcome; and the Joint Chiefs agreed to introduce it that morning after the British General Sir Alan Brooke had completed his comments on the general remarks on global strategy that had been circulated by the Americans the day before.

The U.S. Chiefs presented CCS 219 at the Combined Chiefs' meeting of 14 May and were presented with two British papers in return, one on operations in the European Theater, the other on operations from India in 1943-44.[7] There was no recorded comment on the U.S. paper at that meeting or later in the conference. However, the following day, in a discussion of the agenda for the future work of the Combined Chiefs, Admiral King recommended that the first thing to be done was to set out "agreed basic fundamentals," and it was decided to direct the Combined Staff Planners to prepare

> A statement of agreed essentials for the effective prosecution of the war, which would serve as a background for the formulation of future plans, e.g., security of essential sea communications; security of the citadel of Britain; etc.[8]

The conversation of the Combined Chiefs of Staff moved on to more specific matters, but the planners had their statement ready in time for the CCS meeting two days later. Drafted by the U.S. Joint Staff Planners, it was based in large part on CCS 219.[9] Despite the dissatisfaction expressed by the British Chiefs of Staff with the very similar paper prepared by the JSSC in April, the British planners had questioned only the necessity of keeping China actively in the war and only one addition (paragraph 3d) had been made to the U.S. draft. The statement read as follows:

1. *OVERALL OBJECTIVE OF THE UNITED NATIONS*
   The overall objective of the UNITED NATIONS is:
   In conjunction with RUSSIA and other allies to bring about at the earliest possible date, the unconditional surrender of the AXIS POWERS.
2. *OVERALL STRATEGIC CONCEPT FOR THE PROSECUTION OF THE WAR*
   a. In cooperation with RUSSIA and other allies to bring about at the earliest possible date the unconditional surrender of the AXIS in EUROPE.
   b. Simultaneously, in cooperation with other PACIFIC POWERS concerned, to maintain and extend unremitting pressure against JAPAN with the purpose of continally reducing her military power and attaining positions from which her ultimate surrender can be forced.
   c. Upon the defeat of the AXIS in EUROPE, in cooperation with other PACIFIC POWERS and, if possible, with RUSSIA to direct the full resources of the UNITED STATES and GREAT BRITAIN to bring about at the earliest possible date the unconditional surrender of JAPAN.
3. *ESTABLISHED UNDERTAKINGS IN SUPPORT OF THE OVERALL STRATEGIC CONCEPT*
   Whatever operations are decided on in support of the overall strategic concept, the following established undertakings will

be a fixed charge against our resources, subject to review by the Combined Chiefs of Staff in keeping with the changing situation.

Priority Group 1.

a. Maintain the security and war-making capacity of the WESTERN HEMISPHERE and BRITISH ISLES.

b. Support and maintain the war-making capacity of our forces in all areas to which committed.

c. Maintain vital overseas lines of communication in the ATLANTIC and PACIFIC, with particular emphasis on the defeat of the U-boat menace.

d. Intensify the air offensive from the United Kingdom and concentrate maximum resources in a selected area as early as practicable for the purpose of conducting a decisive invasion of the Axis citadel.

Priority Group 2.

e. Sustain the Soviet Forces by the greatest volume of munitions that can be supplied and transported to RUSSIA without militating against the attainment of the overall objectives.

f. Undertake such measures as may be necessary to provide CHINA with a volume of supplies sufficient to keep CHINA actively in the war against JAPAN.

It was paragraph 2b on which the Joint Chiefs considered it most important to reach agreement, for, in addition to views expressed by the British before the conference, Sir Alan Brooke, in discussion of Admiral Leahy's paper on Global Strategy, had disagreed with the concept of extending pressure against Japan. He argued that it "might well cause a vacuum into which forces would have to be poured and would thereby detract" from the main objective in Europe.[10] As anticipated, paragraph 2b proved a source of difficulty when the Combined Chiefs of Staff discussed the proposed statement of agreed essentials at their meeting of 17 May.[11] The British Chiefs were armed with a memorandum commenting on the draft. Unfortunately no copy of their paper is available. However, paragraph 2b appears to have been the first to which they raised objection, recommending modifying the statement to read, "to maintain, and so far as is consistent with a above, to extend...." They also suggested altering paragraph 3f to read, "Undertake such measures as may be necessary and practicable in order to keep CHINA actively in the war against JAPAN." Both Admiral Leahy and Admiral King pointed out that the Casablanca agreements had in fact provided for extension of operations against Japan and that the only item that was in too short supply to permit sending more forces to the Pacific was shipping. Other necessities were already available. Admiral Leahy emphasized that the defeat of Japan was a vital matter to the U.S. Chief of Staff and that "a situation might arise in which an extension of effort against Japan, if necessary, even at the expense of the

European Theater, would be essential to maintain the integrity of the United States and her interests in the Pacific." Sir Alan Brooke expressed agreement that shipping alone prohibited an equal effort in the Pacific Theater, but he reiterated that he considered it impossible to defeat both Germany and Japan at the same time and that Germany must be defeated first. The matter was not resolved at this meeting and it was finally decided to consider certain paragraphs of the paper, including paragraph 2b, further and to direct the Secretaries to publish a version of the paper which would show the items of agreement and disagreement.[12]

The Secretaries produced their amended version of the paper in time for the CCS meeting the following day,[13] but discussion was postponed. Sir Alan Brooke felt that agreement on essentials in the conduct of the war could more easily be reached if the CCS first agreed on European and Pacific strategy. Admiral Leahy and Admiral King expressed the view that the process should be the other way around and requested that the paper be discussed the following day.[14] However, the U.S. Chiefs were unable to agree among themselves on details of the paper[15] and rather than expose their disagreement to the combined meeting they recommended that the subject be deferred to a later meeting.[16] The paper was not discussed again in that form.

THE FATE OF ANAKIM

At the same time that the Combined Chiefs of Staff directed the preparation of the statement of agreed essentials they asked also for an agenda for the remainder of the conference.[17] The agenda was approved on 17 May, and thereafter the meetings adopted the pattern, although not always the time schedule, which it prescribed.[18] The next two days, 18 and 19 May, were occupied with trying to settle questions related to the defeat of Germany. On the twentieth the CCS turned to the problems of the war against Japan, of which the knottiest was what was to be done in China-Burma-India.

It will be remembered that the British at the second combined meeting at Trident introduced a paper (CCS 225) entitled, "Operations from India, 1943-44." Its contents can have been no surprise to the U.S. Chiefs. Reviewing first the four relevant points on which agreement had been reached at Casablanca,[19] the paper pointed out that only one objective, the preparation of an outline plan for Anakim, had been achieved. As they had already announced, the British Chiefs of Staff had arrived at the conclusion that the full Anakim operation should not be attempted in the winter of 1943-1944. In addition to the earlier objections offered, CCS 225 mentioned apprehension on the part of the British that the Japanese might force unwelcome extension of operations from Burma into Siam and the Malay Peninsula. Nonetheless, the British said, they recognized "that the objects which the Combined Chiefs of Staff had in mind at Casablanca still... [held] good," i.e., increasing air attacks on enemy sea communications, maintaining pressure on enemy forces in the area, and helping China. They suggested discussing alternative operations; concentration on building up the air supply route from Assam to China; limited land operations in Assam to contain Japanese forces and cover the air route; the capture of Akyab; and the capture of Ramree Island. Finally, in order that Anakim's importance could be considered in proper perspective, the British urged again that a plan for achieving the defeat of Japan should be agreed upon at Trident.

At the second combined meeting, Admiral Leahy, pursuing the subject of a long-term plan, suggested that Field Marshal Wavell and General Stilwell be invited to give their views on the method by which Japan should ultimately be defeated. Before they appeared, Sir Alan Brooke elaborated on the British attitude toward operations in Burma. He indicated serious doubts about Anakim, suggesting three alternatives: (1) seizure of the Kra Isthmus to punch through to Bangkok, thereby cutting Japanese communications to Burma and threatening oil traffic; (2) capture of northern Sumatra and Penang; and (3) capture of all of Sumatra and Java. Although he stated that Anakim might prove to be more valuable than any of the alternatives, he immediately offered the same arguments against it and strongly urged development of the air route into China. The only one of the U.S. Chiefs who commented on any of the suggestions specifically was Admiral King, who admitted to being attracted by the Bangkok operation and the resultant severing of the enemy's line of communications. But both he and Admiral Leahy reminded the group that the objective of Anakim was to afford immediate relief to China by opening up land communications over the Burma Road. None of the other operations would achieve that result. In addition Admiral King clearly stated his conviction of the strategic importance of China, both its geographical position and its supply of manpower, without both of which, he insisted, "the task of the United Nations in defeating Japan would be terrific."

The five officers from the Far East (General Stilwell, General Chennault, Field Marshal Wavell, Admiral Sir James Somverville, and Air Chief Marshal Sir Richard Peirse) entered the CCS meeting at that point. The same group accompanied the chiefs to the White House in the afternoon to a meeting with the President and the Prime Minister.[20] The comments on both occasions followed much the same pattern.

The British representatives, as had already been demonstrated, were uniformly convinced that Anakim was impracticable for 1943-1944. Field Marshal Wavell did most of the talking at both meetings describing in some detail conditions in Burma and India and answering the numerous questions put to him. He would undertake Anakim, he said, "only if fully trained and equipped troops were available with the necessary amphibious transport assault and landing ships and specialized equipment. However much shipping was sent now it would not be in time for the forces to be ready in early November." When asked by Admiral Leahy for his opinion as to the best practicable action to keep China in the war, General Wavell replied that increasing the strength of General Chennault's forces "would have more material results than operation Anakim." The other British representatives were in agreement with Field Marshal Wavell, objecting to Anakim particularly because of the extreme difficulty of attacking Rangoon from the sea, and to operations in northern Burma because of the great problem of supplying forces in that area.

The Prime Minister had apparently been much pleased with the President's insistence that air power must be built up in China, for he strongly advocated for 1943 "a *passionate* development of air transport into China, and the build-up of air forces in China." He even suggested that efforts currently directed to developing the Ledo Road and supporting troops in Burma be concentrated on developing the air lift. With considerable eloquence he developed his previous statements, characterizing the prospects for Anakim as "extremely gloomy," and saying that "he could not see how operations in the swamps of Burma would help the Chinese." He put great stress on the statement that the Burma Road could carry only 20,000 tons monthly and that not until 1945 under the current Anakim plan, a statement which no one challenged. Finally, he suggested the seizure of the northern tip of Sumatra as a good way to surprise the enemy in 1944.

There was no concerted effort on the part of the U.S. Chiefs of Staff to win agreement to a full scale Anakim, despite their preconference statements that it must be done. It had been apparent from the beginning that the British were strongly opposed and the President clearly had little more enthusiasm than they for operations in Burma, certainly not for a full scale Anakim in 1943-1944. Whether anyone besides General Marshall had been told that the President was "completely set against any delay in Chennault's program"[21] is not known, but none of the U.S. Chiefs had much to say at either of the meetings. Admiral King, and in a milder way Admiral Leahy, did remind the group of the strategic necessity of keeping China in the war, a course which had been settled for them in any case by Mr. Roosevelt, as Admiral Leahy brought to his colleagues' attention on two occasions during the conference.[22] General McNarney said nothing during the two meetings with the Far East officers, while General Marshall's chief contribution was to urge at the close of the meeting at the White House that General Stilwell's plan be thoroughly explored.

With little or no support from the U.S. Chiefs of Staff, General Stilwell spoke alone in defense of his opinion that "the best way to help the Chinese situation was to reassure the Chinese that a main effort was being made to reopen the supply route from India," in other words, Anakim, or at least an operation in northern Burma. Aware "that the weight of opinion was apparently against him," he stressed the importance of keeping China in the war and of strengthening the Chinese army into a force capable of fighting the Japanese. He admitted that building up the air forces in China would affect Japanese shipping and afford stimulus to Chinese morale, but he warned of the probable reaction of the Japanese army around Kunming to an increased air offensive. General Stilwell insisted that since Chiang had participated in planning for Anakim he expected it to be executed and would feel deserted if it were not. Although it is difficult to reconcile this interpretation with Chiang's delays which had so exasperated General Stilwell in the winter of 1942-1943, with his insistence on an increased air force, and with his lack of concern over the reform of his armies, no one at Trident questioned his interest in reopening of the Burma Road and in the Anakim operation.

The President made it clear at the plenary session that it was Chiang's expressed wishes that he championed, by reiterating that "it must be borne in mind that the Generalissimo was head of the State, as well as Commander in Chief," and "it was difficult from the psychological point of view to tell the Generalissimo that we thought things should be done in some manner different from his ideas." In the course of the discussion Mr. Roosevelt asked General Stilwell and General Chennault what their projects in China would require. When the former told him 2,000 tons a month for the next five months and the latter 4,700 tons for four months and after that 7,000 tons a month, the President "suggested" that the immediate objective for the air supply line should be 7,000 tons monthly by July, considerably above the current maximum of 3,400 tons. The Combined Chiefs of Staff considered this a decision. They agreed at their next meeting, the following day, to direct their commanders in chief in the Far East by despatch to "Give first priority to [the] effort to prepare Assam air fields in order that not less than 7,000 tons per month may be transported to China by 1 July 1943," and further to provide facilities for 10,000 tons monthly not later than 1 September, taking adequate measures to protect the airfield area."[23]

Although this arrangement would certainly affect the program of General Stilwell, it did not settle the question of whether or not to attempt to do Anakim in 1943-1944. By the end of the plenary session, during the course of which the discussion between General Stilwell and Mr. Churchill became quite heated, it was apparent that General Stilwell alone was anxious to undertake the full scale Anakim. It appears from the record that the British would not have been averse to abandoning any idea of operations in Burma. Especially was that true of Mr. Churchill, who had decided before he reached Washington that "going into swampy jungles to fight the Japanese is like going into the water to fight a shark. It is better to entice him into a trap or catch him on a hook and then demolish him with axes after hauling him out on to dry land."[24] Moreover, the Prime Minister did not entirely share the President's view that the Generalissimo's demands must be respected and he bluntly stated that "he was not prepared to undertake something foolish purely in order to placate the Chinese." The U.S. Chiefs, however, still considered it necessary to open land communications to China in some way or other in order to be in position to make the best possible use of China's potentialities as the tide of war advanced. The President also expressed support for future land operations in Burma. While there was no decision at either of the meetings attended by the theater commanders, there was general agreement that Anakim was out for 1943-1944 and the staffs should look into ways of expanding the air route and opening a land route to China. The following morning the Combined Chiefs of Staff directed their planners to report on:

(1) The potentialities of the air route from Assam to China given complete priority for its development except for the minimum requirements of the forces defending the air field areas, and whether any further steps can now be taken to enable these potentialities to be realized.

(2) The most promising operations, having regard to the various considerations brought to light in previous discussions, for the opening of a land route to China, and what resources and conditions are necessary for carrying it out without prejudicing the development of the air route.[25]

The planners found themselves agreed on one thing: the Anakim plan that had been prepared at New Delhi was impracticable, primarily because it envisaged an attack on Rangoon up the Rangoon River.[26] The other members of the committee accepted Admiral Cooke's suggestion of three alternatives which the subcommittee appointed to do the work should examine: (1) opening of the road from Ledo through Myitkyina to Lashio, coupled with operations from Imphal to protect the road; (2) the same, plus operations to secure Akyab and Ramree Island in order to establish air bases along the coast; and (3) a different plan of operations to open the Burma Road from Rangoon including a new method of attacking Rangoon itself.

On 19 May the subcommittee presented a paper on "Operations in Burma to Open and Secure an Overland Route to China."[27] Having examined the various suggestions, the subcommittee recommended the following:

a. *PHASE I*.
(1) Advance into Upper BURMA, starting between 1 November and 15 December 1943.
b. *PHASE II*.
(1) Advance overland to AKYAB, 1-15 November 1943.
(2) Simultaneous amphibious assault on AKYAB, RAMREE, TAUNGUP, and SANDOWAY, 1-15 December 1943.
c. *PHASE III*. (continuous from PHASE II).
(1) Overland advance on PROME.
(2) Long range penetration brigade exploit route AN-CHAUNG-MINBU.

The subcommittee's study had led to the conclusion that Phase II was essential to divert Japanese forces away from the area of operations under Phase I in northern Burma. An overland assault would be of a limited nature, however, and consequently, in order to keep the enemy occupied, it was considered necessary to undertake also the amphibious assaults and the overland advance on Prome. Throughout all phases an air offensive would be carried out in Burma and naval forces in the Pacific would operate to contain the Japanese Fleet. It was estimated that the operation would require 1,088 operational aircraft and 150 transports, 13 Chinese divisions, 6 British divisions, 3 British followup brigades, 3 long range penetration groups, and 5 assault brigade groups, in addition to considerable naval forces.

Completion of this limited operation would open the road to China from Ledo, thereby raising Chinese morale although not greatly increasing the flow of supplies except for gasoline. That would be piped through a line following the road. The operation was also designed to increase the efficiency of the air transport project by providing additional airfields and protection. Longer range results were expected to include increased security for the Kunming area through keeping the enemy occupied in Burma and maintenance of China in the war. Dependent upon the provision of adequate equipment and training of the British and Chinese forces, the operation was expected to pave the way for a final campaign to recapture all of Burma in 1944-1945.

As a preliminary to opening the Burma Road from Rangoon it was decided that if possible during the 1943-1944 season, if not, the following year, an amphibious assault should be made on the coast opposite Bassein preparatory to an overland advance to take that city. After Bassein had been secured, forces would advance on Rangoon while simultaneous offensives were launched southward from Mandalay and from the Taungup-Prome area.

The Combined Staff Planners approved most of the conclusions of their subcommittee.[28] The British members, however, were skeptical of the prospects of success in the attack on Prome and the landings at Taungup and Sandoway because of the strong Japanese forces that could be brought to bear in the region, the lack of suitable British troops, and the difficulties of providing support from other areas. The U.S. planners, on the other hand, thought the difficulties could be surmounted. It was finally decided to submit the paper to the Combined Chiefs of Staff together with a memorandum containing the comments of the CPS.[29] At the same time the planners submitted a report on the potentialities of the air route from Assam into China,[30] which emphasized that the capacity was currently limited by the incomplete status of the airfields in Assam and estimated that 20,000 tons monthly could be achieved by December 1943.

These papers came before the Combined Chiefs of Staff for discussion at their 90th meeting on 20 May 1943.[31] In the five days since assigning the study the chiefs had done nothing about China-Burma-India except to hear the views of Mr. T.V. Soong on 17 May.[32] Mr. Soong had spoken strongly in favor of more aircraft for General Chennault and for execution of the full Anakim operation with adequate naval support. He had emphasized that the Generalissimo was Supreme Commander in the China Theater and his military views "must...be given overriding consideration." The records do not indicate that the chiefs discussed his remarks, or, in fact, that they intended to do more than permit him to address the conference in order to satisfy the Generalissimo's desires to participate.

The officers from the Far East attended the meeting on 20 May, and from the discussion it is apparent that American interest in a ground campaign far exceeded that of the British. Left to their own devices it is doubtful that they would have undertaken any sizable operations in the area, for certainly the aversion of the Prime Minister to operations in jungles and his doubts that it was essential to support Chiang Kai-shek and to keep China in the war were shared by the British Chiefs of Staff. Aware, however, that the Americans felt strongly that something must be done for Chiang and that the JCS, at least, were anxious to reopen ground communications to China, the British could not refuse entirely to contemplate some sort of offensive in Burma.

Sir Alan Brooke set the keynote for the British comments by pointing out the advantages the Japanese enjoyed in their lines of communications in Burma and stating it was his opinion that if an attempt were made to build up the air route to maximum capacity and at the same time to undertake a land offensive neither would be done efficiently. He was in favor of concentrating on the air route and undertaking only limited operations from Ledo and Imphal and to capture Akyab and Ramree.

Field Marshal Wavell, whose responsibility it would be to execute any ground operations, was even more pessimistic. He recommended developing the air ferry route and then building up air supremacy in Burma, after which, if resources were available, advances might be made from Yunnan on Lashio, from Ledo on Myitkyina and Bhamo, and from Imphal into the Chindwin Valley to cover the Myitkyina airfields and the route to Burma. He urged attacking Akyab and Ramree but was opposed to attempting Sandoway and Taungup and to attacking Rangoon through Bassein. He finally said that he was prepared to go ahead as far as possible as long as he could maintain a force equal to the Japanese, but the Chinese must advance simultaneously in order to protect his eastern flank.

These pessimistic comments evoked words from General Marshall, who had participated hardly at all in earlier discussions of Burma. The gist of his remarks was that the project might be difficult but that with hard fighting it could be done. He warned against strong Japanese reaction on the ground to large increases in air operations and emphasized the effect ground offensives in Burma would have on Chinese morale and on operations in the South and Southwest Pacific. His comments were echoed by

Admiral Leahy who, while in some doubt as to how far Allied forces could advance in Upper Burma, believed that the attack should be directed on Mandalay in order to draw off the Japanese from other areas. General McNarney further emphasized the point by insisting that Mandalay and Lashio were essential to provide an air warning system to cover the fighters at Myitkyina who were protecting the air transport route.

The British fairly consistently insisted that a line through Bhamo, Katha, Pinlebo, and Kalewa was as far as the available forces could be expected to advance because of the problem of supply. They made no comment on General Stilwell's remark that if forces could be supplied that far they could be supplied at Mandalay since Katha and Mandalay were both on the Irrawaddy River and Kalewa was upstream on the Chindwin.

In respect to the potentialities of the air route from Assam to China, the Joint Chiefs of Staff, at General McNarney's recommendation, had already agreed that it would be desirable to delete from the planners' paper all mention of a capacity of 20,000 tons over the Hump because it would give the British an argument against the necessity of ground operations in Burma, and because an independent study made at General McNarney's request had in any case revealed that it would be difficult to achieve even 7,000 tons.[33] General McNarney enlarged somewhat on the latter point at the Combined Chiefs' meeting on 20 May, pointing out that it had been premised on the availability of aircraft from production, without consideration of the other demands for them. There was no dispute at the meeting over Sir Charles Portal's suggestion that the facilities be expanded in any event to take care of 20,000 tons and that that figure be made the ultimate goal. Admiral King, however, recommended that 10,000, the figure which the President had established for November, be the present goal, and that anything above that goal be used for ground operations against Mandalay.

There was no decision at the 90th CCS meeting on either the problem of operations in Burma or the expansion of the air transport route. The one thing that was certain was that there was to be no full scale Anakim in 1943-1944, although eventually it might still be undertaken.[34] At 1530 on the same afternoon the Combined Chiefs of Staff met in closed session. There was undoubtedly considerable further discussion of both of the papers concerned with Burma, for the matter had by no means been resolved in the morning session. As a result of the meeting, of which no minutes were published,[35] the following decisions were announced:

    a. The concentration of available resources as first priority within the Assam-Burma theater on the building up and increasing of the air route to China to a capacity of 10,000 tons a month by early fall, and the development of air facilities in Assam with a view to -
      (1) Intensifying air operations against the Japanese in Burma;
      (2) Maintaining increased American Air Forces in China;
      (3) Maintaining the flow of air-borne supplies to China.

b. Vigorous and agressive [sic] land and air operations from Assam into Burma via Ledo and Imphal, in step with an advance by Chinese forces from Yunnan, with the object of containing as many Japanese forces as possible, covering the air route to China, and as an essential step towards the opening of the Burma Road.
　　　c. The capture of Akyab and of Ramree Island by amphibious operations.
　　　d. The interruption of Japanese sea communications into Burma.[36]

　　This decision was approved by the President and the Prime Minister the following day,[37] but not without further discussion. Mr. Roosevelt felt that Rangoon should have been mentioned in order to satisfy the Chinese, and Mr. Churchill suggested that the phrase "with possible exploitation toward Rangoon" be added at the end of point *c*. However, they were persuaded that the Chinese might interpret this as a promise, which was certainly not intended by the British, and only the first three words of Mr. Churchill's suggestion were added. The Prime Minister raised another point in respect to the CCS decision by indicating that he "was unhappy that it did not include any mention of offensive action against Kra, Sumatra, or Penang," in which he had already expressed an interest. He was reminded by Sir Alan Brooke that the Combined Chiefs were still working on a plan for the defeat of Japan in which such operations would be considered. Admiral King expressed doubt that they could be carried out in conjunction with the operations in the Burma Theater because of the shortage of shipping. He, however, thought that they might eventually be indispensable for inducing the Japanese to split their fleet.[38]

　　There is no record that the matter of operations in Burma was discussed again at Trident until 24 May,[39] when, at the next to the last of the plenary sessions, in the course of consideration of the Combined Chiefs' proposed final report to the President and Prime Minister, Mr. Roosevelt asked Mr. Hopkins what he thought the Generalissimo's reactions to the decisions in respect to China-Burma would be. Mr. Hopkins expressed the view that, if Chiang were told, he would not admit that he agreed with the decisions and he would resent not having been consulted. Mr. Hopkins suggested that Chiang be informed that Anakim was to go on. General Marshall thought that he should be told more than that, however, everything in fact except details concerning the capture of Akyab and Ramree. Mr. Churchill suggested a statement to be given to the Generalissimo but decided to prepare it in writing after the meeting.

　　The following day the Prime Minister's suggestion was circulated and discussed by the Combined Chiefs of Staff at their separate meeting and in the final plenary session of the Trident Conference.[40] With the only significant change the identification of the items as "proposals" rather than "decisions" the statement was approved in time for General Marshall to use it in a scheduled talk with Chinese representatives that afternoon.[41]

Except for a few minor modifications in words, the statement to be made to the Chinese differed from the decision of the CCS only in the substitution for the seizure of Akyab and Ramree of the more general item, "amphibious operations against the Burmese coast with the purpose of interrupting Japanese communications between the coast and their northern front." In addition, presumably in view of the Generalissimo's insistence upon the assurance of naval support before agreeing to operations in Burma, a paragraph was added at the end, stating

> For the above purposes all possible measures will be taken to secure the Naval Command of the Bay of Bengal by an adequate force. No limits, except those imposed by time and circumstances, will be placed on the above operations, which have for their object the relief of the siege of China.

It was probably hoped that this would satisfy Chiang Kai-shek that naval forces would be on hand without committing Great Britain or the United States to furnish any specific number of vessels. Should the first sentence prove too inflexible to explain any insufficiency of naval forces in the area, the second was not. It would indeed be difficult to find any elements more inclusive than "time and circumstances." One or the other could certainly serve to explain any change in the program approved at Trident.

STRATEGIC PLAN FOR THE DEFEAT OF JAPAN

By 20 May the two main strategical problems, what was to be done after Husky and what sort of operation was to be undertaken in Burma, had been settled, and the time had come to take up the question of operations in the Pacific area. In preparation for CCS discussion, the secretaries of the conference circulated a U.S. paper containing a "Strategic Plan for the Defeat of Japan."[42] It was the same six-phase plan which the Joint Chiefs of Staff had approved in JCS 287/1 on 8 May,[43] but revised by the Joint Staff Planners to place more emphasis on the necessity of keeping China in the war and to include the over-all strategic concept from CCS 232 still not approved.[44] There was some explanation of the successive phases, but the plan was not a detailed list of projected operations, and the British Chiefs were not satisfied that it spelled out sufficiently the course that should be followed in defeating Japan. Both Sir Alan Brooke and Sir Charles Portal made that clear, and Sir Charles added further, "The facts should be assembled, the objects set out, together with alternative courses of action to achieve these objects with full facts and arguments for and against each course." Admiral Leahy spoke for the U.S. Chiefs on this point, and he could merely explain that the paper was not intended to be a detailed plan. He suggested that it be used as a basis for further study. His suggestion was accepted, and the Combined Chiefs directed the CPS "to initiate a study and prepare for consideration by the Combined Chiefs of Staff an appreciation leading up to an outline plan for the defeat of Japan including an estimate of the forces required for its implementation."[45]

At the final meeting of the conference the chiefs approved a CPS proposal that a U.S. Planning Team should visit London to discuss the problem and assist the British Joint Staff Planners in preparing the British part of the study. Subsequently, a British team was to visit Washington to participate in completion of the plan.[46]

Planning for the defeat of Japan was a long range project on which agreement could be deferred, but operations to be undertaken against Japan in the year ahead were of immediate concern, for it was necessary to provide for material support. Consequently, after revising JCS 304, "Operations in the Pacific and Far East in 1943-44," to take into account the decision made at the 91st meeting in respect to operations in Burma, the Joint Staff Planners circulated it to the Combined Chiefs of Staff on 20 May 1943 as CCS 239,[47] without having received formal approval from the Joint Chiefs of Staff.

The following morning the Joint Chiefs, meeting in preparation for the combined meeting later the same morning, discussed CCS 239 and the oral report Admiral King was to give to the Combined Chiefs on the situation in the Pacific.[48] It is clear from the recorded minutes that the U.S. Chiefs had not previously discussed the paper and it is even indicated that some of them had not read it.[49] Admiral King expressed himself as "not in sympathy with the paper as drafted," but he indicated only two points of disagreement. One was the inclusion in a paper on the Pacific of an item on operations in Burma. The other was the fact that "there was nothing in the paper about attacking Japanese lines of communications." It was finally decided that an item reading, "Intensified action against enemy lines of communications," could be added to the list of specific objectives for 1943-1944. There was practically no comment on his other remarks, and the Joint Chiefs concurred in his proposal to present to the British Chiefs CCS 239 and the U.S. project for the Pacific in 1943-1944 as developments from CCS 168, the paper on operations in the Pacific in 1943 which the JCS had presented at Casablanca,[50] and which had been simply "noted" by the Combined Chiefs of Staff.

The report thus presented to the Combined Chiefs of Staff on 21 May 1943 recommended for 1943-44 a list of objectives that would advance the offensive well along toward the defeat of Japan. Proposed were:

    (1) Conduct of air operations in and from CHINA.
    (2) Operations in BURMA to augment supplies to CHINA.
    (3) Ejection of the Japanese from the ALEUTIANS.

(4) Seizure of the MARSHALL and CAROLINE ISLANDS.

(5) Seizure of the SOLOMONS, the BISMARCK ARCHIPELAGO, and Japanese held NEW GUINEA.

(6) Intensification of operations against enemy lines of communication.

These operations, it was noted, would be restricted by the availability of amphibious craft and trained amphibious divisions.

In discussing CCS 239 at the CCS meeting Admiral King described again his views on strategy in the Pacific, in almost the same terms he had used at Casablanca.[51] The objectives in the Pacific, he thought, should be severing the Japanese lines of communications and recapturing the Philippines. The road to the Philippines lay across the Central Pacific, through Truk and the Marianas; and Truk could be taken in 1944. There was no mention of the strategic importance of the Southwest Pacific. Lest there be any further question of simply holding a line in the Pacific Admiral King emphasized the necessity of maintaining and extending unremitting pressure against Japan. There were two criteria for judging any operation undertaken in the Pacific, he said:

a. Would it further threaten or cut Japanese lines of communication;

b. Would it contribute to the attainment of positions of readiness from which a full-scale offensive could be launched against Japan.

The objectives listed for 1943-44 had been selected with these in mind.

If the British did not like the program Admiral King offered for 1943-44 there is no indication of it in the minutes of the meeting. There was no need to discuss again the desirability of advancing in the Pacific to the extent available forces would permit. The CCS approved CCS 239 with only one change of wording, thus endorsing the offensive in the Central Pacific Area through the seizure of the Carolines.

CONCLUSIONS REACHED AT TRIDENT

In preparation for a scheduled meeting with the President and the Prime Minister at 1700 on 21 May, the Combined Chiefs of Staff at their morning meeting directed the Secretaries to prepare a report to the chiefs of state on what had been accomplished up to that time.[52] The major objectives for the next year had by then been agreed upon and the Secretaries assembled the conclusions of the several papers, seven of which had been approved.[53] In addition to those decisions relating to the war against Japan, which had already been discussed, it had been agreed by the chiefs: (1) that the Azores Islands should be acquired as soon as possible, by diplomatic means if practicable, if not, by military occupation; (2) that an air offensive should be conducted from the United Kingdom designed to accomplish "the progressive destruction and dislocation of the German military, industrial, and economic system, and the undermining of the morale of the German people to a point where their capacity for armed resistance is fatally weakened"; (3) that preparations should be made for an operation from the United Kingdom against the continent of Europe on about 1 May 1944; (4) that the Allied Commander in Chief, North Africa, should be instructed to exploit the situation, after completion of Husky, in the manner best calculated to eliminate Italy from the war; (5) that the French forces in North Africa should be rearmed and reequipped as a secondary commitment; and (6) that the U.S. Army Air Forces should present its plan for bombing the Rumanian oil fields to the Commander in Chief, North Africa, for comment.

As the covering memorandum on this first report of the military decisions pointed out, these conclusions still had to be related to the available resources, particularly of shipping and landing craft. In addition, several matters of over-all significance still remained to be considered, and when the President and the Prime Minister expressed general approval of the report which was presented to them,[54] the Combined Chiefs of Staff returned to the problems that were still unsettled.

The Combined Staff Planners earlier the same day had appointed six subcommittees to prepare "an optimum deployment of the available means of the United Nations to meet the requirements of the basic undertakings and projected operations for 1943-44," considering air, ground, and naval forces, shipping, assault ships and landing craft, and critical items peculiar to specific operations.[55] The reports were combined into a lengthy paper, which, with some amendment by the CPS, was circulated as CCS 244 on 22 May 1943.[56]

The CPS conclusions were as follows:

Ground Forces.
4. All the ground forces required can be made available....
Naval Forces.
5. If a covering force is required for the operations to capture Akyab and Ramree, and if the Italian Fleet has not been eliminated, some diversion of U.S. naval forces may be required.... Subject to this, all naval forces required can be made available.
Air Forces.
6. Broadly there are sufficient air forces to meet all requirements in all theaters.

. . . .

Assault Shipping and Landing Craft.
10. Provided the casualties in operations are no greater than we have allowed for, and provided that the U.S. and British planned productions are maintained, all the assault shipping and landing craft required can be made available.

The "if" in this last item was large, however, for it was stated clearly in the annex dealing with landing craft that the current naval building program already had a deficit of 110,000 tons of steel in the third quarter, and the landing craft program might well have to be cut.

Deficiencies in "critical items" did not appear to the Combined Staff Planners to be serious. Even shipping, which had long been the limiting factor in all strategic planning, appeared to promise better things ahead, for it was concluded that, if losses did not become excessive, personnel shipping would be sufficient to permit optimum deployment of United Nations forces within the limits of cargo shipping. Cargo shipping in turn promised small deficiencies in the third and fourth quarters of 1943 and the first quarter of 1944 with a surplus after that. The deficiencies, with proper distribution among the various programs, were not expected to be "unmanageable." In extenuation of the conclusions presented in CCS 244 were annexes that explained in more detail the information that had been used in making the decisions outlined in the paper and included the figures of requirements and availabilities from which the conclusions were drawn.

Both the JCS and the CCS discussed this important report at some length, concentrating upon shipping in their comments and questions. Ultimately both groups accepted the conclusions of the planners in that matter as in the others. The paper was approved on 23 May 1943, with only a few amendments which had no direct bearing on operations against Japan.[57]

During the last days of the conference the Combined Chiefs of Staff concerned themselves with certain details in respect to operations in the European Theater and such other matters as the movements of the large converted passenger liners, *Queen Mary* and *Queen Elizabeth*. There remained to be approved a final report for presentation to the President and the Prime Minister at the close of the conference. The initial draft of this paper, prepared by the U.S. Joint War Plans Committee,[58] did not simply elaborate on the interim report the chiefs had made on the twenty-first. Instead it followed the general form of CCS 232, the earlier paper on "Agreed Essentials in the Conduct of the War." Thus it was not simply a summary of decisions, but an attempt to relate the decisions to one another and to available resources as outlined in CCS 244. The paper the CPS submitted for circulation to the chiefs on 23 May 1943 (CCS 242/1) was revised by the Combined Secretariat to take into account the decisions made by the CCS that morning, and it was as CCS 242/2 that it was finally presented for discussion.[59]

The Joint Chiefs of Staff, on 24 May, considered the paper in detail, agreeing to recommend a large number of changes in the wording of the text.[60] The point on which the greatest concern was felt was the one that had caused difficulties in the earlier consideration of CCS 232, that is, the matter of extending unremitting pressure against Japan. Since there had been no decision, the item was included in CCS 242/2 with alternate readings, expressing the proposal of the Combined Staff Planners and the changes recommended by the British Chiefs of Staff. Admiral King, ever insistent that the best possible position must be attained in the Pacific in order that United Nations forces would be prepared to move in for a final blow when opportunity offered, "expressed apprehension that the British Chiefs of Staff amendment...was, in effect, a lever which could be used to stress European action at the expense of our Pacific effort." Unfortunately, the official minutes state only that there was "prolonged discussion" of this point, and one can merely speculate as to whether the other members of the group differed with Admiral King in his suspicions of the British intentions, or whether they offered evidence to confirm them, whether there was disagreement within the group as to the merit of Admiral King's policy or whether the chiefs considered other ways of insuring that it was to be followed. Whatever the discussion, Admiral King carried his point, for "it was agreed that the Joint Chiefs of Staff should firmly adhere to the wording...as proposed by the Combined Staff Planners, carrying the question to the highest level if necessary."

CCS 242/2 was given careful consideration at the combined meeting that followed the Joint Chiefs' meeting on the morning of 24 May.[61] Admiral Leahy there brought up the troublesome matter of the extension of pressure in the Pacific, emphasizing as his opinion that the British proposal was "unacceptable since, should the situation in the Pacific become dangerous to U.S. interests or to U.S. itself, it would be necessary to supplement U.S. forces in this theater even at the expense of the early defeat of Germany." Sir Charles Portal responded by denying that the British intended to restrict operations in the Pacific, wishing rather to insure that any surplus forces could be concentrated on the defeat of Germany. General Marshall then spoke up on the question of air forces, reminding the group that they had agreed to send to the United Kingdom the maximum number of air groups that could be maintained there. Consequently, he felt that if there was a surplus they should go to the Southwest Pacific, where small additions could accomplish great results, and where numerical superiority was needed in order to overcome the Japanese advantage of interior lines of communication. Should the Japanese effect a major concentration, he warned, U.S. forces would be in a most difficult situation, and public opinion would not permit major reverses in the Pacific. Air Chief Marshal Portal then agreed that any potential surplus forces should go to the Pacific, to provide for agreed operations or to defend the United States. He said that he had meant that, if all was going well in the Pacific, Germany would be eliminated more quickly if any surplus went either to the United Kingdom or to the Mediterranean. The difficulty was finally overcome by adding to the wording the U.S. Chiefs advocated a clause proposed by Sir Dudley Pound: "The effect of any such extension on the overall objective to be given consideration by the Combined Chiefs of Staff before action is taken." Thus limits were put on the moves that could be made in the Pacific without CCS approval, but the possibility of getting such approval was offered.

After a paragraph-by-paragraph consideration of the paper, during which the Combined Chiefs of Staff made several changes of wording and resolved the differences where the draft showed alternate statements for the two groups, the report was revised and reissued as CCS 242/3. This version was submitted to the President and the Prime Minister at a plenary session in the same afternoon.[62]

The chiefs of state questioned very little in the paper and nothing in respect to operations against Japan. As a result of the discussion, the report was revised slightly and issued again as CCS 242/4. In a separate memorandum, Mr. Churchill made further suggestions which met with the approval of the Combined Chiefs of Staff.[63] At the last plenary session, held at 1130 on 25 May 1943, the President and the Prime Minister gave final approval to the amended version which was then issued as CCS 242/6 the official statement of the Trident decisions.[64]

CCS 242/6 will be treated at greater length in other sections of the History of the Joint Chiefs of Staff[65] and it is not necessary to discuss the entire document here. However, it is desirable to review those portions of the final decisions which had a direct bearing upon the war against Japan.

Once again an attempt had been made to define the over-all objective. For the first time it included the policy Mr. Roosevelt had announced at Casablanca. It read: "In conjunction with RUSSIA and other Allies to bring about at the earliest possible date, the unconditional surrender of the AXIS powers." This was followed by a statement of the over-all strategic concept, part of which has already been discussed:

    1. In cooperation with RUSSIA and other Allies to bring about at the earliest possible date, the unconditional surrender of the AXIS in Europe.

    2. Simultaneously, in cooperation with other PACIFIC Powers concerned to maintain and extend unremitting pressure against JAPAN with the purpose of continally reducing her Military power and attaining positions from which her ultimate surrender can be forced. The effect of any such extension on the overall objective to be given consideration by the Combined Chiefs of Staff before action is taken.

    3. Upon the defeat of the AXIS in EUROPE, in cooperation with other PACIFIC Powers, and if possible, with RUSSIA, to direct the full resources of the UNITED STATES and GREAT BRITAIN to bring about at earliest possible date the unconditional surrender of JAPAN.

Then came a statement of basic undertakings in support of this concept, the same sort of general items that had been listed in similar papers as "a first charge against our resources." The list included maintaining the security of the Western Hemisphere and the British Isles, supporting the war-making capacity of forces in all areas, maintaining lines of communications, intensifying the air offensive in Europe, concentrating forces for an invasion of the Axis citadel, aiding the Russian war effort, preparing the way for participation by Turkey, and aiding the French forces in Africa. It also included undertaking "such measures as may be necessary and practicable in order to aid the war effort of CHINA as an effect Ally and as a base for operations against JAPAN." This was a more definitive statement of the attitude to be maintained toward China than had previously been agreed. It was one of the points on which CCS 242/2 had included two versions, CPS and British, neither of which called for more than keeping China actively in the war. The stronger statement was one of those changes to the paper which the Joint Chiefs of Staff agreed to, and the Combined Chiefs of Staff incorporated, without recording the discussion which produced them.

Following the general objectives for which available resources were to be used were listed the specific operations for 1943-1944 upon which agreement had been reached, with the explanatory comment that no order of priority was necessary since the comparison of operations to resources had indicated that all could be accomplished. There was no provision for the possibility that the estimates of availability and of requirements might prove inaccurate. Thus there was supposed to be no significance in the fact that "operations for the defeat of Japan" came at the end of the list. For the Burma-China Theater the decision of the Combined Chiefs of Staff at their 91st meeting was incorporated, with one significant addition, a fifth item which read:

> The continuance of administrative preparations in INDIA for the eventual launching of an overseas operation of about the size of Anakim.

Where this came from and what its significance was meant to be are not known. It first appeared with the notation, "This has not yet been agreed," in CCS 242/2, the version of the report prepared by the Combined Secretariat. Mr. Churchill had said at the meeting attended by the area officers that "he saw no reason openly to abandon the operation at present. He thought that moves in preparation should continue provided they did not hamper the development of the air route." But there was no recorded discussion then or later, and it can only be surmised that the point was included for appearance's sake, on the theory that planning did not mean preparation for launching. The likelihood of doing Anakim was left in doubt.

Although the official minutes do not indicate that the British Chiefs of Staff had had much to say in respect to specific operations in the Pacific, the final report included the statement that "various courses of action have been examined by the Combined

Chiefs of Staff." Those upon which agreement was reached were those which Joint Chiefs of Staff had decided upon before the conference began:

    (1) Conduct of air operations in and from CHINA.
    (2) Ejection of the Japanese from the ALEUTIANS.
    (3) Seizure of the MARSHALL and CAROLINE ISLANDS.
    (4) Seizure of the SOLOMONS, the BISMARCK ARCHIPELAGO, and Japanese held NEW GUINEA.
    (5) Intensification of operations against enemy lines of communication.

Completion of these objectives would advance United Nations forces far on the road to the defeat of Japan.

With a summary of the availability of resources to meet these commitments, and agreements on equipment for Turkey and the French in North Africa, the paper ended, cancelling any conflicting decisions of the Casablanca Conference and providing for another meeting in July or August "to examine the decisions reached at this Conference in the light of the situation existing at the time."

The President and Prime Minister approved the final report from their staffs at the last meeting on 25 May 1943. Trident was over. The Joint Chiefs of Staff could proceed to develop plans for moving on in the Pacific Theater. The British Chiefs of Staff were to do the same for Burma.

Even before the last word was said the Joint War Plans Committee had started preparing for the next combined conference, to come after Sicily had been captured and the time had come to plan the next move against Germany. By that time the end of the monsoon and the target date for operations in Burma would be closer. Again the question would be raised as to whether they should be undertaken at all. In the Pacific Theater, however, the prospect would be so encouraging that the objectives for 1943-1944 would be extended to the Palaus and the Marianas. With the launching of action in the Gilberts within a few weeks after the conference's close the great offensive that was to stop only with Japan's defeat would be begun.

PART II

THE ADVANCE TO VICTORY

Chapter XVII

STRATEGIC PLANNING FOR THE PACIFIC THEATER IN THE SUMMER OF 1943: QUADRANT

Less than three months were to elapse after the conclusion of the Trident discussions before the American and British leaders met again, this time at Quebec, for the conference known as Quadrant. During the interval the North African conquest was completed with the seizure in June of Pantelleria and Lampedusa, Linosa and Lampione, Italian islands off the coast of Tunisia. In July Husky was launched, and after 38 days of hard fighting, during which the Germans evacuated the bulk of their troops to the mainland of Italy, Sicily was in the hands of the United Nations. Mussolini was overthrown, replaced by Marshal Pietro Badoglio, and rumors reflected secret negotiations for the surrender of Italy. In Russia the Red Army launched a great summer offensive and captured the city of Orel, drove on to Kharkov, and then pushed the Germans back to the Dnieper River by the end of August. U.S. forces in the South Pacific were capturing New Georgia Island and Vella Lavella and occupying Woodlark and Kiriwina without opposition, while forces in the Southwest Pacific were pushing on in New Guinea toward Salamaua.

By the summer of 1943 the initiative lay with the United Nations, but there was still no firm decision as to the route which they should follow to the ultimate goal of unconditional surrender. This was particularly true in respect to the war against Germany, for British and Americans continued to disagree on what was to follow the capture of Sicily and when they should invade the continent of Europe. A long-term plan for the defeat of Japan remained a matter for further study and future decision. The incomplete nature of the Trident decisions was recognized even as they were made by the Combined Chiefs of Staff (CCS), who agreed that another conference would be held during the summer to examine the decisions in the light of the contemporary situation.

In the period between conferences and at the Quadrant meetings the Joint Chiefs of Staff (JCS) considered primarily three strategic problems: operations in the Pacific Theater during 1943-1944; long-term strategy for the defeat of Japan; and what was to be done in China-Burma-India. The first of these involved an area of U.S. strategic responsibility; the decisions were formulated by the U.S. Chiefs and hardly more than corroborated at Quadrant.

414   THE ADVANCE TO VICTORY

The second remained on the combined planning level almost entirely until the Quadrant meetings were well advanced. The third was a continuing problem to the Combined Chiefs of Staff and was a major topic of discussion at Quebec. For the most part the three matters were handled quite independently of one another, and in the interests of clarity they will be treated separately here. It must be borne in mind, however, that all were being considered simultaneously, together with the problems of war with Germany and the numerous other matters which required attention on the top military level.

OPERATIONS IN THE NORTH PACIFIC AREA

The decisions of the Trident Conference had prescribed for 1943-1944 operations in the Aleutians, the Marshall and Caroline Islands, the Solomons, the Bismarck Archipelago, and New Guinea. Even as the meetings were going on, joint U.S. plans for the first of these were being completed.

The North Pacific Area was never an area of major importance in JCS strategic planning for the defeat of Japan, although the possibility was always recognized that developments might render invasion of Japan from the north desirable. This potential significance as well as the demands of U.S. territorial defense made it essential to recapture the positions in the Aleutians occupied by the Japanese in the spring of 1942. By December of that year the staffs of the Commander in Chief, Pacific Fleet, and the Commanding General, Western Defense Command, had begun to plan an operation to recapture the island of Kiska. In March 1943, however, the shortage of shipping and equipment led Rear Admiral Thomas C. Kinkaid, Commander, North Pacific Area, to recommend postponement of the Kiska operation and substitution of an attack on the island of Attu. The change received the approval of the Joint Chiefs of Staff, and landings began on Attu on 11 May 1943.[1]

At the end of May, with the occupation of Attu virtually completed, the Commanding General, Western Defense Command, and the Commander in Chief, Pacific Fleet, asked the Joint Chiefs of Staff to approve a directive for an operation for the reduction of Kiska and Little Kiska.[2] Their project was divided in three tasks: (A) to make the plans and train the occupying force; (B) to reduce and occupy the islands "at the earliest practicable date"; (C) to improve the enemy airfield already there and construct another. The target date was set for 15 August 1943.

Admiral King was in San Francisco for talks with Admiral Nimitz when the two Pacific commanders sent their proposal to Washington, and he approved the project.[3] The War Department gave informal approval to commencement of planning and training and began work on problems of supply, but decision on Tasks B and C was reserved for JCS action.[4] Unlike the Attu operation the Kiska project was formally presented in a JCS paper.

At the JCS meeting of 8 June 1943 no one showed a great deal of enthusiasm for the project.[5] General Marshall, while admitting that he did not know much about it, said he thought it was a matter for naval decision on the basis of whether or not there was a necessity for controlling Kiska. Admiral King suggested that the decision be put up to the Joint Staff Planners (JPS). This was approved, and it was also decided to accept a force, amounting to approximately a regimental combat team, which the Canadian Government had offered for use in the Aleutian offensive.[6]

The Joint Staff Planners based their report on the premise that, since the Combined Chiefs of Staff had agreed at Trident that the Japanese would be ejected from the Aleutians, it was largely a question of when it should be done.[7] They considered the advantages of the operation: the psychological effect on the American people of driving the Japanese from American soil and the effect on the Japanese of another defeat; denial of the base to the enemy; the probable diversion to the Kuriles of Japanese forces from other areas; and the acquisition of a submarine and air base for the United States. Offsetting these was the probability that occupation of Kiska would be a costly operation and that with Japan proper so close to the island it would be necessary to maintain a large garrison. A quick survey of available resources indicated to the planners' satisfaction that the requisite force could be made available in time for the approximate target date of 15 August 1943. Consequently, the Joint Staff Planners recommended and the Joint Chiefs of Staff approved the proposed joint directive to take Kiska, leaving the actual date of execution for the Commander in Chief, Pacific Fleet, and the Commanding General, Western Defense Command, to decide.[8] After extensive preparations U.S. troops landed on Kiska in mid-August, only to find that the enemy had anticipated the move and all Japanese forces had departed. Recapture of the Aleutians became only a problem of reoccupation, and no further sizable military action was undertaken in the area.

OPENING UP THE CENTRAL PACIFIC

Following the Trident Conference the Central Pacific became increasingly the main focus of JCS strategic planning and the scene of major operations. As early as 12 February 1943 the Navy's War Plans Division had completed a "Plan for the Control of the Marshall Islands."[9] At that time, when the theater representatives at the Pacific Military Conference were being told that their plans for future operations in the South and the Southwest Pacific Areas were too ambitious and sufficient supplies could not be provided, attack on the Marshalls was out of the question. By the end of May, however, growing naval strength in the Pacific was encouraging the Navy to think of expanding operations. The Combined Chiefs of Staff at Trident had approved both the Marshalls and the Carolines as objectives for 1944, and planning could begin in earnest.

The Navy planners in February had reached the conclusion that in order to control the Marshall group three atolls, Kwajalein, Wotje, and Maloelap, would have to be occupied. They thought that this could be accomplished in three ways: by direct westward assault, by assault from the north or the south, or by first capturing and consolidating flanking positions. Direct attack was deemed preferable, but no target date was suggested for the operation.

A more general outline of operations in the Marshalls was included in the Trident paper, "Operations in the Pacific and Far East."[10] Not specific as to objectives, this report merely stated that it would be "necessary to occupy or neutralize all of the major atolls in the group and WAKE ISLAND." It was suggested that the Fourth Marine Division, scheduled to leave the United States in December 1943, could be earmarked for the Marshalls, but the other amphibious division required would have to be either one already in the Southwest Pacific or an Army division trained in the United States for amphibious warfare. Consequently the campaign could not be undertaken before early 1944.

Three days after the last of the Trident meetings the Joint War Plans Committee (JWPC), at the instigation of Rear Admiral Charles M. Cooke, Jr., of the Joint Staff Planners, directed its Rainbow Team to prepare by 5 June "an outline plan for advancing into the MARSHALLS, a study of the requirements for the operations recommended, and recommended target dates for initiating the operations."[11] The preliminary report, JPS 205, was circulated to the Joint Staff Planners on 10 June, with the recommendation that no decisions should be made in respect to a specific operation in a specific area of the Pacific without full consideration of all other areas.[12] The paper's authors were not yet decided whether there should be a single line of advance through the Central Pacific, a concentration instead on the route northward from the Southwest Pacific, or a combination of the two. The plan they had evolved for the Marshalls would strongly curtail operations in the Southwest Pacific Area during the ensuing year.

The planners of the Rainbow Team adopted as most feasible and acceptable for a Marshall Islands operation the same course of action which the Navy planners had selected in February, simultaneous assault on Kwajalein, Wotje, and Maloelap, the three atolls which formed the nucleus of the Marshall Islands. They discounted both a step-by-step seizure of a large number of atolls and an advance along the Gilberts-Jaluit-Mille line, judging that the enemy would be alerted and able to disperse his aircraft widely for defense in depth, while U.S. forces became involved in prolonged and costly operations which placed U.S. aircraft in a less strategic position.[13] After the central group of the Marshalls was secured, the planners recommended, capture of Eniwetok and Kusaie should be undertaken, the former because it supported the Eniwetok-Wake-Taongi triangle and the islands of the northern Marshalls and the latter because it supported the Gilberts and the southern Marshalls. Both islands were within medium bomber range of the enemy base on Ponape and heavy bomber range of the infamous Truk. The campaign would be concluded by reduction or neutralization of the entire Wake-Marshalls-Gilberts system.

Recommendation of a target date for this operation was made independently of the availability of means to do it. Reviewing the projects approved for the war against Japan in 1943-1944, the planners decided that it would be particularly desirable to have operations going on elsewhere at the same time the Burma campaign was begun. They recognized that intensifying action in the South-Southwest Pacific would create some diversion of Japanese forces but anticipated that it would not be such a sharp reaction as an attack on the Marshall Islands would evoke. Since the target date for operation in Burma was 1 November 1943, the target date for the Marshalls should be about the same, specifically 29 October, which fell during the dark of the moon.

Attacks on the Marshalls would pose new problems. Not only would a new area of the Pacific be opened to U.S. forces but the island objectives were all reef-fringed coral atolls, different from any of the positions yet attacked in the South and the Southwest Pacific. The forces selected to execute the operation were of great significance, both because of the nature of the objectives and because of the shortage of properly trained troops. The JWPC paper put it thus:

> In view of (1) the importance of this operation, (2) the serious implications of a failure in the initial assaults, (3) the fact that it must be a guide to the effectiveness of far-reaching amphibious operations in the future as now planned, and (4) the fact that this is the first attempt to seize properly defended and supported atolls, *it is considered almost imperative that all troops committed to the assault be battle-tested shock-troops with amphibious training.*

There were only two areas where such troops could be found, and so it was to the South and the Southwest Pacific Areas that the planners looked. The First Marine Division, relieved several months earlier from Guadalcanal, was currently ready for action in the Southwest Pacific but not scheduled for use until late in the year. Assuming that troops exposed in malarious areas required at least four months for rehabilitation, in order for the First Marine Division to be available for action in the Marshalls about 1 November, the planners calculated, it would have to be kept out of action in the South or Southwest Pacific after the end of June. The Second Marine Division, in the South Pacific Area, would be ready about 1 August, and it too would have to be kept from other projects until the Marshalls were attacked. The Seventh Army Division, amphibiously trained, was considered less desirable than the two Marine divisions. In addition there were the trained but not seasoned Third Marine Division in the South Pacific and the Twenty-eighth Army Division in the United States. Although these two could be utilized without affecting operations already scheduled, it was the proven First and Second Marine Divisions that the planners recommended using.

To move the troops selected would of course require amphibious craft, and these also were in limited supply. A JWPC study on the utilization of amphibious assault craft, JCS 311,[14] prepared at the beginning of the Trident Conference, had reached the conclusion that, if the New Guinea-Solomons operations were completed about 1 January 1944, enough assault shipping for two divisions could be moved from the South Pacific to Pearl Harbor for the Marshalls campaign by about 1 April 1944. Such a diversion would mean that no ship-to-shore operations could be conducted in the South-Southwest Pacific until the Marshalls operations were completed. Considerably more disruption could be expected with a target date of 29 October 1943 for the Marshalls operation. In fact, JPS 205 estimated that a cessation of amphibious operations in the South-Southwest Pacific would be required beginning not later than late July. According to the timetable assumed for planning purposes in the absence of any reported from the area, this would permit occupation of Kiriwina and Woodlark Islands, infiltration into New Georgia and/or Santa Isabel, and capture of the Lae-Salamaua-Finschhafen-Madang area of New Guinea.

In addition to troops and amphibious assault craft some of the planes required for the Marshalls operations could be readily found only in the Southwest Pacific Area. Specifically, although in the main carrier aircraft would be used for the occupation, one additional heavy and one medium bomber group were required for garrison duties. Recommendation was made that they come from the Southwest Pacific, where air operations would have to be curtailed accordingly.

On the same day that the JWPC presented this "preliminary report" on the requirements and implications of a campaign in the Marshalls group, Admiral King gave the Joint Chiefs a statement of his own views of what action should next be taken in the Pacific.[15]

Reviewing the decisions of Casablanca and Trident in respect to Pacific operations, Admiral King emphasized how little was actually being done or even scheduled to maintain pressure on the Japanese and retain the initiative against them. As he pointed out, the Buna-Gona campaign on New Guinea had been completed in January, resistance on Guadalcanal had ceased in February, nothing much had been accomplished in Burma, and, in fact, the seizure of Attu was the only real offensive action against Japan in the first half of 1943. Two areas in the South-Southwest Pacific either lightly held by the enemy or not occupied at all were to be captured in late June, but no other dates were set and it was likely that the projected operations would not take place until late in 1943.[16] Consequently, Admiral King urged that the Joint Chiefs decide: to set up firmly timed operations for the Central Pacific Area, specifically (as recommended by the Joint War Plans Committee) for about 1 November; to delegate responsibility to the Commander in Chief, Pacific Ocean Areas, for coordinating timing of offensive operations in the whole Pacific Theater; and to require of the Commander in Chief, Southwest Pacific Area, firm dates and a list of specific operations contemplated in his area. Admiral King also recommended that Admiral Nimitz's original directive to "Prepare for the execution of major amphibious offensives to be launched from the SOUTH PACIFIC Area and SOUTHWEST PACIFIC Area" be augmented by adding, "Coordinate the timing, under the general direction of the U.S. Joint Chiefs of Staff, of major amphibious offensives throughout the PACIFIC THEATER." This suggestion, which would in effect place General MacArthur under Admiral Nimitz, seemed certain to meet with opposition.

Admiral King's memorandum invoked serious discussion among the Joint Staff Planners, whose views were divided.[17] The Navy member, Admiral Cooke, was insistent that the delays and postponements in the Pacific must be ended and the fleet not be permitted to remain idle for any protracted period. Although he indicated that some of the premises of the JWPC report were inaccurate, he urged that an operation in the Marshalls be scheduled for 1 November. He was certain that the requisite forces could be provided without disrupting planned operations elsewhere and that action in the Marshalls would actually assist operations in both Burma and New Guinea.

The Army members, of whom Colonel Frank N. Roberts was the chief spokesman, insisted that operations in the Marshalls at the expense of planned operations in the Southwest Pacific were not to be countenanced. The Army was in favor of a campaign in the Central Pacific, but only after careful planning and examination of its effect on other operations. Colonel Roberts objected strongly to the recommendation that the Commander in Chief, Pacific Ocean Areas, be made responsible for the timing of amphibious operations in the Pacific Theater, despite Admiral Cooke's reminder that it was proposed only for major amphibious operations and that under JCS direction. The colonel pointed out that coordination could hardly be effective unless command of all forces in the Pacific went with it, and this the Army would not approve. Colonel Adrian Williamson even went so far as to suggest that operations in the Southwest Pacific Area be specifically exempted from such timing control. It was apparent that no complete agreement was to be reached on Admiral King's recommendations, and the Joint Staff Planners finally decided to send a split report to the Joint Chiefs of Staff. At the same time they directed the Joint War Plans Committee to prepare a plan for seizure of the Marshall Islands about 1 November or 1 December 1943, predicated on causing no serious interruption to the operations already approved for the South-Southwest Pacific Area (Cartwheel).[18]

In the report on Admiral King's recommendations the planners recommended that firmly timed operations be set up for the Central Pacific, specifically against the Marshalls about 1 November, but that the Marshalls should not be attacked "at such an early date that our resources in men and material will be strained to a critical point."[19] The planners agreed that the Supreme Commander, Southwest Pacific Area, should be required to furnish specific dates for his contemplated operations, even though it might be necessary later to change them. In regard to the coordination of timing of operations in the Pacific, the Army planners recommended that no change be made in the directive to the Pacific commanders, while the Navy planners proposed accepting Admiral King's suggestion for amendment of Admiral Nimitz's directive, adding at the end, major amphibious operations "which involved the support of major naval forces." The Army argued that the Joint Chiefs of Staff could not delegate their authority in the matter, for timing required an over-all knowledge of the global situation. Such delegation, they felt, would in effect give the Commander in Chief, Pacific Fleet, supreme command of the entire Pacific Theater, which the Army did not consider expedient. The Navy planners pointed to the task already included in the directive to the Commander in Chief, Pacific Ocean Areas: "Prepare for the execution of major amphibious offensives to be launched from the SOUTH PACIFIC AREA and SOUTHWEST PACIFIC AREA." Adequately to integrate over-sea operations with sea operations throughout the Pacific, protect sea and air communications in the Pacific Theater, and hold island positions in the Pacific Ocean Areas and the line of communications to Australia while containing Japanese forces within the entire Pacific Theater was a large order, the Navy argued. The Commander in Chief, Pacific Ocean Areas, would have to exercise command of requisite forces and retain control of their movements.

The Joint Chiefs of Staff approved all the recommendations on which the Joint Staff Planners had reached agreement, but they deferred decision on the question of coordination of timing. Admiral Leahy meanwhile indicated that he agreed with the Army view of the matter.[20]

One of the planners' suggestions had already been executed. With the concurrence of "the Navy Department" General Marshall had had a JCS radio sent to General MacArthur informing him that, because of the increased fleet strength anticipated in the Pacific, the Joint Chiefs were considering attacking the Marshalls about 15 November.[21] He was also told that tentative plans contemplated taking the First Marine Division from the Southwest Pacific[22] and the Second Marine Division and considerable naval forces from the South Pacific. A time schedule of operations in the South and Southwest Pacific Area, which had been estimated in Washington since none had come from the theater, was included in the radio with an urgent request for an outline of operations that might affect planning for the Central Pacific.

While awaiting replies from the theater commanders, the Joint War Plans Committee proceeded with preparation of a plan for seizing the Marshalls without interfering with operations in the Southwest Pacific (Cartwheel).[23] The committee did not change the three-phase operation of JPS 205 but merely changed the target date to "not later than 1 December 1943," a date the committee felt would still provide support for the Burma operations, since it seemed highly likely that there would be a delay in getting them underway.[24] The later date, moreover, would permit a diversionary carrier raid on Hokkaido in October, a project which two naval officers, Captain C.J. Moore and Captain C.R. Brown, had recommended to the Joint Staff Planners.[25] On the other hand, it would also mean that, unless necessary amphibious assault craft could be made available from other sources, ship-to-shore amphibious operations in the South-Southwest Pacific would still have to cease by late August 1943. The other recommendations of the revised paper were modified to make potential interference with Cartwheel less obvious. Thus, although it was still pointed out that the assault should be made by battle-tested shock troops and the same divisions were considered available, the First and Second Marine Divisions were not specifically recommended. Nor was the Southwest Pacific Area suggested as the source for the lacking heavy and medium bombardment groups.

In addition to the slightly modified plan for seizure of the Marshalls, the Joint War Plans Committee submitted a second report based on the assumption that the necessary forces could not be made available for the full operation.[26] With considerable hesitation, and reiterating that the Kwajalein-Wotje-Maloelap project was preferable provided the requisite forces could be found, the Joint War Plans Committee proceeded to examine hastily three alternate courses of action designed to secure the Marshalls without interrupting Cartwheel. Two of them, an advance from the north through Wake and an advance from the east by the seizure of key positions in the eastern Marshalls, were rejected for strategic reasons. The third, an advance from the south through the Gilbert Islands with first assault on Nauru and Tarawa, was accepted as a possible alternative to the direct advance into the Marshalls. On the basis of a very incomplete study, however, the planners stated plainly that "the GILBERTS operation is definitely inferior to the MARSHALLS operation...and every effort should be made to carry through the latter operation." The possible tactical advantage of controlling positions in the Gilberts before tackling the Marshalls was not discussed.

No one seems to have been very eager to attack the Gilberts, but to the Army planners at least it appeared that the Navy was ready to back such action mainly to satisfy its desire to "do something."[27] To this the Army objected, believing that the Navy should be satisfied with fleet action in the Pacific without the feeling that every time the fleet did anything some ground had to be gained. In retrospect JPS 205/1 and JPS 205/2 both seem very inadequate, and for the planners at the time, particularly the Army planners, they left many questions unanswered. Consequently, when they came up for discussion by the Joint Staff Planners, Colonel Roberts proposed that the Joint War Plans Committee study all aspects of the problems of operations in the Marshalls and/or the Gilberts rather than going ahead with plans for operations in either one.[28] The Joint Staff Planners approved. Detailed directions were issued to the Joint War Plans Committee and passed in turn to the Rainbow Team. The final paragraph of JWPC's comments indicates the scope of the directive:

> The objective of this study appears to include the determination of the most suitable and feasible operations in the PACIFIC, whether they apply to the MARSHALL-GILBERTS or not.[29]

By this time General Marshall had received a reply from General MacArthur giving information about his plans for operations in the South-Southwest Pacific.[30] In addition to specific dates and forces required, General MacArthur indicated clearly his lack of sympathy with operations in the Central Pacific. He characterized as "disturbing" the information he had received about tentative plans for operations in the Marshalls and pointed out that the capture of Rabaul was the main objective of operations in the South-Southwest Pacific. The limited operations the Joint Chiefs of Staff had approved in March 1943 were merely preliminary thereto. General MacArthur reported that the First Marine Division was scheduled for the attack on New Britain on approximately 1 December. Plans for operations in the South Pacific Area were not yet complete, but he felt that no amphibious division could be spared from there either. While he admitted that a diversionary attack on the Marshalls would support his own operations, he insisted that "the troops for the secondary attack should be drawn from the mainland rather than be subtracted from the main attack to an extent that may result in its collapse."

General MacArthur clearly suspected that the Marshalls project signified a change in basic strategy. Consequently he offered his views:

> From a broad strategic viewpoint I am convinced that the best course of offensive action in the Pacific is a movement from Australia through New Guinea to Mindanao. This movement can be supported by land based aircraft which is utterly essential and will immediately cut the enemy lines from Japan to his conquered territory to the southward. By contrast a movement through the mandated islands will be a series of amphibious attacks with the support of carrier based aircraft against objectives defended by Naval units and ground troops supported by land based aviation. Midway stands as an example of the hazards of such operations. Moreover no vital strategic objective is reached until the series of amphibious frontal attacks succeed in reaching Mindanao. The factor[s] upon

which the old Orange plan[s] were based have been greatly altered by the hostile conquest of Malaya and the Netherlands East Indies and by the availability of Australia as a base.

General MacArthur's views were undoubtedly passed to the various planning groups, but they did not gain universal acceptance. This is hardly surprising, for his ideas ran counter to long-established naval views of how to defeat Japan, and the decision to take prompt action against the Marshalls was already firm. A week after General MacArthur's message arrived the Joint Strategic Survey Committee (JSSC), on its own initiative, produced a paper recommending what General MacArthur had feared, i.e., a change of strategy in the war against Japan.[31] The committee pointed out that in 1942 the necessity of defending positions in the Central and North Pacific and Australia and the line of communications thereto had so completely absorbed available resources that the only offensive moves that could be made against Japan were in the South and Southwest Pacific. This, combined with the psychological and political factors involved, had fostered the strategy of moving against Japan by advancing northward from Australia. In the opinion of the Joint Strategic Survey Committee this reversing of the Japanese route of approach offered tremendous difficulties, for the enemy would be constantly in the better strategical position. In view of this and the increase in naval power in the Pacific the committee advised that the strategic concept for 1943 and early 1944 be revised and the campaign through the Marshalls and Carolines be established as the primary offensive move, according it priority over the operations planned for the South-Southwest Pacific.

The Joint Chiefs of Staff were not yet ready to adopt a policy of full priority for the Central Pacific over the Southwest Pacific Area.[32] Only Admiral King offered complete approval of the JSSC recommendation and urged that the strategy be reviewed. He expressed a preference for "hitching off" and shooting for Luzon through the Mandated Islands and the Marianas rather than continuing frontal attacks and risking being bottled up in the Celebes Sea. The others had little to say. No conclusions were reached, and the paper was referred to the Joint Staff Planners "for examination."

On about 4 July Admiral Nimitz's preliminary plan for operations in the Marshall Islands arrived in Washington and was studied by the Joint War Plans Committee along with the JSSC paper and its own studies of the Marshalls and Gilberts.[33] Admiral Nimitz had rejected the JWPC proposal of directly attacking Wotje, Maloelap, and Kwajalein, primarily because of the difficulties of obtaining adequate photographic reconnaissance. Instead he recommended initial seizure of Tarawa in the Gilberts, and Jaluit and Mille in the southern Marshalls, followed at once by reduction of the remainder of the atolls and capture of Maloelap, Wotje, Kwajalein, Eniwetok, and Kusaie at the earliest practicable date. Photographic reconnaissance of Tarawa, Jaluit, and

Mille could be obtained from bases on Funafuti, and air bases in the United States-held Samoan and Ellice Islands could be used to support the operation. Moreover, the naval covering force would be placed logically south and west of Jaluit, where it could serve to protect the Solomons and the Bismarck Archipelago. Seizure of only Jaluit and Mille in the Marshalls, unfortunately, would leave the enemy temporarily with more land-based air cover than the United States would have in that group, thus necessitating continued carrier-based cover. An attempt to remedy this situation by taking Kwajalein, Wotje, Maloelap at the same time as Jaluit and Mille had been discarded because such an operation, it was estimated, would require all the forces available in the entire Pacific.

Admiral Nimitz also reported that he had "given careful consideration to the command set up and if he followed his personal desires he would exercise direct command to capture the MARSHALL ISLANDS. This would require his presence in the area of operations and would restrict his exercise of strategic control throughout the Pacific Ocean Areas." Without recommending that the command be his, however, he announced plans to move the Commander in Chief, Pacific Fleet, Headquarters westward at opportune times as the campaign progressed.

The Joint War Plans Committee weighed the advantages and disadvantages of four different projects for the Marshalls and Gilberts: (A) the initial seizure of Kwajalein, Wotje, and Maloelap; (B) initial seizure of Nauru, Tarawa, and Makin; (C) initial seizure of Tarawa, Jaluit, and Mille; and (D) seizure of Wake Island.[34] The committee decided that (B) was most desirable.

Plan (B) called for an operation to be mounted either in the Fijis or the Hawaiian area, or both, with the objective capture and consolidation of the Gilberts, to be followed at an indeterminate date by an advance into the Marshalls. This plan offered definite advantages: it could be done with land-based air search and limited land-based support; it required one reenforced division instead of two and less shipping than plan (A); it would provide air bases for reconnaissance and softening up attacks on the Marshalls and for staging short-range aircraft into the Marshalls; operations could be stopped for any period desired following consolidation of Nauru, Makin, and Tarawa; and the naval force covering would also be in position to support operations in the Solomons. On the other hand plan (B) had disadvantages: the first phase would provide only a few air bases against a heavy concentration of enemy bases; the enemy would be alerted against further advance; naval forces would have to remain in covering positions until the air bases were operative; and unless an advanced fleet anchorage were developed at Nukufetau in the Ellice Islands, naval forces would have to operate at great distances from existing bases.

The plan preferred by the JWPC could not be carried out in 1943 without some curtailment of action in the South-Southwest Pacific, although the committee rejected as impossible any such reduction of effort there as the Joint Strategic Survey Committee had proposed. In order to provide for enough amphibiously trained troops for the Central Pacific program the JWPC recommended not subordination of the Southwest Pacific campaign but a revision of the objectives currently set. Specifically the committee advocated elimination of the plan to occpuy western New Britain and substitution of some other operation for the seizure of the Bismarck Archipelago, thereby releasing the First and the Second Marine Divisions for action in the Central Pacific. "If the same ground, sea, and air effort is expended in 'controlling' rather than 'seizing' the BISMARCK ARCHIPELAGO, in advancing in NEW GUINEA, and in seizing MANUS ISLAND and establishing air and naval facilities there," the JWPC suggested, "a more advantageous situation than the holding of RABAUL may be created earlier and at less cost."

The JWPC's conclusions were incorporated in five recommendations: that the directive to the Supreme Commander, Southwest Pacific Area, should be amended to make control rather than seizure of the Bismarck Archipelago the ultimate objective of the Cartwheel operations and to cancel the occupation of western New Britain; that after capture of Kieta and Madang and neutralization of Buka, the objective should be control of the Bismarcks, advance in New Guinea, and establishment of bases in Manus Island; that the First and Second Marine Divisions should be used in the Marshalls-Gilberts; that the seizure of Nauru, Tarawa, and Makin should be adopted for planning with a target date of 1 December 1943; that to draw enemy air forces to Japan the Commander in Chief, Pacific Fleet, should be directed to institute naval demonstrations in the vicinity of Japan.

The Joint War Plans Committee submitted its report to the Joint Staff Planners on 10 July 1943, recommending that it not be implemented unless further investigation had indicated that the effort might be continued to the final objective, capture of all of the Gilberts and Marshalls.

The Joint Staff Planners were not thoroughly pleased.[35] They did not disagree with the concept of advancing into the Gilberts first, but the Army, represented by Colonel Roberts, objected to the absence of provision for carrying on into the Marshalls and the Carolines. "As he understood it, forces were to be withdrawn from the South Pacific only for the limited purpose of acquiring positions in the Gilberts. To go into the Gilberts at the expense of pressure on Rabaul was not acceptable to the Army. This pressure required the capture of Kavieng and Manus Island and the rest of the airfields on New Britain." Admiral Cooke protested that Rabaul could be more rapidly reduced by operations in the Marshalls than by any other means, and he insisted that the Navy did not contemplate stopping with the Gilberts operation. He submitted a memorandum of general comments on operations in the Central Pacific, and at Colonel Robert's suggestion decision was deferred until that paper could be studied. Within the next few days, with some revisions by the Army Operations Division, the paper was approved informally and submitted to the Joint Chiefs of Staff[36] with JPS 205/1, 205/2, 205/3, and a fourth study on the availability of aircraft for Central Pacific Operations.[37]

The paper presented to the Joint Chiefs of Staff was not a plan but rather a listing of pertinent facts in respect to the war against Japan which supported the conclusion that operations against the Gilbert Islands should be undertaken and followed promptly by an advance into the Marshalls. Review of the operations scheduled for the South-Southwest Pacific on the assumption that Rabaul would be neutralized but not captured indicated the advisability of not curtailing operations there but continuing as planned, in order to maintain pressure on Japan. Only the Second Marine Division, scheduled for eventual use against Rabaul, and some naval forces would be needed from the South Pacific for the Gilberts. The rest of the forces would be made available from other sources. Without any supporting figures it was stated that adequate means would be available for a Marshalls operation about 1 February 1944, provided the assault units used in the Gilberts were relieved promptly. Finally, on the basis of all the studies made in Washington, the Joint Staff Planners recommended that the Joint Chiefs of Staff approve a despatch to the Commander in Chief, Pacific Fleet, directing him

> *a.* ...to prepare for the seizure and occupation of the GILBERT Islands and NAURU with a target date of 1 December, this date contingent upon the feasibility of withdrawing required naval forces from South Pacific and naval forces and assault shipping from the North Pacific, the determination of which will be made by the Joint Chiefs of Staff;
>
> *b.* ...to undertake the preparation of outline plans for follow-up operations in the MARSHALLS about 1 February 1944, to be submitted, together with a detailed estimate of forces required, to the Joint Chiefs of Staff before 1 September 1943.

Even before the Joint Chiefs of Staff gave formal consideration to the JPS report, Admiral King had indicated his concurrence by recommending that advantage be taken of the pressure already being exerted on the Japanese through operations in the Solomons and New Guinea and that the target dates be advanced to 15 November for the Gilberts and 1 January for the Marshalls.[38] At the JCS meeting of 20 July he elaborated on his views, stressing the assistance which would be afforded to Cartwheel by diversions caused by the proposed Marshalls-Gilberts operations.[39] Although there still remained some uncertainty as to where the requisite planes would come from General Arnold offered the assurance that "this was an important operation and it would be up to the Army Air Forces to make means available to insure its success."[40] There was no opposition. Admiral Nimitz was directed to take the Gilberts and to prepare plans for capturing the Marshalls, with the target dates Admiral King had suggested.[41]

He was also informed that the operations were to be planned on the assumption that Cartwheel would be carried out and that post-Cartwheel operations for the capture of Wewak, Manus, and Kavieng would be initiated about February 1944, with the objective of gaining control of the Bismarck Archipelago, exerting pressure on the Japanese, and supporting subsequent attacks against the Caroline Islands. These latter operations were currently being studied in Washington.[42]

Admiral Nimitz's directive was sent to General MacArthur for information. On the following day General Marshall told the SWPA Commander that in Washington it appeared that the most feasible operation to follow Cartwheel was the isolation of Rabaul through the capture of Wewak, Manus, Kavieng.[43] If General MacArthur concurred he was asked to submit outline plans to the Joint Chiefs of Staff before 1 September.

General MacArthur's reply was prompt and firm.[44] Making no direct mention of Manus and Kavieng, he explained that the theater plans did not include a direct amphibious attack on Wewak because of its heavy garrison "and other difficulties." Instead he was planning initially to isolate Wewak by seizing the area farther west, which was lightly held. This action was certain to invoke strong naval reactions and consequently would require strong naval support, necessitating an adequate advanced naval base. The only appropriate locality for such a base was Rabaul. Consequently its capture was, General MacArthur considered, "a prerequisite to a move in force along the north coast of New Guinea."

General MacArthur's reply seems to have borne no more weight in Washington than his earlier recommendation against operations in the Central Pacific. By the time his message arrived the Joint War Plans Committee was at work studying the problem of post-Cartwheel operations as part of its preparations for the next combined conference.

OPERATIONS IN THE PACIFIC, 1943-1944

Apparently determined that the rush of preparation that had preceded Trident should not happen again, the Joint War Plans Committee had started to plan for the next combined meetings even before the Trident Conference was concluded. By 5 June the committee had submitted to the Joint Staff Planners a list of suggested topics on which studies should be prepared and secured JPS approval for the whole program.[45] A study of specific operations to be undertaken in the Pacific and the Far East during 1943-1944 was assigned to the JWPC subcommittee known as the Pink Team, comprising two naval officers, Rear Admiral R.E. Schuirmann and Captain G.H. Bahm.[46] The report was supposed to be finished by 7 July, but that objective was not reached, for several other studies were assigned to the same team during the same period.[47]

On 15 July, when it was becoming apparent that the next conference would convene in mid-August, the Rainbow Team was made responsible for the study.[48] Its report was finally approved by the Joint Staff Planners and submitted to the Joint Chiefs of Staff as JCS 446 on 6 August 1943.[49]

JCS 446 was based on a new estimate of the Japanese situation which had just been presented to the Joint Chiefs of Staff as one of the same series of conference studies.[50] The strategic concept, however, followed that outlined in the "Strategic Plan" the U.S. Chiefs had submitted at Trident.[51] In general, it provided for the opening of lines of communication to China by an advance westward across the Pacific and from the south up through the Malacca Straits and the South China Sea, to be followed by an air offensive and finally by an invasion of the Japanese islands. It was assumed that by the end of 1944 U.S. forces could reach a line in the Pacific extending roughly from the Palaus through the Vogelkop, the western tip of New Guinea. The British would by the same time have started to eject the enemy from Burma.

The Joint War Plans Committee had already completed outline plans for most of the operations envisaged from 1943-1944. There were to be five in the Central Pacific Area. First came those already discussed in detail and scheduled for launching later in 1943, namely, seizure of the Gilberts through simultaneous attacks on Nauru, Tarawa, and Makin, followed by capture of the Marshall Islands, including Wake and Kusaie.[52] With these areas secure, the plan was to move westward into the Carolines, taking first Ponape, "the last Japanese strong position protecting TRUK from a westward advance."[53] Truk itself would be next, for with the Carolines controlling the Central Pacific and Truk controlling the Carolines, it was considered by the planners "the key Japanese position in the Central Pacific."[54] Seizure of Truk would require preliminary occupation or neutralization of positions to the southeastward in the Caroline Islands and subsequent reduction of enemy positions as far west as Woleai. The final operation was expected to invoke the strongest enemy resistance, for it was planned to seize the Palau Islands, success in which project "would facilitate operations of any nature, in any direction, against some of the enemy's most vital holdings and lines of communication."[55] The program called for initial seizure of the island of Yap and supporting positions, to be followed by capture or neutralization of all eight of the Palau Islands. From there the next step would be the Philippines.

While these operations were being carried out in the Central Pacific, advances would also be made in the Southwest Pacific Area. Despite General MacArthur's protests that "contemplating capture of Wewak prior to Rabaul would involve hazards rendering success doubtful," and that Rabaul would have to be occupied in order to provide the essential naval base for support of an advance along the north coast of New Guinea,[56] his views were not incorporated in the Joint War Plans Committee's outline plan for operations to follow Cartwheel.[57] It presented a three-phase operation that would result in capture of northern New Guinea as far west as Wewak, occupation of Kavieng, New Ireland, New Hanover, and the St. Matthias Islands of the Bismarck Archipelago, seizure of Manus and the Admiralty Islands, and the neutralization and control of Rabaul. Measures designed to neutralize Rabaul were to be carried out concurrently with assaults on the other objectives. The planners discarded occupation of Rabaul itself, as they had recommended in their study of operations in the Marshalls and Gilberts,[58] on the grounds that it "would prove an intolerable drain on...resources and available manpower. The same ground, sea, and air effort could be expended in *neutralization rather than seizure*, in continuing the advance in NEW GUINEA, in seizing NEW IRELAND and the ADMIRALTIES, and in establishing air and naval facilities in these areas. This would create a more advantageous situation in a shorter time and at a much lower cost." When this three-phase operation was complete, advances were to be made step-by-step along the north coast of New Guinea, culminating in the seizure and consolidation of the Vogelkop.[59]

The Joint War Plans Committee had presented no plans for operations in Burma and China, and JCS 446 summarized those the British were expected to have ready. They were the projects on which agreement had been reached at Trident: limited advances in northern Burma and on the southwest coast following the monsoon in November 1943; an all-out operation to drive the Japanese from Burma, starting at the end of the monsoon season in 1944. As for China, JCS 446 simply stated that operations would be increased as resources permitted, the maximum flow of supplies would be achieved, and larger American air forces maintained.

The planners intended that the operations against Japan should be carried out as rapidly as possible, seeking to maintain momentum and transferring forces or equipment between areas in order that they not remain idle. Should there be conflict between areas, "due weight should be given to the fact that operations in the Central PACIFIC promise more rapid advance." The speed of advance could not be precisely predicted, but JCS 446 did offer a list of target dates which could result in accomplishment of the desired objective by the end of 1944: (See chart on p. 430).

Target Dates	Central Pacific	Southwest Pacific	CHINA BURMA-INDIA
15 Aug. 1943	KISKA	---	---
1 Sep. 1943	---	LAE-MADANG	---
15 Oct. 1943	---	BUIN-FAISI	---
1 Nov. 1943	---	---	(1) Upper BURMA (2) AKYAB-RAMREE
15 Nov. 1943	GILBERTS	---	---
1 Dec. 1943	---	(1) W. NEW BRITAIN (2) KIETA (3) BUKA (Neutralize)	---
1 Jan. 1944	MARSHALLS	---	---
1 Feb. 1944	---	(1) RABAUL (Neutralize) (2) WEWAK	
1 May 1944	---	KAVIENG	---
1 June 1944	PONAPE	MANUS	
1 Aug. 1944	---	HOLLANDIA	
1 Sep. 1944	TRUK	---	---
15 Sep. 1944	---	WAKDE	---
15 Oct. 1944	---	JAPEN	---
1 Nov. 1944	---	---	Complete BURMA
30 Nov. 1944	---	MANOKWARI	---
31 Dec. 1944	PALAU	---	---

This program, JCS 446 stated confidently, was within the means available for 1943-1944, and its completion would "place the UNITED NATIONS in a position to use most advantageously the great air, ground and naval resources which will be at our disposal after GERMANY is defeated." Just in case further action proved feasible, it was announced on the paper's cover sheet that plans for an operation against Paramushiru were under consideration and a plan for the seizure of Guam and the Marianas in connection with Palau-New Guinea operations would be prepared.

Of the Joint Chiefs of Staff only Admiral King objected to any of the contents of JCS 446.[60] He took exception to the prospect of an advance by the British through the Malacca Straits and up through the South China Sea, indicating that "he did not wish to give any comfort to the British on any such concept."[61] Although this concept had been accepted by the Combined Chiefs of Staff in more detailed form as part of the strategic plan for the defeat of Japan approved at Trident,[62] the minutes do not indicate that anyone reminded the chiefs of this fact. Instead Admiral Cooke commented that it seemed likely that there would not be sufficient British forces available to carry out their part of the operations. The British planners had hinted that they "would be very weary after the war in Europe and would be busy doing other things such as providing occupation forces in Europe." In any event, the Joint

Chiefs of Staff decided to eliminate mention of the advance through the Malacca Straits from the paper.

Admiral King also stressed the importance of the Marianas, informing the group "that there was always discussion whether to conduct operations against Palau after Truk, or to go up into the Marianas." Occupation of the Marianas, he told them, would offer a serious threat to Japan, while Palau was a staging point between Hawaii and the Philippines. On his recommendation, the way was left open to modify the program of operations outlined in JCS 446 by incorporation of the following statement:

> ...It may be found desirable or necessary to seize Guam and the Japanese MARIANAS, possibly the BONINS, in conjunction with the seizure of the western CAROLINES, and in particular with the attack on the PALAUS. The MARIANA-BONIN attack would have profound effects on the Japanese because of its serious threat to the homeland.

When the paper had been revised and reissued as a combined paper (CCS 301),[63] General Arnold reminded the Joint Chiefs that, if all the air strength from Europe was going to be transferred to the Pacific after the defeat of Germany, bases for the air force would have to be taken into consideration in planning future operations in the Pacific. There was no disagreement with that, but the paper at hand seemed adequate for presentation to the British, and the Joint Chiefs of Staff approved it as one of those to be offered at Quadrant.[64] As it happened it was the first paper concerning the war with Japan to be discussed at Quadrant, for the over-all study of a long-term plan for the defeat of Japan, which the U.S. Chiefs had insisted should be considered before specific operations were recommended, had not yet been completed.[65]

On 17 August 1943, after the Combined Chiefs of Staff at Quebec had finished their usual general discussion, approved an outline plan for Operation Overlord (the invasion of Normandy), reaffirmed their support of air operations from the United Kingdom, and accepted a strategic concept for the defeat of the Axis in Europe, they turned to the war against Japan and CCS 301.[66]

The British Chiefs of Staff had only three major questions on the program the Joint Chiefs of Staff presented. Was it not unduly pessimistic to assume that Russia would remain at peace with Japan? Might not the collapse of Japan be obtained without invading the Japanese islands? Might it not be better to restrict operations in the Mandated Islands, and thereby possibly release resources for Overlord? Someone, presumably one of the U.S. Chiefs, "pointed out that while Russia had everything to gain by attacking Japan, it might well be that she would wait to do so until the defeat of Japan had been almost completely accomplished." If the desirability of trying to persuade Russia to join forces sooner was discussed, the minutes show no evidence of it. Nor

432   THE ADVANCE TO VICTORY

do they indicate any speculation as to whether or not invasion of Japan itself would prove necessary. They merely state:

> It was also generally agreed that while blockade and air bombardment might produce the collapse of Japan without invasion, it was necessary to plan on the assumption that the country itself would have to be attacked by land forces.

The discussion of whether or not operations in New Guinea could be curtailed to advantage is recorded in greater detail. Admiral King declared that if there should be a cutback he considered that any forces that were released should not be diverted to Overlord but concentrated on the "Island thrust" in the Pacific. But he stood up for the Southwest Pacific operations, for he believed that the two routes of advance were complementary and that both were essential. As he explained, either the two thrusts would converge on the Philippines or the forces in the Central Pacific would swing north from Truk to the Marianas. General Marshall also told the British Chiefs that in any case there could be little or no saving by cutting down in the Southwest Pacific, for most of the requisite forces were already in the New Guinea area and many were of types that could not be used against Germany. Besides, he thought that the New Guinea operations were causing very important losses to the Japanese. There appears to have been no answer to a final comment by Sir Charles Portal

> that it was not considered that operations in New Guinea should be discontinued, but rather that they should be limited to a holding role. The Island advance would cut across the Japanese lines of approach to the south

and so presumably New Guinea need not be entirely recaptured.[67]

One addition was made to CCS 301 at the recommendation of the British. In a brief discussion of China and the value of the Chinese army, Sir Alan Brooke recommended that a paragraph on the air route into China be inserted, for the limited lines of supply through Assam were already looming as an important topic of discussion. Consequently an approximate paraphrase of the Trident agreement was added to the paper:

> Present plans provided for the first priority of resources available in the China-Burma-India Theater, on the building up and increasing of the air routes and air supplies to China, and the development of air facilities, with a view to:
> 1. Keeping China in the War.
> 2. Intensifying operations against the Japanese.
> 3. Maintaining increased U.S. and Chinese Air Forces in China.
> 4. Equipping Chinese ground forces.[68]

Although this paragraph was the only part of CCS 301 given formal approval, the entire paper was tacitly approved at Quadrant by incorporation in the final report to the President and the Prime Minister.[69] Thus when the Quadrant Conference closed, the U.S. Chiefs could plan for operations which by the end of 1944 would advance their forces in the Southwest Pacific Area as far as the Vogelkop, and in the Central Pacific to the line of the Palaus-Marianas. Should the tentative time schedule be bettered, subsequent combined conferences would decide on further moves. There was no longer talk of holding a line in the Pacific until Germany should be defeated.

Chapter XVIII

CHINA-BURMA-INDIA IN THE SUMMER OF 1943: QUADRANT

The U.S. Chiefs of Staff could continue to determine strategy for the Pacific Theater almost independently because the theater was their responsibility and U.S. forces carried the major share of the burden. The problem of what should be done in China, Burma, and India, however, inevitably involved lengthy discussions with the British and the Chinese. In the summer of 1943 as throughout most of the war these discussions resulted in little actual accomplishment.

The objectives adopted for China-Burma-India at Trident in 1943-1944 included buildup of the air route to China, land operations in northern Burma, amphibious landings on the Burma coast, and interruption of Japanese sea communications into Burma.[1] However, American and British views of the importance of operations in Burma had always differed. Target dates for the agreed operations were months ahead, and the Trident decisions were tentative and largely designed to foster plans rather than action. It was the need to determine future objectives in Burma as well as the operations to follow the conquest of Sicily that resulted in the agreement for the Combined Chiefs of Staff to meet again in July or August and examine the Trident decisions in the light of the contemporary situation.

CHIANG KAI-SHEK AND THE TRIDENT DECISIONS

U.S. views of what should be done in Burma were based on two factors, a long-term objective of bombing Japan from bases in China and a firm commitment of aid to China. Since the Generalissimo was not privy to the Trident discussions, one of the first things to be done after conclusion of the conference was for the President to inform him what had been agreed in respect to China-Burma-India. It will be recalled that Chiang's opinion that the major portion of the tonnage flown over the Hump should go to the air forces in China had been approved by President Roosevelt. Even had the divisions of supplies been less advantageous to air Chiang would probably have been pleased that the combined staffs had set buildup of the air route to China as the first objective for the area. He was skeptical, however, of the plans for operations in Burma, and he sent Mr. T.V. Soong a list of questions about them to ask the President.[2]

Most of the Generalissimo's interests were concerned with the matter which had constantly delayed his agreement to participate in land operations in Burma, i.e., what naval support was to be given the operations. "Has Great Britain committed herself," he asked, "to engage her navy in giving effective support for joint action in the Andaman Sea and is she determined to take Rangoon?" Was the United States going to provide the naval strength that General Arnold had indicated when he was in Chungking? Would Great Britain send as much or more? Now that the North African campaign was over, could the naval strength for Anakim be increased in order to expedite the capture of Rangoon? Would the U.S. Army take part, and if so, how many divisions? He did not doubt, he said, that Great Britain could fill its commitments, but he did think it "necessary for the President to exercise his influence continually in order to prevent delay in the execution of the plan." Moreover, the Generalissimo hoped that Mr. Roosevelt would see to it that plans were so made as to synchronize the movements of the Army in the north with amphibious operations in the south of Burma.

Mr. Roosevelt replied orally to these questions when they were presented to him by Mr. Soong and then sent them to the Joint Chiefs of Staff "to read and return." There is no record that the Joint Chiefs ever discussed the questions among themselves, nor have any individual comments been discovered. However, there can have been no doubt in their minds that the Generalissimo was not going to take action in northern Burma unless he was assured of naval support in the south.

Upon Lieutenant General Joseph W. Stilwell's return to Chungking from Washington about the middle of June he presented the Generalissimo with more details of the proposal for Saucy, the campaign in Burma which had been settled upon at Trident, seeking Chiang's agreement to Chinese participation. Almost two weeks later the Generalissimo, in conference with General Stilwell, "intimated general approval" of the operations but made no commitment.[3] Instead he raised again the question of naval support, inquiring just what ships would be allocated to the project and stressing the necessity of taking Rangoon. It was not until 12 July, almost a month from the time General Stilwell presented the proposal to Chiang Kai-shek, that General Stilwell received an answer. It was affirmative:

(1) I agree that the air facilities in the Assam area should be developed. At the same time I believe the air strength should be increased so that with complete air superiority the land and Naval forces will be more sure to win. According to my judgement, the enemy will be able to put 500 planes into Burma, and increase this number, if necessary, to 800 or even 1,000. I hope at the same time that the shipment of materials into China by the Air Ferry will not be affected by this operation, and also that the plan of increasing the tonnage will go on as before.

(2) With the plan for the use of land and air forces after the rains in attacks from Ledo, Imphal, and Paoshan simultaneously, in order to contain as much enemy force as possible, I am in complete agreement. There is no difference here from former plans. On the India side, I hope the US will send strong ground units to join the effort, for in this way we will be more sure of victory. I trust you will forward this idea to the President. In conclusion, the matter of cooperation between Americans, British, and Chinese in timing the operation, and the use of the Air Force in support of Chinese ground troops, should be discussed between the Americans, British, and Chinese, in order to get concrete plans for the operation.

(3) I agree with the estimate of 3 battleships and 8 carriers as the basis of the Naval Force for the control of the Bay of Bengal, and also with the plans for the use of land and Naval Forces to get control of the Burma coast.[4]

Thus it appeared that agreement had at least been reached among the major participants that the first steps toward retaking Burma would be undertaken after the monsoon, in the fall of 1943.

BUILDING UP THE AIRLIFT

The prime requisite for the building up of the air route from Assam into China, first on the list of the Trident projects for the Far East, was completion of the series of airfields in Assam. On 3 June 1943 the British Chiefs of Staff reported to the Combined Chiefs that word had been received from India that not all the hard standings projected could be completed by 1 July.[5] The local authorities had set a goal for that date of five fields with forty hard standings apiece and two with twenty-five and aimed for completion of one more field by 1 September. This program was expected to produce accommodations for the 7,000-ton lift by 1 July and 10,000 by 1 September, provided necessary supplies and personnel could be delivered to Assam. That, the British indicated, would depend upon whether the Americans could clear 1,000 freight cars held up at the Assam end of the railroad line from India.

It was two weeks before the Joint Chiefs of Staff approved this target.[6] In approving it they pointed out that recent reports from the theater showed that progress was considerably short of the construction target for airfields although it was still expected to satisfy requirements. The Joint Chiefs recommended that the local commanders work out solutions to local problems together and that, instead of waiting for trucks to arrive from the United States, the Commanding General, Services of Supply, U.S. Army Forces, procure vehicles required for airdrome construction from the British in India. Approval of the theater target was communicated to the local commanders following CCS approval in mid-June.[7] Progress did not live up to expectation, however. In the month of June only, 2,200 tons were carried into China by the Air

Transport Command (ATC). In July, when 7,000 tons were to have been delivered, the total was still only 4,500, 200 tons less than Major General Claire L. Chennault's share alone.[8] Plans for the advance into north Burma from Imphal and for the amphibious attack on Akyab, in the meantime, had been making slow progress.

SOUTHEAST ASIA COMMAND

There had been considerable dissatisfaction among the top level staffs in Washington over the poor showing which the British had made in the limited operations in Burma in the Spring of 1943. Suspicions that Field Marshal Sir Archibald Wavell was responsible seemed to be verified by the defeatist attitude he showed during the Trident Conference.[9] The British leaders were aware of this feeling of their American colleagues, and shortly after their return to London Mr. Churchill reported to the President his tentative ideas about changing command arrangements in India.[10] He proposed to make Field Marshal Wavell Viceroy of India, a civilian position, and to offer General Sir Claude Auchinleck the position of Statutory Commander in Chief in India, with functions limited to defense of India proper and to discipline, administration, and training of the Indian Army and of British troops in India. "In order to secure the prosecution of the war against Japan with the utmost vigor" he proposed to create a new command in Southeast Asia, possibly under a single Supreme Commander.

About a week later the Prime Minister formally proposed appointment of an Allied Supreme Commander in Chief, independent of and equal to the Commander in Chief, India, and "responsible for the conduct of operations against Japan in East Asia, and for the development of the air route to China."[11] He would have a Deputy Supreme Commander, under whom in turn would be a Naval Commander in Chief, an Army Commander in Chief, two Air Commanders in Chief, and a Principal Administrative Officer. Mr. Churchill's choice for Supreme Commander was Air Chief Marshal Sir Sholto Douglas; for Deputy, an American such as General Stilwell; for Naval Commander in Chief, Admiral Sir James Somerville; for Army Commander in Chief, an undesignated British officer. One of the Air Commanders in Chief would be responsible for "The air war against Japan," while the other took over operation of the air transport route and its terminals in India. For the former the Prime Minister suggested Air Marshal Sir Keith Park, for the latter an American. Mr. Churchill carefully explained that he did not intend to interfere with the existing relationship of General Chennault to the Generalissimo, pointing out that, when the weather was bad in China and good in Burma, General Chennault could "combine his operations with those of both the air commanders in the East Asia Theater."

The Prime Minister suggested that the command organization should follow the MacArthur model as closely as possible. That meant "the Combined Chiefs of Staff would exercise general jurisdiction over grand strategic policy and over such relating factors as are necessary for proper implementation of that policy including the allocation of forces and war materials." In all matters pertaining to operational strategy, however, the British Chiefs of Staff would have jurisdiction. They would issue all instructions to the Supreme Commander, East Asia.

Mr. Churchill passed off the details of "exact frontiers," etc., as matters that could be "thrashed out" by the two staffs, and he gave no indication where he proposed the boundaries of the command should lie. The title, Supreme Commander, East Asia, however, implied inclusion of all East Asia, including China. To this the President objected.[12] Pointing out that the U.S. Air Force was in India expressly for the purpose of supporting China, that a large number of Chinese troops were at Ramgarh, and that eleven Chinese divisions from Yunnan were scheduled to participate in the Burma campaign, he reminded the Prime Minister that the Generalissimo was already Supreme Commander of the China Theater and warned that they would "have a most difficult task in securing the Generalissimo's cooperation to the suggestion of a Supreme Command for all East Asia." The President agreed that unity of command was desirable and approved the suggested appointments with the exception of Sir Sholto Douglas, but he asked the Joint Chiefs of Staff to study the matter "from every angle" before he made a final reply.

Mr. Churchill protested at once that he had not intended to include China in the new command.[13] The eastern boundary, he said, would comprise:

> ...The frontier between China and Burma and between China and Indo China to the Gulf of Tonkin, thence southwards along the coasts of Indo China, Thailand, and Malaya to Singapore: from Singapore south to the north coast of Sumatra: thence round the east coast of Sumatra (leaving the Sunda Strait to the eastward of the line) to a point on the coast of Sumatra at longitude 104 degrees east: thence south to latitude 08 degrees south: thence south easterly towards Onslow, Australia, and, on reaching longitude 110 degrees east, due south along that meridian.

He thought perhaps it would be better to call it Southeast Asia than East Asia. It seemed to him essential that all troops within the area be subject to the Supreme Commander, including the Chinese forces on the Ledo Road and those from Yunnan as soon as they crossed the border into Burma. He also considered it essential that all air forces in the area and all air operations into and from the area be under the control of the Supreme Commander. Perhaps any objections from Chiang Kai-shek to this command arrangement could be overcome by making General Stilwell responsible both to the Generalissimo and to the Supreme Commander, adding to the complexity of his position.

In the meantime the War Department planners had already gone to work on a draft reply to the Prime Minister's first proposal, and

General Marshall submitted it to the Joint Chiefs of Staff for approval on 28 June 1943.[14] In a covering memorandum he informed the other chiefs that not only did he object to the inclusion of China in the command but he also felt that the organization should follow the Eisenhower (North Africa) pattern, which would place the Supreme Commander directly under the Combined Chiefs of Staff, rather than the MacArthur pattern, according to which the British Chiefs of Staff would direct operational strategy and issue all instructions. The avowed U.S. policy of aid to China, he explained, would not permit direct subordination to the British Chiefs of Staff of any command which embraced U.S. means for supporting China. On the other hand, it would be acceptable to have the British Chiefs of Staff act as the executive agency for the Combined Chiefs of Staff.

General Marshall insisted that General Stilwell should be made Deputy Commander but proposed that he should retain command of the forces already assigned to him. General Stilwell's command, said General Marshall, was "somewhat of an independent affair," involving as it did "air forces in India and China, Chinese ground forces supported by U.S. service forces in India and North Burma, and... control of ground forces in Yunnan." He did not believe this mixture could be put under direct British control.

Practically the same information that General Marshall gave to the Joint Chiefs of Staff was incorporated in the radio finally sent to the Prime Minister by the President on 30 June 1943.[15] While the theater boundaries proposed by the Prime Minister in his second message were accepted, firm objection was made to the suggestion that the Supreme Commander have direct control of all forces, particularly of air forces. Chiang Kai-shek, it was pointed out, "would raise serious objection to subjecting Chennault's operations into Burma under any direct supreme command in India other than that provided by the channels already in existence."

The Prime Minister and his staff did not agree with the Americans that the Eisenhower pattern of command was preferable for the new theater, and they continued to urge approval of the MacArthur pattern, subject to CCS control of allocations of American and British resources between the China Theater and the Southeast Asia Command. Somewhat reluctantly Mr. Churchill agreed to try giving General Stilwell command over the forces already assigned to him, pointing out, however, that the British Chiefs of Staff felt that General Stilwell would have enough to do as Deputy Supreme Commander with direct responsibilities to the Generalissimo, responsibility for the operation of the air route to China, and control of discipline and administration of all American forces in Southeast Asia.[16]

Reserving to the Combined Chiefs of Staff control over the allocation of resources was not sufficient to convince the American staff that the command should be patterned after that of General MacArthur, and more arguments were offered through Mr.

Roosevelt.[17] As the tempo of the war against Japan increased, he pointed out to Mr. Churchill, it would be necessary to integrate planned operations in the Southeast Asia Theater more closely with efforts in the entire Pacific. Division of major operational planning and strategic control of the two areas between London and Washington would weaken the entire effort. Moreover, he suggested, chances of securing the cooperation of the Generalissimo might be enhanced by centering control of Southeast Asia in Washington where Chiang had representation on the Pacific War Council if not on the Combined Chiefs of Staff.

While this exchange was going on, the President and the Prime Minister had also been discussing the man to be assigned to the new command. Having announced initially that he was "not prepared at the moment...to accept Sholto Douglas," Mr. Roosevelt suggested Admiral Sir Andrew B. Cunningham as "especially acceptable" and remarked that Air Marshal Sir Arthur Tedder was "also favorably considered."[18] But the Prime Minister felt that neither of these could be spared from the Mediterranean Theater.[19] Instead of offering some other substitute he wrote at length to the President in support of Sir Sholto Douglas, whom the British Chiefs of Staff were strongly backing. Moreover, since no explanation had been given of why the U.S. Chiefs opposed the appointment, the Prime Minister inquired whence came their doubts. Obviously determined to stick by his man, he suggested that, if the President remained unconvinced, he "could make, as a first step, a unified new British Joint South-East Asia Command under Douglas with a thoroughly good liaison with Stilwell and work up to the combined Supreme Command in two stages as confidence grew."

If the British were determined, the Americans were no less so. In still another message prepared in the War Department the President continued to urge Admiral Cunningham and to refuse Sir Sholto Douglas.[20] Without mentioning names he reported that "a number of general officers who have been thrown in contact with Douglas all have gotten the same unfavorable reaction." The new position would require "a man of unusual breadth of vision, moral courage, and personal characteristics that lend themselves to coordinating actions of diverse peoples." He felt that these qualities were present in Admiral Cunningham, in whom the American Chiefs had complete confidence. The President apparently thought that a naval commander might induce the British to send more ships to the area, for he concluded his remarks by saying: "The importance of Cunningham in the Mediterranean is fully realized, but I am hopeful that the situation will be so clarified navally in a short time that his services can be spared as well as some of his ships."

The matter seemed to be at a stalemate on the top level, and on 10 July the British Chiefs of Staff cabled Sir John Dill in Washington, suggesting an approach through General Marshall.[21] They reported that they were seriously considering doing as the

Prime Minister had suggested to the President and giving up the whole idea in favor of a Joint South-East Command. They asked Sir John Dill to call on General Marshall and

> tell him with the utmost frankness that we are surprised and upset that the American Chiefs of Staff should refuse to accept our estimate of Sholto Douglas. We are unanimous and emphatic that he is the best available man for the job and they should surely realize that we are in a far better position to judge than they are. Please add that we ourselves take a very poor view of Stilwell but that we have suppressed our own feelings in deference to the opinion of the American Chiefs of Staff in the interests of Anglo-American co-operation.

By 13 July Rear Admiral Charles M. Cooke, Jr., Assistant Chief of Staff (Plans) to Admiral King, had become considerably concerned that no commander in chief for Burma had yet been designated and that so little progress appeared to have been made in planning the Burma operations. He reminded Admiral King that ten LST's were supposed to leave the United States for India on 27 July and that the time was getting on and something must be done if the United States was going to furnish submarines, destroyers, and possibly carriers also for operations in Burma in November and December.[22] On the same day Admiral King passed to the Joint Chiefs of Staff Admiral Cooke's recommendation that they take up the matter with the President or the British Chiefs of Staff "as a matter of urgency."[23] General Marshall reported, however, that negotiations for designation of a commander were under way on a high level, and the Joint Chiefs deferred action.[24] A week later Admiral Leahy brought the paper up again and both Admiral Cooke and Admiral King expressed concern that planning for the Burma operations was making little progress. Again General Marshall reported that negotiations were in progress and again the Joint Chiefs made no decision.[25]

The following week the British Chiefs of Staff submitted a proposed agenda for the Quadrant Conference, scheduled by then for mid-August, about three weeks away.[26] Included among the items they wished to discuss was the establishment of the Southeast Asia Command and appointments to it. The U.S. Chiefs objected to this further delay in getting things going in Burma and urged that arrangements be completed "at the earliest possible date, without waiting for the conference to convene."[27] Their objections were to no avail. The Prime Minister had already decided that the problem would have to be settled at Quadrant, for there was "much that can only be satisfactorily dealt with by personal discussion."[28]

So it was that on the second day of the conference at Quebec the British Chiefs of Staff introduced a paper (CCS 308) summarizing points relating to the Southeast Asia Command on which the President and the Prime Minister had reached "general agreement" and indicating those still under discussion.[29]

The area was described as embracing French Indochina, Thailand, Burma, Malaya, Sumatra, and the sea areas west of the Southwest Pacific Area, east of the western border of Persia, and south as far as need be.[30] According to the British summary the combined command and staff should be set up "on the lines of the North African Command," with a British Supreme Allied Commander, an American deputy, and undesignated Naval, Army, and Air Commanders in Chief, who would "control all operations and have under their command such Naval, Military and Air forces as may be assigned to the Southeast Asia Theater from time to time." In addition there would be a coordinating Principal Administrative (the British term for logistics) Officer. Conflicts over priorities with the Commander in Chief, India, would be settled by the Viceroy in India, but both of the military commanders would have direct access to the British Chiefs of Staff.

Although a command and staff "on the lines of the North African Command" was mentioned as one of the matters in general agreement, the British Chiefs pointed out that they still favored a setup that would "follow as closely as possible, *mutatis mutandis*, the MacArthur model" rather than the Eisenhower pattern. They explained that the Combined Chiefs of Staff would still have "general jurisdiction over grand strategic policy" and related factors such as the allocation of resources. The British Chiefs of Staff would have jurisdiction over all matters relating to operational strategy and would transmit all instructions to the Supreme Commander.

The responsibilities of General Stilwell as Deputy Supreme Commander remained unsettled despite the Prime Minister's earlier assurance to the President that the British would try what the U.S. Chiefs suggested.[31] In CCS 308 the British Chiefs defined the two views. The Americans proposed that General Stilwell should retain command of all ground and air forces currently under him and any U.S. and Chinese forces that subsequently became available, as well as continuing responsibility for operation of the air transport route and defense of its terminal in India and maintaining direct relations with Generalissimo Chiang Kai-shek. All of this seemed too much to the British Chiefs of Staff, who objected that it would be "very difficult" for General Stilwell to maintain command over part of the land and air forces in Burma while all other elements in the area were under someone else.

In addition to these points of difference the British Chiefs proposed that all such American agencies as the Office of Strategic Services (OSS), the Office of War Information (OWI), the Federal Communication Board (FCB), and the Office of Economic Warfare (OEW), which had representatives in the area, currently under General Stilwell's control, should be coordinated with similar British agencies and operate in conformity with the requirements of the Supreme Commander.

Discussion of the British paper by the Joint Chiefs of Staff at two meetings indicated that some of the details of the proposals were not previously known to them.[32] They expressed surprise that the area would not include India at all. As General Marshall remarked, the new command comprised "an area...entirely under Japanese control and...whoever the commander might be would have to walk on the ocean or conquer Japan." These alternative criteria probably were not being considered in the choice of a commander, but none had yet been selected.[33]

The U.S. Chiefs were not going to object to the area to be included in the new command, but they spent considerable time discussing objections to its form. In response to a direct question from Admiral Leahy, who apparently had endorsed U.S. objections to British proposals in the pre-Quadrant exchanges without fully comprehending the import of the U.S. arguments, General Marshall stated clearly why the U.S. Chiefs should object to following the MacArthur pattern in Southeast Asia:

> the question of our relation with China would make that extremely inadvisable. He explained that under the MacArthur pattern, the latter has no contact at all with the British Government or the British Chiefs of Staff and deals only with the United States Chiefs of Staff. He did not feel that an arrangement whereby the Chinese took their directions directly from the British Chiefs of Staff would be acceptable to the Generalissimo. To overcome this, arrangements would have to be made that they would deal with the British through General Stilwell.

In conversation with the Prime Minister, General Marshall had found strong feeling about the fact that under the MacArthur command set-up the British had not been fully advised of developments in Australia. He had also ascertained that one reason the Prime Minister was anxious to follow the MacArthur pattern in Southeast Asia was in order to insure cooperation between the command and the Indian Government, represented by the Viceroy, in the allocation of resources in India. When Admiral Leahy, Admiral King, and Admiral Cooke seemed disposed to object to agreeing that the Viceroy should have authority to settle conflicts over priorities, they were reminded by General Marshall that the Combined Chiefs of Staff could no more dictate to the Viceroy than they could to the Generalissimo.

On 18 August the Joint Staff Planners turned in a report on CCS 308 in which they emphasized that the objective of all U.S. activity in India was assistance to China.[34] Once north Burma had been captured and a land route opened up, U.S. forces would be moved into China, and U.S. effort, commanded by General Stilwell under the Generalissimo, would concentrate on establishing air bases in China, developing Chinese forces, and deploying maximum air units. On this premise the Joint Staff Planners urged that the U.S. Chiefs should stick to the type of command organization which they had been advocating and that neither the Viceroy nor the Commander in Chief, India, should have any control of lend-lease materials for China. The Joint Staff Planners also recommended that, because of the necessity of maintaining General Stilwell's forces as an entity committed to the China Theater, he should retain control despite the difficulties involved.

On the recommendation of General Marshall the planners' paper was not accepted for presentation to the Combined Chiefs of Staff. Instead it was decided to propose certain changes in the British statement of the relation of the new command to the Combined Chiefs of Staff, changes that would render the organization more like the Eisenhower than the MacArthur pattern. Specifically, where the British sentence read, "The Combined Chiefs of Staff would exercise general jurisdiction over grand strategic policy for the Southeast Asia Theater," it would read instead, "would exercise a general jurisdiction over strategical matters." And the statement, "The British Chiefs of Staff would exercise jurisdiction over all matters pertaining to operational strategy, and would be the channel through which all instructions to the Supreme Commander are passed," would be changed to read, "would exercise jurisdiction over all matters pertaining to operations and would be the channel through which all instructions to the supreme commander [are] passed." No change was proposed in the statement of General Stilwell's position, for the Joint Chiefs of Staff intended to stand by their previously stated views. They would also recommend, however, that decision on the coordination of agencies be deferred, since the matter was under consideration in a different series.[35]

General Wedemeyer tried these suggestions out on two of the British Planners before the U.S. Chiefs met with their British colleagues that afternoon and ascertained that they had no objection.[36] This proved to be the case also with the British Chiefs of Staff, who did not object to this reduction of their control.[37] But they still were not convinced of the desirability of combining under General Stilwell the duties of Deputy Supreme Commander, Chief of Staff to the Generalissimo, and Commander of the U.S. and Chinese forces in the area. The subject was discussed at considerable length. The U.S. Chiefs stressed the necessity of insuring that Chinese forces in Burma would do their part and emphasized that the basic U.S. objective was assistance to China, while the British underlined the complications which would result if part of the forces in Burma were under command separate from that of the Supreme Commander. They finally approved suggestions made by General Arnold and Sir Charles Portal, on the basis of which the Combined Staff Planners (CPS) subsequently revised the statement of General Stilwell's position to read:

> General Stilwell will be Deputy Supreme Allied Commander of the Southeast Asia Theater and in that capacity will command the Chinese troops operating into Burma and all U.S. air and ground forces committed to the Southeast Asia Theater.

The operational control of the Chinese forces operating into Burma will be exercised, in conformity with the overall plan of the British Army Commander, by the Deputy Supreme Allied Commander or by his representative, who will be located with the troops.

The operational control of the 10th Air Force will be vested in the Deputy Supreme Allied Commander and exercised by his air representative located at the headquarters of the Air Commander in Chief.

General Stilwell will continue to have the same direct responsibility to Generalissimo Chiang Kai-shek as heretofore. His dual function under the Supreme Allied Commander and under the Generalissimo is recognized.

The organization and command of the U.S. Army and Navy Air Transport Services in the Southeast Asia area will remain under the direct control of the Commanding General, U.S. Army Air Forces, and of the Commander in Chief, U.S. Fleet, respectively, subject to such supply and service functions as may be by them delegated to the Deputy Supreme Allied Commander. Requests by the Supreme Allied Commander for the use of U.S. troop carrier aircraft for operational purposes will be transmitted to the Deputy Supreme Allied Commander.[38]

In the matter of coordinating American agencies with comparable British ones the chiefs agreed to a U.S. suggestion to set up a Combined Liaison Committee in New Delhi for full and open discussion of quasi-military activities in the area. Before plans for any such operations were put into effect by U.S. agencies, however, the agreement specified that they would have to obtain concurrence of the government of India, the Commander in Chief, India, or the Supreme Commander, Southeast Asia, whichever was appropriate.[39]

On 23 August the Combined Chiefs of Staff met for the second and last time at Quadrant with the President and Prime Minister and presented them with a final report on the decisions they had reached during the conference, including the organization of the Southeast Asia Command.[40] There was considerable discussion of this, in the course of which it was brought out that in the delineation of the new area an important point had been overlooked. When Mr. Roosevelt inquired whether or not Thailand had ever been removed from the Generalissimo's China Theater, no one seemed to know.

Admiral Leahy thought Thailand ought to be in the Southeast Asia Command since troops from the new command might be able to occupy Thailand whereas the Chinese could not. Finally, Admiral King said someone was going to investigate and see whether both Thailand and French Indochina had been removed from the China Theater "in a more recent definition of bounds." No such thing had in fact been done, and the President, when informed of the situation, decided to do nothing about it until some action against Thailand was definitely planned.[41] In the meantime

Thailand was included in the final definition of Southeast Asia Command.

The record is not clear as to when the decision was made to appoint Lord Louis Mountbatten Supreme Commander. Although the minutes of the meeting of the Joint Chiefs of Staff on the morning of 23 August indicate that Lord Mountbatten had been selected, at the plenary session that afternoon the Prime Minister proposed a public announcement which read:

> It has been decided to establish a combined separate Southeast Asia Command. The Supreme Commander will be (here give the officer designated by name).

There is no apparent reason why the name should have been omitted from the record. In any case, at their last meeting the following morning the Combined Chiefs of Staff approved an announcement of the appointment of Vice Admiral Lord Louis Mountbatten to the position.[42] Whatever the method of selection had been, the important point was that Admiral Mountbatten had been appointed and the U.S. Chiefs could feel that progress was being made toward launching the campaign in Burma.

THE CAMPAIGN IN BURMA

The impatience which the U.S. Chiefs had felt at the long delay in setting up the Southeast Asia Command was but one aspect of their dissatisfaction in the summer of 1943 with continuing British reluctance to prepare in earnest for a full-scale campaign in Burma. Although no formal report of the status of planning came from the British until 5 August, as the summer advanced the U.S. Chiefs and the President became increasingly determined that the British should be pinned down to a definite commitment as to when they would move in Burma and what scale of assistance they might be expected to expend in that area.[43]

At the end of July the Joint Strategic Survey Committee, in a survey of the situation and recommendation of the position which the U.S. Chiefs should take at Quadrant, spoke firmly for execution of the operations in Burma upon which agreement had been reached at Trident.[44] The committee was insistent that nothing should be committed to the war in Europe that would interfere with the Trident concept of operations against Japan. Nor should victory in Europe be long delayed, for the war against Japan would not wait indefinitely. The committee urged that planning should be begun for the transfer of resources from the European area to the Pacific after the defeat of Germany. Predicting that the British would favor delaying the Burma campaign, the committee insisted that this tendency should be strongly resisted. Neither operations in Europe nor an attack on Singapore should be allowed to take precedence over operations in Burma. Moreover, the committee thought that the concept of opening a line of communications from Singapore to Hong Kong should be examined critically and weighed against the desirability of combining British and U.S. resources for the advance through the Central Pacific.

The members of the Joint Strategic Survey Committee were obviously impatient with apparent British failure to execute conference decisions wholeheartedly and with dispatch. They undoubtedly recalled the variant interpretations which the two nations had put on the decisions of Casablanca, and they were annoyed at British insistence on operations in the Mediterranean area rather than immediate concentration on invasion of the European continent. As they contemplated the situation which had developed by late July and the outcome of earlier conference decisions, they offered the following candid comment on British conference techniques:

> British method at these conferences is obvious - to compromise when necessary to obtain an agreed document, and then to proceed immediately to undermine that part of the agreement which they orginally opposed, but reluctantly accepted. Their efforts during and since Trident clearly follow this pattern in regard to the Pacific vs. Europe and West Europe vs. the Mediterranean. Opportunity should be made to intimate to the British that aside from any other question that might be raised against this procedure, it definitely affects the firmness of the Conference decisions, and by complicating long range planning, interferes with the effective conduct of the war.

Whether this estimate of British intent is a fair one is open to doubt and without access to British records would be impossible to establish. It is presented here merely as an indication of the interpretation which the Joint Strategic Survey Committee put on British actions. There is no record of comment by the Joint Chiefs of Staff, who merely "noted" the whole paper and referred it to the Joint Staff Planners for consideration in the preparation of papers for Quadrant.[45]

A week later the British Chiefs submitted a report on the progress of their plans for operations from India.[46] They contemplated initiation of the advance from Imphal in November 1943 with the maximum strength to be reached in February 1944, but according to their estimates the assault on Akyab could not take place until 1 January 1944. Fair weather landing strips needed for support might not dry out before mid-December, a "number of training factors," including the late arrival of certain assault vessels, would hold things up, and the long range penetration brigades would be unable to operate until at least the end of December. After they had set these dates, however, the British Chiefs had been informed of floods on the Damodar River in the vicinity of Calcutta, which had broken rail lines and were certain to prejudice military plans.

The "late arrival" of certain vessels, the British Chiefs explained, was caused by "important developments in Crete and in other parts of the Eastern Mediterranean" where it was reported that Italians and Greeks were fighting one another. In view of this circumstance the British were "holding 5 L.S.I.'s and certain other ships" that were scheduled to have left Suez for India and the Akyab assault by 10 August. This action by the British considerably disturbed Admiral King, who felt that it indicated that the British did not consider the Akyab operation a firm commitment. He expressed his dissatisfaction in two letters to Admiral Sir Percy Noble.[47] In the first he refused a request to assign U.S. naval officers to liaison duty with the British Eastern Fleet, for he thought the request anticipated U.S. forces joining the British naval forces for the Akyab operation, and he was opposed to such action. The second letter was in response to a request that thirteen U.S. LCT(5)'s be loaded on British and American LST's as they passed through the Mediterranean en route to India. Transfer of these would cut into Overlord-Post-Husky resources, and Admiral King refused to furnish them unless the British would move the LSI's and accompanying craft to India and furnish LCT's to make up the U.S. requirements for Overlord.

Despite Admiral King's strong reaction to the British delays, the Joint Chiefs did not even discuss the British progress report but informally referred it too to the Joint Staff Planners for consideration and for preparation of comments to be presented at Quadrant.[48]

DISCUSSION AT QUADRANT

The first meeting of the Combined Chiefs of Staff at Quadrant, convened at 1030 on 14 August 1943,[49] was devoted in large part to questions of procedure, routine approval of the same strategic concepts which had been agreed upon at Trident, and establishment of an agenda for the succeeding meetings.[50] The chiefs agreed that all problems of the European Theater would be discussed first. Then those concerned with the war against Japan would be taken up, followed by the U-boat war, miscellaneous matters such as landing craft, the relation of resources to the strategic plans decided on, and finally the report to the chiefs of state.

When the general lines of the conference meetings had been laid out, the Combined Chiefs of Staff began their talk, as they had at previous conferences, with general reports on the current situation in the several combat areas. At the second meeting, on the afternoon of the first day, the U.S. Chiefs spoke on various aspects of the war against Japan, outlining their views in broad terms. First, Admiral King stressed the importance of using airfields in China to take care of the air forces for which island bases would not afford adequate accommodations. His support of the U.S. estimate of China's importance was echoed by General Marshall, who read a telegram from General Stilwell reporting on the training programs for Chinese troops in Ramgarh and Yunnan and urging an early campaign to reopen the Burma Road. General Marshall also spoke, in a context not made clear in the minutes, of four fundamental issues (although apparently he did not say that they should be settled at Quadrant):

...Firstly, what was the value of Chinese troops; secondly, could we afford to take so little action with regard to China that the present government would fall; thirdly, if we employed only air forces from China, would not the Japanese reactions be so strong as to cut the line of communication to them, and, fourthly, in an operation through China was it essential to capture a port for heavy buildup of supplies and thus link up with the naval operations across the Pacific.

Only the fourth of these was considered at any length in the subsequent days of the conference.

General Arnold also talked of the value of Chinese bases and described in some detail the requirements of air forces already in China or allocated there and the possibilities of supplying them. He urged that the Burma Road be reopened and, if possible, a port on the east coast of China, in order to support air operations.

The U.S. view contained two basic points: China must be kept in the war because its bases were needed. In order to keep China active and to supply air forces which would operate from its fields, the Burma Road must be reopened as soon as possible, in accordance with the program already established at Trident. The British Chiefs, however, had different opinions.

Sir Alan Brooke advocated nothing so drastic as giving up all idea of operations in Burma, but he made it clear that the British considered the Trident program still open to discussion. After explaining that it would be necessary to demobilize a large number of British troops after the defeat of Germany, he remarked, "The relative advantages of the opening of the original Burma Road or the seizure of a port in China must be examined, together with the time factor, in relation to the working of the Burma Road at its maximum capacity." He suggested that an operation on the northern tip of Sumatra might be the first step to an attack on Malaya and an advance on Singapore. However, before the Combined Chiefs of Staff looked into this possibility, he recommended that they investigate the effect of the floods in Assam on the planned operations in Burma and on the scheduled dates for launching them.

During the period between Trident and Quadrant the British in India had been developing plans for the three-way advance in northern Burma, from Imphal, Ledo, and Yunnan, and for the amphibious operations on the southern coast. A progress report arrived from General Sir Claude Auchinleck, Commander in Chief, India, just in time for Sir Alan Brooke to introduce it on the first day at Quebec.[51] It was highly pessimistic.

The difficulty was one of transportation in India. As General Auchinleck pointed out, when the decisions on operations in Burma were made at Trident the requirements for delivery of resources to Assam were calculated at 4,300 tons per day. It was thought that this figure might be reduced closer to 3,400 tons per day, the theoretical maximum capacity of existing delivery lines to

Assam. The project was approved on that assumption. However, General Auchinleck reported, actually requirements had increased and deliveries had fallen far short of the theoretical maximum. A total deficiency of 128,000 tons was anticipated by 1 March 1944. While the requirements of various projects might be somewhat reduced and the efficiency of the transportation system somewhat improved, General Auchinleck strongly doubted that the overall deficiency could be eliminated, and he warned of the possibility of having to call off either the advance from Ledo or that from Imphal or both. Cancellation of the former would save an estimated four or five hundred tons per day, the latter about two, the two together six or seven, which would then make remaining requirements, mostly for the air transport line to China, equal delivery.

General Auchinleck was of the opinion that abandonment of the land operations in northern Burma should not affect the overland attack on Arakan in south Burma or the amphibious assault on Akyab. Here again, he had little hope that enough could be delivered in time to build up the supporting airfields in eastern Bengal and to supply the Arakan campaign, without which he considered the Akyab assault extremely hazardous. He was in favor of abandoning the offensives and building up the airfields. He concluded:

> ...The course of planning for even the limited operations intended in Northern Burma has brought me to the conclusion that best military course would be to avoid such operations and to concentrate on supply to China by air, at the same time increasing and conserving strength of India and preparing resources for large scale amphibious operations against Malaya next winter. Preparation for these would enable us to bring training of troops to high standard. If they were definitely decided on for 1944/45 it would be desirable to divert resources earmarked for Akyab to taking Andamans in the late spring of 1944. We are urgently examining the possibility of this and will signal results to you.

An ad hoc committee which was given General Auchinleck's message to study concluded that both the Ledo and the Imphal operations could not be carried out. One would have to be cancelled. Since the Ledo operation was designed to support construction of the road to China, the U.S. members of the committee were in favor of curtailing the Imphal project.[52] Reluctant to abandon any operations in 1943-1944, however, the committee asked General Auchinleck to reexamine the situation on the assumption that preparation for the campaign in northern Burma would be given priority over all other activities in India and that the United States would furnish military personnel to help run the railroad and provide locomotives, freight cars, trucks, towboats, and barges, all in considerable numbers and within the next few months. This assistance, the committee felt, might permit undertaking both projects about 15 February 1944.[53]

While awaiting a reply from General Auchinleck, the Combined Chiefs of Staff adopted a suggestion of Sir Alan Brooke and commenced their consideration of operations from India on the basis of existing plans.[54] The British Chiefs enthusiastically introduced discussion of the technique of jungle fighting which had been developed in India by Brigadier Orde C. Wingate. In the spring of 1943 his "long range penetration group" had achieved some success in a campaign from India across Burma to the east side of the Irrawaddy River. Supported entirely by air drops, this large scale guerrilla operation had caused considerable damage to the enemy's railroad between Mandalay and Myitkyina, although suffering heavy casualties.[55] Brigadier Wingate himself was at Quadrant and explained the tactical employment of this group to the Combined Chiefs of Staff. The British Chiefs heartily endorsed a scheme of employing six long range brigade groups to conduct flanking operations ahead of the three advances into north Burma, to dislocate enemy communications and prepare the way for the full scale operation following. Brigadier Wingate's operations, the British believed, would facilitate the capture by regular forces of enough of northern Burma to open up a road to China. Subsequently, as Sir Alan Brooke suggested, long range penetration groups might be used to operate from the southern coast of Burma to the Mandalay-Rangoon line of communications.

The U.S. Joint Chiefs of Staff were favorably interested in this Wingate technique of jungle warfare.[56] General Marshall went so far as to suggest providing American troops for one of the columns, on the theory that the Chinese might be more inclined to cooperate in the use of long range penetration groups in conjunction with their advance from Yunnan if U.S. units were incorporated in the Wingate command. General Marshall said, "We could cheerfully accept a subordinate role in the Wingate operations for the favorable effect the operations might have on China." Admiral King further pointed out that, if successful, the Wingate operations would lead forces far enough forward to open up prospects of capturing Burma in 1945. The Joint War Plans Committee did not share the Joint Chiefs' enthusiasm for the project.[57] While agreeing that it offered "almost limitless possibilities," the members of the committee pointed out that its adoption would delay initiation of the advance into north Burma. They felt that it was too late for American participation to be practicable and in any case that the project would be an unacceptable drain on resources. Despite their views, however, the long range penetration groups were accepted as an element of the projected campaign.

Another aspect of operations in north Burma was taken up by the Combined Chiefs of Staff on 21 August when General Somervell and General Sir Thomas Riddell-Webster presented a study (CCS 325) of supply routes in northeast India, the area that was proving to be a bottleneck.[58]

U.S. and British representatives had disagreed as to when the road from Ledo to Kunming might be expected to be open for traffic, the former estimating March 1945, the latter March 1946.[59] It was decided, however, that, regardless of the date when the road would be open, it was necessary to start work on expanding the line of communications to Assam to prepare to take the extra tonnage it would have to carry in order to supply and maintain the capacity of the road across Burma.

The planned capacity for the Assam line of communications was 102,000 tons per month by 1 November 1943, an amount which the committee calculated would be enough for minimum maintenance of essential ground and air forces, an air ferry delivery to China of about 10,000 tons, and road construction to keep up with the advance of operations. When the road was completed and carrying 65,000 tons, it was estimated that 118,000 tons per month more, exclusive of petroleum products, would have to be carried through Assam to take care of this and the increase of the air route and of operational forces. Consequently, the two generals recommended that the Supreme Commander, Southeast Asia Command, be directed to develop the Assam route and increase its capacity so that by 1 January 1946 it could carry 220,000 tons per month. The necessary material and personnel for this expansion would be furnished by the United States.

Before presenting their report to the Combined Chiefs of Staff General Somervell and General Riddell-Webster separately secured the support of their respective chiefs.[60] Consequently there was no difficulty in reaching agreement on the recommendations at the combined meeting.

Another factor in the campaign in northern Burma and in the construction of the Ledo Road was a projected pipeline from Calcutta to Kunming. At the second Quadrant meeting the Combined Chiefs of Staff had heard from General Somervell a description of the project, and at the request of Sir Alan Brooke the Joint Chiefs of Staff had directed their Joint Administrative Committee (JAdC) to prepare a study on the subject for British consideration.[61] The committee's report, having been approved by the U.S. Joint Chiefs of Staff and by a special combined ad hoc committee appointed to handle administrative matters, was taken up by the Combined Chiefs on 23 August.[62]

The pipeline project was in effect a dual project, consisting of construction of a six-inch pipeline from Calcutta to Dibrugarh in Assam and of a four-inch line from Dibrugarh via Fort Hertz to Kunming. The first of these was designed to carry 36,000 tons per month and provide gasoline for the air ferry and to supplement the supply of the ground force attacking from Imphal as well as 18,000 tons to go on through the smaller line to Kunming. It was estimated that the first portion of the line would take five months to build and the latter, eight. The 50,000 short tons of equipment required for the project could be carried in available cargo shipping, but additional troop shipping for about 4,000 men would be required. Despite the strain which transportation of the construction materials would put upon the already strained route between

Calcutta and Assam and the necessity of providing adequate protection to prevent the enemy from interrupting construction, the committee concluded that the project was feasible and recommended approval by the Combined Chiefs of Staff. The chiefs apparently were stopped by the "ifs" just mentioned, for the minutes record that "it was pointed out" that if the project was given unqualified approval it might act to decrease the scale of military operations in northern Burma. CCS approval was qualified by making the construction "subject to prior requirements of military operations in Burma."[63]

It was the next to the last day of the conference before General Auchinleck's reaction to the proffered assistance for developing the line of communications through Assam was presented to the Combined Chiefs of Staff. In the meeting that day the British Chiefs of Staff introduced a summary of "a number of telegrams" which they had received from General Auchinleck and which had been informally circulated to some of the U.S. Planners.[64] The British proposed to take the telegrams back to London, have them studied, and then tell the U.S. Chiefs of Staff how much they would like to have.

General Auchinleck expected that, even with the assistance offered by the United States, the estimated deficiency of 128,000 tons by 1 March 1944 could be cut only to 102,000 tons. This would have to be borne either by the Ledo operation or partially by that and partially by the Imphal operation. Even limited operations would, the British Chiefs reported, "apparently" absorb the entire capacity of the line of communications and render long term improvements to the transportation system itself impossible. They concluded that there were three possible courses of action in north Burma in the dry season 1943-1944: (1) a main effort of land and air operations to establish land communications with China and improve the air route, probably at the expense of the air lift, but the British did not estimate what the reduction would be; (2) first priority to increasing air supplies to China, probably undertaking no offensive operations in north Burma; (3) a main effort in developing the line of communications in Assam in order in the 1944-1945 season to make the air route secure and deliver a far greater tonnage to China, curtailing land operations and temporarily accepting a small delivery rate to China. The British Chiefs of Staff favored the first, suggesting

> that the successful conquest of Northern Burma in the coming dry season which should result in our joining hands with the Chinese, should go far to compensate the Generalissimo for a temporary reduction in the supplies he will receive by air. Priorities between the three courses will not be rigid and we therefore propose to instruct the Supreme Commander, in formulating his proposals, to regard this decision as a guide and bear in mind the importance of the longer term development of the L. of C.

Despite the fact that two days earlier the Combined Chiefs of Staff had approved an interim report to the President and Prime Minister which listed the first alternative as an agreed operation,[65] according to the official CCS minutes there was a "full discussion" of this paper before the British recommendation was accepted. Unfortunately there is no available record of what was said, but it is safe to assume that some attention must have been paid to the conflict between this decision and the agreement that had been made at Trident:

> (1) The concentration of available resources, as first priority within the ASSAM-BURMA Theater, on the building up and increasing of the air route to CHINA to a capacity of 10,000 tons a month by early fall, and the development of air facilities in ASSAM with a view to:
>   (a) Intensifying air operations against the Japanese in BURMA;
>   (b) Maintaining increased American Air Forces in CHINA; and
>   (c) Maintaining the flow of air-borne supplies to CHINA.
> (2) Vigorous and agressive [sic] land and air operations at the end of the 1943 monsoon from ASSAM into BURMA via LEDO and IMPHAL, in step with an advance by Chinese forces from YUNNAN, with the object of containing as many Japanese forces as possible, covering the air route to China, and as an essential step towards the opening of the BURMA Road.[66]

Indeed it seems very likely that the change of emphasis was quite intentional, for the dictated decision at Trident which gave almost all Hump tonnage to General Chennault and the Fourteenth Air Force had militated against delivery of large amounts of ground equipment essential to the preparation of the Chinese forces in Yunnan for the coming campaign in northern Burma. The unsatisfactory reaction of those who supported ground operations in northern Burma to the priorities thus established at Trident may be detected in General Marshall's remark at the plenary session of 23 August when the President and the Prime Minister reviewed the CCS agreement to put the main effort in northern Burma into offensive operations.[67] "It was necessary," said General Marshall, "for someone on the ground to have authority to make decisions regarding priorities.... If, for example, it was arbitrarily decided to use the entire capacity of the air transport route to supply General Chennault with gasoline, this very decision might jeopardize the success of the Burma operations which in themselves were essential to keeping China in the war."

Mr. Churchill's immediate reaction to the CCS agreement was to inquire what was meant by the statement that the Supreme Commander "should give priority to operations in Northern Burma but at the same time keep in mind the long-term necessities for improving the lines of communication." Sir Alan Brooke's reply fell far short of explaining how such a procedure would be followed through.

The directive was intended, he said, "to emphasize the importance of the Burma operations and, at the same time, to caution him to take a long-range view of the necessity for building up his lines of communication, without which no communications would be possible." The very vagueness of this statement was to cause considerable confusion in the theater in the ensuing months.

Lest there be misunderstanding of the import of the decision, General Arnold put it on record at the plenary meeting that giving first priority to the reconquest of northern Burma might render it impossible for him to fulfill his responsibility for delivering supplies by air to China. No one else seems to have been greatly concerned.

AMPHIBIOUS OPERATIONS

Decision on what was to be done in northern Burma was simple in comparison with the problem of deciding on the other phase of operations from India, the amphibious assault on Akyab and Ramree. This was intended as the first step toward reopening the original Burma Road, a project the U.S. Chiefs of Staff favored as a means of direct assistance to China and the British Chiefs of Staff opposed as unnecessary and expensive. The British favored instead an advance around through the Malacca Straits to the east coast of China. Mr. Churchill strongly urged an attack on the island of Sumatra as a valuable alternative to the Akyab-Ramree attack. These different views had been inconclusively discussed at Trident, and the conflict between the two consumed considerable time at Quadrant.

An attack on Sumatra was mentioned by Sir Alan Brooke at the second meeting of the conference as a project on which the British had prepared a study and which he thought bore investigation.[68] He also brought it up several days later, when Brigadier Wingate's project was under discussion, as an operation that "might prove necessary were it found that the floods would seriously hamper operations in Burma."[69] Consequently, in preparation for combined discussion the Joint Chiefs of Staff talked about Sumatra at their meeting of 18 August.[70]

No one at the meeting came out entirely in favor of the attack on Sumatra, although General Arnold expressed interest in it. He pointed out that it would yield air bases from which to strike at Singapore and Bangkok and would close off the Straits of Malacca, cutting Japanese communications into Burma. He recognized that it did not lead to anything but thought that there was virtue in the fact that forces in the Far East would at least be doing something. He also said, however, that he thought that the chiefs "should figure out some method to obtain the initiative and drive through Burma."

The only other good word for Sumatra came from Admiral Cooke, who attempted to summarize the British point of view.

...They will say that their method would result in getting supplies into China earlier than through Burma. They are considering the date of April 1944. It is questioned whether it is better to accept an operation in which the British will wholeheartedly take part or one in which they are half-hearted. With regard to the Burma operations, if they are started in February, 1945, the earliest date for obtaining Rangoon would be April, 1945. The monsoon then comes on the 15th of May and consequently no supplies would go over the road until 1946. The British won't agree that the capture of Burma will provide bases for operations against Japan. He felt there was some asset to the desirability of having willing partners. As between Singapore in 1945 and Burma in 1944, he felt it was better to take Burma in 1944. On the other hand, the British point out that there will be no operations between 1944 and 1945 unless Sumatra is undertaken.

General Marshall confessed no firm conviction for either the Akyab-Ramree operation or the Sumatra attack, which presumably would use some of the same forces. From a negative point of view he recognized the difficulties of executing the former operation and of overcoming British reluctance. On the other hand, he was uncertain whether troops could be successfully landed and maintained in Sumatra. He reported, however, that from conversations with various officers and with the Prime Minister he had gained the impression that Mr. Churchill wanted to go to Sumatra but the British Chiefs and their planners did not. In consonance with this, Admiral Leahy, who spoke little, urged that the U.S. Chiefs stand fast for the campaign in Burma, believing that the British would ultimately go along.

Admiral King raised the practical point that, although the British claimed the Sumatra operation would be done with the forces allocated to Akyab-Ramree, the former would certainly require shipping that would not be needed for the latter and would have to be supplied from somewhere else. He also expressed opposition, without explaining his views, to the British desire to go from Sumatra up through the South China Sea to Hong Kong.

The only one who offered substantial arguments in favor of the Akyab-Ramree operation was General Somervell, who stressed the contribution it would make toward the goal of operations against Japan from China bases. This first operation, he said, would lead to the recapture of Rangoon and the reopening of the original Burma Road. The Ledo Road then under construction would provide only 65,000 tons per months plus 50,000 tons of gasoline through the pipeline for China, whereas recapturing Burma and Rangoon to reopen the Burma Road would double that amount. The resources that could then be delivered would support 200,000 European troops and 750,000 Chinese troops in China, who could advance to the east and open up the requisite air bases for operations against Japan.

The Joint Chiefs of Staff talked for a considerable length of time about Sumatra, but they reached no conclusion. Four days later the Joint War Plans Committee reported to the planners that it strongly favored the Akyab-Ramree operations as "essential to any early success in that area."[71] The capture of Sumatra, on the other hand, would require serious and unacceptable diversions of shipping and aircraft carriers from other theaters. The committee's final conclusion was that the Burma operations which had been agreed to at Trident were sound and should be pursued. As for other projects,

> There are numerous variations to our strategy in this theater which have been examined and innumerable possibilities which can yet be explored. Each undoubtedly can be found to provide certain advantages. All appear to have one common feature, the further delay in a re-conquest of Burma.

Whether the Joint Chiefs of Staff ever saw this report is doubtful, for by the time it reached the Joint Staff Planners the discussions by the Combined Chiefs of Staff had gone beyond the point where it could be of use.

After the arrival of President Roosevelt and Prime Minister Churchill at Quebec a plenary session was held to discuss the progress that had been made.[72] There was still little decided in respect to the war against Japan and the progress report which the chiefs presented was concerned primarily with the war against Germany. However, the President and Prime Minister discussed at some length, and as inconclusively as their staffs had been doing, the relative merits of operations against Akyab and against Northern Sumatra. Mr. Churchill waxed eloquent. After warning the chiefs not to feel themselves limited by the results of the planners' study on a long-term plan for the defeat of Japan, he said that "he did not view with favor the idea that a great expedition should be launched to retake Singapore in 1945," for it might paralyze all action in 1944. He made no mention of a campaign to retake all of northern Burma, but instead he expressed approval of a plan to extend the operation of long range penetration groups in that area during the coming winter. This, he thought, should be supplemented by seizure of the northern tip of Sumatra, obviously his pet project. It would be, Mr. Churchill said, "the Torch of the Indian Ocean.... We should be striking and seizing a point of our own choice, against which the Japanese would have to beat themselves if they wished to end the severe drain which would be imposed upon their shipping by the air forces from Sumatra." He was convinced that strategically the Sumatra project was "of highest importance," and he even went so far as to "compare it, in its promise of decisive consequences, with the Dardanelles operation of 1915." "The alternative," he said, "would be to waste the entire year, with nothing to show for it but Akyab and the future right to toil through the swamps of Southern Burma."

Mr. Roosevelt shared the views of the U.S. Chiefs of Staff in respect to Sumatra, and he spoke at some length, although less dramatically than the Prime Minister. Using the same simile that he had employed at Trident when he urged a maximum effort against Japanese shipping,[73] he compared the enemy position to a piece of pie, with Japan at the apex and the island barrier, from Solomons to Burma, forming the outside crust. Rather than nibbling at the crust in Sumatra he favored hitting as close to the apex as possible. To him it seemed that the direct route to Japan lay along the Burma Road to China and through China to Japan. While operations were proceeding in that direction, he pointed out, on the other side of the slice they would be advancing through the Gilberts and Marshalls to Truk. Mr. Roosevelt said that, although the Generalissimo had insisted on the capture of Rangoon, he himself never had thought much of the idea of taking either Akyab or Rangoon. But he thought that "the Sumatra operation would be heading away from the main direction of our advance to Japan."

There was no decision by the heads of state. The following day the Combined Chiefs of Staff turned again to the question of operations in Burma or Sumatra, approaching it from another angle as they took up CCS 313, the planners' summary of their "Appreciation and Plan for the Defeat of Japan."[74] In order to understand the discussion it is desirable to review briefly the development of this study.

STRATEGIC PLAN FOR THE DEFEAT OF JAPAN

Work on the long range strategic plan for the defeat of Japan had been begun immediately after the close of Trident, but it proved to be a long, slow job. The chiefs and their planners discussed the immediate problem of war with Japan during the summer of 1943, as they always had, with only a general notion of the long term strategy for reaching their goal.

In accordance with the Trident agreement "that a U.S. Planning Team should visit London to discuss the grand strategy of the war against Japan, and in particular to assist the British Joint Planners in preparing the British part of this paper,"[75] on 5 June 1943 the Red Team of the Joint War Plans Committee received orders to London.[76] The members were authorized to discuss any features of strategy for the defeat of Japan but were urged to confine that part of the plan prepared in London to broad strategy and to operations in the British sphere of responsibility, Burma and India, on which the U.S. Chiefs were anxious to get a British commitment. U.S. planners in the meantime, as the Joint War Plans Committee had recommended, would continue their own "studies on the defeat of JAPAN, with a view to *retaining* the *initiative* and *leadership* now established in relation to the British."[77] They did not want British interference in Pacific strategy.

The discussions in London revealed clearly to the U.S. representatives that the British simply did not want to fight in Burma and were prepared to argue for several other operations instead. The British estimated quite differently the importance of supporting China in the war, primarily because they did not agree with the predominant U.S. view that Chinese soldiers, properly trained and officered, could operate effectively against the Japanese and make a valuable contribution to the war effort. In the British view the eventual use of China as a base for operations against Japan was not sufficiently important to warrant attempting to strengthen China to the point where its military contribution would be significant. Consequently, agreement on long-term plans was difficult.[78]

The first fruits of the coordinated planning, an estimate or appreciation of the situation, arrived in Washington late in June for study by the Joint Intelligence Committee (JIC) and the Pink Team of the Joint War Plans Committee. They were just completing their reviews of this preliminary report when word came to the Combined Chiefs of Staff that it was hoped to finish the London part of the whole appreciation and plan by 10 July 1943.[79]

It was the British thought that both "Directors of Plans" (Joint Staff Planners) should study the paper independently. Then the British planning team would come to Washington and the plan would be completed there for presentation to the Combined Chiefs of Staff. The British suggested that when the full scale combined conference was held later in the summer the "Directors of Plans" should take advantage of the opportunity to clear the report at their level before submitting it to the Combined Chiefs. The Joint Chiefs of Staff balked at the implication that the plan would not be presented to the Combined Chiefs of Staff until the conference-after-next and were even more disturbed at a report from the planners who had gone to London that the British were considering proposing that nothing but European matters be discussed at the next conference. Consequently, the Joint Chiefs recommended that the plan be completed in Washington as suggested and "that the Combined Staff Planners should place an appreciation before the Combined Chiefs of Staff in order that it may be considered at their next conference."[80] The British Chiefs agreed that speedy completion of the study was desirable.[81] Accordingly, the Joint Staff Planners issued a directive to the Joint War Plans Committee, who in turn passed it to the Red Team, to work with the British team in Washington on the completion of the appreciation and plan for the defeat of Japan.[82]

The conference between British and American planners convened in Washington on 31 July 1943.[83] On 8 August the report, CPS 83, was completed--some 103 pages plus charts.[84] It included first the appreciation already studied in Washington, comprising a survey of the Japanese economy, military strength, psychology, and intentions, plus a discussion of Russia and China and the bearing those two nations had on the war against Japan. Thereafter came special studies on the invasion of Japan, strategic bombing of Japan, the battle of China, amphibious advances, the initial advance from the west, and a summary of basic principles and conclusions including an outline plan.

The planners had concluded that the agreed objective, "unconditional surrender," did not have much reality in the war with Japan. Japanese soldiers were fighting to the death, Japan had never suffered major defeat, and it seemed unlikely that the military regime would ever submit to such terms, certainly not unless U.S. armed forces were actually present in the Japanese home islands. Consequently the planners recommended restatement of the objective as "the destruction of Japanese capacity to resist." Achievement of that objective would involve, first of all, the earliest possible destruction of the Japanese Fleet and Air Forces. It would require heavy and sustained air bombardment of Japan. This of itself might accomplish Japan's surrender but would in any case be an essential prelude to it. For executing such an offensive bases in China and/or Formosa would almost certainly be required. Securing and developing airfields in China would mean acquiring ports, of which Hong Kong seemed most suitable. Therefore, a sea route to China and/or Formosa would be necessary and the Japanese lines of communication to the area would have to be cut, requiring control of the South Japan and South China Seas. To reach that area from the east, the planners concluded the best route would be through the Mandated Islands and then either north of Luzon or through the Celebes and Sulu Seas. From the west the area would be best reached through the Straits of Malacca. This, then, was the general pattern the war should follow.

A timetable of action against Japan conservatively outlined a lengthy campaign, upon several of whose features Americans and British had been unable to agree. (*See* chart on p. 461.)

There was no estimate of when the end of the campaign against Japan might be reached.

By the time this paper was completed the U.S. Joint Staff Planners were about to leave for Quadrant. Before their departure they sought comments from the Joint Chiefs of Staff, although the Combined Staff Planners had not yet had an opportunity to discuss the report.[85] The Joint Chiefs only "noted" the paper, but their reaction during discussion was one of dissatisfaction. Admiral Cooke, who himself had not studied the whole report, brought it to the chiefs' attention that the British, in the appended lists of forces available, reported a deficiency in most items, and that they seemed indisposed to undertake the recapture of Burma or to use British forces against Japan in any strength before Germany was defeated. Admiral Leahy, at least, shared Admiral Cooke's doubts as to what the British would actually do, for he insisted several times that they should be asked directly what their intentions were. Various other comments were made, but although Lieutenant General Joseph T. McNarney said he did not think the paper worthy of consideration, and Admiral Leahy suggested telling the planners that it did not meet with approval, the chiefs reached no conclusions.

Before presenting the report to the Combined Chiefs of Staff, the Combined Staff Planners at Quebec discussed it at considerable

CHINA-BURMA-INDIA, SUMMER 1943: QUADRANT

Action in the West			Action in the West
Serial 1 - Up to November 1943			
Development of air routes to China. Holding operation in North Burma and China.			Offensive operations against Solomons and New Guinea. Offensive operations against the Aleutians.
Serial 2 - November 1943 to May 1944			
Offensive operations in Northern Burma and on Arakan Coast. Developing Northern routes to China.			Offensive operations against Gilberts and Marshalls. Subsidiary operations in Solomons and New Guinea and air operations from the Aleutians.
Serial 3 - June 1944 to November 1944			
Holding operations in Burma.			Offensive operations against Carolines. Subsidiary operations in the New Guinea area.
Serial 4 - November 1944 to May 1945			
Course B (Favored by U.S.) Offensive Operations in North. [*sic*] Burma and capture of Rangoon.	Course C (Favored by British) Offensive operations in North Burma. Offensive operations against Northern Sumatra and Malaya.		Offensive operations against the Pelews and possibly Marianas.* Subsidiary operations in the New Guinea area. Commence offensive operations against South Philippines.**
Serial 5 - June 1945 to November 1945			
Holding operations in Burma.	Holding operations in North Burma. Continue offensive operations in Malaya and against Japanese communications to Burma.	Continue offensive operations against the South Phiippines.	OR Offensive operations against Luzon, Formosa or Ryukyus.
Serial 6 - November 1945 to May 1946			
Complete offensive operations to clear Burma. Offensive operations against N. Sumatra and Malaya.	Offensive operations against North Burma and Rangoon, subsequently clearing the whole of Burma. Offensive operations against Camranh Bay.**	Continue offensive operations against South Philippines.	OR Launch offensive operations against Hong Kong or Formosa (if not already captured).
Serial 7 - During the remainder of 1946			
Complete capture of Malaya.	Launch offensive operations against Luzon, Formosa, Hong Kong, Hainan and/or Ryukyus from East and West.		OR Establish the strategic bombing force in China and/or Formosa.
Serial 8 - From 1947 onwards			
Establish the strategic bombing force in China and/or Formosa. Bomb Japan. Invade Japan.			

*The British Planning Staff attach more importance to this operation than the U.S. Planners.
**If conditions are favorable, it may prove feasible to by-pass this objective.

length on five occasions.[86] U.S. disappointment settled principally upon the apparent British reluctance to undertake the campaign in Burma. It had been hoped that this appreciation and plan, prepared as it was for the most part by the British, would at last contain a full account of what they would do in Burma and what forces they would have available to do it with. Instead, however, as Admiral Cooke pointed out, the British were rejecting the operation and proposing instead an operation against Singapore on a much larger scale, over a prohibitively long period of time, and apparently to be carried out in large part with American forces. Admiral Cooke felt that the United States would be well occupied in the Pacific areas and that the British should contribute to Japan's defeat by action in Burma and Malaya. He urged the importance of operations in Burma, not only to open the supply route to China, but to enable the deployment of aircraft from China bases against targets in the Pacific.

In reply, Captain A.W. Buzzard, RN, explained that the bypassing of south Burma by an operation against Singapore was considered to be an important way of speeding up the war. He believed that Singapore might be captured in the fall of 1945 and a rendezvous effected between British forces from the south and U.S. forces from the east in the Hong Kong-Formosa area during the following winter (1945-1946). Captain H.B. Slocum, USN, one of the U.S. Planners who had worked on the paper but who had apparently not agreed with all the British concepts, pointed out that, with great successes, U.S. forces might be able to reach Formosa from the east by the spring of 1945, but up to that point very little assistance would have come from British operations to the southward. If, however, all of Burma were captured as the U.S. Planners advocated, the air bases in China which could then be supplied would be of great help to U.S. forces during the westward advance across the Pacific.

Admiral Cooke also took issue with the estimated length of time between completion of the war against Germany and the defeat of Japan. In so doing he offered a unique interpretation of the Trident objective of defeating all three Axis members in the shortest possible time: "If the United Nations could foresee the defeat of Germany in 1944, and that of Japan in 1948, or alternatively by a redistribution of resources, the defeat of both Germany and Japan in 1946, then the latter alternative would be the one to choose in accordance with that overall directive." In any event, he thought it would be impossible to maintain popular support for the war against Japan until 1948. Consequently, "unless we set up a plan for the defeat of Japan one year after the collapse of Germany, he felt we would never achieve our object."

Admiral Cooke objected to the characterization of operations in the Southwest Pacific as subsidiary, stating that "he viewed those operations as part of a long, continuous front, on the parts of which the emphasis varied with the situation."

The Combined Staff Planners finally decided to submit the summary of the paper to the Combined Chiefs of Staff with a covering memorandum indicating the divergent views of the U.S. and British Planners.⁸⁷ Both approved the basic concept and the general lines of advance toward the Japanese homeland. But they disapproved the long time lapse before Japan would be defeated. On how long it should be, however, they disagreed. While the U.S. Planners recommended that the defeat of Japan twelve months after the defeat of Germany should be set as a controlling objective, the British thought that this "would necessitate an entirely new concept of operations involving an assault on the Japanese homeland without the preparatory bombing from bases in China and/or Formosa which they believe will be required." They would agree only that intensified study should be given to ways and means of shortening the war.

The planners also differed on the matter of relegating action in the Solomons and New Guinea to a subsidiary position, as well as on the significance of operations in Burma. The U.S. Planners maintained that it was essential to recapture south Burma beginning in November 1944, both in order to improve the supply line to China and as a preliminary to an advance through the Straits of Malacca. They objected to the British plan which provided no action between the recapture of northern Burma in 1943-1944 and an attack on Malaya in March 1945. The British countered that the recapture of Rangoon and south Burma would be "a small strategic gain for the expenditure of great effort." On the other hand, they characterized the recapture of Singapore before Rangoon as "a full and correct application of sea and air power." It would, they said, "electrify the Eastern world and have an immense psychological effect on the Japanese." Moreover, it would threaten enemy communications to Thailand and to Burma, enable direct attack on the Dutch oil fields, flanking the whole Japanese defense structure in Southeast Asia and furnishing a base for naval and air forces. Above all, they argued, it would provide "for an advance complementary to that being undertaken by the U.S.A. from the East, and converging upon the same objectives, i.e., the capture of HONG KONG or FORMOSA and the control of the SOUTH CHINA SEA." With these split recommendations the planners circulated the plan to the Combined Chiefs of Staff, whose discussions at Quadrant had arrived at the same difference of opinion.⁸⁸

Before discussing the paper with their British colleagues the Joint Chiefs of Staff, on the morning of 20 August, considered the planners' report among themselves.⁸⁹ Admiral King, who had never favored the Singapore-Hong Kong advance via the South China Sea, now expressed strong opposition to it. He was joined by Admiral Leahy, who professed that he did not believe that Hong Kong could be taken by sea alone. There would have to be some attack on land. Admiral King said that, in view of the large amounts of troop lift, shipping, and landing craft that would be required for operations against Sumatra and then up through the South China Sea to Hong Kong, it seemed to him that "it would be doing things the hard way." He pointed out that the route would be flanked by the Japanese in Borneo, and he questioned the value of Hong Kong as an entrance into China. He thought the operation must have been planned largely for the employment of the British Navy. Apparently he was not very anxious to have the British Navy in the Pacific. When General Marshall asked, "If the British Navy were not employed against Hong Kong, how would it be employed? Furthermore, if the British Navy were so employed, would that not permit greater concentration of the U.S. Navy?" Admiral King's recorded reply was cryptic: "Our forces could lend a hand on either side." Rather than agreeing to the Sumatra operation and becoming involved in the Singapore-Hong Kong project, he recommended that an operation against Bangkok, which would cut the Japanese line of communications to Burma and obviate the necessity of taking Rangoon, be substituted. A landing below Moulmein had indeed been contemplated in a plan prepared by the Army six months before and informally offered at Trident, but, as General Wedemeyer reported, the British had not been much interested in it.

These discussions by the Joint Chiefs of Staff resulted in a proposal to the Combined Chiefs of Staff to modify the CPS recommendations.[90] Specifically, instead of recommending approval of the lines of advance set forth in the planners' "Appreciation and Plan," they proposed

> Direct examination of lines of advance, including a study of the feasibility and desirability of operations through the Moulmein area or Kra Peninsula in the direction of Bangkok with the object of isolating Rangoon and facilitating the capture of Singapore.

The U.S. Chiefs also recommended approval of planning for operations either in south Burma or toward Singapore, the plans to be revised at the next CCS meeting (presumably the next full-scale conference). In the other recommendations the Chiefs of Staff followed the suggestions of the U.S. Planners in the split report, except that the employment of Dominion forces was not specifically outlined but left for decision among all governments concerned.

At the combined meeting that afternoon General Marshall spoke out in favor of recapturing all of Burma in order to reopen the main road to China.[91] He urged the capture of Akyab and Ramree before the next monsoon and described Sumatra as "a diversion from the main effort which must be concentrated with a view to clearing Burma."

Sir Alan Brooke then calmly defined the point at issue. First north Burma must be recaptured and the Ledo Road opened. Then either the Akyab operation should be undertaken in March 1944 or northern Sumatra in May. Apparently a port in China could be opened at approximately the same time, whether it was done by an overland advance through China or by seaborne attacks from Singapore. After Admiral Leahy and Admiral King suggested the desirability of attacking the Kra Isthmus to take Bangkok instead of

Singapore, Sir Alan Brooke inquired whether one of these or operations in southern Burma would most assist the U.S. thrust in the Pacific. To this Admiral King confessed that he did not think an attack on Rangoon would divert many Japanese forces, but he did feel that an attack on the vital center of Bangkok or into China to develop the air offensive would elicit strong reaction. There was considerable discussion and general agreement that the air facilities in India and northern Burma must be built up and that there would be tremendous quantities of air forces available once Germany had been defeated. No decision was reached at this meeting, however.

The following day General Marshall admitted to the Joint Chiefs of Staff that "the more he heard about conditions in India, the less realistic operations against Akyab and Ramree appeared to be--especially as to their probability and the questionable success to be obtained."[92] He had not decided where the attack should be made, but he was not certain that it should be on Akyab and Ramree. Admiral King seemed to be weakening somewhat also, for he said "his interest in the Akyab-Ramree operations centered on its usefulness towards operations against Rangoon." But Admiral Cooke informed the chiefs that "the War Planning Team [presumably those who had worked on CPS 83] considered that implications of not carrying out the Akyab-Ramree operations would have serious effects." They felt the project was essential to secure Imphal and to protect Ledo. And General Arnold observed that the only way proper air support could be provided for Moulmein operations was from Ramree. The Joint Chiefs decided to request a closed session of the Combined Chiefs of Staff to discuss their recommendation on CCS 313, but at the next meeting matters took a different turn.[93]

In the form of a progress report for the President and Prime Minister the British Chiefs of Staff submitted for consideration a memorandum covering all the general points that had been brought out in reference to the war against Japan.[94] It included all those on which agreement had been reached, and either attempted to compromise on those still at issue or postponed any decision at all. It also assumed agreement on some non-controversial matters of which the minutes record no discussion. Since the paper was accepted with only a few alterations and served as the basis for the final report to the chiefs of state, it is well to examine it in detail.

The Combined Chiefs of Staff had concluded that "the dependence of Japan upon air power and shipping for maintaining her position in the Pacific and Southeast Asia," the consequent need of "applying the maximum attrition" to those two factors, and the advantage that might be gained and the time saved by more extensive use of the superior air resources at the disposal of the United Nations required particular emphasis. As general principles these were not likely to be disputed. There was no attempt to indicate how best they might be emphasized.

Next came a paragraph covering the unconventional types of warfare which had been discussed:

> The Combined Chiefs of Staff consider that great advantage can be obtained by modern and untried methods from the vast resources which, with the defeat of Germany, will become available to the United Nations. They have in mind:
>
> *a.* A project rapidly to expand and extend the striking power of the United Nations air forces in China as well as of the ground troops for their defense by employing the large numbers of load carrying aircraft available to open an 'air road' to China without waiting for the opening of the Burma Road proper.

The last phrase was removed in subsequent revision of the paper, and it may probably be assumed that it was done at the insistence of the U.S. Chiefs because of the implication that opening the Burma Road was not a major objective.

The paragraph continued:

> *b.* The reconquest of areas in Southeast Asia by the employment of lightly equipped jungle forces, dependent entirely upon air supply lines.
>
> *c.* The use of special equipment such as artificial harbors, Habbakuks etc.,[95] to enable the superior power of the United Nations to be deployed in unexpected and undeveloped areas.
>
> Although from every point of view operations should be framed to force the defeat of Japan as soon as possible after the defeat of Germany - even within twelve months of that event - decisions which will insure a much more rapid course of events than that envisaged in the plan laid before us must await further examination on the lines indicated above.

Sir Charles Portal expressed opposition to the U.S. view that planning should proceed on the basis of defeating Japan within twelve months after the defeat of Germany. He felt that would be too restrictive, particularly since the planners had concluded that the campaign against Japan would take four or five years. Moreover, he thought it might result in withdrawing forces prematurely from the European Theater. General Marshall, however, argued for the provision, for he "felt that we were under necessity of pressing for as expeditious a way as possible of forcing an issue and bringing the war to a successful conclusion." Naturally it should be up to the Combined Chiefs of Staff to decide when resources would be taken from the European Theater. Planning for an early victory seemed to him to have psychological value also, for he thought that by prescribing twelve months "military thought would be spurred on and given every incentive to devise the best ways and means of bringing the war with Japan to a successful conclusion as early as possible." The British gave in on the point and the phrase between dashes was changed to a declarative sentence, "Planning should be on the basis of accomplishing this within twelve months of that event." This apparently was one point on which the views of the British Chiefs were not coordinated with those of the Prime Minister, for when the report was submitted to him and the President, Mr. Churchill singled out this point as one he was glad to see and one that "discouraged planning on the basis of a long war of attrition."[96]

In respect to the forces to be used in the war against Japan, three points were made. Forces should be deployed in accordance with the over-all objective and strategic concept defined at Trident. Reorientation from the European Theater to the Pacific should be started as soon as the Combined Chiefs of Staff thought the situation allowed. (Again, a qualifying phrase, "without necessarily waiting for an armistice," was removed in revision.) Forces in the east were to be provided by the United States, and forces in the west by Great Britain, except for special types which the United States would furnish. Use of Dominion forces would be discussed by all governments concerned.

At this point the British memorandum began to set aside for further discussion problems on which agreement had not been reached:

> The Combined Chiefs of Staff are convinced that the issues raised in the plan...that had been submitted are so large and complicated that it would be impracticable to arrive at all the necessary decisions for operations in the war against Japan in 1943-44 during the few days of Quadrant which remain. They therefore propose that, as soon as the necessary further examinations have been made, a Combined Chiefs of Staff Conference should be held wherever may be most convenient, unless agreement is reached through ordinary channels.

There were certain matters on which the chiefs "felt able" to make decisions at once. First, they approved the U.S. proposals for operations in the Pacific in 1943-1944.[97] However, the British Chiefs, still not convinced that the operations in the Southwest Pacific were essential, recommended a qualification which read, "it being understood that the operations in New Guinea will be kept constantly under review to ensure that the results likely to be obtained are commensurate with the effort involved." To this the U.S. Chiefs objected, saying that this would be done in any case, and, if General MacArthur were told of the action, "it would have a disheartening effect upon him, which would merely add to the disappointment he has already suffered owing to resources asked for and being refused to him." The British "had no idea that this particular report would be forwarded to General MacArthur," but they agreed to removal of the qualification.

The second point in agreement was that operations would be carried out to recapture upper Burma "in order to improve the air route and establish overland communications with China." The extent of the operations would be dependent on the effect of the recent floods. The U.S. Chiefs made an unsuccessful attempt to remove the last reservation, presumably fearing that it might afford an "out." But the British Chiefs reported that they had had telegrams which "left no conclusion possible but that the floods would to some degree, at least, affect the operations planned....they felt it their duty to make this clear to the President and Prime Minister."

The third point was stated indefinitely as, "To continue preparations for an amphibious operation in the spring of 1944 on the scale already contemplated." In order that there should be no misunderstanding on this, the U.S. Chiefs insisted that the operation should be identified as the capture of Akyab and Ramree. The record does not indicate that the British Chiefs objected to this addition, but Sir Charles Portal did ask why the U.S. Chiefs thought the capture of Akyab was essential in the spring of 1944. Admiral Leahy explained that they believed that if the Japanese were in Akyab they could flank the operations in northern Burma. General Arnold said he thought the Akyab operations would draw enemy troops away from north Burma. Moreover, he said, it would be a base from which to attack Rangoon and the line of communications to Burma. Both Sir Charles Portal and Sir Alan Brooke said they had never thought that Akyab's capture was essential to the north Burma campaign, especially in view of the terrain between. They proposed that the operation be carefully studied before any commitment was made, in order to be sure that it was clearly necessary. Thus the U.S. Chiefs of Staff failed to get a firm agreement to execute the operation, but they did keep the subject open for further study.

One other point was included on the list of agreed decisions. It, too, was indefinite, but no attempt seems to have been made to change the statement: "To continue the preparation of India as a base for the operations eventually contemplated in the Southeast Asia Command."

The problems on which no decision had been reached were all on a list of studies to be prepared after the conference. These included the two conflicting projects, Sumatra, with a target date of spring 1944, and operations southward from north Burma, with a target date of November 1944. As alternatives, "the feasibility and desirability" of attacking through the Moulmein area or the Kra Isthmus toward Bangkok or through the Malacca Straits and Malaya to take Singapore were to be studied. Finally, on the assumption that Germany was defeated in the fall of 1944 a study was to be made of the "potentialities and limitations" of the air route to China, expanded to use all the heavy bomber and transport aircraft likely to be available thereafter.

At the next meeting the Combined Chiefs of Staff approved construction of a four-inch pipeline from Assam to Kunming and a six-inch pipeline from Calcutta to Assam.[98] They also agreed that the main effort from India should go into offensive operations to open land communications with China and improve the air route, but that these priorities were not rigid and the new Supreme Commander should keep in mind the importance of long-term development of the lines of communication. With no further significant changes the whole paper became a part of the final report to the President and the Prime Minister.[99]

Mr. Soong was invited to the final meeting of the Combined Chiefs on 24 August 1943 and given a report of the conference decisions, well couched in generalities. He was told of the pipeline and the estimated capacity of the Ledo Road (65,000 tons). Sir Alan Brooke carefully avoided saying how many British troops could be expected to participate in the proposed operations in Burma, indicating that the number was dependent upon the effect of the floods on the line of communications through Assam. Similarly, in respect to the date for starting the advance, he revealed only that it was later than originally envisaged. Moreover, when questioned about the amphibious operations which the Generalissimo had always wanted in Burma, Sir Alan Brooke said only that the amphibious assault "was to take place from India and would have a direct bearing on operations in Burma and Western China." However, both Admiral Leahy and General Marshall stressed the importance of Chinese cooperation. "Only thus could success be achieved and without it all our efforts would be futile."

In addition to this meeting of Mr. Soong with the Combined Chiefs of Staff and an earlier conference he had with the President and the Prime Minister, at the conclusion of Quadrant the chiefs of state reported the general decisions in respect to China-Burma-India directly to Generalissimo Chiang Kai-shek.[100] Presented as "proposals that have been advanced as to operations in your theaters and areas contiguous thereto" were: (1) acceleration of the buildup of the air freight route into China; (2) improvement of the lines of communication from Calcutta to Assam; (3) an attack from Assam into Burma in the coming dry season, via Imphal and Ledo, coordinated with an advance from Yunnan, all preceded by long range penetration groups, and (4) amphibious attacks against an undetermined objective. The Generalissimo was not told that the decision to execute the campaign in north Burma and the requirements to improve the line of communications into Assam would probably result in temporary reduction of the deliveries by air lift into China. Nor was the need for cooperation stressed as it had been to Mr. Soong. Only in connection with the announcement of the appointment of Lord Mountbatten was Chiang told that it was hoped that the new command would produce unity in the combined effort in Burma, unity which "must be achieved if success is to be attained."

PRACTICABILITY OF THE DECISIONS

As had been the case at Trident one of the last things to be discussed at Quadrant was whether or not there would be enough available to carry out all the operations on which agreement had been reached. The Combined Staff Planners had conducted fairly extensive studies of availabilities, which they presented in a series of annexes and appendices to a paper in which they concluded that in most respects requirements could be met.[101] There would be enough ground troops for operations from the United Kingdom, in the Mediterranean, and in the Pacific, but "searching investigations" were still being made to determine whether or not requisite forces for north Burma could be found by mid-February 1944. Naval forces would be on hand for everything but Bullfrog, the attack on Akyab and Ramree. It had already been estimated at Trident that the United States would have to provide certain naval forces for that operation.[102] The Quadrant study still indicated that the British would be unable to furnish them all, being short one escort carrier (at Trident they had asked for five, plus two fleet carriers), twenty-one destroyers, eight escorts, and six submarines. There was no indication that the deficit would be made up by the United States. As a matter of fact, it was stated in the annex that operations in the Central Pacific would probably occupy all U.S. naval forces. As for air forces, these too were available for everything, except for a possible deficiency that might arise in the Pacific if additional resources were not made available by conclusion of the war with Germany, and subject to using only allocated air resources in the Mediterranean Theater. Assault shipping and landing craft would be in adequate supply until the summer of 1944, but the planners cautioned that they would be "the bottleneck limiting the full scope of assault in the approved operations." Shipping, long the controlling factor in strategic planning, was now loosened up, and the planners reported that, except for a small deficit in the Pacific, to be met by the end of the first quarter of 1944, there was enough personnel shipping to meet known requirements, and careful operation should assure sufficient cargo shipping for "all essential commitments." There was no consideration, however, of auxiliaries, depot, and repair ships which would be needed by the British Navy in the area of Southeast Asia.

AIR PLAN FOR THE DEFEAT OF JAPAN

Mention should be made of one more paper that was introduced at the Quadrant Conference, for it marked the beginning of combined recognition of a new factor in the war against Japan. This was a study prepared by the Air Forces planners and submitted by General Arnold via the Joint Chiefs of Staff to the Combined Chiefs of Staff.[103] Under the title, "Air Plan for the Defeat of Japan," the paper discussed employment of the very long range bombers, the B-29's, soon to be available for operation. The air planners who had prepared the paper had arrived at the conclusion that

> The destruction of Japanese resources to such a point that the enemy's capacity for effective armed resistance is substantially exhausted can be accomplished by sustained bombing operations of 10-20 B-29 groups based in an area of Unoccupied China within 1500 miles of the center of the Japanese industrial zone.

The details of the plan will not be discussed until later in this section, for, in accordance with the paper's own recommendations, the Combined Chiefs of Staff agreed to refer it to the Combined Staff Planners for study, requesting "an appropriate report" not later than 15 September 1943.[104]

CONCLUSION

The last meeting of the Combined Chiefs of Staff at Quadrant was held on 24 August 1943, ten days after the first. From the U.S. point of view the sum total of the discussions of the war with Japan was that the desired program for operations in the Pacific area in 1943-1944 had been given combined approval, and "operations for the capture of Upper Burma" had been agreed to, with a target date of mid-February 1944 instead of November 1943, subject to the limiting effect of floods whose extent was still undetermined and to an increase in the capacity of the line of communications to Assam. A Supreme Commander, Southeast Asia, had been selected and the outline of his organization agreed to. Buildup of the air supply route to China, given first priority at Trident, was to be continued, but the main effort was to be put into the offensive operations on the ground in north Burma. The amphibious operations in southern Burma had not been abandoned, but neither had they been approved. They, like various potential alternatives, were subject to later decision. In short, the Quadrant Conference had not decisively resolved the strategical problems of the combined areas of the Far East.

Chapter XIX

THE FALL OF 1943: QUADRANT - SEXTANT

    During the period between the Quadrant Conference and the next combined meetings, held in late November and early December at Cairo and Teheran, developments in strategic planning followed closely the pattern that had been drawn between Trident and Quadrant. Like Trident, Quadrant concluded with an agreement to meet soon again and carry on with the continuing problems that awaited operational developments and with those on which only tentative decisions had been reached. Thus, shortly after the return of the Joint Chiefs of Staff from Quebec, preparations were begun for the next conference even as the first moves were made to implement the Quadrant decisions. Again the joint staff prepared a series of papers for background or for presentation to the British when the two groups met. As before these included plans for extending operations in the Pacific, to which the British would be expected to give almost routine approval. Both joint and combined groups of planners considered anew the larger problem of strategy aimed at achieving the final defeat of Japan. The important developments related to both of these came during during the autumn months and neither would be a matter for lengthy consideration at Cairo. As in the past it would be the British plans for operations in Southeast Asia and the role of Burma, China, and India in the war against Japan that would evoke extensive discussion when the combined groups reconvened.

EMPLOYMENT OF BRITISH NAVAL FORCES

    Prime Minister Churchill remained for a time in Canada after the conclusion of Quadrant and then proceeded to Washington for a stay at the White House. During his visit in the U.S. capital the surrender of Italy was announced. The following day, 9 September 1943, the Italian battle fleet sought refuge at the British port of Malta. Acquisition of these vessels and the concurrent release of British vessels from the necessity of watching them in the Mediterranean offered the United Nations a new source of naval power, which Mr. Churchill immediately brought to the attention of his associates. This was the first serious move by the British to participate with a sizable force in the war in the Pacific.
    At noon on 9 September the Prime Minister summoned General Marshall to the White House and presented him with a memorandum

on the strategic situation resulting from Italy's collapse, indicating that he intended to discuss it with the President and the Combined Chiefs of Staff late that afternoon.[1]

Mr. Churchill's paper turned at once to the question of naval forces.

> Assuming we get the Italian Fleet, we gain not only that fleet, but the British Fleet, which has hitherto contained it. This very heavy addition to our naval power should be used at the earliest possible moment to intensify the war against Japan. I have asked the First Sea Lord to discuss with Admiral King the movement of a powerful British battle squadron, with cruisers and ancillaries, to the Indian Ocean via the Panama Canal and the Pacific. We need a strong Eastern Fleet based on Colombo during the amphibious operations next year. I should be very glad if it were found possible for this fleet to serve under the American Pacific Command and put in at least four months of useful fighting in the Pacific before taking up its Indian Ocean station. We cannot afford to have idle ships. I do not know however how the arrival of such reinforcements would enable the various tasks assigned to United States forces in the Pacific to be augmented. Apart from strategy, from the standpoint of high policy His Majesty's Government would desire to participate in the Pacific war in order to give such measure of assistance as is in their power, not only to their American Allies, but on account of the obligations to Australia and New Zealand. Such a movement of our ships to and through the Pacific would undoubtedly exercise a demoralising effect upon Japan, who must now be conscious of the very great addition of naval weight thrust against her, and besides this it would surely give satisfaction in the United States as being a proof positive of British resolve to take an active and vigorous part to end in the war against Japan.

Admiral King at least was not impressed with the proffered "proof positive," for as the Joint Chiefs of Staff talked together before proceeding to the White House to discuss the memorandum with the two heads of state he remarked that as he saw it, "no useful purpose would be served by the employment of the British units in the Pacific."[2] It would be the responsibility of the U.S. Navy to find occupation for these vessels and to provide logistic support while they were in the Pacific. This prospect seemed to him fraught with problems far outweighing any advantages to be gained. He had already heard of the project from the Prime Minister and requested comments from naval commanders in the Pacific, although the idea was decidedly unattractive to him. He pointed out, for example, that the British did not plan to send enough destroyers to safeguard the larger vessels (three or four battleships and three or four cruisers). The ships were too heavy for use in the narrow waters around Rabaul, whose neutralization was to be completed during this period. In any case the vessels were not needed, for the United States already had fourteen modern battleships as well as eight older ones. Support of an additional naval force of such proportions would be a strain on the trooplift supply at a time when personnel shipping was already scarce. On the one hand, Admiral King doubted that there would be any considerable fleet action for the vessels to participate in during the three or four months they would be there; on the other, he feared that they might just go to Australia and New Zealand, "stay in port and show the flag," thereby complicating the logistic problem considerably. Admiral King would be delighted, he said, to have the British Fleet go out to the Bay of Bengal. He could see no reason why the ships should not go to Colombo by the way of the Pacific, but he did not want them staying east of the Java Sea for any length of time.

Admiral Leahy was inclined to favor the project or at least to seek some useful purpose in such a visit. He suggested that the British ships might relieve some U.S. forces, or some might be sent to General MacArthur and used in that area rather than in the Pacific Ocean Areas. To this Admiral King replied that he could not see how they would be of much use in the short time they would be there, and once they were detached the chiefs might expect requests from General MacArthur for replacements. General Marshall seems to have been almost neutral on the matter, although his staff had reported to him favorably on it.[3] He raised several questions to Admiral King and accepted his comments without argument. These were all expressions of opinion without decisions, for the chiefs suspected that in any case they might "have their hands forced in this matter."

Late that afternoon, when the Combined Chiefs met with the President and the Prime Minister, they found Mr. Roosevelt enthusiastic about the use of British ships in the Pacific, even beyond what Mr. Churchill had proposed. Cautioning the Chiefs of Staff to consider the political implications of sending forces released from Europe at once to join the war against Japan, the President went so far as to suggest that "with the help of British naval vessels it might be possible to use all four routes to Japan: that from the Kuriles, the middle route by Hawaii, a third route by the Marshall Islands, and a fourth route northward from the Solomons. He appreciated, however, that logistical considerations might prevent full utilization of such vessels as the British Navy could make available."

The Prime Minister did not echo the President's enthusiastic suggestion for extensive use of British naval forces in the Pacific, a suggestion which must have made more than one of the Combined Chiefs of Staff gasp inwardly at the revisions of plans and the tremendous logistic problems involved. Admiral King quickly picked up Mr. Roosevelt's last remark, added the comment that weather was a limiting factor in increasing the naval strength in the Pacific, and pointed out the need for an adequate destroyer complement for escort purposes. He agreed, however, that it would be "entirely feasible for that part of the British Navy released from the Mediterranean to proceed to its station in the Indian Ocean via the Panama Canal and the Pacific."[4]

There was no decision on the matter at this meeting, and the Combined Chiefs were directed to look into it further and report to the Prime Minister before he left.

Mr. Churchill's memorandum was turned over to the Combined Staff Planners in time for a meeting at 2045 the same evening.[5] There was not much discussion, for at Admiral Cooke's suggestion it was agreed that the two basic problems, the movement of a British squadron to the Far East and the aftermath of Italian surrender, should be referred to subcommittees. Admiral Cooke did most of the talking, saying little that was new beyond expressing "some doubt about the degree of usefulness of a British squadron operating in the Bay of Bengal next winter" and making the interesting, if vague, observation that "when we were ready to employ all of our forces against the Japanese, a British fleet operating from the New Hebrides could be very helpful."

The subcommittees went right to work on the report and had it ready at 0800 the next morning for review by the Combined Staff Planners, who in turn amended it in some particulars and passed it on to the Combined Chiefs of Staff in time for their special meeting at 1100.[6]

The planners had stressed the two major drawbacks to using British naval forces in the Pacific, the necessity that the group sent should be a balanced unit and not require destroyers from the U.S. Pacific Fleet, and the formidable task of supporting a large British force for a protracted period. Assuming that these obstacles could be overcome, the planners recommended that the best use that could be made of a British squadron in the Pacific would be in support of the Solomon Islands-New Britain-New Guinea operations, pointing out that the British ships might divert Japanese forces from the Gilberts-Marshalls area and that their presence in that region would have beneficial political effects on Australia and New Zealand. The planners also assumed that some British submarines could be released from the Mediterranean and prove useful in the Java Sea and off the Malayan coast.

The Combined Chiefs of Staff recognized that the final word could not be given without further study of the problems involved. After some discussion General Sir Hastings Ismay went to work on a draft memorandum for the Prime Minister which he presented to the CCS for comment later in the meeting.[7] The Combined Chiefs agreed that it was "most desirable that a powerful British battle squadron should proceed at the earliest possible date to the Indian Ocean via the Panama Canal and the Pacific," but their hearty acceptance of Mr. Churchill's project was considerably restricted by their directives to the British Admiralty and the U.S. Navy Department to look into the balanced composition of the squadron, the date on which it would sail, and how it would be used in the Pacific. The chiefs' report was acceptable to the Prime Minister, who announced that the Admiralty had indicated that the ships would have to be refitted anyway and given more anti-aircraft before they could be sent to the Pacific. Despite all obstacles, however, Mr. Churchill remained convinced that the principle was a good one and "that the difficulties would be overcome."[8] Still it was to be some time before British naval vessels contributed significantly to the war in the Pacific.

PLANS FOR THE GILBERTS AND MARSHALLS

Preparations for offensive operations in the Pacific Theater were being rushed as the Quadrant meetings ended. Forces were already assembling for the attack on the Gilbert Islands and Nauru for which the Joint Chiefs of Staff had issued a directive on 20 July 1943.[9] At the same time Admiral Nimitz's planners were working on "outline plans for follow-up operations to capture, occupy, defend and develop bases in the Marshalls about 1 January 1944." Upon the chiefs' return from Quebec they found the theater plan had arrived in Washington and the Joint Staff Planners were ready to present it with comments at the first post-Quadrant meeting of the Joint Chiefs of Staff.[10]

In summary the theater plan was this:

   (a) Simultaneous seizure of key islands on the KWAJALEIN, WOTJE, and MALOELAP atolls, followed at once by the reduction of the remainder of the islands of those atolls.
   (b) Contain and neutralize JALUIT and MILLE.
   (c) Mount operation both from OAHU and South Pacific bases.
   (d) Use ELLICE and GILBERT positions as staging points.
   (e) Employ NAURU, GILBERT positions, and BAKER for photographic reconnaissance, search, and for repeated air strikes to soften up the MARSHALLS.
   (f) Target date 1 January 1944.

Information about the Marshalls was still inadequate, however, and until photographic reconnaissance was obtained the objectives and the plan for attacking them would have to remain tentative.

The scope of this operation was narrower than the planners in Washington thought proper, for the breakdown of Pacific operations in the final decision at Quadrant had included Wake and Kusaie with the Marshalls as it had Nauru with the Gilberts.[11] Extension of action to those islands, lying strictly speaking outside the Marshall group, and to Eniwetok, which lies between Wake and Kusaie, would place U.S. forces in position to carry on to the Carolines and the Marianas rather than, as in the Pacific theater plan, simply consolidating a position in the center of the Marshall Islands. Incidentally, inclusion of the additional objectives would push the advance that much closer to the Western Pacific without the complications of issuing another directive. So to the proposed directive that had accompanied the theater plan the Joint Staff Planners added a task to follow or accompany the capture and consolidation of bases in the Marshalls, "seize or control Wake, Eniwetok, and Kusaie."

As it had been for so long, the availability of an adequate supply of shipping was a significant factor in planning the Marshalls operation. Of the estimated forces required, the Joint Staff Planners questioned only the provision of enough amphibious assault vessels. Barring losses it appeared that there would be a shortage in the Central Pacific on 1 January 1944 of nine APA's and ten AKA's. There was a prospect that some of the deficit would be made up from training forces in the Atlantic, and additional ships could be transferred from the South and the Southwest Pacific on 1 December. Substitution of other types of ships would further ease the situation. Apparently the Navy planners were satisfied that these measures would provide enough in time. The Army planners, however, insisted that the assigned target date of 1 January 1944, "contingent upon the successful completion of the Gilbert operations," be made contingent also "upon the availability of shipping."

Here was a potential conflict of demands between operations in the Marshalls and operations in the South-Southwest Pacific (Cartwheel), where the final steps before neutralization of Rabaul (seizure of western New Britain and Kieta on Bougainville and neutralization of Buka) were scheduled for 1 December 1943. As Admiral King pointed out, if the Joint Chiefs did not decide at once which operation was to have priority on the available shipping, they would have to do so eventually. The implication of the Army's proposed phrase was that the operation in the Marshalls "might be postponed until the necessary shipping could be made available from something else." Admiral King was in favor of making 1 January a firm target date for the Marshalls, possibly cutting back on operations in the Southwest Pacific Area.

Admiral Cooke informed the group that the Marshalls operation could be done all right if Cartwheel were successfully completed and enough combat loaders were made available from that operation. Perhaps all nine of the APA's would not be needed. There was an additional possibility that certain ships might be made available instead from Italian sources after the surrender details were worked out. Admiral Cooke was firm that postponement of the target date for the Marshalls to 15 January "would be bad as far as the...buildup was concerned," but the record does not make clear what aspects of it he had in mind.

General Marshall apparently did not see the urgency of the earlier target date as strongly as did the naval officers, but he accepted the assurances of the planners that it could be met if Cartwheel were finished on time. Recognizing, too, the desirability of giving Admiral Nimitz a firm date for planning, he agreed to removal of the qualication proposed by the Army planners.

Accordingly Admiral Nimitz was directed to prepare to take the Marshalls, Wake, Kusaie, and Eniwetok with a target date of

1 January 1944, assuming "continuance of currently planned Cartwheel operations and that post-Cartwheel operations will be initiated about February 1944 for further advances in New Guinea and against New Ireland and the Admiralty Islands."[12]

Establishment of the target date for the Marshalls operation was not the final word on the availability of shipping. General Marshall was struck with the large amount for which the plan called, larger than that used by Lieutenant General George Patton for landing 34,000 troops in Torch. Accordingly he recommended that the Joint Staff Planners be directed to study the effect the operations in the Central Pacific would have on other troop movements and operations in other areas of the Pacific.[13] The other chiefs had no objection, and the study was made.

There was no problem with cargo shipping, but personnel shipping was scarce. Admiral Nimitz's plan called for the use of nine AP's between October and February. Their absence from other projects in the Pacific would be increasingly felt, but a program for converting certain cargo vessels to troop transports, recently recommended by the Joint Military Transportation Committee (JMTC), was expected to provide replacements soon. No material interference with scheduled operations was anticipated.[14] This appraisal by the planners satisfied the Joint Chiefs, who accepted the report and pursued the subject no further.[15]

Completion of the operations in the Gilberts still remained a condition on the target date for the Marshalls of 1 January 1944. As was the case with most of the islands of the vast Pacific, scant geographical information about the Gilberts was available before war broke. In order to obtain more and to ascertain the extent to which the Japanese had fortified the islands, photographic reconnaissance planes were early sent out over the area. The results of their work and reports of a British engineer who had lived on Nauru Island some time previously convinced the amphibious commanders in the Pacific that an entire division would be required to wrest Nauru from the Japanese, for its physical contour alone was a strong defense. Consequently Admiral Nimitz recommended to the Joint Chiefs of Staff that Nauru not be taken, predicting that the assault would "involve losses of personnel and material and a logistic burden which outweigh advantages." He proposed substituting Makin Island, north rather than west of the Gilberts, closer to the Marshalls, and apparently within the capability of available forces.[16]

Admiral Nimitz's recommendation arrived in Washington with the prior approval of Admiral King, who was in Pearl Harbor at the time. Colonel Roberts of Army OPD reported to General Marshall that the only apparent disadvantage in substituting Makin would be that it was not close enough to Ponape for air reconnaissance. But either Bougainville or Buka was near enough for that. So was Tarawa, first objective in the Gilberts, provided the air strip already known to be there was lengthened. General Arnold was concerned about giving up Nauru, where air facilities were already installed, for Makin, "with only potential air base capacities, especially since the latter action includes the possibility of losses to our fleet from the Japanese land-based air forces from bases in the Marshalls." General Marshall reported his comment to Admiral King, but officially the War Department concurred in the substitution, and Admiral Nimitz proceeded with plans for the new objective.[17]

By the end of October studies made in preparation for the two operations in the Central Pacific convinced Admiral Nimitz that he could not be ready to move into the Marshalls on the target date of 1 January 1944 without curtailing troop training and the rehabilitation of ships used in the Gilberts campaign to an extent that would jeopardize the success of the Marshalls operation.[18] Consequently he recommended that the target date be changed to 31 January, with the recognition that if excessive battle damage were sustained in the Gilberts the attack might have to be postponed still further.

Upon receipt in Washington of Admiral Nimitz's recommendation for delay, the members of the Joint War Plans Committee investigated the matter. They decided that although the month's lag in the momentum of the Central Pacific program would extend the vulnerability of the Gilberts to attack from bases in the Marshalls and provide opportunity for the Japanese to improve their defenses, the disadvantages involved in the delay were outweighed by the advantages of more adequate preparation for the Marshalls campaign. The planners also pointed out that the date closer to the target date for the advance against Wewak in New Guinea (1 February) would permit a greater degree of mutual support between the two operations. They recommended approval of the new target date of 31 January 1944 for the Marshall campaign.[19]

Through the Joint Staff Planners the recommendation was forwarded to the Joint Chiefs of Staff, and a paper was circulated informally for approval of the four members.[20] Admiral Leahy, Admiral King, and General Arnold were in favor of accepting the postponement, but General Marshall suggested that instead of agreeing outright to a delay of thirty days they should aim for an earlier date and direct initiation of the operation "as soon as possible after 1 January 1944." "It was the duty of the Joint Chiefs of Staff," he said, "in judging such matters, to decide the relation between urgency and perfection." Admiral King agreed with this suggestion and himself proposed the additional phrase, "and not later than 31 January 1944," in order to safeguard against a further postponement. So the Marshalls campaign was scheduled for some time in the first month of 1944, and Admiral Nimitz was reminded by Admiral King "that you will spare no effort to speed up training and other preparations, and thus get on with the war."[21]

JOINT COMMAND IN THE PACIFIC

Inauguration of a campaign in the Central Pacific Area inevitably involved creation of new forces and new commands and expansion of the staff of Admiral Nimitz. There had been dissatisfaction in the Army over the original assignment of Admiral Nimitz to the dual position of Commander in Chief, Pacific Ocean Areas, and Commander in Chief, Pacific Fleet. The disproportionate representation of Army officers on his staff became of more significance than it had previously been as operations in the Marshalls and Gilberts presented requirements for larger numbers of Army troops.

Late in June 1943 Admiral King suggested to General Marshall that, in order to reduce uneconomical uses of personnel and make more assault troops available for operations in the Central Pacific, Army troops be sent to relieve some 9,000 Marine Corps troops currently assigned to garrison duty on the islands of Tutuila, Wallis, Upolu, and Palmyra, all far removed from action.[22] In further preparation for opening up the Central Pacific he suggested to General Marshall that additional Army officers should be attached to the staff of the Commander in Chief, Pacific Fleet, and to a new Central Pacific Force which would have to be established for the operations then projected for the Marshalls. His recommendation was limited, however, to two colonels or lieutenant colonels, one ground and one air, for each staff.[23] It was mid-July when General Marshall's formal reply was sent, apparently after some informal discussion of the command situation in the Pacific.[24] General Marshall recommended that the requirements of the rear area bases for garrisoning should be examined before Army forces were indiscriminately tied down there and that the redistribution of the forces in the Pacific should be a function of Admiral Nimitz and his staff. This led General Marshall to point out that Admiral Nimitz had under his command in the Central and South Pacific about 300,000 Army troops, 80,000 Marines, and 80,000 to 100,000 shore based naval personnel. Preliminary action toward supplying him with a joint staff by assigning a few Army officers to it did not seem sufficient to General Marshall, for in his view it was "superimposed, somewhat as an excrescency, on the Pacific Fleet Staff." So he proposed that Admiral Nimitz be relieved of command of the Pacific Fleet, established as a Theater Commander, and provided "with the least practicable delay" with a "complete operational joint staff."

About ten days before this Admiral King had suggested to the Pacific Fleet commander that some change in his command setup might be desirable.[25] Admiral King had pointed out that the expansion of operations in the Pacific would mean large increases in forces and require over-all coordination by the Commander in Chief, Pacific Ocean Areas, distinct from the purely naval functions of the Commander in Chief, Pacific Fleet. Admiral King sought comment from Admiral Nimitz on the desirability of establishing a distinction between the staff work done for him in his two capacities and on the relationship between the over-all command of the Pacific Ocean Areas and the commands of the three areas that comprised it.

Admiral Nimitz had seen little to recommend a division between his two staffs.[26] It would, he pointed out, require more staff officers, slow down business, require more files and more space, and tend to grow in size. The only advantage he could see was that it would facilitate a change if expanding operations should require the establishment of commands subordinate to the Commander in Chief, Pacific Fleet, and the Commander in Chief, Pacific Ocean Areas, for any specific purpose. It would also be useful if the former should decide to go afloat. He recommended that his "span of control" as Commander in Chief, Pacific Fleet, should not be increased but rather decreased "by appointing officers who in turn will command several subordinates now on the same echelon of command." This led him to recommend the appointment of a Commander, Central Pacific, and some expansion of his current planning staff instead of a two-staff organization.

In replying to General Marshall, Admiral King took cognizance of the remarks of the Pacific Fleet commander. He agreed that the expansion of activities in the Pacific Ocean Areas might well make it necessary to relieve Admiral Nimitz from his duties as commander of the fleet.[27] However, he reminded General Marshall that "the command area in the PACIFIC OCEAN AREAS was set up by the Joint Chiefs of Staff, with full cognizance that he was also the Commander in Chief, Pacific Fleet." Up to that time the setup had been working well and, Admiral King thought, "utilized our best talent to the best advantage." He preferred to let things remain as they were until some change became really necessary.

The War Department, however, was hearing from Army personnel of inadequacies in the Nimitz staff arrangements and displeasure over the lack of a strong joint headquarters command.[28] General Marshall's reaction to Admiral King's reminder that the Joint Chiefs of Staff had set up Admiral Nimitz's command that way was to recommend that the directive be changed and that Admiral Nimitz be made a theater commander with full responsibility for the Central and the South Pacific Areas.[29]

To strengthen his case General Marshall obtained from General Eisenhower, then Commander in Chief, Allied Forces in Europe, and American Theater Commander, a description of that staff organization, which he presented to Admiral King to illustrate what he meant when he advocated a similar joint staff for Admiral Nimitz in a Pacific Theater.[30] Unfortunately for General Marshall's argument, an analysis of General Eisenhower's staff organization indicated that not only was his own position complicated, and not only did he have direct command of ground forces, but his staff showed a predominance of ground officers and relatively little naval and air representation. It was hardly convincing evidence that Admiral Nimitz's commands should be separated and he be made a theater commander.

The anxiety of the War Department for a joint command arrangement in the Pacific did achieve some results. Early in September Admiral King sent to Admiral Nimitz an outline drawn by the Navy planners of the process of planning the Pacific war campaign and a draft plan for a joint staff, explaining, "I plan to keep command of the Pacific Fleet and the command of the Pacific Ocean Areas vested in one person, - you. However, I have been pressed by Marshall for some months to separate the two and set up a joint staff that would give the Army a greater participation in the direction of the PACIFIC Campaign. This diagram for command and staff set-up are [sic] efforts by the Plans Division to compose the conflicting aspects of this problem."[31] But Admiral Nimitz had already taken steps and decided to form a joint staff under a Deputy Commander in Chief, Pacific Ocean Areas (he requested a vice admiral), and a Chief of Joint Staff. It was to have four divisions, two of which, plans and operations, would be headed by naval officers; an Army officer would head logistics and Admiral Nimitz requested another for the intelligence division.[32] General Marshall was "gratified" when informed of the new organization, but he continued to feel that Admiral Nimitz should be a theater commander and made "responsible for operations, including logistical support, of all Army and Naval forces in the North, Central and South Pacific Areas."[33] With Admiral Nimitz's own arrangements, however, the matter rested.

THE NORTH PACIFIC AREA

The main tide of advance in the Pacific was to be in the Central and Southwest Pacific Areas; but there were sizable U.S. forces deployed in the North Pacific Area also. After Kiska was occupied on 15 October 1943 came the question of what was to be done next. It was apparent that the Japanese had abandoned the Aleutians and consequently the defense force should be reduced. The problem was whether the advantage then held in the area should be exploited by pushing on to Paramushiru and down into Hokkaido, northernmost of the islands of Japan. For some time there had been talk of such a project and a general feeling that in an indefinite future it would be desirable. Now that the danger that Japan would attempt to wreak havoc with an advance in force in the reverse direction seemed past, a successful campaign against Paramushiru and the Kuriles began to appear possible. It would be a large operation, however, and require considerable preparation and a large amount of troops and supplies. Proportionate cutbacks would have to be made in the other campaigns already scheduled for the areas of the Pacific.

While the Joint Chiefs of Staff were at Quebec in August 1943 Admiral King suggested that, since "there had not been much trouble with Kiska, the possibility might now be considered of going on into Paramushiru."[34] Oddly enough General Marshall was hesitant about the operation because he thought it "a rather formidable naval proposition." There was also the question which General Handy mentioned of adequate bases in the Aleutians and Alaska from which to launch an attack on Paramushiru, and of shipping availabilities, raised by General Somervell. The discussion turned away from the campaign in the Kuriles to the size of the garrison forces that should be maintained in the Aleutians. Admiral King took the lead in this matter also, suggesting that Attu was overgarrisoned, that if the Japanese had actually left the Aleutians fewer troops would be needed there, and "that the chief thing to do was to get Central Pacific operations rolling as soon as possible." Perhaps, said General Marshall, the 7th Division could be removed from Kiska to "help out towards improving the target date in the Central Pacific." There was no further talk of Paramushiru and only on the last matter did the chiefs take action, directing the Joint Staff Planners to look into the possibilities of moving the 7th Division to the Central Pacific in shipping then available in the Aleutians. In the fall the transfer was made, and the 7th Division participated the following February in the attack on Kwajalein in the Marshalls.[35]

The Quadrant decisions left the way open for "consideration of operations against Paramushiru and the Kuriles."[36] Lieutenant General John L. DeWitt, Commanding General, Western Defense Command, in a letter that arrived in Washington early in August, had recommended such action for April or May 1944,[37] and the members of the Joint War Plans Committee considered his views as they studied the problem as one of their post-Quadrant assignments. Before they had developed a report, however, the Joint Chiefs of Staff had gone further into the matter of garrison forces in Alaska and the Aleutians.

General Marshall raised the issue early in September, pointing out to the chiefs that "the large forces involved...were a great burden, a heavy morale problem, and a naval problem rather than an air problem." The Army proposed to reduce the garrison forces by about 20,000 by 1 January 1944 and another 20,000 by the following July.[38] There seems to have been general sympathy with General Marshall's remarks, the only uncertainty being to what extent forces should be maintained in the area for operations against Paramushiru. There was still no firm decision to attack Paramushiru, but Admiral Cooke for one thought that it would come, for he pointed out that the JPS would consider "whether it would be preferable to keep large forces in the Aleutians and mount operations against Paramushiru from there, or whether such operations should be mounted from the United States." However, in turning the matter over to the planners, the chiefs included the qualifying, "if such operation is decided upon."

Lieutenant General Simon B. Buckner, the army commander of the Alaskan Sector, and Rear Admiral John W. Reeves, naval commander in the same area, were summoned to Washington to give the Joint Staff Planners their views on the requirements of the region. As long as there was no decision about further operations there was inevitable uncertainty about what troops would be needed in the area. As would be expected the theater commanders were not advocating considerable reductions. General Buckner favored "going on from Paramushiru to force a showdown action." He thought the operations would take an initial force of two divisions already in the area (which would be replaced by green troops from the United States) and two additional divisions trained for amphibious operations. He spoke too of "a chain of bases for air operations" and reported that two fields suitable for B-29's were already being built, although in mid-September there was no agreement that B-29's would be used from the Aleutians. It was his view that Russia would "be influenced" by activity in the Kuriles, but that it would have to "go full blast...if we are to break the present Russia-Japan balance and influence the Russians to join us." Admiral Reeves for the most part seconded the statements of his army colleague, as did Captain Oswald S. Colclough, aide to Vice Admiral Thomas C. Kinkaid, Commander North Pacific Force. Captain Colclough, however, urged that a target date be set and preparations made for the Paramushiru operation, recommending 15 May 1944.[39]

By 21 September the JWPC report had been approved by the Joint Staff Planners for presentation to the Joint Chiefs of Staff.[40] The JWPC had strongly urged "prompt and clear-cut decisions" about future operations, about a large base planned for construction at Adak, and about the ceiling on garrison forces. But the JPS pointed out that there could be no firm decision "pending the completion of current studies as to the merits and possibilities, including timing, of operations against Paramushiru and the Kuriles." Still the planners recommended approval of the most important conclusions of the study: construction of a troop staging and supply base "of appropriate capacity" at Adak; completion of projected construction in the area, especially the bases for B-29's, allocation of two B-29 groups "if operational and available" to the Alaska Defense Command "at such time as best to assist in the over-all plan for the defeat of Japan"; no immediate reduction in Alaskan forces if operations were to be conducted against Paramushiru in the spring of 1944; reduction of the forces to approximately 80,000 by 1 July 1944 if there were to be no operations until the spring of 1945, which seemed more feasible. There was a difference of opinion among the planners on the last point. The Navy planners recommended keeping 100,000 troops on hand on the remote possibility of hostilities between Russia and Japan, in which event "it would be most important that Paramushiru be taken before the Japanese take Petropavlovsk." This was too slight a possibility for the Army planners, however, who thought "the maintenance of extra forces in Alaska in anticipation thereof is not justified, especially in view of the pressing need elsewhere for service troops and the over-all manpower problem now confronting the Army."

In presenting their study the members of the Joint War Plans Committee made a rare comment about the impact of post-war possibilities upon their problem. Stressing the significance of "a clear understanding of the great strategic importance of the region," they pointed out that it

reaches deep into a region of the world in which not only our
enemy, JAPAN, but also our ally, RUSSIA, is keenly interested.
No one can forecast the pattern of our future relationships
with either of these powers. Come what may during or after
this war - the justification or not for large or small garrisons, the requirement or not to furnish support to RUSSIA on
short notice should she go to war with JAPAN, whether or not
operations are conducted against PARAMUSHIRU, whether or not
RUSSIA or JAPAN or both are strong or weak, friendly or unfriendly in the post war period, etc. - common sense demands
that we properly organize this area for defense and for offense,
and at the earliest practicable date.[41]

From this the planners concluded that the proposed base at Adak and an appropriate number of B-29 bases should be completed without delay.

At the same time this report was submitted the Joint Strategic Survey Committee was making recommendations to the chiefs that the categories of defense of various parts of the Alaska-Aleutians area be reduced. When the JWPC paper was submitted to the members of the Joint Strategic Survey Committee for comment the latter suggested that the proposals they had already made would answer the question of what garrison forces should be retained. Alaska would be put in a revised Category A, probably free from attack. The Adak Subsector of the Aleutians would be changed from Category D, possibly subject to major attack, to C, in all probability subject to minor attack. The Unalaska Subsector would move from D to B, possibly subject to minor attacks.[42] If the Paramushiru operation was not to take place before the spring of 1945, and the JSSC considered no earlier date practicable, the committee thought that the forces of the Alaska Defense Command should be reduced to 80,000 troops by 1 July 1944, that only staging and supply areas for the Paramushiru campaign should be constructed, with the exception of bases for two to three groups of B-29's to be completed by the following spring.

The Joint Chiefs of Staff made some changes in the recommendations of the Joint Strategic Survey Committee, proposing to reduce the garrisons sooner than 1 July 1944 "if shipping and construction requirements permit," and, at General Arnold's suggestion, not specifying the number of groups of B-29's.[43] But they made no decisions immediately, apparently agreeing with Admiral Leahy, "that the Joint Chiefs of Staff were not in a position at this time to determine when Paramushiru was to be done." At a subsequent meeting on 5 October 1943, Admiral King, who had not been present when the paper was first discussed, argued that the Aleutians should not be taken out of Category D, "that Adak is an area of probable contact with the Japanese and that it was within their capabilities to return to the Aleutians in force." He thought that even so the garrisons need not be so large. However, General Marshall thought "that the retention of the Aleutian Islands in Category D was a concession of superhuman powers to the

486   THE ADVANCE TO VICTORY

Japanese," and General Handy pointed out that "General Buckner would be quite justified in feeling that sufficient forces should be retained in the islands to repel such major attacks." Admiral King objected no more, and the chiefs approved the recommendations of the Joint Strategic Survey Committee.[44]

Thus on 5 October 1943 the Joint Chiefs of Staff had approved a cutback in the number of troops who would remain in the dreary, quiescent area of Alaska and the Aleutians. In so doing they had indirectly approved the premise that operations against Paramushiru and the Kuriles would not be feasible until the spring of 1945. This conclusion had been reached at about this time by the Joint War Plans Committee in its study of a plan for such operations. The committee's review of the situation and of the effect of operations against Paramushiru and the Kuriles had produced a largely negative viewpoint:

> a. That operations against the KURILES should not be mounted unless our capabilities will allow the offensive action thus initiated to be sustained.
> b. That the initiation of an *acceptable* operation against the KURILES in 1944 prior to the defeat of the European AXIS, would definitely halt offensive operations in other PACIFIC Areas which are dependent upon the support of major naval forces.
> c. That no operations to seize any of the KURILES should be undertaken in 1944.
> d. That operations in the North PACIFIC for 1944 should be limited to harassing air strikes within the limitations of the 11th Air Force, sweeps by light naval task forces against Japanese shipping, continuation of submarine warfare, air and submarine reconnaissance of the KURILES and HOKKAIDO, and possible naval carrier raids against the KURILES and HOKKAIDO.
> e. That due to the magnitude of the forces involved, with the consequent effect on other operations in the PACIFIC, further study of operations against PARAMUSHIRU and the KURILES should be based on the "Short Time" Plan for the Defeat of JAPAN now undergoing study by the Combined Staff Planners.[45]

The Army Air Forces member of the Joint Staff Planners disagreed with these conclusions, holding the view that it was highly desirable to establish bases for B-29's in the Kuriles.

This report was never presented to the Joint Chiefs of Staff and so never received official sanction, remaining in the files for a call that never came. Its contents, however, were known to the planners and to the members of the Joint Strategic Survey Committee, who were making proposals to the chiefs in respect to the forces to be retained in the Alaskan-Aleutian area, accepting the thesis that the spring of 1945 would be the earliest practicable time for pushing on to the Kuriles. That was how the matter stood at the end of 1943, a negative sort of conclusion that nothing would be done in 1944, but whether Paramushiru would be attacked

PUSHING AHEAD IN THE SOLOMONS AND NEW GUINEA

after that no one knew.[46] Actually that operation was never to be undertaken.

Since March 1943 General MacArthur in the Southwest Pacific and Admiral Halsey in the South Pacific had been directing their operations toward placing U.S. forces in southern Bougainville and western New Britain, where they would be in a position to threaten the important Japanese base at Rabaul. During the summer forces from the South Pacific Area captured Munda and its airfield on the island of New Georgia, northwest of Guadalcanal. They then jumped over a strong Japanese position on Kolombangara and took the island beyond it, Vella Lavella. Admiral Halsey's next move was to be against Buin at the southern tip of Bougainville and the island of Faisi across the straits to the south.

General MacArthur's forces had spent the summer (winter in the southern latitudes, but it made no difference, close as they were to the equator) moving up the coast of New Guinea, pushing the Japanese from one position to another on the almost uninhabitable shore. By mid-September they had gotten as far as the strategic post of Lae, taking almost at the same time Salamaua, both important spots for naval and air bases. After seizing Nadzab and Finschhafen General MacArthur planned to move across to Cape Gloucester in western New Britain, where his forces could threaten Rabaul at the opposite end of the island.

As the target date for the Buin-Faisi operation approached, it became clear that the Japanese were concentrating forces in that area and that a direct attack would meet with stiff opposition. Consequently Admiral Halsey recommended to General MacArthur that the program be changed and Admiral Halsey move instead into the more lightly held Treasury Islands, lying southwest of Buin-Faisi, and into Choiseul to the northeast. From these positions air and naval forces could effect "the strangulation" of southern Bougainville. In return General MacArthur suggested that Admiral Halsey consider the possibility of obtaining airfields on Bougainville itself, fields from which fighter planes could reach Rabaul in time to support the attack on Cape Gloucester in December. Not without misgivings Admiral Halsey tentatively selected Empress Augusta Bay on the west coast of Bougainville as a feasible objective, albeit "a hazardous major operation."

The Joint War Plans Committee made a study of this change of plans and concluded that it was within the terms of the current directive and required no action by the Joint Chiefs of Staff.[47] But the committee awaited with considerable interest General MacArthur's answer to a request for his plans for moving on to Kavieng and the Admiralties and advancing to the Vogelkop in New Guinea, in accordance with the decisions reached at Quadrant.[48]

Preparations had begun for the Sextant Conference by the time the theater plan, Reno III, reached Washington, and the planners considered it in connection with a study of specific operations against Japan for the following year.[49] Reno III had as an objective the isolation of Japan from the area of Malaya and the Netherlands East Indies by the invasion of the Philippines. The program would be developed in five phases:

    I Seize bases in the BISMARCKS and to the northwest of VITIAZ STRAIT to isolate RABAUL and for support of subsequent operations to occupy the GEELVINK BAY-VOGELKOP area.
   II Advance northwestward along the north coast of NEW GUINEA, accompanied by establishment of protection in the ARAFURA SEA area for the left flank of subsequent operations to occupy the GEELVINK BAY-VOGELKOP area.
  III Seize and establish in the GEELVINK BAY-VOGELKOP area the major bases required for subsequent operations to occupy MINDANAO.
   IV Seize areas contiguous to Western NEW GUINEA required for flank protection and support of subsequent operations to occupy MINDANAO.
    V Occupy MINDANAO and consolidate the Southern PHILIPPINES in preparation for subsequent operations to sever Japanese communications with the MALAYA-N.E.I. area.

The idea was to push the line of bomber bases gradually westward and into the Philippines, bypassing enemy positions wherever possible, protecting the flanks of the advance by air operations and establishment of advanced naval bases. It was estimated that if Phase I were initiated on 1 February 1944 Phase V could be launched on the same day of the following year. To do this, however, would require retention under General MacArthur's command of the forces currently attached to the South Pacific Area, a disposition by no means agreed in Washington. There would also have to be some other additions, specifically six infantry divisions, some eighteen air groups of various kinds, and an assortment of escort carriers, destroyers, PT boats, attack transports, and landing craft.

Reno III's extensive program of operations in the Arafura Sea and the areas west of New Guinea was not at all in line with current thinking in Washington, where the general concept currently preferred was that the entire program in the Southwest Pacific Area should be aimed toward the Philippines and to a considerable extent serve the purpose of protecting the flank of the main advance in the Central Pacific. A campaign in the Netherlands East Indies would inevitably be considered of lesser importance to the early defeat of Japan. There was no discussion of Reno III by the Joint Chiefs (if, indeed, they saw the plan at all), but the Joint War Plans Committee looked into it as part of its whole plan for operations against Japan in 1944.

SPECIFIC OPERATIONS FOR 1944

By November 1943 it seemed probable that during the following year great progress would be made toward the defeat of Japan. All the materials of war and the trained troops to use them were becoming more plentiful. Even the supply of shipping, while still short, was gradually growing. So it was that as part of the preparation for Sextant the Joint War Plans Committee drafted and the Joint Staff Planners sent to the Joint Chiefs of Staff a report on specific operations against Japan in 1944, aimed at "obtaining positions and reducing Japan's military strength to such an extent as will permit the eventual invasion of Honshu not later than the spring of 1946, in order to force her unconditional surrender at the earliest practicable date."[50]

Following the pattern of the program approved at Quadrant, the new plan included operations in both the Central Pacific and the New Guinea-NEI-Philippines area, with the latter giving way when conflicts between the two arose. The planners had studied Reno III and they incorporated parts of it that could be carried out with available forces. For China the B-29 program was to be the main effort. Upper Burma was to be captured and additional offensive operations undertaken to keep pressure on the enemy, destroy as much as possible of his strength, and cause him to disperse his forces. In the North Pacific activity would be confined to bombing and naval raids, while preparations were to be made for entering the Kuriles if Russia went to war with Japan and to support a westward advance into Hokkaido in 1945. The year 1944 would be a busy one, as witness the schedule of operations. (See chart on p. 490.)

The chiefs considered this paper as they were travelling across the Atlantic for the conference at Cairo. The minutes of their meeting indicate that they had little constructive to offer.[51] Admiral King emphasized the importance of operations in the Central Pacific, with which, he said, "nothing should interfere." There was the usual discussion of what the British were going to do in Southeast Asia. "Very little had been achieved to date," said Admiral Cooke. Admiral King recommended "strenuous action" there, but General Somervell reminded the group "that the British claim that the water in that area is too shoal for the British Navy to operate in effectively, and apparently they are therefore stimying plans for that area." After a few more similar remarks the chiefs turned the paper back to the Joint Staff Planners.

By this time the long range plan for the defeat of Japan had been completed and received comments both from the chiefs and from the Joint Strategic Survey Committee.[52] Accordingly the JPS revised the 1944 program, emphasizing as the first conclusion, "that every effort should be exerted to bring the U.S.S.R. into the war against JAPAN at the earliest practicable date."[53] The planners also removed reference to invasion of Honshu and revised the objective to "obtaining strategic objectives and bases from which to conduct further operations to force the unconditional surrender of JAPAN at the earliest practicable date." The B-29 projects, omitted entirely from the original schedule, were included in the

490   THE ADVANCE TO VICTORY

Target Dates	Central Pacific	Southwest Pacific	Southeast Asia Command and China
1-31 Jan. 1944	Seizure of the Marshalls, including Eniwetok and Kusaie.	Complete the seizure of Western New Britain; continue neutralization of Rabaul.	
15 Jan. - 15 March 1944			Operations in Upper Burma, Arakan Region and China.
1 Feb. 1944		Seizure of Hansa Bay area.	
20 Mar. 1944		Capture of Kavieng.	
20 Apr. 1944		Seizure of Manua.	
1 May 1944	Seizure of Ponape.		
1 June 1944		Seizure of Hollandia. (Humboldt Bay)	
20 July 1944	Seizure of Eastern Carolines (Truk Area).		
15 Aug. 1944		Advance to westward along north coast of New Guinea to include Vogelkop.	
1 Oct. 1944	Seizure of Guam and Japanese Marianas.		
1 Nov. 1944 (end of monsoon)			Intensification of offensive operations in the Southeast Asia Command.

*   *   *   *   *   *   *   *   *   *   *

31 Dec. 1944	Seizure of the Palaus.		

revised program, operations from China to start 1 May 1944. Amphibous operations in Southeast Asia during the first quarter of the year, subsequently called Buccaneer, were also added.

The Joint Chiefs of Staff talked over the revised version in more detail than they had the original schedule of operations for 1944, and all but Admiral Leahy had a revision to suggest.[54] General Marshall, who had had little to say on the earlier occasion, now questioned whether the chiefs could say at the time whether or not they wished to go into Ponape and Truk. This was to become a matter for some discussion later on, but in November 1943, as Admiral Cooke pointed out, "these were objectives for planning purposes only." In other words the schedule was to provide a rough idea of where the forces of the United Nations might be by the end of 1944, subject to change if some other objectives offered greater advantages.

Admiral King apparently did not favor the occupation of the Palaus, and he suggested that the item be deleted. On the other hand, General Marshall wondered whether it did not actually belong in the program for the Southwest Pacific as well as for the Central Pacific Area. The time was distant, and as Admiral Cooke had reminded everyone the plan was tentative. The Palaus item was removed.

Except for the established project for the use of B-29's from bases in China, their potential uses were still a matter for speculation. At General Arnold's suggestion it was agreed to set 31 December 1944 as the date for initiation of very long range bombing from bases in the Marianas. However, when Rear Admiral Bernhard H. Bieri suggested using B-29's to bomb oil refineries in the Netherlands East Indies, General Arnold disapproved. He was dubious about both the basing of the planes and the significance of the targets in that area. Still Major General Richard K. Sutherland had reported that B-29's could be flown from fields in northern Australia, and General Arnold finally agreed to scheduling the initiation of B-29 bombing of targets in the Netherlands East Indies for 20 July 1944. It was to be with the understanding, however, that it was "for planning purposes only and not a commitment."

As was frequently the case there had been only a rough attempt to relate the program of operations to the availability of the means to execute it. Consequently, after the program had the approval of the Joint Chiefs of Staff, the Joint Logistics Committee (JLC) studied it to see whether the schedule was feasible.[55] The committee concluded that the operations for the first half of the year could be carried out all right, except for the B-29 bombing from bases in the Chengtu area of China. Troop shipping could not be provided for that without cutting into troop lift to other areas. If Germany were defeated by the first of July 1944, there would be no difficulty with the operations scheduled for the remainder of the year. Otherwise shipping would be short and there might be fewer heavy bombers than required for the Southwest

Pacific Area. In sum, for a tentative plan such as this was it was presumed that enough could be found to start off with and there was a good chance of carrying through the whole program.

There was nothing but routine approval by the Joint Chiefs of the report from the Joint Logistics Committee. The program for 1944 was submitted to the Combined Chiefs at Sextant on 6 December and approved without discussion, with the exception of Operation Buccaneer, which had by then been cancelled.[56] Thus, whereas at Quadrant the operations that had been approved were to put United Nations forces at the end of 1944 in the Carolines and Palau, the Sextant plans would put them into the Marianas by October and have very long range bombers operating from that area by the end of the year. Whereas at Quadrant it was planned that forces in the Southwest Pacific Area would get as far as Manokwari on the eastern shore of the Vogelkop at the end of November, at Sextant the advance westward from Hollandia to include the entire Vogelkop was scheduled to begin on 15 August. Only in Southeast Asia had the program been slowed down, delaying the operations in Upper Burma from November 1943 to the first quarter of 1944 and discounting completely the project for completing the recapture of Burma. The acceleration on paper had been considerable; in execution it was to be even greater.

LONG RANGE PLANNING FOR THE DEFEAT OF JAPAN

Strategic plans for a year in advance were one portion of the whole strategic plan that would culminate in the defeat of Japan, the long range plan that had been occupying the attention of combined planners since the Trident Conference. It will be recalled that the "Appreciation and Plan for the Defeat of Japan" presented by the CPS to the CCS at Quadrant[57] had not been accepted. Aside from its other shortcomings, two new ideas that had been introduced at the conference necessitated reconsideration of the whole problem. First was the concept that Japan should be defeated within twelve months of the defeat of Germany; second was the presentation by General Arnold of the new "Air Plan for the Defeat of Japan."[58] In the closing days of the Quadrant meetings the U.S. Staff Planners were directed to review the air plan by 15 September and prepare by 15 October a new plan for the defeat of Japan twelve months after Germany's collapse.[59]

The "Air Plan for the Defeat of Japan" (CCS 323) had been drafted hastily in order to bring the matter to the attention of the chiefs at Quebec and to insure further study of the part that would be played in the war against Japan by the new very long range bombers, the B-29's, soon to be available. There had been no previous consultation with the theater commanders and no detailed study of the program's practicability. In fact the plan was drawn almost solely from the estimated 1,500-mile range of the new planes, and the shorter range of the smaller B-24's already in use. Whether the plan was feasible remained for the joint planners to determine.

CCS 323 was based on the assumption that Germany would collapse in the fall of 1944 and that Japan should be defeated within twelve months of that event. So it was estimated that an effective bomber offensive against Japan would have to be launched not later than the fall of 1944. The possibility of using bases in the Maritime Provinces of Siberia was removed by the uncertainty as to whether or not Russia would enter the war against Japan as well as by the tremendous logistic complications involved in that area. It was assumed that no bases for B-29's would be available in the islands of the Pacific as early as 1944-1945. Hence the only available area within reach of the Japanese islands was the mainland of China. The area around Changsha was selected as being 1,500 miles from the most vital targets.

The opening up of airfields in China and a large scale program of offensive operations would place a new and a considerable demand upon the air transport route across the Hump from India, for there was little prospect that ports on the China coast would be available in time to help support the bomber offensive, and the ground route across Upper Burma would be neither finished nor adequate to supply the project. With transport planes in short supply the Air Forces planners proposed to convert B-24's into cargo planes and tankers. Four thousand of these, they estimated, could supply the twenty groups of B-29's (twenty-eight to a group) that would be available by May 1945. The planners predicted that with that many bombers in operation "the degree of destruction of Japanese resources essential to crush the enemy's capacity for effective armed resistance...[would] have been fully accomplished" by 31 August 1945. Twenty-eight B-29 groups operating for six months were expected to "reduce the Japanese war effort to impotency."

This large bombing program would require construction of new bases in India as well as in China; it would also pose problems of defense for the base areas, for the Japanese seemed certain to react violently to the bomber offensive. The Air planners concluded, however, that simultaneous operations in the Pacific, in Burma, and perhaps in Sumatra would prevent Japan from substantially increasing its air forces in China. Initiation of the program was expected to stimulate Chinese morale and it was confidently "believed...that Chinese forces, reasonably equipped and supplied, aided in leadership, supported by the U.S. 10th and 14th Air Forces, will be able to defend the air base areas." Thus easily was the defense problem disposed of.

The Air Forces offered a program in two phases. Between October 1944 and April 1945 sustained bombing by B-29's would "accomplish the destruction of selected strategic Japanese industrial systems, including aircraft factories and ship yards." Between May and August 1945 an all-out attack on other strategic objectives, augmented by attacks by two groups of B-29's based in the Aleutians, was "to accomplish the destruction of Japanese resources which are an essential preliminary to an occupation of the Japanese homeland by United Nations forces." The whole project, the originators believed, would "vastly strengthen our Chinese Allies, and...bring about a decisive defeat of Japan within twelve months after the defeat of the Axis powers in Europe."

Having presented the plan to the chiefs, General Arnold sent a summary of it to General Stilwell and his staff, asking for comments.[60] He also asked them a series of questions about the best locations for airfields, the time it would take to build them, the supporting fighter forces that would be required, and the adequacy of the supply route through India to support the operations.[61] It took time to prepare answers to all these and other similar questions, and the deadline for the Joint Staff Planners approached before a reply came from the theater. It made little difference, however, for the information available in Washington had already convinced the planners that the plan as written was not feasible.

On 11 September the Joint War Plans Committee reported to the Joint Staff Planners that the program could not "be implemented on the scale envisaged to complete the bombing offensive against the Japanese homeland, by 1 October 1945."[62] In the first place, it appeared that the shipping necessary to carry cargo and personnel to India to make preparations for the project could not be provided until after Germany had been defeated. Then, the planners discovered that the number of B-24's required had been calculated without recognizing that the route from Calcutta to Kunming to Changsha would be longer than that usually taken over the Hump from Assam to Kunming. The fuel requirements would be increased and the number of missions reduced accordingly. This meant 3,084 B-24's would be required in June 1944 and 7,164 in May 1945 instead of the original estimate of 2,000 in October 1944 and 4,000 in May 1945. As long as Germany remained a belligerent these planes would not be forthcoming. Accordingly the JWPC recommended that the Air plan be dropped as a separate study and that a study of just what could be done strategically and tactically with large numbers of aircraft in the India-China theater be made in conjunction with the long range plan for defeating Japan.

The U.S. Joint Staff Planners apparently were prepared to accept the conclusions and recommendations of the JWPC, but they found the British planners in favor of presenting the results more bluntly.[63] The latter proposed to state that the "logistical study here of the lift required to maintain the bomber force forward, as conceived in C.C.S. 323, shows us conclusively that the plan as envisaged is incapable of achievement on this score alone.... We therefore see no need to examine further at this stage the many other factors involved, such as shipping, capacity of ports, etc. on which only incomplete information is as yet available." Their recommendation was more limited: "that the study of the extent to which air attack on Japan can be brought to bear by utilizing bombers as transports should be continued as part of the general study."

The official minutes of the meeting at which the Joint Staff Planners discussed the British comments are terse and give no indication of how they were received beyond a single statement: "COL. WILLIAMSON [Colonel Adrian Williamson, representing Brigadier General Laurence S. Kuter] did not agree with the suggestions proposed by the British Planners."[64] The nature of the objection is not recorded, and the minutes of the meeting of the combined planners the following day shed no light. The report that went to the Combined Chiefs of Staff included the greater part of the blunt British statements. However, a reply had come from General Stilwell by that time, doubting the practicability of the original plan but offering an alternative prepared by Major General George E. Stratemeyer. So the Combined Chiefs were informed that "some modified form of the plan may be feasible."[65]

The Combined Chiefs of Staff agreed to drop the separate air plan, and deleting the restricting phrase, "utilizing bombers as transports," they directed the Combined Staff Planners to investigate the extent to which air attacks could be brought to bear on Japan.[66]

There had been little time to study General Stratemeyer's plan, and it was not presented to the chiefs at once. The proposal, dubbed Twilight, was unique:

> Twilight plan consists of the basing of long range bombers at a rear adequately prepared air base [in the Calcutta area]. At this base the bomber is completely equipped and prepared for assault mission, less bombs. The airplane is completely serviced (7,666 gallons). It then proceeds to advanced airdrome (1500 to 1600 miles) where bombs are loaded and excess fuel, approximately 1,183 gallons, is off loaded and placed in storage and final preparation is made for assault mission. The aircraft is flown to staging area by flight crew with combat crew aboard obtaining as much rest and relaxation as possible. At staging airdrome the combat crew takes over and after being properly briefed proceeds on the mission. The flight crew remains at advanced airdrome until the aircraft returns from mission, when flight crew takes over and flies bomber to its rear base carrying combat crew. Sufficient fuel is serviced at advanced airdome after the assault mission for the bombers return to rear base airdrome. Upon landing at rear base flight crew is relieved for rest, wounded evacuated to hospital and aircraft turned over to ground crew for preparation for next mission.[67]

The B-29's were to be self-supporting, except for bombs and the ground supplies for their advance bases, which would be hauled by 45 converted B-24's and 367 C-54's or C-87's. The difficult job of maintaining the heavy bombers would be accomplished at secure bases in India, and supplies and personnel for ground support would not have to be transported far across the Hump into China.

This new idea appealed to the planners of the Air Forces. After slight modification, including recommendation that the feasibility of bases in the less exposed Chengtu area be considered, they presented it to the Joint War Plans Committee early in October for consideration in preparation of the plan for the defeat of Japan.[68] "Strategic bombing operations against Japanese mainland objectives from China," said the Air planners, "logically constitute the major United Nations air offensive in the period immediately following the defeat of Germany, unless relations between Russia and Japan alter. Strategic and transport air forces required can be provided, the logistic needs come within the capacity of the facilities available, and the operations contemplated would contribute heavily to accelerating the collapse of Japan."

As yet there were no B-29's in operation, but there soon would be, and it was expected that twenty-eight groups would be in action by August 1945. The new plan for China did not accommodate all of these, and the Air Forces planners looked about for other base areas within range of the islands of Japan. Quadrant had paved the way for occupation of the Mariana Islands by the end of 1944, primarily to secure bases from which to project operations still farther toward Japan. By mid-September, as an outline plan for the campaign was completed, it began to appear possible to advance the date for attacking the Marianas. The potentialities of that area for bases for very long range bombers had become a matter of considerable interest.[69]

The Air planners recommended to the JWPC that "plans for the acceleration of the defeat of Japan should place emphasis upon the seizure of the Marianas at the earliest possible date, with the establishment of heavy bomber bases as the primary mission, together with the provision of adequate defense forces."[70] These were to be advance staging bases, and the B-29's would be maintained in the rear area of the Marshalls and the Carolines. The Air planners contemplated putting more of the very long range bombers in the Aleutians with staging bases in the area of Paramushiru, whence they could reach down from the north into Japan. The value of the Bonins as fighter bases was also recommended to the JWPC, as was the importance of getting Russia into the war against Japan, for B-17's or B-24's could reach Japan from bases in the Maritime Provinces of Siberia. All of these scattered air forces, the Air planners were insistent, would have to be under "a cohesive over-all control." Like the Navy the Air Forces did not look with favor upon dispersing their components under a variety of unsympathetic commands.

These recommendations went into the fund from which U.S. and British planners were evolving the plan for the defeat of Japan; but long before that was completed the Air Forces planners independently had worked out a modification of the Twilight plan for operating B-29's out of China. The new plan, submitted to the Joint Staff Planners at the beginning of November, was designed to strike at the heart of Japan's coke industry, thereby disrupting the production of steel.[71] Fourteen to fifteen hundred miles from the major part of the coke-producing area was the region near Chengtu in China. Bases in that area would bring the targets within the radius of action of the B-29, newly re-estimated at about 1,600 miles. Supply bases would be built near Calcutta and the big bombers would carry their own supplies in to the forward bases in China, thereby making no demands on other activities in the area. With 150 planes to be available by March 1944 and 150 more by September it was estimated that the first attack on Japanese objectives could be mounted by April 1944. Thereafter a minimum of one mission of 100 planes per month could be flown, increasing to three for the last four months of the year. There was no extravagant claim for this expensive plan. "Such sustained though limited operations against Japanese mainland objectives, in conjunction with continuous destruction of Japanese critical resources elsewhere," the Army Air Forces suggested, "may well accelerate the collapse of that country." At any rate the project was considered of sufficient value to warrant the recommendation that first priority be given to the production of B-29's.

The Joint Staff Planners, about to depart for the Sextant Conference, were hesistant about accepting this new plan without further study. The naval representative, Captain Austin K. Doyle, at the 9 November meeting, cautioned the JPS that granting over-riding priority to B-29 production "might upset the delicate balance of manpower and material allocated to the aircraft industry.... The result might be a failure of the Navy to meet strategic commitments in the Pacific owing to lack of sufficient air power." Aware of the numerous other problems of logistics, shipping, and personnel, the JPS accepted Captain Doyle's recommendations that the JWPC be directed to make a thorough study of the plan, forwarding a summary by cable to the planners at Cairo. In the meantime the Air Forces member would "take steps" to propose to the Joint Chiefs that, without accepting the plan, they take necessary action with the British and Chinese authorities to obtain authorization to build the bases the project required.[72]

The Joint Staff Planners submitted a formal paper to the Joint Chiefs of Staff, recommending that they expedite arrangements for the construction of airfields both in India and in China "by May 1944 insofar as practicable consistent with the commitments already placed on the Allied Commanders in those areas."[73] Before the paper even reached the JCS, however, work on the project had received the sanction of President Roosevelt. On the day after the Air Forces paper was discussed by the planners the President told Mr. Churchill about the project and asked him to ask the Government of India "to render every possible assistance" to speed the construction of the bases near Calcutta. At the same time he asked Generalissimo Chiang Kai-shek to provide the labor and materials, while the United States furnished the money under lend-lease, for the construction of five advanced bases in the Chengtu area.[74]

Despite Mr. Roosevelt's action, the Joint Chiefs spent a considerable amount of time on the planners' recommendations at their meeting of 15 November.[75] The net result of their discussion was the optimistic agreement that the airfields should be constructed not "*by* May 1944," but "*not later than* May 1944," and postponement of action on General Arnold's recommendation "that 4 aviation engineer battalions be sent to Calcutta at the earliest possible moment to assist in the construction of air bases." Two days later they approved sending not only these four battalions but four dump truck companies and two pipeline laying companies as well "by first available transport."[76] At Sextant the Combined Chiefs of Staff agreed to expedite the airfield construction, to the extent that U.S. units would arrive in Calcutta by 15 January and "that certain resources [would] be diverted from Ledo, which would result in delaying progress of road construction for a period of six weeks to two months."[77]

While the last formalities of agreement were being completed the Home Team of the Joint War Plans Committee, remaining in Washington, was correlating reports from various other joint committees and submitting conclusions by cable to the JWPC at Cairo.[78] The project did not look very impressive as the planners delved deeper into the problems of carrying it out. They found, for example, that the bases at Calcutta and Chengtu and the arrangements for personnel and equipment probably could not be completed until July 1944. They figured out that the system of using the B-29's to carry their own supplies in to the bases in China would mean that only 14 per cent of the total number of flights would be strikes against the enemy. Defense of the advance bases appeared certain to be more costly than anticipated. Delivery of the forces and equipment would require extensive adjustment of available shipping, cutting down "to the extent of 64,000 troops to Bolero or Central Pacific, or 48,000 to South-Southwest Pacific, in addition to the postponement of the movement of 4,000 troops already scheduled for the China-Burma-India area." These figures would be increased if more antiaircraft and service troops were supplied. The planners found, too, that the target set in the plan, Japan's coke industry, was a long-term project and could not be expected to contribute quickly and effectively to the defeat of Japan. This was partly because of the small number of missions that would be flown, and largely because flight tests had shown the estimated radius of action of the B-29 to be closer to 1,304 miles than to the 1,625 originally planned on. A considerable proportion of the targets would be out of range.

Subject to these limitations the Joint War Plans Committee concluded that the plan was feasible and that construction should be rushed on the airfields at Calcutta and Chengtu. But the planners recommended that no firm commitment should be made on the deployment and use of the B-29's and the current plan should not be submitted to the Combined Chiefs of Staff until further study had been made of the optimum use for the new bombers. This in effect was what had been agreed upon by the Combined Chiefs, and they were already considering other uses for the new bombers in connection with the over-all plan for the defeat of Japan which was finally presented to them in the last days of the Sextant Conference.[79]

It will be remembered that the U.S. planners had been directed at Quadrant to prepare by 15 October a plan for Japan's defeat. Subsequent agreement that the plan should be coordinated with the British at the level of the Combined Staff Planners and delays in the arrival of British planners in Washington had delayed completion of the project. It was 25 October before the combined teams submitted their report to the CPS.[80]

The plan presented in October concluded that the Japanese home islands would have to be invaded in order to accomplish unconditional surrender, but that invasion and defeat by the fall of 1945 was highly unlikely. First there would have to be bombing from bases yet to be obtained, destruction of the Japanese fleet, air forces, and shipping, and the program of offensive action for 1944 decided upon at Quadrant. There seemed little prospect that any of the objectives could be bypassed or the Japanese Fleet brought to action "with a desirable superiority."

Assuming completion of the offensive program already set, the planners foresaw four alternatives:

Course W. To aim at the invasion of Hokkaido in the summer of 1945, and, failing this, the capture of Formosa from the Pacific in the spring of 1945....

Course X. To aim at the capture of Formosa from the Pacific in the spring of 1945, retaining the option to undertake FIRST CULVERIN [North Sumatra] in the autumn (or possibly spring) of 1945 if the Formosa operation has to be postponed....

Course Y. To aim at the capture of Singapore by the end of 1945 to enable Formosa to be attacked from both the Pacific and the South China Seas in the winter of 1945-46....

Course Z. To undertake a major diversion in Southeast Asia (FIRST CULVERIN) in the spring of 1945 (or possibly autumn 1944) and to aim at the capture of Formosa from the Pacific in the winter of 1945-46.

In all four courses supporting operations were to be continued from New Guinea toward the Philippines, from northern Burma against southern, and from China by air against Japan. The British Fleet was expected to make a considerable contribution, although with limited forces, under W and X concentrating in the Pacific after 1944, in Y operating in the Indian Ocean, in Z combining action in both areas.

Favoring Course X as the "most promising way of finishing the war comparatively soon" with the minimum of risks, the planners offered a program:

THE ADVANCE TO VICTORY

CHINA - SOUTHEAST ASIA	PACIFIC

General

Throughout the war, continuous and increasing submarine and air attack on Japanese shipping.

Build up Chinese Army with object of securing airfields and capturing a port.

1944 and Early 1945

CHINA - SOUTHEAST ASIA	PACIFIC
Northern Burma ...Secure line of road Ledo-Myitkina-Paoshan (1943-44)	Mandated islands, with Marianas at earliest possible date (Target July 1944).
...Secure approx. line Pakkoku-Mandalay-Lashio (1944-45)	Northern New Guinea and Bismarck Archipelago.
Bomb targets in Yellow Sea area from China (Chengtu)	Bomb Japan from Marianas.

Spring 1945 - Spring 1946

Throughout this period watch situation in order to seize earliest possible opportunity of invading Japan.

CHINA - SOUTHEAST ASIA	PACIFIC
Exploit in Burma	Formosa (spring 1945)
Bomb targets in Yellow Sea Area from China (Chengtu), and possibly bomb Japan from Kweilin.	Failing Formosa, Luzon (spring 1945)
Possibly diversion in Northern Sumatra - FIRST CULVERIN (autumn 1945) if South Philippines is main effort in Pacific.	Failing Luzon, South Philippines from New Guinea area and gain control of Celebes-Sulu Sea area (spring 1945). (This advance will take place in any case to the extent which resources permit after providing for the main effort.)
Exploit into Sumatra and Malaya. (Subject to the requirements of the main effort.)	Exploit through Philippines.
	(Formosa in winter 1945-46, if not already captured.)
	Bomb Japan and cut sea communications south of Formosa.
	Note: Northern Kuriles might be undertaken as a diversion or after collaboration with Russia.

Summer 1946 Onwards

CHINA - SOUTHEAST ASIA	PACIFIC
	Hokkaido (summer 1946), followed by early attack on Honshu (autumn 1946), with diversion against South Japan from Formosa-China area.
Mop up throughout area.	Mop up remaining Japanese held areas.

This suggested program was highly tentative, as the appended discussion showed. If it should prove possible to accelerate the schedule in the Central Pacific, bypassing Truk and going directly to the Marianas from the Gilberts and Marshalls, the whole timetable would be speeded up. Whether or not the British Fleet would be available, how much of it, and when, whether Russia would enter the war, all were important questions that would help to determine the development of the program. The use of carrier-based aircraft against the Japanese home islands was a method yet untried, as were the B-29's, and the degree to which these new weapons would prove successful would affect the timing of strategic movements. The effectiveness of U.S. submarines against Japanese shipping, the progress of action in the New Guinea-Philippines area, these and many other factors would establish the date when invasion of Hokkaido, deemed the easiest target of the Japanese islands, could be undertaken.

Even before the Combined Staff Planners had a chance to discuss this report the Senior Team of the Joint War Plans Committee expressed dissatisfaction with it.[81] "Present directives should aim for the quickest way of defeating Japan," said the Senior Team, and they favored Course W. They did not agree that "There is no prospect of defeating Japan by October 1945." They also objected to the part assigned to the British Fleet and the stress put upon the help it would offer in the Pacific. The senior group insisted that British forces sent there would have to be balanced and be able to support themselves, not an inadequate assortment of vessels that would be a drain on U.S. facilities. Moreover the Senior Team thought that before any British ships went to the Pacific they should be put to good use in the Indian Ocean, the same old objection "that the British are not prepared to make full use of their capabilities in the S.E. Asia area."

Neither the Joint nor the Combined Staff Planners showed any enthusiasm for their workers' report.[82] Practically everyone seemed to have some objection or at least some uncertainty. At the JPS meeting Brigadier General Haywood S. Hansell said he thought the problem of maintaining B-29's in China could be solved and he "was not sure that invasion was necessary to accomplish Japan's defeat." Admiral Bieri was of the opinion that "too little emphasis had been placed in the report on the destruction of [the] Japanese battle fleet as a primary objective and prerequisite to victory." He warned the Combined Staff Planners "against too pessimistic a view of future operations." "When the full weight of our air and naval power is deployed against her," he said, "We may find the road much easier than anticipated." Captain Doyle urged that careful study should be made of the potentialities of carrier-based air power within the next few months. "He considered that results might even indicate the practicability of conducting a carrier campaign designed to whittle down Japanese strength in their homeland." There was general dissatisfaction with the target date for invasion of

Hokkaido and considerable question as to whether or not Formosa should be seized.

In the end the U.S. planners worked up answers to four questions posed by the British:

(1) Is it agreed that Hokkaido or Formosa in the Summer or Spring of 1945 provides the best hope for speeding the war?

(2) Is it agreed that, to stand a reasonable chance of capturing either in the Spring or Summer 1945, the British Fleet and amphibious effort is required in the Pacific for both the operations themselves and for the 1944 Pacific operations?

(3) Is it agreed that the chances of achieving one or other of these objectives would be increased by deciding now which one we should chiefly aim for?

(4) Anyhow, if subsequent investigations should show this to be the case, is it agreed that Formosa in Spring 1945 is the one to go for?

To the first of these the answer was "successful capture and occupation of Hokkaido." The JPS said "No" to the second, reminding their British colleagues:

The U.S. Staff Planners do not consider that even the small portion of the British Fleet and amphibious forces available in 1944 can be logistically supported in the Central or North Pacific areas. It is believed that the greatest contribution by the British naval and amphibious forces to the over-all effort in the war against Japan would be to undertake continuing offensive operations in the southeast Asia area.

Obviously British naval forces were not going to be welcomed in the Central Pacific Area, but the JPS did think British ships might support General MacArthur's operations and recommended that logistical facilities be established as soon as possible in the Australian area. The answer to the third question cancelled the fourth, for the planners proposed to decide at once on the capture and occupation of Hokkaido in the summer of 1945, taking Honshu if possible the following spring.[83]

There was no combined agreement on the plan at once. The British planners made it clear that they could not agree to send appreciably larger naval forces to the Far East in the near future, for most of the British Fleet had been operating continuously for five years and would require some extensive overhaul before being transferred. There was some discussion of the plan, but no decision, as the Combined Staff Planners deferred action, noting "that a satisfactory exchange of information on certain aspects of C.P.S. 86/2 had taken place."[84]

The U.S. Joint War Plan Committee in the meantime had gone ahead and prepared a report on the subject which the Joint Staff Planners forwarded to the Joint Chiefs of Staff.[85] It included the recommendation that Hokkaido be invaded in 1945 and Honshu the following spring. In the near future the Mandated Islands of the Central Pacific were to be captured and a strategic bombing force established in Guam, Tinian, and Saipan. General MacArthur would continue to advance into the Philippines. Preparations would be made to occupy the Kuriles in case the Russians came into the war. Upper Burma was to be captured and additional unspecified operations undertaken by ground, sea, and air, "for the purposes of maintaining pressure on the enemy, forcing dispersion of his forces, and attaining the maximum attrition practicable on his air and naval forces and shipping." In China air operations were to have first priority, while the Chinese Army was to be built up to defend the airfield areas.

This report and the original paper drew forth some interesting comments. The Sextant Conference was close at hand, and in a preparatory paper the Joint Strategic Survey Committee spoke out in a vein somewhat unlike that commonly expected from "elder statesmen."[86] They called the plan too conservative, saying "we are now over-estimating the Japs and underestimating our potentialities. Their efforts during the past year bear clear evidence of either lack of resources, poor strategic sense, or both.... the best evidence obtainable indicates that the scale of their defeats is increasing at a cumulative rate." The JSSC believed that "the key to the early defeat of Japan lies in all-out operations through the Central Pacific, with supporting operations on the northern and southern flanks - using all forces, naval, air and ground, that can be maintained and employed profitably in these areas. We believe that this principle and the related principle that operations from the west (via Singapore) should be of diversionary nature, have not been sufficiently recognized and emphasized." As for the use of British naval forces, the committee recommended that the principle should be to employ them to supplement U.S. forces, "to the extent that they can expand what would otherwise be restrictive factors in the main effort across the Pacific."

Vice Admiral Russell Willson of JSSC further enlarged upon these views in a memorandum to Admiral King.[87] He strongly doubted that invasion of the Japanese islands would be necessary, feeling that Japan could be isolated by a sea and air blockade, its fleet whittled down, and its vulnerable cities and factories wiped out by air bombardment. He saw signs that Russia would enter the fight promptly after the collapse of Germany, and he was optimistic enough to suggest that inasmuch as "the tide [was] running more strongly in our favor in Europe than we had previously considered probable" there was justification for making a new study on the defeat of Japan, assuming that Germany could collapse by the spring of 1944.

As the Joint Chiefs of Staff, en route to Cairo, studied the reports of the planners and the comments of the JSSC, Admiral King admitted that he was "astounded" at the plan for invading Hokkaido rather than Formosa in 1945.[88] Hokkaido did not "loom up as important" in any of the campaigns then being planned and he did not understand how the planners proposed to reach it. They would come straight in from the Pacific, General Handy explained, and in twelve months instead of the eighteen that would be required to take Formosa. Why not Khushu, Admiral King suggested, for that island was nearer the earlier objectives of the Pacific campaign and would more logically follow the step-by-step advance that had been the strategic pattern. The planners had thought of that, but Admiral Cooke said they had discarded the idea on the supposition that the Japanese buildup there would be too great, and there would not be enough landing craft available to carry the necessary troops to take the island.

None of the chiefs was much pleased with the report. General Arnold had little to say about it, but Admiral Leahy questioned whether Japan could be invaded and defeated in a single year. General Marshall raised the question of the use of aircraft carriers again and suggested that not enough consideration was being given to the effects of depriving Japan of oil. They all agreed with Admiral King that the plan should be reconsidered.

It was late in the conference at Cairo before the Combined Staff Planners finally prepared a report to the CCS. The first days of Sextant were occupied with discussions with Generalissimo Chiang Kai-shek and the representatives of Southeast Asia Command and China-Burma-India and with preparations for the long-awaited meetings with the Russians at Teheran. While the heads of state and the Combined Chiefs of Staff were away talking with the Soviets, the Combined Staff Planners worked on a revision of the plan for the defeat of Japan.[89]

There were numerous new angles to be explored and new points to be included in order to hope for CCS approval. The possibility that Germany might collapse in the spring of 1944 was being seriously considered at the time, and it seemed probable that the USSR would enter the war against Japan promptly after Germany's collapse. There was a question as to which of the Japanese islands would be the best to attack first as well as whether invasion would be necessary at all. The British naval and air forces that would be available for the Pacific and for the Indian Ocean required further study. How British vessels would be used and supported in the Pacific had not been determined. The air programs for China and India and the capabilities of the two nations to support them remained undecided, as did the larger question of the relation of the efforts in Southeast Asia to the main program in the Pacific. After a series of discussions among the planners and the logistics experts and a series of preliminary papers, a report, CCS 417, was finally presented to the Combined Chiefs of Staff on 2 December.[90]

The aim of this final plan was "to obtain objectives from which we can conduct intensive air bombardment and establish a sea and air blockade against Japan, and from which to invade Japan proper if this should prove to be necessary." This would mean an advance via New Guinea-NEI-Philippines and through the Central Pacific in time for a major assault in the area of Formosa-Luzon-China in the spring of 1945 from an unspecified "distant base." The two lines of advance through the Pacific were to be "mutually supporting," forces would be interchanged and operations simultaneous. Should there be conflicts, "due weight should be accorded to the fact that operations in the Central Pacific promise at this time a more rapid advance toward Japan and her vital lines of communication; the earlier acquisition of strategic air bases closer to the Japanese homeland; and, of greatest importance, are more likely to precipitate a decisive engagement with the Japanese Fleet." Operations in all other areas would support the main action in the Central and Southwest Pacific.

Annexed to the plan was a note on preparations that should be made for the entry of Russia into the war, including building up supplies, strengthening Russia's defenses, preparing to move U.S. air forces into Siberia, provided the Russians would permit it, and generally keeping plans flexible enough to allow for Russia's entry. There were tables of British naval forces available in the Indian Ocean after capture of the Andamans and of U.S. and British air forces that could be deployed to the Pacific after Germany was defeated. Finally there was a summary of what had been named the "Drake" Plan for bombing Japan with B-29's "supplied [by B-24's] through India and operating through forward airfields in the Kweilin area of China."

The concept of equal stress on operations in the Central and in the Southwest Pacific Areas, it will be remembered, had been discussed frequently in the preceding months of the war against Japan. In the preparation of the earlier versions of long range plans for the defeat of Japan the British had urged that the program in the Southwest Pacific should be made subordinate to the direct advance in the Central Pacific area. On the other hand, when informed of the developing plans for the Gilberts and Marshalls, General MacArthur had recommended that these be made supporting operations for his major advance into the Philippines from the southwestern regions of the Pacific. The members of the Joint Strategic Survey Committee in the early months of 1943 had proposed that everything be subordinated to the Central Pacific, and they renewed their recommendations when CCS 417 came to their attention. "The history of our discussions with the British concerning the strategic concept for Europe," JSSC remarked, "clearly demonstrates the continuous difficulties which arise when the primacy of the operations in one part of a theater is not clearly set forth and accepted--but remains the subject of debate, whenever operations are being considered in another part of the same theater. It is most desirable that we should profit by this experience and have no question in our own minds as to where the primary effort is to be made in the Pacific."[91]

The opposite side of the story was brought to the Joint Chiefs of Staff orally by General Sutherland of General MacArthur's staff at the meeting at which the chiefs discussed CCS 417.[92] General Sutherland argued for the supremacy of operations from the Southwest

Pacific into the Philippines over those through the Pacific islands, characterizing the latter as "a slow process of frontal attrition which does not in itself produce any vital strategic results," and a course which would not "employ in effective combination the three essentials of modern combat: land, sea and air power." He argued strongly for General MacArthur's plan, Reno III, which would place U.S. forces in Mindanao on 1 February 1945 even with the limited means remaining after allocations were made to the competing operations in the Central Pacific. "All available means should be provided for that purpose [Reno III]," he urged, "avoiding wasteful dissipation and concentrating on the most advantageous axis of advance the forces necessary to drive rapidly forward to the vital strategic objective."

General Sutherland's enthusiasm had no more immediate effect on the Joint Chiefs' action than did the advice of the Joint Strategic Survey Committee. The chiefs were not ready to concentrate the major effort on either the Central or the Southwest Pacific Area to the exclusion or minimizing of the other. Compromise remained the rule. Even before General Sutherland spoke, Admiral King had expressed satisfaction with CCS 417. He disliked some of the phrasing, but he thought "it constituted an evolution of the former approach to the problem and, in his opinion, it should be embodied in the Sextant Conference." General Marshall agreed, and, after hearing General Sutherland's remarks, almost without comment the Joint Chiefs recommended approval of CCS 417 with only slight changes.

The British were pleased with the statement in CCS 417 that the main effort against Japan was to be in the Pacific; it offered them another argument against large-scale operations in Burma. Lord Mountbatten had apparently alarmed them by reporting to the group at Sextant that he thought "that once the operations in North Burma were undertaken, either they would have to be continued to complete the capture of the whole of Burma or, alternatively, our forces would have to withdraw when the monsoon stopped." Sir Alan Brooke reminded the Combined Chiefs of Staff of this statement as they discussed CCS 417, expressing a fear "that Burma might become a huge vacuum and if this were the case, it would not fit in with the strategic concept set out in the plan under consideration, i.e., that the main effort should be made in the Pacific." With no objection from the U.S. Chiefs he proposed including a statement in the plan that a full campaign might prove necessary in Burma. Again the Combined Staff Planners got the plan back to see what effect this statement would have.[93]

Among the revisions the CPS decided were necessary was a statement that land forces in the Southeast Asia Command up to the end of 1944 were "unlikely to be sufficient to extend the area of occupation or even to maintain the position reached." This was considered a calculated risk which must be accepted. "On no account should we allow ourselves to be committed to a campaign for the recapture of the whole of Burma until this can be done without prejudice to our main effort in the Pacific even if this means that we might eventually have to abandon the reopening of the Burma Road."[94] This has all the appearance of another attempt by the British to head off any commitment to large-scale operations in Burma. Just what was to be done in those areas, however, was still the subject of discussion, and General Marshall, speaking for the U.S. Chiefs, disagreed with this definitive statement. It was ruled out. The Combined Chiefs approved CCS 417 "in principle... as a basis for further investigation and preparation, subject to final approval of the Combined Chiefs of Staff."[95] This was hardly full, wholehearted acceptance, but it did provide a guide upon which subsequent shorter range planning and operational planning could be based. At long last there was a pattern on paper for the continuation of the campaign against Japan. However, this pattern would soon be outmoded, as the speed of advance in the Pacific was accelerated.

Chapter XX

THE FAR EAST AND THE SEXTANT CONFERENCE

The problems of China-Burma-India and the role of that region in the war against Japan continued in the fall of 1943, complicated rather than simplified by the establishment of the Southeast Asia Command (SEAC). This was, of course, the only area in which to any considerable extent the United States shared the fight against the Japanese with other nations. The other problems of that war could be settled unilaterally or with scarcely a question from the British Chiefs of Staff; but the problems of the Far East were a major issue at every combined conference and generally the only one on which there was any protracted discussion. The Sextant Conference was no exception.

CHINA-BURMA-INDIA

Southeast Asia Command

The formal agreement at Quadrant to create a new command in Southeast Asia set the Supreme Allied Commander, Vice Admiral Lord Louis Mountbatten to work studying the complex problems of the area and assembling a staff to take out there with him. By 21 September a directive had been completed in London and submitted by the British Chiefs to the Combined Chiefs of Staff for approval.[1] A supplementary memorandum followed a week later.[2] Although these papers were turned over at once to the Joint Staff Planners for study "as a matter of urgency," it was weeks before a report reached the Joint Chiefs of Staff.[3]

On 28 September the Joint War Plans Committee completed a report for the JPS, recommending a few changes in the draft directive notably a clearer delineation of the relationship between the new commander and the Combined Chiefs of Staff and the exclusion of Indochina from the area as agreed at Quadrant, but otherwise advising approval of the British draft.[4] The Joint Staff Planners seemed disposed to accept the recommendations, but action was postponed to give Colonel Roberts a chance to read the paper.[5] Over two weeks went by, and dissatisfaction with the British draft increased. Finally on 17 October Colonel Roberts offered the Joint Staff Planners a draft of his own.[6] After some discussion, during which Admiral Bieri said he did not see why any directive was necessary, action was deferred until the next meeting three days later.[7] Subject to some amendment and revision the paper was finally approved on this occasion, but it was 6 November before the modifications had been made and the final report reached the Joint Chiefs of Staff.[8]

The JPS had finally concluded that the British draft directive was unacceptable for six reasons. It made the Supreme Commander "responsible to the British Chiefs of Staff rather than to the Combined Chiefs of Staff *through the British* Chiefs of Staff." There was no clear definition of General Stilwell's functions as Deputy or of the operational control of U.S. units in the area. There was insufficient provision for the integration of Chinese effort. There was inadequate provision for the allocation of forces by the Commander in Chief, India. There was too much emphasis "on the importance of India as a base, serving to de-emphasize the importance of offensive operations." Indochina was included in SEAC although the CCS decision had excluded it. The planners enclosed a draft directive of their own, incorporating the points mentioned above.

While the Joint Staff Planners were working on their report they had learned that the British Chiefs of Staff were themselves revising their original draft directive. Admiral Mountbatten had gone out to India early in October, and on the twenty-first the Prime Minister sent him a directive which had been prepared by the British Chiefs of Staff without consulting their American colleagues. On 8 November a copy of it was presented to the Combined Chiefs of Staff.[9] Thus the Joint Chiefs of Staff received the *fait accompli* at the same time they had their own planners' recommendations on an obsolete draft.

Admiral Mountbatten's directive made him "responsible to the British Chiefs of Staff, who are authorized by the Combined Chiefs of Staff to exercise jurisdiction over all matters pertaining to operations and will be the channel through which all Directives will be issued to you." His duties were given in general terms, with reference to the pertinent decisions of the Quadrant Conference. Thus, his "prime duty" was

> to engage the Japanese as closely and continuously as possible in order by attrition to consume and wear down the enemy's forces, especially his Air Forces, thus making our superiority tell and forcing the enemy to divert his forces from the Pacific Theater; and secondly, but of equal consequence, to maintain and broaden our contacts with China, both by the Air route and by establishing direct contact through Northern Burma inter alia by suitably organized, Air-supplied ground forces of the greatest possible strength.

The directive promised a battle fleet at least four weeks before the first major amphibious operation, "sufficient in strength to fight a general engagement with any force which, in the opinion of His Majesty's Government, it is reasonable to suppose the Japanese could afford to detach from the Pacific." As resources became available Admiral Mountbatten was to form a Combined Striking Force "as the foundation of whatever amphibious descent is eventually chosen."

Annexed to the directive was a revised version of the memorandum submitted earlier, outlining the organization of the Southeast Asia Command and its staff and its relationship to commands already existing in the area. The points important for this study, including General Stilwell's position and command arrangements for U.S. and Chinese forces, were taken verbatim from the Quadrant agreement and have been discussed elsewhere.[10]

The unilateral action of the British in sending Admiral Mountbatten a directive on which comments had not even been invited from the U.S. Chiefs must have been at least surprising to the Joint Chiefs of Staff, although the long delay in commenting on the original draft certainly does not indicate a high pitch of interest. The minutes of the JCS meeting of 9 November at which the British paper and the now obsolete recommendations from the Joint Staff Planners were included on the agenda give no indication of JCS reactions beyond a matter-of-fact statement of the development by Admiral Leahy. The two papers were turned over to the planners "for study and recommendation."[11]

The Army planners at once expressed dissatisfaction with the British directive on the grounds that it did not follow their interpretation of the Quadrant decisions in four particulars:

 a. It emphasizes amphibious operations, not necessarily in support of a North Burma campaign,
 b. It limits the extent of ground operations in Upper Burma to those that can be air supplied.
 c. By so doing it glosses over the importance which we attach to driving a land route of supply to China across North Burma,
 d. and thus minimizes the American objectives and deployments in China, Assam, and North Burma to the advantage of British interests in Southeast Asia.

OPD objected also to the interpretation of the relationship of the new command to the Combined Chiefs of Staff.[12]

The Joint War Plans Committee found fault only with the last point and with the fact that the directive to a command that was supposed to be under CCS control was issued not by the Combined Chiefs of Staff, through the British Chiefs of Staff, but by the Prime Minister and Minister of Defense, establishing "a militarily undesirable precedent." The JWPC recommended that the Joint Chiefs point out the irregularity to the President and suggest that he request the Prime Minister to substitute the wording of the Quadrant statement:

 The Combined Chiefs of Staff will exercise a general jurisdiction over strategy for the Southeast Asia Theater, and the allocation of American and British resources of all kinds between the China Theater and the Southeast Asia Command. The

British Chiefs of Staff will exercise jurisdiction over all matters pertaining to operations, and will be the channel through which all instructions to the Supreme Commander are passed.[13]

No action was taken on the JWPC report, for it had already been overtaken by other events.[14] The British directive stood.

Stilwell Crisis - October 1943

Admiral Mountbatten had arrived in the Far East in October to find himself confronted with numerous knotty problems, not the least of which was centered upon the ranking U.S. officer in the area, General Stilwell. As has already been seen, General Stilwell's complicated status with responsibilities in many directions and his undiplomatic personality had caused friction. The details of this unsavory story are beyond the scope of this account. The situation had been tense for some time when Admiral Mountbatten arrived in India.[15]

On 15 September 1943, Mr. Soong, the Chinese Foreign Minister, presented to President Roosevelt a plan for complete reorganization of the China Theater, eliminating General Stilwell.[16] In view of the new Southeast Asia Command, Mr. Soong suggested, General Stilwell's position should be reexamined.

> At present he is Chief of Staff of the China Theater and has independent command of the U.S. Air Force in China, India, and Burma. He also commands the SOS in India and China, Air Transport Command between India and China, and the Chinese Ramgarh divisions, and has some undefined authority over the Chinese Expeditionary Troops now in Yunnan. In addition he had been given authority by the War Department, without the concurrence of China, over the Chinese lend-lease program. The straddling of authority over such multifarious spheres is making for friction which may dangerously imperil future campaigns.

Mr. Soong also urged again that China be represented on the Combined Chiefs of Staff and on the Munitions Assignments Board (MAB). He was, of course, not strictly accurate in his charge that the War Department independently had given General Stilwell authority over lend-lease for China. There is no available evidence that his proposals were taken seriously, but the following month General Stilwell's relations with the Generalissimo became so strained that there was serious consideration in Washington of removing General Stilwell from his difficult spot.

Early in October General Somervell went to Chungking as a special emissary from the President. At his first meeting with Generalissimo Chiang Kai-shek he learned that Chiang wanted General Stilwell removed. Such action would place Admiral Mountbatten in the odd spot of having the man who had been in command of most of the Chinese troops that would participate in operations in

Burma removed just before the operations began, a situation Admiral Mountbatten was not eager to have thrust upon him. His objections reenforced those of General Somervell. With considerable help from Madame Chiang and her sister, Madame Kung, the Generalissimo was mollified and General Stilwell restored to favor. By 25 October General Somervell was able to report that General Stilwell's position with the Chinese was "stronger than it has been."[17]

When Admiral Mountbatten assumed command in Southeast Asia,[18] General Stilwell's status was further complicated. As described later by Admiral Mountbatten in his final report:

> As Deputy Supreme Allied Commander, Lieut.-General Stilwell's allegiance was to me; and in my absence from the theater he was directly responsible, through the British Chiefs of Staff, to the Combined Chiefs of Staff. As Chief of Staff to the Supreme Commander of the China theatre, his allegiance was to the Generalissimo. He therefore had to consider Chinese policy and interests, although these sometimes conflicted with the requirements of South-East Asia strategy--particularly since the Generalissimo and the armed forces of China were independent of the Combined Chiefs of Staff. Thirdly, as U.S. Commanding General, C.B.I., Lieut.-General Stilwell was responsible to the U.S. Joint Chiefs of Staff: reporting to, and receiving administrative orders directly from, the War Department at Washington. As I had operational control of forces in South-East Asia, and the Generalissimo had operational control of forces in the China theatre, when opposite arguments were submitted about the employment of all resources in S.E.A.C. in order to aid China, Lieut.-General Stilwell had either to remain silent or oppose the policy of one or other of his superiors.[19]

General Stilwell could write to his wife that he was relieved to have Admiral Mountbatten on hand, that "Somebody else is responsible and it's a grand feeling."[20] But the new organization would by no means bring simplification to the confused tangle that had developed in China-Burma-India nor readily provide agreement on operations in the area.

Interpreting the Quadrant Decisions

It will be remembered that at Quadrant the Combined Chiefs of Staff had agreed

> a. That the main effort [in North Burma] should be put into offensive operations, with the object of establishing land communications with China and improving and securing the air route.
>
> b. That priorities cannot be rigid and that therefore the Supreme Commander should be instructed that in formulating his proposals he should regard the decision in a above as a guide and bear in mind the importance of the longer term development of the lines of communication.[21]

Even as they made this general decision the chiefs themselves acknowledged that it was only a beginning. Still they made no attempt to delve deeper into the significance of the words, leaving it to the Supreme Commander, Southeast Asia Command, to work out the details of priorities. In the interim before Admiral Mountbatten's arrival, it fell to the Commander in Chief, India, General Sir Claude Auchinleck, to apply this rough formula and to prepare the British forces in India for participation in the forthcoming operations in Burma. On him also lay the responsibility for the decrepit and woefully inadequate line of communications which delivered from Calcutta to Assam all the supplies for the Ledo Road, the ground offensive from Imphal, the airfields from whence flew the transports which were the communication lines to China, and the material, including their own requirements, carried by those same planes. This bottleneck soon caused critical difficulties.

General Auchinleck studied the general decisions communicated to him after Quadrant and concluded that by implication the various projects in his area were placed in the following priority:

1. Reoccupation of Northern Burma;
2. Development of air routes and facilities;
3. Development of lines of communication, including pipelines;
4. Amphibious operations on the scale planned for the Arakan coast, exact objectives to be selected later;
5. Development of India as base for future operations.[22]

On this basis he decided that only 134 long tons per day of the tonnage laid down in Assam could be allocated to all air ferry route operations and all operations of the Tenth Air Force in India. This would mean "negligible tonnage for China." The engineers required to prepare for the operations in North Burma would have to be taken from amphibious forces and from those working on the airfields of the ferry route. If, as seemed logical, an offensive into southern Burma were to follow the occupation of northern Burma, the entire capacity of the Assam delivery route would be involved, leaving "nothing for China or long range development." These implications were serious, for already there was serious dissatisfaction with the tonnage that had been reaching China.

Since the Trident decision which assigned the first 4,700 Hump tons to General Chennault, deliveries into China had been picking up slowly. Tonnage had risen from 3,190 in June to 4,570 in July and 5,729 in August, but it was not enough for the ambitious program of the Fourteenth Air Force.[23] Moreover some of the planes promised to that command at Trident in May had not arrived by September, and the promises of performance by the Fourteenth Air Force could not be fulfilled. At the beginning of September General Chennault sent one of his staff to Washington "to explain our situation personally," taking advantage of the opportunity to send along personal letters to the President and Mr. Hopkins, telling them that the Fourteenth Air Force had not delivered as promised because he had not "been given the tools to do the job."[24] Said General Chennault, "After trying to form the most impartial judgment possible in my situation, I feel that postponement of the China air offensive will be downright tragic. I am ready to pledge my reputation, such as it is, that the return on the investment will cripple the enemy's total airpower and weaken the sea communications on which his whole system of conquest demands."[25]

What answer if any was sent to General Chennault is not known, but on 16 September General Stilwell delivered to Madame Chiang Kai-shek a letter from President Roosevelt, explaining the difficulties that had prevented larger deliveries to China, promising the delayed planes, and pledging to "drive ahead to reach our goal of 10,000 tons per month as soon as it is within our power to do so."[26]

There would be obstacles in the way of achieving 10,000 tons in the immediate future, not the least of them General Auchinleck's literal interpretation of the decision at Quadrant to give priority to ground operations in northern Burma, and particularly to the British operations from the Imphal area. As he saw it the first thing to be done was to build a road from the British base into Burma, and that meant transferring some of the engineer units working on additional airfields in Assam. He was certain that those already constructed could support a lift of up to 7,000 tons monthly and thought it highly unlikely that more than this could be delivered for China over the inadequate communications line into Assam. This was a serious situation and one to which Major General Raymond A. Wheeler, in charge of the Hump program of supply, took strong exception. As far as he knew the goal of 10,000 tons set at Trident still held and he could not believe that the full implications of assigning first priority to ground operations had been explained to the Combined Chiefs of Staff and the President. Moreover he thought it "uneconomical" to take resources away from a task that was almost finished. Eventually, he believed, they would need "all the airfields we can get in Assam" both for the transports to China and for operations in northern Burma.[27]

For October General Auchinleck announced a big cut in supplies delivered to Assam for projects other than the British 4th Corps and their ground operations. Brigadier General Benjamin Ferris, General Stilwell's deputy at New Delhi, reported to General Marshall with considerable concern that by careful planning and cutting into stockpiles in Assam it seemed possible to support the Tenth Air Force, the Ledo Road, and the Chinese Corps in India and to deliver 8,000 to 9,000 tons monthly to China. But this could not long be continued, and, reported General Ferris,

General Auchinleck "stated in so many words that in extreme case there would be no tonnage for China." The British general did not seem to appreciate the connection between his ground operations and the efforts of the Chinese Yunnan force and the Fourteenth Air Force, both of which were dependent upon the Hump transport line.[28]

General Auchinleck's interpretation of the Quadrant agreement was definitely not that of the War Department or the Joint Chiefs of Staff. Upon receipt of General Ferris's report that the engineers were to be transferred at once, the chiefs sent a despatch to the British Chiefs of Staff requesting that General Auchinleck "be informed of the great importance of making an all-out effort to improve and develop the lines of communication in eastern India and Assam to the extent that a 10,000 ton per month air lift to China may be reached at the earliest possible moment."[29] Perhaps, the U.S. Chiefs suggested, the movement of British engineers from the airfields could be so timed that American units could take over part of the work. "In view of political implications with China, our objective of maintaining China in the war, and commitments previously made to the Generalissimo by the President that we will attain a monthly lift of 10,000 tons this fall," the chiefs continued, "it is desired prior to any action being taken to reduce tonnage allocations for the US and Chinese forces inclusive of air transport requirements, that the matter with all implications be presented to the Combined Chiefs of Staff for decision." The Joint Chiefs of Staff figured that such problems would be resolved in the theater when the Southeast Asia command was in operation, but until that day they "desired that future matters which may operate to reduce the tonnage to China be referred to the Combined Chiefs of Staff."

The British Chiefs, who held different views of the importance of supporting China, pointed out at once that it had been clearly recognized at Quadrant that giving priority to ground operations "would probably mean some reduction in the air lift to China."[30] The British had themselves indicated as much when they recommended that course of action, and General Arnold had announced that he probably could not accomplish the 10,000-ton goal. Events were proving that 10,000 tons monthly could not be achieved, and, said the British Chiefs of Staff, "We feel that this is the effect of the Quadrant decision and that it must be faced." Moreover, they thought General Auchinleck had "acted fully in accordance with the policy agreed upon by the Combined Chiefs of Staff at Quadrant." Until Admiral Mountbatten actually assumed command the Commander in Chief, India, would have to make operational decisions in his behalf. The British Chiefs requested that their U.S. colleagues endorse General Auchinleck's action and explain the Quadrant policy to General Stilwell and his deputies at New Delhi.

The U.S. Chiefs remained unconvinced. In a reply prepared in the War Department they quoted from the final report of the Quadrant conference the agreement to continue the build-up of air routes and to increase the delivery of supplies by air to China.[31]

Clearly the only way to gain the 10,000-ton objective and still put the maximum effort into offensive operations would be "to bend every effort to improving and developing the lines of communications in Eastern India and Assam." The Joint Chiefs pointed out that as long as the lines of supply to China went through India-Burma questions involving the sacrifice of the supply for one for the benefit of the other were necessarily matters for CCS consideration. When General Stilwell became Deputy Supreme Commander he could present China's needs to Admiral Mountbatten and such decisions could be made in the Southeast Asia Command. If the Commander in Chief, India, were given the last word, it would mean that General Auchinleck would be controlling the deliveries to the China Theater, and the U.S. Chiefs disapproved. They proposed again that the Combined Chiefs of Staff urge upon Generals Stilwell and Auchinleck the necessity of building up the lines of communications into Assam and continuing construction of the airfields and ask them to submit mutual recommendations of "the minimum lift to China to be maintained together with the implications."

When the whole thing came up for discussion at the Combined Chiefs' meeting on 1 October there was still disagreement.[32] The British continued to think that General Auchinleck was the one best able to decide how needs should be rated in order to cut down the least on the tonnage to China and that he was in fact doing his best "to make both the Burma Operation and the air lift possible to the fullest practicable extent." General Marshall did admit that "General Auchinleck was justified in taking his decision in the light of the directive," but the Chief of Staff did not suggest that the directive be changed or made more definitive. Whatever it said, he pointed out, President Roosevelt's earlier decision in regard to the air lift had to be taken into consideration. General Handy spoke up for the Chinese forces in Yunnan who were also to participate in the northern Burma campaign and who needed supplies that could be delivered only by air. The two groups did not get together on who should control the decisions, but they finally agreed that the British Chiefs should draft a despatch to the two commanders to be considered informally by the CCS and sent by the U.S. Chiefs to General Stilwell and by the British to General Auchinleck.

It was a week before the British draft was received.[33] There was no mention of airfields or of the transportation into Assam. Instead the emphasis was put upon the Chinese forces in Yunnan. "In allocating supplies in accordance with the Quadrant decision between offensive operations into Burma and the air ferry route," the draft said, "the Combined Chiefs of Staff assume that the fact that operations of ground and air forces from Yunnan into Burma form part of this main effort and are themselves to some extent dependent on the air lift to China, is not being lost sight of." The question of a minimum air lift to China also was tied to the Yunnan forces, and the two generals were to be informed that it was "most desirable" that they get together and submit "at the earliest possible date an agreed recommendation as to the minimum air lift to China that should be maintained to nourish the Yunnan advance."

By the time the British draft reached the United States, Admiral Mountbatten had arrived in India. Nevertheless the U.S. Chiefs accepted the recommendation of General Handy that the directive still be sent to General Auchinleck and Stilwell and to Admiral Mountbatten as well. They also adopted General Handy's suggestions that the Yunnan operations be characterized as "almost entirely dependent" upon the Hump lift and that the requested recommendation include tonnage to nourish the Fourteenth Air Force as well as the Yunnan advance.[34] The British did not object and the message went to General Stilwell on 11 October, presumably also to the two British officers, although the JCS records do not indicate whether such action was taken.[35]

This was the end of this particular episode as far as the Combined Chiefs of Staff were concerned, but by no means the end of the problem of the air transport to China. The President grew exceedingly concerned over the delays in getting supplies into China and supporting the Fourteenth Air Force, as reports came in from Chinese sources that General Chennault was not being adequately supported and that he was seriously considering resigning as Chief of the Chinese Air Staff.[36] There were many reasons why the Hump deliveries were slow in being built up, as General Marshall explained to Mr. Roosevelt: inexperienced personnel, both pilots and maintenance people on the ground; bad weather; unanticipated difficulties with the new C-46's which had been sent out for use on this most difficult of runs without first working out the inevitable adjustments of a new type of plane; and the inadequacies of the railroad in Assam.[37] The President made two moves in an attempt to remedy the situation. He cabled the Prime Minister, pointing out that the British controlled the supplies being carried from Calcutta to Assam and expressing a wish that Mr. Churchill "would take a personal part in this business because I am a bit apprehensive that with our new project in Burma our air force in China will be forgotten and I think that is a great mistake." And he recommended to General Marshall that he wire General Somervell, already in China, "to give this whole business his special consideration and attention."[38]

What action if any was taken by the Prime Minister is not known, but General Somervell went at the problem in the theater with some success. When a member of the Railway Commission told him naively "that they could secure more tonnage but that the reason that more had not already been secured was that they had never been asked to move more than the figure previously furnished by the India Command," the problem of increasing deliveries into Assam began to resolve itself. After a conference with interested officials General Somervell reported confidence that enough additional tonnage could be carried not only to keep Hump deliveries at 12,000 tons monthly but to provide more for Ledo or for Imphal operations.[39] The weather was improving in the meantime and concurrently the problems of inexperienced personnel and untried planes were diminishing with a corresponding rise in the tonnage being carried over the Hump. The increases started during the visit of General Somervell continued, and it was not long before the 10,000-ton goal was reached and left far behind.

Operations in SEAC: Buccaneer

The day before the British directive to Lord Mountbatten was published in Washington the British Chiefs had circulated a report on their plans for operations in Southeast Asia.[40] Aware that the U.S. Chiefs interpreted differently the statement of British jurisdiction in Southeast Asia, the British Chiefs introduced their report by presenting their views. It was, they thought, "for them to consider what operations should be carried out in this theater, presenting their conclusions to the Combined Chiefs of Staff in exactly the same way as the U.S. Chiefs of Staff present theirs for the Central and Southwest Pacific. In their view, it [was] wrong in principle that details of these operations should be thrashed out by combined machinery." They would, of course, consult the CCS in matters of grand strategy. Presumably the British thought this would mean an end to the protracted arguments as to what should be done in Burma and the repeated attempts of the U.S. Chiefs to get the British to participate in large scale operations in that area.

Having stated their position, the British Chiefs reported only briefly on the alternative operations they had considered for Southeast Asia. They rejected as impracticable an advance southward from Yunnan and Assam to take all of Burma because of the immense difficulties of supporting such an operation. They considered a combination of an airborne and seaborne assault on Rangoon and "strong pressure from the north" possible but questionable because it would require large numbers of amphibious forces and equipment which would have to be released from other theaters. Similarly they concluded that Singapore could not be recaptured until after Germany was defeated. They rejected operations in the direction of Bangkok as impracticable to support and extremely difficult because of the nature of the country. They decided that although they might capture Bassein they could not hold it. They concluded that Akyab was no longer valuable for air bases or essential to any of the operations currently under consideration and that in any case it was doubtful that it could be taken by an amphibious operation.

"The operation in the Spring of 1944 most likely to further the war against Japan," agreed the British Chiefs, "is the capture of Northern Sumatra [FIRST CULVERIN].... It would provide us with the only air base from which effective blows can be struck direct at Japanese resources; and an air offensive from this area would not only inflict shipping losses which Japan can ill afford but also contain and destroy air forces which would otherwise be available in the Pacific area." There was a drawback, however. Although the forces already allotted to the Akyab operation would be enough for the core of First Culverin, there would have to be "a considerable measure of assistance from the United States," including two cruisers, six escort carriers, twenty-four LST's, plus other ships and landing craft and an assault brigade, two commandos, two beach groups, and three airfield construction groups.

The only operation the British Chiefs estimated practicable with the resources allotted at Quadrant was the capture of the Andaman Islands (Buccaneer), which they thought could be done in early March 1944. It would, they pointed out, give extended photographic reconnaissance and intelligence facilities, offer a better position for developing operations later on against Lower Burma or Northern Sumatra, and "keep the Japanese guessing as to our further intentions, thus imposing upon them further dispersion of effort." The British asked for U.S. views as to the possibility of helping out with First Culverin or agreeing formally to the mounting of Buccaneer.

The Joint Strategic Survey Committee recommended that the chiefs agree to Buccaneer, for although it was "relatively small," it was "the first definite amphibious commitment in this area which the British had been willing to undertake."[41] Strengthened by some false operation along the Arakan coast, JSSC thought, Buccaneer would succeed in pinning down Japanese forces in southern Burma while operations were in progress up north. As for First Culverin, the committee did not agree that it was "most likely to further the War against Japan," but in any case they considered it not feasible to divert U.S. forces from the Pacific for such a purpose.

Reviewing the British interpretation of their jurisdiction in Southeast Asia, the JSSC recommended that the U.S. Chiefs try to clarify the relationship "along the lines of the U.S. concept." The committee pointed out that it had been agreed at Quadrant that the "Combined Chiefs of Staff would exercise a general jurisdiction over strategy for the Southeast Asia Theater."[42] Certainly decision among four courses of action was a matter of strategy.

The Joint Staff Planners agreed with the conclusions of JSSC and seconded that group's recommendations to the Joint Chiefs of Staff.[43] At the same time they added a few comments, summarizing the interests of the United States in the area and suggesting that the Combined Chiefs had the same right of guidance and decision on operations in the Pacific as in Southeast Asia. The Joint Staff Planners incorporated the recommendations in a draft memorandum to the British Chiefs and proposed that Admiral Mountbatten be asked to recommend additional operations that could be undertaken in support of Buccaneer.

520   THE ADVANCE TO VICTORY

The Joint Chiefs agreed with their committees, although Admiral King termed Buccaneer "wholly inadequate," and the proposed memorandum was submitted to the CCS at Sextant, where Buccaneer was to be a major issue.[44]

SEXTANT

In the fourth week of November 1943 U.S. Marines were fighting their way ashore at Tarawa and Army troops were taking Makin nearby, to inaugurate the campaign in the Gilberts and start U.S. forces on the road across the Central Pacific. On the opposite side of the world military and political leaders of the three nations most deeply involved in the war against Japan, the United States, Great Britain, and China, were meeting for the first time at Cairo in Egypt.

Prime Minister Churchill had started as soon as he returned to London after Quadrant to try to arrange a three-way meeting with Premier Stalin and President Roosevelt, a meeting of which there had long been discussion but which had never proved feasible.[45] At the end of October Secretary of State Cordell Hull, Foreign Secretary Anthony Eden, and Foreign Minister V.M. Molotov concluded successful preliminary talks on political matters at Moscow.[46] Shortly thereafter plans were completed for a meeting of the three heads of state at Teheran in Iran late in November. It was planned that the Americans and British should meet first at Cairo, and Mr. Roosevelt took the initiative in arranging that they should be joined there by Generalissimo Chiang Kai-shek and some of the military commanders from the Far East.

Many of the papers that would be presented at Sextant, as the conference was to be called, had been prepared or were in the process of preparation before the time and place for the meetings were settled upon.[47] By 22 October the Joint Strategic Survey Committee, after discussions with the Joint Staff Planners and the Joint Logistics Committee, was recommending what should be discussed when the two groups met.[48] The JSSC advised endorsing the statements of concept and objectives agreed upon at Quadrant and then proceeding to reports from all theaters and discussion of major theater problems, taking up European-Mediterranean matters first, then those relating to the war with Japan. The Joint Chiefs accepted the JSSC's suggestions.

Five days before the U.S. party sailed aboard the *Iowa* for Cairo the Combined Chiefs of Staff reaffirmed the over-all objective, the strategic concept for the prosecution of the war, and the basic undertakings in support of the over-all concept, which had been accepted at Quadrant.[49] Only the basic undertakings were revised, to provide that getting Turkey into the war should not conflict with requirements for operations in Europe, that assistance would be extended to the Italian forces who had recently become "co-belligerents," and that preparations would be made to "reorient forces from the European Theater to the Pacific and Far East as soon as the German situation allows."

The ocean voyage gave the Joint Chiefs of Staff opportunity to discuss among themselves and with the President the numerous problems that would be taken up at Cairo and at Teheran, specific matters to be presented to the British, and general problems to be considered with Generalissimo Chiang Kai-shek and Premier Stalin.

The presence of Generalissimo Chiang Kai-shek at Cairo introduced several complications. President Roosevelt's belief in China's importance and insistence upon China's status as a Great Power, which had led him to invite Chiang, were not shared by the Prime Minister. Mr. Churchill would have preferred that Chiang not attend the conference. Aside from the political problems, Chiang seemed certain to make a bid for assistance which the United States and Britain were not prepared to give and to demand operations in southern Burma on which the two nations were not themselves agreed. Chiang would undoubtedly have to be told something of future plans, but how much was difficult to decide, for as General Somervell put it, "information seemed to have a way of leaking out in China."[50] Despite the Generalissimo's obvious interest in plans for defeating Japan, General Somervell suggested that the U.S. representatives "might wish to state only that the war effort is progressing as rapidly as we are able to advance it in order to attack Japan by air, sea, and land when we are in a position to do so." Admiral Leahy suggested trying to ascertain the Chinese attitude toward Russian participation in the war against Japan, but Mr. Roosevelt pointed out that the Chinese wanted equal rights with the Russians in Outer Mongolia and were anxious to get Manchuria back. The President thought discussion would undoubtedly cause trouble.[51] The Joint Staff Planners proposed an agenda for the President's conversations with the Generalissimo, but since there are no official records of those meetings it is not known whether it was used.

Because of the Generalissimo's presence, as well as the presence of most of the top commanders from the area (Admiral Mountbatten, General Stilwell, General Wheeler, General Wedemeyer, lately sent to be Deputy Chief of Staff, SEAC, General Stratemeyer, and General Chennault), the British suggested on the first day of the conference that they turn first to a discussion of operations in Southeast Asia and then get on with the war against Europe in preparation for the meetings at Teheran.[52] For the first three days the chiefs discussed little that was not concerned with the Far East, to the considerable annoyance at least of Prime Minister Churchill, who has since written:

> What we had apprehended from Chiang Kai-shek's presence now in fact occurred. The talks of the British and American Staffs were sadly distracted by the Chinese story, which was lengthy, complicated, and minor. Moreover,...the President, who took an exaggerated view of the Indian-Chinese sphere, was soon closeted in long conferences with the Generalissimo. All hope of persuading Chiang and his wife to go and see the Pyramids and

enjoy themselves till we returned from Teheran fell to the ground, with the result that Chinese business occupied first instead of last place at Cairo.[53]

Indeed Mr. Churchill is right, for in informal discussions among various ones of those attending the conference and in the formal, officially recorded meetings themselves it was apparent that the three national groups had quite different ideas of the significance of the campaign in Burma and of the other tangled problems of the Far East. American and British Chiefs had been arguing about Burma almost since the war began, but this was the first opportunity for them and the President and Prime Minister to experience at first hand the difficulties of trying to obtain the cooperation of the Chinese. The attempts to reach agreement were very time-consuming.

The Generalissimo offered his ideas of China's role in the defeat of Japan the day before the first plenary session in a paper presented by General Stilwell:

> c. Continue to train and improve combat effectiveness of Chinese Army - Current.
> d. Initiate intensive bombing of Japan by V.L.R. bombers - Early 1944 -
> e. Recapture Canton and Hongkong - Nov. 1944 - May 1945.
> f. Carry out intensive bombing of Formosa and P.I., deny use of Straits of Formosa and South China Sea to Japan and furnish land-based air support to any U.S. Navy activities in these areas - Oct. 1944 -
> g. Attack Formosa if required - May 1945 - Nov. 1945.
> h. Offensive operations towards Shanghai - Nov. 1945.[54]

This long range program was supposedly based upon the decisions of Quadrant, but it went far beyond the program agreed upon for the China Theater. Amazed at the requirements of the ambitious program, the Joint Staff Planners recommended that the whole thing be disapproved on the basis that China's role in the future course of the war would be adequately covered in the larger plans for action against Japan.[55]

The Joint Chiefs of Staff discussed the paper on the morning of the twenty-third and generally agreed that only the first four points were consistent with agreed concepts.[56] General Marshall showed some enthusiasm for the program, pointing out that it in fact "constituted a milestone in the prosecution of the war in the East." For the first time the Generalissimo was agreeing to make use of China's manpower, and General Marshall, well aware of the difficulties General Stilwell had been encountering in trying to get Chiang's cooperation, thought the Generalissimo should be encouraged. The U.S. Chiefs finally endorsed the first four items and adopted General Marshall's proposal that the others be given "detailed examination and study because of logistic involvements." Later in the day the Combined Chiefs of Staff agreed and turned the paper over to those working on the long range plan for the defeat of Japan. By that time the conference had become involved in more specific plans for operations in Burma.[57]

At 1100 on 23 November the Combined Chiefs of Staff met with the President, the Prime Minister, and Generalissimo Chiang Kai-shek at the villa of Ambassador Alexander Kirk at Cairo.[58] After the President had opened the meeting Admiral Mountbatten described in some detail the proposed plan for SEAC operations, Tarzan, and the over-all plan for the next few months in Burma, Champion. The 15th Corps would advance on the Arakan front along the coast in western Burma, while the 4th Corps started southeast from Imphal toward Sittang. The Chinese Army in India at the same time would move down through the Hukawng Valley toward Myitkyina to link up with the Chinese forces from Yunnan advancing westward. Long range penetration groups would support both of the latter actions, and parachute troops would be flown in to take the airfield at Indaw, to be maintained by air until they could be joined by General Stilwell's forces from Ledo. If the Generalissimo approved, the Chinese Ledo force would operate under the British 14th Army Commander until it reached Kamaing, when General Stilwell would take over. Chiang Kai-shek said only that he would like to see it all on a map.

Admiral Mountbatten then turned to a very touchy subject, the tonnage to be delivered over the Hump. The goal of 10,000 tons per month had not yet been reached, but he expected that for November and December deliveries would come to 9,700. In January and February they would drop to 7,900 tons because of the requirements of the Burma campaign and rise again in March to 9,200. Chiang had told Admiral Mountbatten in Chungking that he understood the necessity for reducing deliveries to China, but he certainly did not favor it.

Prime Minister Churchill spoke next, saying that "he had high hopes of these operations, the success of which largely depended on surprise and secrecy and ignorance on the part of the enemy as to the lines of approach and the points of attack." He promised "a formidable British Fleet" in the Indian Ocean--"no less than 5 modernized capital ships, 4 heavy armored carriers, and up to 12 auxiliary carriers, together with cruisers and flotillas." By spring Admiral Mountbatten would have an amphibious force "for use in such amphibious operations as might ultimately be decided upon." This was all very well, said the Generalissimo, but the success of the Burma campaign depended "not only on the strength of the naval forces established in the Indian Ocean, but on the simultaneous coordination of naval action with the land operations."

The Generalissimo's conviction that only naval operations could prevent the Japanese from reenforcing Burma and that without them the campaign in northern Burma would not be successful was not new. He had always insisted upon naval operations in the Bay of Bengal. Despite Mr. Churchill's view that the connection was not close and that a strong fleet would suffice to prevent Japanese reenforcement in strength, Chiang neither accepted nor rejected Admiral Mountbatten's proposals and continued to insist on naval operations.

Just what would satisfy the Generalissimo apparently was not clear from his remarks at this first meeting. General Stilwell told the Combined Chiefs of Staff that afternoon that he thought Chiang would be satisfied if naval security could be guaranteed in the Bay of Bengal, a situation which Admiral Cunningham felt he could not ensure.[59] Admiral Mountbatten, on the other hand, thought from his conversations with the Generalissimo that Chiang was insisting upon the amphibious operation in the Andaman Islands, Buccaneer. But the status of this project was no more definite at the moment than the size of the British Fleet that would be sent to the Bay of Bengal.

It will be remembered that the U.S. Chiefs of Staff had approved the British proposal for Buccaneer, refusing the additional forces required for Culverin, and remarking that the Combined Chiefs of Staff should consider things other than grand strategy in relation to Southeast Asia Command. The Combined Chiefs approved these U.S. comments at their meeting on 23 November but suspended decision on Buccaneer "in order to allow the operation to be considered in relation to the other operations to be undertaken."[60] It was already apparent that Buccaneer would be a sticky problem.

The Chinese military representatives came in toward the end of the CCS meeting, but they had not been briefed by the Generalissimo and had no comments to offer.[61] Since they were obviously going to say nothing at all, General Stilwell talked about the condition of the Yunnan force, and Generals Chennault and Stratemeyer told what plans had been made to coordinate air and ground effort.

Before the next CCS meeting General Marshall had a talk with Chiang. He found the Generalissimo opposed to Admiral Mountbatten's plan "which he [Chiang] felt would lead to heavy losses and possibly defeat."[62] Chiang insisted upon an amphibious operation simultaneous with the land campaign and argued that all the advances in northern Burma should be aimed at an east-west line running through Mandalay, which would carry them considerably farther than was currently planned. When General Marshall reported the Generalissimo's ideas to the Combined Chiefs, Admiral Mountbatten opposed them strongly. He thought his program would carry the advance as far as it could be supported by the beginning of the April monsoon. When the monsoon was over in the fall, it would be necessary either to advance farther or retreat before the Japanese could counterattack. Sir Alan Brooke pointed out that in starting into Burma at all the Allies were committing themselves to taking the whole thing, probably with a final airborne attack on Rangoon and amphibious operations as well. He suggested trying instead to open the Straits of Malacca. Admiral King mentioned that another alternative would be to try to sever the

Japanese lines of communication by attacking Bangkok, but no one seemed interested in pursuing the idea.

Again the Chinese military representatives came into the CCS meeting, this time prepared to present the Generalissimo's views and primed with questions prepared by General Stilwell.[63] All the questions were seeking information and commitments from the British, the number of purely British units in the India-Burma area, the fighting experience of the troops, plans for British forces, etc. Although Admiral Mountbatten answered them, he was clearly annoyed. Even the terse official minutes give a strong hint of his feelings. He is reported to have requested

> an explanation with regard to the questions asked as to the numbers of British and Indian troops engaged. Did the Chinese Representatives wish to infer that the fighting qualities of the Indian troops were bad? This suggestion he most strongly refuted. The Indian divisions had fought magnificently in the North African campaigns. If, on the other hand, the Chinese representatives wished to imply that British troops were remaining in India without playing an active part in the operations, he wished it to be clearly understood once and for all that this was not the case.[64]

General Marshall also became annoyed with the Chinese insistence on what they had to have before they would cooperate in Burma and what had to be delivered over the Hump.[65] He pointed out that the Chinese were talking about American planes and American personnel and American material and reminded them that "the present campaign was designed to open the Burma Road, for which the Chinese had asked, and that the opening of the Road was for the purpose of equipping the Chinese Army."[66] But Chiang had instructed his representatives that there should be no drop below 10,000 tons and had directed General Stilwell to say that the needs of the Chinese Air Force should be met. Inasmuch as General Chennault estimated that the needs of the Chinese Air Force and the needs of the Fourteenth U.S. Air Force would come to 10,000 tons, it was hard to see where the ground forces would fit in at all. The meeting decided only that Admiral Mountbatten should go and talk with the Generalissimo.

The next day the U.S. Chiefs speculated among themselves as to the possibility of stepping up the airlift.[67] General Marshall was firm that there could be no more planes for it. It seemed probable, however, that as a result of General Somervell's investigations the efficiency of the lift could be increased from the current 55 per cent to at least 75 per cent. It was generally agreed that Chiang should not be told of this lest it not be fulfilled. The Joint Chiefs were obviously impatient with Chiang's refusal to accept the Mountbatten plan, but only Admiral Leahy suggested that Chiang be told he could take that or no Burma campaign at all. (He said it twice.) Perhaps there was too much likelihood that the Chinese would take the second alternative.

At a meeting attended only by the Combined Chiefs Admiral Mountbatten reported on his visit to the Generalissimo and one between Chiang and the Prime Minister which Admiral Mountbatten had attended.[68] The Generalissimo had insisted upon his own plan for a campaign in Burma despite Admiral Mountbatten's view that the 535 transport planes that had been estimated necessary to support it could not be found. Chiang finally agreed to participate in Tarzan provided the British Eastern Fleet was in the Bay of Bengal and an amphibious operation was conducted simultaneously. First, however, he insisted that the Combined Chiefs of Staff be asked formally to provide the 535 transports.

As Admiral Mountbatten had expected, the chiefs did not for a moment consider it possible to produce 535 more planes. "Possibly 25," said General Arnold, but "the figure of 535 might be impossible to find without taking aircraft away from other operations to which they had already been allotted." After some discussion about the allocation of Hump tonnage and the necessity for reducing deliveries during the Burma campaign, which Chiang had refused to accept, the Combined Chiefs of Staff decided that Admiral Mountbatten should draft a paper to submit to the Generalissimo, seeking his written agreement to SEAC's plan for operations in Burma. Later in the day Admiral Mountbatten submitted six "Points on which Generalissimo's Agreement Should Be Obtained:"

1. Since the Combined Chiefs of Staff are unable to find the 535 additional transport aircraft which are required for the MANDALAY plan, it is agreed that the plan presented by Admiral Mountbatten at the first Plenary session shall be accepted.

2. The stipulation which the Generalissimo has made that an amphibious operation is to be carried out in March is noted, and will be taken into consideration by the Combined Chiefs of Staff when amphibious operations in all parts of the world are reviewed in about a week's time. Meanwhile preparations are being pushed forward in the South East Asia Theater for an amphibious operation to meet this date, should approval be subsequently given.

3. A fleet of adequate strength to cover such an operation and to obtain command of the Bay of Bengal will be assembled by the beginning of March.

4. That the air needs of the North Burma campaign must have first priority during the battle, and that discretion is given to the Supreme Allied Commander to use the air forces including A.T.C. as necessary for the battle. He has given an undertaking that he will use his best endeavors to see that 8,900 tons per month are passed over the hump on an average over the next six months.

5. The Supreme Allied Commander is delegating his command over the Chinese-American Task Force starting from Ledo to

Lieutenant General Slim, commanding the 14th British Army, until the main body reaches KAMAING, when he will place the force under the command of Lieutenant General Stilwell.

6. It is understood that the necessary resources will be made available to enable further offensive operations to be undertaken in October, 1944, when the monsoon stops.[69]

Recognizing the Generalissimo's reluctance to admit that operations in Burma would need transports for support at the expense of deliveries to China, General Marshall proposed a substitute paragraph 4 which seemed more likely to meet with Chinese approval:

The Supreme Commander, South East Asia Command will be authorized to divert not more than an average of 1,100 tons per month from tonnage over the "hump" to the requirements of the Burma campaign. Diversions in excess of this figure may be made by him only to meet sudden and critical emergencies of the battle or by permission of the highest authority. The Air Transport Command will use its utmost energy to raise the efficiency of its operation and increase the "hump" tonnage to a full 10,000 tons per month into China by the late winter and a further increase in the spring.

There was no objection to this modification nor to a less binding final paragraph proposed by the British:

It is the intention to resume the offensive in October 1944, when the monsoon stops; it is, however, too far ahead to decide the precise resources which will be available.

The chiefs decided that the six points should be forwarded to the Generalissimo by Admiral Mountbatten "without delay."[70]

Precisely what happened on 26 November, the last day of the first meetings at Cairo, is difficult to trace. It appears that even as the chiefs had been receiving the "six points" the night before, Chiang Kai-shek, in conversation with President Roosevelt, was rejecting the agreements that had seemed to be reached. On the morning of 26 November the Generalissimo summoned Generals Arnold, Stilwell, Somervell, Stratemeyer, Wheeler, and Merrill to a meeting with himself and his military advisors and insisted that the Hump deliveries would have to be maintained at 10,000 tons per month for China. The U.S. officers explained that all available C-46's were being assigned to the Hump, that the efficiency of the line was going to be increased, that they were trying to find twenty-five C-47's to take care of Admiral Mountbatten's needs in north Burma, and that with these arrangements the tonnage "in due course" would probably actually exceed the 10,000-ton figure. The U.S. representatives also pointed out that Admiral Mountbatten's figure of 8,900 was only 1,100 short of 10,000 and that with the increases it might be possible both to provide 1,100 tons for him and 10,000 for China. They promised to make every effort to do so. Chiang still insisted that his demands and those of Admiral

Mountbatten could be kept separate, but he finally agreed to "accept the figures given to him with the understanding that the ATC would devote its best endeavors to securing the greatest possible increase in the tonnage."[71]

That afternoon the President and Prime Minister met with the Generalissimo and Madame Chiang. Mr. Churchill had with him the CCS's six points but did not present the paper. Although there are no minutes of the meeting, it appears that harmony was achieved, for at a tea party that afternoon Chiang told Admiral Mountbatten that he had agreed to everything. This the Supreme Commander, Southeast Asia Command, interpreted to mean:

(a) Operation TARZAN was approved.
(b) It was decided to accept the revised 'Hump' tonnage figures following on the approval of operation TARZAN.
(c) The carrying out of an amphibious operation was approved, the latter to be synchronised with operation TARZAN. In point of fact the Generalissimo made the carrying out of a synchronised amphibious operation the condition of the Chinese forces taking part in operation TARZAN.[72]

There is some evidence that the Generalissimo's acquiescence was not complete, but that is of comparatively little consequence in respect to the final outcome, for the British had already begun to speak of the possible curtailment or sacrifice of the amphibious operation in the Bay of Bengal.[73]

It is difficult to determine from the official records how firm an agreement to do Buccaneer was made during the time the Generalissimo was in Cairo, for there was no written record and no minutes were kept of the numerous informal meetings between the heads of state. From the beginning Chiang had made an amphibious operation in the Bay of Bengal the condition of his agreement to participate in Tarzan, and it is apparent that at some time President Roosevelt, with or without the concurrence of Prime Minister Churchill, committed the combined forces to such an operation. Certainly the Generalissimo left Cairo with the understanding that some amphibious operation would be done, and all the others at Sextant were aware of the fact.[74]

At the CCS meeting on the afternoon of 26 November the British Chiefs gave clear evidence that they did not recognize a final commitment to Buccaneer. In preparation for the approaching meetings with the Russians at Teheran the chiefs discussed at length operations in the Mediterranean and their relationship to operation Overlord.[75] Mr. Churchill had expressed the view at the second plenary session two days before that Overlord "should not be such a tyrant as to rule out every other activity in the Mediterranean" and had advocated a program comprising "Rome in January, Rhodes in February, supplies to the Yugoslavs, a settlement of the Command arrangements and the opening of the Aegean, subject to the outcome of an approach to Turkey; all preparations for Overlord to go ahead full steam within the framework of the foregoing policy for the Mediterranean."[76] In a memorandum the next day the British Chiefs explained that they did "not in any way recoil from, or wish to sidetrack, our agreed intention to attack the Germans across the Channel in the late spring or early summer of 1944." They simply did not want to "regard Overlord on a fixed date as the pivot of our whole strategy on which all else turns."[77]

Advocating attacking the Germans "remorselessly and continuously in any and every area where we can do so with superiority," the British Chiefs proposed six courses of action in the Mediterranean: unification of command; maintenance of the offensive in Italy until the line across the neck of the boot from Pisa to Rimini was secured; strengthening guerrilla efforts in Yugoslavia, Greece, and Albania; bringing Turkey into the war; opening the Dardanelles as soon as possible; and undermining resistance in the Balkans. Should this program make it necessary to put back the date upon which the forces for Overlord would be available in the United Kingdom the British proposed to accept it, for it would not necessarily follow that the date of the invasion of France would be retarded correspondingly.

The Joint Staff Planners advised the Joint Chiefs to go slow in accepting these proposals, pointing out that they were "couched in the broadest of terms."[78] The British had not attempted to assess the cost of the program to agreed operations elsewhere, and the planners reminded the chiefs that they knew "from experience that to approve an eccentric operation, however attractive in itself, is to invite a situation requiring additional military means far in excess of those originally allotted."

It was on the limited supply of landing craft that the Mediterranean projects would make demands that could be met only at the expense of operations already agreed. The British paper spoke only of delay in Overlord, but the Combined Chiefs had discussed the paper the day before in closed session and they had heard enough of the views of Mr. Churchill to know that the British were also thinking of the vessels allotted to India and to Buccaneer. Admiral King put the question directly to the U.S. Chiefs-- if they decided to accept the British proposals, would they agree to postpone both Buccaneer and Overlord, or only one? This was a question in which the chiefs could not in fact give an unqualified answer. They certainly did not favor delaying Overlord any longer. There had been so many obstacles in the way of a firm commitment on that. But the agreement on Buccaneer had been made by higher authority, and General Marshall had "received the impression that the President would not accept any British withdrawal of their landing craft from Buccaneer." Of course, General Marshall suggested, if the British took theirs away the Americans could remove theirs also and use them in the Pacific. The political implications were significant, but all the Joint Chiefs agreed that regardless of them Buccaneer should be mounted.[79]

Some decision had to be made on the British Mediterranean proposals, for the group was to leave after the meeting of 26 November for the conference at Teheran and it was essential to have an agreement as a basis for discussion with the Soviet staff. The U.S. Chiefs decided to accept the proposals as such a basis, but with the understanding that they included the opening of the Dardanelles and the capture of Rhodes, requiring the retention of landing craft in the Mediterranean. Such retention "would in no way interfere with the carrying out of Operation Buccaneer."[80]

All right, said Sir Alan Brooke, speaking for the British Chiefs, "if the capture of Rhodes and Rome and Operation Buccaneer were carried out, the date of Overlord must go back." Although General Marshall acknowledged this, he thought "that it was essential to do Operation Buccaneer, for the reasons that firstly, not only were the forces ready but the operation was acceptable to the Chinese; secondly, it was of vital importance to operations in the Pacific; and, thirdly, for political reasons it could not be interfered with."

The discussion at this combined meeting must have been extremely interesting, for both U.S. and British officers were firm in their views of what should not be done. The British were persuaded that Buccaneer should be sacrificed and the CCS should be in a position to tell the Russians that Overlord would come off as soon as possible. The U.S. Chiefs, on the other hand, conscious of the touchy situation vis-a-vis Chiang Kai-shek, and themselves advocates of the strategic advantages of Buccaneer, were not enthusiastic about further commitments in the Mediterranean. The official minutes reflect the discussion only dimly, for they read:

> In the course of a full discussion the following points were made.
> a. SIR ALAN BROOKE said that it might be necessary to consider earnestly the possibility of putting off Operation BUCCANEER since by so doing the full weight of our resources could be brought to bear on Germany, thus bringing the war as a whole to an end at the earliest possible date. The matter should be looked at from a purely strategical aspect.
> b. SIR CHARLES PORTAL felt that the Russians might well say that not only did they agree with the proposed course of action outlined by the British Chiefs of Staff and tentatively accepted by the United States Chiefs of Staff but also that they required Operation OVERLORD at the earliest possible date. In this case we must surely consider the possibility of putting off Operation BUCCANEER. He did not believe this Operation essential to the land campaign in Burma.
> c. ADMIRAL KING considered it unsound to bring back landing craft from BUCCANEER. In his view the land campaign in Burma was not complete without Operation BUCCANEER. Our object was to make use of China and her manpower and the delay of a year in achieving this object must most certainly delay the end of the war as a whole.

d. GENERAL MARSHALL stressed the U.S. contribution to the war in Europe. He believed that the suggestion that putting off the Operation BUCCANEER would shorten the war was an overstatement. The United States Chiefs of Staff were most anxious that BUCCANEER should be undertaken. They had gone far to meet the British Chiefs of Staff views but the postponement of BUCCANEER they could not accept.

e. ADMIRAL LEAHY said he wished it clearly understood that the United States Chiefs of Staff were not in a position to agree to the abandonment of Operation BUCCANEER. This could only be decided by the President and the Prime Minister.

In closed session the chiefs agreed to accept the British proposals tentatively for discussion with the Soviets, accepting the fact that the target date for Overlord would be delayed and "certain landing craft" would have to be retained in the Mediterranean. The U.S. Chiefs put it on record that they "could not accept the abandonment of the BUCCANEER operation." If further discussion should indicate that postponement was desirable, it would have to be taken up with the heads of state.

So matters stood as the Combined Chiefs of Staff and the President and Prime Minister set off from Cairo for the city of Teheran. The talks at Cairo had actually produced no firm decisions in respect to the war against Japan. Although the situation had looked promising at last for Chinese cooperation in Burma, it was apparent that when the chiefs returned to Cairo the whole question of amphibious operations would have to be reopened.

EUREKA - THE MEETINGS AT TEHERAN

The conference at Teheran, Eureka, long hoped for by Mr. Roosevelt and Mr. Churchill, was primarily a political conference, although the Combined Chiefs of Staff attended most of the meetings and some of the most important decisions had to do with military matters. The chiefs had anticipated this and had agreed early in the conference at Cairo that they would prepare no formal agenda for military discussions at Teheran, "because the military problems to be considered would arise from the political discussions which would be held at the start of the conference."[81] The U.S. Chiefs, however, did have their planners prepare a summary of "broad lines of action [to] be adopted" in the talks with the Soviets.[82] Included with the statement of general attitudes was a proposed agenda of the most important subjects to be taken up: bases for shuttle bombing; Soviet strategic bombing of targets in Germany; air transport routes; weather information; Overlord; current plans for Italy; propaganda; and matters dealing with Japan. The last of these was based on acceptance of Mr. Stalin's assurance to Mr. Hull during the conference of Foreign Ministers at Moscow that Russia would enter the war against Japan after Germany had been defeated. Five things were to be sought from the Russians:

a. Request Soviets to furnish combat intelligence information concerning JAPAN....

b. Request Soviets to indicate whether they consider it desirable at this time to set in hand arrangements to base Soviet submarine force in U.S. territory.

c. Request Soviets to indicate what direct or indirect assistance they will be able to give, if it is found possible to launch an attack on the Northern Kuriles.

d. Soviets to indicate what ports, if any, they could allow the U.S. Navy to use....

e. Soviets to indicate what air bases, if any, they could allow our air forces to use for operations against Japan, and what facilities, including gasoline and bombs, could be supplied....

Discussing this paper with the Joint Chiefs of Staff before it was presented for combined consideration, Admiral Leahy spoke of "instructions recently received by the Joint Chiefs of Staff from the President that the subject of the Japanese war was not to be discussed with the Soviets."[83] How or when these instructions were given is not known; nor are the circumstances that evoked them. However, the chiefs agreed in general that if the Soviets were to bring up the question of the war with Japan they would not be bound by the Presidential instructions and would take up the points recommended in this paper. Even under those conditions, however, the chiefs were wary of introducing this touchy matter with their Russian allies "because of the sensitiveness of the Soviets and their tendency to misunderstand." General Marshall suggested that "if the discussions were conducted by all of the Chiefs, difficulties were sure to ensue." Perhaps the discussions might be delegated to Ambassador W. Averell Harriman or Major General John R. Deane. Admiral King proposed that the questions and their answers should all be given in writing. What the British Chiefs of Staff thought on the subject is not recorded. However, the CCS adopted the U.S. paper "as a basis for the agenda at the forthcoming conference with the U.S.S.R."[84] The problem was purely academic, for the occasion never arose for the military staff to discuss the war with Japan.

There are several published accounts of the conference at Teheran, written by the participants and by other historians of the war.[85] The political discussions were of considerable importance, and the problems of war in Europe consumed a large part of the time of the three leaders of state. Other sections of the History of the Joint Chiefs of Staff will deal in detail with the issues and the discussions at the conference, and it is neither necessary nor desirable to recount them at any length here. There was only one item of direct significance in the war against Japan and that was a very important matter indeed.

At the first plenary session of the three chiefs of state and their military staffs (only Admirals Leahy and King represented the U.S. Chiefs of Staff), President Roosevelt gave "a general survey of the war and of the meaning of the war...from the American point of view."[86] In it he stressed, as the JCS had recommended in their tentative agenda, the demands of the Pacific war upon the interests and the resources of the United States. His account of U.S. accomplishments and plans for the war in the Pacific and in Southeast Asia elicited an important comment from Premier Stalin:

> Unfortunately we [the Soviets] have not so far been able to help because we require too much of our forces on the Western Front and are unable to launch any operations against Japan at this time. Our forces now in the East are more or less satisfactory for defense. However, they must be increased about three-fold for purposes of offensive operations. This condition will not take place until Germany has been forced to capitulate. *Then* by our common front we shall win.

Here was the first commitment of Marshal Stalin himself to the President and the Prime Minister that Russia would ultimately join the fight to defeat Japan. It was given orally, to be sure, but it was well witnessed and it appears in the official minutes of the conference at Teheran. From this point on the Combined Chiefs of Staff could count on Russian participation after the collapse of Germany, if only they could figure out when that was likely to come.

The minutes of the plenary sessions contain no further discussion of this commitment or of the other problems of war with Japan. At the one recorded meeting of a military committee of the three nations (Admiral Leahy, General Marshall, General Sir Alan Brooke, Air Chief Marshal Sir Charles Portal, and Marshal Voroshilov) the entire discussion centered upon operations against Germany, particularly the timing of Overlord and related actions. Talking alone with Marshal Stalin, however, President Roosevelt gave him two memoranda requesting information on the points the chiefs had suggested. Mr. Stalin promised to study them after his return to Moscow.[87]

On 1 December 1943 the President, the Prime Minister, and Marshal Stalin signed a paper which listed the military conclusions of the Eureka Conference. The three:

> (1) Agreed that the Partisans in Yugoslavia should be supported by supplies and equipment to the greatest possible extent, and also by commando operations:
>
> (2) Agreed that, from the military point of view, it was most desirable that Turkey should come into the war on the side of the Allies before the end of the year:
>
> (3) Took note of Marshal Stalin's statement that if Turkey found herself at war with Germany, and as a result Bulgaria declared war on Turkey or attacked her, the Soviet would immediately be at war with Bulgaria. The Conference further

took note that this fact could be explicitly stated in the forthcoming negotiations to bring Turkey into the war:

(4) Took note that Operation Overlord would be launched during May 1944, in conjunction with an operation against Southern France. The latter operation would be undertaken in as great a strength as availability of landing-craft permitted. The Conference further took note of Marshal Stalin's statement that the Soviet forces would launch an offensive at about the same time with the object of preventing the German forces from transferring from the Eastern to the Western Front:

(5) Agreed that the military staffs of the Three Powers should henceforward keep in close touch with each other in regard to the impending operations in Europe. In particular it was agreed that a cover plan to mystify and mislead the enemy as regards these operations should be concerted between the staffs concerned.[88]

None of these, it will be noted, mentioned the war against Japan. Most of them would have no direct influence on events there. The fourth decision, however, as developments had already indicated probably would happen, was to conflict immediately upon the return of the group to Cairo with the plans for Buccaneer.

CAIRO AGAIN

Back to Cairo went the Combined Chiefs of Staff and the President and Prime Minister to work again on some of the problems yet unsolved. It was soon apparent that solution would not be entirely simple.

The crux of the difficulty was the importance of Buccaneer. Before Teheran there had been discussion of the possibilities and the requirements of operations in the eastern Mediterranean, particularly seizure of the island of Rhodes, and the British Chiefs of Staff had indicated their view that such action was of enough importance to require the transfer of landing craft, always in short supply, from the Southeast Asia Command. At Teheran interest in Rhodes had waned as talk centered upon an operation in southern France (Anvil) as a corollary to Overlord. Although no one had more than a general idea of what such an attack would involve, it had appealed to the group and especially to Marshal Stalin and had been included in the final military agreement of the Teheran meetings. If Rhodes had threatened to conflict with Buccaneer, the larger assault on southern France was certain to. At the first CCS meeting after the return from Teheran the problem presented itself.[89]

As has been said no one knew how large Anvil would have to be in order to be successful and there was no decision at Teheran as to how much should be allotted to it. Raising the question at the 3 December meeting, Sir Alan Brooke suggested that the entire landing craft situation be investigated to see where enough for a two-divisional assault on the south of France could be found. Admiral

King at once objected that the agreement had not been on a two-divisional assault, but on as large a one as possible with the available landing craft. Sir Alan simply replied that "he regarded a two-divisional assault as the minimum which could be accepted." Sir Charles Portal backed him up with the hope "that the United States Chiefs of Staff agreed with them, that an assault with less than two divisions would be asking for failure." He reminded the chiefs that the plan that had been considered at Teheran "envisaged something in the neighborhood of a two-divisional assault with an advance up the Rhone by some ten divisions." If that was to be successful, in the opinion of Sir Charles other operations would have to suffer. He considered that the Combined Staff Planners would have to have an indication of the strength of the attack if they were to study the landing craft situation.

Admiral King continued to insist that there was no previous agreement on two divisions and that the planners could work from the available craft to the practicable strength of the operation. Whether by prearrangement or lack of concern none of the other U.S. Chiefs said much on this issue, although no one disputed the fact that the size of the assault had not been settled. Both Admiral Leahy and General Marshall insisted that whatever happened there should be no interference with Overlord. "What was required," said General Marshall, "was a report on the landing craft necessary for a successful operation against the South of France without affecting Operation Overlord. This operation could not be planned on a lavish scale." Admiral King finally gave in on his fight to stay within resources already available, and the Combined Chiefs directed their planners to examine the proposed operation on the assumption that it would be "carried out with a minimum of two assault divisions."

The next morning, Saturday, the combined group joined the Prime Minister and the President for a plenary session at which the chief topic of discussion was Buccaneer and its relation to Anvil and Overlord.[90] Early in the meeting Mr. Churchill put in a plea for an Anvil operation "as strong as possible...planned on the basis of an assault force of at least two divisions." He expressed concern over the large requirements Admiral Mountbatten had submitted for Buccaneer. "Operations in Southeast Asia," he said, "must be judged in their relation to the predominating importance of Overlord." He felt that the situation had changed significantly since the Generalissimo left Cairo under the impression that Buccaneer was to be done. First, "the Soviets had declared themselves ready to go to war with Japan immediately Germany collapsed." Overlord had been scheduled for May, and Anvil had been agreed upon. "Operations in the Southeast Asia Command had lost a good deal of their value."

The British Chiefs of Staff strongly supported their Prime Minister in his questioning of the value of Buccaneer and of the numbers of troops which Admiral Mountbatten was contemplating for the operation. Admiral King alone of the U.S. Chiefs spoke out for Buccaneer, pointing out "that landing craft and assault shipping for a two-division assault was already in sight, subject to certain complications." It had been arranged, he said, to divert to the United Kingdom for Overlord some of the landing craft previously scheduled for the Pacific. Admiral King also told the group that Buccaneer would help operations in the Pacific, for Japanese fighter aircraft would be absorbed by Buccaneer at the same time that Rabaul was being attacked.

President Roosevelt, like Mr. Churchill, was impressed by the size of the force Admiral Mountbatten wanted, and the President suggested that the admiral be told to use what he had. This suggestion Admiral Leahy took up, suggesting "that if it could be decided:

> a. that ANVIL should go ahead on the basis of a two-division assault; and,
> b. that Admiral Mountbatten should be instructed to do the best he could with the resources already allocated to him; the picture would begin to be filled in. Of course, if Admiral Mountbatten said that he could do nothing, some of his resources could be taken away from him for other purposes.

This simplification was not given serious consideration. Mr. Churchill at once suggested that Buccaneer might be postponed until fall, after the monsoon. To this Admiral King objected, reminding the group that "there was a definite commitment to the Generalissimo that there should be an amphibious operation in the spring." Mr. Churchill protested. The Generalissimo could have no illusions about where *he* stood, he said, for when Chiang had insisted that there had to be an amphibious operation simultaneous with the north Burma campaign (Tarzan), the Prime Minister "had said quite firmly that he could not agree." That he was strongly opposed to Buccaneer is evident from the minutes of this meeting where he and his two officers, Sir Charles Portal and Sir Alan Brooke, raised all sorts of arguments for increasing the forces in the European Theater and procuring the additions at the expense of Buccaneer. As Sir Charles reminded the meeting, so far "nobody knew whether a two-division assault would, or would not, be enough for Anvil. Perhaps the lift for an entire division would have to come from the Southeast Asia Command. Sir Alan Brooke pointed out that only three and a half divisions were to be used in the Overlord assault and at present only two at Anvil. "Surely it would be better to employ all the Buccaneer resources to strengthen up the European front."

Mr. Churchill argued the advantages of operations in the Aegean. Finally

> THE PRIME MINISTER suggested that it might be necessary to withdraw resources from BUCCANEER in order to strengthen up OVERLORD and ANVIL.
> THE PRESIDENT said that he could not agree with this. We had a moral obligation to do something for China and he would

not be prepared to forego the amphibious operation, except for some very great and readily apparent reason.

THE PRIME MINISTER said that this "very good reason" might be provided by Overlord. At present the assault was only on a $3\frac{1}{2}$ division basis, whereas we had put 9 divisions ashore in Sicily on the first day. The operation was at present on a very narrow margin.

FIELD MARSHAL DILL thought it was impossible for us to be strong at both OVERLORD AND ANVIL.

ADMIRAL LEAHY agreed that, from the military point of view, there was everything to be said for strengthening up OVERLORD and ANVIL at the expense of other theaters; but there were serious political issues at stake.

GENERAL MARSHALL agreed with Field Marshal Dill and Admiral Leahy. He pointed out, however, that the difficulties in abandoning or postponing Buccaneer were not merely political. If Buccaneer was cancelled, the Generalissimo would not allow Chinese forces to take part in TARZAN. There would be no campaign in Upper Burma, and this would have its repercussion on the operations in the Pacific. There would be a revulsion of feeling in China; the effect on Japan would be bad, and the line of communication [to] Indochina would be at hazard.

THE PRIME MINISTER observed that he had never committed himself to the scale or timing of the amphibious operation in the Southeast Asia Theater. Perhaps it might be advisable to revert to Akyab or Ramree.

THE PRESIDENT said that the Generalissimo was anxious that we should secure a base from which the supply line from Bangkok could be bombed.

ADMIRAL KING, in reply to a question from the Prime Minister, said that he had no fear of the Japanese being able to retake the Andamans once we had occupied them. He added that any increase in the scale of Buccaneer was out of the question.

The meeting concluded with an injunction from the President and Prime Minister to their respective staffs to meet together and try to reach agreement on the points at issue in the light of the discussion which had taken place.

It can hardly be said that the issues were clearly defined at the close of this plenary session. There was no question but that Overlord would be done and little doubt that there would be some form of Anvil. Even during the course of the meeting, however, the British, originally advocating a minimum of two divisions for Anvil, had enlarged their position and were urging concentrating everything upon Anvil and Overlord, to the point of cancelling or at least of postponing Buccaneer. The U.S. representatives, while also supporting Overlord and Anvil, had not yielded in their insistence upon Buccaneer, although the operation had been limited to the capabilities of available resources. Interestingly, though, they were arguing for it primarily for political reasons, that the Generalissimo was expecting it and should not be disappointed, lest he refuse to participate in the more significant ground campaign. The Americans did not attempt on this occasion to justify it strategically.

The Combined Chiefs of Staff met that afternoon and worked through various other matters with which they were concerned, including the over-all plan for the defeat of Japan, reviewing the discussion of the plenary session as the last item of a long afternoon.[91] It is impossible to tell from the extremely summary minutes how the discussion went, but the differences remained unresolved. The chiefs decided that the two groups should draft separate papers on "high policy regarding the European Theater and the Southeast Asia Command."

The two drafts were exchanged that evening.[92] They agreed only in the statement that Overlord and Anvil were the supreme operations for 1944 and that they must be carried out in May. To the British Chiefs this meant "that any other operations which may interfere with or prejudice the success of Overlord or Anvil must be postponed or cancelled. Consequently, Operation Buccaneer must be postponed until after the monsoon, and such resources now allocated to it as are required for European operations must be made available." The political implications of such postponement the British would leave to the President and the Prime Minister. The Americans recommended doing "everything practicable" to increase the strength of Overlord and if necessary provide additional resources for Anvil. Additional landing craft, however, should come not from Buccaneer but from "accelerated building and conversion." For, said the U.S. Chiefs:

> Political and military considerations and commitments make it essential that Operation TARZAN and a simultaneous amphibious operation should take place in March. Apart from political considerations, there may be serious military repercussions if this is not done, not only in Burma and China, but also in the Pacific.

Admiral Mountbatten, they proposed, "should be told that he must do the best that he can with the resources already allocated to him."

Meeting at 0900 the following morning, the Joint Chiefs of Staff concentrated on attempting to define the military considerations that made Buccaneer essential.[93] There was no disagreement among the group (at least none is recorded) as General Marshall and Admiral King enumerated ways in which abandonment of Buccaneer and the almost certain corollary abandonment of Tarzan would react to the disadvantage of the United Nations. General Marshall suggested that "the failure to do TARZAN hazarded the entire air lift to China," despite the British view that the air line could be protected even if Tarzan were not done. "If TARZAN was abandoned," added Admiral King, "the Japanese would be able to divert forces for employment against the main lines of advance through the South and Southwest and Central Pacific." General Somervell interposed his belief "that a failure to carry out the Burma campaign would be bitterly resented by the Chinese." Apparently Admiral King was sympathetic with Chiang's view, for he expressed the opinion that "an amphibious operation was essential to the success of the North Burma operation and must be mounted."

The emphasis the U.S. Chiefs put upon the military significance of Buccaneer at their meeting with the British Chiefs immediately following the joint session came as a surprise to the British, who had thought the disagreement was almost entirely on the political aspects.[94] The discussion thus took quite a different turn from any of the earlier ones, with comments back and forth on the implications of failure to do Tarzan and the advantages of holding the Andaman Islands. It was an inconclusive exchange in which neither side yielded. The chiefs had only a half hour before moving on to a plenary session, and they finally submitted their unresolved views to the President and Prime Minister.[95]

Again the conference at Cairo took up in plenary session the problem of Buccaneer.[96] Prime Minister Churchill suggested a new solution, advancing the date for the operation perhaps to January; but General Marshall at once announced that this would be impossible. Alternatively Mr. Churchill suggested postponing Buccaneer until fall, after the monsoon, and informing the Generalissimo "that, as a result of developments arising from the discussion with the Russians, we could not carry out Buccaneer as originally contemplated." But President Roosevelt was skeptical of this course. "Suppose," said he, "Marshal Stalin was unable to be as good as his word; we might find that we had forfeited Chinese support without obtaining commensurate help from the Russians."

Mr. Hopkins, who had attended the previous session but had taken little or no part in the discussions, stepped into this one, ascertaining by asking a number of pertinent questions that as yet there had been no detailed study as to whether a two-divisional assault would be adequate for Anvil and that if more were necessary there would have to be more landing craft from somewhere.

Otherwise the talk covered many of the same points that had been discussed before. Admiral King continued to have the most to say in support of the operation, but it was the British and particularly Prime Minister Churchill who did most of the talking. To mollify Chiang Kai-shek, Mr. Churchill suggested,

> the Generalissimo should be informed that Admiral Mountbatten had now said that he wanted more forces than had been contemplated when he, the Generalissimo, had been in Cairo. It was therefore proposed to postpone BUCCANEER until after the monsoon. Meanwhile, TARZAN would go forward. The postponement of BUCCANEER would not effect [sic] TARZAN. If the Generalissimo expressed surprise and threatened to withhold the Yunnan forces, we should say that we would go on without them. Alternatively, we could say that the inaction of the Yunnan forces would allow more supplies to go over the "hump."

Once again the meeting broke up with the problem unresolved. The group accepted a suggestion from the Prime Minister that the Combined Chiefs of Staff "consult with the Force Commanders of Buccaneer" and then ask Admiral Mountbatten what lesser amphibious operations he could do "if the bulk of landing craft and assault shipping were withdrawn from Southeast Asia during the next few weeks."

The Combined Chiefs met that afternoon with the British Force Commanders for Buccaneer, Lieutenant General J. Stopford, Rear Admiral T. Troubridge, and Air Vice Marshal J.W. Baker, and with Major General A.C. Wedemeyer.[97] From the Force Commanders' statements the chiefs concluded that there were enough resources for Buccaneer already available in Southeast Asia with the exception of some 120 carrier-borne aircraft. These promised no difficulty, however, for Admiral King thought it highly probable that four to six CVE's could be made available from U.S. sources. The chiefs agreed to send a despatch to Admiral Mountbatten for an estimate on an alternative amphibious operation and in the meantime to put the SEAC representatives at Cairo, in consultation with the Combined Staff Planners, to work on one for discussion the following morning. By the next morning the situation had changed.

Some time in the afternoon of 5 December Mr. Roosevelt finally made up his mind to give in to the insistence of the Prime Minister and bring the long discussion to an end by agreeing to postpone if not cancel Buccaneer.[98] Mr. Churchill was delighted with the decision, but not so the U.S. Joint Chiefs of Staff. They all believed, and Admiral King in particular insisted, that Chiang Kai-shek would not continue to agree to do Tarzan without Buccaneer, and, as will be shown, they were quite correct. But of course President Roosevelt's decision held. With the concurrence of Mr. Churchill he informed the Generalissimo:

> Conference with Stalin involves us in combined grand operations on European continent in late spring giving fair prospect of terminating war with Germany by end of summer of 1944. These operations impose so large a requirement of heavy landing craft as to make it impracticable to devote a sufficient number to the amphibious operation in Bay of Bengal simultaneously with launching of Tarzan to insure success of operations.
>
> This being the case: Would you be prepared [to] go ahead with Tarzan as now planned, including commitment to maintain naval control of Bay of Bengal coupled with naval carrier and commando amphibious raiding operation simultaneous with launching of Tarzan? Also there is the prospect of B-29 bombing of railroad and port Bangkok.
>
> If not, would you prefer to have Tarzan delayed until November to include heavy amphibious operation. Meanwhile concentrating all air transport on carrying supplies over the hump to air and ground forces in China.

I am influenced in this matter by the tremendous advantage
to be received by China and the Pacific through the early
termination of the war with Germany.[99]

The same evening the Combined Staff Planners reported that,
after making a general survey of the possibilities of an amphibious operation in Southeast Asia without most of the landing craft,
they had concluded that there might be some merit in operations
along the Arakan coast or in capturing the northern tip of Ramree
Island.[100] But this was hardly a recommendation, for those who
made the survey were far removed from the theater of operations.
There was nothing that the CCS could do but note the paper.[101]
The Combined Chief also approved a statement of the situation in
the form of four decisions proposed by the U.S. Chiefs:

    a. Delay major amphibious operations in the Bay of Bengal
until after the next monsoon and divert the landing craft now
assigned to BUCCANEER to Operations ANVIL and OVERLORD.

    b. Make all preparations to conduct TARZAN as planned, less
BUCCANEER, for which will be substituted naval carrier and amphibious raiding operations simultaneous with the launching of
TARZAN; and carry out air bombardment of the Bangkok-Burma
railroad and the harbor of Bangkok, in the meantime maintaining naval control of the Bay of Bengal, or, alternatively,

    c. Postpone TARZAN, increase to a maximum with planes available the air lift to China across the "hump," and intensify the
measures which will enable the B-29's to be brought to bear on
the enemy.

    d. The choice between alternatives *b* and *c* above will be
made at a later date by the Combined Chiefs of Staff after obtaining an expression of opinion by the Generalissimo and the
Supreme Allied Commander, Southeast Asia Command.

Admiral Mountbatten later that day turned down any other amphibious operation as impracticable and advised the CCS that a
revision of Tarzan would be required in the light of Chiang's
probable refusal to participate, a decision which the chiefs accepted as inevitable.[102] Buccaneer was off, and with it went the
recently engendered hope of the U.S. Chiefs for enthusiastic
British cooperation in action in Burma. The repercussions of
the reversal in China and in Southeast Asia were significant but
will remain for discussion in a later chapter.

With the removal of this roadblock the Sextant Conference would
come to an early conclusion. At the meetings of 6 and 7 December
1943 the CCS cleared up the last of the papers remaining, including the over-all plan for Japan's defeat and specific operations
for 1944 in the war against Japan. The chiefs also adopted a
recommendation made by General Arnold that seemed likely to resolve the problem of the allocation of Hump tonnage. In order
that Admiral Mountbatten should have control over the resources
assigned to him and at the same time that there should be firm
commitments of tonnage for the next six months, fixed numbers of

planes were assigned to Tarzan and to deliveries to China and a specified number of tons for China was set for the next six months. If this did not give Chiang what he had asked at least it insured that China would be provided for.[103]

FINAL REPORT

On 6 December 1943 the Combined Chiefs presented the heads of state with a final report on the conclusions of the Sextant Conference.[104] It had much the same form as the Quadrant report and in fact incorporated much of the wording of that document *in toto*. Included were all the decisions of the Teheran meetings as well as those which had been worked out at Cairo. At the last plenary session President Roosevelt commended the Combined Chiefs of Staff upon their report, while Mr. Churchill dubbed it "a masterly survey of the whole military scene. He gave it as his opinion that when military historians came to adjudge the decisions of the Sextant Conference, they would find them fully in accordance with the classic articles of war."

There remained the inevitable last-minute rough estimate of whether or not available resources were sufficient for the operations which had been set up at Sextant.[105] As to ground forces there was no question. Naval forces "so far as can be foreseen" would be available. There might be a deficiency of troop carrier squadrons in the Mediterranean, of land-based aircraft in the Pacific if the war with Germany lasted too long, and of transport aircraft for China if forces in North Burma required too many. The production of LST's and LCT's continued "to be the bottleneck limiting the scope of operations against the enemy," but it was considered that there should be enough for approved operations in 1944 if carefully used. This was taking cognizance of the fact that a month's production of LST's previously assigned to the Pacific and destined for use at Truk was to be sent instead to the European Theater for use in Anvil. By pooling resources within the Pacific Theater it was hoped that the deficiency in the Pacific could be cancelled.

If all went well, 1944 would see the long-awaited attack on the northwest coast of Europe, combined with a newly planned assault upon the southern shores of France. The troops already battling in Italy would push on as far as the Pisa-Rimini line. Together these operations should bring Germany close to capitulation by the end of the year. In the Pacific the new B-29 programs would be launched both from China and from bases in the Marianas, for by October 1944 the advance was to take in Guam and other points in the Marianas, while General MacArthur's forces in the Southwest Pacific were to have occupied the Vogelkop of New Guinea and be poised for action in the Philippines. Only in Southeast Asia were the projects for which the U.S. Chiefs had expected approval when Sextant opened left in a state of uncertainty. Elsewhere 1944 was to register strong punches upon the weakening Axis.

Chapter XXI

MONTHS OF CRITICAL DECISION, JANUARY-MAY 1944

By the beginning of 1944 the production of war materials in the United States was reaching high gear. Critical items that were not yet available were at least expected to be available within a calculated space of time. In both the European and the Pacific Theaters United Nations forces were prepared to take the offensive. The long-awaited cross-Channel invasion of Europe was scheduled for the spring of 1944, and forces of hitherto unequalled proportions were being rapidly assembled in the British Isles. In the Mediterranean area plans were maturing for a landing at Anzio in an attempt to turn the flank of the German line of defense in Italy and speed the capture of Rome. Farther ahead lay the landings in southern France which were to be keyed in with the major attack in the north. The campaign in the South-Southwest Pacific to seize vital points in the Solomons, New Britain, and New Guinea in order to neutralize Rabaul was nearing completion. Central Pacific forces had completed operations in the Gilbert Islands and were shortly to attack key positions in the Marshalls. In Southeast Asia the Chinese Ledo force under General Stilwell was moving into Upper Burma. British forces at Imphal were preparing for limited operations in the west. Future plans for the area had just been radically changed by the decision at Cairo to transfer landing craft to the Mediterranean.

The general outline of the program that would eventually bring Japan to its knees had been drawn, and tentative objectives for 1944 had been approved. The time had come to make the decisions that would convert the long range plans and estimates into tangible and practicable directives to the commanders whose responsibility it was to carry them out.

MOVING ON IN THE PACIFIC

At the end of 1943 General MacArthur's forces in the Southwest Pacific were rapidly consolidating positions around Rabaul from the southwest while the forces under Admiral Halsey in the South Pacific Area were moving upon the same objective from the southeast. As the action moved out of the original geographic limits of the South Pacific Area it would seem logical to expect that that command would cease to be operational and the combat forces assigned there would be transferred either to the neighboring Southwest Pacific or to the Central Pacific. At the least there would have to be some decision and some directive to General MacArthur for operations to follow the isolation of Rabaul.

Early in December the members of OPD of the War Department proposed to their naval counterparts a message to be sent by the Joint Chiefs to General MacArthur.[1] OPD suggested that General MacArthur be asked to recommend a directive for operations following Cartwheel (action culminating in the isolation of Rabaul). It should, the planners suggested, be based on certain assumptions: that operations in the Central Pacific would continue under the command of Admiral Nimitz, while General MacArthur controlled those in the Southwest Pacific Area; that air and ground forces currently allocated to the South Pacific Area should be transferred to the Southwest Pacific Area in accordance with mutual recommendations from General MacArthur, Admiral Nimitz, and Admiral Halsey; that elements of the Third Fleet from the South Pacific Area would be consolidated with the Seventh Fleet in the Southwest Pacific Area; that only garrison and maintenance forces would remain in the South Pacific; that supply, staging, training, and rehabilitation in the South Pacific Area would be made available as required to the Commander in Chief, Southwest Pacific Area, and similar facilities in the Southwest Pacific would be available to the Commander in Chief, Pacific Ocean Areas.

These suggestions did not meet with approval in the Navy Department. In the first place, as Admiral Bieri informed Brigadier General Frank N. Roberts, the naval planners considered it undesirable to ask General MacArthur for his recommendations, especially when there was probably no agreement within the Pacific Theater.[2] "The establishment of the relationship between areas," said Admiral Bieri, "is a responsibility of the J.C.S. and can be settled without getting into an inter-theatre discussion." He took exception to most of OPD's assumptions, making it evident that he did not favor transferring the South Pacific forces wholesale to the Southwest Pacific. As Admiral Bieri saw it the immediate problem was to establish a basis for coordinating the operations about to be launched in the Pacific. Sometime later it could be decided what forces would be transferred from the South Pacific Area after completion of operations in the Bismarck Archipelago. Admiral Bieri proposed a directive to General MacArthur to proceed into the Bismarck Archipelago and along the north coast of New Guinea, with support and cover by forces under Admiral Nimitz's command. Immediate command of the operation against Kavieng on the northwest end of New Ireland would be reserved to the Commander, South Pacific, as had been provided in the earlier Elkton plans.

It was almost a month before a final directive went from the JCS to General MacArthur. In the meantime plans and preparations were being made by General MacArthur and Admiral Nimitz, the former to attack Manus Island in the Admiralties and Kavieng on

24 March, the latter to cover for this action by a strong carrier attack upon Japanese Fleet units at Truk.[3] General MacArthur was insistent that command for the operations in the Bismarck Archipelago must be undivided, a point upon which apparently there was misunderstanding but no disagreement, and that the allocation of forces should be controlled by the Joint Chiefs of Staff rather than by himself or by Admiral Nimitz. After an exchange of memoranda General Marshall and Admiral King agreed to this provision. Directives were sent to General MacArthur and Admiral Nimitz on 23 January 1944.[4] Operations "for seizure or control of the BISMARCK ARCHIPELAGO" were assigned a target date of 1 April. The timing for the advance along the north coast of New Guinea was left to the local commander for determination.

The air attack on Truk which was to provide cover for the seizure of Manus Island and Kavieng (or Emirau Island, which Admiral Halsey and Admiral Nimitz favored) was expected in naval circles to prove perhaps "even more important in the prosecution of the war" than the operations for which it would provide a diversion.[5] At the least it would yield intelligence information of the atoll's fortifications and strength. It was strongly hoped that important units of the Japanese Fleet might also be surprised there and perhaps destroyed. But the forces required for such an attack and others needed in the Bismarcks operation could not be provided by the Pacific Fleet without affecting the schedule for operations in the Central Pacific. Completion of the campaign in the Marshalls would have to be postponed; seizure of Kusaie, Eniwetok, and Wake, deferred until the first of May.[6]

With the Marshalls under U.S. control, what would come next? In January 1944 no one was sure. When Admiral King flew to Pearl Harbor at the beginning of the month, he was apprised of the views of the staff of the Commander in Chief, Pacific Ocean Areas, which had been incorporated in the plan, Granite.

Granite was based upon the program set at Sextant in CCS 417/2, translating that program into a schedule of operations for the year ahead. It contemplated obtaining control of the Marshalls in two steps, capturing Kwajalein and Eniwetok and neutralizing the remainder of the Marshalls, Wake, and Kusaie. Then would come the Carolines. With Ponape bypassed, at least one all-out carrier strike would be made against Truk. About 1 August the Mortlock Islands would be taken, concurrent with or followed by the seizure of Truk. Guam and the Japanese Marianas would be taken about 1 November; Tinian, Saipan, and Guam would be captured simultaneously if possible. Granite recognized that it might prove possible to bypass Truk and take Palau and the Marianas *seriatim* or simultaneously, but no target date was proposed. After completion of this program, Central Pacific forces would cooperate with those from the Southwest Pacific Area to reoccupy the Philippines and establish sea communications to China. For operations up to 1 August 1944 forces were available in the Pacific. After that date more heavy bombers would be needed.[7]

Admiral King seems to have agreed with the views of the local planners. He reminded the group that the objective of the drive across the Pacific was China, because of its strategical position and supply of manpower. He said again, as he had frequently said before, that the key to the Pacific was the Mariana Islands, whose possession would not only cut the Japanese line of communications to the more southerly islands but would furnish bases from which U.S. forces could strike at Japan. With the capture of the Marshalls the Marianas would be much nearer. Rear Admiral Forrest Sherman suggested that if it should prove possible to bypass the much-dreaded Truk perhaps Central Pacific forces could go directly to Saipan, Tinian, and Guam. Admiral King returned to Washington with the impression that his opinions had been endorsed by the Pacific planners.

The question of what was to come after the Marshalls and the Bismarck Archipelago were taken was discussed at considerable length at a conference of representatives of the various areas of the Pacific at Pearl Harbor at the end of January. The main purpose of the meeting was to arrange for coordinating efforts in the impending operations in the Southwest and Central Pacific Areas, and the talk of future plans was indecisive. It was nonetheless interesting.[8]

There was general agreement among the group that the ultimate objective of the Pacific advance was China and that the road to China lay through the Philippines. Admiral Nimitz and his planners were uncertain what the next move after completion of the Marshalls campaign should be, whether to Truk, to Palau, or to the Marianas. As Admiral Sherman later explained their attitude, it was "to keep our minds open and not make any commitments in regard to the situation as it develops. The way to make progress in the Pacific Campaign is to commit ourselves to one operation at a time, and each time be prepared to exploit as much as possible any favorable development that may occur."

It appeared increasingly possible that Truk could be bypassed and Palau be made the next objective in the Central Pacific. If Palau could be taken by fall, Rear Admiral Charles H. McMorris predicted, "it should be possible to be in the Philippines by the end of the year." Such progress would be dependent upon developments in the Southwest Pacific Area, and the representatives from General MacArthur's staff had some ideas about that. General Sutherland, Chief of Staff, spoke strongly in favor of pooling all available resources in the Pacific and concentrating upon operations in the Southwest Pacific Area. "If Central Pacific will move against Palau as the next operation after the Marshalls," he said, "and make available to SWPA the amphibious force now contemplated for Truk, we can take all of New Guinea, the Kai and Tanimbars, and Halmahera in time to join you in amphibious movement to Mindanao this year." Concentrating resources in the Pacific upon the Southwest Pacific Area rather than dividing the effort on two axes was a concept long advocated by General

MacArthur. There was considerable support for it at the Pearl Harbor conference, and the Southwest Pacific Area group was encouraged by the trend of the discussion. "The responsible people," Admiral Nimitz, Admiral McMorris, and Admiral Sherman, did not offer arguments against it. On the other hand neither did they speak in favor of transferring the bulk of the resources of the Pacific Ocean Areas to the Southwest Pacific.

Admiral King's enthusiasm for the Marianas was not shared by the group attending the Pearl Harbor conference. The general reaction was, in fact, opposition, particularly opposition to the potential use of the islands as bases for B-29's. Admiral McMorris said he doubted if long range bombing from the Marianas would cause the capitulation of Japan; Lieutenant General George C. Kenney, Commanding General of Allied Air Forces, Southwest Pacific Area, spoke of the bombing project as "just a stunt." Vice Admiral John H. Towers, Commander Air Force Pacific, recommended that if the Marianas were in fact not going to be useful as bases for long range aircraft the strategy should be completely reoriented. Vice Admiral Thomas C. Kinkaid, Commander, Seventh Fleet, remarked that "any talk of the Marianas for a base leaves me entirely cold." Even Admiral Sherman had much to say about the costliness of operations in the Marianas and the limitations of the harbors they afforded. The strategic importance of the islands for protection of the line of communications to the Philippines and neutralization of the Carolines, the point Admiral King stressed, was not even mentioned.

As has been said, there were no strategic decisions made at the conference at Pearl Harbor. Decisions would have to be made in Washington, and almost at once Admiral Sherman and General Sutherland were both to present their views there to the Joint Chiefs of Staff and their planners.

As the Pearl Harbor conference concluded, forces were poised to strike at the Marshall Islands, to seize Majuro and Kwajalein. It had been agreed at the meetings that the next action after completion of this operation would be on 26 March when a task fleet consisting of all available fast carriers and battleships plus supporting forces would attack Truk. Two carrier divisions would then be transferred to the South Pacific Force to participate in the Kavieng-Manus operations, while the other naval forces covered the operation, if possible engaging the enemy fleet. By about 14 April all of these would be released again to the Central Pacific to participate in the final phase of the Marshalls campaign, the seizure of Eniwetok.[9]

Breaking off thus in the midst of the Marshalls operation to lend support to the South-Southwest Pacific can hardly have been desired by the planners of the Pacific staff. At the least it would give the enemy a chance to strengthen his position. But bases in the Admiralties were highly important for staging future operations and for supporting the westward advancing fleet, especially since Rabaul was to be bypassed. It was then assumed that they would not be acquired without additional help from the Pacific Fleet, although this support subsequently proved unnecessary. The Kwajalein operation, begun on 31 January, went so well that on 2 February it was nearly concluded, with considerably smaller losses than anticipated and having involved only part of the forces prepared. Consequently the Joint Chiefs of Staff told Admiral Nimitz that, if he wanted to go ahead at once with the seizure and occupation of Eniwetok, they would accept a short delay in the Kavieng-Manus operation. On 18-19 February U.S. forces took Eniwetok, two months ahead of schedule.[10]

Acceleration of the campaign in the Marshalls made it even more imperative that decision be made as to what was to be done next and what route was to be followed across the Pacific. The latest plan received in Washington from General MacArthur was Reno III, a program which, utilizing his own forces and those in the South Pacific Area plus support from the Pacific Fleet, would secure for General MacArthur control of all of New Guinea and the nearby islands of the Netherlands East Indies as far as Mindanao in the Philippines. This program, it will be recalled, had not been accepted in its entirety at Sextant. No decision had been made that would provide to the Commander in Chief, Southwest Pacific Area, the requisite forces for such a campaign. That he was still thinking in those strategic terms had been brought out at the Pearl Harbor meetings, but no revision of Reno III had been presented to Washington. As the Joint Chiefs and their planners prepared to restudy the problem of Pacific operations, General MacArthur was asked again for his plans and a redefinition of his needs.[11]

On 2 February a long cable from General MacArthur was received in the War Department. In it he predicted that, if all mobile forces of the South and Southwest Pacific Areas were used, the Geelvink Bay-Vogelkop movement projected in Reno III could not be begun before 1 October 1944 and entrance into the Philippines no sooner than March 1945. Even that schedule would require more air and amphibious forces by 1 October. The possibility that the forces of the South Pacific Area might not be transferred to his command was simply unthinkable. They had been under his strategic direction since mid-1943 and the Reno plans were drawn on the assumption that they would be available. "While it can be understood that additional means can not be provided if they are not available to the War and Navy Departments under existing commitments," said General MacArthur, "I must state that any reduction in the forces presently engaged in the Southwest Pacific by actual withdrawal of forces of any category would be incomprehensible. It would unquestionably prolong the war and would have the most profound psychological effect."[12] This led General MacArthur to present his views of the strategic concept being followed in the Pacific:

> ...There are now large forces available in the Pacific which with the accretions scheduled for the current year would permit

the execution of an offensive which would place us in the Philippines in December if the forces were employed in effective combination. However, under the plan of campaign that has been prepared in Washington, the forces will be employed in two weak thrusts which can not attain the major strategic objective until several months later resulting at best in the delay of future operations that would entail conflict with the rainy season in the Philippines with a consequent overall delay in the conduct of the war of 6 additional months. ...Move through the mandated islands does not attain a major strategic objective nor can it prepare for the assault against the major objective of the Philippines because it is impossible to secure land based air support or to prepare a fleet base therein due to the lack of adequate land areas for such installations and to the distances involved. All available ground, air and assault forces in the Pacific should be combined in a drive along the New Guinea-Mindanao axis supported by the main fleet based at Manus Island and other facilities already available in these waters. This axis provides the shortest and most direct route to the strategic objective and is the only one that permits of an effective combination of land, sea and air forces. I propose that with the completion of the operations in the Marshalls, the maximum force from all sources in the Pacific be concentrated in my drive up the New Guinea coast to Mindanao, to be coordinated with a Central Pacific operation against the Palaus and the support by combatant elements of the Pacific Fleet with orders to contain or destroy the Japanese Fleet.

This program inevitably aroused strong resistance from Admiral King. He had just received the minutes of the Pearl Harbor conference of 27-28 January and read them "with indignant dismay."[13] "The idea of rolling up the Japanese along the NEW GUINEA coast, through HALMAHERA and MINDANAO, and up through the PHILIPPINES to LUZON, as our major strategic concept, to the exclusion of clearing our CENTRAL PACIFIC line of communications to the PHILIPPINES," he said, "is to me absurd. Further, it is not in accordance with the decisions of the Joint Chiefs of Staff." Admiral King assumed that Admiral Nimitz was in agreement with his own strategic ideas, and he told the Commander in Chief, Pacific Ocean Areas, "I'm afraid...that you have not...maintained these views sufficiently positively vis-a-vis the officers from the SOUTH and SOUTHWEST PACIFIC." Lest there be some doubt as to what his views were, he commented at length on the importance of the Marianas and the Carolines and outlined his own strategic concept for the defeat of Japan:

    (1) - Japan will ultimately be forced to her "inner ring" of defense - Japan, Korea, Manchuria, Shantung, etc.
    (2) - Everything that we do must be related to (1).
    (3) - (1) requires use of China as a base - and of Chinese manpower to secure and maintain the base.

(4) - (3) requires availability of ports in China - none of which are accessible north of Formosa.
(5) - LUZON is the key point for opening up sea routes to ports in China.
(6) - Central Pacific general objective is LUZON.
(7) - (6) requires clearing Japs out of Carolines, Marianas, Pelews - and holding them.
(8) - (7) cuts Jap lines of communications to Netherlands East Indies east of Philippine Islands - also protects flank of advance from S.W. Pacific to Mindanao.
(9) - (7) has priority over advance from S.W. Pacific to Mindanao.
(10) - Occupation and use of Mindanao will not open communications with ports in China - Mindoro Strait is controlled from Luzon - Balabac Strait is too far to southward.
(11) - Occupation and use of Mindanao is primarily to effect reoccupation of Philippine Islands which will roll-up against tremendous difficulties.
(12) - (10) and (11) emphasize (5), (6), (7), (8).

If the naval officers attending the conference at Pearl Harbor had seemed half-hearted in their support of the above strategy, General MacArthur in his cable of 2 February certainly was not half-hearted, and Admiral King expressed strong disagreement with the general's views.[14] Apparently, said Admiral King, General MacArthur had not accepted the decisions of the Combined Chiefs of Staff at Sextant. Admiral King reminded General Marshall that the chiefs had decided (in CCS 417) that

> the advance in the Pacific shall be simultaneous along both axes and shall be mutually supporting, that when conflicts in timing and allocation of means exist, due weight should be accorded to the fact that operations in the Central Pacific promise at this time a more rapid advance toward Japan and her vital lines of communication.

Admiral King expressed the view that it was not a propitious time to revise the agreed strategy. Moreover he thought the people in the Southwest Pacific Area were unduly optimistic about the rate of their advance in New Guinea. There certainly had not yet been any long or rapid forward strides. Furthermore he could not see that the presence of the entire Pacific Fleet or even a considerable part of it was essential to the New Guinea campaign. Nor was he convinced that it would prove necessary to fight all the way north through the Philippines. In short, Admiral King recommended that General MacArthur be required to submit his plans immediately for executing the CCS decisions for operations for 1944.

On the same day Admiral King sent these remarks to General Marshall, General Sutherland and Admiral Sherman attended the meeting of the Joint Chiefs of Staff to discuss future operations in the Pacific.[15] General Sutherland urged the concentration of forces on the New Guinea-Mindanao axis, predicting that the Reno program could be accelerated and Mindanao occupied by 1 December 1944. Asked by Admiral King what would come next, General Sutherland recommended that the Philippine Islands should be reconquered; then would come the move to China.

The plan Admiral Sherman discussed was an accelerated Granite. If Eniwetok was to be taken in February instead of April the next major operation would be done in June. Since it was highly unlikely that the Southwest Pacific advance would have gotten far enough to support occupation of Palau, the June objective would be either the Carolines or the Marianas, depending on whether or not the Japanese Navy had been materially reduced or driven back. This plan, too, called for reconquest of the Philippine Islands but differed in that Luzon would be occupied at the same time an attack was being made on Mindanao.

These discussions and the progress of operations in the theater led General Marshall to recommend that it was time to reexamine Pacific strategy.[16] With both of the area commanders proposing plans that would employ the forces of the South Pacific Area, clearly there would be conflicts unless the chiefs made some clear-cut decision on the scale and timing of future operations. Consequently General Marshall suggested that the Joint Strategic Survey Committee be asked for its advice on the general line of action that should be pursued in the Pacific. Admiral King agreed readily and the committee went to work.[17] On 16 February JSSC presented its report, JCS 713.[18]

The Joint Strategic Survey Committee was still convinced that "the primary effort against Japan should be made from the East, across the Central Pacific." Operations in other areas, the Southwest Pacific, the North Pacific, China and Burma, should be coordinated with and support the primary effort. The JSSC considered the ultimate objective of Pacific strategy to be to crack "the Japanese citadel"--Japan, Korea, Manchuria, and Shantung--using China as a base. The goal of the westward advance would be the line Luzon-Formosa-China coast, with Formosa the center of the area for attacking the citadel of Japan. The most direct and fastest route to this area led across the Central Pacific.

The Southwest Pacific concept had been supported principally on the grounds that it would employ sea, land, and air power in the best combination, but with this argument the committee took issue. It appeared, JCS 713 contended, that the SWPA concept would involve large land masses and require large land forces to counter the great Japanese strength on land. Naval power could not be fully employed in the area, but enough of it would be required to prevent full employment in the Central Pacific. As for air, there would be no early use at all for the B-29's. The committee also doubted the contention that it would prove easier to support the Reno campaign logistically but offered no figures, merely saying that the basic question was not which would be easier but whether the most promising course could be supported.

Completion of the Reno program would see U.S. forces in Mindanao. But Mindanao would be only the entrance to the Philippines, and it would be necessary to fight the full length of the islands in order to attain the desirable strategic position. This was not the best way to fight Japan, said the Joint Strategic Survey Committee. The chiefs should establish clearly:

>(1) That the primary effort against Japan will be made from the east across the Central Pacific, with a view to the early seizure of the Formosa, Luzon, China coast area, as a base from which to attack the citadel of Japan.
>
>(2) That operations in the Southwest Pacific along the New Guinea-Mindanao axis, in coordinated support of the primary effort through the Central Pacific, will be continued with all resources that can be made available, such availability to be determined from time to time by the Joint Chiefs of Staff in order to insure the continuous and most effective employment of all forces.
>
>(3) That operations in Southeast Asia and China will be maintained and supported to the extent to which they are practicable and contribute to the over-all concept of the earliest possible defeat of Japan.
>
>(4) That operations in the North Pacific will support the primary effort in the Central Pacific, the kind and extent of such operations to be related to and coordinated with Russia's action in regard to Japan.

Approved plans for the capture of the Admiralty Islands should be carried out. Then would come the capture of the Marianas and the neutralization or capture of the Carolines, followed by the seizure of Palau. From the Palau-Marianas line forces would move to Formosa, directly, or via Luzon, taking Mindanao if necessary as an intermediate objective.

While agreeing that the Luzon-Formosa-China coast area constituted the first major objective of the Pacific campaign, General Marshall called attention to the fact that the Joint Strategic Survey Committee had left some of the most important questions unanswered. For example, how should amphibious craft be allocated? And how would land-based and carrier-based air power best be employed? He stressed the desirability of keeping plans for successive operations flexible. The Army planners had inferred from JCS 713 that the Southwest Pacific Area would get what was left over after the requirements of the Central Pacific were satisfied. There was not even an indication of the relative timing of operations in the two areas. General Marshall proposed that the Joint Staff Planners be asked for recommendations on timing and on the most feasible approach to the major objective and be directed to investigate the availability of resources. He also recommended that both General MacArthur and Admiral Nimitz be asked to make plans and suggestions for succeeding operations in their areas, the latter also being asked for his views as to whether Truk should be taken.[19]

Admiral King reminded General Marshall that the early success at Kwajalein had opened the way to accelerating the campaign in the Central Pacific. Admiral King urged that the momentum be sustained by directing Admiral Nimitz to prepare his forces to take Truk in order to secure control of the Carolines, or to bypass Truk if possible, "seizing, occupying, defending, and developing bases in the Marianas, and/or the Pelews" instead.[20] Admiral King offered no target date, but Admiral Nimitz had in fact already begun to prepare forces, for the Truk operations or an alternate one, with a tentative target date of 15 June 1944.[21] From General MacArthur in the meantime had come a message addressed to General Sutherland protesting the possibility that South Pacific forces might be removed from his control and insisting that "the Philippines remained the key to the Pacific situation."[22]

Clearly there would have to be some decision in Washington as to what the route to the far Pacific was to be, but before that was achieved the area commanders in the Pacific Theater could well be alerted that it was likely to come. Admiral Bieri and General Handy consulted on the message General Marshall had proposed, eliminating the request for Admiral Nimitz's views on Truk, since they were likely to be forthcoming in any case, and agreeing that the despatch should be sent as a clarification of CCS 417, on Admiral Bieri's suggestion that the theater commanders not be sent something "out of the blue."[23] With the approval of General Marshall, Admiral King, and the other chiefs the message was sent:

> In clarification paragraph 5 CCS 417/2, the Joint Chiefs of Staff have decided that our first major objective in the war against Japan will be the vital Luzon-Formosa-China coast area. Strategy will be directed to attain this objective by the most direct and expeditious course possible. Direction of such strategy, including allocation of means, continues to be the function of the Joint Chiefs of Staff. As indicated in Paragraph 7 F CCS 417/2 planning should be conducted on a basis which will permit flexibility in adjusting operations to the developing situation. To this end, plans should be prepared for all probable operations. Timely recommendations regarding the adjustment of succeeding operations to the changing situation will be required by Chiefs of Staff.[24]

The despatch settled nothing. It was just one of those general statements of policy to set the background for more tangible strategic decisions. It was such a decision that the chiefs were called upon to make. Upon agreement between General Marshall and Admiral King the Joint Staff Planners were put to work on the studies General Marshall had recommended, and the Joint Strategic Survey Committee was directed to review JCS 713 in the light of General Marshall's comments.

Assignment of these long range studies did not satisfy Admiral King's impatience to get on with the war in the Pacific. The capture of Eniwetok had been completed on 23 February; the Marshalls were in U.S. control; Admiral King was anxious to keep going in the Central Pacific Area. As he approved the despatches to General MacArthur and Admiral Nimitz and the directives to the Joint Staff Planners and the Joint Strategic Survey Committee, Admiral King reminded General Marshall of his proposed directive to prepare to take Truk, saying:

> I am as anxious as you are to have a comprehensive plan for operations against the Japanese, but I feel that we should not put off decision as to what is to be done in the immediate future, at this time when our tremendously powerful forces can be thrown against an enemy who is obviously bewildered by recent events. The GYMKHANA-ROADMAKER [Mortlock-Carolines] operation will, I think, be an essential part of any plan that is produced and I think it essential that planning for this operation be started without delay.[25]

General Marshall, however, did not wish to rush into a commitment to proceed in the Central Pacific. Admiral Nimitz was about to come to Washington for consultation, and the Chief of Staff, U.S. Army, recommended waiting to get his views before issuing any further directive. If Truk was going to be bypassed, there would be amphibious equipment available, and perhaps it would be better to use it to accelerate operations in the Southwest Pacific Area.

Acceleration of operations was precisely what General MacArthur and his staff had on their minds at this time. SWPA forces had achieved unexpected success in the Admiralties, where what was intended to be a reconnaissance in force on 29 February had developed into a successful invasion. Probably also inspired by Lieutenant General Richard K. Sutherland's reports from Washington that the Southwest Pacific Area seemed to be getting second billing, General MacArthur recommended to the Joint Chiefs of Staff on 5 March that the Hansa Bay operation scheduled for about 22 April be omitted and he move instead farther up the coast to Hollandia.[26] He proposed to use the forces of the South and Southwest Pacific Areas as they were augmented from the Central Pacific Area for the Kavieng-Manus operation, including the aircraft carriers loaned for cover. Establishment of forces around Hollandia, said General MacArthur, would have wide implications, hopelessly isolating "some 40,000 of the enemys [sic] ground forces along the New Guinea coast," securing "airfields from which our land based air forces can dominate the Vogelkop," and hastening the westward advance by several months.

This revised timetable was part of a new Reno plan, which was just being completed and which reached Washington within a couple of days. It proposed operations in four phases: (1) northwestward advance along the north coast of New Guinea to seize and establish in the Humboldt Bay and the Geelvink Bay areas the bases required for subsequent operations to occupy Mindanao; (2) establishment of air forces in the Arafura Sea area for strategic bombing in the Netherlands East Indies and support of subsequent operations into the Vogelkop and Halmahera; (3) seizure of areas in the western tip of the Vogelkop and in Halmahera for flank protection and support of operations to occupy Mindanao; (4) occupation of Mindanao and establishment of bases for attack upon the Formosa-China coast area.[27]

Acceleration of operations in the Southwest Pacific by the retention of forces from the Central Pacific Area after the capture of Kavieng and Manus would throw off the Central Pacific timetable, as Admiral Nimitz, in Washington for consultation, hastened to point out.[28] "This proposal would involve," said he, "stopping the Central Pacific Campaign, losing its momentum, deferring movement into the MARIANAS until the approach of the typhoon season, and by allowing the enemy additional time to strengthen his defenses in the CAROLINES and MARIANAS would jeopardize our ability to reach the LUZON-FORMOSA-CHINA Area in early 1945 as now planned." Admiral Nimitz suggested two possible schedules for the rest of 1944: (1) capture of Truk on 15 June; capture of the southern Marianas on 1 September in order to acquire the airfields Truk did not afford; capture of Palau on 15 November to support the advance from the Southwest Pacific Area into Mindanao; or (2) capture of the southern Marianas on 15 June; capture of Woleai on 15 July to neutralize Truk from the west; capture of Yap on 1 September to provide the harbors lacking in the Marianas; capture of Palau on 1 November. Reserving decision as to whether or not Truk should be bypassed, Admiral Nimitz asked for a directive to prepare a secure control of the Carolines and Marianas with a target date of 15 June 1944.

In addition to submitting his memorandum Admiral Nimitz, accompanied by Admiral Sherman, attended the JCS 150th meeting on 7 March 1944 to present his views in person. The chiefs listened and asked questions and "took note" of what was said. As a result of comments as to the length of time involved in the second schedule Admiral Nimitz decided that the capture of Yap could be deferred until Palau had been taken and then the desired harbor at Ulithi could be occupied without having to take Yap at all. This would push the target date for Palau to 1 October.[29]

The Joint War Plans Committee had been discussing all of these proposals and comments, and on 8 March the committee reported to the Joint Staff Planners its recommendations for future operations in the Pacific.[30] The JWPC had decided that the most feasible way to reach the Luzon-Formosa-China coast area was via the Central Pacific to Palau, "thence, with the assistance of land-based air previously established in Mindanao to neutralize enemy air on Luzon, direct to Formosa." This shortcut program would include: seizure of Hollandia on 15 April; seizure of Mortlock and Greenwich on 15 May to neutralize the Carolines; seizure of the Palaus and Woleai on 15 July; seizure of Mindanao on 15 September by joint forces from both areas of the Pacific; and seizure of Formosa from bases in the Palaus and Mindanao on 1 January 1945. Perhaps, the JWPC suggested, it might prove desirable to delay the Formosa operation for six weeks and to take either the Marianas or, more probably, Luzon after Mindanao. It was recommended that the Kavieng operation be cancelled since U.S. forces already controlled the Bismarck Sea.

It should be noted that in this plan: (1) Truk was to be bypassed. (2) Formosa was to be the final objective. The JWPC pointed out that only Formosa was strategically significant in and of itself and that neither Luzon nor China would provide a base that would control Japan's line of communications. (3) The Marianas were to be neutralized. The committee ruled them out as an objective because their capture would delay the attack on Palau and would serve no necessary function in the operations against Formosa. Formosa was thought to furnish better space for B-29 airfields with only slight delay in construction. (4) From Hollandia forces of the Southwest Pacific Area were to bypass northwestern New Guinea, the Arafura Sea, and Halmahera to participate directly in the Mindanao operations.

The Joint Staff Planners did not approve this rapid program.[31] Admiral Bieri pointed out at once that it did not provide proper staging areas for the Formosa campaign. More serious than that, leaving both Truk and the southern Marianas in the enemy's hands placed the enemy in a position "to harass and even interdict our line of communications [to Palau] to a greater extent than we would be able to exert similar pressure on him." Moreover the program called for preliminary air bombardment of the Palaus from Hollandia, a distance of 800 miles, and Admiral Bieri doubted that this could be effective.

Admiral Sherman, who was attending the meeting, informed the group that the staff of the Commander in Chief, Pacific Ocean Areas, had abandoned the plan for taking Mortlock and Greenwich to neutralize Truk because no more than one airfield could be established on Mortlock. The only way to neutralize Truk was by interruption of its air pipeline through occupation of the Marianas.

The Joint War Plans Committee revised the plan after this discussion to make the schedule: Hollandia on 15 April, Southern Marianas on 15 June, Palaus on 1 September, Mindanao on 15 October, and Formosa on 15 January 1945.[32] Still the Joint Staff Planners were not satisfied. Admiral Bieri thought there had not been sufficient consideration of timing between the southern Marianas, the Palaus, and Mindanao to allow for fleet support and the problems of repair, supply, and rehabilitation. He suggested changing the dates to: Marianas, 15 June; Palaus, 15 September; Mindanao, 1 November; Formosa, 31 January.[33] In any case he was opposed to issuing directives for operations too far in advance lest later it prove advisable to cancel them. Moreover he thought that an alternate operation against Truk should be included in case the Marianas assault proved inadvisable. To this General Roberts objected, pointing out that an alternative operation would throw the program out of balance and that a change could be made when the time came if it seemed desirable. General Hansell expressed the view that the planners were thinking conservatively, not driving themselves hard enough. Far from agreeing, Admiral Bieri advised that the Mindanao date should be made 15 November to allow for rehabilitation of fleet forces. General Hansell urged the appointment of a commander for the Joint Pacific Theater, but this knotty problem was deferred by mutual consent lest the whole plan be delayed while an attempt was made to settle it.

As a result of all these discussions, on 10 March the Joint Staff Planners submitted a report to the Joint Chiefs of Staff.[34] Admiral Bieri's recommendations had been adopted, and Mindanao was moved to 15 November with Formosa postponed to 15 February. Included was a draft directive to Admiral Nimitz and General MacArthur, informing them of the program and directing them to prepare for seizure of the Marianas and Hollandia respectively.

The following day the Joint Chiefs discussed the report at a meeting attended by Lieutenant General Stanley D. Embick and Admiral Willson of the Joint Strategic Survey Committee, by Admiral Nimitz, and by General Sutherland, representing General MacArthur.[35] The only strong dissatisfaction with the plan was expressed by General Sutherland. General Embick said he thought it was "as wise a one as can be made at the present time." Admiral Nimitz concurred with the report, "with the provision that if he found it necessary to take Woleai or Mortlock in order to neutralize Truk, and could do this without prejudice to other operations in the area, he should be allowed to do so." Admiral Sherman said the plan represented "the optimum employment of forces of the Southwest Pacific Area and Pacific Ocean Areas, subject to two reservations." His first was that it might prove unnecessary "to extend to the southwest from the Southern Marianas to cut off Truk at once....[The] second reservation was that if the enemy estimate of the situation be the same as ours, the Japanese can move heavier forces into the Marianas to prevent us from bypassing Truk." But General Sutherland commented, "the Planners have disregarded General MacArthur's estimate of what can be done with the forces in the Southwest Pacific Area and...their paper presents an incorrect picture."

General Sutherland pointed out two major fallacies. First there was no provision for land-based air support for the assault on Formosa from the Palau-Guam line. The second error was the assumption that Mindanao could be taken on 15 November in a move from Hollandia 1,000 miles away. Hollandia was in fact an inadequate base, he said. There were no others provided for, and hence the movement would have to be based on Milne Bay, 900 miles behind Hollandia. He argued that the proposal to take out the Marianas and

Palau could take all of 1944 and not land forces in Mindanao until April 1945, just in time for the rainy season. However, if Truk could be bypassed to the south and all forces combined to advance along the line Admiralty Islands-Mindanao-Formosa, Mindanao could be occupied by November and Luzon by June 1945.

General Sutherland objected to the proposal to cancel operations against Kavieng. If Manus were to be used as a naval base, Kavieng would be needed as an air base, he argued. It was moreover, 600 miles from Truk. Despite the doubts of the Pacific Ocean Area representatives that Kavieng and Hollandia could be done in rapid succession and the vital transports returned to the Central Pacific Area in time for the Marianas campaign, General Sutherland expressed the opinion that Kavieng could be taken on 1 April and Hollandia between 15 and 24 April. There was considerable discussion as to how much of a threat Japanese possession of Kavieng would actually constitute since the enemy already had little freedom of movement in New Britain and New Ireland. Admiral Nimitz reported that by the end of March bombers would be hitting Truk from Eniwetok and the flow of planes to Kavieng would not last much longer. He was strongly supported by Admiral Bieri, who described the attacking of Kavieng as "a serious error" that might unnecessarily tie up both Army and Navy forces that were needed elsewhere.

Although General Sutherland spoke at considerable length in support of the Southwest Pacific Area plan, he persuaded no one. General Roberts reported for the planners that they did not expect the Southwest Pacific area attack to stop at Hollandia but to continue along the coast. Moreover they had always considered that an attack on Mindanao would be mounted from bases farther to the rear than Hollandia, perhaps even as far as Espiritu Santo. Admiral Nimitz spoke out most strongly for the necessity of controlling the Marianas, Carolines, and Palaus in order to protect the line of communications into the Philippines. This feeling was clearly shared by Admiral King, who urged, "Ultimately the Marianas, Carolines, and Palaus must be cleared. It is to our advantage to do this as early as possible and then have only attacks from the Netherlands East Indies area to fear. Since the Marianas, the Carolines, and the Palaus must be cleared sooner or later, it should be done now."

General Marshall and Admiral Leahy (General Arnold was not present) confined their marks almost entirely to questioning the theater officers and the planners. But there was no doubt that Admiral King shared the views of the men from the Pacific Ocean Areas. Immediately after the meeting of 11 March he circulated a memorandum in answer to General Sutherland's remarks, outlining the general scheme for mounting an amphibious operation against the Luzon-Formosa-China Area from Hawaii, Suva, Guadalcanal-Russells, Manus, Noumea, Espiritu Santo, Efate, and Milne Bay, possibly using Palau, Yap, Ulithi, and Guam for staging equipment and some troops.[36]

Before the JCS meeting Admiral King had prepared a revision of the proposed directives to the theater commanders.[37] He emphasized the primacy of operations in the Central Pacific, making it clear that the forces loaned to the Southwest Pacific Area to assist and support the Hollandia operation would be returned to the Pacific Ocean Areas in ample time for use in the Marianas campaign. If this was discussed at the JCS meeting on 11 March, there is no mention of it in the official minutes, but the Joint Strategic Survey Committee was directed to turn to at once and submit their comments on it and on the Joint Staff Planners' report.

The conclusion of the JSSC was unequivocal:

> Whatever our exact objective in the Formosa-Luzon-China Area – and whenever or however it is to be attained, a fundamental strategic prerequisite is our control of the Marianas, Carolines, Palau Ocean Area. In seizing such control as soon as we can, we are taking a step that must be taken if we are to reach the citadel of Japan.[38]

The committee suggested adopting Admiral King's proposed directives, with a few clarifying changes.

The Joint Chiefs of Staff held a special meeting the following morning, 12 March 1944, to discuss the problem of Pacific strategy.[39] Unfortunately it was a closed session, no official minutes were kept, and it is impossible to tell even the length of the discussion. Two decisions were recorded. Just "for the record in connection with planning" the JCS approved the statement:

> Items of moment in connection with paragraph 6 of the approved message are: the release of the 3rd Marine Division to the Commander in Chief, Pacific Ocean Areas, and the matter of the APD's and LST's which were loaned for the Rabaul campaign.

With some amendments the Joint Chiefs approved Admiral King's proposed directive to the two area commanders.[40] Thus on 12 March 1944 General MacArthur and Admiral Nimitz were officially informed of the strategy the Joint Chiefs of Staff had adopted:

> Para. 1. With reference to our dispatch of March 2...the Joint Chiefs of Staff have further decided that the most feasible approach to the Formosa-Luzon-China area is by way of Marianas-Carolines-Palau-Mindanao area, and that the control of the Marianas-Carolines-Palau area is essential to the projection of our forces into the former area, and their subsequent effective employment therefrom. Examination leads us to the decision that effective lodgment in the former area will be attained by the following main courses of action:
>
>   *a.* Cancellation of FOREARM [Kavieng]. Complete the isolation of the Rabaul-Kavieng area with the minimum commitment of forces.
>
>   *b.* Early completion of Manus occupation and development as an air and fleet base.

      c. Occupation of Hollandia by CINCSOWESPAC, target date April 15, 1944. The objective is the establishment of heavy bombardment aircraft for preliminary air bombardment of the Palaus and neutralization of western New Guinea-Halmahera area.
      d. Establish control of Marianas-Carolines-Palau area by POA forces-
         (1) By neutralization of Truk.
         (2) By occupation of the southern Marianas, target date June 15. The objective is to secure control of sea communications through the Central Pacific by isolating and neutralizing the Carolines and by the establishment of sea and air bases for operations against the Japanese home land.
         (3) Occupation of the Palaus by POA forces, target date September 15. The objective is to extend the control of the eastern approaches to the Phillippines [*sic*] and Formosa, and to establish a fleet and air base and forward staging area for the support of operations against Mindanao, Formosa and China.
      e. Occupation of Mindanao by SOWESPAC forces, supported by the Pacific fleet, target date November 15. The objective is establishment of air forces to reduce and contain Japanese forces in the Philippines preparatory to a further advance to Formosa either directly or via Luzon, and to conduct air strikes against enemy installations in the N.E.I.
      f. Occupation of Formosa, target date February 15, 1945, or occupation of Luzon should such operations prove necessary prior to the move on Formosa, target date February 15, 1945. Planning responsibilities as follows: Formosa-CINCPOA; Luzon-CINCSOWESPAC.

Admiral Nimitz and General MacArthur were directed to proceed accordingly with this program, conferring and planning for coordination and mutual support. The course was set and the time established for the next and greatest advances yet toward the defeat of Japan.

SHIPPING

    Island-to-island operations in the Pacific necessarily required great amounts of shipping, not only to deliver the troops and supplies from the United States to the bases in the Pacific, but to move them from a base area to the military objective. Two days after the JCS directive was sent to the theater commanders Admiral King reported to the Joint Chiefs that in order to carry out the program Admiral Nimitz would have to have some additional ships under his operational control: two AP's (EC2 type) and eighteen AK's in April; seventeen AP's, sixteen AP's (EC2 type), and eighteen AK's in May; seventeen AK's in June. Admiral King recommended that the chiefs direct the Joint Military Transportation Committee to provide the Commander in Chief, Pacific Ocean Areas, with these ships, varying the number in accordance with changes in plans.[41] This proposal, as was the case increasingly with JCS papers, was circulated for informal approval by the four Chiefs of Staff. Admiral Leahy was in favor of it, but General Marshall was unwilling to approve the allocations without further investigation. He proposed that the JMTC be directed "to study and recommend to the Joint Chiefs of Staff the measures that should be taken for best implementing the requirement to" provide the ships.[42] Admiral King accepted the modification.[43]

After looking into the situation the Joint Military Transportation Committee concluded that enough troop shipping could be found without having to disrupt current shipping schedules. Cargo shipping also could be furnished, but it would be necessary drastically to curtail programs in the Pacific not directly related to immediate operations.[44]

The availability of shipping was considerably affected by the Pacific commanders' practice of holding ships in their theaters, to an extent that seemed excessive to Washington planners. It was felt that some of these could be returned and the shipping shortage relieved to that extent. At the end of March, General Marshall suggested to the Army commanders in the Pacific Area that they review the situation in their theaters to ascertain whether some of the ships they were operating locally might be released and returned to the Pacific Coast. General MacArthur replied that, on the contrary, the new program of operations would necessitate that he have many more cargo vessels than were currently assigned under his control.[45] While some supplies could be delivered directly to operational areas, he said, much of his material was procured on the Australian mainland and had to be shipped about 2,200 miles to forward bases. He would send ships back as quickly as he could, but with the newly approved program he would have to keep more than twice as many as had yet been authorized. At General Marshall's request the JMTC restudied Admiral Nimitz's needs together with those of General MacArthur.[46]

The JMTC investigation disclosed that, although enough cargo vessels could be supplied for both the Commander in Chief, Pacific Ocean Areas, and the Commander in Chief, Southwest Pacific, in April, under current allocations there would be a deficit in sailings from the Pacific Coast of fifty-six in May, eighty-five in June, and thirty-five in July, about a third of the total requirements for those months.[47] The JMTC urged that the Pacific commands review their requirements to be sure there was no duplication and to ascertain whether any reductions could be made. If the cargo shipping was to be supplied, it would be "only by a sterner approach to the doctrine of bare necessities." At the committee's recommendation the Joint Chiefs of Staff approved the allocations for April (it was too late to change them in any event) and directed the theater commanders to send representatives to Washington to discuss the shipping situation.[48]

By the time the Pacific Shipping Conference convened in Washington on 18 April 1944 the problem of finding cargo shipping had been eased somewhat by developments in the European Theater. Operations in Italy subsequent to the landings at Anzio had not been making the progress anticipated, and it was increasingly apparent that two divisions could not be spared from Italy for Anvil, the amphibious attack on southern France which was originally scheduled for approximately the same date as Overlord in May 1944. After a lengthy interchange of papers the Combined Chiefs of Staff finally agreed that, rather than attempt a smaller operation in France, they should postpone the target date of Anvil until July. With the possibility thus presented of transferring shipping from the Atlantic, the Pacific Shipping Conference was able to cut down considerably on the deficit in availabilities for the Pacific Theater, reducing it, for example, to nine in May, twenty-seven in June, and thirty-eight in July. These were still significant figures, however, for as the conference report pointed out, they amounted to 13 per cent of the net Pacific requirements for June and 20 per cent for July. In submitting the conclusions of the conference the Joint Military Transportation Committee recommended that they be reviewed by the Joint Staff Planners, that the area commanders be asked to set up priorities on the basis of (1) indispensable cargoes, (2) necessary cargoes, and (3) desirable cargoes, and that the Commander in Chief, Pacific Ocean Areas, be informed immediately whether he would be furnished with the shipping he had requested for the Marianas campaign.[49]

The Joint Staff Planners were obviously suspicious that General MacArthur was asking to retain shipping to support operations that were not essential to the program approved by the Joint Chiefs of Staff or to add to excessive stockpiles or over-ambitious construction projects. Major General Richard J. Marshall, the representative from the Southwest Pacific Area, was questioned closely as to the uses to which the required shipping would be put and the projects planned for the area. As yet no plan of operations under the directive approved in JCS 713/4 had been received in Washington. The tabulated breakdown of shipping requests appeared to indicate more extensive plans than that directive had authorized, and the planners did not wish to sanction them indirectly by recommending shipping allotments.[50]

After several days of discussion the Joint Staff Planners submitted their comments to the Joint Chiefs of Staff on 5 May 1944.[51] It was evident that there simply was not enough shipping to go around and to provide for all the requests from the Pacific Ocean Areas and the Southwest Pacific. The planners therefore recommended that first of all the operations already approved by the Joint Chiefs of Staff should be provided for: Hollandia, the Marianas, Palau, Mindanao, and operation of B-29's from the Marianas. Then the remaining shipping should be divided among the

Pacific areas, including China-Burma-India, in direct proportion to the requirements. The planners favored approval of the requested retentions for the next three months and for planning purposes for August to December, subject to final approval of the operations to be conducted in the Southwest Pacific Area prior to the assault on Mindanao. Having ascertained from the Joint Military Transportation Committee that its recommendations for shipping allotments had not reduced the availabilities for Anvil to such a point as to render it impracticable, the planners urged that, after providing enough insurance so that Anvil could be mounted between July and September, every effort be made to provide additional shipping for the Pacific.[52]

The Joint Chiefs of Staff approved the planners' report. General MacArthur, Admiral Nimitz, and Admiral Halsey were directed to set up shipping priorities in the three categories. The Joint Military Transportation Committee was told to revise its report. General MacArthur was asked to submit "without delay" his plan for carrying out the directive of 12 March.[53]

Subsequently additional transfers from the Atlantic further reduced the shipping deficit in the Pacific. With the remaining shortage apportioned among the several areas, the Joint Military Transportation Committee was able to report to the Joint Chiefs on 7 June 1944 that, although the requests could not be fully met until November, the deficits could be adjusted in such a way that they could be absorbed without affecting operations.[54]

PROBLEMS OF COMMAND

The decision of the Joint Chiefs of Staff to continue operations in both the Central and the Southwest Pacific Areas under separate commands but with "mutual coordination" inevitably involved complications that would not have been present had there been but one command in the Pacific Theater. In the spring of 1944 a contretemps over the base to be built at Manus Island resulted in clarification of one of the important aspects of coordination.

The capture of Manus was strongly recommended by the staff of the Commander in Chief, Pacific Ocean Areas, for it promised to afford a naval base for supporting future campaigns, in the Carolines and Palaus particularly, and advance operations of the Pacific Fleet. At the end of January it was agreed at the Pearl Harbor conference that Manus would be taken by forces from the Southwest Pacific Area, but the construction of a naval operating base would be the responsibility of the Commander, South Pacific. In the JCS directive of 12 March 1944 General MacArthur was told to expedite the development of a base in the Admiralties.[55] A second directive from General Marshall on 20 March informed the Commander in Chief, Southwest Pacific Area, that facilities in the South Pacific Area were to be "rolled up" to the maximum extent, and instructed him to develop the base at Manus "insofar as practicable" from means available in the South Pacific. Since the base was to be adequate for supporting a large task force of the

Pacific Fleet as well as naval forces of the Southwest Pacific Area, General Marshall "suggested" that the responsibility for developing the base be delegated to the Commander, South Pacific Area.[56]

Behind this calm suggestion lay a matter that was extremely controversial in the Pacific Theater and known in Washington, the question of who should build and what forces should use the base at Manus.[57] General MacArthur promptly reported his side of the story, without indicating that there was another.[58] The base was being developed from means in the South Pacific Area, he said, and Admiral Nimitz was being kept informed. But the Commander Allied Naval Forces, Southwest Pacific Area, was doing the work, for it was "essential that the work be carried out by an agency operating within this command." General MacArthur's idea as to who was to use the base was that, since it lay "in an operational area where the coordination of all forces is required, it would be violative of basic principles to introduce any agency other than a transient Naval Force which is not part of the command." As for the South Pacific Force, it had been "projected into operations in the Southwest Pacific Area through the artificiality of extending it forward through the Solomons to Emirau," which had been substituted for Kavieng. He could see "no further justification for its continued operation beyond the geographical boundaries that have been fixed by international agreement." General MacArthur strongly recommended that the South Pacific forces be broken up and reallocated to active areas.

The other side of the problem was strongly championed in Washington by Admiral King. He pointed out that, whereas General MacArthur had reported that for his future operations he would not need any bases in the South Pacific Area, Admiral Nimitz had said that he would have use for several, for staging and rehabilitation and for logistic support of Central Pacific operations. Manus would serve as a major fleet operating base. Its development should be coordinated with the rolling up of bases in the South Pacific Area, and until a recent sudden change was made by General MacArthur it had been scheduled to be developed by the Commander, South Pacific. Admiral King thought the Joint Chiefs of Staff ought not to accept General MacArthur's statements that there could be no further justification for continuing the operation of the South Pacific Force and that only a transient naval force should cross geographical boundaries. This was not in line with existing policies, and he mentioned the contemplated uses of B-29's and the fact that the chiefs proposed to mount troops for future operations wherever it was most practicable to do so. He quoted from a JCS directive of May 1942:

> Boundary lines of ocean areas...are designed to give a general definition to usual fields of operations; they are not designed to restrict or prevent responsible commanders from extending operations outside their assigned areas when such

action will assist or support friendly forces, when it is necessary to accomplish the task in hand, or when it will promote the common cause.[59]

Admiral King recommended that General MacArthur be directed to delegate the development of naval facilities at Manus to the Commander, South Pacific, and be told that the Joint Chiefs could not accept "any restriction on the use of facilities in one area by the forces of another."

General Marshall saw the matter differently. General MacArthur had reported that Admiral Nimitz was informed of the plans for Manus and had been asked for suggestions, and the Chief of Staff, U.S. Army, did not agree that matters in respect to Manus were, as Admiral King had said, "in a confused and unsatisfactory state." General Marshall could not see that General MacArthur had any intention of placing restrictions on the flexibility of operations or the use of the facilities at Manus. Accordingly he recommended that the Joint Chiefs of Staff simply accept the plans already made for developing the base at Manus.[60]

"The fact remains," said Admiral King, "that this matter is in an unsatisfactory state to the Commander in Chief, U.S. Fleet, and Chief of Naval Operations because of the unilateral sudden shift in arrangements and because, with the responsibility to supply many means from the U.S., the detailed plans which I expected to receive and pass on have not been received or passed upon here." Furthermore, "the coordination of rolling up the South Pacific facilities and building up the Manus facilities and those further west would have been more expeditiously handled and with less difficulty, from the naval point of view, by keeping this development under the Naval Commander experienced in this work and who handled it previously and will again handle it at Palau."[61] Nevertheless Admiral King was willing to concede and suggested simply amending the despatch proposed by General Marshall to request General MacArthur's plans, including the facilities he expected to move up from the South Pacific Area. However, Admiral King recommended that the Joint Staff Planners be asked to draft a reply to General MacArthur's statement that only a transient naval force should be introduced at Manus, and to refer the draft for comment to the Joint Strategic Survey Committee.

It was three weeks before the Joint Staff Planners completed their report and another five days before the Joint Strategic Survey Committee had approved it and the result was submitted to the Joint Chiefs of Staff.[62]

Recognizing that there would inevitably be situations in which forces from one area would have to use bases in another area of the Pacific, the planners recommended sending a despatch to General MacArthur and Admiral Nimitz, clarifying the command relationships involved:

> a. The situation and the scope of operations may require forces of any category of one area, under their own commanders

and retaining their normal command relationships to stage through, or mount from bases in another area in order to take maximum advantage of all available facilities and to employ forces most effectively.

 b. Fleet units in the Pacific, retaining their normal command relationships, must be free to operate from available bases in both the Southwest Pacific and Pacific Ocean Areas.

 c. Occasions may arise where it will be more expedient for a commander engaged in an operation in one area to employ temporarily a part of his own air force from bases in an adjacent area. In such cases, the air elements so operating should be given their missions by their own commander. The local coordination of their operations, including defense measures, with operations of the forces assigned to the area must then be the responsibility of the commander of the area from which they operate. This area commander is charged with the coordination of matters affecting the administration, maintenance, servicing, and supply of these units during the period of their operation. Except in a strategical or tactical emergency demanding such action, such air forces will not be utilized for purposes other than their assigned missions.

This general statement of policy was approved informally by the Joint Chiefs of Staff on 1 May and sent at once to the two commanders in chief in the Pacific.[63] General MacArthur conferred with Admiral Halsey and others and withdrew his restrictive order.

REDEPLOYMENT OF THE SOUTH PACIFIC FORCES

After the seizure of the Bismarck Archipelago and Hollandia, New Guinea, by no stretching of the South Pacific Area boundaries could that area be considered operational. What would become of the forces assigned there was a complicated question, for General MacArthur was no less reluctant to release those which had been operating under his control or cooperating with SWPA action than was Admiral Nimitz to permit a permanent transfer of forces from that portion of the Pacific Ocean Areas to the SWPA. While the program of operations in the Pacific for 1944 was being discussed at length the Joint War Plans Committee had been considering the disposition to be made of the forces of the South Pacific Area.[64] The committee report, originally circulated to the Joint Staff Planners on 10 February, was revised several times in the light of comments from the planners, from the services individually, and from the Joint Logistics Committee, and in accordance with the strategic discussions and decisions that resulted in the 12 March directive to the Pacific commanders. On 17 March recommendations were finally presented to the Joint Chiefs of Staff, three days before troops from the South Pacific Area occupied Emirau.[65]

The planners proposed that, after the capture of Hollandia, all Army ground units except garrison and maintenance forces required for the South Pacific Area should be transferred to the control of the Supreme Commander, Southwest Pacific Area. This meant six divisions plus smaller combat and service units. Other Army forces would follow as bases in the South Pacific were reduced or closed. The 3rd New Zealand Division would remain in the South Pacific until its future employment had been determined by negotiations with the New Zealand Government. All Marine Corps troops, two divisions, one regiment, seven defense battalions, would go to the control of the Commander in Chief, Pacific Ocean Areas, to participate in the amphibious operations scheduled for the Central Pacific Area.

In recommending redeployment of naval forces the planners listed the numbers and types of ships that should constitute the Seventh Fleet, already attached to the Southwest Pacific Area, and proposed that the Commander in Chief, Pacific Ocean Areas, provide for any current deficiencies and losses of destroyers and smaller vessels. All other major naval units in the South Pacific would revert to the control of the Commander in Chief, Pacific Ocean Areas.

It would be necessary to retain some naval air patrol squadrons for antisubmarine and patrol purposes, and other air units, including the Thirteenth Air Force, until the completion of active operations and for the neutralization of the Kavieng-Rabaul area. As soon as practicable, however, the Thirteenth would be transferred to the Southwest Pacific Area. The planners incidentally recommended that the Commander in Chief, Southwest Pacific, be instructed that his air forces should support operations in the Central Pacific Area, and when the Joint Chiefs of Staff so directed be transferred temporarily to the Commander in Chief, Pacific Ocean Areas. Naval and Marine air units would remain under the control of the Commander in Chief, Pacific Ocean Areas, and be withdrawn as required for use in the Mandates. Units of the Royal New Zealand Air Force would remain in the South Pacific Area for garrison and local defense duties.[66]

The theater commanders had not been formally consulted in the development of this report, but it had been worked up while some of the theater representatives were in Washington and written with the future schedule of operations in the Pacific Theater in mind. Most of the amphibious and naval forces deployed in the South Pacific Area were to remain under the control of Admiral Nimitz, while General MacArthur acquired principally ground troops which would be most helpful in the land campaigns in New Guinea and the Philippines. The Joint Chiefs of Staff approved the scheme of redeployments with little or no discussion, and the theater commanders were directed on 25 March 1944 to "make arrangements as to availability for transfer of command and assistance in the physical movement of forces."[67]

With combat operations assigned to the South Pacific Forces nearing completion, and plans approved for their redeployment, it was but a matter of time before the South Pacific Area would cease all participation in active operations. Technically the Commander, South Pacific, still retained responsibility for some of the bases beyond the original geographic limits set up for the

Guadalcanal operation. When Admiral King visited Pearl Harbor early in May, he found Admiral Nimitz and his staff anxious to achieve a clear-cut separation of the South Pacific from the Southwest Pacific and of the Third Fleet from the former.[68] By 21 May transfer arrangements had progressed to the point that General MacArthur and Admiral Halsey could recommend to Admiral King and General Marshall that on 15 June, the date tentatively set during Admiral King's visit, the Commander in Chief, Southwest Pacific Area, should take over command of all units and installations west of 159° East. Admiral Halsey was to retain command of the Third Fleet, turning over to Vice Admiral John H. Newton command of the South Pacific Area east of 159° East. The chiefs approved the date, apparently without discussion. Bases in the South Pacific Area continued to be used, but combat had left the area behind.[69]

Chapter XXII

SEAC and Burma in Early 1944

STRATEGIC DISCUSSIONS

When Lord Louis Mountbatten assumed the position of Supreme Commander, Southeast Asia, it was planned that a road would be driven across North Burma to Kunming or Chungking by a series of operations that included: a southeasterly advance of the two Chinese Ramgarh divisions from Ledo; a southeasterly advance by three British Indian divisions from Imphal on the Kalemyo-Kalewa area; operations by ten Chinese divisions from Yunnan against the Myitkyina-Bhamo area; a move of three British Indian divisions down the Arakan coast toward Akyab; and a supporting amphibious operation against the Andaman Islands.

The Joint Chiefs of Staff had supported the campaign in Burma because it promised a way into China over which supplies could be delivered by land to strengthen the Chinese Army and prepare for support from the mainland for amphibious landings from the east on the China coast. The long struggle to achieve British, Chinese, and American cooperation in Burma seemed for a time to have ended at Cairo, for the Generalissimo agreed to order his troops in Yunnan across the Salween River into Burma in return for the pledge of an amphibious operation in the Bay of Bengal. But President Roosevelt had finally given in to British pressure to transfer landing craft from the Southeast Asia Command to the Mediterranean for use in the newly planned landings in southern France. He was thereby put in the position of having to tell Chiang that the amphibious operations in southern Burma could not be carried out. So doing, he offered the Generalissimo the alternative of going ahead with the land campaign, supported by carrier and commando raids in the Bay of Bengal, or of delaying land operations until November when an accompanying amphibious operation of some size might be practicable.[1]

Chiang's answer was not long in coming.[2] Expressing himself as aware of the "tremendous advantages to be reaped by China as well as by the United Nations as a whole in speedily defeating Germany first," the Generalissimo pointed out that China's collapse "would have equally grave consequences on the global war." Consequently he would accept the President's recommendation and wait for amphibious support. Both the military and the economic situation in China would make it impossible to wait until November 1944, said Chiang. The only remedy would be "to assure the Chinese people and Army of your sincere concern in the China theater of war by assisting China to hold on with a billion gold dollar loan to strengthen her economic front and relieve her dire economic needs."[3] This was not the whole price, however. "In order to prove our resolute determination to bring relentless pressure on Japan, the Chinese Air Force and the American Air Force stationed in China should be increased, as from next Spring, by at least double the number of aircraft already agreed upon, and the total of air transportation should be increased, as from February of next year, to at least twenty thousands tons a month to make effective the operation of the additional planes." Although Chiang said that Japan could be expected to launch an all-out offensive against China in the coming year, he did not ask for any additional support for the Chinese Army.

After talking with General Stilwell, the Generalissimo sent a second message to President Roosevelt, again asking for financial assistance and more aircraft. He had concluded, he said, that it would be best to defer the Burma campaign until November when a full-scale amphibious operation could be launched but to prepare at full speed for the land campaign so that it could be undertaken at any time enough ships were concentrated for "a grand scale landing on the enemy's flanks."[4]

Information available in the War Department did not indicate that China's economic plight was as serious as the Generalissimo had pictured it.[5] The demands accompanying Chiang's conditional acceptance of President Roosevelt's suggestion that the campaign in Burma might be delayed until November must certainly have irritated those concerned in the War Department, and the President endorsed the firm reply drafted there for the Generalissimo. Chiang was told that the President considered the best contribution to China's economic difficulties would be to open a land supply route across Burma into China. This would also insure the security of air transport and improve the situation of General Chennault's forces by increasing the flow of supplies to them.[6]

While President Roosevelt and Generalissimo Chiang Kai-shek had been exchanging messages, Admiral Mountbatten and his staff had been looking more thoroughly into the possibilities of an amphibious operation with the forces that were to be left in Southeast Asia. The British Chiefs of Staff on 21 December circulated without comment a recommendation from the Southeast Asia Command for an operation aiming to destroy the Japanese in the area of Mayu and subsequently to capture Akyab.[7] It would involve an advance down the Kaladan Valley and an amphibious landing on the southern part of the Mayu Peninsula. SEAC recommended executing this operation, called Pigstick, simultaneously with a modified Tarzan.

The chiefs took no action on Pigstick at once, but the SEAC

staff went ahead with plans and preparation. However, Pigstick also was to be sacrificed for the campaign against Germany. At about this time it was decided, with the approval of the Prime Minister and the President, to conduct an amphibious operation on the coast of Italy in order to attack the enemy's flank and put Allied forces well along the way to Rome.[8] This operation, dubbed Shingle, scheduled for 20 January, would require landing craft, more than were available in the Mediterranean. On 30 December the British Chiefs reported that they had been "considering whether we can afford to leave in South East Asia sufficient resources to enable Admiral Mountbatten to undertake operation Pigstick."[9] Cancellation of Pigstick would release three fast LST's and six smaller landing craft that the British thought could be helpful for the operations in the Mediterranean, both Shingle and the larger attack on southern France, Anvil. As for Pigstick, although the British Chiefs thought it had considerable merit, they pointed out that it was still in the planning stage and inevitably would require more than was currently estimated. They recommended that Admiral Mountbatten be told it would not be done and that such of the landing vessels as could be used be sent to the Mediterranean.

The immediate reaction of the Joint Staff Planners was opposition to this proposal. They did not see that three LST's could mean success or failure for Shingle, and they were highly dubious that these ships would have a significant effect upon Overlord and Anvil.[10] On the other hand, without the LST's Admiral Mountbatten could not undertake any significant amphibious action and the President would be placed in the embarrassing position of having to tell the Generalissimo that even the smaller amphibious operation would have to be called off. The JPS recommendation "that plans and preparations for Pigstick continue on the basis of no further withdrawals of assault shipping or landing craft from the Southeast Asia Theater" was accepted by the Joint Chiefs, who presented it to the British in CCS 452/1.[11]

The reply of the British Chiefs of Staff is very interesting.[12] They were strongly of the opinion that it would not be possible to recruit sufficient landing craft for Shingle from the Mediterranean. The U.S. Chiefs had recommended reconditioning some that were in the eastern Mediterranean, but, said the British, these were worn out and could not possibly be used. Already, the British Chiefs reported, they had heard from Admiral Mountbatten that he would need escort carriers that could not possibly be sent to him and, as they had pointed out in the beginning, his requirements were certain to increase. There was clearly no margin either for Shingle or for Anvil and certainly none for Overlord. "Having regard to the emphasis which was laid upon Anvil and Overlord at Sextant and to the importance attaching to early success in Italy," the British Chiefs assumed that the U.S. Chiefs would "see the danger of our undertaking a new commitment and would agree that the advantages to be gained from Pigstick should be sacrificed in favor of Shingle and Anvil." So sure had the British been that as a matter of fact they had ordered the three LST's back from Southeast Asia "a few days ago" so that they would get to the Mediterranean in time for Shingle! Despite this obvious *ex post facto* report the Representatives of the British Chiefs in Washington concluded their memorandum by reporting that their seniors in London had asked them "to say how very much they hope that the Combined Chiefs of Staff will accept that Pigstick cannot be undertaken!"

Later the same day the British Representatives circulated another memorandum reporting that Admiral Mountbatten had informed them that "even if Pigstick were now ordered it would be too late to catch the last favorable period this season."[13] Consequently he had stopped the mounting of Pigstick.

That the U.S. Chiefs of Staff were surprised and far from pleased by this action of the British Chiefs of Staff is very apparent in the recorded minutes of the next CCS meeting.[14] Admiral Leahy said that as far as he could see there was no action practicable except to take note of the situation. Sir John Dill thought it necessary to apologize for the failure to keep the U.S. Chiefs properly informed and said, "If it was the desire of the U.S. Chiefs of Staff to revoke the decision to recall the three LST's he would be happy to transmit this to the British Chiefs of Staff." The U.S. Chiefs did not want to do that, but Admiral King said he would like to know to what extent Admiral Mountbatten's decision to cancel Pigstick resulted from the recall of the three LST's. General Marshall requested information as to just what was going to be undertaken in North Burma as well as any other operations Admiral Mountbatten contemplated with the resources available to him. Once again it was apparent that the British had no enthusiasm for operations in Burma.

On 21 January the British Chiefs circulated a report on Admiral Mountbatten's limited plans for Southeast Asia.[15] The Chinese Ledo force was to advance to Mogaung-Myitkyina. Operations were to be carried out by the forces based on Imphal to secure the area around Tiddim, dominate the hills south of Tamu-Sittang, and raid down into the Kabaw Valley, while long range penetration brigades operated east of the Chindwin. In the Arakan region two brigades were to advance down the Kaladan Valley to gain additional air strips and generally improve the SEAC position. Since none of this area was very far east of the border of India, the program would hardly contribute greatly to the operations of the Ledo force in Upper Burma.

Despite the modest scale of this plan the Joint Staff Planners favored its approval.[16] Its single outstanding merit, they said, was that it maintained an Allied offensive. It also would create a diversion of enemy air strength and shipping from the Pacific. But there were numerous questions left unanswered: What line would be held during the 1944 monsoon? What were the target dates? How would the Eastern Fleet be used? These and several other questions the U.S. Chiefs submitted to the British, deferring comment on the SEAC program.[17]

The limited operations projected in the Southeast Asia Command in the first half of 1944 were indicative that developments since Sextant necessitated a change in the plans for operations in Burma. Resources upon which some of the plans had been based had been taken away; the amphibious operation, Buccaneer, had been cancelled; even the smaller Pigstick had been given up; and the Generalissimo had declared himself unwilling to allow the Yunnan force to participate in a campaign in Upper Burma without amphibious support. The SEAC staff reviewed the plans for long-term strategy, and at the beginning of January the Supreme Commander recommended to the British Chiefs of Staff that:

  a. The Ledo Road be driven only to Myitkyina.
  b. The support of the 14th Air Force and Matterhorn should be the main contribution of the South East Asia Command (SEAC) to the war effort this year.
  c. Only limited advances be made in Burma, in the Chin Hills and toward Akyab.
  d. His major effort be made toward Sumatra in 1944-1945.[18]

There was almost unanimous agreement among the members of the SEAC staff that an assault on Sumatra and Malaya and an advance to the coast of China would be of greater assistance to China than the expenditure of vast amounts of men and resources in building and supporting the Ledo Road across Upper Burma. This was the old Culverin proposal to which the Joint Chiefs of Staff had always been cool. It was also quite counter to the agreed strategy of the Combined Chiefs of Staff at Sextant and would mean cancellation or at least curtailment of the project long supported by the U.S. Chiefs of opening up a land route into China.[19]

Of those in the theater to whom the new plan was presented, General Stilwell, as would be expected, protested most strongly. A copy of his written comments was received in Washington early in February.[20] Attacking details of the project, General Stilwell summarized: "The difficulties of a campaign in BURMA are known. There will at least be no surprises on that score. The difficulties of a campaign in SUMATRA are not known, and it may well prove to be a far more formidable undertaking." His views of the desirability of attacking the Japanese on the flank in Burma rather than frontally via Sumatra were shared by the Joint Staff Planners, who were in favor of pushing ahead with the strategy already approved for the theater. After reviewing the reports from SEAC and General Stilwell's comments, the Joint Staff Planners reminded the Joint Chiefs that the United States was "committed to a policy of developing China as a base for support of the Pacific advances," and that large assignments of service troops and material had been made to that end. The planners were of the opinion that the only way the objective could be accomplished was by opening a land route to China. Should that fail an increase of the transport lift over the Hump would yield a limited buildup of air and ground strength in China. Expressing their concern lest nothing at all be accomplished in Burma in the spring of 1944, the planners urged the Joint Chiefs of Staff to present a memorandum to their British colleagues:

> We are apprehensive that further delay in issuing a clear cut directive to Admiral Mountbatten to reach definite objectives in North Burma this spring will result in little being accomplished before the onset of this monsoon. Time is fleeting and a decision must be reached as soon as possible.
>
> We believe that it is essential to use China as a base to support to the greatest extent possible our advance against Japan from the Pacific. In order to prepare the China base in time to support our main effort against the Formosa-China-Luzon area, every means available to us for operations in North Burma must be employed now. The seizing and holding of Myitkyina this dry season is considered a minimum objective.
>
> General Stilwell is confident that the Chinese-American force from Ledo can capture and hold Myitkyina, provided the British IV Corps will cross the Chindwin in force and seize and hold the Shwebo-Monywa area.
>
> We have been informed that Admiral Mountbatten is planning and preparing for an attack during 1944-1945 against Sumatra. We consider that Admiral Mountbatten should be definitely directed to undertake offensive operations in Upper Burma this dry season using all means at his disposal. A failure to do this, or the withholding of forces necessary for the success of these operations in order to prepare for an operation the resources for which are not yet in sight, cannot in our opinion be justified.
>
> We recommend, therefore, that the Combined Chiefs of Staff direct Admiral Mountbatten to commence operations without delay to seize and hold Myitkyina and the Shwebo-Monywa area, using all means now at his disposal.[21]

The Joint Chiefs accepted their planners' recommendations and passed the memorandum to their British colleagues on 17 February.[22]

The British forwarded the remarks of the U.S. Chiefs to Admiral Mountbatten but themselves deferred comment. They were already engaged in talks in London with a mission from SEAC, Axiom, which had been sent to present the SEAC proposals in the hope of gaining their acceptance by the Combined Chiefs of Staff.[23]

The differences of view between General Stilwell and Admiral Mountbatten were of considerable concern to the general and his CBI staff. Hence it was decided to send a separate mission from CBI to present General Stilwell's views in Washington and insure against the U.S. Chief's receiving a distorted account of them from the Axiom group. The CBI mission, headed by Brigadier General Benjamin G. Ferris, Deputy Chief of Staff, U.S. Army Forces,

CBI, arrived in Washington before the Axiom people, headed by Major General A.C. Wedemeyer, had come from London.

On 23 February the CBI representatives attended a meeting of the Joint Staff Planners.[24] The CBI group insisted that General Stilwell was "doing his utmost to carry out the directives of the Combined Chiefs of Staff," and in particular the decisions made at Quadrant and Sextant. General Ferris pointed out that the reopening of land communications with China would provide a flow of 40,000 to 50,000 tons monthly into China plus 16,000 tons of gasoline to be carried in the accompanying pipeline. Of more importance, he said, it would ensure protection of the air route into China. Northern Burma, however, could not be taken without the assistance of the British forces in the Imphal area. General Stilwell and Brigadier Wingate, commanding the long range penetration groups, were reported to be "convinced that a show of strength by the Imphal, Ledo and Yunnan forces would result in a Japanese withdrawal from Northern Burma to a line roughly on an axis east and west of Mandalay."

The Stilwell group would have another opportunity to present their case, but in the meantime the Axiom Mission arrived in Washington with the SEAC proposals carefully and elaborately prepared.[25] In papers circulated to the Joint Chiefs of Staff the SEAC planners reviewed the current mission of the command and the possible courses of action for the future. The mission, it will be remembered, was twofold:

> 'A' To maintain and broaden our contacts with CHINA, both by the air route and by establishing direct contact through NORTH BURMA.
>
> 'B' To engage the Japanese so as best to achieve attrition and diversion of their forces from the Pacific.

Military and eningeering demands of the Ledo Road were reported to be interfering with the priority accorded to the air transport line. That part of the road which had to date been built, however, was not thought wasted, for it was essential for the limited military operations to defend the air route. Completion of the road, on the other hand, would be long delayed, involve the reconquest of Burma, and be slower in supplying China with large amounts of material than a route by the sea. Clearance of the entire area of Burma would require forces much beyond those available in SEAC, whose actions "would be relatively ineffective in quickening the tempo of a PACIFIC advance, and ill-placed to develop an alternative major thrust against JAPAN." If operations in northern Burma were limited to minor ones to defend the air route, however, resources would be available for another project, and SEAC recommended a breach of the Malay-Netherlands East Indies Barrier by an attack on North Sumatra in November 1944. It would, said the report, "remove a corner stone in the Japanese defensive perimeter and strangle some of her sources of raw material, so that she would be compelled to meet it by a diversion of her Forces." The paper concluded:

> 17. Land contact with CHINA through N. BURMA will gain no timely advantage to us or to CHINA, and will commit us in BURMA to costly and sterile effort, thus retarding rather than hastening the defeat of JAPAN. On the other hand, the air route commits us only to the limited operations necessary for its defense, thereby freeing forces for more productive effort against JAPAN.
>
> 18. It is concluded that:
>   (a) Operations in BURMA should be limited to reasonable defence of the air route and bases, and to containing the Japanese.
>   (b) Appropriate effort should be made to increase air operations based in CHINA.
>   (c) Further construction of the LEDO Road should be restricted to the minimum requirements for the defence of the air route.
>   (d) An assault on N. SUMATRA should be launched in November 1944.

The project outlined by the Axiom group was well received in London, as might be expected. On 26 February the British Chiefs of Staff reported to the CCS that they had ascertained that, contrary to suspicions of the CBI staff, Admiral Mountbatten was not withholding any forces for a future attack on Sumatra but was using the maximum that could be supported in the land campaign from Imphal. However, he did not share General Stilwell's view that the British forces could take the Shwebo-Monywa area before the monsoon, nor, indeed, that the Ledo force could capture Myitkyina. The British Chiefs were convinced that the Ledo Road could not be completed to Kunming soon enough to prepare a base in China before the Pacific drive reached China from the east. Consequently they recommended that all efforts be applied to developing the air route and maintaining the maximum air force possible in China until the naval campaign had reached China's shores. Admiral Mountbatten would accordingly be instructed "to develop, maintain and protect the air link with China."[26] This was not a full endorsement of the SEAC proposals, but it was a clear indication that British sympathy was not with General Stilwell and the Ledo Road.

The next step was to hear in Washington the case of the Axiom Mission. On 3 March the group attended a meeting of the Combined Chiefs of Staff.[27] General Wedemeyer, as the chief spokesman for the mission, explained the SEAC proposals, stressing the changed circumstances which necessitated revision of the original directive to the Supreme Commander. With Chinese help refused because of the cancellation of Buccaneer, the staff had concluded that Upper Burma could not be denied to the enemy and the Ledo Road could not be built in 1944 and should not even be attempted.

SEAC AND BURMA IN EARLY 1944

Consequently they had concentrated on the security of the air ferry route. Briefly, what SEAC was proposing was

> to continue to support the maximum the air effort from China, which was achieving most valuable results; to increase the capacity of the air ferry route; and to undertake land operations to secure the air ferry route and to deny freedom of action to the enemy. One further point: It was proposed to construct an oil pipeline through to China by one of two alternative routes.

In the questioning that followed General Wedemeyer's presentation it was brought out that the pipeline would stretch approximately 1,000 miles across very difficult country. Nevertheless, it was reported by Major General D. Harrison that the engineers estimated that it could be completed in eight to twelve months.

The chiefs had numerous questions as to the feasibility and the desirability of the SEAC proposals. They merely "noted" the statements of the Axiom group, however, and agreed to await the views of the British Chiefs of Staff in their capacity as executives for the theater.[28]

By this time a considerable number of papers had accumulated and many words had been spoken on the matter of strategy in Southeast Asia. The studies submitted by the Axiom Mission had been presented for consideration to the Joint Staff Planners. On 16 March that group produced for the chiefs a report of its investigation.[29] Observing in the first place, "Basic differences exist between United States and British strategical trends in Southeast Asia and China," the paper presented a clear statement of those differences which it will be profitable to repeat in considerable detail.

> *a.* The Americans consider that while the China Theater will increase in military usefulness in support of the final advance on Japan, the Southeast Asia Theater will decrease in strategic value once a lodgment is gained in the Formosa-Luzon-China Coast area. This view is apparently not shared by the British.
>
> *b.* The British have considered the QUADRANT decisions and the Prime Minister's directives pertaining to opening communications to China, under the assumption that this is to be accomplished in order to develop timely and decisive air and land offensives against Japan *from* China.... The Americans consider the need for establishing communications to China as a means for developing China as a base for *support*, principally by air, of the main effort in the Pacific (SEXTANT).
>
> *c.* In the development of overland communications from India to China the British measure the results to be gained in terms of the road only, and have not weighed fully the value of the pipelines to be laid along the road...not only in support of the initial entry into the Formosa-China Coast area, but in continued support of the subsequent air operations from China against Japan proper as well....

578   THE ADVANCE TO VICTORY

The project for a pipeline without the road was deemed impracticable by the Americans. Despite General Harrison's optimistic estimate of eight to twelve months for completion of the line, Lieutenant General Raymond A. Wheeler had told the Joint Logistics Committee it could not be done before November 1945. Even the Axiom group estimated 1 January 1945 as the most optimistic date for the capture of Upper Burma and thought gasoline would be flowing through the pipeline by 1 May.

   d. The British are satisfied to maintain the existing air transport capacity of 13,000 tons a month, whereas the Americans are striving to increase this capacity to as much as 20,000 tons per month.

While the British were emphasizing protection, the Americans were stressing expansion, and expansion could come only by taking the airfields at Myitkyina, thereby allowing a more southerly route at a lower altitude.

   e. The British assume that the capture of Upper Burma will eventually necessitate the seizing of Rangoon and all of Burma. The Americans consider that Upper Burma can be held by advancing our forces to the line Kalewa-Shwebo-Katha-Lashio. They feel further that securing this line will accomplish the immediate Allied objectives in Asia, and that the remainder of Burma, as well as other Japanese occupied countries, will fall after our lodgment in the Formosa-China Coast-Luzon area.

Whereas the Americans argued for vigorous action to take Upper Burma in order to increase deliveries to China and thereby insure effective air support from China for the advance to Formosa, the British felt that the tremendous logistical problems could not be solved, that the Ledo Road would not deliver enough, and that there was not time to develop China as an effective base. Instead the British argued for an operation against Sumatra late in 1944. But they were counting on amphibious resources from the European Theater, and the Americans could not see how, with the current planning date for Germany's defeat October 1944, resources could be available for an attack before March 1945 with a subsequent delay in the capture of Singapore until December 1945, long after Formosa had been reached from the east.

The Joint Staff Planners concluded their study with a recommendation that the Joint Chiefs of Staff inform the British that they could not agree to the Sumatra campaign and urge again "that the necessary directive be issued to Admiral Mountbatten to undertake the most vigorous action to capture Upper Burma during the remainder of this dry season, throughout the monsoon, and next fall, in order to increase the capacity of the air transport line to China and expedite the laying of a pipeline to that country." This, the planners felt, would best support the main effort against Japan, the Pacific advance to China-Formosa-Luzon.

The JPS report had been drafted with only informal discussion with the members of the Axiom Mission, and it was four days after completion of the paper that the group from SEAC attended a full meeting of the Joint Staff Planners.[30] On the following day the group was invited in for questioning by the Joint Chiefs of Staff, who were considering the JPS report.[31] Both of these appearances seem to have been purely perfunctory, for, although General Wedemeyer and his colleagues gave considerable additional information to the planners, the planners did not change their paper; and, although the chiefs asked a number of detailed questions, after the Axiom group had left the JCS meeting the Joint Chiefs approved the JPS recommendations with no further discussion.[32]

Thus in the last week of March the Axiom Mission left Washington, without having convinced the U.S. Chiefs of the desirability of undertaking an operation in North Sumatra. There was as yet no new directive for the Supreme Commander, Southeast Asia, as the British Chiefs forwarded to him the JCS recommendations, asking for his comments.[33]

A NEW DIRECTIVE FOR SEAC

Admiral Mountbatten was not pleased with the recommendations made by the Joint Chiefs of Staff. By mid-April General Stilwell's Ledo force had made such good progress that it looked as if it would soon reach Mogaung en route to Myitkyina. Taking and holding Myitkyina, however, would depend upon what forces the Japanese could bring to bear and how much help would be given by the Chinese Yunnan forces. Admiral Mountbatten had concluded that it would be impossible to gain control of Upper Burma down to the line Katha-Bhamo by the end of 1944 as the U.S. Chiefs advocated. Indeed he thought the project was unsound and should not be attempted. With the acceleration of U.S. operations in the Pacific, he felt, construction of a road and a pipeline to China across northern Burma was more than ever out of step with global strategy. They could not be built in time to assist in the attack on Formosa and the China coast and would not be necessary once the sea route to China had been opened up. Admiral Mountbatten thought that if Myitkyina were taken it could be exploited either by construction of a pipeline through there into China or by construction of a line that far and use of Myitkyina as an oil head and staging area for aircraft flying into China from India. That was the objective he had currently set for himself. After considering the U.S. recommendations he proposed to the British Chiefs that his directive in respect to North Burma "continue to be to develop, maintain, broaden and protect the air link to China."[34]

Although Admiral Mountbatten's remarks were received on 15 April, it was almost a month before the British Chiefs of Staff sent any comments to Washington. In the meantime the U.S. Chiefs had gone ahead with planning on the assumption that Myitkyina and a protective zone south of there would be secured by 1 January 1945. With attainment of that objective they foresaw an increase of Hump tonnage to 20,000 tons monthly, completion of a six-inch pipeline from Calcutta to Dibrugarh by January 1945, completion of a four-inch pipeline from Dibrugarh to Kunming by May, construction of a single track gravel road from Ledo to Myitkyina and subsequent development to a two-track road, minimum road construction from Myitkyina to Kunming, and finally construction of a four-inch pipeline from Kunming to Tushan to permit delivery of 100 octane gasoline to Kweilin.[35]

The British Chiefs of Staff continued to doubt the value of trying to open a land route across Upper Burma or even of building a pipeline through Myitkyina into China. While they were delaying comment on the U.S. proposals for future operations in Southeast Asia, the U.S. Chiefs issued a directive to General Stilwell to concentrate his efforts toward amassing supplies in China in order to support the attack on Formosa and landings on the China coast, whenever they might come. This to the British Chiefs of Staff seemed an argument against building a road or a pipeline through Myitkyina into China, for they were convinced that neither could be completed in time to be of value. Clearly there would have to be an increase in the amount of supplies delivered to China, but the British Chiefs favored accomplishing that by air, preferably by flying long range aircraft from Calcutta directly into China.

When the British finally submitted their comments on Admiral Mountbatten's despatch on 10 May, it was to recommend that he be charged with developing, maintaining, broadening, and protecting the air route to China in order to provide a maximum flow of petroleum products and other supplies.[36]

After studying the British paper the JWPC concluded that the directive proposed by the British Chiefs of Staff was in fact in agreement with the U.S. Chiefs' own views that the Southeast Asia Command should work to increase the air lift to China in order to provide support for the advance in the Pacific.[37] The planners discounted the possibility of providing long range transports (C-54 and C-87) to increase the deliveries to China by flying directly from Calcutta, however. Instead they proposed acceptance of a plan suggested by the Air Transport Command to use Myitkyina as an advanced fighter base that could provide protection for a more southerly air route without itself requiring as much defense in depth as a transport base. To the Joint Staff Planners the JWPC recommended acceptance of the directive to Admiral Mountbatten proposed by the British Chiefs of Staff.

Before this paper reached the Joint Chiefs of Staff the draft directive to Admiral Mountbatten had been revised twice. In the first place General Roberts of the Joint Staff Planners objected that a minimum objective should be set for SEAC operations, preferably the securing of the Myitkyina area. Then General Somervell, Commanding General, Army Service Forces, pointed out that General Stilwell's advance in Upper Burma was doing so well that it might actually prove feasible to put the first four-inch pipeline through to Kunming by 1 December 1944. He was insistent that no premature decision be made to abandon the road or the pipeline. In fact, if the SEAC directive was to be changed, he thought it should include constructing the Ledo-Kunming Road and pipelines. The directive finally recommended to the Joint Chiefs of Staff set neither the securing of Myitkyina nor the completion of the pipeline as objectives but urged the seizure of opportunities leading to the attainment of either with forces already available. Admiral Mountbatten would be directed

> To develop, maintain, broaden and protect the air link to China in order to provide maximum and timely flow of POL and stores to China in support of Pacific operations; to press advantages against the enemy by exerting maximum effort, ground and air, particularly during the current monsoon season; and in pressing such advantages to be prepared to exploit the development of overland communications to China. These operations must be dictated by the forces at present available or firmly allocated to SEAC.[38]

That General Somervell's recommendation was not adopted in full was largely because the U.S. Chiefs, no less than the British, were determined that no substantial forces would be sent to Burma and India until after the defeat of Germany. Without them the theater commanders reported that the road and the pipeline into China could not be completed.

Ten days before the Joint Chiefs of Staff approved the planners' paper for presentation to the British an advance force of General Stilwell's command had occupied the airstrip at Myitkyina.[39] It appeared that with help from the Chinese or from the British farther west in Burma, Myitkyina might very soon be in friendly hands for exploitation as an air base and as a major point on the road to China. There was little evidence that help or even interest was to be forthcoming from either source, however, and General Stilwell's elation at having acquired a toehold was strongly tempered. His impatience with the apparent apathy of the British in SEAC toward operations in Burma and his disgust with two years of procrastination by the Chinese were further complicated by the directive that had reached him at the beginning of the month to focus his efforts toward providing maximum support to the advance upon Formosa, Luzon, and the coast of China.[40] He had been working for two years under a directive to increase the combat efficiency of the Chinese Army in order to fight the Japanese on the mainland of Asia. This had involved supplying the Chinese with American weapons and supplies, and the opening of a route into China on the ground had seemed a requisite. Now he was being told that his efforts were to be concentrated on supporting air operations and that Hump tonnage to other projects would have to be cut back. What effect the new directive was to have on his original mission General Stilwell did not know, and on 24 May he sought information on the subject from General Marshall.[41]

In reply General Marshall explained that if possible Japan should be defeated without a major campaign on the mainland of Asia.[42] As General Stilwell had already been told, priority for the next several months was to be given to building up the air effort in China. Since the demands of the war against Germany precluded the sending to CBI of the troops necessary for reopening ground communications immediately, deliveries to China would have to be made by air. Therefore General Stilwell should devote his "principal effort to support of the Hump, its security, and the increase in its capacity with the view to development of maximum effectiveness of the 14th Air Force consistent with minimum requirements for support of all other activities in China." This did not mean abandonment of the road or the pipeline project. General Stilwell's directive on that subject was no more definite than that proposed for Admiral Mountbatten: "In pressing the advantages against the enemy you should be prepared to exploit the development of overland communications to China."

Precisely what the Joint Chiefs of Staff envisaged as they talked of exploiting the development of overland communications to China is not clear. In any event they had come to the view that the major objective in Upper Burma must be the increase of tonnage delivered over the Hump for the support of air rather than ground operations. When on 2 June the Combined Chiefs took up the directive recommended by the U.S. Chiefs, Sir John Dill suggested emphasizing the importance of the timely increase of air transport as Admiral Mountbatten's main object by saying that other efforts would be carried out "so far as is consistent with" the main one of developing the air link. The U.S. Chiefs accepted this modification with no objection, and the directive was finally sent in that form to Admiral Mountbatten on 3 June 1944. This was the most definite directive he was to receive before September.[43]

TRANSPORT AIRCRAFT

While the question of long-term strategy in Southeast Asia was being discussed on the highest echelons, the British forces fighting in eastern India had been encountering Japanese opposition. In Arakan the XV Corps, headed for Akyab, ran into difficulties as Japanese forces launched an offensive against them. The enemy succeeded in closing the Ngakyedauk Pass, cutting off the 7th Division from the rest of the corps, and it became necessary to fly supplies in to the troops by air. Inasmuch as one of the long range penetration brigades had already started down the Hukawng Valley and the remaining two were scheduled to be flown in early in March, all to be entirely dependent upon air supply, the transport aircraft assigned to SEAC were not adequate for the new emergency. Admiral Mountbatten cabled the British Chiefs of Staff for permission to divert planes from the Hump temporarily to meet the situation.[44]

The SEAC staff had calculated that at the peak period of operations there would be a deficiency of about thirty-eight

C-47's. If that number of planes were diverted from India and an equivalent number of C-46's transferred from the Hump to India, deliveries to China would be reduced about 100-114 tons per day or about 3,000-3,500 tons per month. Lest it be necessary to cancel the operations of the long range penetration groups, Admiral Mountbatten requested permission from the Combined Chiefs to divert up to thirty-eight C-47's. His request was forwarded by the British Chiefs of Staff on 21 February, with a strong recommendation for the temporary transfer.

One can well imagine that this situation was greeted with dismay by the U.S. Chiefs, for the Hump traffic was finally being built up to effective strength. At General Arnold's suggestion, however, they agreed to the temporary diversion of thirty C-47's and crews from the Air Transport Command, with the understanding that any future deficiencies would be made up from British sources.[45]

Before word of this approval could reach Admiral Mountbatten another message arrived from him, indicating that the C-46's being used on the Hump had proved to be feasible for dropping supplies. Consequently it would not be necessary to go to the anticipated trouble of transferring C-46's to the trans-India route to release C-47's for supplying the troops in Burma. He was changing his request to twenty-seven C-46's.[46] The British Chiefs agreed, assuming approval by the U.S. Chiefs of Staff.[47] The U.S. Chiefs objected. They had approved thirty C-47's. Twenty-seven C-46's would carry tonnage equivalent to forty C-47's, unnecessarily reducing the Hump deliveries. Consequently they told the British Chiefs that if the C-46's had already been diverted they should be sent back, exchanged for not more than thirty C-47's.[48]

This had hardly been straightened out, the 7th Division rescued and the transports returned, when another emergency arose. This time the Japanese were found to be concentrating forces along the border of India near Imphal, apparently preparing for an offensive. Admiral Mountbatten decided that in order to hold the Imphal Plain it would be necessary to send reenforcements to the area by air, again diverting about thirty C-47's or the equivalent number of C-46's from the Hump. Admiral Mountbatten took the initiative and ordered the C-47's transferred, asking the British Chiefs for concurrence with his conclusion that the emergency was a continuing one, though not telling them that the diversion had already been ordered.[49] He also asked for blanket authority to divert aircraft from the Air Transport Command when he deemed it necessary for protection of the air transport route.[50]

Although the U.S. Chiefs were reluctant to cut further into Hump tonnage, they foresaw potential profits in the Imphal operations and recognized the serious threat by the Japanese. Consequently they agreed to the diversion of thirty C-47's or the equivalent number of C-46's, to be returned "at the earliest possible time." However, they refused any blanket authority for diversions, on the grounds that "the primary mission of the planes is to serve the China Theater." If any more transports were needed, the U.S. Chiefs recommended, the British Chiefs should provide them.[51]

As a further measure to ease the Imphal crisis General Stilwell and Admiral Mountbatten recommended to their respective Chiefs of Staff that the President and the Prime Minister bring pressure to bear on Generalissimo Chiang Kai-shek to order the forces in Yunnan to cross the Salween River and fight in Burma.[52] President Roosevelt acted at once and sent off a message drafted hastily in the War Department.[53] Describing in some detail the successes being won by the Ledo force in Upper Burma and the difficulties already facing the Japanese in that area, the President represented the situation as a great opportunity for the Chinese Yunnan force to achieve a substantial victory. Politely he concluded, "I am communicating my views to you at length and in considerable detail in the hope that you will give orders to the commander of your Yunnan force to cooperate in developing what appears to be a great opportunity."

The Generalissimo replied ten days later. China simply was not strong enough to maintain defenses within the China Theater and prepare for the eventual arrival of Allied forces on the China coast. "I am of the opinion," said Chiang, "that as long as our line of defences has not been adequately strengthened, it is impossible for our main forces to undertake an offence from Yunnan.... I realize that reinforcements should be sent to Burma in view of the military situation there and that although this does not fall within scope of our work, still we should do what we can in compliance with your request. I have therefore decided to dispatch to India by air as many of our troops in Yunnan as can be spared in order to re-enforce the troops in Ledo, thus enabling the latter to carry on their tasks of defeating the enemy."[54]

The Generalissimo's "No!" was not taken as the last word in Washington. When General Stilwell reported three days later that part of the Japanese 56th Division had been removed from the Yunnan front to oppose the Ledo force and the long range penetration groups, President Roosevelt again wrote to Chiang in emphatic terms:

> The present offensive by the Japs in the Imphal area is directed primarily against the L-of-C which makes possible the transportation of materials to China. If the Japanese succeed in their intentions in this drive, they can then concentrate against and destroy the Ledo Force and turn against your "Y" Force at their leisure....
>
> While heavy fighting is in progress in West Burma and on the Arakan Coast, the Salween front has remained quiet and as a result the Japanese have been able to divert elements of the

56th Division to meet Stilwell's thrust down the Mogaung Valley and the threat of the long range penetration groups in North Burma. It is inconceivable to me that your "Y" Forces, with their American equipment, would be unable to advance against the Japanese 56th Division in its present depleted strength. To me the time is ripe for elements of your 71st Army Group to advance without further delay and seize the Tengchung-Lungling areas....

To take advantage of just such an opportunity, we have, during the past year, been equipping and training your "Y" Forces. If they are not to be used in the common cause our most strenuous and extensive efforts to fly in equipment and to furnish instructional personnel have not been justified. They should not be held back on the grounds that an amphibious operation against the South Burma coast is necessary prior to their advance. Present developments negate such a requirement. The Jap has deployed the bulk of 7 divisions in his operations on the Arakan, the Chindwin, and in the Mogaung Valley. *I do hope you can act.*[55]

It was ten days before an answer came, and then it was not direct from the Generalissimo. General Ho Ying-chin, Chinese Chief of Staff and Minister of War, told General Marshall on 14 April that part of the Yunnan force would move across the Salween. The decision, he said, had been made "on [the] initiative of [the] Chinese without influence of outside pressure, and was based on [the] realization that China must contribute its share to the common war effort."[56]

This final agreement to participate in action in Upper Burma had not come soon enough to cause any spectacular change in the situation, which had already developed further crises. On the same day the Generalissimo's first reply was received Admiral Mountbatten reported that the Japanese were threatening the rail line between Dimapur and Ledo, the only means of communication with most of the Hump air bases and with General Stilwell's base at Ledo.[57] In the hope of scoring a decisive victory Admiral Mountbatten proposed to fly the 7th Indian Division up from Arakan and to fly in two more long range penetration brigades to the rear of the enemy. This would mean an estimated 100 C-47's or their equivalent. So Admiral Mountbatten requested permission to retain the twenty C-46's for a longer period, asking that some arrangements be made for the remainder by the next favorable period of the moon, 4 April. The British Chiefs accordingly proposed that he be authorized to take 70 more C-47's or the equivalent off the Hump, unless some of the 400 transports promised by General Arnold for later in the year could be delivered ahead of time.[58]

The Joint Chiefs of Staff agreed that Admiral Mountbatten might keep the twenty C-46's he already had, but they could see no justification for taking any more planes off the Hump. Nor could

General Arnold's air staff find any more U.S. transports elsewhere to send to Southeast Asia.[59] However, information available in Washington indicated that the British themselves had 219 two-engine transports in the Middle East and India. The U.S. Chiefs were inclined to think that perhaps the British could find more help for Admiral Mountbatten if they tried a little harder.[60]

The British did look a little farther and reported that they could spare twenty C-47's from the United Kingdom and possibly twenty-five from the Mediterranean. The March quota, twelve planes, was already en route to Southeast Asia. Until these arrangements should become effective the British Chiefs recommended that the U.S. Chiefs approve a temporary diversion from the Hump to meet Admiral Mountbatten's requirements.[61]

The U.S. Chiefs were glad to accept a new proposal from General Arnold: that one U.S. troop carrier group (sixty-four planes) be diverted from the Mediterranean to SEAC for not more than thirty days while the British were sending the transports they had mentioned, including the Mediterranean squadron. The remaining deficit--thirteen planes--would be taken from the Air Transport Command in India, to be replaced by diversions from British allocations in April.[62] This proposal was accepted by the British. With some protest from the Mediterranean commander, arrangements were made to send from the Mediterranean the U.S. group and an RAF squadron with fifteen planes, a number that proved temporarily satisfactory to Admiral Mountbatten.[63] In the first week of April they were on their way.

The temporary diversion of aircraft from the Mediterranean Theater was not a solution to the problem. As April advanced it became clear that at the end of the thirty-day loan period the forces fighting in the Mogaung-Myitkyina area and around Imphal and the long range penetration brigades in Central Burma would still be dependent upon air for supply. Consequently Admiral Mountbatten on 25 April requested to be allowed to keep the transports and that they be replaced at once in the Mediterranean Theater with an equal number of the first assignment to him of the 400 transports promised by General Arnold on 24 March. Forwarding his message to the Combined Chiefs of Staff, the British Chiefs expressed the view that it was essential for the U.S. and RAF planes to be returned in order to be available for the vital battle in Italy. They recommended that unless 79 of the first 100 transports could be sent to the Mediterranean by mid-May, Admiral Mountbatten be allowed to call on the 20 C-46's which he had recently returned to the Hump and re-divert Hump aircraft until the arrival of the first 100 planes in Southeast Asia.[64]

Since the transports allocated to Southeast Asia were not suitable for use in the Mediterranean Theater, the Joint Chiefs of Staff decided that the seventy-nine planes should be returned. The first 100 planes could leave the United States by about 22 May. If an emergency arose before that, the JCS suggested, Admiral Mountbatten might use any of the twenty C-46's he had just returned to the Hump.[65] When the Supreme Allied Commander, Mediterranean, subsequently agreed to extend the date of loan of his planes until 31 May the problem seemed to be solved.[66]

In the large picture of the war against Japan these recurrent emergencies in Burma form a small part in a remote area. Their significance lies not in their immediate effect on the campaign to defeat Japan but in the amount of attention they demanded from the Joint Chiefs of Staff and in the illustration they afford of the difficulties encountered by the JCS and CCS as they attempted to focus activity in the area upon the development of the air link with China.

Chapter XXIII

CHINA'S ROLE IN THE PACIFIC CAMPAIGN

FUTURE PLANS FOR CHINA

The problems of Burma could not be entirely divorced from the problems of China, for as had been reiterated again and again it was the U.S. purpose to keep China in the war. Just what part China would and could play in the final phases of the fight, however, was undetermined in the spring of 1944.

China had always been the stated objective of the advance across the Pacific. Plans repeatedly included mention of the use of Chinese bases in the ultimate thrust against Japan. But 1944 found the military situation within China little if any stronger than it had been when the Japanese attacked Pearl Harbor. Transport by air over some of the roughest territory in the world was still the only way of getting supplies into the country. General Stilwell's efforts to carry out his original directive to assist in improving the combat efficiency of the Chinese Army had been largely thwarted by the Generalissimo, who put more faith in air than in ground forces. B-29 bases in China were nearing completion. But a further study of the complications of operating the huge planes at the end of the long supply route and surveys of the potentialities of other bases soon to be acquired in the island-to-island advance in the Pacific resulted in a shift of the major plans for B-29 operations from China to the Marianas. There remained the Fourteenth Air Force in China under command of General Chennault, who continued to urge that his force be enlarged and a heavy blow be struck at Japan by attacks upon Japanese aircraft and ships.[1]

General Chennault's proposals were not adopted, for they were more ambitious than anything contemplated by the planners in Washington and would have involved extensive revision of current plans and supply schedules for China-Burma-India. Still the Fourteenth Air Force did have a part to play in the approaching showdown with Japan. It was this part and the uses to be made of other forces in China and Chinese bases themselves that came up for serious discussion in the first months of 1944.

In a study of the Pacific program, made in March by the Joint Staff Planners, China's contribution to the drive to reach Formosa and the coast of China itself by 15 February 1945 was considered to be limited to support by the Fourteenth Air Force and the Chinese-American Wing and by the B-29's based in the Chengtu area.[2] No larger effort could be supplied, for neither the advance against Sumatra advocated by the British nor the road and pipeline construction backed by the Americans could be completed in time. "It would seem most logical then," the planners recommended, "that all efforts in that area should be directed towards nourishing the air forces in China so that they, by an all-out effort, can support our assault from the Pacific." The original concept under which General Stilwell had been directed to improve the efficiency of Chinese ground forces, that is, that ultimately the Japanese Army would have to be defeated on the mainland of Asia, no longer seemed valid in the light of rapid advances across the Pacific.

It was estimated in Washington that, if essential supplies were carefully and secretly stocked in the forward China area during the next year by diverting 5,000 tons a month from the Hump, it should be possible to operate three groups of medium bombers and six fighters for thirty days to support amphibious operations in Formosa. Shortly after the directive of 12 March was sent to the Pacific commanders, General Arnold alerted General Stratemeyer in New Delhi to plan for such a project and asked for information as to transportation into the east China area.[3] An exchange of messages followed as the CBI planners clarified the assumptions upon which their plans should be drawn.[4]

It was during this period that President Roosevelt was endeavoring to persuade Generalissimo Chiang Kai-shek to permit his troops in Yunnan to cross the Salween River and participate in the fighting in Burma. When Chiang made no reply to the second message from the President, General Marshall suggested to General Stilwell that, if the Yunnan force was not going to move, he might "consider diverting the HUMP tonnage going to them, or at least a major portion of it, to Chennault's air or to the activities of the B-29's."[5] Here was a potential source of supply for the air forces that were to support the Formosa operation. In a paper prepared by the Joint War Plans Committee on 12 April it was proposed that only those Yunnan divisions which would definitely participate in operations should continue to receive supplies via the Hump.[6] The planners recommended that General Stilwell be given a general directive, "reaffirming to him the concept of Pacific operations, and directing that he commence now to stock and conserve supplies in China in order that the air forces based there can furnish adequate support for the assault on Formosa with a target date of February 1945, and support, to some extent, for the attack against Mindanao."

There was some question among the planners as to whether such a directive should go to General Stilwell at all and whether he should be told to consider necessary steps or actually start in on stockpiling for the Formosa operation. After several discussions and exchanges of memoranda, however, the Joint Staff Planners finally agreed on a paper, including a draft directive, and submitted it to the Joint Chiefs on 28 April 1944.[7] By this time General Marshall had learned from General Ho Ying-chin that part of the Yunnan force would cross the Salween.

The report finally submitted to the Joint Chiefs took note of General Ho's promise but still recommended that Hump tonnage for ground forces be provided only to those actually participating in operations. In the proposed directive the "how" of the stockpiling was left to General Stilwell's decision.

General Stilwell was to be "charged with responsibility for air support from China against such targets as Formosa, the Ryukyus, the Philippines, and the China Coast prior to and during the advance on Formosa." To as great an extent as proved practicable he was also to furnish support for the attack on Mindanao in November 1944. General Stilwell was to estimate the extent of the air effort he would be able to furnish, assuming there would be no reenforcements beyond those currently scheduled, but allowing for the coordinated use of the XX Bomber Command and temporary use of part of the Tenth Air Force. Said the JPS draft:

> It is recognized that major curtailment of "hump" support to ground forces in China and to such other activities as do not directly support an air effort will be required. We are prepared to authorize such curtailment on the basis of your recommendations on this matter.
>
> Pending submission and approval of your plans, the Joint Chiefs of Staff consider it necessary to commence immediately the progressive stock piling in China of supplies to be used for these supporting operations.

The Joint Chiefs of Staff were in favor of sending the message to General Stilwell. Admiral King, however, expressed his view that the Hump was "of vital importance and the Chiefs of Staff should retain control of it." He felt that General Stilwell should be instructed rather than asked for his recommendations for curtailing the Hump tonnage. The others[8] agreed with Admiral King, and the sentence concerning General Stilwell's recommendations on the matter was deleted. With some slight clarifying amendments proposed by Major General Laurence S. Kuter, the message was approved and sent to the CBI commander.[9] Addition of this new demand on the transport line over the Hump would inevitably complicate the already involved problem of tonnage allocation.

THE TWENTIETH AIR FORCE

Still another problem was being added to the many in China-Burma-India and still another demand was being placed upon the supply line in the spring of 1944 with the arrival of the first very long range bombers. This new weapon not only introduced a new project for supply and support but presented a new complication of command in that area where nothing was simple.

In preparation for the imminent arrival of the first B-29's in India General Marshall proposed to General Stilwell at the beginning of January 1944 that he, as Commanding General, U.S. Army Forces, China-Burma-India, should exercise direct control of the B-29 force assigned there (the XX Bomber Command), using the facilities of the Tenth and the Fourteenth Air Forces for administrative and operational control. The XX Bomber Command would operate under "general directives" from the Joint Chiefs of Staff.[10] General Stilwell concurred in this arrangement, and the Joint Chiefs of Staff approved it informally on 17 January.[11] But the command problem was not so easily solved.

Arrangements for command of the very long range bomber force had not been discussed with the British. When Admiral Mountbatten received General Stilwell's General Order No. 16 defining the setup, he protested to the British Chiefs of Staff.[12] General Stilwell had retained direct "command and control" of the XX Bomber Command, assigning to General Stratemeyer, Commanding General, Army Air Forces, India-Burma Sector, responsibility for logistics and transportation "and for recommendations to the Theatre Commander after consultation with the Commanding General 20th Bomber Command for missions in the South East Asia-China-Area." General Chennault was made responsible for defending the airfields in China, for supporting the bombers while there, "and for recommendations to the Theatre Commander through the Air Adviser after missions... from China bases." Admiral Mountbatten objected that there would have to be more specific provision for coordination of the operation of the big bombers "with the theatre commanders from, through and in whose theatres they operate." Unless the theater people were all "put in the picture" before the missions were assigned, he anticipated a clash of priorities between theater operations and the operations of the B-29's. Admiral Mountbatten recommended that the Joint Chiefs of Staff retain direction of the very long range bombers, but "the Chiefs of Staff concerned [i.e., presumably the British Chiefs for missions in SEAC] will issue directives assigning missions for VLR bombing simultaneously to the commander of the VLR Bomber Force (i.e. General Stilwell) and the commanders of all theatres concerned, i.e. theatre in which bombers will be based, theatres over which they fly and theatres in which targets lie." Coordination would be the responsibility of the force commander, who would not dispatch the missions until arrangements had been made with all theater commanders.

The British Chiefs of Staff endorsed Admiral Mountbatten's comments, passing them along to the Combined Chiefs with the remark "that it would be a quite unworkable arrangement to give General Stratemeyer, as a subordinate commander of Air Marshal Peirse and Admiral Mountbatten, independent command of air forces based in China under the independent direction of the U.S. Joint Chiefs of Staff and General Stilwell." The British recommended also that the theater commanders be instructed to be mindful of a serious threat to the air route over the Hump or to the B-29 bases themselves once the air operations started.[13]

The British proposal was turned over to the Joint War Plans Committee for study. That group was so busy with other matters at the time, however, that the Army Air Staff and Operations Division prepared a draft reply and a directive to General Stilwell, which General Arnold submitted on 6 March directly to the Joint Chiefs of Staff. Advance elements of the XX Bomber Command had already arrived in India and China.[14]

The paper presented by General Arnold had incorporated some of the substance of a separate JPS report that was being circulated to the Joint Chiefs at the same time. The Joint War Plans Committee had undertaken in January 1944 a study of the best use and deployment of the new B-29's, concluding that the most satisfactory bases for long range bombing operations would be found in the Marianas.[15] Recognizing, however, that the Marianas would not be available until late in the year, JWPC recommended that the first four groups of B-29's be employed from bases in the Southwest Pacific against targets in the Netherlands East Indies, a plan strongly championed by General MacArthur.[16] The next four groups would go to India-China for operations against Japanese industrial targets (the Matterhorn project). The following twelve would go to the Marianas as soon as possible, being assigned in the interim either to the Southwest Pacific or to Chengtu, whichever proved more profitable.

The members of the staff of the Army Air Forces were not enthusiastic about attacking the Netherlands East Indies but felt that it was more important to hit the Japanese industrial areas in Manchuria. They thought too, that the JWPC had not paid sufficient heed to the problem of command. Consequently they drafted a separate report, to the considerable annoyance of Admiral Bieri, who pointed out that the Joint Staff Planners were in fact a joint committee and JPS reports were supposed to represent "a balanced view." They could be amended or rewritten by the planners, or revised by the subcommittee, or submitted with divergent views. But he objected to a separate report by one of the services.[17]

Discussion went on among the Joint Staff Planners during the entire month of February. It was 1 March when they finally approved a report after several revisions, including in it most of the points upon which the Army Air Forces had been insistent, and submitting it to the Joint Chiefs as JCS 742.[18]

The Joint Staff Planners had accepted the conclusion of the Joint War Plans Committee that the principal targets in the Japanese home islands would not be within reach until bases had been developed in the Marianas. They had recognized, however, that the first eight groups of B-29's available would go to the Matterhorn project in China, since it already had the approval of the Combined Chiefs of Staff. It was perhaps from the inevitability of this assignment that the Navy and Army Planners had accepted the order of priority upon which their air colleagues were most insistent:

> a. Against iron and steel in the form of coke ovens, and shipping in congested harbors, from available bases in China, and,
>
> b. Against the petroleum refineries in the N.E.I., primarily those at Palembang, from bases in Australia or Ceylon.

It would be largely the responsibility of the Matterhorn group to cover the oil refineries, for the JPS recommended that the next twelve groups available go to the Marianas and be sent to the Southwest Pacific temporarily only in the event the Marianas bases were not yet ready. Perhaps eventually two groups might be sent to the Aleutians.

Lest there be confusion over theater responsibilities or U.S. and British jurisdiction the Joint Staff Planners recommended:

> Control, including deployment, of VLR bombers be retained directly under the Joint Chiefs of Staff in order that VLR forces may be employed and deployed to meet the developments in the strategic situation.

General Arnold's draft directive to General Stilwell incorporated many of the points in JCS 742.[19] General Stilwell was assigned command of the bombing forces "based in the CBI area, in operations under the operational control of the Joint Chiefs of Staff." The objectives set for B-29 operations were those advocated by the Air planners:

> a. Coke ovens in Manchuria, Korea and Japan.
> b. Japanese industrial and urban areas.
> c. Shipping concentrations in main Japanese shipping centers.
> d. Key aircraft industrial targets in Japan.

In addition the bombers were to undertake one or more missions against the Pladjoe oil refineries at Palembang, but this was clearly a secondary task. These strategic bombing operations were to be the initial step of a sustained air bombardment designed "to achieve the progressive destruction and dislocation of the Japanese military, industrial and economic systems, and the undermining of the morale of the Japanese people to a point where their capacity for armed resistance is fatally weakened."

General Arnold proposed no such complicated system of coordination as had Admiral Mountbatten but recommended that B-29 operations be coordinated with those of the Chinese Air Force and the Fourteenth Air Force in China. In operations from bases in the Southeast Asia Command or against objectives in its area of responsibility General Stilwell was to consult with the Supreme Commander to insure coordination with theater air forces.

Finally, General Arnold included the important provision that in an emergency "theater commanders may, at their discretion, utilize the strategic air forces, which are based within their respective theaters, for purposes other than their primary mission, informing the U.S. Chiefs of Staff."

The Joint Chiefs of Staff discussed General Arnold's draft at some length, concentrating particularly upon the allowance for diversion of the very long range bombers in the event of an emergency. Admiral Bieri, maintaining that it was not clear how Admiral Mountbatten would get control of the planes, had recommended a change to read:

> Should an emergency arise requiring the use of the strategic air forces for purposes other than their regularly assigned missions, they should be made available to the theater commander concerned for such purposes and the U.S. Chiefs of Staff informed.

General Arnold approved this revision before the JCS meeting of 7 March, but both he and General Hansell, the Air Planner, were reluctant to admit the need for clarification, pointing out that a similar situation existed in the Mediterranean, where it was provided for by an identical directive.[20]

Admiral King suggested that the situation was different in CBI, and he proposed asking the Joint Staff Planners to consider the problem. By the end of the discussion, however, the Joint Chiefs accepted a recommendation from Admiral King that the paper be approved with the new statement and some other minor alterations proposed by the Navy planners. The directive went out to General Stilwell the following day.[21]

At the same JCS meeting the JCS report on optimum use of very long range bombers was also under consideration. Neither General Arnold nor Admiral King was satisfied with the statement on command as it stood and both of them had suggested amendments before the Joint Chiefs met. General Arnold recommended that he be made "executive agent of the Joint Chiefs of Staff, to exercise general direction of the VLR bomber forces engaged in the war against Japan," when necessary coordinating matters with General Marshall and Admiral King.[22] Admiral King suggested substituting for the indefinite "control" a more precise definition of JCS jurisdiction, "strategic deployment and the designation of missions." Coordination of the B-29 operations with other theater activities would be the responsibility of the area commander.[23] Admiral King thought General Arnold's proposals might be "out of step with the Planners' recommendations," and the Joint Chiefs decided to send the paper back to the planners for reconsideration.[24]

Once again the Joint Staff Planners took up the problem of B-29's. Admiral Bieri suggested that telling the Commanding General of the Army Air Forces to coordinate the operations of the very long range bombers was "in effect telling him to execute his normal functions." Coordination of logistic support was the province of the theater commanders. His weak case against the executive provision was supported by Rear Admiral Donald B. Duncan, who suggested that General Arnold's functions would overlap those of Admiral King and General Marshall and confuse the entire picture.[25] However, General Hansell argued that since the Joint

Chiefs intended to shift the bombers from one theater to another coordination was necessary. The executive would have to decide on targets and the type and number of attacks and other operational details. The JPS finally decided, at Admiral Duncan's suggestion, that what General Arnold wanted was direct access to the aircraft in a given theater. Consequently they recommended reserving to the Joint Chiefs "strategic control, including deployment and the designation of missions" and authorizing the Commanding General, Army Air Forces, "to communicate directly with VLR bomber forces in the field for purposes of coordinating their operations."[26] This was not the full executive authority General Arnold would have preferred, but apparently it was not in line either with what Admiral King thought should be done, for he recommended that the whole collection of papers be turned over to the Joint Strategic Survey Committee for comment.[27]

If the Joint Strategic Survey Committee had any views on the command and control of B-29's, they do not appear in the official record. In that connection the committee recommended only inclusion of a provision for the theater commanders to use the B-29's in their areas in case of emergency. Otherwise JSSC took note of the accelerated program for Pacific operations which had been decided upon two weeks previous and recommended that four of the B-29 groups assigned to Matterhorn be sent instead to the Marianas, whence they might be expected to strike directly at "the vitals of Japan."[28] Although messages were received at this time from both General MacArthur and Admiral Nimitz urging that B-29's be sent to Darwin to attack the oil refineries in the Netherlands East Indies, the JSSC report did not even mention them. The Joint Staff Planners did study the matter subsequently, however, and reached the conclusion that the results would not be commensurate with the cost of maintaining B-29's in Australia, a conclusion approved by the Joint Chiefs.[29]

The subject of command was not closed, despite omission by the Joint Strategic Survey Committee of any comment. On 28 March General Arnold reported at the JCS meeting that Admiral King had suggested to him that "the most satisfactory solution would be to create an air force, known as the Joint Chiefs of Staff Air Force, to be commanded by the Commanding General, Army Air Force, who will be the executive agent of the Joint Chiefs of Staff. The Joint Chiefs of Staff would determine its employment and deployment. The Commanding General, Army Air Forces, would be responsible for its logistic support, administration and transfers."[30] The question had apparently been settled before the meeting, for there was no further discussion of it, and General Arnold had already prepared an outline of how it would be arranged.[31] With the Joint Chiefs' approval the Twentieth Air Force was activated on 4 April 1944, adding one more to the complex of commands in the war against Japan.[32]

The JCS sent the problem of deployment of B-29's back to the Joint Staff Planners, this time as a matter of urgency, for the first planes were almost ready to leave for India. The planners incorporated the JSSC recommendation that the second four groups of B-29's be sent to the Marianas. They also proposed that when bases on Formosa became available the B-29's be transferred there from both the Marianas and Chengtu to the full capacity of the Formosan airfields.[33] The Joint Chiefs of Staff approved this proposed deployment on 10 April.[34]

The JCS decision to activate the Twentieth Air Force, reserving command of it in Washington, necessitated revision of the directive which had been sent to General Stilwell early in March. Accordingly, on 14 April General Arnold proposed a new directive, limiting General Stilwell's responsibility for the XX Bomber Command primarily to logistic support, to provision and defense of bases for the B-29's, and to coordination of their operations with those of local forces.[35] The Joint Chiefs of Staff gave this their approval and reported their decisions to the British Chiefs of Staff.[36] The British, however, proved reluctant to accept the command arrangement under the U.S. Joint Chiefs of Staff. The British themselves were anxious to participate in the control of the very long range bombers. They offered two arguments: first, the bombers were to operate from bases in India and Ceylon and would be under British responsibility for logistic support and for defense; second, the British hoped after conclusion of the war against Germany to participate themselves in very long range operations, with bombers "which it was hoped would compete in range with that of the B-29's." The British urged that General Arnold remain in command of the Twentieth Air Force, but under the Combined Chiefs of Staff. There was little chance the U.S. Chiefs of Staff would approve such a proposal, for the command was currently entirely American and the future operations of B-29's were to be largely from bases in the U.S.-controlled Pacific Theater. The discussion dragged on until the middle of June, when the British Chiefs finally agreed to the setup under the U.S. Chiefs, provided that if more than four very long range groups should be sent to CBI the British were to be consulted, that if RAF planes should participate in the operations of the Twentieth Air Force the British Chiefs should participate in its strategic control, and that if operations were undertaken against objectives in the Southeast Asia Command the Supreme Commander should be consulted.[37]

ALLOCATING HUMP TONNAGE

Although there had as yet been no decision between Formosa and Luzon, arrangements were being made in the summer of 1944 to provide for supporting operations from bases in China. In the middle of May, shortly after General Stilwell was given a directive to stockpile material in China for operations in support of the Formosa campaign, the Joint War Plans Committee completed a draft plan for the seizure of Formosa with a target date of 11 February.[38] This plan, based on the assumption that Luzon would be bypassed, called for support by two groups of bombers, four groups of fighters, and three squadrons of reconnaissance of the Fourteenth Air Force in China, one group of bombers and two of fighters of the Chinese-American Wing, eight squadrons of bombers and eight of fighters of the Chinese Air Force, and the four groups of B-29's of the XX Bomber Command. Because of the complications of weather and supply, however, the plan did not count heavily upon these forces in China for air support, relying more strongly upon planes based in the Marianas, Palau, and Mindanao.

A theater plan for support for the Formosa operation, sent by General Sultan from New Delhi on 28 May, provided for a total of six bomber groups, two heavy and four medium, four fighter groups plus two squadrons, two reconnaissance squadrons, and one troop carrier squadron, in addition to the XX Bomber Command.[39] This force could be supported for thirty days, however, only if the Air Transport Command were built up to carry 29,000 tons over the Hump monthly by December 1944 so that 57,713 tons could be stockpiled by February 1945. If no more planes were furnished to ATC, it was proposed to divert the 7th Bomber Group to act as transports about 1 July. With that arrangement only 13,925 tons could be accumulated in China by February. This would permit the operation for thirty days of a task force of the Tenth Air Force, consisting of one heavy and two medium bomber groups, one fighter group, two fighter squadrons, and one reconnaissance squadron. The CBI staff urged that the Hump be provided with more planes.[40]

There seemed little likelihood in Washington at the time that more transports could be sent to the area. On 20 June the theater commanders were told that their first plan was not practicable and that they should submit a new one as soon as it was decided how many planes could be sent.[41]

Five days later General Stratemeyer reported from New Delhi, "If they decided that assistance from air units in CBI is essential for Pacific operations in early 1945, it is imperative that we have some commitment or ATC augmentation in order that bases may be provided."[42] Bases could not be built overnight. Nor could a stockpile in China be assembled at the last moment. If the project was considered of sufficient importance, General Stratemeyer suggested, the Combined Chiefs of Staff should be able to make at least a tentative commitment.

Plans for operations in the Pacific were very much unsettled at that moment, but on 7 July General Arnold presented to the Joint Chiefs of Staff a tentative plan to send more transports to the India-China Division of the Air Transport Command, aiming for delivery of as much as 31,000 tons by December 1944.[43] The chief obstacle was the supply of gasoline. At General Arnold's suggestion the Joint Logistics Committee looked into that problem. Despite a current critical shortage JLC concluded that ATC's requirements were small in comparison with those of the United Kingdom and in relation to anticipated dividends. Consequently the committee recommended that the necessary gasoline be supplied.

General Arnold in turn recommended that the Joint Chiefs of Staff approve his plan for sending more transports to the theater. Approval was given informally on 25 August, on the same day that the Joint Chiefs agreed on a statement for General Stilwell as to how the Hump tonnage should be used.[44]

The need of an authoritative statement of priorities on Hump tonnage had become apparent as plans for accumulating a stockpile of material in China conflicted with the demands occasioned by a critical military situation. The Japanese advance into eastern and southern China which had begun in April was renewed with greater strength in June with the enemy pushing on from Hankow. By 18 June Changsha had fallen. Next on the list was Hengyang. Chinese defenses there were more effective, and it was only after a long siege that the city was finally taken on 8 August. Eastern China and the airfields, real and potential, in that area were under Japanese control.[45]

The diversion of transports from the Hump route occasioned by the crises in Burma in the spring of 1944 had cut into the amount carried into China. Unusually good weather in June, however, pushed the tonnage from ten to fifteen thousand tons. By August 23,677 tons reached China.[46] Still the demands exceeded the supply.

The continuing calls upon Hump tonnage--General Chennault's Fourteenth Army Air Force, the Chinese ground forces, other Chinese projects--were increased by the requirements of resisting the Japanese attack. Added to these were the stockpile program and the needs of the XX Bomber Command, for the original plan to make the B-29's self-supporting had not worked out. The Air Transport Command was called upon to help carry material to the bases around Chengtu. These accumulations of supplies for future operations appeared to those involved in fighting the Japanese in east China a ready source for gasoline and other supplies.

At the beginning of June Generalissimo Chiang Kai-shek appealed to President Roosevelt and General Marshall to turn over the gasoline and other stocks stored at Chengtu to General Chennault and the Fourteenth Air Force to help meet the emergency in east China. Chiang urged that both the Fourteenth and the Chinese Air Force be strengthened and that 8,000 rocket launchers each with 100 rounds of ammunition be supplied to the ground forces in China.[47] In response action was taken to ship 500 rocket launchers and 50,000 rockets, but U.S. supplies were not sufficient to spare all that Chiang asked for. There was no question of building up the Chinese Air Force at the expense of other projects, for it had to date proved utterly worthless. However, with JCS approval General Stilwell diverted to the Fourteenth Air Force 1,500 tons allotted to the XX Bomber Command for June. He also diverted a heavy bomber group of the Tenth Air Force to carry supplies for the Fourteenth.

The Joint Chiefs of Staff opposed any cutting into supplies already assembled for the B-29's in China, reasoning that the weak Chinese ground troops could not prevent the Japanese from going where they pleased, that experience in Italy indicated that air forces alone could not hold ground forces, and that the future operations of the XX Bomber Command would contribute much more to future action to defeat Japan than the Fourteenth Air Force could.[48] Thus when General Chennault appealed the first week of August for the use of some of the B-29's themselves to bomb Hankow and Wuchang, where the Japanese were shipping supplies for a final push at Hengyang, General Marshall took the attitude that air forces already available could do considerable damage and the B-29's had better be devoted to the projects already set for them.[49]

In mid-July General Arnold presented the AAF plan for increasing Hump tonnage to 31,000 tons by December and recommended that enough of this to permit 225 combat sorties a month from Chengtu bases be allocated to the B-29 project. Beyond that he proposed that combat supplies be delivered to the hard-pressed Chinese armies and the air forces in China to insure that China would remain in the war against Japan.[50]

The Joint War Plans Committee, to whom General Arnold's paper was circulated at his request, did not agree that the XX Bomber Command should have first priority of Hump deliveries. The rapidly changing tactical situation in China and Burma, as had been clearly illustrated in the preceding months, was certain to continue to produce emergency needs that would have to be met by the theater commander as they arose. However much the Hump tonnage was increased, said JWPC candidly, "it should be recognized that demands on 'hump' tonnage will always exceed capacity." Consequently the committee strongly recommended that the Commanding General, U.S. Army Forces, China-Burma-India, be given a guide as to the relative importance of the projects in China. In a suggested list of priorities JWPC put the Fourteenth Air Force first. Second they placed "stockpiling of aviation supplies in China to permit air support of scheduled Pacific operation by the XX Bomber Command and the Fourteenth Air Force with full consideration to the reduced effectiveness of the latter without east China fields." The requirements of the XX Bomber Command for a program of 225 sorties per month came third on the list. Last were the requirements of Chinese air and ground forces.[51]

The Joint Staff Planners were not entirely satisfied with this order of priorities. General Roberts expressed the opinion that the Chinese ground forces should have first call on the allocation of Hump tonnage, for with the assistance of the Fourteenth Air Force they were the best assurance for holding vital air bases in the areas of Kweilin and Kunming. Colonel Richard C. Lindsay suggested that with the increased capacity of the Hump route it was no longer necessary to stockpile far in advance. Total volume later should take care of all requirements. The JPS amended the directive the JWPC had recommended for General Joseph W. Stilwell accordingly and directed that the paper go to the Joint Chiefs of Staff.[52]

Before the JPS paper was presented to the Joint Chiefs, General Marshall asked General Stilwell whether he felt he needed additional guidance for the allocation of Hump tonnage.[53] This inquiry resulted not only from the planners' study, of which General Marshall was informed, but also from a report sent to General Arnold by Lieutenant General Barney M. Giles, who was in the Far East on an inspection trip.[54] General Giles had submitted a series of recommendations for increasing Hump tonnage to 21,320 tons monthly. He advocated allocating 6,300 tons of this to the XX Bomber Command, 13,200 to the Fourteenth Air Force, China Air Force, and other agencies in China as decided by the theater commander, and 1,820 tons to stockpile for Pacific operations, provided it would not seriously interfere with the security of bases in eastern China. Should the total deliveries fall short, said General Giles, all the allocations should be reduced proportionately.

Replying for General Stilwell, Major General Daniel I. Sultan admitted that the theater staff was finding it difficult to assess the demands of the XX Bomber Command and the stockpile project alongside the other requirements of the theater, partly because there were no specific directives as to relative urgency. General Sultan did not think it wise for the Joint Chiefs of Staff to make precise allocations of tonnage, for there had to be continual adjustments. "We would be assisted considerably, however," he said, "by a statement from the Joint Chiefs of Staff which would indicate the relative importance of 20th Bomber Command, the stockpile program, and the current operations in China."[55]

Such a statement had been incorporated in the proposed directive circulated with the report by the Joint Staff Planners on 14 August. The order of importance was stated to be:

    a. For maintenance, development, broadening and securing of the air link to China to insure the operation and defense of adequate air bases in China from which to support the Pacific campaign against Japan:

        First, in support of operations to attain this objective, the supply of the Fourteenth Air Force (including the Chinese-American Wing) to develop the maximum effectiveness consistent with minimum requirements for support of other activities in China and Burma.

        Second, stockpiling of necessary aviation supplies in China at such time as will permit air support of scheduled Pacific operations by the XX Bomber Command and the Fourteenth Air Force with full consideration to the reduced effectiveness of the latter without east China fields.

    b. For implementation of MATTERHORN at an optimum rate of 225 sorties per month. In this connection guaranteed deliveries of tonnage in exchange for transport aircraft formerly assigned to the XX Bomber Command and since transferred to Army Transport Command should be considered firm unless required to meet an emergency need for *a* above.

> c. For requirements of Chinese air and ground forces other than those covered in a.[56]

None of the chiefs disagreed seriously with this list. A week after the paper was circulated, however, General Arnold pointed out that as worded it did not guard against stockpiling for operations that did not have JCS approval. Consequently he recommended revising the statement to read:

> Second, the stockpiling in China of such quantities of aviation supplies as are necessary to permit that support by the XX Bomber Command and the Fourteenth Air Force required in Pacific operations approved by the Joint Chiefs of Staff. In this connection full consideration will be given to the reduced effectiveness of the Fourteenth Air Force in the event that East China fields are not available.[57]

Without recorded discussion the Joint Chiefs approved the paper.[58] In general terms General Stilwell was thus informed of the significance placed by the JCS on CBI support for operations in the Pacific, even though agreement on what those operations were to be had yet to be made.

PAC-AID

In August revised plans for air operations from China in support of the advance in the Pacific were received in Washington from the China-Burma-India Theater.[59] There were three of them: Pre-Pac-Aid, a plan for operations of the Fourteenth Air Force prior to the initiation of support of Pacific operations; Pac-Aid, a plan for supporting operations in the event all bases remained in friendly hands; and Alternative-Pac-Aid, a plan based on the supposition that the southeast China air bases had been lost to the Japanese.

Pre-Pac-Aid was a summary of the operations already under way or planned to October 1944. These included bombing attacks and reconnaissance by B-29's; attacks on enemy shipping, mining, support of Chinese ground troops, and defense of air bases in China, by the Fourteenth Air Force; and defense of the Hump and of air bases and ground forces in the Myitkyina area.

Pac-Aid was out of date by the time it was received in Washington, for the Japanese already virtually controlled U.S. air bases east of the Hankow-Hengyang-Canton line and stood ready to advance either to Kweilin, where there were more air bases, or toward the Hankow-Canton overland communications.

Alternative-Pac-Aid was based more realistically on the situation as it currently existed or a worse one in which all air bases east of the line Changsha-Kweilin-Nanning-Hanoi would be in Japanese hands. In either case the plan provided for counter air action to deny to the Japanese use of the bases they had acquired and of the land lines of communication from northern China to French Indochina; continuous attrition of enemy shipping; and provision of support to Chinese ground forces. Under the existing conditions heavy bombers with fighter escorts could operate effectively against shipping and land targets in the Formosa area. If the enemy advanced further, U.S. operations would be limited to preventing his using bases in China proper to reenforce Formosa; to supporting the Chinese ground troops; and to defending remaining U.S. bases.

The XX Bomber Command, under Alternative-Pac-Aid, would make approximately 400 bombing sorties over a period of one month including 15 days prior to D Day for Formosa, aimed at bombing vital industrial targets and port facilities and at long range reconnaissance.

The Pac-Aid plans called for a task force built up from the Tenth and the Fourteenth Air Forces, comprising two heavy bomber groups, four medium bomber groups, four fighter and fighter-bomber groups, one twin engine fighter squadron, one night fighter squadron, two photo reconnaissance squadrons, and one troop carrier squadron. For the support of this force 67,779 tons of supplies would be accumulated in China.

The Joint Staff Planners studied these plans when they arrived in Washington and on 11 September recommended to the Joint Chiefs of Staff that Pre-Pac-Aid and Alternative-Pac-Aid be approved in principle.[60]

Since the Joint Chiefs of Staff were at Octagon when the JPS report was circulated, it went to the Joint Deputy Chiefs of Staff. They approved it, apparently without joint discussion, but subject to some limitations recommended by General McNarney.[61] There would be no resources beyond those available or already committed; no forces would go to China unless the Commanding General, U.S. Army Forces, CBI, thought they could be profitably used there and their removal from India-Burma would not endanger operations in Burma; the 7th Bomber Group, assigned to supplying the Fourteenth Air Force, would go back to combat operations as soon as other means were available to meet supply requirements; the XX Bomber Command was to continue its program of 225 sorties monthly until D minus 15 of the Formosa operation.[62]

The message sent to General Stilwell, Admiral Nimitz, and General MacArthur, and to Admiral Mountbatten for information, charged General Stilwell and General Arnold, as Commanding General, Twentieth Air Force, with responsibility for providing air support from China in accordance with requirements set by Admiral Nimitz and General MacArthur. Preparations were to be made for Alternative-Pac-Aid. How much of it was to be put into execution would depend upon how much farther the Japanese advanced in China, upon how much assistance the commanders in the Pacific felt they needed, and upon whether or not it was finally decided to occupy Formosa. The last question was currently very much on the minds of the Joint Chiefs and their staffs.

Chapter XXIV

LUZON OR FORMOSA

One of the major strategic problems confronting the Joint Chiefs of Staff in 1944 was the question of whether the U.S. forces advancing in ever-greater strength against the Japanese in the Pacific should move on to Luzon and the Philippines, bypass the Philippines and strike at Formosa and the coast of China, or attack objectives in both areas. This problem in all its ramifications was discussed repeatedly by the Joint Chiefs themselves and by their planners until October 1944, when there remained barely time to prepare for carrying out the directive that finally went to the Pacific commanders.

The choice between Luzon and Formosa was a complicated one. Luzon represented the whole Philippine archipelago, which had been lost in the early months of the war and for whose recapture there were strong political arguments. Officially these were largely discounted by the Joint Chiefs, who consistently drew a careful line between military and political considerations. But General MacArthur placed great emphasis upon the obligation of the United States to liberate the Filipino people and repeatedly reminded the Joint Chiefs of that obligation. All Southwest Pacific Area plans implicitly if not specifically held the recapture of the islands to be their chief objective. In Washington, however, there was less conviction as to the necessity of recapturing the Philippines, particularly as the tempo of advance and the strength of U.S. forces increased. Among the Joint Chiefs of Staff and their planners considerable discussion was held of the practicability of a campaign in the Philippines, of the strategic advantages of positions in the Philippines and particularly in Luzon, in comparison with other possible operations, of which the most discussed was the capture of Formosa.

The seizure of Formosa was a project backed primarily by naval planners, with Admiral King the outspoken advocate. It implied not alone the occupation of the island but the acquiring of control of the Formosa Straits and a landing on the adjacent China coast, probably in the vicinity of Amoy. The object was to be not only the acquiring of territory for air and naval bases and the opening of a port through which they could be supplied, but more importantly the securing of an area which would successfully cut the sea and air lines of communications from Japan to the rich areas of the Netherlands East Indies and Southeast Asia, establishing a blockade that might of itself compel the Japanese to surrender.

On 2 March 1944, it will be remembered, the Joint Chiefs had announced to the commanders in the Pacific that the "first major objective" of strategy in the Pacific was to be "the vital Luzon, Formosa, China Coast Area." A tentative target date of 15 February 1945 was set for the occupation of Formosa, with the possibility that Luzon would be taken instead on the same date "should such operations prove necessary prior to the move on Formosa." Decision between the two was deferred. It was this absence of a decision that caused protracted and sometimes heated discussion during the succeeding months of 1944.[1]

By May 1944 the situation in the Pacific looked most hopeful. Landings had been made at Hollandia on 22 April almost without opposition. Within a month Southwest Pacific forces had jumped to Sarmi and Wakde and then moved two hundred miles farther west to Biak in the Schouten Islands. Central Pacific forces, having consolidated their positions in the Marshalls, were preparing to move into the Marianas and land on Saipan in the middle of June. Next would come the Palaus. The advance had gained momentum. Seemingly nothing short of Japan's defeat would stop it.

Late in May the Joint Strategic Survey Committee reported to the Joint Chiefs of Staff on a study of operations in the Pacific to follow seizure of the Marianas.[2] The overwhelming success being achieved in the Pacific had given the committee pause. Possibly, the JSSC suggested, "less force could have been used, thus accelerating the advancing schedule and providing for additional essential operations at the same time." Specifically, perhaps the Palau campaign could be advanced a few weeks.

Examining two tentative plans produced by the JWPC, one for the occupation of Formosa, the other for occupation of Mindanao with an advance north into Luzon, the JSSC was concerned about the timing and interrelation of the two projects. The seizure of Formosa no longer seemed so difficult as the JSSC had first conceived it. On the other hand the JWPC studies seemed to indicate that seizure of Mindanao and Luzon would be more so, especially because the Japanese were known to be concentrating in the area of Halmahera-Mindanao. The members of the JSSC concluded that there should be "a prompt, searching and open-minded reexamination of our plans for operations subsequent to the occupation of the Marianas," presumably by themselves and the JWPC, with a view to taking all possible short cuts. It might even prove feasible to take Formosa before Mindanao, avoiding the danger of bogging down in the southern Philippines.

Without comment the JCS approved JSSC's recommendation for a restudy of plans.[3] Two days later Japanese troops in China pushed south from Hankow on the second phase of their attempt to gain control of airfields in east China. This renewed campaign raised doubts, particularly in the minds of Army planners, of the feasibility of planning to land on the coast of China. With the coastal area in enemy hands such action seemed likely to involve Allied forces in a costly land campaign whose results would be entirely disproportionate to the effort that would be expended. If China was not to be attacked from the sea, then the question arose as to whether Formosa would be needed. These doubts were not immediately reflected in joint war plans, but the JSSC was sufficiently concerned about the implication of the new Japanese moves to go on record to the JPS with the opinion "that the deterioration of conditions in China...would seem to have an increasingly important bearing on the question of doing the Formosa operation as soon as possible."[4]

The first step toward speeding the campaign was to find out what the Pacific commanders were planning to do under current directives. On 6 June Admiral King called the attention of the other chiefs to the absence of detailed plans and estimated requirements for General MacArthur's program in the Southwest Pacific, pointing out the danger that his intentions might interfere with projects already approved.

In response to an earlier request for information to assist in the allocation of shipping, General MacArthur had submitted a timetable that read: 21 May--Wakde; 1 June--Biak; 1 August--Northern Vogelkop; 15 September--Halmahera; 15 November--Mindanao.[5] The first of these had already been accomplished, a few days ahead of schedule. There were serious doubts among Washington planners, however, as to the necessity of undertaking what promised to be an expensive operation in Halmahera, and even of making a large scale attack on Mindanao.[6] General MacArthur's estimated requirements were entirely unknown. After some discussion the Joint Chiefs decided to have a message sent asking for General MacArthur's plans for future operations.[7]

Before any word came from the Southwest Pacific commander, the Joint Staff Planners presented the chiefs with a preliminary survey made by the JWPC of the possibility of speeding up the campaign in the Pacific. It could be done, the planners pointed out, in one of two ways: advancing target dates for currently scheduled operations, or bypassing objectives previously selected. They recommended that Admiral Nimitz and General MacArthur be asked what they thought of using either or both methods to expedite the advance from the Marianas.[8]

All the chiefs but Admiral Leahy were in London at this time in order to be at hand to make a quick decision in case it proved necessary to withdraw the troops that had just landed in Normandy. Consequently General McNarney acted for General Marshall and proposed a third possibility for accelerating the Pacific campaign, namely, bypassing objectives currently selected, including Formosa, and choosing new ones, perhaps even Japan itself. This suggestion met with general approval and was incorporated in a request for recommendations that went to the Pacific commanders on 13 June.[9]

General MacArthur replied promptly and vehemently to the suggestion that the Philippines might be bypassed.[10] He disagreed strongly with any thought of attacking Formosa directly across the Pacific from the Hawaiian Islands without land-based air support. In order for the attack on Formosa to be successful, he said, Luzon would have to be occupied and bases established there to provide support and to prevent the enemy from flanking the operation. As for bypassing even Formosa and directly attacking the mainland of Japan, General MacArthur thought that idea was "utterly unsound." Even if there were enough shipping for such an operation, he did not think it could possibly succeed without air support. It was about the Philippines that General MacArthur had the most to say.

> It is my opinion [he said] that purely military considerations demand the reoccupation of the Philippines in order to cut the enemy's communications to the South and to secure a base for our further advance. Even if this were not the case and unless military factors demanded another line of action, it would in my opinion be necessary to reoccupy the Philippines. Philippines is American Territory where our unsupported forces were destroyed by the enemy. Practically all of the 17,000,000 Filipinos remain loyal to the United States and are undergoing the greatest privation and suffering because we have not been able to support or succor them. We have a great national obligation to discharge. Moreover if the United States should deliberately bypass the Philippines, leaving our prisoners, nationals and loyal Filipinos in enemy hands without an effort to retrieve them at earliest moment we would incur the gravest psychological reaction. We would admit the truth of Japanese propaganda to the effect that we had abandoned the Filipinos and would not shed American blood to redeem them; we would undoubtedly incur the open hostility of the people; we would probably suffer such loss of prestige among all the peoples of the Far East that it would adversely affect the United States for many years. I feel also that a decision to eliminate the campaign for the relief of the Philippines, even under appreciable military considerations, would cause extremely adverse reactions among the citizens of the United States. The American people I am sure would acknowledge this obligation.

That General MacArthur felt strongly on the subject there can be no doubt. "If serious consideration is being given to [attacking Formosa or Japan directly]," he said, "I request that I be accorded the opportunity of personally proceeding to Washington to present fully my views."

These representations from General MacArthur were considered by the Joint War Plans Committee in its study of the possibility of accelerating the Pacific campaign. Despite his views the committee continued to feel that Mindanao and all the Philippines might well be bypassed. The JWPC thought the threat presented by U.S. forces on the line Marianas-Palau-New Guinea would serve to contain the Japanese forces in the Philippines and prevent their participation in subsequent operations in the Pacific without the necessity of fighting a costly campaign. Current Pacific Ocean Areas plans for the seizure of Formosa did not call for land-based support from Luzon such as General MacArthur envisaged, but rather for the reduction of enemy air capabilities there. The primary purpose in occupying Mindanao was to be to neutralize the air strength of Luzon. The JWPC thought there was a good possibility that this purpose could be achieved through the use of carrier based planes and the Twentieth Air Force. If so, the need for taking Mindanao would be eliminated.

The Joint War Plans Committee incorporated these views in a preliminary report to the Joint Staff Planners, concluding that there was little likelihood of speeding up the schedule of the Pacific campaign. The JWPC recommended that its conclusions be noted by the Joint Chiefs and that no directive be issued to the theater commanders until receipt of Admiral Nimitz's comments.[11]

This JWPC paper was not based on thorough study of logistics problems or careful analyses of the capabilities of the Twentieth Air Force and carrier based planes or complete estimates of the Japanese strength in the Philippines and Formosa. It was rather a summary of probabilities that accepted the tentative conclusions of the Pacific Ocean Areas planners. The comments of the Joint Staff Planners as the paper came to them for discussion were at least equally speculative. It was apparent that the matter needed more study and that Admiral Nimitz's comments on accelerating his schedule should be awaited.[12]

Having had no reply from Admiral Nimitz by 29 June, Admiral King asked him for an interim response, allowing for the impracticability of forecasting the situation that would follow occupation of the Marianas.[13] In reply, far from proposing any speeding up, Admiral Nimitz said he probably could not achieve the target dates set in the 12 March directive.[14] Enemy garrisons in the Marianas and Palau were known to have increased. He was considering a modification of the Palau operation that would include taking only Angaur, Peleliu, Yap, and Ulithi "in order to obtain air base and anchorage facilities which though not completely satisfactory may be obtained without excessive delay." Admiral Nimitz reported that representatives of his staff had learned from General MacArthur's representatives that the Southwest Pacific Commander was planning to occupy Morotai Island in early September, Sarangani Bay in Mindanao in late October, Leyte about 15 November, Legaspi and Aparri in Northern Luzon in mid-January, to attack Mindoro in February, and to make a major assault on Luzon through Lingayen Straits about 1 April. Admiral Nimitz commented that this timing seemed optimistic.

General MacArthur's program was not known in such detail in Washington, and accordingly General Marshall asked him at once for further information.[15] On 8 July General MacArthur sent a summary of his latest plan, the fifth version of Reno.[16] With the objective of furnishing adequate support for the operations against Formosa and the China coast, he aimed for the occupation or control of central and northern Luzon prior to the 1945 rainy season. He planned initially to bypass the enemy's strong points in Halmahera and Davao, landing by way of the Vogelkop and Morotai in southern Mindanao. Thence he would advance along the eastern coast of the Philippine archipelago, using Pacific Fleet support to the maximum, seizing bases to support the main effort through the Balingtang Channel, north of the islands, into Lingayen Gulf to Manila and the Central Plain area. He set target dates of 8 September 1944 for Morotai, 25 October 1944 for Sarangani Bay, mid-January 1945 for southeastern Luzon, and 1 April 1945 for the main effort in Lingayen Gulf.

To carry out the Reno V program General MacArthur would need more amphibious lift, carrier-based air support, and fleet bombardment. The final phase would require full support by all elements of the Pacific Fleet.

Reno V was conceived as the major campaign plan for the Pacific. As such Admiral King objected to it. Writing to the head of the Navy's War Plans Division, he said:

> McArthur's [sic] recent despatch re so-called 'Reno V' appears to omit any considerations other than McArthur's views and desires. It assumes that CinCPOA's forces are at his beck and call regardless of what JCS have laid down for CinCPOA to do. The 'end-around' into Lingayen Gulf is, to my mind, a 'vision'. In fact, the whole concept smacks of views and desires predicated on beating CinCPOA's already outlined tasks from JCS.[17]

Admiral King was anxious that the comments of General MacArthur and Admiral Nimitz be studied by the JPS for discussion at the next JCS meeting, for he was to leave for Pearl Harbor on 11 July for another conference with Admiral Nimitz.[18] Although the official minutes of the JCS meeting of 11 July do not indicate any discussion of Pacific strategy, the planners' views were undoubtedly presented orally to the chiefs so that Admiral King left aware of current Washington thinking. At the same time the planners, still working on the study of the acceleration of the campaign in the Pacific, were informed of the views of the Joint Chiefs of Staff.

The weeks that followed saw much inconclusive discussion on the planning level as the JWPC attempted to develop a study that the JPS would forward to the Joint Chiefs of Staff. Seeking the quickest and best route to Japan's defeat, the JWPC concluded that there were two possibilities: through the Philippines, Formosa, the Ryukyus, Kyushu, and Honshu, or through the Bonins,

Kyushu, and Honshu, perhaps eliminating Kyushu. Decision between them would be affected by the availability of ground and army air forces, the ability to take objectives without prior bombardment by land-based air other than B-29's and the ability to carry out amphibious operations without direct support from land-based air power. The full potentiality of carrier-based air would not be known, the JWPC pointed out, until the Japanese Navy was neutralized and the Pacific Fleet could enjoy sufficient freedom of action to test the practicability of advancing without land-based air support.

The Joint War Plans Committee decided that until the war with Germany was over and the Japanese Fleet was out of the war there would not be enough U.S. forces to proceed from the Marianas to the Bonins, Kyushu, and Honshu. However, the longer route could be followed through Formosa. If the fleet were gone but war with Germany still continued the JWPC recommended taking the longer route but giving immediate consideration to bypassing Mindanao. Rather than advocating a decision between the two routes the JWPC suggested that its study be sent to the two Pacific commanders and Admiral Nimitz be asked to prepare campaign plans through the invasion of the Tokyo Plain.

Some of the Joint Staff Planners were not convinced that the two routes described by the JWPC were mutually exclusive. General Roberts suggested at the next JPS meeting that the Mindanao operation would be useful in itself as a means of weakening the enemy as well as providing a base that would assist in neutralizing Japanese air forces on Luzon. Arguing against taking Mindanao, however, Colonel C. Stanton Babcock of JWPC mentioned again the possibility that forces might bog down in Mindanao. Admiral Duncan suggested that strategically it might be preferable to omit Mindanao and attack Luzon from the north at the same time as Formosa. It was another inconclusive discussion and the JWPC took the paper back for further study.[19]

Before pursuing further the question of speeding up the campaign against Japan the JWPC took a look at the complete plan Reno V, which had reached Washington in July. The committee concluded that it was adequate for accomplishing the reoccupation of the Philippines, assuming that that was necessary prior to seizing Formosa. However, in its entirety Reno V would mean that Formosa, which in current JCS directives was still the objective of the advance across the Pacific, could not be taken as scheduled on 15 February but would have to be postponed until October after the typhoon season. The program through the occupation of Mindanao would support a direct attack on Formosa, but the final phases, specifically the occupation of Luzon, could be undertaken only as an alternative to the Formosa operation. The JWPC recommended only that the theater commanders be asked for plans for the possible alternate operations.[20]

The comments of the Joint Staff Planners on this report on Reno V and on a further revision of the study on the "means and methods of accelerating the war in the Pacific" indicate that, as Admiral Duncan suggested at the JPS meeting of 26 July, it was time for the Joint Chiefs of Staff to decide whether Formosa should be attacked directly or whether Luzon should be taken first.[21] The target date for seizure of Formosa had been set by the chiefs in March as 15 February 1945, reserving the possibility that Luzon might have to be occupied before Formosa could be taken.[22] The series of studies on the possibility of moving faster in the Pacific had raised a number of questions as to which operations were essential and which could be drastically cut or entirely eliminated. Seemingly the seizure of Formosa was fixed. But the chiefs had left unanswered the question of whether Luzon should be taken and as yet had shown no anxiety to make the decision.

In an attempt to arrive at some conclusion on the planning level the Joint Staff Planners sent the JWPC reports back for further study and approved a message to the planning staffs of Admiral Nimitz and General MacArthur. In it they sought information for planning purposes, based upon the assumption that Formosa was to be taken before Luzon and that the primary purpose of the Leyte-Mindanao operations was to reduce enemy air strength in Luzon in support of the assault on Formosa.[23] It was further assumed for planning purposes that the eventual reoccupation of the Philippines would be undertaken without direct support of the Pacific Fleet, that landing craft would be transferred to the Southwest Pacific Area from the Central Pacific for shore-to-shore operations, and that air, ground, and service forces from the Southwest Pacific would participate in the Formosa campaign. A target date was suggested for Formosa of at least early March 1945 and for Leyte of not later than 1 December 1944.

When this planning message reached the Southwest Pacific Area headquarters, General MacArthur was at Pearl Harbor talking with President Roosevelt. That conference followed closely a visit by Admiral King in which he had spoken strongly to Admiral Nimitz's staff in favor of bypassing Luzon and going straight to Formosa. The record shows no lengthy discussion of the point, although Admiral Raymond A. Spruance and Vice Admiral Richmond K. Turner did venture the view that Luzon should be taken first in order to provide bases for the fleet. Admiral King was not invited to stay for the President's visit, but he left assured that Admiral Nimitz knew what his views were.[24]

Admiral Leahy was the only one of the Joint Chiefs of Staff present as General MacArthur and Admiral Nimitz described to the President what they thought should be done in the Pacific. Although they agreed they could either take Luzon first or go straight to Formosa, Admiral Nimitz spoke for the latter on the grounds that it would be easier for the fleet and would expedite the advance against Japan; General MacArthur argued for Luzon first, an easier operation for the army and one with political significance. Both agreed that in any case the decision would not have to be made immediately but could be postponed until fall.

After listening to the two presentations Mr. Roosevelt expressed a preference for the course outlined by General MacArthur and assured him that the Philippines would be taken. However he did not rule out Formosa. Nor did he make a final decision as to which operation should come first.[25]

Reassured by the President's comments, General MacArthur returned to his headquarters to find the JPS planning message based upon the assumption that Luzon would be bypassed. General MacArthur quickly despatched a message to General Marshall spelling out his views.[26]

Expressing his "strongest noconcurrence" in the assumption that the initial lodgment in the Philippines was for the purpose of neutralizing enemy air in Luzon and "that Southwest Pacific forces are to be drained away to augment Formosa forces leaving the remainder to maintain pressure, continue attrition and extend holdings to the limit of such resources as may be left," General MacArthur stated:

> The initial major strategic objective in the Far East is the Philippines and Luzon is the most important element thereof. This objective is of first importance not only strategically but from the higher viewpoint of national policy. Strategically the occupation of the Philippines will deny the enemy access to Malaya, the NEI, Borneo and South China. For this purpose the capture of Formosa is not necessary. On the other hand the occupation of Formosa without the Philippines would not accomplish the purpose. The occupation of the Philippines and the establishment of bases in [sic] an essential prerequisite to any campaign in the Far East that will employ large numbers of troops. The Formosa campaign itself can not be supported logistically without adequate bases in the Philippines. I consider that from the strategical standpoint alone the occupation of the Philippines is essential and it is my opinion that after that has been accomplished and bases have been established, an assault upon Formosa will not be necessary. With Luzon properly organized it will be possible to bypass Formosa and strike deeper into enemy territory against objectives that can be attained with less bloodshed and which would be of greater value, thus accelerating the time schedule of the campaign. It is presumed the objects of the planning being undertaken are to shorten the war and to reduce losses. An attempt to execute a great campaign in the far reaches of the Pacific without the establishment of adequate bases would be fraught with the gravest danger of disaster, which, if incurred, would greatly lengthen the war and multiply losses. Such a line of action is not justified. We have fought thus far in the hostile outpost and delaying position and are now about to effect a penetration in the center of his main defenses. The lodgment must be effected and solid preparation, tactical and logistical, must be completed before

continuing the strategical maneuver that will exploit the initial victory.

General MacArthur's objections were not entirely from the standpoint of strategy, however.

> From the highest point of view of national policy the liberation of the Philippines is essential. The Philippine Archipelago is American territory which we failed adequately to defend, with the resultant loss and untold suffering of its loyal people and the death of many thousands of its soldiers and civilians. It is a national obligation to recover the Philippines at the earliest possible date. The President of the United States has acknowledged that obligation and has stated that the Philippines would be redeemed as soon as possible. The enemy has stated repeatedly to all races of the Far East that the United States would not shed the blood of its soldiers in redemption of the Filipinos. To adopt a course of action that would tend to support the correctness of the Japanese assertion would destroy the honor and prestige of the United States throughout the Far East and bring us into disrepute throughout the world. The campaign proposed by the Navy and outlined through the assumptions indicated by the Joint Staff Planners not only violates the strategic aspects and the national obligations of the country but also carries with it a deeper and more sinister implication.
>
> The occupation of a portion of the Philippines and the bypassing of the remainder by an assault on Formosa would impose upon the Philippines a complete blockade. The Philippine Islands are not self sufficient in food and are dependent upon considerable importations. Even now the people are suffering severely from malnutrition and are barely above the starvation level. The imposition of a blockade would immediately cause a major famine in the Philippines that would result in the death of millions of Filipinos. The failure of the United States to liberate its people would be a blot upon its honor but the imposition of a blockade that would result in the death by starvation of those loyal people presents a course of action that should not be considered by any government even if it were proposed by the military. It is a line of action that would exceed in brutality anything that has been perpetrated by our enemies.

General Marshall quietly admonished General MacArthur for commenting to him on a planning level message and assured the Southwest Pacific Area commander that no directive would be issued until the return of Major General J.E. Hull, who was currently visiting General MacArthur's headquarters at Brisbane.[27]

General MacArthur's comments were added to the material being studied by the Joint War Plans Committee, but they had no visible effect on current planning. The JWPC had recently received

Admiral Nimitz's plan for future operations, Granite II. The committee was surprised to find that it provided for only a limited operation in southern Formosa, to be followed promptly by occupation of Amoy on the China coast. Occupation of all of Formosa, Admiral Nimitz advised, would require an estimated 208,000 more men. Despite this development the JWPC concluded that Granite II was in line with the directive of the preceding March, and the committee recommended a directive to the theater commanders to occupy the Leyte-Mindanao area not later than 1 December, temporarily bypass Luzon, and attack Formosa by 1 March 1945.[28]

This idea of taking part of Formosa and moving to the China coast was in consonance with the naval view of the significance of the operation, that is, the control of Formosa Strait and the cutting of Japanese sea lanes to the South. However, it was disquieting to the Army planners. General Roberts was particularly skeptical. He considered that Formosa was to be taken to provide air bases and that, if only a bridgehead were to be secured there, probably more could be accomplished by taking Luzon. He was insistent that the requirements of the Formosa campaign be given further study.[29]

The JPS were clearly too uncertain themselves as to what should next be done to make any formal recommendations to the Joint Chiefs of Staff. But Admiral King at least had firm convictions on the subject. On 18 August he recommended to General Marshall that the JCS issue a directive for the advance of the forces of the Southwest Pacific Area into the central Philippines to be followed by the establishment of the forces of the Pacific Ocean Areas in the Formosa Strait region with a target date of 15 February 1945.[30] This was in accordance with a recommendation from Admiral Nimitz in which he expressed confidence that with his forces established in the Formosa Strait area the advance of General MacArthur's forces into Luzon would cause no delay in the progress of the war and would meet with minimum resistance.[31] It was also essentially the conclusion the JWPC had reached from its study of Reno V and Granite II. But it met with no immediate approval.

By this time Major General John E. Hull, Lieutenant General Barney M. Giles, and Colonel William L. Ritchie had reported to General Marshall on their talks with General MacArthur at Brisbane. He had no confidence, they reported, that the air forces of the Southwest Pacific Area from Leyte or Mindanao could neutralize enemy air power based on Luzon. He had spoken of the seizure of Formosa as "a massive operation, extremely costly in men and shipping, logistically precarious and time consuming." Luzon, he thought, would have to be taken in any case, but Formosa could be bypassed if Luzon were seized first. General MacArthur was willing to predict that his losses in a Luzon campaign would be "inconsequential." He sent General Marshall "his personal guarantee that the Luzon campaign could be completed in a maximum of six weeks, and that he was confident it would be completed in less than thirty days after the landing at Lingayen."[32]

At this stage General Marshall was unwilling to agree to a directive involving assault on Formosa without further investigation. Accordingly on 22 August he proposed to Admiral King that they issue a firm directive for the operations in the southern and central Philippines but ask for more study about the availability of forces for the Formosa campaign.[33] At a special meeting of the JCS on the same day Admiral King argued the merits of an occupation of Formosa.[34] He believed it would have to be accomplished sooner or later and delay would only make it more difficult. Formosa, he felt, offered the greatest facilities for airfields for supporting the invasion of Japan as well as providing an important link in the vital seaway to China. On the other hand he could visualize no operation at all following an all-out effort on Luzon. Moreover for strategic reasons he was opposed to an amphibious operation through the Lingayen Gulf with a Japanese-held Formosa on the flank.

General Marshall thought that "the Luzon operation would be somewhat less difficult in view of the friendly population that would be encountered there." From Luzon he foresaw a move either to Formosa or to the tip of Japan itself. On the other hand, if Formosa were taken first the next move would have to be southward to Luzon. General Marshall was inclined to favor bypassing Formosa entirely and going to Kyushu, from which "there was little doubt that the Japanese communications could be dealt a decisive blow."

The discussion at this meeting centered entirely upon three major operations, on Luzon, Formosa, or Kyushu. There was no mention at all of the significance or even the possibility of action in the Ryukyus or the Bonins preliminary to the invasion of Japan. Instead it was a question of whether the move could be made directly to the Japanese islands of whether Formosa or Luzon would be taken first.

From the few recorded remarks of General Arnold and Lieutenant General T.T. Handy, who was attending the meeting, it is apparent that they shared General Marshall's doubts of the desirability of tackling Formosa and his preference for supporting General MacArthur in the seizure of Luzon. Admiral Leahy was doubtful about all the proposed operations, for none provided an adequate base for the fleet. His inclination was to make plans for everything and decide among them later. Admiral Cooke, however, urged that a prompt decision be made among Luzon, Formosa, and Kyushu in order that plans and preparations could be made and the Formosa operation, if there was to be one, could be completed by 1 March 1945.

The JCS reached no decision, and the JPS continued with the discussion of what should be done. Almost a week after the JCS meeting the planners met with General Hull and with Admiral Sherman and Brigadier General H.C. Mandell of Admiral Nimitz's Staff.[35] The Pacific planners were closely questioned by the JPS as to the requirements of the Formosa operation as planned by the Commander in Chief, Pacific Ocean Areas, the possibilities of reducing the shortage of service troops below the estimated 120,000, and the feasibility of attacking Formosa without Luzon, of going into Lingayen Gulf, and of taking Kyushu after Leyte without occupying either Luzon or Formosa.

Admiral Sherman gave a detailed account of the plan for occupying part of the island of Formosa and establishing a base at Amoy, then moving from there to another position farther forward, such as Okinawa. He was doubtful that Kyushu could be attacked directly without preliminary bases close enough to provide land-based air support. Although he presented the arguments for the Granite II concept, Admiral Sherman did not argue against Luzon. In fact he expressed the opinion that detailed estimates would probably show similar requirements and shortages for either the assault on Luzon or the attack on Formosa.

Admiral Sherman spoke at length about the requirements and availability of forces for the Formosa operation as planned by the Commander in Chief, Pacific. Nevertheless he failed to convince the Army planners of the feasibility of taking only part of Formosa. They felt it unlikely that the Japanese on the rest of the island would cooperate to the extent of allowing U.S. forces to remain unchallenged. They also feared that the enemy would send reenforcements and force what was intended to be an operation to secure a beachhead to become a major campaign. Moreover they questioned the strategic value of holding only a portion of Formosa, where the room for B-29 bases would be very limited, certainly less than that available on Luzon.[36] After a long discussion, the JPS meeting ended with no decisions.

On 1 September Admiral Sherman reviewed the problem before the JCS.[37] Time was getting on, and there was still no directive to proceed beyond the Palaus. The Marianas were already under U.S. control, following completion of the occupation of Saipan on 9 July and capture of Tinian and Guam by the middle of August. Southwest Pacific forces meanwhile had occupied the island of Noemfoor west of Biak and succeeded on New Guinea in cutting the Japanese garrisons into isolated segments which were no longer a serious menace. Operations in the Palaus were scheduled to begin later in September. Surely it was time for the chiefs to issue a new directive, for launching of an operation of the magnitude considered for Luzon or Formosa would require many months of assembling troops and materiel and planning details of timing and organization.

Again the JCS went through the arguments of Luzon vs. Formosa. Again Admiral King asked what could follow the occupation of Luzon. Such a project, he said, "would be merely delaying the operations that would be finally necessary for the defeat of Japan." Actually "the real decision was to be whether or not the operation would be against Formosa and thereafter against the mainland of Japan" or whether Formosa would be omitted. General Marshall had a different view. "If a decision were taken now on the facts as they are apparent," he said, "the operation against Luzon would, of necessity, have to be selected." In his opinion the shortage of troops for the Formosa campaign was a strong argument against it. He urged going slow in any case until the outcome of the operations in Europe was clearer and the resources that could be transferred to the Pacific were fixed.

It was apparent that there would be no easy decision between Luzon and Formosa, and Admiral Leahy recommended that at least a directive for the occupation of Leyte be drawn in order that preparations could proceed. This was not a simple matter. Admiral King felt strongly that if there was to be a directive for Leyte alone it should state plainly that the purpose of the operation was to attain air superiority in the Philippines, including Luzon, or to prepare for the next operation. The rest of the group seemed to feel that decision on what was to follow Leyte could be deferred. Ultimately the chiefs directed the JPS to prepare directives for the Leyte operation "as a matter of urgency."

Instead of limiting the objective to Leyte, the JWPC immediately offered the JPS a draft directive for a series of operations culminating in the establishment of U.S. forces in the Formosa-Amoy area.[38] General Roberts independently drafted a second directive that would leave the choice between Luzon and Formosa unsettled. When the 2 March directive was written, he argued, Formosa seemed the logical primary intermediate objective. The situation had changed. "The interim directive must leave the way clear for a later decision and therefore should not point to or stress either objective." Admiral Duncan insisted that there would have to be a decision in order that logistic preparations could go forward and the main operation not be delayed. The planners finally compromised and left the way open by including in their draft (JCS 713/9) the statement:

> Preparation of plans, logistic preparations and the disposition of forces and resources will be such as to permit the advance to Formosa by Pacific Ocean Areas forces, target date 1 March 1945, or the reconquest of Luzon by SWPA forces, target date 20 February 1945, whichever should next be ordered by the Joint Chiefs of Staff.[39]

The Commander in Chief, Southwest Pacific Area, was to occupy the Leyte-Surigao area, with a target date of 20 December 1944, occupy bases in the central Philippines necessary for either an advance to Formosa or the seizure of Luzon, and submit plans for both of the latter contingencies. The Commander in Chief, Pacific Ocean Areas, would furnish support for the Southwest Pacific operations and submit plans for a Formosa campaign as well as for support of a Luzon operation. Both were to coordinate plans with the Commanding General, U.S. Forces, China-Burma-India, and with the Commanding General, Twentieth Air Force.

Admiral King objected.[40] "Such a directive," he said, "would aggravate the indecision" that had been incorporated in the directives back in March. Final decision had at that time been postponed primarily because there was question as to the feasibility of going directly to Formosa. Now, Admiral King pointed out, the Marianas as well as the Marshalls and New Guinea had been occupied. Under such pressure the Japanese could be expected to strengthen such important positions as Formosa. Greatest speed should be used to "beat the Japanese to the punch in this area," thereby making early contact with China, coordinating the forces of the Pacific Ocean Areas with the Fourteenth Air Force, and establishing air and naval forces in position to cut Japanese traffic to the south, to establish air forces to attack Japan, and to build "bases for the speedy and effective further advance of our forces to the complete defeat of the JAPANESE war machine." He urged that the JCS make a decision to carry out the Formosa operation. "Continued postponement of decision on this matter cannot but have an adverse and delaying effect on the progress of our operations in the JAPANESE WAR."

The directive proposed by the JPS would not do for Admiral King. He recommended instead one drafted by the Navy planners in accordance with his understanding of the last JCS meeting, that is, with no provision for logistic preparations for the Luzon operation. Instead General MacArthur would occupy Morotai, Talaud, Sarangani Bay, and Misamis between 15 September and 7 December, then take the Leyte-Samar area while Admiral Nimitz provided cover and support and made plans for Formosa. The operations would be designed "to provide for a direct move to FORMOSA...target date 1 March 1945, in the event the Joint Chiefs of Staff should specifically so direct at a later date."

Admiral King enlarged upon his comments on the draft directive by submitting two more papers to the JCS, both dealing with the troop requirements of the Formosa operation.[41] One enclosed a memorandum from Lieutenant General A.A. Vandegrift, Commandant of the Marine Corps. General Vandegrift reported that many of the service forces the commander-designate of the Formosa campaign, General Buckner, said were required for the support of the Marines were in fact already organic parts of the Fleet Marine Force or else were not suited to the Marine Corps type of amphibious warfare. The other paper enclosed a recommendation from Admiral Sherman that the shortages estimated by General Buckner be reviewed. He suspected they would prove to be overly pessimistic and in large part could be made up by transfers from other areas of the Pacific. After the actual availabilities were calculated, Admiral Sherman thought the Commander in Chief, Pacific Ocean Areas, should proceed to plan an operation.

General Handy, chief of Army's Operations Division, was not pleased with Admiral King's proposed directive and particularly the implication that Formosa was to have priority over Luzon.[42] The chiefs had in fact agreed at the last meeting only to issue a directive for the Leyte operation. They had deferred any decision on what was to come next. Consequently General Handy recommended to General Marshall that Admiral King's draft be amended to direct the Commander in Chief, Southwest Pacific Area, to prepare for a move into Luzon with a target date of 20 February 1945, in case the chiefs should decide on that operation.

At the JCS meeting of 5 September General Marshall submitted a new draft directive, modified in accordance with General Handy's recommendation.[43] At the same time he expressed concern over the concept of taking only part of Formosa, for he was uncertain as to the significance of the new plan, what it would accomplish and what it would require and how it would compare with an assault on Luzon. "He felt that the ideal operation would be to seize Formosa and then move back to the Luzon operation." But General Marshall was not yet ready to make a binding decision on the matter.

Once again the JCS talked over the problem of what should be done after the occupation of Leyte and what sort of directive should be sent to the Pacific commanders. Admiral Leahy had apparently been thinking the matter over before the meeting, and he gave the chiefs a long summary of his conclusions, the high points of which were:

> There appear to be under consideration only three courses of military action by American ground troops against Japan after Leyte:
> From south to north -
> 1. Occupation of the Philippines including Luzon.
> 2. Occupation of southwestern Formosa and Amoy.
> 3. Occupation of the southern end of Kyushu.
> Of these three, occupation of the Philippines can be accomplished with the forces available.
> Occupation of southwestern Formosa and Amoy will require Army and Marine forces totalling 500,000 men. Service troops to the number of about 100,000 are not now available for this operation, but probably can be made available.
> Occupation of Southern Kyushu will eventually require about the same force as the Formosa-Amoy operation. It has the advantage of promising less enemy resistance to the first landing - and the disadvantage of being close to the Japanese fleet based in the Inland Sea, and the shore based air forces in Japan proper, both of which may be expected to make serious difficulties for the landing of troops after the first wave.
>
> . . . .
>
> It appears evident that of these three operations, seizure of the Philippines would be less costly in life and resources and not more costly in time than either of the other two.
>
> . . . .
>
> A successful and sustained occupation of the Philippines, of Formosa, or of Kyushu will succeed in shortening the war with Japan.
> The last two...hold some risk of failure with a certainty of high cost in life; while a strangulation of Japan by an effective

> sea and air blockade will probably require a longer time to
> bring the war to an end, but with less cost to us in life and
> material because of our overwhelming sea and air supremacy.
>
> . . . .
>
> My conclusion is that America's least expensive course of
> action is to continue and intensify the air and sea blockade,
> with an intensified air bombardment of Japan's war industry,
> and at the same time to reoccupy the Philippines.
> My second choice would be the Formosa-Amoy campaign.
> My third choice would be Kyushu.
>
> . . . .
>
> It seems necessary that the Joint Chiefs of Staff should
> obtain a decision on the highest political level as to whether
> we should take a shorter course toward the already certain
> defeat of Japan at greater cost in life and material, or a
> longer course at a much less cost.

Only General Marshall expressed agreement with the suggestion that decision be sought at a higher level. But neither he nor Admiral Leahy proposed any tangible step in that direction. The discussion continued after Admiral Leahy's presentation virtually as though it had not been made, as all present offered comments on the problem confronting them. General McNarney made the interesting suggestion that Luzon and Amoy be taken and Formosa neutralized. The strategic effect, he thought, would be much the same as taking Luzon and Formosa and the cost would be less. The idea did not appeal to Admiral King, for he could see no sequel to it. General Arnold doubted the necessity of invading Formosa, but General Marshall still favored that operation. He was insistent, however, that Luzon would have to be taken, although he remained uncertain which operation should come first.

Again the JCS meeting ended with no decision. Again the chiefs referred the problem to the JSSC, requesting a review of the various draft directives and a recommendation "as a matter of urgency."

The JSSC remained convinced that securing the Formosa-Amoy area as provided in the directive of 2 March 1944 was essential for further operations against Japan.[44] Hence the only question was whether or not it was necessary to go into Luzon first. The committee considered only two criteria--the availability of resources and the cost in lives. Assuming that Luzon would be occupied sooner or later, the JSSC feared that if undertaken first the Luzon campaign might delay the end of the war as much as six months, whereas a previous seizure of Formosa-Amoy would reduce Japanese support of the Philippines and facilitate their seizure. As for resources, the JSSC thought that the likelihood was so great that sufficient force could be made available from units scheduled for Europe[45] and by reexamination of requirements and availabilities in the Pacific that a directive for the southern Formosa-Amoy operation with a target date of 1 March 1945 should be issued at once. A firm directive was essential for planning purposes, but the JSSC cautioned that "later review in the light of the developing situation may result in amendment."

The directive recommended to the JCS was that proposed by General Marshall, amended to provide that the Commander in Chief, Southwest Pacific Area, should make plans for a move into Luzon "in case the progress of events indicates that adequate resources can not be made available by 1 March 1945 for the operation against Formosa, and for that reason it is considered necessary by the Joint Chiefs of Staff that the occupation of Luzon precede the move on Formosa." In two other places in the directive, where the Army draft had proffered an alternative between Luzon and Formosa subject to the future direction of the Joint Chiefs, the JSSC gave preference to Formosa, *unless* the chiefs should order Luzon first.

The chiefs were not pleased with the result of the JSSC study.[46] General Marshall in particular objected to the assumption that the Formosa operation had to be mounted. He noted the absence of reference to an operation against Kyushu or heavy bomber attacks on the Japanese homeland, and he urged again that no decision be made at present. Admiral King recommended that that portion of the report concerning the availability of resources be sent to the JLC for consideration. He also suggested that the chiefs go back to the original directive proposed by the JPS on 2 September for occupation of the Leyte-Surigao area and development of bases in the Central Philippines and for the preparation of plans for Formosa or Luzon. However, Admiral King recommended deleting from the draft the final paragraph, which had directed preparations such that either Formosa or Luzon could be attacked, "whichever should next be ordered by the Joint Chiefs of Staff." On this suggestion the chiefs agreed. On 9 September 1944 General MacArthur was directed to occupy the Leyte-Surigao area, with a target date of 20 December 1944 and to develop necessary bases and forces in the Central Philippines to support a further advance to Formosa by Pacific Ocean Areas forces on 1 March 1945 or to seize Luzon on 20 February 1945. He was to submit plans for his part in both operations. Admiral Nimitz was to provide him with fleet support and assault shipping for the Leyte-Surigao operation and to submit plans for occupying and developing Formosa and if necessary Amoy and for supporting the alternate assault on Luzon. Both were to arrange for coordination and mutual support, not only with each other but with the Commanding General, U.S. Forces, China-Burma-India, and with the Commanding General, Twentieth Air Force.[47]

The situation rested here until after the return of the JCS from the Octagon Conference at Quebec. During these meetings, however, the chiefs had made a decision that advanced the timetable for Pacific operations. The fast carrier task forces of Admiral Halsey's Third Fleet had been operating in the Central Philippines in support of the Palau and Morotai operations. They had met with such success and so little opposition that on 13 September Admiral Halsey recommended that the whole Palau operation, scheduled to begin two days later, be dropped and the Philippines be made the next objective. This would mean omitting the seizure of Peleliu and Angaur on 15 September and Yap and Ulithi in the western Carolines on 5 October. The last of these, however, Admiral Halsey thought essential for future operations and in any case considered easy to take and defend.[48]

Admiral Nimitz was immediately agreeable to bypassing Yap, but he pointed out to Admiral Halsey that Palau was necessary not only to support the Philippine occupation and other future operations but to complete the neutralization of the Carolines. Omission of the Yap operation would release the XXIV Army Corps, which Admiral Nimitz promptly offered to General MacArthur for use in the Leyte campaign.[49]

At this point the Joint Chiefs of Staff, who had received information copies of these messages at Quebec, advised General MacArthur to accept the offer. This plan, they said, was "highly to be desired and would advance the progress of the war in your theater by many months as well as simplifying the arrangements for further operations."[50]

General MacArthur's first reaction was hesitation because his own intelligence sources indicated stronger Japanese installations on Leyte than Admiral Halsey had reported. However, in the evening of 14 September the Joint Chiefs of Staff were called from a formal dinner to discuss a message from General MacArthur, reporting that he was prepared to attack Leyte with a target date of 20 October, cancelling his previously scheduled operations on Talaud and Mindanao. The chiefs immediately acquiesced, and orders to proceed were on their way at once. By this rapid decision two months were cut from the Pacific timetable.[51]

Although the operations in the Palaus and Morotai were already under way when the chiefs returned to Washington, and the attack on Leyte was only a month in the future, there was no immediate move by the JCS to decide what should be done after the conclusion of the Leyte operation. Air attacks were being made on objectives in the Philippines during this period. The success they were having and intelligence from other sources led General MacArthur to decide that it would be feasible to proceed directly from Leyte to Luzon, leaving the Aparri area to be taken later. On 21 September he reported to General Marshall that he was modifying his plans accordingly.[52]

With support from the entire Pacific Fleet General MacArthur contemplated seizing a beachhead in the Lingayen area. Then would follow an overland campaign to take Manila and a period of consolidation to complete the occupation of Luzon. Combining resources of the two areas in the Pacific and exploiting Japanese weaknesses should, General MacArthur felt, permit the occupation of Manila by February. Operations already contemplated to the northward of the Philippines could then go ahead on schedule, with the great advantage of land-based air support from Luzon. The Formosa operation would be rendered unnecessary and a direct move could be made to Kyushu, particularly if the Bonins were attacked previously. Southwest Pacific forces meanwhile would proceed to reconquer Borneo and the Netherlands East Indies.

General MacArthur's message struck a responsive note in the War Department, where the planners were becoming impatient that no decision had yet been made about Luzon.[53] On 22 September General Marshall proposed to the JCS that a target date of 20 December be set for Luzon and that plans and preparations be made to occupy Formosa as soon as possible thereafter.[54] He recommended, however, that all Army resources be made available to General MacArthur and that *he* be directed to plan for Formosa instead of Admiral Nimitz. This was in furtherance of the Army's contention that for protracted land campaigns ground forces should be under Army command.

General Marshall did not recommend bypassing Formosa, but he argued strongly against going there first. The taking of Luzon, he contended, would permit a flexibility that possession of Formosa never would. If Formosa were taken first, Pacific Ocean Areas forces would be committed there and Southwest Pacific forces tied down short of Luzon until the Formosa-Amoy situation, which might be difficult, was cleared up. It seemed logical to secure Luzon, which General MacArthur estimated could be done in December and would take six weeks, then concentrate on Formosa, which promised to take much longer. The time would be shorter if resources from both areas were combined to do it. Perhaps in the last stages, General Marshall suggested, Admiral Nimitz could get ready to take objectives in the Bonins and Ryukyus.

The memorandum inevitably evoked unfavorable comment from Admiral King.[55] He at once recommended that if there were to be a single command it should be under Admiral Nimitz. Until the sea lanes to the coast of Asia were in U.S. control, he argued, the Navy could not avoid responsibility for the operations necessary to secure them. Whereas General Marshall had spoken of shortages of Army service troops, Admiral King pointed out that amphibious forces had always been in shortest supply and that in 1943 he had recommended consolidation of the Pacific commands under Admiral Nimitz, partly in order to insure efficient use of amphibious resources. As for flexibility, surely Admiral Nimitz had illustrated his abilities in that direction by cutting out the Yap operation just a week before.

Admiral King did not oppose the seizure of Luzon, but he specified that it should be accomplished "in a manner that will best contribute to the over-all campaign necessary for the defeat of Japan." If the operation was to be done with a major amphibious movement into Lingayen Gulf, he felt it would best be supported from airfields on southern Formosa. The estimate of six weeks to complete the occupation he considered optimistic. In any event, he argued, it would be unsound to try to keep the Pacific Fleet that long in a position where it could control the airfields of southern Formosa and still expect it to be ready to meet the Japanese Fleet. Admiral King recommended that Luzon be taken, but that it be taken by shore-to-shore operations from the south. Since Luzon was considered a relatively easy target and the operation would not involve the whole fleet, he thought Formosa could be seized about 1 February 1945.

In a second memorandum to the JCS Admiral King listed seventeen points that argued for occupying Formosa-Amoy while continuing operations for occupation of the Philippines instead of completing the seizure of Luzon first.[56]

Again at the JCS meeting on 26 September the chiefs reached no decision. Since Admiral King was leaving almost at once for a conference with Admiral Nimitz, it was deemed best to await his return before attempting to settle the matter. In the meantime the Army sought information from General MacArthur with which to meet Admiral King's chief argument against taking Luzon, the inadvisability of holding the Pacific Fleet for six weeks in a vulnerable spot in support of the Lingayen operation.[57] Admiral King's fears, it turned out, were not valid, for the plan for the Lingayen operation did not call for direct support by the Pacific Fleet. Instead the fleet was to be used to cover the operation, the escort carriers and part of the Seventh Fleet remaining in direct support while the other fleet elements struck wherever were found Japanese forces that might conceivably be used to reenforce the Japanese defense of Luzon. Rather than being tied down in a dangerous area the fleet was to roam as far as need be to carry the offensive to the enemy. General MacArthur explained this concept in detail, but by the time Admiral King returned from the Pacific further refutation was unnecessary.[58]

Admiral King's conference with Admiral Nimitz at the end of September finally convinced him that the proposal to take Formosa was impracticable.[59] He found Admiral Nimitz prepared to accept General Buckner's estimates of requirements and shortages and to abandon the idea of attempting to take Formosa. Instead he recommended accepting General MacArthur's plan for taking Luzon via Lingayen Gulf with a target date of 20 December. At the same time Admiral Nimitz said, Pacific Ocean Areas forces could prepare to seize islands in the Nanpo Shoto (Bonins) on 20 January 1945 and the Nansei Shoto (Ryukyus) on 1 March. He looked hopefully at the possibility of drawing out the Japanese Fleet by these operations and he pointed out that the Bonins would furnish fields from which fighters could support the B-29's, a protection much desired by the Army Air Forces.

After much discussion of Admiral Nimitz's views and the implications of his recommendations Admiral King reluctantly accepted them. Promptly upon his return to Washington on 2 October he circulated a draft directive for the two Pacific commanders, embodying the recommendations of the Commander in Chief, Pacific Ocean Areas. There was one important reservation, however. With the intention of avoiding the risk of fleet operations in the area between Luzon and Formosa, Admiral King included the provision, "movements of major amphibious forces into the CHINA SEA north-about of LUZON will not be carried out without the specific prior approval of the Joint Chiefs of Staff."[60] As General Handy pointed out to General Marshall, this had the effect of reducing the authority granted in the preceding part of the directive and allowing merely the making of plans and preparations to seize Luzon. It seemed to General Handy that the commanders on the spot were better able than the Joint Chiefs of Staff to tell whether the situation in that region was unsafe at the time the operation was launched. Consequently he proposed substituting:

> CINCSOWESPAC and CINCPOA will keep the air situation affecting the movement of assault forces north of Luzon under continuous review, and if they consider the enemy air situation such as to make this movement unacceptable, they will report immediately to the Joint Chiefs of Staff making appropriate joint recommendations.[61]

General Handy also recommended changing Admiral King's draft to make General MacArthur responsible for an operation in Formosa in case there was to be one.

This last recommendation did not meet with approval at the JCS meeting on 3 October, and it was decided simply to state that "directions regarding plans for possible operations against Formosa, the Pescadores, Amoy and other points on the China Coast will be issued later." The other recommendation was adopted, but the wording was changed to read, "If either considers the enemy air situation such as to make this movement unduly hazardous, he will report immediately to the Joint Chiefs of Staff with appropriate recommendations."[62]

With the issuance on 3 October of the directive for General MacArthur to seize and occupy Luzon with a target date of 20 December 1944 and for Admiral Nimitz to provide fleet cover and support, the question of whether Luzon or Formosa should be taken first was finally settled. Formosa was not yet eliminated as a possible objective. However, the orders to Admiral Nimitz to occupy one or more positions in the Bonins and in the Ryukyus virtually rendered the occupation of Formosa and of positions on the China coast unnecessary for a naval and air blockade of the Japanese islands. No one yet knew whether they would be needed to stage an invasion of Japan itself.

Chapter XXV

THE OCTAGON CONFERENCE

Ten months elapsed between the conclusion of the conference at Cairo and the start of the next combined meetings, known as Octagon, at Quebec in September 1944. In the intervening months the desirability of another conference had been discussed from time to time, but it was not until August that it was finally decided to meet the following month.[1]

There was no such flurry of planning as had preceded some of the earlier conferences. Instead of the scramble to prepare numerous papers on projects the United States wished to present and on projects it was expected the British would offer, there was an attempt by the combined staffs to complete action on as many pending papers as possible before the conference and to reach agreement upon a simplified agenda that would cover the main points at issue and could be completed within a few days. Much that might otherwise have been the business of Octagon was accomplished ahead of time.

On 22 August the Joint Chiefs of Staff sent the British two recommendations, one for an agreement on basic policies, the other a list of subjects for discussion at Quebec. The first of these was a reaffirmation of the statements of over-all objective, strategic concept, and basic undertakings approved at Sextant, the last revised in accordance with developments since the end of 1943. In respect to the war against Japan this meant making the reorientation of forces from the European Theater to the Pacific and the Far East a matter of highest priority as soon as permitted by the situation in Europe. It meant also addition of another point in line with U.S. planning, that is, "Continue operations leading to the earliest practicable invasion of the industrial heart of Japan."[2] At the time of Sextant invasion had been set as an objective only if it should prove necessary; but by the time of Octagon the continuing successes in the Pacific, the superiority in air and sea forces, and the prospects for more following Germany's collapse were encouraging the planners to urge a firm decision to invade Japan.

The British Chiefs of Staff had no objection to the new statement on operations. They were unwilling to commit themselves, however, to transferring forces wholesale to the Pacific as soon as Germany surrendered, apprehensive lest insufficient strength be left for postwar requirements in Europe. Consequently they recommended including the provision, "having regard to other inescapable commitments," in the statement on reorientation of forces.[3] To this the Joint War Plans Committee saw no objection, since the CCS would have to approve any highest priority commitment that affected the reorientation.[4] General Roberts, the Army member of the Joint Staff Planners, however, feared that the British might find "inescapable commitments" in order to avoid reorienting their forces to the war against Japan. At Admiral Duncan's suggestion the Joint Staff Planners recommended that the Joint Chiefs propose changing the wording to "agreed commitments."[5] The British clung to their suggestion, arguing that they could not avoid returning Dominion forces to their homelands, for example, an inescapable commitment but not necessarily an agreed one. Ultimately the U.S. Chiefs abandoned any advantage the planners may have hoped to gain, by adopting wording suggested by Admiral King, "having regard to other agreed and/or inescapable commitments."[6]

The list of subjects the U.S. Chiefs of Staff proposed for consideration at Octagon on 22 August was brief:

    a. *The war against Germany*.
        (1) Operations for the defeat of Axis powers in Europe.
        (2) Occupation of Germany, its satellites, and Axis-occupied countries.
    b. *The war against Japan*.
        (1) Operations for the defeat of Japan.
        (2) British participation in the war against Japan after the defeat of Germany.
    c. Redeployment of forces reoriented from Europe to the war against Japan.[7]

Having first secured agreement to enlargement of the scope of b (2) by removing "after the defeat of Germany," on 2 September the British submitted a proposed agenda. On it were included progress reports on operations in Southeast Asia Command and in the Pacific, an estimate of the enemy situation, strategy for Japan's defeat, including Russian participation, British participation in the war against Japan, and the redeployment of forces to the Pacific.[8] The Joint Chiefs of Staff disapproved a comment of the Joint Staff Planners that progress reports were unnecessary and on 7 September accepted the agenda proposed by the British.[9] When the first meeting of the Octagon Conference convened at Quebec on 12 September 1944 the agenda was all decided and the Combined Chiefs of Staff could approve a schedule that would cover everything in five days.

The action taken at Quebec in relation to the war against Japan for the most part resolved problems that had been awaiting decision for weeks or even months. Consequently it will be necessary to start the account of each major topic some months before the Americans and British gathered at Quebec.[10]

A NEW STRATEGIC CONCEPT FOR THE WAR AGAINST JAPAN

On the last day of June 1944 the Joint Staff Planners presented to the Joint Chiefs of Staff a long report (JCS 924) entitled, "Operations against Japan Subsequent to Formosa," their answer to a directive to consider the strategy of the war in Asia and to combine it with the strategic plan for the Pacific area in a new plan for the defeat of Japan.[11] The membership of the Joint Staff Planners and the Joint War Plans Committee had changed considerably in the year since the first long range plan was completed, and U.S. forces had shown their mettle in victory after victory in the Pacific. Whereas the earlier planners had set the objective of the war at the blockade of Japan and invasion "if necessary," doubting that it would prove so, in JCS 924 the objective was defined as "invasion of the industrial heart of Japan and the seizure of objectives therein, in order to force the unconditional surrender of Japan." Investigating the various intermediate objectives that might be attacked in order to accomplish the final victory, the paper concluded that "the suitable, feasible and acceptable concept of operations for the main effort to bring about the unconditional surrender of Japan" would be:

  a. Concurrent advances through the Ryukyus Bonins and Southeast China coast for the purpose of intensifying the blockade and air bombardment of Japan and creating a situation favorable for:
  b. An amphibious assault on Kyushu for the purpose of further reducing Japanese capabilities by engaging and fixing major enemy forces and establishing a tactical condition favorable to:
  c. A decisive stroke against the industrial heart of Japan by means of an amphibious attack through the Tokyo plain assisted by continued pressure from Kyushu.

Although this program did not require Russian participation, it was hoped that the Russians could contain and defeat the Kwantung Army in Manchuria and permit U.S. planes to use Siberian air bases. The British part would be to breach the Malay Barrier, preferably through the Sunda Straits, soon after the assault on Formosa, attaining "a position to project our forces into the Malay Peninsula, Indo-China, Southeastern China, or that part of the East Indies not under our control, whichever, at the time would be most profitable." At best such operations would afford direct assistance to the main advance in the Pacific. At worst they would increase contacts with the enemy, hasten the time when resources of the Netherlands East Indies would become available, and mark the first step of a mopping-up campaign that eventually would have to be undertaken. By keeping these operations a British responsibility the planners sought to avoid the complications of combined command.

For air attacks on the Japanese homeland and invasion of the Bonins and the Ryukyus the JWPC assigned target dates of from about 1 April 1945 to 30 June 1945. Positions would be consolidated through the summer months while British forces moved into the South China Sea. The final phase would start with assault of Kyushu on 1 October 1945 and culminate in assault of the Tokyo Plain at the end of December. Such a timetable was considered conservative, however, as the planners anticipated the possibility of an invasion of Kyushu or even the Tokyo Plain as early as 1 July 1945.

Recommending that this concept of operations be accepted as a basis for planning, the JWPC suggested that the Combined Chiefs of Staff agree upon a restatement of the over-all objective for the Pacific, specifically:

> To force the unconditional surrender of Japan by:
> (1) Lowering Japanese ability and will to resist by establishing sea and air blockades, conducting intensive air bombardments, and destroying Japanese air and naval strength.
> (2) Invading and seizing objectives in the industrial heart of Japan.

Only one of the chiefs recorded a comment on this long study. Admiral King recommended inclusion of a statement that in order to have air operations from Siberian fields there would have to be naval operations to open a sea route to the Maritime Provinces of Siberia. Approval of his proposal as well as of the recommendations of the planners in their report was given by the JCS without further comment.[12]

The British Chiefs of Staff did not accept the revised objective so readily. Rather than the full report, they received from the U.S. Chiefs only a recommendation that the objective be restated, together with the explanation that with the preponderance of forces available or to be available after the defeat of Germany it was deemed advisable to plan to invade the industrial heart of Japan, avoiding the "unacceptable delay" involved in attempting to defeat Japan "by sustained aerial bombardment and the destruction of her sea and air forces."[13]

The British Chiefs agreed to accept the new statement, but in so doing they sought assurances: first, that the new objective in no way affected the priority of measures for the defeat of Germany; second, that the change "should not imply authorisation for an extension of operations in the Pacific which has not hitherto received the final approval of the Combined Chiefs of Staff."[14]

The British Chiefs argued the need of combined authorization for the extension of operations in the Pacific on the basis of a "sentence" in the final report to the President and the Prime Minister at Sextant, reading: The effect of any such extension of unremitting pressure against Japan on the over-all objective to be given consideration by the Combined Chiefs of Staff before action is taken."[15] The members of the Joint War Plans Committee, to whom the British comments were referred, were incensed at this interpretation.[16] It was "unwarranted," they said. Such a meaning "must be read into the sentence in C.C.S. 426/1 to which they invited attention." The Combined Chiefs of Staff were not supposed to approve an extension of operations in the Pacific but only consider the effect of such on the over-all objective. As for the other British reservation, the planners could not see how the British could consider that the new objective would have an adverse effect on the priority of measures for Germany's defeat. The JWPC recommended a memorandum from the U.S. Chiefs, calmly stating that they "were mindful of the agreement" that the supreme operations for 1944 were Overlord and the invasion of the southern coast of France, currently named Dragoon, and that nothing would be done to risk failure. The second point was dismissed with the statement that the JCS would "continue to advise the Combined Chiefs of Staff concerning the extension of operations in the Pacific in order that consideration may be given to the effect on the over-all objective." For unrecorded reasons Admiral Duncan of the Joint Staff Planners changed both of these remarks to simple non-committal affirmation of the "existing agreements" relating to the priority of Overlord and Dragoon and "to the effect on the over-all objective of extension of operations in the Pacific."[17]

The Joint Chiefs passed the recommended reply to the British Chiefs of Staff on 4 August but received no answer.[18] In preparation for the Octagon Conference the U.S. Chiefs raised the matter again the following month, recommending that the CCS formally record their approval of the restated objective.[19] There was no question of the meaning behind the U.S. assurances and no further discussion of the matter, as the Combined Chiefs of Staff, through the Secretariat, recorded formal approval of the restated objective, thereby authorizing invasion of Japan as the goal of operations in the Pacific.[20]

The new statement of concept was incorporated by the Joint Staff Planners in a brief summary paper on U.S. intentions in regard to Japan, presented by the U.S. Chiefs at Octagon following a general report on the progress of the war in the Pacific.[21] The paper included a schedule of major operations in pursuance of the over-all objective, a schedule based upon the directives to General MacArthur and Admiral Nimitz that were still under discussion as the JPS paper was written.[22] Because there had been no decision between Formosa and Luzon the timetable was highly tentative:

Target Date	Objective
15 October 1944	Talaud
15 November 1944	Sarangani Bay
20 December 1944	Leyte-Surigao Area
1 March 1945	Formosa-Amoy Area
or	
20 February 1945	Luzon

If Formosa was to be done, for planning purposes the Bonins had been approved for April, the Ryukyus for May, the China coast March to June 1945, southern Kyushu in October, and the Tokyo

Plain in December. What would follow a Luzon operation remained undetermined. Undoubtedly at least the Bonins would be on the schedule, for the Army Air Forces wanted them for fighter bases to cover the operations of B-29's.[23] None of the dates was considered fixed, and all possible short cuts were recommended.

The British Chiefs of Staff were anxious not to be committed to a program that did not mention anything about British participation. When the U.S. paper came up for discussion at the second meeting at Quebec, Sir Alan Brooke asked the Combined Chiefs to take note that this was not the whole story. There would be British operations, not yet approved, that would have to be taken into consideration when production plans were made. What he had in mind was the British Fleet's participation in Pacific operations, the British Task Force in the Southwest Pacific, or the operation in southern Burma, all of which the British intended to bring up later in the conference. With this understanding, then, the schedule was accepted as a basis for planning.[24]

BRITISH PARTICIPATION IN THE PACIFIC

The over-all plan for the defeat of Japan, approved in principle at Sextant "as a basis for further investigation and preparation, subject to final approval by the Combined Chiefs of Staff," included the assumption that a sizable British naval force would be available for operations in the Pacific by June 1944.[25] There was, however, no commitment as to how such a force would be used.

Developments in the European Theater during January indicated to the British that some of their vessels could be spared from there sooner than anticipated. Consequently Admiral Noble proposed to Admiral King that a British task force be sent to the Pacific some time in April.[26] In U.S. naval circles the prospect of British naval participation in the Pacific Theater was viewed with less than enthusiasm. Thus far the U.S. Navy had been getting along all right without British help and there was reluctance to permit the British to get into the closing phases of the war when U.S. forces were strong enough to carry on alone. Addition of another national force promised more complications of command and logistics than help. Moreover there was a strong feeling that the British should concentrate on the Indian Ocean and the Bay of Bengal and some doubt that British ships could safely be spared at all before the launching of Overlord and Anvil. The lack of bases for more naval forces gave Admiral King ample grounds for replying to Admiral Noble that the proffered ships could not be handled effectively until August or September.

Admiral Noble's overture, while representing the views of the British Chiefs of Staff, did not represent the views of the Prime Minister and the British War Cabinet.[27] Mr. Churchill held that, rather than sending a small naval contingent to fight from Australian bases under U.S. command, the British should advance a task force from the Bay of Bengal eastward to the Malay Peninsula and into the Netherlands East Indies according to the Culverin concept. The differences were unresolved during the first months of 1944.

Late in February the main Japanese Fleet withdrew from the Central Pacific to Singapore, thereby putting an end to any idea of the British attacking Sumatra, while making it highly desirable that British naval forces attempt to hold the enemy in the area as long as possible.[28] Despite this development the British Chiefs of Staff continued to insist in London that the U.S. Chiefs were expecting British naval assistance in the Pacific in June. On 10 March Prime Minister Churchill sought to settle the problem by asking President Roosevelt whether there was "any specific American operation in the Pacific, (a) before the end of 1944 or (b) before the summer of 1945, which would be hindered or prevented by the absence of a British Fleet detachment."[29]

Mr. Churchill was quite right in this instance. The U.S. planners had not been counting on British participation in the campaigns in the Pacific. Commenting on his questions, the Army's Operations Division remarked that "operations by a strong British naval detachment in the Pacific will be the opening wedge toward putting the direction of the Pacific war on a Combined, rather than a Joint level, with the attendant slow-down of operations."[30] The naval planners' thoughts undoubtedly ran much the same way. Mr. Roosevelt's reply assured Mr. Churchill that no operation would suffer from the absence of a British Fleet detachment in 1944. In fact, he said, there seemed little likelihood that British ships would be needed before the summer of 1945.[31]

On the strength of this reply Mr. Churchill informed the British Chiefs that, barring unforeseen events, the center of gravity for the British and the Imperial war effort against Japan would be the Indian Theater and the Bay of Bengal. There preparations would be made for amphibious action with the ultimate objective reconquest of Singapore.[32] The Prime Minister closed the question, but he left the loophole of "unforeseen events."

In June 1944, when the U.S. Chiefs were in London, discussion came up with the British Chiefs of the contribution the British could make to the war against Japan. Admiral King urged that existing British forces be used to maintain pressure on Burma-Malaya-Sumatra in order both to protect the supply line to China and to contain Japanese forces in the area. If the British wished to participate in operations in the Pacific, said Admiral King, it was "desirable to have concrete proposals including objectives, forces to be used, and timing, together with definite provision for giving logistic support to the proposed operations. Such support cannot be furnished by [the] United States without interference with their own projected operations."[33]

The British Chiefs were clearly eager to operate British naval forces from bases in Australia. Sir Alan Brooke pointed out that facilities in India could not support operations beyond those currently planned nor a large enough force to operate in both the

Bay of Bengal and the Southwest Pacific. Sir Andrew Cunningham predicted that a British task force operating from Australian bases could attack Amboina in January 1945. He recommended Amboina as a first objective and Borneo second. In the beginning British naval forces would be expected to work under General MacArthur with Australian land and air forces. What might come later is not recorded. At the conclusion of the discussion Sir Alan Brooke agreed that the British Chiefs would draw up a program for operations on General MacArthur's left flank, using available British naval forces.

Admiral King reported these conversations to Admiral Nimitz at Pearl Harbor in July. He also left behind for General MacArthur, soon to arrive for conference with President Roosevelt, a summary of the British ideas communicated in London.[34] Admiral King warned that the British might propose to extend the boundaries of the Southeast Asia Command to include most of the Netherlands East Indies, where British forces might hope to operate after Southwest Pacific Area forces had moved on into the Philippines. However, Admiral King thought the European war would be over before the British would be in a position to send major forces to the Pacific.

General MacArthur had already suspected that the British had designs on part of the Southwest Pacific Area, and he told the President plainly of his opposition to any such plan.[35] Replying to Admiral King's memorandum on 21 July he spelled out his views.[36] After describing the progress made under the existing command arrangement General MacArthur said:

> The British have contributed nothing to this campaign and, in fact, opposed the Australian proposal to make available Australian troops for the defense of their own country.[37] They now propose to enter this theatre at the moment when victory lies clearly before us in order to reap the benefits of our successes. It is anticipated that they intend to provide only the command structure, supplanting the American commander who has been entrusted with this duty for more than two years. They would not be able to provide forces in strength before a long lapse of time if, indeed, they contemplate so doing....
>
> ...We have carried the responsibility for the defense and initiation of the counteroffensive and it is not just that we should be relieved by the British immediately following the decisive strategic victory in order to permit them to reap the benefits of the final blows. It would be destructive of American prestige in the Far East and would unquestionably have the most deleterious effect upon future economic trends.

Let the British operate in their own area against Burma, Malaya, Sumatra, and the east coast of Asia, said General MacArthur. With the unlimited supply of labor in India they should be able to expand facilities there to accommodate their forces. He had himself given up planned operations in the Arafura Sea because of lack of amphibious means, and he intended to strike at Borneo and the Netherlands East Indies from the rear at the earliest opportunity. A frontal assault from Australia such as the British had in mind would be "more costly and time-consuming." If the British wanted to add their means to the Southwest Pacific Area forces they would be most welcome, but they "should flow in under the command set-up and the strategic control that has been agreed upon and which has been in successful operation for so long."

General Marshall promptly told General MacArthur he was confident that the British actually planned to put their forces under the existing command. This was, in fact, just what the British proposed to the CCS on 15 August.[38] In the meantime, however, they had introduced discussion of the participation of ground and air as well as naval forces.

In mid-July the British representatives in Washington informed the Combined Chiefs of Staff that from their correspondence with their chiefs in London it was apparent that the latter were expecting to provide six British divisions plus two British-trained Dutch divisions for the war in the Pacific.[39] It was upon this supposition that they had submitted requests during the spring for equipment and particularly for landing craft from U.S. production.[40] In order to overcome U.S. reluctance to allocate production before there was decision as to where it would be used, the British representatives proposed that the CCS record a decision that they would contribute six divisions plus two Dutch ones to the war against Japan, and that they would need assault lift for three divisions. Production planning, they urged, should be based on this expectation.

It was mid-August when the Joint Logistics Committee finished studying the problem and made recommendations to the Joint Chiefs of Staff.[41] In order for the British to be supplied with new equipment for jungle warfare, the committee pointed out, U.S. requirements would have to be cut into, for there was little prospect of increased production. However, there seemed a good possibility that some of the necessary stock would become available after the defeat of Germany. In principle the JLC felt that the need for equipment could not be adequately judged without operational plans. Consequently the committee urged that the British Chiefs of Staff be encouraged to hasten the presentation of their plans to the CCS and submit requirements based on agreed plans.

When presented with this report Admiral Leahy recommended that nothing be done until after the next combined conference, scheduled for September. Admiral King on the other hand thought that it would be profitable to let the British Chiefs know how the U.S. Chiefs felt.[42] General McNarney, acting for General Marshall, redrafted the memorandum the JLC had proposed submitting to the British. He did not approve the idea of holding out for the British operational plans but rather recommended that Britain be urged to compute requirements as the United States did, upon the basis of operational plans and availability of equipment after the defeat of Germany. This memorandum met with approval from the Joint Chiefs and was sent to the British on 29 August 1944.[43] There was no reply to it before the Quebec Conference, for the British did not feel so strongly about contributing ground forces to the war in the Pacific as they did about Royal Navy vessels.

Two weeks before this the British Chiefs of Staff reported to the CCS that in the Bay of Bengal they were building up a strong fleet, most of which would not be required for SEAC operations.[44] It was their "desire in accordance with His Majesty's Government's policy that this fleet should play its full part at the earliest possible moment in the main operations against Japan wherever the greatest Naval strength is required, and thereafter its strength should be built up as rapidly as possible...under United States Command." It was the "distinct preference" of the British Chiefs that the fleet participate in the main operations in the Pacific. However, if the U.S. Chiefs could not accept this, the British would be "willing to discuss an alternative." Their suggestion would be "formation of a British Empire Task Force under a British Commander consisting of British Australian and New Zealand land sea and air forces to operate in the South West Pacific Theatre under General MacArthur's Supreme Command." There it would be in a position to reenforce the U.S. Pacific Fleet if that should be desired.

From the beginning the first choice of the British Chiefs was virtually ruled out in the U.S. discussion of the paper. Commenting to General Marshall, Admiral King never mentioned it but took exception to the second choice, for the British Commander in Chief, Eastern Fleet, Admiral Bruce-Fraser, would automatically be senior to Vice Admiral T.C. Kinkaid, Commander, Seventh Fleet, the ranking naval officer in the Southwest Pacific Area.[45] Admiral King suggested replacing Admiral Kinkaid with Admiral Royal E. Ingersoll, who was senior to the British commander. General Marshall consulted General MacArthur but found him reluctant to lose Admiral Kinkaid, and it was decided to let the matter rest until the British Fleet's arrival in the area was imminent.[46]

In Washington, meanwhile, the Joint Strategic Survey Committee was recommending just what General MacArthur dreaded, that the British progressively take over control of the Australian area.[47] In a memorandum to the Joint War Plans Committee, which was studying the British proposal, the JSSC reiterated an opinion already stated in May that the British should have sole responsibility for an advance from the Sumatra area, extending control eventually to include all of Australia and New Guinea, some time after General MacArthur's forces had moved to the Philippines. The JSSC pointed out that this arrangement

> would reduce United States involvement in the knotty problems of participation by Dutch, Portuguese, and French and the restoration of their former territories. It would also help to

minimize United States military involvement in British-Chinese conflicts of interest over Hongkong and similar matters. Finally, and of great importance, if such a British area is established, it will avoid throwing the detailed operational control of the war against Japan into the Combined Chiefs of Staff as would be likely by extension if a major Combined command should be established within the present Southwest Pacific area.

The Joint War Plans Committee relayed the recommendations of the Joint Strategic Survey Committee to the Joint Staff Planners on 26 August in the form of a planning paper for the next Allied staff conference.[48] The following day there came a message from General MacArthur reporting his own objections and those of the Prime Minister of Australia to transferring control of part of the Southwest Pacific Area to the British.[49] He feared lest formation of a British Empire Task Force in the Southwest Pacific Area prove to be an entering wedge for a separation of territory from his command. However, he was willing to accept British forces to be amalgamated servicewise into the existing setup.

Despite General MacArthur's views the Joint War Plans Committee still favored the gradual transfer of part of the Southwest Pacific Area to British command. The committee recommended that the chiefs make no immediate decision on the matter, first requesting from the British more information as to when and what forces would be available and how they thought the forces might be used. With revisions by the Joint Staff Planners the report was circulated to the Joint Chiefs of Staff on 4 September.[50]

Besides recommending requests for further information the JPS report concluded that the best solution seemed to be: First, to continue to use the British Eastern Fleet in the Indian Ocean-Bay of Bengal area as long as the Southeast Asia Command operations required it. Second, that the Joint Chiefs should not directly refuse to permit British fleet units to operate in the Pacific Ocean Areas but should insist on knowing what units would be available in the form of a balanced task force. Third, that British land and air forces might be used in the Southwest Pacific Area but they would have to be amalgamated under General MacArthur's command. Fourth, if the British should bring up the question of extending the Southeast Asia Command area they should be told that it would have to be done progressively, that it would have to be cleared with all the governments who approved the establishment of the Pacific Theater, and that it would be influenced by established strategy.

As the Joint Chiefs considered this report Admiral Leahy expressed fear that the British would be deterred by such questioning from giving any assistance at all. He recommended that the chiefs record acceptance of the offer of a fleet "with alacrity and without conditions."[51] General Marshall agreed. When General McNarney said that integration of the Australian, New Zealand, Dutch, and other units into a British Empire Force would remove from General MacArthur resources on which he was planning for his program of operations, General Marshall reminded him that the force would not be available until April or May 1945. Ignoring the first choice of the British Chiefs the JCS agreed on the following reply:

> The United States Chiefs of Staff accept the British proposal... for the formation of a British Empire task force under a British commander, consisting of British, Australian, and New Zealand land, sea, and air forces to operate in the Southwest Pacific Theater under General MacArthur's supreme command. It is noted that this will enable the British Fleet to be well placed to reinforce the U.S. Pacific Fleet if this should later be desired.[52]

It must have been no surprise to the U.S. Chiefs that the British were displeased with this answer. As the combined staffs assembled at Quebec for the Octagon Conference the British Chiefs circulated a request for a formal expression of U.S. views on the employment of the British Fleet in the main campaign against Japan.[53]

The Joint Staff Planners, in proposing a reply to the British Chiefs, stressed the necessity that a British naval task force in the Pacific would have to be balanced and self-supporting.[54] Such a force, the JPS suggested, would be welcomed, to be used initially on the southern flank of operations in the Pacific Ocean Areas. For planning purposes the JPS thought the British should submit a quarterly schedule showing what forces would be available and indication that they would be supported.

The Joint Chiefs of Staff did not approve the emphasis put by the JPS upon logistical support for the British naval forces. Admiral Leahy thought in fact that "the British should be informed immediately that the U.S. Chiefs of Staff would be pleased to have the assistance of any force that they could provide in the Pacific." His opinion that details of size and maintenance could be discussed later was not shared by the other chiefs. Still they approved a memorandum proposed by General Marshall that gave greater appearance of cordiality by removing the request for assurance of logistical support. The U.S. Chiefs of Staff, it read, would welcome a British naval task force to participate in the main operations against Japan, initially on the western flank of the advance in the Southwest Pacific. The chiefs assumed that the task force would be balanced and self-supporting, but they asked no details.[55]

The question of British participation in the Pacific Theater was raised by the British Prime Minister at a plenary session that same morning, before the U.S. reply had reached the desks of the British Chiefs of Staff.[56] Somewhat to the surprise of his own Chiefs of Staff and undoubtedly with no previous warning to the U.S. Chiefs, Mr. Churchill concluded a broad summary of the war situation with the statement:

There were certain elements inimical to Anglo-American good relations which were putting it about that Great Britain would take no share in the war against Japan once Germany had been defeated. Far from shirking this task, the British Empire was eager to play the greatest possible part. They had every reason for doing so. Japan was so much the bitter enemy of the British Empire as of the United States. British territory had been captured in battle and grievious [sic] losses had been suffered. The offer he, the Prime Minister, now wished to make, was for the British Main Fleet to take part in the main operations against Japan under United States Supreme Command.

The President, the record reads, responded "that the offer was accepted on the largest possible scale."

That the Prime Minister had in mind the operation of a British Fleet under Admiral Nimitz's command cannot be doubted, for he remarked "that the placing of a British fleet in the Central Pacific would not prevent a detachment being made to work with General MacArthur in the Southwest Pacific if this was desired." However, the minutes do not show that he succeeded in getting a commitment as to where British ships would be used or how. When he subsequently asked specifically about the use to be made of the British Fleet, Mr. Roosevelt replied generously that "his thought was to use it in any way possible." Admiral King said only that the matter was being studied. Still Mr. Churchill made it quite clear in the record that he offered the use of the British Fleet and the President accepted the offer.

The British Chiefs of Staff were not pleased with the paper they received that day from the U.S. Chiefs. The following morning a heated argument developed at the CCS meeting as the British attempted to get a commitment from the U.S. Chiefs, and in particular from Admiral King, that the British Fleet would be used in the main operations against Japan.[57] Agreement was reached on deletion from the paper of the expectation that British forces would operate initially in the Southwest Pacific, but that was not enough.

As the British sought specific agreements, Admiral King insisted that he was in no position then to commit himself as to where the British Fleet could be used. The practicability of its use, he felt, should be discussed from time to time. He wished to accept the fleet in principle, "but it would be entirely unacceptable for the British Main Fleet to be employed for political reasons in the Pacific and thus necessitate withdrawal of some of the United States Fleet."

All of the British Chiefs argued that the British Fleet should be used in the main operations in the Pacific, that that was what the Prime Minister had had in mind and that was what the President had accepted. Sir Andrew Cunningham understood that "the Prime Minister and President were in agreement that it was essential for British forces to take a leading part in the main operations against Japan." His recollection was shared by the other British

Chiefs, but Admiral King remembered no such thing. Indeed the minutes of the plenary session indicate only an acceptance of participation and no mention of a leading role. Admiral King's strong stand against a commitment to use the British Fleet as a major element in the operations in the Central Pacific was not seconded by the other U.S. Chiefs, who took little or no part in the discussion. Admiral Leahy did attempt to smooth things over by suggesting that where the fleet should be used could be decided later, provided it was self-supporting. Ultimately this was what was accepted, as the CCS

 a. Agreed that the British Fleet should participate in the main operations against Japan in the Pacific.
 b. Took note of the assurance of the British Chiefs of Staff that this fleet would be balanced and self-supporting.
 c. Agreed that the method of the employment of the British Fleet in these main operations in the Pacific would be decided from time to time in accordance with the prevailing circumstances.
 d. Took note that in the light of *a* above, the British Chiefs of Staff withdraw their alternative proposal to form a British Empire task force in the Southwest Pacific.

An offer of British air power for use in the Pacific made by the Prime Minister at the same time encountered no such stormy reception, as the British Chief of Air Staff agreed to make a general estimate of the contribution that might be offered by the Royal Air Force.

From the difficult question of what contribution the British would make in the Pacific the Combined Chiefs of Staff turned to the question of what was to be done in the British area of responsibility, Southeast Asia.

OPERATIONS IN BURMA

During the summer of 1944 there was a great deal of activity in Burma as Chinese and British forces pushed ahead despite the continuous rains of the monsoon. The British were moving east from Imphal toward the Chindwin. The forces from Ledo under General Stilwell's command were attempting to consolidate and extend their positions in northern Burma and to capture the town of Myitkyina. The airfield had been in Allied hands since May. From the east the Chinese Yunnan force that had finally crossed the Salween River was encountering slow going. All of these operations were partly if not entirely dependent for support upon supplies brought in by air, for the farther into Burma they advanced the poorer were the roads behind them.

General Arnold, it will be recalled, had informed the Combined Chiefs of Staff on 24 March 1944 that four groups of transport aircraft, a total of 400 planes, and two air commando groups would be ready by September and could be made available to the Southeast Asia Command.[58] The needs of the Southeast Asia Command for transports to supply by air units that were remote from bases had led to a series of temporary solutions, the last of which was the loan of seventy-nine U.S. and British aircraft from the Mediterranean Theater in April 1944. The period for retention of these planes in SEAC was extended twice, despite protests from the Supreme Allied Commander, Mediterranean,[59] while the first group of 100 combat cargo planes was being prepared for departure from the United States ahead of original schedules.[60]

Discussing the situation in Burma and the needs of other areas of the war with Japan in mid-May 1944, the Joint Staff Planners recommended, and the Joint Chiefs of Staff approved, that, General Arnold's original statement notwithstanding, no further commitments of combat cargo units would be made to the Southeast Asia Command until receipt of a plan for future operations that would indicate clearly the use to which the planes would be put.[61] In their discussions with the British Chiefs in London in June the U.S. Chiefs made it plain that they had no intention of sending more transports until they knew how they would be used.[62] In a subsequent cable Admiral Mountbatten insisted that in order to carry out his directive of 2 June he would need four combat cargo groups by about 1 December.[63] Nevertheless, the Joint Chiefs on 3 July approved a recommendation of the Joint Staff Planners that the combat cargo group to be ready in August be allocated to Southeast Asia Command and that the two air commando groups and the other two combat cargo groups be tentatively allocated to the Southwest Pacific pending receipt of plans for their employment.[64]

The British Chiefs of Staff immediately protested the temporary assignment of the groups to the Pacific area. Their request that firm decision be delayed until further word was received from Southeast Asia Command was followed by a cable direct from Admiral Mountbatten to General Marshall and General Arnold.[65] Admiral Mountbatten reported that plans were being prepared for liquidating the enemy at least in upper Burma and should be forwarded by the end of the month. He could have submitted plans earlier, he said, but he insisted that they be realistic. "It would now appear," he protested, "that because I have waited...I am being penalized and the resources which you so kindly offered and which we felt at last would present the opportunity to carry out our directive may be diverted elsewhere." "I do hope," he continued, "that you appreciate my position and accept the suggestion that the allocation to other theatres of the remaining 200 combat cargo planes and the air commandos will not be made firm until our specific requirements for planned operations can be considered." Specific plans were precisely what the U.S. Chiefs of Staff were waiting for before making firm commitments, and General Marshall so informed the Southeast Asia commander.[66]

A preliminary report of the plans developed in Southeast Asia Command was sent to General Marshall by General Sultan following an area conference on 22 July 1944. On 31 July the British Chiefs circulated the outline plans themselves.[67] There were two alternative projects: the first, Plan "Y" or Capital,[68] was an offensive from Imphal across the Chindwin complemented by airborne operations to take Kalewa and the entrance to the Mandalay Plain, while the Ledo and Yunnan forces advanced from the north, the objective being to occupy upper Burma including Mandalay; the second project, Plan "Z" or Dracula, was for a combined seaborne and airborne attack to capture Rangoon and push north, while vigorous operations were undertaken in upper Burma.

The Americans in Southeast Asia Command strongly favored the first of these as most likely to open an overland route to China and so support the major operations in the Pacific Theater. They were of the opinion that the Rangoon plan was not in accordance with the Southeast Asia Command directive recently issued and moreover that it would involve substantial resources not yet allocated to the area. Admiral Mountbatten on the other hand preferred the Rangoon plan. He suggested as he submitted it that a sizable operation in southern Burma might result in drawing off some of the Japanese that were currently offering strong resistance in northern Burma. If such developed the plan would indirectly comply with his directive and lead to the reopening of ground communications to China. Plan "Z" would certainly require more resources than the Mandalay operation, but Admiral Mountbatten did not think the requirements were prohibitive.

The Joint War Plans Committee and the Joint Staff Planners, having studied the messages from Admiral Mountbatten, agreed with the American commanders in the theater that Plan "Y" was preferable. The operations therein envisaged they found to be in accord with the Southeast Asia Command directive as well as "suitable and feasible, and...within the capabilities of the forces and resources that are now, or can be made available to the Southeast Asia Command." Reasoning that allocating the additional combat cargo group and the air commando group that the Southeast Asia Command's Mandalay plan required might induce the British to maintain a strong offensive in upper Burma whereas withholding them might provide a reason for reneging, the planners recommended that the planes be promptly allocated.[69]

Before the Joint Chiefs (except for Admiral King, who had approved them) took action on the planners' recommendations, the British Chiefs of Staff submitted their own comments.[70] They had accepted the recommendations of Admiral Mountbatten. Painting a highly unpleasant picture of operations in northern Burma, the British said that continuing to fight the Japanese there would "merely lead to a continuation of the present unsatisfactory state of affairs." They felt bound to reject such a program. On the other hand, capture of Rangoon and of Pegu twenty miles away would at a single stroke cut the main lines of communication to the interior of Burma by road, rail, and river. This would lead to an end of the operations in Burma. Consequently the British asked that the Combined Chiefs of Staff approve the Rangoon plan in principle and make every effort to provide the remaining forces that would be needed to carry it out. A few days later the British reported that they could probably provide all the assault shipping and craft required for the Rangoon plan and possibly the land forces. To fill the air requirements the United States would be expected to send the last two combat cargo groups plus 362 transports and 584 gliders.[71]

General Wedemeyer, in Washington in mid-August, reported to Admiral Mountbatten, who was then in London, that he found from conversations with the Joint Chiefs of Staff that they were willing to agree to the initiation of Plan "Y" as soon as possible after the monsoon. Provided that the enemy lines of communication through the Mandalay area were severed, the U.S. Chiefs would agree to curtailing the northern operation and using resources made available by the capitulation of Europe for a strengthened attack on Rangoon in mid-March.[72]

Possibly taking a cue from this report the British Chiefs of Staff on 22 August pointed out to the Combined Chiefs of Staff that their previous estimates of forces available were based on the execution of the first two phases of the Mandalay operation before undertaking to capture Rangoon.[73] They would cut off phase two at the line Kalewa-Yeu-Shwebo-Indaw-Katha-Bhamo-Loiwing instead of carrying it to the line Shwebo-Mogok-Lashio as originally proposed by Admiral Mountbatten. In a report to the Joint Staff Planners the Joint Strategic Survey Committee pointed this out, recommending acceptance of the British proposal, but with the larger objective. The JSSC also advised agreeing to the attack on Rangoon, on the assumption that resources would be available from Europe and the assurance that the operation would not interfere with the attainment of the objectives in northern Burma.[74]

With some modification by the Joint Staff Planners, notably the addition of seizure of the Yeu-Shwebo area to the minimum operations in northern Burma, the JSSC recommendations were passed on to the Joint Chiefs of Staff on 29 August 1944 and by them in turn approved and circulated to the British two days later. The British promptly proposed that in addition to the directive preferred by the U.S. Chiefs for Admiral Mountbatten to execute Plan "Y" he be told to start planning to launch Plan "Z" in mid-March, "on the clear understanding that such preparations will not jeopardise the early attainment of the objectives of Phase One and Phase Two of Plan Y."[75] The U.S. Chiefs were agreeable.[76] On the strength of this campaign to insure reestablishment of ground communications to China they finally decided to send to Admiral Mountbatten one of the combat cargo groups and one air commando group, the remainder going to the Southwest Pacific Area.[77]

At Octagon the British Chiefs of Staff circulated a draft directive to Admiral Mountbatten, setting as his primary object the recapture of all Burma at the earliest date.[78] It provided for "the stages of Operation Capital necessary to the security of the air route" and for Operation Dracula with a target date of

15 March. If Dracula had to be postponed beyond the monsoon of 1945 he was to exploit Capital as far as possible. There was a good chance that Dracula would have to be postponed, for, as Sir Charles Portal reminded the chiefs at Quebec, Admiral Mountbatten had only 448 transport aircraft and he would need 1,200 in order to execute the Rangoon operation. The British could supply 190 more, but the rest would have to come from U.S. sources, such as the fourth combat cargo group which it had just been announced would go to the Southwest Pacific Area. Even this would not be enough, said General Arnold. There just would not be enough available until hostilities ended in Europe. There was general agreement that this was the case. Still, the Combined Chiefs noted, the prospects of providing enough aircraft seemed good.

At the recommendation of the U.S. Chiefs, ever mindful of their commitment to support China and fearful that it might be lost sight of, the CCS agreed to specify that operations to recapture all Burma must not prejudice the opening of land communications and that Capital should be carried out at least far enough to achieve that objective.[79]

The object assigned to Admiral Mountbatten was modified during discussion of the proposed directive with the heads of state at the second plenary meeting of the Octagon Conference. Instead of giving to the Southeast Asia Command the task of recapturing all of Burma the new directive set the objective at "destruction or expulsion of all Japanese forces in Burma at the earliest date." It looked at least as if, provided aircraft could be supplied, Burma might be freed.[80]

LOGISTICS PROBLEMS

The Octagon agenda did not include consideration of the availability of means for the operations under discussion as Sextant had done. There were two main reasons for this: first, it was a short conference and only topics that required combined discussion at the top level were included; second, there were no longer shortages of such proportions as to limit drastically the program that could be carried out. Planning for production and allocation of resources was a problem for the logistics committees and did not so urgently require top level discussion.

Two matters related to logistics did come to the attention of the Combined Chiefs at Octagon, however. One of them, the redeployment of forces from the European Theater, was set aside for consideration by the logistics planners after completion of the conference.[81] The other, the question of when the war against Japan might be expected to end, received only slightly more attention from the Combined Chiefs of Staff.

The British Chiefs felt that in order to plan for the redeployment of forces and for production and the allocation of manpower it would be highly desirable to set a planning date for the end of the war in the Far East. In order to allow for contingencies, they suggested, the CCS should accept a date two years after the defeat of Germany.[82]

The U.S. Chiefs had been planning for some time on the basis of defeat of Japan one year after the collapse of Germany, and they saw no need of extending the anticipated interval to two. As General Somervell pointed out, current plans were to invade the Tokyo plain in December 1945. It would undoubtedly take three months to reduce Japanese resistance. General Marshall recommended that they set the planning date for Japan's defeat at eighteen months after the defeat of Germany. Inasmuch as no one knew when that event would take place and current indications were that the Japanese would fight practically to the last man, that did not seem excessive. Yet it allowed for moving troops and equipment from the European Theater and using them in the final stages of the campaign. The British had no quarrel with the shortened period or the recommendation of the U.S. Chiefs that the estimate be adjusted periodically as the war progressed. Consequently eighteen months after the defeat of Germany was set at Octagon as the planning date for the end of the war against Japan.[83]

CONCLUSION OF OCTAGON

All of the conclusions reached by the Combined Chiefs of Staff at Quebec were incorporated in a report to the heads of state and presented to them on 16 September.[84] In addition to the matters that have been discussed there had of course been problems relating to the war against Germany. The main business in respect to that theater had been to approve proposals for future operations and distribution of forces and to discuss possible additional projects later developments might make feasible. At the final meeting of the conference the President and Prime Minister went over the report of decisions point by point, commenting on most, approving the majority, amending some.

Mr. Churchill apparently was still worried about the possibility of bogging down in Burma, for he warned against overinsuring the security of the air route and the opening of overland communications with China lest Dracula be ruled out. He was most anxious to put an end to operations in Burma and get on to something more profitable elsewhere. With this in mind he called upon the United States to provide two divisions to participate in the Rangoon campaign, possibly sending two that were scheduled for late transportation to Europe. His suggestion was not accepted. As General Marshall pointed out, all U.S. divisions were allocated, the last scheduled to sail for Europe either the last week in January or the first week in February. As a matter of fact General Stilwell had asked for some that he was not likely to get. If there were to be more ground forces for Dracula, they would not be supplied by the United States.

The President and Prime Minister approved the work done by their military staffs and the conference adjourned. Brief summary reports were sent to Stalin and to the Generalissimo[85] and a communique to the press, the latter exuding confidence to the point of smugness:

> The President and the Prime Minister, and the Combined Chiefs of Staff held a series of meetings during which they discussed all aspects of the war against Germany and Japan. In a very short space of time they reached decisions on all points both with regard to the completion of the war in Europe, now approaching its final stages, and the destruction of the barbarians of the Pacific.
>
> The most serious difficulty with which the Quebec Conference has been confronted has been to find room and opportunity for marshalling against Japan the massive forces which each and all of the nations concerned are ardent to engage against the enemy.[86]

Chapter XXVI

THE RECALL OF GENERAL STILWELL

The summer and fall of 1944 saw the friction that had existed almost from the beginning between General Stilwell and Generalissimo Chiang Kai-shek increase to such an extent that President Roosevelt finally recalled the American general from an impossible situation. Action from Washington in this crisis originated almost entirely in the War Department or the White House. However, the Joint Chiefs were occasionally formally involved, and they were kept informed of developments as General Marshall acted with JCS sanction. Consequently it is necessary to summarize the story.[1]

In June 1944 there was pressure both from Burma and from China to do something about the command setup in China-Burma-India. While General Stilwell held the post of Deputy Supreme Commander, Southeast Asia Command, at the same time he was in the field commanding the Chinese troops pushing across northern Burma. For military operations he came directly under Admiral Mountbatten, an awkward situation since all other military forces in the area were under the British Lieutenant General William J. Slim. Admiral Mountbatten was anxious to have all field forces under a single command. By June the complicated command arrangements, combined with difficulties of General Stilwell's personality, had convinced the British that a change should be made. Consequently Sir Alan Brooke took advantage of General Marshall's visit to London to urge that General Stilwell be removed.[2]

In China in June 1944 the security of Chungking itself was in doubt as the Japanese continued to advance in the east. Chinese armies, for the most part poorly organized and ill-equipped, had proved no match for the enemy. The past reluctance of the Generalissimo to build up his ground forces and the squabbles over Hump tonnage left observers in Washington no confidence that supplies flown into China to attempt to hold the line would be delivered to proper destinations or effectively used. Consequently there was growing belief that someone should be put in authority to see that the armies of China received equipment when and where it would do the most good. On 1 July General Marshall sought General Stilwell's opinion, suggesting that he turn over the position of Deputy Supreme Commander to General Sultan once the Myitkyina-Mogaung situation was secure and transfer his attention to China.

There he would concentrate on "the rehabilitation and in effect the direction of the leadership of the Chinese forces in China proper."[3]

General Stilwell was hardly enthusiastic about going to China and stated frankly that unless he were given complete authority over the Chinese Army he would not attempt the job. That would not be easy to attain. General Stilwell recommended that "the President...send...a very stiff message, emphasizing our investment and interest in China, and also the serious pass to which China has come due to mismanagement and neglect of the Army, and insisting that desperate cases require desperate remedies." Perhaps then, said General Stilwell, "the Generalissimo might be forced to give me a command job."

Even under ideal conditions of command General Stilwell could see only one possibility of saving the situation in east China. That was to use the Chinese Nationalist troops that were stationed in northwest China watching the Chinese Communists and attack through Loyang toward Chengchow and Hankow. Action would have to be quick and radical, General Stillwell insisted, and to get help from Chiang the picture would have to be painted for him in the strongest terms.[4]

Whether General Marshall had discussed his message to General Stilwell with the Joint Chiefs of Staff before sending it is not known. On 4 July he talked over both communications with them and obtained their approval of asking the President to send the Generalissimo such a message as General Stilwell had mentioned.[5]

With the help of a description of the desperate situation in China and the sad state of the Chinese armies, President Roosevelt was convinced of the desirability of entrusting the remaining military resources to one individual, and he sent the Generalissimo the strong message that had been drafted for his signature in the War Department. "The extremely serious situation which results from Japanese advances in Central China, which threaten not only your Government but all that the U.S. Army has been building up in China," he told Chiang "leads me to the conclusion that drastic measures must be taken immediately if the situation is to be saved. The critical situation which now exists, in my opinion calls for the delegation to one individual of the power to coordinate all the allied military resources in China, including the communist forces." Mr. Roosevelt recommended that Chiang recall General Stilwell from Burma "and place him directly under you in command of all Chinese and American Forces, and...charge him with the full responsibility and authority for the coordination and direction of the operations required to stem the tide of the enemy's advances." "I feel that the case of China is so desperate," he said, "that if radical and promptly applied remedies are not immediately effected, our common cause will suffer a disastrous set-back."

This was strong language from the head of one state to the head of another. It must be supposed that it was hardly pleasing to the Generalissimo to be told that he should put General Stilwell, for whom his feelings were somewhat short of affection, in command of all the armies in China. Nevertheless he immediately notified President Roosevelt that he "agreed in principle" with the suggestion that General Stilwell be put in command of Chinese and American army forces in China.[6] This did not mean Chiang was going to adopt any such arrangement at once. He hastened to point out that "Chinese troops and their internal political conditions are not as simple as those in other countries." It would be a bigger problem than directing the Chinese Ledo force. If the change were made in haste there would be misunderstanding and confusion. Consequently Chiang proposed "a preparatory period in order to enable General Stilwell to have absolute command of the Chinese troops without any hindrance."

The Generalissimo also repeated a suggestion made to Vice President Henry A. Wallace in June, that President Roosevelt send to China "an influential personal representative who enjoys your complete confidence, is given with full power and has a farsighted political vision and ability, to constantly collaborate with me and he may also adjust the relations between me and General Stilwell so as to enhance the cooperation between China and America."

It was entirely true that Chinese troops and their political conditions were unlike those in any other country. Many of the Chinese war lords had their own armies that cooperated with the Nationalist Government only at their commanders' discretion. It was also reasonable to suppose that making arrangements for General Stilwell's command would take a little time. But to General Marshall these proposals seemed designed to delay action on the command rearrangements. He recommended avoiding involvement in the question of personal representatives and drafted a reply that promised merely to give the suggestion consideration. Mr. Roosevelt apparently did not share General Marshall's concern that there would be no action until the representative was sent, for he changed the draft and told the Generalissimo that he was looking for the right man for the job. At the same time he urged Chiang "to take all steps to pave the way for General Stilwell's assumption of command at the earliest possible moment."[7]

It was two weeks before the Generalissimo replied to President Roosevelt's message, in a memorandum that the President did not see until his return in mid-August from his trip to the Pacific.[8] Chiang reported that he had decided that certain factors were essential for putting the command plan into effect: "(1) Due regard should be given to the political circumstances obtaining in China; (2) The psychology of the Chinese Army and people should be taken into account; (3) General Stilwell should be enabled, under the command of the Generalissimo, to direct military affairs in the most effective manner for the actual furtherance of the joint war effort." Certain conditions would have to be met: First, the forces would be those of the National Government serving at the front. This left out the war lords' forces and the Chinese

Communists, unless they agreed to submit faithfully to the central government. Second, General Stilwell's functions and authority, his title, and his relationship to the Generalissimo should be clearly defined before he assumed command. Third, the Chinese Government or its commander in chief should have authority over the distribution and disposal of all military lend-lease supplies. Finally, Chiang still hoped that President Roosevelt would send "a personal representative in whom the President has full confidence, and with whom the Generalissimo can talk as if personally with the President."

During Mr. Roosevelt's absence, General Marshall and Secretary of War Henry L. Stimson selected a candidate for Presidential representative. Their choice was Brigadier General Patrick J. Hurley, who had been in China the previous year, sent by the President to prepare for the Generalissimo's trip to Sextant. General Stilwell was agreeable to General Hurley's appointment. President Roosevelt approved, and on 9 August General Marshall sent a message to the Generalissimo in the President's name, informing him of the decision. With General Hurley would go Mr. Donald Nelson, just being replaced as head of the War Production Board (WPB).[9]

General Hurley and Mr. Nelson arrived in India on 4 September 1944. With General Stilwell, they proceeded to Chungking two days later. Thereafter followed a series of conferences with the Generalissimo in which General Hurley tried to make arrangements for setting up the command under General Stilwell.[10] The discussions were long and tortuous as the Americans tried to sell their views of how the command should be organized and what General Stilwell's responsibilities would be. It appeared that everything was practically settled, that the Generalissimo would appoint General Stilwell with full authority, when suddenly the situation exploded.

The spark that set off the explosion was apparently a report General Stilwell sent to Washington on 15 September. Having just ascertained at first hand that there was little prospect of holding Kweilin, he was told by the Generalissimo that the Yunnan force should be withdrawn from Burma, where it was making progress, to defend Kunming. Chiang also thought the weary Chinese troops that had just occupied Myitkyina should push on at once to Bhamo. He threatened to withdraw the Yunnan force if the move to Bhamo was not made. General Stillwell reported his discouragement with the whole situation to General Marshal, concluding:

> ...I am now convinced that he regards the South China catastrophe as of little moment, believing that the Japs will not bother him further in that area, and that he imagines he can get behind the Salween and there wait in safety for the U.S. to finish the war. Our conferences on command are dragging, and tomorrow we are going to try some plain talk with T.V. Soong, in the hope of getting to the Gmo some faint glimmer of the consequences of further delay and inaction.

THE RECALL OF GENERAL STILWELL

Word of this threat to the campaign in northern Burma arrived when the Combined Chiefs of Staff were meeting at Quebec, where they approved the directive to Admiral Mountbatten to proceed with Capital and Dracula. The Army's Operations Division team drafted a reply, which was approved by the Joint Chiefs of Staff and sent by the President on 16 September 1944. At a plenary session on that afternoon General Marshall reported the incident in general terms and informed the group that the President had told the Generalissimo that if the Yunnan force were withdrawn he would have to accept full responsibility.[11]

It was a blunt message that went to Chungking from Quebec on 16 September.[12] "After reading the last reports on the situation in China," it read, "my Chief of Staff and I are convinced that you are faced with the disaster that I have feared." The Japanese in east China had been eager to force a withdrawal of the Yunnan force across the Salween and delay opening of the land route to China. "If you do not repeat not provide manpower for your divisions to north Burma, and if you fail to reinforce the Salween forces and withdraw the army," said the President, "you will lose all chance of opening land communications with China and immediately jeopardize the air route over the Hump. For this you must be prepared to accept the consequences and to assume the personal responsibility."

At a time when Chiang had failed to put General Stilwell in command of all the forces in China, the message went on, the loss of a critical area in east China was threatened, with possible catastrophic consequences. "Only drastic and immediate action on your part alone can be in time to preserve the fruits of our long years of struggle and the efforts we have been making to support you; otherwise, military and political considerations alike are going to be swallowed up in military disaster." Said the President, "I am certain that the only things you can do now in an attempt to prevent the Japs from achieving their objective in China is to reinforce your Salween armies immediately, press their offensive while at the same time placing General Stilwell in unrestricted command of all of your forces."

This message reached Chungking at a moment when General Hurley appeared to have achieved success and was in fact in conference with the Generalissimo over the preparation of a commission for General Stilwell in his new position. Delivery of the President's message by General Stilwell put an end to that day's conversations with Chiang. From then on negotiations deteriorated. It seemed to General Hurley and General Stilwell until 25 September that the discussions would ultimately be successful, but on that day General Hurley was given an aide memoire which he sent at once to the President.[13] In it the Generalissimo agreed to the appointment of an American general as commander in chief of Chinese-American forces fighting against Japan in China. However, he stated emphatically that he could not "confer this heavy responsibility upon General Stilwell." He would "have to ask for his resignation as chief of staff of the China theater and his relief from duty in this area."

Chiang had believed that the President's message of 16 September was sent at General Stilwell's request. He interpreted it as indication that General Stilwell had no intention of cooperating with him, that in fact General Stilwell considered Chiang under his command. "If, ignoring reason and experience, I were to appoint General Stilwell, as field commander," said Chiang, "I would knowingly court inevitable disaster.... Almost from the moment of his arrival in China, he showed his disregard for that mutual confidence and respect which are essential to the successful collaboration of allied forces." He continued, "Far from leading to an intensified effort against the common enemy, the appointment of General Stilwell as field commander would immediately cause grave dissensions in the new command and do irreparable injury to the vital Chinese-American military cooperation." Any other qualified American officer, Chiang would take. But not General Stilwell.

It was about ten days before the Generalissimo received a reply from Washington to this aide memoire. General Marshall and Secretary Stimson were in favor of a firm refusal to relieve General Stilwell, but President Roosevelt disagreed. The Joint Chiefs of Staff discussed the matter, and several draft replies were prepared before any was accepted. The message finally sent was a compromise.[14]

President Roosevelt accepted Chiang's proposal that General Stilwell be removed as Chief of Staff and be relieved of responsibility for lend-lease matters. The President was now "inclined to feel," he said, "that the United States Government should not assume the responsibility involved in placing an American officer in command of your ground forces throughout China." Maintenance of tonnage deliveries over the Hump was of such importance to the stability of the Chinese Government, however, the President continued, "that the continuance of a reasonably secure situation regarding operations over the Hump demands that Stilwell be placed in direct command under you of the Chinese forces in Burma and of all Chinese ground forces in Yunnan Province, it being understood that adequate support in replacements and supplies be furnished these armies by you." If this were not done, the President was confident "that the Hump tonnage will be interrupted by Japanese action." There would have to be adjustments in other phases of command in the area, but Mr. Roosevelt expressed the hope that Chiang would accept the proposals promptly, "because I feel that should we remove Stilwell from the Burma campaign the results would be far more serious than you apparently realize."

The Generalissimo's reply was a demand that General Stilwell be recalled.[15] After a long conversation with General Hurley, in which the President's representative, although handicapped by lack of intimate knowledge of past events in the theater, did his best to defend General Stilwell, Chiang presented General

Hurley with an aide memoire and a formal note to the President. "So long as I am head of the State and Supreme Commander in China," the aide memoire read, "it seems to me that there can be no question as to my right to request the recall of an officer in whom I can no longer repose confidence." In some detail Chiang placed the blame upon General Stilwell for the loss of east China, accused him of withholding lend-lease materials from Chinese ground forces, of pursuing a totally wrong strategic concept in Burma, and in general of incompetence and faulty military judgment. It was lengthy and unjust, but there was nothing to be gained in refuting it.

General Hurley forwarded the Generalissimo's papers to Washington, himself commenting that he was convinced that Chiang Kai-shek and General Stilwell were "fundamentally incompatible" and that the choice lay between the two. Two days later, on 13 October, he sent the President a detailed account of the situation as he saw it and the problems involved in trying to reconcile the differences between General Stilwell and Generalissimo Chiang Kai-shek. While expressing sympathy and admiration for General Stilwell, General Hurley reported that he was convinced that command under General Stilwell would not work. "I respectfully recommend," he said, "that you relieve General Stilwell and appoint another American general to command all the land and air forces in China under the Generalissimo."[16]

In view of the Generalissimo's firm request and General Hurley's recommendation there was nothing to be done but to recall General Stilwell. On 18 October President Roosevelt communicated that decision to Chiang Kai-shek.[17] So doing he stated plainly that "General Stilwell was not responsible for the decisions with respect to attacking in North instead of South Burma." The decision was made by the Combined Chiefs of Staff with his approval and that of the Prime Minister. But setting the record straight on who was responsible for the military decisions for which General Stilwell had been blamed did not remedy the situation. General Stilwell was to be removed. His departure would hasten the decision that had been under discussion for some time, to divide the theater in two parts. President Roosevelt proposed to name General Wedemeyer Chief of Staff to the Generalissimo and Commander, U.S. Forces, China Theater. In India-Burma General Sultan would take over command. General Chennault would continue in command of the Fourteenth Air Force in China under General Wedemeyer.

So ended a mission that had been virtually impossible from the beginning. The tasks assigned to the two men who would replace General Stilwell were described in a directive circulated to the Joint Chiefs by General Marshall for approval on 23 October. Only Admiral King had comments to make on the draft. His were minor and concerned with insuring that the U.S. Navy Group, China, under Rear Admiral Milton E. Miles, not be placed under command of General Wedemeyer.[18]

A single message sent on 24 October 1944 informed General Wedemeyer and General Sultan of their new assignments.[19] General Wedemeyer was told:

> a. Your primary mission with respect to Chinese Forces is to advise and assist the Generalissimo in the conduct of military operations against the Japanese.
>
> b. Your primary mission as to U.S. combat forces under your command is to carry out air operations from China. In addition you will continue to assist the Chinese Air and Ground Forces in operations, training and in logistical support.
>
> c. You will not employ United States resources for suppression of civil strife except in so far as necessary to protect United States lives and property.

The Commanding General, U.S. Forces, China Theater, was also to keep a guiding hand on allocations of lend-lease material, by controlling supplies delivered into China by U.S. facilities.

General Sultan, as Commanding General, U.S. Forces, India-Burma Theater, was given the primary mission of supporting the China Theater. This was to include "the establishment, maintenance, operation and security of the land L of C to China, and the security of the air route to China." He was to participate in and support the Southeast Asia Command operations as directed by the Combined Chiefs of Staff, placing forces involved under his command under Admiral Mountbatten's operational control for the purpose. General Sultan was also given responsibility for the logistic and administrative support of all U.S. Army forces in his theater. Like General Wedemeyer he was cautioned against using U.S. resources for the supression of civil strife.

In an attempt to avoid conflicts between the two halves of what had once been a single command both officers were directed to coordinate their activities and cooperate with one another.

With the issuance of these directives a new era began in the Far East.

Chapter XXVII

PLANNING, FROM OCTAGON TO ARGONAUT

In the months following the conference at Quebec victory over both Germany and Japan was almost in sight. Although progress in Europe was slower than had been hoped, United Nations forces were advancing on all fronts. The German offensive in the Ardennes in December 1944 was only temporarily successful. U.S. forces were able to reverse the tide the following month and push on into Germany. In the Pacific September and October saw occupation of Morotai and the Palaus, followed on 21 October by the invasion of Leyte in the Philippines. Two days thereafter began the naval Battle of Leyte Gulf, which ultimately resulted in an overwhelming American victory. From Leyte General MacArthur moved on to Mindoro and finally Luzon. In northern Burma the advance continued and resulted at last in the reopening of a road to China at the end of January 1945. Meanwhile British operations against Akyab and Ramree had met with success. Only in China in the fall of 1944 were the Japanese making progress. Chinese cities fell one after another, including the important air base at Kweilin. By mid-December Japanese pushing south met Japanese moving north from Indochina and completed a land link from Korea to Malaya.

The invasion of the Japanese home islands had been set as the ultimate objective in the war against Japan, and the operational program was established through the capture of Luzon and of positions in the Bonins and the Ryukyus. It remained to be decided what intermediate operations, if any, should follow the seizure of the Ryukyus and which of the islands of Japan should be assaulted. For combined consideration operations in Southeast Asia Command and the availability of forces in the area continued to occupy the chief's attention. Increasingly during the fall of 1944 these and the numerous contingent problems were settled "by informal action," generally by exchanges of papers, occasionally by informal discussion. Fewer and fewer JCS and CCS meetings were held. The system of keeping and publishing minutes was almost entirely abandoned. In regard to the war against Japan this lack is not very keenly felt by the historian, for few of the remaining problems were as controversial or as complicated as those that had confronted the JCS in the preceding years.[1]

BRITISH AIR ASSISTANCE IN THE PACIFIC

As the war against Japan approached its final phase the British Chiefs of Staff were anxious that plans be drawn with the expectation that British naval and air forces would participate. Immediately upon the conclusion of the Octagon Conference they reported to the Combined Chiefs that, depending upon the availability of bases, forty squadrons of Lancaster bombers would be ready for action in the Pacific by October 1945. Twenty of these squadrons would have to serve as tankers, for by refuelling in flight Lancasters were supposed to be capable of a radius of action of 1,500 miles with 4,000 pounds of bombs. This was less than the range and capacity of the U.S. B-29's, and the British Chiefs thought it would probably restrict the British planes to bases on Formosa or the nearby coast of China.[2]

The first reaction of the Joint War Plans Committee to this offer, as the committee studied it for the Joint Chiefs, was to recommend that the British Chiefs be told that all heavy bomber bases within range of Japan would be needed for the more effective B-29's. From bases in the Southeast Asia Command and the Southwest Pacific Area Lancasters would strike vital targets in the Malay Barrier and the Netherlands East Indies. Eventually they might be moved closer, the JWPC suggested, but at present the British should be asked to plan to use their bombers in Southeast Asia and the Southwest Pacific.[3]

On the recommendation of the Army and Air Forces planners the JWPC thought again about the desirability of British participation in the main air operations against Japan, both for British prestige and for reducing commitments of U.S. resources. The committee still agreed that Lancasters should not displace B-29's. It was finally decided to recommend that the Joint Chiefs of Staff be noncommittal, welcoming the British offer but appending the statement:

> The deployment of Lancasters either as heavy bombers or flight-refueling bombers against targets in Japan proper must, of course, be governed by the availability of air bases within effective radius of Japan. Determination of the specific areas, numbers and dates of availability of bases for the use of Lancasters must await developments of the situation in the Pacific and the firming of plans.

Since the Joint Chiefs of Staff adopted the JWPC's suggestion, their reply to the British on 26 October gave the impression of eager acceptance of British assistance but reserved the privilege of indefinitely postponing any use of it.[4]

The following March the British Chiefs of Staff pursued the matter further, with a request based upon information received in staff discussions in Washington, that the Cagayan River area in northern Luzon be made available for airfield construction for the British Lancasters.[5]

Investigation revealed, however, that access to that area was extremely difficult and the expense of constructing bases there would far outweigh the military value of operations that distance from Japan. The Joint Staff Planners gave some consideration to allocating to British use the island of Miyako Jima in the Ryukyus, a suggestion that appealed to the British Chiefs, who were prepared to provide the construction crews and go to work almost at once.[6] This too went by the board when it was decided not to take Miyako but to concentrate on developing Okinawa. From there the greatest distance to the Tokyo area was only 800 miles, a circumstance that led to a new proposal that the British provide a force that could be used for tactical as well as strategical operations, including smaller planes that could provide direct support to the invasion of Japan. The British readily accepted a suggestion that ten squadrons be sent out and at once went to work planning their logistical support and arranging for convoys to carry necessary construction personnel to the area. Like many another project this one was caught unfinished by the Japanese surrender and British land-based planes did not participate in the final phases of the war in the Pacific.[7]

OPERATIONS FOR THE DEFEAT OF JAPAN

The anticipated use of a British air force in the final phases of the war in the Pacific was one of the factors taken into consideration by the Joint War Plans Committee in the months following Octagon as it studied the question of how best to strike the final blow at Japan.[8] That Japan would surrender before the vital industrial area of Honshu had been invaded seemed to the JWPC highly doubtful. In any event the committee felt such an operation would have to be included in strategic planning. It was, however, too formidable an undertaking to be contemplated without some preliminary occupation of one of the other Japanese islands. For this the JWPC selected Kyushu, ruling out Hokkaido, where weather conditions would prevent landings earlier than May and where an attack would have to be made from the north, sacrificing all the advantages of the approach already under way from the south.

With no fixed terminal date for the end of the war against Germany, the JWPC estimated September 1945 to be the earliest that necessary forces and equipment from the European Theater could be expected to be in the Pacific. Accordingly the planners assigned the assault on Kyushu a target date of September 1945 and scheduled the invasion of Honshu for December. This would leave an interval of uncertain duration between the Ryukyus operation and the Kyushu assault, which, the JWPC suggested, might well be occupied with attacks on the China coast, Formosa, or the northern Kuriles, depending upon the strategic situation and the availability of forces.

The decision to eliminate Hokkaido as an objective was questioned immediately by General Roberts as the JWPC report came up for discussion by the Joint Staff Planners. He was of the opinion that Hokkaido might be taken as an intermediate objective in the period between the Ryukyus and Kyushu operations. The other members of the committee did not agree. Brigadier General W.W. Bessell pointed out that means for an attack on Hokkaido would not be available before May or June, which would be too close to the date for the attack on Kyushu. Commodore E.W. Burrough reminded the group that the six-month interval was supposed to be used for softening up Japanese air, naval, and industrial strength. Besides, he pointed out, it would be extremely difficult for the Navy to support an attack on Hokkaido because of the lack of intermediate bases and of good ports. Admiral Duncan added that an operation against Hokkaido would require all available resources and could not be undertaken as an interim affair. Moreover, it would put the Navy in a very vulnerable position by splitting naval supporting forces between Hokkaido and the Bonins and Ryukyus.[9]

As a result of the JPS comments the Joint War Plans Committee completely reworked the paper, adding more arguments against the selection of Hokkaido as a substitute for Kyushu. The committee also explored the possibility that in order to soften up Japan for invasion it might be necessary to undertake contributory operations before attempting to attack Kyushu. These would be major projects, dependent upon troops from the European Theater, and would probably delay the invasion of Honshu. Possible objectives might be Formosa, Hokkaido, positions on the coast of China north of Swatow, or the northern Kuriles.[10]

At the next JPS meeting Brigadier General Richard C. Lindsay, who had not been present for the earlier discussion, reopened the question of retaining Hokkaido as an alternative to Kyushu.[11] He contended that Hokkaido would not take so much effort as Kyushu and could perhaps be attacked early in 1945. Such an operation would surprise the Japanese, he said, and provide more air bases from which to conduct air attacks on Honshu.

In what appears from the minutes to have been a lively exchange Admiral Duncan presented again all the arguments already used against Hokkaido. In a further revision of the paper General Lindsay's points were included, but Kyushu was still considered the preferable objective. The paper did contain a proposed operational concept, however, in which Hokkaido was listed as alternate to Kyushu.

The planners' report was circulated to the Joint Chiefs of Staff on 27 October 1944.[12] In commenting upon it Admiral King urged that during the period between the Ryukyus and Kyushu operations the objective should be to lower "Japanese ability and will to resist by establishing sea and air blockades, conducting intensive air bombardment, and destroying Japanese air and naval strength." Positions should be seized that would broaden the base for bombing Japan by air and for cutting Japanese communications with the Asiatic mainland. This would mean maintaining pressure on Japan, in short establishing a blockade that might render it unnecessary to invade the Japanese home islands. Hokkaido, Admiral King agreed, should not be a major objective.[13]

General Arnold agreed with Admiral King that it was essential to have more bases in order to prepare Honshu by air attack before attempting an amphibious landing. His recommendation, however, was to take Hokkaido in May 1945. General Arnold discounted the naval objection to dividing the fleet between support of Hokkaido and support of the Ryukyus and Bonins. The Japanese Fleet had suffered a major defeat at Leyte, he pointed out, and was no longer a significant threat to the lines of communication. Besides, he argued, occupation of Hokkaido would assure a line of communications to Russia when and if Russia came into the war.[14]

In the light of the chiefs' comments the Joint War Plans Committee and the Joint Staff Planners worked over the study, presenting the JCS with a new version on 23 November.[15] In it the JPS pointed out that, until Germany had been defeated and forces redeployed to the Pacific, extensive operations could not be undertaken without risking delay in the invasion of Japan. Perhaps such delay would be necessary in order further to soften up Honshu for attack. In that event the planners considered invading Hokkaido, but they cautioned that this could not be done as early as May-June 1945 and no land-based air support could be used. Formosa was also considered a possible objective, but the northern Kuriles were omitted. Positions in the Kuriles, said the planners, might be required to support the Russian effort, but they would not contribute directly to the main campaign and could be taken only at the expense of further operations in the Ryukyus or on the China coast. Such operations as those were much to be preferred, for they would maintain pressure on Japan, sustain momentum, and furnish more air bases for supporting the invasion. Objectives on the China coast, however, would have to be limited to isolated positions where Allied forces could not be drawn into a major operation.

The JCS approved this report for planning purposes and sent a summary to the CCS.[16] Thus the planners could assume that the Ryukyus campaign in March would be followed by limited but unspecified operations in June, and assault on Kyushu in September, and invasion of the Tokyo Plain in December 1945. The last two dates would depend upon the transfer of forces from Europe and upon the adequacy of the earlier operations to prepare the main Japanese islands for the assault.

On the same day the JCS report was circulated to the CCS General MacArthur reported to General Marshall that the construction of airfields on Leyte had been delayed by exceptional weather conditions. He had been forced to postpone the Mindoro operation and the operation in Lingayen Gulf which was to open the Luzon campaign, the latter to 9 January.[17] This three-week delay would in turn affect the target dates for the Bonins and the Ryukyus assaults, for forty days would be required after Lingayen for upkeep of the covering forces. Admiral Nimitz at once reported the situation to Admiral King and recommended postponing seizure of the Bonins to 19 February and of the Ryukyus to 1 April. In the circumstances the Joint Chiefs could merely accept the theater recommendations.[18]

By this time the Pacific Ocean Areas plan for the Ryukyus operation had been received in Washington. It was a three phase project known as Iceberg, designed to contribute significantly to "broadening the base" of operations in the manner strongly championed by Admiral King. There would be little time between its completion and the assault on Kyushu. On 1 April 1945 Okinawa was to be attacked. Positions there would be consolidated and Ie Island taken by D plus 30. Then four other islands would be taken successively--Okino Daito, Kume, Miyako, and Kikai, the last with a target date of D plus 120, presumably about 1 August.[19]

In addition to the occupation of the Ryukyus the Pacific Ocean Areas planners were studying other operations that would help to prepare the situation for the invasion of the Japanese home islands. "The establishment of a truly effective sea and air blockade of Japan," they contended, and the deployment of air forces adequate for an intensive air bombardment of Japan require that our forces be established in additional positions from which vital Japanese areas can be reached by medium range aircraft and from which Japanese communications with central China and with Manchuria and Korea can be cut." This meant a minimum of a base area in eastern China, possibly one in the Shantung Peninsula, and one in Korea, to be secured in that order. In East China the most favorable target seemed to be the Chusan Archipelago-Ningpo Peninsula area in Chekiang province. For operations there the Pacific Ocean Areas planners tentatively suggested a target date of 20 August 1945.[20] The Joint Staff Planners had also been considering this area a desirable objective, but they thought suitable positions there could be taken as early as June 1945.[21]

In January the Joint Staff Planners reviewed the Pacific Ocean Areas plan for Iceberg and subsequent projects and their own study of operations on the China coast. To the JCS they recommended approval of the Iceberg concept. If forces and resources for a sizable operation in the Chusan Archipelago-Ningpo Peninsula area were not readily available, however, the JPS decided it might be preferable to undertake a smaller operation such as seizure of Tai Shan and the Changtu Islands, assuming that the Kyushu invasion was to be carried out in 1945. Consequently they recommended that planning for operations on the China coast continue but no immediate decision be made.[22]

There had not yet been any decision by the Joint Chiefs of Staff beyond that of November 1944 that Kyushu should be attacked in September and Honshu probably in December. JCS approval of the Iceberg program was promptly given, but the chiefs did not consider it necessary to make a commitment on what should be done between its completion and the invasion of Kyushu. Unwilling to decide either for or against landings on the coast of China, the JCS instructed Admiral Nimitz to go ahead and make plans for an operation in the Chusan-Ningpo area but not to start actual preparations.[23]

AIR FORCES FOR THE PACIFIC

The air bases whose seizure was the chief objective of the several possible operations prior to the invasion of Kyushu would be useful only in proportion to the availability of planes to use them. There was no longer a serious shortage of aircraft such as had complicated strategic planning in the first years of the war. Still for the concluding phases of the war large numbers of planes would be needed and it was essential to make arrangements to get them to the area, either from the United States or from the European Theater of Operations, and to plan for enough planes for the available bases as well as enough bases for the essential planes. At the end of September 1944 the Joint Staff Planners completed for the JCS a study entitled "Tactical Air Forces Required to Accomplish Earliest Possible Conclusive Defeat of Japan." Including a reserve of 3,132 land-based aircraft, it called for 1,140 land-based naval planes, 4,938 carrier-based, 1,692 Marine Corps, and 9,055 Army, a total of 16,825.[24]

General Arnold was not wholly pleased with the JPS estimates. The report was all right, he said, if it was "merely to outline the maximum number of airplanes that can be used against Japan under the most favorable circumstances - with a later revision in mind." He did not think 16,000 planes could be used profitably in daily operations but felt that a large percentage would have to be kept back in rear areas. With all the large land masses around Germany, he pointed out, only about 17,000 planes were in operating combat units there.[25]

The Joint Staff Planners did not attempt to defend their figures on the basis of actual strategic necessity. Rather they protested that they had considered currently estimated airfield capacities and had increased the number of planes by 30 per cent to provide for increased capacities, rehabilitation, reequipment, and rotation of units. The figure they had arrived at seemed to the planners the largest number that could be effectively employed.[26] Apparently this explanation satisfied General Arnold, for on 14 October the Joint Chiefs informally approved the report for planning purposes.[27]

This study had not included the B-29's that were supposed to be used for strategic bombing aimed at "the destruction of selected industrial systems, primarily in Japan proper, to undermine her war-making capacity to a point where it is fatally weakened." On 11 November the planners circulated a second study on this phase of operations against Japan.[28]

In order effectively to attack Japan's aircraft and electronics industries and the six most important urban areas, to provide for mining ship lanes and attacking part of the coke industry, the planners estimated, 700 B-29 sorties from Chengtu, 5,500 from the Philippines, and 13,500 from the Marianas would be required. These could be accomplished by 1 October 1945 if four B-29 groups were deployed in China through January and twelve were built up in the Marianas and seventeen in the Philippines by September. In order to keep areas neutralized and to attack new objectives a total of forty-seven groups would be required eventually in the Marianas and the Philippines or equivalent bases such as the Ryukyus or northern Formosa.

In approving this JPS report General Arnold pointed out that some of its statements and assumptions were already outdated.[29] Admiral King's approval was given with the understanding that the allocation of forces and resources would "be integrated with and adjusted to the requirements of all other forces employed in the war against Japan."[30] With these qualifications this study joined the other as background for planning.

A more practical problem in the use of air power against Japan was introduced to the JCS by General Arnold on 6 December.[31] The air planners were currently considering deploying forty-eight very long range bomber groups in the Marianas, Luzon, and the Ryukyus. Two wings of B-29's (eight groups) were scheduled to be ready for deployment in the first six months of 1945 with as yet no decision as to where they should be sent. Although the Marianas seemed the best prospect the logistic problems had not been thoroughly studied. General Arnold recommended that the Joint Logistics Committee look into the logistics requirements and "the integration of those requirements with the overall requirements for the Pacific theater." At the same time he asked that the committee investigate the feasibility of planning to move the XX Bomber Command with its four B-29 groups from China to Luzon or the Ryukyus as soon as possible, a transfer that was being recommended from China by General Wedemeyer and that had in fact been under consideration in Washington for some time.

General Marshall had asked General MacArthur in early October when bases for the XX Bomber Command could be available either on Leyte or Luzon and which would be preferable. General MacArthur reported that Leyte could accommodate the four groups about 1 June and Luzon, which he preferred, between 15 May and 15 August.[32] These dates were still far distant and nothing was done about the move.

At the end of October, shortly after General Stilwell's recall, Major General Patrick J. Hurley had recommended from Chungking that the B-29's be removed from China, where, he said, they were getting the greatest portion of supplies, and that the maximum Hump tonnage be made available to the tactical operations of the Fourteenth Air Force. General Wedemeyer commented at the time that General Hurley's report on the amount of tonnage the B-29's were receiving was exaggerated and his remedy too drastic. But by December he was convinced that great dividends could be realized in the critical situation in eastern China if the tonnage currently allocated to the XX Bomber Command went to the ground forces and the Fourteenth Air Force instead. "For every ton of supplies sent to the Chengtu areas to support the 20th Bomber Command effort," he reported, "we could move two and one half tons into the Kunming area to insure the security of our bases and to maintain China in the war effort." He recommended that the very long range bombers be removed from the area as soon after 15 January as possible.[33]

The Joint Logistics Committee made no immediate report on the feasibility of transferring the XX Bomber Command but reported on 20 December that the two new B-29 wings could be supported in the Marianas approximately as soon as they became available, without interfering with other operations. The Joint Chiefs approved that deployment, subject to the understanding stipulated by Admiral King "that the necessary adjustment with regard to shipping can be made without detriment to approved operations in the Pacific theater."[34] They had already told General Wedemeyer that he had better plan his allocations of Hump tonnage on the basis of the B-29's remaining in China.[35]

In mid-January General Wedemeyer renewed his request, urging that the XX Bomber Command be moved by the first week in February. This time General Arnold recommended that the Joint Chiefs approve the withdrawal. He suggested that the four groups could be operated temporarily from bases in India and moved in April to the bases in the Marianas scheduled to receive the first four new groups from the United States. The latter would undoubtedly profit from the extended training period they would thus receive.[36] With the approval of the Joint Chiefs of Staff the XX Bomber Command was ordered to leave China immediately.[37] So ended the first mission of the very long range bombers.[38]

OPERATIONS IN SOUTHEAST ASIA

The problems of China and of operations in Southeast Asia continued to claim JCS and CCS attention in the fall and winter of 1944-1945. The outlook in Burma in October 1944 did not look promising. Shortly after the conclusion of Octagon the British Chiefs of Staff reported that they had reluctantly accepted the apparent fact that the target date of 15 March 1945 for Dracula, the operation in southern Burma, could not be met. In the European Theater U.S. and British forces, just at the frontier of Germany, were meeting with stiff resistance. There seemed little likelihood that the situation would ease sufficiently to permit troops and aircraft for Dracula to be moved to Southeast Asia. Consequently the British recommended that Admiral Mountbatten be told to exploit the operations in northern Burma, Capital, throughout 1945 and to submit new plans for carrying out Dracula as soon as possible after the 1945 monsoon season.³⁹ Admiral Mountbatten's directive had provided for such a development. Consequently the Joint Chiefs of Staff merely concurred in the British recommendation.⁴⁰

Postponement of Dracula did not mean idleness in Southeast Asia. At the conclusion of Prime Minister Churchill's visit to Moscow he summoned Admiral Mountbatten to Cairo to discuss what could be undertaken with forces already available in Burma and India. Mr. Churchill was anxious to attack the Kra Isthmus as a step toward recapture of Singapore. There was also talk of taking the Andaman or Nicobar Islands or Sabang in northern Sumatra, but there the conference ended with no decision.⁴¹

After Admiral Mountbatten's return to Southeast Asia he and his staff developed a program of operations designed to retake Singapore as rapidly as possible. Following completion of phases one and two of Capital with occupation of the line Kalewa-Shwebo-Mogok-Lashio, the Southeast Asia Command forces were to move on Akyab (Talon) and to clear the Arakan (Romulus) in December and January. In March 1945 two divisions would undertake an amphibious operation to establish a forward naval and air base on the Kra Isthmus. Dracula would come after the 1945 monsoon. This program, Admiral Mountbatten thought, not only represented sound strategy and complied with his current directive but made the best use of resources in the theater and promised a considerable contribution to the war against Japan.⁴²

The British Chiefs of Staff welcomed the idea of occupying Akyab and the Arakan but were in some doubt as to whether there would be enough resources for the Kra Isthmus operation. On 25 November they reported to the CCS that they had approved Talon and Romulus as being within the terms of the CCS directive.⁴³ The Arakan operation was launched on 12 December. Planning for the Kra Isthmus attack proceeded but hopes of executing it dimmed rapidly.⁴⁴

Even before the British had officially approved Talon and Romulus Admiral Mountbatten received word that Generalissimo Chiang Kai-shek had decided to withdraw some of the Ramgarh-trained Chinese divisions from northern Burma to try to hold the Japanese then threatening Kunming. These were the most seasoned troops in the area, and Admiral Mountbatten protested.⁴⁵ Weakening of the Northern Combat Area Command of which these divisions were a part would jeopardize the entire Capital operation, he reported. An amphibious operation would be out completely. Moreover, he said, during the lengthy, complicated process of transferring troops and equipment to China they would be making no contribution whatever to the war.

Admiral Mountbatten urged the Combined Chiefs of Staff to see that "the strongest representations" were made to Chiang not to withdraw Chinese troops but to contrive to readjust his forces in China to meet the emergency. The Supreme Allied Commander, Southeast Asia, did not feel he could himself assess the situation in

China, but he was quite certain that removal of Chinese forces from Burma "would endanger the accomplishment of my directive and undermine the whole policy of aid to China which has governed Allied strategy in South East Asia."

Admiral Mountbatten's protest was seconded by Prime Minister Churchill, who proposed to President Roosevelt a joint message to the Generalissimo earnestly requesting him to reconsider any idea of weakening his "gallant forces which are cooperating so successfully with ours with the intention of reestablishing firm communications between China and her Allies."[46]

On the same day Mr. Churchill's message was forwarded to the Joint Chiefs of Staff for preparation of a reply, word came from General Wedemeyer that he considered the Generalissimo's decision to call his troops back to China necessary. He was impressed with the serious threat to the Kunming area of China, the end of the Hump supply line. Its loss, he pointed out, would completely nullify the purpose of operations in Burma. General Wedemeyer sought from the Joint Chiefs of Staff "as a matter of urgency" a decision on the relative over-all priorities of operations in China, India, and Burma. He recommended that Admiral Mountbatten be instructed "that Capital and Romulus operations will be conducted only in such manner and to a degree that will not militate against the measures required to insure the defense of the Kunming area."[47]

General Marshall accepted General Wedemeyer's estimate that the move of two divisions to China was necessary. At his recommendation the Joint Chiefs of Staff informed the CCS that the U.S. Chiefs felt they must at once approve the troops' withdrawal. The Generalissimo had made the decision in any case, and the U.S. Chiefs did not consider themselves in a position to oppose his wish to use his own forces to meet the threat to China's very existence. They suggested, however, that divisions not heavily engaged in Burma might be substituted for those the Generalissimo had specified.[48]

In a directive to General Wedemeyer for which the JCS sought British concurrence the chiefs instructed him to work out a selection of units for transfer that would cause the least interference with Admiral Mountbatten's operations in North Burma. The JCS also proposed to direct General Wedemeyer to "call on [Lieutenant General D.I.] Sultan for any U.S. Air Forces including ATC and other U.S. resources required for the transport and support of the two divisions and to meet other requirements arising out of the present emergency in China."

This "blank cheque on United States Air Forces, including transport aircraft, in South East Asia" drew objection from the British Chiefs of Staff. They could not countenance a constant threat of removal of air transport forces at a critical moment in Burma to meet unknown requirements in China. They insisted on knowing first what effect the use of these aircraft to move and support the two divisions would have on Capital and Romulus. Instead of the blanket statement proposed by the U.S. Chiefs the British recommended that General Wedemeyer be told to consult with General Sultan and report what aircraft would be needed to move and support the two Chinese divisions.[49]

To General Marshall this seemed to necessitate an unwarranted delay in transferring the troops. On his recommendation the Joint Chiefs told the British they believed postponement might well be disastrous. They were sending the directive to General Wedemeyer but telling him "to limit his demands for transport aircraft to those not at present actively employed and urgently required for the supply of Southeast Asia Command (SEAC) forces engaged with the enemy, unless no other means of meeting his emergency requirements can be found." Movement of the 14th Chinese Division by air from Myitkyina to Kunming was begun on 4 December.[50]

The British Chiefs of Staff felt that this JCS limitation on General Wedemeyer's demands for transport aircraft still permitted the possibility that he might feel compelled to call for planes whose removal from Southeast Asia Command would adversely affect operations there. Consequently they recommended that General Wedemeyer be instructed to tell Admiral Mountbatten about all calls he proposed to make on the Southeast Asia Command aircraft, that Admiral Mountbatten report any that interfered adversely with his operations, and that the Combined Chiefs of Staff make the final decision as to whether the planes should be taken.[51]

This was too broad an agreement for the U.S. Chiefs of Staff, who considered the situation in China too critical to delay emergency transfers of aircraft while awaiting authority of the Combined Chiefs of Staff. Approving an agreement reached between General Wedemeyer and Admiral Mountbatten to transfer two combat cargo groups to China, the U.S. Chiefs insisted on reserving the right, already agreed by the CCS the preceding January, to transfer units from the Tenth U.S. Air Force in Burma to the Fourteenth in China.[52]

Following communication of these views by the British representatives on the CCS to the British Chiefs of Staff there came a protest from London that the situation had changed since January. Most significant was the division of the two theaters so that the U.S. commander in China had no direct responsibility for operations in Burma. The British Chiefs said they had no objection to minor adjustments between the two U.S. forces, and they understood the earlier reservation to apply to minor transfers. They could not approve major transfers that might affect the ability of the Supreme Commander, Southeast Asia Command, to carry out CCS directives. They felt that substantial variations in the forces allocated to operations approved by the Combined Chiefs of Staff should be made only with CCS concurrence. Accordingly they asked the U.S. Chiefs to agree:

> a. Where a definite allocation of resources from Southeast Asia Command to China has been agreed by Combined Chiefs of Staff, e.g. the two Chinese divisions, it is proper for

General Wedemeyer to communicate direct with General Sultan
repeating to Admiral Mountbatten for information.

    b. Where no definite allocation has been made, but a tentative earmarking only, the question is one of allotment of resources between two strategic theatres and must be dealt with in the first place direct between General Wedemeyer, as representing the Generalissimo, and Admiral Mountbatten as Supreme Allied Commander, Southeast Asia Command.

    c. Although most questions will be of course solved by direct communications between General Wedemeyer and Admiral Mountbatten should any conflict of opinion arise it must be referred to the Combined Chiefs of Staff.[53]

Studying this British view the Joint Staff Planners decided that this was not a problem of the allocation of resources between theaters, properly subject to CCS agreement. The U.S. Chiefs of Staff had always intended that the U.S. forces and resources in India-Burma should constitute a reserve for China where they could not all be maintained. It was all right to agree that allocation of anything other than air forces between Southeast Asia Command and China Theater should be subject to CCS approval. But air units could be moved quickly and would be needed first in an emergency. Moreover there were more U.S. air forces in the area. The Joint Staff Planners felt that the U.S. Chiefs of Staff should retain authority to move U.S. air units from the Tenth Air Force to the Fourteenth.[54]

With some changes of wording recommended by General Marshall the Joint Chiefs forwarded to the CCS the memorandum drafted by the planners. The JCS agreed that General Wedemeyer should tell Admiral Mountbatten his future requirements for U.S. resources from India-Burma, and that Admiral Mountbatten should tell the CCS what effect such transfers would have on SEAC operations. However, the JCS pointed out, U.S. air forces that could not be maintained in China had been deployed to India for the specific purpose of assisting China. This was entirely distinct from the general question of allocations between theaters, and the U.S. Chiefs did not consider it a matter for control by the Combined Chiefs of Staff. Consequently, they informed the British, they did not feel free to waive the reservation that U.S. forces could be moved as needed from the Tenth to the Fourteenth Air Force.[55]

In a closed session on 22 December the Combined Chiefs of Staff finally reached a compromise, agreeing

    that should the Supreme Allied Commander, Southeast Asia report that proposed diversions of resources to China from his theater would materially limit the execution of Operation Capital, the decision on such a move would lie with the Combined Chiefs of Staff. Should, however, a situation develop in China which, in the opinion of the United States Joint Chiefs of Staff is one of extreme emergency, such a diversion could be made on the decision of the United States Joint Chiefs without awaiting the final decision of the Combined Chiefs of Staff.[56]

Subsequently the British Chiefs of Staff recommended that Capital not be specifically mentioned, since it was but one of the operations in Southeast Asia. They proposed substituting "approved operations or place any substantial part of his forces in jeopardy" in order to put a further check on removals of aircraft.[57]

Two days after this proposal was circulated and before it was acted on, Akyab was occupied without opposition. The Southeast Asia Command forces in northern Burma were making good progress. The Fourteenth Army from the west was about to enter the Mandalay Plain with a possibility that the advance might be pushed farther south. However, the amount of progress that could be made was limited by the necessity for supply by air.

In December Admiral Mountbatten had agreed to send three combat cargo squadrons to help meet the emergency in China, on the understanding that they would be replaced from outside Southeast Asia Command by 1 March.[58] He had also loaned a fourth to be returned or replaced by 1 February. The planes had gone, but there was no guarantee as to when they would be replaced. On 4 January the British Chiefs of Staff asked that the CCS decide at once that the three combat cargo squadrons would be returned by 1 March 1945.[59] This request was still being studied by the Joint Staff Planners two weeks later when the British reported that they had modified their views.

It looked as if the advance in the Mandalay area might be continued even to the point of taking Rangoon by land, eliminating Dracula altogether. In order to continue operations, however, Admiral Mountbatten was asking for more transport aircraft, two squadrons by 1 February, one by the middle of the month, and a fourth by 1 March, the last to compensate for the absence of the other three since mid-December. The British Chiefs felt there was much to be gained by exploiting the success in Burma. They were prepared to send out a transport squadron from those currently with the Allied Air Forces in the Mediterranean. Since the Japanese threat in China was receding by this time, they asked the U.S. Chiefs of Staff to instruct General Wedemeyer to send back two combat cargo squadrons to Southeast Asia Command by 1 February and a third by 14 February.[60]

Upon being consulted by the Joint Chiefs of Staff General Wedemeyer agreed to the return of two combat cargo squadrons by 1 February but reported that he would have to retain one for continued use in China. General Sultan reported from India that in any case this was about all that could be used effectively in support of projected operations. Consequently the Joint Chiefs of Staff approved the British proposal to transfer a squadron from the Mediterranean and General Wedemeyer's decision to return two from China. "With complete development of the other logistical facilities and organizations of the lines of communication and with maximum utilization of each available transport aircraft," the JCS suggested, Admiral Mountbatten should be able to support his offensive in Burma.[61]

Upon British approval of this JCS decision the specific problem of air transports was settled. But the British Chiefs remained unsatisfied about General Wedemeyer's authority to call on forces from India-Burma without CCS approval. Their recommendation of 2 January had not been acted upon. It was a matter of principle and one they felt would seriously affect developments in Southeast Asia. When the American and British military staffs met at Malta at the end of January the British Chiefs took advantage of the occasion to reopen the question of transferring forces.

Chapter XXVIII

RUSSIAN PARTICIPATION IN THE WAR AGAINST JAPAN

Whether or not the USSR would enter the war against Japan and what the Russian contribution would be were major unknowns in all long range planning for Japan's defeat. Marshal Stalin's announcement at the tripartite meeting at Teheran that Soviet forces would move against Japan after Germany had been defeated did little to change the situation. Planning for Russian participation continued to be a story of frustration and of estimates based on suppositions as U.S. representatives tried in vain to secure information from the Soviets or to achieve some measure of coordination in planning. There was hope that the sending of General Deane to Moscow in October 1943 as head of a Military Mission would result in closer cooperation. But General Deane tried for months with virtually no results to arrange to discuss with Soviet military authorities what Russia could contribute in the Far East and what facilities in Soviet territory might be made available to U.S. forces. Even information as to what supplies Russia would need from the United States when it entered the war against Japan was not readily forthcoming.[1]

It had been generally agreed from the beginning of the war that Russian intervention against Japan was desirable, although the possible effect of such intervention on the whole strategic situation was not clear. As the advance across the Pacific neared its final phases evidence grew that the Soviets could make the greatest contribution by moving forces from Siberia into Manchuria to contain the powerful Japanese Kwantung Army and prevent its return to reenforce the defenses of Japan against the invasion scheduled for the fall of 1945.

In September 1943 the Joint Strategic Survey Committee made its strongest statement in favor of Russian intervention, stating that a cardinal factor of "a national policy...aligned realistically with the military capabilities and interest of the United States" was "the great importance to the United States of Russia's full participation in the war against Japan after the defeat of Germany." It was, said the JSSC, "essential to the prompt and crushing defeat of Japan at far less cost to the United States and Great Britain."[2] A year later General Embick of that committee went so far as to suggest that U.N. advances in the Pacific be slowed down when they came within air range of the Japanese home islands until Russia had been persuaded to move in the Far East. He feared that if the Soviets thought the United States would go on alone to invade Japan in any case, they would sit back and not get into the war until Japanese troops had been removed from Manchuria and that area could be occupied at minimum cost. General Embick sent his suggestion to the War Department, but it did not gain acceptance.[3]

Despite the absence of information as to what the Soviets would be prepared to contribute to the war against Japan some plans had to be made for U.S. procedure when that development came. In the months following the meetings at Teheran the Joint War Plans Committee made a study of possible courses of action in the North Pacific assuming the collaboration of the USSR. In general terms the JWPC proposed:

(1) Soviet offensives against Japanese ground forces in Manchuria and Southern Sakhalin.
(2) Attacks by Soviet aircraft and submarines against Japanese shipping and land targets.
(3) The establishment of U.S. forces and air bases in Kamchatka, and air forces and bases on the Siberian mainland, north of Vladivostok.
(4) Attacks by U.S. heavy and VLR bombers against targets in the Kuriles and Japan proper.[4]

The Joint War Plans Committee deplored the lack of information concerning Russian capabilities and intentions in the Far East and recommended that General Deane pursue the attempt to get answers to a series of questions that had been given him at Sextant. The committee also recommended that he seek agreement for U.S. personnel to survey air and port installations in the Maritime Provinces and Kamchatka. Until this information was available the JWPC felt plans should be based upon the supposition that Russia would remain neutral and upon the recognition that without Russian cooperation there was no useful purpose in planning to operate U.N. forces from Siberia.

The JWPC paper was sent to General Deane in February, but despite his repeated efforts it was June before Marshal Stalin gave any cause to expect discussions of some of these problems.[5] On the basis of a conversation of Ambassador Harriman with Stalin, General Deane took hope that military talks might soon be arranged. On 19 June he sent General Arnold an agenda he proposed to follow when and if talks on air collaboration became possible.[6] Before proceeding he sought the views of air planners in Washington as to the size of the air force to be sent to Siberia and the administrative and command arrangements to be made for it.

The reaction of the Joint War Plans Committee, when sought by the JCS, was that the United States should make no commitments until Russian intentions and capabilities were definitely known. When information was obtained from the Russians, existing plans could be restudied to determine whether or not the current concept of deploying no major U.S. forces in the North Pacific should be changed. The committee's recommendation that General Deane initiate discussions with this idea in mind, although seconded by the Joint Staff Planners, did not meet with the approval of the Joint Chiefs of Staff.[7]

General Arnold, presumably with at least General Marshall's approval, replied independently directly to General Deane, reminding him of a study the Air Staff had made earlier of the logistical problems involved in basing heavy bombers in Siberia.[8] The staff had concluded that ten heavy bomber groups and ten fighter groups could be moved into the area and that six of each should be operated by Americans under U.S. command while four were operated by the Russians. General Arnold recommended that General Deane take this as his objective. Its attainment would depend upon the Soviets' capabilities of supporting these forces, including construction of air bases of sufficient capacity.

General Marshall proposed to the Joint Chiefs of Staff that General Deane be directed to emphasize in his discussions with the Russians that the United States wished to operate U.S. planes from bases in Siberia at an early date. Again he suggested seeking detailed information as to Russian intentions and capabilities and urging early preparation for U.S. air forces in Siberia.[9] At the recommendation of Admiral King a request for information necessary for planning to open and secure a sea route to the Maritime Provinces was added to the draft message prepared by General Marshall, and the message was sent to General Deane on 5 July.[10] However, the first meeting General Deane was able to secure with a Russian military representative was at the beginning of August, on the day before he left for a trip to Washington. Like many others the meeting was unproductive.

After the Octagon Conference hopes of progress toward combined military discussions were raised again. When Ambassador Harriman and Ambassador Sir Archibald Clark-Kerr of Great Britain called on Marshal Stalin to deliver a report of the conference the Soviet leader promised to instruct his military chiefs to meet with General Deane within a few days.[11] In anticipation of discussions General Deane sought from the Joint Chiefs of Staff a statement of the broad strategic concept of how Soviet aid could be used to the best advantage in the war against Japan. He himself suggested:

    (1) Securing the Trans-Siberian Railroad and the Vladivostok Peninsula.
    (2) Setting up American and Soviet strategic air forces for operation against Japan from the Maritime Provinces.
    (3) Securing the Pacific supply route....
    (4) Defeat of the Japanese army in Manchuria.

The Joint Chiefs of Staff approved this statement, adding the Kamchatka Peninsula to item (2), inserting as the third item "Interdiction of lines of communications between Japan proper and the Asiatic mainland," and placing the Pacific supply route last on the list. Once again the chiefs reminded General Deane to try to get the long-sought information and to find out when the Soviets thought their entry into the war against Japan would be most effective.[12]

No American-Soviet discussions developed from the post-Octagon talks with Marshal Stalin, but in early October the arrival of Prime Minister Churchill and Mr. Anthony Eden in Moscow for conferences presented another opportunity. Ambassador Harriman and General Deane took advantage of it to give Marshal Stalin a broad summary of JCS strategic plans for the war against Japan and to seek information of Russian plans. For once their attempts were successful.[13]

After a series of meetings attended by various U.S. and British representatives General Deane was able to report some details of Russia's intentions. He had learned from Marshal Stalin and from General Antonov, Soviet Deputy Chief of Staff, that there were currently thirty Russian divisions in Siberia. That number would have to be doubled before they would attack the Japanese forces in Manchuria. Although Marshal Stalin would not say precisely when they would enter the war he did specify that it would be three months or more after the defeat of Germany, commenting that "the political aspects of the situation have not been fully considered." Once the Russians were in he expected the end of the war would come quickly. Consequently a stockpile of supplies for two or three months in Siberia would suffice.

Marshal Stalin agreed to several things the United States had been seeking for months: to make bases available to an American Strategic Air Force in the Maritime Provinces and Kamchatka, with the stipulation that the bases should be built and stocked but the planes not sent to the fields until about ten days before they were to start operations; to make available a naval base at Petropavlovsk at some indeterminate time; to permit small U.S. parties to survey the area for air and naval facilities; and to direct his military leaders to get together with General Deane to discuss details.

The most tangible result of the conversations was the presentation by Marshal Stalin of a list of supplies required from the United States for the two-month stockpile in Siberia. The total came to 860,420 tons of dry cargo and 206,000 tons of liquid, a large amount for delivery by 30 June 1945 and across the Pacific, since the Trans-Siberian Railway would be occupied carrying men and equipment from Russia.

As the October meetings came to an end there seemed every hope that at last planning could be coordinated. The supply list was approved in the United States and deliveries began. But even with that there were long delays on the part of the Russians whenever problems of nomenclature, priority, or availability arose. Military planning progressed no farther than Marshal Stalin's promises, for the combined discussions never eventuated.

As November 1944 saw still no coordinating of U.S. and USSR plans for action against Japan the Joint War Plans Committee on its own initiative prepared a study of when Russia might be expected to declare war on Japan and the significance of such a development. The committee's paper, after revision by the Joint Staff Planners, reached the Joint Chiefs of Staff as JCS 1176 on 23 November 1944.[14]

JCS 1176 acknowledged the general view that it would be desirable to add the weight of force that Russia could contribute to hasten the defeat of Japan. On the other hand, the paper pointed out, implicit in current war planning was the conviction that Japan could be defeated without Russian help and that consequently no support could be given Russia that would prejudice the main effort in the Pacific. There was no doubt that Russia would eventually come into the war. "Russia's interests in the Far East and in post-war world politics," said the planners, "will undoubtedly force her entry." The timing would depend upon when Germany was defeated, upon when Soviet strength in Siberia was sufficient to offer good prospects for defeating the Kwantung Army, and upon when or whether speedy and conclusive defeat of Japan seemed imminent. There was no illusion that anything but Soviet self-interest would determine when the decision would be made. However, the planners thought the timing might be influenced through U.S. assistance in building up supplies in the Far East.

Strategically the JPS felt the timing of Russia's entry was important. Should hostilities break out before the Russians were prepared to launch and maintain a strong offensive against the Kwantung Army the Japanese could seize the initiative, cut the Trans-Siberian Railway, throw the Russians off balance, and perhaps even defeat them. From the U.S. point of view the best time for a Russian move would be at least three months before the invasion of Kyushu. This would insure the commitment of the Kwantung Army in Manchuria when U.S. troops landed in Japan. From the Soviet point of view, however, it would be preferable to delay action until after the invasion of Kyushu, when troops might be removed from Manchuria to reenforce the Japanese islands.

Russia's contribution to the war effort was still expected to be primarily containing and defeating the Kwantung Army. Besides that the Soviets might develop a strategic air force capable of intensive air bombardment of Japan and perhaps interdict the lines of communication between Japan and the mainland of Asia. The United States probably would not be expected to commit U.S. forces in Siberia but could assist the Russians by delivering supplies to Siberia, establishing and maintaining sea and air routes to Siberia, maintaining the security of Kamchatka, creating a Soviet strategic air force, and permitting Soviet submarines and light naval craft to operate from the Aleutians. Again there was no way of knowing whether these measures were actually feasible and would be encouraged by the Russians. The JPS recommended initiating negotiations to find out as much as possible, including the sending of technical observers to the Kamchatka, Vladivostok, and Amur River areas. They also recommended delivery of the maximum possible amount of supplies to Russia and creation and training of a Soviet strategic air force.

In summary the JPS proposed a statement of principles basic to the whole policy toward Russia's entry into the war against Japan:

a. We desire Russian entry at the earliest possible date consistent with her ability to engage in offensive operations and are prepared to offer the maximum support possible without prejudice to our main effort against Japan.

b. We consider that the mission of Russian Far Eastern Forces should be to conduct an all-out offensive against Manchuria to force the commitment of Japanese forces and resources in North China and Manchuria that might otherwise be employed in the defense of Japan, to conduct intensive air operations against Japan proper and to interdict lines of communication between Japan and the mainland of Asia.

JCS 1176 was, said General Arnold as he approved it, "a basic paper limited to an expression of broad principles and policies."[15] While recognizing the difficulty and in some cases the impossibility of detailed planning without more information about Russia's intentions and capabilities, General Arnold urged that the planners prepare studies on various phases of Russian participation in the war, the securing of a passage through the Kurile Islands, for example, or the establishment of bases for strategic air operations from Kamchatka. With these in hand, he pointed out, it would be possible to negotiate with the Russians more realistically, telling at once what a specific project would entail. He also recommended that the planners work up a paper on U.S. views to be presented to the Russians at the next staff conference.

Admiral King's comments on JCS 1176 as he, too, approved it, set the planners to work studying the merits of an operation in the Kuriles.[16] Added incentive for such a study was given with the receipt from Admiral Nimitz of a summary of a plan, Keelblocks II, prepared by a joint staff representing various elements of the Pacific Ocean Areas and the North Pacific Area.[17]

Keelblocks II aimed to establish sea and air communications with the Soviet Maritime Provinces promptly upon the entry of Russia into the war against Japan. This would involve a two-phase operation: (1) the occupation of Kamchatka and installation of an air force there and establishment of light naval forces at Petropavlovsk and in the Gulf of Amur; (2) the occupation of southern Paramushiru. Admiral Nimitz sought approval of the outline for planning purposes and for preliminary preparations in order that Phase I could be executed without delay when the occasion offered.

Again the Joint Staff Planners were hampered by lack of information. Although the North Pacific was considered strategically important because it might be necessary to supply Russian forces over Pacific supply routes, they pointed out, it was not really known whether the necessity existed or would develop. They urged that Russia be pressed for information as to whether supplies would have to be carried in that way.

The occupation of Kamchatka seemed to the planners of doubtful suitability. It would depend on whether Russia could defend the area and whether the United States wished to stage and mount forces there for subsequent operations in the Kuriles. In comparison with other base areas already scheduled for development the planners thought Kamchatka least suitable, if for no other reason because it was so far from strategic targets in Japan.

Nor were the Joint Staff Planners enthusiastic about operations in the Kuriles. If they were undertaken before Russia entered the war they might lead Japan to close communication lines to Vladivostok and other ports or even declare war on Russia before the Soviets were ready. After the beginning of hostilities the Japanese could be expected to cut off communications with Vladivostok anyway. Since the other Siberian ports were open only from June to October, the planners pointed out, unless a Kurile Strait were opened during that period it would not be profitable. Climatic conditions would render operations in the Kuriles difficult and costly, and the Joint Staff Planners felt that those islands would not provide bases strategically superior to others already planned.

Although the planners concluded that operations in Kamchatka or the northern Kuriles would not be worth the cost, they acknowledged that available information was insufficient to make a final decision. Consequently they recommended trying to find out to what extent the Russians would be dependent upon a Pacific supply route, what help, if any, they would need for defending Kamchatka, and the potentialities of Kamchatka for basing ground, air, and light naval forces. Pending receipt of such information the JPS recommended that planning for a small operation in Kamchatka proceed and that no decision be made about operations in the northern Kuriles.[18] The Joint Chiefs of Staff approved their planners' recommendations, apparently without question.

All of the preceding studies contributed toward the preparation of a report completed by the Joint Staff Planners on 18 January 1945, partially in response to General Arnold's recommendation but specifically for surveying U.S. views prior to tripartite meetings scheduled for early February.[19]

Virtually no further information had been obtained from the Russians by mid-January than had been at hand in November. A special planning group that had been sent to Moscow to meet with a corresponding Soviet group had not yet succeeded in arranging even one conference. The Russians had approved the sending of a survey party to Kamchatka but had postponed and complicated plans for an actual visit to the area. One significant bit of information had been received, a negative one from General Antonov. He had informed General Deane that Soviet requirements would preclude the basing of any U.S. air or naval forces in the Maritime Provinces. This news came as a surprise, inasmuch as Marshal Stalin himself had agreed earlier that U.S. forces might operate from that area.[20]

In the new study the Joint Staff Planners reaffirmed the statement of basic principles from JCS 1176 in regard to Soviet entry into the war against Japan. They again recommended seeking the information requested in the study on the Kuriles and Kamchatka operations as well as any new factors from the Russian viewpoint as to the optimum timing for Soviet action or new concepts of Soviet operations against Japan. Although the JPS recommended attempting to ascertain the feasibility and necessity for undertaking the courses of action to support Russia that had been suggested in JCS 1176, the paper advised against wholesale commitments. The United States should, said the JPS:

> Indicate to the Russians that any operations by us to open sea routes to Sea of Okhotsk-Amur River ports will be extremely costly and at the expense of our own efforts toward Japan from the south; that because of limitation of means, the probability of amphibious operations in the North Pacific in 1945 is remote.
>
> ...Emphasize that if we are to conduct a difficult campaign to open a sea route of only limited capacity the U.S. and U.S.S.R. should insure that the use made of the route will be that which will bring about the earliest defeat of Japan.
>
> ...Indicate clearly that if a supply route is opened and maintained by the diversion of U.S. forces and resources, in order to gain full advantage of this effort, we expect Russian agreement to the basing of U.S. strategic air forces in eastern Siberia.

Accompanying the JPS report was a draft memorandum for the President, repeating the statement of basic principles, reporting the status of negotiations with the Russians on various military problems, and indicating the objectives the planners thought should be achieved at the coming conference. In view of later developments it is significant to note that these were primarily concerned with acquiring information for strategic planning. There was no question of negotiating to secure a Soviet declaration of war on Japan.

The Joint Chiefs of Staff approved the planners' paper, but subject to some amendments. Most important was the addition to the memorandum for the President of a recommendation that Marshal Stalin be asked to agree to provide adequate weather stations in Siberia and the Mongolian Plateau to furnish weather reports that would support future operations against the Japanese.[21]

This, then, was the report of the Joint Chiefs of Staff to the President as preparations for top level discussions with the

Russians were completed. In order to provide maximum assistance to the program scheduled for the Pacific it was necessary for Russia to enter the war against Japan "at as early a date as possible consistent with her ability to engage in offensive operations." The United States would support Soviet efforts to the maximum as long as they did not interfere with the main effort against Japan. Russia should make the greatest effort to defeat the Japanese in Manchuria, should conduct air operations against Japan proper in collaboration with U.S. air forces based in Siberia, and should interfere as much as possible with sea traffic between Japan and the Asiatic mainland.

It would be desirable to obtain information for planning from the Russians, said the Joint Chiefs: "a better estimate than we have received to date of the timing and planning of their operations"; the extent to which they would be dependent upon deliveries across the North Pacific; as much as possible about their distribution facilities for supplies; agreement in principle to the establishment of U.S. air forces in Siberia; the need for U.S. assistance to defend Kamchatka; what if any bases the Russians would need in the Aleutians; whether adequate weather stations could be provided in Eastern Siberia and the Mongolian Plateau. In addition the chiefs included a suggestion "that Marshal Stalin be asked that necessary administrative steps be taken to make collaboration between the U.S. and U.S.S.R. work more efficiently and more rapidly."

All of these, said the Joint Chiefs in conclusion, were matters for discussion "on the broadest basis." Details should be worked out by the two staffs. When the U.S. and USSR military chiefs met at Yalta in February 1945 the Joint Chiefs particularly sought information on the points outlined in this report.

Chapter XXIX

THE ARGONAUT CONFERENCE

The conference called Argonaut was in reality two conferences--an American-British conference held at Malta from 30 January to 2 February 1945 and a tripartite conference including Soviet representatives at Yalta from 4 to 11 February 1945. The first of these was almost entirely military. At the second the most significant discussions were political. The Joint Chiefs of Staff had little or nothing to do with those decisions made at Yalta which have since become highly controversial.[1]

In preparation for the meetings at Malta, on 9 January 1945 the British representatives in Washington sent the Joint Chiefs of Staff a tentative list of subjects for combined discussion.[2] For the most part they were general topics, including for the war against Japan: progress reports on operations in Southeast Asia Command and in the Pacific, further objectives in both areas, allocation of resources between Southeast Asia Command and China, and an estimate of the enemy situation.

The Joint War Plans Committee, looking over these suggestions, approved all except the progress reports. "No useful purpose is served in the presentation of progress reports by theater and area commanders at these conferences," said the JWPC, "particularly because the preparation of these reports places an unnecessary burden on the theater commanders." To the list proposed by the British the JWPC added an appreciation of the situation in China and a report on General Wedemeyer's future plans for the China Theater. They also recommended that the over-all objective, the strategic concept for the prosecution of the war, and basic supporting undertakings approved at Octagon be reaffirmed.[3]

The Joint Staff Planners and the Joint Chiefs of Staff in turn approved the JWPC recommendations. The Combined Chiefs were informed of the proposed changes on 15 January.[4]

In general the British approved the revised list of topics. They felt, however, that they could reaffirm the basic undertakings only on the understanding that it was "without prejudice to decisions which have yet to be taken as a result of the examination of the cargo shipping review." At their insistence upon its urgency, a study of the shipping problem was added to the list, even though it increased the number of people that would have to attend the meetings.[5]

The agenda finally agreed upon included four topics relating specifically to the war against Japan: strategy in Southeast Asia Command; allocation of resources between Southeast Asia Command and China; Pacific operations; and a planning date for the end of the war against Japan. A planning date for the end of the war against Germany was also included.[6] With the agenda established before the conference convened, one of the first items of business at the opening meeting at Malta was the adoption of a time schedule for considering each topic.[7]

SOUTHEAST ASIA

At Malta, as was customary, the Combined Chiefs of Staff first took up matters relating to the war against Germany. At the second meeting, on 31 January, they came to two papers related to the Southeast Asia Command. The first was a draft directive for Admiral Mountbatten, circulated by the British Chiefs of Staff. The other was a statement of U.S. views.[8]

The British proposed to set as the first object for the Southeast Asia Command the liberation of Burma at the earliest possible time. The next main task would be the liberation of Malaya and the opening of the Straits of Malacca. The Supreme Commander was to be told to aim at the accomplishment of the first objective with the forces already at his disposal. Although reenforcements might be sent from the European Theater he was not to plan on them.

Included among the forces currently in Southeast Asia Command were some U.S. troops and resources and some Chinese divisions which in the U.S. view should be available for use in China and could not necessarily be depended upon by Admiral Mountbatten for his operations. So the proposed directive raised again the question of authority to transfer forces from Southeast Asia Command.

The comment submitted by the U.S. Chiefs on the British draft directive was written by the Joint Staff Planners and was included in a study of JCS policy for the area that was intended to guide the Joint Chiefs in their combined discussions.[9] The primary interest of the United States in the Far East area, the JPS pointed out, was to continue aid to China on a scale such as to maintain and defend the air and land routes to China, insure the defense of the most important parts of China, notably Kunming and Chungking, and permit preparations for the Chinese to assume the offensive in the summer of 1945. This was consistent with General Wedemeyer's plans for the China Theater. However, he would need more forces than were then available, some from Southeast Asia Command and some from outside the theater. Insofar as practicable, the JPS concluded, his needs should be met, by withdrawing U.S. forces and resources and Chinese divisions from India and Burma as rapidly as they could be deployed in China.

In the memorandum presented to the CCS the Joint Chiefs of Staff summarized the view that the function of U.S. resources deployed in India-Burma was to provide direct or indirect support for China. When use of U.S. forces in Southeast Asia Command would not interfere with this primary object, Admiral Mountbatten would be permitted to employ them. The Joint Chiefs proposed that if any U.S. plans for removal of forces from Southeast Asia Command would, in the opinion of the British Chiefs of Staff, "jeopardize British forces engaged in approved operations in Burma, the transfer will be subject to discussion in the Combined Chiefs of Staff." Admiral Mountbatten, the U.S. Chiefs suggested, should be apprised of their policy lest he count too heavily upon having permanent use of U.S. and Chinese forces.

At the Argonaut meeting of 31 January General Marshall talked at length about the U.S. views and the situation in China-Burma-India.[10] The British were neither disposed to accept nor immediately inclined to reject the U.S. paper. After an inconclusive discussion the British Chiefs circulated a memorandum calling attention to the political and military importance of their stake in operations in Burma. They felt compelled, they said, "to reopen the question and to ask that no transfer of forces to the China theatre from the India-Burma theatre which is not acceptable to Supreme Allied Commander, Southeast Asia Command should be made without the agreement of the Combined Chiefs of Staff."[11]

The question at issue, as General Marshall pointed out at the JCS meeting the following day, was "whether the United States Chiefs of Staff can order transfers of resources when they do not jeopardize British forces engaged in approved operations in Burma or whether every transfer requires agreement by the Combined Chiefs of Staff as proposed by the British."[12] General Marshall thought the U.S. proposal amply covered the situation. He recommended that the U.S. Chiefs urge its acceptance. The JCS Secretary, Brigadier General A.J. McFarland, meanwhile, had received word that the British would withdraw their most recent comment if the U.S. Chiefs would delete the words, "British forces engaged in," making the removal of forces from Southeast Asia Command a matter for CCS discussion if it would "jeopardize approved operations in Burma." This elicited an immediate objection from Brigadier General G.A. Lincoln of the JPS, who pointed out that, whereas jeopardy to the forces engaged in an operation was easily established, the question of jeopardy of approved operations would be difficult to determine. There might be considerable and involved differences of opinion. General Lincoln suggested substituting "the" for the word "British."

The Joint Chiefs decided to stand by their original paper. At the CCS meeting later that day General Marshall presented General Lincoln's arguments against the British proposal. However, Sir Charles Portal pointed out that the British were simply asking for a discussion before a move was ordered that would jeopardize the success of an approved operation without the CCS being fully aware of the consequences of the transfer of forces. It was finally decided to approve the U.S. statement of policy, changing the last sentence to read:

Any transfer of forces engaged in approved operations in progress in Burma which is contemplated by the United States Chiefs of Staff and which, in the opinion of the British Chiefs of Staff, would jeopardize those operations, will be subject to discussion by the Combined Chiefs of Staff.[13]

The directive proposed by the British was sent to Admiral Mountbatten from Argonaut, together with the statement of U.S. policy, in order that he should be aware that U.S. and Chinese resources in Southeast Asia Command might be removed from his control and transferred to China.

THE WAR IN THE PACIFIC

Combined discussion at Malta of Pacific operations was limited to a detailed oral presentation by Admiral King and General Marshall and to circulation of a paper prepared by the JWPC summarizing U.S. plans.[14] The presentation made by the U.S. Chiefs at the CCS meeting on 1 February enlarged upon the JCS memorandum and explained the factors that determined the program laid out for the defeat of Japan.[15] The chiefs outlined plans to attack Iwo Jima in the Bonins on 19 February 1945 and Okinawa and other objectives in the Ryukyus from 1 April to August 1945 with the prospect of seizing a position in the Chusan-Ningpo area and invading Kyushu-Honshu in the winter of 1945-1946, depending upon the availability of forces redeployed from Europe. There was nothing controversial in the JCS report, and it was simply noted by the Combined Chiefs of Staff.

This was the last CCS discussion of the war against Japan at Malta, and indeed during the entire Argonaut Conference. However, when the CCS presented a preliminary report to the President and Prime Minister on 2 February Mr. Churchill went at some length into the question of what was to be done in the Far East and in particular what the British contribution would be.[16]

"The main object of the operations to clear the enemy from Burma," said Mr. Churchill, "was to liberate the important army engaged there for further operations against Japan." He wondered whether the combined staffs had decided what these further operations should be. The Prime Minister suggested that small detachments might be able to go to Java or Sumatra and liberate those countries. With some feeling, however, he remarked that he wanted British forces "to go where a good opportunity would be presented of heavy fighting with the Japanese, particularly in the air, as this was the only way which the British had been able to discover of helping the main American operations in the Pacific." Actually there had been no CCS decision on such operations, and Sir Alan Brooke told the Prime Minister that the chiefs were waiting to see Admiral Mountbatten's plans before making any.

It is apparent from the minutes that Mr. Churchill was not satisfied with the small part the British forces in the Far East seemed scheduled to play in the final phase of the war. American and British operations appeared to be diverging, with U.S. effort going on into China and British effort turning south. The Prime Minister inquired whether there had been any thought of moving British or Indian divisions to China. Such a possibility had not been considered, at least not by the CCS. As Sir Alan Brooke pointed out, there were no facilities in China to support British troops. His comment was seconded by General Marshall and Admiral Leahy, but the Prime Minister made it quite clear that if the Americans decided they wanted British troops in China he would certainly be prepared to consider sending them.

The President and the Prime Minister approved the schedule for operations in the Pacific that the U.S. Chiefs had presented to the CCS. In accepting the final report of the Combined Chiefs, which incorporated this program, Mr. Churchill made one significant suggestion: that the United States, the British Empire, Russia, and China issue an "ultimatum calling upon Japan to surrender unconditionally, or else be subjected to the overwhelming weight of all the forces of the four powers."[17] This was not a matter for military discussion, although the suggestion was made at the final plenary session of the combined staffs at Yalta. On the other hand, adoption of such a course would have a considerable effect upon future military operations against Japan. However, Mr. Roosevelt was not enthusiastic about the idea, and no action was taken. Military planners continued to assume that the Japanese probably would not surrender until the island of Honshu had been invaded.

PREPARATIONS FOR THE YALTA CONFERENCE

At the same time an agenda was being developed for the CCS meetings to be held at Malta, a second list of topics was being prepared for discussion with the Soviet military leaders at the tripartite meetings that would follow at Yalta. On 11 January the Joint War Plans Committee presented the Joint Staff Planners with a proposed list. Its major emphasis was on coordinating effort in the war against Germany and preparing to establish military occupation following Germany's defeat. The planners also proposed an exchange of information about enemy dispositions and intentions in the Far East and a discussion of Russian participation in the war against Japan. Whether the U.S. Chiefs or their representatives would meet with the Soviet military leaders without the British in attendance was not known. Should such meetings occur, the JWPC proposed that the questions pertaining to the Japanese war and to shuttle bombing in Europe serve as an agenda.[18]

Before forwarding the JWPC report to the Joint Chiefs of Staff, the Joint Staff Planners enlarged upon the subjects that would probably call for discussion in respect to Soviet collaboration in the Far East. These would include, for example, the use of Kamchatka as a base, the development of a Soviet strategic air force, the installation of both Soviet and U.S. strategic air forces in Kamchatka and eastern Siberia, and Russia's specific need to have supplies transported across the North Pacific.[19]

With JCS approval this proposed list of subjects for discussion with the Russians was sent to the British Chiefs of Staff and to General Deane in Moscow for presentation to the Chief of the Soviet General Staff.[20] The British approved, but no comment came from Moscow.[21] How many military meetings would be held, who would participate, and what subjects would be discussed were not decided until the staffs assembled at Yalta.

THE DISCUSSIONS AT YALTA

The Yalta Conference was primarily a meeting of the heads of state of the United States, Great Britain, and the USSR. Consequently the most important discussions were political. The Joint Chiefs of Staff did not participate in the political meetings and were neither consulted beforehand nor informed afterward of what had taken place. There were, however, several meetings attended only by the military staffs.

Two main problems concerning the war against Japan were discussed at Yalta. The first was the conditions under which Russia would enter the war in the Far East. The second concerned practical details of Soviet participation. The former was entirely a matter for discussion between the heads of state. The latter was primarily a matter for discussion by the military staffs.

Long before the meetings at Yalta it was well established that the Soviet Union would enter the war against Japan after the defeat of Germany. At Teheran in November 1943 Marshal Stalin had announced eventual Soviet participation and had spoken of the Russian desire for a warm water port in the Far East. Subsequently, in conversation with Ambassador Harriman and General Deane he had mentioned "political aspects of Russia's participation."[22] The first clear indication of what political aspects Marshal Stalin had in mind was given to Mr. Harriman in December 1944. As he recorded it later, the ambassador was told by Marshal Stalin:

> Russia's position in the East should be generally reestablished as it existed before the Russo-Japanese War in 1905. The lower half of Sakhalin should be returned to the Russians, as well as the Kurile Islands, in order to protect Soviet outlets to the Pacific. The Russians wished again to lease the ports of Dairen and Port Arthur and to obtain a lease on those railroads in Manchuria built by the Russians under contract with the Chinese, specifically, the Chinese Eastern Railway, which was the direct line from the Trans-Siberian Railroad through the Vladivostok, and the South Manchurian Railroad making a connection to Dairen. He stated that the Soviet Union would not intereferee [sic] with the sovereignty of China over Manchuria. In addition Stalin asked for the recognition of the status quo in Outer Mongolia.

Mr. Harriman reported the Soviet proposals to the President, but the Joint Chiefs of Staff were not informed of them.[23] It was not until a meeting of the JCS with President Roosevelt, Secretary of State Edward R. Stettinius, and Ambassador Harriman at Yalta on 4 February 1945 that the chiefs were told that Marshal Stalin would probably raise the question of what the Russians would get out of the war in the Far East. This was not a military matter. The Joint Chiefs of Staff had already told the President that Soviet participation was much to be desired. The minutes do not indicate any discussion of whether concessions should be made to secure that participation, and decision was not within the responsibility of the JCS.[24]

The first tripartite plenary meeting at Yalta was convened on 4 February 1945 at 1700. Thereafter followed a series of smaller meetings, most of them dealing with political problems concerning the war in Europe and postwar cooperation. It was not until the afternoon of 8 February that Marshal Stalin announced at a meeting with President Roosevelt, Mr. Harriman, and Mr. Molotov and two interpreters "that he would like to discuss the political conditions under which the USSR would enter the war against Japan." Thereupon he presented the same points he had made to Mr. Harriman, explaining that if these conditions were not met he and Mr. Molotov would find it hard to explain to the Soviet people why Russia was going to war with Japan.

There was not much discussion of the Russian proposals. Mr. Roosevelt concerned himself chiefly with how they could be arranged, suggesting that Dairen not be leased outright from the Chinese but be made a free port under some sort of international commission. He also made a similar suggestion about the use of the Manchurian railways. At Marshal Stalin's insistence that there should be a written agreement Mr. Harriman met with Mr. Molotov on 10 February and was given a proposed draft. He made some suggestions at the time, and the statement was further revised later in the day through conversation between President Roosevelt and Marshal Stalin. On 11 February the agreement was signed by Prime Minister Churchill as well as by the two other heads of state.[25] The Joint Chiefs of Staff were not told of it at the time.

While the political discussions were going on the military staffs of the three nations had been holding separate meetings. There were two tripartite military sessions, one on 5 February, the other the following day. After discussion of the war against Germany the American Chiefs summarized U.S. plans for future operations against Japan, answering a few questions interposed by the Russians. Any question of Russian plans for the Far East was turned off with the comment, "It would be more convenient to discuss questions concerning the Far East after this matter had been considered by the Heads of State."

In hopes of eventual U.S.-Soviet staff talks the Joint Chiefs of Staff had developed a list of the questions for which they were particularly seeking answers. The Joint Staff Planners and General Deane both prepared such lists, seeking much of the same information, most of which had repeatedly been asked for during the preceding year.[26] Two problems the Joint Chiefs of Staff considered of paramount importance and sent to the President with the recommendation that he seek answers directly from Marshal Stalin. They were:

    a. Once a war breaks out between Russia and Japan, is it essential to you that a supply line be kept open across the Pacific to Eastern Siberia?
    b. Will you assure us that United States air forces will be permitted to base in the KOMSOMOLSK-NIKOLAEVSK or some more suitable area providing developments show that these air forces can be operated and supplied without jeopardizing Russian operations?[27]

Mr. Roosevelt duly forwarded the questions to the Soviet leader, but he received no reply. Subsequently Marshal Stalin told the President "that he recognized the importance of these supply routes and...that he had no objection to the establishment of American bases in the Maritime provinces."[28]

On 8 February the U.S. Chiefs finally met with the Soviet military leaders to discuss Soviet participation against Japan. The four U.S. Chiefs were unaccompanied by secretary or interpreter. Three secretaries and a naval aide attended with the three representatives of the Soviet Union.[29]

The Joint Chiefs had decided, before going to the meeting, to present General Deane's list of questions and some from the list prepared by the Joint Staff Planners.[30] Accordingly, Admiral Leahy opened the discussion by reading ten questions for which the U.S. Chiefs sought answers. Soviet comments followed, but although General Antonov's replies were helpful he made it quite clear "that his comments represented his own personal opinion and views and further that he would refer the questions to Marshal Stalin the same day and would arrange to provide complete and authoritative answers as quickly as possible."[31]

On the afternoon of 9 February the U.S. Chiefs, except for Admiral Leahy, met again with the Russians. Having discussed all the questions with Marshal Stalin, General Antonov was prepared with official answers as follows:

    Q. Have there been any changes in Soviet projected plans of operations in the Far East from those described to Mr. Harriman and General Deane in October?
    A. None, except that troops on the European front were being delayed in departure for the Far East.
    Q. Will the Soviets require a Pacific supply route after Soviet-Japanese hostilities start?
    A. Yes, particularly for food and petroleum products.
    Q. Will agreement be given for operation of U.S. air forces in the Komsomolsk-Nikolaevsk area?

A. Yes. Reconnaissance can now be made.
Q. Will U.S. forces be required for defense of Kamchatka?
A. "U.S. assistance will be very useful."
Q. Will the Soviets make pre-hostility preparations including construction and reception and storage of U.S. stockpiles in Kamchatka and Eastern Siberia?
A. When requirements are determined preparations will be made by the Soviets. Material assistance from the United States may be needed.
Q. Can the Kamchatka survey party depart from Fairbanks by 15 February 1945?
A. For security the Kamchatka survey would have to be delayed until the last moment.
Q. Will the Soviets occupy southern Sakhalin and when? If so, will they cover passage of LaPerouse Strait?
A. This will be one of the first operations. LaPerouse Strait will be covered.
Q. Will combined planning in Moscow be vigorously pursued?
A. Yes. "We shall fulfill on our side the plan which was made."
Q. How would weather and the season of the year affect beginning operations in Eastern Siberia?
A. For ground forces September. October, November are most favorable. For sea forces, July, August, September.
Q. Can weather information from more stations in Eastern Siberia be made available to the United States?
A. Yes.

The discussion of these questions and answers was followed by an exchange by General Kuter and Marshal of Aviation Khudyakov of information about air matters, particularly the basing of U.S. air units in Siberia.

This was the end of the participation of the Joint Chiefs of Staff in the conference at Yalta. Together with the British Chiefs they had already submitted the final report of CCS accomplishments to the President and Prime Minister that morning.[32] In the next day or two the chiefs departed in various directions.

From the military point of view the accomplishments of the meetings at Yalta were not of major significance. To be sure, information that had long been sought was finally obtained. There was another assurance that combined planning could proceed. But for the most part the answers were general and there were no written military agreements. As long as the date of Germany's surrender and hence of Russia's entry into the war in the Far East remained unknown, planning for cooperation in military operations would have to proceed on assumptions and uncertainties.

Chapter XXX

ARGONAUT TO TERMINAL

The two best-remembered events of the spring of 1945, the death of President Roosevelt on 12 April and the surrender of Germany on 8 May, did not have a profound effect upon strategic planning for the war still to be won against Japan. The end of the war in Europe meant that forces from that theater could be transferred to the Pacific to assist in the final operations of the long campaign. Target dates that had previously been based upon an estimated date for the German surrender could now be calculated upon a fixed basis. The change of presidents meant only the instruction of a new man in a course already for the most part laid out.

In the short period between the conference at Yalta and the final wartime meetings at Potsdam in July, two major objectives in the Pacific were seized, first Iwo Jima, then Okinawa. The Joint Chiefs of Staff and their committees were working on plans for the final phase of the war, on the redeployment of forces from Europe to participate in it, on the question of what operations might be expected most speedily to induce Japanese surrender, and on the knotty problem of command arrangements. The JCS devoted much time and thought also to planning for the cessation of hostilities and the numerous postwar readjustments in the Pacific areas, adjustments very different from those already being made in the European Theater. Other portions of the History of the Joint Chiefs of Staff will discuss postwar planning in detail. This and the succeeding chapters of this volume will concentrate upon the final phases of strategic planning for Japan's defeat.

REORGANIZATION OF COMMANDS IN THE PACIFIC

Although no directive for the invasion of the Japanese home islands had been agreed upon at the beginning of 1945, the progress of the campaign in the Pacific had reached a point where it was apparent that some readjustment in the command arrangements would have to be made. The Japanese archipelago lay within the original Pacific Ocean Areas under Admiral Nimitz's command. Invasion of those islands, however, would involved a major land campaign and would require large forces from the Southwest Pacific Area. The continued existence of the two areas seemed anomalous when the bulk of the forces assigned to both would be concentrated in a single final action.

Responsible officers in both the Army and the Navy recognized that some change in the command setup in the Pacific was desirable, but it was the Army that felt more strongly. There was intense opposition to permitting the land battles anticipated on Kyushu and Honshu to be waged under an over-all naval command. Moreover, with the occupation of Luzon General MacArthur's forces would have reached the northernmost limits of the original Southwest Pacific Area. He would either have to be given authority beyond those limits or turn his attention to mopping up operations and minor actions in the Netherlands East Indies with those forces not required for the invasion of Kyushu. It seemed more profitable to focus upon the main axis of advance and avoid any possibility of becoming involved in side operations that would not contribute significantly to Japan's collapse.

Both at General MacArthur's headquarters and in Washington in the summer and fall of 1944 wide acceptance was being given to the idea of consolidating all Army forces in the entire Pacific Theater under a single commander. Naval forces would be similarly consolidated, actually a minor adjustment since Admiral Nimitz in his role of Commander in Chief, Pacific Fleet, had some degree of control of all naval forces in the Pacific. However, although Army planners in the War Department worked over the idea with a view to presenting a paper for joint consideration, it was never completed.[1] A suggestion of the Joint War Plans Committee, possibly Army-inspired, in August that the Joint Strategic Survey Committee study the boundaries within the Pacific Theater with the idea of forming a single forward area and appointing a Supreme Commander for Pacific operations made no progress either, for the Joint Staff Planners were unwilling to pursue the matter.[2]

The first recorded discussion by the Joint Chiefs themselves of the matter of command came in September 1944 in connection with the problem of whether Luzon or Formosa was to be taken first. At that time General Marshall recommended that all Army forces in the Pacific should be combined under a single commander, with a view to minimizing shortages and assuring the most effective use of available resources. He proposed that "all Army resources in the Pacific be made available to CINCSWPA, except those essential for Pacific Ocean Areas defense and logistical requirements," and that General MacArthur be directed "to occupy Luzon on 20 December and make plans and preparations to occupy Formosa as soon as possible thereafter."[3]

Admiral King objected to this proposal primarily because it would give the Army responsibility for the Formosa operation, which he conceived as part of the Navy's responsibility for achieving control of the sea lanes to the coast of China. He recommended in turn that, if there were to be unification of command "with a view to attaining maximum flexibility of employment of resources," both areas of the Pacific Theater should be put under the command of CINCPOA.[4]

At the time the Joint Chiefs of Staff did not discuss the problem any further. The choice between Luzon and Formosa was enough for one time. With the issue of a directive to General MacArthur to seize Luzon and to Admiral Nimitz to move into the Bonins and Ryukyus that problem was solved, and the question of command beyond that was set aside.

As the Leyte occupation was nearing completion and successful landings were being made on Mindoro in mid-December, General MacArthur sent to General Marshall "as a matter of the most immediate and gravest urgency" his "views and recommendations with regard to the command structure." With large-scale land operations in the offing, he said, "we are so handicapped by the artificial area boundaries and command that the ultimate success of the war against Japan is in gravest jeopardy." The solution he proposed was to place all of the naval forces under a single commander and all of the Army forces under a single commander under the direction of the Joint Chiefs of Staff. They would appoint the commander for a specific operation in accordance with the principle of paramount interest.[5]

When General Marshall told him that the Army planners were working upon a similar proposal to present to the Joint Chiefs of Staff, General MacArthur responded with a stronger plea.[6] "Disaster is as certain under the present nebulous and faulty command structure with completely non strategic area boundaries as anything that can be predicted for future military operations," he said. He considered the problem of command "perhaps the gravest issue in the Pacific." Most strongly he urged "that if necessary the whole issue be placed before The President so that the responsibility for what may happen may not rest upon the Army."

Despite General MacArthur's plea for prompt action General Marshall made no formal presentation of the command problem to the Joint Chiefs of Staff. For one reason or another the time did not seem quite right. The German offensive in the Ardennes was making unexpected demands for forces that had been scheduled to go to the Pacific, and the possibility seemed real that the timetable for Japan's defeat would have to be lengthened. Another factor tending to postpone discussion of command changes was the tripartite conference being planned for the beginning of February. If this should result in a decision for prompt Soviet entry into the war against Japan it would change the entire strategic picture in the Far East.

Although General Marshall did not raise the question of rearranging commands, in connection with another problem he did make a suggestion to the JCS which appears to have been intended as an entering wedge for the establishment of a unified command of all Army forces. Commenting on a JPS report on redeployment from the European Theater to the Pacific, General Marshall accepted its recommendations with the understanding that General MacArthur would be responsible for the troop basis planning for Army forces in all Pacific areas, collaborating as necessary with Admiral Nimitz and the Twentieth Air Force.[7]

Admiral King objected to this restriction, arguing that General MacArthur had not been assigned responsibility for accomplishing any objectives outside the Southwest Pacific Area. Admiral King would not agree to any theater or area commander's doing troop basis planning for any theater or area for which he had no responsibility. He in turn suggested setting up a planning command for the invasion of Japan or the landings on the China coast. Like the command that had been organized well in advance of the Normandy invasion this would include a real joint staff and represent all the land, sea, and air forces involved.

General Marshall's reply was that troop basis planning was an administrative function of the War Department and he had mentioned General MacArthur's part in it solely for information. He made no comment on Admiral King's suggestion for a planning command. Thus again the problem was touched upon and dropped.[8]

Shortly after this exchange some interest in the command problem was aroused in the Navy Department by the receipt of Admiral Nimitz's views. He recommended that the Pacific Ocean Areas, exclusive of Japan, should constitute a single theater under unified command. "When land operations involving large armies are undertaken in Japan," Admiral Nimitz proposed, "the land area of Japan should constitute a new theater with a theater commander responsible direct to the Joint Chiefs of Staff." CINCPOA would command the amphibious phase of the operations.[9]

This proposal struck a responsive chord in the Navy's War Plans Division, where it was further suggested that the Philippines be included in the Pacific Ocean Areas, since they would form the main base for support of the invasion of Japan. Although it was recommended that Admiral King submit Admiral Nimitz's proposal to the JCS, however, no presentation was made.[10]

On 26 February 1945 General Marshall finally put the question of a change in the command structure in the Pacific squarely before the Joint Chiefs of Staff. He made the recommendation by then widely advocated in the Army, that all Army forces in the Pacific Theater be placed under a single Army commander and all naval forces under a single Navy commander, each to "plan and conduct his own service's part in the Pacific war," under JCS direction. The Joint Chiefs would continue to prescribe the command for major operations.[11]

General Marshall's proposal brought forth a more far-reaching one from General Giles, who was substituting for General Arnold. He recommended "that the command organization best adapted to the tempo and strategy of the Pacific operation is one which provides for a Supreme Commander for the war against Japan and which places under his complete and direct control, on a coordinate and co-equal basis, the land, sea and air forces involved in that war." Should this prove impracticable, however, and the system proposed by General Marshall be accepted, General Giles recommended that it be with the stipulation that the Twentieth Air Force would continue to operate under the Joint Chiefs of Staff.[12]

The following week Admiral King went to the West Coast for a conference with Admiral Nimitz, who confirmed his view of the importance of operations on the coast of China.[13] Upon his return he presented the JCS with a summary of his ideas on command.[14]

Basing his proposals on the principle that command questions could not be divorced from the operations to be carried out, Admiral King recommended that the Commander in Chief, Pacific Ocean Areas, be assigned the following tasks:

(1) Complete the occupation of such positions in the Ryukyus as are essential to the success of subsequent operations.

(2) Occupy positions in the Chusan Archipelago and the eastern portion of the Ningpo Peninsula with a target date of 20 August, 1945.

(3) Make plans and preparations for operations to keep open a sea route to La Perouse Strait, including the seizure of Matsuwa if required, with a target date of 15 September, 1945.

(4) Make plans for the occupation of a position in the Shantung Peninsula following the occupation of the Chusan-Ningpo positions.

(5) Provide naval cover and support for the operations of the Southwest Pacific Area.

For the Commander in Chief, Southwest Pacific Area, Admiral King proposed:

(1) Complete the occupation of Luzon and only such other positions in the Philippines as are essential to the accomplishment of the overall objective in the war against Japan.

(2) Occupy North Borneo, including Brunei Bay, using Australian combat and service troops. Units of the British Pacific fleet will be allocated for this operation.

(3) Provide support for the operations of the Pacific Ocean Areas....

(4) Establish bases in Luzon to support further advances for the accomplishment of the over-all objective in the war against Japan.

(5) Make available to CINCPOA for use in the operations directed...above, a corps of three divisions complete with service and supporting troops,...to be ready for mounting one each in May, June, and July, or later as required by CINCPOA.

To provide for the ultimate invasion of Japan, Admiral King proposed establishment of a Japan Area (JAPA), bounded by the shoreline perimeter of Kyushu, Shikoku, Honshu, Hokkaido, and other islands included therein. The Commander in Chief, Japan Area, would have administrative responsibility for all Army forces in the Pacific, with the title, Commanding General, Army Force, Pacific Theater. He would:

(1) Provide Army forces for the operations directed to be

conducted by CINCPOA and CINCSWPA, and, consistent therewith, make preparations for the invasion of Japan.

(2) Prepare plans for the land campaign in Japan. Cooperate with CINCPOA in the preparation of plans for the naval and amphibious phases of the invasion of Japan.

Discussing these proposals at a closed session of the JCS on 8 March, General Marshall objected in several respects. In the first place, he thought CINCJAPA should have command of the land areas to the south, in order to coordinate resources and the operation of land-based air. In the second place, General Marshall was not at all convinced of the necessity or the desirability of undertaking an operation in Chusan before attacking Kyushu. He thought that, except for service forces, there were enough resources in the Pacific Theater to carry out a successful landing on Kyushu without waiting for transfers from the European Theater. Chusan, he feared, might prove to be a drain on the resources for the invasion of Japan, and he recommended that no commitment be made until 1 May, when scheduled operations would have progressed farther. Finally, General Marshall did not believe that Admiral King's proposed command arrangement would solve the problem of allocation of resources, especially of service troops.

General Marshall offered instead a draft directive incorporating the Army views. It provided for designation of General MacArthur and Admiral Nimitz as Commander in Chief, Army and Naval Forces respectively, for the entire Pacific Area. Cooperating closely, they were to "conduct operations in the Pacific Area aimed at attainment of the over-all objective," the former with responsibility for functions normally pertaining to land operations, the latter for those pertaining to sea operations. General Marshall included also a directive for the Commander in Chief, Pacific Ocean Areas, and for the Commander in Chief, Southwest Pacific Area, with tasks differing from those proposed by Admiral King primarily in the restriction of Admiral Nimitz to planning instead of preparation for such operations as the seizing of positions in the Chusan Peninsula. A significant substitution was made also for paragraph (5) of General MacArthur's tasks:

> Prepare plans and make preparations for the campaign against the mainland of Japan. Cooperate with CINCPOA in the preparation of plans for the naval and amphibious phases of the invasion of Japan.

Following the JCS discussion Admiral King drafted a new directive, attempting to cover the important points that had been raised. This, together with the other drafts and a summary of General Marshall's comments at the JCS meeting, was turned over to the Joint Staff Planners "for study and report."

Once a day for the next week the Joint Staff Planners met and discussed various phases of the problem of command in the Pacific.[15] The talk was confined almost entirely to Admiral Duncan and General Lincoln, representing respectively the Navy and Army viewpoints. Apparently they did not interpret their directive to "study and report" as meaning to reach agreement, for, although they talked at considerable length and discussed every point in the draft directives, at the end of the week their chief accomplishment was to narrow down and more clearly define the area of disagreement.

On 16 March the Joint Staff Planners submitted to the Joint Chiefs of Staff two draft directives, one a revision of that introduced by Admiral King, the other a revision of General Marshall's.[16] Explaining that the committee did not consider that it could resolve the basic difference between the two, the JPS described the disagreement thus:

> ...The Navy proposal continues the emphasis on area command, control and responsibility for operations under the principle of unified command, creates a third area in the Pacific, and leaves Commanders in Chief of the Army forces and the Navy forces in a role which is primarily administrative and logistical. The Army proposal places emphasis, including command responsibility for operations (to be undertaken under the principle of unified command), on the role of the Commanders in Chief of the Army forces and Navy forces respectively and while retaining for the present the two area commands, concentrates most of the command and control of forces and operations in two commanders.

The differences that the Joint Staff Planners had been unable to resolve were not easily resolved by the Joint Chiefs of Staff either. General Marshall remained intent on avoiding naval command of the invasion of Japan and insistent that all Army forces in the Pacific should be under a single command. Admiral King was apprehensive that the Army system would result in removing control of the Ryukyus campaign and any operations in China from the Commander in Chief, Pacific Ocean Areas. He continued to argue for an area command for the Japanese invasion, controlling base defense, allocation, shipping, supplies, and other logistic matters as well as the operations themselves. When there seemed no immediate prospect of reconciling the two views, Admiral King recommended that at least directives such as he had proposed for current and future operations should be sent to the theater commanders.[17] However, this suggestion was not accepted.

During the days that followed, Army and Navy planners as well as the chiefs themselves continued to discuss the problem in all its aspects. The Army planners rejected the Navy's idea of issuing a directive for the operations and settling the problem of command and control at a later time. Papers were exchanged and many discussions held as the planners gradually evolved a solution. Finally, on 3 April, two days after landings were made on Okinawa, agreement on a directive was reached.[18]

It was basically the Army proposal that was adopted. The directive called for two force commanders, with the Supreme Commander, Southwest Pacific Area, also designated Commander in Chief, U.S. Army Forces, Pacific, and the Commander in Chief, U.S. Pacific Fleet and Pacific Ocean Areas, in his first capacity assigned command of all naval forces. The Joint Chiefs of Staff were to issue operational directives, assigning missions and command responsibility for major operations and campaigns. Normally CINCAFPAC would be charged with responsibility for land campaigns and CINCPAC for sea campaigns. Admiral King's fear that Admiral Nimitz would be removed from control of the Ryukyus operation was calmed by inclusion of a provision that the two theater commanders would continue to command forces of the other services currently allocated to them until they passed to other commands by mutual agreement or by JCS direction.

The operational directive approved by the chiefs on the same day charged Admiral Nimitz with: completing operations in the Ryukyus in accordance with his current directive; continuing "such operations for securing and maintaining control of the sea communications to and in the Western Pacific as are required for the accomplishment of the over-all objective"; continuing planning for taking positions in the Chusan Archipelago and the Ningpo Peninsula, limiting assembly of special equipment so as not to jeopardize preparations for the invasion of Japan; making plans to keep open a sea route to La Perouse Strait; providing forces and supporting operations in the Philippines under General MacArthur; planning and preparing "for the naval and amphibious phases of the invasion of Japan" in cooperation with CINCAFPAC. General MacArthur was to "complete the occupation of Luzon and conduct such additional operations in the Philippines as required for the accomplishment of the over-all objective in the war against Japan"; make plans to occupy North Borneo using Australian troops; provide forces and support for the Ryukyus operations; plan and prepare for the land campaign in Japan, cooperating with CINCPAC.

According to this directive the Twentieth Air Force was to remain under General Arnold's command and he was to cooperate with both theater commanders in preparations for the invasion. General Arnold, however, was not satisfied with the existing arrangement of the Twentieth Air Force or with the several air commands in the Pacific. By late spring of 1945 there were already 800 B-29's in the Pacific Theater, commanded from Washington, but dependent upon the theater or area commanders for logistical and administrative support. The time seemed to have come to transfer the command and operational control from Washington to the Pacific and to form a single command of all strategic bombing that would smooth out some of the complicated relations with Army and naval commands in the area. Consequently General Arnold recommended establishment of a U.S. Army Strategic Air Force (USASTAF) built initially around the Twentieth Air Force and its supporting elements plus any others the Pacific commanders or the Joint Chiefs of Staff prescribed. The new organization would follow the pattern developed in the European Theater, and General Arnold recommended that General Carl Spaatz be put in command.[19]

As proposed by General Arnold, the USASTAF would be independent of CINCPAC and CINCAFPAC, would cooperate with them, and would have equal representation with them on agencies concerned with the allocation of shipping space. This complete operational independence brought forth an objection from Admiral Leahy. He promptly commented that he thought it essential in the interests of efficiency that operational control of USASTAF be placed directly under CINCAFPAC, who was responsible for the end results.[20]

After discussion at a JCS luncheon meeting on 29 May 1945 General Arnold withdrew his original proposal and offered a revised draft directive that instead of setting up a new organization transferred the Headquarters, Twentieth Air Force, to the Pacific and changed its name to USASTAF. Under USASTAF were to be the XX Bomber Command, redesignated the Eighth Air Force, and the XXI Bomber Command, redesignated the Twentieth Air Force. USASTAF planes were to be available in an emergency to CINCAFPAC or CINCPAC upon request. "This arrangement," the directive read, "will enable COM GEN USASTAF to present to CINCAFPAC and CINCPAC his requirements so that adjustments necessary to meet changing conditions will whenever possible be made in the Pacific."[21]

Upon recommendation of Admiral King, before issuing a directive to the theater commanders the Joint Chiefs of Staff asked for comments from General MacArthur and Admiral Nimitz.[22] The latter approved, but General MacArthur had reservations. The Pacific was limited, he pointed out, in the areas where planes could be deployed and in the targets for those places to hit. Under the proposed setup there would be working within the area the Far East Air Force, the Strategic Air Force, Navy land-based air forces and carrier-based air forces. General MacArthur urged that the efforts of all land-based planes be coordinated by placing them under the general control of a single commander who would presumably be under him.[23]

General Arnold felt that the presence in the theater of General Spaatz as commander of USASTAF would help to smooth out problems and ease the difficulties General MacArthur feared. Admiral King, however, was of the opinion that something should be done in response to General MacArthur's comments. He did not propose to put all land-based air forces under a single command. Instead he recommended that, since theater plans for the invasion of Japan had been based upon the existing arrangement of the Twentieth Air Force, title and all current directives be retained and the command simply transferred to the theater. In effect there would be no change.[24]

General Arnold was on an inspection tour of the Pacific Theater for most of the month of June. He returned more strongly convinced than ever that there should be a single strategic air command. At a JCS meeting on 2 July he obtained agreement on a new version of the directive, which was finally approved and sent a week later. It provided for establishment of USASTAF very much in the form General Arnold had originally advocated, including combat and service units of the Twentieth and Eighth Air Forces and other elements agreed upon by the theater commanders or the JCS. Its commander was "charged with the primary responsibility for the conduct of land-based strategic air operations against Japan with the object of accomplishing the progressive destruction and dislocation of Japan's military, industrial and economic systems to a point where her capacity for armed resistance is fatally weakened." He was to be independent of the other commands in the Pacific, but he was to cooperate with them and they were to meet his logistic requirements. The Joint Chiefs of Staff, through General Arnold, would continue to issue directives to the new command.[25]

The establishment of USASTAF completed the rearrangements of U.S. commands in the Pacific Theater. Simultaneously, however, negotiations had been under way with the British to effect a change in the Southwest Pacific Area.

THE FUTURE OF THE SOUTHWEST PACIFIC AREA

The campaign that had led to the invasion of Luzon and was oriented northward toward Japan itself had resulted in the bypassing of the largest portions of the Netherlands East Indies. Although rich in resources for war, notably oil, rubber, and manganese, strategically the islands were of minor importance in the pattern set for the defeat of Japan. The Japanese depended upon them for vital supplies; but U.S. forces did not need them sufficiently to warrant diverting resources to occupy any of the islands.

At the beginning of February 1945, as the end of the major campaign in the Philippines came in sight, General MacArthur began to think of the desirability of seizing Borneo and acquiring its oil for use in the attack on Kyushu and Honshu. To the Joint Chiefs of Staff, then at Yalta, he reported that he was planning amphibious operations into Borneo that would be launched about 1 April 1945, using Australian troops. Staging the forces in the area of Hollandia-Morotai would require more shipping than was currently assigned to the Southwest Pacific Area, and General MacArthur sought JCS permission to retain forty-eight Liberty ships and ten trans-Pacific troop ships for it. The operation itself would take more, but how much had not been determined.[26]

General MacArthur's request arrived at a time when American and British shipping experts were searching for cargo vessels to fill the major commitments. Consequently, although the JCS looked with favor upon the use of Australian troops rather than American for mopping up the Netherlands East Indies, they considered the prospect of getting appreciable supplies of oil from Borneo too slight to warrant providing cargo shipping from the limited world supply. With JCS approval General Marshall refused General MacArthur's request, asking him to consider what could be done with what he had and perhaps a little more at some time in the future.[27] General Marshall suggested taking the island of Hainan, west of Luzon, off the coast of Indochina. Control of Hainan, he pointed out, would close off the China Sea, provide direct air communications to China, and allow air control of the Japanese land routes through South China.

In response to General Marshall's message General MacArthur reported his plans for the completion of operations within the Southwest Pacific Area. He was firmly opposed to trying to take Hainan, for, he said, it "would not produce strategic benefits that would be commensurate with the means required nor the risks involved." His idea was to clear out the Philippine Islands with U.S. forces, concluding with the occupation of Mindanao about 12 April. On 18 May Australian forces would start the reconquest of the Netherlands East Indies by seizing Balikpapan, then occupying an area of southern Borneo in order to install fighter aircraft. About 27 June they would move directly to the Batavia area to reconstitute the Dutch government of the NEI.[28]

Once again General MacArthur tried to convince the Joint Chiefs of Staff of the political importance of a campaign he wished to undertake. Under the international agreement that established the Southwest Pacific Area, he said, the United States was obligated to free the Netherlands East Indies. "To eliminate consideration of the Netherlands East Indies after freeing Australian and United States territories and reestablishing governments therein would be invidious and would represent a failure on the part of the United States to keep faith." Moreover, "the reestablishment of the Netherlands East Indies Government in Batavia would bring about the most favorable repercussions throughout the Far East and would raise the prestige of the United States to the highest level with results that would be felt for a great many years." As a final argument, General MacArthur reported that the Australians were becoming restive because their troops were not in action.

The Joint Chiefs of Staff, who turned General MacArthur's message over to the Joint Staff Planners for study, were not impressed with the political necessity of retaking the Netherlands East Indies. However, they recognized that the area had potential value for employing and deploying forces of their Allies. When the theater commands were rearranged in April 1945 General MacArthur was directed to make plans for occupying North Borneo, including Brunei Bay, with Australian troops. Admiral King in particular looked upon this as a good potential base for the British Pacific Fleet, adequate in size and located so that British naval forces would not use facilities required by the U.S. Navy and could participate, if it seemed desirable, in operations to the north.

General MacArthur fitted the Brunei Bay operation into his original plan and set a target date for it of about 25 June, following occupation of Tarakan on 29 April and Balikpapan on 18 May. After Admiral King objected that this would be too long delayed and that it was not necessary to take Balikpapan, the date was advanced to 23 May. Subsequently General MacArthur received JCS approval to retain the assault on Balikpapan, after pointing out that Australian troops would execute the operation and it would have no effect upon the operations against the Japanese islands.[29]

The discussion of operations in Borneo and a base for the British Pacific Fleet revived talk of turning over to the British responsibility for the larger part of the Southwest Pacific Area. This had been on the minds of the planners at least since the Octagon Conference, when it was discussed as part of the larger question of British participation in the war against Japan.[30] Now, in mid-April 1945, it seemed desirable to direct General MacArthur's attention more squarely to the north and to give some of the Southwest Pacific to the British to add to their Southeast Asia Command. Consequently, the JPS directed the JWPC to prepare a study on the matter, even as the Joint Chiefs themselves brought it up at one of the now rare meetings of the Combined Chiefs of Staff.[31]

During the course of the CCS conversation (unfortunately not recorded), the U.S. Chiefs told the British representatives that they felt the situation in the Southwest Pacific Area was reaching a point where at least part of it should become an area of British responsibility. The area transferred might be bounded by a line approximately from a point on the China coast between Indochina and China southeastward through the Balabac Strait to the Equator and thence eastward. The U.S. Chiefs thought that possibly during June 1945, after Brunei Bay had been occupied, the transfer could be undertaken.

This apparently was the first the British had heard of the plan to make Brunei Bay a base for their Pacific Fleet. They objected strongly. While recognizing that it was within an area of U.S. strategic responsibility they were unhappy that they had not been informed sooner of the plans to take British territory with Australian troops. They considered Brunei Bay undesirable as a base because it was too far from the main theater of operations against Japan, undoubtedly suspecting the U.S. Chiefs of trying to keep British naval forces out of that theater. Moreover, they estimated that the base could not be developed until the beginning of 1946. Finally, there were other equivalent sites nearer the main base in Australia. What the British really wanted was a suitable anchorage much closer to Japan, in the Philippines, for example. They preferred to continue using Manus rather than to establish a base at Brunei Bay. If the main purpose of operations in Borneo was to be the building of an air base the British seriously questioned whether the expenditure of resources was justified.[32]

The U.S. Chiefs, in a reply prepared by Admiral King, said that they did not consider that Brunei Bay was far removed from the main theater of operations, for the main theater extended from the Kuriles to the Malay Barrier. Besides, operations in the Netherlands Indies and the Malay Peninsula would be supported by naval operations in the South China Sea, for which a base at Brunei Bay would be most desirable. Moreover, there were no sites available in the Philippines, and Manus was too far from the main theater. British naval forces based at Brunei Bay could still be used anywhere they were needed. "The seizure of the Brunei Bay area is considered a desirable operation whether or not it is utilized for an advanced British base," said the JCS, without explaining why they thought it so.[33] With this argument, however, they asked the British Chiefs to reconsider their objection.[34]

Still the British continued to believe that developing Brunei Bay would be a waste of constructional resources, especially since Singapore might well have been captured before the base was completed. They could foresee no "operations in the South China Sea which would require in Borneo more than advanced anchorage with very limited shore facilities."[35]

Landings at Brunei Bay proceeded on 10 June 1945. The question of what use would be made of the base was dropped as CCS attention focused on the larger problem of reorganizing the command of the whole Southwest Pacific Area.

The British Chiefs of Staff clearly were not eager to assume strategic responsibility for the Southwest Pacific. Before replying to the suggestion of the U.S. Chiefs at the CCS meeting of 13 April, they sought further information about U.S. intentions for the area. Would they, for example, leave all Australian forces there? If so, would they continue to provide the equipment and logistics support the Australians could not furnish and leave the base installations and administrative personnel? Would the United States leave in the area amphibious lift for at least one division? What about allocations of merchant shipping for operational and maintenance needs? To what extent would the U.S. Chiefs continue to depend upon the civil resources of Australia?[36]

The Joint Staff Planners and the Joint Logistics Committee, studying these questions, decided some concessions should be made, inasmuch as the United States would have to continue to support the area if the British refused to take responsibility. Despite British eagerness for a prompt reply it was two weeks before the planners produced answers for JCS consideration. Even then they recommended that the views of the Commander in Chief, Southwest Pacific Area, be sought before any reply was given to the British Chiefs of Staff.[37]

Another week passed before the Joint Chiefs sent the message to General MacArthur. His concurrence arrived on 30 May and it was not until 7 June that the Joint Chiefs finally answered the British questions.[38]

The general tenor of the reply was that the United States proposed to leave Australian and other Allied forces in the area of the Southwest Pacific but to remove all U.S. forces and mobile equipment that would be needed for the operations to the north. After the British had assumed responsibility the United States did not plan to provide supplies but would seriously consider requests under lend-lease or through CCS channels for the allocation of amphibious craft, shipping, etc. The JCS accepted General MacArthur's proposal of 15 August as the target date for releasing Allied forces and transferring tactical responsibility to the British, with gradual turn-overs of installations thereafter. The area would be bounded thus:

> Beginning on the coast of Indo-China at 15° north, through Balabac Strait along the 1939 boundary line between the Philippines and Borneo to latitude 05° north; thence east to 05° north 130° east; thence south to the equator; thence east to 140° east; thence generally southeast to 02° 20' south 146° east; thence east to 02° 20' south 159° east; thence south.

Part of the irregularity was required by the location of the islands in the area. Part was the result of U.S. insistence that the Admiralty Islands and specifically the extensive naval base at Manus should remain under U.S. control.

The British Chiefs of Staff were not enthusiastic. They themselves had little to send to the area, and the amount the U.S. was intending to provide was disappointing. Nor was the idea attractive of assuming strategic responsibility for the Southwest Pacific to which they had access only from bases in Australia and up the coast of New Guinea. British planning had centered on the recapture of Singapore and the opening of the Straits of Malacca to gain entrance from Southeast Asia Command to the South China Sea and the area to the north. The British did not care to become bogged down in the Netherlands East Indies and risk having no part at all in the main operations against Japan. Consequently they did not hasten to reply to the U.S. report.[39]

On 9 July, when the British Chiefs finally answered the U.S. paper, they proposed to extend the boundaries of the Southeast Asia Command as far as the Moluccas and the Lesser Sunda Islands, including on the west all of Indochina and Thailand, which had not been included in the U.S. area. To the eastward would be established an Australian command, bounded on the north by the Equator from the Moluccas to the International Date Line, thus including all Australian mandated territories. This area would be under an Australian commander appointed by the Australian Chiefs of Staff, and the chain of command would run through the British to the Combined Chiefs of Staff.

The most important point raised by the British Chiefs, however, was a proposal to take over some of the responsibility for higher strategic control in the war against Japan. They put it this way:

> We feel that the time has now come when we should take upon ourselves a greater share of the burden of strategic decisions which will be required before Japan is defeated. Although our contribution in the Pacific must always remain small in comparison with that of the United States, it is natural that our interest and concern should grow as more of our forces begin to be deployed in the Pacific area. Moreover, when the Straits of Malacca have been opened, there will no longer be the same

natural geographical division between SEAC and the Pacific. All operations in the war against the Japanese would then form one strategic concept.

The British Chiefs proposed that the Combined Chiefs of Staff should "exercise general jurisdiction over strategic policy and the proper coordination of the Allied efforts in all theatres engaged against the Japanese." For all matters pertaining to operations in the Pacific Ocean area and China the U.S. Chiefs of Staff would exercise jurisdiction, acting as agents of the CCS. The British Chiefs would function similarly in respect to Southeast Asia Command and Southwest Pacific Area. Finally, the CCS would have jurisdiction over the allocation of forces and war materials among all theaters engaged against the Japanese.[40]

The British proposals were first considered by the Joint Staff Planners and the Joint Strategic Survey Committee in connection with a study of the future of the CCS organization and the feasibility of forming some similar group with Chinese and Russian representatives. The first proposal of the JSSC was to reduce the functions of the CCS, dissolving agencies no longer necessary to the war program, and limiting it in general to the exchange of views on a consultative basis. Chinese and Russian representatives would be included when appropriate, either in full session or more often on a bilateral basis.[41]

The JSSC approved a JPS recommendation that the area originally proposed for British control not be extended, either on the west to include Indochina, whose status vis-a-vis the Chinese Theater was uncertain, or on the east to encompass the Admiralty Islands and reach to the International Date Line. The subdivision of the area, they agreed, should be determined by the British.

A few days after the circulation of the JSSC report the chiefs decided the JPS should study further the relation of the JCS to other nations participating in the war against Japan.[42] As a result, in a new revision the JPS dropped the discussion of the reorganization of the CCS and emphasized that any change in the current system of controlling the war against Japan that would mean added complications and more cumbersome procedures was unacceptable. The committee suggested readjusting the status of the Southeast Asia Command in relation to the CCS, in view of decreased U.S. interest in operations in that area. "Increased participation of the Combined Chiefs of Staff in the Pacific theater" would be "impracticable."[43]

When the Joint Chiefs presented this report to the CCS at Terminal the British Chiefs agreed to the boundaries on the east of the area for transfer. They recommended, however, that the President and the Prime Minister be asked to urge the Generalissimo to agree to the transfer of Indochina to the Southeast Asia Command.[44]

The British Chiefs of Staff still felt that they should be given a larger share in the control of the war against Japan. They pointed out that the United States and Great Britain were the two major powers allied against Japan and should consult freely on all matters of major strategic importance. The British Chiefs were responsible to the British Government for advice on how British forces should be used and they felt they should be better informed of strategic plans. What they were asking was to be consulted on major strategic policy. They were entirely confident in General MacArthur and Admiral Nimitz and had "no intention of suggesting interference with the operational control now accorded" them.

At the Terminal meeting of 18 July the Combined Chiefs of Staff approved in principle the transfer of responsibility for the Southwest Pacific Area to the British Chiefs of Staff. Whether or not Indochina should be included was left unsettled after General Marshall suggested that it be divided in two and the northern half be left in the China Theater. The British Chiefs wished to consider this further. The time for the transfer was also left for further discussion, as the British Chiefs expressed doubt that Admiral Mountbatten would be ready to take over as early as 15 August.[45]

On the matter of control in the war against Japan General Marshall explained that it was extremely difficult to conduct the strategy of the Pacific war because of the great distances and the enormous forces employed there. The U.S. Chiefs did not feel they could also "shoulder the burden of debating the pros and cons of operational strategy with the British Chiefs of Staff." General Marshall suggested that the U.S. Chiefs would be glad to tell the British what they proposed to do and if the British objected they might remove their forces. The Joint Chiefs felt, however, that they had to have freedom to decide ultimately what should be done.

The Combined Chiefs finally agreed that the U.S. Chiefs would retain control of operational strategy, promptly and fully informing the British Chiefs of future plans. They would consult the British on matters of general strategy, but if there were disagreement the U.S. Chiefs would decide what should be done. The British were to give adequate advance notice if they were going to withdraw any forces.[46]

It was not until 10 August that the British Chiefs reported when they could assume control of the Southwest Pacific Area. They could not arrange for a complete transfer in the immediate future, they said, but they recommended that the first move be begun immediately by giving Admiral Mountbatten responsibility for future operational planning in the area.[47] This suggestion was still under consideration by the Joint War Plans Committee when the fighting ended on 15 August.

OLYMPIC

Although after the Octagon Conference the agreed over-all objective for the war against Japan provided for "invading and seizing objectives in the industrial heart of Japan" preceded by "establishing sea and air blockades, conducting intensive air bombardment, and destroying Japanese air and naval strength,"[48] in the spring of 1945 there was still some uncertainty in the JCS as to the ultimate necessity and desirability of invading the Japanese islands. The records do not reveal clear-cut opposition to planning for invasion or intensive argument in support of a plan to bring about Japan's collapse by blockade. Rather they show a reluctance, particularly on the part of Admiral King and Admiral Leahy of the JCS, to consider invasion inevitable, a continuing enthusiasm for extension of the campaign in the Ryukyus to other objectives in that area and to the coast of China, and, in negative fashion, a compulsion on the part of the Joint Staff Planners to justify the Kyushu operation.

It was decided in January 1945 that Admiral Nimitz should be directed to make plans for an operation in the Chusan-Ningpo area of China but not to start preparations for landing there.[49] A similar provision was incorporated in the operational directive sent to Admiral Nimitz at the beginning of April when the change in command arrangements in the Pacific Theater was effected.[50] By this time, however, operations in the Ryukyus had already begun with landings on Okinawa. The question of whether Kyushu should be the next objective or whether an air and sea blockade of Japan should be completed by the seizure and development of positions on the coast of China or elsewhere needed to be settled in order to make theater planning realistic.

At the end of April the Joint Staff Planners completed for presentation to the Joint Chiefs of Staff a study of Pacific strategy in which they stressed the desirability of invading the Japanese islands.[51] Unconditional surrender, the planners pointed out, had been set as the aim of the war against Japan. That it could be accomplished was questionable, however, for it was a concept foreign to the Japanese nature and up to this point in the war no organized Japanese units had surrendered. After a campaign of bombardment and blockade the planners foresaw only a possible negotiated peace. If even that failed of accomplishment it would be necessary to turn from blockade to a costly and time consuming invasion after all. A campaign of invasion, on the other hand, could be carried through if necessary to absolute defeat, if there were no surrender.

Current intelligence estimates further supported the plan for invasion. The Japanese Fleet and air arms seemed incapable of more than an all-out suicide defense; Japan's resources were obviously drastically reduced; potential reenforcements from Asia were estimated to be a maximum of one division a month. As for casualties, one of the chief arguments against attempting to invade the islands of Japan, the planners made no estimates. They pointed out, however, that in seven amphibious campaigns in the Pacific the casualty rate had run 7.45 per thousand per day, whereas in the protracted land warfare in the European Theater of Operations it had been only 2.16. From this they concluded that amphibious operations should be limited, that land campaigns would be less costly, and that consequently invasion was preferable to a series of amphibious actions.

Current studies indicated that by December 1945 systematic bombing of Japan would have created a situation suitable for invasion, and sufficient forces and resources would be available to launch the invasion of Kyushu (Olympic) and Honshu (Coronet). Thus it seemed to the JCS unnecessary to undertake a campaign of blockade and bombardment that would require twenty-eight divisions in comparison to the thirty-six needed for Olympic-Coronet and that moreover could not be completed until about the fall of 1946 as compared with an estimated June 1946 for the invasion program.

As a final argument, the planners pointed out that invading Kyushu and Honshu would prevent the necessity of seizing bases in eastern China and would probably result in the capitulation of Japanese forces in China at less cost and without becoming embroiled in political difficulties with the Chinese Communists and the Nationalist Government of Chiang Kai-shek. Moreover, by control of the air Japanese troops would be prevented from moving to and from the mainland of China and it would no longer be necessary to depend upon the Russians to contain the Kwantung Army.

In concluding, the planners recommended the following course:

    a. Apply full and unremitting pressure against Japan by strategic bombing and carrier raids in order to reduce war-making capacity and to demoralize the country, in preparation for invasion.

    b. Tighten blockade by means of air and sea patrols, and of air striking force and light naval forces to include blocking passages between Korea and Kyushu and routes through the Yellow Sea.

    c. Conduct only such contributory operations as are essential to establish the conditions prerequisite to invasion.

    d. Invade Japan at the earliest practicable date.

    e. Occupy such areas in the industrial complex of Japan as are necessary to bring about unconditional surrender and to establish absolute military control.

The JPS recommended that a "declaration of intentions" should be made to the Japanese in order that they might know what lay ahead for them if resistance continued and what "unconditional surrender" would entail.

The only JCS comment on this report came from Admiral King, who disagreed with the argument but not the conclusions. In particular he objected to the comparison of casualties between the two theaters. There were so many differences in the character of the fighting and the enemies in the Pacific and the European theaters that Admiral King felt the casualty figures proved nothing and it would be wrong to judge the relative cost of amphibious and land campaigns by them. However, he approved the course of action the JPS recommended. Following his lead the Joint Chiefs of Staff officially noted the paper, in effect agreeing to the program as a basis for planning.[42]

Admiral King's approval of the JPS conclusions did not mean that he had been convinced that Japan would have to be invaded. He still felt that the preliminary application of pressure and tightening of the blockade might achieve victory without the necessity of committing forces to a land campaign. However, recognizing the need of the theater commanders for more definite instructions in order to plan realistically, he recommended to the Joint Chiefs of Staff at the end of April that a directive for Olympic be issued at once, setting the target date proposed by both General MacArthur and Admiral Nimitz, 1 November 1945. As late as August or September, Admiral King pointed out, the decision could be reversed if it seemed desirable. In any event, he thought, the operation should be submitted to the President for approval.[53]

In accordance with Admiral King's proposal the Joint Staff Planners at once attempted to prepare a directive for Olympic and were immediately confronted with the problem of command. Both Admiral Duncan and General Lincoln offered drafts, the former assigning command to Admiral Nimitz until the Army was established ashore, when it would go to General MacArthur, the latter placing General MacArthur in command of the entire operations. They reached no conclusion, and the directive submitted to the JCS on 14 May incorporated the difference of concept in the form of alternate wording.[54]

Directing the invasion of Kyushu with a target date of 1 November 1945, the JPS draft charged CINCAFPAC-CINCSWPA with responsibility for conduct of the campaign in Kyushu and with planning for continuation of the campaign in Japan, cooperating with CINCPAC in plans and preparations for the naval and amphibious phases. CINCPAC-CINCPOA was charged with responsibility for the naval and amphibious phases of the operation, according to the naval version coordinating his plans with CINCAFPAC-CINCSWPA's plan for the land campaign, or, according to the Army version conducting the naval and amphibious phases in conformity with the plan for the land campaign. The Army version was based on the belief that all phases of the campaign should be built back from and adjusted to support the land battle and that it would be unsound to treat them separately. The Navy planners recognized the necessity of building back from the land campaign to the naval and amphibious phases but felt that the land campaign must fit in with the practical aspects and possibilities of the amphibious operations. They believed that the arrangement advocated by the Army and Air Forces planners would "remove from Admiral Nimitz all control as to decision on a plan for the success of which he is responsible."[55]

The Joint Chiefs of Staff did not easily settle this difference. At a luncheon meeting on 15 May they agreed tentatively on a modification of the directive proposed by General Marshall, charging CINCAFPAC-CINCSWPA "with the responsibility for the conduct of the campaign in Kyushu including control of the amphibious assault through the appropriate naval commander." CINCPAC-CINCPOA would be responsible for the conduct of the naval phases of Olympic and correlate (instead of the Navy planners' "coordinate") his plans with those for the land campaign.[56]

Admiral King's tentative approval of this directive was withdrawn the following day after he had consulted the naval planners. Thereupon, as had frequently been the case during the war with Japan, he and General Marshall tried to settle the problem in an exchange of memoranda.

Admiral King first proposed that, in the interests of issuing a directive promptly, the Joint Chiefs simply direct the Pacific commanders to execute the operation on the basis of the directives they already had, with a target date of 1 November 1945. Any problems they could not resolve would be considered separately by the JCS.

To this General Marshall objected, feeling that the difficulties the chiefs were having would be repeated at great cost in the theater unless command responsibility were clearly and unmistakably defined. The directive modifying command arrangements in the Pacific had plainly stated that the JCS would assign missions and fix command responsibility for specific major operations, with CINCAFPAC normally responsible for land campaigns and CINCPAC for sea. Since Olympic would be a land campaign General MacArthur should have primary responsibility. General Marshall thought that, through the naval commander, he should also control the naval resources involved in putting the troops ashore. To Admiral King's brief directive General Marshall proposed to add that "primary responsibility for this operation, including control of the amphibious assault through the appropriate Naval commander, is assigned CINCAFPAC."

Admiral King disagreed. He pointed out that CINCPAC had been charged with completing the seizure and development of positions in the Ryukyus, continuing "such operations for securing and maintaining control of the sea communications to and in the WESTERN PACIFIC as are required for the accomplishment of the over-all objective," and making plans and preparing for the naval and amphibious phases of the invasion of Japan. In Admiral King's opinion this constituted an integrated and continuing sea campaign, requiring the employment of practically the entire Pacific Fleet. The operations could be coordinated and commanded only from an adequate naval command setup under CINCPAC. Of course, said Admiral King, the naval operations would have to be planned to fit in with the ultimate land campaign, and the plans already prepared by Admiral Nimitz had in fact been adjusted to it. Admiral King could not agree that General MacArthur should control any part of the amphibious operations, but in order to avoid misunderstanding he suggested adding to the JPS directive or to his own shorter one a statement that:

> The land campaign and requirements therefor are primary in

the Olympic Operation. Account of this will be taken in the preparation, coordination, and execution of plans.

General Marshall commented that apparently he and Admiral King were in complete disagreement as to whether CINCAFPAC's responsibility for the campaign in Kyushu should include the amphibious assault and as to the necessity for designating a commander with primary responsibility for the whole campaign. He proposed that they take up these differences at once with the Joint Chiefs of Staff and settle them. But Admiral King felt there was some misunderstanding of what was meant by primary responsibility and by control of the amphibious assault. At his suggestion Admiral Cooke and General Hull discussed the matter. When they were unable to reach a conclusion, however, General Marshall recommended a JCS meeting.

Ten days after their first discussion of a directive for Olympic the Joint Chiefs of Staff took up the problem again. There are no minutes of this meeting, but it may be assumed that there was much talk before a decision on CINCAFPAC's responsibility was finally reached. The wording finally settled upon must have been more pleasing to the Navy than to the Army. Far from specific, it limited CINCAFPAC-CINCSWPA to "primary responsibility for the conduct of operation Olympic including control, in case of exigencies, of the actual amphibious assault through the appropriate naval commander." Otherwise CINCPAC-CINCPOA was to be responsible for the naval and amphibious phases of the operations. What would constitute an exigency warranting CINCAFPAC's control was not indicated.

On 25 May 1945 the directive for Olympic was finally sent by the JCS to General MacArthur, Admiral Nimitz, and to the Commanding General, Twentieth Air Force, General Arnold, who was to "cooperate in the plans, preparations, and execution of operation Olympic and in the continuance of the campaign in Japan." The JCS was to determine when the Twentieth Air Force should come under one or the other of the theater commanders. About this part of the directive there had been no dispute.[57]

Plans and preparations for Olympic, the largest campaign of the war against Japan, proceeded in the late spring and early summer of 1945 but always with the understanding that the whole project was subject to review and even cancellation if the situation warranted. In mid-June, as President Truman prepared for the tripartite meetings at Postdam, he reopened the question of whether or not to proceed with plans and preparations for Olympic. At a meeting with the Joint Chiefs of Staff and the Secretaries of War and the Navy the President called upon each of those present for his views as to whether Olympic should be undertaken. This was not a discussion of the possibility of an early Japanese surrender but of the desirability of proceeding to plan on a campaign that was certain to take a large price in American lives and treasure.[58]

General Marshall read to the group a brief of a memorandum prepared by the JPS giving the reasons for selection of Kyushu and discussing the feasibility of the target date, the forces to be used, and the impracticability of trying to estimate casualties. He also read a message from General MacArthur that spoke of Olympic as "the most economical...[operation] in effort and lives that is possible," then gave his own view that it "was the only course to pursue...the only way the Japanese could be forced into a feeling of utter helplessness." Admiral King said he was impressed with Kyushu's strategic location, "the key to the success of any siege operations." Lieutenant General Ira C. Eaker, substituting for General Arnold, urged that there be no delay. Secretary Stimson said the JCS plan was "the best thing to do, but he still hoped for some fruitful accomplishment through other means." Secretary James Forrestal also agreed that it was a sound decision to proceed with the operations against Kyushu. With this unanimous support President Truman agreed they should continue to prepare for Olympic.

The JCS did not issue a directive for Coronet, the invasion of Honshu and the seizure of the Tokyo Plain. It was not yet necessary to do so in order to complete preparations for this much-dreaded operation in time for the tentative target date of March 1946. To a large extent Coronet would be a follow-up of Olympic, using some of the same forces, and planning could proceed without a final directive from the JCS to the theater commanders. Finally, hopes were strong that by the time Olympic was launched the situation might have changed to an extent that would render it preferable to change the concept of Coronet if not to eliminate the operation altogether. Since Japan did surrender well in advance of the target date for Olympic the order of 25 May to prepare for that operation was the last strategic directive issued by the Joint Chiefs of Staff in the war against Japan. The joint staff and departmental planners in Washington as well as the theater commands would be busy with detailed planning. But as had been the case with all wartime operations the issuance of the directive for Olympic concluded the direct participation of the JCS as a unit in that project.

PRIORITIES AND REDEPLOYMENT

Olympic and Coronet were conceived as operations far larger than any that had yet been undertaken against Japan, involving tremendous forces, many of which would have to be transferred from the European Theater of Operations to the Pacific before the operation could be launched. Planning for these transfers, estimates of the dates of availability of forces, calculations of the numbers that would be required in order to undertake the operations, all of these were complicated problems that occupied several of the joint committees during the last year and a half of the war.

The prewar decision that Germany was to be defeated first made it inevitable that after the German collapse attention would be focused upon defeating Japan and that many of the troops that had achieved victory in Europe would have to be moved to the Pacific to participate in the war to be brought to a conclusion there. The planners could and necessarily had to start well in advance of Germany's defeat to plan these wholesale transfers, but as long as the terminal date of the war in Europe was not known plans had to be tentative.

Following the agreement made at Sextant to "prepare to reorient forces from the European Theater to the Pacific and Far East as soon as the German situation allows"[59] combined planning was begun. But the problem did not seem particularly urgent, and in any case it would be primarily a matter of redeploying U.S. forces. Consequently most of the work on it was done by U.S. planners.

There were many problems contingent to that of redeployment to be considered. Probably the most basic was the question of what forces would actually be needed for the final phases of the war against Japan. But it was not then a matter of ordering the requisite numbers from one theater to the other, for the conclusion of hostilities in Europe would not automatically release all the forces that had been involved there. Some would have to be retained for the military occupation and others would be needed for the rehabilitation of the areas where war had been fought. There was also the problem of finding shipping to transport the forces from one theater to the other. Finally there was the desirability of permitting troops long overseas a period of leave at home before sending them on their way to the Pacific Theater.

In the course of study of the problems of redeployment during 1944 and 1945 a number of joint papers were evolved, some of which were ultimately presented to the Joint Chiefs of Staff. They normally approved the reports or simply took notice of them as tentative plans contingent upon the time and circumstances of Germany's defeat. Such, for example, was JCS 521/6, completed in June 1944, a study of the worldwide deployment of forces of the United States to the end of September 1945.[60] This periodic revision of a continuing study included lists of deployments and was based upon the assumption that Germany remained undefeated, that Germany was defeated by 1 October 1944, or that Germany was defeated by 1 January 1945. The Joint Chiefs, without discussion, approved JCS 521/6 for planning purposes.[61] Upon the basis of this study detailed plans for redeployment were prepared by agencies of the War Department. These lacked validity, however, for there was no coordination with the British, who would certainly be expected to have views on the forces to be retained or transferred and the personnel and cargo shipping that could be available to move them. Consequently, at the Octagon Conference the U.S. Chiefs of Staff recommended that a combined study be made of the whole redeployment problem.[62] It was the following April before that report was ready. In the meantime the JPS study on deployment of U.S.

forces had been revised twice, the last time upon the assumption
that the war in Europe ended 1 July 1945.[63] Although neither Admiral King nor General Marshall was pleased with all the figures
in the last revision, because time was getting short the chiefs
agreed to accept it for planning purposes until a further revision
had been issued.[64]

The study submitted by the Combined Staff Planners in April 1945
did not pretend to be any more conclusive than the U.S. studies of
strategic deployment had been. It covered only the question of
personnel shipping and was submitted for approval "only for use in
planning employment of troop shipping in accomplishing redeployment."[65] At the insistence of the U.S. planners, however, it included a statement upon the priority to be accorded to operations
in Japan which elicited a CCS discussion of that basic problem.

U.S. eagerness to turn as quickly as possible from the fight
in Europe to the campaign in the Pacific was not entirely shared
by the British Chiefs of Staff. They were apprehensive that U.S.
aid and interest in the problems of Europe might come to a sudden
end with the surrender of Germany and that all U.S. effort would
be devoted to the war in the Pacific with no thought of the continuing problems of Southeast Asia. Consequently the British
planners objected when the Americans insisted upon including in
the shipping study the statement that:

> Operations against the Japanese homeland and preliminary operations connected directly therewith will have first priority in
> the allocation of resources in the war against Japan. In the
> event of conflict with other requirements, shipping resources
> must be allocated on the required scale to assure that these
> operations can be executed at the earliest practicable date.

After studying the split report of the Combined Staff Planners
the British Chiefs of Staff, on 14 April, informed the CCS that
they felt that to give overriding priority to Olympic and Coronet
"would have implications which might in the outcome be detrimental to our war effort."[66] The British suggested that the same
policy be followed as had been adopted in respect to the major
operations on the European Continent and that the statement read:

> Operations Olympic and Coronet, and preliminary operations
> directly connected therewith are the supreme operations in the
> war against Japan. No other operations must be undertaken
> which hazard the success of these main operations.

As yet there had been no firm directive for Olympic and Coronet,
and there was still a possibility that some other operation would
be substituted or undertaken first. Consequently, in commenting
upon the British proposal the JWPC suggested designating "the invasion of Japan and operations directly connected therewith" as
the supreme operations. The committee also proposed substituting
the strong "nothing" for "no other operations" in the second sentence.[67] To this the Joint Staff Planners added "or delays" after

"hazards" and forwarded the recommendation to the Joint Chiefs of Staff.[68]

When the paper was circulated informally to the JCS, Admiral Leahy objected to introducing the question of delay. Admiral King in turn objected to its deletion. After some informal discussion Admiral Leahy withdrew his disapproval and the JCS reply was presented to the CCS.[69]

The British Chiefs of Staff approved the less specific designation of the main operations, but they objected to both of the other changes. They felt they could not agree that nothing which might hazard the success of the main operations should be undertaken, for they had certain commitments they considered inescapable that might interfere. Moreover they felt that the inclusion of "or delays" might lead to misunderstandings.[70]

Upon reconsideration the Joint Staff Planners continued to feel that "or delays" should not be deleted, lest resources not be made available as soon as possible. On the other point, however, they decided that the British recommendation might be adopted, since the chief area of conflict was troop shipping and supplies. The British had offered the use of three of their biggest troop ships for six months, and that problem was consequently minimized. Others could be settled as they arose.[71]

The Joint Chiefs of Staff accepted their planners' recommendations and presented them to the CCS on 16 May. On 1 June the CCS informally approved the redeployment study. The statement of priority as approved by the U.S. Chiefs was incorporated in the agreement on basic policies in the final report at the Terminal Conference.[72] Detailed redeployment plans worked out by the War and Navy Departments were already operative.

FUTURE OPERATIONS IN SOUTHEAST ASIA COMMAND

Operations in Southeast Asia during the first half of 1945 had been making great progress. The campaign to clear all of Burma continued successful beyond expectation. By mid-February, when some of the Washington planners en route back from Yalta stopped to talk with Admiral Mountbatten, he spoke of taking Rangoon before the monsoon that spring and then moving on to Singapore.[73] On 24 March the British Chiefs of Staff, having themselves approved SEAC's plans, formally sought CCS approval.[74]

Admiral Mountbatten was planning three major operations to follow closely the completion of the campaign in Burma: in early June 1945 an amphibious attack with at least two divisions in the area of Phuket about midway down the Malay Peninsula; in October 1945 amphibious operations with five divisions in the Port Swettenham/Port Dickson area of Malaya; and between December 1945 and March 1946 amphibious, overland, and airborne operations to take Singapore. Approval by the British Chiefs of Staff was contingent on the understanding that the action not be undertaken until the fall of Rangoon was clearly imminent.

The Joint War Plans Committee, directed to study the British request, was reluctant to recommend approval until more was known about the reenforcements needed to carry out the program. The Joint Staff Planners agreed that the Southeast Asia Command proposals "would probably require extensive allocation of resources by the United States with consequent adverse effect on main operations against Japan." Until it could be shown that this would not be the case, they recommended, the Joint Chiefs of Staff should not approve the program.[75]

The Joint Chiefs of Staff consequently informed the British that they did not feel they could approve the proposed schedule until it was established that the proposed scale of operations was necessary and could be carried out "without interfering with preparations for, and the execution of, the main operations against Japan." Because Roger, the Phuket operation, was relatively small and the target date close, the JCS approved this operation, subject to the agreement made in CCS 452/37 at Yalta limiting the use of U.S. resources.[76]

The British Chiefs, however, considered the three operations a series that should be approved without delay, with the understanding that the provision of the necessary resources would not hazard the early success of Olympic and Coronet. On this basis the Joint Chiefs of Staff finally approved the whole program on 11 May 1945. Ten days later the British Chiefs reported a change in plans.[77]

Rangoon had been taken the first week in May, earlier than had been expected, and there was every evidence that Japanese defenses throughout Southeast Asia were deteriorating as a result of the operations in the Pacific and the insecurity of Japanese lines of communication. Consequently Admiral Mountbatten decided to take advantage of the situation and strike more directly at Singapore, cutting out the assault on Phuket and advancing the date of the other two operations. The second half of August 1945 was set as the target date for the assault on the Port Swettenham-Port Dickson area. It appeared that Singapore would soon be in British hands again.[78]

GENERAL WEDEMEYER'S PLANS FOR CHINA

Although there was still serious consideration of landings on the coast of China in early 1945, there was no longer thought of using U.S. forces in sizable land campaigns there, with or without outside assistance. In March General Wedemeyer came to Washington and presented a plan of operations for Chinese forces in the China Theater. It envisaged a main thrust from the west to the Nanning-Liuchow area on 1 August 1945 followed by seizure of the Canton-Hongkong port Area on 1 December. From Nanning-Liuchow an air transport route to Luzon could be established, offering another avenue of supply to China. Capture of Hongkong would at last provide an entrance from the coast.[79]

General Wedemeyer was insistent that no operations within China should interfere with the main operations against Kyushu and Honshu. His program was strongly endorsed by Generalissimo Chiang Kai-shek and was treated in Washington as an agreed project, not one requiring JCS approval. Discussion of it by the Joint Staff Planners and the Joint Logistics Committee was primarily concerned with supply and support.

Although most of the required resources were already available or allocated to the theater there was a further build-up of the Air Transport Command and a problem of shipping and of redeploying forces after the defeat of Germany that would have to be considered in relation to other projects. Consequently the planners recommended establishment of a relative priority for the campaign in China (Rashness). They pointed out that it would contribute more directly to the Olympic-Coronet program than would those in the Southeast Asia Command and that the support of China was recognized as firm U.S. policy. In view of this, the planners recommended, and on 20 April the Joint Chiefs approved, "the provision of United States resources for operation Rashness in a priority below that for operations in the Pacific and above that for operations in Southeast Asia Command."[80]

When the Combined Chiefs of Staff assembled with the heads of state at Potsdam in July 1945 their plans were for a major campaign in Japan, with other operations of lesser magnitude in China, in Southeast Asia, and in the Netherlands East Indies. There was no way of foreseeing that much of the planning would be set aside unused as the war against Japan came swiftly to a close.

Chapter XXXI

TERMINAL - THE POTSDAM CONFERENCE

THE JAPANESE SITUATION

The conference held at Potsdam in July 1945 was primarily an occasion for meetings of the heads of state of the United States, Great Britain, and the USSR. Plans for the political conference were well advanced before it was finally decided, in mid-June, that the Combined Chiefs of Staff would meet for discussions of military problems, and if possible for talks with the Russian military chiefs, while the tripartite political meetings were in progress.[1]

When the Combined Chiefs of Staff met at Potsdam on 16 July the situation of the Japanese looked completely hopeless. A CIC paper "noted" by the chiefs at this first meeting summarized it thus:

> Recent advances in the western Pacific, culminating in the capture of Okinawa, provide the Allies with bases from which effective air attacks can be directed against all important areas under Japanese control. Furthermore, the Allies are now in possession of potential forward bases for an invasion of the Japanese home islands, Korea, or the central China coast. Air bases in the interior of China are being recaptured and may be more fully utilized. In addition, increasing Soviet forces in the Maritime Provinces and along the Amur River threaten Manchuria and the areas bordering the Japan Sea.
>
> On the continent the Japanese are now forced to depend upon inadequate and vulnerable land communications. Japan's seaborne communications with all areas south of the Yangtze River had been practically severed. Sea traffic between Japan proper and ports from Shanghai northward to southern Korea is limited to hazardous runs along the Korean and North China coasts. Even the relatively short shipping routes across the Sea of Japan and the Tsushima Straits are increasingly menaced by Allied mining, aerial, and submarine activities.
>
> The southern areas are not only cut off from the home islands, but the Japanese find it increasingly difficult to maintain communications between the various territories in the south which are still in their possession.

714   THE ADVANCE TO VICTORY

> Sea and air operations have virtually destroyed the capability of the Japanese naval and air forces for other than suicide operations against our forces. Blockade, and air attacks on productive capacity and concentrated reserves of materiel, are seriously impairing remaining Japanese defensive capabilities. The incendiary bombing attack of Japanese cities has had a profound psychological and economic effect on the Japanese. The complete destruction of major areas in all of the important war production centers is placing a tremendous strain upon residual economy, substituting appreciably for the lack of high combat expenditures and producing a chaotic condition in administration and control, which will greatly accelerate the effects of subsequent all-out attacks upon transportation. On the other hand, stocks of ammunition and ammunition production facilities still require intensive and extremely heavy attacks to produce any shortage significant to the interests of invasion and occupation.[2]

Despite this bleak outlook for Japan, however, the CIC saw no prospect of surrender until the army leaders acknowledged defeat, either because of the physical defeat of the main Japanese armies or through a desire to salvage enough to maintain the military tradition of Japan and ultimately permit the resurgence of a military nation.

Against this background, so dark for Japan, the progress reports presented to the CCS at the first Terminal meeting were bright indeed. In Southeast Asia, the Central Pacific, the Philippines, the strategic bombing program, everywhere operations were meeting with success. U.S. plans to continue pounding the Japanese islands from the air and blockading them from the sea and to land forces on Kyushu in November 1945 emphasized even more clearly how completely the initiative in military operations was in U.S. hands.[3] Nevertheless, at a later meeting of the Potsdam Conference the Combined Chiefs approved 15 November 1946 as the date for the end of organized resistance by Japan upon which to base planning for production and the allocation of manpower.[4]

The second CCS meeting held at Potsdam, on 17 July 1945, was occupied entirely with a discussion of the contribution to be made by the British in the final phases of the war against Japan. This was a subject in which the British were much more interested than the Americans, for U.S. forces could be made available in sufficient strength to carry out the program for the Pacific. Before the conference the British Chiefs of Staff had proposed that British participation take four forms: first, the British Pacific Fleet; second, a very long range bomber force of ten squadrons to be increased to twenty when airfields became available; third, a British Commonwealth Force (British, Indian, and Dominion) of three to five divisions, supported by the East Indies Fleet and a tactical air force of some fifteen squadrons, to participate under American command in Coronet, the invasion of

Honshu; fourth, operations in the outer zone to maintain pressure against the Japanese across the Burma-Siam frontier.

The British reported that the availability of the land force would depend in part upon the date of the recapture of Singapore. Although its exact size and composition would have to be determined later, the British Chiefs suggested that it might be (a) a force of one or two divisions in the assault plus two or three in the build-up, logistically largely self-supporting; (b) a force of three divisions in the assault and one or two in the build-up relying in large part on American logistic aid; or (c) up to five divisions in the build-up, largely self-supporting. "We should naturally prefer," said the British Chiefs, "a course which allowed us to take part in the assault."[5]

General Marshall sent a summary of the British proposals to General MacArthur for comment and immediately received an adverse reply. The addition of a mixed force with different organization, equipment, and procedures as well as language seemed to promise tremendous complications. General MacArthur objected strongly to trying to work into his plans a force whose availability could not be firmly known until after the capture of Singapore in November 1945. He urged particularly that the chiefs discourage its use in the assault phase of Coronet. He also opposed the introduction of a small British tactical air force which would probably offer more complications than assistance.

As a counter-proposal General MacArthur suggested that the participation of British forces be limited to one corps of three amphibiously trained divisions, British, Canadian, and Australian. The British and Australians would be given American equipment (plans for a Canadian division had already been made) and supported from the United States, to be concentrated by 1 December in the Borneo-Morotai area or possibly the United States. The corps would be carried to the objective area in British shipping about Y plus 10, to serve as an integral corps within a U.S. army as the AFPAC assault reserve afloat.[6]

As a result of General MacArthur's comments the recommendation of the Joint War Plans Committee, revised by the Joint Staff Planners and adopted by the Joint Chiefs of Staff, was that the British offer be accepted in principle "subject to satisfactory resolution of operational problems by Commander in Chief, U.S. Army Forces, Pacific, and Commander in Chief, U.S. Pacific Fleet, and to the clarification of certain factors which the United States Chiefs of Staff believe will be controlling."[7] This was agreed to by the Combined Chiefs of Staff, who thus went on record at Potsdam as favoring in principle the use of British land forces in the Honshu operation.[8]

The controlling factors in the project that gave the JCS concern were much the same as the points raised by General MacArthur--the availability and composition of the forces and the problems of their operation and logistic support. At the CCS meeting the British Chiefs commented on most of the points raised by their American colleagues, again expressing the hope that British troops might participate in the assault on Honshu and not just in the follow-up operations. However, their offer was accepted only in principle. As a first step toward working out details an agreement was made that appropriate commanders and a staff of such a force as the British proposed to provide should visit General MacArthur and Admiral Nimitz and draw up a concrete plan for submission to the Combined Chiefs of Staff. A second step was General Arnold's agreement, as a result of the remarks of Sir Charles Portal, to investigate further the possibility of using a British tactical air force.

This discussion at Potsdam of the participation of a British land force contrasted sharply with the heated exchanges between U.S. and British Chiefs at Octagon over the question of using a British naval force in the Pacific. In part the calmer reaction of the U.S. Chiefs may be explained by the fact that the logistical problem posed by the ground force would not be so great and U.S. plans would not be affected to the same extent. Then, too, the details were not to be settled until some later date. No directive for Coronet had yet been issued. It was highly possible that the operation would never have to be executed.

PARTICIPATION OF OTHER NATIONS

The British were not the only ones anxious to have a part in the final phases of the war in the Pacific. The French, Dutch, and Portuguese also from time to time had expressed a desire to use their forces to the maximum for the liberation of their own territories. Now that the fighting in Europe was over there would be troops available and their use in colonial areas would have great propaganda value. Obviously it was impracticable to engineer an operation by these forces alone. Most of the logistical arrangements would have to be worked out by the United States. The difficulties of transporting and maintaining a small disparate force and undertaking to recapture islands that were not strategically essential to the main campaign against Japan dampened any enthusiasm the Joint Chiefs of Staff might have had for encouraging other nations to participate.

In April 1945, when operations in the Netherlands East Indies were being considered and mopping up action in other bypassed areas began to seem more practicable, the British Chiefs of Staff recommended that the CCS should agree on a general policy in regard to French and Dutch participation in the war against Japan. The British suggested that, particularly in operations aimed at the liberation of French and Dutch territories, the nations might contribute to the extent of supplying token forces, technical experts, and members of the civil administration. The British recommended also that the French and Dutch should be kept informed of CCS plans that might affect their national interests in the Far East.[9]

The U.S. Chiefs did not answer the British suggestion until July, when they reported their agreement in principle. They were

not enthusiastic, however, and the statement of policy that the
CCS approved, apparently with little discussion, at the third
meeting at Potsdam can hardly have given the French and Dutch
much encouragement.

> While it is at present impracticable due chiefly to logistical difficulties for French or Netherlands armed forces to take a major part in the immediate operations in the Far East, the provision of such assistance which may be synchronized with operations will be taken into account by the Combined Chiefs of Staff. The use of such forces will depend solely on military considerations. French or Netherlands forces so accepted must operate under the complete control of the commander in chief concerned.[10]

A similar feeling is evident in a letter approved by the CCS
on the same day for the Department of State and the Foreign Office
in respect to Portuguese participation in the recapture of Timor.
The CCS agreed to accept Portuguese assistance for such operations,
but that was not to be interpreted to mean approval of the use of
Portuguese troops anywhere else or to be a commitment to retake
Portuguese Timor.[11]

DIRECTIVE FOR SUPREME COMMANDER, SOUTHEAST ASIA

The agreement in principle to the employment of a British Commonwealth land force in Coronet was incorporated by the British Chiefs in a draft directive to Admiral Mountbatten, with advance notice that he would be expected to provide part of the force and that filling its requirements would have priority over all his other tasks. The directive also informed the Supreme Commander, Southeast Asia, that the boundaries of his command would be extended in accordance with the CCS agreement to include Borneo, Java, and the Celebes.

The operational directive proposed for Admiral Mountbatten reflected the progress that had finally been made in the most controversial of areas. The primary task was to be the opening of the Straits of Malacca, long talked of but never before within reach. Specific operations were to include the completion of the liberation of Malaya, the maintenance of pressure on the Japanese across the frontier of Burma-Siam, the capture of key areas of Siam, and the establishment of bridgeheads in Java and/or Sumatra in preparation for subsequent clearance of the whole area.[12]

There was little in this directive that had not already received CCS approval and, subject to the stipulation it contained that the main operations in the Pacific were to have priority, nothing in the operations it outlined to which the U.S. Chiefs had any objection. The reallocation of areas and command in the Southwest Pacific had not yet received the approval of the Australian, New Zealand, and Dutch Governments, but obtaining that seemed hardly more than a formality and certain to be completed by the time of transfer. The U.S. Chiefs proposed some changes in the wording of the British draft, but in substance they approved it with very little discussion.

Admiral Mountbatten himself arrived in Potsdam in time for the final CCS meeting on 24 July. His account of what had been done and what remained to be finished in the Southeast Asia Command led to an amiable discussion. With the U.S. aim of opening a land route to China long since realized, and the main campaign in the Pacific nearing its conclusion, the U.S. Chiefs did not oppose any operation for which Southeast Asia Command forces were considered adequate.[13]

The rest of the CCS meetings at Potsdam were taken up with a variety of problems, some having to do with postwar matters in the European Theater, others relating to details of the war in the Pacific. As at all earlier conferences the chiefs prepared a report for the heads of state, summarizing the agreements they had reached. Like all the previous conference reports it included a statement of basic objectives, strategy, and policies, but in this instance the Combined Chiefs of Staff had been unable to agree.

The first week in May, even before the surrender of Germany, the Joint War Plans Committee had prepared for the Joint Staff Planners a revised statement of broad principles regarding prosecution of the war, recommending that the Combined Chiefs of Staff agree upon a new statement in accordance with the changed situation resulting from Germany's collapse. The committee's aim in the revision was to eliminate irrelevant material and to emphasize clearly that the chief objective was to bring about the unconditional surrender of Japan. In form and wording the new statement followed closely the agreement that had been made at the Argonaut Conference.[14]

The JWPC report underwent several revisions at the hands of the Joint Staff Planners before it was finally presented to the Joint Chiefs of Staff on 24 May 1945.[15] With some slight amendments the JCS approved it and presented it to the Combined Chiefs of Staff on 14 June. Thereafter followed a series of exchanges as the Americans and the British tried to secure acceptance of a statement that would represent their separate views of where CCS interest should lie.[16]

It was not difficult to agree that the over-all objective should be "in conjunction with other Allies to bring about at the earliest possible date the unconditional surrender of Japan." The over-all strategic concept also was readily agreed to be:

> In cooperation with other Allies to bring about at the earliest possible date the defeat of Japan by: lowering Japanese ability and will to resist by establishing sea and air blockades, conducting intensive air bombardment, and destroying Japanese air and naval strength; invading and seizing objectives in the Japanese home islands as the main effort;

conducting such operations against objectives in other than the Japanese home islands as will contribute to the main effort; establishing absolute military control of Japan; and liberating Japanese-occupied territory if required.

In respect to the European Theater the only thing to be done was "to establish and maintain, as necessary, military control of Germany and Austria." It was on the matter of basic undertakings and policies for the prosecution of the war that the CCS could not reach agreement.

The chief difference the Combined Chiefs of Staff were unable to resolve was in large part the result of the sharp separation in the U.S. Government of matters military from matters political. It was the problem of lend-lease that caused the difficulty. Whereas the Americans felt they could commit themselves to support of their Allies only insofar as it would further the war against Japan, the British considered it essential to assure continuing lend-lease aid not only for the war effort of the British Commonwealth but also for rehabilitation and the requirements of military occupation. The JCS did not have authority to make the broad interpretation of policy the British Chiefs desired.

After several attempts to reach agreements, the U.S. Chiefs finally stated their position thus:

> The United States Chiefs of Staff...consider that the basic undertakings should be confined to broad statements concerning the military conduct of the war. As a result of the changed circumstances arising from the defeat of Germany and the practical capability of the British Commonwealth to support its own forces in the field, they are operating on the basis that approval of the issue to Allied Governments of Lend-Lease munitions of war and military and naval equipment will be limited to that which is to be used in the war against Japan and which will not be used for any other purpose. They do not propose to subscribe to any statements which deviate from this principle. They consider that occupation forces are not a subject for combined military commitments. Matters relating to post-war armies are also not susceptible to combined military commitments. Any arrangements which the British wish to make on these subjects are beyond the purview of the United States Chiefs of Staff and should be taken up on the governmental level.[17]

With discussion at an impasse it was agreed, upon British recommendation, to present both versions of the statement to the heads of state for settlement. Consequently at the plenary meeting held on 24 July, the only one at Terminal, approval of the CCS report hinged upon the question of to what extent U.S. lend-lease support could be promised for uses not directly connected with the prosecution of the war against Japan.[18]

Feeling that the Congressional intent behind the latest renewal of the Lend-Lease Act bound him to a strict interpretation,

President Truman could not agree to commitments for such purposes as reconstruction and rehabilitation of the United Kingdom. He did, however, decide to consider the military occupation of Germany and Austria a part of the war and agreed that U.S. support could be expected for that.

The statement of basic undertakings finally approved was couched as was customary, in very general terms. Instead of the firm emphasis upon furtherance of the war against Japan it incorporated the broader needs of military occupation as well. Three undertakings were considered fundamental:

    a. Maintain the security and war-making capacity of the Western Hemisphere and the British Commonwealth as necessary for the fulfillment of the strategic concept.

    b. Support the war-making capacity of our forces in all areas, with first priority given to those forces in or designated for employment in combat areas in the war against Japan.

    c. Maintain vital overseas lines of communication.

The President and Prime Minister without question approved the remainder of the report of the CCS agreements at Terminal.

MEETINGS WITH THE SOVIETS AT POTSDAM

It was not until the afternoon of 24 July, the day of the CCS meeting with the heads of state, that the Combined Chiefs of Staff finally met with the Soviet military chiefs.[19] There was no longer a question of urging the USSR to enter the war against Japan. Since the Yalta Conference conviction had grown among U.S. leaders that Russian participation was not at all essential. However, no urging was necessary. The Soviets had denounced their five-year neutrality pact with Japan in mid-April. The only question was when hostilities would begin. General Antonov at the outset of the tripartite military meeting announced that Soviet troops "would be ready to commence operations in the last half of August. The actual date, however, would depend upon the result of conferences with Chinese representatives which had not yet been completed."[20]

The remainder of this tripartite meeting was occupied with a general summary by General Antonov of Russian plans and with reports by the U.S. and British Chiefs of Staff of the situation as it appeared in the war against Japan, both the capabilities of the Japanese and the accomplishments and potentialities of forces of the United Nations. Most of the discussion was concerned with the areas where U.S. and Soviet forces might be expected to come in contact and with information that would be helpful to the Russians after they commenced hostilities. The plans for coordinating efforts for which the U.S. Chiefs had hoped had never been arranged. By this time, however, they were no longer eager to attempt to base U.S. forces in the Maritime Provinces or to become involved in operations in the Kuriles or the area north of the Japanese Archipelago. These were thought to be diversions which might jeopardize the major operations against Japan and would probably contribute little to their success.[21]

Although the U.S. Chiefs no longer sought specific information as to Russian intentions such as they had asked for at Yalta, they had prepared five questions which General Marshall presented at the tripartite meeting. Two days later the Soviet Chiefs discussed their answers at a meeting attended only by the U.S. Chiefs and their staffs. They were most cooperative.[22]

The first question had to do with weather information, a vital factor for operations against Japan. President Truman had already recommended to Generalissimo Stalin that weather liaison groups be established in Petropavlovsk and Khabarovsk to insure the supply of essential data to U.S. forces. The Soviet reply to a query as to whether the High Command had received any instructions on the subject was that radio stations would be set up in the two places, using facilities supplied by the United States. However, it was considered wiser to use Soviet personnel to operate them. When Admiral King expressed disappointment at this and belief that the employment of American personnel would increase the efficiency of the effort, General Antonov immediately agreed to their use.

The second and third questions were chiefly concerned with the areas in which U.S. naval and air forces would operate. The Russians accepted most of the U.S. recommendations on this, although drawing a slightly different line through the Sea of Japan and excluding the Sea of Okhotsk and Inner Mongolia from unhampered U.S. operations. In the area north and west of the boundary line U.S. forces would have to be subject to coordination, presumably arranged in the theater. The same would apply to Soviet operations to the south and east.

In response to the fourth question the Soviets agreed to send liaison groups to the commands in the Far East and to Washington and in turn to receive American liaison groups for the staffs of the Soviet commanders in the Far East.

The fifth question had been a request for a specific list of repair facilities for ships and planes in distress in Soviet territory. The Soviet reply listed both ports and airfields that could be made available.

This meeting and the amiable agreements made at it marked the conclusion of JCS participation in the Potsdam Conference. Compared with the other conferences of the war period there had been little CCS business to transact and very little that was controversial in the problems that were taken up. Military planning continued to be based on the premise that it would probably be necessary to fight to a finish and a hope that it would not. Developments on the political level at Potsdam were hastening the achievement of that hope.

Chapter XXXII

VICTORY

The two decisions made at Potsdam in July 1945 that had the greatest effect upon the war against Japan were technically not conference decisions at all. One was made by President Truman; the other jointly by him, Prime Minister Churchill, and Generalissimo Chiang Kai-shek. The Combined Chiefs of Staff participated in an advisory capacity.

In order of revelation, the first of these decisions was to publish a statement warning Japan to capitulate and explaining what was meant by unconditional surrender. Issuance of such a statement was by no means a new idea at Potsdam. It will be recalled, for example, that Prime Minister Churchill had made a similar suggestion at Yalta. In the intervening period several such statements had been issued with JCS endorsement by the various agencies concerned with psychological warfare. The idea for the stronger declaration that was released during the Potsdam Conference had originated with General Marshall and had been recommended by the JCS, the State-War-Navy Coordinating Committee (SWNCC), and the State Department early in June for publication by President Truman. He, however, had preferred to discuss it with the other heads of state at Potsdam rather than taking unilateral action.[1]

Inasmuch as Russia was not yet at war with Japan, the question of an ultimatum or any similar declaration was not one for discussion at the tripartite meetings. At the first CCS meetings, however, the British Chiefs of Staff brought up the subject, recommending that an explanation of the term "unconditional surrender" be made to the Japanese as a means of hastening the end of the war. Immediately the U.S. Chiefs, although agreeing with the British suggestion, pointed out that it was a political matter beyond their jurisdiction and up to the President and the Prime Minister to act upon.[2]

From a draft written by Secretary of War Stimson, President Truman and Secretary of State James Byrnes worked out a statement that met with the approval of Prime Minister Churchill and Generalissimo Chiang Kai-shek. This "Potsdam Declaration" was published by the three heads of state on 26 July 1945, before Mr. Churchill's return to London.[3]

"We—the President of the United States, the President of the National Government of the Republic of China, and the Prime Minister of Great Britain, representing the hundreds of millions of our countrymen," the proclamation read, "have conferred and agreed that Japan be given an opportunity to end this war." Thereafter followed a statement that was both a warning and an explanation.

Futher resistance was worse than futile, Japan was told, for the three nations were prepared to unleash their land, sea, and air forces to strike the final blows against Japan. "The full application of our military power, backed by our resolve will mean the inevitable and complete destruction of the Japanese armed forces and just as inevitably the utter devastation of the Japanese homeland."

Urging Japan "to decide whether she will continue to be controlled by those self-willed militaristic advisers whose unintelligent calculations have brought the empire of Japan to the threshold of annihilation, or whether she will follow the path of reason," the Potsdam Declaration stated the terms upon which Japan's surrender would be accepted. These included: the elimination of irresponsible militarism; temporary occupation of points in Japanese territory; limitation of Japanese sovereignty to the islands of Honshu, Hokkaido, Kyushu, Shikoku, and minor islands; the return of Japanese military forces to their homes; the punishment of war criminals; the maintenance of industries to sustain Japanese economy and permit the exaction of reparations in kind; eventual participation in world trade relations; and occupation by Allied forces until a peacefully inclined and responsible government had been established in Japan.

Concluding, the three heads of state called "upon the Government of Japan to proclaim now the unconditional surrender of all Japanese armed forces, and to provide proper and adequate assurances of their good faith in such action. The alternative for Japan is prompt and utter destruction."

This proclamation contained no hint of the other significant decision made by President Truman at Potsdam, that is, to use the atomic bomb. During the war years the Joint Chiefs of Staff had been generally aware of the development of atomic research, although this very secret project was not under their authority and JCS discussion of it, if there was any, was never recorded. As long as the potentialities of the bomb were unknown and the reactions to be expected from its use in Japan could not be determined, JCS strategic plans had necessarily assumed a fight to the finish, although recognizing the possibility of Japanese surrender at any time, and had shown no evidence at all of the possible availability of a mighty new weapon. By the spring of 1945 the Army Air Forces had begun to make preparations and to train units to carry atomic bombs in the event they became available. However, once the bombs were developed, it was the President's responsibility to determine whether they should be used. In considering this momentous problem he consulted the members of the JCS, and particularly General

Marshall and General Arnold; but it was President Truman who gave the word that would send the planes on their way.[4]

Events moved rapidly after the chiefs' return from Potsdam. Even before they arrived in Washington it had been announced from Tokyo that the Japanese Government intended to ignore the Potsdam ultimatum.[5] While the scheduled program of full scale bombing of the Japanese islands by the Army Air Forces and the Navy continued, and preparations for the invasion of Kyushu went ahead, the first atomic bomb was dropped on Hiroshima on 5 August. On 8 August Russia finally declared war against Japan, sending Soviet troops across the Manchurian border the next morning. The second bomb fell on Nagasaki on 9 August, and the following day the Japanese offered to accept the terms of the Potsdam Declaration, provided the Emperor's sovereignty was maintained. After being informed that the authority of the Emperor would be subject to the Supreme Commander of the Allied Powers, the Japanese agreed. On 14 August 1945 the fighting war was over.

Japan's surrender did not take the Allied governments entirely by surprise. Intelligence reports for some time had indicated that Japan could not hold out for long, and an increasing number of more or less authentic peace feelers had been reported from various neutral sources. The mechanism of surrender had been a topic of conversation at Potsdam and a subject for discussion and planning on military and political levels for some weeks before the surrender came. Plans from both General MacArthur and Admiral Nimitz for the occupation of the islands of Japan and other Japanese-held territory in the Far East had been worked over by the joint staff in Washington. On 11 August the Joint Chiefs of Staff issued a procedural directive to the two theater commanders and sent to General MacArthur, who was to be designated Supreme Commander for the Allied Powers, drafts of the instrument of surrender, a proclamation to be made by the Emperor of Japan, and a naval and military General Order No. 1, to be issued upon Japan's capitulation. The joint staff had been working on the preparation of all these documents since early summer.[6]

Japan's acceptance of the Allied surrender terms set in motion a new train of events and created a completely different atmosphere, in which military preparations for the culminating operation of the long campaign in the Pacific were set aside and the anticipated invasion of the Japanese islands became instead a peaceful occupation.

It had been a long, hard fight to victory from the dark morning of 7 December 1941, and many were those who had participated in it. The defeat of Japan could only in small part be credited to the planning teams in Washington and the theaters of war whose part has been described in the preceding pages. It was the valiant efforts of the fighting men that had achieved the victory-- the men of the great naval forces, submarines, carriers and planes, amphibious craft, and all the many fighting and support vessels that by August 1945 comprised the largest Navy in the world; the hardhitting Marines who wrested island after island from stubborn Japanese defenders; the men of the Army Air Forces, those who supported ground and sea forces and those who went on ahead and bombed from bases scattered over the Pacific and the continent of Asia; and the men of the Army, who fought long, weary battles on land in the Pacific islands and in Asia and built bases ever nearer the enemy shores. Without all of these the strategic pattern developed often thousands of miles from the fighting would have had no validity.

Responsibility for the strategy by which Japan was defeated lay with the Joint Chiefs of Staff after the combined agreement made in the spring of 1942 gave them strategic control of the Pacific Theater as executives for the Combined Chiefs of Staff. The CCS kept a restraining hand on operations through control of material means and officially accepted strategic plans, almost always without question. It was the Joint Chiefs of Staff who approved strategic plans, decided between alternate courses of action when their staffs were unable to reach agreement, and issued directives to the theater commanders. Since JCS decisions were always unanimous, it is difficult, except in general terms, to determine the part played in the direction of the war by the four men who were the U.S. Joint Chiefs of Staff.

Admiral King stands out clearly as the JCS member whose influence upon the course of events in the Pacific was greatest. This was inevitable in a war that was largely amphibious and whose strategy had for many years been a major topic of study and discussion in naval circles. To him should go the major share of the credit for convincing the other top military men as well as the heads of state that the defensive in the Pacific should not be static but that constant pressure should be maintained upon the Japanese and every opportunity for improving the U.S. position should be capitalized upon. Although his efforts to get a fixed percentage of available means assigned to the war against Japan were not successful, they did help to insure the availability of sufficient resources to keep the offensive in motion in the Pacific Theater while the major effort was being made to defeat Germany. At the same time it should be pointed out that Admiral King strongly supported the agreed concept that Germany's defeat should come first and that, although in problems of supply and support he was inclined to show a stubborn naval bias, his contributions to the strategic decisions of the Joint Chiefs of Staff went far beyond the limitations of his service interests or the war in the Pacific.

Admiral King's role in the development of strategy for defeating Japan is very difficult to evaluate in detail. Officially he approved or disapproved recommendations that came to him as Commander in Chief, U.S. Fleet, and Chief of Naval Operations and as one of the Joint Chiefs of Staff, from his own naval planners, from the theater commanders, and from the joint planners in Washington. Frequently these recommendations had already been influenced by his own views. Still many of the objectives he preferred, most notably Formosa, were bypassed, and much of the time his recommendations were only in terms of areas or island groups. He accepted without question the specific objectives deemed by the operating commands most suitable.

The one who came closest to Admiral King in his basic view that the Japanese should be kept under constant pressure was not a member of the Joint Chiefs of Staff but the Supreme Commander, Southwest Pacific Area, General MacArthur. Although his role was to recommend and then to accept a decision from the JCS, and many of his views on strategy differed sharply from those endorsed by the JCS, his repeated efforts to get more support for his area of command and to push ahead as rapidly and with as much force as possible helped to insure that the war against Japan did not become a forgotten war and were largely responsible for the development of the advance on two axes.

The other members of the Joint Chiefs of Staff were not so closely connected with the war in the Pacific as was Admiral King in his role as top naval officer. Although to some extent General Marshall represented General MacArthur and his views to the JCS, much of the time he did not champion them against opposing ones advanced by the joint staff, the naval planners, or Admiral King. Once convinced of the wisdom of maintaining pressure in the Pacific through adoption of an offensive as quickly as possible, he strongly backed that principle in discussions with the British and seldom questioned strategic plans that came up for JCS approval. He did, however, exert a restraining influence, particularly in the early stages of the war, by insisting in case of conflicting demands that the first priority on men and materiel should be accorded to the war against Germany. This attitude was stronger in General Arnold, whose first concern was for the creation of overwhelming air power in the European Theater. In discussions of strategy in the war against Japan General Arnold's views were seldom expressed. Admiral Leahy was not much more vocal than General Arnold. When there was a difference of opinion on Pacific strategy, more often than not he sided with Admiral King, but he seldom advanced original views of his own. His chief function was to keep the JCS and the President informed of each other's positions.

The relatively small number of instances in which the Joint Chiefs argued among themselves the merits of one line of strategy against another in the war against Japan is evidence of the effectiveness of the joint staff in working out solutions between conflicting views on lower levels. It was the joint staff who studied the situation, in detail, reviewed the plans of the theater commanders, and made recommendations to the chiefs from which they determined the strategy to be adopted. Cooperation within the JCS organization was not perfect. Service interests and lifetimes of experience in unilateral thinking inevitably influenced the views of the individual workers as well as those of the Joint Chiefs. Nevertheless, to a remarkable degree, despite prolonged and often heated discussions, the joint committees resolved their differences and submitted to the chiefs recommendations which bore no evidence of unilateral authorship.

The strategic pattern of the war against Japan was not drawn in detail in the beginning but evolved gradually under JCS direction as the war progressed. In its early stages it was shaped by the disasters with which the United States and its Allies had been plunged into the fight. Even the basic principle, "Defeat Germany First," approved long before the blow struck at Pearl Harbor, could not be strictly followed in the beginning because of the overwhelming force of that first attack. Although the major effort subsequently was put into the war against Germany, an offensive was adopted against Japan much sooner than prewar plans had contemplated. The availability of forces, the broad reach of Japanese expansion, and the command organizations in the Pacific determined the steps to be taken in that offensive.

The first objective in the Pacific Theater was to establish a line of defense that could be held against further Japanese aggression. Immediately upon the outbreak of war, reenforcements were rushed to the area in order to establish such a line. But it was not to remain a static line. Inevitably theater commanders, supported in Washington particularly by Admiral King and the naval planners, soon began looking for opportunities to improve their positions and to unleash the forces that had been assembled. The action begun at Guadalcanal became a chain reaction of increasing size and speed. As U.S. production lines and training camps began to turn out forces and equipment designed for island-to-island warfare, strategic plans became more ambitious. With fewer shortages it became easier to win JCS and CCS approval for maintaining constant pressure upon the enemy and for pushing the offensive in the Pacific concurrently with the conduct of large-scale operations in Europe. Thus, by the time Germany surrendered, Japan, too, was close to final defeat.

The strategic pattern that thus evolved for the Pacific had the great advantage of flexibility. Directives were never issued by the Joint Chiefs of Staff far in advance of target dates and sometimes were so close as to allow barely sufficient time for preparation. From the point of view of strategy this was highly commendable, for it permitted plans not yet firm to be changed to take advantage of opportunities as they developed, omitting operations entirely or changing their scope as the situation warranted. To those charged with the procurement and supply of men and equipment, however, the absence of a long-term plan for the war against Japan from which requirements could be calculated with some degree of accuracy was a real hardship. The CCS practice of approving operations for the various areas of war at the same time without first ascertaining whether available resources were sufficient for everything can hardly be said to have eased the burden of the logistics planners.

Besides resulting in a rush of resources to the Pacific Theater and an incentive for a turn from the defensive to the offensive, the force and wide extent of the initial Japanese attacks influenced the direction that the offensive would take. The flood of enemy forces across the islands of the southwestern Pacific, threatening Australia and the line of communications to it as well as the Hawaiian Islands, drew attention to that area and immediately resulted in the establishment of the ill-fated ABDA Command. Political as well as strategical considerations made it inevitable that the British Dominions be held even though the defense of the islands of the southwestern Pacific failed. No strategic pattern for fighting Japan could be developed without giving serious consideration to the needs and potentialities of that area. The establishment there of a separate command under General MacArthur resulted from this initial Japanese menace and in turn insured that maintaining the defensive would not long be the order of the day.

While there is much to be said for striking the enemy wherever possible and keeping him occupied on several fronts, the division of the Pacific Theater between two major commands complicated the problems of war and undoubtedly reduced the efficiency with which the war was fought. There could be no single line of advance in the Pacific as long as there were two equivalent commands, in each of which plans were being developed and strongly championed for attacking vital Japanese positions and pushing on to the main Japanese islands. On the other hand concentration solely upon either the direct westward advance through the Central Pacific or the advance from the southwest to the Philippines would have left the enemy in control of strategic positions on the flanks and might well have resulted in a slower rate of progress and a longer war. The MacArthur program and the Nimitz program were in fact mutually supporting. The full benefits of that circumstance could have been better realized, however, had the entire Pacific Theater been under a single command. With one command responsible for the whole Pacific Theater, operations in the two areas could have been better coordinated both in planning and in execution, fewer facilities duplicated, and less time spent by the Joint Chiefs of Staff in settling conflicting views of strategy and according priority on the limited stocks of planes, landing craft, shipping, and other resources.

Thus far comments on the strategy followed to defeat Japan have intentionally been limited to the strategic program of the Pacific Theater. Whereas the combined operations of the Southwest Pacific Area and the Pacific Ocean Areas led directly to Japan's defeat, it is difficult indeed to discover any essential military contribution of the other region of the war, China-Burma-India. Certainly its contribution did not balance the effort expended. Had there been no potential strategic importance in that area, the U.S. Chiefs would still have been bound by political considerations to support China and, since the only supply route to China lay through India and Burma, would have become involved in their problems as well. As it was, China was considered to be the objective toward which the advance across the Pacific was headed, an area essential for air and naval bases and a possible source of troops as well for the final blow against Japan. As the war progressed, however, China's strategic significance decreased. The political commitment to continue to support China was an unrewarding drain on military resources as it became apparent that Chinese bases were of doubtful strategic importance and that Chinese forces were incapable of making a large contribution toward Japan's defeat. Complicated by British reluctance to recapture Burma and open a land route to China instead of retaking Singapore and opening a sea lane to the Pacific from India, the problems of China, Burma, and India certainly did not repay in strategic gain the mental, physical, and financial effort that went into them.

The Joint Chiefs of Staff and their subordinate committees had fought the war to a victorious conclusion. The organization forged in war had not been a perfect one. Joint ways of thinking had not always come easily and often not at all. Eight years after Japan's surrender it is not difficult to point to things that might have been done differently. Despite many rough spots, however, the JCS had achieved cooperation among representatives of the services to an extent never before considered possible.

NOTES

N.B. For present locations of the documents cited, see Bibliographic Essay.

Footnotes are generously employed in these volumes for authentication of the historical text. They are designed with particular attention to the needs of students and staff officers who may wish to make a closer investigation of the records underlying any portion of the account. Although shortened where possible by the use of abbreviation, the notes contain full guidance to the identification of the cited papers.

The references to published works, periodicals, newspapers, and public documents follow the generally recognized usage. No such standardization exists in the matter of citing official correspondence and committee papers, and the Historical Section has necessarily developed a style manual tailored to its own purposes. The elements of these citations are described below, in the order in which they normally appear.

1. *Classification*. The symbols (TS), (S), (C), and (R) are easily recognized as abbreviations for the four standard security classifications, while (U) designates an unclassified item. The security classification given in footnotes is the one appearing on the document when it was consulted. Where subsequent downgrading was actually recorded on the document it has been indicated, as by the notation (S dg R), but no attempt has been made to keep abreast of the continuing process of reclassification of the official records. Where the security level of material cited in footnotes is higher than the SECRET classification of this history, the references have been cleared and certified by appropriate authority.

The notation (UNK) for "unknown" has also been used occasionally when a document appears originally to have warranted, and probably borne, a security classification which was not indicated on the copy seen by the author.

2. *Character of the document*. An abbreviated term indicates whether the paper is a letter, memorandum, report, note, message, or memorandum for record (ltr, memo, rpt, etc.). For joint and combined committee papers the short title is the first element of this characterization, such as JCS 1627/3 or CPS 98/1/D.

3. *Writer or reporting agency*.

4. *Addressee*. This is of course a vital element in the citation of correspondence and messages, but for CCS, JCS, and other

committee papers no addressee appears; the short title is usually a sufficient indication of the disposition of the paper.

5. *Subject*. The subject or title is treated as a quotation, using the exact wording without abbreviation. Where no subject appears on the document, this item is omitted.

6. *Serial number*. If there are additional identifying numbers that may be helpful in locating the paper in certain records collections, these are given. This is particularly applicable to some naval documents, and to the CM-IN or CM-OUT number of messages sent through War Department channels.

7. *Date*.

8. *Source*. Normally the file number alone satisfies this requirement. In a few instances where the records are difficult to find or are not in a standard archive in the Washington area, a more specific locational reference is given in the footnote. A general discussion of the physical location of the records most consulted appears later in this statement.

In the interest of brevity and simplification no file reference has been included for two main classes of JCS documents. The first, the weekly Compilation of Decisions (CD) is filed in the CCS 016 series. The second, minutes of the Joint and Combined Chiefs of Staff and all their regular committees, is found in a CCS 334 file bearing the name of the particular organization.

The official records of basic importance to this history are those of the Joint Board and the Joint and Combined Chiefs of Staff. They are maintained by the JCS Research and Records Analysis Section. Some inactive files of the wartime period have been retired to the Departmental Records Branch, Adjutant General's Office, in Alexandria, Virginia, but remain under JCS control. The Joint Board, JCS, and CCS serial papers in the JCS records section comprise the central and official files of the three organizations. Other copies of the same papers may be found, however, in records collections of the Army and the Navy, under differing index systems. When appearing there, the papers are not necessarily accompanied by the same supporting materials as are found in the JCS files, but these service records in turn contain other commentary that is often useful.

The Army collection of joint and combined papers for the wartime period bears the designation "ABC" and was originally developed by the Strategy & Policy Group of the War Department Operations Division (OPD). The ABC files are located in the Departmental Records Branch, AGO, in Alexandria, but are available only through application to the Assistant Chief of Staff, G-3, General Staff, U.S. Army. The same is true of the WPD and OPD files, which are the records of the War Plans Division, 1921-March 1942, and its successor, the Operations Division, March 1942-June 1946. Another collection of unusual interest, the OPD Executive file, is ultimately the responsibility of G-3 but is currently in the custody of the Office of the Chief of Military History, Department of the Army. The records center in Alexandria maintains other significant

Army files which may be consulted directly. Those of the Chief of Staff (designated OCS or WDCSA) are foremost in this category.

Most of the official naval records used in the preparation of this history are in the custody of the Office of Naval Records and History. These include the Secret-Confidential (SC) and Super-Secret (SS) files of CominCh and CNO, Admiral King's own office files which may be consulted only by direct permission of the Chief of Naval Operations, and a miscellaneous collection of records of the War Plans Division (WPD) of the Office of CominCh. Some use has also been made of the general files of CinCPac currently at the Naval Records Management Center at Alexandria, Virginia.

CHAPTER I

[1] (S) MSS, JCS Hist, *Evolution of Global Strategy* and *War Against Germany and Its Satellites*.

[2] (U) Ltr, Recorder JB to Presidents, Army War College and Navy War College, 24 Dec 04, JB 325 (ser 19). For detailed discussion of the Joint Board, see (S) MS, JCS Hist, *Evolution of Global Strategy*.

[3] (S) Rpt, JPC to JB, encl "Joint Army and Navy Basic War Plan - Orange," 12 Mar 24, JB 325 (ser 228). This was based on a joint estimate of the situation approved by the JB the year before. (S) Ltr, JPC to JB, "Synopsis of the Joint Army and Navy Estimates of the Orange Situation," 25 May 23, JB 325 (ser 207); (S) Mns, JB Mtg, 7 Jul 23.

[4] The total strength, officers and enlisted, in 1924 was 141,618. Mark S. Watson, *U.S. Army in World War II, Chief of Staff: Prewar Plans and Preparations* (Washington, 1950), p. 16.

[5] (S) Mns, JB Mtg. 7 Jun 24; (S) Rpt, JPC to JB. "Joint Army and Navy Basic War Plan - Orange," 20 Jun 24, JB 325 (ser 228A); (S) Mns, JB Mtg, 10 Jul 24; (S) Ltr, JPC to JB, "Joint Army and Navy Basic War Plan - Orange," 16 Jul 24, JB 325 (ser 228B); (S) Mns, JB Mtg, 15 Aug 24; (UNK) Ltr, JB Secy to SecNav, "Joint Army and Navy Basic War Plan - Orange," 5 Sep 24, JB 325 (ser 228).

[6] (S) Ltr, Sen Mbr JB to SecWar, "Joint Army and Navy Basic War Plan - Orange," 14 Jun 28; (C) Ltr, Secy Navy WPD to Secy JB, "Action on Joint Board Report," 19 Jun 28; (S) Ltr, Secy GS USA to Secy JB, 10 July 28. All in JB 325 (ser 280).

[7] For discussion of Army strength, see Watson, pp. 1-5, 15-31. Naval figures are in E.J. King, *U.S. Navy at War* (Washington, 1946), pp. 5-6.

[8] (S) Ltr, JB to SecWar, "Revision of Joint Army and Navy Basic War Plan - Orange," 8 May 35; (S) Ltr, JB Secy to SecNav, same subj, 10 May 35. Both in JB 325 (ser 546).

[9] (S) Ltr, JB to SecWar, "Revision of Joint Army and Navy Basic War Plan - Orange," 19 May 36, JB 325 (ser 570). For discussion of the inadequacies of Philippine defenses, see Watson, pp. 414ff.

[10] (S) Memo, JB to JPS, "Joint Army and Navy Basic War Plan - Orange," 10 Nov 37, JB 325 (ser 617).

[11] (S) Ltr, Navy Mbrs JPC to JB, "Joint Army and Navy Basic War Plan - Orange," 29 Nov 37; (S) Ltr, Army Sec JPC to JB, same subj, 30 Nov 37. Both in JB 325 (ser 617). (S) Ltr, JPC to JB, same subj, 27 Dec 37; (S) "Joint Army and Navy Basic War Plan - Orange (1938)," 28 Feb 38. Both in JB 325 (ser 618).

[12] (S) Mns, JB Mtg, 9 Nov 38.

[13] (S) JB 325 (ser 634), "Exploratory Studies," 21 Apr 39.

[14] For discussion of the "Rainbow" series, see (S) MSS, JCS Hist, *Evolution of Global Strategy* and *War Against Germany and Its Satellites*, ch I.

[15] (C) JB 325 (ser 670), "National Defense Policy for the United States," 21 Dec 40. Fuller discussion is in (S) MS, JCS Hist, *War Against Germany and Its Satellites*, ch I.

[16] (S dg U) ABC-1, "United States-British Staff Conversations," 27 Mar 41, *Hearings before the Joint Committee on the Investigation of the Pearl Harbor Attack* (Washington, 1946) (hereinafter: PHA), pt 15, pp. 1485-1542.

[17] (S) B.U.S. (J)(41)13, 11 Feb 41, ABC papers in file of Adm R.L. Ghormley, NR&H.

[18] For further discussion, see (S) MS, JCS Hist, *Evolution of Global Strategy*.

[19] (S dg U) "Joint Army and Navy Basic War Plan - Rainbow No. 5," 14 May 41, JB 325 (ser 642-5). Reprinted in *PHA*, pt 18, pp. 2908-2926.

[20] (S) Ltr, Pres to SecWar and SecNav, 9 Jul 41, JB 355 (ser 707); (S) JB 355 (ser 707), "Army and Navy Estimate of United States Over-all Production Requirements," 11 Sep 41; (S) MS, JCS Hist, *Procurement and Allocation of Material Means*.

[21] (MS) Brit Doc, M.M. (J)(41)1, "Directive to British Representatives at Singapore Conference" 13 Apr 41; (S) Ltr, Secy US Staff Comm to Brit NA, ser 011512-17, 16 Apr 41. Recommendation for such a conference appeared in the letter of transmittal to CNO, CofS USA, and BCOS accompanying ABC-1. (S) Ltr, CinCAF to CNO, FF6/A8/A16-3 (S-43), 29 Apr 41. All in CNO(WPD) file "*A.D.B. FILE*." The original suggestion was made by RAdm R.M. Bellairs in a letter to RAdm R.L. Ghormley, 9 Feb 41, Ghormley papers, NR&H.

[22] (S) Ltr, CofS Asiatic Flt to CNO, "Report of NEI-USA Staff Discussions at Batavia," FF6/A16-3(S-6), 19 Jan 41; (S) Msg, CNO to CinCAF, 15 Feb 41; (S) Ltr, CinCAF to CNO, S-22, w/encl, "Despatch Report on Anglo-Dutch-Australian Conference Held at Singapore February 22-25 1941," 5 Mar 41. All in CNO(WPD) file "*A.D.B. FILE*."

[23] (MS dg U) "American-Dutch-British Conversations, Singapore, April, 1941 (Short Title--'A.D.B.')," 27 Apr 41, *PHA*, pt 15, pp. 1551-1584. When the U.S. naval representative, Capt W.R. Purnell, left for the conference, CinCAF, Capt Purnell's commanding officer, had not yet received a copy of ABC-1 and had seen one only briefly. (S) Ltr, CinCAF to CNO, "American-Dutch-British Conversations, April 1941," FF6/A16-3(S-43), 29 Apr 41, CNO(WPD) file "*A.D.B. FILE*."

[24] (S) Ltr, CNO and CofS USA to Spec Nav and Army Observers, London, "Comment on the report of the American-Dutch-British Conversations, Singapore, April 1941," (SC)A16-1/RF13-13, ser 075112, 3 Jul 41, *PHA*, pt 15, pp. 1677-1679; (S) Memo, CNO and CofS USA to Pres, "Estimate Concerning Far Eastern Situation," 5 Nov 41, *PHA*, pt 14, pp. 1061-1062; (S) Memo, CNO and CofS USA to Pres, "Far Eastern Situation," 27 Nov 41, *PHA*, pt 14, p. 1083.

[25] (S) Ltr, CNO and CofS USA to Spec Nav and Army Observers, London, "Comment on the report of the American-Dutch-British Conversations, Singapore, April 1941," (S) A16-1/RD13-13, ser 075112, 3 Jul 41, *PHA*, pt 15, pp. 1677-1679. Statement of RAdm R.K. Turner, *PHA*, pt 4, pp. 1931-1933.

[26] (S) Mns, Admty Liaison Cmte, 22 Aug 41, Ghormley Papers, NR&H.

[27] (S) Ltr, Spenavo London to CNO, "ADB-2 - Comments on," ser 00281, 1 Sep 41; (S) Ltr, Spenavo London to WPD, "Comments on ADB-2," ser 00288, 2 Sep 41; (S) Ltr, RAdm R.K. Turner to RAdm V.H. Danckwerts, ser 011512-72, 3 Oct 41; (S) Msg, Spenavo London to CNO, 251922 Oct 41; (S) Msg, CNO to Spenavo London, 052030 Nov 41; (MS) Msg, Admty to BAD, 253, 1559A, 5 Nov 41; (S) Ltr, Secy for Collab to Jt Secys BJSM, "U.S.-British Commonwealth Cooperation in the Far East Area," ser 011512-104, 11 Nov 41. All in CNO(WPD) file.

[28] (MS) BCOS Doc, "General Strategy Review," 31 Jul 41, JB 325 (ser 729).

[29] (S) JB 325 (ser 729), 25 Sep 41.

[30] 55 Stat (1941), pt 1, p. 31.

[31] (S) Ltr, CNO to CinCUS, 27 May 40, *PHA*, pt 14, p. 943. For similar reasons fleet detachments had been sent to Australia at Presidential request. (S) Ltr, CNO to CinCUS, 4 Apr 41; (S) Ltr, CNO to CinCUS, 19 Apr 41. Both reprinted in *PHA*, pt 16, pp. 2160-2165. Fuller discussion in (S) MS, JCS Hist, *Evolution of Global Strategy*.

[32] (S) Ltr, CNO to CinCPac, 4 Apr 41, w/encl, CNO Memo to Pres, *PHA*, pt 16, p. 2162.

[33] (S) Memo, CNO to SecNav, "Discussion of existing strategic situations in the Pacific Ocean," ser 066912, 10 Jun 41, *PHA*, pt 9, p. 4299.

[34] Watson, pp. 414-452; (C) Msgs, HighComPhil to Int Dept for Pres, 547, 6 Aug 40; 548, 7 Aug 40; 738, 14 Oct 40; 739, 16 Oct 40; 747, 16 Oct 40. All in JB 306 (ser 672).

[35] The JB sent the recommendation to the Pres via SecWar and SecNav at the end of Jan 41. He passed it to the SecInt who approved it and a despatch, subsequently sent by Pres Roosevelt to Pres Quezon, informing him in greater detail than the Army and Navy wished of their plans. (S) Ltr, SecWar and SecNav to Pres, 30 Jan 41; (U) Memo, SecInt to Pres, 10 April 41; (U) Ltr, SecInt to SecWar, 24 Apr 41. All in JB 305 (ser 672). (S) Memo, Sec War to SecNav [encl memo for Pres] 24 Apr 41; (S)

Memo, SecNav to SecWar, ser 050812, 5 May 41. Both in CNO(SC) file "A16-1/EG12 to A16-1/EG52."

[36] Proposed legislation was approved by the DCofS, WD, on 30 Jun but not recommended to Congress until Sep. In the meantime $10,000,000 had been borrowed from the AAF funds and $15,000,000 from the President's Emergency Fund. A bill appropriating the originally estimated $52,000,000 plus $10,000,000 to repay the President's Fund was finally introduced in Congress on 19 Dec 41 and passed four days later as Public Law 371. Six days before, the Third Supplemental National Defense Appropriation Act, 1942, had been passed, including $269,000,000 for the Army of the Philippines. (UNK) Memo, Actg ACofS USA to CofS, "Legislation for Improving the Defenses of the Philippine," 26 Jun 41, OCS 20891-90. (U) Gen G.C. Marshall, Official Report, 8 Sep 43, pp. 5-6. (S) Memo, Actg ACofS USA to CofS, "Funds for Philippine Army," 17 Sep 41; (C) Memo, CG Budget and Legislative Planning Branch, "Funds for Philippine Army," 22 Sep 41. Both in WPD 3251-58.

[37] (S) Mns, JB Mtg, 12 Jul 41.

[38] On 11 Dec 40 the Pres had approved a draft of an order to nationalize the armed forces of the Philippines, but it was not signed. (S dg U) Ltr, Dir BurBud to SecWar, 11 Dec 40, *PHA*, pt 20, p. 4370.

[39] Note comments of Adm Hart: "The induction of the Philippine Army and the building up of the USAFFE was...accompanied with much publicity,-which condition continued throughout." (C) T.C. Hart, MS, *Narrative of Events, Asiatic Fleet Leading up to War and from 8 December 1941 to 15 February 1942* (NR&H, 11 Jun 42), p. 20.

[40] (S) Ltr, SecWar to Pres, 25 Jul 41, *PHA*, pt 20, p. 4366. Draft of a proposed executive order was cleared by the BurBud and the Atty Gen, but at the President's suggestion it was changed to a military order. (U) Ltr, Actg SecWar to Dir BurBud, 18 Jul 41; (S) Ltr, Asst Dir BurBud to AG, 21 Jul 41; (U) Ltr, Actg AG to Pres, 21 Jul 41; (U) Ltr, Asst Dir BurBud to AG, 25 Jul 41. All reprinted in *PHA*, pt 20, pp. 4368-4371.

[41] (S) Msg, Marshall to MacArthur, 26 Jul 41, WPD 3251-50.

[42] W.F. Craven and J.L. Cate, eds, *The Army Air Forces in World War II* (hereinafter: *AAF in WW II*), vol I, *Plans and Early Operations* (Chicago, 1948), p. 178. Footnote reference, Memo, Arnold to Marshall, 18 Jul 41, not seen by this author.

[43] (U) Memo, Marshall to Stark, 12 Sep 41, *PHA*, pt 33, p. 1170. Gen Marshall reports reenforcements sent or to be sent to the PI: 26 Aug: part of AA rgt and "some reserve supplies"; 8 Sep: rest of AA rgt, tank bn of 50 tanks, 50 pursuit planes, and personnel; 18 Sep: 50 cannon mounts, 50 more tanks; 12 Sep: 9 Flying Fortresses landed in Manila; 30 Sep: 26 Flying Fortresses to leave San Francisco; Oct: first of a total of 130 pursuit planes; Nov: probably reserve of 6-9 B-24's; Dec: some 35 Flying Fortresses; also to go: some 54 dive bombers, some 130 pursuit plus two additional squadrons.

737   NOTES TO CHAPTER I

An Army WPD "Estimate of Situation, Philippines," 2 Oct 41 (WPD 3251-60), predicted that the Philippines could not be defended against a maximum Japanese effort but that with the authorized reenforcements they could be held against a strong attack and that the added strength probably would deter the Japanese. No corroboration has been found for the statement of Secy Stimson that, "Now it began to seem possible to establish in the Philippines a force not only sufficient to hold the Islands but also, and more important strong enough to make it foolhardy for the Japanese to carry their expansion southward through the China Sea." Henry L. Stimson and McGeorge Bundy, *On Active Service in Peace and War* (New York, 1947), p. 388.

[44] (S) JB 325 (ser 642-5) (Rev), "Proposed changes in Joint Army and Navy Basic War Plan - RAINBOW No. 5," 19 Nov 41. Louis Morton, MS, *The Fall of the Philippines* (OCMH, 1952), pp. 127-131.

[45] (S) Ltr, Jt Secys BJSM to Secy for Collab, "United States-British Commonwealth Co-operation in the Far East Area," N.O. 119/41, C.S. (47) 53, CNO(WPD) file "Pacific & Far East Area, British Joint Staff 1941."

[46] (S) Msg, CinCAF to CNO, 271130 Oct 41, Hart, *Narrative*, p. 25.

[47] (S) Ltr, CNO to CinCAF, "Reenforcement of British Naval Forces in the Far East Area," ser 0126612, 7 Nov 41, CNO(WPD) file "*A.D.B. FILE*"; (S) Msg, CNO to CinCAF, 182125 Nov 41, WPD 3251-68; Hart, *Narrative*, p. 28; (S) Msg, CinCAF to CNO, 080121 Dec 41, CNO(WPD).

[48] (S) Msg, Admty to CNO, 281717 Oct 41, CNO(WPD) file "*A.D.B. FILE.*" Establishment of a similar command above, rather than in place of, CinC, China, had been suggested in ADB-1 and by the British Chiefs of Staff to the CNO and CofS USA on 21 May 41. (S) M.M. (J)(41)21, "Comments of British Chiefs of Staff on Singapore Report," CNO(WPD) file "*A.D.B. FILE.*" In both cases the U.S. Chiefs questioned the value of creating a superior echelon of command. (S) Msg, Spenavo London to CNO, 251922 Oct 41, CNO(WPD) file "*A.D.B. FILE.*"

[49] (U) Ltr, CNO to CinCPac, 23 Sep 41, *PHA*, pt 33, pp. 1168-1169; (MS) Msg, Admty to BAD, 253, 5 Nov 41, CNO(WPD) file "*ABC-Pacific and Asiatic Dispatches.*"

[50] Hart, *Narrative*, pp, 34-36; (S dg U) Msg, CinCAF to CNO, 070327 Dec 41, *PHA*, pt 19, p. 3547; pt 4, p. 1933.

[51] (S) Msg, CNO to CinCAF, 080121 Dec 41, CNO(WPD).

[52] As Adm Hart put it on his return to Washington:

Looking back at this time, the lack of preparation for joint action between the three Navies in that area was really seriously disadvantageous in only two particular factors;-the personnel of the Asiatic Fleet had acquired no familiarity with the N.E.I. and Malayan waters and preparations for joint tactical operations were quite incomplete. There was also the lack of personal acquaintance as among officers of the three Fleets; but the most disadvantageous circumstance was American lack of familiarity with the waters in which they later had to fight....
Hart, *Narrative*, pp. 2-3.

[53] For the extent of Japanese conquest of China by the end of 1941 and for a description of conditions in the Chinese Army, see Charles F. Romanus and Riley Sunderland, *U.S. Army in World War II: China-Burma-India: Stilwell's Mission to China* (Washington, 1953), ch I.

[54] E.R. Stettinius, Jr., *Lend-Lease, Weapon for Victory* (New York, 1944), pp. 109-118; Romanus-Sunderland, *Stilwell's Mission*, pp. 10ff; C.L. Chennault, *Way of a Fighter* (New York, 1949), pp. 90-104.

[55] Fuller discussion in Romanus-Sunderland, *Stilwell's Mission*, ch I.

[56] (C) Ltr, SecWar to JB, "Aircraft Requirements of Chinese Government," 13 May 41, JB 355 (ser 691).

[57] (C) Ltr, Currie to SecNav, 28 May 41, JB 355 (ser 691).

[58] (S) JB 355 (ser 691), Rpt by JPC, "Aircraft Requirements for the Chinese Government," 9 Jul 41.

[59] (S) Mns, JB Mtg, 12 Jul 41.

[60] (S) Ltr, Patterson and Knox to Pres, 18 Jul 41, w/comment, "OK-but restudy Military Mission versus the Attache method. F.D.R.," 23 Jul 41, JB 355 (ser 691). Representatives of the Army and the State Dept looked into the advantages of attaches rather than a military mission. They decided against the former. (S) Memo, Brig Gen L.T. Gerow to RAdm R.K. Turner, 28 Aug 41, WPD 4389-17. The JB also discarded a suggestion from the Navy that naval representatives be included in the mission. (S) Memo (2), Gerow to Turner, 28 Aug 41, WPD 4389-17.

[61] G-2 recommended on 14 Jul that Gen Magruder be ordered to prepare to head a Military Mission (OCS 20241-178). On 11 Aug SecWar unofficially ordered Gen Magruder to organize a mission. Official instructions were issued by SecWar on 27 Aug (OCS 21300-5).

[62] (S) JB 354 (ser 716), "United States Military Mission to China," 12 Sep 41.

[63] Cordell Hull, *The Memoirs of Cordell Hull* (New York, 1948), vol II, pp. 982-1037, 1054-1094.

[64] (S) Memo, Gerow to Marshall, "Immediate Aid to China," 1 Nov 41; (S) Memo, Col Bundy for Rec, "Immediate Aid to China," 1 Nov 41; (S) "Notes on Conference with Mr. Currie at the State Department, 12:45 p.m.," 1 Nov 41. All in WPD 4389-27. (S dg U) Memo, CNO and CofS USA to Pres, "Estimate Concerning Far Eastern Situation," ser 0130012, 6 Nov 41, *PHA*, pt 14, pp. 1061-1062; (S dg U) Memo, CNO and CofS USA to Pres, "Far Eastern Situation," *PHA*, pt 14, p. 1083.

[65] Statement of ex-SecState Hull, 23 Nov 45, *PHA*, pt 2, p. 431.

[66] For further discussion of manpower and mobilization, see (S) MS, JCS Hist, *Mobilization and Demobilization of Military Manpower*.

CHAPTER II

[1] (S) Memo, Actg ACofS WPD (L.T. Gerow) to CofS, "Brief Current

Strategic Estimate," 12 Dec 41, WPD 4622-37. Adm Harold R. Stark, USN (Ret), CNO in Dec 41, in an interview with the author on 17 Jun 49, expressed certainty that there was a comparable Navy estimate, but unfortunately the earliest one that has so far been found was written a week later in preparation for the Arcadia Conference. He had no adverse comments on the Army's study, and consequently it has been used here to illustrate military views as close as possible to the outbreak of war. VAdm Vincent R. Murphy, USN(Ret), Assistant War Plans Officer, Staff of CinCPac on 7 Dec 41, told the author on 19 Apr 49 that an estimate of the situation was drawn up in CinCPac Hq at Pearl Harbor on 8-10 Dec 41 and given to SecNav Frank Knox on his arrival. Although SecNav brought it back to Washington, it has not been found in Navy files.

[2] Adm Stark told CinCPac on 9 Dec 41 that he expected the Japanese to follow up the attack on Pearl Harbor and render Hawaii untenable, and he thought the Japanese had forces suitable to occupy Oahu, Midway, Maui, and Hawaii. He also questioned whether Midway could be held and hoped that Johnston, Palmyra, and Samoa might be. (S) Msg, CNO to CinCPac, 091812 Dec 41, in (TS) CominCh file "CinCPac Despatches - Jan - thru June 1942."

[3] (U) ABC-1, "United States-British Staff Conversations Report," 27 Mar 41, *PHA*, pt 15, pp. 1485-1541; (U) "The Joint Army and Navy Basic War Plan--Rainbow No. 5," *PHA*, pt 18, pp. 2908-2920.

[4] Sunk or damaged, some very badly, were: 8 battleships, 3 light cruisers, 3 destroyers, 1 repair ship, 1 minelayer, 1 seaplane tender, and 1 target ship. *PHA*, pt 12, p. 354. In addition, 87 Navy and Marine Corps planes and 63 Army planes were destroyed in the initial attack. For itemized lists of Navy losses, see *PHA*, pt 12, pp. 354-358; for Army losses, *PHA*, pt 12, p. 323.

[5] (U) ABC-1, "United States-British Staff Conversations Report," 27 Mar 41, *PHA*, pt 15, pars 55 & 57, pp. 1526-1527. U.S. Gibraltar Force to be transferred consisted of: 3 battleships, 1 carrier, 4-8" cruisers, 13 destroyers, and 12 patrol seaplanes. Force "H" comprised: 1 battleship, 1 battle cruiser, 1 aircraft carrier, 1-6" cruiser, and 8 destroyers.

[6] An itemized list of transfers from the Pacific to the Atlantic between 1 Feb 41 and 7 Dec 41 is contained in (U) Memo, Cdr J.F. Baecher to Mr. Seth W. Richardson, 29 Apr 46, *PHA*, pt 11, p. 5505.

[7] (S) Mns, JB Mtg, 8 Dec 41; (S) Ltr, Secy for Collab to CSO BJSM, "*ABC-1; modification of*," ser 011512-118, 16 Dec 41, CNO(WPD) file "Pacific and Far East Area, British Joint Staff 1941."

[8] It was the opinion of G-2 that Japan's next objective might be major fleet units, installations on the West Coast, Alaska, or the Panama Canal, and that "of these objectives, the loss of the Panama Canal and the major elements of the fleet would be the most disastrous to the United States." (S) Memo, Lt Col P.M. Robinett, ACofS G-2 to CG FF, WPD 4544-28.

[9] (S) Mns, JB Mtg, 9 Dec 41; also, 8, 10, 13, and 17 Dec 41.

[10] (S) Ltr, CofS USA to CNO, "Defense of Oahu," 12 Dec 41, WPD 4544-29; (S) Mns, JB Mtg, 13 Dec 41.

[11] Both Brig Gen L.T. Gerow and Brig Gen B.B. Somervell reported to Gen Marshall on 12 Dec 41 that two ships carrying troops, pursuit aircraft, and ammunition were ready to sail for Hawaii the following day, but that efforts to get the Navy to cooperate in convoying them had produced unsatisfactory results. Gen Gerow suggested that Gen Marshall take up the matter with Adm Stark. (S) Memo, Gerow to CofS, "Reinforcements for Hawaii," 12 Dec 41; (S) Memo, Somervell to CofS, "Lack of Effort of Navy Department to Speed up Dispatch of 21 Knot Convoy to Copper," 12 Dec 41. Both in WPD 4622-39. The other side of the story was told to the author by VAdm Vincent R. Murphy in an interview on 19 Apr 49. To him the Army appeared to have no appreciation of the desirability of forming convoys rather than wasting the limited supply of escort vessels on individual ships.

[12] (S) Mns, JB Mtgs, 9 and 13 Dec 41.

[13] (C) "Joint Action of the Army and the Navy, 1935," (JAAN), pars 9b(2) and 10.

[14] WPD 2917-26 to 47 contains most of the documents exchanged in this discussion. Cf. also (C) JB 350 (ser 678), Ltr, CNO to JB, ser 015012, "'Joint Action of the Army and the Navy, 1935,' proposed revision of Coastal Frontiers," 11 Feb 41; (C) Memo, Lt Col J.L. McKee and Lt Col L.H. Slocum to Gen Gerow, "'Joint Action of the Army and the Navy November 1935,' Proposed Revision of Coastal Frontiers," 4 Oct 41, JB 350 (ser 678); (U) Memo, Gerow to CofS, "Method of Coordination of Command in Coastal Frontiers," 17 Nov 41, WPD 2917-32, *PHA*, pt 15, pp. 1482-1483.

[15] Apparently no Navy representatives were present. (UNK) Memo, Actg ACofS (Gerow) to Stark, 12 Dec 41, WPD 2917-34. Enclosed are a draft proposal for command control in Panama and the Caribbean, a page from ch II, JAAN, and a map of the Panama and Caribbean Coastal Frontiers with notations by "FDR." Memo indicates "attached are the papers on unity of command that were discussed at the White House today," implying that Adm Stark was not present at the discussions. Note on memo indicates papers were delivered to Adm Stark at 7:15 p.m., 12 Dec 41. In conversation with the author on 17 Jun 49, Adm Stark was unable to recall whether or not he was present at the meeting.

[16] (S) Mns, JB Mtg, 13 Dec. 41.

[17] (S) Mns, JB Mtg, 17 Dec 41; (S) Memo, CNO to CofS, USA, "Unity of Command," 17 Dec 41, WPD 2917-38. Adm Stark accepted an Army proposal, with modification to indicate that unity of command was established on the initiative of the Secretaries of War and Navy, rather than by direction of the President. The reason for this is not clear. The memo to which this was a reply has not yet been located by the author.

[18] (S) Mns, JB Mtg, 17 Dec 41; (P&C) Memo, CofS to ComGenHawDept, 20 Dec 41, WPD 2917-35; (S) Msg, CNO to CinCPac, 172355 Dec 41,

WPD 2917-37; (S) Msg, CofS to ComGenHawDept, 693, 17 Dec 41, WPD 2917-38; (P&C) Ltr, CofS to ComGenHawDept, 20 Dec 41, *PHA*, pt 15, p. 1483.

    Instructions...were issued a few days ago assigning unity of command to the Navy in Hawaii. At the same time unity of command was assigned to the Army in Panama.

    For your confidential information, this action was taken in the following circumstances: In the first place, the Secretary of War and the Secretary of the Navy were determined that there should be no question of future confusion as to responsibility. Further, the efforts I have been making for more than a year to secure unity of command in various critical regions had been unavailing....Both Stark and I were struggling to the same end, but until this crash of December 7th the difficulties seemed, at least under peacetime conditions, almost insurmountable.

[19] (S) Msg, CNO to CinCPac, 090139 Dec 41, (TS) CominCh file "CinCPac Despatches."

[20] (S) Mns, JB Mtg, 8 Dec 41.

[21] (S) Ltr, Secy for Collab to CSO BJSM, "ABC-1; modification of," ser 011512-118, 16 Dec 41, CNO(WPD) file "Pacific and Far East Area British Joint Staff 1941."

[22] (S) Memo, Gerow to CofS USA, "Reinforcement of the Philippines," 14 Aug 41, WPD 3251-55; (U) Memo, CofS USA to CNO, 12 Sep 41, Exh. 12 to Navy Ct. of Inq., PHA, pt 33, p. 1170. Navy planners and Adm Stark had for some time been urging an increase of Army forces, particularly planes. (S) Ltr, Stark to Hart, 23 Dec 40, PHA, pt 14, p. 984.

[23] USSBS (Pacific), *The Campaigns of the Pacific War* (Washington, 1946), p. 28. Commanders have given conflicting accounts of the events in the Japanese attacks, and it has been difficult to explain these considerable losses. The best discussions are in *AAF in WW II*, vol. I, pp. 201-204, and Walter D. Edmonds, "What Happened at Clark Field," *Atlantic Monthly*, vol 188, no. 1 (Jul 51), pp. 19-33.

[24] For a full account of the campaign in the Philippines, see Louis Morton, MS, *The Fall of the Philippines* (OCMH, 1952).

[25] (S) Mns, JB Mtg, 8 Dec 41.

[26] (S) Mns, JB Mtg, 9 Dec 41.

[27] (S) Mns, JB Mtg, 10 Dec 41; (S) Msg, US CofS to CG USAFFE, 776, 12 Dec 41, WPD 4628, lists ships in convoy and their cargo.

[28] (S) Msg, CofS to Barnes, 12 Dec 41, WPD 4628.

[29] (S) Msg, CofS to Brett, 31, 17 Dec 41, WPD 4628; (MS) Pers Msg for FDR from Sayre, 15 Dec 41, WPD 4622-38; (S) Msg, CofS to Brink, MO Singapore, 59, 15 Dec 41, WPD 4544-31; Stimson and Bundy, pp. 395-397.

[30] (S) Msg, AG to Brett, 31, 17 Dec 41, JB 325 (ser 738); (S) Msg, CofS to Brett, 34, 21 Dec 41, WPD 4630-1.

[31] (S) JB 325 (ser 738), "Agreement on Organization and Coordination of Army and Navy Support for Army and Navy forces in the Philippines, the Netherlands East Indies, and Australia," 21 Dec

41. There is no evidence in JB minutes, and none has been found elsewhere, of the circumstances under which this study was undertaken by JPC.

[32] (S) Msg, SecWar to Brett, 21 Dec 41, JB 325 (ser 738).

[33] (S) Msg, Brereton to AG, 251501 Dec 41 (Navy channels), WD WPD MC 1494; (S) Msg, CG USAFFE to AG, 25 Dec 41, WD WPD MC 1462; *AAF in WW II*, pp. 220ff; Lewis H. Brereton, *The Brereton Diaries* (New York, 1946), pp. 60-67.

[34] The decision was made independently of the naval forces present, and Adm Hart was not informed until removal had commenced. The surface forces of the Asiatic Fleet had been sent south under RAdm Glassford on the 8th, according to plan. Only submarines remained in the islands, operating from the tender *Canopus* after destruction of the naval facilities at Cavite on 10 December. (C) Hart, *Narrative of Events*, pp. 36-46; WDGS, *The World at War, 1939-1944* (Washington, 1945), pp. 116-119; Gen G.C. Marshall, *The United States at War*, Official Report, p. 11.

[35] (S) Msg, CG USAFFE to CofS, 2 and 3, 1 Jan 42, WPD 4639-2.

[36] (S) Msg, CofS USA to CG USAFFE, 913, 2 Jan 42, WPD 4639-2. Under the old Orange plans it had been assumed that the fleet might be able to regain control of the western Pacific in time for a combined naval and military expedition to relieve the Philippine garrison within six months of the outbreak of war. After 1937 it was recognized that one or two years might elapse before such relief could reach the Philippines. The Rainbow studies of 1939-40 assumed that a strong British Fleet in the southwest Pacific might permit the Philippines to be held and relieved before the garrison was overwhelmed. Rainbow No. 5 contained no provision for relieving the Philippines.

[37] Memo, Pres to SecWar, 30 Dec 41, quoted in Robert E. Sherwood, *Roosevelt and Hopkins* (New York, 1948), p. 454.

[38] (S) Memo, Army WPD (sgd L.T. Gerow, ACofS) to CofS, "Relief of the Philippines," 3 Jan 42, WPD 4639-3. ABC-4/3 was produced at Arcadia. For discussion see below, pp. 55-57.

[39] The trip was planned on 7 Dec 41 when the PM called the Pres after learning of the attack on Pearl Harbor. Sherwood, p. 439.

[40] The JB was not an exact parallel to the BCOS organization and was already proving far from ideal for direction of war strategy. Adm King was not a member of it. Except for some preparatory work before the conference, it did not participate in Arcadia. For more detailed discussion of Arcadia organization and membership see (S) Vernon E. Davis, *History of the Joint Chiefs of Staff in World War II: Organizational Development* (Washington, 1953), vol I, ch V. Problems considered at the conference which were not directly concerned with the war against Japan are discussed in (S) MSS, JCS Hist, *Evolution of Global Strategy* and *War Against Germany and Its Satellites*.

[41] Winston S. Churchill, *The Grand Alliance* (Boston, 1950), p. 641. (S) Brit Doc COS (42) 79, "Washington War Conference,"

Feb 42, photostat in JCS HS. Anns I to VI are minutes of British staff meetings. In a letter to Gen Marshall on 2 Jan 42 (WPD 4389-57) Lt Gen Sir Colville Wemyss reported that "the policy is that the security of Singapore and Burma and sea communications to the Indian Ocean are second in importance only to the security of Great Britain and her sea communications...." Mr. Churchill predicted on 23 Dec that Singapore would hold out for six months.

[42] (S) "British Memorandum of 18 Dec 1941," JB 325 (ser 729) General Strategy -- Review by the British Chiefs of Staff. (Hereinafter: JB 325 [ser 729].) The BCOS had determined upon these points at a meeting on 13 Dec 41. (S) Mns, BCOS Mtg, 13 Dec 41, Ann I to Brit Doc, "Washington War Conference December 1941-January 1942," C.O.S. (42) 79, Feb 42, photostat in JCS HS.

[43] (S) Memo for Rec, by Col W.P. Scobey, 21 Dec 41; (S) "Paper A, Tentative U.S. Views on Subjects of British Memorandum, Dec 19"; (S) Paper B, Dft, "Broad Military Decisions," nd. All in JB 325 (ser 729). According to Col Scobey's memo the two papers were approved by JB on 21 Dec 41. They "constitute the approved view by The Joint Board on general strategy, and served as the basis for presentation by the Chief of Staff and Chief of Naval Operations of the War and Navy Departments' recommendations to the President on December 21, 1941." Several drafts, including one prepared by SecWar, are in WPD 4402-136. Internal evidence (handwritten changes, sizes of type) indicates that the Navy prepared the initial draft of Paper B, while the Army prepared the initial draft of Paper A, and the two were rather hastily combined in the final paper.

[44] (S) "Brief Joint Estimate of the Military Situation of the Associated Powers," 20 Dec 41, JB 325 (ser 729). A note signed W.P.S[cobey] states that it is one of the development papers for Paper B. The size of type and SECRET stamp indicate naval origin, although the paper is not specifically identified.

[45] This position was emphatically stated to the author by Adm Harold R. Stark, USN(Ret) in an interview on 17 Jun 49.

[46] For discussion of the Victory Program prepared in the summer of 1941 see (S) MSS, JCS Hist, *Evolution of Global Strategy* and *Mobilization and Demobilization of Military Manpower*.

[47] (S) Memo, by SecWar, "Memorandum of Decisions at White House, December 21, 1941," WPD 4402-136, sec 10, env; (S) Memo, Actg ACofS to CofS USA, "General Strategic Review," 23 Dec 41, WPD 4402-136, sec 10.

[48] *The Grand Alliance*, pp. 663-665. Present were Mr. Cordell Hull, Mr. Sumner Welles, Mr. Harry Hopkins, Lord Beaverbrook, and Lord Halifax.

[49] (S) Marshall, "Notes of Meeting at the White House with the President and Prime Minister Presiding," 23 Dec 41, WPD 4402-136.

[50] (S) Mns, Arcadia 1st Mtg, 24 Dec 41. Minutes of this and the subsequent meetings have been reproduced and bound in a volume bearing the title of the conference, a copy of which is in JCS R&RA. Separate minutes were kept by the British and are included

as annexes to (S) Brit Doc COS (42) 79, "Washington War Conference," Feb 42, photostat in JCS HS.

[51] This statement was probably made by one of the British Chiefs of Staff, for the next sentence states, "The Prime Minister had quoted Stalin as saying that Russia was not ready to enter the war in the Far East now, but perhaps would be able to do so in the spring." This information had been obtained through Mr. Anthony Eden, who was just concluding conversations in Moscow with Stalin. *The Grand Alliance*, p. 631. SecState Cordell Hull had also been told as early as 11 Dec 1941 by Soviet Ambassador Maxim Litvinov that Russia was not then in a position to cooperate against Japan. Hull, vol II, p. 1111.

[52] (S) Memo by BCOS, "Probable Maximum Scale of Enemy Attack on West Coast of North America," nd, Ann 2 to Mns, Arcadia 1st Mtg, 24 Dec 41.

[53] (S) WW-1, Memo by BCOS (rev by US CsofS), "American-British Strategy," nd, Ann 1 to Mns, Arcadia 1st Mtg, 24 Dec 41.

[54] The paper in final form, dated 31 Dec 41, is appended to the bound Arcadia minutes.

[55] The original British version read, "the collapse of Italy and Japan must speedily follow." At the suggestion of some unidentified person at the first meeting it was decided that it would be better to omit the adverb. (S) Brit Mns, Arcadia 1st Mtg, item III.

[56] (S) IB 166, "Japanese Potentialities against Singapore," MID, G-4, 33782, 22 Dec 41.

[57] (S) Memo, Brig L.C. Hollis to US CsofS, 24 Dec 41, WPD 4402-136.

[58] (S) Mns, Arcadia 2nd Mtg, 25 Dec 41, items 3 and 4; (S) Brit Mns, Arcadia 2nd Mtg, 25 Dec 41, item 3.

[59] The American-British Planning Committee rather than the old JPC of the Joint Board. The final form of the directive was drawn up by the Secretaries and Adm Pound on the basis of drafts offered at Arcadia meeting by various members of the group.

[60] (S) ABC-4/3, Rpt by Jt Plng Cmte, "Supporting Measures for the Southwest Pacific," 28 Dec 41, *Arcadia*.

[61] This paper seems to have been prepared mainly by the U.S. members of the Joint Planning Committee. (S) Memo, RAdm R.K. Turner, "Suggested procedure for drafting report of Southwest Pacific Area," 26 Dec 41; (MS) Uniden, "Study of the Supporting Measures in Favor of the Philippines, Malaya and the NEI," 25 and 26 Dec 41. Both in ABC 381 Southwest Pacific Area (1-12-42). The only evidence of the origin of the latter paper is a U.S. Navy reference number on p. 7 (OP-12A-4-aw). In somewhat lengthier form it contains essentially the same points as ABC-4/3.

[62] Cf. above, pp. 47-51.

[63] (S) Mns, Arcadia 7th Mtg, 31 Dec 41, item 3.

[64] (S) Msg, CofS USA to Brink, 59, 15 Dec 41, WPD 4544-31. This was one of three conferences which Mr. Roosevelt proposed, at Singapore, Chungking, and Moscow, to report to Washington during

the Arcadia Conference the problems and views of officials in the three areas. Plans for the Singapore Conference apparently were made by the War Dept and the Pres. CNO, in directing CinCAF to send a representative, reported first learning of the conferences after instructions had been sent to Col Brink, (S) Msg, CNO to CinCAF, 160035 Dec 41, CNO(WPD). A Chinese representative was invited but none came.

[65] (S) Rpt, Brink to CofS USA, "Inter-Allied Conference, Singapore, December 18th and 20th, 1941," 25 Dec 41, WPD 4544-31.

[66] (MS) Msg from Cooper, no adee, 20 Dec 41, WPD 4402-137; (UNK) Msg, MA Singapore to WD, 21 Dec 41, rpted in (S) Memo for Pres, no sig, "Situation in the Philippines," 24 Dec 41, OCS 18136-179.

[67] (S) Msg, CinCAF to CNO, 220815 Dec 41, CNO(WPD).

[68] (S) Msg, MA Singapore to WD, 21 Dec 41, rpted in (S) Memo for Pres, "Situation in the Philippines," 24 Dec 41, OCS 18136-179.

[69] (S) Memo, Rogers to ACofS WPD, "Preliminary Report of Singapore Conference by Col Brink," Dec 41, WPD 4544-31.

[70] (S) Mns, Arcadia 2nd Mtg, 25 Dec 41.

[71] In a memo on this conference drawn up by Brig Gen Eisenhower, it is recorded that "No other individual, except Admiral King made any remarks in favor of attempting, immediately, to set up a unified command in the Southwestern Pacific." (S) Memo for File, 28 Dec 41, WPD 4639. British minutes of the meeting record that "Admiral King said that it would certainly be better to decide at home the general line of action to be followed in the Southwest Pacific area than to have it discussed by a Committee on the spot. If there were to be a single Commander, it would be very difficult for him to reconcile the various national interests." (S) Brit Mns, Arcadia 2nd Mtg, 25 Dec 41. Adm Stark was strongly in favor of unified command. Conv, Adm Stark with author, 17 Jun 49.

[72] (S) Mns, WH Conf, 26 Dec 41, WDCSA 334 Meetings & Conferences (1-28-42) I, "Informal Conferences Held during the Visit of the British Chiefs of Staff in Washington, Notes on," OCS Super-Secret file, DRB AGO; (S) Brig Gen L.T. Gerow, "Notes on Conference at White House, British & American Staffs," 26 Dec 41, OPD Exec 4, item 13.

[73] Gen Marshall's meeting with the PM was arranged by Mr. Hopkins, who had been advised by Lord Beaverbrook during the meeting that the PM could be persuaded. Sherwood, p. 457.

[74] (S) Mns, Mtg, US CsofS, CNO's office, 27 Dec 41 (SS) WDCSA 334 Meetings & Conferences (1-28-42) I.

[75] (S) Mns, Brit Staff Conf, 27 Dec 41, Brit Doc C.R. 22, photostat in JCS HS; *The Grand Alliance*, p. 673.

[76] (S) Mns, Brit Staff Conf, 28 Dec 41, Brit Doc C.R. 23, JCS HS.

[77] (S) Memo for file by Gen Eisenhower, "Notes Taken at Joint Conference of Chiefs of Staff on Afternoon, December 25," 28 Dec 41, WPD 4639. This includes an outline of instructions from Gen Marshall to draw up a document

to take the form of a letter of instructions to a supreme commander, giving him his mission, defining his authority and placing upon his authority specific limitations so as to exclude his interference from anything that was strictly the business of any particular government. The purpose of these rigid restrictions was to convince the other members of the conference that no real risk would be involved to the interests of any of the Associated powers, while on the other hand great profits should result.

[78] (S) Mns, Arcadia 4th Mtg, 27 Dec 41, item 5.

[79] (UNK dg U) Msgs, PM to Lord Privy Seal, 28 and 29 Dec 41, *The Grand Alliance*, pp. 674-676; Sherwood, pp. 466-467. Having outlined the proposal, the PM stated, "I have not attempted to argue the case for and against our accepting this broadminded and selfless American proposal, of the merits of which as a war winner 1 have become convinced." (S) Mns, WH Conf, Pres, SecWar, SecNav, ASecWar, US CsofS, Turner, Gerow, Hopkins, Sexton, 28 Dec 41, in (SS) WDCSA 334 Meetings & Conferences (1-28-42).

[80] Memo [for record?] by Hopkins, 30 Dec 41, Sherwood, p. 469. Mr. Hopkins further reported:

As a matter of fact I suggested the words to the Prime Minister when I found he was getting all set to issue all the directions himself. It seemed to me so essential to get the unity of command through in the South West Pacific that rather than try to define what the "appropriate body" would be, I urged both the Prime Minister and the President to send it along and decide the make-up of the "appropriate joint body" later.

It now develops that everybody and his grandmother wants to be on the joint body and it now looks as if it would end by having the joint British and American staffs assist the President. At any rate they will run it.

[81] (S) Mns, Arcadia 5th Mtg, 29 Dec 41, item 5.

[82] (S) Memo by BCOS, "Proposed Method of Handling Matters concerning the Southwest Pacific," 29 Dec 41, Ann 2 to (S) Mns, Arcadia 5th Mtg, 29 Dec 41.

[83] (S) Mns, Arcadia 5th Mtg, 29 Dec 41, item 5.

[84] (S) Memo, Hopkins to Stark, 30 Dec 41, with encl, Ann 1 to (S) Mns, Arcadia 6th Mtg, 30 Dec 41.

[85] (S) Mns, Arcadia 6th Mtg, 30 Dec 41, item 1; (S) Memo, US CsofS to Pres, "Higher Direction of War in the ABDA Area," 30 Dec 41, Ann 2 to (S) Mns, Arcadia 6th Mtg, 30 Dec 41.

[86] For discussion of Pacific War Council, see below pp. 79-80.

[87] (S) Mns, Arcadia 4th Mtg, 27 Dec 41, item 5.

[88] (S) Mns, JPC 5th Mtg, 29 Dec 41. It is merely stated: "Following an examination of the situation and a discussion of the various features incidental to the problem the Committee agreed to the [draft directive] and directed it be sent to the Chiefs of Staff Committee." Since there are no further details and no

planning papers are available, it is not possible to determine the contributions of the various members to the final draft. (S) U.S. ABC-4/5, Brit WW (JPC) 5, CCS 381 (12-29-41).

[89] (S) U.S. ABC-4/5, Brit Ser WW-3, "Draft Directive to the Supreme Commander in the ABDA Area," 30 Dec 41, ann 3 to (S) Mns, Arcadia 6th Mtg, 30 Dec 41.

[90] (S) U.S. ABC-4/5, Brit WW-6 (approved), "Directive to the Supreme Commander in the ABDA Area," 10 Jan 42, Ann 1 to Mns, Arcadia 8th Mtg, 10 Jan 42.

[91] Gen Marshall's original draft used the designation ADBU; in the draft submitted by the planners ABDU was used. At the mtg of 30 Dec it had become ABDA.

[92] For fuller discussion see below, ch III.

[93] (S) Ltr, Lt Col Vogel, G.S.(Brit), to Brig Gen Gerow, 15 Dec 41, WPD 4402-132.

[94] (S) Brit Doc CR 37, Mns, BCOS Mtg, 1 Jan 42, item 1; (S) Brit Doc CR 38, Mns, BCOS Mtg w/PM, 1 Jan 42. Both in JCS HS.

[95] (S) Brit Mns, WH Conf, 1 Jan 42, in (SS) WDCSA 334 Meetings and Conference (1-28-42). The boundaries of the new commands were outlined in an annex to the directive.

On the North:...the boundary between India and Burma, thence eastward along the Chinese frontier and coastline to the latitude of 30 degrees North, thence along the parallel of 30 degrees North to the meridian of 140 degrees East. Note: Indo-China and Thailand are not included in this area.

On the East:...the meridian of 140 degrees East from 30 degrees North, to the Equator, thence east to longitude 141 degrees East, thence south to the boundary of Dutch New Guinea on the South Coast to the meridian 143 degrees East, then south down this meridian to the coast of Australia.

On the South:...the northern coast of Australia from the meridian of 114 degrees East, thence northwestward to latitude 15 degrees South, longitude 92 degrees East.

On the West:...the meridian of 92 degrees East.

[96] (S) Mns, Arcadia 6th Mtg, 30 Dec 41, item 2. The PM reported to the Lord Privy Seal on 28 Dec that Gen Brett would probably be Deputy and an American admiral would command the naval forces. (S) Msg, PM to LPS, encl to Ann XIII, COS (42) 79, "Washington War Conference December 1941 - January 1942," photostat in JCS HS.

[97] (S) U.S. ABC-4/3, Brit WW(JPC)3, "Supporting Measures for the Southwest Pacific," 28 Dec 41, Arcadia. See above, pp. 56-57.

[98] (S) ABC-4/5, "Draft Directive to Supreme Commander in the ABDA Area," 29 Dec 41, in (TS) CominCh file "ABC-4/1 to ABC-4/9 inclusive." Corrections in Adm King's handwriting include indication that the change in this instance was an Army proposal, with the note, "Safeguard against British 'piecemeal' air tactics - to avoid weakening of squadrons by scattering.

[99] (S) ABC-4/5 (Approved), "Directive for the Supreme Commander, Approved by the President and the Prime Minister," 2 Jan 41 [sic], CNO (WPD) file "*Comdr. McDowell--J.P.C. Reports.*"

748   NOTES TO CHAPTER II

[100] FAdm King and Adm Stark were both questioned on this point. Neither could recall why the statement was revised, but neither took exception to the suggestion above. Adm Stark did point out that it conformed to previous over-all plans. Comments of both men are on file in JCS HS.

[101] Cf. above, p. 56.

[102] By Telegram on 2 Jan, Gen Wavell informed the BCOS of his view of objectives for the area:

> attack on enemy shipping by air and submarine and on enemy air bases by air should be our primary objectives; and that to secure the line of naval and air bases Port Darwin-Timor-Java-Southern Sumatra-Singapore would probably represent the limit possible with the resources likely to be immediately available. I did not consider air bases in Northern Sumatra could be held with the enemy already established in Penang. The Chiefs of Staff...agreed generally with my views on the objectives to be aimed at, except that they considered air bases in Northern Sumatra must be held.

(S) Wavell, "Despatch on Operations in South-West Pacific, January 15th - February 25th, 1942," CCS 381 (12-29-41).

[103] "In practice, however, it became necessary for the Intendant General's Branch of ABDACOM staff to make all administrative arrangements in respect of many units and details which arrived in the Netherlands Indies during the later stages of the existence of ABDACOM," (S) Brit Doc No. B-3198, Archibald P. Wavell, "ABDACOM," p. 7, CCS 381 (12-29-41).

[104] (S dg U) ABC-4/5, "Directive to the Supreme Commander in the ABDA Area," 10 Jan 42, *Arcadia*.

[105] (S) Mns, Arcadia 8th Mtg, 10 Jan 42; (U) Ltr, Pres to Marshall, 9 Jan 42, *F.D.R.: His Personal Letters* (1928-1945 - II), p. 1271; (UNK) Ltr, Hollis to Hopkins, 5 Jan 42; (UNK) Ltr, Sumner Welles to Pres, 5 Jan 42. Both in (TS) Sherwood, Catalog of Papers of Harry Hopkins (hereinafter: Hopkins Catalog), I, bk IV, items 14, 15.

[106] (S) Mns, Arcadia 8th Mtg, 10 Jan 42.

[107] (S) Mns, Arcadia 9th Mtg, 11 Jan 42, item 2.

[108] (S) Mns, Arcadia 9th Mtg, 11 Jan 42, item 2. The identity of the "shipping experts" is not clear from the Arcadia papers. They probably were not formally organized as a committee.

[109] (S) Ann 1, "Memorandum of Proposed Shipping Adjustments," Mns, Arcadia 10th Mtg, 12 Jan 42.

[110] (S) Mns, Arcadia 10th Mtg, 12 Jan 42, item 1.

[111] (S) Memo, CofS USA to ACofS WPD, G-3, G-4, 13 Jan 42, CNO (WPD) file "C.O.S. & J.P.C. Mns."

[112] (S) Mns, JB Mtg, 26 Nov 41; (S) JB 349 (ser 735), "Alternate Route in the Pacific for Movement of Land-Based Airplanes to Far East," 28 Nov 41. Responsibility for development of the route from Hawaii as far as the Solomons was given to ComGenHawDept, while CG USAFFE was made responsible for bases from the Solomons to the Philippines. Negotiations with New Caledonia

749   NOTES TO CHAPTER II

were complicated by the political situation in regard to France and construction had not actually begun there. On the other islands work had commenced, and it was contemplated that the route would be fully operational by mid-January 1942. For details see material in WD WPD files 3718 and 4571.

[113] Cf. above, pp. 30-31.

[114] (UNK) Msg, CominCh to CinCPac, 301740 Dec 41, rpted in comments of FAdm King on MS, this ch, cy in JCS HS; (S) Memo, ACofS (Plans) to CominCh, ser 01912, 5 Jan 42, CominCh (SC) file "A16-3 (18)."

[115] (S) Mns, BCOS Mtg, 29 Dec 41, JCS HS; (S) Brit Doc M.M. (41) 234, "Pacific Islands Route - Defence Arrangements," 30 Dec 41, WPD 4571-23. The final paper submitted to CCS was based on the draft in the latter document.

[116] (S) Mns, JPC 6th Mtg, 3 Jan 42; (S) Memo, Cdr R.E. Libby to King, "Brief of Working Committee Memorandum for Planning Committee, subj: Security of Island Bases between Hawaii and Australia," 2 Jan 42, in (TS) CominCh file "ABC-4/1 to ABC-4/9 inclusive."

[117] (S) ABC-4/8, "Defense of Island Bases between Hawaii and Australia," 10 Jan 42, *Arcadia*.

[118] (S) Mns, Arcadia 9th Mtg, 11 Jan 42, item 4.

[119] (S) Memo, CominCh to CNO, JJ7(002), "Fuel Station in Society Islands; Borabora," 1 Jan 42, WPD 4571-21.

[120] (S) Mns, BCOS Mtgs, 1 and 2 Jan 42, JCS HS.

[121] (S) Statement by Adm King in Mns, WH Conf, 1 Jan 42, in (SS) WDCSA 334 Meetings and Conferences (1-28-42).

[122] Ann 3, "The Australian and New Zealand British Naval Stations west of Longitude 180° and south of the equator," par 29 *PHA*, pt 15, p. 1516.

[123] (S) Memo, ACofS (Plans) to CominCh, "Patrol of Ocean Triangle Outlined by Australia-New Zealand-Fiji," 01912, 5 Jan 42, (SC) A16-3(18).

> ...From the longitude of Torres Strait eastward along the Equator to longitude 170° east; thence southeasterly to latitude 20° south, longitude 175° west; thence south along the meridian of 175° west longitude.

[124] (S) Ltr, CominCh to Pound, 8 Jan 42, CNO(WPD) file "ANZAC."

[125] The reason for the Australian delay is not known. The subject does not appear in the minutes of the last meetings at Arcadia, and it has not been possible to ascertain the date on which the proposal was submitted to the Australians. There is a complete hiatus of documentary evidence on this subject between CominCh's ltr of 8 Jan and the Australian reply of 23 Jan.

[126] (S) Msg, Aust Govt to PM, 23 Jan 42, encl to CCS 7, 23 Jan 42, CCS 045.4 (1-23-42).

[127] (S) Mns, CCS 1st Mtg, 23 Jan 42, item 2.

[128] (S) CCS 15, "Institution of the ANZAC Area," 29 Jan 42, CCS 381 (1-24-42) sec 1; (S) Msg, CCS to ABDACOM, DBA 7, 30 Jan 42, CCS 320.2 (1-28-42). A CominCh memo in (TS) CominCh

file "Vice Chief of Naval Operations," indicates Adm Leary was to assume command on or about 2 Feb 42. (S) Msg, CominCh to CinCPac, 292110 Jan 42, (TS) CominCh file "CinCPac Despatches."

[129] "Beginning at longitude 141° East at the Equator eastward along the equator to longitude 170° East thence southeasterly to point in latitude 20° South longitude 175° West thence due South; from point of beginning South along Meridian 141° East to South coast of New Guinea thence eastward along said coast to Meridian 143° East thence due South in sea areas only."

[130] Later the President's Chief of Staff was to complete the membership. For detailed discussion of the evolution of CCS and JCS, see (S) Davis, *Organizational Development*, vol I, chs V-VII.

[131] *New York Times*, 6 Jan 42, p. 6; 12 Jan 42, p. 5; 26 Jan 42, p. 4. (S) Msg, PM to Pres, 27 Jan 42, OPD Exec 8, item 3.

[132] Plans for PWC were announced by the PM to the House of Commons on 27 Jan 42. *New York Times*, 28 Jan 42, p. 10. PM Curtin's comment was: "A war council centered in London and working with service chiefs who would make recommendations for transmission to Washington would not be acceptable to Australia." The first meeting was held on 10 Feb 42. *New York Times*, 10 Feb 42, p. 6. Winston S. Churchill, *The Hinge of Fate*, pp. 8, 18-19. (S) Davis, *Organizational Development*, vol I, ch VI, pp. 288-297.

CHAPTER III

[1] These officers, with the exception of the Chief of Staff, had been appointed by the CCS. For a detailed discussion of the organization of ABDACOM, see official British report, (S) Wavell, "ABDACOM." Principal commands in Far East were summarized for Gen MacArthur in (S) Msg, CofS USA to CGUSAFE, 991, 30 Jan 42, WPD 4628-25:

> Gen Wavell's headquarters has five staff divisions, each with American, British, Dutch, and Australian members as appropriate and available. In addition to staff heads, Brereton has headquarters in Java and commands all U.S. operating forces in ABDA and in Australia assigned to service in or in support of ABDA. The War Department does not know the exact locations of the elements of his command. Command of U.S. base forces and facilities in Australia is under Gen Barnes with HQ at Melbourne....

The American commanders themselves were not certain as to the limits of their powers. For series of despatches attempting to define their authority, cf. WPD 4628-20 to 25.

[2] The original directive to Gen Wavell contained instructions to set up headquarters in Java. This was not specifically stated in the final directive but by separate message he was instructed to do so. (S) Mns, Arcadia 8th Mtg, 10 Jan 42; Hart, *Narrative*, pp. 54-55; Wavell, "ABDACOM," sec II; (S) Wavell, "Despatch on Operations in South-West Pacific, January 15th - February 25th, 1942," pp. 2-3, CCS 381 (12-29-41). Adm Hart later expressed

751   NOTES TO CHAPTER III

regret that he had not followed Adm Helfrich's recommendation and set up headquarters at Batavia.

[3] (S) Msg, ABDACOM to Brit and US CsofS, 00048, 14 Jan 42, CNO(WPD) file "ABDA."

[4] (S) Msg, CominCh to CinCAF for Wavell, 160418 Jan 42; (S) Memo, King to Brit and US CsofS, "Assumption of ABDA Command by General Wavell," 16 Jan 42. Both in WPD 4639-19.

[5] (S) Memo, Marshall to Stark, King, and Arnold, 16 Jan 42, photostatic copy with "OK FDR" in WPD 4639-19; (S) Memo, CofS USA to King, "Assumption of Command in the ABDA Area," nd, contains msg to be sent via CinCAF to ABDACOM, CNO(WPD) file "ABDA." Gen Marshall urged immediate implementation since official approval from London, the Australian and the New Zealand Governments would probably entail a dangerous delay.

[6] (S) Msg, CofS to CGUSAFFE, 930, 11 Jan 42, WPD 4639-14.

[7] (S) Ltr, Secy for Collab to Secy BJSM, 16 Jan 42, ser 011512-142, encl A, Msg, CCS to ABDACOM, approved by Admty 17 Jan 42, CNO(WPD) file "ABDA."

[8] (S) Wavell, "ABDACOM," p. 16.

[9] *Campaigns of the Pacific War*, ch III and apps 10-14.

[10] (S) Wavell, "ABDACOM," pp. 16-17.

[11] In Malaya were some three Imperial Divisions, with three others en route, two of which, Australian Divisions from the Middle East, arrived too late and were diverted to Burma and the N.E.I. Some 40,000 troops were under American command in the Philippines and 3 Dutch divisions in Java.

[12] (S) Wavell, "ABDACOM"; (C) T.C. Hart, *Narrative of Events* (Supplementary Narrative), cys in NR&H; *The Brereton Diaries*, pp. 88-89.

[13] (S) Encl A to CominCh ser 011512-142 to BJSM, 16 Jan 42, Msg, CCS to ABDACOM, CNO(WPD) file "ABDA,"

> No restrictions as to time and locality are placed upon your employment of forces to accomplish the purposes set forth in your directive. It is intended that you will utilize your forces to carry out the missions laid down in your directive in a logical sequence to be determined by you in the light of the changing situation.

[14] (S) JB 325 (ser 738), 21 Dec 41.

[15] The southern boundary was defined as "the northern coast of Australia from the meridian of 143° East, westward to the meridian of 114° East, thence northwestward to latitude 15° South, longitude 92° East."

[16] (S) Wavell, "ABDACOM," p. 4.

[17] (S) Mns, Arcadia 9th Mtg, 11 Jan 42.

[18] (S) CCS 8, "Inclusion of Port Darwin in the ABDA Area," 24 Jan 42, CCS 381 (1-24-42) sec 1; (S) Msg, CCS to ABDACOM, DBA 2, 24 Jan 42, in JCS file DBA & CCOS Radios to ABDACOM; (S) Mns, CCS 2nd Mtg, 27 Jan 42, item 6.

[19] (S) CCS 14, "Malaya-New Guinea Situation," 27 Jan 42, CCS 371 (1-27-42).

NOTES TO CHAPTER III

[20] (S) Mns, CCS 2nd Mtg, 27 Jan 42, item 8; (S) Msg, CCS to ABDACOM, DBA 5, 29 Jan 42, CCS 320.2 (1-28-42).

[21] (S) Msg, ABDACOM to CCS, 00649, 1 Feb 42, CCS 320.2 (1-28-42).

[22] (S) Mns, CCS 1st Mtg, 23 Jan 42, item 10.

[23] (S) Mns, CCS 3rd Mtg, 3 Feb 42, item 7 (S) Msg, CCS to ABDACOM, DBA 8, 3 Feb 42; Msg, CofS USA to ABDACOM, rptd in memo to Brig Dykes, 6 Feb 42; (S) Msg, CofS USA to ABDACOM, 5 Feb 42. All in JCS file DBA & CCOS RADIOS TO ABDACOM.

[24] (S) CCS 29, "Naval, Air, and Land Forces of the United Nations in or Assigned to the ABDA and ANZAC Areas," 5 Feb 42, CCS 320.2 (1-28-42). Rpted in App.

[25] (S) CCS 30, "Air Requirements for Australia and New Zealand," 5 Feb 42, CCS 452.1 (2-5-42).

[26] (S) Mns, CCS 4th Mtg, 10 Feb 42, item 7; (S) CCS 30/1, Memo by JCS, "Air Requirements for Australia and New Zealand," 10 Feb 42, CCS 452.1 (2-5-42).

[27] (S) JPS 12, changed to JPS 2/1, "Directive to JUSSC," 11 Feb 42, CCS 381 (1-30-42) sec 1. Cf. below, ch V, pp. 106ff.

[28] (S) Msg, CofS USA to Brett to AG, 5 ABDA 152, 31 Jan 42; (S) Msg, CofS USA to Brett, 69, 2 Feb 42. Both in WPD 4639-28.

[29] (UNK) Dft Memo, Actg ACofS G-2 to CofS USA, "Japanese Acquisition of Commercial Air Base on Portuguese Timor," 10 Nov 41, WPD 4295-2.

[30] (UNK) Memo, Col C.W. Bundy to Exec WPD, 12 Nov 41, WPD 4295-2.

[31] (S) Msg, Brett to AG, Navy CinCAF to OpNav, 150300, WDMC 832, Jan 42, ABDACOM Desp 00058, 15 Jan 42.

[32] (S) Msg, CCS to ABDACOM, DBA 6, 30 Jan 42; (S) CCS 16, "Portuguese Timor," 27 Jan 42. Both in CCS 660.2 (1-27-42) sec 1.

[33] (S) Wavell, "ABDACOM," p. 58; (S) Msg, ABDACOM to CCS, CCOS 21, 24 Feb 42, in JCS file Radios from ABDACOM, GHQ Java, etc.

[34] (S) Msg, CofS USA to Brett, 2 Feb 42, CCS 21368-21.

[35] (S) CCS 25, "Defense of Timor," 2 Feb 42, CCS 660.2 (1-27-42) sec 1.

[36] (S) Msg, Brett to CofS USA, ABDA 208, 4 Feb 42, in JCS file Radios from ABDACOM, GHQ Java etc; (S) Wavell, "ABDACOM," p. 59; (S) CCS 25/1, "Defense of Timor," 6 Feb 42, CCS 660.2 (1-27-42) sec 1; (S) Msg, ABDACOM to CGS Aust (Sturdee), 00576, 31 Jan 42, in JCS file Radios from ABDACOM (Wavell Only).

[37] (S) Wavell, "ABDACOM," p. 60.

[38] (S) Msg, CCS to ABDACOM, DBA 19, 20 Feb 42, in JCS file DBA & CCOS Radios to ABDACOM; (S) Msg, ABDACOM to CCS, CCOS 17, 22 Feb 42, in JCS file Radios from ABDACOM, GHQ Java etc; (S) Wavell, "ABDACOM," p. 72.

[39] As listed in (S) Wavell, "ABDACOM," p. 18, ABDA naval forces comprised:

	Cruisers	Destroyers	Submarines	Sloops
U.S.	4	11	26	--
British	6	5 (plus 4 old small DDs at Singapore)	2	2
Dutch	3	8	8 (plus 3 local defense submarines)	--

Adm Hart in 1949 remembered the number of U.S. cruisers as 2 or 3, destroyers as 12. Conv, Adm Stark with author, 17 Jun 49.

[40](S) CCS 2, BCOS Msg, "Naval Reinforcements for ABDA Area," 19 Jan 42, CCS 045.4 (1-19-42).

[41](S dg U) Ltr, CNO and CofS USA to Spenavo London, "Comment on the report of the American-Dutch-British Conversations, Singapore, April, 1941," 075112, 3 Jul 41, *PHA*, pt 15, pp. 1677-1679.

[42](S dg U) Msg, CinCAF to CNO, 070327 Dec 41, *PHA*, pt 18, p. 3547.

[43](S) Msg, TROOPERS to EASFAR, MIDEAST, ADMINDIA, *et al.*, 61519, 1 Jan 42, rpted in (S) Wavell, "ABDACOM," p. 17. Gen Brereton, Deputy CinC of ABDACOM air staff, had similar differences with his senior, Air Marshal Peirse, RAF. Gen Brereton advocated concentrating bomber efforts against Japan in Macassar Strait, while Air Marshal Peirse was inclined to employ them piecemeal in Malaya. *The Brereton Diaries*, pp. 88-89.

[44](S) CCS 2/1, Memo by JCS, "Naval Reinforcements for ABDA Area," 20 Jan 42, CCS 045.4 (1-19-42). Reply drawn up by naval members, approved by Army CofS. (S) Memo, ACofS (Gerow) to CofS USA, "Naval Reinforcements for ABDA Area," 20 Jan 42, WPD 4639-21; (S) Mns, CCS 1st Mtg, 23 Jan 42, item 2.

[45](S) Mns, CCS 2nd Mtg, 27 Jan 42, item 1; (S) Mns, CCS 3rd Mtg, 3 Feb 42, item 3.

[46](UNK) Ltr, Sumner Welles to Pres, 5 Jan 42, summary in Hopkins Catalog, bk V, Command in ABDA Area, item 14.

[47](UNK) Msg, PM to Pres, 1 Feb 42, summary in Hopkins Catalog, bk V, item 17.

[48](S) Msg, CominCh to CinCAF, 302350 Jan 42; (S) Msg, CinCAF to CominCh, 011055 Feb 42. Both in (TS) CominCh file "ComSoWestPac Despatches - Jan. '42 thru Dec. '43."

[49](S) Msg, CominCh to CinCAF, 041740 Feb 42; (S) Msg, CinCAF to CominCh, 050425 Feb 42. Both in (TS) CominCh file "ComSoWestPac Despatches - Jan. '42 thru Dec. '43." In addition to the documents cited other sources for the account of the relief of Adm Hart are: his own account; (C) T.C. Hart, *Narrative of Events* (passim and Supplementary Narrative); Conv, Capt T.B. Kittredge USNR, JCS HS, with Adm Stark, Sep 47; and Conv, Adm Stark with author, 17 Jun 49. FAdm King and Adms Stark and Hart have read a draft of this chapter, and this passage has been revised to accord with their recollections. Both FAdm King and Adm Stark were insistent that it was through no shortcoming of Adm Hart, physical or otherwise, but because of political pressure that he was replaced. Comments on file in JCS HS.

[50](S) CCS 32, "Naval Command ABDA Area," 7 Feb 42, CCS 210.33 ABDA Area (2-7-42); (S) Mns, JCS 1st Mtg, 9 Feb 42, item 2; (S) Mns, CCS 4th Mtg, 10 Feb 42, item 10.

[51]Gen Marshall informed Gen Brett that "we are unanimous in our desire to avoid unnecessary intrusion into matters in which General Wavell's wishes should be decisive, but to insure successful operation of unified command in its initial application it is

essential that homeland support of countries affected be sustained. ..." He expressed it as his personal opinion that "any other solution would involve the most profound political repercussions in this country and could not possibly be accepted." (S) Msg, CofS USA to Brett, 73, 4 Feb 42, WPD 4628-27. The question of an American air commander was discussed at some length by the U.S. Chiefs. The President's message to the PM in which it was recommended was prepared in the War Dept (draft dtd 30 Jan 42 in WPD 4629-26). After it was forwarded by the PM to Gen Wavell, Gen Brett suggested that his own authority be extended to include supply and maintenance of US forces in the area, and that a US admiral continue in command of the combined naval forces. (S) Msg, Brett to CofS USA, 8, 3 Feb 42, AG 371 (2-3-42). It appears that Gen Wavell disapproved the US proposal, although no documentary evidence has yet been discovered.

[52] (U) Msg, PM to Wavell, 23 Jan 42, *The Hinge of Fate*, p. 134.

[53] *The Hinge of Fate*, p. 133.

[54] For fuller discussion of prewar relations with China, see above, ch I, and (S) MS, JCS Hist, *Evolution of Global Strategy*.

[55] (S) Paraphrase of msg from American Amb at Chungking to State Dept, 8 Dec 41, WPD 4389-2.

[56] (S) Mns of Conf, Magruder, Gimo, Mme Chiang, Gen Chang Shen, Col MacMorland, at Chungking, 10 Dec 41, in file "Magruder Mission (AMMISCA) War Diary, 8 Dec 41-June 42." OCMH files. (S) Msg, AMMISCA to AGWAR, 95, 10 Dec 41, "Conference File Dec 1941," Hq China Theater, CT 23, Dr 2, RAC, AGO, St. Louis, Mo.; (S) Msg, Owen Lattimore to Lauchlin Currie, from Chungking, 11 Dec 41, WPD 4389-47.

[57] Sherwood, p. 439.

[58] (S) Msg, CofS USA to Brett, 71, 15 Dec 41, WPD 4389-54. Gen Brett was just arriving in Burma to survey the possibilities of supplying bomber bases in China by air. The conference was called for 17 Dec but delayed because of Gen Brett's and Gen Wavell's late arrival. Romanus-Sunderland, *Stilwell's Mission*, pp. 51-56.

[59] This (S) paper, mentioned in the conf minutes, is probably to be identified as "The General Scheme of the Associated Operation of United States, Great Britain, Union of Socialist Soviet Republic of Russia, Netherland and China," which is included with the minutes of the Chungking Conf in folder, "Conference File Dec. 1941," file Hq China Theater, Ct 23, Dr 2, RAC, AGO, St. Louis, Mo. There is no evidence that it was even forwarded to Washington.

[60] (S) Mns of the Chungking Conf are in folder "Conference File, Dec. 1941," file Hq China Theater, CT 23, Dr 2, RAC, AGO, St. Louis, Mo.; (S) Copy of Gen Brett's cabled report of 27 Dec 41, WPD 4389-58.

[61] On 15 Dec 41, Burma had been transferred from the Far East Command with headquarters at Singapore to GHQ (India).

[62] Wavell msg, "Operations in Burma from 15th December 1941, to 20th May, 1942," supp to *London Gazette*, 11 Mar 48, OCMH.

[63] (S) Memo, no sig to CofS USA, "Transfer of Chinese Lend-Lease Stores to Burma," 13 Dec 41, WPD 4389-27.

[64] (S) Msg, SecWar to AMMISCA, 70, 14 Dec 41, WPD 4389-47.

[65] (S) Mns of Conf, Chungking, 26 Dec 41, Gimo, Mme Chiang, Gen Magruder, Col MacMorland, Owen Lattimore, Gen Shang Chen; (S) Msg, AMMISCA to SecWar and CofS, 129, 27 Dec 41; (UNK) Msg, Amb Gauss to SecState, 543, 29 Dec 41. All in folder "Conference File Dec 1941," file Hq China, CT 23, Dr 2, RAC, AGO, St. Louis, Mo. Romanus-Sunderland, *Stilwell's Mission*, pp. 57-60.

[66] (U) Memo, Brig Gen L.T. Gerow, ACofS WPD, to Col Handy, 28 Dec 41, WPD 4389-61. Gen Gerow requested a paper on the subject of a joint body in Chungking, "as imposing as possible. The President is interested."

[67] (S) Mns of Mtg in office of SecWar, 29 Dec 41; (S) Memo for Gerow, encl dft memo for Pres, 29 Dec 41. Both in WPD 4389-61. Sherwood, p. 458.

[68] (S) Mns, Arcadia 5th Mtg, 29 Dec 41, item 6, and Ann 3 to mns.

[69] (S) Msg, CNO to ALUSNA, Chungking, 300327 Dec 41, *Arcadia*.

[70] Note Mr. Hopkins' comments on the final copy that went to the Pres: "I personally don't think Chiang Kai-shek is getting much of a command out of this. In fact, all he is getting that he has not already got is that any of our or British troops in China will fight under him." Hopkins Catalog, I, bk V, Command in ABDA Area.

[71] Stimson and Bundy, p. 529. A paper prepared by Brig Gen Raymond E. Lee predicted a Japanese invasion of Burma in the near future and estimated that, unless heavy ground and air reenforcements could reach Burma, Rangoon could be captured in not to exceed five weeks, spelling the end of delivery of supplies overland to China. (S) Memo, Actg ACofS G-2 to ACofS WPD, "Japanese Attack against Burma," 28 Dec 41, WPD 4544-35.

[72] (UNK) Memo, "The China Proposal," in possession of Lt Gen Drum; notes thereon courtesy of Mr. Riley Sunderland, CBI Sec, OCMH. The remark was made by the Pres at the time that Gen Marshall was jumped over Gen Drum to be Chief of Staff. For fuller discussion, see Romanus-Sunderland, *Stilwell's Mission*, pp. 63-70.

[73] *Ibid*.

[74] The work appears to have been instigated by SecWar Stimson who, in a memo to Gen Marshall on 6 Jan 42, outlined his views of Gen Drum's projected command and recommended that the approval of the Pres and the PM be obtained before the British left for London. (S) Memo, Stimson to Marshall, 6 Jan 42, OPD 314.7 CTO sec 3, ch 3, Washington Pre Planning.

[75] (S) Ltr, Soong to ASec War McCloy, 6 Jan 42, confirming previous conversation, WPD 4389-64. Gen Drum records that the possibility of such an appointment had already been discussed with Soong before he (Gen Drum) was summoned to Washington. Hence, it is highly possible that it had been suggested to the Gimo that he make such a proposal.

[76] (S) ABC-4/CS2, Memo for BCOS, "Immediate Assistance to China," 8 Jan 42; 2nd dft of same, 9 Jan 42, CCS 091.711 China (1-20-42) sec 1. The second draft is labelled "Ad. Turner." It includes some revisions which presumably were made after discussion with Navy planners.

[77] (S) ABC-4/CS2, Memo for BCOS, "Immediate Assistance to China," 8 Jan 42, CCS 091.711 China (1-20-42) sec 1. Recommendations almost identical to those outlined above were made by Gen Magruder in a msg to MID, 5 Jan 42, in (TS) CominCh file "Memoranda to Admiral - 1942."

[78] (S) U.S. ABC-4/9, Brit WW (JPC) 9, Rpt by JPC, "Immediate Assistance to China," 10 Jan 42, CCS 091.711 China (1-20-42) sec 1; (S) Mns, JPC 8th Mtg, 9 Jan 42, CNO(WPD) file "Cdr McDowell - CCS & JPC Minutes."

[79] (S) Mns, Brit Staff Mtg, 10 Jan 42, C.R. 55, Ann XXVII, item 6. "Immediate Assistance to China," JCS HS.

[80] (S) Mns, Arcadia 8th Mtg, 10 Jan 42, item 4; (S) U.S. ABC-4/9, "Immediate Assistance to China," 10 Jan 42, CCS 091.711 China (1-20-42) sec 1. The minutes give few details of the discussion of this paper but indicate that it went on "at some length."

[81] (UNK) Memo, Drum, "The China Proposal," nd; (S) Memo, Drum to SecWar and CofS USA, "Strategic and Operational Conception of the U.S. Effort to Assist China," 8 Jan 42; (S) Paper by Drum, "Analysis of General Staff Memorandum for British Chiefs of Staff," 8 Jan 42; (S) Memo, Drum to SecWar and CofS USA, "Vital considerations relative to my proposed trip to China," 10 Jan 42. All in WPD 4389-71.

[82] Joseph W. Stilwell, *The Stilwell Papers* (New York, 1948), pp. 26-27.

[83] (S) Mns, CCS 1st Mtg, 23 Jan 42, item 4. (S) CCS 4, Paper by JCS, "Employment of A.V.G. in Burma and China," 20 Jan 42; (S) Msg, CCS to ABDACOM, DBA 1, 24 Jan 42. Both in CCS 091.711 China (1-20-42), sec 1.

[84] (S) Mns, CCS 2nd Mtg, 27 Jan 42 (S) Msg, CofS USA to Chinese Mil Mission, China, 149, 27 Jan 42; (S) Msg, Magruder to CofS USA, 231, 29 Jan 42; (S) Msg, CofS USA to Magruder, 168, 1 Feb 42. All in WPD 4626-7. (S) Msg, CCS to ABDACOM, DBA 11, 6 Feb 42, in JCS file DBA & CCOS Radios to ABDACOM; (U) Msg, PM to Pres, 31 Jan 42, *The Hinge of Fate*, p. 152.

[85] (S) Memo, Soong to McCloy, 29 Jan 42, WPD 4389-89. The Gimo's message is described as the reply to a telegram in which he was asked whether China was receiving any war materials from Russia and whether British and Chinese forces could hold northern Burma even if Rangoon was lost. The circumstances under which that telegram was sent and the telegram itself have not been discovered.

[86] (S) CCS 22, Army Paper, "Cooperation with Chiang Kai-shek," 2 Feb 42, CCS 091.711 China (1-20-42) sec 1.

[87] (S) Msg, CCS to ABDACOM, DBA 10, 4 Feb 42, in JCS file DBA & CCOS Radios to ABDACOM. Churchill had always favored accepting Chinese help for the defense of Burma. (U) Msg, PM to Wavell, 23 Jan 42, *The Hinge of Fate*, pp. 133-134.

NOTES TO CHAPTER III

[88] (S) Msg, ABDACOM to CCS, 00885, CCOS 3, 7 Feb 42, in CCS file Radios from ABDACOM.

[89] (S) Ltr, ASecWar to Soong, 15 Jan 42; (S) Msg, Gimo to Soong, 21 Jan 42; (S) Ltr, SecWar to Soong, 23 Jan 42; (S) Ltr, Soong to SecWar, 23 Jan 42; (S) Ltr, SecWar to Soong, 29 Jan 42; (C) Ltr, Soong to SecWar, 30 Jan 42. All in WPD 4389-64. Apparently Mr. Soong did not keep the Gimo informed of these negotiations, for it became necessary six months later to outline for him just what had been agreed when Gen Stilwell was originally sent out.

[90] (S) Ltr, CofS USA to Stilwell, "Instructions as United States Army Representative in China," 2 Feb 42, WPD 4389-64.

[91] CCS was informed of Gen Stilwell's appointment in a paper by the US Army CofS. (S) CCS 27, "Immediate Assistance to China," 4 Feb 42, CCS 091.711 China (1-20-42) sec 1.

[92] (S) Wavell, "ABDACOM," p. 60ff.

[93] Orders for the raids were issued by Adm Nimitz, CinCPac, on 9 Jan 42. (C) ONI Combat Narrative, "Early Raids in the Pacific Ocean," Jan 43.

[94] See his numerous operation reports. Adm Hart, in *Narrative of Events*, complains of Gen Wavell's over-optimism and implies that the rapid fall of Singapore was a shock within ABDA as well as outside. On 8 Feb, Gen Brereton announced to the Staff that he was prepared to recommend to the War Dept that the remnants of the Far East Air Force be withdrawn to Burma or Australia. He was criticized by Gen Wavell and Gen Brett for what appeared to them to be a somewhat unwarranted and pessimistic attitude. *The Brereton Diaries*, p. 88.

[95] (S) Msg, ABDACOM to CCS, 00488, 29 Jan 42, in JCS file Radios from ABDACOM (Wavell Only).

[96] (S) Msg, ABDACOM to CCS, CCOS 7, 13 Feb 42, in JCS file Radios from ABDACOM, GHQ Java etc.

[97] (S) Msg, ABDACOM to CCS, CCOS 8, 15 Feb 42, in JCS file Radios from Wavell, GHQ Java etc.

[98] Gen Wavell later reported that the first division of it could not have been wholly operative until 21 March. Wavell, "ABDACOM," p. 71.

[99] (S) Msg, ABDACOM to PM and Dill, 01288, 16 Feb 42, in JCS file Radios from ABDACOM, GHQ Java etc.

[100] (S) Mns, CCS 5th Mtg, 17 Feb 42, item 1.

[101] (S) Msg, CCS to ABDACOM, DBA 17, 17 Feb 42, in JCS file DBA and CCOS Radios to ABDACOM; (S) Msg, ABDACOM to CCS, CCOS 14, 19 Feb 42, in JCS file Radios from ABDACOM, GHQ Java etc; (S) Msg, CCS to ABDACOM, DBA 21, 21 Feb 42, in JCS file DBA & CCOS Radios to ABDACOM.

[102] Exchange of msgs, Pres and PM Aust, in P&O file of "Msgs CCS to and from Gen Wavell et al. Jan-Feb-Mar 42"; Sherwood, p. 508; *The Hinge of Fate*, pp. 155-166.

[103] (MS) Msg, Admty to CCS, COS(W)58, 18 Feb 42, in JCS file Radios from C's/S London & Admiralty to B.A.D.

[104] This amounted to 3 weak Dutch divisions, comprising 17 battalions, little artillery, and a few light tanks and armored cars; 1 squadron British Hussars with 25 light tanks; less than 3,000 Australians; 2 heavy and 3 light regiments of British AA Artillery, one of each having lost its equipment in South Sumatra, totalling some 5,500 men; 1 regiment U.S. field artillery. These were supported by 3 to 4 cruisers and about 10 destroyers, about 75 fighters, 40 medium bombers, 20 Dutch Glenn Martins, 14 U.S. dive bombers, and 20 B-17's. Against this the Japanese could bring an estimated 400-500 planes, unlimited naval resources, and a landing force of some six divisions. Wavell, "ABDACOM," pp. 71-72.

[105] (S) Msg, CCS to ABDACOM, DBA 19, 20 Feb 42, in JCS file DBA & CCOS Radios to ABDACOM.

[106] (S) Msg, ABDACOM to CCS, CCOS 16, 21 Feb 42, in JCS file Radios from ABDACOM, GHQ Java etc.

[107] (S) Memo, Marshall and Arnold to Stark and King, "Reply to ABDA No. 01864 of February 21st," 21 Feb 42, CCS 381 (1-24-42) sec 1. Memo has all four signatures.

[108] (S) Msg, CCS to ABDACOM, DBA 20, 21 Feb 42, in JCS file DBA & CCOS Radios to ABDACOM; (S) Mns, CCS 7th Mtg, 21 Feb 42.

[109] (S) Msg, CCS to ABDACOM, DBA 22, 22 Feb 42, in JCS file DBA & CCOS Radios to ABDACOM.

[110] (S) Msg, CofS USA to Brett, 185, 21 Feb 42, CCS 381 (1-24-42) sec 1.

[111] (S) Msg, ABDACOM to CCS, CCOS 19, 22 Feb 42; (S) Msg, ABDACOM to CCS, CCOS 20, 23 Feb 42. Both in CCS 381 (1-24-42) sec 1.

[112] (P&C) Msg, Van Mook to Marshall, 22 Feb 42, P&O file of "Msgs CCS to and from Wavell et al." His final plea was, "For God's sake take the strong and active decisions and don't stop sending materials men pending deliberations as time factor more pressing than ever."

[113] (S) Mns, CCS 8th Mtg, 23 Feb 42; (S) Msg, CCS to ABDACOM, DBA 23, 23 Feb 42, in JCS file DBA & CCOS Radios to ABDACOM.

[114] See below, ch V.

[115] (S) Msg, ABDACOM, to CCS, 02418, 25 Feb 42; (S) Msg, JSM to CsofS London, JSM 73, 24 Feb 42; (S) Msg, Admty to BAD, (W) 89, 25 Feb 42; (S) Memo, ACofS G-2 to CofS, "Psychological effect of the dissolution of ABDA Command," 24 Feb 42. All in CCS 381 (1-24-42) sec 1. (S) Msg, CCS to ABDACOM, DBA 25, 23 Feb 42; (S) Msg, JSM to ABDACOM, DBA 26, 24 Feb 42, gives PM's reasons: "Any announcement will not only give the enemy the impression that we are throwing up the sponge in Java but will also sensibly add to danger of journey of General Wavell and his Staff"; (S) Msg, CCS to ABDACOM, DBA 27, 24 Feb 42. All in JCS file DBA & CCOS Radios to ABDACOM.

[116] (S) Msg, BCOS to JSM (W)92, 26 Feb 42; (S) Msg, BCOS to JSM, (W)96, 2 Mar 42; Press Release - 2 Mar 42. All in CCS 381 (1-24-42) sec 1.

NOTES TO CHAPTER IV

CHAPTER IV

[1] It is recorded in minutes of a meeting of the War Department War Council on 16 Feb that "There has been a gentleman's agreement between us and the British that should the Japanese take Sumatra and thus split the ABDA area, we will have to place Australia under this area and make two commands, one for the Burma area and one for the ABDA Australian area." Mr. Stimson recommended that an American officer should command both areas. (S) Mns, SecWar Conf, Vol II, War Council, 16 Feb 42, WDCSA file. Membership on the War Council included SecWar, USecWar, ASecWar, CofS, DCofS, ACsofS, and CG's, Ground Forces, Air Forces, and Services of Supply.

[2] Sherwood, pp. 502-503.

[3] (S&P) Msg, Pres to PM, 10b, 18 Feb 42, ABC 323.31 Pacific Ocean Area (1-29-42) sec 1-A. Paper is initialled by Gen Marshall, with a note that the SecWar had seen it.

[4] (S) Mns, CCS 5th Mtg, 17 Feb 42, item 1; (S) Memo, King to CCS, "Changes in ABDA and/or ANZAC Areas evolving from developments in the Far East," 17 Feb 43, CCS 381 (1-24-42) sec 1. Pencil draft in Adm King's handwriting, dtd 17 Feb 42, is in (TS) CominCh file "Memos to U.S. Chiefs of Staff."

[5] (S) JPS 12/1 (changed to JPS 2/2), Rpt by JUSSC, "Review of the Strategic Situation in the Japanese Theater of War," 18 Feb 42, CCS 381 (1-30-42).

[6] (S) JPS 12/1(A) [changed to JPS 2/2(A)], Minority Rpt, "Review of the Strategic Situation in the Japanese Theater of War," 18 Feb 42, CCS 381 (1-30-42).

[7] (S) Memo, Note by Secy, nd, CCS 381 (1-24-42) sec 1, with handwritten notation, "Discussed in meeting of 2-21-42 CCS (TWH [ammond])." Mns of JCS, CCS, and JPS contain no specific mention of it. The subject was discussed, however, by the CCS on 23 Feb. Establishment of an "Australian Command" under the best available Australian general was recommended by RAdm R.K. Turner in (S) Memo, ACofS (Plans) to CominCh, "Recommended new strategic deployment against Japan," 17 Feb 42, cy minus p. 4 in CNO(WPD) file "A16-3(4) Pacific Ocean Areas (whole)."

[8] (S) Mns, CCS 8th Mtg, 23 Feb 42, item 1.

[9] (S) Msg, Admty to BAD Washington, (W)76, 23 Feb 42, CCS 381 (1-24-42) sec 1.

[10] (S) Mns, CPS 5th Mtg, 25 Feb 42, item 6; (C) CCS 53, "Demarcation of New Strategic Areas in the Japanese War Zone," 28 Feb 42, CCS 381 (1-24-42) sec 1.

[11] Someone in Army WPD raised the same point in an undtd memo of notes on CPS 19/D, the directive to the CPS. It was also noted that forces defending Australia would have to operate in the sea areas west of the continent which, in the British plan, were within the Indian Ocean Area. These points were probably raised in the CPS meeting of 25 Feb when the British plan was discussed. Copy of memo is in ABC 323.31 Pacific Ocean Area (1-29-42) sec 1-A.

760   NOTES TO CHAPTER IV

[12] It is interesting to note that no mention is made of possible future offensives against the Japanese. The operations envisaged are entirely with forces available "against military and naval communication lines, and against lines of cargo vessels engaged in transporting strategic materials to Japan."

[13] (S) Mns, CCS 9th Mtg, 3 Mar 42, item 2:

the dividing line between the Indian Ocean and Pacific Ocean Areas should run from Singapore south to the North coast of Sumatra, thence round the East coast of Sumatra (leaving the Sunda Strait to the eastward of the line) to a point on the coast of Sumatra longitude 104° East, thence South to latitude 8° south, thence to Onslow in Australia, thence south along the coast of Australia to longitude 117° East, thence due south.

The official minutes record "a full discussion" with no further comment. It would be interesting to know more fully how the earlier views of the British (i.e., a dividing line from Singapore through the Java Sea, Flores Sea, and Bandar Sea to 129° East, thence due south to Australia) were reconciled with those in CCS 53.

[14] (S) Msg, CG USAFFE to CofS, 2 and 3, 1 Jan 42, WPD 4639-2. On 25 Jan 42 the question was raised again by representatives of the State Dept., who persuaded military officials to consult Gen MacArthur. No evidence has been found that a request for his opinion was actually sent. Possibly it went from the State Dept. There seems to be no connection between the discussion of 25 January and the request from Gen MacArthur on 2 February for transportation for Pres Quezon. (S) Memo, ACofS to CofS USA, "Summary of conversation between Gen Eisenhower, Capt Glover, Mr. Stanley Hornbeck, and Mr. Hamilton," 25 Jan 42, WPD 3251-74.

[15] (S) Msg, MacArthur to Marshall, 187, 2 Feb 42, WPD 3251-74.

[16] (S) Msg, Marshall to MacArthur, 2 Feb 42, WDCSA Super-Secret file 370-05 Philippines; (S) Msg, CominCh to ComSoWesPacFor, 16 Feb 42, WPD 3251-74.

[17] (S) Msg, MacArthur to Marshall, 226 and 227, 8 Feb 42, WDCSA Super-Secret "File on Philippine Situation," 381 (2-17-42).

[18] (S) Mns, JCS 1st Mtg, 9 Feb 42, item 1; Stimson and Bundy, pp. 397-405.

[19] Stimson and Bundy, pp. 400-403.

[20] (S) Msg, MacArthur to Pres, 252, 11 Feb 42, WDCSA Super-Secret "File on Philippine Situation," 381 (2-17-42).

[21] (S) Msg, MacArthur to Marshall, 296, 16 Feb 42; (S) Msg, Marshall to CG USAFFE, 16 Feb 42. Both in WDCSA Super-Secret "File on Philippine Situation," 381 (2-17-42). On 4 Feb Gen MacArthur had been told that if Bataan were lost he might be needed more elsewhere and orders would come from the President. (SS) Msg, Marshall to MacArthur, 4 Feb 42, WDCSA Super-Secret 370.05 Philippines (3-17-42).

[22] (S) Msg, Marshall to MacArthur, 21 Feb 42, WDCSA Super-Secret 370.05 Philippines (3-17-42). Gen MacArthur's opinion was requested, but apparently it had been decided to remove him before any reply was received.

[23] Sherwood, p. 509; (S) Msg, Marshall to MacArthur, 1078, 22 Feb 42, WDCSA Super-Secret 370.05 Philippines (3-17-42).

[24] (S) Msg, MacArthur to Marshall, 358, 24 Feb 42, WDCSA Super-Secret 370.05 Philippines (3-17-42).

[25] (S) CCS 56, "Message from Prime Minister on Current Situation," 5 Mar 42, CCS 381 (3-5-42).

[26] Initial discussion of the PM's message was at a conference of the CCS with the President, Mr. Stimson, and Mr. Hopkins. (S) Mns, file CCS 031 (3-5-42). The *New York Times* reports meetings of the President with Gen Marshall on 6 Mar and with Mr. Stimson, Mr. Knox, Gen Marshall, Gen Arnold, Adm Stark, and Adm King on 7 Mar. No minutes of these two meetings are available. A summary of the views of the President on the 7th is in (S dg C) JCS 19, Note by Secys, "Strategic responsibility of the United Kingdom and the United States," 9 Mar 42, CCS 381 (1-24-42) sec 3. They were also discussed at the JCS 5th Mtg, 9 Mar 42, item 1. CPS draft of reply in (S) CCS 56/1, "Message from Prime Minister on Current Situation," 6 March 42, CCS 381 (3-5-42) (2). (S) Ltr, Pres to PM, 115, 9 Mar 42, CCS 381 (3-5-42).

[27] (S) JCS 19, Note by Secys, "Strategic Responsibility of the United Kingdom and the United States," 9 Mar 42, CCS 381 (1-24-42) sec 3; (S) CCS 56/1, "Message from Prime Minister on Current Situation," 6 Mar 42, CCS 381 (1-5-42) (2).

[28] (C) JCS 19/1, Memo by CofS USA, "Strategic Responsibility of the United Kingdom and the United States," 9 Mar 42, CCS 381 (1-24-42) sec 3. This paper was prepared by Gen Eisenhower of OPD and apparently formed the basis for discussion by Gen Marshall with the President on the 8th. At this time a specific recommendation that the PWC be moved to Washington was removed.

[29] (S) Mns, JCS 5th Mtg, 9 Mar 42, item 1; (S) Mns, CCS 12th Mtg, 17 Mar 42, item 7; (S) Mns, CCS 13th Mtg, 24 Mar 42, item 4; (S) CCS 57/2, Memo by JCS, "Strategic Responsibility of the United Kingdom and the United States," 24 Mar 42, CCS 381 (1-24-42) sec 3.

[30] Adm King told JCS on 16 Mar that the President had not yet had a reply from the Prime Minister, although Mr. Hopkins "had received a despatch in which there was a phrase which might be construed to indicate that the ideas proposed by the President were acceptable, and further statements from which might be inferred that the Prime Minister desired to retain the Pacific War Council in London." On 9 Jun 42 Lt Col J.C. Holmes reported to Brig Gen W.B. Smith, U.S. Secy of CCS, that there was no indication that the matter was ever referred to the British in London, or, if so, that a reply was received. (S) Memo, Holmes to Smith, "Strategic Responsibility of the United Kingdom and

United States," 9 Jun 42, CCS 381 (1-24-42) sec 3. He further stated that the provisions of CCS 57/2 were "embodied in a proposed message approved by the United States Joint Chiefs of Staff to be sent by The President to the Prime Minister. It was subsequently learned that this message was not dispatched." The Secretariat tried unsuccessfully again when Gen Marshall and Adm King went to London in July 1942 to have the paper approved. (S) Memo, Secy JCS to US CsofS, "Status of Agreements Concerning Strategic Responsibility of the United States and the United Kingdom," 15 Jul 42, CCS 381 (1-24-42) sec 3, with notation, "Taken to London but not used." A copy of CCS 57/2, in ABC 323.31 Pacific Ocean Area (1-29-42) sec 2, has a note by A.M.[iller], indicating that nothing had been done by 8 May 45.

[31] (S&P) Msg, PM to Pres, 46, 17 Mar 42, CCS 031 Personal Message File.

[32] (S) Msg, PM to Pres, 54, 20 Mar 42; (S) Msg, PM to Pres, 58, 24 Mar 42; (S) CCS 57/1, "Australian Views on Strategic Control in the Pacific Area," 22 Mar 42. All in CCS 381 (1-24-42) sec 2 pt 1.

[33] The Australians preferred that the western boundary of the Pacific Theater run from 005°S not to Onslow but to 110°E and south along that meridian. This was the line ultimately adopted. They also thought that China should be in the Indian Ocean Theater. For political reasons it was placed in the Pacific Theater.

[34] (S) Msg, PM to Pres, 58, 24 Mar 42, CCS 381 (1-24-42) sec 2 pt 1.

[35] (S) Mns, JCS 7th Mtg, 23 Mar 42, item 1.

[36] (S dg C) JCS 19, Note by Secys, "Strategic Responsibility of the United Kingdom and the United States," 9 Mar 42, CCS 381 (1-24-42) sec 3.

[37] (S) Memo, CofS USA to Pres, 24 Mar 42, CCS 381 (1-24-42) sec 2 pt 1. The Pres asked Gen McNarney to send it to the PM on 7 Apr if Gen Marshall had not already done so, but Gen McNarney replied that the same information was included in the directives to the Pacific commanders which had by that time been approved by Australia and New Zealand. (UNK) Memo, Pres to McNarney, 7 Apr 42; (UNK) Memo, Actg CofS to Pres, "Pacific Strategic Areas," 8 Apr 42. Both in WDCSA 381 Australia.

[38] (S) Mns, JCS 8th Mtg, 30 Mar 42, item 8:

> It was brought to the attention of the Chiefs of Staff that a recent public radio broadcast had been made to the effect that a Pacific War Council would be set up in Washington, composed of representatives of the U.S., Australia, New Zealand, Canada, N.E.I., and China. GENERAL MARSHALL stated that he had heard unofficially that President Roosevelt would assume the Presidency of the Council.

Creation of the council was announced on 30 Mar, but an Army OPD memo of the same day outlines the differing views of the British and Americans as still existent. (S) OPD Memo, "Summary of Status with respect to spheres of strategic responsibility," 30 Mar 42, ABC 323.31 Pacific Ocean Area (1-29-42) sec 1-B.

NOTES TO CHAPTER IV

[39] *New York Times*, 21 Mar 42, p. 3; 31 Mar 42, p. 1; 1 Apr 42, p. 1; 2 Apr 42. Present at the first meeting were T.V. Soong (China), Nash (New Zealand), Evatt (Australia), Halifax (Great Britain), Roosevelt (U.S.), Wrong (Canada), Loudon (Netherlands), and Hopkins. The final decision to establish the council was made by the Pres on the advice of Hopkins. (U) Memo by Hopkins, 1 Apr 42, Sherwood, pp. 515-517.

[40] (MS) Msg, Evatt to Curtin, 23 Apr 42, CCS 320.2 (1-28-42).

[41] (S) Mns, JCS 3rd Mtg, 2 Mar 42, item 5. The minutes include the island of Yap, but this appears to be an error inasmuch as Yap was in Japanese possession and far removed from the other islands. Comments on this chapter by FAdm E.J. King, JCS HS.

[42] (MS) Msg, JSM to BCOS, 76, 25 Feb 42, CCS 381 (1-24-42) sec 1.

[43] (S) CCS 53/1, Memo by BCOS, "Demarkation of New Strategical Areas in the Japanese War Zone. Command in Northern Australia," 5 Mar 42; (S) Memos, JCS Secy Smith to Stark, etc., "Command in Northern Australia," 5 Mar 42. Both in CCS 381 (1-24-42) sec 1.

[44] (S) Msg, Brett to CofS USA (CG-217), 87, 27 Feb 42, rptd in JPS 17, 1 Mar 42; (S) Msg, CofS USA to CG USAFIA, 479, 28 Feb 42. Both in CCS 381 (1-24-42) sec 1. Gen Brett's preliminary report included "A new appreciation of the limits of the ANZAC Area in view of the dissolution of the ABDA Area," a plan for joint strategic action, recommendation of an American for supreme commander, and a summary statement of the new commander's primary functions.

General Marshall made reference to a message from Gen Brett, numbered CG-205, no copy of which has yet been discovered, which apparently mentioned Gen MacArthur specifically as the choice for Supreme Commander. On 2 Mar 42 the Sydney *Telegraph* recommended Gen MacArthur's appointment. (UNK) Memo, Col Black to Gen Smith, 2 Mar 42. Gen Brett also sent Gen Marshall the directive which the Australian and New Zealand Chiefs of Staff prepared, recommending that "Unified command with definite strategical plans" be established without further delay. This was essentially the directive submitted officially by the Australian Government on 7 Mar (see below). (S) Msg, Brett to Marshall, 467, 3 Mar 42, CCS 381 (1-24-42) sec 1.

[45] (S) CCS 57, Memo by BCOS, "Governmental and Strategical Control and Commands in the ANZAC Area," 7 Mar 42, CCS 381 (1-24-42) sec 1.

[46] (S) Mns, CCS 10th Mtg, 7 Mar 42, item 3.

[47] Comments of FAdm E.J. King on draft of this chapter, JCS HS.

[48] (S) JCS 18, Note by Secys, "Governmental and Strategical Control and Commands in the Anzac Area," 8 Mar 42, CCS 381 (1-24-42) sec 1. Limits of the Australian Area are defined as:
From Cape Camau (Indo-China) along the eastern coast of Thai and Malaya to Singapore, thence south on Longitude 105° East and the east coast of Sumatra, to Latitude 7° South, thence southeasterly to Onslow, thence along the western and south

coasts of Australia to Longitude 117° East, thence south; beginning at the starting point of Cape Camau, easterly to Latitude 5° North, Longitude 129° East, thence south to the equator, thence east to Longitude 165° East, thence south to Latitude 10° South, thence southwesterly to Latitude 17° South, Longitude 160° East, thence south.

A draft copy of JCS 18 in the same file has extensive pencil corrections by "K[ing]."

[49] (S) JCS 18/2, Memo by CofS, "Creation of Southwest Pacific Area," 9 Mar 42, CCS 381 (1-24-42) sec 2 pt 1.

[50] (S) Mns, JCS 5th Mtg, 9 Mar 42, item 1.

[51] (S) Mns, JCS 5th Mtg, 9 Mar 42, item 1. The minutes read:

Admiral King went on to say that the Samoan, Fiji, and Solomon Islands are closely related to the actual defense of Australia and should be considered as strong points for eventual offensive action toward the northwest; the New Hebrides and other islands which lie to the east of the dividing line proposed by the Navy are primarily concerned with the protection of the lines of communication between the U.S., Australia, and New Zealand.

Inasmuch as Samoa and Fiji lie to the east of the line and fit logically into the second category rather than the first, it must be concluded that the statement has been incorrectly recorded.

[52] (S) Mns, JCS 6th Mtg, 16 Mar 42, item 3; (S) Mns, CCS 12th Mtg, 17 Mar 42, item 7; (S) Memo, JCS Secy to Brig Dykes, 16 Mar 42, (TS) CominCh file "Memos to Secretariat, Jan '42 to Oct '42"; (S) Msg, CominCh to ComSWPacFor and ComAnzacFor, 171640 Mar 42, (TS) CominCh file "ComSoWestPac Despatches - Jan '42 thru Dec '43."

[53] (S) Msg, Marshall to Brett, 613, 10 Mar 42, OPD Exec 10, item 10. This instructs Gen Brett, upon the arrival of Gen MacArthur, to call within one hour upon the PM of Australia, tell him of Gen MacArthur's arrival and propose that the Australian Government nominate Gen MacArthur to the post. (S) Msg, CofS USA to CG USAFFE, 18 Mar 42, CCS 381 (1-24-42) sec 2 pt 1. This is Gen MacArthur's notification. Gen Brett's letter to PM Curtin was published in the *New York Times* on 18 Mar 42.

[54] (S) Memo, King to Marshall, "Command Areas in Pacific Theater," 19 Mar 42, (TS) CominCh file #24 "Army - Re Unity of Command." The Navy planners recommended establishing both commands simultaneously because they feared that the Army might object to putting Army garrisons and aircraft under naval command in the POA and that a strong move might be made to enlarge the SWPA to include most of the South Pacific. (S) Memo, Turner to King, 19 Mar 42, CNO(WPD) file "A16-3(4) Pacific Ocean Areas (whole)."

[55] (S) Memo, King to Marshall, "Proposed Directives for Supreme Commanders in the South West Pacific Area, and the North and South Pacific Areas," 20 Mar 42, CNO(WPD) file "A16-3(4) Pacific Ocean Areas (whole)."

[56] Comments of FAdm E.J. King on draft MS of this chapter. Adm King felt certain that the planners and Gen Marshall and himself had discussed these directives thoroughly before they were approved. Col A. Franklin Kibler told Gen Handy that the drafts assigned tasks more detailed than the Army would have desired but that the Navy insisted "and the Army can agree." (S) Mns, JCS 8th Mtg, 30 Mar 42, item 8.

[57] Signed copies are in CCS 381 (1-24-42) sec 2 pt 1.

[58] (S) Memo, CCS Secy (Smith) to King, "Pacific Directives," 4 Apr 42, CCS 381 (1-24-42) sec 2 pt 1.

...Apparently London is very literal minded in their interpretation of the extent of the international agreement.... You will note that this does not change anything, but simply confines the statement as to the international agreement to the basic fact that the Pacific Area is a United States strategic responsibility. Under that basic agreement we assume the authority to make such subdivisions as we see fit and to give such missions to our commanders as the situation indicates.

A note on the altered paragraph of a copy of the directives in the same file indicates that it was approved by Adm King and Gen Eisenhower on 4 Apr 42.

The designation "Pacific Ocean Area" is used throughout in the directive. When this became "Areas" is not clear. The first recorded use of the plural is in a summary of decisions of the JCS 10th Mtg, 13 Apr 42, item 3. The minutes use the singular. Adm King used the plural in a draft memo to the President on 14 Apr 42 (not sent).

[59] Boundaries of the SWPA, as defined in Annex 1:

From Cape Kami in the Luichow Peninsula around the coast of the Tonkin Gulf, Indo-China, Thailand, and Malaya to Singapore: from Singapore south to the north coast of Sumatra, thence round the east coast of Sumatra (leaving the Sunda Strait to the eastward of the line) to a point on the coast of Sumatra at Longitude 104° East, thence south to Latitude 08° South, thence southeasterly towards Onslow, Australia, and on reaching Longitude 110° East, due south along that meridian.

...The north and east boundaries...: From Cape Kami...south to Latitude 20° North; thence east to Longitude 130° East; thence south to the Equator; thence east to Longitude 165° East; south to Latitude 10° South; southwesterly to Latitude 17° South, Longitude 160° East; thence south.

The Southeast Pacific Area was bounded by a line "from the Mexican - Guatemala western boundary southwesterly to Latitude 11° North, Longitude 110° West; thence south." The Pacific Ocean Area was divided at the Equator and 42° North in a North, a Central, and a South Pacific Area.

[60] The following provisions of the ABDA directive were omitted: required consent of local commander or government to transfer land forces from that government's territory; required notice

from government concerned prior to reduction of forces assigned or committed to area; statement of duty of coordinating operations of all forces, assigning missions, forming task forces, etc.; responsibility for disposition of reenforcement; authorization to require reports and make recommendations to other governments; control through subordinate commanders of national forces; right of subordinate commanders to appeal direct to their own governments.

[61](S) Memo, Memo of Interv, Col C.H. Donnelly and Col L.M. Guyer with Gen Marshall, 11 Feb 49, JCS HS.

[62](S) Memo, Turner to King, 19 Mar 42, CNO(WPD) file "A16-3(4) Pacific Ocean Areas (whole)." Adm Turner said he thought the tasks give a "clear strategic picture of what is required in that Area. If you omit any of these, I believe that you will find the Supreme Commander will tend to use his naval forces and air forces in a wrong manner, since he has shown clearly unfamiliarity with proper naval and air functions." (This reflects dissatisfaction in naval quarters with the tendency of Gen MacArthur both before and during the war up to this point to consider naval and air forces valuable primarily for tactical cooperation with ground forces.)

[63] Absence of a statement of strategic concept such as had been included in the ABDA directive is not surprising since this is a U.S. joint directive issued with the approval of the other governments. Definition of strategic policy was a function of a higher echelon. There had been no statement approved since the Arcadia Conference.

[64](S) Memo, CominCh-CNO to CofS USA, "Offensive Operations in South and Southwest Pacific Areas," 26 Jun 42, OPD 381 SWPA #80.

[65](SS) JCS 353/1, Rpt by JPS, "Future Campaign Operations in the Pacific Ocean Areas," 14 Jun 43, CCS 381 Pac. Ocean Areas (6-10-43) sec 1.

[66] Gen MacArthur inquired almost at once: "(1) The nature of the offensive that is contemplated to be launched from this and adjacent areas. (2) The size of the force that is expected to be eventually alloted [sic] for its accomplishment. (3) An approximate idea of the date when such and [sic] operation could be expected to [be] initiated." (S) Msg, MacArthur to Marshall, 558, 1 May 42, CCS 320.2 (1-28-42). No reply has yet been located.

[67](S) Memo, CofS USA and CominCh to Pres, 30 Mar 42, submitting drafts of the two directives, bears the notation, "Approved, Franklin D. Roosevelt," and "Approval given March 31, 1942 JCH [?]," CCS 381 (1-24-42) sec 2 pt 1.

[68](S) Memo, RAdm Stoeve and Maj Gen Dijxhoorn to CCS, 8 Apr 42, CCS 381 (1-24-42) sec 2 pt 1.

[69] In an undtd tel to Evatt, fwded by the Pres to the JCS indiv on 3 Apr 42, the PM of Australia repeated the arguments of the Australian Chiefs of Staff:

767 NOTES TO CHAPTER IV

> Australian line of communications with the United States in [sic] through New Zeland [sic] Fiji and New Caledonia and the most effective and economic use of forces available to defend the whole area depends upon there being united command so that speedy reinforcement of any new points threatened can be affected [sic] as necessary.

In a reply drafted by the Joint Secretariat and revised by Adm Turner, Adm King reiterated the belief of himself and Gen Marshall that

> ...Australia proper and the New Zealand-line of communications area are two separate strategic entities. The defense of Australia is primarily a land-air problem for which the best possible naval support is a fleet free to maneuver without restrictions imposed by the local situation. New Zealand, on the other hand, is the key point for the support of the Pacific line of communications, the security of which is a naval responsibility. New Zealand has no relation to the defense of Australia in current circumstances.

(S) Memo, Smith to King, 4 Apr 42 w/dft reply to President's memo of 3 Apr, CCS 381 (1-24-42) sec 2 pt 1, bears comments of Adms King, Willson, and Turner.

[70](S) Tel, Aust PM to Evatt, 31, 7 Apr 42, CCS 381 (1-24-42) sec 2 pt 1. The Australian Chiefs of Staff insisted "that any power to move our troops out of Australian territory should be subject to prior consultation and agreement with the Commonwealth Government," and that right of communication of commanders with their governments be guaranteed. Fwded w/dft reply to Adm King by Secy Smith, 9 Apr 42. Reply in (S) Ltr, King to Evatt, 10 Apr 42, quoting from (S) Memo, CofS USA to Pres, 24 Mar 42. Objections of New Zealand Government in (UNK) Ltr, Nash to King (following conv on 11 Apr), 14 Apr 42, encl (MS) Msg, PM NZ to Nash, 105. It is indicated that: "We note with regret that these proposals consolidate the division, to which we have always been and still are firmly opposed, between Australia and New Zealand which in our opinion form one strategic whole." Further, "it should be understood...that any...power to move troops from the Dominion should be subject to prior consultation and agreement of the New Zealand Government." Reply in (S) Ltr, King to Nash, 14 Apr 42. All corres was conducted by Adm King in the absence of General Marshall, in London, seeking British acceptance of a project for an offensive in the European Theater.

[71] Revised form of directives with memo for record, 5 Jan 44, CCS 381 (1-24-42) sec 2 pt 1.

[72](U) Ltr, Evatt to King, 14 Apr 42; (U) Ltr, Nash to King, 15 Apr 42; (S) Msg, McNarney to MacArthur, 1273, CM-OUT-2483, 14 Apr 43; (S) Msg, MacArthur to Marshall, AG 327, CM-IN-4719, 18 Apr 42; (S) Msg, MacArthur to Marshall, AG 366, CM-IN-5052, 19 Apr 43. All in CCS 381 (1-24-42) sec 2 pt 1.

[73] (S) Mns, JCS 9th Mtg, 6 Apr 42; (S) Mns, JCS 10th Mtg, 13 Apr 42. Comments of VAdm V.R. Murphy, USN(Ret), to author, 19 Apr 49, JCS HS.

CHAPTER V

[1] (S) ABC 4/CS1, "American-British Strategy," 31 Dec 41, *Arcadia*.

[2] For discussion of Gymnast, see (S) MS, JCS Hist, *War Against Germany and Its Satellites*. The U.S. planners agreed with the British conclusions and were supported by the CMTC, which had been investigating the shipping situation. (S) ABC-4/2, Rpt by JPC, "Northwest Africa project," 25 Dec 41; (S) ABC-4/2A, "Operation Super-Gymnast," 13 Jan 42. The British early expressed the opinion that combined forces available would be insufficient to cope even with "no more than slight unco-ordinated resistance" from the French in Africa, for which allowance had originally been made, and they recommended that "the plan for Super-Gymnast must be based on the whole hearted co-operation of the French in North Africa and on active assistance from the Vichy French Fleet. (S) CPS 2, Memo by BCOS, "Super-Gymnast," 22 Jan 42. U.S. members of CPS expressed agreement in (S) CPS 2/1, 1 Feb 42. Following studies of the harbor facilities of Casablanca and over-all demands on U.S. and British shipping, the British recommended setting aside invasion plans. (S) Memo by BCOS, "The Possibility of Executing Operation - Super Gymnast"; (S) CCS 5/2, "Super-Gymnast," 3 Mar 42. All in CCS 381 (1-20-42).

[3] (S) CCS 54, "Appreciation of German Intentions for 1942," 26 Feb 42, CCS 381 Germany (2-3-42) sec 1. An appreciation by CIC estimated that the most probable major move by the Germans in 1942 would be designed to destroy the Russian Army and gain access to the Caucasus. Agreed by CCS at 9th Mtg, 3 Mar 42.

[4] (S) Mns, CCS 5th Mtg, 17 Feb 42, item 2.

[5] For discussion of the extent of the shipping shortage and the reasons for it, see (S) MS, JCS Hist, *Ships, Shipping, and Strategy*, pt I.

[6] (S) CCS 30, Memo by BCOS, "Air Requirements of Australia and New Zealand," 5 Feb 42, CCS 452.1 (2-5-42). The total requirements were originally estimated at 306 for Australia, 36 for New Zealand, later modified to 250 for Australia and 4 formed squadrons for New Zealand. The paper was apparently referred to the Army, presumably via the U.S. Chiefs and the JPS. A first draft reply was sent by Maj Gen M.F. Harmon for Gen Arnold to WPD, who revised it and submitted it via the CofS USA. (S) CCS 30/1, Memo by JCS, "Air Requirements for Australia and New Zealand," 10 Feb 42, CCS 452.1 (2-5-42).

[7] (S) ABC-4/8, Rpt by JPC, "Defense of Island Bases between Hawaii and Australia." 13 Jan 42, *Arcadia*.

[8] (S) CPS 8, Brit Memo, "Air Defense of Fiji and New Zealand," 31 Jan 42, CCS 660.2 (1-31-42).

[9] For fighters, reply was made in CCS 30/1, submitted by the JCS, 10 Feb, after preparation in the War Dept. It included the following summary of allocations of estimated U.S. production from Feb to Dec 42:

	US AAF	British	USSR	NEI	China	Total
1-Engine	2911	3383	680	100	141	7215
2-Engine	1235	467				1702
	4146	3850	680	100	141	8917

U.S. Requirements
  Required for tactical units - 2108
  Attrition and reserves   - 2760
                              4868
            (Shortage 722)

Reply for the bomber request was made by the JPS in CPS 8/1, 13 Feb 42. February production of bombers was allocated as follows:

Type	British	U.S.	Others
Bombers (L)	191	65	100
Bombers (M)	65	45	55
Bombers (H)	47	60	-

Figures on British production, allocations, and commitments were not available to the United States. Such figures were requested in CCS 30/1.

[10] (S) Mns, CPS 3rd Mtg, 14 Feb 42, item 3. (S) CPS 8/1, Memo by JPS, "Air Defense of Fiji and New Zealand," 13 Feb 42; (S) CCS 45, Memo by CPS, "Air Defense of Fiji and New Zealand," 18 Feb 42. Both in CCS 660.2 (1-31-42).

[11] (S) Mns, CCS 4th Mtg, 10 Feb 42, item 7; (S) Mns, CCS 8th Mtg, 23 Feb 42, item 3. The MAB report on aircraft resources of the United Nations was submitted to CPS as CPS 14/2 on 24 Feb 42 and revised at various times subsequent thereto. For fuller discussion, see (S) MS, JCS Hist, *Procurement and Allocation of Material Means*, pt III.

[12] (S) CPS 12, Memo by JUSSC, "Reinforcement of Australia by 12 Heavy Bombers," 5 Feb 42, CCS 452.1 (2-5-42).

[13] (S) CPS 12/1, Brit redft, "Reinforcement of Australia by 12 Heavy Bombers," 5 Feb 42, CCS 452.1 (2-5-42).

[14] (S) Mns, CPS 3rd Mtg, 14 Feb 42, item 7. (S) Msg, Marshall to Brett, 20 Feb 42; (S) Msg, Brett to Marshall, 24, 18 Feb 42. Both in ABC 452.1 (1-22-42) sec 1. The British planners had proposed that the bombers be placed under Australian strategic command, and the Australians indicated their desire to command any American air forces assigned to defense of Australia. But the U.S. planners were opposed, and the bombers were attached to ANZAC.

[15] (S) Mns, CPS 3rd Mtg, 14 Feb 42, item 7; (S) Mns, CPS 4th Mtg, 23 Feb 42, item 1; (S) CCS 49, Rpt by CPS, "Reinforcement of Australia by 12 Heavy Bombers," 23 Feb 42, CCS 452.1 (2-5-42); (S) Mns, CCS 9th Mtg, 3 Mar 42, item 3.

[16] (S) CCS 33, "Additional Fighter Type Airplanes to the Netherlands East Indies," 7 Feb 42, CCS 452 (2-7-42); (S) Mns, CCS 4th Mtg, 10 Feb 42, item 8. These are presumably the same 36 P-40's which were returned to the disposition of the U.S. on 21 Mar 42, because the NEI no longer had use for them. (S) Ltr, Exec Secy, Neth Puch Comm, to Secy MAB, 21 Mar 42, CCS 452 (3-21-42) sec 1.

[17] (S) CCS 34, Note by BCOS, "The Economical Employment of Air Forces against Japan," 9 Feb 42, CCS 381 (2-9-42).

[18] (S) JPS 12, changed to JPS 2/1, "Directive to Joint U.S. Strategic Committee," 11 Feb 42, CCS 381 (1-30-42) (1); (S) Mns, CCS 4th Mtg, 10 Feb 42, item 6. On 30 Jan 42 JUSSC received a directive to prepare a study of world strategy. This had apparently been approved by JPS on 28 Jan at a meeting called by Adm Turner to discuss it. (S) JPS 2, Dir to JUSSC, "Strategic Deployment of the Land, Sea and Air Forces of the United States," 30 Jan 42; (S) Memo, no adee, sgd R.K. Turner, 26 Jan 42, CCS 381 (1-30-42) (1). There is no indication in the CCS minutes or in the directive that the initiative came from them. No minutes of meetings of the U.S. Chiefs are available for the period prior to formation of the JCS organization. In the directive of 11 Feb JUSSC was charged with making recommendations for deployment of forces in the Pacific, to "be based on agreed concepts of grand strategy, but [they] should take cognizance of the further development of the strategic situation in the Pacific." Specifically they were to consider four papers: CCS 34, The Economical Employment of Air Forces against Japan; CCS 30, Air Requirements for Australia and New Zealand; CCS 33, Additional Fighter Type Aeroplanes to the Netherlands East Indies; CCS 29, Naval Air and Land Forces of the United Nations in or assigned to ABDA and ANZAC Areas.

[19] (S) JPS 4-A, "Agreed Concepts of Grand Strategy," 14 Feb 42, CCS 381 (2-2-42) (1); (S) Mns, JPS 2nd Mtg, 19 Feb 42, item 1.

[20] (S) JPS 12/1, changed to JPS 2/2, Rpt by JUSSC, "Review of the Strategic Situation in the Japanese Theater of War," 18 Feb 42; (S) JPS 12/1(a), changed to JPS 2/2/(A), "Minority Report," 18 Feb 42. Both in CCS 381 (1-30-42). It has not been possible to establish authorship of the dissenting report although the opinions seem to point to a member of the Army Air Forces. There were at the time ten members on JUSSC. A roster dated 20 Feb 42 is in file CCS 334 (2-20-42).

[21] CCS had agreed on 26 Jan that the first two U.S. Heavy Bombardment groups should be assigned to operate from U.K. bases. As Adm King remarked, "apart from purely strategical considerations it was obviously necessary for political reasons, in order to stress solidarity of purpose between the United Nations, that at least certain of these aircraft should operate from bases in the United Kingdom at the earliest possible date." (S) Mns, CCS 2nd Mtg, 26 Jan 42, item 11.

[22] The recommended courses of action were:

(a) While holding Java and Sumatra as long as possible:

(1) Concentrate the maximum locally available land and air forces in Burma, Assam, and Bengal to resist the Japanese advance on land.

(2) (Majority) Prepare the ground and air defenses of Australia and its sea and air communications with the United States, using the minimum force required, and hold Australia as a base for current and future operation.

(Minority) Defend Australia and its sea and air communications with the United States, using the minimum force required.

(b) Exert maximum pressure against the Japanese by operations of strong naval forces based in Mid-Pacific, including attack on vital Japanese sea communications and exposed positions, and attack on Japanese naval forces under conditions favorable to increasing our relative strength.

(c) Reinforce strongly the British Eastern Fleet and operate it from bases in the Indian Ocean against Japanese naval and expeditionary forces; adding to it appropriate units of ABDA naval forces as they are forced to withdraw from Malaysia.

[23] (S) Mns, JPS 2nd Mtg, 19 Feb 42, item 2; (S) Mns, JPS 3rd Mtg, 21 Feb 42 (1100 and 1700) and 24 Feb 42, item 1.

[24] (S) Memo, Turner to JPS, "Review of the Strategical Situation of the Japanese War," 23 Feb 42, ABC 370 (1-28-42). He recommended that the paper be dropped and JUSSC be directed to prepare answers to the following questions:

(a) On the assumption that a decision is reached to hold Australia, New Zealand, and the Middle Pacific islands, what is the strength and distribution of the land, sea and air forces required: 1. Within the next three months? 2. Within the succeeding six months? 3. At the end of 18 months from now?

(b) What proportion of these various forces should be supplied by the United States, and what proportion by the British Commonwealth?

(c) Will the required forces, in the strengths indicated, be available during the three periods mentioned, and can they be transported to these positions and thereafter be maintained...?

(d) What would be the effect, if these deployments were made, on the ability of the United States to: 1. Relieve British troops in Iceland? 2. Provide planned reinforcements to the United Kingdom? 3. Build up and maintain in India United States air forces in the strengths now contemplated? 4. Provide air reinforcements in the Middle East? 5. Provide expeditionary forces in northwest Africa? 6. Improve the security of the sea communications in the Western Atlantic?

(e) Under a second assumption that it is decided that the United States will guarantee sea communications to Australia, and provide land and air forces in Australia and New Zealand only in the strengths now planned, what would be the strengths and distribution of United States forces required?

772   NOTES TO CHAPTER V

(f) For this plan, provide additional answers to questions (b), (c) & (d).

[25] (S) Unsgd Army Memo for JPS, "Admiral Turner's Memorandum, February 23, on J.P.S. 'Review of the Strategical Situation of the Japanese War,'" Feb 42, ABC 370 (1-28-42). The remark is made that Adm Turner's proposal "practically amounts to sabotaging of some two or three weeks' work of the Strategic Committee," and such a study would not "eliminate controversial questions." It was recommended that the JPS "proceed with a consideration of the paper....If we cannot agree, the issues should be presented clearly to the Joint U.S. Chiefs of Staff. If this can be done, the paper will have served a very useful purpose."

[26] (S) JPS 2/4(D), Dir to JUSSC, "Strategic Deployment of the Land, Sea and Air Forces of the U.S.," 24 Feb 42, CCS 381 (1-30-42) (1).

[27] (S) JPS 2/5, Rpt by JUSSC, "Strategic Deployment of the Land, Sea and Air Forces of the U.S." 6 Mar 42; (S) JPS 2/6, Rpt by JUSSC, same subj, 6 Mar 42. Both in CCS 381 (1-30-42) (1). JPS 2/5 combined JPS 2/2 and 2/2(A). JPS 2/6 was a new study of minimum requirements.

[28] General courses of action for the Pacific Theater were outlined in both JPS 2/5 and 2/6 in essentially the same terms:

(a) Secure the Territory of North and South America and their coastal communications.

(b) Secure the major base areas of Hawaii, the Mid-Pacific Islands, Australia and New Zealand and their sea and air communications with the United States.

(c) From these base areas, exert pressure against the Japanese by operations of naval and air forces including attack on vital Japanese sea communications, and attack on Japanese naval forces under conditions favorable to increasing our relative strength.

(d) Stop the Japanese advance through Burma; and secure India and her essential sea and air communications, together with the sea routes to the Red Sea and Persian Gulf.

(e) Maintain land and air communications between India and China.

[29] The author has been unable to find copies of the draft recommendations. However, from an unsigned document entitled "Comments on the Attached Draft of Committee Recommendations for J.P.S. 2/5," in ABC 370 (1-28-42), it may be concluded that they were essentially the same as the alternate conclusions subsequently included in JCS 23. (See below.)

[30] (S) CCS 56, "Message from Prime Minister on Current Situation," 5 Mar 42, CCS 381 (3-5-42) (2). Further details on the need for additional shipping were sent from BCOS to BJSM (Admty COS(W)105, 5 Mar 42) for presentation to the U.S. Chiefs. (S) CPS 23 (D), "United States Shipping for Transportation of British Troops to the Indian Ocean and Middle East," 5 Mar 42, CCS 381 (3-5-42) (2). CMTC had been studying the shipping situation since receipt of a memo from the British on 14 Feb. (S) CCS 38, "Relation of Merchant Shipping Losses to the Prosecution of the

War," 14 Feb 42, CCS 540 (2-12-42) sec 1. At the CCS 5th meeting, 17 Feb 42, Sir John Dill reported that the BCOS had requested that it be emphasized to the U.S. Chiefs "that unless it was found possible to produce more shipping, particularly personnel shipping from U.S. sources, we might shortly be faced with the choice of risking either the Middle East or Far East." CMTC reported that there was insufficient shipping available to meet all demands, that the British war effort and reenforcement of the Indian Ocean area were suffering, that U.S. shipping was all assigned in 1942, primarily for "outbound Defense Aid or military," and that although the U.S. economy would not suffer particularly, any diversion of U.S. shipping to offset British losses would affect the U.S. military effort or defense aid. (S) CCS 39/1, Rpt by CMTC & CPS, "Relation of Merchant Shipping Losses to the Prosecution of the War Effort," 14 Mar 42, CCS 540 (2-12-42) sec 1. When CCS finally discussed the report, on 17 Mar, they instructed CMTC to keep the matter under continuing review. For fuller discussion, see (S) MS, JCS Hist, *Ships, Shipping, and Strategy*, pt I.

[31] (S) Mns, WH Conf, 5 Mar 42, CCS 031 (3-5-42); (S) CCS 56/1, "Message from Prime Minister on Current Situation," 6 Mar 42, CCS 381 (3-5-42) (2); (S) Mns, CPS 7th Mtg, 6 Mar 42; (S) Mns, JCS 4th Mtg, 7 Mar 42, item 1. Following the JCS meeting the chiefs went to the White House. (S) Mns, CCS 10th Mtg, 7 Mar 42 (1530), item 1. JCS discussed the draft reply alone and with the President before it was considered by CCS. The message in final form is annexed to the CCS minutes of the 10th meeting.

[32] (S) CPS 23/1, "United States Shipping for Transportation of British Troops to the Indian Ocean and Middle East," 6 Mar 42, CCS 381 (3-5-42) (2).

[33] (S) Mns, JPS 4th Mtg, 11 Mar 42, items 4 and 5; (S) Mns, JPS 5th Mtg, 14 Mar 42, item 1.

[34] (S dg R) JCS 23, Rpt by JPS, "Strategic Deployment of Land, Sea, and Air Forces of the United States," 14 Mar 42, CCS 381 (1-30-42) (1).

[35] On 17 Feb 42 Adm Turner, alarmed by the rapid Japanese advance and believing that the Russians could hold in Europe and that operations against the Japanese would at least release the pressure against Russia from the east, had recommended to Adm King that all further reenforcement of Iceland and the U.K. be postponed and sufficient amounts of men and materiel be sent to the Pacific to insure its defense. (S) Memo, ACofS (Plans) to CominCh, "Recommended new Strategic deployment against Japan, 17 Feb 42, CNO(WPD) file "A16-3(4) Pacific Ocean Areas (whole)"; (S) WPD "Notes on JCS 23," no sig, nd, ABC 370 (1-28-42). An untitled, unsigned paper in the same file repeats (2) as it appeared in JCS 23 with a note attached, "The Air Corps members of the Joint Staff Planners are in complete accord with this concept," and is signed by H.S. Hansell for Gen Spaatz. The third view may represent that of a member of JUSSC although

more radical than the dissenting report made earlier by one of that committee. The unknown author of "Comments on the Attached Draft of Committee Recommendations for J.P.S. 2/5" [ABC 370(1-28-42)] remarked:

> It is believed that all [the Joint Staff Planners] felt that forces in addition to those now in the Southwest Pacific should be moved there, such additional forces to be substantially as those recommended by the JUSSC. Nor do I believe it is correct to say that any of the Committee members were convinced that Germany would completely defeat Russia in 1942 unless we moved all possible forces to the United Kingdom for an offensive this year.

[36] JUSSC was concurrently working on a study on priorities for munitions production. In a preliminary report, dtd 24 Feb 42, to JPS, JUSSC recommended:

> the Committee is of the opinion that useful recommendations cannot be submitted until after there is available a United States strategical concept, including a decision as to the theater in which the major effort of the United Nations is to be made immediately and in the long range view. Such information is necessary because the war in the Pacific Theater will be largely a naval, amphibious, and air effort while the war in the European Theater will be chiefly an air and land effort.

(S) Memo, JUSSC to JPS, "Directive for study of: Priorities in Production of Munitions Based on Strategical Considerations," 24 Feb 42, CCS 400.17 (2-20-42) sec 1.

[37] (S) Mns, JCS 6th Mtg, 16 Mar 42, item 4.

[38] (S) JCS 23, "Strategic Deployment of Land, Sea and Air Forces of the United States," 14 Mar 42, CCS 381 (1-30-42) (1).

[39] (MS) Brit Doc J.P.(41) 1028, "Operation 'ROUND-UP'," 24 Dec 41, CCS 381 (3-23-42) pt 1; (S) Mns, CCS 13th Mtg, 24 Mar 42, item 9.

[40] Recommended by W.B. Smith (CCS Secy) in (S) Memo to Marshall, 23 Mar 42, CCS 381 (3-23-42) pt 2; (S) Mns, JCS 7th Mtg, 23 Mar 42, item 7; (S) Mns, CCS 13th Mtg, 24 Mar 42, item 9.

[41] For a fuller discussion, see (S) MS, JCS Hist, *War Against Germany and Its Satellites*.

[42] *Campaigns of the Pacific War*, p. 31; *The World at War*, p. 116; Sherwood, p. 525; Samuel E. Morison, *The Rising Sun in the Pacific, 1931 - April 1942* (Boston, 1948), pp. 381-386.

[43] (MS) Brit Doc C.O.S. (42) 97(0), "Comments on General Marshall's Memorandum," 13 Apr 42, CCS 381 (3-23-42) pt 3; (S) Msg, Marshall (London) to McNarney, 14 Apr 42, (TS) CominCh file "President; Prime Minister - Jan. 1942 - "

[44] Msgs, PM to Pres, 7 Apr 42, 15 Apr 42, *The Hinge of Fate*, pp. 181, 183-184.

[45] (S) Msg, McNarney to Marshall (London), 320, 14 Apr 42, re Marshall's 2398 of 14 Apr; (S) Msg, PM to Pres, 69, 15 Apr 42; (S) Msg, Pres to PM, 16 Apr 42; (S) Msg, PM to Pres, 71, 18 Apr 42. All in (TS) CominCh file "President; Prime Minister -

Jan 1942 -." (S) Memo, ACofS(P) to CominCh, "Situation in Indian Ocean," 16 Apr 42, (TS) CominCh file #35, "Ass't Chief of Staff (Plans - F-1)." *Campaigns of the Pacific War*, p. 31.

[46] (S) Note, nd, by R.K. Turner, CNO(WPD) file "Directives to SC, SWPA and to CinCPOA," atchd to paper dtd 26 Mar 42 on Strategic Deployment.

[47] (S) Memo, CNO (prepared by Adm Turner) to CofS USA, "Strategic Deployment in the Pacific Against Japan," 29 Mar 42, CominCh file "A16-3(1)"; (S) Memo, Actg CofS to King, "Strategic Deployment in the Pacific against Japan," 6 Apr 42, (TS) CominCh file "Memos from Gen. Marshall 15 Jan 42 - 1 Sept. 44."

[48] The question had been raised at the 1st meeting of the PWC, of which minutes are not available to furnish further details. (S) Memo, Capt J.L. McCrea to Marshall, King, and Arnold, 2 Apr 42, CCS 660.2 (4-2-42) sec 1.

[49] (S) Army and Navy drafts of memos for Pres on adequacy of defenses of Fiji and New Caledonia, in CCS 660.2 (4-2-42) sec 1. These were apparently prepared independently, not for the JPS. (S) Mns, JPS 10th Mtg, 4 Apr 42, item 5; (S) Mns, JCS 9th Mtg, 6 Apr 42, item 6.

[50] (S) Memo, King to Pres, "Adequacy of the Defenses of the Fiji Islands and New Caledonia," 7 Apr 42; (S) JPS 21/5/D, "Defense for the Island Bases along the Lines of Communication between Hawaii and Australia," 7 Apr 42. Both in CCS 660.2 (4-2-42) sec 1.

[51] The subcommittee consisted of JUSSC plus Col DeW. Peck, USMC, Capt R.O. Glover, USN, Lt Cdr G.W. Anderson, Jr., USN, and Lt Col E.H. McDaniel, USA. (S) JPS 21/6/D, "Defense for the Island Bases along the Lines of Communication between Hawaii and Australia," 9 Apr 42, CCS 660.2 (4-2-42) sec 1.

[52] (S) Mns, JPS 13th Mtg, 22 Apr 42, item 5; (S) Mns, JPS 14th Mtg, 25 Apr 42, item 2; (S) Mns, JPS 15th Mtg, 29 Apr 42, item 5; (S) JPS 21/7, "Defense for the Island Bases along the Lines of Communication between Hawaii and Australia," 18 Apr 42; (S dg R) JCS 48, same subj, 2 May 42. Both in CCS 660.2 (4-2-42) sec 1.

[53] (S) Msg, Marshall to MacArthur, 1493, 26 Apr 42; (S) Msg, MacArthur to Marshall, 139, 27 Apr 42; (S) Msg, Marshall to MacArthur, 1512, 27 Apr 42. All in CCS 660.2 (4-2-42) sec 1.

[54] (S) OPD "Notes on JPS 13th mtg, 22 Apr 42, JPS 21/7 - Defense of Island Bases," ABC 381 Pacific Bases sec 2 (1-22-42).

[55] (S) Memo, Pres Naval Aide to JCS, "Aircraft and Troops for Australia," 1 May 42, CCS 381 (5-1-42)(1). The question may have arisen as a result of Dr. Evatt's presentation of PM Curtin's and Gen MacArthur's opinions. Cf. below.

[56] (S) Memo, CofS USA (prepared by DDE) to Pres, 4 May 42, CCS 381 (5-1-42) (1).

[57] (S) Memo, King to JCS, "J.C.S. 48 - Defense of Island Bases in the Pacific," nd, App I to Mns, JCS 13th Mtg, 4 May 42.

[58] (S) Mns, JCS 13th Mtg, 4 May 42, item 3. It is interesting to note, and indicative of Gen Arnold's position in JCS, that

although the problem concerned air forces, and although Gen Arnold had certainly discussed it with Gen Marshall, the minutes record no direct participation by Gen Arnold in the discussion at the JCS meeting beyond a brief statistical statement.

[59] (S) Memo, CofS to Pres, "The Pacific Theatre versus 'Bolero'," 6 May 42, CCS 381 (5-1-42) (1).

[60] (S) Memo, Pres to Marshall, 6 May 42, CCS 381 (5-1-42) (1).

[61] (SS) Memo, Pres to Stimson, Marshall, Arnold, Knox, King, and Hopkins, WDCSA SS file "381 File I." "...not to be circulated or used beyond the above group." Memo outlines the situation on 6 May 42 and was written because "I always think it well to outline in simple terms and from time to time complex problems which call for over-all planning." He considered it of primary importance to help the Russians, by maintaining the flow of goods and by organizing a second front. "As regards timing, the general strategic plan in the Pacific Theatre, in the India-Burma Theatre, and in the Near East Theatre calls for a continuous day to day maintenance of existing positions and existing strength in these theatres at least for the next few months. The Atlantic Theatre general plan calls, however, for very great speed in developing actual operations. . .The necessities of the case call for action in 1942--not 1943."

[62] (S) Memo, ACofS (Eisenhower) to Smith (Secy JCS), "U.S. Army Objectives in the Pacific," 13 May 42; (S) Note, Cdr Libby to King, 30 May 42. Both in (TS) CominCh file "Memoranda to Admiral - 1942."

[63] (S) Mns, SecWar Confs, War Council, Vol II, 23 Mar 42, in CofS recs. Shortly before this CIC had estimated that it was unlikely that the Japanese would attack the Australian mainland. (S) CCS 18/1, "Possible Japanese Action against Australia and New Zealand," 13 Mar 42, CCS 381 (1-31-42).

[64] *New York Times*, 20 Mar 42 et seq; Sherwood, pp. 508-509; *The Hinge of Fate*, pp. 155-166.

[65] *New York Times*, Mar 42. A typical remark of an unidentified officer of Gen MacArthur's staff is quoted in *New York Times*, 30 Mar 42. "We are all through with the fire-and-fall-back policy.... This is as far south as we are going. From now on we are going north." (S) Msg, MacArthur to Marshall, 59, 2 Apr 42, CCS 320.2 (1-28-42). In Gen MacArthur's words, "The general public attitude to defeatism is being replaced by a growing feeling of confidence and self reliance."

[66] (S) Msg, MacArthur to Marshall, 70, 4 Apr 42, CCS 660.2 (3-14-42) sec 1; (S) Msg, MacArthur to AGWAR, AG 286, 16 Apr 42, CCS 320. 2 (1-28-42). (S) Msg, MacArthur to Marshall, AG 453, 24 Apr 42; (S) Msg, MacArthur to Marshall, AG 470, 25 Apr 42. Both in CCS 045.4 (1-29-42).

[67] See above, ch IV, p. 143.

[68] (S) Mns, CCS 11th Mtg, 10 Mar 42, item 3.

[69] (C) Ltr, Exec Secy, Neth Purch Comm, to Exec Secy MAB, 21 Mar 42, CCS 452 (3-21-42) sec 1.

[70] (S) Memo, Secy MAC(A) to Secy MAB, "Policy Regarding Disposal of N.E.I. Airplanes," 26 Mar 42, CCS 452 (3-21-42) sec 1. There is no indication in the memo of what should be done with ten other bombers already completed. Mr. R.G. Casey, in a letter to Maj Gen J.H. Burns, gave it as his understanding that the ten were to be sent also when certain modifications had been made. (U) Ltr, Casey to Burns, 27 Mar 42, CCS 452 (3-21-42) sec 1. Dr. Evatt, however, had been told that six were to go to Brazil.

[71] (S) Note by R.K. Turner, nd (atchd to paper dtd 26 Mar 42), CNO (WPD) file "Directive to SC, SWPA and to CinCPOA."

[72] (S) Ltr, Evatt to Marshall, 31 Mar 42, ABC 452.1 (1-22-42) sec 1.

[73] (S) Mns, CCS 14th Mtg, 31 Mar 42, item 3.

[74] (S) Mns, JCS 9th Mtg, 6 Apr 42, item 7; (S) CCS 60, Memo by JCS, "U.S. Aircraft Allocated to the N.E.I.," 7 Apr 42, CCS 452 (3-21-42) sec 1; (S) Mns, CCS 15 Mtg, 7 Apr 42, item 4. The problem is difficult to follow in the official documents. It appears that the U.S. Chiefs were anxious to get these planes for the U.S. Army and Navy without having to divide them with the British, while the British were eager to have some of the planes sent elsewhere than to the Pacific Theater. Although the British, and Adm King, seem to have assumed that the planes would go to the Pacific, such an intention was not recorded, and the recommendation that reallocation should be a U.S. responsibility was based rather on the original assignment of the planes to the Dutch. MAB subsequently reassigned them by nations rather than areas. (S) Memo, Secy MAC(A) to Exec MAB, "Reassignment of N.E.I. Airplanes," 20 Apr 42, CCS 452 (3-21-42) sec 1.

[75] (S) CCS 30/2, Msg by BCOS, "Provision of Fighter Aircraft for Australia," 6 Apr 42, CCS 452.1 (2-5-42); (S) Mns, JCS 9th Mtg, 6 Apr 42, item 7; (S) Mns, CCS 15th Mtg, 7 Apr 42, item 4.

[76] (S dg R) CCS 61/1 "Aircraft Situation of the United Nations," 22 Jun 42, cy w/relevant papers in CCS 452 (4-8-42) sec 1. For a fuller discussion of the A-S-T agreement, see (S) MSS, JCS Hist, *Procurement and Allocation of Material Means* and *War Against Germany and Its Satellites*.

[77] (MS) Msg, Evatt to Curtin, E.S. 17, 23 Apr 42, CCS 320.2 (1-28-42).

[78] (S) Memo, Capt J.L. McCrea, USN, to JCS, 21 Apr 42; (S) Msg, Evatt to Curtin, E.S. 17, 23 Apr 42. Both in CCS 320.2 (1-28-42). It is impossible to tell from the available records why the question was raised by Dr. Evatt at this particular meeting. Neither the PWC minutes nor the exchange of messages between Dr. Evatt and PM Curtin prior to the meeting is available. It is probable that PM Curtin's S.W. 29 directed Dr. Evatt to investigate the aircraft situation and outlined Gen MacArthur's views as to the requirements of his command. How much Gen MacArthur knew of the exchanges between the two Australians is impossible to tell from the documents. He subsequently denied

NOTES TO CHAPTER V

all knowledge, and it is probable that he at least never saw the messages.

[79] (S) Msg, Marshall to MacArthur, 1188, 9 Apr 42, CCS 320.2 (1-28-42).

[80] (S) Memo, W.B. Smith to McCrea, "Air Forces for Australia," 22 Apr 42; (S) Ltr, W.B. Smith to Evatt, 22 Apr 42. Both in CCS 320.2 (1-28-42).

[81] (MS) Msg, Curtin to Evatt, S.W. 34, 28 Apr 42, CCS 320.2 (1-28-42).

[82] (S) Ltr, Evatt to Hopkins, 29 Apr 42, CCS 320.2 (1-28-42). It may be inferred from the ltr that Dr. Evatt had also discussed the matter at the PWC meeting of the same day, although it is not directly so stated.

[83] (S) Msg, PM to Pres, 82, 29 Apr 42, Exec 10, item 52.

[84] (S) Msg, Marshall to CinCSWPA, 8, 30 Apr 42, CM-OUT-6034, CCS 320.2 (1-28-42).

[85] (S) Memo, Smith to McCrea, 1 May 42, CCS 320.2 (1-28-42), encl Marshall-MacArthur msgs 14-30 Apr 42; (S) Memo, Marshall to Pres, 29 Apr 42, Exec 10, item 53.

[86] (S) Msg, MacArthur to CofS USA, 151, CM-IN-0667, 3 May 42, CCS 320.2 (1-28-42).

[87] (S) Memo, Pres to CofS USA, 5 May 42, WDCSA (SS) 381 Australia. Memo contains draft of message for Gen MacArthur. It was returned by Gen Marshall with comments on 6 May.

[88] (S) Msg, MacArthur to Marshall, 176, CM-IN-2333, 8 May 42, Exec 2, item li.

[89] (U) Ltr, King to G.P. Hayes, 20 Nov 51, JCS HS files; Morison, *The Rising Sun in the Pacific*, pp. 389-398; *AAF IN WW II*, vol I, pp. 438-444. The AAF volume incorrectly suggests that Pres Roosevelt had a hand in it "although it is not possible to determine its original author."

[90] *Ibid*. Naval War College, Analysis, *The Battle of the Coral Sea*, 1947.

[91] (S) JIC Daily Summary, 19 Feb 42, 24 Feb 42, *et seq*.

[92] (S) Msg, CominCh to CinCPac and ComSoWesPacFor, 182032 Apr 42, (TS) CominCh despatch file.

[93] *Campaigns of the Pacific War*, pp. 52-55.

[94] (S) Msg, CinCPac to CominCh, 102347 May 42, (TS) CominCh file "CinCPac Despatches."

[95] Orders were in fact issued by Imperial General Headquarters on 18 May to occupy strategic points in New Caledonia, Fiji, and Samoa. IGHQ Navy Order No. 19, 18 May 42, in file of Japanese Navy Orders, 8-5.1 CH, OCMH. IGHQ Army Order No. 633, 18 May 42, in file of Japanese Army Orders, 8-5.1, CF, V2, OCMH.

[96] (S) Ltr, CominCh to CofS USA, "Situation in South Pacific and Southwest Pacific Areas as of the end of May, 1942," 12 May 42, (TS) CominCh file "Memos to Gen. Marshall - 15 Jan 42 - 1 Sept 44"; (S) Mns, JCS 14th Mtg, 11 May 42, item 8.

[97] (S) Memo, Marshall to Eisenhower, 12 May 42, WDCSA 381 Southwest Pacific. Informing Gen Eisenhower of the agreement,

Gen Marshall said: "Involved in this would be two squadrons to a total of about sixteen 4-engine bombers." Adm King's aide recorded that it was "tentatively agreed Army would provide (a) 16 Heavy Bombers in SUVA (b) 13 Medium Bombers in SUVA (c) 13 Medium Bombers in New Caledonia." (S) Memo, Cdr Libby to VAdm Willson, RAdms Edwards and Turner, "Shore-based aircraft for South Pacific Islands," 12 May 42, (TS) CominCh file "#33, Chief of Staff." Army progress reported in (S) Memo, Marshall to King, "Situation in South Pacific," 13 May 42, WDCSA 381 Southwest Pacific.

[98] (S) Memo, CominCh to CofS USA, "Strength of Hawaii and Alaskan Defenses," ser 00384, 18 May 42, Exec 10, item 67A; (S) Msg, CofS USA to CG HawDept, 3829, 20 May 42, OPD 381 PTO sec 1.

[99] Samuel E. Morison, *Coral Sea, Midway and Submarine Actions, May 1942-August 1942* (Boston, 1949), pp. 160-166; (S) Msg, Marshall to DeWitt, CM-OUT-4284, 21 May 42, OPD Exec 10, item 14; Edwin M. Snell and Maurice Matloff, MS, *Strategic Planning for Coalition Warfare: 1939-1942* (OCMH), ch IX, pp. 22-23.

[100] (S) Msg, MacArthur to Marshall, 199, 23 May 42, OPD 381 PTO sec 1.

[101] (S) Memo, CominCh-CNO to CofS USA, "Reply to Australia Despatch #199," ser 00415, 24 May 42; (S) Memo, Col J.R. Deane, Secy GS, to WPD Msg Ctr, 24 May 42. Both in WDCSA 381 Southwest Pacific.

[102] (S) Memo, King to Marshall, "Situation in the Pacific," ser 00421, 24 May 42, WDCSA 381 Southwest Pacific Area.

[103] *North Carolina*, one unidentified heavy cruiser, one 5" cruiser, plus *Wasp* Detachment (already ordered), *Washington* Detachment, including two heavy cruisers, four destroyers.

[104] (S) Memo, Marshall to King, "Situation in Pacific, Reference Your Memorandum of May 24th," nd, OPD 381 PTO sec 1.

[105] (S) JIC Daily Summary, 51, 30 Jan 42.

[106] (S) Msg, CG USAFFE to CofS USA, 10 Dec 41, WPD 4544-26; (MS) Msg, ABDACOM to CCS, 00278, 23 Jan 42, CCS file, Radios from ABDACOM (Wavell Only).

[107] (S) Memo, Stark to Pres, 13 Dec 41, ser 0145612, 4557-32. Army opinion to contrary in rough drafts of an unused memo prepared for Gen Marshall in same file.

[108] (S) Memo, Pres to Stark and Marshall, "United Nations Action in Case of War between Russia and Japan," 4 Mar 42, encl to JCS 16, 6 Mar 42, CCS 381 (3-5-42) (1). What prompted the President to send this memo is not known.

[109] (S) Memo, Maj E.P. Curtis, Secy Air Staff, to Actg ACofS WPD, "Airport Information, Nome-Moscow," 28 Oct 41; (S) Memo, Actg ACofS Gerow to CofS USA, "Airport Information, Russia," 29 Oct 41; (S) Memo, SecWar to SecState, 31 Oct 41; (S) Memo, Gerow to CofS USA, 8 Nov 41. All in WPD 4557-15. (UNK) Memo, Lt Col C.L. Bissell to Col Handy, 10 Jan 42; (S) Memo, H.L. George, ACofAS, to ACofS WPD, "Proposed Air Service to Siberia via Alaska," 26 Jan 42; (S) Ltr, SecWar to Pres, 14 Jan 42;

(S) Memo, Curtis to CofS USA, "Siberian Air Bases," 16 Jan 42; (S) Memo, ACofS Gerow to CofS USA, "Siberian Air Bases," 26 Jan 42. All in WPD 4557-43.

[110] (S) Mns, JPS 7th Mtg, 21 Mar 42; (S) Mns, JPS 8th Mtg, 25 Mar 42; (S) JPS 19/2, Paper by JUSSC, "United Nations Action in Case of War between Russia and Japan," 20 Mar 42. Army OPD draft papers on subject are in ABC 381 (1-23-42).

[111] (S) Memo, RAdm Turner to JPS, "United Nations Action in Case of War Between Russia and Japan," 28 Mar 42, CCS 381 (3-5-42) (1). Fwded as JCS 16/1, 29 Mar 42.

[112] (S) Mns, JCS 8th Mtg, 30 Mar 42, item 7; (S) Memo, CofS USA and ComInCh to Pres, 30 Mar 42, CCS 381 (3-5-42) (1). A note attached to the memo indicates that it was returned without comment. It is possible that the President discussed the matter with the chiefs orally. Whether he took any action might be learned from White House files.

[113] (S) Mns, JCS 13th Mtg, 4 May 42; (S) Mns, JCS 19th Mtg, 9 Jun 42, item 12.

[114] (Trans) Cross's rec of mtg, Pres, Molotov, Hopkins, 1 Jun 42, in Sherwood, p. 572. Memo by Hopkins, 9 Jun 42, *ibid.*, p. 584.

[115] (S) Msg, Mayer (Chungking) to Milid, 191, 5 Jun 42, CCS 381 (3-5-42) (1); (S) JIC Daily Summary, 179, 7 Jun 42.

[116] *Campaigns of the Pacific War*, pp. 78-81; *AAF IN WW II*, vol II, pp. 462-468.

[117] (S) JCS 61, "Estimate of Situation in the North Pacific Area June 13, 1942," 14 Jun 42, CCS 381 North Pacific Area (6-13-42).

[118] (S) Mns, JCS 20th Mtg, 15 Jun 42, item 4.

[119] (S) Msg, Pres to Stalin, 171704 Jun 42, CCS 381 (3-5-42) (1). The President seems to have talked first with Amb Litvinov.

[120] (S) Mns, JCS 21st Mtg, 23 Jun 42, item 7; (S) Msgs, Pres to Stalin, 240015, 240018 Jun 42, CCS 381 (3-5-42) (1). There is no indication that the second message was discussed at the JCS meeting, and no preliminary drafts have yet been seen. From the detailed discussion which it contains of plans for the ferry route, it is apparent that the President had discussed its formulation at least with Gen Arnold or some other air force representative.

[121] (S) Msgs, Standley to SecState, 227, 231, 2 Jul 42, in OCS file RUSSIA.

[122] (S) Ltr of Instructions, SecWar to Maj Gen F. Bradley, 20 Jul 42. From the President, Bradley carried instructions to "tell Stalin to let us know what he wants and in what priorities and show us how to get it to him...there was practically no limit to the aid we would furnish the Russians if they would do this." (S) Memo, Maj Gen F. Bradley to CofS USA, "Visit with the President," 22 Jul 42. Both in OCS file RUSSIA. The report of these discussions has not been seen by the author.

[123] Memo, Lt(jg) H. Wilmerding to Lt Col R.L. Vittrup, 13 Jun 42; (S) JPS 31/D, "United States Aid to Russia in Case of Attack by Japan," 15 Jun 42. Both in CCS 381 (3-5-42) (1).

[124] (S) JPS 31/1, "United States Aid to Russia in Case of Attack by Japan," 16 Jun 42; (S) JCS 16/2, same subj, 19 Jun 42. Both in CCS 381 (3-5-42) (1). (S) Mns, JPS 20th Mtg, 17 Jun 42, item 7.

CHAPTER VI

[1] (S dg U) ABC-1, "United States-British Staff Conversations," 27 Mar 41, *PHA*, pt 15, pp. 1485-1541; (S dg U) NBWP-Rainbow No. 5 (WPL-46), *PHA*, pt 18, pp. 2877-2941. For fuller discussion of these documents in relation to the war against Japan, see above, ch I. U.S. Army members of the ABC-1 Conference had felt that possible extension of operations into the Carolines would involve more Army forces than they could furnish. But the Navy maintained that the way should be open for taking advantage of any possible Japanese weakness to extend U.S. positions closer to the Japanese lines of communications. (S) Mns, Army & Navy Sections, 19 Feb 41, 09212-15, in Ghormley papers, NR&H; Comments of VAdm V.R. Murphy, USN (Ret), 19 Apr 49, on this chapter, JCS HS.

[2] (S) Ann "J" to Ltr, CominCh-CNO to CinCPac, "Information and Instructions Relative to the Pacific Campaign (WPL-46-PC)," 00298, 23 Apr 42, CNO(WPD) file "WPD-46-PC-#990." (TS) CominCh file "Digest of Despatches Embodying Operating Policy or Directives."

[3] (S) Msg, CominCh to CinCPac, 122000 Feb 42; (S) Ann "J" to Ltr, CominCh-CNO to CinCPac, 00298, 23 Apr 42. Both in CNO(WPD) file (WPL-46-PC-#990." Comments of VAdm V.R. Murphy, USN(Ret), in conversation with the author, 19 Apr 49, JCS HS files. (S) Encls to Ltr, Cdr W.R. Denekas, USN, to Col C.H. Donnelly, USA, 25 Jan 50, JCS HS files.

[4] (S) JCS 5, Note by Secy, "Defense Force for an Advance Base in Ellice Island Area," 5 Feb 42, CCS 660.2 Ellice Island (2-5-42). The enclosure has become detached from the cover sheet and is not identified as such in the JCS file. It is quite probable that this study developed in WPD from the combined study made during Arcadia on "Defense of Island Bases" (ABC-4/8), although no direct evidence has been found. The date is of interest because JCS had not yet held its first formal meeting.

[5] (S) "Notes on J.C.S. 5," WPD Paper, nd; (S) Memo, ACofS Gerow to CofS USA, "Defense For an Advance Base in Ellice Island Area," 10 Feb 42. Both in ABC 381 Ellice Islands (2-5-42).

> Each island garrison necessitates diversion of Army combat resources (air and ground), the utilization of our limited shipping and the employment of naval forces for escort and relief in case of attack....We are not yet in a position to undertake a sustained offensive across the Pacific. Until we can carry out such an offensive, our island commitments should be limited to those necessary to secure our routes to critical areas.

Occupation of Funafuti was ultimately approved at JCS 6th meeting, 16 Mar 42, item 10.

782   NOTES TO CHAPTER VI

⁶(S) Memo, King to CCS, "Changes in ABDA and/or ANZAC Areas Evolving from Developments in Far East," 17 Feb 42, CCS 381 (1-24-42) sec 1.

⁷(S) Ltr, CominCh to CNO and CofS USA, "Establishment of United States garrison in Efate, New Hebrides Island," ser 00105, 18 Feb 42, (SC) CominCh file "FF1/A16-3/F-1."

⁸(S) Memo, Marshall to King, "Establishment of U.S. Garrison in Efate, New Hebrides Islands," 24 Feb 42, (SC) CominCh file "A16-3(1)." That some of the Navy planners did indeed feel that the over-all strategy should be reversed is evidenced by a memo written by RAdm R.K. Turner on 17 Feb, in which he urged that no further reenforcements be sent to Iceland and the United Kingdom until fall, but go rather to Australia and New Zealand. He argued that available resources were not sufficient to sustain a divided effort, and that if both continued the United States would probably be defeated in the Pacific. (S) Memo, Turner to King, "Recommended new strategic deployment against Japan," 17 Feb 42, CNO(WPD) file "A16-3(4) Pacific Ocean Area (whole)."

⁹(S) Memo, CominCh to CofS USA, "Establishment of U.S. Garrisons in Efate, New Hebrides; and at Tongatabu in the Tonga Islands," 00149, 2 Mar 42, (SC) CominCh file "A16-3/1"; (S) Mns, JCS 4th Mtg, 2 Mar 42, item 5; (S) Memo, King to Pres, 5 Mar 42, ABC 323.31 Pacific Ocean Area (1-29-42) sec 1-A.

¹⁰(S) Mns, Mtg, Pres and CCS at White House, 5 Mar 42, CCS 031 (3-5-42). The President stated it as an established fact that activity in the Pacific would follow the Navy's general scheme. Adm King outlined the plan to him in a memo on 5 Mar 42, ABC 323.31 Pacific Ocean Area (1-29-42) sec 1-A. Whether this was presented before the meeting, whether the President discussed it with Adm King or the others, and what comments, if any, the President made are not indicated in available documents. The JCS minutes contain no details of the discussion of the question of these garrisons and no specific statement of agreement. Undated papers, "Status of Joint Plan for the Occupation and Defense of Efate, New Hebrides, (Roses)," and "...of Tongatabu (Bleacher)," in ABC 381 (3-2-42), state that joint plans were being developed. Pencilled notations on the papers indicate that action was taken at the JCS 5th meeting, 9 Mar 42. Orders from the Army Chief of Staff to CG, New Caledonia, to send a detachment to Efate as a temporary measure before establishing a permanent garrison were relayed in (S) Msg, CominCh to CTG 12.1, 081905 Mar 42, (SC) CominCh file "A16-3(1)." (S) Ltr, CominCh to Dist List, encl "Joint Basic Plan for the Occupation and Defense of Tongatabu," 00178, 12 Mar 42; (S) Memo, ACofS Eisenhower to CGAF, CGGF, CGSOS, AG, "Joint Basic Plan for the Occupation and Defense of Tongatabu," 15 Mar 42. Both in OPD 381 Tonga Tabu, sec 1.

¹¹On 26 Mar 42, Adm Turner advised Adm King that an attempt to establish bases by assault in the Solomons, as projected for the future, would at that time result in failure. To assure success, he recommended consolidating and strengthening

the positions already occupied before undertaking an offensive. (S) Memo, ACofS(P) to CominCh, "Strategic Deployment in the Pacific against Japan," 26 Mar 42, CNO(WPD) file "A16-4(4) Pacific Ocean Area (whole)."

[12] (S) Memo, ACofS(P) to CominCh, "Pacific Ocean Campaign Plan," 16 April 42, CNO(WPD) file "A16-3(4) Pacific Ocean (whole)", (S) Ltr, CominCh-CNO to CinCPac, "Information and Instructions Relative to the Pacific Campaign," 00298, short title WPL-46-PC, 23 Apr 42, CNO(WPD) file "WPL-46-PC #990."

[13] (S) Exchange of Memos, King and Sir John Dill, Apr 42, (TS) CominCh file "Memos to/from British - 1941."

[14] A memo drawn up by Army OPD on 21 Apr included the statement:
> No indication has been given to the Operations Division as to the extent or the timing of the operations the Navy is contemplating. We do not know major fleet elements are to operate in the region, prepared to support the island bases, or whether these islands are to be mere outposts in hit-and-run tactics.

It was recommended that no additional forces be committed to the area and that troops already there be used for occupation *after* bases had been seized by Navy and amphibious troops. (S) Memo, Eisenhower to Marshall, "Strategic Conceptions and their application to Southwest Pacific," 21 Apr 42, OPD 384 PTO (4-21-42) (4-2-42), #11.

[15] (S) Uniden Paper, "Estimate Southwest Pacific Offensive," 22 Jun 42, OPD 381 SWPA.

[16] Cf. above, ch V.

[17] IGHQ Navy Order No. 20, 11 Jul 42, in file of Japanese Navy Orders, 8-5.1, CH, OCMH; (S) Ltr, CominCh to CofS USA, "Situations in South Pacific and Southwest Pacific Areas as of the end of May 1942," 12 May 42, (TS) CominCh file "Memos to Gen. Marshall - 15 Jan 42 - 1 Sept 44"; (S) Msgs, CominCh to CinCPac, 152130, 152136, 172220, 211930 May 42, (TS) CominCh despatches; (S) Msg, Emmons to Marshall, 16 May 42, CCS 381 (3-27-42); Morison, *Coral Sea*, pp. 69-159, 166-184; *AAF in WW II*, vol I, pp. 451-462; *Campaigns of the Pacific War*, pp. 58-60.

[18] (S) Msg, CinCPac to ComAmphibForPac, info MarCorpsHQ, CominCh, 252349 May 42; (S) Msg, CinCPac to SC SWPA, info CominCh, 280351 May 42. Both in (TS) CominCh file "CinCPac Despatches."

[19] (S) Msg, CominCh to CinCPac, 010100 Jun 42; (S) Msg, SC SWPA to CinCPac, info CominCh, 291335 May 42; (S) Msg, CinCPac to CominCh, 300419 May 42; (S) Msg, CinCPac to SCSWPA, 020455 Jun 42. All in (TS) CominCh file "CinCPac Despatches."

[20] (S) Memo, Marshall to King, "Early attack on Japanese Advance Bases," 6 Jun 42, (TS) CominCh file "Memos from Gen Marshall 15 Jan. '42 - 1 Sept '44"; (S) Msg, MacArthur to Marshall, AG 913, 8 Jun 42, WDCSA SPA. Gen MacArthur's earlier requests for an additional carrier or two had been turned down. (S) Msg, MacArthur to Marshall, AG 453, 24 Apr 42; (S) Msg, Marshall to MacArthur, 1499, 26 Apr 42. Both in CCS 045.4 (1-19-42).

[21] (S) Msg, CofS USA to SC SWPA, 198, 8 Jun 42, OPD 381 SWPA (6-8-42), #51; (S) Memo, CominCh-CNO to CofS USA, "General

784 NOTES TO CHAPTER VI

MacArthur's Despatch AG 913 of June 8, 1942," 11 Jun 42, (SC) CominCh file "A16-3(1) Overflow #2." A thorough search of the JCS records has revealed no papers pertaining to operations in the New Guinea-New Britain-Solomons area prior to discussion of the project at the JCS meeting of 10 Jul 1942.

[22] (S) MS, JCS Hist, *War Against Germany and Its Satellites*.

[23] (S) Mns, Plen Sess, WH, 21 Jun 42, CCS 334 Conference (6-21-42).

[24] (S) Memo, Marshall to King, "Operations in the Southwest Pacific," 12 Jun 42, OPD 381 SWPA, #73. Gen Marshall estimates that a force sufficient for the operation could be assembled in Brisbane by about 5 Jul 42. (S) R&R, AFCAS to AFAEP, "Plan for Raboul [sic]," 15 Jun 42; (S) Memo, Col R.G. Breene, Dir Tech Servs, to Brig Gen N.F. Twining, "Overall Capture of Rabaul," 17 Jun 42; (S) Memo, no orig to Arnold, "Plan for Capture of Rabaul," 20 Jun 42; (S) Memo, Maj Gen M.F. Harmon, CofAS, to ACofAS Plans, "Plan for Capture of Raboul [sic]," 22 Jun 42; (S) Memo, Col Frank Everest to Twining, 23 Jun 42; (S) Memo, Col O.A. Anderson, ACofAS (Plans) to CofAS, "Plan to Capture Rabaul," 25 Jun 42. All in AF HS file, "Material Brought Down from Col. Williams File Sept. 10, 1943. Material dated from May, 1942 to November, 1942." (S) Memo, Col W.L. Ritchie to Gen Streett, "Offensive Operation in the Southwest Pacific," 23 Jun 42; (S) Memo, Handy to Marshall, "Operations in Southwest Pacific," 24 Jun 42. Both in OPD 381 SWPA.

[25] Col. W.L. Ritchie, Col E.H. McDaniel, Capt R.O. Glover.

[26] In the Pacific Fleet as of 15 Jun 42 were four carriers—*Saratoga*, *Enterprise*, *Hornet*, and *Wasp*. Morison, *Coral Sea*, p. 257.

[27] Comments of FAdm King on draft MS of this chapter on file in JCS HS.

[28] (S) Msg, Marshall to MacArthur, 277, 23 Jun 42; (S) Memo, Ritchie to Streett, 23 Jun 42; (S) Memo, Handy to Marshall, 24 Jun 42; (S) Msg, CominCh to CinCPac, 242306 Jun 42. All in OPD 381 SWPA.

[29] (S) Msgs, CominCh to CinCPac, 231255, 242306 Jun 42, OPD 381 SWPA #80.

[30] (S) Memo, CominCh-CNO to CofS USA, "Offensive Operations in the South and Southwest Pacific Areas," 25 Jun 42, OPD 381 SWPA #80.

[31] (S) Msg, MacArthur to Marshall, 248, CM-IN-7976, 24 Jun 42, WDCSA file Southwest Pacific Area.

[32] (S) Memo, CofS USA to King, "Offensive Operations in the South and Southwest Pacific Areas," 26 Jun 42, OPD 381 SWPA #80.

[33] (S) Memo, CominCh-CNO to CofS USA, "Offensive Operations in South and Southwest Pacific Areas," 26 Jun 42, OPD 381 SWPA #80.

[34] (S) Memo, Marshall to King, 29 Jun 42, OPD 381 SWPA #80.

[35] (S) Ltr, CinCPac to VAdm Ghormley, "Instructions relative to duties as Commander South Pacific Area and South Pacific Force," 090W, file A16-3/P-17, 12 May 42, OPD 384 PTO (4-2-42)

NOTES TO CHAPTER VI

#15. Comments of VAdm V.R. Murphy on draft MS of this chapter, Apr 41.

[36] It appears that Gen Marshall and Adm King met on both 29 and 30 Jun and that the second proposal was offered as a substitute when the first was not accepted and then became Adm King's preference. In a memo to Adm King on 1 Jul Gen Marshall speaks of "going back" to the idea of transferring command after discarding Adm King's proposal of "yesterday" for conduct of the whole operation under JCS. (S) Memo, Marshall to King, 1 Jul 42, WDCSA 210.72 South Pacific Area (7-1-42).

[37] (S) Msg, MacArthur to Marshall, 254, CM-IN-9329, 28 Jun 42, OPD TS Msg file.

[38] (S) Memo, Marshall to King, 1 Jul 42, w/2 encls, OPD 381 SWPA #80.

[39] (S) Memo, King to Marshall, 2 Jul 42, OPD 384 PTO (7-2-42).

[40] (S) Msg, CominCh to CinCPac, 022100 Jul 42, CCS 381 (1-24-42) sec 2 pt 1.

[41] *Ibid.*

[42] (S) Ltr, CG HawDept to CofS USA, "Army Command in South Pacific Area," 20 May 42; (S) Memo, Handy to Marshall, "Army Command - South Pacific Area," 25 Jun 42; (S) Ltr, Marshall to King, "Army Command - South Pacific Area," 26 Jun 42; (S) Ltr, King to Marshall, "Army Command - South Pacific Area," ser 00580, 2 Jul 42; (S) Msg, Marshall to Emmons, 4 Jul 42. All in OPD 384 PTO. (S) Msg, Marshall to Emmons, 4630, 1 Jul 42, OPD 381 PTO sec 2, 65.

[43] (S) Memo, ACofS (Handy) to CofS, "Army Command - South Pacific Area," 25 Jun 42; (S) Ltr, CofS USA to CominCh, "Army Command - South Pacific Area," 26 Jun 42; (S) Ltr, CominCh to CofS USA, "Army Command - South Pacific Area," ser 00580, 2 Jul 42. All in OPD 384 PTO.

[44] (S) Msg, Marshall to MacArthur, 334, CM-OUT-0677, 3 Jul 42, OPD TS Msg file.

[45] (SS) Msg, MacArthur and Ghormley to CominCh and CofS USA, 081012 Jul 42, so-called "Seven-part Despatch," (TS) CominCh file "ComSoWesPac Despatches - Jan. '42 thru Dec. '43."

[46] (S) Memo, Cooke to King, "MacArthur-Ghormley Seven-Part Despatch 081012, Offensive Operations in the Southwest Pacific," 9 Jul 42, (TS) CominCh file #35, "Ass't Chief of Staff (Plans-F-1)."

[47] (S) Memo, King to Marshall, "MacArthur-Ghormley Seven Part Despatch 081012 on Southwest Pacific Offensive Operations," 10 Jul 42, OPD 381 SWPA #87.

[48] (S) Mns, JCS 24th Mtg, 10 Jul 42, item 3.

[49] (SS) Msg, CofS USA and CominCh to ComSoWesPacArea and ComSoPacFor, 102100 Jul 42, OPD 381 SWPA.

[50] (S) Msg, War Cab Officers to BJSM, Wash, C.O.S.(W) 217, 8 Jul 42, CCS 381 (3-23-42) pt 3 sec 2; *The Hinge of Fate*, p. 434.

[51] (SS) Dill's proposed tel to HMG re C.O.S.(W) 217 of 8 Jul, WDCSA 381 File I.

[52] (S) Mns, JCS 24th Mtg, 10 Jul 42, item 1.

[53] (S) Memo, CofS USA and CominCh to Pres, 10 Jul 42, CCS 381 (3-23-42) pt 3 sec 2. Adm King's comments on the draft MS of this chapter (in JCS HS files) indicate that he was not very enthusiastic about leaving the British and turning to the Pacific.

[54] (SS) Memo, Marshall to Pres, "Latest British Proposals Relative to Bolero and Gymnast," 10 Jul 42, (TS) CofS file "Bolero."

[55] (S) Memo, J.R. Deane to King, 12 Jul 42, CCS 381 (3-23-42) pt 3 sec 2.

[56] (S) Memo, JCS to Pres, "Pacific Operations," 12 Jul 42, CCS 381 (3-23-42) pt 3 sec 2. This is a copy including a letterhead of CominCh but gives no indication where the memo was drafted.

[57] (SS) Msg, Pres to Marshall, 14 Jul 42, (TS) CofS file "Bolero"; (S) Memo, Marshall to King, 15 Jul 42, WDCSA 381 War Plans.

[58] (S dg U) Memo, Pres to Hopkins, Marshall, and King, "Instructions for London Conference - July 1942," 16 Jul 42, Sherwood, pp. 602-605.

[59] *Ibid.*

[60] For fuller discussion of the preceding episodes, see (S) MS, JCS Hist, *War Against Germany and Its Satellites*, ch III. Also, Snell-Matloff MS, ch XII.

[61] Cf. (S) MS, JCS Hist, *War Against Germany and Its Satellites*, ch VI.

CHAPTER VII

[1] (S) Memo, W.B. Smith to JCS, "Notes of a conference held at the White House at 8:30 P.M., July 1942," 1 Aug 42, CCS 381 (7-24-42) sec 1.

[2] Note, for example, (S) JCS 23, Rpt by JPS, "Strategic Deployment of Land, Sea and Air Forces of the United States," 14 Mar 42, CCS 381 (1-30-42) (1). Also, (C) CCS 50/2, CPS Dir to MAB, "Directive for Assignment of Munitions," 23 Mar 42, CCS 400.3 (2-17-42).

[3] (S) Mns, CCS 15th Mtg, 7 Apr 42, item 2; (S) CPS 28/D, Dir, "Strategic Policy for the United Nations," 8 Apr 42, CCS 381 (3-27-42).

[4] For fuller discussion, see (S) MS, JCS Hist, *Procurement and Allocation of Material Means.*

[5] (S) Mns, CCS 15th Mtg, 7 Apr 42, item 3; (S) CCS 61/D, "Aircraft Situation of the United Nations," 9 Apr 42, CCS 452 (4-8-42) sec 1.

[6] (S) Mns, CPS 14th Mtg, 14 Apr 42, item 1; (S) CPS 28/1, "United States-British Strategy," 8 Apr 42, ABC 381 (9-25-41) sec 1.

[7] In an OPD brief (author unknown) for discussion at the JPS meeting of 20 May it was pointed out that existing commitments would absorb all aircraft allocated to the Army Air Forces in 1942, and leave none for the projected U.S. Air Force in Europe. (S) "Notes on JPS 17th mtg, 20 May 42," ABC 381 (9-25-41) sec 1.

[8] (S) CPS 28/D, Memo, JUSSC to JPS, "Strategic Policy for the United Nations," 14 May 42, CCS 381 (3-27-42).

[9] (S) Mns, JPS 17th Mtg, 20 May 42, item 8; (S) Mns, CPS 18th Mtg, 5 Jun 42, item 1; (S) Mns, CPS 19th Mtg, 11 Jun 42, item 4.

[10] (S) CCS 61/1, "Aircraft Situation of the United Nations," 22 Jun 42, CCS 452 (4-8-42) sec 1.

[11] (S) Mns, JCS 21st Mtg, 23 Jun 42, item 1. Air Vice Marshal Slessor's action was apparently a surprise even to Gen Arnold. Gen Arnold had, however, discussed its contents previously with both PM Churchill and Pres Roosevelt. H.H. Arnold, *Global Mission* (New York, 1949), pp. 309-321. For further discussion, see (S) MS, JCS Hist, *Procurement and Allocation of Material Means*.

[12] (R) CCS 61/1, "Aircraft Situation of the United Nations," 22 Jun 42, CCS 452 (4-8-42) sec 1.

[13] See below, pp.

[14] (S) Mns, JCS 21st Mtg, 23 Jun 42, item 1; (S) Mns, CPS 23rd Mtg, 27 Jun 42, item 1.

[15] (S) CPS 28/3, "Strategic Policy and Deployment of United States and British Forces," 24 Jun 42; (S) JPS Info Memo 6, "Detailed Deployment of Air Forces in the Pacific," 25 Jun 42; (S) CCS 91, "Strategic Policy and Deployment of United States and British Forces," 7 Jul 42. All in CCS 381 (6-24-42) sec 1.

[16] This had appeared last on the list presented by the subcommittee, with the "major combined offensive against Germany" not further defined.

[17] Whether the loose phrase, "based on the availability of units," means "based on units available," i.e., "on hand or definitely scheduled" or "based on the units estimated to be available" is not clear. It appears, however, that an attempt had been made to produce a practicable deployment plan and to utilize concrete figures of units scheduled by the services for readiness at the designated times.

[18] The reduction of shipping for Bolero resulting from sending 6 additional air groups to the Middle East and 2 medium bomber squadrons to India was reported on and approved by CCS in connection with CCS 91. (S) CCS 87/2, "Shipping Implications of Proposed Air Force Deployment," 10 Jul 42, CCS 452 (4-8-42) sec 1. (S) Mns, JCS 25th Mtg, 14 Jul 42, item 2; (S) Mns, CCS 31st Mtg, 16 Jul 42, item 2.

[19] Cf. above, ch V.

[20] (S) OPD Memo on CCS 91; (S) JPS Info Memo 8, "Study on C.C.S. 91," 15 Jul 42, CCS 381 (6-24-42) sec 1; (S) Mns, JCS 25th Mtg, 14 Jul 42, item 1.

[21] (S dg C) JCS 69, "Arnold-Slessor-Towers Agreement," 3 Jul 42, CCS 452 (6-26-42) sec 1. Fwded as CCS 92, "Dominion Air Forces," 12 Jul 42.

[22] (S) Mns, JCS 23rd Mtg, 7 Jul 42, item 4; (S) Mns, JCS 25th Mtg, 14 Jul 42, item 1; (S) Mns, CCS 31st Mtg, 16 Jul 42, item 1.

[23] (S) Msg, Marshall to CinCSWPA, 16 Jul 42, WD 410; (S) Msg, SC SWPA to CofS USA, 19 Jul 42, C-136, CCS 452 (6-26-42) sec 1. It has not been determined where the idea of replacing US pilots with Australian originated.

[24] Par 7 provided: "When the strategic requirements of these

NOTES TO CHAPTER VII

Dominions have been approved by the Combined Chiefs of Staff, the United States will make the necessary allocations of aircraft, through the machinery of the Combined Munitions Assignment Board. Allocations to the Dominions will be a matter for agreement by the Combined Munitions Assignment Board."

[25] (S) JPS 37/1, "Dominion Air Forces," 28 Jul 42, CCS 452 (6-26-42) sec 1.

[26] (C) CCS 92/1, "Dominion Air Forces," (incl Ann I, "Dominion Air Requirements," by CofAS, 24 Jul 42), 29 Jul 42, CCS 452 (6-26-42) sec 1.

[27] (S) Mns, JPS 25th Mtg, 30 Jul 42, item 2.

[28] (S) Memo, Anderson, ACofAS (Plans), to JPS, "Dominion Aircraft Requirements," 5 Aug 42, CCS 452 (6-26-42) sec 1.

[29] (S) Mns, JPS 26th Mtg, 5 Aug 42, item 5.

[30] (S) JCS 80, "Study of C.C.S. 91 and C.C.S. 92," 9 Aug 42, CCS 452 (6-26-42) sec 1.

[31] (S) Mns, JCS 28th Mtg, 11 Aug 42, item 9.

[32] (S) CCS 91 (Rev Anns, pt II), 12 Aug 42, CCS 381 (6-24-42) sec 1; (S) Mns, CCS 36th Mtg, 13 Aug 42, item 6.

[33] (S) JCS 80/1, "Study of C.C.S. 91 and C.C.S. 92," 18 Aug 42, CCS 452 (6-26-42) sec 1; (S) Mns, JCS 29th Mtg, 18 Aug 42, item 8. The messages to the local commanders were sent by agreement of the JCS at this meeting, as CofS to CinCSWPA, 1061, 20 Aug 42, and CofS to ComSoPac, no No., 20 Aug 42. Replies: CinCSWPA to CofS, C-337, 24 Aug 42; Necal to War, 129, 24 Aug 42. Both in CCS 452 (6-26-42) sec 1. (S) Memo, Aust Min Dixon to CofS, "Memorandum Concerning Allocation of Aircraft to the Royal Australian Air Force," 28 Aug 42, doc WDCSA 452.6 Aust, WDCSA file "Australia - Secret Files."

[34] (S) CCS 91/1, "Strategic Policy and Deployment of United States and British Forces," 1 Sep 42; (S) CCS 91/2, same subj, 3 Sep 42; (S) CCS 91/3, same subj, 14 Sep 42. All in CCS 381 (6-24-42) sec 1. (S) Mns, CCS 39th Mtg, 4 Sep 42, item 2.

[35] (S) Mns, CCS 37th Mtg, 21 Aug 42, item 1.

[36] The first meeting of the MRP was held on 26 May 42. Its agenda consisted primarily of reports given by the various members of the activity in their particular areas of major interest. Minutes are on file in JCS, file CCS 334. For further discussion, cf. (S) Davis, *Organizational Development*.

[37] (S) Ltr, Curtin to Pres, 31 Aug 42, CCS 660.2 (3-14-42) sec 2.

[38] (S) CPS 47/D Memo, CCS Sect to CPS Sect, "Reinforcements for Southwest Pacific Area," 12 Sep 42; (S) CCS 113/1, Dft Reply, Pres to Curtin, "Reinforcements for Southwest Pacific Area," 13 Sep 42; (S) Memo, Hammond to ACofS OPD, 16 Sep 42, informs Pres had signed proposed reply and sent it to PM Curtin. All in CCS 660.2 (3-14-42) sec 2.

[39] (S) JPS 75/D, Dir to JPS, encl Msg, Curtin to Pres, "Strength of Armed Forces in Australia," 22 Oct 42, CCS 320.2 Australia (10-22-42).

[40] (S) CIC 10, Rpt by CIC, "Japanese Intentions," 5 Oct 42, CCS 381 Japan (4-23-42) sec 1. This was subsequently revised and submitted to the CCS on 8 Nov 42 as Info Memo 25. The British JIC took exception to the extent of considering an attack on Port Darwin a possibility.

[41] (S) JCS 135/1, Rpt by JPS, "Strength of Armed Forces in Australia," 26 Oct 42; (S) Memo, Cdr W.L. Freseman, Aide to Leahy, to Deane, 28 Oct 42. Both in CCS 320.2 Australia (10-22-42). (S) Mns, JCS 39th Mtg, 27 Oct 42, item 6.

[42] (S) Memo, Deane to Leahy, Marshall, King, and Arnold, 19 Nov 42, CCS 320.2 Australia (10-22-42).

[43] *Ibid.*

[44] (S) Mns, CCS 4th Mtg, 20 Nov 42, item 7. The U.S. Secretariat prepared the draft reply for the President. (S) Memo, Leahy to Pres, 23 Nov 42, CCS 320.2 Australia (10-22-42). Pencilled note states sent by President on 2 Dec.

[45] (S) Mns, CCS 50th Mtg, 27 Nov 42, item 5.

[46] (S) CCS 130, Rpt by CPS, "Return of the Australian and New Zealand Divisions from the Middle East," 4 Dec 42, CCS 320.2 Australia (10-22-42).

[47] (S) Mns, CCS 51st Mtg, 4 Dec 42, item 3; (S) CCS 130/1, Rpt by CPS (rev), "Return of the Australian and New Zealand Divisions from the Middle East," 4 Dec 42, CCS 320.2 Australia (10-22-42).

[48] See above, ch V.

[49] (S) Mns, CCS 51st Mtg, 4 Dec 42, item 3.

[50] (S) Memo, McCrea to Leahy, encl Msg, Curtin to Pres, 18 Dec 42; (S) Rpt by JPS, "Return of Equipment of the 9th Division," 20 Dec 42. Both in CCS 320.2 Australia (10-22-42). (MS) Ltr, Dill to Marshall, 26 Dec 42, OPD 336.2 Australia.

CHAPTER VIII

[1] The three tasks were: (1) seizure and occupation of Santa Cruz Islands, Tulagi, and adjacent positions; (2) seizure and occupation of the remainder of the Solomon Islands, of Lae, Salamaua, and the northeast coast of New Guinea; (3) seizure and occupation of Rabaul and adjacent positions in the New Guinea-New Ireland area. (S) Msg, ComInCh to CinCPac, 022100 Jul 42, CCS 381 (1-24-42) sec 2 pt 1; (S) Memo, RAdm Cooke, ACofS (Plans), to Capt Corn, "Directive for Future Planning Section," 6 Jul 42, CNO(WPD) file "A16-3(5) War Plans."

[2] (S) Msg, CofS USA and ComInCh to CinCPac and ComSoWesPacFor, 102100 Jul 42, OPD 381 SWPA #87.

[3] (UNK) Memos, Arnold to Hopkins, 13 Sep 42, 7 Oct 42, Hopkins Catalog, vol II, bk V; (U) JCS 152, Memo by CG AAF, "Strategic Policy for 1943," 16 Nov 42, CCS 381 (11-16-42); *Global Mission*, pp. 337-350.

[4] William D. Leahy, *I Was There* (New York, 1950), pp. 116-119.

[5] For delineation of tasks, see fn 1.

⁶On 11 Jul, after being informed that the JCS were insistent on launching Task One even though Tasks Two and Three could not follow immediately, ComSoPac informed CominCh that he considered the available means sufficient for accomplishment of Task One, provided that ComSoWesPac had enough successfully to interdict the Japanese aircraft based in the New Britain-New Guinea-Northern Solomons area. (SS) Msg, ComSoPac to CominCh, 112000 Jul 42, (TS) CominCh file "ComSoPac Despatches - 26 May thru Aug. 1942."

⁷(S) Memo, CominCh-CNO to CofS USA, "Garrison Forces for Solomon Islands Area," 00641, 15 Jul 42, WDCSA file "Southwest Pacific Area."

⁸(S) Memo, CofS USA to CominCh, "Garrison Forces for the Solomon Islands Area," 16 Jul 42; (S) Memo, King to Marshall, 16 Jul 42; (S) Memo, ACofS (Handy) to CofS USA, "Garrison Force for the Solomon Island Area," 17 Jul 42. All in WDCSA file "Southwest Pacific Area." (S) Msg, CofS USA to CinCSWPA, 334, 3 Jul 42, OPD 381 SWPA #85.

⁹(S) Memo, CominCh (Russell Willson, CofS) to CofS USA, "Reinforcements for Holding Occupied Positions in the South Pacific," 22 Jul 42, WDCSA file "Southwest Pacific Area."

¹⁰*Ibid*. (S) Memo, ACofS (Handy) to CofS USA, "Reinforcements for Holding Occupied Positions in the South Pacific," 24 Jul 42, OPD 381 PTO 381, sec 2, #76. Encl to above sent by Actg CofS to CominCh, 27 Jul 42; (S) Memo, Handy to CofS USA, "Antiaircraft Regiments for the Solomon Islands Area," 23 Jul 42, WDCSA file "Southwest Pacific Area." Encl to above sent by Actg CofS McNarney to CominCh, 27 Jul 42.

¹¹(S) CCS 94, "Operations in 1942/43," 24 Jul 42, CCS 381 (7-24-42) sec 1.

¹²Two unsigned sheets of pencil notes on White House stationery apparently given to Gen Marshall on 15 Jul (OPD Exec 10, item 35). Matloff - Snell MS, p. XI-22. Cf. Sherwood, p. 503.

¹³(S) Mns, JPS 35th Mtg, 16 Sep 42, item 4.

¹⁴(UNK) Ltr, Marshall to Eisenhower, 30 Jul 42; Matloff - Snell MS, p. XII-24.

¹⁵(S) Memo, CominCh to CofS USA, "Reenforcements for holding occupied positions in the South Pacific," 00724, 1 Aug 42, OPD 320.2 PTO sec II.

¹⁶(S) Memo, ACofS (Handy) to CofS USA, "Reinforcements for Holding Occupied Positions in the South Pacific," 5 Aug 42; (S) Memo, G.F.S. (uniden) to CofS USA, "Reinforcements for Pacific Area," 3 Aug 42; (S) Handwritten Memo, GCM to Handy, undtd. All in OPD 320.2 sec II #32.

¹⁷(S) Memo, King to CofS USA, "Japanese Operations, Northeast Coast of New Guinea," 00719, 31 Jul 42, OPD 381 SWPA #92.

¹⁸(S) Msg, Marshall to MacArthur, 384, 31 Jul 42; (S) Msg, MacArthur to CofS USA, Q-147, 2 Aug 42, OPD 381 SWPA #92.

¹⁹(SS) Msg, ComSoPac to CinCPac and CominCh, 050730 Aug 42, OPD 320.2 PTO sec II.

[20] (S) Memo, CominCh to CofS USA, "Minimum Army Reinforcements ...," 00768, 8 Aug 42, OPD 320.2 PTO sec II #37.

[21] (S) Memo, CominCh-CNO to CofS USA, "Reinforcements for South Pacific and Hawaiian Areas," 00790, 13 Aug 42; (S) Memo, ACofS to CofS USA, "Reinforcements for South Pacific and Hawaiian Areas," 15 Aug 42; (S) Memo, CofS USA to CominCh, "Reinforcements for South Pacific and Hawaiian Areas," 20 Aug 42. All in OPD 320.2 PTO, sec II #37. Actually twenty of the B-25's were still being prepared at modification centers, per (S) Memo, ACofS to CofS USA. "Availability of Heavy Bombardment Groups for Pacific," 14 Aug 42, WDCSA file "Southwest Pacific Area."

[22] (S) Memo, CominCh-CNO to CofS USA, "Early Initiation of a Limited Task Two," 00838, 20 Aug 42, OPD 381 PTO sec 2 #84.

[23] (S) Memo, Marshall to SOS, 20 Aug 42; (S) Memo, Actg ACofS to CofS USA, "Shipping Capabilities for Reinforcement of the South Pacific," 22 Aug 42; (S) Memo, CofS USA to CominCh, "Early Initiation of Limited Task Two," 24 Aug 42. All in OPD 370.5 PTO sec 2 #9. (S) Memo, CominCh-CNO to CofS USA, "Transportation of 13,000 Army Troops," 00872, 27 Aug 42, OPD 381 PTO sec 2 #84.

[24] Approximately 10,000 Marines had been landed on Guadalcanal in the initial operation. The Japanese later reported that they had 2,230 troops on the island when the Marines attacked. However, the assault plans of Adm Turner and Gen Vandegrift were based on an estimate of about 7,000 enemy troops. Info supplied by Dr. John Miller, Hist Div, WDSS, to Lt. G.P. Hayes, USN, JCS HS, 13 Jun 49.

[25] (S) Memo, CofS USA to CominCh, "Early Initiation of Limited Task Two," 14 Aug 42, OPD 381 PTO sec 2 #84; (S) Msg, CominCh to CinCPac, ComSoPac, ComSWPA, 151951 Aug 42, (TS) CominCh file "CinCPac Despatches."

[26] (S) Msg, ComSoPac to CinCPac and CominCh, 170230 Aug 42, (TS) CominCh file "CinCPac Despatches."

[27] (S) Msg, MacArthur to Marshall, C381, 30 Aug 42, encl to (S) JCS 96, "Japanese Intentions in the Pacific Theater," 31 Aug 42, CCS 381 Japan (4-23-42) sec 1.

[28] (S) Ltr, Curtin to Pres, 31 Aug 42, CCS 660.2 (3-14-42) sec 2.

[29] (S) JCS 96, "Japanese Intentions in the Pacific Theater," 31 Aug 42, CCS 381 Japan (4-23-42) sec 1.

[30] (S) JCS 96/1, "Japanese Intentions in the Pacific Theater," 1 Sep 42, CCS 381 Japan (4-23-42) sec 1.

[31] (S) Mns, JCS 31st Mtg, 1 Sep 42, item 9.

[32] (S) Memo, Davis to Vittrup, "Japanese Intentions in the Pacific Theatre," 8 Sep 42, CCS 381 Japan (4-23-42) sec 1.

[33] Cf. above, p. 249.

[34] (S) Memo, Cooke to Vittrup, "Japanese Intentions in the Pacific Theater," 14 Sep 42, CCS 381 Japan (4-23-42) sec 1.

[35] (S) Mns, JPS 35th Mtg, 16 Sep 42, item 4.

[36] Cf. above, p. 249.

[37] *Ibid.*

[38] (S) JCS 96/2, "Japanese Intentions in the Pacific Theater," 24 Sep 42, CCS 381 Japan (4-23-42) sec 1; (S) Mns, JCS 35th Mtg, 29 Sep 42, item 8; (S) Mns, JCS 44th Mtg, 1 Dec 42, item 5; (S) Mns, JPS 36th Mtg, 23 Sep 42, item 2; (S) Ltr, Handy to Harmon, 12 Sep 42, OPD 381 PTO sec III #100.

[39] Cf. above, ch VII, "Attempt to Define a Strategic Policy."

[40] (S) Memo, JPS Secy (Vittrup) to Secy JUSSC, "Detailed Deployment of Aircraft in the Pacific Theater," 20 Aug 42, CCS 381 (6-24-42) sec 1. The preliminary study had been circulated as JPS Info Memo 6, 25 Jun 42, same file. At the JCS 29th meeting on 18 Aug 42, Adm King reiterated his views in regard to defense of the line of communications in the Pacific. Neither in those minutes nor in the minutes of the JPS meeting of 19 Aug is there mention of this directive to the JUSSC.

[41] (S) JPS 48, Rpt by JUSSC, "Detailed Deployment of U.S. Air Forces in the Pacific Theater," 28 Aug 42, CCS 381 (6-24-42) sec 1.

[42] (S) Mns, CCS 35th Mtg, 6 Aug 42, item 3; (S) Mns, CPS 28th Mtg, 7 Aug 42, item 3; (S) CCS 100, Rpt by CPS, "General Order of Priority of Shipping Movements," CCS 452 (4-8-42) sec 1; (S) Mns, JCS 28th Mtg, 11 Aug 42, item 7; (S) Mns, CCS 36th Mtg, 13 Aug 42, item 3.

[43] (S) JPS 48, "Detailed Deployment of U.S. Air Forces in the Pacific Theater," 28 Aug 42, CCS 381 (6-24-42) sec 1. (S) OPD Paper, "Notes on 32nd mtg JPS, 2 Sep 42, Detailed Deployment of U.S. Air Forces in the Pacific Theater"; (S) Memo, CG AAF to CofS USA, "Air Force Employment," 29 Jul 42. Both in ABC 381 (9-5-41) sec III.

[44] (S) Mns, JPS 33rd Mtg, 2 Sep 42, item 12; (S) JCS 97, Rpt by JPS, "Detailed Deployment of U.S. Air Forces in the Pacific Theater," 5 Sep 42, CCS 381 (6-24-42) sec 1.

[45] (S) Memo, CominCh-CNO to CofS USA, "Air Reinforcements for Guadalcanal-Tulagi Area," 00912, 3 Sep 42, WDCSA file "Southwest Pacific Area."

[46] It is interesting to note that the *AAF Statistical Digest of World War II* gives the following figures for aircraft in the POA on 31 Aug 42: heavy bombers - 40; medium bombers - 22; light bombers - 7; fighters - 234.

[47] (S) Dft of memo for CominCh, prepared for sig of Gen Arnold, "Air Reinforcements for the Guadalcanal-Tulagi Area," 5 Sep 42, AF Hist Div file No. 8092-27; (S) Identical memo, Actg CofS USA to CominCh, "Air Reinforcements for the Guadalcanal-Tulagi Area," 5 Sep 42, WDCSA file "Southwest Pacific Area." The latter superseded one dtd 3 Sep 42, which differed in the numbers of aircraft listed.

[48] Adm King was out of Washington on 8 Sep. Info supplied by Cdr W.R. Denekas, USN, Aide to FAdm King, on 14 Jun 49.

[49] (S) Memo, Dep CominCh (Willson) to Jt US Sect, "J.C.S. 97 - Detailed Deployment of U.S. Air Forces in Pacific Theater," 7 Sep 42, CCS 381 (6-24-42) sec 1; (S) Mns, JCS 32nd Mtg, 8 Sep 42, item 1.

NOTES TO CHAPTER VIII

[50](S) JCS 97/1, "Relationship between Torch and Air Operations from the Middle East and the United Kingdom," 11 Sep 42, CCS 452 (9-8-42).

[51](S) Memo, CominCh-CNO to CGAAF, "Need for Army Aircraft in the Current Solomons Operation," 5 Sep 42, encl to (S) JCS 97/2, "Detailed Deployment of U.S. Air Forces in the Pacific Theater," 15 Sep 42, CCS 381 (6-24-42) sec 2.

[52](S) Memo, CGAAF to CominCh-CNO, "Need for Army Aircraft in the Current Solomons Operation," 14 Sep 42, encl to (S) JCS 97/2, 15 Sep 42, CCS 381 (6-24-42) sec 2.

[53](S) JCS 97/2, "Detailed Deployment of U.S. Air Forces in the Pacific Theater," 15 Sep 42; (S) JCS 97/3, same subj, 15 Sep 42. Both in CCS 381 (6-24-42) sec 2.

[54](S) Mns, JCS 33rd Mtg, 15 Sep 42, item 3.

[55](S) Mns, JCS 36th Mtg, 6 Oct 42, item 2.

[56](S) Mns, JPS 38th Mtg, 7 Oct 42, item 10; (S) Mns, JPS 39th Mtg, 9 Oct 42, item 1; (S) Mns, JPS 40th Mtg, 12 Oct 42, item 1; (S) Mns, JCS 37th Mtg, 13 Oct 42, item 6; (S) Mns, JPS 41st Mtg, 14 Oct 42, item 3. (S) JCS 97/4 Rpt by JPS, "Detailed Deployment of U.S. Air Forces in the Pacific Theater," 16 Oct 42; (S) Memo, Cdr McDowell to ACofS OPD and Aide to CominCh, "Detailed Deployment of U.S. Air Forces in the Pacific Theater," 16 Oct 42; Handwritten Note, Deane to Leahy, 16 Oct 42, informing him of approval of paper. All in CCS 381 (6-24-42) sec 2.

[57](S) JCS 97/5, "Deployment of U.S. Air Forces in the Pacific Theater," 22 Oct 42, CCS 381 (6-24-42) sec 2; (S) Mns, JCS 39th Mtg, 27 Oct 42, item 7.

[58]Joint orders issued to theater commanders in May (Navdis 041819 May 42, CofS USA and CominCh to CinCPac et al.) had forbidden permanent transfers from assigned stations of units of a service to which the commander did not belong. Adm King submitted to the JCS a draft directive for CinCPac modifying this in accordance with the JCS agreement, authorizing transfer of aircraft, pilots, or service personnel. (S) Memo, King to JCS, "Deployment of U.S. Air Forces in the Pacific Ocean," ser 001342, 6 Nov 42. This was modified by Gen Marshall to confine CinCPac's authority to deploying and redistributing units, rather than individual pilots and aircraft, in order to maintain the integrity of AAF units in the Pacific. (S) Memo, Marshall to Deane, "Deployment of U.S. Air Forces in the Pacific Theater," 11 Nov 42. CinCPac was informed in (C) Msg, CofS USA and CominCh to CinCPac, 141928 Nov 42. All in CCS 381 (6-24-42) sec 2.

[59](S) OPD Paper, "Brief, J.C.S. 97/5 - Deployment of U.S. Air Forces in the Pacific Theater," 26 Oct 42, CCS 381 (6-24-42) sec 2.

[60](S) Mns, JCS 38th Mtg, 20 Oct 42, item 5.

[61](S) Mns, JCS 39th Mtg, 27 Oct 42, item 7.

[62](S) JPS 84/D, Dir, "Continuing Study of Aircraft Requirements in All Theaters," 13 Nov 42, CCS 381 (6-24-42) sec 2.

[63] (S) JCS 112, Memo by CominCh, "J.C.S. Directive for Joint Operations in the Southwest Pacific Area," 21 Sep 42, CCS 381 SW Pacific Area (7-10-42).

[64] Late in Sep Adm King received a letter from Adm Ghormley, dated 6 Aug 42, containing the estimates, previously submitted by message, of himself and Gen Harmon of the forces required for the South Pacific. It had been forwarded by Adm Nimitz on 6 Sep 42, with his own recommendations. Although Adm King sent it on to Gen Marshall with his endorsement of the recommendations, the Army took no action. (S) Ltr, ComSoPac to CominCh, 0048, 6 Aug 42, file A16-3, w/end No. 1, CinCPac to CominCh, 6 Sep 42, w/end No. 2, CominCh-CNO to CofS USA, 23 Sep 42, OPD 320.2 PTO sec II.

[65] JIC Daily Summaries during the first week of October reported concentrations of over 30 vessels in the harbor of Rabaul as well as smaller numbers elsewhere in the area.

[66] (S) Memo, King to Leahy and Marshall, "Military Situation in the Pacific," 3 Oct 42, WDCSA file "Southwest Pacific Area." Gen Arnold was absent on an inspection tour of the Pacific at this time.

[67] (S) JCS 112/1, Memo by CominCh-CNO, "Military Situation in the Pacific," 14 Oct 42, CCS 381 SW Pacific Area (7-10-42).

[68] On 11 Oct the JIC Daily Summary reported that at least 51 vessels had been observed at Rabaul two days before. By 16 Oct the concentration had shifted southeast to the Bougainville-Shortlands area, where the presence of about 40 vessels was reported.

[69] On 26 Oct there were 26 fighters, 16 dive bombers, and 1 torpedo bomber at Henderson Field.

[70] (S) Msg, CG SPA to CofS USA, 639, CM-IN-06202, 15 Oct 42; (S) Msg, CofS USA to CG Haw Dept, 720, CM-OUT-5129. Cf. (S) D/F, OPD 320.2 PTO sec II #62.

[71] *Enterprise* had been damaged in the battle of 23-25 Aug. *Saratoga* had sustained a torpedo hit on 31 Aug and was out of action. *Wasp* had been sunk by an enemy submarine on 15 Sep.

[72] (S) Msg, CofS USA to CinCSWPA, 16 Oct 42, 2716, WDCSA file "Southwest Pacific Area." Gen Marshall stated that he had just gone over Navy charts of the situation in the South Pacific, and it appeared evident that the explanation which he relayed to Gen MacArthur had been given to him by the Navy planners.

[73] (S) Msg, MacArthur to CofS, eyes only, C-731, 17 Oct 42, in OPD Exec file "From MacArthur." Cy has written note on distribution of five copies.

[74] (S) Mns, JCS 24th Mtg, 10 Jul 42, item 3; (MS) Cunningham to Willson, 25 Jul 42, and reply, 00696, 27 Jul 42, (SC) CominCh file "A16-3(1), Overflow File No. 2." (S & P) Msg, First Sea Lord to Adm Little, 18 Jun 43, (TS) CominCh file "Memos to/from British - 1942."

[75] (S) Ltr, Curtin to Pres, 31 Aug 42; (S) CPS 47/D, Memo, CCS Sect to CPS Sect, "Reinforcements for Southwest Pacific," fwds 2 ltrs, Curtin to Pres for dft reply. Both in CCS 660.2 (3-14-42) sec 2.

NOTES TO CHAPTER VIII

[76] (MS) Msg, Admty to BAD, 501, 23 Oct 42, (TS) CominCh file "Memos to/from British - 1942."

[77] (S) Memo, Capt J.L. McCrea to Marshall, 14 Oct 42, OPD 381 SWPA #101.

[78] Gen Arnold's views of the advisability of building up air forces in the United Kingdom and diverting only an absolute minimum from that project had been presented to Mr. Hopkins in at least 3 memos and would presumably have been discussed with the President. Summaries of memos, Arnold to Hopkins, 3 Sep 42, 13 Sep 42, 7 Oct 42, Hopkins Catalog, vol II, bk V, *Torch and Air Offensive*.

[79] (S) Memo, 24 Oct 42, CCS 381 (6-24-42) sec 2.

[80] (S) Memo, Marshall to Pres, "Situation in the South Pacific," 26 Oct 42, OPD 381 PTO sec III #107.

[81] (S) Memo, King to Pres, "Diversion of Munitions, including Aircraft, to the South Pacific," 26 Oct 42, OPD 381 PTO sec III #107.

[82] Attached to a smooth copy of Gen Marshall's memo in the OPD file is a typed copy of a handwritten note from Gen Marshall to Adm (Leahy?), in which he says, "I would like to talk it over with you before it goes to the President, if at all. I think later, and before anything goes to the President, the U.S. Chiefs of Staff should talk the entire matter over, this afternoon if possible." OPD 381 PTO sec III #107. No specific record of any discussion of these memos has been found.

[83] (S) Memo, Leahy to Deane, 26 Oct 42, CCS 540 SWPA (10-26-42). File also contains copy of ltr to Mr. Douglas, dtd 26 Oct 42, stamped out by CCS mail room at 0015, 27 Oct 42.

[84] (S) Memo, Land and Douglas to Pres. "Requirements for Additional Tonnage," 27 Oct 42, CCS 540 SWPA (10-26-42). The file is confusing as to whether this memo was sent directly to the President or enclosed with the letter to Adm Leahy discussed below. The latter appears likely, from the filing arrangement.

[85] (S) Ltr, Douglas to Leahy, 28 Oct 42, CCS 540 SWPA (10-26-42).

[86] (S) Memo, Deane to JPS, 29 Oct 42; (S) JPS 78/D, "Allocation of Twenty Additional Ships for Use in the Southwest Pacific," 29 Oct 42. Both in CCS 540 SWPA (10-26-42).

[87] (U) Rpt by JPS, "Allocation of Twenty Additional Ships for Use in the Southwest Pacific," 5 Nov 42, CCS 540 (10-26-42). A previous paper with the same number was submitted on 2 Nov but withdrawn when it was discovered that some of the ships assigned to Alaska were of smaller tonnage. Cf. (S) Mns, JCS 40th Mtg, 3 Nov 42, item 2.

[88] (S) Memos, Deane to Leahy, Marshall, King, "Allocation of twenty additional ships for use in the Southwest Pacific," 5 Nov 42, origs with indicated approval of JCS in CCS 540 SWPA (10-26-42).

[89] (S) Ltr, Douglas to Leahy, 9 Nov 42, CCS 540 SWPA (10-26-42).

[90] (U) Ltr, CSAB to CCS, 9 Nov 42, CCS 540 SWPA (10-26-42).

[91] (S) Mns, JCS 42nd Mtg, 17 Nov 42, item 6.

[92] (S) Ltr, Douglas to Leahy, 17 Nov 42; (S) Memo, McDowell to Secys CMTC, "Allocation of twenty additional ships for use in the

Southwest Pacific," 18 Nov 42; (S) Mns, CMTC 47th Mtg, 18 Nov 42, item 1; (U) JCS 143/3, Rpt by CMTC, "Allocation of Twenty Additional Ships for Use in the Southwest Pacific," 19 Nov 42; (S) Memo, Deane to Jt Exec Offs, CSAB, 28 Nov 42. All in CCS 540 SWPA (10-26-42).

[93] *Campaigns of the Pacific War*, pp. 125-126.

CHAPTER IX

[1] John Fischer, "Vinegar Joe's Problem," *Harpers Magazine*, vol 190, no. 1135 (Dec 44), pp. 92-93.

[2] (S) Msg, BCOS to BJSM, (W)70, 21 Feb 42, CCS file Radios from C's/S London & Admiralty to B.A.D.

[3] See above, ch III.

[4] (S) Msg, Gimo to Soong, 21 Jan 42, OPD Exec 8, bk 2.

[5] *The Stilwell Papers*, p. 51.

[6] (S) Msg, Gimo to Soong for Pres, 10 Mar 42, OPD Exec 10, item 19.

[7] Sherwood, pp. 511-512. No direct reply from the PM to the President's message of 10 Mar 42 has been found by the author.

[8] (S) Msg, Pres to Gimo, 11 Mar 42, OPD Exec 10, item 19. Attached to copy of message is a note from Gen Eisenhower, ACofS WPD, to CofS: "I explained to the President that I brought it to him personally because it was a mere temporizing measure; he understood the necessity of this...."

[9] (S) Msg, PM to Pres, 49, 17 Mar 42, OPD Exec 10, item 62.

[10] (S) Memo, Marshall to Dill, 19 Mar 42, OPD Exec 10, item 62; (U) Msg, Pres to PM, 20 Mar 42, *The Hinge of Fate*, p. 169.

[11] (S) Msg, Stilwell to Marshall and Stimson, 448, CM-IN-0772, 3 Apr 42, CCS 091.711 China (1-20-42) sec 1. Before his departure from Washington, Gen Stilwell had outlined his views of what should be done in the CBI:

> The long-range objective is to build up the combat efficiency of the Chinese Army and prepare a land base of operations in China, Burma and India for a final offensive against Japan. At least one corps of American troops should ultimately participate, and the necessary preparations should be kept in mind. The placing of a few small American units in India now would facilitate security of supply and the organization of a base which could ultimately serve both China and the Near East.

(S) Memo, Stilwell to CofS, 31 Jan 42, OPD 314.7 CTO sec 3, ch 3, Wash. Pre Planning.

[12] Gen Stilwell was told by Gen Marshall that "there are no immediate prospects of dispatching an American division to India." (S) Msg, Marshall to Stilwell, 3 Apr 42, OPD Exec 10, item 21.

[13] For fuller details, see Romanus-Sunderland, *Stilwell's Mission*, chs III and IV. Also, *The Stilwell Papers*, ch 3, pp. 43-106.

[14] Stettinius, ch X; (S) Summary, "Chinese Ordnance Requirements," no sig, 5 Feb 42, CCS 400.3295 China (3-17-42) sec 1.

NOTES TO CHAPTER IX

[15] In one of his first conversations with the Gimo, on 9 Mar 42, Gen Stilwell asked whether the thirty divisions had been selected. He was told Chiang would select them when he knew when the equipment was going to arrive. Gen Stilwell insisted they should be selected first, but it was many months before they were actually designated. (S) Notes on Conv, Stilwell with Gimo, 9 Mar 42, JCS HS.

[16] (UNK) Memo, Soong to Pres, 30 Jan 42, WPD 4389-90.

[17] Claire L. Chennault, *Way of a Fighter* (New York, 1949), p. 233; Vern Haugland, *The AAF against Japan* (New York, 1948), p. 197.

[18] (S) Msg, Brereton to Marshall, Navy 260730 Feb 42; (S) Msg, Brereton to Marshall, 251005 Feb 42. Both in CCS 323.361 (2-23-42). Gen Brereton's initial command included eight heavy bombers, six from Java and two diverted while en route there, eight bomber crews, and a few staff officers. *AAF in WWII*, vol 1, p. 483.

[19] *The Brereton Diaries*, p. 109; (S) Msg, Marshall to Stilwell, 28 Feb 42, OPD 381 CTO (2-28-42).

[20] *AAF in WW II*, vol I, pp. 497-498, 507-508.

[21] See p. 198.

[22] (S) Ltr, CNO (Horne) to BuShips, BuOrd, BuAer, and BuSandA, "Project 'Friendship' - Establishment of," 11 Mar 42, ser 0302823, L8-3, SACO file, S3 IN, 2 Feb 42 to 9 Dec 42, NR&H; Memo of Conv, RAdm Miles with author, 23 Jun 50, JCS HS.

[23] On 5 Feb 42 the (S) JIC Daily Summary carried this item: "A government spokesman states that it will require a year for Chinese transportation facilities to distribute the military supplies already received from the UNITED STATES." The JIC comment is most interesting: "The implication of this remark, in the context of the interview, is that CHINA is already sufficiently supplied to carry on her war effort for a year or two after existing outside communications are cut, allowing time to replace them."

[24] (S dg C) JCS 9, Encl, Ltr, Soong to McCloy, "Transportation of Military Supplies to China," 9 Feb 42, CCS 540 China (2-9-42).

[25] (S) Mns, JCS 7th Mtg, 23 Mar 42, item 5.

[26] (S) Ltr, Soong to McCloy, 12 Feb 42, CCS 540 China (2-9-42).

[27] (S dg C) CCS 50/2, CPS Dir to MBW, "Directive for Assignment of Munitions," 23 Mar 42, CCS 400.3 (2-17-42); (S) Mns, CCS 13th Mtg, 24 Mar 42, item 7.

[28] (S) Ltr, Soong to McCloy, 6 Mar 42, CCS 540 China (2-9-42).

[29] *AAF in WW II*, vol I, pp. 510-511.

[30] (C) CCS 52, Memo by RBCOS, "Air Transportation for Maintenance of Forces in Burma," 28 Feb 42, CCS 360 (2-28-42); (S) Mns, CCS 9th Mtg, 3 Mar 42, item 4.

[31] (S) Mns, CCS 15th Mtg, 7 Apr 42, item 6.

[32] (S) Msg, Marshall to Stilwell or Bissell, 449, CM-OUT-2193, 12 Apr 42, CCS 400.3295 China (3-17-42).

[33] For detailed discussion of this, see ch V, pp. 115-116.

[34] (S) Msg, Marshall (London) to McNarney, 2401, CM-IN-3720, 14 Apr 42, OPD Exec 1, item 5; (S) Msg, Marshall to Stilwell or Bissell, 479, CM-OUT-2708, 15 Apr 42, CCS 091.711 China (1-20-42) sec 1; (S) Memo, Eisenhower to WDCMC, "Far Eastern Situation," 16 Apr 42, OPD Exec 1, item 5.

[35] (S) Msg, Bissell to Marshall, 540, CM-IN-4903, 18 Apr 42, CCS 091.711 China (1-20-42) sec 1.

[36] *AAF in WW II*, vol I, pp. 503-504.

[37] (S) Msg, Marshall to Stilwell, WD 713, CM-OUT-5022, 24 May 42, CCS 091.711 China (1-20-42) sec 1.

[38] (S) CCS 52/1, Req from MAB, "Cargo Transport Aircraft for Burma," 24 Apr 42; (S) CCS 52/2, Memo by RBCOS, "Transport Aircraft for India and Burma," 24 Apr 42. Both in CCS 360 (2-28-42).

[39] (S) Mns, JCS 12th Mtg, 27 Apr 42, item 3; (S) Mns, CCS 17th Mtg, 28 Apr 42, item 1; (S) Mns, CCS 18th Mtg, 5 May 42, item 2. At the JCS mtg it was stated that the 1st Ferry Group, under Gen Stilwell, would be built up to a total of 50 transports by 20 Jun 42. At the 17th CCS mtg, Sir John Dill reported 4 transports (presumably British, but not so stated) in Burma and 24 in India. Gen Arnold reported 34 planes en route to the Burma-China theater as part of a total of 75 committed there. It is not clear how these figures fit with his later statement at the same meeting that there were

> three types of transport service now in being in India:-
>   (1) A special service from the U.S. to India and China,... controlled directly from the U.S.
>   (2) Transport planes destined for China, of which there were now forty-four, with expectation of an increase to a total of seventy-five by this summer. These were under the direction of General Stilwell.
>   (3) The trans-India service, where he expected to have twenty in May and forty in the late summer, under direct control of General Brereton.

The picture is further confused by Gen Arnold's statement the next week that Gen Stilwell had a total of 16 planes, 6 under CNAC and 10 under his own control. Nineteen more were en route and 23 about to leave the US. Gen Brereton had 4 with 1 more at Khartoum and 5 en route. In addition he would soon have 8 which had been loaned to Gen Stilwell. It was hoped that by the middle or latter part of June Gen Brereton would have 25 and General Stilwell 40.

[40] See pp. 206.

[41] A case in point is the famous Doolittle raid on Tokyo of which Chiang was not fully informed in advance, although he was asked to have airfields prepared in North China.

[42] For discussion of the PWC, see ch IV.

[43] For a fuller discussion of the question of representation of other nations on the CCS, see (S) Davis, *Organization Development*, vol I, ch VI.

[44] (S) Ltr, Gimo to Pres, 10 Mar 42; (S) Memo, Pres, no sig,

undtd, filed w/msg, Gimo to Soong, 19 Apr 42. Both in OPD Exec 10, item 19b. A summary of the memo, apparently repeated in a letter from Soong to Hopkins, 20 Apr 42, appears in Hopkins Catalog. The President passed the memo to Gens Marshall and Arnold and Mr. Hopkins for preparation of a reply.

[45] (S) Msg, Gimo to Soong, 19 Apr 42, OPD Exec 10, item 19b.

[46] (S) Msg, Marshall to AMMISCA for Gimo from Pres, 19 Apr 42, OPD Exec 10, item 21.

[47] These were United States, Great Britain, Australia, New Zealand, Netherlands, China, Canada. For fuller discussion, see (S) Davis, *Organizational Development*.

[48] (S) Ann to Mns, MRP 1st Mtg, 26 May 42, circ as CCS 74, 29 May 42, CCS 334 MRP (5-18-42).

[49] (MS) Msg, BCOS to BJSM, W 191, 2 Jun 42, CCS 334 MRP (5-18-42); (S) Mns, CCS 22nd Mtg, 2 Jun 42, item 1.

[50] (U) Memos, Cdr R.D. Coleridge, BJSM, to Gen Smith, 5 Jun, 8 Jun 42; (S dg R) JCS 58, Note by Secys, "Chinese Concept of Conduct of Present War," 8 Jun 42; (S) Ltr, Marshall, King, and Dill to Hsiung, 13 Jun 42. All in CCS 334 MRP (5-18-42). (S) Mns, JCS 19th Mtg, 9 Jun 42, item 8.

[51] (S) Ltr, Hsiung to Marshall, King, and Dill, 26 Jun 42, CCS 334 MRP (5-18-42).

[52] (C) Ltr, Gen Shang Chen, Chief, Chinese Mil Mission, to Leahy 3 Jul 45, Encl to (C) JCS 1407, Note by Secys, "Chinese Representation on the Combined Chiefs of Staff," 3 Jul 45, CCS 334 MRP (5-18-42).

[53] (S) Msg, Stilwell to AGWAR, AMMISCA 437, CM-IN-1434, 1 Apr 42, CCS 400.3295 (China) (3-17-42) sec 1; (S) JIC Daily Summary, 127, 16 Apr 42.

[54] For difficulties over command of the ferry route from India to China see *AAF in WW II*, vol I, pp. 506-507. (S) Msg, Brereton to Arnold, AQUILA 393, CM-IN-1928, 19 Apr 42; (S) Msg, Arnold to AQUILA, WD 195, CM-OUT-3982, 21 Apr 42. All in CCS 360 (2-28-42).

[55] (S) Msg, Stilwell to Marshall, 520, CM-IN-3962, 15 Apr 42, CCS 400.3295 China (3-17-42) sec 1.

[56] (C) Memo, Maj Gen J.H. Burns, Exec MAB, to Hopkins, "Shipments to China," 22 Apr 42, CCS 540 China (2-9-42).

[57] (S) Msg, Marshall to Stilwell, 566, CM-OUT-5680, 29 Apr 42, CCS 540 China (2-9-42).

[58] (S) Msg, Stilwell to Marshall, 629, CM-IN-0513, 2 May 42, CCS 540 China (2-9-42).

[59] (S) Mns, MAC(G) 27th Mtg, 11 May 42; (S) Ltr, Aurand to Exec MAB, "Chinese Emergency Air Transportation Program," 11 May 42, Encl No. 2 to Mns, MAB 15th Mtg, Case No. G-11.

[60] It is not clear what was meant by a route "farther west." It seems likely, however, that the possibility envisaged was that the route might have to start from Dibrugarh, which was considered a possible terminal point during early surveys.

[61] (S) 1st Ind to MAB 15th Mtg, Agenda, 11 May 42, MAB TO MAC(G), 14 May 42, CCS 540 China (2-9-42); (S) Memo, Eisenhower to Brig Gen H.J. Malony, Asst Exec, MAB, "Air and Ground Routes India to China," 12 May 42. Both in CCS 400.3295 China (3-17-42) Sec 1.

NOTES TO CHAPTER IX

[62] (S) Mns, MAB 15th Mtg, 13 May 42, item 6. Introduction of the practice of making a representative of the US Army the consignee of lend-lease goods in certain areas had been considered by the MAC(G) in March when it had proved desirable but well-nigh impossible to transfer jurisdiction of unused items in certain areas, of which India and China were outstanding examples. The UK representative, while recognizing the utility of such a procedure in certain areas, had objected because of the uncertainty of ultimate delivery to the nation concerned. (S dg R) Mns, MAC(G) 11th Mtg, 19 Mar 42, minute No. 112; (S) Ltr, Col R.C. Benner, Secy MAC(G), to Exec MAB, "Shipping to U.S. Representatives for Countries Concerned," 23 Mar 42, Case No. G-5, Agenda MAB 8th Mtg, CCS 334 MAB (3-11-42). MAB, on 25 Mar, "authorized the Chairman to appoint a Committee with power to consider and decide the...[case]." The report of that committee does not show in the MAB minutes.

[63] (S) Msg, Marshall to Stilwell and Wheeler, 809 and 365, CM-OUT-2032 and 2033, 9 Jun 42, CCS 400.3295 China (3-17-42) sec 1.

[64] (UNK) Memo, McCloy to Soong, 19 May 42, ASW 400.336 China. On 15 May CDS reported 156,102 long tons awaiting shipment. (UNK) Rpt of Subcmte, MAC(G), "Summary of material awaiting shipment," App MAC(G) 29th Mtg, 18 May 42, DRB AGO.

[65] (S) Memo, Capt McCrea to JCS, 25 May 42, encl Msg, Madame to Currie, 23 May 42, CCS 091.711 China (1-20-42) sec 1.

[66] (S) Msg, Gimo to Pres, 1 Jun 42; (S) Memo, Malony to Hopkins, 13 Jun 42. Both in CCS 400.3295 China (3-17-42) sec 1.

[67] (S) Msg, Brereton to AGWAR, 17H6, 10 Jun 42, Encl 1 to MAB Case No. G-15, filed w/Mns, MAB 21st Mtg, CCS 334 MAB (5-20-42).

[68] (S) Msg, Stilwell to Marshall, AMMISCA 834, 18 Jun 42; (S) Msg, Wheeler to Marshall, 347W610, 19 Jun 42. Both in CCS 334 MAB (5-20-42).

[69] (S) Mns, MAC(G) 35th Mtg, 22 Jun 42; (S) Ltr, Chm MAC(G), to Exec MAB, "July Assignments to China," 23 Jun 42, Case No. G-15 in Agenda for MAB 21st Mtg. Ltr was referred by MAB at 21st Mtg, 24 Jun 42, to a special committee whose recommendation to refer the question to the CCS was approved at the MAB 22nd Mtg, 2 Jul 42.

[70] (UNK) Ltr, Soong to McCloy, 18 Jun 42, ASW 400.336 China; (UNK) Ltr, Soong to Hopkins, 20 Jun 42, *Hopkins Catalog*, bk V, note by R. Sunderland, OCMH DA.

[71] (UNK) Memo, Soong to Hopkins, 25 Jun 42, *Hopkins Catalog*, bk V. China had no representation on either committee and the source of Mr. Soong's information is not known to the writer.

[72] *The Brereton Diaries*, p. 141; *AAF in WW II*, vol I, p. 341. At the 17th mtg of the JCS, 1 Jun 42, Gen Marshall referred to this force as "a squadron of twenty-six airplanes." Since these were not being given to China under lend-lease, their detainment was not inconsistent with the President's earlier assurance to the Gimo that no lend-lease planes would be taken away from China without his consent.

[73] In a preliminary draft of a message from the President to the Generalissimo prepared by OPD the statement was included: "The paramount importance to your theater of holding Egypt made by decisions inevitable." This was crossed out before the msg was sent. OPD Exec 10, item 19. The concept that India was linked strategically with the Middle East had several times been voiced. Cf. (S) Memo, Eisenhower to Marshall, "Strategic Conceptions and their Application to Southwest Pacific," 21 Apr 42, ABC 381 (9-25-41) sec 1. Gen Eisenhower said,

> we must...defend the Indian-Middle East theater firmly. We must *insist* that England take this problem [securing the support of the Indian population] in hand, now--in view of the deadly danger the region faces--there is no more important problem demanding immediate solution by the CCS.

[74] (S) Msg, Marshall to Stilwell, 888, CM-OUT-5699, 23 Jun 42, CCS 370.5 Middle East (6-22-42); (S) Mns, CCS 29th Mtg, 25 Jun 42. Exactly how and by whom the decision to order Gen Brereton to the Middle East was made has not been determined to the writer's satisfaction. An indication that it was made in the White House conferences, if not by the President himself, is found in Mr. Churchill's remark to Gen Brereton at Cairo on 9 Aug 42: "I was in the President's office the day it was decided to whistle you from India over here to the Middle East." *The Brereton Diaries*, p. 145. Note also Gen Marshall's later remark that the transfer "was caused by urgent British requests for...[it]." (S) Mns, JCS 23rd Mtg, 7 Jul 42, item 1.

[75] (S) Msg, Marshall to Stilwell, Brereton, *et al.*, 896, CM-OUT-6075, 24 Jun 42, CCS 370.5 Middle East (6-22-42). *AAF in WW II*, vol I, p. 339.

[76] (S) Msg, Stilwell to SecWar and Marshall, 873, CM-IN-8586, 26 Jun 42, CCS 091.711 China (1-20-42) sec 1. Verbatim minutes of Gen Stilwell's conference with the Gimo and Madame indicate clearly how angry the Chinese were. After asking twice how many transports Gen Brereton would take and being told by Gen Stilwell that he did not know, Chiang said:

"The President informed me he had ordered the 10th Air Force to China. Is that correct?"

Stilwell - "The 10th Air Force was placed under my orders and I ordered it to China."

Chiang - "You are my Chief of Staff, and the 10th Air Force is under your orders; therefore it is under my orders. Why was I not consulted about the removal of the heavy bombers to Egypt? I did not consent and protest."

Stilwell - "The heavy bombers can't be accommodated in China."

Chiang - "The President should notify me before taking away what he had given me. The Chinese are being defeated too."

Madame - "Each time the British have a defeat, materials are diverted from China. Do the Allies want China to make peace? China can't keep fighting without air support."

Stilwell - "I know, and I objected. I made an issue of the diversion when they attempted to put the 10th Air Force under Wavell."

. . . .

Chiang - "Do the Allies want the China theater? I want a one word answer - yes or no. China has done her part for the Allied cause. China can't be expected to do more. Have the Allied nations done their part toward China? [No answer]
For five years China has fought the war for America and Britain, as well as China. There will be a serious reversal of feeling by the Chinese when they learn of these diversions."
The Chiangs continued on, accusing Gen Stilwell of not asking for materials needed in China and so being responsible for their not arriving. (S) Mns, Conf, Stilwell, Gimo, Madame, in Chungking, 26 Jun 42, 1100, in Folder, "Memos for Madame, Correspondence, May to Sept 1942," Hq China Theater, CT 23, Dr 2, RAC, AGO, St. Louis, Mo.

[77] (S) Msg, Pres to Gimo, CM-OUT-7014, 28 Jun 42, OPD Exec 10, item 9.

[78] Note that the figure 500 had appeared in a strategic estimate of uncertain origin which arrived through Mr. Currie before the Joint Board in May 41. (C) Memo, Lt Col E.E. MacMorland to Secy GS, "Chinese Aircraft Requirements," 12 May 41, Encl to (S) JB 355 (ser 691) 9 Jul 41.

[79] (S) Msg, Stilwell to Marshall, 894, CM-IN-0560, 1 Jul 42, OPD Exec 10, item 22. At a meeting with Gens Stilwell, Bissell, Chennault, the Chinese Gens Chow, Mow, Huang, and Tong on 2 Jul 42, Madame Chiang took the matter of airplanes in her own hands. Her decision was that the Chinese Air Force should have 150 pursuit and 50 bombers, Gen Chennault 200 pursuit and 100 bombers. These figures Gen Stilwell was directed to recommend to the War Department. (By an interesting bit of logic, Gen Bissell pointed out that the Chinese already had their 150 pursuit--144 P-66's in or en route to India and "the remainder of the 150 were P-43's in China!") As for transports, she directed that two fields be completed within two months, and if still more were needed she would take steps to have them established. (S) Mns, Mtg of 2 Jul 42, in Folder, "Memos for Madame, Correspondence May to Sept 1942," Hq China Theater, CT 23, Dr 2, RAC, AGO, St. Louis, Mo.

[80] (S) Mns, SecWar Confs, War Council, 6 Jul 42, CofS Recs. Chiang had suggested a visit from Mr. Hopkins.

[81] (S) Memo, Maj Gen R.C. Moore to CofS, 27 Jun 42, in WDCSA (S) file China. Gen Moore, representing the CofS on the MAB, supported his view that the 3,500 tons should be allocated. However, he remarked: "I realize the political aspects of this problem and the necessity for our point of view at this time. However, I feel that sooner or later we must take a realistic attitude toward the possibilities of delivery of equipment to China in our allocations."

[82] (S) Rpt of Spec Cmte appointed by MAB in its 21st Mtg, 24 Jun 42, Tab B to Memo, Gen Burns, Exec MAB, to Secy CCS, "July Assignments to China," 2 Jul 42: (S) CCS 90, Memo from MAB, "July Assignments to China," 2 Jul 42. Both in CCS 400.3295 China (3-17-42) sec 1.

[83] (S) Mns, JCS 23rd Mtg, 7 Jul 42, item 3; (S) Memo, Smith to Dykes, 9 Jul 42; (S) CCS 90/1, Memo by RBCOS, "July Assignments for China," 10 Jul 42. Both papers in CCS 400.3295 China (3-17-42) sec 1. (S) Mns, JCS 25th Mtg, 14 Jul 42, item 4; (S) Mns, CCS 31st Mtg, 16 Jul 42, item 4; (S) Msg, Marshall to Stilwell, 1033, CM-OUT-5475, 18 Jul 42, CCS 400.3295 China (3-17-42) sec 1. The British were afraid that additional allotments of Bren guns to China would cut into British quotas of that item.

[84] (S) Ltr, AM Evill to Arnold, 3 Jul 42, CCS 323.361 (2-23-42).

[85] (S) Mns, JCS 23rd Mtg, 7 Jul 42, item 1; (S) Ltr, Arnold to Evill, 8 Jul 42, CCS 323.361 (2-23-42).

[86] (S) Mns, JCS 29th Mtg, 18 Aug 42, item 9; (S dg U) JCS 84, Memo by CG AAF, "Employment of 10th Air Force," 18 Aug 42; (S) Ltr, Arnold to Evill, 20 Aug 42. Both in CCS 323.361 (2-23-42).

[87] (MS) Msg, BCOS to BJSM, 26 Sep 42; (MS) Dill to Marshall, 28 Sep 42. Both in OPD 381 CTO sec 2.

[88] For fuller discussion of this, cf. ch X, pp. 236-237.

[89] (S) Msg, Madame to Currie, 6 Mar 42, OPD Exec 10, item 19b.

[90] (S) Memo, Stilwell to Chiang, Encl w/Msg, Gimo to Soong, 5 Jul 42, OPD Exec 10, item 19; *The Stilwell Papers*, pp. 120-123.

[91] (S) Msg, Gimo to Soong, 5 Jul 42, OPD Exec 10, item 19b; *The Stilwell Papers*, pp. 126-147.

[92] (S) Msg, Pres to Gimo, 14 Jul 42, OPD Exec 10, item 19. The message was drafted for the President in the WD.

[93] (S) Memo, McCloy to McNarney, 27 Jul 42, WDCSA (S) file China.

[94] How Mr. Soong's action was discovered is not known to the author. On 24 Jul Gen Marshall reported to Gen Stilwell that the WD had been informed that the President's message was not sent. (S) Msg, Marshall to Stilwell, eyes only, CM-OUT-6863, 24 Jul 42, Personal File, bk 1, DRB AGO. *The Stilwell Papers*, p. 130. Mr. Soong on 26 Jul told Mr. McCloy (fn 93) what he had sent the Gimo. How Mr. Soong happened to tell him, whether spontaneously or on demand, Mr. McCloy did not record.

[95] (S) Msg, Currie to CofS for Pres, 998, CM-IN-9776, 28 Jul 42, OPD Exec 10, item 19; (S) Msg, Marshall to Stilwell, 1094, CM-OUT-8454, 29 Jul 42, OPD Exec 10, item 21. Mr. Soong reported to Mr. McCloy on 27 Jul that he had had a message from the Gimo apparently reporting that Gen Stilwell had shown him a copy of the President's original message. According to Mr. Soong, Chiang said that

> if any message such as General Stilwell had presented to him as being en route to him from the President should be sent, and if this position was upheld, on receipt of such a telegram he would be forced to resign as the Supreme Commander of

804   NOTES TO CHAPTERS IX AND X

the Chinese area and abolish the Chinese area entirely; that he was quite firm in this position and that his position should be stated firmly to the American authorities.
(S) Memo, McCloy to McNarney, 27 Jul 42, WDCSA (S) file China.

[96] (U) Lauchlin Currie, "Report on Visit to China," 24 Aug 42, CCS microfilm 20840-83.

[97] (S) Ltr, Currie to Marshall, 14 Sep 42, OPD Exec 10, item 22; (C) Memo, Pres to Marshall, 3 Oct 42, OPD 381 CTO sec 2.

[98] (S) Memo, Marshall to Pres, "Situation relative to General Stilwell," 6 Oct 42, OPD 381 CTO sec 2.

[99] Note that by Dec 42 Mr. Joseph Alsop, a great admirer of Gen Chennault, on a visit to the CBI as an official of China Defense Supplies, Inc., sent to his good friend in the White House, Mr. Hopkins, the first of a number of letters that were to continue later when he returned to the theater on General Chennault's staff. In this, written from India on 10 Dec, before he had gotten to China, he stated that he was "much more than half convinced that a situation exists which is grossly dishonoring to the Army, to the President, and to the country."

[100] (S) Memo, Handy to Marshall, "Three minimum requirements for the China Theater submitted by Generalissimo Chiang Kai-shek," 14 Aug 42, OPD 381 CTO sec 2.

[101] (S) Memo, Handy to Marshall, "Support of China," 4 Sep 42, Encl (S) Memo, Marshall to Pres, "Support of China," sent 11 Sep 42, OPD 381 CTO sec 2. The draft msg for the Gimo is not included with the carbon of the memo for the President.

[102] (S) Ltr, Currie to Marshall, 14 Sep 42; (S) Msg, Marshall to Stilwell, 1398, CM-OUT-8582, 25 Sep 42. Both in OPD Exec 10, item 22.

[103] (S) Msg, Stilwell to Marshall, 1180, CM-IN-10737, 23 Sep 42; (S) Msg, Stilwell to Marshall, 1196, CM-IN-13086, 28 Sep 42. Both in OPD Exec 10, item 22.

[104] (S) Memo, Handy to Marshall, 4 Sep 42, Tab C, OPD 381 CTO sec 2.

[105] (S) Memo, Marshall to Pres, "Support of China," 2 Oct 42, OPD 381 CTO sec 2. Copy has notation that encl memo was accepted by the President on 10 Oct. *Stilwell Report*, p. 59, indicates that he received the message as No. 1469 on 12 Oct 42.

[106] (S) Msg, Gimo to Pres, 14 Nov 42, CCS 091.711 China (1-20-42) sec 2; (S) Msg, Pres to Gimo, 1 Dec 42, OPD Exec 10, item 54.

CHAPTER X

[1] It is impossible to give accurate figures on the number of troops employed by either side in Burma. It appears, however, that the British and Chinese employed a total of about 80,000 troops, while the Japanese used a total of about 50,000 men, during the Burma campaign. At the beginning of hostilities in December the British had 25,000-30,000 troops in Burma while the Japanese opened their campaign there with 24,000. The Japanese air strength, however, greatly exceeded that of the Allies. See

Romanus-Sunderland, *Stilwell's Mission*, p. 102. A fuller discussion appears in the history prepared in the CBI Theater. (S) *History of C-B-I Theater, 21 May 1942 to 25 October 1944*, sec 3, ch IV, OPD 314.7 CTO.

[2] (S) Memo, Brig Gen R.W. Crawford, Actg ACofS, to CofS USA, "Keeping China in the War," 26 May 44, OPD 381 CTO sec 1.

[3] (S) Msg, Stilwell to AGWAR, NR 98, CM-IN-7490, 28 Apr 42, OPD Exec 10, item 21; (S) Msg, Gruber to AGWAR, 621, CM-IN-174, 1 May 42. Both in CCS 091 China (1-20-42) sec 1. Romanus-Sunderland, *Stilwell's Mission*, ch III.

[4] (S) Msg, Marshall to Stilwell, 567, CM-OUT-5677, 29 Apr 42; (S) Msg, Marshall to Stilwell, 575, CM-OUT-6033, 30 Apr 42. Both in CCS 091.711 China (1-20-42) sec 1.

[5] (S) Msg, Gruber to Marshall, 630, CM-IN-0535, 2 May 42, CCS 091.711 China (1-20-42) sec 1.

[6] (S) Msg, Gruber to AGWAR, 621, CM-IN-174, 1 May 42, CCS 091.711 China (1-20-42) sec 1; *The Stilwell Papers*, pp. 163-164.

[7] (SS) Ltr, Dill to Marshall, 19 Oct 42; (S) Memo, Marshall to Pres, 5 Nov 42. Both in WDCSA (SS) file 381 China. Gen Marshall informed the President:

> ...I had the British Chiefs of Staff in London practically force the British Foreign Office to instruct the Viceroy in England to permit Wavell to agree to a corps of 30,000 Chinese troops at Ramgarh, and also I forcibly impressed T.V. Soong with the fact that the great issue was Burma (not merely a harmonious group at Chungking); which meant a properly trained Chinese force at Ramgarh, an improved or selected Chinese force in Yunnan and a practical basis of cooperation with the British in such an operation - in other words Stilwell.

[8] Gen Stilwell first proposed the project in April. The Gimo did not give final consent until 29 Jun. Even after that the British were reluctant to agree. By mid-October, however, the training program had made such progress that with some reluctance both the Gimo and the BCOS agreed to expansion to many thousand more men than had originally been proposed. *The Stilwell Papers*, pp. 136-138; *CBI History*, p. 65; (S) Memo, Eisenhower, ACofS, to Malony, "Air and Ground Routes India to China," 12 May 42, CCS 400.3295 China (3-17-42) sec 1; (S) Msg, Stilwell to Marshall, 893, CM-IN-570, 2 Jul 42, OPD Exec 10, item 22; (S) Msg, Marshall to Stilwell, 2 Jul 42, OPD Exec 10, item 21; (S) Msg, Marshall to Stilwell, eyes only, 75, CM-OUT-4877, 14 Oct 42, OPD CTO sec 2.

[9] For employment of the Tenth AF under British direction, see above, ch IX, pp. 217-218. AVG equipment and the few members of the Group who volunteered were transferred to the Tenth AF on 4 Jul 42 as the China Air Task Force. For Brereton's air plans, see *The Brereton Diaries*, pp. 125-126.

[10] (S) Msg, Stilwell to Marshall, NR 61, CM-IN-7037, 25 May 42, CCS 091.711 China (1-20-42) sec 1; *CBI History*, pp. 88-89.

[11] (S) Memo, Capt McCrea to JCS, 25 May 42, encl cy of Msg, Mme Chiang to Currie, 23 May 42; (S) Mns, JCS 16th Mtg, 25 May

42, item 8; (S) Memo, Brig Gen W.B. Smith to Capt McCrea, 26 May 42. Both papers in CCS 091.711 China (1-20-42) sec 1.

[12](S) Memo, Gen Crawford, Actg ACofS, to WD Msg Ctr, "Far Eastern Situation," 28 May 42, OPD 381 CTO (2-28-42). Sent as (S) Msg, Marshall to Stilwell, 745, CM-OUT-5991, 28 May 42.

[13](S) Memo, Gruber to CofS USA, "The Situation in the China Theater," 28 Jul 42, OPD 381 CTO sec 2.

[14](S) Mns, JCS 28th Mtg, 11 Aug 42, item 6. During discussion of a strategic hypothesis for 1944, Gen Marshall remarked that "actually the big issues to be decided were whether the major U.S. effort was to be made in the Pacific as against Europe and the Middle East." (S dg C) JCS 85, Rpt by JUSSC, "Strategic Policy of the United Nations and the United States on the Collapse of Russia," 24 Aug 42, CCS 381 (6-1-42).

[15](S) CPS 35/D, Dir to CPS, "Production Requirements," 17 Jul 42, CCS 400.17 (7-6-42) sec 1. For more detailed treatment, see (S) MS, JCS Hist, *Procurement and Allocation of Material Means*, pt III, ch III.

[16](S dg R) CCS 97, Rpt by CPS, "Strategic Hypothesis for Deployment of Forces in April, 1944," 24 Jul 42. A British document on the same subject, from which CCS 97 was developed, had stated, "Any offensive from India against Burma or China to be confined so as not to take shipping away from the North Atlantic." (S) CPS 35/1, Brit Paper, "Strategic Hypothesis for April, 1944," 15 Jul 42. Both in CCS 400.17 (7-6-42) sec 1.

[17](S) Mns, JCS 26th Mtg, 28 Jul 42, item 2; (S) Mns, CCS 34th Mtg, 30 Jul 42, item 1.

[18](S) Mns, JCS 27th Mtg, 4 Aug 42, item 8; (S) Mns, CCS 35th Mtg, 6 Aug 42, item 6; (S) CPS 35/3/D, Dir to CPS, "Strategic Hypothesis for Deployment of Forces in April 1944," 6 Aug 42; (S) Mns, CPS 28th Mtg, 7 Aug 42, item 5; (S dg R) CCS 97/2, Rpt by CPS, "Strategic Hypothesis for Deployment of Forces in April 1944," 8 Aug 42. Both papers in CCS 400.17 (7-6-42) sec 1.

[19](S) Mns, JCS 28th Mtg, 11 Aug 42, item 6.

[20](S dg R) CCS 97/2 (Proposed Revision), including changes proposed by JCS, 12 Aug 42, CCS 400.17 (7-6-42) sec 1. At the suggestion of Sir John Dill at the next CCS meeting, the words "strategic defensive" were deleted. (S) Mns, CCS 36th Mtg, 13 Aug 42, item 2.

[21](S) Memo, Handy to CofS USA, "Three minimum requirements for the China Theater submitted by Generalissimo Chiang Kai-shek," 14 Aug 42, OPD 381 CTO sec 2; (S) Mns, OPD Policy Cmte, 29 Aug 42, ABC 334.3 Policy Cmte (1 Aug 42) sec 1.

[22](S) Mns, CCS 27th Mtg, 19 Jun 42.

[23](S) Mns, Comb Staff Conf, 10 Downing St., 20 Jul 42, CCS 381 (3-23-42) pt 3 sec 2. In a general discussion of all the war theaters, the PM raised the question of Operation Anakim. "He read out the circumstances in which the Operation might be launched." Although copies of this plan were subsequently made available to the CPS (see below, pp. 234-235) the author has

been unable to discover that the JCS had copies at the time Gen Marshall's memo was written.

[24] See ch VII, pp. 157ff. (S) CCS 91, "Strategic Policy and Deployment of United States and British Forces," 7 Jul 42, CCS 381 (6-24-42) sec 1.

[25] (S) CCS 104, Memo by CofS USA, "Retaking of Burma," 25 Aug 42, CCS 381 Burma (8-25-42).

[26] (S) Mns, JCS 30th Mtg, 25 Aug 42, item 7.

[27] (S) Mns, CCS 38th Mtg, 28 Aug 42, item 4; (S) CCS 101, Memo by CIC, "The Situation in China," 23 Aug 42, CCS 381 China (6-23-42).

[28] The Gimo's approval was said by Mr. Currie to be conditioned on despatch of at least one American division to the theater and progress toward the goal of 500 planes and 5,000 tons of air freight per month. Gen Stilwell had submitted a plan for a "Pacific Front" to the Gimo on 29 Jul 42. It was probably a copy of this, entitled "Proposed Plan for Opening a Second or Pacific Front," and containing the same points as the plan Mr. Currie brought back, differently stated, which Gen Stilwell sent to Gen Marshall on 30 Jul 42. Available evidence does not indicate when this was received in the WD. However, it was not until 14 Sep 42 that Brig Gen A.C. Wedemeyer forwarded it to the CPS. (S) Memo, Wedemeyer to Sect CPS, "General Stilwell's Plan," 14 Sep 42, CCS 381 Burma (8-25-42) sec 1. The plan itself is in ABC 384 Burma sec II, 8-25-42. Cf. (S) *CBI History*, pp. 127-129. Lt Col Frank Dorn (at that time Artillery Officer at Gen Stilwell's Hq at Chungking) sent a copy of an "uncensored" version of the "Gimo's Plan" to Gen Handy on 4 Aug 42 (OPD 381 CTO sec 3).

[29] (S) Memo, Pres to Leahy w/encls, 26 Aug 42, circ as (S) CCS 104/1, "Retaking of Burma," 29 Aug 42, CCS 381 Burma (8-25-42) sec 1.

[30] These were to be predominantly British soldiers, "not the usual hodge-podge of Punjabis, Burmese, Assamites, and Indians, all of whom have proven themselves to be more or less undependable." The latter qualification was omitted when the plan was circulated to the CCS, as was the statement that, without an American division, "it is believed that it will be impossible to goad the British in India into any serious offensive operation."

[31] The uncensored version submitted by Col Dorn contained the warning, "The Burma phase of the land operations must *not* under any conditions fall under British command. It has long since become obvious that the British simply do not know how to command, and their ponderous hesitancy and timidity would jeopardize the entire position." OPD 381 CTO sec 3.

[32] For more detailed accounts of his accomplishments, see Romanus-Sunderland, *Stilwell's Mission*, chs II, IV; also Chennault, chs 9-13.

[33] (U) Msg, Chennault to Stilwell, 13 Aug 42, quoted in Chennault, pp. 210-211.

NOTES TO CHAPTER X

[34] (S) Brit Doc, nd, photostat copy in CCS 381 Burma (8-25-42) sec 1. Another copy in ABC 384 Burma (8-25-42) sec 1-B has the date in pencil, 12 Jun 42.

[35] (S) Mns, CPS 31st Mtg, 4 Sep 42, item 4; (S) CCS 104/2, Rpt by CPS, "Plan for the Recapture of Burma," 9 Sep 42, CCS 381 Burma (8-25-42) sec 1.

[36] (S) Mns, CCS 40th Mtg, 18 Sep 42, item 2; (S) Mns, JCS 33rd Mtg, 15 Sep 42, item 8; (S) OPD Brief of CCS 104/2, 13 Sep 42; (S) Msg, Marshall to Stilwell, 1367, CM-OUT-6610, 19 Sep 42. Both papers in CCS 381 Burma (8-25-42) sec 1.

[37] (S) Memo, Vittrup, Secy CPS, to Col F.N. Roberts, et al., "Plan for Retaking of Burma," 19 Sep 42; (S) Memo, Wedemeyer, Strategy & Policy Grp, OPD, to Sec CPS, "General Stilwell's Plan," 14 Sep 42. Both in CCS 381 Burma (8-25-42) sec 1. Cf. fn 28 above.

[38] (S) Msg, BCOS to BJSM, 26 Sep 42, OPD 381 CTO sec 2.

[39] (S) Ltr, Dill to Marshall, 28 Sep 42, OPD 381 CTO sec 2.

[40] (S) Memo, Handy to Marshall, "Employment of 10th Air Force in Burma Operations," 1 Oct 42; (S) Ltr, Marshall to Dill, 1 Oct 42; (S) Memo, Handy to Marshall, "Burma Operations," 1 Oct 42. All in OPD 381 CTO sec 2.

[41] (S) Memo, Handy to Marshall, "Burma Operations," 1 Oct 42, OPD 381 CTO sec 2; (S) Memo, CofS USA to Pres, 10 Oct 42, OPD Exec 10, item 54.

[42] (S) Msg, Stilwell to Marshall, eyes only, 1115, CM-IN-1704, 4 Sep 42, OPD Exec 10, item 22.

[43] (S) Memo for Rec, Lt Col W. Krueger, Jr., "British obstruction to increase in Chinese training project in India," 6 Oct 42, OPD 381 CTO sec 2; (S) Mns, JCS 37th Mtg, 13 Oct 42, item 7; *The Stilwell Papers*, pp. 162-164.

[44] (S) Msg, Pres to Gimo, 10 Oct 42, CCS 381 Burma (8-25-42) sec 1.

[45] (UNK) Note of agreements made at conf, Stilwell and Wavell, 27 Oct 42, JCS HS files.

[46] (S) Msg, Stilwell to Marshall, 1384, CM-IN-5176, 11 Nov 42, CCS 381 Burma (8-25-42) sec 2.

[47] (S) Memo, Marshall to Pres, 5 Nov 42, WDCSA (SS) 381 China.

[48] *CBI History*, p. 95. (S) Msg, BCOS to BJSM, COS(W) 315, 20 Oct 42; (S) Msg, Wavell to BCOS, 28 Oct 42, Tab "A" to OPD notes on JCS 40th Mtg. Both in ABC 384 Burma (8-25-42) sec I-A. (S) Msg, Stilwell to Marshall, 1356, CM-IN-1965, 4 Nov 42, OPD Exec 10, item 22. (S) Memo, McCrea to CCS, 15 Nov 42, encl Msg, Soong to Hopkins, 13 Nov 42; (S) Msg, Stilwell to Marshall, eyes only, 1384, CM-IN-5176, 11 Nov 42; (S) Msg, Stilwell to AGWAR, 1478, CM-IN-1197, 3 Dec 42. All in CCS 381 Burma (8-25-42) sec 2. (S) Mns, OPD Policy Cmte 18th Mtg, 5 Dec 42, ABC 334.3 Policy Cmte (1 Aug 42) sec 1. *The Stilwell Papers*, pp. 166-168.

[49] (S) Mns, CPS 36th Mtg, 29 Oct 42, item 4; (S) CPS 43/2, Rpt by Subcmte, "Plan for Retaking of Burma," 24 Oct 42, CCS 381 Burma (8-25-42) sec 1; (S) CCS 104/3, Rpt by CPS, "Plan for Retaking of Burma," 30 Oct 42, CCS 381 Burma (8-25-42) sec 2.

NOTES TO CHAPTER X

[50] See ch XIV. (S) Brief, no orig, CCS 104/3, 2 Nov 42, CCS 381 Burma (8-25-42) sec 2; (S) Suppl Mns, JCS 40th Mtg, 3 Nov 42, item 8; (S) Memo, Col Roberts to Wedemeyer, 6 Nov 42, ABC 384 Burma (8-25-42) sec 1-A; (S) Mns, CCS 47th Mtg, 6 Nov 42, item 2; (S) CCS 104/4, Rpt by CPS, "Plan for Retaking of Burma," 16 Jan 43, CCS 381 Burma (8-25-42) sec 2.

[51] Although the larger project for retaking Burma and reopening the whole land route from Rangoon to the Burma Road had by no means been abandoned, it appears that it had now been decided that a reasonably adequate supply route could be built up from India to China via the road on which work had already been begun from Ledo across north Burma to meet the Burma Road. This project had not been advanced in the larger program since that would have resulted in reopening the old route from Rangoon. With that objective postponed indefinitely, establishment of a substitute route seemed a legitimate objective for a limited operation. The tenor of thought in the theater is outlined in an unofficial (S) "Estimate of the Situation," dated 16 Nov 42 which was prepared by Lt Col E.D. Merrill of Gen Stilwell's staff following Joint British-American Staff Committee discussions. Col Merrill pointed out that the theater mission was to defend available US supply routes to China and reestablish a land route. The only existing line was by air from Karachi to Dinjan to Kunming. Means were not available for reopening the Burma Road from Rangoon. However, they would permit a north Burma campaign which would result in establishment of a land route from Ledo. A copy of Col Merrill's study is in CCS 381 Burma (8-25-42) sec 2. Whether Col Timberman brought it back with him is not known.

[52] (S) Mns, OPD Policy Cmte 18th Mtg, 5 Dec 42, ABC 334.3 Policy Cmte (1 Aug 42) sec 1.

[53] (S) Memo for Rec, nd; (S) Msg, Marshall to Stilwell, eyes only, 1724, CM-OUT-7378, 21 Nov 42, OPD 381 CTO sec 2, item 100; *The Stilwell Papers*, p. 171. The authorship of this message has not been determined. It went over Gen Marshall's name.

[54] (C) Msg, Stilwell to Timberman, 1463, nd [c. 28 Nov 42], in Radios - Personal File, Book #1, Stilwell's Files, DRB AGO. Conv, Brig Gen T.S. Timberman with author, 27 Feb 50.

[55] (S dg U) JCS 162, Memo by CofS USA, "Operations in Burma, March 1943," 7 Dec 42, CCS 381 Burma (8-25-42) sec 2.

[56] (S) Suppl Mns, JCS 45th Mtg, 8 Dec 42, item 6.

[57] (S dg U) JCS 162/1, Rpt by JPS, "Operations in Burma, March 1943," 11 Dec 42; (S dg U) JCS 162/2, Memo by JSSC, same subj, 11 Dec 42. Both in CCS 381 Burma (8-25-42) sec 2. (S) Suppl Mns, JCS 46th Mtg, 15 Dec 42, item 5. The JSSC agreed that the proposed operation was "strictly in accord with the basic strategic concept of the Committee" and that "the results attained should be far more than commensurate with the effort expended." The JPS recommended that provision of forces required by General Stilwell be accelerated.

[58] (S) Msg, Marshall to Stilwell, 88, CM-OUT-7065 and 7066,

810   NOTES TO CHAPTER X

21 Oct 42; (S) Msg, Marshall to Stilwell, 92, CM-OUT-7429, 22 Oct 42. Both in OPD (TS) Cable files, 12 May 42-31 Oct 42.

[59] (S) Msg, Stilwell to Marshall, eyes only, 1500, CM-IN-3814, 8 Dec 42. CCS 381 Burma (8-25-42) sec 2.

[60] (S) Msg, Stilwell to Marshall, eyes only, 230, CM-IN-7215, 16 Dec 42. CCS 381 Burma (8-25-42) sec 2.

[61] (S) Suppl Mns, JCS 45th Mtg, 15 Dec 42, item 5; (S dg U) JCS 162/1, Rpt by JPS, "Operations in Burma," 11 Dec 42, CCS 381 Burma (8-25-42) sec 2.

[62] (S dg C) JCS 175, Memo by CofS USA, "General Stilwell," 21 Dec 42; (S dg C) JCS 175/2, Note by Secys, "General Stilwell," 30 Dec 42. Both in CCS 323.361 (12-21-42). (S) Suppl Mns, JCS 47th Mtg, 22 Dec 42, item 10.

[63] (C) Memo, Lt Col E.E. MacMorland to Secy GS, "Chinese Aircraft Requirements," 12 May 41, Encl to (S) JB 355 (ser 691), 9 Jul 41. Memo forwards paper received from Mr. Currie, of undesignated origin.

[64] Chennault, pp. 212-216; (S) Memo, Handy to CofS USA, "Report by the Naval Attache in Chungking reference operations U.S. Forces, China-Burma-India," 12 Dec 42, OPD 381 CTO sec 3.

[65] (S) Mns, OPD Policy Cmte 18th Mtg, 5 Dec 42, ABC 334.3 Policy Cmte (1 Aug 42) sec 1.

[66] (S) Suppl Mns, JCS 45th Mtg, 8 Dec 42, item 6.

[67] (S) Uniden Memo to Marshall, 30 Dec 42, ABC 384 Burma (8-25-42) sec 2. Cy in WDCSA 381 China (SS) has note that Gen Deane brought the memo to Gen Marshall from Adm Leahy.

[68] (S) Memo, Marshall to Leahy, "Chennault," 4 Jan 43, OPD 381 CTO sec 3.

[69] (S) Memo, Arnold to CofS USA, "Establishment and Assignment of Mission to Separate Air Force in China," 6 Jan 43, WDCSA 381 China (SS).

[70] (S) Memo, Handy to CofS USA, "Separate Air Force in China," 13 Jan 43, WDCSA 381 China (SS).

[71] (S) Msg, Stilwell to Marshall, 234, CM-IN-8024, 17 Dec 42; (S) Msg, Stilwell to Marshall, 242, CM-IN-9617, 21 Dec 42. Both in CCS 381 Burma (8-25-242) sec 2.

[72] (MS) Ltr, Dill to Marshall, 10 Dec 42, WDCSA China (S); (S) Msg, Wavell to Dill, 31969/COS, 18 Dec 42, CCS 381 Burma (8-25-42) sec 2. (S) Memo, Marshall to Dill, 18 Dec 42; (MS) Ltr, Dill to Marshall, 19 Dec 42. Both in OPD Exec 10, item 65.

[73] On 18 Jul 42 Gen Stilwell had recommended to the Gimo that he agree to furnish 20 divisions to invade Burma, provided the British would cooperate by putting enough naval strength in the Bay of Bengal to control it, by invading Burma via the Chindwin toward Shwebo and Mandalay, and by landing at Rangoon. (S) Memo, Stilwell to Gimo, 18 Jul 42, JCS HS files.

[74] (S) Msg, Chiang to Pres, AMMISCA 1556, 28 Dec 42, CM-IN-12657 (30 Dec 42); (S) Msg, Stilwell to Marshall, 1562, 28 Dec 42, CM-IN-12796 (30 Dec 42). Both in OPD Exec 10, item 22.

NOTES TO CHAPTERS X AND XI

[75] (S) Msg, Dill to BCOS, 2 Jan 43, OPD Exec 10, item 22; (S) Ltr, Dill to Marshall, 2 Jan 43 (date on memo is incorrectly "1942"), (TS) CominCh file "U.N. Strategy - Post-Torch, PreANFA."

[76] (S) Msg, Pres to Gimo, 2 Jan 43, CCS 381 Burma (8-25-42) sec 2.

[77] (S) Memo, Marshall to Leahy, King, & Arnold, "Burma Operations," 5 Jan 43, OPD Exec 10, item 22; (S) Mns, WH Mtg, JCS & Pres, 7 Jan 43. Presumably this message was sent, since the President did not disagree with it. No concrete evidence of its despatch has been seen by the author.

[78] (S) Msg, Gimo to Pres, eyes only, 31, CM-IN-3980, 9 Jan 43, OPD Exec 10, item 22.

[79] (S) Msg, Pres to Stilwell for Gimo, 9 Jan 43, OPD Exec 10, item 70.

CHAPTER XI

[1] "...Germany is still the prime enemy and her defeat is the key to victory. Once Germany is defeated the collapse of Italy and the defeat of Japan must follow....It should be a cardinal principal of A-B strategy that only the minimum of force necessary for the safeguarding of vital interests in other theatres should be diverted from operations against Germany." (S) ABC-4/CS1, "American-British Strategy," *ARCADIA*.

[2] See ch VII, pp. 157ff. (S) CCS 91, Rpt by CPS, "Strategic Policy and Deployment of United States and British Forces," 7 Jul 42, CCS 381 (6-24-42) sec 1.

[3] (S) Dft of Dir to CPS, "Production Requirements," nd, [c. 6 Jul 42], CCS 400.17 (7-6-42) sec 1.

[4] (S) Mns, CPS 25th Mtg, 13 Jul 42, item 2; (S) CPS 35/1, Brit Note, "Strategic Hypothesis for April 1944," 15 Jul 42, CCS 400.17 (7-6-42) sec 1.

[5] (S) Mns, JPS 23rd Mtg, 17 Jul 42, item 5; (S) Mns, JPS 24th Mtg, 2 Jul 42, item 2.

[6] (S) Mns, CPS 26th Mtg, 24 Jul 42, item 1; (S) CCS 97, Rpt by CPS, "Strategic Hypothesis for Deployment of Forces in April, 1944," 24 Jul 42, CCS 400.17 (7-6-42).

[7] (S) CCS 94, Memo by CCS, "Operations in 1942/43," 24 Jul 42, CCS 381 (3-23-42) pt 3 sec 2; (S) MS, JCS Hist, *War Against Germany and Its Satellites*, ch III, pp. 70-71.

[8] (S) Mns, JCS 26th Mtg, 28 Jul 42, item 2; (S) Mns, CCS 34th Mtg, 30 Jul 42, item 1.

[9] (S) CCS 97/1, Rpt by CPS, "Strategic Hypothesis for Deployment of Forces in April 1944," 1 Aug 42, CCS 400.17 (7-6-42) sec 1; (S) Mns, JCS 27th Mtg, 4 Aug 42, item 8; (S) Mns, CCS 35th Mtg, 6 Aug 42, item 5; (S) Ann to Mns, CCS 35th Mtg.

[10] (S) Mns, CPS 28th Mtg, 7 Aug 42, item 5; (S) CCS 97/2, Rpt by CPS, "Strategic Hypothesis for Deployment of Forces in April 1944," 8 Aug 42, CCS 400.17 (7-6-42) sec 1.

[11] (S) Mns, JCS 28th Mtg, 11 Aug 42, item 6.

12 (S) Mns, CCS 36th Mtg, 13 Aug 42, item 2; (S) CCS 97/3, "Strategic Hypothesis for Deployment of Forces in April, 1944," 14 Aug 42, CCS 400.17 (7-6-42) sec 1.

13 (S) JPS 43, Rpt by JUSSC, "Strategic Policy of the United Nations and the United States on the Collapse of Russia," 8 Aug 42, CCS 381 (6-1-42). It is therein stated that the study was prepared in compliance with a memo directive from Adm Turner and Gen Eisenhower, 20 May 42. The directive is not in this folder. The bulky annex (331 pages) is missing from JCS files but can be found in ABC 384 USSR (6-1-42).

14 (S) Mns, JPS 27th Mtg, 12 Aug 42, item 1; (S) Mns, JPS 29th Mtg, 19 Aug 42, item 2; (C) JCS 85, Rpt by JUSSC, "Strategic Policy of the United Nations and the United States on the Collapse of Russia," 24 Aug 42, CCS 381 (6-1-42).

15 Adm Leahy went so far as to call it "an excellent statement of policy."

16 (S) Mns, JCS 30th Mtg, 25 Aug 42, item 3. It is of interest that an "Air War Plan" drafted by the air planners on 24 Aug 42, apparently with Gen Arnold's approval, stated that "Collapse of Russia does not in any way necessitate the abandonment of our original concepts." The paper was sent by Col Elmer J. Rogers (E.J.R.) to Gen Wedemeyer ("AL") for comment, with a note that it had not yet been signed by Gen Arnold. ABC 384 USSR (6-1-42).

17 (C) JCS 85/1, JPS Rev, "Strategic Policy of the United Nations and the United States on the Collapse of Russia," 4 Sep 42, CCS 381 (6-1-42).

18 (S) Mns, JCS 32nd Mtg, 8 Sep 42, item 3.

19 (U) Ltr, Dill to King, 7 Nov 42, with Encl, "American-British Strategy," (TS) CominCh file "Memos to/from British-1942." Mr. Oliver Lyttelton was just coming to Washington to discuss matters pertaining to the Combined Production and Resources Board (cf. (S) MS JCS Hist, *Procurement and Allocation of Material Means*) and the short version had been prepared to give him background for his talks. FM Dill informed the JCS, "I want you to know the sort of strategical background he has."

20 (UNK) Note, Cooke to King, nd, filed with Dill's memo (fn. 19). Adm Cooke and his Army colleagues felt the JCS should take action.

21 Those versions presently available consist of marginal notes on the Navy's copy and a formal memo signed by Gen Handy presenting OPD's views. In most instances these are compatible, and it seems highly probable that the OPD paper was prepared after close consultation with the Navy planners, if not with their complete concurrence.

In a note to Adm King included with a copy of the British document in Adm King's file, Adm Cooke said: "Army planners went in huddle on this Sunday afternoon. So did we. I have a draft of proposed comment by J.C.S. which will be written up by about 10 00. Will confer further with Army. Consider it important and urgent that J.C.S. act today or tomorrow on this." No copy of such a paper for the JCS has been seen. It is possible that it was developed along the lines of the OPD paper here discussed. There is no indication that the JCS formally considered the matter.

[22] (S) Memo, ACofS USA (Handy), "American-Britsh Strategy," 8 Nov 42, WDCSA 381.

[23] (S) Memo, Handy to CofS, "American-British Strategy," 8 Nov 42, ABC 381 (9-25-41) sec III.

[24] (U) JCS 152, Memo by CG AAF, "Strategic Policy for 1943," 16 Nov 43, CCS 381 (11-16-42).

[25] For details of the JSSC, see (S) Davis, *Organizational Department*, vol II, ch X; (S) Mns, JCS 42nd Mtg, 17 Nov 42, item 7.

[26] (S) Unsgd copy of a paper headed, "*Action Recommended*, J.C.S. 152 - *Admiral Leahy's recommendations:*", CCS 381 (11-16-42). Existence of numerous similar papers on other subjects indicates that this was what Adm Leahy used during discussions at JCS meetings.

[27] (S) Notes on JCS 42nd Mtg, 17 Nov 42, "JCS 152," prepared by Col Lincoln, ABC 381 (9-25-41) sec III.

[28] (S) Mns, JPS 46th Mtg, 18 Nov 42, item 4.

[29] (S) Mns, CPS 38th Mtg, 26 Nov 42, item 2; (S) CPS 35/7, Note by Brit JPS, "Strategic Deployment of United States and British Forces as of April 1, 1944," 2 Dec 42, CCS 400.17 (7-6-42) sec 4; (S) Mns, CPS 40th Mtg, 3 Dec 42.

[30] (S) Mns, JCS 42nd Mtg, 17 Nov 42, item 8.

[31] (S) Mns, CPS 40th Mtg, 3 Dec 42, item 5; (S) Mns, CPS 41st Mtg, 4 Dec 42, item 1; (S) Mns, CPS 42nd Mtg, 17 Dec 42, item 2; (S) CPS 49/1, Rpt by Subcmte, "Planning for Operations Subsequent to 'TORCH,'" 27 Nov 42; (S) CPS 49/3, same subj, 8 Dec 42. All papers in CCS 381 (11-16-42).

[32] (S) JUSSC Dft of JCS 134/2, "U.S. War Production Objectives, 1942," 23 Nov 42, CCS 400.17 (7-6-42) sec 3. This statement was deleted for unknown reasons before the paper was presented to the JCS, but nevertheless it is a good illustration of the effects of top level action or inaction on those trying to work out the details of war planning. For fuller discussion of this paper, see (S) MS, JCS Hist, *Procurement and Allocation of Material Means*, pt I, ch II.

[33] (S) Mns, JCS 42nd Mtg, 17 Nov 42, item 8.

[34] (S) JCS 167, Rpt by JSSC, "Basic Strategic Concept for 1943," 11 Dec 42, CCS 381 (8-27-42) sec 2. In the succeeding pages the discussion concentrates on those portions of these papers which concerned the war against Japan. The discussion of the war against Germany, which in most instances was handled in greater detail in the papers themselves, is treated in (S) MS, JCS Hist, *War Against Germany and Its Satellites*, ch V.

[35] What apparently was the working draft copy bearing some handwritten corrections is in file CCS 381 (8-27-42) sec 1. A search of JSSC files on 17 Mar 50 failed to produce any others.

[36] Adm Leahy's concluding statement that there were many points in the statement of Gen Stratemeyer on which he could not agree is the only evidence that the general spoke.

[37] Just what Adm Leahy meant by the last statement is not too clear. It seems probable that he was questioning whether it might not be advisable to concentrate first on Japan, although the only comment he made on the war against Japan was to question why only "limited" operations were scheduled in Burma. On the other hand he also questioned whether the transfer of excess forces from Africa to the United Kingdom was acceptable strategy. Did this mean he was not so strongly opposed as were some of his colleagues to moving on into southern Europe? It is interesting to note that some time before this the President had suggested to the PM that the next move might well be made in Sardinia, Sicily, or southern Italy. See (S) MS, JCS Hist, *War Against Germany and Its Satellites*, ch V, pt 3.

[38] (S) JCS 167/1, Paper by JSSC, "Basic Strategic Concept for 1943," 26 Dec 42, CCS 381 (8-27-42) sec 1.

[39] (S) "Draft of Suggested Changes in J.C.S. 167/1," (Adm King), 22 Dec 42, CCS 381 (8-27-42) sec 1.

[40] (S) Mns, JCS 47th Mtg, Dec 42, item 9; (C) CCS 135, Memo by JCS, "Basic Strategic Concept for 1943," 26 Dec 42, CCS 381 (8-27-42) sec 1.

[41] (C) CCS 135/1, Memo by BCOS, "Basic Strategic Concept for 1943 - The European Theater," 2 Jan 43; (C) CCS 135/2, "American-British Strategy in 1943," 3 Jan 43. Both in CCS 381 (8-27-42) sec 1.

[42] Since these papers were both concerned primarily with the war against Germany, they are discussed at greater length in (S) MSS, JCS Hist, *War Against Germany and Its Satellites*, Ch V, as well as in *Evolution of Global Strategy*.

[43] (S) JCS 167/3, Rpt by JSSC, "Basic Strategic Concept for 1943," 5 Jan 43, CCS 381 (8-27-42) sec 1.

[44] (S) JCS 167/4, Ltr, JSSC to JCS, dtd 31 Dec 42, "Basic Strategic Concept for 1943 - Operations Subsequent to Torch," 10 Jan 43, CCS 381 (8-27-42) sec 1. JSSC recommended firmly that JCS "oppose any proposals to occupy Sardinia and Sicily during the year 1943."

[45] (S) Mns, JCS 49th Mtg, 5 Jan 43, item 10.

[46] (S) JPS 106, Rpt by JUSSC, "Basic Strategic Concept for 1943," 7 Jan 43, CCS 381 (8-27-42) sec 1.

[47] (S) JCS 167/5, Rpt by JSSC, "Basic Strategic Concept for 1943," 10 Jan 43, CCS 381 (8-27-42) sec 1.

[48] The comparison, in two sections, 20 and 12 pp., is in file CCS 381 (8-27-42) sec 1. Their authorship is not indicated.

[49] See ch VIII, pp. 186ff.

[50] (S) Memo, Arnold to CofS USA, "One Commander for the Pacific Theater," 6 Oct 42, OPD 384 (4-3-42). A penned note has been added: "OPD - G.C.M."

[51](S) Memo, Streett to Wedemeyer, "One Commander for the Pacific Theater," 9 Oct 42, OPD 384 (4-3-42).

[52](S) Memo, Wedemeyer to Streett, "Supreme Commander in the Pacific Theater," 11 Oct 42, OPD 384 (4-3-42).

[53](S) Memo, Streett to Handy, "Command in the Pacific," 31 Oct 42, OPD 384 PTO sec II.

[54](S) Memo, Marshall to Pres, "Situation in the South Pacific," 26 Oct 42, OPD 381 PTO sec III.

[55](SS) Msg, CominCh to CinCPac, ComSoPac, ComSoWesPac, 291906 Nov 42, WDCSA SWPA. John Miller, Jr., *Guadalcanal: The First Offensive* (Washington, 1949), p. 212.

[56](S) Memo, CofS USA to CominCh, "Proposed Joint Directive for Offensive Operations in the Southwest Pacific Area," 1 Dec 42, CCS 381 SWPA (7-10-42).

[57](S) Memo, no sig, "Efforts to Gain Unity of Command in the Pacific," 20 Feb 42, in Capt A.E. Smith's file "Mac #1," CNO(WPD). (Capt Smith's file has since been lost or destroyed.) Capts Glover and Smith of WPD had informed OPD by phone that the Navy was favorable toward Gen Marshall's suggestion and predicted that the joint directive would probably be sent on 3 or 4 Dec. (S) Memo for Rec, "Relief by Army Troops of MC Ground and Avn Units now on Garrison Duty in Samoan and the Hawaiian Area," 19 Dec 42, OPD 320.2 PTO (12-3-42).

[58](SS) Msg, CominCh to CinCPac and ComSoPac, 301915 Nov 42, (TS) CominCh file "CinCPac Despatches."

[59](SS) Msg, CinCPac to CominCh & ComSoPac, 020235 Dec 42, (TS) CominCh file "CinCPac Despatches."

[60](S) Memo, Cdr V.D. Long to Leahy, Marshall, Willson, Deane, "Future Operations in the Solomons Sea Area," 001515, FF1/A16-3(1), 15 Dec 42, encl cy CinCPac Ltr, 0259W, A16-3, 8 Dec 42, CCS 381 SWPA (7-10-42).

[61]Adm Nimitz summarized the situation in respect to amphibious forces:

1st Marine Division - now being removed from Guadalcanal, and will require until about March 1st to be ready again for active operations. It is being assigned to the Southwest Pacific Force. Whether it will be available for future operations in the Solomons is not known.

2nd Marine Division - two regiments now at Guadalcanal; will probably be relieved by the 25th Army Division; should be ready 1 February. One regiment in New Zealand which is probably ready now.

3rd Marine Division - should be ready as a division on 1 March; one regiment ready 1 January; another on 1 February.

Army Divisions - none in training, or even assigned, therefore none can be ready in less than three months.

[62](S) Memo, CofS USA to CominCh, "Strategic Direction of Operations in the Southwest Pacific," 21 Dec 42, OPD 381 SWPA sec II.

[63] (S) Ltr, CominCh-CNO to CofS USA, "Relief by Army Troops of Marine Corps Ground and Aviation Units now on Garrison duty in the Samoan and Hawaiian Areas," 3 Dec 42, 001463, WDCSA SWPA. The units included: 2 reinforced regiments, 7 defense battalions, 3 fighter squadrons, and 2 dive bomber squadrons.

[64] (S) Memo, CofS USA to CominCh-CNO, "Relief of Marine Corps troops in Samoa and Hawaii," 24 Dec 42, WDCSA SWPA.

[65] (S) JCS 97/7, "Deployment of U.S. Air Forces in the Pacific Theater," 21 Dec 42, CCS 381 (6-24-42) sec 2.

[66] (S) Mns, JCS 47th Mtg, 22 Dec 42, item 3.

[67] (S) JPS 48/4, "Deployment of U.S. Air Forces in the Pacific Theater," 6 Jan 42, CCS 381 (6-24-42) sec 2.

[68] (S) Mns, JPS 54th Mtg, 13 Jan 43, item 1.

[69] (S) JCS 97/8, "Deployment of U.S. Air Forces in the Pacific Theater," 16 Jan 43; (S) Memo, Capt Forrest B. Royal, JCS Dep Secy, to CofAS, Dep CofS USA, VCNO, same subj, 16 Feb 43. Both in CCS 381 (6-24-42) sec 2.

[70] (S) Prelim Dft Memo, King to CofS USA, "Strategic Direction of Operations in Southwest Pacific," dtd (in pencil) 23 Dec 42, OPD Exec 10, item 67B.

[71] (S) Memo, Handy to Conolly, 29 Dec 42, OPD 384 PTO.

[72] An undtd memo signed "AES[mith]" indicates that several draft replies were prepared in the Navy's WPD. One of these, dtd 30 Dec 42, was included with the memo. Apparently, however, it was not sent. Both documents are in CNO(WPD) file "A16-3(1) Unity of Command."

[73] (S) Ltr, King to Marshall, 6 Jan 43, (TS) CominCh file "Memos to Gen. Marshall - 15 Jan 43-15 Sep 44." The Navy recognized that the 2 Jul directive specified that Gen MacArthur would command Tasks Two and Three but was reluctant to change commands. Cdr R.E. Libby, Aide to Adm King, recommended just before the above memo was sent: "...if agreement of the Army to a modified directive satisfactory to us cannot be obtained, then our only recourse appears to be to insist that operations continue as an extension of Task One rather than passing to Task Two--an admittedly weak position for us to take in view of the specific statements of Tasks in the directive." (S) Memo, Libby to King, "Command Problem in South and Southwest Pacific," 4 Jan 43, (TS) CominCh file "Memos to Admiral - Sept. 42 - June 43."

[74] (S) Memo, CofS USA to CominCh, "Strategic Direction of Operations in the Southwest Pacific," 8 Jan 43, OPD 384 PTO sec II.

[75] (UNK) Ltr, King to Marshall, 8 Jan 43, (TS) CominCh file "Memos from Gen. Marshall 15 Jan 42-1 Sept 44." (S) Msg, CofS USA to SC SWPA, 192, 8 Jan 43, OPD 381 PTO sec III.

[76] For fuller discussion, see ch V.

[77] (S) Memo, ACofS (Handy) to CofS, "General DeWitt's Plan for Operations in Alaska," nd [c. 27 Jul 42], OPD 381 AGD sec 1.

[78] (S) Msg, CofS to CG WDC, 1578, CM-OUT-1651, 6 Aug 42; (S) Msg, CofS to CG ADC, 672, CM-OUT-2968, 10 Aug 42; (S) Memo,

Streett to Handy, 9 Sep 42; (S) Memo, R.L. Conolly, Actg ACofS (Plans) to Handy, 18 Dec 42. All in OPD 381 ADC sec 1.

[79] (S) Ltr, CofS USA to CominCh, "Amphibious Operations against Kiska," 17 Oct 42, OPD 381 ADC sec 1. (S) Memo, Lt. Gen S.D. Embick, Sen USA Mbr, PJBD, to CofS, "Garrisons in Alaska," 26 Nov 42; (S) Memo, Handy to CofS, "General DeWitt's Letters of 27 November and 5 December concerning Employment of the 44th Division and 184th Infantry in Connection with the Reduction of Boodle," 15 Dec 42. Both in OPD 381 ADC sec 2.

[80] (S) Memo, CominCh to CofS USA, "Direction to occupy Amchitka in order subsequently to expel Japanese from Kiska and all of Aleutians," 001514, 15 Dec 42; (S) Memo, CofS USA to CominCh, same subj, 16 Dec 42 (?). Both in OPD 381 ADC sec 2. (S) Memo, R.L. Conolly, Actg ACofS (Plans), to Handy, 18 Dec 42, OPD 381 ADC sec 1.

[81] (S) Memo, King to JCS, "Campaign against Japan via the Northern Route," 21 Sep 42, CCS 381 Japan (8-25-42) sec 1.

[82] (S) Memo, McDowell to Libby, "Campaign against Japan via the northern route," 22 Sep 42, (TS) CominCh file "Memos to Secretariat, Jan '42 to Oct '42."

[83] (S) JCS 182, Rpt by JPS, "Campaign against Japan via the Northern Route," 1 Jan 43, CCS 381 Japan (8-25-42) sec 2.

[84] (S) Mns, JCS 49th Mtg, 5 Jan 43, item 5.

[85] (S) JCS 180, Memo by CofS USA, "Bradley Mission," 27 Dec 42, CCS 373 U.S.S.R. (7-2-42).

[86] (S) Mns, JCS 48th Mtg, 29 Dec 42, item 1.

[87] (S) Msg, Bradley to CofS USA, 90, CM-IN-2940, 5 Oct 42, CCS 373 U.S.S.R. (7-2-42).

[88] (S) Memo, Leahy to Pres, "Survey of Air Force Facilities in the Far East," 30 Dec 42, CCS 373 U.S.S.R. (7-2-42).

[89] (Pers & Conf) Msg, Stalin to Pres, 5 Jan 43, CCS 373 U.S.S.R. (7-2-42).

[90] (S) Msg, Roosevelt to Stalin, 8 Jan 43, CCS 373 U.S.S.R. (7-2-42).

[91] (Priv & Conf) Msg, Stalin to Roosevelt, 13 Jan 43, CCS 373 U.S.S.R. (7-2-42); (S) Mns, JCS Sp Mtg (Anfa), 16 Jan 43; (S) Mns, JCS 53rd Mtg, 17 Jan 43.

[92] (S) Dft Msg (not used), Pres to Stalin, nd, OPD Exec 20, item 1. Attached to the draft is a pencilled note signed by Gen Handy: "File this. We may need it later in case they decide to get hard with Joe."

[93] (S) Mns, CCS 47th Mtg, 6 Nov 42, item 2. *See* ch X, pp. 239-240.

[94] (S) CPS 43/3, Rpt by Subcmte to CPS, "Plan for the Retaking of Burma," 15 Dec 42, CCS 381 Burma (8-25-42) sec 2.

[95] (S) Mns, CPS 42nd Mtg, 17 Dec 42, item 3.

[96] (S) CPS 43/5, "Plan for the Retaking of Burma," 23 Dec 42; (S) CPS 43/6, "Plan for the Retaking of Burma," 9 Jan 43. Both in CCS 381 Burma (8-25-42) sec 2. (S) Mns, CPS 43rd Mtg, 24 Dec 42, item 3; (S) Mns, CPS 44th Mtg, 14 Jan 43, item 2.

[97] Essentially the same operation was outlined in a radio sent to Gen Marshall in North Africa on 12 January. (S) Msg, "Anfi Casablanca Young" to Lt Col Frank McCarthy for Marshall, 6, CM-OUT-3941, 12 Jan 43, CCS 381 Burma (8-25-42) sec 2. Although it was stated that this was the minimum action which JPS felt could be accepted without completely abandoning land operations in north Burma. no mention of this is found in the JPS minutes.

CHAPTER XII

[1] On the fourth day of the conference Brig Gen John E. Hull and Col Charles K. Gailey of OPD joined Gen Wedemeyer and were helpful in the rest of the conference work. For further details of the organization of the conference and the attendance at the meetings, see (S) MS, JCS *Hist*, *Organizational Development*, ch XV.

[2] On 9 Nov 42 Brig Gen W.B. Smith reported to Gen Marshall that Mr. Churchill wanted Gen Marshall and possibly Adm King to come to London to discuss future strategy. (UNK) Msg, Smith to Marshall, 9 Nov 42, Hopkins Catalog, bk V, Torch, item 19.

[3] (S) Msg, BCOS to BJSM, Nr. C.O.S.(W)433, 7 Jan 43, CCS 381 (8-27-42) sec 1.

[4] The use of the codeword "Ravenous" on the JCS and CCS level is confusing. In this as in numerous other cases the records are not clear as to when the name was adopted or to just which form of operation it applied. It appears, however, that Ravenous, like Anakim, was a name originally adopted by the British to designate the British operations in southern Burma and the Chindwin Valley. The term was used loosely at Casablanca for both the purely British and the combined projects in various forms, all short of the full-scale operation to retake all of Burma which was Anakim.

[5] (S) Memo, CominCh-CNO to Sec CCS, "Agenda for SYMBOL Conference," 0052, 8 Jan 43, CCS 381 (8-27-42) sec 1. Gen Marshall's suggestions and two others from Adm King were combined with those of the BCOS and an agenda was issued as CCS 140 on 8 Jan 43.

[6] (S) Mns, JCS 50th Mtg (Casablanca), 13 Jan 43.

[7] (S) Mns, CCS 55th Mtg, 1030, 14 Jan 43. The official minutes of the JCS 51st meeting state that it was held at the same hour. Presumably, however, it preceded the CCS meeting.

[8] (S) Mns, CCS 56th Mtg, 1430, 14 Jan 43.

[9] (S) MNs, 2nd ANFA Mtg, 1700, 18 Jan 43, *Casablanca*, p. 144.

[10] (S) Mns, JCS 52nd Mtg, 16 Jan 43.

[11] (S) CCS 153, "Situation to be Created in the Eastern Theatre (Pacific and Burma) in 1943," 17 Jan 43, CCS 381 Eastern Theatre (1-17-43). The original cover sheet stated that "A" had been prepared by the U.S. JPS and "agreed to in principle by the British Joint Planning Staff," while "B" had "not been concurred in by the British." This was revised to state that "A" had been prepared by the U.S. JPS and "discussed at a meeting of the Combined Staff Planners," while "B" had merely been "prepared by the Joint U.S. Staff Planners." There is no recorded explanation of this change.

12(S) CCS 153/1, Memo by Brit JPS, "Situation to be Created in the Eastern Theatre (Pacific and Burma) in 1943," 17 Jan 43, CCS 381 Eastern Theatre (1-17-43).

13(S) Mns, JCS 54th Mtg, 18 Jan 43.

14(S) Mns, CCS 60th Mtg, 18 Jan 43.

15No copy of the original note has been found. In revised form, however, it was circulated as (S) CCS 155, "Conduct of the War in 1943," 18 Jan 43, CCS 381 (8-27-42) sec 1.

16(S) Mns, CCS 61st Mtg, 19 Jan 43, item 1.

17(S) CCS 155/1, Memo by CCS, "Conduct of the War in 1943," 19 Jan 43, CCS 381 (8-27-42) sec 2.

18(S) CCS 156, Note by Secys, "Suggested Procedure for Dealing with the Agenda of Conference," 18 Jan 43, CCS 381 (8-27-42) sec 2.

19See ch X, pp. 232ff.

20Gen Marshall estimated the chances of success with Ravenous at "better than fifty-fifty." (S) Mns, JCS Mtg w/Pres, 15 Jan 43, item 5.

21As has been noted, CCS 104/4 was not presented by the CPS in Washington until after the Casablanca discussions had begun and there is no evidence that the chiefs made any use of it. Nor was the minimum operation which the U.S. JPS had relayed by radio to Gen Marshall at Casablanca discussed.

22(S) Mns, CCS 59th Mtg, 17 Jan 43, item 1. Also (S) Mns, CCS 55th Mtg, 14 Jan 43; (S) JCS Mtg w/Pres, 15 Jan 43, item 5.

23(S) Mns, JCS 52nd Mtg, 16 Jan 43. Also (S) Mns, CCS 59th Mtg, 17 Jan 43, item 1.

24(S) Mns, JCS Mtg w/Pres, 15 Jan 43; (S) Mns, JCS Mtg w/Pres, 16 Jan 43.

25(S) Mns, JCS 53rd Mtg, 17 Jan 43.

26(S) Mns, CCS 59th Mtg, 17 Jan 43, item 1.

27(S) Mns, JCS 54th Mtg, 18 Jan 43; (S) Mns, Conf, King, Pound, Cunningham, 18 Jan 43, 1400, (TS) CominCh file "Memos to Admiral-Sept. '42-June '43."

28(S) CCS 154, "Operations in Burma, 1943," 17 Jan 43, CCS 381 Burma (8-25-42) sec 2.

29(U) Ltr, PM to War Cabinet, 20 Jan 43, *Hinge of Fate*, p. 683.

30(S) Mns, CCS 60th Mtg, 18 Jan 43.

31(S) Mns, CCS 65th Mtg, 21 Jan 43, item 4; (S) CCS 164, Rpt by Brit JPS, "Operation Anakim - Provision of Forces," 20 Jan 43; (S) CCS 164/1, same subj, rev of CCS 164, 21 Jan 43. Both in CCS 381 Burma (8-25-42) sec 3.

32(S) Mns, JCS Mtg w/Pres, 15 Jan 43, item 5.

33(S) Mns, JCS Mtg w/Pres, 16 Jan 43.

34(S) Mns, ANFA Plen Sess, 18 Jan 43.

35(S) Mns, 3rd Plen Sess, 23 Jan 43.

36Notes dictated by Mr. Hopkins of conversation with Gen Arnold at Casablanca, 19 Jan 43, Sherwood, p. 681.

37*Hinge of Fate*, p. 693.

38(S) CCS 170/2, "SYMBOL, Final Report to the President and Prime Minister," 23 Jan 43, *Casablanca*.

[39] (S) CCS 168, Memo by JCS, "Conduct of the War in the Pacific Theater in 1943," 22 Jan 43, CCS 381 Eastern Theatre (1-17-43).
[40] (S) Mns, CCS 67th Mtg, 22 Jan 43, item 1.
[41] *Ibid.*
[42] (S) CCS 170/1, Memo by CCS, "Report to the President and Prime Minister," 23 Jan 43, CCS 381 (8-27-42) sec 2.

CHAPTER XIII

[1] (S) Memo, Lt Col E.H. McDaniel to Brig Gen A.C. Wedemeyer, "Strategic Plan for Offensive Operations against Japan," 10 Aug 42, CCS 381 Japan (8-25-42) sec 1.
[2] Various working papers and correspondence in regard to the study are in CCS 381 Japan (8-25-42) sec 1. Outline is in (S) JIC 45/M, Request by JPS, "Strategic Plan for the Defeat of Japan, Estimate of the Situation," 28 Aug 42, CCS 381 Japan (8-25-42) sec 1.
[3] See ch XI, pp. 260-261.
[4] (S) JPS 67/2, Note by Secys, "Proposed Directive for a Campaign Plan for the Defeat of Japan," 4 Jan 43, CCS 381 Japan (8-25-42) sec 2.
[5] (S) OPD "Notes on JPS 53rd mtg, 6 Jan 43," ABC 381 Japan (8-27-42) sec 1.
[6] (S) Mns, JPS 53rd Mtg, 6 Jan 43, item 6.
[7] Col Maddocks had previously suggested in a memo to Adm Bieri that the over-all strategic study be *substituted* for JPS 67/2. (S) Memo, Maddocks to Bieri, 10 Jan 43, ABC 381 Japan (8-27-42) sec 1.
[8] (S) Mns, JPS 54th Mtg, 13 Jan 43, item 6.
[9] (S) (Ltd Dist) JPS 67/3, Rpt by JUSSC, "Operations in the South and Southwest Pacific Areas during 1943," 15 Feb 43, CCS 381 Japan (8-25-42) sec 2.
[10] Japan was estimated to have 132,000 troops in the Solomons-New Guinea-Arafura Sea-Banda Sea area and 60,000 more en route. Air strength was estimated at 547 planes. Naval strength was limited only by escort requirements and the needs of the home islands for defense.
[11] (S) Mns, JPS 60th Mtg, 17 Feb 43, item 3; (S) Mns, JPS 61st Mtg, 24 Feb 43, item 4.
[12] (S) Msg, CominCh to CinCPac, 022100 Jul 42, CCS 381 (1-24-42) sec 2 pt 1.
[13] (UNK) Ltr, King to Marshall, 8 Jan 43, (TS) CominCh file "Memos from Gen. Marshall 15 Jan '42 - 1 Sept '44."
[14] (S) Msg, Marshall to MacArthur, 164, CM-OUT-2273, 7 Jan 43, in OPD Msg files, TS OUT, 1 Jan 43-30 Apr 43; (S) Msg, Marshall to MacArthur, 192, 8 Jan 43, OPD 381 PTO sec 3.
[15] I.e., Gen Marshall and Adm King. Gen Arnold had gone on to India and China.
[16] (SS) Msg, MacArthur-Ghormley to CominCh-CofS, 081012 Jul 42, (TS) CominCh file "ComSoWestPac Despatches-Jan '42 thru Dec '43."
[17] (S) Msg, MacArthur to CofS, C-251, CM-IN-12553, 27 Jan 43, CCS 381 SWPA (7-10-42).

[18] (S) Memo, King to Marshall, "Operations in SW Pacific for Prosecution of Rabaul Campaign," 00240, 6 Feb 43, OPD 381 PTO sec 3.

[19] (S) Memo, Cdr V.D. Long, USN, Aide to King, to Leahy, Marshall, Willson, Deane, "Future Operations in the Solomons Sea Area," 001515, A16-3(1), 15 Dec 42, encl Ltr, CinCPac to CominCh, 8 Dec 42, CCS 381 SWPA (7-10-42).

[20] (SS) Msg, ComSoPac to ComSoWesPac, info CominCh, 170510 Dec 42, (SC) CominCh file "A16-3(4)-File #1, Warfare Operations, SWPac 1943."

[21] (SS) Msg, CominCh to ComSoPac, 182159 Dec 42, (SC) CominCh file "A16-4(4)-File #1, Warfare Operations, SWPac 1943."

[22] Several draft operational plans and memoranda on possible operations in the Gilbert and Ellice Islands were formerly in Capt A.E. Smith's file, "Mac #1," in Navy Plans Division. That file has, however, disappeared and seems to have been destroyed. Several papers on the subject are in WPD file "n," Pacific, safe 184, NR&H. See also, (S) memo, Col F.A. Hart, USMC, to ACofS (Plans), "Estimated Forces for Gilbert Islands Plan and Logistics Therefore," 9 Feb 43, CNO(WPD) folder #1, "Future Plans Section Memos," safe 183, NR&H.

[23] Before war began, Capt C.J. Moore, USN, of Navy WPD had recommended fortification of Makin, but his proposal was turned down. Conv, RAdm C.J. Moore with author, 29 Jan 52.

[24] (SS) Msg, CominCh to ComSoPac, 092200 Feb 43, (TS) CominCh file "CinCPac Despatches."

[25] (SS) Msg, ComSoPac to CominCh info CinCPac, 110421 Feb 43, (TS) CominCh file "ComSoPacFor Despatches, Jan 43-May 43."

[26] (UNK) Msg, CinCPac to CominCh, 112237 Feb 43, quoted in Memo, ACofS(Plans) to King, 12 Feb 43, CNO(WPD) file "Pacific."

[27] (SS) Msg, CominCh to CinCPac info ComSoPac, 131250 Feb 43, in Navy WPD, Capt Smith's file, "Mac #1," now missing.

[28] (SS) Msg, ComSoPac to CominCh, 170617 Feb 43, in Navy WPD, Capt Smith's file, "Mac #1," now missing.

[29] (S) Msg, MacArthur to Marshall, C-447, CM-IN-7418, 15 Feb 43, CCS 381 SWPA (7-10-42).

[30] (S) Memo, CofS USA to CominCh, "Operations in the Southwest Pacific for Prosecution of Rabaul Campaign," 17 Feb 43, OPD 381 PTO sec 3. Apparently Adm King was out of town or otherwise occupied when Gen MacArthur's message came in, for the proposal was discussed by the Army and Navy staffs and a joint despatch sent out before Gen Marshall informed Adm King of it in this memo.

[31] (S) Memo, King to Marshall, "Development of Operations in South-Southwest Pacific," 00313, 18 Feb 43, OPD 381 PTO sec 3.

[32] (S) Memo, CofS USA to CominCh, "Development of Operations in South-Southwest Pacific," 19 Feb 43, OPD 381 PTO sec 3.

[33] Discussion of the problem continued in Navy WPD, although no solution was reached. Not all of the planners shared Adm King's views in the matter. A memo by Capt A.E. Smith, "Effort

to Gain Unity of Command in the Pacific," 20 Feb 43, in CNO(WPD) file "Pacific," for example, pointed out that the Army had been consistent in holding to unity of command under the SC SWPA, for Tasks Two and Three. However, "CominCh's position has been regularly inconsistent. When it came time to execute Task Two, General Marshall sent over a directive copied from 022100 July and giving General MacArthur command for Task Two. AC/S (Plans) sent it to Admiral King with his concurrence. Admiral King did not approve and since that time none of CominCh's proposals have been acceptable to the Army." Adm Edwards, Deputy CominCh, in an undated memo at this same time (CNO(WPD) file "Pacific") advised Adm King that the JCS "had better keep control of matters involving SOPac and SWPac joint-ly [sic]." To this advice, Adm King indicated agreement.

[34] (S) Mns of all six meetings, including lists of officers attending, are filed in CCS 334 Pacific Military Con. (3-12-43).

[35] (S) Mns, PMC 1st Mtg, 12 Mar 43, 1030.

[36] (S) Mns, PMC 3rd Mtg, 13 Mar 43.

[37] (S) PMC 1, Note by Secys, "'ELKTON' Plan," 11 Mar 43, encl Plan dtd 28 Feb 43, CCS 381 (2-28-43) sec 1.

[38] (S) Mns, PMC 2nd Mtg, 12 Mar 43, 1430; (S) Memo, ACofS (Plans) to King, "Procedure for Pacific-Southwest Pacific Conference," 12 Mar 43, (TS) CominCh file #35, "Asst Chief of Staff (Plans-F-1)."

[39] (S) Memo, ACofS Handy to Pacific Conferees, "Deployment of Forces," 13 Mar 43, CCS 381 (2-28-43) sec 2.

[40] The figures were listed as "planned initial equipment strength." Replacements were to be planned at the rate of 20 per cent of initial equipment per month, except for transports, which were to be replaced as required. In most types of planes there was no change in the numbers listed for the three succeeding quarters of the year.

[41] A study submitted to JPS by a subcommittee on the same day, 13 Mar 43, listed 487, 728, and 850 U.S. Army planes for the Central, South, and Southwest Pacific Areas, respectively, as of 1 Jan 44. The paper was not approved. (S) JPS 142, "Strategic Deployment of U.S. Forces for 1943," 13 Mar 43, CCS 381 (2-8-43) sec 1.

[42] (S) JCS 218, Rpt by JSSC, "Personnel and Deployment" 12 Feb 43, CCS 320.2 (2-4-43) sec 1; (S) Mns, JCS 62nd Mtg, 16 Feb 43, item 7.

[43] (S) Mns, PMC 3rd Mtg, 13 Mar 43.

[44] (S) Memo, Sutherland and Harmon to JPS, 14 Mar 43, CCS 381 (2-28-43) sec 2.

[45] (S) CCS 155/1, Memo by CCS, "Conduct of the War in 1943," 19 Jan 43, *Casablanca*, p. 18.

[46] See above, p. 317.

[47] Papers relating to this are filed in CCS 452 (8-27-42) secs 1 and 2. See also (S) MS, JCS Hist, *Evolution of Global Strategy*.

823 NOTES TO CHAPTER XIII

⁴⁸These figures were taken from a paper prepared by the Air Forces planners, (S) AWPD-42, "Requirements for Air Ascendancy," 9 Sep 42, Tab B-4-a, cy in files of SecWar, DRB AGO. The figures for the South Pacific Area given by Adm Cooke include some naval planes attached to the South Pacific Area and both Army and Navy planes assigned to "Pacific Attack Forces." In light bombers, however, these add up to 536 rather than 576 as quoted at the PMC meeting.

⁴⁹(S) Memo, RAdm Cooke to Pacific Conferees, "Availability of Navy Forces," 13 Mar 43, CCS 381 (2-28-43) sec 2.

⁵⁰Why Gen Anderson was not to have a hand in this is not clear, unless it was felt that more progress would be made without the possibility of reopening the discussion just concluded.

⁵¹(S) JCS 238, Memo by JPS, "Plan for Operations for the Seizure of the Solomon Islands-New Guinea-New Britain-New Ireland Area," 16 Mar 43, CCS 381 (2-28-43) sec 2.

⁵²(S) (Ltd Dist) Suppl Mns, JCS 66th Mtg, 16 Mar 43, item 1.

⁵³(S dg U) JCS 238/1, Rpt by JPS, "Plan for Operations for the Seizure of the Solomon Islands-New Guinea-New Britain-New Ireland Area," 18 Mar 43, CCS 381 (2-28-43) sec 2.

⁵⁴(S) (Ltd Dist) Mns, JCS 67th Mtg, 19 Mar 43, item 1.

⁵⁵Adm Cooke said that since the problem related primarily to allocations of Army ground and air forces the Army representatives had set forth two proposals in the matter. An otherwise unidentified paper, entitled "Outline History of Pacific Military Conference," in Capt A.E. Smith's file, "Mac #1," formerly in the Navy War Plans Division, remarked of this: "The Army was...very definitely opposed to allocating any more planes to the South West Pacific or the South Pacific. Eventually, through devious means, the Navy Staff Planner was able to get before the JCS three plans for additional allocations of aircraft and troops."

⁵⁶As in numerous other instances the official minutes of this meeting are not complete and the approval is simply listed at the end as a *fait accompli*, without indication of how the decision was reached. The "Outline History of Pacific Military Conference" (see fn. 55) enlarges on this a bit:

> ...The Joint Chiefs of Staff accepted the plan which gave the greatest increase in air. General Stratemeyer, who represented General Arnold in the latters [sic] absence, did not concur. The Army Staff Planner had recommended the acceptance of the least reinforcements. The conference was satisfactory up to this point from the Navy viewpoint.

⁵⁷(SS dg U) Memo, Sutherland, Spruance, and Browning to JCS, "Offensive Operations in the South and Southwest Pacific Areas during 1943," 20 Mar 43, circ as JCS 238/2, CCS 381 (2-28-43) sec 2.

⁵⁸(S) (Ltd Dist) Mns, JCS 68th Mtg, 21 Mar 43, item 1.

⁵⁹Conv, Col E.H. McDaniel with author, 12 Feb 52.

⁶⁰(SS) Memo, CominCh-CNO to CofS USA, "Operations Against Attu," 22 Mar 43, OPD 381 Security, sec II, case #54.

61 (S) Memo, Handy to King, 22 Mar 43, OPD 381 Security, sec II, case #54.

62 (SS) Memo, King to Marshall, "Offensive Operations in the Solomons-New Guinea Area," 19 Mar 43; (SS) Memo, Cooke to King, 19 Mar 43. Both in (TS) CominCh file "Memos to Gen. Marshall-15 Jan 42-1 Sept 44."

63 (SS) Memo, Cooke to Wedemeyer, 22 Mar 43, encl Dft Dir, OPD Exec 2, item 1a, tab O. In the same file (tab M) is a draft identified as Army Proposal #1, dtd 20 Mar 43. There is no indication, however, that this was submitted to the Navy for comment.

64 (SS) Memo, Cooke to Handy, 22 Mar 43, encl Dft Dir, OPD Exec 2, item 1a, tab K.

65 (SS) Memo, Cooke to Handy, "Command in the Pacific," 23 Mar 43, OPD Exec 2, item 1a.

66 (SS) Memo, Cooke to Handy, 24 Mar 43, encl Dft Dir, OPD Exec 2, item 1a, tab H.

67 (SS dg U) Memo, King to JCS, "Directive for Operations in the South and Southwest Pacific," 27 Mar 43, CCS 381 (2-28-43) sec 2. No known copy of this has indication of the date on which it was prepared or submitted. Consequently it might be supposed that it was not drafted until later and was modeled on Gen Marshall's draft. However, a comparison of the Army's three proposed directives with the Navy versions of the same alternatives, indicating the origin of each, shows clearly that Gen Marshall's was a modification of the Navy directive to give command to CinCPOA. Doc filed with (S) Memo, Handy to Cooke 25 Mar 43, OPD Exec 2, item 1a, tab G.

68 (S) Memo, Handy to Cooke, 25 Mar 43, OPD Exec 2, item 1a, tab G.

69 (S) Memo, no sig [Cooke?] to Handy, 25 Mar 43, OPD Exec 2, item 1a, tab G; (SS) Memo, ACofS(Plans) to King, 25 Mar 43, (TS) CominCh file "Memos to Admiral - Sept. '42 - June '43." Adm Cooke remarked that the directive was not susceptible to patching, but at Gen Handy's urging he had indicated some of the unsatisfactory parts, "but always telling him that this directive is not satisfactory in any case."

70 (S) Memo, Marshall to JCS, "Directive," 26 Mar 43, CCS 381 (2-28-43) sec 2.

71 (SS) Memo, Deane to King, "Directive for Operations in the South and Southwest Pacific," 27 Mar 43; (SS) Memo, Deane to Marshall, "Proposed directive for operations in the South and Southwest Pacific," 27 Mar 43. Both in CCS 381 (2-28-43) sec 2.

72 (SS dg U) App "B" to JCS 238/4, "Plan for Operations for the Seizure of the Solomon Islands-New Guinea-New Britain-New Ireland Area," 27 Mar 43, CCS 381 (2-28-43) sec 2.

73 *Ibid.*, App "C."

74 (SS) Mns, JCS 70th Mtg, 28 Mar 43.

75 (SC) Msg, JCS to MacArthur, Nimitz, Halsey, CM-OUT-11091, 11092, 11093, 29 Mar 43, CCS 381 (2-28-43) sec 2.

[76] An otherwise unidentified document entitled "Outline History of Pacific Military Conference," formerly in the file of Capt A.E. Smith, Navy WPD, included the closing statement:

> I have come to the conclusion that Admiral King considers his relations with General Marshall of such a successful plan in the conduct of the war that there are some matters in which he will not proceed to their logical accomplishment believing that even if he succeeded he would damage the relationship mentioned beyond repair. One of these items is the unification of command in the CinCPac including the efforts of General MacArthur up the New Guinea coast.

CHAPTER XIV

[1] (S) CCS 155/1, Memo by CCS, "Conduct of the War in 1943," 19 Jan 43, *Casablanca*.

[2] Cf. (S) MSS, JCS Hist, *Evolution of Global Strategy* and *War Against Germany and Its Satellites*.

[3] (S) Mns, CCS 60th Mtg, 18 Jan 43, item 1.

[4] (S) Mns, CCS 65th Mtg, 21 Jan 43, item 4; (S) CCS 170/2, Final Rpt to Pres and PM, "Symbol," 23 Jan 43, *Casablanca*.

[5] When Sir John Dill reported on the trip to the CCS he said that they had gone "armed with clear instructions approved by the President and Prime Minister as to the extent and importance of operations in Burma." (S) Suppl Mns, CCS 72nd Mtg, 19 Feb 43, item 5. No written instructions have been found by the author. For more detailed account of the discussions, see Romanus-Sunderland, *Stilwell's Mission*, pp. 272-277.

[6] (S) USB 7, Mns, 1st Mtg, New Delhi, 1 Feb 43, Encl to CCS Info Memo 43, 22 Feb 43, CCS 381 Burma (8-25-42) sec 3 pt 1. Since the minutes of all the meetings are enclosed with the same memo, it will not subsequently be cited. (U) Ltr, Pres to Gimo, 25 Jan 43; *Global Mission*, p. 415.

[7] (S) JPS No. 47, Summary, nd, CCS 381 Burma (8-25-42) sec 3 pt 1.

[8] (S) USB 7, Mns, 1st Mtg, 1 Feb 43, CCS 381 Burma (8-25-42) sec 3 pt 1. Gen Arnold is recorded as saying that it was to prepare for direct attack on Japan from China, "and also to avoid a prolonged advance from island to island in the Pacific, that the Burma plan had been given priority; and he felt that it was now only necessary to state clearly what was required for the resources to be made available." This very optimistic view seems ill-supported by the agreement as stated at Casablanca.

[9] *Ibid*. British officers attending were FM Wavell, FM Dill, RAdm A.F.E. Palliser, Lt Gen E.L. Morris, Air Marshal J.E.C. Baldwin. U.S. officers were Gen Arnold, Brig Gen C. Bissell, Brig Gen B.G. Ferris, Col J.E. Smart.

[10] Gen Stilwell expressed disappointment at the slow rate at which the Chinese divisions for the Yunnan group were being assembled despite his strong urging that the Generalissimo get on with the program. Because of the status of that project,

826   NOTES TO CHAPTER XIV

Gen Stilwell reported, his original plan for an offensive of some weight in the spring would have to be modified to very limited action. (S) Memo, Stilwell to Gimo, 28 Jan 43 (cy in JCS HS files.)

[11] Maj Gen R.A. Wheeler, in charge of the construction of the Ledo Road, indicated that he hoped that before serious raids began the road would reach within thirty miles of Shingbwiyang

[12] FM Wavell explained that the British IV Corps would advance via the roads to Imphal and Tiddim and it might be possible to attack the Kalewa-Kalemyo area from both places by the end of March or the beginning of April.

[13] *The Campaign in Burma* (HMSO, London, 1946), prepared for SEAC by Central Office of Information, pp. 31-32.

[14] (S) USB 22, "Decisions taken at the American-British Conferences held on February 1, 2, 3, 1943," CCS 381 Burma (8-25-42) sec 3 pt 1.

[15] (S) USB 9, Mns, 2nd Mtg, 2 Feb 43, CCS 381 Burma (8-25-42) sec 3 pt 1.

[16] (S) CCS Info Memo 44, "Chinese-British-American Conferences," 22 Feb 43, CCS 381 Burma (8-25-42) sec 3 pt 1. At this meeting only Chiang, Gen Arnold, Mr. Soong, and Col L.R. Parker were present. The subsequent meetings, minutes of which are included in the same Info Memo, were attended by various of the following in addition: FM Dill and Maj Gen Grimsdale, British; Gens Stilwell, Wedemeyer, Bissell, and Chennault, American; Gens Ho Yingchin, Chow, and Mo, Chinese.

[17] (S) CCS Info Memo 45, "Chinese-British-American Conference, Calcutta, India, February 9, 1943," 22 Feb 43, CCS 381 Burma (8-25-42) sec 3 pt 1.

[18] (MS) Msg, Wavell to BCOS, info CinCEF, BJSM, 10 Feb 43, CCS 381 Burma (8-25-42) sec 3.

[19] (S) Memo, JCS Secy Deane to ACofS OPD & Aide to ComInCh, "Operation Anakim," 12 Feb 43, CCS 381 Burma (8-25-42) sec 3.

[20] (SC) Msg, Wedemeyer to Marshall, eyes only, CM-IN-8057, 16 Feb 43, CCS 381 Burma (8-25-42) sec 3.

[21] (S) Suppl Mns, CCS 72nd Mtg, 19 Feb 43, item 5.

[22] *Global Mission*, pp. 407-409. Except for the minutes of the meetings, Gen Arnold, FM Dill, and Gen Somervell made no written report or comment to the CCS.

[23] See ch IX, pp. 221-223.

[24] *Ibid.*

[25] See ch X, p. 246.

[26] (S) Memo, Actg CofS McNarney to CG AAF, "Separate Air Force in China," c. 16 Jan 43. Gen McNarney was replying to a memo received from Gen Arnold commenting on the President's suggestion and recommending "that the principle of the establishment of a separate air force in China with an assigned mission be accepted." (S) Memo, CG AAF to CofS USA, "Establishment and Assignment of Mission to Separate Air Force in China," 6 Jan 43. Both in (SS) WDCSA 381 China.

[27] (U) Ltr, Pres to Gimo, 25 Jan 43, *Global Mission*, p. 415.

28(S) Memos, Arnold to Stilwell, "Air Transport Command Operations India to China," "Operations of Heavy Bombers in China," "Aid to Chinese Air Force," 7 Feb 43, OPD Exec 10, item 58.

29(S) Memo, CG AAF to CofS USA, "Establishment and Assignment of Mission to Separate Air Force in China," 6 Jan 43, (SS) WDCSA 381 China.

30See ch X.

31All above discussion in (S) CCS Info Memo 44, "Chinese-British-American Conferences," 22 Feb 43, CCS 381 Burma (8-25-42) sec 3 pt 1.

32(S) Ltr, Gimo to Pres, 7 Feb 43, OPD Exec 10, item 58.

33(S) Msg, Marshall to Stilwell, eyes only, 2170, CM-OUT-6939, 19 Feb 43, OPD Msg file, TS OUT, 1 Jan 43-30 Apr 43. Details of how the decision was made have not been discovered. Gen Marshall informed Gen Stilwell: "As Arnold forecast to you, the Chennault situation has come to a head. Decision has been made..."

34(S) Memo, CofS to Pres, "Chinese Theater," 22 Feb 43, encl Dft Msg, Pres to Gimo, (SS) WDCSA 381 China.

35(S) Memo, Leahy to Marshall and Arnold, 24 Feb 43, (SS) WDCSA 381 China.

36(S) Memo, Marshall to Pres, "Reply to Generalissimo's Memorandum," 27 Feb 43, CCS 400.3295 China (3-17-42) sec 2.

37(S) Msg, Pres to Gimo, 6 Mar 43, CCS 091.711 China (1-20-42) sec 2.

38(UNK) Ltrs, Joseph Alsop to Harry Hopkins, 1, 3, 5, 26 Mar 43; (C) Ltr, Soong to Hopkins, 25 Mar 43. All in Hopkins Catalog, bk VII, Chinese Affairs (5).

39(S) Memo, Marshall to Pres, 18 Feb 43, (SS) WDCSA 381 China.

40(S) Memo, Pres to Marshall, 8 Mar 43, OPD Exec 10, item 58.

41(S) Memo, Marshall to Pres, "Your note to me of March 8th reference China," 16 Mar 43, (SS) WDCSA 381 China.

42(S) Msg, Marshall to Stilwell, 2373, 27 Mar 43, CofS Log, Mar 43. The reason for Gen Marshall's delay in sending the word to Gen Stilwell is not known. Nor has record been found of the occasion of the President's stipulation.

43Gen Stilwell interpreted this to mean 3/8 of the tonnage delivered and he was not told otherwise. (S) Msg, Stilwell to Marshall, AG 271, CM-IN-16733, 31 Mar 43. OPD Exec 10, item 22.

44(UNK) Ltr, J. Alsop to Hopkins, 26 Mar 43, Hopkins Catalog, bk VII, Chinese Affairs (5).

45C) Ltr, T.V. Soong to Hopkins, 25 Mar 43, Hopkins Catalog, bk VII, Chinese Affairs (5) item 31.

46(S) Memo, Marshall to Pres, 10 Apr 43, (SS) WDCSA 381 China.

47(SS) Memo, CofS to Pres, "The Generalissimo's request for Chennault to report to Washington," 12 Apr 43, (SS) WDCSA 381 China.

48(S) Memo, Pres to CofS, 12 Apr 43; (S) Msg, Marshall to Stilwell, eyes only, 2498, CM-OUT-5624, 14 Apr 43. Both in (SS) WDCSA 381 China. Gen Marshall informed Gen Stilwell that the President had refused to include Gen Bissell, but did not say why.

828 NOTES TO CHAPTER XIV

[49] (S) Suppl Mns, CCS 73rd Mtg, 26 Feb 43, item 7.
[50] (S) Suppl Mns, CCS 74th Mtg, 5 Mar 43, item 2. For detailed discussion of Husky and its conflicting demands, see (S) MS, JCS Hist, *War Against Germany and Its Satellites*, ch VIII, pt A.
[51] (S) Mns, CCS 73rd Mtg, 26 Feb 43, item 9; (S) CCS 183, Note by Secys, "Review of the Availability of United Nations Shipping," 28 Feb 43, CCS 540 (2-28-43).
[52] (S) CCS 183/1, Memo by RBCOS, "Review of the Availability of United Nations Shipping," 12 Mar 43, CCS 540 (2-28-43).
[53] (S) Suppl Mns, CCS 75th Mtg, 12 Mar 43, item 6.
[54] (S) Mns, CMTC 61st Mtg, 15 Mar 43, item 1. Maj Gen Charles P. Gross discussed at some length the U.S. Army's views of what shipping was to be provided to the British. Initially, it had been understood (by the Army) that the U.S. contribution would be limited to replacement of British losses. At Casablanca, shipping allocations and operational plans had been based on this assumption. Since Casablanca, however, the British import program had come to the fore and it had been assumed that thirty sailings a month would be required. By mid-March it was more apparent that the British wanted a firm figure of 7 million tons of cargo for the year. The CSAB, it appeared, was planning for U.S. aid to the British import program on that basis. This, the British representatives hastened to point out, was based on a letter from the President to the Prime Minister on 30 Nov, in which he had assured "that sufficient American tonnage would be made available out of U.S. shipbuilding to meet U.K. imports, the supply and maintenance of the British Armed [sic] forces and other services essential to maintaining the war effort of the British Commonwealth to the extent that they cannot be transported by the fleet under British control." The discussion at this meeting showed clearly that U.S. and British members had different understandings of what had been decided at Casablanca, what was agreed in the first place, and what the current basis for allocation of U.S. shipping was. It was finally decided to assume that 7 million tons were to be furnished to the British and to estimate the implications of supplying that amount.
[55] (S) CCS 183/2, Rpt by CMTC, "Review of the Availability of United Nations Shipping," 18 Mar 43, CCS 540 (2-28-43).
[56] (S) Mns, CCS 76th Mtg, 19 Mar 43, item 5.
[57] (SS) JCS 243, Rpt by JSSC, "Survey of Present Strategic Situation," 23 Mar 43, CCS 381 (8-27-42) sec 2.
[58] (SS) JCS 243/1, Rpt by JSSC, "Survey of Present Strategic Situation," 25 Mar 43, CCS 381 (8-27-42) sec 2.
[59] (S) Suppl Mns, JCS 69th Mtg, 23 Mar 43, item 10.
[60] (SS dg C) JCS 243/2, Memo by CominCh-CNO, "Survey of Present Strategic Situation," 27 Mar 43, CCS 381 (8-27-42) sec 2.
[61] (S) Suppl Mns, JCS 71st Mtg, 30 Mar 43, item 7.
[62] Cf. (S) MS, JCS Hist, *War Against Germany and Its Satellites*, ch III.
[63] (SS) Memo, Marshall to Handy, 30 Mar 43, ABC 384 Burma (8-25-42) sec II.

[64] *Ibid.*

[65] (S) Memo, Handy to Marshall, "Anakim vs. Bolero," 31 Mar 43, OPD Exec 10, item 57.

[66] (S) Memo, Marshall to King and Leahy, 3 Apr 43, OPD (SS) 381 Security sec II, case 75. No minutes of such a meeting have been found. In the covering memo to Adms King and Leahy, Gen Marshall said, "Apropos of our discussion of yesterday afternoon and the information that the President had already dispatched a message regarding Anakim to the Prime Minister, herewith is the final draft of my memorandum to him on the subject." Since reference is made in the draft to the President's comments the preceding day, it may be assumed that Gen Marshall, Adm Leahy, and Adm King had met with him. There is no indication of Gen Arnold's presence or absence. No copy of the President's message to the Prime Minister nor clear indication of its contents has been found.

[67] (S) Memo, Leahy to Marshall, 3 Apr 43, OPD (SS) 381 Security sec II.

[68] (SS) Memo, King to Marshall, 3 Apr 43, OPD (SS) 381 Security sec II.

[69] (SS) Memo, Marshall to Pres, 3 Apr 43, OPD (SS) 381 Security sec II.

[70] (TS) Msg, PM to Pres, c. 6 Apr 43, OPD (SS) Security sec II. For full discussion of the message, see (S) MS, JCS Hist, *War Against Germany and Its Satellites*, ch VIII, pt A, pp. 127-138.

[71] (S) Mns, Sp JCS Mtg w/Pres and Hopkins, 6 Apr 43, item 2.

[72] Of Adm Leahy the minutes record only that he "pointed out that whether the operation was a success or not it was bound to divert considerable Japanese forces from the South and the Southwest Pacific."

[73] The reason for inclusion of the Aleutians is not clear.

[74] (S) Memo, Macready to Marshall, 13 Apr 43, (S) WDCSA Anakim. The committee's report has not been seen by the author.

[75] (SS dg R) JCS 260, Dft Memo, JCS to CCS, "Status of Anakim," 12 Apr 43, CCS 381 Burma (8-25-42) sec 3.

[76] (SS dg U) JCS 253, Memo from CG AAF, "Allocation of Aircraft to the India-China-Burma Theater," 6 Apr 43, CCS 381 Burma (8-25-42) sec 3.

[77] (S) Suppl Mns, JCS 74th Mtg, 13 Apr 43, item 2.

[78] (SS dg R) CCS 198, Memo by JCS, "Status of 'Anakim' (Allocation of Aircraft)," 13 Apr 43; (SS dg R) CCS 198/1, Memo by JCS, "Status of 'Anakim,'" 13 Apr 43. Both in CCS 381 Burma (8-25-42) sec 3.

[79] (MS) Ltr, Macready to Marshall, 13 Apr 43, (S) WDCSA Anakim.

[80] (S) Suppl Mns, CCS 80th Mtg, 16 Apr 43, item 7.

[81] (S) Memo, Leahy to RBCOS, "C.C.S. Conference with Commanders of India-Burma-China Theaters," 19 Apr 43, CCS 381 Burma (8-25-42) sec 3.

[82] (SS) JCS 243/3, Rpt by JSSC, "Survey of Present Strategic Situation," 9 Apr 43, CCS 381 (8-27-42) sec 2.

[83] (S) JCS 243/4, Rpt by JSSC, "Survey of Present Strategic Situation," 26 Apr 43, CCS 381 (8-27-42) sec 2.

[84](S) Suppl Mns, JCS 74th Mtg, 13 Apr 43, item 4; (SS dg S) CCS 199, Memo by JCS, "Survey of Present Strategic Situation," 13 Apr 43, CCS 381 (8-27-42) sec 2.

[85](S) Suppl Mns, CCS 81st Mtg, 23 Apr 43, item 5.

[86]Published as (SS dg S) CCS 199/1, Memo by RBCOS, "Survey of Present Strategic Situation," 23 Apr 43, CCS 381 (8-27-42) sec 2.

[87](S) JCS 243/4, Rpt by JSSC, "Survey of Present Strategic Situation," 26 Apr 43, CCS 381 (8-27-42) sec 2.

[88](S) Suppl Mns, JCS 76th Mtg, 27 Apr 43, item 3; (SS dg S) CCS 199/2, Memo from JCS, "Survey of Present Strategic Situation," 27 Apr 43, CCS 381 (8-27-42) sec 2.

[89](S) Suppl Mns, CCS 82nd Mtg, 30 Apr 43, item 8.

[90]At the JCS 76th mtg, 27 Apr, Gen Marshall "raised the question as to what effect a controversy regarding an interpretation of the Casablanca decisions would have on the next conference. He indicated that it might be well to refrain from a 'preliminary skirmish' if it would weaken our position in the conference that was to come."

CHAPTER XV

[1](S) Mns, JCS 78th Mtg, 8 May 43, item 5.

[2]For a more detailed account of the origin and development of the JWPC, see (S) Davis, *Organizational Development*, vol II, ch XI, and various papers in file CCS 334 JSPG (4/23/43) sec 1. The Senior Team at the outset consisted of Capt C.J. Moore, USN, Col J. Smith, USAAF, and Col W.W. Bessell, USA. Whether the JWPC knew from the beginning that the conference was likely to be held before summer is not clear from the records.

[3]The date seems to have been fixed as a result of a message from the Prime Minister to the President on 29 Apr in which he reported that he thought he could manage to get to Washington by 11 May. *Hinge of Fate*, p. 783. For more detailed discussion of how and why the decision was made, see (S) MSS, JCS Hist, *Evolution of Global Strategy* and *War Against Germany and Its Satellites*, ch VIII, pt C.

[4](S) Memo, Jt Secys JWPC to Secy JPS, "J.W.P.C.-3, Agenda for Next United Nations Conference," 24 Apr 43; (S) JWPC 3, "Agenda for Next United Nations Conferences," 24 Apr 43; (S dg R) JCS 272, Rpt by JCS, "Agenda for Next United Nations Conference," 26 Apr 43. All in CCS 381 (4-24-43) sec 1 pt 1.

[5](S) OPD "Notes on JCS 76th mtg, 26 April 1943," ABC 337 (26 Apr 43).

[6](S) Suppl Mns, JCS 76th Mtg, 27 Apr 43, item 1.

[7](S) JWPC 4, "General Plan for the Preparation of Studies, Plans and Data for the Next Series of United States-British Staff Conferences," 28 Apr 43, CCS 381 (4-24-43) sec 1 pt 1.

[8](S) Memo by JWPC for Red, White, and Blue Planning Teams, 1 May 43, CCS 381 (4-24-43) sec 1 pt 1.

[9](SS) JWPC 4/2/D, Dir, "General Plan for the Preparation of Studies, Plans and Data for the Next Series of United States-

British Staff Conferences," 3 May 43; (SS dg R) JCS 272/1, Rpt by JPS, "Agenda for Next United Nations Conference," 5 May 43. Both in CCS 381 (4-24-43) sec 1 pt 1.

[10] (SS) JCS 283, Rpt by JSSC, "Current British Policy and Strategy in Relationship to That of the United States," 3 May 43, CCS 381 (4-24-43) sec 3. For fuller discussion, see (S) MS, JCS Hist, *Evolution of Global Strategy*.

[11] (SS) JCS 243/3, Rpt by JSSC, "Survey of Present Strategic Situation," 9 Apr 43, CCS 381 (8-27-42) sec 2.

[12] (SS) Suppl Mns, JCS 77th Mtg, 4 May 43, item 12.

[13] (S dg R) JWPC 10, "Global Estimate of the Situation," 2 May 43, rev as (S dg R) JWPC 10/1, "Global Estimate of the Situation, 1943-44," 5 May 43, CCS 381 (4-24-43) sec 2.

[14] (SS) JWPC 9/1, Rpt by JWPC, "Operations in the Pacific & Far East in 1943-44," 5 May 43, CCS 381 (4-24-43) sec 6 pt 1.

[15] (SS) JWPC 15, Rpt by JWPC, "A Strategic Plan for the Defeat of Japan," 3 May 43, CCS 381 (4-24-43) sec 6 pt 1.

[16] (S) Mns, JPS 61st Mtg, 24 Feb 43, item 4. Cf. ch XIII, p. 307.

[17] (S) (Ltd Dist) JPS 67/4, Rpt by JUSSC, "Strategic Plan for the Defeat of Japan," 28 Apr 43; (S) Memo, Jt Secys JWPC to Secy JPS, "Strategic Plan for the Defeat of Japan," 27 Apr 43, CCS 381 Japan (8-25-42) sec 2.

[18] (SS) JWPC 15, Rpt by JWPC, "A Strategic Plan for the Defeat of Japan," 5 May 43, CCS 381 (4-24-43) sec 6 pt 1.

[19] This last modification apparently resulted from an objection expressed by Capt C.J. Moore, USN, of the JUSSC, and senior naval member of the JWPC, that in JPS 67/4 "the relative merits of the Central and South Pacific routes were compared with primary consideration of relative position only, and...a combination of the two routes was not considered at all." It was his view that intermediate objectives should be determined in the light of the whole situation shortly before the operations were to be initiated. Despite the traditional naval predilection for the central route, Captain Moore's opinion was certainly practical in view of the dual command set-up in the Pacific. (S) Memo, Moore to JPS, "Strategic Plan for the Defeat of Japan," 27 Apr 43, CCS 381 Japan (8-25-42) sec 2.

[20] (SS) JWPC 9/1, Rpt by JWPC, "Operations in the Pacific & Far East in 1943-44," 5 May 43, CCS 381 (4-24-43) sec 6 pt 1.

[21] The President had set 10,000 tons as the goal in his message to the Generalissimo on 6 Mar 43. OPD Exec 10, item 58.

[22] It is not clear whether the JWPC was in fact accepting Gen Chennault's claims for a force of 455 planes. The statement actually reads: "It is believed that the operation of this force will accomplish the following objectives: ..." Since there is no indication to the contrary it may probably be assumed that the JWPC accepted the claims.

[23] (SS dg R) JCS 290, Rpt by JPS, "Conduct of the War in 1943-1944," 7 May 43, CCS 381 (4-24-43) sec 1 pt 1. Accompanying it

was (SS) JWPC 14, "Conduct of the War 1943-44," 7 May 43, which amplified some of the conclusions. It is impossible to ascertain from available records which members of the JWPC worked on this paper and how closely the various teams worked together in their hurry to complete the job.

[24] See ch XIV, p. 358.

[25] (S) Mns, JCS 78th Mtg, 8 May 43, item 6.

[26] The President had already indicated his preference for air rather than ground operations in China. Cf. below, pp. 384-385.

[27] Reissued as (SS dg R) JCS 287/1, "Strategic Plan for the Defeat of Japan," 8 May 43, CCS 381 (4-24-43) sec 6 pt 1. Both of these modifications may perhaps be explained by the nature of the papers, viz., statements of the U.S. position to be presented to the British Chiefs of Staff. British interests were concerned, and British support was needed in the recapture of Burma and the preparations for air operations from China bases. In the other case it may have been thought that the implication that Japan might be defeated without invasion would weaken the position of the JCS as they asked for more advances in the Pacific area. An additional explanation is perhaps the decision made but not announced by the President at this time to support Gen Chennault's air program.

[28] (SS) JWPC 9/2, "Operations in the Pacific and Far East in 1943-44," 11 May 43; (SS dg C) JCS 304, same subj, 12 May 43. Both in CCS 381 (4-24-43) sec 7 pt 1.

[29] (SS dg S) JCS 286, Rpt by JCS, "Recommended Line of Action at Coming Conference," 6 May 43, CCS 381 (4-24-43) sec 3; (SS) Msg, BCOS to BJSM, COS (W) 598, 031941 May 43, CCS 381 (4-24-43) sec 1 pt 1. At the JCS 77th Mtg, 4 May 43, Adm Leahy "suggested the U.S. Chiefs of Staff have no objections to the proposed agenda." Brig Gen A.C. Wedemeyer, however, reminded the group that the JPS were preparing a more detailed agenda and the JCS recorded neither approval nor disapproval.

[30] Cf. above pp. 365-366.

[31] (S) Mns, JCS 78th Mtg, 8 May 43, item 6c; (SS) Memo, Leahy to Pres, "Recommended line of action at coming conference," 8 May 43, CCS 381 (4-24-43) sec 3.

[32] (SS) JWPC 22, "Operations in Burma - 1943-44," 10 May 43, circ as (SS) JCS 297, same subj and date; (SS) JWPC 26, "Outline Plan for A Revised Anakim," 10 May 43, circ as (SS) JCS 303, same subj and date. Both in CCS 381 (4-24-43) sec 6 pt 1.

[33] Cf. ch XIV, p. 353.

[34] The text of the paper stated that the third quarter of the year was when the shipping could be supplied. The next month appeared in the conclusions.

[35] These points were made more strongly in a (S) Memo prepared by Col F.A. Hart, USMC, to Capt Moore, on 6 May 43, entitled, "Conclusions Reached by Sub-committee on Prospects of Successfully Completing Anakim in the Next Dry Season." (Navy WPD folder #1, "Future Plans Section Memos.") JCS 297, of which the actual

authors have not been identified, was obviously based on this memo. Col Hart recommended that one US division be made available to Gen Stilwell in India by 1 Sep. He also took a realistic view of the likelihood of the British meeting their commitments:

There is a great deficiency in British personnel and logistic requirements to be provided from outside India. The difficulty of meeting these requirements can *possibly* be overcome, but, the *probability* of accomplishment is very doubtful; due primarily to the British belief that, at this time, the prosecution of our combined effort against Germany is more necessary than the execution of Anakim.

[36] (MS) Memo, Brig H. Redman, Secy BJSM, to Gen Deane, JCS Secy, 5 May 43, CCS 381 (4-24-43) sec 1 pt 1.

[37] (S) Mns, JCS 80th Mtg, 12 May 43, item 9.

[38] *Ibid.*, item 1.

[39] (SS) JCS 306, Rpt by JWPC, "Operations in Sumatra," 15 May 43, CCS 381 (4-24-43) sec 6 pt 2.

[40] JCS 283, "Current British Policy and Strategy in Relationship to That of the United States"; JCS 285, "Form of Summary of Decisions of Prospective Conference"; JCS 286, "Recommended Line of Action at Coming Conference"; JCS 272, "Agenda for Next United Nations Conference"; JCS 287, "Strategic Plan for the Defeat of Japan"; JCS 288, "Invasion of the European Continent from Bases in the Mediterranean in 1943-44"; JCS 289, "Outline Plan for the Seizure of Sardinia"; JCS 290, "Conduct of the War in 1943-44"; JCS 291, "Invasion of the European Continent from the United Kingdom in 1943-44"; JCS 293, "Limited Operations in the Mediterranean in 1943-44."

[41] (SS) Suppl Mns, JCS 79th Mtg, 10 May 43, item 5; (SS) Memo, JSSC Secy to Leahy, "Suggested Opening Remarks on Global Strategy of the War," 10 May 43, CCS 381 (4-24-43) sec 2.

[42] (SS) Suppl Mns, JCS 79th Mtg, 10 May 43, item 17. Although Gen Arnold was absent from this meeting Gen McNarney attended in his capacity as Deputy Chief of Staff. Beginning with the next JCS meeting and throughout the Trident Conference he substituted for Gen Arnold, who had been taken sick.

[43] (SS) JCS Info Memo 70, 10 May 43, CCS 381 (4-24-43) sec 1 pt 1; (S) Mns, JCS 80th Mtg, 12 May 43, item 5.

[44] (S) Mns, JCS 80th Mtg, 12 May 43, item 9.

[45] (UNK) Ltr, Soong to Hopkins, 29 Apr 43, Hopkins Catalog, bk VII, quoted in Romanus-Sunderland, *Stilwell's Mission*, pp. 319-320.

[46] (S) Chennault, "Notes on Strategic Possibilities of a Small American Air Force in China," encl to CCS 104/1, "Retaking of Burma," 29 Aug 42, CCS 381 Burma (8-25-42) sec 1. Cf. ch X, pp. 233-234.

[47] (S) Ltr, Chennault to CG AAF, "A Plan for Operation of Air Forces in China," 1 May 43, encl Plan dtd 30 Apr 43, OPD 381 Security, case 124. Chennault, pp. 221-222.

[48] *Ibid.*

[49] (SS) Memo, Stilwell to CofS, 1 May 43, ABC 381 Japan (8-27-42) sec 1. The same attitude is recorded in *The Stilwell Papers*, p. 204. Also (UNK) Memo, Stilwell to CofS, 1 May 43; (UNK) Memo, Stilwell to Pres, 1 May 43, cys in JCS HS file. It is not known whether or not the last two memos were ever sent.

[50] In view of later developments in China it is interesting to note Gen Stilwell's comments on the Communist armies in northwest China. Reporting that the Generalissimo had posted 16 of the best Chinese divisions to do nothing but watch the Communists and see that no supplies got to them, he characterized the Chinese Red as "a man who would like to see taxes reduced to where they are bearable and the legal rate of interest reduced to about 10% a month." He further stated,

> The Generalissimo is rabid on this subject. There is apparently no hope that he will soften in any way. He pretends to deal with the Reds - he has an office for that in Chungking - but I personally have been warned about mentioning the subject to him in any way. I was in hope we could get some of those units but I was told if I mentioned it to him he would fly into a rage so there is very little hope for a united Chinese front.

(S) Mns, Conf w/Stilwell and Chennault, 30 Apr 43, WDCSA (S) "China."

[51] (S) Suppl Mns, JCS 88th Mtg, 4 May 43, item 1.

[52] They are discussed in greater detail, as is the entire episode, in Romanus-Sunderland, *Stilwell's Mission*, pp. 320-321.

[53] *Ibid.*, passim. Sherwood, p. 731. Madame Chiang also was in Washington at about this time.

[54] Adm Leahy alone of the JCS was in favor of sending all Hump tonnage to Gen Chennault. Leahy, p. 158.

[55] (SS) Memo, Marshall to Stilwell, 3 May 43, WDCSA 381 China.

[56] Ltr, Soong to Hopkins, encl dft of tel to Gimo, 18 May 43, Hopkins file, quoted in Romanus-Sunderland, *Stilwell's Mission*, p. 327.

CHAPTER XVI

[1] (S) Mns, 1st Plen Sess, Trident, 12 May 43. Minutes of all the meetings which the chiefs attended, including those numbered as CCS meetings, and all the approved papers are bound in the CCS volume *Trident*.

[2] (S) Memo by JCS, "Global Strategy of the War," Ann "A" to Mns, CCS 83rd Mtg, 13 May 43.

[3] (SS) JCS 243/3, Rpt by JSSC, "Survey of Present Strategic Situation," 9 Apr 43, CCS 381 (8-27-42) sec 2. Cf. ch XIV, pp. 358ff.

[4] (S) Memo by BCOS, "Conduct of the War in 1943-44," Ann "B" to Mns, CCS 83rd Mtg, 13 May 43.

[5] (S) Mns, JCS 81st Mtg, 14 May 43, item 3.

[6] (S) CCS 219, Memo by JCS, "Conduct of the War in 1943-44," 14 May 43, *Trident*.

[7] (S) Mns, CCS 84th Mtg, 14 May 43, item 2. (S) CCS 224, Memo by BCOS, "Operations in the European Theater between 'Husky' and

"Roundup'"; (S) CCS 225, Memo by BCOS, "Operations from India, 1943-44." Both in *Trident*.

[8] (S) Mns, CCS 85th Mtg, 15 May 43, item 2.

[9] (SS) CCS 232, Rpt by CPS, "Agreed Essentials in the Conduct of the War," 16 May 43, CCS 381 (4-24-43) sec 2.

[10] (S) Mns, JCS 83rd Mtg, 17 May 43, item 4; (S) Mns, CCS 84th Mtg, 14 May 43, item 2.

[11] (S) Mns, CCS 86th Mtg, 17 May 43, item 5.

[12] The original version of the minutes [cy in CCS 334 CCS (2-5-43) (Meetings-70th thru 88th)] stated that the chiefs had approved CCS 232 subject to certain changes, including deletion of paragraphs on which there had not been agreement, and that they had agreed to consider these paragraphs further "with a view to their being recorded later should agreement be reached regarding the questions at issue." To this Adm King expressed objection at the JCS 84th meeting (18 May 43, item 4), particularly to the idea of actually deleting the items. Gen Marshall also objected, saying that "he had been advised that our agreement, made in the manner it was, was an error of the first magnitude because it appeared that the U.S. had approved the British aims and the British had not approved the U.S. aims. Because this paper is a background document, it gives the British an advantage which was not intended." Consequently, the JCS at their meeting with the BCOS the following day pointed out their differences with the minutes as written and it was agreed that the minutes should be revised to indicate only that certain changes were to be made in the paper, including publication of an amended version showing items of agreement and disagreement, and that certain paragraphs were to be considered further. (S) Mns, CCS 87th Mtg, 18 May 43, item 1.

[13] (SS) CCS 232/1, Note by Secys, "Agreed Essentials in the Conduct of the War," 18 May 43, CCS 381 (4-24-43) sec 2.

[14] (S) Mns, CCS 87th Mtg, 18 May 43, item 3.

[15] (S) Mns, JCS 85th Mtg, 19 May 43, item 1.

[16] (S) Mns, CCS 88th Mtg, 19 May 43, item 2.

[17] (S) Mns, CCS 85th Mtg, 15 May 43, item 2.

[18] (S) Mns, CCS 86th Mtg, 17 May 43, item 6; (S) CCS 233/1, "Agenda for the Remaining Conference," 17 May 43, *Trident*.

[19] (S) CCS 170/2, Final Rpt to Pres & PM, sec 5 (b), 23 Jan 43, CCS 381 (8-27-42) sec 2.

[20] (S) Mns, 2nd Plen Sess, Trident, 14 May 43, 1400.

[21] (SS) Memo, Marshall to Stilwell, 3 May 43, (SS) WDCSA 381 China.

[22] (S) Mns, JCS 82nd Mtg, 15 May 43, item 1, (S) Mns, JCS 83rd Mtg, 17 May 43, item 4.

[23] (S) Mns, CCS 85th Mtg, 15 May 43, item 5.

[24] *Hinge of Fate*, pp. 786-788.

[25] (S) Mns, CCS 85th Mtg, 15 May 43, item 3.

[26] (S) Mns, CPS 56th Mtg, 16 May 43, item 1.

[27] (SS) CPS 69, Rpt by Subcmte, "Operations in Burma to Open and Secure an Overland Route to China," 19 May 43, CCS 381 Burma (8-25-42) sec 3.

[28] (S) Mns, CPS 59th Mtg, 19 May 43, item 2.

[29] (SS) CCS 231, Rpt by CPS, "Operations in Burma to Open and Secure an Overland Route to China," 19 May 43; (SS) CCS 238, Memo by CPS, "Operations in Burma 1943-44," 19 May 43. Both in CCS 381 Burma (8-25-42) sec 3.

[30] (S) CCS 229, Rpt by CPS, "Potentialities of Air Route from Assam to China," 19 May 43, CCS 360.4 (5-19-43).

[31] (S) Mns, CCS 90th Mtg, 20 May 43, item 4.

[32] (S) Mns, CCS 86th Mtg, 17 May 43, item 3.

[33] (SS) Mns, JCS 86th Mtg, 20 May 43, item 4.

[34] Note that in CCS 242/6, the final report to the President and Prime Minister, provision was made to continue "administrative preparations" for an eventual operation "about the size of Anakim." See below, p. 408.

[35] If minutes were kept, their whereabouts is not known to the author.

[36] (S) Mns, CCS 91st Mtg, 20 May 43.

[37] It was presented to them in (SS) CCS 242, Memo by CCS, "Draft of Agreed Decisions," 21 May 43, CCS 381 (4-24-43) sec 1 pt 1.

[38] (S) Mns, 4th Plen Sess, Trident, 21 May 43, item 4.

[39] (S) Mns, 5th Plen Sess, Trident, 24 May 43.

[40] (SS) Unnumbered Memo by CCS, "Suggested Statement to be Made to the Chinese," 25 May 43, CCS 381 Burma (8-25-42) sec 3; (S) Mns, CCS 96th Mtg, 25 May 43, item 4; (S) Mns, 6th Plen Sess, Trident, 25 May 43, item 3.

[41] (SS) Memo, Deane to Marshall, "Visit of General Chu," 24 May 43, CCS 381 Burma (8-25-42) sec 3; (S) Mns, CCS 96th Mtg, 25 May 43, item 4. There is no indication in available records that Gen Marshall actually made the statement to the Chinese representatives, but since it was agreed at the plenary session "that the President and General Marshall should make use of the form of words contained in the Annex to these Minutes in conversation with Dr. Soong and General Chu respectively, and should hand them copies of the document for their retention," it may be assumed that they did.

[42] (SS) CCS 220, Memo by JCS, "Strategic Plan for the Defeat of Japan," 14 May 43, CCS 381 Japan (8-25-42) sec 3; (S) Mns, JCS 86th Mtg, 20 May 43, item 3.

[43] Cf. ch XV, pp. 368-369; 372-373.

[44] Cf. above, pp. 390-392.

[45] (S) Mns, CCS 90th Mtg, 20 May 43, item 3.

[46] (S) Mns, CCS 96th Mtg, 25 May 43, item 5; (S) CCS 251/1, Memo by CPS, "Proposals for Improving Combined Planning," 25 May 43, CCS 300 (1-25-42) sec 2.

[47] (SS) CCS 239, Rpt by JPS, "Operations in the Pacific and Far East in 1943-44," 20 May 43, CCS 381 Japan (8-25-42) sec 3. The circumstances under which the paper was submitted are not clear

NOTES TO CHAPTER XVI

from the record. The covering memo by the U.S. Chiefs, however, states that "the enclosed report, prepared by the United States Joint Staff Planners, is submitted for consideration by the Combined Chiefs of Staff." Although the paper was originally submitted to them on 12 May, the JCS apparently had not found time to discuss it before the conference discussion reached the point when the subject was to be considered. It is interesting to note that CCS 220 was submitted with the memo that it "meets with the approval of the United States Chiefs of Staff." CCS 239 was not.

[48] (S) Mns, JCS 87th Mtg, 21 May 43, item 1.

[49] Note, for example: "In response to a question from Admiral Leahy, Admiral King said the paper was intended for 1943 and 1944." "He [Adm Leahy] then asked if the conclusions of CCS 219 were the same as the conclusions of CCS 239." "General Marshall thought the paper commencing with Part I appeared to be done in considerable detail."

[50] (S) CCS 168, Memo by JCS, "Conduct of the War in the Pacific Theater in 1943," 22 Jan 43, *Casablanca*. Whether this was part of Adm King's dissatisfaction with the paper or whether he was simply discussing the organization of the remarks he was to make later to the CCS in not clear from the minutes.

[51] (S) Mns, CCS 92nd Mtg, 21 May 43, item 4.

[52] (S) Mns, CCS 92nd Mtg, 21 May 43, item 5.

[53] (SS) CCS 242, Memo by CCS, "Draft of Agreed Decisions," 21 May 43. The JSSC had prepared a draft of a report for the President and Prime Minister the day before, but the Secretaries did not use it. (SS) JCS 325, Rpt by JSSC, "Tentative Draft on Decisions of the Trident Conference," 20 May 43. Both in CCS 381 (4-24-43) sec 1 pt 1.

[54] (S) Mns, 4th Plen Sess, Trident, 21 May 43.

[55] (SS) Dir by CPS, no number, "Implementation of Assumed Basic Undertakings and Specific Operations for the Conduct of the War - 1943-1944," 21 May 43, CCS 370 (5-21-43) sec 1. The "basic undertakings and projected operations for 1943-44" are listed in an appendix in the same form as the JSSC draft report to the chiefs of state which was not used. This fact and the fact that mention is made of a projected meeting of the CPS at 1300, 21 May, indicate that the directive was issued before the plenary session and probably before the morning meeting of the CCS. There is no mention of the directive in the CCS minutes.

[56] (SS) CPS 72, Rpt by Cmte, "Implementation of Assumed Basic Undertakings and Specific Operations for the Conduct of the War - 1943-1944," 22 May 43; (S) Mns, CPS 61st Mtg, 23 May 43, item 1; (SS) CCS 244, Rpt by CPS, same subj, 22 May 43. Both papers in CCS 370 (5-21-43) sec 1.

[57] (S) Mns, CCS 94th Mtg, 23 May 43, item 5. For fuller discussion, see (S) MS, JCS Hist, *Evolution of Global Strategy*.

[58] (SS) CPS 73, Rpt by JWPC, "Draft Report to the President and Prime Minister," 23 May 43, CCS 381 (4-24-43) sec 1 pt 2.

[59] Both papers are entitled "Draft Report to the President and

Prime Minister," are dated 23 May 43, and are filed in CCS 381 (4-24-43) sec 1 pt 2.

[60] (S) Mns, JCS 90th Mtg, 24 May 43, item 3.

[61] (S) Mns, CCS 95th Mtg, 24 May 43, item 2.

[62] (SS) CCS 242/3, Memo by CCS, "Final Report to the President and Prime Minister," 24 May 43, CCS 381 (4-24-43) sec 1 pt 2; (S) Mns, 5th Plen Sess, Trident, 24 May 43.

[63] (SS) CCS 242/5, Memo by Secys, "Final Report to the President and Prime Minister," 25 May 43, CCS 381 (4-24-43) sec 1 pt 2; (S) Mns, CCS 96th Mtg, 25 May 43, item 2.

[64] (S) Mns, 6th Plen Sess, Trident, 25 May 43, item 2; (SS) CCS 242/6, Final Rev, "Final Report to the President and Prime Minister," 25 May 43, CCS 381 (4-24-43) sec 1 pt 2.

[65] (S) MSS, JCS Hist, *Evolution of Global Strategy* and *War Against Germany and Its Satellites*.

PART II: THE ADVANCE TO VICTORY

CHAPTER XVII

[1] (S) ONI Combat Narrative, "The Aleutians Campaign," 1945 pp. 65-71; (SS) Msg, CominCh to CinCPac, 221939 Mar 43, JCS HS files; (SS) Memo, King to Marshall, "Operation Against Attu," ser 00516, 22 Mar 43, OPD 381 Security, sec II, case 54.

[2] (SS) Msg, CinCPac-CG WDC to CominCh, 292248 May rptd in (SS) JCS 346, Note by Secys, "Operation 'Cottage'," 3 Jun 43, CCS 381 North Pacific Area (6-13-42).

[3] Conv, Cdr. F.H. Schneider, Aide to FAdm King, with Hayes.

[4] (SC) Msg, WD to CG WDC, 3514, CM-OUT-172, 1 Jun 43, rptd in JCS 346, Note by Secys, "Operation 'Cottage'," 3 Jun 43, CCS 381 North Pacific Area (6-13-42).

[5] (SS) Suppl Mns, JCS 91st Mtg, 8 Jun 43, item 5.

[6] (SC) Msg, Marshall to Dewitt, eyes only 3549, CM-OUT-1804, 4 Jun 43, CCS 381 North Pacific Area (6-13-42).

[7] (SS) JCS 346/2, Rpt by JPS, "Operation 'Cottage'," 11 Jun 43, CCS 381 North Pacific Area (6-13-42).

[8] (U) Memo, no sig, indicating time approval received from each chief; (SS) Msg, CominCh to CinCPac, 142219 Jun 43. Both in CCS 381 North Pacific Area (6-13-42).

[9] (S) "Brief of Plan for the Control of the Marshall Islands Dated February 12, 1943," 15 Feb 43, in CNO(WPD) file "Marshall Islands Plan," case 183. The plan itself is also there.

[10] (S) CCS 239/1, Rpt by JCS, "Operations in the Pacific and Far East in 1943-44," 23 May 43, *Trident*, pp. 127-155.

[11] (S) Memo, JPS to JWPC, "Examination into Pacific Theater," 27 May 43, ABC 384 Marshall Islands (6-10-43) sec 1. Memo was signed by Adm Cooke and had notation, "Concurred in by Gen Wedemeyer. CMC." (SS) JWPC 39/D, Dir to Rainbow Team, "Operations against the Marshall Islands," 28 May 43, CCS 381 Marshall Islands (5-28-43) sec 1.

NOTES TO CHAPTER XVII

[12] (SS) JPS 205, Prelim Rpt by JWPC, "Operations against the Marshall Islands," 10 Jun 43, CCS 381 Marshall Islands (5-28-43) sec 1.

[13] The paper reads, "This would force our aircraft to operate at greater distances than from the center position." The above interpretation seems most logical.

[14] (SS dg C) JCS 311, Rpt by JWPC, "Mobility and Utilization of Amphibious Assault Craft," 15 May 43, CCS 560 (5-15-43).

[15] Circ as (SS) JCS 353, Memo by CominCh, "Future Campaign Operations in the Pacific Ocean Areas," 11 Jun 43, CCS 381 Pacific Ocean Area (6-10-43) sec 1. Adm King sent a copy of his memo to Gen Marshall the same day with the note: "If you and I had been able to visit the CENTRAL, SOUTH, and SOUTHWEST PACIFIC in May, as we planned, we might have been able to resolve the problems set forth in this paper. We were unable to do so [because of Trident]. I now feel that the urgency of these problems will permit of no further delay in the taking of effective action to solve them." (SS) Memo, King to Marshall, ser 001150, 11 Jun 43, in (TS) CominCh file "Memos to Gen. Marshall 15 Jan 42-1 Sept 44."

[16] Information currently received from Gen MacArthur indicated that operations against Kiriwina and Woodlark were scheduled for 30 Jun, against Lae-Salamaua for 1 Sep, against southern Bougainville following that, and western New Britain and Buka still later. (SC) Msg, MacArthur to Marshall, C-2727, CM-IN-17166, 27 May 43, CCS 381 (2-28-43) sec 3; (SS) JWPC 54, "Sequence of Certain Pacific Operations," 14 Jun 43, CCS 381 Marshall Islands (5-28-43) sec 1.

[17] (SS) Memo, Capt F.B. Royal, DSecy JCS to Secy JPS, "Future campaign operations in the Pacific Ocean Areas," 11 Jun 43, CCS 381 Pac. Ocean Area (6-10-43) sec 1; (SS) Mns, JPS 80th Mtg, 13 Jun 43, item 1.

[18] (SS) JWPC 54/1/D, Dir to Pink Team, "Sequence of Certain Pacific Operations," 14 Jun 43, CCS 381 Marshall Islands (5-28-43) sec 1.

[19] (SS) JCS 353/1, Rpt by JPS, "Future Campaign Operations in the Pacific Ocean Areas," 14 Jun 43, CCS 381 Pac. Ocean Area (6-10-43) sec 1.

[20] (SS) Mns, JCS 92nd Mtg, 15 Jun 43, item 8.

[21] (S) Msg, JCS to MacArthur, 4769, CM-OUT-6093, 14 Jun 43, CCS 381 (2-28-43) sec 3.

[22] Adm King recommended to Gen Marshall on 14 Jun that the 1st Marine Division be removed from the Southwest Pacific where it was not scheduled for use until fall, and replaced by two more Army Divisions. (S) Memo, King to Marshall, "Withdrawal of the First Marine Division and Change of Allocation of Two (2) Army Divisions to Southwest Pacific Area from Tentative to Firm Assignment (J.C.S. 238/3)," 14 Jun 43, ABC 370.26 (7-8-42) sec 1. After hearing from Gen MacArthur, however, Gen Marshall rejected the idea, on the grounds that it was essential for the planned

assault on New Britain. (S) Memo, Marshall to King, same subj, 23 Jun 43, WDCSA South Pacific Area.

[23] (SS) JWPC 54/1/D, Dir to Pink Team, "Sequence of Certain Pacific Operations," 14 Jun 43, CCS 381 Marshall Islands (5-28-43) sec 1.

[24] (S) JPS 205/1, Rpt by JWPC. "Operations against the Marshall Islands," 17 Jun 43, CCS 381 Marshall Islands (5-28-43) sec 1.

[25] (SS) Mns, JPS 80th Mtg, 13 Jun 43, item 1.

[26] (SS) JPS 205/2, Rpt by JWPC, "Operations Against the Marshall Islands," 18 Jun 43, CCS 381 Marshall Islands (5-28-43) sec 1.

[27] (SS) Memo, Col W.W. Bessell, Jr., to Col F.N. Roberts, "JPS 205/2 - Operations Against the Marshall Islands," 18 Jun 43, in OPD Exec 2, item 1i, vol VI.

[28] (S) Mns, JPS 82nd Mtg, 23 Jun 43, item 2.

[29] (SS) JWPC 58/D, Dir to Rainbow Team, "Operations in the Central Pacific," 25 Jun 43, CCS 381 Marshall Islands (5-28-43) sec 1.

[30] (SC) Msg, MacArthur to Marshall, C3302, CM-IN-13149, 20 Jun 43, CCS 381 (2-28-43) sec 3.

[31] (SS dg S) JCS 386, Memo by JSSC, "Strategy of the Pacific," 28 Jun 43, CCS 381 Pac. Ocean Area (6-10-43) sec 1.

[32] (SS) Suppl Mns, JCS 94th Mtg, 29 Jun 43, item 6.

[33] (S) Ltr, CinCPac to CominCh, "The Seizure of the Marshall Islands," ser 0096, [1 Jul 43], in CNO (WPD) file "Operations-Marshalls-Flintlock," 0-11, env 62, safe 139. In (SS) Msg, CinCPac to CominCh, 030021 Jul 43, CinCPac informed CominCh that the plan would be delivered by Capts James M. Steele and Donald C. Bingham on 4 Jul. It has not been possible to discover whether these two men actually came. The presence of Capt Forrest Sherman at the JPS 85th Mtg, 14 Jul 43, seems to indicate that he came then or shortly thereafter to discuss the project.

[34] (SS) JPS 205/3, Rpt by JWPC, "Operations Against the Marshalls-Gilberts," 10 Jul 43, CCS 381 Marshall Islands (5-28-43) sec 1. CinCPac's plan is not listed among the references cited in the paper, and no copy of the plan has been found in JCS files. However, both (C) and (D) (see text) are identified as "developed by the Commander in Chief, U.S. Pacific Fleet."

[35] (SS) Mns, JPS 85th Mtg, 14 Jul 43, item 2.

[36] *Ibid*. Adm Cooke's memo has not been identified as such, but it appears to be the first draft of JCS 386/1, a copy of which is in ABC 384 Pacific (6-28-43) together with a revision by OPD and note that the Navy concurred in the revision. The paper was issued as (SS dg U) JCS 386/1, Rpt by JPS, "Strategy in the Pacific," 19 Jul 43, CCS 381 Pac. Ocean Area (6-10-43) sec 1.

[37] (SS) JPS 205/4, Rpt by JWPC, "Operations in the Central Pacific," 15 Jul 43, CCS 381 Marshall Islands (5-28-43) sec 1.

[38] (SS dg S) JCS 386/2, Memo by CominCh-CNO, "Strategy in the Pacific," 20 Jul 43, CCS 381 Pac. Ocean Area (6-10-43) sec 1.

[39] (S) Suppl Mns, JCS 97th Mtg, 20 Jul 43, item 9.

⁴⁰JCS 386/1 stated that two heavy bomber and two medium bomber squadrons would come from the North Pacific if operations there were completed in time. A JWPC paper of 15 Jul on deployment of forces provided for transfer of ½ group heavy bombers and ½ group medium bombers from the North Pacific Area to the Western Defense Command in order to release a group of each from the WDC to the Central Pacific in the last quarter of 1943. No earlier mention of this plan has yet been found. (SS dg S) App "A" to Encl "A" to JPS 193/1, Rpt by JWPC, "Strategic Deployment of U.S. Forces to 1 July 1944," 15 Jul 43, CCS 381 (2-8-43) sec 1.

⁴¹(SS) Msg, ComInCh to CinCPac, 202204 Jul 43, CCS 381 Pac. Ocean Area (6-10-43) sec 1.

⁴²Cf. below, pp. 428ff.

⁴³(SC) Msg, Marshall to MacArthur, 5972, CM-OUT-08604, 21 Jul 43, CCS 381 S.W.P.A. (6-5-43).

⁴⁴(SC) Msg, MacArthur to Marshall, C4183, CM-IN-16149, 23 Jul 43, CCS 381 S.W.P.A. (6-5-43).

⁴⁵(SS) JPS 189/1, Rpt by JWPC, "Preparations for the Next U.S.-British Staff Conference," 4 Jun 43, CCS 381 (5-25-43) sec 1.

⁴⁶(SS) JWPC 45/D, Dir to Pink Team, "Specific Operations in the Pacific and Far East, 1943-44," 5 Jun 43, CCS 381 Japan (8-25-42) sec 4.

⁴⁷(SS) JWPC 44/D, Dir to Pink Team, "Operations in the New Guinea-Rabaul Area Subsequent to Cartwheel," 5 Jun 43, CCS 381 S.W.P.A. (6-5-43); (SS) JWPC 54/D, Dir to Pink Team, "Sequence of Certain Pacific Operations," 14 Jun 43, CCS 381 Marshall Islands (5-28-43) sec 1; (SS) JWPC 46/1/D, Dir to Pink Team, "Outline Plan for the Defeat of Japan," 29 Jun 43, CCS 381 Japan (8-25-42) sec 4.

⁴⁸The Pink Team may have been an ad hoc committee and may have gone out of existence in mid-Jul. For further details of the organization of JWPC, see (S) Vernon E. Davis, *History of the Joint Chiefs of Staff in World War II: Organizational Development* (Washington, 1953), vol II, ch XII.

⁴⁹(SS) JPS 245, Rpt by JWPC, "Specific Operations in the Pacific and Far East, 1943-44," 5 Aug 43, fwded as (SS dg R) JCS 446, same subj, 6 Aug 43, CCS 381 Japan (8-25-42) sec 6.

⁵⁰(S dg C) JCS 440, Rpt by JPS, "Estimate of the Enemy Situation 1943-1944, Pacific-Far East Area," 4 Aug 43, CCS 381 (6-4-43) sec 2 pt 1. Cf. ch XV, pp. 368-369.

⁵¹(S) CCS 220, Memo by JCS, "Strategic Plan for the Defeat of Japan," 14 May 43, *Trident*, pp. 31-36.

⁵²Cf. above, pp. 415-427.

⁵³(SS) JPS 234, Plan by JWPC, "Operations for the Seizure of Ponape," 31 Jul 43, CCS 381 Ponape Island (7-31-43).

⁵⁴(SS) JPS 235, Plan by JWPC, "Operations Against the Caroline (Truk Area)," 31 Jul 43, CCS 381 Caroline Islands (7-15-43).

⁵⁵(SS) JPS 236, Plan by JWPC, "Operations Against the Palau Islands," 31 Jul 43, CCS 381 Palau Islands (7-15-43).

⁵⁶(SC) Msg, MacArthur to Marshall, C4183, CM-IN-16419, 23 Jul

43, CCS 381 S.W.P.A. (6-5-43). Since this is filed with the JWPC plan it may be assumed that Gen MacArthur's views were known by the planners.

[57] (SS) JPS 243, Plan by JWPC, "Operations in the New Guinea-Bismarck Archipelago-Admiralty Islands Area, Subsequent to Cartwheel," 5 Aug 43, CCS 381 S.W.P.A. (6-5-43).

[58] Cf. above, pp. 425-426.

[59] (SS) JPS 244, Plan by JWPC, "Plan of Operations in New Guinea Subsequent to the Bismarck Archipelago-Admiralty Islands Operations and the Seizure of Wewak," 8 Aug 43, CCS 381 S.W.P.A. (6-5-43).

[60] (SS) Mns, JCS 101st Mtg, 7 Aug 43, item 5. Adm Leahy was not present. Gen Marshall "outlined the paper" but made no comment.

[61] Apparently Adm King objected to the strategy of operations in the South China Sea where they would be flanked by the Japanese in Borneo, and he thought the British Navy would be more profitably employed in the Bay of Bengal or the Andaman Sea. These views came out at the JCS meeting of 20 Aug. (SS) Mns, JCS 109th Mtg, 20 Aug 43, item 4. Cf. ch XV, p. 368.

[62] (S) CCS 220, Memo by JCS, "Strategic Plan for the Defeat of Japan," 14 May 43, CCS 381 Japan (8-25-42) sec 3.

[63] (SS dg R) CCS 301, Memo by JCS, "Specific Operations in the Pacific and Far East, 1943-44," 9 Aug 43, CCS 381 Japan (8-25-42) sec 6.

[64] (SS) Suppl Mns, JCS 102nd Mtg, 9 Aug 43, item 2.

[65] (SS) JCS 422/2, Rpt by JPS, "Proposed Agenda for Quadrant," 27 Jul 43, CCS 381 (5-25-43) sec 1.

[66] (S) Mns, CCS 110th Mtg, 17 Aug 43, item 4.

[67] The British Chiefs of Staff raised the question again later in the conference in connection with an interim report of progress to the President and the Prime Minister. See ch XVIII, p. 467. (SS) CCS 319/1, Memo by BCOS, "Progress Report to the President and Prime Minister," 21 Aug 43, CCS 381 (5-25-43) sec 2; (SS) Uncirc Mns, CCS 114th Mtg, 21 Aug 43, item 2.

[68] The Secretaries first submitted a draft to which the JCS objected and for which they recommended a substitute. (SS dg R) CCS 301/1, Note by Secys," Specific Operations in the Pacific and Far East, 1943-44," 18 Aug 43, CCS 381 Japan (8-25-42) sec 6; (SS dg S) CCS 301/2, Memo by JCS, same subj, 20 Aug 43, CCS 381 Japan (8-25-42) sec 7; (S) Mns, CCS 114th Mtg, 21 Aug 43, item 4.

[69] (S) CCS 319/5, "Final Report to the President and Prime Minister," 24 Aug 43, *Quadrant*, pp. 249-263.

CHAPTER XVIII

[1] (S) Mns, 6th Plen Sess, Trident, 25 May 43, item 3.

[2] (SS) Memo, Pres to CofS, 5 Jun 43, encl Msg, Gimo to Pres, 29 Mar 43, and Msg, Gimo to Soong, 29 May 43, CCS 381 Burma (8-25-42) sec 3.

[3] (S) Msg, Stilwell to Marshall, eyes only, 590, CM-IN-16837,

26 Jun 43; (S) Msg, Stilwell to Marshall, eyes only, 602, CM-IN-19124, 30 Jun 43. Both in CCS 381 Burma (8-25-42) sec 3.

[4] (S) Msg, Stilwell to Marshall, eyes only, 647, CM-IN-9919, 13 Jul 43, CCS 381 Burma (8-25-42) sec 3; Joseph W. Stilwell, *The Stilwell Papers* (New York, 1948), p. 212.

[5] (S) CCS 221, Memo by RBCOS, "Assam Airfields," 3 Jun 43, CCS 381 Burma (8-25-42) sec 3. Comparison between the local estimate and the requirements agreed in Washington on 25 May, as indicated in a chart annexed to CCS 221, reveals that the theater goal was ahead of the Washington estimate. No copy of the latter has been found by the author.

[6] (SS) Memo, Marshall to Secy JCS, "Assam Airfields," nd; (S) CCS 221/1, Memo by JCS, "Assam Airfields," 16 Jun 43. Both in CCS 381 Burma (8-25-42) sec 3. Draft of CCS 221/1 accompanying Gen Marshall's memo is dated 10 Jun. The reason for the delay is not known.

[7] (S) Mns, CCS 98th Mtg, 18 Jun 43, item 13; (SS) Msg, CCS to Stilwell, 18 Jun 43, CCS 381 Burma (8-25-42) sec 3.

[8] (SC) Msg, Wheeler to Marshall, CM-IN-14002, 22 Jun 43, CCS 381 Burma (8-25-42) sec 3; W.F. Craven and J.L. Cate, eds, *The Army Air Forces in World War II* (hereinafter: *AAF in WW II*), vol IV, pp. 443-444; Charles F. Romanus and Riley Sunderland. *U.S. Army in World War II: China-Burma-India Theater*, *Stilwell's Mission to China* (Washington, 1953), chart 6, p. 284.

[9] William D. Leahy, *I Was There* (New York, 1950), p. 172; Winston S. Churchill, *The Hinge of Fate* (Boston, 1950), p. 801; (C) Ltr, no sig, to Mr. Speed, "Account of off-the-record mtg with King on 25 Jul 43," 26 Jul 43, JCS HS files.

[10] (TS) Msg, PM to Pres, 311, 13 Jun 43, OPD Exec 10, item 24. Apparently the two men had discussed the situation during Trident, for the message starts: "I thought you would like to know the way in which my mind has moved about the South East Asia (or Japan) front."

[11] (S) Msg, PM to Pres, 320, 19 Jun 43, CCS 323.361 (6-19-43) sec 1.

[12] (S) Msg, Pres to PM, 24 Jun 43, CCS 323.361 (6-19-43) sec 1. This was apparently written in the War Dept.

[13] (S) Msg, PM to Pres, 332, 28 Jun 43, CCS 323.361 (6-19-43) sec 1.

[14] (S) Memo, Marshall to JCS, "Supreme Command, Asiatic Theater," 28 Jun 43, CCS 323.361 (6-19-43) sec 1. This was not circulated formally and only a carbon is in the JCS files. Presumably copies were sent individually to the chiefs.

[15] A copy of a "Proposed Radio to the Prime [Minister] from the President" is filed with Gen Marshall's memo to the JCS of 28 Jun 43 in CCS 323.361 (6-19-43) sec 1 and labeled "Encl. #3." It bears the notation, "Change copy written by Adm. Cook [*sic*] and Col Timberman 29 June '43." This ambiguous statement appears to indicate that the draft which bears it is the one Gen Marshall submitted; the one finally sent, considerably rephrased,

was the revision of Adm Cooke and Col Timberman. (SS) Msg, Pres to PM, 298, 30 Jun 43, CCS 323.361 (6-19-43) sec 1.

[16] (SS) Msg, PM to Pres, 342, 3 Jul 43, encl to Memo, Deane to JCS, 5 Jul 43, CCS 323.361 (6-19-43) sec 1.

[17] (S) Msg, Pres to PM, 311, 9 Jul 43, CCS 323.361 (6-19-43) sec 1; (UNK) Memo for Rec, OPD Exec 10, item 63A.

[18] (S) Msg, Pres to PM, 24 Jun 43; (SS) Msg, Pres to PM, 298, 30 Jun 43. Both in CCS 323.361 (6-19-43) sec 1.

[19] (S) Msg, PM to Pres, 345, 6 Jul 43, CCS 323.361 (6-19-43) sec 1.

[20] (U) Memo, WDL[eahy] to Deane, 7 Jul 43, CCS 323.361 (6-19-43) sec 1; (S) Msg, Pres to PM, 8 Jul 43, OPD Exec 10, item 25.

[21] (SS) Msg, BCOS to FM Dill, eyes only, 10 Jul 43, OPD Exec 10, item 25.

[22] (SS) Memo, Cooke to King, "Designation of Commander in Chief for the BURMA AREA," 13 Jul 43, in (TS) CominCh file #35 "Ass't Chief of Staff (Plans-F-1)."

[23] (SS dg U) JCS 409, Memo by CominCh-CNO, "Designation of Commander in Chief for Burma Operations," 13 Jul 43, CCS 323.361 (6-19-43) sec 1.

[24] (S) Suppl Mns, JCS 96th Mtg, 13 Jul 43, item 12.

[25] (SS) Suppl Mns, JCS 97th Mtg, 20 Jul 43, item 6.

[26] (SS dg S) CCS 288, Memo by RBCOS, "Proposed Agenda for Quadrant," 26 Jul 43, CCS 381 (5-25-43) sec 1.

[27] (SS) JCS 422/2, Rpt by JPS, "Proposed Agenda for Quadrant," 27 Jul 43, CCS 381 (5-25-43) sec 1; (SS) Suppl Mns, JCS 98th Mtg, 27 Jul 43, item 3.

[28] (SS dg S) CCS 288/2, Memo by RBCOS, "Proposed Agenda for Quadrant," 29 Jul 43, CCS 381 (5-25-43) sec 1.

[29] (SS dg C) CCS 308, Memo by BCOS, "South East Asia Command," 15 Aug 43, CCS 323.361 (6-19-43) sec 1.

[30] *Ibid.*

   a. *Eastern Boundary*

   From the point where the frontier between China and Indo China reaches the Gulf to Tonking [sic], southwards along the coast of China, Thailand, and Malaya to Singapore; from Singapore south to the North Coast of Sumatra; thence round the East Coast of Sumatra (leaving the Sunda Strait to the eastward of the line) to a point on the coast of Sumatra at longitude 104 degrees East; then South to latitude 08 degrees South; thence Southeasterly towards Onslow, Australia, and, on reaching longitude 110 degrees East, due South along that meridian.

   b. *Northern Frontier*

   From the point where the frontier between China and Indo China reaches the Gulf of Tonkin westwards along the Chinese frontier to its junction with the Indo-Burma border; thence along that border to the sea; thence round the Coast of India and Persia (all exclusive to the Southeast Asia Command) to meridian 60 degrees East.

c. Western Boundary

Southward along meridian 60 degrees East to Albatross Island, thence Southeastward to exclude Rodriguez Island and thence due southward.

[31] Cf. above, p. 439.

[32] (SS) Mns, JCS 105th Mtg, 16 Aug 43, item 4; 106th Mtg, 17 Aug 43, item 6. The JCS first referred CCS 308 to the JPS for study but discussed it themselves at the next meeting when they found the CCS were to take it up a day sooner than originally planned in the place of the "Appreciation and Plan" which was not yet finished.

[33] U.S. objection to Sir Sholto Douglas had finally been accepted. Adm Sir Andrew Cunningham had been considered and rejected at his own recommendation. The JCS seem to have known nothing further than that.

[34] (SS dg C) JCS 476, Rpt by JPS, "Southeast Asia Command," 18 Aug 43, CCS 323.361 (6-19-43) sec 1.

[35] (S) CCS 196/2, Memo by RBCOS, "Intelligence and Quasi Intelligence Activities in India," 9 Aug 43, CCS 385 India (4-8-43).

[36] (S) Memo, Wedemeyer to Marshall, 18 Aug 43, CCS 323.361 (6-19-43) sec 1.

[37] (S) Mns, CCS 111th Mtg, 18 Aug 43, item 5.

[38] (SS) CPS 85/D, Note by Secys, "Southeast Asia Command," 19 Aug 43; (SS dg C) CCS 308/1, Rpt by CPS, "Southeast Asia Command," 21 Aug 43. Both in CCS 323.361 (6-19-43) sec 1.

[39] (SS dg C) CCS 308/2, Memo by JCS, "Southeast Asia Command," 21 Aug 43, CCS 323.361 (6-19-43) sec 1; (S) Mns, CCS 114th Mtg, 21 Aug 43, item 3.

[40] (S) Mns, 2nd Plen Sess, Quadrant, 23 Aug 43; (SS dg S) CCS 319/3, "Draft Final Report to the President and Prime Minister," 22 Aug 43, CCS 381 (5-25-43) sec 2.

[41] (S) Memo, TST[imberman] to Handy, 23 Aug 43; (U) Memo, FNR[oberts] to Wedemeyer, 23 Aug 43; (SS dg C) JCS 470, Memo by CominCh-CNO, "Boundary of Chinese Theater," 6 Sep 43; (S) Memo, Leahy to Pres, "Boundaries of the Chinese Theater," 7 Sep 43, w/note, dtd 14 Sep 43, sgd "William D. Leahy." All in CCS 323.361 (6-19-43) sec 1.

[42] (S) Mns, CCS 116th Mtg, 24 Aug 43, item 7.

[43] (SS) Mns, JCS Sp Mtg, 26 Jul 43, item 1; (S) Mns, JCS 103rd Mtg, 10 Aug 43, item 6; (S) Mns, Mtg, Pres & JCS, 10 Aug 43, item 2.

[44] (SS) JCS 422/1, Memo by JSSC, "Quadrant," 25 Jul 43, CCS 381 (5-25-43) sec 1.

[45] (SS) Suppl Mns, JCS 98th Mtg, 27 Jul 43, item 2.

[46] (SS) CCS 298, Memo by RBCOS, "Progress of Plans and Preparations for Operations from India," 5 Aug 43, CCS 381 Burma (8-25-42) sec 4.

[47] (SS) Ltr, King to Noble, 5 Aug 43; (SS) Ltr, Noble to King, 5 Aug 43; (SS) Ltr, King to Noble, 6 Aug 43. All in CominCh (SS) "(A) File #1."

[48] (S) Mns, JCS 100th Mtg, 6 Aug 43, item 6.
[49] (S) Mns, CCS 106th Mtg, 14 Aug 43. Minutes of all Quadrant meetings of the CCS are in the bound Quadrant volume, together with copies of the papers in their final form.
[50] (S) CCS 288/3, "Agenda," 14 Aug 43, *Quadrant*, pp. 31-33.
[51] (SS) CCS 305, Msg, from Auchinleck, "Effect of Indian Floods on Burma Campaign," 14 Aug 43, CCS 381 Burma (8-25-42) sec 4; (S) Mns, CCS 107th Mtg, 14 Aug 43.
[52] (SS) Mns, JCS 107th Mtg, 18 Aug 43, item 2.
[53] (S) Mns, CCS 107th Mtg, 14 Aug 43. Members of the committee were Gen Sir Thomas Riddell-Webster, Maj Gen P. Mallaby, Lt Gen Brehon B. Somervell, USA, and RAdm Oscar C. Badger, USN. (S) Msg, Quadrant to War Cabinet Offices to CinC India, 158, 16 Aug 43; (SS) CCS 305/1, Ad Hoc Cmte Rpt, "Effect of Indian Floods on Burma Campaign," 18 Aug 43. Both in CCS 381 Burma (8-25-42) sec 4.
[54] (S) Mns, CCS 110th Mtg, 17 Aug 43, item 5.
[55] Frank Owen, *The Campaign in Burma* (London, HMSO, 1946), pp. 34-42; British Air Ministry, *Wings of the Phoenix* (London, HMSO, 1949), pp. 30-31.
[56] (SS) Mns, JCS 107th Mtg, 18 Aug 43, item 2.
[57] (SS) JPS 260/1, Rpt by JWPC, "Operations against Japan 1943-44 (from India)," 22 Aug 43, CCS 381 Burma (8-25-42) sec 4.
[58] (SS dg R) CCS 325, Note by Secys, "Supply Routes in Northeast India," 21 Aug 43, CCS 401 (8-19-43).
[59] (SS) App IV to CPS 83, "Appreciation and Plan for the Defeat of Japan," 8 Aug 43, CCS 381 Japan (8-25-42) sec 6; (S) Dft Memo, Ad Hoc Cmte to CCS, 17 Aug 43, CCS 401 (8-19-43). The memo, of which this is a carbon copy, apparently was not submitted, but formed part of the developing material for CCS 325. It discusses problems of construction and maintenance as well as the two views on the time of completion, which are stated thus:

> The United States view is that an all-weather road from Ledo via Myitkyina - Paoshan to Kunming should be opened by March, 1945. By July, 1945, this will be brought to its full estimated capacity of 80,000 short tons per month delivered to Kunming. By March, 1945, two four-inch pipe lines should be constructed from Digboi to Kunming, one by Fort Hertz to supply aviation gasoline, and the other along the road to provide the necessary motor transport gasoline with some reserve for use in the interior of China. In addition the six-inch line between Calcutta and Digboi should be in full operation.
>
> The British view is that an all-weather road from Ledo via Myitkyina and Paoshan to Kunming might be completed by March, 1946, and the pipe lines by the same date. The British view on the six-inch line from Calcutta to Digboi and thence via Fort Hertz into China coincides with the American view, to

wit, that work can be completed during the first eight months of 1944, provided air transport can be made available.

The divergence of views expressed above was temporarily settled in conference by the Administrative Committee by the adoption of a compromise figure of 65,000 tons monthly for delivery into Kunming. The timing for the completion of the work is tied into the conception of the tactical operations which is still under consideration by the Combined Chiefs of Staff....

The minutes of the Combined Administrative Committee (CAdC) give no indication that the subject was even discussed. No further information has as yet been discovered as to how this odd compromise figure was reached.

[60] (SS dg R) JCS 480, Memo by Somervell, "Supply Routes in Northeast India," 19 Aug 43, CCS 401 (8-19-43); (SS) Mns, JCS 109th Mtg, 20 Aug 43, item 9.

[61] (S) Mns, CCS 107th Mtg, 14 Aug 43; (S) Memo, Deane to JAdC, "Pipe Line from India to China," 14 Aug 43, CCS 678 (8-14-43).

[62] (S) JCS 475, Rpt by JAdC, "Pipeline from India to China," 17 Aug 43; (S) CCS 312, same subj, 18 Aug 43; (SS) Mns, JCS 107th Mtg, 18 Aug 43, item 8; (S) CCS 312/1, Memo by Ad Hoc Cmte, "Pipeline from India to China," 21 Aug 43. All papers in CCS 678 (8-14-43).

[63] (S) Mns, CCS 115th Mtg, 23 Aug 43, item 4.

[64] (S) Mns, CCS 115th Mtg, 23 Aug 43, item 5; (SS) CCS 327, Memo by BCOS, "Operations from India," 23 Aug 43, CCS 381 Burma (8-25-42) sec 4; (S) Msg, Auchinleck to BCOS, 66688 COS 19th Aug 200825 Aug 43, ABC 400 N.E. India (8-21-43). An attached note from Gen Somervell to Gen Wedemeyer states that copies had gone to Maj Gen T.T. Handy, Brig Gen W.A. Wood, RAdm O.C. Badger, and Col Strong.

[65] Cf. below, pp. 465-469.

[66] (S) CCS 242/6, "Final Report to the President and Prime Minister," 25 May 43, item 3, *Trident*, p. 175.

[67] (S) Mns, CCS 115th Mtg, 23 Aug 43, item 2; (SS dg S) CCS 319/3, "Draft Final Report to the President and Prime Minister," 22 Aug 43, CCS 381 (5-25-43) sec 2. CCS 319/4 was the revision of CCS 319/3 incorporating the decision on CCS 327 but apparently it was not typed up in time to be given in anything but rough form at the meeting the same afternoon. (S) Mns, 2nd Plen Sess, Quadrant, 23 Aug 43.

[68] (S) Mns, CCS 107th Mtg, 14 Aug 43.
[69] (S) Mns, CCS 110th Mtg, 17 Aug 43, item 5.
[70] (SS) Mns, JCS 107 Mtg, 18 Aug 43, item 2.
[71] (SS) JPS 260/1, Rpt by JWPC, "Operations Against Japan 1943-44 (from India)," 22 Aug 43, CCS 381 Burma (8-25-42) sec 4.
[72] (SS dg S) CCS 319, "Progress Report to the President and Prime Minister," 19 Aug 43, CCS 381 (5-25-43) sec 2; (S) Mns, 1st Plen Sess, Quadrant, 19 Aug 43, 1730.

848 NOTES TO CHAPTER XVIII

[73] (S) Mns, 1st Plen Sess, Trident, 12 May 43, 1430.
[74] (S) Mns, CCS 113th Mtg, 20 Aug 43, item 5; (S) CCS 313, Memo by CPS, "Appreciation and Plan for the Defeat of Japan," 18 Aug 43, *Quadrant*, pp. 154-170.
[75] (S) CCS 251/1, Memo by CPS, "Proposals for Improving Combined Planning," 25 May 43, *Trident*, pp. 245-248.
[76] (SS) JWPC 46/D, Dir to Red Team, "Conference with British Joint Planning Staff," 5 Jun 43, CCS 381 Japan (8-25-42) sec 4.
[77] (S) JPS 189, Memo by JWPC, "Preparations for the Next U.S.-British Staff Conference," 25 May 43, CCS 381 (5-25-43) sec 1.
[78] (SS) JWPC 46/3, Msgs to & from Red Team, "Outline Plan for the Defeat of Japan," 6 Jul 43, CCS 381 Japan (8-25-42) sec 4. Conv, Col E.H. McDaniel with Hayes, 12 Feb 52.
[79] (SS) JWPC 46/1/D, Dir to Pink Team, "Outline Plan for the Defeat of Japan," 29 Jun 43; (SS) JIC 122/M, Memo of Request, "Appreciation and Plan for the Defeat of Japan," 30 Jun 43; (SS) JIC 122/1, Rpt by Subcmte, "Appreciation and Plan for the Defeat of Japan," 6 Jul 43; (SS) JWPC 46/4, Rpt by Pink Team, "Outline Plan for the Defeat of Japan," 13 Jul 43; (S) CCS 269, Memo by RBCOS, "Appreciation and Plan for the War Against Japan," 5 Jul 43. All in CCS 381 Japan (8-25-42) sec 4.
[80] (SS) Suppl Mns, JCS 95th Mtg, 6 Jul 43, item 14; (S) Mns, CCS 101st Mtg, 9 Jul 43, item 10; (S) Mns, JCS 96th Mtg, 13 Jul 43, item 9; (S) CCS 269/1, Memo by JCS, "Appreciation and Plan for the War Against Japan," 13 Jul 43, CCS 381 Japan (8-25-42) sec 4.
[81] (S) Mns, CCS 102nd Mtg, 16 Jul 43, item 4; (S) CCS 269/2, "Appreciation and Plan for the War against Japan," 17 Jul 43, CCS 381 Japan (8-25-42) sec 4.
[82] (SS) JWPC 46/6, Dir to Red Team, "Appreciation and Outline Plan for the Defeat of Japan," 23 Jul 43, CCS 381 Japan (8-25-42) sec 4.
[83] (SS) Mns, CPS 70th Mtg, 31 Jul 43, item 1.
[84] (SS) CPS 83, Dft, "Appreciation and Plan for the Defeat of Japan," 8 Aug 43, CCS 381 Japan (8-25-42) sec 6. The summary is in Pt IX, pp. 60-67.
[85] (SS) Mns, JCS 102nd Mtg, 9 Aug 43, item 3.
[86] (SS) Mns, CPS 72nd Mtg, 13 Aug 43, item 1; 73rd Mtg, 14 Aug 43, item 1; 74th Mtg, 15 Aug 43, item 4; 75th Mtg, 16 Aug 43, item 1; 76th Mtg, 18 Aug 43, item 1.
[87] (S) CCS 313, Memo by CPS, "Appreciation and Plan for the Defeat of Japan," 18 Aug 43, CCS 381 Japan (8-25-42) sec 6.
[88] See above, p. 448.
[89] (SS) Mns, JCS 109th Mtg, 20 Aug 43, item 4.
[90] (SS) CCS 313/1, Memo by JCS, "Appreciation and Plan for the Defeat of Japan," 20 Aug 43, CCS 381 Japan (8-25-42) sec 7.
[91] (S) Mns, CCS 113th Mtg, 20 Aug 43, item 5.
[92] (S) Mns, JCS 110th Mtg, 21 Aug 43, item 2.
[93] (S) Mns, CCS 114th Mtg, 21 Aug 43, item 2. The meeting was attended only by the four U.S. Chiefs of Staff, the three

British, Sir John Dill, and the Combined Secretaries and apparently conducted as an executive session. Only the decisions are published in the Quadrant volume. A fuller account of the discussion on CCS 319/1 appears in uncirculated minutes of which a copy is filed in CCS 334 Comb Chiefs of Staff (8-17-43).

[94] (SS dg S) CCS 319/1, Memo by BCOS, "Progress Report to the President and Prime Minister," 21 Aug 43, CCS 381 (5-25-43) sec 2; (SS) Uncirc Mns, CCS 114th Mtg, 21 Aug 43, item 2.

[95] Habbakuks were "floating seadromes or giant aircraft carriers" designed to serve as advance landing fields. Of three varieties the British were particularly enthusiastic about Habbakuk II, which was supposed to be constructed of a frozen mixture of water and wood pulp called pykrete, which the British inventor demonstrated at one of the meetings. The U.S. Chiefs of Staff were not enthusiastic about devoting the necessary facilities to developing these untried schemes, but finally agreed to further study of the project and to construction of a section of Habbakuk II. (S) Mns, CCS 112th Mtg, 19 Aug 43, item 3; (S) CCS 315, Memo by BCOS, "Habbakuks," 18 Aug 43; (S) CCS 315/2, Note by Secys, "Habbakuks," 29 Aug 43. Both in *Quadrant*, pp. 185-199.

[96] (S) Mns, 2nd Plen Sess, *Quadrant*, 23 Aug 43, item 5.

[97] See ch. XVII, p. 431-432.

[98] (S) Mns, CCS 115th Mtg, 23 Aug 43, items 4 & 5.

[99] (S) Mns, CCS 116th Mtg, 24 Aug 43; (S) Mns, 2nd Plen Sess, Quadrant, 23 Aug 43; (S) CCS 319/5, "Final Report to the President and Prime Minister," 24 Aug 43, *Quadrant*, pp. 249-263.

[100] (S) Msg, Pres & PM to Gimo, 25 Aug 43, rptd in CCS Info Memo 128, 30 Aug 43, CCS 381 (5-25-43) sec 2.

[101] (S) CCS 329/2, Rpt by CPS (rev), "Implementation of Assumed Basic Undertakings and Specific Operations for the Conduct of the War 1943-1944," 26 Aug 43, *Quadrant*, pp. 325-386.

[102] (S) CCS 244/1, Rpt by CPS, "Implementation of Assumed Basic Undertakings and Specific Operations for the Conduct of the War 1943-1944," 25 May 43, *Trident*, pp. 183-228.

[103] (SS dg R) CCS 323, Memo by JCS, "Air Plan for the Defeat of Japan," 20 Aug 43, CCS 373.11 Japan (8-20-43) pt 1.

[104] (S) Mns, CCS 114th Mtg, 21 Aug 43, item 6.

CHAPTER XIX

[1] (SS) Mns, JCS Sp Mtg, 9 Sep 43, item 1; (SS) CCS 341, Note by Secys, "Review of Strategic Situation in Light of Italian Collapse," 9 Sep 43, CCS 381 (9-9-43); Winston S. Churchill, *Closing the Ring* (Boston, 1951), pp. 134-137.

[2] (S) Mns, JCS Sp Mtg, 9 Sep 43, item 1.

[3] (TS) Memo, Actg CofS Hull to CofS USA, 9 Sep 43, OPD 300.6 Sec.

[4] (SS) Mns, Mtg, Pres and PM w/CCS, 1700, 9 Sep 43.

[5] (SS) Mns, CPS 80th Mtg, 9 Sep 43, item 1; (SS) Memo, Comb Sect to CPS, "Review of Strategic Situation in light of Italian Collapse," 9 Sep 43, CCS 381 (9-9-43).

[6] (SS) CPS 87, Rpt by Subcmte, "Review of Strategic Situation in the Light of the Italian Collapse," 9 Sep 43; (SS) CCS 341/1, Rpt by CPS, same subj, 10 Sep 43. Both in CCS 381 (9-9-43). (SS) Mns, CPS 81st Mtg, 10 Sep 43, item 1.

[7] (SS) Suppl Mns, CCS 118th Mtg, 10 Sep 43, item 1. Adm King by that time had left to attend a meeting with Mr. Churchill for discussion of Habbakuks, the floating airfields, and accordingly the memo was sent to him in final form for presentation to the Prime Minister. (S) Mns, Mtg, King et al. w/PM, 10 Sep 43, CCS 334 CCS (8-17-43). (SS) Memo, Cooke to King, 19 Sep 43; (SS) CCS 341/2, Rpt by CCS, "Review of Strategic Situation in the Light of the Italian Collapse," 10 Sep 43. Both in CCS 381 (9-9-43).

[8] (S) Mns, WH Mtg, CCS w/PM, 11 Sep 43, item 1.

[9] (SS) Msg, CominCh to CinCPac, 202204 Jul 43, CCS 381 POA (6-10-43) sec 1.

[10] (S) Mns, JPS 97th Mtg, 27 Aug 43, item 1. (SS dg R) JPS 262, Rpt by JWPC, "The Seizure of the Marshall Islands," 28 Aug 43; (SS dg R) JCS 461, Rpt by JPS, same subj, 30 Aug 43. Both in CCS 381 Marshall Islands (5-28-43) sec 2. (SS) Suppl Mns, JCS 112th Mtg, 31 Aug 43, item 12.

[11] (S) CCS 319/5, "Final Report to the President and Prime Minister," 24 Aug 43, *Quadrant*, pp. 249-263.

[12] (SS) Msg, JCS to CinCPac, 012115 Sep 43, CCS 381 Marshall Islands (5-28-43) sec 2.

[13] (SS dg R) JCS 471, Memo by CofS USA, "Pacific Operations and Availability of Shipping," 6 Sep 43, CCS 540 Pacific Ocean Area (9-6-43) sec 1; (S) Suppl Mns, JCS 113th Mtg, 7 Sep 43, item 10.

[14] (S dg R) JCS 471/1, Rpt by JPS, "Pacific Operations and Availability of Shipping," 23 Sep 43, CCS 540 Pacific Ocean Area (9-6-43) sec 1; (S dg R) JCS 493, Rpt by JMTC, "Provision of Adequate Trooplift for the Movement of U.S. Forces Overseas," 10 Sep 43, CCS 561.4 (8-13-43).

[15] (S) Suppl Mns, JCS 116th Mtg, 28 Sep 43, item 8.

[16] (S) Msg, Nimitz to JCS, 260439 Sep 43, OPD Msg file. Before 7 Dec 41 Capt C.J. Moore, USN, then in Navy WPD, had recommended garrisoning of Makin, then held by the British. Conv, Moore with Hayes, 29 Jan 52.

[17] (SS) Memo, Roberts to Handy, "Substitution of Makin for Nauru in Operation Galvanic," 27 Sep 43, ABC 384 Pacific (6-28-43); (SS) Memo, CofS USA to CominCh, same subj, 27 Sep 43, OPD Exec 2, item 1b.

[18] (SS) Ltr, CinCPac to CominCh, ser 00247, 25 Oct 42, CNO(WPD) file "Operations-Marshalls Flintlock 0-11," env 62, case 139, NR&H.

[19] (S) JPS 205/5, Rpt by JWPC, "Operations in the Central Pacific Area," 30 Oct 43, CCS 381 Marshall Islands (5-28-43) sec 2.

[20] (S) Mns, JPS 110th Mtg, 30 Oct 43, item 7; (SS dg R) JCS 559, Rpt by JPS, "Operations in the Central Pacific Area," 1 Nov 43, CCS 381 Marshall Islands (5-28-43) sec 2.

[21] (SS) Suppl Mns, JCS 121st Mtg, 2 Nov 43, item 20; (SS) Msg, CominCh (JCS) to CinCPOA, 042125 Nov 43, CCS 381 Marshall Islands (5-28-43) sec 2; (SS) Memo, CominCh to CinCPOA, "Delay in Flintlock," ser 002415, 4 Nov 43, CNO(WPD) file "Operations-Marshalls-Flintlock 0-11," env 62, case 139, NR&H.

[22] (S) Memo, King to Marshall, "Relief by Army Troops of Marine Corps Ground and Aviation Units now on Garrison and Defense Duty at Tutuila, Wallis, Upolu, and Palmyra," ser 001256, 24 Jun 43, OPD 370.5 Security, sec VII, case 240.

[23] (TS) Ltr, CominCh-CNO to CofS USA, "Assignment of Army Officers to the Staffs of the Commander in Chief, U.S. Pacific Fleet and the Commander Central Pacific Force," ser 001272, 25 Jun 43, CNO(WPD) file "Joint Army-Navy Staff for CinCPOA-ComSoPac," J-2, env 43, safe 139, NR&H.

[24] (S) Memo, Marshall to King, "Relief by Army Troops of Marine Corps Ground and Aviation Units now on Garrison and Defense Duty at Tutuila, Wallis, Upolu and Palmyra," 13 Jul 43, OPD 370.5 Security, sec VII, case 240.

[25] (SS) Msg, CominCh to CinCPac, 021437 Jul 43, in (TS) CominCh Despatch file.

[26] (S) Ltr, CinCPac to CominCh, "Commander in Chief, U.S. Pacific Fleet's Command and Staff Organization for Pacific Ocean Areas," ser 00111, 12 Jul 43, CNO(WPD) file "Joint Army-Navy Staff for CinCPOA-ComSoPac," J-2, env 43, safe 139, NR&H.

[27] (SS) Memo, King to Marshall, "Relief by Army Troops of Marine Corps Ground and Aviation Units now on Garrison and Defense Duty at Tutuila, Wallis, Upolu, and Palmyra," 19 Jul 43, OPD 384 PTO sec II.

[28] (S) Ltr, Brig Gen Edmond H. Leavey to Somervell, 29 Jul 43, OPD 384 PTO sec II, 55.

[29] (SS) Memo, Marshall to King, "Relief by Army Troops of Marine Corps Ground and Aviation Units now on Garrison and Defense Duty at Tutuila, Wallis, Upolu, and Palmyra," 2 Aug 43, OPD 370.5 Security, sec VII, case 240.

[30] (S) Msg, Eisenhower to Marshall, W-6285, CM-IN-814, 1 Aug 43; (S) Ltr, King to Marshall, ser 001800, 30 Aug 43. Both in CNO(WPD) file "Joint Army-Navy Staff for CinCPOA-ComSoPac," J-2, env 43, safe 139, NR&H.

[31] (SS) Ltr, King to Nimitz, ser 001889, 6 Sep 43, CNO(WPD) file "Joint Army-Navy Staff for CinCPOA-ComSoPac," J-2, env 43, safe 139, NR&H.

[32] (S) Ltr, Nimitz to King, "Command Relationships and Staff of Commander in Chief, Pacific Ocean Areas and U.S. Pacific Fleet - Reorganization of," ser 00168, 9 Sep 43, CNO(WPD) file "Joint Army-Navy Staff for CinCPOA-ComSoPac," J-2, env 43, safe 139, NR&H.

[33] (S) Memo, Handy to Cooke, "Joint Staff for Admiral Nimitz," 20 Sep 43; (S) Memo, Marshall to King, 24 Sep 43. Both in OPD 384 PTO sec II, 53.

[34] (S) Mns, JCS 108th Mtg, 19 Aug 43, item 10.

[35] Correspondence in OPD 370.5 Security, case 264.

[36] (S) CCS 319-5, "Final Report to the President and Prime Minister," 24 Aug 43, *Quadrant*, pp. 249-263.

[37] (S) Ltr, DeWitt to CofS USA, "Plan for Suggested Offensive Operations in the Northwestern Pacific," 30 Jul 43; (S) Ltr, DeWitt to Marshall, 2 Aug 43. Both in CCS 381 Northwestern Pacific Area (7-30-43) sec 1.

[38] (S dg U) JCS 474, Memo by CofS USA, "Garrisons in Alaska," 7 Sep 43, CCS 320.2 (2-4-43) sec 1; (SS dg U) Suppl Mns, JCS 113th Mtg, 7 Sep 43, item 16.

[39] (S) Mns, JPS 101st Mtg, 15 Sep 43, item 1.

[40] (S dg U) JCS 474/1, Memo by JPS, "Garrisons in Alaska," 21 Sep 43, CCS 320.2 (2-4-43) sec 1.

[41] When the documents on this matter were declassified in the fall of 1946 for presentation to the Senate's Special Committee Investigating the National Defense program, this passage alone remained "secret."

[42] (S dg U) JCS 474/2, Memo by JSSC, "Garrisons in Alaska," 21 Sep 43; (S) JCS 474/3, Rpt by JSSC, "Garrisons in Alaska," 25 Sep 43. Both in CCS 320.2 (2-4-43) sec 1. (S dg U) Suppl Mns, JCS 115th Mtg, 21 Sep 43, item 6. For description of Categories of Defense see *Joint Action of the Army and the Navy, 1935*, ch V, sec III.

[43] (SS dg U) Suppl Mns, JCS 116th Mtg, 28 Sep 43, item 10.

[44] (SS dg U) JCS 474/5, Memo by CominCh-CNO, "Change in Category of Defense in Hawaiian and Aleutians Islands," 5 Oct 43, item 5.

[45] (SS) JPS 291, Rpt by JWPC, "Operations against Paramushiru and the Kuriles," 30 Sep 43, CCS 381 Northwestern Pacific Area (7-30-43) sec 1.

[46] It might be noted that on 26 Oct the JCS approved a conclusion of the Joint Production Survey Committee that the Canol Project, for building an oil pipeline from the Norman Wells oil fields in Canada to Alaska was "necessary to the war effort." For further details, see CCS 678 Yukon (9-20-43) sec 1. Also, *Additional Report of the Special Committee Investigating the National Defense Program*, "The Canol Project," 8 Jan 44; *ibid.*, "Fifth Annual Report," 3 Sep 46, pp. 23-25.

[47] (SS) JPS 275, Rpt by JWPC, "Operations in the South-Southwest Pacific Area," 18 Sep 43; (SS) JPS 275/1, Rpt by JWPC, same subj, 21 Sep 43. Both in CCS 381 (2-28-43) sec 3.

[48] (SC) Msg, Marshall to MacArthur, 8162, CM-OUT-9252, 18 Sep 43, CCS 381 S.W.P.A. (6-5-43); (S) CCS 319/5, "Final Report to the President and Prime Minister," 24 Aug 43, *Quadrant*, pp. 249-263.

[49] Reno III, "Outline Plan for Operations of the Southwest Pacific Area to Reoccupy the Southern Philippines," 20 Oct 43, ABC 384 Pacific (1-17-43) sec 8-A.

[50] (S) JWPC 115/1, Rpt by JWPC, "Specific Operations for the

Defeat of Japan, 1944," 7 Nov 43, CCS 381 Japan (10-22-43). Submitted to JCS as JCS 581.

[51] (SS) Mns, JCS 123rd Mtg, 15 Nov 43, item 9.

[52] See below, pp. 499ff.

[53] (SS dg S) JCS 581/1, "Specific Operations for the Defeat of Japan, 1944," 16 Nov 43, CCS 381 Japan (10-22-43).

[54] (SS) Mns, JCS 124th Mtg, 17 Nov 43, item 5.

[55] (SS) Mns, JLC 14th Mtg, 3 Dec 43, item 1; (SS dg S) JCS 581/3, Rpt by JLC, "Specific Operations for the Defeat of Japan, 1944," 4 Dec 43, CCS 381 Japan (10-22-43).

[56] (SS) Mns, CCS 137th Mtg, 6 Dec 43, item 5.

[57] (S) CCS 313, Memo by CPS, "Appreciation and Plan for the Defeat of Japan," 18 Aug 43, CCS 381 Japan (8-25-42) sec 6.

[58] (SS dg R) CCS 323, Memo by JCS, "Air Plan for the Defeat of Japan," 20 Aug 43, CCS 373.11 Japan (8-20-43) pt 1.

[59] (SS) Mns, CPS 78th Mtg, 24 Aug 43, item 3; (SS) CPS 86/D, Dir, "Preparation of Studies on the Defeat of Japan," 26 Aug 43, CCS 381 Japan (8-25-42) sec 7; (S) CCS 319/5, "Final Report to the President and Prime Minister," 24 Aug 43, *Quadrant*, pp. 249-263.

[60] (SC) Msg, Arnold to Stilwell *et al.*, 3246, CM-OUT-10990, 26 Aug 43, CCS 373.11 Japan (8-20-43) pt 1.

[61] (SC) Msg, Arnold to Stilwell, 3267, CM-OUT-12229 through 12233, 29 Aug 43, CCS 373.11 Japan (8-20-43) pt 1.

[62] (SS) JPS 271, Interim Rpt by JWPC, "Studies on the Defeat of Japan," 11 Sep 43, CCS 373.11 Japan (8-20-43) pt 1.

[63] (SS) CPS 86/1, Rpt by JPS, "Studies on the Defeat of Japan," 13 Sep 43; (SS) Memo, Secy CPS to JPS Mbrs, "Studies for the Defeat of Japan," 14 Sep 43. Both in CCS 373.11 Japan (8-20-43) pt 1.

[64] (S) Mns, JPS 101st Mtg, 15 Sep 43, item 11.

[65] (SS) Mns, CPS 82nd Mtg, 16 Sep 43, item 1; (SS) CCS 348, Rpt by JPS, "Studies for the Defeat of Japan," 16 Sep 43, CCS 373.11 Japan (8-20-43) pt 1.

[66] (SS) Mns, CCS 119th Mtg, 17 Sep 43, item 10.

[67] (SC) Msg, Stilwell to Marshall for Arnold, 2106, CM-IN-9027, 11 Sep 43, CCS 373.11 Japan (8-20-43) pt 1.

[68] (SS) JWPC 79/1/D, Dir to Red Team, "Preparation of Studies on the Defeat of Japan (Air Plan)," 30 Sep 43; (SS) JPS 288, Memo by AAF Mbr, "Plans for the Defeat of Japan within 12 Months after the Defeat of Germany," 4 Oct 43. Both in CCS 381 Japan (8-25-42) sec 7. (S) Mns, JPS 104th Mtg, 29 Sep 43, item 21.

[69] (SS) JPS 264, Plan by JWPC, "Outline Plan for the Seizure of the Marianas, Including Guam," 6 Sep 43, CCS 381 Marianas (8-6-43). The plan gives in the summary a target date of 31 Dec 45, but details in the enclosures indicate this to be a misprint.

[70] (SS) JPS 288, Memo by JPS, "Plans for the Defeat of Japan within 12 Months after the Defeat of Germany," 4 Oct 43, CCS 381 Japan (8-25-42) sec 7.

[71] (SS) JPS 320, Plan by AAF, "Early Sustained Bombing of Japan," 9 Nov 43, CCS 373.11 Japan (8-20-43) pt 2.

[72] (S) Mns, JPS 113th Mtg, 9 Nov 43, item 1.
[73] (SS dg R) JCS 600, Rpt by JPS, "V.L.R. Airfields (B-29) in the China-Burma-India Area," 11 Nov 43, CCS 373.11 Japan (8-20-43) pt 2.
[74] (TS) Msg, Pres to Gimo, 10 Nov 43, OPD Exec 10, item 63B.
[75] (SS) Mns, JCS 123rd Mtg, 15 Nov 43, item 10.
[76] (SS) Mns, JCS 124th Mtg, 17 Nov 43, item 6.
[77] (S dg R) CCS 401/2, Note by Secys, "V.L.R. Airfields (B-29) in the China-Burma-India Area," 6 Dec 43, CCS 373.11 Japan (8-20-43) pt 2.
[78] (SS) Memo, JWPC Secy to Col C.R. Peck, "Message to Sextant," 17 Nov 43; (SC) Msg, Home Team to JWPC, 579, CM-OUT-7503, 19 Nov 43; (SC) Msg, Home Team to JWPC, 1010, CM-OUT-8334, 20 Nov 43; (SS) JPS 320/1, Rpt by JWPC, "Early Sustained Bombing of Japan," 3 Dec 43. All in CCS 373.11 Japan (8-20-43) pt 2.
[79] (SC) Msg, JWPC to Home Team, 10094, CM-IN-1139, 2 Dec 43, CCS 373.11 Japan (8-20-43) pt 2.
[80] (SS) Suppl Mns, CCS 120th Mtg, 24 Sep 43, item 4; (SS) CPS 86/2, "The Defeat of Japan within Twelve Months after the Defeat of Germany," 25 Oct 43, CCS 381 Japan (8-25-42) sec 8.
[81] (SS) JWPC 120, "Comments on the Defeat of Japan within Twelve Months after the Defeat of Germany," 26 Oct 43, CCS 381 Japan (8-25-42) sec 8.
[82] (SS) Mns, JPS 109th Mtg, 27 Oct 43, item 1; (SS) Mns, CPS 88th Mtg, 28 Oct 43, item 1.
[83] (S) Memo by US Mbrs of CPS, "The Defeat of Japan within Twelve Months after the Defeat of Germany," encl to (S) Memo, US Secy CPS to Capt L.E. Porter, RN, Brig J.K. McNair, Air-Commo P. Warburton, RAF, "The Twelve Months Plan for the Defeat of Japan," 1 Nov 43, CCS 381 Japan (8-25-42) sec 8.
[84] (SS) Mns, CPS 89th Mtg, 4 Nov 43, item 4.
[85] (SS) JWPC 120/2, "The Defeat of Japan within Twelve Months after the Defeat of Germany," 2 Nov 43; (SS dg R) JCS 564, Rpt by JPS, same subj, 4 Nov 43. Both in CCS 381 Japan (8-25-42) sec 8. (SS) Mns, JPS 111th Mtg, 3 Nov 43, item 8.
[86] (S) JCS 533/5, Rpt by JSSC, "Recommended Line of Action at Next U.S.-British Staff Conference," 8 Nov 43, CCS 381 (10-17-43) sec 1.
[87] (SS) Memo, Willson to King, "Plans for Defeat of Japan," 11 Nov 43, CCS 381 Japan (8-25-42) sec 9.
[88] (SS) Mns, JCS 123rd Mtg, 15 Nov 43, item 8.
[89] (SS) Mns, CPS 90th Mtg, 26 Nov 43.
[90] (SS dg S) CCS 417, Rpt by JPS, "Overall Plan for the Defeat of Japan," 2 Dec 43, CCS 381 Japan (8-25-42) sec 9. Minutes of the various meetings and the several preparatory papers are in the same file. (S) Brit paper, J.C. (Sextant) 11, "Overall Plan for the Defeat of Japan," 26 Nov 43, ABC 381 Japan (8-27-42) sec 6.
[91] (SS dg S) JCS 614, Rpt by JSSC, "Plan for Defeat of Japan," 2 Dec 43, CCS 381 Japan (8-25-42) sec 9.

[92] (SS) Ann to Mns, JCS 133rd Mtg, 3 Dec 43, item 5.
[93] (S) Mns, CCS 134th Mtg, 4 Dec 43, item 4.
[94] (SS dg S) CCS 417/1, Rpt by CPS, "Over-all Plan for the Defeat of Japan," 5 Dec 43, CCS 381 Japan (8-25-42) sec 9.
[95] (SS) Mns, JCS 136th Mtg, 6 Dec 43, item 3; (S) Mns, CCS 137th Mtg, 6 Dec 43, item 4.

CHAPTER XX

[1] (SS dg C) CCS 308/4, Memo by BCOS, "Directive to the Supreme Allied Commander, South East Asia," 21 Sep 43, CCS 323.361 (6-19-43) sec 1.
[2] (SS dg C) CCS 308/5, Memo by RBCOS, "The Reorganization of Command in India and Southeast Asia," 27 Sep 43, CCS 323.361 (6-19-43) sec 1.
[3] (SS) Memo, DSecy JCS to Secy JPS, "Directive to the Supreme Allied Commander, South East Asia," 23 Sep 43, CCS 323.361 (6-19-43) sec 1.
[4] (SS) JPS 258/3, Rpt by JWPC, "Directive to the Supreme Allied Commander, South-East Asia," 28 Sep 43, CCS 323.361 (6-19-43) sec 1.
[5] (SS) Mns, JPS 104th Mtg, 29 Sep 43, item 20.
[6] (SS) Mns, JPS 107th Mtg, 17 Oct 43, item 11. No copy of Col Roberts' draft has been found. Adverse comment had also been made by Maj Gen W.D. Styer of ASF in a memo to Gen Handy, "Attached draft of Directive to the Supreme Allied Commander and Deputy Supreme Allied Commander, Southeast Asia Theater and to the Commander in Chief India," 2 Oct 43, OPD 384 TS, cases 1-18.
[7] (SS) Mns, JPS 108th Mtg, 20 Oct 43, item 1.
[8] (S) Memo, Handy to Marshall, 23 Oct 43, OPD Exec 10, item 25; (S dg C) JCS 476/2, Rpt by JPS, "Directive to the Supreme Allied Commander, Southeast Asia," 6 Nov 43, CCS 323.361 (6-19-43) sec 1.
[9] (SS dg C) CCS 308/6, Memo by RBCOS, "Reorganization of Command in India and Southeast Asia," 8 Nov 43, CCS 323.361 (6-19-43) sec 1.
[10] See ch XIV.
[11] (SS) Suppl Mns, JCS 122nd Mtg, 9 Nov 43, item 4.
[12] (TS) Memo, Handy to CofS, "Prime Minister's Directive to Admiral Mountbatten," 9 Nov 43, OPD 384 TS, cases 1-18.
[13] (SS) JPS 258/7, Study by JWPC, "Directive to the Supreme Allied Commander, Southeast Asia," 23 Nov 43, CCS 323.361 (6-19-43) sec 2.
[14] The JPS directed their Secretary to tell the JCS the report had been prepared but would not be forwarded. (SS) Mns, JPS 115th Mtg, 24 Nov 43, item 3.
[15] Romanus-Sunderland, *Stilwell's Mission*, pp. 371 ff; (UNK) Ltr, Joseph Alsop to Hopkins, 1 Sep 43, Hopkins Papers, bk VII.
[16] Romanus-Sunderland, *Stilwell's Mission*, pp. 374-375, 376.

[17] (S) Msg, Somervell to Marshall, 2810 KM 2683, CM-IN-15125, 25 Oct 43, CCS 381 Burma (8-25-42) sec 4; Romanus-Sunderland, *Stilwell's Mission*, pp. 377-379; *The Stilwell Papers*, pp. 224-238; Lord Louis Mountbatten, *Report to the Combined Chiefs of Staff by the Supreme Allied Commander South-East Asia, 1943-1945* (London, 1951), p. 5 (hereinafter: Mountbatten Report), copy in CCS 311.5 (6-9-42) BP.

[18] (MS) Msg, Mountbatten to BCOS et al., OZ 3758, 16 Nov 43, CCS 323.361 (6-19-43) sec 2; Mountbatten Report, pp. 1-11.

[19] Mountbatten Report, p. 7. Despite the agreement by the CCS at Quadrant that Gen Stilwell was to be Deputy SAC SEAC apparently the appointment was not considered firm until Adm Mountbatten should have assembled his staff and although Gen Stilwell acted in that capacity he never received official orders. (MS) Ltr, Redman to Leahy, 30 Sep 43, CCS 323.361 (6-19-43) sec 1. Romanus-Sunderland, *Stilwell's Mission*, pp. 379-380.

[20] *The Stilwell Papers*, p. 231.

[21] (S) Mns, CCS 115th Mtg, 23 Aug 43, item 5, p. 481; (S) CCS 319/5, "Final Report to the President and Prime Minister," 24 Aug 43, par 41, *Quadrant*, p. 257.

[22] (SC) Msg, Ferris to Marshall, eyes only, AG 1718, CM-IN-6163, 8 Sep 43, CCS 381 Burma (8-25-42) sec 4.

[23] (S) Msg, WD to Arnold (Sextant), 1008, 20 Nov 43, OPD Msg file; (S) Memo, Handy to CofS, "When the 308th Heavy Bombardment Group in China Can Be Self Sustaining," 27 Aug 43, CofS file "China S." Figures are from the first. The latter says 4,544 tons were delivered in Jul. Claire L. Chennault, *Way of a Fighter* (New York, 1949), p. 247, says "Hump tonnage for July fell 1,700 tons short of our 4,700-ton priority."

[24] Chennault, pp. 252-253; (C) Ltr, Chennault to Hopkins and Pres, 5 Sep 43, Hopkins Papers, bk VII, item 61.

[25] Apparently much the same report had been sent to FM Dill by the British Military Attache in Chungking, for on 10 Sep Gen Marshall wrote to FM Dill:

> My reaction to the Military Attache's message is that General Chennault has either directly or indirectly influenced him to send it to you. The statements he made in the message could only have been based on information obtained from Chennault and are almost identical with statements previously made by Chennault in other correspondence.
>
> General Chennault is an intrepid and inspiring leader who can direct very effectively the operations of combat aircraft; but his methods of influencing his proposals present a very serious problem for me. His action results in indirectly subverting Stilwell and Stratemeyer, who have been doing everything in their power to advance the arrangements for the support of his activities.

(TS) Ltr, Marshall to Dill, 10 Sep 43, OPD 384 TS, cases 1-18.

[26] Romanus-Sunderland, *Stilwell's Mission*, p. 374; (SS) Memo, Marshall to Pres, "Telegram to Madame Chiang," 10 Sep 43, WDCSA (SS) 381 China.

[27] (MS) Msg, Auchinleck to Stilwell, 72666, 22 Sep 43, CCS 381 Burma (8-25-42) sec 4.

[28] (S) Msg, Ferris to Marshall, eyes only, AG 1929, 23 Sep 43, CCS 381 Burma (8-25-42) sec 4.

[29] (MS) Msg, BJSM to BCOS, 1202, 24 Sep 43, CCS 381 Burma (8-25-42) sec 4. Apparently this was drafted in the War Dept and processed informally for approval by the other chiefs. (SS dg S) Msg, Marshall to Ferris, CM-OUT-12707, 27 Sep 43, OPD 400 TS sec III, case 85.

[30] (SS) CCS 327/1, Memo by RBCOS, "Operations from India," 28 Sep 43, CCS 381 Burma (8-25-42) sec 4.

[31] (SS) Suppl Mns, JCS 116th Mtg, 28 Sep 43, item 13; (SS) CCS 327/2. Memo by JCS, "Operations from India," 30 Sep 43, CCS 381 Burma (8-25-42) sec 4.

[32] (SS) Suppl Mns, CCS 121st Mtg, 1 Oct 43, item 6.

[33] (S) Dft, CCS 327/3, Memo by RBCOS, "Operations from India," 8 Oct 43, CCS 381 Burma (8-25-42) sec 4. Apparently this was not formally circulated as a CCS paper.

[34] (SS) Memo, Handy to Royal, "Operations from India," 10 Oct 43, CCS 381 Burma (8-25-42) sec 4. Memo has written "OK's" by Gen Marshall, Adm King, and Adm Leahy.

[35] (SS) Msg, JCS to Stilwell, 3516, 3517, CM-OUT-4722, 4723, 11 Oct 43, CCS 381 Burma (8-25-42) sec 4.

[36] (C) Msg, Alsop to Soong, 26 Sep 43, Hopkins Papers, bk VII, Chinese Affairs (11), item 65; (S) Memo, Pres to Marshall, 15 Oct 43, CofS file "China S."

[37] (S) Memo, Marshall to Pres, "Air Cargo - India to China," 4 Oct 43, CofS file "China S."

[38] (UNK) Msg, Pres to PM, 389, 15 Oct 43, w/fwding note to Gen Marshall, CofS file "China S."

[39] (S) Msg, Somervell to Marshall, eyes only, 2810 KB 2683, CM-IN-15125, 25 Oct 43; (S) Memo, Marshall to Pres, 25 Oct 43, encl Msg, Somervell to Marshall, 23 Oct 43. Both in CCS 381 Burma (8-25-42) sec 4.

[40] (SS dg R) CCS 390, Memo by RBCOS, "Future Operations in South East Asia Command," 7 Nov 43, CCS 381 Burma (8-25-42) sec 4.

[41] (S dg R) JCS 582, Rpt by JSSC, "Future Operations in the Southeast Asia Command," 9 Nov 43, CCS 381 Burma (8-25-42) sec 4.

[42] (S) CCS 308/3, "Southeast Asia Command," 21 Aug 43, *Quadrant*, p. 127.

[43] (SS) JPS 316/1, Rpt by JWPC, "Future Operations in Southeast Asia Command," 14 Nov 43; (SS dg C) JCS 582/1, Rpt by JPS, same subj, 16 Nov 43. Both in CCS 381 Burma (8-25-42) sec 5.

[44] (SS) Mns, JCS 124th Mtg, 17 Nov 43, item 8.

[45] *Closing the Ring*, pp. 306-320.

[46] *Ibid.*, pp. 284ff; Cordell Hull, *The Memoirs of Cordell Hull* (New York, 1948), vol 2, pp. 1274-1318.

[47] (SS) JCS 533, Note by Secys, "Preparation for the Next United States-British Staff Conference," 18 Oct 43. Apparently the code name Pentagon was originally assigned to the Cairo conference and presumably dropped to avoid confusion. (S) Memo, JWPC Secys to Sen Team, "Preparations for the next conference," 21 Oct 43. Both in CCS 381 (10-17-43) sec 1.

[48] (SS) JCS 533/1, Rpt by JSSC, "Preparations for the Next United States-British Conference," 22 Oct 43, CCS 381 (10-17-43) sec 1.

[49] (SS) CCS 380/1, Memo by JCS, "Basic Policies for the Next United States-British Staff Conference," 3 Nov 43, CCS 381 (10-17-43) sec 1; (S) Sp Suppl Mns, JCS 120th Mtg, 20 Oct 43; (SS) Suppl Mns, CCS 126th Mtg, 5 Nov 43, item 11.

[50] (SS) Mns, JCS 126th Mtg, 19 Nov 43, item 3.

[51] (SS) Mns, Mtg, JCS w/Pres, 19 Nov 43, item 5.

[52] (S) CCS 404/1, Memo by RBCOS, "'Sextant' Agenda," 22 Nov 43, CCS 381 (10-17-43) sec 2; (S) Mns, CCS 127th Mtg, 22 Nov 43, item 2.

[53] *Closing the Ring*, p. 328. Note comments of Adm Mountbatten:

This conference is going all hay wire. I had expected to put my proposals before the British Chiefs of Staff, at the same time as my Deputy Chief of Staff, Al Wedemeyer put the same plans before the American Chiefs of Staff. I had then naturally supposed that the plans would be considered in my presence by the Combined Chiefs of Staff.

Having worked out that all resources I was asking for could be made available, I then presumed there would be a meeting among the Combined Chiefs of Staff, and the Chinese Military Staff.

Fourthly and finally, I presumed the matter would be dealt with on the highest level at a Plenary meeting between the President, Prime Minister and Generalissimo and the Combined... Chiefs of Staff.

Believe it or not, but these four meetings were held in the reverse order since it was considered of utmost importance that the Generalissimo should not be kept waiting to join in the discussion.

(UNK) Extract from SAC SEAC Personal Diary, Hq SACSEA War Diary, 23 Nov 43 (hereinafter: *SEAC Diary*).

[54] (SS) CCS 405, Memo by Stilwell, "Role of China in Defeat of Japan," 22 Nov 43, CCS 381 Japan (10-22-43).

[55] (SS) JPS 351, Rpt by JWPC, "Role of China in the Defeat of Japan," 23 Nov 41, CCS 381 Japan (10-22-43).

[56] (SS) Mns, JCS 128th Mtg, 23 Nov 43, item 2.

[57] (S) Mns, CCS 128th Mtg, 23 Nov 43, item 2.

[58] (S) Mns, 1st Plen Sess, 23 Nov 43, *Sextant*, p. 377; Leahy, p. 200; *The Stilwell Papers*, p. 245; *SEAC Diary*, 23 Nov 43.

[59] (S) Mns, CCS 128th Mtg, 23 Nov 43, item 2.

[60] *Ibid.*, item 4.

[61] *SEAC Diary*, 23 Nov 43; *The Stilwell Papers*, p. 245.

[62] (S) Mns, CCS 129th Mtg, 24 Nov 43, item 5.

[63] *The Stilwell Papers*, p. 246.

[64] (S) Mns, CCS 129th Mtg, 24 Nov 43, item 7; *SEAC Diary*, 24 Nov 43.

[65] *The Stilwell Papers*, p. 255.

[66] (S) Mns, CCS 129th Mtg, 24 Nov 43, item 7.

[67] (SS) Mns, JCS 130th Mtg, 25 Nov 43, item 6.

[68] (S) Mns, CCS 130th Mtg, 25 Nov 43, item 1; *SEAC Diary*, 24 Nov, 25 Nov 43.

[69] (SS dg R) CCS 411, Note by Secys, "Operations in the South East Asia Command," 25 Nov 43, CCS 381 Burma (8-25-42) sec 5.

[70] (S) Mns, CCS 131st Mtg, 26 Nov 43, item 1; (SS dg R) CCS 411/2, Note By Secys, "Operations in the South East Asia Command," 2 Dec 43, CCS 381 Burma (8-25-42) sec 5.

[71] Informal notes of conference, 26 Nov 43, CCS 381 Burma (8-25-42) sec 5; Henry H. Arnold, *Global Mission*, (New York, 1949), p. 464; *The Stilwell Papers*, pp. 246-247.

[72] *SEAC Diary*, 26 Nov, 27 Nov 43. Apparently the contents of the six-point note were communicated to the Generalissimo by Gen Stilwell the following day. Stilwell Diary, unpublished section, 27 Nov 43. Gen Wedemeyer later reported, "It is understood that the paper was explained to the Generalissimo but was not handed to him." (SS dg R) CCS 411/3, Memo by DCofS SEAC, "Operations in the South East Asia Command," 4 Dec 43, CCS 381 Burma (8-25-42) sec 5.

[73] Gen Stilwell recorded (unpublished diary entry of 27 Nov 43), "I am to stick out for Toreador and 10,000 tons." Adm Mountbatten wrote in his diary, "Joe Stilwell absolutely staggered me by coming in and saying that the Generalissimo had that morning rejected all the points which he had agreed to at the last Plenary meeting the previous evening, and had instructed Stilwell to try and obtain a complete reversal of every point." *SEAC Diary*, 27 Nov 43.

[74] There are numerous references in secondary sources to the agreement. Adm Mountbatten reports that "the President and Prime Minister now gave him an assurance that the operation would take place, and that a large Allied fleet would be in the Bay of Bengal." Mountbatten Report, p. 27. Churchill reports, "The President, in spite of my arguments, gave the Chinese the promise of a considerable amphibious operation across the Bay of Bengal within the next few months." *Closing the Ring*, p. 328. Adm Leahy speaks of it as President Roosevelt's decision. Leahy, p. 201. See also (MS) Msg, Mountbatten to Wedemeyer, 89006, 30 Nov 43, OPD 300.6 Sec (OCS Papers).

[75] (S) Mns, CCS 131st Mtg, 26 Nov 43, item 4.

[76] (S) Mns, 2nd Plen Sess, 24 Nov 43, *Sextant*, p. 383; *Closing the Ring*, pp. 329-334.

[77] (SS) CCS 409, Note by BCOS, "'Overlord' and the Mediterranean," 25 Nov 43, CCS 381 (3-23-42) pt 6.

[78] (SS dg C) JCS 611, Rpt by JPS, "'Overlord' and the Mediterranean," 26 Nov 43, CCS 381 (3-23-42) pt 6.

[79] (SS) Mns, JCS 131st Mtg, 26 Nov 43, item 3.

[80] (S) Mns, CCS 131st Mtg, 26 Nov 43, item 4B.
[81] (S) Mns, CCS 129th Mtg, 24 Nov 43, item 4.
[82] (SS) JPS 354, Rpt by JWPC, "Collaboration with U.S.S.R.," 24 Nov 43; (SS) JCS 606/2, same subj, 25 Nov 43; (SS) CCS 407, same subj, 25 Nov 43. All in CCS 381 (10-17-43) sec 2.
[83] (SS) Mns, JCS 130th Mtg, 25 Nov 43, item 3.
[84] (S) Mns, CCS 131st Mtg, 26 Nov 43, item 5.
[85] *Closing the Ring*, pp. 347-407; Robert E. Sherwood, *Roosevelt and Hopkins* (New York, 1948), pp. 776-799; Leahy, pp. 203-212; *Global Mission*, pp. 465-471.
[86] (S) Mns, 1st Plen Sess, Eureka, 28 Nov 43, *Sextant*, pp. 513-525.
[87] Sherwood, pp. 784-785. (S) Memo of Conf, Pres and Stalin, 29 Nov 43; (S) Memo of Conv, Pres, Stalin, Harriman, and Molotov. 1 Dec 43. Both in *Tehran* (State Dept doc).
[88] (S) CCS M-165, "Military Conclusions of the 'Eureka' Conference," 2 Dec 43, *Sextant*, pp. 375-376.
[89] (S) Mns, CCS 133rd Mtg, 3 Dec 43, item 2(4).
[90] (S) Mns, 3rd Plen Sess, 4 Dec 43, *Sextant*, pp. 389-396.
[91] (S) Mns, CCS 134th Mtg, 4 Dec 43, item 8.
[92] (SS) CCS 423, Memo by BCOS, "Draft Agreement by the Combined Chiefs of Staff," 4 Dec 43; (SS) CCS 423/1, Memo by JCS, same subj, 4 Dec 43. Both in CCS 381 (10-17-43) sec 3. The file contains a draft labelled "Ismay's draft" and modified in Adm King's handwriting to the form in which CCS 423/1 was presented. CCS 423 was obviously based on the same draft but modified somewhat before formal presentation.
[93] (SS) Mns, JCS 135th Mtg, 5 Dec 43, item 2.
[94] (S) Mns, CCS 135th Mtg, 5 Dec 43, item 2.
[95] (S) CCS 423/2, Rpt by CCS, 5 Dec 43, CCS 381 (10-17-43) sec 3.
[96] (S) Mns, 4th Plen Sess, 5 Dec 43, *Sextant*, pp. 397-404.
[97] (S) Mns, CCS 136th Mtg, 5 Dec 43, item 1.
[98] *Closing the Ring*, pp. 411-412; Sherwood, pp. 800-801; Leahy, pp. 213-214. Adm Leahy incorrectly gives the date as 6 Dec. (C) Ltr, King to Col C.H. Donnelly, 11 Oct 49, JCS HS files.
[99] (U) Memo, FDR to PM, 5 Dec 43, CCS 381 Burma (8-25-42) sec 5. Also printed in Sherwood, pp. 801-802.
[100] (SS) CCS 427, Rpt by CPS, "Amphibious Operations in South East Asia Alternative to 'Buccaneer,'" 5 Dec 43, CCS 381 South East Asia (12-5-43).
[101] (SS) Mns, CCS 137th Mtg, 6 Dec 43, item 6.
[102] (SS) CCS 427/1, Note by Secys, "Amphibious Operations in Southeast Asia Alternative to 'Buccaneer,'" 6 Dec 43, CCS 381 South East Asia (12-5-43); (S) Mns, CCS 138th Mtg, 7 Dec 43, item 3.
[103] (SS dg R) CCS 411/5, Memo by JCS, "Operations in Southeast Asia Command," 7 Dec 43, CCS 381 Burma (8-25-42) sec 5; (S) Mns, CCS 138th Mtg, 7 Dec 43, item 8.
[104] (SS) CCS 426/1, Rpt by CCS, "Report to the President and Prime Minister," 6 Dec 43, CCS 381 (10-17-43) sec 3; (S) Mns, 5th Plen Sess, 6 Dec 43, *Sextant*, pp. 405-407.

[105] (S) CCS 428 (Rev), Note by Secys, "Relation of Available Resources to Agreed Operations," 15 Dec 43, *Sextant*, pp. 315-373.

CHAPTER XXI

[1] (S) Memo, Hull to Roberts, "Suggested JCS Directive," nd, CNO (WPD) file "Agenda for Pacific Conference Dec '43," env 130, case 140, NR&H.

[2] (SS) Memo, Bieri to Roberts, "Directives to CinCSWPac and CincPOA," 26 Dec 43, CNO(WPD) file "Agenda for Pacific Conference Dec '43," env 130, case 140, NR&H.

[3] (SS) Msg, MacArthur to Com 3rd Flt, CinCPac, info CominCh and CofS USA, 061127 Jan 44, (TS) CominCh file "COMSOWESPAC Despatches Jan-Jun '44"; (SS) Msg, CinCPOA to CinCSoWesPac, 070521 Jan 44, (TS) CominCh file "CINCPAC DESPATCHES - Jan. '44 thru Feb. '44."

[4] (SS) Memo, Marshall to King, 20 Jan 44; (SS) Memo, King to Marshall, "Directive for Seizure or Control of BISMARCK ARCHIPELAGO," ser 00226, 22 Jan 44. Both in OPD Exec 10, item 68. (SS) Memo, Marshall to King, "Directive for Seizure or Control of BISMARCK ARCHIPELAGO," 23 Jan 44; (SS dg C) Msg, JCS to CINCSWPA, 231510 Jan 44; (SS dg C) Msg, JCS to CINCPOA, 231515 Jan 44. All in CCS 381 (2-28-43) sec 3.

[5] (SS) Memo, King to Marshall, "Directive for Seizure or Control of BISMARCK ARCHIPELAGO," ser 00226, 22 Jan 44, OPD Exec 10, item 68.

[6] (SS) Mns, PH Conf, King, Nimitz, *et al.*, 3 Jan '44, ff., CNO(WPD) file "Agenda for Pacific Conference Dec. '43," env 130, case 140, NR&H.

[7] (SS dg C) CinCPOA, "Campaign Plan GRANITE," 27 Dec 43. Summary in (S) JPS 390, "Campaign Plan 'GRANITE,'" 5 Feb 44, CCS 381 Japan (10-22-43).

[8] (SS) Mns, Pacific Conf, 27-28 Jan 44, CNO(WPD) file, env 131, case 140, NR&H; (SS) Mns of Conf, Sherman and Navy Dept Planners, 5 Feb 44, CNO(WPD) file "Conference Minutes and Agenda - Notes," env 142, safe 140, NR&H; (SS) Msg, Nimitz to King, 291839, 291852 Jan 44, (TS) CominCh file "CINCPAC Despatches Jan. '44 thru Feb. '44." (S) Memo, Col W.L. Ritchie to Handy, "Brief of Pacific Conference, held at Pearl Harbor 27-29 January 1944," 4 Feb 44; (S) Memo for File, nd; (S) Memo, Handy to Marshall, 7 Feb 44. All in OPD 334.8 Security, case 111. (SS) Ltr, Nimitz to King, "Assignment of Naval Forces and Assault Shipping to Third and Seventh Fleets for Operations Against The Bismarck Archipelago," ser 00014, 30 Jan 44, ABC 384 Pacific (1-17-43) sec 3-A. George C. Kenney, *General Kenney Reports* (New York, 1949), pp. 347-349.

[9] (SS) Ltr, Nimitz to King "Assignment of Naval Forces and Assault Shipping to Third and Seventh Fleets for Operations Against the Bismarck Archipelago," ser 00014, 30 Jan 44, ABC 384 Pacific (1-17-43) sec 3-A.

[10] (SC) Msg, CominCh-CNO to CinCPOA, 021936 Feb 44, WD CM-IN-1854, OPD TS Msg file; J.A. Isely and P.A. Crowl, *The U.S. Marines and Amphibious War* (Princeton, 1951), pp. 291-292.

[11] (SC) Msg, Marshall to MacArthur, 3406, CM-OUT-9541, 24 Jan 44, (TS) CominCh file "COMSOWESPAC Despatches Jan-Jun '44"; (SC) Msg, JCS to MacArthur and Nimitz, 3631, CM-OUT-12133, 30 Jan 44, CCS 045.9 (1-30-44).

[12] (SC) Msg, MacArthur to Marshall, C-1217, CM-IN-1443, 2 Feb 44, CCS 045.9 (1-30-44).

[13] (SS) Memo, King to Nimitz, ser 00409, 8 Feb 44, CominCh file "Secret Security A File - 1944."

[14] (SS) Memo, King to Marshall, "CinCSWPac Despatch C121702 February 1944," 8 Feb 44, OPD 384 TS, case 38.

[15] (S) Suppl Mns, JCS 145th Mtg, 8 Feb 44, item 7.

[16] (SS) Memo, Marshall to King, 10 Feb 44, OPD Exec 2, item 1b.

[17] (SS) Memo, King to Marshall, "1944 Operations in the Pacific Area," ser 00451, 11 Feb 44, OPD Exec 2, item 1b; (SS) Memo, JCS Secy to JSSC Secy, "Broad question of Pacific Strategy," 12 Feb 44, CCS 381 Pac. Ocean Area (6-10-43) sec 2.

[18] (S dg R) JCS 713, Rpt by JSSC, "Strategy in the Pacific," 16 Feb 44, CCS 381 Pac. Ocean Area (6-10-43) sec 2.

[19] (SS) Memo, Marshall to Leahy and King, 24 Feb 44, ABC 384 Pacific (1-17-43) sec 3-A.

[20] (SS) Memo, King to Marshall, "Proposed Joint Chiefs of Staff Directive to Commander in Chief, Pacific Ocean Areas, to Secure Control of the Carolines," ser 00629, 24 Feb 44, OPD Exec 10, item 68.

[21] (SS) Msg, Nimitz to King, 142253 Feb 44, (TS) CominCh file "CINCPAC Despatches - Jan '44 thru Feb '44"; (SS&P) Ltr, Nimitz to King, 22 Feb 44, CNO(WPD) file "Operations - Miscellaneous Central Pacific 0-12," env 63, case 139, NR&H.

[22] (SC)Msg, MacArthur to Marshall to Sutherland, eyes only, C1741, CM-IN-10909, 16 Feb 44, OPD TS Msg file.

[23] (SS) Memo, Bieri to Handy, 26 Feb 44, ABC 381 Japan (8-27-42) sec 6.

[24] (SS) Memo, King to Marshall, "J.C.S. 713," ser 00667, 27 Feb 44, OPD Exec 2, item 1b. (SS) Memo, Marshall to King, "Your Memorandum of 24 February on Proposed Directive to CINCPOA and Memorandum of 27 February on JCS 713," 1 Mar 44; (SS) Memo, King to Marshall, 1 Mar 44; (SS) Memo, Lt Col F.T. Newsome to McFarland, 2 Mar 44; (SC) Msg, JCS to MacArthur and Nimitz, 4785 & 729, CM-OUT-682, 2 Mar 44. All in CCS 381 Pac. Ocean Area (6-10-43) sec 2.

[25] (SS) Memo, King to Marshall, 1 Mar 44, CCS 381 Pac. Ocean Area (6-10-43) sec 2.

[26] (SC) Msg, MacArthur to JCS, C2473, CM-IN-3318, 5 Mar 44, CCS 381 Pac. Ocean Area (6-10-43) sec 2. Cf. (SS) Memo, Sutherland to Marshall "Post-KAVIENG Operations," 5 Mar 44, ABC 384 Pacific (1-17-43) sec 3-A.

²⁷(SS) RENO IV, "Outline Plan for Operations of the Southwest Pacific Area to Include the Reoccupation of the Southern Philippines," 6 Mar 44, CNO(WPD) file, env 68, case 184, NR&H.

²⁸(SS) Memo, CinCPac, no adee, "Sequence and Timing of Operations, Central Pacific Campaign," 7 Mar 44, circ as JCS Info Memo 200, 7 Mar 44, CCS 381 Pac. Ocean Area (6-10-43) sec 2.

²⁹(S) Memo, Nimitz to King, "Sequence and Timing of Operations, Central Pacific Campaign," 8 Mar 44, CCS 381 Pac. Ocean Area (6-10-43) sec 2.

³⁰(S) JWPC 186/1/D, Dir to White Team, "Future Operations in the Pacific," 2 Mar 44; (S) JWPC 186/3, Rpt by JWPC, same subj, 8 Mar 44. Both in CCS 381 Pac. Ocean Area (6-10-43) sec 2.

³¹(S) Mns, JPS 133rd Mtg, 8 Mar 44, item 1.

³²(S) JWPC 186/4, Rpt by JWPC, "Future Operations in the Pacific," 9 Mar 44, CCS 381 Pac. Ocean Area (6-10-43) sec 2.

³³(S) Mns, JPS 134th Mtg, 9 Mar 44, item 15; 135th Mtg, 10 Mar 44, item 1.

³⁴(S dg R) JCS 713/1, Rpt by JPS, "Future Operations in the Pacific," 10 Mar 44, CCS 381 Pac. Ocean Area (6-10-43) sec 2.

³⁵(S) Mns, JCS 151st Mtg, 11 Mar 44.

³⁶(S dg R) JCS Info Memo 203, Memo by CominCh-CNO, "Mounting an Invasion Force for Luzon-Formosa-China Area," 11 Mar 44, CCS 381 Pac. Ocean Area (6-10-43) sec 3.

³⁷(S dg R) JCS 713/2, Memo by CominCh-CNO, "Future Operations in the Pacific," 11 Mar 44, CCS 381 Pac. Ocean Area (6-10-43) sec 3.

³⁸(SS dg R) JCS 713/3, Rpt by JSSC, "Future Operations in the Pacific," 11 Mar 44, CCS 381 Pac. Ocean Area (6-10-43) sec 3.

³⁹(S) Mns, JCS 152nd Mtg, 12 Mar 44, item 1.

⁴⁰(SC) Msg, JCS to MacArthur and Nimitz, 5171 & 989, CM-OUT-5137, 12 Mar 44, CCS 381 Pac. Ocean Area (6-10-43) sec 3.

⁴¹(S dg U) JCS 762, Memo by CominCh, "Amended Shipping Requirements for Pacific Operations," 14 Mar 44, CCS 540 Pac. Ocean Area (9-6-43) sec 1.

⁴²(S) Memo, McFarland to Leahy, "Amended shipping requirements for Pacific Operations," 14 Mar 42; (TS) Memo, Newsome to Sect JCS, "JCS 762 - Amended Shipping Requirements for Pacific Operation," 16 Mar 44. Both in CCS 540 Pac. Ocean Area (9-6-43) sec 1.

⁴³(TS) CD-10, 20 Mar 44.

⁴⁴(TS dg U) JCS 762/1, Rpt by JMTC, "Amended Shipping Requirements for Pacific Operation," 29 Mar 44, CCS 540 Pac. Ocean Area (9-6-43) sec 1.

⁴⁵(S) Msg, Marshall to MacArthur, WAR-16504, CM-OUT-16504, 30 Mar 44; (S) Msg, Marshall to Harmon, WAR-16505, CM-OUT-16505, 30 Mar 44; (S) Msg, Marshall to Richardson, WARX-16506, CM-OUT-16506, 30 Mar 44; (TS) Msg, MacArthur to Marshall, C-10245, 31 Mar 44, rptd in (TS) JMT 50/2/D, Note by Secy, "Amended Shipping Requirements for Pacific Operations," 1 Apr 44. All in CCS 540 Pac. Ocean Area (9-6-43) sec 1.

46 (TS) Memo, McFarland to Leahy, Arnold, Horne, "Amended Shipping Requirements for Pacific Operations," 1 Apr 44, CCS 540 Pac. Ocean Area (9-6-43) sec 1.

47 (TS dg U) JCS 762/2, Rpt by JMTC, "Amended Shipping Requirements for Pacific Operations," 4 Apr 44, CCS 540 Pac. Ocean Area (9-6-43) sec 1.

48 (TS) Suppl Mns, JCS 156th Mtg, 4 Apr 44, item 1; (TS dg C) Msg, JCS to MacArthur and Nimitz, WARX-18510, CM-OUT-18510, 4 Apr 44, CCS 540 Pac. Ocean Area (9-6-43) sec 1.

49 (TS dg U) JCS 962/3, Rpt by JMTC, "Shipping Requirements and Availabilities for Pacific Operations," 25 Apr 44, CCS 540 Pac. Ocean Area (9-6-43) sec 1. Minutes of the Pacific Shipping Conference are in the same file. For discussion of ANVIL, see CCS 465/12 through /20, CCS 381 (1-11-44) sec 3. Cf. *Closing the Ring*, pp. 511-515.

50 (TS) Mns, JPS 148th Mtg, 30 Apr 44, item 1; 149th Mtg, 2 May 44, item 1.

51 (TS dg C) JCS 762/4, Rpt by JPS, "Shipping Requirements and Availabilities for Pacific Operations," 5 May 44, CCS 540 Pac. Ocean Area (9-6-43) sec 2.

52 (TS) JMT 50/6, Rpt by JMTC, "Shipping Requirements and Availabilities for Pacific Operations," 4 May 44, CCS 540 Pac. Ocean Area (9-6-43) sec 2.

53 (TS) CD, JCS 762/4, 6 May 44. (TS dg C) Msg, JCS to MacArthur, Nimitz, Halsey, WARX-33051, CM-OUT-33051, 6 May 44; (TS) Memo, DSecy JCS to JMTC, "Shipping requirements and availabilities for Pacific operations," 6 May 44; (TS dg C) Msg, JCS to MacArthur, WAR-33050, CM-OUT-33050, 6 May 44. All in CCS 540 Pac. Ocean Area (9-6-43) sec 2.

54 (TS dg U) JCS 762/7, Rpt by JMTC, "Shipping Requirements and Availabilities for Pacific Operations," 7 Jun 44, CCS 540 Pac. Ocean Area (9-6-43) sec 2.

55 (SS) Msg, Nimitz to King, 291852 Jan 44, (TS) CominCh file "CINCPAC Despatches Jan '44 thru Feb '44." (SS) Mns of Conf, Sherman and Navy Dept Planners, 5 Feb 44, CNO(WPD) file "Conference Minutes and Agenda - Notes," env 142, safe 140, NR&H.

56 (TS) Msg, Marshall to MacArthur, 5448, CM-OUT-8237, 20 Mar 44, CCS 045.9 (1-30-44).

57 Leahy, pp. 228-230.

58 (TS) Msg, MacArthur to Marshall, C3227, CM-IN-15706, 22 Mar 44, CCS 045.9 (1-30-44).

59 (TS dg U) JCS 790, Memo by CominCh-CNO, "Naval Bases in South Pacific Areas for Supporting Future Operations," 27 Mar 44, CCS 045.9 (1-30-44).

60 (TS dg U) JCS 790/1, Memo by CofS USA, "Naval Bases in South Pacific and Southwest Pacific Areas for Supporting Future Operations," 30 Mar 44, CCS 045.9 (1-30-44).

61 (TS dg U) JCS 790/2, Memo by CominCh-CNO, "Naval Bases in South Pacific and Southwest Pacific Areas for Supporting Future Operations," 31 Mar 44, CCS 045.9 (1-30-44).

⁶²(TS) JPS 427/2, Rpt by JPS, "Command and Control of Bases in the Southwest Pacific Area Being Utilized by Forces from Other Areas," 21 Apr 44; (TS dg U) JCS 790/3, Rpt by JPS, same subj, 26 Apr 44. Both in CCS 045.9 (1-30-44).

⁶³(TS) CD, JCS 790/3, 8 May 44; (TS dg C) Msg, JCS to MacArthur and Nimitz, WARX-30441, CM-OUT-30441, 1 May 44, CCS 045.9 (1-30-44).

⁶⁴(SS) Memo, JPS Secy to JWPC Sect, "Deployment of Forces Now assigned to the South Pacific After Completion of FOREARM and MERCANTILE," 14 Jan 44, CCS 370 South Pac. Area (1-14-44) sec 1.

⁶⁵(TS dg R) JCS 713/5, Rpt by JPS, "Redeployment of Forces in the Pacific Following Operation 'RECKLESS,'" 17 Mar 44, CCS 370 South Pac. Area (1-14-44) sec 1. All preliminary drafts are in the same file.

⁶⁶This provision was subsequently modified when the New Zealand authorities objected to the removal of their air forces from combat operations, and part of them were transferred to the Southwest Pacific. Cf. (TS dg R) JCS 884/2, Rpt by JPS, "Employment of Royal New Zealand Air Force Squadrons," 10 Jun 44, CCS 373 New Zealand (5-29-44).

⁶⁷(TS) Memo, Grave to ACofS OPD and Aide to CominCh, "Redeployment of forces in the Pacific following operation RECKLESS," 25 Mar 44; (TS) Msg, Marshall to MacArthur, WARX-14572, CM-OUT-14572, 25 Mar 44. Both in CCS 370 South Pac. Area (1-14-44) sec 2.

⁶⁸(TS) Mns, Pacific Conf, 5 May 44, CNO(WPD) file "Pacific Conference Agenda - May 1944," env 133, safe 140, NR&H.

⁶⁹(TS) Memo, Col J.H. Baumann to Handy, 20 May 44; (TS) Msg, CinCSWPA to CinCPOA, CominCh, War Dept, 210747 May 44; (TS) Memo, King to Marshall, "Commander in Chief, Southwest Pacific Area Despatch 210747, Copy Attached," 6 Jun 44; (S) Memo, Marshall to King, 6 May 44; (TS) Msg, CofS USA and CominCh, to CinCSWPA, 6 Jun 44. All in OPD 384 TS, case 40.

CHAPTER XXII

¹(U) Msg, Pres to Gimo, 5 Dec 43, quoted in Sherwood, p. 802.

²(S) Msg, Gimo to Pres, eyes only, 919, CM-IN-5966, 9 Dec 43, OPD Exec 10, item 58.

³In copies of the message in CCS 381 South East Asia (12-5-43) and CCS 381 Burma (8-25-42) sec 5 the word "billion" has been omitted.

⁴(UNK) Msg, Gimo to Pres, 17 Dec 43, quoted in Charles F. Romanus and Riley Sunderland, MS, *U.S. Army in World War II: China-Burma-India Theater, Stilwell's Command Problems*, pp. 11-52.

⁵(SS) Memo, McNarney to Leahy, "Loan to China," 20 Dec 43, OPD Exec 10, item 64.

⁶(UNK) Msg, Pres to Gimo, 4092, 20 Dec 43, OPD Exec 10, item 58.

⁷(S) CCS 411/6, Memo by BCOS, "Operations in South East Asia Command," 21 Dec 43, CCS 381 Burma (8-25-42) sec 6.

⁸*Closing the Ring*, pp. 427-441.
⁹(SS dg S) CCS 452, Msg by BCOS, "Cancellation of Operation 'PIGSTICK,'" 30 Dec 43, CCS 381 Burma (8-25-42) sec 6.
¹⁰(SS) Mns, CPS 103rd Mtg, 1 Jan 44, item 1; (SS) Mns, JPS 119th Mtg, 1 Jan 44, item 1.
¹¹(SS dg S) CCS 452/1, Memo by JCS, "Cancellation of Operation 'PIGSTICK,'" 4 Jan 44, CCS 381 Burma (8-25-42) sec 6.
¹²(SS dg S) CCS 452/2, Memo by RBCOS, "Cancellation of Operation 'PIGSTICK,'" 6 Jan 44, CCS 381 Burma (8-25-42) sec 6.
¹³(SS dg C) CCS 452/3, Memo by RBCOS, "Cancellation of Operation 'PIGSTICK,'" 6 Jan 44, CCS 381 Burma (8-25-42) sec 6.
¹⁴(S) Suppl Mns, CCS 140th Mtg, 7 Jan 44, item 1.
¹⁵(SS dg C) CCS 452/4, Memo by RBCOS, "Operations in Burma, 1944," 21 Jan 44, CCS 381 Burma (8-25-42) sec 6.
¹⁶(SS dg R) JCS 678, Rpt by JPS, "Operations in Burma, 1944," 25 Jan 44, CCS 381 Burma (8-25-42) sec 6.
¹⁷(SS dg C) CCS 452/5, Memo by JCS, "Operations in Burma, 1944," 25 Jan 44, CCS 381 Burma (8-25-42) sec 6.
¹⁸(S dg R) JCS 678/1, Rpt by JPS, "Operations in South East Asia," 16 Feb 44, CCS 381 Burma (8-25-42) sec 6; Mountbatten Report, pp. 30-31; (MS) Msg, SACSEA to BCOS, info BJSM, SEACOS 61, 8 Jan 44, SEAC Diary.
¹⁹(MS) Mns, SACSEA 50th Mtg, 26 Jan 44, item 6; 52nd Mtg, 31 Jan 44, item 1. Both in SEAC Diary.
²⁰(S dg R) App "B" to JCS 678/1, 16 Feb 44, CCS 381 Burma (8-25-42) sec 6.
²¹(SS dg R) JCS 678/1, Rpt by JPS, "Operations in South East Asia," 16 Feb 44, CCS 381 Burma (8-25-42) sec 6.
²²(UNK) CD, JCS 678/1, 17 Feb 44; (SS dg C) CCS 452/6, Memo by JCS, "Operations in Southeast Asia," 17 Feb 44, CCS 381 Burma (8-25-42) sec 6.
²³(SS dg C) CCS 452/7, Memo by RBCOS, "Operations in Southeast Asia," 20 Feb 44, CCS 381 Burma (8-25-42) sec 6.
²⁴(SS) Mns, JPS 130th Mtg, 23 Feb 44, item A.
²⁵(SS) JCS Info Memo 193, "South East Asia Command Strategy in SEAC," 23 Feb 44, CCS 381 Burma (8-25-42) sec 6; (S) "Information Book S.E.A.C.," CCS 381 Burma (8-25-42) BP.
²⁶(SS dg C) CCS 452/8, Memo by RBCOS, "Operations in Southeast Asia," 26 Feb 44, CCS 381 Burma (8-25-42) sec 7; (S) Ltr, Wedemeyer to Mountbatten, 16 Feb 44, SEAC Diary.
²⁷(S) Mns, CCS 148th Mtg, 3 Mar 44, item 1.
²⁸(U) Memo, Brig H. Redman to Col A.J. McFarland, "Strategy in Southeast Asia Command - *Directive to Combined Staff Planners*," 4 Mar 44, CCS 381 Burma (8-25-42) sec 7.
²⁹(TS dg R) JCS 774, Rpt by JPS, "Strategy in Southeast Asia Command," 16 Mar 44, CCS 381 Burma (8-25-42) sec 7.
³⁰(TS) Mns, JPS 139th Mtg, 20 Mar 44, item 1.
³¹(TS) Suppl Mns, JCS 154th Mtg, 21 Mar 44, item 1.
³²(TS dg C) CCS 452/10, Memo by JCS, "Strategy in Southeast Asia Command," 21 Mar 44, CCS 381 Burma (8-25-42) sec 7.

[33] (TS) Msg, BCOS to SACSEA, COSSEA-80, CM-IN-17975, 25 Mar 44, CCS 381 Burma (8-25-42) sec 7.

[34] (TS) Msg, Mountbatten to BCOS & BJSM, SEACOS-137, 14 Apr 44, CM-IN-11044 (15 Apr 44), CCS 381 Burma (8-25-42) sec 7.

[35] (TS) Msg, Marshall to Sultan, WARX-23614, CM-OUT-23614, 15 Apr 44, CCS 381 Burma (8-25-42) sec 7. The reason for the delay by the British is not apparent from available records. The comments finally sent did not refer to any documents subsequently received.

[36] (TS dg C) CCS 452/11, Memo by RBCOS, "Strategy in Southeast Asia Command," 10 May 44, CCS 381 Burma (8-25-42) sec 8; (S) Ltr, Wedemeyer to Mountbatten, 4 Apr 44, SEAC Diary, indicates the Prime Minister at least still hoped for some form of Culverin.

[37] (TS) JPS 406/3, Rpt by JWPC, "Strategy in Southeast Asia Command," 16 May 44, CCS 381 Burma (8-25-42) sec 7.

[38] (TS) Mns, JPS 152nd Mtg, 17 May 44, item 9; 153rd Mtg, 24 May 44, item 14. (TS dg R) JCS 774/1, Rpt by JPS, "Strategy in Southeast Asia Command," 20 May 44, with corrigenda dated 22 May and 25 May 44, CCS 381 Burma (8-25-42) sec 8. (TS) Memo, Somervell to Handy, "Strategy in Southeast ASIA Command, JCS 774/1," 22 May 44; (TS) Memo, Handy to Somervell, "Strategy in Southeast Asia Command, JCS 774/1," 24 May 44. Both in OPD 384 TS, case 6.

[39] Romanus-Sunderland MS, *Stilwell's Command Problems*, ch VI, pp. 32-40.

[40] (TS) Msg, JCS to Stilwell, WARX-31202, CM-OUT-31202, 2 May 44, CCS 481 Burma (8-25-42) sec 8.

[41] (TS) Msg, Stilwell to Marshall, 240240 May 44, CM-IN-18256, CCS 381 Burma (8-25-42) sec 8.

[42] (TS) Msg, Marshall to Stilwell, eyes only, WARX-42202, CM-OUT-42202, 26 May 44, CCS 381 Burma (8-25-42) sec 8.

[43] (TS) Msg, CCS to SACSEAC, COSSEA-108, 3 Jun 44, CM-IN-2665 (4 Jun 44), CCS 381 Burma (8-25-42) sec 8; (TS) Suppl Mns, CCS 161st Mtg, 2 Jun 44, item 5.

[44] (MS) Msg, Mountbatten to BCOS, SEACOS-92, 14 Feb 44, SEAC Diary; (SS) CCS 494, Memo by RBCOS, "Diversion of Transport Aircraft to Arakan from Air Lift to China," 21 Feb 44, CCS 452 Burma (2-18-44) sec 1.

[45] (SS) Memo, Col W.E. Todd to Capt Forrest B. Royal, 22 Feb 44; (SS) CCS 494/1, Memo by JCS, "Diversion of Transport Aircraft to Arakan from Air Lift to China," 22 Feb 44. Both in CCS 452 Burma (2-18-44) sec 1. (S) Suppl Mns, JCS 148th Mtg, 22 Feb 44, item 9.

[46] (SC) Msg, Mountbatten to BCOS, SEACOS-101, 23 Feb 44, CCS 452 Burma (2-18-44) sec 1.

[47] (MS) Msg, BCOS to Mountbatten, COSSEA-65, 24 Feb 44, CCS 452 Burma (2-18-44) sec 1.

[48] (S) CCS 494/2, Memo by JCS, "Diversion of Transport Aircraft to Arakan from Air Lift to China," 25 Feb 44, CCS 452 Burma (2-18-44) sec 1.

[49] Mountbatten Report, pp. 45-46; (TS) Msg, SACSEA to BCOS, SEACOS-112, CM-IN-11270, 16 Mar 44, CCS 452 Burma (2-18-44) sec 1.

[50] (TS) Msg, Mountbatten to BCOS, SEACOS-113, CM-IN-11302, 15 Mar 44, CCS 452 Burma (2-18-44) sec 1.

[51] (TS) Msg, Maj Gen Daniel I. Sultan to Marshall, AG-1602, CM-IN-11275, 16 Mar 44; (TS) CCS 494/4, Memo by JCS, "Diversion of Transport Aircraft from Air Lift to China," 17 Mar 44. Both in CCS 452 Burma (2-18-44) sec 1. (TS) Mns, JPS 138th Mtg, 16 Mar 44, item 2; (S) Suppl Mns, CCS 150th Mtg, 17 Mar 44, item 13. PM Churchill also cabled Pres Roosevelt about Adm Mountbatten's situation, concluding, "We trust that US Chiefs of Staff will agree." (TS) Msg, PM to Pres, 622, 17 Mar 44, OPD Exec 10, item 63c.

[52] (MS) Msg, Mountbatten to BCOS, SEACOS-116, 17 Mar 44, SEAC Diary; Romanus-Sunderland MS, *Stilwell's Command Problems*, ch VIII, pp. 14-29.

[53] (TS) Msg, Pres to Gimo, WAR-4762, 17 Mar 44, OPD Exec 10, item 55.

[54] (UNK) Msg, Gimo to Pres, 27 Mar 44, quoted in Romanus-Sunderland MS, *Stilwell's Command Problems*, ch VIII, pp. 19-20.

[55] (TS) Msg, Pres to Gimo, CM-OUT-17956, 3 Apr 44, atchd to Memo, Marshall to Pres, 3 Apr 44, OPD Exec 10, item 55. The message was drafted in the War Dept, but the last sentence was added by the President.

[56] (UNK) Msg, Ho Ying-chin to Marshall, 14 Apr 44, quoted in Romanus-Sunderland MS, *Stilwell's Command Problems*, ch VIII, p. 28.

[57] (TS) Msg, Mountbatten to BCOS, SEACOS-123, CM-IN-19251, 27 Mar 44, CCS 452 Burma (2-19-44) sec 1.

[58] (TS) CCS 494/7, Memo by RBCOS, "Diversion of Transport Aircraft from Air Lift to China," 27 Mar 44, CCS 452 Burma (2-18-42) sec 1; (TS) Suppl Mns, CCS 151st Mtg, 24 Mar 44, item 3; (TS) Msg, BCOS to SACSEAC, 021620, 251620 Mar 44, SEAC Diary.

[59] (TS) Msg, Arnold to Portal, WAR-14633, CM-OUT-14633, 26 Mar 44, CCS 452 Burma (2-18-44) sec 1.

[60] (TS) CCS 494/6, Memo by JCS, "Diversion of Transport Aircraft from Air Lift to China," 27 Mar 44, CCS 452 Burma (2-18-44) sec 1.

[61] (TS) CCS 494/8, Memo by RBCOS, "Diversion of Transport Aircraft from Air Lift to China," 28 Mar 44, CCS 452 Burma (2-18-44) sec 1.

[62] (TS) CCS 494/9, Memo by JCS, "Diversion of Transport Aircraft from Air Lift to China," 28 Mar 44, CCS 452 Burma (2-18-44) sec 1; (TS) Suppl Mns, JCS 155th Mtg, 28 Mar 44, item 10.

[63] (TS) CCS 494/10, Memo by RBCOS, "Diversion of Transport Aircraft from Air Lift to China," 2 Apr 44, CCS 452 Burma (2-18-44) sec 1.

[64] (TS) CCS 494/11, Memo by RBCOS, "Diversion of Aircraft from Air Lift to China," 29 Apr 44, CCS 452 Burma (2-18-44) sec 1.

[65] (TS) CCS 494/12, Memo by JCS, "Diversion of Aircraft from Air Lift to China," 5 May 44, CCS 452 Burma (2-18-44) sec 1.

[66] (TS) CCS 494/13, Memo by RBCOS, "Diversion of Aircraft from Air Lift to China," 6 May 44, CCS 452 Burma (2-18-44) sec 1.

CHAPTER XXIII

[1] (UNK) Ltr, Chennault to Pres, 26 Jan 44, Hopkins Papers.

[2] (SS dg R) JCS 713/1, Rpt by JPS, "Future Operations in the Pacific," 10 Mar 44, CCS 381 Pac. Ocean Area (6-10-43) sec 2.

[3] (TS) Msg, Arnold to Stratemeyer, 4752, 5034, CM-OUT-6678, 15 Mar 44, CCS 381 Formosa (7-15-43) sec 1.

[4] (TS) Msg, Kuter to Arnold, W-813, CM-IN-14364, 20 Mar 44; (TS) Msg, Arnold to Kuter, 5091, CM-OUT-8657, 21 Mar 44; (TS) Msg, Arnold to Stratemeyer, WAR-13790, CM-OUT-13790, 24 Mar 44; (TS) Msg, Stratemeyer to Arnold, W-885, CM-IN-19205, 27 Mar 44; (TS) Msg, Stratemeyer to Arnold, 834, CM-IN-7524, 11 Apr 44. All in CCS 381 Formosa (7-15-43) sec 1.

[5] (TS) Msg, Marshall to Stilwell, WAR-20146, CM-OUT-20146, 7 Apr 44, CCS 381 Formosa (7-15-43) sec 1.

[6] (TS) JWPC 207/1, Rpt by JWPC, "Directive to Commanding General, U.S. Army Forces, China, Burma, and India," 12 Apr 44, CCS 381 Formosa (7-15-43) sec 1.

[7] (TS) Mns, JPS 145th Mtg, 12 Apr 44, item 11; 146th Mtg, 19 Apr 44, item 9; 147th Mtg, 26 Apr 44, item 5. (TS) Memo, no sig, to Roberts, "J.W.P.C. 207/1," 15 Apr 44; (TS) Memo, JWPC Secy to JPS Secy, Proposed Directive to CGUSAFCBI," 25 Apr 44; (TS dg C) JCS 839, Rpt by JPS, "Instructions to Commanding General, U.S. Army Forces in China-Burma-India, Regarding Air Support of Pacific Operations," 28 Apr 44. All in CCS 381 Formosa (7-15-43) sec 1.

[8] Gen McNarney was representing Gen Marshall at this meeting. Gen Kuter was representing Gen Arnold. Adm Leahy was not present.

[9] (TS) Suppl Mns, JCS 161st Mtg, 2 May 44, item 2; (TS dg C) JCS 839/1, Msg, "Instructions to Commanding General, U.S. Army Forces in China-Burma-India, Regarding Air Support of Pacific Operations," 2 May 44, CCS 381 Formosa (7-15-43) sec 1; (TS) Msg, JCS to Stilwell, WARX 31202, CM-OUT-31202, 2 May 44, CCS 381 Burma (8-25-42) sec 8.

[10] (S dg R) JCS 665, Memo by CofS USA, "Commanding Relationships, VLR Units, India-China," 15 Jan 44, CCS 323.361 (1-14-44) sec 1.

[11] (S dg R) JCS 665/1, Note by Secys, "Command Relationships, VLR Units, India-China," 18 Jan 44, CCS 323.361 (1-14-44) sec 1.

[12] (MS) Msg, Mountbatten to BCOS, SEACOS-105, 26 Feb 44, CCS 323.361 (1-14-44) sec 1. This was the second GO issued by Gen Stilwell. The first, GO 13, dated 30 Jan 44, delegated control to Gen Stratemeyer. Gen Stilwell and Brig Gen K.B. Wolfe, CG, XX Bomber Command, agreed to change it because they feared that Gen Stratemeyer was too closely connected with Adm Mountbatten

in SEAC and that he might arrange to give Gen Chennault practical control of the XX Bomber Command. Both Adm Mountbatten and Gen Chennault were eager to control the B-29's. Romanus-Sunderland MS, *Stilwell's Command Problems*, ch III, pp. 49-50; (UNK) Ltr, Chennault to Pres, 26 Jan 44, Hopkins Papers.

[13] (TS dg S) CCS 501, Memo by RBCOS, "Method of Control, 20th Bomber Command," 28 Feb 44, CCS 323.361 (1-14-44) sec 1.

[14] (SS) Memo, JPS Secy to Sect JWPC, "Method of Control, 20th Bomber Command," 1 Mar 44; (U) Remark on routing slip sgd CRP[eck]; (SS dg S) JCS 747, Memo by CG AAF, same subj, 6 Mar 44. All in CCS 323.361 (1-14-44) sec 1.

[15] (SS) JPS 381, Rpt by JWPC, "Optimum Use, Timing and Deployment of V.L.R. Bombers in the War against Japan," 24 Jan 44; (SS) JIC 152/2, same subj, 18 Jan 44. Both in CCS 373.11 Japan (8-20-43) pt 3.

[16] (SC) Msg, MacArthur to Marshall, C-1217, CM-IN-1443, 2 Feb 44, CCS 045.9 (1-30-44). Adm King also was inclined at the time to the view that "the earliest effective employment of the B-29" would be from bases in northwestern Australia. (SS) Memo, King to Marshall, "CinCSWPac Despatch C121702 February 1944," 8 Feb 44, OPD 384 TS, case 38.

[17] (S) Mns, JPS 131st Mtg, 24 Feb 44, item 2.

[18] (S) Mns, JPS 123rd Mtg, 26 Jan 44, item 12; 127th Mtg, 9 Feb 44, item 1; 128th Mtg, 16 Feb 44, item 10; 131st Mtg, 24 Feb 44, item 2; 132nd Mtg, 1 Mar 44, item 2. (SS) JPS 381/1, Rev Rpt by JWPC, "Optimum Use, Timing and Deployment of V.L.R. Bombers in the War against Japan," 15 Feb 44; (SS) JPS 381/2, Memo by AAF Planner, same subj, 27 Feb 44; (SS dg S) JCS 742, Rpt by JPS, same subj, 2 Mar 44. All in CCS 373.11 Japan (8-20-43) pt 4.

[19] (SS dg S) JCS 747, Memo by CG AAF, "Method of Control, 20th Bomber Command," 6 Mar 44, CCS 323.361 (1-14-44) sec 1.

[20] (SS) Suppl Mns, JCS 150th Mtg, 7 Mar 44, item 7.

[21] (SC) Msg, Arnold to Stratemeyer, Wolfe, Kuter, 4916, CM-OUT-3058, 8 Mar 44, CCS 323.361 (1-14-44) sec 1.

[22] (SS dg R) JCS 742/1, Memo by CG AAF, "Optimum Use, Timing and Deployment of V.L.R. Bombers in the War against Japan," 6 Mar 44, CCS 273.11 Japan (8-20-43) pt 4.

[23] (SS dg R) JCS 742/2, Memo by CominCh, "Optimum Use, Timing and Deployment of V.L.R. Bombers in the War against Japan," 6 Mar 44, CCS 373.11 Japan (8-20-43) pt 4.

[24] (S) Suppl Mns, JCS 150th Mtg, 7 Mar 44, item 4.

[25] (S) Mns, JPS 137th Mtg, 15 Mar 44, item 3.

[26] (TS dg R) JCS 742/3, Rpt by JPS, "Optimum Use, Timing, and Deployment of VLR Bombers in the War against Japan," 16 Mar 44, CCS 373.11 Japan (8-20-43) pt 4.

[27] (U) Memo, Capt E.D. Graves to McFarland, 25 Mar 44, CCS 373.11 Japan (8-20-43) pt 4.

[28] (TS dg R) JCS 742/4, Rpt by JSSC, "Optimum Use, Timing, and Deployment of VLR Bombers in the War against Japan," 27 Mar 44, CCS 373.11 Japan (8-20-43) pt 4.

[29] (TS) Msg, MacArthur to Marshall, C10100, CM-IN-18550, 26 Mar 44, CCS 373.11 Japan (8-20-43) pt 4; (TS) Msg, CinCPac to CominCh, 260833 Mar 44, CNO(WPD) file "South East Asia Command Matters S-2 (1)," env 48, safe 139, NR&H; (TS) JCS 797/1, Rpt by JPS, "Bombing of Refineries at Balikpapan, Palembang and Surabaya," 20 Apr 44, CCS 373.11 Japan (8-20-43) pt 5.

[30] (TS) Suppl Mns, JCS 155th Mtg, 28 Mar 44, item 6.

[31] (TS dg R) JCS 742/5, Note by Secys, "Command and Control of VLR Bomber Forces in the War against Japan," 1 Apr 44, CCS 373.11 Japan (8-20-43) pt 4.

[32] (S) Ltr, Brig Gen R.H. Dunlop, Actg AG, to CG AAF, "Constitution and Activation of the Headquarters, Twentieth Air Force," 4 Apr 44, CCS 373.11 Japan (8-20-43) pt 4.

[33] (TS dg S) JCS 742/6, Rpt by JPS, "VLR Bombers in the War against Japan," 6 Apr 44, CCS 373.11 Japan (8-20-43) pt 5.

[34] (TS) CD, JCS 742/6, 10 Apr 44.

[35] (TS dg S) JCS 747/2, Memo by CG AAF, "Method of Control, 20th Bomber Command," 14 Apr 44, CCS 323.361 (1-14-44) sec 1. Two earlier drafts were submitted to the JCS Sect and one of them circulated as JCS 747/1 on 11 Apr. All are in the same file, but there is no indication why the successive replacements were made.

[36] (TS dg S) CCS 501/3, Memo by RBCOS, "Method of Control, 20th Bomber Command," 15 Apr 44; (TS dg S) JCS 747/3, Note by Secys, same subj, 19 Apr 44; (TS dg S) CCS 501/4, Memo by JCS, same subj, 19 Apr 44. All in CCS 323.361 (1-14-44) sec 1.

[37] (TS) Suppl Mns, CCS 156th Mtg, 21 Apr 44, item 3; (TS) Mns, CCS 166th Mtg, 15 Jun 44, item 5.

[38] (TS dg R) JPS 267/1, Rpt by JWPC, "Seizure and Occupation of Formosa," 16 May 44, CCS 381 Formosa (7-15-43) sec 1 pt 1.

[39] (TS) Msg, Sultan to JCS, CRA-4415, CM-IN-22117, 29 May 44; (TS dg S) JPS 406/6, Note by Secys, "Strategy in Southeast Asia Command," 8 Jun 44. Both in CCS 381 Formosa (7-15-43) sec 2.

[40] For development of the theater plan Enterprise for building up Hump tonnage, see (C) AF (MSTS)MS, *A History of the India-China Division Air Transport Command, Year 1944* (hereinafter: MSTS MS), vol I, pp. 31-43.

[41] (TS) Msg, Marshall(?) to Sultan, Stilwell, Mountbatten, WARX-53610, CM-OUT-53610, 20 Jun 44, extract in CCS 381 Formosa (7-15-43) sec 2.

[42] (TS) Msg, Stratemeyer to Arnold, CABX-2629, CM-IN-21099, 26 Jun 44, CCS 381 Formosa (7-15-43) sec 2.

[43] (TS dg R) JCS 940, Memo by CG AAF, "Augmentation of India-China Division, Air Transport Command," 7 Jul 44, CCS 381 Formosa (7-15-43) sec 2.

[44] (TS dg R) JCS 940/1, Rpt by JLC, "Augmentation of India-China Division, Air Transport Command," 11 Aug 44; (TS dg R) JCS 940/2, Memo by CG AAF, same subj, 14 Aug 44. Both in CCS 381 Formosa (7-15-43) sec 3. (TS) CD, JCS 940/2, 25 Aug 44.

[45] Romanus-Sunderland MS, *Stilwell's Command Problems*, chs VIII-XI.

[46] Figures are from MSTS MS, vol I, p. 44.

[47] (TS) Ltr, Gen Shang Chen to Marshall, 31 May 44; (TS) Memo for Rec, "Air Shipment of supplies to China," 13 Jun 44. Both in OPD 336 TS sec IV, case 78.

[48] (TS) Aide-Memoire, Shang Chen to Pres, 31 May 44, OPD Exec 10, item 61; (TS) Memo, DCofS to Leahy, "Generalissimo's Request for Assistance," 12 Jun 44, w/encls, OPD Exec 10, item 64; (S) Memo for Rec, "Conference between Chiang Kai-shek and Stilwell, 5 Jun 44," Stilwell Papers, Hoover Library; (TS) Mns, CCS 162nd Mtg, 10 Jun 44; (TS) Msg, McNarney to Stilwell, 11 Jun 44, OPD 336 TS sec IV, case 78.

[49] (TS) Msg, Chennault to Sultan, CAKX-5769, 3 Aug 44, CM-IN 2362, CCS 373.11 Japan (8-20-43) pt 6. (TS) Msg, Marshall to Stilwell, WAR-75599, CM-OUT-75599, 4 Aug 44; (TS) Msg, Stilwell to Marshall, TST-525, CM-IN-4176, 5 Aug 44. Both in OPD TS Msg file.

[50] (TS dg R) JCS 959, Memo by CG AAF, "Strategy in China-Burma-India," 15 Jul 44, CCS 381 Burma (8-25-42) sec 9.

[51] (TS) JPS 406/15, Rpt by JWPC, "Strategy in Southeast Asia," 31 Jul 44, CCS 381 Burma (8-25-42) sec 9.

[52] (TS) Mns, JPS 162nd Mtg, 10 Aug 44, item 3.

[53] (TS) Msg, Marshall to Stilwell, WAR-78509, CM-OUT-78509, 10 Aug 44, OPD TS Msg file.

[54] (TS) Msg, Giles sgd Stratemeyer to Arnold, CABX-4039, CM-IN-1539, 2 Aug 44, OPD TS Msg file.

[55] (TS dg S) Msg, Sultan to Marshall, CRA-10808, CM-IN-12874, 14 Aug 44, CCS 373.11 Japan (8-20-43) pt 6.

[56] (TS dg R) JCS 959/1, Rpt by JPS, "Strategy in China-Burma-India," 14 Aug 44, CCS 381 Burma (8-25-42) sec 10.

[57] (TS) Memo, Arnold to Secy JCS, "Strategy in China-Burma-India," 21 Aug 44, CCS 381 Burma (8-25-42) sec 11.

[58] (TS) CD, JCS 959/1, 25 Aug 44; (TS) Msg, JCS to Stilwell, WAR-87086, CM-OUT-87086, 26 Aug 44, CCS 381 Burma (8-25-42) sec 11.

[59] (TS dg S) JPS 507/D, Dir w/encl, "Outline Plans for China Based Air Support of Pacific Operations," 21 Aug 44, CCS 381 Formosa (7-15-43) sec 3.

[60] (TS dg R) JCS 839/2, Rpt by JPS, "Outline Plan for China Based Air Support of Pacific Operations," 11 Sep 44, CCS 381 Formosa (7-15-43) sec 4.

[61] (TS) Memo Sweeney to Horne and McNarney, "Outline Plans for China Based Air Support of Pacific Operations," 14 Sep 44; (TS) Memo, ADCofS O.L. Nelson to Sect JCS, same subj, circ as (S dg C) DA JCS 839/2, 22 Sep 44. All in CCS 381 Formosa (7-15-43) sec 4.

[62] (TS dg C) Msg, JCS to Stilwell, Nimitz, and MacArthur, WARX-34928, CM-OUT-34928, 22 Sep 44, CCS 381 Formosa (7-15-43) sec 4.

CHAPTER XXIV

[1] (SC) Msg, JCS to MacArthur and Nimitz, 4785 & 729, CM-OUT-682, 2 Mar 44, CCS 381 Pac. Ocean Area (6-10-43) sec 2

873 NOTES TO CHAPTER XXIV

[2] (TS dg R) JCS 713/6, Rpt by JSSC, "Future Operations in the Pacific," 29 May 44, CCS 381 Pac. Ocean Area (6-10-43) sec 3.

[3] (S) CD, JCS 713/6, 1 Jun 44.

[4] (U) Memo, Secy JSSC to JPS, "Effect of Current China Situation on Planning for Operations against Japan," 3 Jun 44, CCS 381 Pac. Ocean Area (6-10-43) sec 4.

[5] (TS) Msg, MacArthur to JCS, C-12287, CM-IN-6163, 8 May 43, CCS 381 Pac. Ocean Area (6-10-43) sec 3.

[6] (TS) JPS 404/3, Rpt by JWPC, "Future Operations in the Pacific," 3 Jun 43, CCS 381 Pac. Ocean Area (6-10-43) sec 4; (TS) Mns, Pacific Conf, Pearl Harbor, 6 May 44, CNO(WPD) file "Pacific Conference Agenda - May 1944," env 133, safe 140, NR&H.

[7] (TS) Mns, JCS 166th Mtg, 6 Jun 44, item 4; (TS) Msg, JCS to MacArthur, 48198, CM-OUT-48198, 8 Jun 44, CCS 381 Pac. Ocean Area (6-10-43) sec 4.

[8] (TS) JPS 404/3, Rpt by JWPC, "Future Operations in the Pacific," 3 Jun 43; (TS dg R) JCS 713/7, Rpt by JPS, same subj, 8 Jun 44. Both in CCS 381 Pac. Ocean Area (6-10-43) sec 4. (TS) Mns, JPS 155th Mtg, 7 Jun 44, item 8.

[9] (TS dg S) Msg, JCS to CinCPOA and CinCSWPA, 50007, CM-OUT-50007, 13 Jun 44, CCS 381 Pac. Ocean Area (6-10-43) sec 4.

[10] (TS) Msg, MacArthur to Marshall, CX-13891, CM-IN-15058, 18 Jun 44, CCS 381 Pac. Ocean Area (6-10-43) sec 4.

[11] (TS) JPS 404/5, Rpt by JWPC, "Future Operations in the Pacific," 23 Jun 44, CCS 381 Pac. Ocean Area (6-10-43) sec 4.

[12] (TS) Mns, JPS 157th Mtg, 28 Jun 44, item 3.

[13] (TS) Msg, CominCh-CNO to CinCPOA, 291746 Jun 44, WD CM-IN-2980, 4 Jul 44. CinCPOA had sent CominCh a message addressed to CinCSWPA asking for information about his plans and remarking that his own comments on expediting the Pacific campaign could not be submitted until the Marianas were in hand. (TS) Msg, CinCPOA to CinCSoWesPac and CominCh-CNO, 252223, 290455 Jun 44, WD CM-IN-23957. Both in CCS 381 Pac, Ocean Area (6-10-43) sec 5.

[14] (TS) Msg, CinCPOA to CominCh, 040400 Jul 44, CNO(WPD) file "Agenda for Pacific Conference - July '44," env 134, case 140, NR&H.

[15] (TS) Msg, Marshall to MacArthur, WAR-60580, CM-OUT-60580, 5 Jul 44, CCS 381 Pac. Ocean Area (6-10-43) sec 5.

[16] (TS) Msg, MacArthur to Marshall, C-14608, CM-IN-6202, 8 Jul 44, CCS 381 Pac. Ocean Area (6-10-43) sec 5.

[17] (U) Pencilled Memo, King to F-1, 9 Jul 44, CNO(WPD) file "Memoranda--Admiral King's action," env 179, case 137, NR&H.

[18] (U) Memo, King to F-1, 8 Jul 44; (U) Memo, Cooke to King, "Exploration of Future Operations in the PACIFIC," 8 Jul 44. Both in CNO (WPD) file "Memoranda--Admiral King's action," env 179, case 137, NR&H.

[19] (TS) Mns, JPS 158th Mtg, 12 Jul 44, item 2.

[20] (TS) Mns, JPS 404/8, Study by JWPC, "Future Operations in the Pacific," 20 Jul 44, CCS 381 Pac. Ocean Area (6-10-43) sec 6.

[21] (TS) Mns, JPS 159th Mtg, 26 Jul 44, item 4.

874   NOTES TO CHAPTER XXIV

[22] (S dg R) JCS 713/4, Note by Secys, "Future Operations in the Pacific," 12 Mar 44, CCS 381 Pac. Ocean Area (6-10-43) sec 3.

[23] (TS) Msg, JPS to Staff Planners of CinCPOA and CinCSWPA, WARX-71483, CM-OUT-71483, 27 Jul 44, CCS 381 Pac. Ocean Area (6-10-43) sec 6.

[24] (TS) Mns, Pacific Conf, CinCPOA HQ, 13-22 Jul 44, CNO(WPD) file "Agenda for Pacific Conference - July '44," env 134, case 140, NR&H. E.J. King and W.M. Whitehill, *Fleet Admiral King* (New York, 1952), pp. 561-568. Note that Gen MacArthur told Col Ritchie during the latter's visit to Brisbane in Aug 44 "that CINCPOA's headquarters had tried, on three occasions, to make a dicker with him whereby Luzon would be taken out by the Marines prior to Formosa. That they had consistently expressed the conviction that Luzon was essential to further advance against Japan. It was only after he had turned down their proposition and after Admiral King had gone to Pearl Harbor that they decided that Luzon could be by-passed." (TS) Memo, no sig, "Notes for Discussion with General Marshall," nd, ABC 384 Pacific (1-71-43) sec 5.

[25] (U) Interv, FAdm W.D. Leahy, USN, with Hayes, 25 Nov 52, memo in JCS HS files. Leahy, pp. 250-251. Gen MacArthur told a visitor at his headquarters shortly after his return to Brisbane that "the President had indicated to him that he did not feel we could ever by-pass Luzon and that it should be taken out at the first opportunity." (TS) Memo, no sig, "Notes for Discussion with General Marshall," nd, ABC 384 Pacific (1-17-43) sec 5. (TS) Ltr, Lt Gen R.C. Richardson to Marshall, 1 Aug 44, OPD Exec 9, bk 21, item 1065. R.L. Eichelberger, *Our Jungle Road to Tokyo* (New York, 1950), pp. 165-167. Adm Nimitz reported to Adm King, "The general trend of the discussion, like our own, was along the line of seeing MacArthur into the Central Philippines, thereafter going direct to the Formosa Strait, and leaving the SWPA forces to work into Luzon under cover of the Formosa operation. It was made clear that the time has not yet arrived for firm decisions on moves subsequent to Leyte." (TS) Memo, King to Marshall and Arnold, 9 Aug 44, OPD Exec 10, item 68. This memo quotes a letter from Adm Nimitz of 31 Jul, no copy of which has been found. That no decision was made as to which should come first is clear from the events described below.

[26] (TS) Msg, MacArthur to Marshall, eyes only, C-15689, CM-IN-2479, 3 Aug 44, CCS 381 Pac. Ocean Area (6-10-43) sec 7.

[27] (TS) Msg, Marshall to MacArthur, eyes only, WAR-75632, CM-OUT-75632, 4 Aug 44, OPD TS Msg file.

[28] (TS) CinCPac-CinCPOA, "Campaign Plan Granite," ser 00071, 3 Jun 44, ABC 384 Pacific (1-17-43) sec 3-B-b; (TS) JPS 404/10, Rpt by JWPC, "Future Operations in the Pacific," 29 Jul 44, CCS 381 Pac. Ocean Area (6-10-43) sec 6; (TS) Mns, JPS 160th Mtg, 2 Aug 44, item 4.

[29] (TS) JPS 404/11, Rpt by JWPC, "Future Operations in the Pacific," 4 Aug 44, CCS 381 Pac. Ocean Area (6-10-43) sec 7. (TS) Mns, JPS 162nd Mtg, 10 Aug 44, item 5; 163rd Mtg, 16 Aug 44, item 1; 164th Mtg, 23 Aug 44, item 1. (TS) Memo, Duncan to Cooke, "Future Operations in the Pacific," 7 Aug 44, CNO(WPD) file "Memoranda--Admiral King's action," env 179, case 137, NR&H.

[30] (TS) Memo, King to Marshall, "Future Operations in the Pacific," ser 002356, 18 Aug 44, OPD Exec 10, item 68.

[31] (TS) Msg, CinCPOA to CominCh, 180437 Aug 44, OPD Exec 10, item 68.

[32] (TS) Memo, no sig, "Notes for Discussion with General Marshall," nd; (TS) Memo, no sig, "Notes on Conference August 7 at GHQ, SWPA," 16 Aug 44. Both in ABC 384 Pacific (1-17-43) sec 5. Both were probably written by Col Ritchie. The quotations are from the first. (TS dg S) Ltr, Giles to Arnold, 10 Aug 44, OPD 319.1 TS sec VI, case 228; (TS) Memo, Roberts to Duncan, et al., "Future Operations in the Pacific," 8 Aug 44, ABC 384 Formosa (8 Sep 43) sec 1-D.

[33] (TS) Memo, Marshall to King, "Future Operations in the Pacific," 22 Aug 44, ABC 384 Formosa (8 Sep 43) sec 1-D.

[34] (TS) Mns, JCS Closed Sess, 22 Aug 44. This may have been the meeting at which Adm Leahy reported on the discussions at Pearl Harbor. It is apparent from the minutes that nothing he said about the President's preference was interpreted by the chiefs as a directive to take Luzon first.

[35] (TS) Mns, JPS 165th Mtg, 28 Aug 44, item 1.

[36] (TS) OPD "Notes for JPS 166th Mtg," 30 Aug 44; (TS) Memo, Hull to Handy and Roberts, "Pacific Strategy," 2 Sep 44. Both in ABC 384 Pacific (1-17-43) sec 5.

[37] (TS) Mns, JCS 171st Mtg, 1 Sep 44, item 2.

[38] (TS) Memo, Donnelly to Duncan, Roberts, Lindsay, and Fife, "Future Operations in the Pacific; Directive to CINCSWPA and CINCPOA for Leyte Operation," 2 Sep 44, CCS 381 Pac. Ocean Area (6-10-43) sec 7; (TS) Mns, JPS 167th Mtg, 2 Sep 44, item 1.

[39] (TS dg R) JCS 713/9, Rpt by JPS, "Future Operations in the Pacific," 2 Sep 44, CCS 381 Pac. Ocean Area (6-10-43) sec 7.

[40] (TS dg R) JCS 713/10, Memo by CominCh-CNO, "Proposed Directive to Commander in Chief, Southwest Pacific Area, and Commander in Chief, Pacific Ocean Areas," 4 Sep 44, CCS 381 Pac. Ocean Area (6-10-43) sec 7.

[41] (TS dg R) JCS 713/11, Memo by CominCh-CNO, "Employment of Marine Divisions in 'Formosa' Operation," 4 Sep 44; (TS dg R) JCS 713/12, Memo by CominCh-CNO, "Troops for the Occupation of Formosa," 4 Sep 44. Both in CCS 381 Pac. Ocean Area (6-10-43) sec 7.

[42] (TS) Memo, Handy to Marshall, "Operations in the Western Pacific," 5 Sep 44, ABC 384 Pacific (1-17-43) sec 5.

[43] (TS) Mns, JCS 172nd Mtg, 5 Sep 44, item 2; (TS dg R) JCS 713/13, Memo by CofS USA, "Proposed Directive to Commander in Chief, Southwest Pacific Area, and Commander in Chief, Pacific Ocean Areas," 5 Sep 44, CCS 381 Pac. Ocean Area (6-10-43) sec 8.

876   NOTES TO CHAPTER XXIV

⁴⁴(TS dg R) JCS 713/14, Rpt by JSSC, "Proposed Directive to Commander in Chief, Southwest Pacific Area, and Commander in Chief, Pacific Ocean Areas," 7 Sep 44, CCS 381 Pac. Ocean Area (6-10-43) sec 8. See ch XXI, pp. 553.

⁴⁵The JSSC believed that there was a "strong probability of a collapse of Germany, or at least of a very substantial reduction in the strength of German resistance, prior to the end of the current year." Note that the Combined Intelligence Committee (CIC) was currently predicting the end of organized resistance under the German High Command by 1 Dec 1944. (S) CCS 660/1, Rpt by CIC, "Prospects of a German Collapse or Surrender," 9 Sep 44, *OCTAGON*, pp. 81-90.

⁴⁶(TS) Mns, JCS 173rd Mtg, 8 Sep 44, item 1.

⁴⁷(TS) Msg, JCS to MacArthur and Nimitz, WARX-27648, CM-OUT-27648, 9 Sep 44, CCS 381 Pac. Ocean Area (6-10-43) sec 8.

⁴⁸(TS) Msg, Com 3rd Flt to CinCPOA, info CinCSWPA and ComInCh, 130300 Sep 44; (TS) Msg, same orig and adees, 130230 Sep 44. These were forwarded from Washington to Adm King at Octagon as 131507 and 131443 Sep 44. Both in (TS) ComInCh file "CINCPOA Despatches - September 1944." Isely and Crowl, *U.S. Marines and Amphibious War*, pp. 393-394; *Fleet Admiral King*, pp. 570, 572; George C. Marshall, *The Winning of the War in Europe and the Pacific*, Biennial Rpt, CofS USA, 1 Jul 43 to 30 Jun 45, to Sec War, p. 71; *Global Mission*, pp. 527-528.

⁴⁹(TS) Msg, CinCPOA to CinCSWPA, info ComInCh and Com 3rd Flt, 130813 Sep 44; (TS) Msg, CinCPOA to Com 3rd Flt, info ComInCh and CinCSWPA, 130747 Sep 44; (TS) Msg, same orig and adees, 132100 Sep 44. All in (TS) ComInCh file "CINCPOA Despatches - September 1944." These were forwarded to Adm King at Octagon as 131605, 131537, and 141347, Sep 44.

⁵⁰(TS) Msg, JCS to MacArthur, info Nimitz, Halsey, 24,CM-IN-12198, 13 Sep 44, CCS 381 Pac. Ocean Area (6-10-43) sec 8.

⁵¹(TS) Msg, MacArthur to JCS and CinCPOA, CX-17697, CM-IN-12636, 14 Sep 44; (TS) Msg, MacArthur to JCS, C17744, CM-IN-13415, 15 Sep 44; (TS) Msg, JCS to MacArthur and Nimitz, 31A, CM-IN-13500, 15 Sep 44. All in CCS 381 Pac. Ocean Area (6-10-43) sec 8. The last had been wrongly assigned to a DTG of 150746. The correct one is 150258. Robert R. Smith, *U.S. Army in World War II: The Approach to the Philippines* (Washington, 1953), p. 492.

⁵²(TS) Msg, MacArthur to Marshall, C-18103, CM-IN-19803, 21 Sep 44, CCS 381 Pac. Ocean Area (6-10-43) sec 8.

⁵³(TS) Memo, G.A.L[incoln] to Roberts, "What Do We Do in the Pacific After Leyte?" 18 Sep 44; (TS) Memo T.T.H[andy] to Marshall, "Pacific Operations," nd. Both in ABC 384 Pacific (1-17-43) sec 5.

⁵⁴(TS dg R) JCS 713/15, Memo by CofS USA, "Future Operations in the Pacific," 22 Sep 44, CCS 381 Pac. Ocean Area (6-10-43) sec 5.

[55] (TS) Memo, Lincoln to Handy, 22 Sep 44; (TS) Memo, King to Marshall, 23 Sep 44. Both in ABC 384 Pacific (1-17-43) sec 5. (TS) Memo, McFarland to Chiefs, "Future Operations in the Pacific," 23 Sep 44; (TS dg R) JCS 713/16, Memo by CominCh-CNO, same subj, 25 Sep 44. Both in CCS 381 Pac. Ocean Area (6-10-43) sec 8.

[56] (TS dg R) JCS 713/17, Memo by CominCh-CNO, "Future Operations in the Pacific," 25 Sep 44, CCS 381 Pac. Ocean Area (6-10-43) sec 8.

[57] (TS) Msgs, Maj Gen Marshall to MacArthur, WAR-37000, 37001, CM-OUT-37000, 37001, 27 Sep 44, OPD TS Msg file; (TS) Mns, JCS 179th Mtg, 26 Sep 44, item 9.

[58] (TS) Msg, MacArthur to Marshall, C-18496, CM-IN-26358, 28 Sep 44, OPD TS Msg file.

[59] (TS) Mns, Conf, King, Nimitz, et al., San Francisco, 29 Sep-1 Oct 44, CNO(WPD) file "Agenda for Pacific Conference-Sept. '44," env 135, case 140, NR&H.

[60] (TS dg C) JCS 713/18, Memo by CominCh-CNO, "Future Operations in the Pacific," 2 Oct 44, CCS 381 Pac. Ocean Area (6-10-43) sec 9; (TS) Memo, Handy to Marshall, same subj, 2 Oct 44, ABC 384 Pacific (1-17-43) sec 5; (TS) Memo of conv, Roberts and Duncan, 2 Oct 44, ABC 384 Formosa (8 Sep 43) sec 1-D.

[61] (TS) Memo, Handy to Marshall, "Future Operations in the Pacific (JCS 713/18)," 3 Oct 44, ABC 384 Formosa (8 Sep 43) sec 1-D. Memo has pencilled note, "Most of this read to U.S. Chiefs of Staff 10/3/44. G.C.M."

[62] (TS) Mns, JCS 180th Mtg, 3 Oct 44, item 4; (TS) Msg, JCS to MacArthur and Nimitz, WARX-40782, CM-OUT-40782, 3 Oct 44, CCS 381 Pac. Ocean Area (6-10-43) sec 9.

CHAPTER XXV

[1] (S) JWPC 192, Rpt by JWPC, "Preparations for Next Allied Staff Conference," 14 Feb 44; (TS) JWPC Info Memo 19, "Readiness of Planning Papers for Next Interallied Conference," 19 Mar 44. Both in CCS 381 (2-14-44) sec 1.

[2] (TS dg U) JCS 729/1, Rpt by JPS, "Preparation for Next Allied Staff Conference," 21 Aug 44; (TS) CCS 654, Memo by JCS, "Basic Policies for the Next United States-British Staff Conference," 22 Aug 44. Both in CCS 381 (1-14-44) sec 1. (S) CCS 426/1, "Report to the President and Prime Minister," 6 Dec 43, *SEXTANT*, pp. 297-306.

[3] (TS) CCS 654/1, Memo by RBCOS, "Basic Policies for the Next United States-British Staff Conference," 2 Sep 44, CCS 381 (2-14-44) sec 1.

[4] (TS) JPS 517, Rpt by JWPC, "Basic Policies for the Next United States-British Staff Conference," 2 Sep 44, CCS 381 (2-14-44) sec 1.

[5] (TS) Mns, JPS 168th Mtg, 4 Sep 44, item 9; (TS dg U) JCS 729/3, Rpt by JPS, "Basic Policies for the Next United States-British Staff Conference," 4 Sep 44, CCS 381 (2-14-44) sec 1.

NOTES TO CHAPTER XXV

[6] (TS) CCS 654/8, Note by Secys, "Basic Policies for the Octagon Conference," 12 Sep 44, CCS 381 (2-14-44) sec 22. (TS) Mns, CCS 171st Mtg, 8 Sep 44, item 6; 173rd Mtg, 13 Sep 44, item 7.

[7] (TS) Memo, Secy JCS to Secy BJSM, "Preparations for the next Allied Staff Conference," 22 Aug 44, CCS 381 (2-14-44) sec 1.

[8] (TS) Memo, Cornwall-Jones to McFarland, 25 Aug 44; (TS) CCS 654/2, Memo by RBCOS, "Agenda for the Next United States–British Staff Conference," 2 Sep 44. Both in CCS 381 (2-14-44) sec 1. (TS) Suppl Mns, JCS 170th Mtg, 29 Aug 44, item 1.

[9] (TS dg U) JCS 729/4, Rpt by JPS, "Agenda for the Next United States-British Staff Conference," 4 Sep 44; (TS) Memo, McFarland to Leahy, King, Arnold, same subj, 6 Sep 44; (TS) CCS 654/3, Memo by JCS, same subj, 7 Sep 44. All in CCS 381 (2-14-44) sec 1.

[10] A summary of the status of the major problems for discussion was prepared by JPS and circulated as (TS) JCS Info Memo 302, "Outline and Summary of Important Subjects for Use at the Octagon Conference," 11 Sep 44, CCS 381 (2-14-44) sec 2.

[11] (TS dg R) JCS 924, Rpt by JPS, "Operations against Japan Subsequent to Formosa," 30 Jun 44, CCS 381 Pac. Ocean Area (6-10-43) sec 5.

[12] (TS) Memo, King to JCS, "Operations Against Japan Subsequent to Formosa," 7 Jul 44, CCS 381 Pac. Ocean Area (6-10-43) sec 5; (TS) CD, JCS 924, 11 Jul 44.

[13] (TS) CCS 417/3, Memo by JCS, "Over-all Objective in the War Against Japan," 11 Jul 44, CCS 381 Pac. Ocean Area (6-10-43) sec 6.

[14] (TS) CCS 417/4, Memo by RBCOS, "Over-all Objective in the War Against Japan," 29 Jul 44, CCS 381 Pac. Ocean Area (6-10-43) sec 6.

[15] (S) CCS 426/1, Rpt by CCS, "Report to the President and Prime Minister," 6 Dec 43, *SEXTANT*, p. 299.

[16] (TS dg C) JPS 495/1, Rpt by JWPC, "Over-all Objective in War Against Japan," 31 Jul 44, CCS 381 Pac. Ocean Area (6-10-43) sec 6.

[17] (TS dg R) JCS 924/1, Rpt by JPS, "Over-all Objective in the War against Japan," 1 Aug 44, CCS 381 Pac. Ocean Area (6-10-43) sec 7.

[18] (TS) CCS 417/5, Memo by JCS, "Over-all Objective in War Against Japan," 4 Aug 44, CCS 381 Pac. Ocean Area (6-10-43) sec 7.

[19] (TS) CCS 417/7, Memo by JCS, "Over-all Objective in the War Against Japan," 6 Sep 44, CCS 381 Pac. Ocean Area (6-10-43) sec 8.

[20] (TS) CCS 417/9, Note by Secys, "Overall Objective in the War Against Japan," 11 Sep 44, CCS 381 Pac. Ocean Area (6-10-43) sec 8.

[21] (TS dg R) JCS 924/4, Rpt by JPS, "Operations for the Defeat of Japan, 1944-45," 6 Sep 44; (TS dg R) CCS 417/8, same subj, 9 Sep 44; (TS dg U) CCS 676, Memo by JCS, "General Progress Report on Recent Operations in the Pacific," 12 Sep 44. All in CCS 381 Pac. Ocean Area (6-10-43) sec 8.

[22] See above, ch XXIV.

[23] (TS) Memo, Secy JPS to Duncan, Roberts, Fife, "Fighter Escort for VLR Bombers," 21 Jul 44, CCS 373.11 Japan (8-20-43) pt 6.

[24] (TS) Mns, CCS 173rd Mtg, 13 Sep 44, item 6.
[25] (S) CCS 417, Rpt by CPS, "Over-all Plan for the Defeat of Japan," 2 Dec 43, *SEXTANT*, pp. 254-267; (S) Mns, CCS 137th Mtg, 6 Dec 43, item 4.
[26] (SS) Memo, Bieri to King, "Comments on British Proposals to Send Carrier Task Forces to the Pacific in April," 24 Jan 44, (TS) CominCh file #35 "Ass't Chief of Staff (Plans - F-1)"; (SS) Msg, King to Nimitz and MacArthur, 251303 Jan 44, (TS) CominCh file "CINCPAC Despatches Jan '44 thru Feb '44."
[27] *Closing the Ring*, pp. 571-579.
[28] (S) CCS 498 series, "Effect of the Move of the Main Japanese Fleet to Singapore," 26 Feb-6 Mar 44, CCS 381 Indian Ocean (2-26-44).
[29] *Closing the Ring*, p. 577.
[30] (SS) Memo, C.K.G[ailey] to Handy, 11 Mar 44, encl Memo by Col W.E. Todd, "British Naval Operations in the Pacific," 11 Mar 44, OPD Exec 10, item 63c.
[31] (U) Msg, Pres to PM, 13 Mar 44, *Closing the Ring*, p. 578.
[32] *Closing the Ring*, p. 579.
[33] (TS) Mns, CCS 165th Mtg, 14 Jun 44, item 2; (TS) Informal Notes, CCS 165th Mtg, 14 Jun 44, filed with CCS mns.
[34] (TS) Mns, Pacific Conf, CinCPOA HQ, 13-22 Jul 44, CNO(WPD) file "Agenda for Pacific Conference - July '44," case 140, env 134, NR&H; (TS) Memo, King to MacArthur, 21 Jul 44, OPD Exec 10, item 68.
[35] Leahy, pp. 251-252; (S) Memo, Col Frank McCarthy, Secy GS, to Col Park, 1 Aug 44, OPD Exec 10, item 64.
[36] (TS) Ltr, MacArthur to King, 5 Aug 44, OPD Exec 10, item 68.
[37] He was undoubtedly referring to the Australian requests in early 1942 that their troops in the Middle East be returned. See above, ch III.
[38] (S) Memo, McCarthy to Park, 1 Aug 44, OPD Exec 10, item 64; (TS) Msg, Marshall to MacArthur, WAR-82717, CM-OUT-82717, 18 Aug 44, OPD TS Msg file.
[39] (TS dg C) CCS 619, Memo by RBCOS, "Scale of British Army Effort in the Pacific after The Defeat of Germany," 15 Jul 44, CCS 370 Great Britain (7-15-44) sec 1.
[40] CCS 538 series, CCS 561 (8-18-43) (2).
[41] (TS dg C) JCS 992, Rpt by JLC, "Scale of British Army Effort in the Pacific after The Defeat of Germany," 11 Aug 44, CCS 370 Great Britain (7-15-44) sec 1.
[42] (TS) Memo, McFarland to Leahy, Marshall, Arnold, "Scale of British Army Effort in the Pacific after the Defeat of Germany," 25 Aug 44, CCS 370 Great Britain (7-15-44) sec 1.
[43] (TS dg C) JCS 992/2, Memo by Actg CofS USA, "Scale of British Army Effort in the Pacific after the Defeat of Germany," 27 Aug 44, circ to British as CCS 619/1, 29 Aug 44, CCS 370 Great Britain (7-15-44) sec 1; (TS) Mns, JCS 170th Mtg, 29 Aug 44, item 1.
[44] (TS dg C) Pars 9 & 10 of CCS 452/18, Memo by RBCOS, "British Participation in Far Eastern Strategy," 15 Aug 44, CCS 381 Burma (8-25-42) sec 10.

[45] (TS) Memo, King to Marshall, "Naval Command in Southwest Pacific Area," ser 002350, 17 Aug 44, OPD Exec 10, item 68.

[46] (S) Memo, Marshall to King, nd (c. 1 Sep 44), OPD Exec 10, item 68.

[47] (TS) JWPC 187/20, Note by Secys, encl Rpt by JSSC, "Plans for Operations in Burma," 26 Aug 44, CCS 381 Burma (8-25-42) sec 11.

[48] (TS) JWPC 259/8, Rpt by JWPC, "Preparations for Next Allied Staff Conference (British Participation in the War Against Japan)," 26 Aug 44, CCS 381 Burma (8-25-42) sec 11.

[49] (TS) Mns, JPS 165th Mtg, 28 Aug 44, item 3; (TS) Msg, MacArthur to Marshall, C16679, CM-IN-24955, 27 Aug 44, CCS 381 Burma (8-25-42) sec 11.

[50] (TS) JWPC 259/8 (Rev), Rpt by JWPC, "Preparations for Next Allied Staff Conference (British Participation in the War Against Japan)," 1 Sep 44; (TS dg C) JCS 992/3, Rpt by JPS, "British Participation in the War Against Japan," 4 Sep 44. Both in CCS 381 Burma (8-25-42) sec 11.

[51] (TS) Mns, JCS 173rd Mtg, 8 Sep 44, item 2.

[52] (TS dg C) CCS 452/25, Memo by US CsofS, "British Participation in the War Against Japan," 8 Sep 44, CCS 381 Burma (8-25-42) sec 11.

[53] (TS dg C) CCS 452/26, Memo by BCOS, "British Participation in the War against Japan," 11 Sep 44, CCS 381 Burma (8-25-42) sec 11.

[54] (TS dg C) JCS 992/6, Rpt by JPS, "British Participation in the War against Japan," 12 Sep 44, CCS 381 Burma (8-25-42) sec 12.

[55] (TS) Mns, JCS 175th Mtg, 13 Sep 44, item 6. (TS dg C) CCS 452/27, Memo by JCS, "British Participation in the War Against Japan," 13 Sep 44. The JLC had in the meantime made a study of the logistics problem with the conclusion that a British task force could be maintained in the SWPA but not in POA. (TS dg C) JCS 992/7, same subj, 13 Sep 44. Both in CCS 381 Burma (8-25-42) sec 12.

[56] (TS) Mns, 1st Plen Mtg, 13 Sep 44, *OCTAGON*, pp. 235-242. Sir Andrew Browne Cunningham, *A Sailor's Odyssey* (London, 1951), p. 611.

[57] (TS) Msg, CCS 176th Mtg, 14 Sep 44, item 5.

[58] (TS) Suppl Mns, CCS 151st Mtg, 24 Mar 44, item 3.

[59] See above, ch XXII, pp. 214-220.

[60] (TS) CCS 494/12, Memo by JCS, "Diversion of Aircraft from Air Lift to China," 5 May 44, CCS 452 Burma (2-18-44) sec 1; (TS) Msg, SACMED to BCOS, MEDCOS 111, CM-IN-13791, 18 May 44, CCS 452 Burma (2-18-44) sec 2.

[61] (TS dg U) JCS 864, Rpt by JPS, "Additional Combat Cargo Units for Southeast Asia Command," 19 May 44, CCS 452 Burma (2-18-44) sec 2; (TS) CD, JCS 864, 27 May 44.

[62] (TS) Mns, CCS 166th Mtg, 15 Jun 44, item 4.

[63] (TS) Msg, SAC SEAC to BCOS, SEACOS 180, 16 Jun 44, CM-IN-14122 (17 Jun 44), CCS 381 Burma (8-25-42) sec 9.

[64] (TS dg R) JCS 774/2, Rpt by JPS, "Strategy in Southeast Asia Command," 28 Jun 44, CCS 183 Burma (8-25-42) sec 9; (TS) CD, JCS 774/2, 3 Jul 44.

NOTES TO CHAPTER XXV

[65] (TS dg C) CCS 452/14, Memo by JCS, "Strategy in Southeast Asia Command," 3 Jul 44; (TS dg C) CCS 452/15, Memo by RBCOS, same subj, 6 Jul 44; (TS) Msg, Mountbatten to Marshall and Arnold, SAC 4013, 8 Jul 44, CM-IN-8218 (10 Jul 44). All in CCS 381 Burma (8-25-42) sec 9.

[66] (TS) Msg, Marshall to Mountbatten, WAR-65845, CM-OUT-65845, 15 Jul 44, CCS 381 Burma (8-25-42) sec 9.

[67] (TS) Msg, Sultan to Marshall, TST-362, 22 Jul 44, CM-IN-19066 (23 Jul 44); (TS dg C) CCS 452/17, Memo by RBCOS, "Plans for Operations in Burma," 31 Jul 44. Both in CCS 381 Burma (8-25-42) sec 9.

[68] See map, not in this edition.

[69] (TS) JPS 406/17, Dft Memo by JWPC, "Plan for Operations in Burma," 5 Aug 44; (TS) JPS 406/18, Note by Secys with encl, same subj, 8 Aug 44; (TS dg R) JCS 774/3, Rpt by JPS, same subj, 10 Aug 44. All in CCS 381 Burma (8-25-42) sec 10.

[70] (TS dg C) CCS 452/18, Memo by RBCOS, "British Participation in Far Eastern Strategy," 15 Aug 44, CCS 381 Burma (8-25-42) sec 10; (TS) Memo, McFarland to Leahy, "Plan for Operations in Burma," 17 Aug 44, CCS 381 Burma (8-25-42) sec 11.

[71] (TS dg C) CCS 452/19, Memo by RBCOS, "Plans for Operations in Burma," 20 Aug 44, CCS 381 Burma (8-25-42) sec 11.

[72] (TS) Msg, Wedemeyer to Mountbatten, WAR-83031, CM-OUT-83031, 18 Aug 44, CCS 381 Burma (8-25-42) sec 11. Gen Wedemeyer arrived in Washington on 15 Aug. (S) Msg, CG Harmon Field Nfld, to CG ATC Gravelly Pt, 150634 Aug 44, CM-IN-13520, OPD TS Msg file.

[73] (TS dg C) CCS 452/20, Memo by RBCOS, "Plans for Operations in Burma," 22 Aug 44, CCS 381 Burma (8-25-42) sec 11.

[74] (TS) JWPC 187/20, Rpt by JWPC, "Plans for Operations in Burma," 26 Aug 44, CCS 381 Burma (8-25-42) sec 11.

[75] (TS dg C) CCS 452/22, Memo by RBCOS, "Plans for Operations in Burma," 2 Sep 44, CCS 381 Burma (8-25-42) sec 11.

[76] (TS dg R) JCS 774/5, Rpt by JPS, "Plans for Operations in Burma," 3 Sep 44; (TS dg C) CCS 452/24, Memo by JCS, same subj, 7 Sep 44. Both in CCS 381 Burma (8-25-42) sec 11.

[77] (TS dg R) JCS 774/7, Rpt by JPS, "Allocation of the Two Remaining Combat Cargo Groups and the Two Remaining Air Commando Groups," 12 Sep 44; (TS dg C) CCS 452/29, Memo by JCS, same subj, 14 Sep 44. Both in CCS 381 Burma (8-25-42) sec 12.

[78] (TS dg C) CCS 452/28, Memo by RBCOS, "Directive to SACSEA," 13 Sep 44, CCS 381 Burma (8-25-42) sec 12. (TS) Mns, CCS 174th Mtg, 14 Sep 44, item 4.

[79] (TS) Mns, JCS 176th Mtg, 14 Sep 44, item 4; (TS dg C) CCS 452/30, Note by Secys, "Directive to Supreme Allied Commander, Southeast Asia Command," 14 Sep 44, CCS 381 Burma (8-25-42) sec 12.

[80] (TS) CCS 452/31, Note by Secys, "Directive to Supreme Allied Commander, Southeast Asia Command," 22 Sep 44, *OCTAGON*, pp. 45-47.

[81] (TS dg C) CCS 679, Memo by JCS, "Redeployment of Forces after the End of the War in Europe," 14 Sep 44, CCS 370 (1-13-44) sec 2; (TS) Mns, CCS 175th Mtg, 15 Sep 44, item 4.

[82] (TS) CCS 678, Memo by BCOS, "Planning Date for the End of the War against Japan," 13 Sep 44, CCS 370 (1-13-44) sec 1.

[83] (TS) Mns JCS 176th Mtg, 14 Sep 44, item 7; (TS) Mns, CCS 174th Mtg, 14 Sep 44, item 5.
[84] (TS dg S) CCS 680/1, "Report to the President and Prime Minister," 15 Sep 44, CCS 381 (2-14-44) sec 2; (TS) Mns, 2nd Plen Mtg, 16 Sep 44, OCTAGON, pp. 243-349.
[85] (TS) CCS 681/2, "Communication of the Results of OCTAGON Conference to Marshal Stalin and Generalissimo Chiang Kai-shek," 15 Sep 44, CCS 381 (2-14-44) sec 2.
[86] (TS) Ann II to Mns, 2nd Plen Mtg, 16 Sep 44, OCTAGON, p. 252.

CHAPTER XXVI

[1] The story of the recall is told in considerable detail in Romanus-Sunderland MS, *Stilwell's Command Problems*, pt III.
[2] Romanus-Sunderland MS, *Stilwell's Command Problems*, ch X, pp. 28-29. At Sextant Adm Mountbatten had recommended that CBI be divided and Gen Stilwell be sent to China. (S) Msg, Mountbatten to Dill, SAC 1022, 13 Mar 44, OPD Exec 10, item 57.
[3] (TS) Msg, Marshall to Stilwell, WAR-59012, CM-OUT-59012, 1 Jul 44, OPD Exec 10, item 64.
[4] (TS) Msg, Stilwell to Marshall, CHC-1241, CM-IN-2088, 3 Jul 44, OPD Exec 10, item 64. Quoted in Romanus-Sunderland MS, *Stilwell's Command Problems*, ch X, p. 32.
[5] (TS) Memo, Handy to Leahy, King, Arnold, 3 Jul 44; (S) Memo, Leahy to Pres, 4 Jul 44. Both in OPD Exec 10, item 64. The second is quoted in full in Romanus-Sunderland MS, *Stilwell's Command Problems*, ch X, pp. 34-35. The minutes of the JCS meeting held on 4 Jul contain no mention of discussion of this subject.
[6] (U) Ltr, Gimo to Pres, 8 Jul 44, quoted in Romanus-Sunderland MS, *Stilwell's Command Problems*, ch X, pp. 40-41.
[7] (TS) Memo, Marshall to Leahy, 13 Jul 44, encl Dft Msg to Gimo, OPD Exec 10, item 64; (S dg C) Msg, Pres to Gimo, 25, 13 Jul 44, JWS "Oklahoma File, Stilwell Papers," DRB AGO. The President may have been influenced by a message from Ambassador Clarence E. Gauss urging such an appointment. (S) Msg, Gauss to Pres, 11 Jul 44, OPD Exec 10, item 59.
[8] (TS) Memo, Gimo to Pres, 23 Jul 44, OPD Exec 9, bk 22; (TS) Memo, Hopkins to Marshall, 16 Aug 44, OPD 384 TS, case 47.
[9] (TS) Msg, Marshall to Stilwell, WAR-75342, CM-OUT-75342, 4 Aug 44, OPD TS Msg file; (C) Msg, Hopkins to Pres, 8 Aug 44, Hopkins Papers, bk IX, Explosion in WPB, item 4; (S) Msg, Pres to Gimo, 9 Aug 44, OPD Exec 10, item 49; Romanus-Sunderland MS, *Stilwell's Command Problems*, ch XI, pp. 27-29.
[10] *The Stilwell Papers*, pp. 325-349; Romanus-Sunderland MS, *Stilwell's Command Problems*, chs XI and XII; 82 Cong, 1 sess, H. Cmte on Armed Services and S. Cmte on For Rels, Hrgs, "Military Situation in the Far East," Testimony of Gen P.J. Hurley, 21 Jun 51, pp. 2863-2881 (hereinafter: Hurley Testimony).
[11] (TS) Mns, 2nd Plen Mtg, 16 Sep 44, item 1i, OCTAGON, p. 247; (TS) Mns, JCS 178th Mtg, 16 Sep 44, item 6; (TS) Mns, CCS 176th Mtg, 16 Sep 44, item 5.

¹²Quoted in full in Hurley Testimony, pp. 2867-2868; Romanus-Sunderland MS, *Stilwell's Command Problems*, ch XII, p. 5-6. Also in CCS 381 (2-14-44) sec 2.

¹³Hurley Testimony, pp. 2874-2876; Romanus-Sunderland MS, *Stilwell's Command Problems*, ch XII, pp. 17-19; (TS) Msg, Stilwell to Marshall, CFB-22995, CM-IN-20497, 22 Sep 44, OPD TS Msg file.

¹⁴H.L. Stimson and McGeorge Bundy, *On Active Service in Peace and War* (New York, 1947), pp. 536-538; Romanus-Sunderland MS, *Stilwell's Command Problems*, ch XII, pp. 19, 27-28; (TS) Msg, Marshall to Stilwell, eyes only, 3465, CM-OUT-41875, 5 Oct 44, OPD 384 TS, case 47.

¹⁵Romanus-Sunderland MS, *Stilwell's Command Problems*, ch XII, pp. 30-33; Hurley Testimony, pp. 2869-2871.

¹⁶(TS dg U) Msg, Hurley to Pres, 13 Oct 44, quoted in full in Hurley Testimony, pp. 2879-2881; Romanus-Sunderland MS, *Stilwell's Command Problems*, ch XII, pp. 37-38.

¹⁷Romanus-Sunderland MS, *Stilwell's Command Problems*, ch XII, pp. 40-42; *The Stilwell Papers*, pp. 344-345.

¹⁸(TS) Memo, Marshall to Leahy, King, Arnold, 23 Oct 44; (TS) Memo, King to Marshall, "Directives for the China Theater and for the India-Burma Theater; Comment on," ser 003099, 23 Oct 44. Both in CCS 323.361 (10-23-44) sec 1.

¹⁹(TS) Msg, JCS to Wedemeyer and Sultan, WARX-51593, CM-OUT-51593, 24 Oct 44; (TS dg R) JCS Info Memo 335, "Organization of the China and India-Burma Theaters," 24 Oct 44. Both in CCS 323.361 (10-23-44) sec 1.

CHAPTER XXVII

¹For fuller discussion of JCS meetings and procedures, see (S) MS, JCS Hist, *Organizational Development*, ch XIV, pp. 3-4.

²(TS dg C) CCS 691, Memo by BCOS, "British Participation in V.L.R. Bombing of Japan," 18 Sep 44, CCS 373.11 Japan (9-18-44) sec 1.

³(TS) JPS 526/3, Rpt by JWPC, "British Participation in V.L.R. Bombing of Japan," 6 Oct 44, CCS 373.11 Japan (9-18-44) sec 1.

⁴(TS) JPS 526/4, Rpt by JWPC, "British Participation in V.L.R. Bombing of Japan," 17 Oct 44; (TS dg C) JCS 1120, Rpt by JPS, same subj, 19 Oct 44; (TS dg C) CCS 691/1, Memo by JCS, same subj, 26 Oct 44. All in CCS 373.11 Japan (9-18-44) sec 1. (TS) Mns, JPS 174th Mtg, 11 Oct 44, item 1; 175th Mtg, 18 Oct 44, item 1.

⁵(TS) CCS 691/2, Memo by BCOS, "British Participation in V.L.R. Bombing of Japan," 29 Mar 45, CCS 373.11 Japan (9-18-44) sec 1.

⁶(TS) Msg, MacArthur to Marshall, CA-51492, CM-IN-8975, 10 Apr 45; (TS) JPS 526/6, Rpt by JWPC, "British Participation in V.L.R. Bombing of Japan," 17 Apr 45; (TS dg C) CCS 691/3, Memo by RBCOS, same subj, 2 May 45. All in CCS 373.11 Japan (9-18-44) sec 1. (TS) Mns, JPS 198th Mtg, 18 Apr 45, item 10; 199th Mtg, 25 Apr 45, item 6.

[7] (TS dg C) JCS 1120/1, Rpt by JPS, "British Participation in V.L.R. Bombing of Japan," 10 May 45; (TS dg C) CCS 691/4, Memo by JCS, same subj, 29 May 45; (TS dg C) CCS 691/5, Memo by RBCOS, same subj, 5 Jun 45; (TS dg C) CCS 691/6, Memo by RBCOS, same subj, 4 Jul 45; (TS dg C) CCS 691/8, Memo by JCS, same subj, 14 Jul 45. All in CCS 373.11 Japan (9-18-44) sec 1.

[8] (TS) JPS 404/14, Rpt by JWPC, "Operations for the Defeat of Japan," 7 Oct 44, CCS 381 Pac. Ocean Area (6-10-43) sec 8.

[9] (TS) Mns, JPS 174th Mtg, 11 Oct 44, item 3.

[10] (TS) JPS 404/15, Rpt by JWPC, "Operations for the Defeat of Japan," 18 Oct 44, CCS 381 Pac. Ocean Area (6-10-43) sec 9.

[11] (TS) Mns, JPS 176th Mtg, 25 Oct 44, item 4.

[12] (TS dg R) JCS 924/5, Rpt by JPS, "Operations for the Defeat of Japan," 27 Oct 44, CCS 381 Pac. Ocean Area (6-10-43) sec 9.

[13] (TS dg R) JCS 924/6, Memo by CominCh-CNO, "Operations for the Defeat of Japan," 3 Nov 44, CCS 381 Pac. Ocean Area (6-10-43) sec 10.

[14] (TS dg R) JCS 924/7, Memo by CG AAF, "Operations for the Defeat of Japan," 6 Nov 44, CCS 381 Pac. Ocean Area (6-10-43) sec 10.

[15] (TS dg R) JCS 924/8, Rpt by JPS, "Operations for the Defeat of Japan," 23 Nov 44, CCS 381 Pac. Ocean Area (6-10-43) sec 10.

[16] (TS) Memo w/Routing Slip, McFarland to Leahy, "Operations for the Defeat of Japan," 23 Nov 44; (TS) CCS 417/10, Memo by JCS, same subj, 1 Dec 44. Both in CCS 381 Pac. Ocean Area (6-10-43) sec 10.

[17] (TS) Msg, MacArthur to Marshall, C-54164, CM-IN-506, 1 Dec 44, CCS 381 Pac. Ocean Area (6-10-43) sec 10.

[18] (TS) Msg, CinCPOA to CominCh, 030215 Dec 44; (TS) Msg, CominCh-CNO to CinCPOA, 052032 Dec 44. Both in CCS 381 Pac. Ocean Area (6-10-43) sec 10.

[19] (TS dg R) JCS 924/9, Memo by CominCh-CNO, "Operations Against Chusan Archipelago and Ningpo Peninsula," 4 Dec 44, CCS 381 Pac. Ocean Area (6-10-43) sec 10.

[20] *Ibid*.

[21] (TS dg C) JCS 1215, Rpt by JPS, "Contributory Operations on the China Coast North of Swatow," 31 Dec 44, CCS 381 Chinese Theater (12-7-43) sec 4.

[22] (TS dg R) JCS 713/20, Rpt by JPS, "Future Operations in the Pacific," 11 Jan 45, CCS 381 Pac. Ocean Area (6-10-43) sec 11; (TS dg R) JCS 924/10, Rpt by JPS, "Operations in the Ningpo-Chusan Archipelago Area," 19 Jan 45, CCS 381 Chinese Theater (12-7-43) sec 5.

[23] (TS dg S) Msg, JCS to Nimitz, WARX-22012, CM-OUT-22012, 16 Jan 45, CCS 381 Pac. Ocean Area (6-10-43) sec 11.

[24] (TS dg R) JCS 1079, Rpt by JPS, "Tactical Air Forces Required to Accomplish Earliest Possible Conclusive Defeat of Japan," 29 Sep 44, CCS 373.11 Japan (8-20-43) pt 6.

[25] (TS) Memo by CG AAF, "Tactical Air Forces, etc.," 4 Oct 44, CCS 373.11 Japan (8-20-43) pt 7.

885 NOTES TO CHAPTER XXVII

[26] (TS) Memo by JPS, "Tactical Air Forces, etc.," 11 Oct 44, CCS 373.11 Japan (8-20-43) pt 7.

[27] (TS) CD, JCS 1079, 14 Oct 44.

[28] (TS dg R) JCS 1165, Rpt by JPS, "Weight of Strategic Air Effort Required in Operations Leading to the Earliest Possible Conclusive Defeat of Japan," 11 Nov 44, CCS 373.11 Japan (8-20-43) pt 7.

[29] (TS) Memo, Arnold to Secy JCS, "Weight of Strategic Air Effort, etc.," 22 Nov 44, CCS 373.11 Japan (8-20-43) pt 8.

[30] (TS) Memo, King to Sect JCS, "JCS 1165," 18 Nov 44, CCS 373.11 Japan (8-20-43) pt 8.

[31] (TS dg R) JCS 1190, Memo by CG AAF, "Planned Deployment of VLR Bomber Groups," 6 Dec 44, CCS 373.11 Japan (8-20-43) pt 8.

[32] (TS) Msg, Marshall to MacArthur, WAR-43247, CM-OUT-43247, 7 Oct 44; (TS) Msg, MacArthur to Marshall, C-19686, CM-IN-17061, 18 Oct 44. Both in CCS 373.11 Japan (8-20-43) pt 7.

[33] (TS) Msg, Wedemeyer to Marshall, eyes only, CFB-25886, CM-IN-10154, 10 Nov 44, OPD TS Msg file; (TS) Extract from Msg, Wedemeyer to Marshall, CFBX-28167, 4 Dec 44, CCS 373.11 Japan (8-20-43) pt 8.

[34] (TS dg R) JCS 1190/1, Rpt by JLC, "Planned Deployment of VLR Bomber Groups," 20 Dec 44; (TS dg R) JCS 1190/2, Note by Secys, "Deployment of the 315th and 316th VLR Bomber Wings," 26 Dec 44. Both in CCS 373.11 Japan (8-20-43) pt 8.

[35] (TS) Msg, Wedemeyer to Marshall, CFB-29071, CM-IN-13530, 14 Dec 44; (TS) Msg, JCS to Wedemeyer, WARX-77678, CM-OUT-77678, 15 Dec 44. Both in CCS 373.11 Japan (8-20-43) pt 8.

[36] (TS dg C) JCS 1190/4, Memo by CG AAF, "Movement of XX Bomber Command from China," 15 Jan 45, CCS 373.11 Japan (8-20-43) pt 8.

[37] (TS) Msg, JCS to Wedemeyer, WARX-21782, CM-OUT-21782, 16 Jan 45, CCS 373.11 Japan (8-20-43) pt 9.

[38] For a detailed account of the achievements of the XX Bomber Command, see *AAF in WW II*, vol V.

[39] (TS dg C) CCS 452/32, Memo by RBCOS, "Future Operations in Burma," 5 Oct 44, CCS 381 Burma (8-25-42) sec 12.

[40] (TS dg C) CCS 452/31, "Directive to Supreme Allied Commander, Southeast Asia Command," 22 Sep 44; (TS dg R) JCS 774/8, Rpt by JPS, "Future Operations in Burma," 9 Oct 44; (TS dg C) CCS 452/33, Memo by JCS, same subj, 10 Oct 44. All in CCS 381 Burma (8-25-42) sec 12. (TS) Mns, JCS 181st Mtg, 10 Oct 44, item 5.

[41] Mountbatten Report, p. 84.

[42] *Ibid*. (TS dg S) Msg, Sultan to Hull, CRAX-18492, CM-IN-784, 1 Nov 44; (TS dg S) Msg, Sultan to Hull, CRA-19139, CM-IN-7481, 8 Nov 44. Both in CCS 381 Burma (8-25-42) sec 12.

[43] (TS dg S) Msg, Sultan to Hull, CRA-19978, 16 Nov 44, CM-IN-16661 (17 Nov 44); (TS dg C) CCS 452/34, Memo by RBCOS, "Future Operations in Burma," 25 Nov 44. Both in CCS 381 Burma (8-25-42) sec 12. Mountbatten Report, p. 107.

[44] (TS) Msg, SACSEA to BCOS, SEACOS-275, 6 Dec 44, CM-IN-6527 (7 Dec 44), (TS) Msg, BCOS to BJSM, COS(W) 502, 9 Dec 44, CM-IN-10960 (11 Dec 44). Both in 381 Burma (8-25-42) sec 12.

[45] (TS) Msg, SACSEA to War Cab Offices, SEACOS-263, 23 Nov 44, CM-IN-24369 (25 Nov 44), CCS 370.01 Burma (11-6-44) sec 1; (TS) Msg, SACSEA to JCS, SEACOS-265, 28 Nov 44, CM-IN-28715 (29 Nov 44), CCS 381 Burma (8-25-42) sec 12.

[46] (TS) Msg, PM to Pres, 29 Nov 44, CCS 370.01 Burma (11-6-44) sec 1.

[47] (TS) Msg, Wedemeyer to JCS, CFBX-27686, CM-IN-29542, 30 Nov 44, CCS 370.01 Burma (11-6-44) sec 1.

[48] (TS) Memo, Marshall to Chiefs, "Withdrawal of Chinese Divisions from North Burma," 30 Nov 44; (TS) CCS 740, Memo by JCS, same subj, 1 Dec 44. Both in CCS 370.01 Burma (11-6-44) sec 1.

[49] (TS) CCS 740/1, Memo by RBCOS, "Withdrawal of Chinese Divisions from North Burma," 2 Dec 44, CCS 370.01 Burma (11-6-44) sec 1.

[50] (TS) Memo, McFarland to Leahy, "Withdrawal of Chinese Divisions from North Burma," 3 Dec 44; (TS) CCS 740/2, Memo by JCS, same subj, 3 Dec 44; (TS) Msg, Sultan to Marshall, CRA-21615, CM-IN-4002, 4 Dec 44. All in CCS 370.01 Burma (11-6-44) sec 1.

[51] (TS) CCS 740/3, Memo by RBCOS, "Withdrawal of Chinese Divisions from North Burma," 5 Dec 44, CCS 370.01 Burma (11-6-44) sec 1.

[52] (TS) Mns, CCS 179th Mtg, 8 Dec 44.

[53] (TS dg S) CCS 747, Memo by RBCOS, "Allocations of Resources between the India-Burma and China Theatres," 12 Dec 44, CCS 370.01 Burma (11-6-44) sec 1.

[54] (TS dg U) JCS 1201, Rpt by JPS, "Allocation of Resources between the India-Burma and China Theater," 17 Dec 44, CCS 370.01 Burma (11-6-44) sec 1.

[55] (TS dg S) CCS 747/1, Memo by JCS, "Allocation of Resources between the India-Burma and China Theaters," 21 Dec 44, CCS 370.01 Burma (11-6-44) sec 2.

[56] (TS) Mns, CCS 180th Mtg, 22 Dec 44, item 7.

[57] (TS dg S) CCS 747/3, Memo by RBCOS, "Allocation of Resources between the India-Burma and China Theaters," 2 Jan 45, CCS 370.01 Burma (11-6-44) sec 2.

[58] (TS) Msg, Mountbatten to BCOS, SEACOS-281, 13 Dec 44, CM-IN-14412 (15 Dec 44), CCS 370.01 Burma (11-6-44) sec 1.

[59] (TS dg S) CCS 747/4, Memo by RBCOS, "Allocation of Resources between India-Burma and China Theatres," 4 Jan 45, CCS 370.01 Burma (11-6-44) sec 2.

[60] (TS dg S) CCS 747/5, Memo by RBCOS, "Allocation of Resources between India-Burma and China Theatres," 20 Jan 45, CCS 370.01 Burma (11-6-44) sec 2.

[61] (TS) Msg, Marshall to Wedemeyer, WARX-24309. CM-OUT-24309, 20 Jan 45; (TS) Msg, Wedemeyer to JCS, CFBX-31720, 21 Jan 45, CM-IN-20784 (22 Jan 45); (TS) Msg, Sultan to Marshall, eyes only, CRA-1984, CM-IN-23263, 24 Jan 45; (TS dg S) CCS 747/6, Memo by JCS, "Allocation of Resources between India-Burma and China Theaters," 25 Jan 45. All in CCS 370.01 Burma (11-6-44) sec 2.

[1] A detailed and interesting account of Gen Deane's difficulties in trying to deal with the Russians appears in John R. Deane, *The Strange Alliance* (New York, 1947), chs XIII-XVI.

[2] (S dg C) Ann A to Encl A to JCS 506, Rpt by JSSC, "Instructions Concerning Duty as Military Observer at American-British-Soviet Conference," 18 Sep 43, CCS 337 (9-12-43) sec 1.

[3] (S) Memo, Embick to Marshall, "U.S. Policy in re Russian Participation in the War against Japan," 30 Sep 44, OPD 381 TS, sec XVIII, case 533. (S) Summary of Embick paper by Roberts sgd Handy, same subj, 1 Oct 44, ABC 384 U.S.S.R. (9-25-44) sec 1-A.

[4] (S) JWPC 104/1, Rpt by JWPC, "U.S.S.R. Collaboration against Japan," 28 Feb 44, CCS 381 Japan (10-4-43) sec 1.

[5] The Russians did agree to the exchange of naval information--the subject on which, as JIC pointed out, they had the least to offer and the U.S. the most. (SS) Msg, ALUSNA Moscow to JCS, 291349 Feb 44; (S) JIC 171/1, Rpt by JIC, "Exchange of Japanese Naval Information with the U.S.S.R.," 3 Mar 44. Both in CCS 350.05 (2-29-44).

[6] Deane, pp. 231-232. (TS) Msg, Deane to Arnold, 718, 19 Jun 44, CM-IN-16680 (21 Jun 44), CCS 381 Japan (10-4-43) sec 2.

[7] (TS dg U) JCS 919, Rpt by JPS, "U.S.S.R. Collaboration against Japan," 23 Jun 44, CCS 381 Japan (10-4-43) sec 2.

[8] (TS) Msg, Arnold to Deane, WAR-56070, 23 Jun 44, CM-OUT-56070 (25 Jun 44), CCS 381 Japan (10-4-43) sec 2.

[9] (TS) Memo, Newsome to Sec JCS, "USSR Collaboration against Japan (JCS 919)," 28 Jun 44, CCS 381 Japan (10-4-43) sec 2.

[10] (TS) Memo, King to JCS, "U.S.S.R. Collaboration Against Japan," 3 Jul 44; (TS) Msg, JCS to Deane, WAR-60689, CM-OUT-60689, 5 Jul 44. Both in CCS 381 Japan (10-4-43) sec 2.

[11] Deane, pp. 240-242. (TS) Msg, Deane to JCS, 241846 Sep 44, CCS 381 Japan (10-4-43) sec 3; (TS & P) Msg, Harriman to Pres, 240533 Sep 44, ABC 384 U.S.S.R. (9-25-44) sec 1-A.

[12] (TS) Msg, JCS to Deane, WAR-38050, CM-OUT-38050, 28 Sep 44. A draft of this message was circulated in (TS) JWPC 275/1, "Soviet Participation in the War against Japan," 26 Sep 44. Both in CCS 381 Japan (10-4-43) sec 3. This was substantially revised by the JPS before it was sent. (U) Memo, Handy to Marshall, 27 Sep 44, OPD Exec 10, item 55.

[13] Deane, pp. 243-249. A series of reports from Gen Deane and Amb Harriman is in CCS 381 Japan (10-4-43) sec 3.

[14] (TS) JWPC 286/1, Rpt by JWPC, "Russian Participation in the War against Japan," 8 Nov 44; (TS dg S) JCS 1176, Rpt by JPS, same subj, 23 Nov 44. Both in CCS 381 Japan (10-4-43) sec 3. (TS) Mns, JPS 179th Mtg, 16 Nov 44, item 3; 180th Mtg, 22 Nov 44, item 2.

[15] (TS dg S) JCS 1176/1, Memo by CG AAF, "Russian Participation in the War against Japan," 5 Dec 44, CCS 381 Japan (10-4-43) sec 4.

[16] (TS dg S) JCS 1176/2, Memo by CominCh-CNO, "Operations in the Kuriles," 11 Dec 44, CCS 381 Japan (10-4-43) sec 4.

[17] (TS) Memo, Nimitz to King, "Future Operations - North Pacific," ser 000162, 10 Dec 44, CCS 381 Japan (10-4-43) sec 4.

888 NOTES TO CHAPTERS XXVIII AND XXIX

[18] (TS dg S) JCS 1176/4, Rpt by JPS, "Suitability and Feasibility of Operations in the Kuriles-Kamchatka Area," 6 Jan 45; (U) Routing Slip, 15 Jan 45. Both in CCS 381 Japan (10-4-43) sec 5.

[19] (TS dg S) JCS 1176/6, Rpt by JPS, "Russian Participation in the War against Japan," 18 Jan 45, CCS 381 Japan (10-4-43) sec 6.

[20] (TS) Msg, Deane to JCS, M-22050, CM-IN-16728, 16 Dec 44; (TS) Msg, Deane to JCS, M-22261, CM-IN-4013, 4 Jan 45. Both in CCS 381 Japan (10-4-43) sec 4.

[21] (TS) Memo, Arnold to Secy JCS, "Installation of USAAF Weather Reporting Stations in the USSR," nd, CCS 381 Japan (10-40-43) sec 6.

CHAPTER XXIX

[1] Gen Arnold was not present at Argonaut. He was represented by Gen Kuter. For fuller discussion of the conference arrangements, see (S) Vernon E. Davis, "The Combined Chiefs of Staff at the International Conferences" (Sp Study, JCS HS, Jun 53).

[2] (TS dg R) JCS 1227, Memo by RBCOS, "Subjects Proposed for Discussion by the Combined Chiefs of Staff," 9 Jan 45, CCS 381 (1-9-45) sec 1.

[3] (TS) JWPC 312/1, Rpt by JWPC, "Preparation for the Next U.S.-British-U.S.S.R. Staff Conference," 10 Jan 45, CCS 381 (1-9-45) sec 1.

[4] (TS dg R) JCS 1227/1, Rpt by JPS, "Agenda for Next U.S.-British Staff Conference," 11 Jan 45; (TS) CCS 765, Memo by JCS, same subj, 15 Jan 45. Both in CCS 381 (1-9-45) sec 1.

[5] (TS) CCS 765/2, Memo by RBCOS, "Agenda for the Next U.S.-British Staff Conference," 18 Jan 45; (TS) CCS 765/3, Memo by JCS, same subj, 19 Jan 45; (TS) CCS 765/5, Memo by RBCOS, same subj, 22 Jan 45; (TS) CCS 765/6, Memo by RBCOS, same subj, 22 Jan 45. All in CCS 381 (1-9-45) sec 1.

[6] (TS) CCS 765/8, Memo by RBCOS, "Agenda for Next U.S.-British Staff Conference," 25 Jan 45, CCS 381 (1-9-45) sec 1.

[7] (TS) Mns, JCS 183rd Mtg, 30 Jan 45, item 1; (TS) Mns, CCS 182nd Mtg, 30 Jan 45, item 2.

[8] (TS dg C) CCS 452/35, Memo by BCOS, "Operations in Southeast Asia Command," 30 Jan 45; (TS dg C) CCS 452/36, Memo by JCS, same subj, 31 Jan 45. Both in CCS 381 Burma (8-25-42) sec 13.

[9] (TS dg R) JCS 1238, Rpt by JPS, "Strategy in Southeast Asia, India-Burma, and China," 30 Jan 45, CCS 381 Chinese The. (12-7-44) sec 1.

[10] (TS) Mns, CCS 183rd Mtg, 31 Jan 45, item 5.

[11] (TS dg S) CCS 747/7, Memo by BCOS, "Allocation of Resources between India-Burma and China Theaters," 31 Jan 45, CCS 370.01 Burma (11-6-44) sec 2.

[12] (TS) Mns, JCS 185th Mtg, 1 Feb 45, item 4.

[13] (TS dg C) CCS 452/37, Note by Secys, "Operations in Southeast Asia Command," 1 Feb 45, CCS 381 Burma (8-25-42) sec 13.

NOTES TO CHAPTER XXIX

[14] (TS) JWPC 272/14, Rpt by JWPC, "Operations for the Defeat of Japan," 17 Jan 45; (TS dg R) JCS 924/11, Rpt by JPS, same subj, 19 Jan 45; (TS dg R) CCS 117/11, Memo by JCS, same subj, 22 Jan 45. All in CCS 381 Pac. Ocean Area (6-10-43) sec 11.

[15] (TS) Mns, CCS 184th Mtg, 1 Feb 45, item 5.

[16] (TS) CCS 776/1, Rpt of CCS, "Interim Report to the President and Prime Minister," 2 Feb 45, CCS 381 (1-9-45) sec 2; (TS) Mns, 1st Plen Mtg, 2 Feb 45, *Argonaut*, pp. 287-294.

[17] (TS) Mns, 2nd Plen Mtg, 9 Feb 45, *Argonaut*, pp. 295-297; (TS) CCS 776/2, "Draft of Final Report to the President and Prime Minister," 8 Feb 45, CCS 381 (1-9-45) sec 2.

[18] (TS) JPS 592/1, Rpt by JWPC, "Preparation for the Next U.S.-British-U.S.S.R. Staff Conference," 11 Jan 45, CCS 381 (1-9-45) sec 1.

[19] (TS dg R) JCS 1227/2, Rpt by JPS, "Preparations for Next U.S.-British-U.S.S.R. Staff Conference," 13 Jan 45, CCS 381 (1-9-45) sec 1.

[20] (TS) CCS 765/1, Memo by JCS, "Subjects for Consideration at the Next U.S.-British-U.S.S.R. Staff Conference," 17 Jan 45; (TS) Msg, JCS to Deane, WAR-22611, CM-OUT-22611, 17 Jan 45. Both in CCS 381 (1-9-45) sec 1.

[21] (TS) CCS 765/4, Memo by RBCOS, "Subjects for Consideration at the Next U.S.-British-U.S.S.R. Staff Conference," 20 Jan 45, CCS 381 (1-9-45) sec 1.

[22] (S) Mns, Mtg of Pres, PM, and Stalin, 30 Nov 43, *TEHRAN* (State Dept doc). Deane, p. 247. Statement of W. Averell Harriman, 13 Jul 51, 82 Cong, 1 Sess, Hrgs before S. Armed Services and For Rels Cmtes, "Military Situation in the Far East," 17 Aug 51, pt 5, app NN, pp. 3328-3342. (TS) Msg, Deane to Marshall, M-21391, CM-IN-15444, 16 Oct 44, CCS 381 Japan (10-4-43) sec 3.

[23] Conv, FAdm King's aide with Hayes, 27 May 53; Ltr, FAdm Leahy to Hayes, 27 May 53, JCS HS files.

[24] (TS) Mns, JCS Mtg w/Pres, 4 Feb 45 (Yalta). FAdm King subsequently said that he was opposed to making concessions in order to secure Russian cooperation but had felt that perhaps southern Sakhalin might be given as a "sop." He thought the other chiefs had agreed with him. *Fleet Admiral King*, pp. 591-592. A memo by FAdm King including his recollections of the Yalta conference was shown Lt Hayes by FAdm King's aide on 27 Jun 51.

[25] (TS) Harriman, Notes on Convs, 10 Feb 45, regarding the Far East, "Crimean Conference - Reports and Documents." The full text of the agreement has been published in several places, including 82 Cong, 1 Sess, Hrgs before S. Armed Services and For Rels Cmtes, "Military Situation in the Far East," 17 Aug 51, pt 5, app NN, pp. 3333-3334; Dept of State, *United States Relations with China* (Washington, 1949), pp. 113-114.

[26] (TS) Ltr, Deane to Antonov, 24 Jan 45; (TS dg R) JCS 1227/3, Memo by JPS, "Agenda for 'ARGONAUT'," 4 Feb 45; (TS dg R) JCS 1227/4, Memo by JPS, "Subjects for First U.S.-U.S.S.R. Staff Meeting," 7 Feb 45; (TS dg R) JCS 1227/5, Memo by CG USMILMIS Moscow, same subj, 7 Feb 45. All in CCS 381 (1-9-45) sec 2.

[27] (TS) Mns, JCS 188th Mtg, 5 Feb 45, item 4.
[28] (TS) Memo, Pres to Stalin, 5 Feb 45, CCS 381 Japan (10-4-43) sec 7; (TS) Mns, Mtg, Pres w/Stalin, 8 Feb 45, "Crimea Conference - Reports and Documents."
[29] As early as 3 Feb Gen Antonov was asked if permission could be obtained for the American staff to discuss with the Soviets details of possible Russian participation in the war against Japan. No answer to this request has been found. Adm Leahy suggested to the President on 6 Feb that he try to obtain such permission from Marshal Stalin. Presumably approval was obtained, for on 7 Feb Adm Leahy informed Gen Antonov of the U.S. Chiefs' desire "for a most secret discussion" the following afternoon. This time the reply was affirmative. (TS) Memo, no sig, for Antonov, 3 Feb 45; (TS) Memo, Leahy to Pres, 6 Feb 45. Both in CCS 381 (1-9-45) sec 2. (TS) Ltr, Leahy to Antonov, 7 Feb 45; (TS) Ltr, Antonov to Leahy, 7 Feb 45. Both in CCS 381 (1-9-45) BP.
[30] (TS) Mns, JCS 190th Mtg, 8 Feb 45, item 4.
[31] There are no official minutes of this meeting or the one on 9 Feb. Informal minutes were dictated by Gen Kuter after the meetings. These were supplemented by memoranda by FAdm King and by an unidentified author, probably Gen Marshall. The last is in CCS 381 Japan (10-4-43) sec 7. Photostatic copies of the others are in JCS HS file, "Minutes-U.S.-U.S.S.R. Mtgs. Yalta." Leahy, p. 307.
[32] (TS) Mns, 2nd Plen Mtg, 9 Feb 45, *Argonaut*, pp. 295-297; (TS) CCS 776/2, "Draft of Final Report to the President and Prime Minister," 8 Feb 45, CCS 381 (1-9-45) sec 2.

CHAPTER XXX

[1] (TS dg S) Ltr, Giles to Arnold, 10 Aug 44, OPD 319.1 TS, sec IV, case 228; (TS) Notes for discussion with General Marshall, nd, ABC 384 Pacific (1-17-43) sec 5. (TS) Memo, Ritchie to Hull, 8 Jul 44; (TS) Memo, Arnold to Hull, "Proposed Memorandum by the Chief of Staff," 8 Nov 44; (TS) Memo, Hull to Marshall, "Command in the Pacific," 26 Nov 44. All in ABC 323.31 Pac. Ocean Area (1-29-42) sec 3-A. (TS) Memo, Bessell to Handy, "Command Organization for the War against Japan," 16 Aug 44, OPD 384 TS, case 40; (TS) Memo, Arnold to Marshall, "Organization of Air Forces, Pacific Ocean Areas," 27 Oct 44, OPD Exec 10, item 68; (TS) Memo, Arnold to Handy, "Command in Pacific after Reoccupation of Philippines," 22 Nov 44, OPD Exec 10, item 57.
[2] (TS) JWPC 260, Rpt by JWPC, "Command Organization and Area Boundaries for the War against Japan," 18 Aug 44, CCS 323.261 POA 8-18-44) sec 1; (S) Mns, JPS 164th Mtg, 23 Aug 44, item 9.
[3] (TS dg R) JCS 713/15, Memo by CofS USA, "Future Operations in the Pacific," 22 Sep 44, CCS 381 Pac. Ocean Area (6-10-43) sec 8. For further discussion of this paper, see ch XXIV, p. 622.
[4] (TS dg R) JCS 713/16. Memo by CominCh-CNO, "Future Operations in the Pacific," 25 Sep 44, CCS 381 Pac. Ocean Area (6-10-43) sec 8.

891 NOTES TO CHAPTER XXX

[5] (TS) Msg, MacArthur to Marshall, C-55018, CM-IN-16870, 17 Dec 44, OPD TS Msg file.

[6] (TS) Msg, MacArthur to Marshall, WAR-79291, CM-OUT-79291, 19 Dec 44, cy in JCS HS file; (TS) Msg, MacArthur to Marshall, C-55268, 22 Dec 44, CM-IN-25619 (27 Dec 44), OPD TS Msg file.

[7] (TS dg R) JCS 521/10, Memos by CofS USA and CominCh-CNO, "Strategic Deployment of U.S. Forces Following the Defeat of Germany," 17 Jan 45, CCS 381 (2-8-43) sec 7.

[8] (TS dg R) JCS 521/11, Memo by CofS USA, "Strategic Deployment of U.S. Forces Following the Defeat of Germany," 22 Jan 45, CCS 381 (2-8-43) sec 7; (TS) Memo, J.E. H[ull] to Marshall, 16 Jan 45, ABC 323.31 Pac. Ocean Area (1-29-42) sec 3-A. A similar recommendation for a planning staff was made by Gen Somervell in Feb as a means of aiding procurement planning. (TS) Summary by Hull of Memo, Somervell to Marshall, "Procurement Planning for Pacific Operations," 26 Feb 45, ABC 384 Pacific (1-17-43) sec 7.

[9] (TS) Ltr, CinCPac-POA to CominCh, "Future Operations," ser 000134, 24 Jan 45, CNO(WPD) file "Command-During the War, C-7," env 31, safe 139, NR&H.

[10] (TS) Memo, M.M. Dupre, "Future Operations," 5 Feb 45, CNO(WPD) file "Command-During the War, C-7," env 31, Safe 139, NR&H.

[11] (TS dg C) JCS 1259, Memo by CofS USA, "Command in the Pacific," 26 Feb 45, CCS 323.361 (2-26-45) sec 1.

[12] (TS dg C) JCS 1259/1, Memo by CG AAF, "Command in the Pacific," 28 Feb 45, CCS 323.361 (2-26-45) sec 1.

[13] (TS) Mns, CominCh-CinCPac Conf, 6 Mar 45, CNO(WPD) file, env 137, case 140, NR&H.

[14] (TS dg C) JCS 1259/2, "Directive for Reorganization and Future Operations in the Pacific Theater," 10 Mar 45, CCS 323.361 (2-26-45) sec 1.

[15] Minutes of all the meetings are filed together in CCS 323.361 (2-26-45) sec 1.

[16] (TS dg C) JCS 1259/3, Rpt by JPS, "Directive for Reorganization and Future Operations in the Pacific Theater," 16 Mar 45, CCS 323.361 (2-26-45) sec 1.

[17] (TS) Memo, Marshall to Hull, 19 Mar 45, ABC 384 Pacific (1-17-43) sec 9; (TS) Memo, King to JCS, "Directive for Reorganization and Future Operations in the Pacific Theater," 20 Mar 45, CCS 323.361 (2-26-45) sec 1.

[18] (TS) CD, JCS 1259/3, 3 Apr 45; (TS dg C) JCS 1259/4, Note by Secys, "Command and Operational Directives for the Pacific," 3 Apr 45, CCS 323.361 (2-26-45) sec 1. There are no minutes of the discussions on JCS 1259/3. Comments on planners' discussions are in (TS) Memo, Lincoln to Hull, 26 Mar 45, and (TS) Memo, no sig (Col T.D. Roberts) to Cooke, 28 Mar 45. Both in ABC 323.31 Pac. Ocean Area (1-29-42) sec 3-A.

[19] (TS) Memo, Arnold to Leahy, Marshall, King, 25 May 45, CCS 373.11 Japan (3-20-43) pt 11.

[20] (TS) Memo, Leahy, no adee, 27 May 45, CCS 373.11 Japan (8-20-43) pt 11.

[21] (TS) Memo, Arnold to Leahy and King, 30 May 45, CCS 373.11 Japan (8-20-43) pt 11.

[22] (TS dg R) JCS 742/10, Memo by CominCh-CNO, "Establishment of United States Army Strategic Air Force in Pacific," 31 May 45; (TS) Msg, JCS to MacArthur and Nimitz, WARX-10463, CM-OUT-10463, 1 Jun 45. Both in CCS 373.11 Japan (8-20-43) pt 11.

[23] (TS) Msg, MacArthur to Marshall, CX-17638, CM-IN-2386, 3 Jun 45, CCS 373.11 Japan (8-20-43) pt 12.

[24] (TS dg R) JCS 742/11, Memo by CominCh-CNO, "Transfer of Headquarters Twentieth Air Force to the Pacific," 8 Jun 45, CCS 373.11 Japan (8-20-43) pt 12.

[25] (TS) Msg, JCS to MacArthur, Nimitz, Spaatz, WARX-29978, CM-OUT-29978, 10 Jul 45, CCS 373.11 Japan (8-20-43) pt 13.

[26] (TS) Msg, WD to Argonaut, 5 Feb 45, Ann "A" to Mns, JCS 189th Mtg, 7 Feb 45.

[27] (TS) Mns, JCS 189th Mtg, 7 Feb 45, item 7, and Ann "B".

[28] (TS) Msg, MacArthur to Marshall, CA-50688, CM-IN-27255, 26 Feb 45, CCS 381 Pac. Ocean Area (6-10-43) sec 11.

[29] (TS) Msg, JCS to MacArthur, WAR-63958, CM-OUT-63958, 5 Apr 45; (TS) Msg, MacArthur to Marshall, CAX-51420, CM-IN-6002, 7 Apr 45; (TS dg C) JCS 1307, Memo by CominCh-CNO, "Plans for Occupying North Borneo," 9 Apr 45; (TS) Msg, JCS to MacArthur, WAR-66056, CM-OUT-66056, 10 Apr 45; (TS) Msg, MacArthur to Marshall, CA-51543, CM-IN-10915, 12 Apr 45; (TS) Msg, King to Nimitz, 131644 Apr 45; (TS) Msg, JCS to MacArthur, WAR-70717, CM-OUT-70717, 20 Apr 45. All in CCS 381 Pac. Ocean Area (6-10-43) sec 11.

[30] (TS dg C) JCS 992/3, Rpt by JPS, "British Participation in the War against Japan," 4 Sep 44; (TS dg C) JCS 992/5, Rpt by JSSC, same subj, 8 Sep 44. Both in CCS 381 Burma (8-25-42) sec 11. (TS) Mns, JPS 184th Mtg, 27 Dec 44, item 7.

[31] (TS) Mns, JPS 197th Mtg, 11 Apr 45, item 10; (TS) Mns, CCS 190th Mtg, 13 Apr 45, item 3.

[32] (TS) CCS 847, Memo by RBCOS, "Naval Base for British Pacific Fleet," 28 Apr 45, CCS 045.9 P.O.A. (4-28-45).

[33] At Gen Marshall's recommendation "a desirable" had replaced "an essential" in Adm King's draft.

[34] (S) CCS 847/1, Memo by JCS, "Naval Base for British Pacific Fleet," 12 May 45, CCS 045.9 P.O.A. (4-28-45).

[35] (TS) CCS 847/2, Memo by RBCOS, "Naval Base for British Pacific Fleet," 25 May 45, CCS 045.9 P.O.A. (4-28-45).

[36] (S) CCS 852, Memo by BCOS, "Reorganization of Command in the Southwest Pacific Area," 3 May 45, CCS 325.361 POA (8-18-44) sec 1.

[37] (TS dg R) JCS 1357, Rpt by JPS, "Reorganization of Command in the Southwest Pacific Area," 17 May 45; (S) Memo, Brig A.T. Cornwall-Jones to McFarland, 11 May 45. Both in CCS 323.361 POA (8-18-44) sec 1.

[38] (TS) Msg, MacArthur to JCS, C-17386, CM-IN-28587, 30 May 45; (S) Memo, Cornwall-Jones to McFarland, 29 May 45; (TS dg R) JCS 1357/1, Rpt by JPS, "Reorganization of Command in the Southwest Pacific Area," 1 Jun 45; (TS dg S) CCS 852/1, Memo by JCS, same subj, 7 Jun 45. All in CCS 323.361 POA (8-18-44) sec 1.

[39] (TS) Memo, Lincoln to Hull, 6 Jul 45, ABC 323.31 Pac. Ocean Area (1-29-42) sec 3-B.

[40] (TS dg S) CCS 890, Memo by BCOS, "Command and Control in the War against Japan," 9 Jul 45, CCS 323.361 POA (8-18-44) sec 1.

[41] (TS dg S) JCS 1407/2, Rpt by JSSC, "Future Command and Control by the Combined Chiefs of Staff," 11 Jul 45, CCS 323.361 POA (8-18-44) sec 1. For further discussion, see (S) MS, JCS Hist, *Organizational Development*, vol III.

[42] (TS) Mns, JCS 195th Mtg, 16 Jul 45, item 12.

[43] (TS dg S) JCS 1407/3, Rpt by JPS, "Control and Command in the War against Japan," 16 Jul 45, CCS 323.361 POA (8-18-44) sec 1.

[44] (TS) Mns, JCS 196th Mtg, 17 Jul 45, item 4. (TS dg S) CCS 890/1, Memo by JCS, "Control and Command in the War against Japan," 17 Jul 45; (TS dg S) CCS 890/2, Memo by BCOS, same subj, 18 Jul 45. Both in CCS 323.361 POA (8-18-44) sec 1.

[45] (TS) Mns, CCS 195th Mtg, 18 Jul 45, item 4.

[46] (TS) Mns, CCS 195th Mtg, 18 Jul 45, item 5.

[47] (TS dg S) CCS 852/2, Memo by RBCOS, "Reallocation of Areas and Command in the Southwest Pacific and Southeast Asia Areas," 10 Aug 45; (TS) JWPC 355/2/D, Dir, same subj, 13 Aug 45. Both in CCS 323.361 POA (8-18-44) sec 1.

[48] (TS) CCS 680/2, "Report to the President and Prime Minister," 16 Sep 44, *Octagon*, pp. 129-139.

[49] Cf. above, ch XXVII, pp. 658-659.

[50] (TS dg C) JCS 1259/4, Note by Secys, "Command and Operational Directives for the Pacific," 3 Apr 45, CCS 323.361 (2-26-45) sec 1.

[51] (TS) JWPC 332/1, Rpt by JWPC, "Pacific Strategy," 21 Apr 45; (TS) JWPC 332/2, Rpt by JWPC, same subj, 23 Apr 45; (TS) Mns, JPS 199th Mtg, 25 Apr 45; (TS dg R) JCS 924/15, Rpt by JPS, same subj, 25 Apr 45. All in CCS 381 Pac. Ocean Area (6-10-43) sec 12.

[52] (TS dg R) JCS 924/16, Memo by CominCh-CNO, "Pacific Strategy," 2 May 45; (TS) CD, JCS 924/15, 10 May 45. Both in CCS 381 Pac. Ocean Area (6-10-43) sec 12.

[53] (TS dg C) JCS 1331, Memo by CominCh-CNO, "Proposed Issue of 'Olympic' Directive," 30 Apr 45, CCS 381 Pac. Ocean Area (6-10-43) sec 12.

[54] (TS) Mns, JPS 200th Mtg, 2 May 45, item 14; (TS) Memo, Lincoln to Duncan, "Draft Directive," 2 May 45, ABC 323.31 Pac. Ocean Area (1-29-45) sec 3-A.

[55] (TS dg C) JCS 1331/2, Rpt by JPS, "Directive for Operation 'Olympic,'" 14 May 45, CCS 381 Pac. Ocean Area (6-10-43) sec 12.

[56] All the papers exchanged in the subsequent discussion of the directive are attached to (TS) Memo, Lincoln to McFarland, "Directive for Operation Olympic," 25 May 45, CCS 381 Pac. Ocean Area (6-10-43) sec 13.

[57] (TS) Msg, JCS to MacArthur, Nimitz, Arnold, WARX-87983, CM-OUT-87983, 25 May 45, CCS 381 Pac. Ocean Area (6-10-43) sec 13.

[58] (TS) Memo, Leahy to JCS, 14 Jun 45, CCS 381 Japan (6-14-45) sec 1; (TS) Mns, Mtg, JCS w/Pres, 18 Jun 45, item 1.

[59] (S) CCS 426/1, "Report to the President and Prime Minister," 6 Dec 43, *Sextant*, pp. 297-306.
[60] (TS dg R) JCS 521/6, Rpt by JPS, "Strategic Deployment of U.S. Forces to 30 September 1945," 11 Jun 44, CCS 381 (2-8-43) sec 5.
[61] (TS) CD, JCS 521/6, 26 Jun 44.
[62] (TS dg C) CCS 679, Memo by JCS, "Redeployment of Forces after the End of the War in Europe," 14 Sep 44, CCS 370 (1-13-44) sec 2.
[63] (TS dg R) JCS 521/9, Rpt by JPS, "Strategic Deployment of U.S. Forces Following the Defeat of Germany," 23 Dec 44, CCS 381 (2-8-43) sec 7; (TS dg R) JCS 521/12, Rpt by JPS, same subj, 29 Mar 45, CCS 381 (2-8-43) sec 8.
[64] (TS dg R) JCS 521/15, Memo by CominCh-CNO, "Strategic Deployment of U.S. Forces Following the Defeat of Germany," 11 Apr 45; (TS dg R) JCS 521/16, Memo by CofS USA, same subj, 11 Apr 45; (S dg R) CD, JCS 521/16, 22 Apr 45. All in CCS 381 (2-8-43) sec 9.
[65] (TS dg C) CCS 679/1, Memo by CPS and CAdC, "Redeployment of U.S. and British Forces after the Defeat of Germany," 2 Apr 45, CCS 370 (1-13-44) sec 3.
[66] (TS dg R) CCS 824, Memo by RBCOS, "Operational Priorities for the Continuation of the War against Japan," 14 Apr 45, CCS 381 Pac. Ocean Area (6-10-43) sec 11.
[67] (TS dg R) JPS 647/1, Rpt by JWPC, "Operational Priorities for the Continuation of the War against Japan," 17 Apr 45, CCS 381 Pac. Ocean Area (6-10-43) sec 11.
[68] (TS) Mns, JPS 198th Mtg, 18 Apr 45, item 7; (TS dg R) JCS 1316, Rpt by JPS, "Operational Priorities for the Continuation of the War against Japan," 19 Apr 45, CCS 381 Pac. Ocean Area (6-10-43) sec 11.
[69] (TS) Handwritten Note on Memo, McFarland to Leahy, "Operational Priorities for the Continuation of the War against Japan," 19 Apr 45, CCS 381 Pac. Ocean Area (6-10-43) sec 11; (TS) Memo, McFarland to Marshall, King, Arnold, same subj, 26 Apr 45, with note attached; (TS dg R) CCS 824/2, Memo by JCS, same subj. All in CCS 381 Pac. Ocean Area (6-10-43) sec 12.
[70] (TS dg R) CCS 824/4, Memo by RBCOS, "Priorities for the Continuation of the War against Japan," 3 May 45, CCS 381 Pac. Ocean Area (6-10-43) sec 12.
[71] (TS) Mns, JPS 201st Mtg, 9 Apr 45, item 3; (TS dg R) JCS 1316/1, Rpt by JPS, "Priorities for the Continuation of the War against Japan," 10 May 45, CCS 381 Pac. Ocean Area (6-10-43) sec 12.
[72] (TS dg R) CCS 824/5, Memo by JCS, "Priorities for the Continuation of the War against Japan," 16 May 45, CCS 381 Pac. Ocean Area (6-10-43) sec 13; (TS) CCS 900/3, "Report to the President and Prime Minister," 24 Jul 45, *Terminal*, pp. 247-268.
[73] (TS) Msg, Lincoln sgd Stratemeyer to Marshall for Hull, CABX-2996, CM-IN-17886, 17 Feb 45; (TS) Msg, Cooke to King, TST-1586, CM-IN-18606, 19 Feb 45. Both in CCS 381 Burma (8-25-42) sec 13.

895 NOTES TO CHAPTERS XXX AND XXXI

[74] (TS) Msg, SACSEA to BCOS, SEACOS-317, 26 Feb 45, CM-IN-29128 (28 Feb 45); (TS) CCS 802, Memo by RBCOS, "Future Operations by Southeast Asia Command," 24 Mar 45; (TS) Memo, Maj J.A. Davison, Brit Secy, CPS, to U.S. Secy, CPS, "Future Operations in South East Asia Command," 28 Mar 45. All in CCS 381 Burma (8-25-42) sec 13.

[75] (TS) JPS 636/1, Rpt by JWPC, "Future Operations by Southeast Asia Command," 29 Mar 45; (TS) JCS 774/9, Rpt by JPS, same subj, 2 Apr 45. Both in CCS 381 Burma (8-25-42) sec 13.

[76] (TS) CCS 802/1, Memo by JCS, "Future Operations by Southeast Asia Command," 6 Apr 45, CCS 381 Burma (8-25-42) sec 13. For discussion of CCS 452/37, sec ch XXIX, pp. 678-680.

[77] (TS) CCS 802/3, Memo by RBCOS, "Future Operations by Southeast Asia Command," 14 Apr 45; (TS) JCS 774/10, Rpt by JPS, same subj, 5 May 45. Both in CCS 381 Burma (8-25-42) sec 13. (TS) CCS 802/4, Memo by JCS, same subj, 11 May 45, CCS 381 Burma (8-25-42) sec 14.

[78] (TS) CCS 802/6, Memo by RBCOS, "Change in Plans for Future Operations by Southeast Asia Command," 21 May 45, CCS 381 Burma (8-25-42) sec 14.

[79] (TS) Mns, JPS 191st Mtg, 7 Mar 45, item 1; (TS) Mns, JCS 192nd Mtg, 13 Mar 45, item 1.

[80] (TS) JPS 628, Rpt by CG CT, "Requirements for Operation 'BETA,'" 13 Mar 45, CCS 381 Chinese Theater (12-7-43) s. 6. (TS) JLC 280/1, Rpt by JLC, "Requirements for Operation 'Rashness,'" 4 Apr 45; (TS) JLPC 4/15, Rpt by JLPC, same subj, 4 Apr 45; (TS) JPS 628/1, Rpt by JLPC & JWPC, same subj, 9 Apr 45; (TS dg R) JCS 924/14, Rpt by JPS & JLC, "Priority of Resources for Operations 'Rashness,'" 14 Apr 45. All in CCS 381 Chinese Theater (12-7-43) s. 7. (TS) Mns, JLC 110th Mtg, 6 Apr 45, Item 1; (TS) Mns, JPS 197th Mtg, 11 Apr 45, item 4; (TS) CD, JCS 924/14, 20 Apr 45.

CHAPTER XXXI

[1] (TS) Ltr, H. Maitland Wilson to Leahy, 12 Jun 45, CCS 381 (6-15-45) sec 1.

[2] (S) CCS 643/3, Rpt by CIC, "Estimate of the Enemy Situation," 8 Jul 45, CCS 381 (6-4-43) sec 2 pt 4; (TS) Mns, CCS 193rd Mtg, 16 Jul 45, item 2.

[3] (TS) CCS 892, Rpt by SACSEA, "Progress Report on Operation in the Southeast Asia Command," 15 Jul 45; (S) CCS 893, Memo by JCS, "General Progress Report on Recent Operations in the Pacific," 16 Jul 45; (TS dg R) CCS 894, Memo by JCS, "Report on Army Air Operations in the War against Japan," 16 Jul 45. All in CCS 381 (6-15-45) sec 2. (TS dg S) CCS 880/4, Memo by JCS, "Development of Operations in the Pacific," 29 Jun 45, CCS 381 Pac. Ocean Area (6-10-43) sec 13; (TS) Mns, CCS 193rd Mtg, 16 Jul 45, items 3, 4, & 5.

[4] (TS) Mns, CCS 196th Mtg, 19 Jul 45, item 5.

[5] (TS dg R) CCS 889, Memo by RBCOS, "British Contribution to the Final Phase of the War against Japan," 6 Jul 45, CCS 370 Great Britain (7-15-44) s. 1.

⁶(TS) Msg, Marshall to MacArthur, WAR-28274, CM-OUT-28274, 7 Jul 45; (TS) Msg, MacArthur to Marshall, C-24215, CM-IN-8305, 9 Jul 45. Both in CCS 370 Great Britain (7-15-44) s. 1.

⁷(TS) JPS 717/2, Rpt by JWPC, "British Participation in the Final Phase of the Campaign against Japan," 10 Jul 45, CCS 370 Great Britain (7-15-44) s. 1; (TS dg R) JCS 1424, Rpt by JPS, "British Participation in the War against Japan," 16 Jul 45, CCS 373.11 Japan (9-18-44) sec 1; (TS dg R) CCS 889/1, Memo by CCS, same subj, 17 Jul 45, CCS 370 Great Britain (7-15-44) s. 2; (TS) Mns, JCS 196th Mtg, 17 Jul 45, item 3.

⁸(TS) Mns, CCS 194th Mtg, 17 Jul 45, item 2.

⁹(TS) CCS 842, Memo by RBCOS, "French and Dutch Participation in the War against Japan," 25 Apr 45, *Terminal*, pp. 68-70.

¹⁰(TS) CCS 842/1, Memo by JCS, "French and Dutch Participation in the War against Japan," 10 Jul 45; (TS) CCS 842/2, Memo by JCS, same subj, 18 Jul 45. Both in *Terminal*, pp. 71-74. (TS) Mns, CCS 195th Mtg, 18 Jul 45, item 2.

¹¹(TS) CCS 462/25, Memo by JCS, "Staff Conversations with Portugal," 16 Jul 45; (TS) CCS 462/26, Memo by BCOS, same subj, 18 Jul 45. Both in *Terminal*, pp. 2-6. (TS) Mns, CCS 195th Mtg, 18 Jul 45, item 3.

¹²(TS) CCS 892/1, Memo by BCOS, "Directive to the Supreme Allied Commander Southeast Asia," 20 Jul 45, CCS 381 Burma (8-25-42) sec 14.

¹³(TS) Mns, CCS 200th Mtg, 24 Jul 45.

¹⁴(TS) JWPC 353/1/M, Memo to JPS, "Basic Objectives, Strategy, and Policy," 5 May 45, CCS 381 (5-2-45).

¹⁵(TS dg C) JCS 1366, Rpt by JPS, "Basic Objectives, Strategy, and Policy," 24 May 45, CCS 381 (5-2-45).

¹⁶(TS dg C) CCS 877, Memo by JCS, "Basic Objectives, Strategy, and Policies," 14 Jun 45, CCS 381 (5-2-45). The subsequent comments exchanged by the U.S. and British Chiefs were published as papers in the same series and are filed in the same folder. See also Leahy, pp. 376-377, 387, 410-411.

¹⁷(TS dg C) CCS 877/5, Memo by JCS, "Basic Objectives, Strategy, and Policies," 21 Jul 45, CCS 381 (5-2-45).

¹⁸(TS) Mns, CCS 198th Mtg, 21 Jul 45, item 2; (TS) Mns, Plen Sess, 24 Jul 45, *Terminal*, pp. 307-312; Leahy, p. 414.

¹⁹(TS) Mns, Tri Mil Mtg, 24 Jul 45, *Terminal*, pp. 313-323.

²⁰Walter Millis, ed, *The Forrestal Diaries* (New York, 1951), p. 11; Leahy, p. 353.

²¹In a pre-Potsdam study of the opening of a sea route to Siberia the JPS had strongly recommended against introducing that subject in conversation with the Russians and in favor of telling them if necessary that "(1) The U.S. is not prepared to commit itself to any action that would jeopardize major operations against Japan. (2) The U.S. is not prepared to commit itself to any diversionary effort, such as the opening of a sea route to Siberia, until the military effectiveness of such efforts is reasonably assured." Although the JCS merely noted this paper there can be

no doubt that they approved this policy. (TS dg S) JCS 1176/13, Rpt by JPS, "Opening of a Sea Route to Siberia," 9 Jul 45, CCS 381 Japan (10-4-43) sec 9. (TS) Mns, JCS 199th Mtg, 20 Jul 45, item 1.

[22](TS) Mns, US-USSR Mil Mtg, 26 Jul 45, *Terminal*, pp. 325-337.

CHAPTER XXXII

[1](TS dg R) JCS 1340, Memo by Marshall, "Immediate Demand for the Unconditional Surrender of Japan," 9 May 45. (TS dg R) JCS 1340/1, Rpt by JPS and JIC, same subj, 14 May 45; (TS) SWNCC 149, Memo by Secy JCS, same subj, 9 Jun 45. All in CCS 387 Japan (5-9-45). (S) MSS, JCS Hist, *History of Psychological Warfare*, pt II, ch V, *Evolution of Global Strategy*, unnumbered chapter, "Victory and Peace Objectives: II Japan." (TS) Dept of State, *Handbook of Far Eastern Conference Discussions* (Washington, 1949), pp. F-3 - F-6.

[2](TS) Mns, CCS 193rd Mtg, 16 Jul 45, item 2.

[3]Stimson and Bundy, *On Active Service*, pp. 619-625. James F. Byrnes, *Speaking Frankly* (New York, 1947), p. 206. Leahy, pp. 418-419. (U) SWNCC 149/1, Note by Secys, "Immediate Demand for the Unconditional Surrender of Japan," 3 Aug 45, CCS 387 Japan (5-9-45).

[4]*Global Mission*, pp. 585, 589-590; King & Whitehill, *Fleet Admiral King*, pp. 620-621; *AAF in WW II*, vol V, pp. 704-713.

[5]An interesting and plausible account of the Japanese reaction to the Potsdam statement is contained in William J. Coughlin, "The Great *Mokusatsu* Mistake, Was This the Deadliest Error of Our Time?" *Harper's*, vol 206 (Mar 53), pp. 31-40. Mr. Coughlin contends that by an error in translation of the Japanese word, *mokusatsu*, the Japanese Government was reported to have decided "to ignore" the Potsdam ultimatum rather than the intended "to withhold comment."

[6]The essential documents in preparation for Japan's surrender are in CCS 386.2 Japan (4-9-45). For detailed discussion of pre-surrender preparations, see (S) MS, JCS Hist, *Evolution of Global Strategy*, tentative chapters 96 and 97, "Tripartite Cooperation against Japan: The Potsdam Conference: July 1945," and "The Japanese Surrender: Occupation of Japan (14 August - 1 September 1945)."

BIBLIOGRAPHIC ESSAY

by Dean C. Allard, U.S. Naval Historical Center

RECORDS AND MANUSCRIPTS

In this admirable history, Grace Person Hayes describes and interprets the role of the Joint Chiefs of Staff (JCS) in formulating World War II strategy in the Pacific and China-Burma-India theaters. Although Mrs. Hayes completed these volumes more than a quarter of a century ago, her extensive research into the records of this organization remains unmatched by other historians of the Pacific war. In addition, Mrs. Hayes consulted key series of Army and naval files reflecting the strategic thinking of General of the Army George C. Marshall and Fleet Admiral Ernest J. King, who represented their services on the JCS, and the outlook of other senior planners. As noted in the original preface to this work, the author also obtained comments on the manuscript from several major figures, including Admiral King who, in many respects, emerges as the central figure in the history.

When the Hayes volumes appeared in 1953 and 1954, almost all of the basic archival resources still had security classifications and hence were accessible only to official historians. In the intervening years, however, the records have been declassified virtually without exception and shifted to public repositories where they are available to all scholars.

The records of the JCS, the Combined Chiefs of Staff (CCS), the most basic source material for the Hayes study, and the Joint Board, now are in the custody of the Modern Military Branch of the U.S. National Archives, Washington, D.C. They are designated as Record Group 218. The Modern Military Branch also has the files of various components of the War Department General and Special Staff (Record Group 165), including the joint and combined papers of the Strategy and Policy Group of the Operations Division, which are referred to in the author's footnotes as ABC; other files of the Army's Operations Division (OPD) and its predecessor, the War Plans Division (WPD); and series of records maintained by the Office of the Chief of Staff (OCS) and the War Department Chief of Staff (WDCSA).

When the author prepared this history, the secret-confidential and super-secret office files of Admiral King in his capacity as Commander in Chief, U.S. Fleet (CominCh), and Chief of Naval Operations (CNO) were in the custody of the Office of Naval Records and

and History. Today, this declassified collection is in the Operational Archives of the Naval Historical Center, Washington Navy Yard, Washington, D.C. That repository has the World War II files of the Navy's War Plans Division (WPD), also. The general files of the Commander in Chief Pacific (CinCPac), which the author consulted in the Naval Records Management Center at Alexandria, Virginia, are now in the keeping of the General Archives Division of the National Archives, in Suitland, Maryland.

Although the archival series consulted by the author represent the most significant documents for a history of the Joint Chiefs of Staff, a contemporary scholar may consult a number of more specialized sources that have become available over the last two decades. Among these are the papers of individual members of the JCS, including the files of General Marshall, which have been donated to the George C. Marshall Research Library in Lexington, Virginia. The private papers of Admiral King are in the Manuscript Division of the Library of Congress, Washington, D.C., which division has similar collections from the other two World War II members of the JCS, General of the Army Henry H. Arnold and Fleet Admiral William D. Leahy. Groups of personal-official files maintained by Admirals King and Leahy are now in the Naval Historical Center's Operational Archives. The Wisconsin Historical Society in Madison, Wisconsin, had another collection of Admiral Leahy's personal papers.

Extensive materials pertaining to the nation's senior civilian leaders are available. Of notable importance are the records of President Franklin D. Roosevelt and President Harry S. Truman which, together with the files of many of their associates, are held at the Franklin D. Roosevelt Library in Hyde Park, New York, and the Harry S. Truman Library at Independence, Missouri. The Yale University Library, New Haven, Connecticut, has the significant papers of Secretary of War Henry L. Stimson. Stimson's counterparts in the Navy, Frank Knox and James V. Forrestal, are represented by collections held in the Manuscript Division of the Library of Congress and Princeton University, respectively. Of particular value in the Forrestal collection are his original diaries, which start in 1944. Official series of records for the secretaries of both the Army and the Navy can be found in the Modern Military Branch and the Navy and Old Army Branch of the National Archives.

Below the level of these officials and of the members of the Joint Chiefs of Staff were the principal U.S. Commanders in the Pacific region. As noted previously, the records of Fleet Admiral Chester W. Nimitz's Pacific Ocean Area are in the General Archives Division of the National Archives. That organization has similar files from General of the Army Douglas MacArthur's Southwest Pacific Command and from U.S. Army forces in the China-Burma-India theater under the successive command of Generals Joseph W. Stilwell and Albert C. Wedemeyer. Personal papers of most of these leaders have been deposited in several centers. Those of Admiral Nimitz are in the Operational Archives, Naval Historical Center, while those of General MacArthur are at the MacArthur Memorial

Library in Norfolk, Virginia. A collection of General Stilwell's personal papers is at the Hoover Institution on War, Revolution, and Peace in Stanford, California.

Aside from these groups, there are numerous private papers from other leaders in the Pacific theater and key members of the planning staffs in Washington and elsewhere. Among the most important repositories are the Manuscripts Division of the Library of Congress; the Hoover Institution at Stanford; the Albert F. Simpson Historical Research Center, Maxwell Air Force Base, Alabama; the Naval Historical Center's Operational Archives; the U.S. Army Military History Institute, Carlisle Barracks, Pennsylvania; and the Marine Corps Historical Center in Washington, D.C. All these organizations have aids to finding specific documents in their holdings. In addition, there are the following overall guides to Air Force and naval papers deposited in major American repositories: Lawrence J. Paszek, compiler, *United States Air Force History: A Guide to Documentary Sources* (Washington, D.C.: Office of Air Force History, 1973) and Dean C. Allard, Martha L. Crawley, and Mary W. Edmison, editors, *U.S. Naval History Sources in the United States* (Washington, D.C.: Government Printing Office, 1979).

OFFICIAL HISTORIES AND OTHER PUBLICATIONS

As indicated in the author's footnotes, *The War Against Japan* is one of several staff histories that were being written in the Joint Chiefs of Staff organization at the end of World War II. Aside from Mrs. Hayes's work, the only manuscript in this series that has been completed is Vernon E. Davis's *Organizational Development* (Washington, D.C.: JCS, 1953), a detailed and authoritative account of the origin and evolution of the JCS and CCS structures through 1945. Copies of the Davis history are in the Modern Military Branch of the National Archives. The document also appears in a commercial microfilm publication entitled *Strategic Planning in the U.S. Navy: Its Evolution and Execution, 1891-1945* (Wilmington, Delaware: Scholarly Resources, Inc., 1978). Most of the remaining JCS histories referred to by Grace Hayes are partial drafts and are held in the Modern Military Branch of National Archives.

Considering the close integration of military and diplomatic policy in a total war, it is not surprising that the U.S. Department of State's publication, *Foreign Relations of the United States* (Washington, D.C.: Government Printing Office, various dates) reprints a number of the basic documents cited in the Hayes history. Many of these documents are to be found in the several volumes that deal exclusively with the meetings of the Combined Chiefs of Staff in conjunction with summit conferences of their national leaders. The main *Foreign Relations* series, organized by geographic region, makes more general reference to military matters. Although the originals of these materials are available in the National Archives, the State Department publications make them readily accessible to scholars unable to visit that institution and allow students to correlate the civil and military aspects of wartime policy.

A good starting place for researchers seeking to assess the roles of the individual services is Walter Millis, editor, *The War Reports of General of the Army George C. Marshall, General of the Army H.H. Arnold, and Fleet Admiral Ernest J. King* (Philadelphia: J.B. Lippincott, 1947). These reports made by the senior uniformed representatives were released to the press during the war years and inevitably reflect some of the public relations goals of the Army, the Army Air Corps, and the Navy. Nevertheless, they provide insight into the overall direction of the war.

Much more comprehensive accounts began to be prepared by the military services in the postwar years. At the time Grace Hayes completed her study, the distinguished official history entitled *U.S. Army in World War II* (Washington, D.C.: Government Printing Office, 1947-) had not been completed. Among the key volumes published since 1954 that provide insight on Pacific policy is *Strategic Planning for Coalition Warfare, 1943-1944* (Washington, D.C.: Government Printing Office, 1959) by Maurice Matloff. Another history with the same title, but covering the first two years of American participation, was written by Matloff and Edwin M. Snell, and appeared in 1953. Louis Morton's *Strategy and Command: The First Two Years* (Washington, D.C.: Government Printing Office, 1962) relates exclusively to the Pacific and is another exceptionally valuable study on policy. Unfortunately, no comparable study covering 1944 and 1945 was prepared by the Army's historians.

Other basic titles in the army's series are the two-volume *Global Logistics and Strategy* (Washington, D.C.: Government Printing Office, 1955 and 1968) by Richard M. Leighton and Robert W. Coakley; two studies of the defense of the Western Hemisphere, including the eastern Pacific region, entitled *The Framework of Hemisphere Defense* (Washington, D.C.: Government Printing Office, 1960) and *Guarding the United States and Its Outposts* (Washington, D.C.: Government Printing Office, 1964), by Stetson Conn and other authors; and the three-volume *The China-Burma-India Theater* (Washington, D.C.: Government Printing Office 1953-1959) by Charles F. Romanus and Riley Sunderland. Finally, many individual volumes concerning the major campaigns in the Central and Southwest Pacific are available in the Army's history. Although they deal primarily with operations, these sometimes shed light on strategy.

There are two important publications outside the main Army series. One is Kent Roberts Greenfield, editor, *Command Decisions* (Washington, D.C.: Government Printing Office, 1960), which contains a number of penetrating essays by official historians. Among the subjects covered are the American withdrawal to Bataan early in the war, policy involving the invasion of the Admiralty Islands and Luzon, and the decision to use nuclear weapons in 1945. Of equal interest is the so-called MacArthur History, published in four volumes as the *Reports of General MacArthur* (Washington, D.C.: Government

Printing Office, 1966). This account includes valuable narratives of the campaign in the Southwest Pacific contributed by both American and Japanese authors.

Although they give greater stress to operations than does the Army's series, the histories of other services contain some useful data on the formulation of strategy in the Pacific. The Navy is covered in Samuel E. Morison's semiofficial *History of United States Naval Operations in World War II* (Boston: Little, Brown and Co., 1947-1962). Nine of the fifteen volumes in the classic Morison series relate to the Pacific. A more specialized contribution to the Navy's historical program is George C. Dyer's two-volume *The Amphibians Came to Conquer: The Story of Admiral Richmond Kelly Turner* (Washington, D.C.: Government Printing Office, 1972). In addition to discussing the hard-driving Turner's career as a senior amphibious commander in the Pacific from 1942 to 1945, Dyer assesses Turner's tour as the director of the Navy's War Plans Division from 1941 to 1942. The other major series concerning the services are also multi-volume works: *History of U.S. Marine Corps Operations in World War II* (Washington, D.C.: Government Printing Office, 1958-1971), and Wesley Frank Craven and James Lea Cate, editors, *Army Air Forces in World War II* (Chicago: University of Chicago Press, 1948-1958).

Aside from these accounts of the individual services, several other agency publications supplement Grace Hayes's volumes. The Atomic Energy Commission's *The New World, 1939-1946* (University Park: Pennsylvania State University, 1962) by Richard G. Hewlett and Oscar E. Anderson, Jr., is an outstanding study that contains some coverage on the decision to drop nuclear weapons on Japan. Another key development in 1945 was the participation by the Soviet Union in the Pacific war. A well-researched historical account, *The Entry of the Soviet Union into the War Against Japan, Military Plans, 1941-1945*, was prepared by the Department of Defense and issued as a press release in 1955. Copies of this document are available in the history department of the office of the Secretary of Defense and other specialized military repositories.

Grace Hayes has noted that useful insight into Japanese policy is contained in the publications of the U.S. Strategic Bombing Survey, including *The Interrogations of Japanese Officials* (Washington, D.C.: Government Printing Office, 1946). Since 1954, more detailed coverage of this all-important aspect has become available in a mimeographed series of translated *Japanese Monographs* originally prepared for the General Headquarters, Far East Command, by former Japanese officers and officials. A full set of the *Monographs* is held by the U.S. Army's Center of Military History. Approximately one-fourth of the 184 titles in this series have been reprinted in a fifteen-volume set entitled *War in Asia and the Pacific, 1937-1949: Japanese and Chinese Studies and Documents*, edited by Donald S. Detwiler and Charles B. Burdick (New York: Garland Publishing, 1979). Unfortunately, the exhaustive official history prepared over the last two decades by the Japanese Defense Agency's War History Section, published under the general title *Senshi Sosho*, is to be found only in Japanese. There apparently are no plans to translate the approximately 100 volumes of this major source into English.

Finally, reference should be made to the *History of the Second World War* prepared for the British government under the general editorship of J.R. M. Butler. Two sub-series are of particular relevance for students of strategy in the Pacific. One is a six-volume work entitled *Grand Strategy* (London: Her Majesty's Stationery Office, 1956-) written by J.R.M. Butler and several other authors. The second sub-series, which relates exclusively to the Pacific but focuses more on operations, is H. Woodburn Kirby *et al.*, *The War Against Japan* (London: Her Majesty's Stationery Office, 1957-1969) published in five volumes. Both of these histories present accounts from a British perspective of much of the material covered by Grace Hayes.

MEMOIRS, BIOGRAPHIES, AND OTHER PERSONAL SOURCES

A notable biography of a major American strategist is Forrest C. Pogue's *George C. Marshall* (New York: Viking, 1963-), three volumes of which have appeared to date. Another standard source, Ernest J. King and Walter M. Whitehill, *Fleet Admiral King: A Naval Record* (New York: Norton, 1952), was available at the time Grace Hayes wrote her history. It may now be supplemented by Thomas B. Buell's *Master of Sea Power: A Biography of Fleet Admiral Ernest J. King* (Boston: Little, Brown and Co., 1980), which stresses King's contribution to strategy in the Pacific. Two more concise appreciations of the admiral have been written by Robert W. Love, Jr. His essays appear in Kenneth J. Hagan, editor, *In Peace and War: Interpretations of American Naval History* (Westport, Conn.: Greenwood Press, 1978) and a volume under the general editorship of Love entitled *The Chiefs of Naval Operations* (Annapolis: Naval Institute Press, 1980). Students of the Navy's role also will find much useful material in the numerous oral histories of senior naval officers prepared since 1969 by John T. Mason, Jr. of the U.S. Naval Institute. More than one hundred volumes containing transcripts of the interviews are available at the institute's offices in Annapolis and at the Naval Historical Center in Washington, D.C.

Unfortunately, the other members of the Joint Chiefs of Staff have not been assessed in recent works. Until such volumes appear, students of the war must depend upon the older memoirs produced by Admiral Leahy and General Arnold published as *I Was There* (New York: Whittlesey House, 1950) and *Global Mission* (New York: Harper, 1940), respectively. General Alexander A. Vandegrift was not a member of the Joint Chiefs but, as Commandant of the Marine Corps in 1944 and 1945 and a senior commander in the Pacific before that time, he was a figure of central importance. In cooperation with Robert P. Asprey, the general wrote *Once a*

Marine (New York: Norton, 1964), an overall account of his eventful career.

Among the nation's civilian leaders, Franklin D. Roosevelt is of paramount importance. Useful accounts of his activities as commander in chief appear in James MacGregor Burns, *Roosevelt: Soldier of Freedom* (New York: Harcourt, Brace, Jovanovich, 1970) and William R. Emerson's essay in Ernest R. May, editor, *The Ultimate Decision: The President as Commander in Chief* (New York: Braziller, 1960). The older *Roosevelt and Hopkins: An Intimate History* (New York: Harper, 1948) by Robert S. Sherwood, is still useful. *Memoirs: Years of Decision* (New York: Doubleday, 1955), written by Roosevelt's successor, Harry S Truman, continues as one of the basic sources on World War II.

For the British side, Winston S. Churchill's *The Second World War* (Boston: Houghton Mifflin, 1948-1953) is both a history and a personal memoir. Another revealing title is Arthur Bryant, *The Turn of the Tide: A History of the War Years Based on the Diaries of Field Marshal Lord Alanbrooke, Chief of the Imperial General Staff* (London: William Collins and Sons, 1957).

The civilian secretaries of the American armed services are discussed in a number of books. The influential Henry L. Stimson, in cooperation with McGeorge Bundy, wrote *On Active Service in Peace and War* (New York: Harper, 1947), a standard account that was available when Grace Hayes was working on her history. The secretaries of the Navy were not as important in the development of strategic policy. Nevertheless, students of the Pacific War will find useful coverage on Frank Knox in an essay by George H. Lobdell in *American Secretaries of the Navy*, a two-volume work edited by Paolo E. Coletta, Robert G. Albion, and K. Jack Bauer (Annapolis: Naval Institute Press, 1980). *Forrestal and the Navy* by Robert G. Albion and Robert H. Connery (New York: Columbia University Press, 1962), and Walter Millis, editor, *The Forrestal Diaries* (New York: Viking, 1951) provide useful coverage of Knox's successor, even though the latter does not present the complete Forrestal diary, which is available in the secretary's private papers at Princeton.

Turning to the highest-ranking American commanders in the Pacific, reference should be made to General MacArthur's own *Reminiscences* (New York: McGraw Hill, 1964) and the collection of his papers in *A Soldier Speaks* (New York: Praeger, 1965). These accounts may now be assessed in the light of an outstanding critical biography by Clayton D. James, *The Years of MacArthur* (Boston: Houghton Mifflin, 1970-). The two James volumes published to date bring the general through the end of World War II. Admiral Nimitz refused to write his memoirs but, after the admiral's death, the Nimitz family cooperated with his principal biographer, E.B. Potter, author of *Nimitz* (Annapolis: Naval Institute Press, 1976). An older work that continues to have some merit is Edwin P. Hoyt's *How They Won the War in the Pacific: Nimitz and His Admirals* (New York: Weybright and Talley, 1970). The Japanese naval leader who was Nimitz's approximate counterpart, Admiral Isoroku Yamamoto, is assessed in a perceptive biography by Hiroyuki Agawa published in English as *The Reluctant Admiral: Yamamoto and the Imperial Navy* (Tokyo: Kodansha International Ltd., 1979).

On the Asian mainland, General Joseph W. Stilwell and General Albert C. Wedemeyer served as the senior American military representatives. A collection of original documents, *The Stilwell Papers*, was edited by Theodore H. White (New York: Sloane, 1948) and is one of the sources cited in the Hayes history. A more complete and recent documentary source is Charles F. Romanus and Riley Sunderland, editors, *Stilwell's Personal File* published in five volumes (Wilmington, Delaware: Scholarly Resources, Inc., 1976). Barbara W. Tuchman's *Stilwell and the American Experience in China* (New York: Macmillan, 1970) synthesizes much previous work on this colorful leader. Wedemeyer's own memoir, *Wedemeyer Reports* (New York: Henry Holt, 1958), is the essential source on the general. There is no definitive account of Lord Mountbatten, the magnetic commander of the Southeast Asia Command in the last two years of the war. But, a recent anecdotal biography is Richard Hough's *Mountbatten: Hero of Our Time* (London: Weidenfeld and Nicolson, 1980).

Examples of personal sources available for other important individuals include Alfred D. Chandler, Jr., and Stephen E. Ambrose, editors, *The Papers of Dwight David Eisenhower* (Baltimore: Johns Hopkins University Press, 1970). This five-volume series includes papers on the Pacific generated during Eisenhower's assignment as a planning officer on the War Department's General Staff in the early months of World War II. Milton E. Miles's *A Different Kind of War* (Garden City: Doubleday, 1967) is an important memoir by the commander of Naval Group, China, that includes frank discussions of the complex civil-military relationships in China. The commander of the land-based aerial bombardment campaign against the Japanese home islands, Curtis E. LeMay, joined with McKinlay Kantor to prepare an overall memoir, *Mission With LeMay* (Garden City: Doubleday, 1965).

For the many other memoirs and biographies that are part of the voluminous literature of World War II, readers are referred to the comprehensive bibliographic essays in *A Guide to the Sources of United States Military History* (Hamden, Conn.: Archon Books, 1974) and to the scheduled five-year updates of that volume.

SECONDARY SOURCES

Over the last thirty-six years a tidal wave of literature touching in some way upon the strategy and policy of the Pacific War has appeared from presses in this country and abroad. Among these contributions are many works by diplomatic historians that, although primarily concerned with the broad political aspects of World War II, relate military strategy to more general developments. Considering the priority given by wartime leaders to the defeat of

Germany, the relatively limited participation of British forces in the Pacific before 1945, and the overriding importance of U.S.-Soviet relations in the postwar years, it is not surprising that these historians give special attention to events in Europe. Nevertheless, such standard works as Herbert Feis, *Churchill, Roosevelt, Stalin: The War They Waged and the Peace They Sought* (Princeton: Princeton University Press, 1957) make reference to the Pacific in the context of European strategic developments. There is some coverage of the Pacific War in the writings of the New Left, or revisionist, historians who, in the 1960s, began a critique of U.S. policy based on their belief that American leaders sought to assure American economic and political domination in the postwar world. Typical of these books is Gabriel Kolko's *The Politics of War: The World and United States Foreign Policy, 1943-1945* (New York: Random House, 1968). A more recent volume, John L. Gaddis's *The United States and The Origins of the Cold War* (New York: Columbia University Press, 1972), is particularly valuable because it includes a judicious appraisal of both the revisionist and the traditional schools.

Following the defeat of Germany, it became evident that the Soviet Union planned to enter the war against Japan and also that British forces would be freed to participate in that conflict. Hence, in their discussions of events after May 1945, diplomatic historians pay greater attention to the Pacific. Among the specific issues addressed are American attitudes toward Soviet participation, the influence of the doctrine of unconditional surrender on the Japanese, and the decision to employ nuclear weapons. As for the earlier period, the works of Herbert Feis, which combine sound research with the author's personal insight as a former foreign affairs official, are standard accounts: they include *Between War and Peace: The Potsdam Conference* (Princeton: Princeton University Press, 1960) and *The Atomic Bomb and the End of World War II* (Princeton: Princeton University Press, 1966). The revisionists have addressed the same material, but reach different conclusions. An extreme example is Gar Alperovitz in *Atomic Diplomacy: Hiroshima and Potsdam* (New York: Simon and Schuster, 1965). Alperovitz believes that the primary reason for dropping the atomic bomb was not to subdue an already-defeated Japan, but to coerce the Soviet Union into accepting American plans for a peacetime world. In his book mentioned above, John Gaddis presents a balanced critique of this thesis.

Of relevance to the general strategy in the Pacific are two helpful books that concentrate on American-British relations. James R. Leutze's *Bargaining For Supremacy: Anglo-American Naval Collaboration, 1937-1941* (Chapel Hill: University of North Carolina Press, 1978) provides many insights into the evolution of Anglo-American policy before the attack on Pearl Harbor, including the Anglo-American outlook on the Pacific. This study is carried forward by Christopher Thorne's *Allies of a Kind: The United States, Great Britain, and The War Against Japan, 1941-*

1945 (New York: Oxford University Press, 1978). As is true of Leutze, Thorne sees tensions in the British-American relationship, although neither author ignores the areas of agreement between the two nations.

Other specialized diplomatic histories deal with politico-military developments in China and therefore can be seen as supplementing Grace Hayes's treatment from the perspective of the Joint Chiefs of Staff. Two representative titles are Herbert Feis, *The China Tangle* (Princeton: Princeton University Press, 1953), and a somewhat revisionist critique of U.S. policy by Michael Schaller entitled *The U.S. Crusade in China* (New York: Columbia University Press, 1979).

A number of important books also have been produced by historians whose primary interest is military institutions, as opposed to international politics. The Army's former chief historian, Kent Roberts Greenfield, is the author of *American Strategy in World War II: a Reconsideration* (Baltimore: Johns Hopkins University Press, 1963) which covers the Pacific. Samuel Eliot Morison, who might be viewed as Greenfield's naval counterpart, wrote a brief, interpretive essay entitled *Strategy and Compromise* (Boston: Little, Brown and Co., 1958). Two other titles in the same category are Russell F. Weigley's often brilliant overall account of American strategy, *The American Way of War: A History of United States Military Strategy and Policy* (New York: Macmillan, 1973), and Allan Millett's recent history of the Marines, *Semper Fidelis: The History of the United States Marine Corps* (New York: Macmillan, 1980). Both Millett and Weigley provide a useful view of the planning and conduct of the Pacific war within the context of more general historical developments.

A remarkable number of books deal with land, sea, and air operations in World War II. Although very few provide original details on the national and international strategy that are the particular concern of Grace Hayes, some exceptions deserve notice. These include the standard account by Jeter A. Isely and Philip A. Crowl, *The U.S. Marines and Amphibious War: Its Theory and Its Practice in the Pacific* (Princeton: Princeton University Press, 1951). Clark G. Reynolds in *The Fast Carriers: The Forging of an Air Navy* (New York, McGraw-Hill, 1968) relates another category of Pacific warfare to broad strategic considerations.

I would like to conclude this essay by singling out three titles: John B. Lundstrom, *The First South Pacific Campaign: Pacific Fleet Strategy, December 1941-June 1942* (Annapolis: Naval Institute Press, 1976), Edward Van Der Rhoer, *Deadly Magic: A Personal Account of Communications Intelligence in World War II in the Pacific* (New York: Charles Scribner's Sons, 1978), and W.J. Holmes, *Double-Edged Secrets: U.S. Naval Intelligence Operations in the Pacific During World War II* (Annapolis: Naval Institute Press, 1979). Lundstrom, who presents one of the few fresh accounts of Pacific policy to appear in recent years, argues that the U.S. Navy was seeking a decisive fleet action with the Japanese during the first six months of the war. Among the new materials he consulted were recently released files revealing the use by military planners of intercepted Japanese communications. The role of radio intercepts in shaping the Pacific campaign is the primary concern of Van Der Rhoer and Holmes, both of whom were participants in the process. As information on communications intelligence continues to be released and assessed by historians, it is possible that an important explanatory element for certain aspects of strategy will be brought forth, as has been the case already for the European theater. It seems unlikely, however, that the broad outline of American grand strategy depicted with so much skill by Grace Hayes will see basic revision in the years to come.

INDEX

A-29 Lockheed Hudson, 215
Abadan, 115
ABC Conversations, 8-9
ABC-1, 9-12, 17-18, 27-28, 30, 55-58
ABC-4/3, 35
ABC-4/CS1, 41-42
ABCD, 73
ABCDR, 73
ABDA
   aircraft for, 63, 66-67, 107
   Australia as part of, 64-66
   dissolution of, 84-87, 90-97
   establishment of, 44-53
   naval forces, 63, 752n39, 67, 69, 70
   objectives 748n102
   Supreme Commander, 61
ABDA Command (ABDACOM), 36, 44-53, 57, 59, 61-72, 75, 77, 81, 89,
      93, 96, 100, 103, 110, 137, 200, 203
ABDAFLOAT, 61
ABDAIR, 61
Adak Island 273, 484-45
ADB-1, 13-14
Admiralty Islands, 139, 329, 370, 429, 478, 544, 552, 554, 558, 563,
      699, 700
   bases, 547
   Japanese in, 140
Aegean Sea, 536
Africa, 141, 408. *See also* North Africa
Agattu Island, 274, 284, 328
Airborne operations
   Kalewa, 640
   New Guinea, 142
   Rangoon, 338, 524
Air commando groups, 638-41

Aircraft. *See also* B-29s.
  allocation, 54, 67, 106-7 117-20, 122-23, 128-29, 130, 155-56, 159-63, 182, 205, 207, 217-19, 269, 316-20, 325-26, 769n9
  availability, 426, 470, 659
  delivery, 116
  deployment, 31, 110-11, 116, 182-88, 264, 314, 317-20
  diversion from Europe, 107, 153
  ferrying to Russia, 132-34
  for the South Pacific Area, 174, 184-88, 269, 313-34, 319
  for the Southwest Pacific Area, 163, 186, 264, 191, 313-14, 319
  from BOLERO, 119-20, 130, 153, 173, 176, 182-88
  in ABDA, 63
  production, 67, 106-7, 155, 344-45
  shortage, 54, 106, 130, 317
  troop carrier, 445
Air deliveries to China. *See* Hump tonnage.
Airfields, adequacy in South Pacific, 117-18
Air Force, U.S.
  Eighth, 349, 694
  Ninth, 357
  Tenth, 116, 203, 205-7, 209, 214-19, 223, 227, 237, 344, 357, 445, 493, 513-14, 590-91, 597-98, 602, 664-65
    transfer to Egypt, 215-16, 218
  Eleventh, 486
  Thirteenth, 567
  Fourteenth, 203, 345, 380, 385, 454, 493, 513-15, 517, 525, 573, 582, 588-89, 591, 593, 597-602, 617, 651, 660-61, 664-65
  Twentieth, 590-96, 607, 616, 620, 688-94, 706
  tactical, 659
Air offensive
  European theater, 408
  from China. *See* China, air operations from
  from North Africa, 259-60, 264
  from Sumatra, 518-19
  from the United Kingdom, 154-170, 181, 185-87, 257-59, 264, 289, 318-28, 324-26, 350, 366, 390-91, 403, 431. *See also* SICKLE.
  in Burma, 235
Airpower, 180-81
Air reenforcements, 175-77, 180-88
Air superiority, 51-52
Air supremacy in the Admiralties, 370
Air Transport Command (ATC) 242, 385, 436-37, 511, 526-27, 580, 583, 586, 597-98, 663, 712
Air transports, 223
  conversion of medium bombers, 232
  for Burma, 205, 663
  for India, 205
  for SEAC, 638

Akyab, 235-37, 239, 277, 280, 285, 289, 295, 338, 341-42, 353, 356,
    363, 376, 378, 393, 396, 398, 400, 430, 437, 447-48, 450,
    455-58, 464-65, 468, 470, 518-19, 537, 569, 570, 573, 582,
    653, 662, 666. See also CANNIBAL; RAVENOUS.
Alaska, 12, 37, 42, 94, 158, 300
  air route to Russia, 131
  communications, 133, 260
  defense of, 129, 259
  garrison forces, 483, 485
  Japanese in, 380
Alaska Defense Command, 484-85
Aleutian Islands, 27, 32, 129, 131, 140, 272-73, 284, 300, 306, 327,
    356, 366, 371, 402, 409, 414-15, 461, 484-86, 493
  B-29 bases, 493, 496, 593
  capture of, 372
  intelligence, 133
  Japanese threat to, 157
  Russian bases, 676
  Russian naval operations, 672
Alexander, Lt. Col. E.H., 233
Alexander, Gen. Sir Harold, 154, 201
Allocation of aircraft. See Aircraft, allocation.
Allocation of forces, 37, 39, 46-47, 154-67
Allocation of resources, 43, 279-81, 285, 359, 439, 443, 712
  proportionate between Europe and the Pacific, 104, 108, 111-14,
    116, 119-20, 137, 182-83, 254, 260, 262-63, 279-81
ALTERNATIVE PAC-AID, 601-2
Amboina, 632
Ambon Island, 97
Amchitka Island, 273
American Volunteer Group (AVG), 20, 79, 203, 206, 208-9, 212-13, 227,
    245
Amherst, 239
Ammunition shortage, 194
Amoy, 603, 613, 615-16, 618-20, 622-24, 629
Amphibious craft, 403, 418, 421, 552, 699
Amphibious Force, South Pacific, 147
Amphibious forces, 118, 141-42, 146, 148, 158, 175, 240, 286, 288,
    403, 416-18, 425, 523, 578, 622-23
Amphibious Forces, Pacific Fleet, 140
Amphibious operations, 102, 108, 230, 236, 239-40, 266, 295, 307, 330,
    354, 396, 400-401, 419-20, 455-58, 468-69, 509-10, 523, 526,
    589, 614, 695, 703-4
Amur, Gulf of, 673
Amur River, 673, 675, 713
An, 396
ANAKIM, 230, 247, 261-63, 278, 281-82, 288-301, 306-7, 321, 323,
    335-36, 339, 341-42, 347-60, 363, 369, 371, 373-74, 376,
    378, 382, 386-89, 392-93, 395-96, 398-400, 408, 435

ANAKIM (Cont'd)
  alternatives to, 367
  forces for, 286-89, 336-37
  landing craft, 289, 293-97, 307
  Modified, 369
  shipping, 287, 296, 352-56, 359, 377
Andaman Islands, 192, 450, 505, 519, 524, 537, 539, 569, 662. *See also* BUCCANEER.
Andaman Sea, 435
Anderson, Col, O.A., 151, 179-81, 252, 269, 315-20
Anfa Conference. *See* Casablanca.
Angaur, 607, 621
Antiaircraft equipment and facilities, 29, 35, 38, 118
Antiaircraft regiments, 129, 172
Antisubmarine warfare, 261, 351
Antonov, General, 671, 675, 684, 721
ANVIL, 534, 541, 630
ANVIL or BUCCANEER, 541
ANZAC area, 58, 70, 89, 90, 96-97, 107, 109, 112
ANZAC Command, 59
ANZAC Council, 97
ANZAC naval force, 56, 59
Aparri, 607, 621
Arafura Sea, 455, 488, 556, 632
Arakan, 450, 461, 523, 582, 585, 662
Arakan coast, 277, 337, 338, 513, 519, 541, 569, 584
Arakan region, 490
ARCADIA, 36-60, 64-65, 72, 77, 88, 199, 291
ARCADIA agreement, 104, 114, 251, 254-55, 291
Argentia, Newfoundland, 14
ARGONAUT agreement, 718
Armaments, production, 40-41
Army
  British Fourteenth, 523, 527, 666
  Chinese, 526, 569
  Chinese Fifth, 80, 202
  of the Philippines, 736n36
Army Air Staff, 592
Army Air Transport Command. *See* Air Transport Command.
Army Air Transport Service, 445
Army Corps, U.S. XXIV, 621
Army Group, Chinese 71st, 585
Army Transport Command, 600. *See also* Air Transport Command.
Arnold, Lt. Gen. Henry H., 36, 66, 129, 181, 184-85, 187-88, 193, 212, 218, 232, 246-47, 254, 259, 265, 278-79, 281, 326, 336-37, 339-48, 350, 354, 356-57, 386, 426, 431, 435, 449, 455, 465, 468, 470, 478-79, 485, 491-92, 494, 497, 504, 558, 583, 585-86, 589, 592-602, 638-39, 642, 657, 659-61, 669-70, 673-74, 689, 693-95, 706-7, 724, 726

>   and allocation of aircraft, 117, 155, 162-63, 170, 205, 207, 257, 345, 357, 585, 597-98
>   and British air participation, 716
>   and Chennault, 246, 281, 298, 336
>   and Doolittle raid, 127
>   and Hump tonnage, 212, 340, 343, 515, 541-42, 527, 597, 599
>   and independent air force in China, 246, 343-45
>   and invasion of Formosa, 614, 619
>   and mobile air force, 117, 170, 257
>   and Stilwell, 444, 593
>   and strategic air offensive against Germany, 170, 185-87, 257, 348
>   and unified command in the Pacific, 265
>   commander of the Twentieth Air Force, 590-96, 693-94
>   meeting with Soviet representatives, 132-33
>   trip to Chungking, 336, 339-40, 343-44
>   trip to New Delhi, 336-39, 341
>   views on strategy, 170, 257

Arnold-Evill-Towers report, 155
Arnold-Portal Agreement, 155, 161
Arnold-Slessor-Towers Agreement, 123, 156-57, 159, 162, 218
Artificial harbors, 466
Asia for the Asiatics, 74, 199, 227
Asiatic Fleet, 6, 14, 18, 33, 40, 45, 69, 94
Assam, 200, 202, 226, 230, 232, 277, 393, 432, 451, 453, 449-50, 468-69, 494, 510, 513, 518
>   advance from, 239
>   airfields, 353, 387, 395-97, 399, 435-36, 454, 514
>   air route to China, 396-97, 436
>   floods, 449, 467-69
>   line of communications to, 471
>   route to China, 157

Assault shipping, 295-96, 404, 418, 470, 477-78, 536, 540, 641. *See also* Landing craft.
>   withdrawal from BUCCANEER, 540

Assault ships, 404, 447, 477
Associated Powers, 75
Atom bomb, 723
Attrition, 300, 387
Attu Island, 272, 414, 483
>   Japanese in, 133, 140, 328
>   seizure of, 371, 418

Auchinleck, Gen. Sir Claude J.E., 215, 437, 449-50, 453, 513-16
Aurand, Brig. Gen. H.S., 211
Australasia, 137-38
Australia, 8, 14, 18, 32, 35-36, 39-40, 42-45, 50, 52-53, 55-61, 63-71, 73, 83-85, 88-90, 93, 95-101, 103, 106, 109-10 117, 119, 122, 126-27, 232, 256, 422, 443
>   air bases in, 142
>   aircraft for, 66-67, 106-7, 111, 122, 124-25, 159-60, 176

Australia (Cont'd)
  air forces in, 119
  allocations to, 111, 126
  and Supreme War Council, 207
  as a base, 423
  B-29 bases in, 491, 593
  British naval bases in, 630-32
  British obligation to, 473
  communications to, 137-38, 140, 147, 180, 259-60, 299, 300, 372, 420
  defense of, 11, 111, 124, 126, 158, 161, 163-67
  diversion of aircraft to, 129
  forces and equipment for, 123, 165, 167
  garrisons for Solomons from, 147
  Japanese attacks on, 139, 353, 366
  security of, 259
  shipping for, 124, 195
  threat to, 121, 140, 157
  U.S. forces for, 93, 112-13, 140, 165-66
  U.S. forces in, 40
Australian Area, 98, 634
Australian Command, 89, 699
Australian Commonwealth Naval Board (ACNB), 59
Australian Corps, 83
Australian forces, 139, 634-36, 715
Australian mobile air force, 148, 170
Australian troops, 690, 693, 695-97, 751n11
  diversion of to Burma, 83-84, 121, 167
  in Java, 84-85
  in the Middle East, 112, 164
  in the Netherlands East Indies, 695-97
  return of from the Middle East, 121, 165-67
Australian War Cabinet, 66
Australian War Council, 165
AXIOM, 574-76, 578-79

B-17s
  for bases in Siberia, 496
  sent to Alaska, 129
B-24s, 214, 234, 492-96
B-25s, 122, 127, 234
B-29s, 299, 470-71, 484, 489, 492-93, 495-98, 501, 505, 540-41, 551, 564, 590, 592-99, 601, 609, 623, 630, 654, 659-60, 693.
    See also MATTERHORN.
  bases for, 299, 485-86, 491, 588-89, 597
    in the Aleutians, 493, 496, 593
    in the Carolines, 496
    in Ceylon, 593, 596
    in the Chengtu area, 497-98, 589, 592-93, 596, 598-99, 660
    in Formosa, 556, 596, 615, 660

		in India, 497-98, 588, 596, 660-61
		in the Kuriles, 486
		in Leyte, 660
		in Luzon, 660
		in the Marianas, 492-93, 496, 542, 547, 562, 592, 595-96, 660-61
		in the Marshalls, 496
		in the Ryukyus, 660
		in SEAC, 590-96
	British and, 596
	command of, 591-96, 693
	operating from Australia, 491, 593, 595
	operating from China, 299, 489, 491, 493-95, 497, 588. *See also* China, air operations from.
	removal from China, 660-61
	use against the Netherlands East Indies, 491, 592, 595
Babcock, Col. C. Stanton, 609
Badoglio, Marshal Pietro, 413
Bahm, Capt. G.H., 427
Baker, Air Vice Marshal J.W., 540
Baker Island, 476
Balabac Strait, 550, 697, 699
Bali, 82, 85
Balikpapan, 69, 696-97
Balingtang Channel, 608
Bandar Sea, 90
Bandoeng, 61
Bangkok, 393, 456, 464, 468, 518, 525, 537, 540-41
Barnes, Brig. Gen. Julian F., 33
Basmata, 267
Basra, 34
Bassein, 235, 239, 337-38, 376, 378, 397-98, 518
Bassein River, 378
Bataan Peninsula, 34, 42, 62, 91, 93, 127, 139
Batavia, 61, 696
Battalions, U.S.
	First Marine Raider, 141
	76th Coast Artillery (AA), 172
Bauxite, 185
Bengal, 157
	airfields in, 450
	Bay of, 115, 122, 157, 206, 235, 247, 280, 294, 339, 355, 401, 436, 474-75, 523-24, 526, 528, 540-41, 569, 630-32, 634-35
	Japanese in Bay of, 122, 205
Bering Sea, 133
Bering Strait, 273
Bessell, Brig. Gen. W.W., 656
Bhamo, 232, 240, 353, 398-99, 579, 641, 648
Biak, 604, 605, 615
Bieri, Rear Adm. Bernhard H., 305, 307, 491, 501, 508, 544, 553, 556-58, 592, 594

Bilin River, 81
Bismarck Archipelago, 24, 107, 138-39, 261, 268, 271, 300, 332,
    370-74, 403, 409, 414, 424-25, 427-28, 500, 544-46, 566
Bismarck Islands, 137, 488
Bismarck Sea, 556
Bissell, Brig. Gen. Clayton L., 206, 208, 222, 233-34, 243, 245,
    340, 343, 347
Blockade, 108, 136, 299, 604, 619, 624, 627-28, 656, 658, 702-4,
    713-14, 718
  of the Philippines, 33, 612
BOLERO, 114-16, 119-20, 130, 149-51, 181, 206, 261-64, 301, 348-54,
    359, 361, 365, 374, 386
  aircraft from, 153, 173, 176, 182-88, 252
  redeployment of forces, 173
  shipping, 158, 173, 348, 359
BOLERO-ROUNDUP, 142
Bomber Command, U.S.
  XX, 590-92, 596-602, 660-61, 694
  XXI, 694
Bomber Group, U.S. 7th, 597, 602
Bomber offensive against Germany, 322-26, 335, 348, 366. *See
    also* Air offensive
Bombers, long range, 117-19, 129, 147-48, 154
Bonin Islands, 431, 496, 608-9, 614, 622-24, 627, 629-30, 653,
    656-58, 680, 688
Bora Bora, 57, 119, 172
Borneo, 37, 42, 62, 82, 152, 463, 611, 622, 632-33, 693, 695-99,
    715, 717
Borneo, East, 18
Borneo, North, 62, 690
Bougainville, 143, 306, 309, 312-13, 216-27, 332, 477-78, 487
  Japanese in, 140, 191
Bradley, Maj. Gen. Follett, 134, 274-75
Brereton, Maj. Gen. Lewis H., 34, 42, 61, 63, 203, 206-7, 213,
    215, 227
Brett, Maj. Gen. George H., 33-34, 51, 61, 65, 67-69, 71, 73, 85,
    97, 99
BRIMSTONE, 262, 279, 292, 295
  vs. ANAKIM, 263
Brink, Lt. Col, Francis G., 44-46
Brisbane, 32-34
British air operations in the Pacific, 680. *See also* British
    participation.
British air power in the Pacific, 638. *See also* British participation.
British Cabinet, 48
British-Chinese relations, 74
British command, SWPA, 635
British Commonwealth Force, 714
British cooperation, 139
British Defense Committee, 66

British Dominions, aircraft for, 156-57, 159-63
British Eastern Fleet, 90, 108, 115, 130, 164, 191-92, 240, 247,
    280-82, 285, 293-94, 337-38, 448, 473, 526, 572, 635
  Commander in Chief, 59
  Curtin's view of, 164
  role of, 192
  support of Burma operation, 240
  U.S. liaison officers for, 448
  U.S. reenforcement of, 115, 338, 448
British Empire Task Force, 634-35
British Far Eastern Fleet, 18, 45
British Fleet, 501, 630-31, 634, 637, 714
  in the Pacific 463-64, 472-76, 502, 635-38
British import program 348-49
British Joint Planners, 155
British Joint Planning Staff (JPS), 106, 296-97, 337, 402
British Joint Staff Mission, 377
British Main Fleet 637
British Naval Commander in Chief, China, 58
British naval forces, 69-70, 192, 247, 282
  King's views of use of in the Pacific, 430, 463-64
British Pacific Fleet, 690, 697
British participation, 282, 501-4, 630-38, 654-55, 680-81, 697-99,
    714-16
British Planning Staff, 461
British Staff Planners, 106, 296-97, 337, 402
British strategic concept, 255, 360
British Task Force, 630
British territory, occupation of, 139
Brooke, Gen. Sir Alan, 280-82, 286-88, 290, 388, 390-93, 398, 400-401,
    432, 449-52, 454-55, 464-65, 468-69, 506, 524, 530, 533-36,
    630-32, 645, 680-81
Brown, Cdr. C.R., 162, 181, 421
Browning, Capt. M.R., 316, 326, 328
Bruce-Fraser, Adm., 634
Brunei Bay, 690, 696-98
Byrnes, SecState James, 722
BUCCANEER, 491-92, 518-20, 524, 528, 531, 534-41, 573, 576
  landing craft, 529-30
  vs. ANVIL and OVERLORD, 530-31, 534-40
Buckner, Lt. Gen. Simon B., 483-84, 486, 617, 623
Buin, 197, 267, 309, 313, 327, 430, 487
Buka Island, 267, 308, 313, 425, 430, 477-78
  Japanese airfield, 148
BULLFROG, 470
Buna, 178
  Japanese base, 142, 175
  Japanese landings
Buna Bay, 142
Buna-Gona campaign, 418

Buna-Guadalcanal line, 312
Burma, 20, 26, 35, 39-40, 42-43, 50, 52, 63, 71, 75, 78-79, 81,
       83-84, 87-89, 110, 112, 121, 126, 198-249, 284-85, 291-99,
       306, 336-42, 352, 631-32, 679, 715. *See also* ANAKIM;
       RAVENOUS.
  air bases, 236, 357, 465
  aircraft for, 83, 205-7, 246, 663
  amphibious operation, 226, 230, 235, 239, 400, 449, 468-69, 471,
       510, 524, 526, 528, 536-37, 540, 569-70, 573, 640-41, 662
  Australian troops for, 84, 167
  AVG in, 79
  British plan, 234-35
  Chinese troops in, 79, 80, 279, 444, 449
  Churchill's views, 394-95
  command in, 278
  defense of, 71, 202, 259, 372
  in ABDA, 50-51, 71, 75, 83
  Japanese attacks on, 353, 366
  Japanese communications to, 235, 380, 393, 400, 434, 455, 464,
       468, 525, 711
  King's views of, 260
  loss of, 202
  naval support for, 435, 470, 523-24, 526
  operations, 261, 276, 280-81, 285, 352, 393, 402, 409, 417, 419,
       428-30, 433-34, 436, 441, 446-48, 454-59, 461-63, 467-68,
       470, 489-90, 492-93, 499-500, 503, 506, 513-14, 516, 519,
       521, 523, 526-27, 539, 543, 569, 630, 640, 643, 710
  recapture of, 158, 224, 235, 239-40, 290, 337, 346, 368, 372, 376,
       388
  U.S. plan for, 239-40
  U.S. troops in, 678-80
Burma Road, 19, 71, 74, 77-78, 80, 202, 204, 210, 230-31, 248, 253,
       256, 262, 277, 285-86, 294-95, 297-98, 306, 344, 355, 368,
       388, 393-97, 400, 448-49, 454-56, 466, 507
  British plans for, 234-35, 276-77, 285
  capacity of, 344, 394, 456
  loss of, 226, 231
  reopening of, 230-32, 236-37, 239, 253, 256, 289, 306, 368, 449,
       456, 525
  Roosevelt's view of, 248, 458
Burrough, Commo. E.W., 656
Butler, Brig. Gen. W.O., 129
Buzzard, Capt, A.W., RN, 462

C-46s, 517, 527, 583, 585-86
C-47s, 206, 527, 583, 585-86
C-53s, 202
C-54s, 213, 495, 580
C-87s, 242-43, 495, 580
Cagayan River area, 654

Cairo, 34, 472, 489
Calcutta, 205, 340, 447, 453, 468-69, 494, 497-98, 513, 517, 580
   air base at, 495, 497
   Japanese bombing of, 353
   pipeline from, 468-69, 452, 579
   shipping route to, 293
Camranh Bay, 381, 461
Canada
   aircraft, 160
   allocations to, 123
   and China, 73
   and Supreme War Council, 207
   local defense forces, 31
Canadian forces, 415, 715
CANNIBAL, 289, 295, 338, 350
Canton, 228, 232, 522, 601, 711
   Japanese airdrome, 381
Canton Island, 55, 57
Cape Gloucester, 308, 326-27, 487
Capetown, 94
CAPITAL, 640-41, 649, 661-63, 665-66
Caroline Islands, 6, 8, 11, 24, 30-31, 136, 139, 285, 290, 310, 372-74, 403, 409, 414, 416, 423, 425, 427, 431, 461, 476, 490, 492, 496, 545, 547, 549-52, 554-55, 558-60, 563, 621
Carpentaria, Gulf of, 65
Carrier-based air, 140, 142, 374, 501
CARTWHEEL, 419, 421, 425-26, 477-78, 544
Casablanca, 264, 317
Casablanca decisions, 306-7, 315-28, 335-36, 339, 348-52, 356, 358-62, 367, 371, 377, 388, 391-92, 409, 418
Casey, R.G., 121
Casualties, 188, 451, 703
   estimated, 707
Casualty rate, 702
Caucusus, 111, 113
CCS 57/2, 161
CCS 91, 157-60, 182-83, 186, 251
CCS 91/1, 163
CCS 92, 162
CCS 94, 173, 182, 184-85, 187, 252-53
CCS 97, 229
CCS 97/1, 229
CCS 97/2, 230
CCS 97/3, 253
CCS 104/3, 276
CCS 104/4, 277
CCS 135, 261
CCS 135/1, 261
CCS 135/2, 261
CCS 153, 284-85
CCS 154, 294

922   INDEX

CCS 155/1, 290-91, 301, 307, 317-20, 322-25, 356, 259-61, 367
CCS 168, 301, 402
CCS 199, 360-61
CCS 199/1, 362
CCS 199/2, 362
CCS 219, 389-91
CCS 225, 392
CCS 232, 401, 405
CCS 239, 402-3
CCS 242/1, 405
CCS 242/2, 405-6, 408
CCS 242/3, 407
CCS 242/4, 407
CCS 242/6, 407
CCS 244, 404-5
CCS 301, 431-32
CCS 308, 441-43
CCS 313, 458, 465
CCS 323, 492-94
CCS 417, 504-7, 550, 553
CCS 417/2, 545, 553
CCS 426/1, 628
CCS 452/1, 571
CCS 452/37, 711
Celebes, 62, 82, 368, 373, 717
Celebes Sea, 368, 423, 460, 500
Central Pacific Area, 96, 101-12, 136-37, 139, 280, 310, 312, 314, 373
Ceram, 373
Ceylon, 84, 110, 115, 126, 157-58, 206, 218
  B-29 bases, 593, 596
CHAMPION, 523
Changsha, 493-94, 598, 601
Changtu Islands, 658
Chaung, 396
Chekiang Province, 658
Chen, Col. T.T., 341
Chengchow, 646
Chengtu, 491, 496-98, 500, 592, 598-99, 660
  B-29s, 589, 592-93, 596, 598-99, 660
Chennault, Col. Claire L., 19, 79, 90, 198, 203, 222-23, 226, 233, 243-46, 281, 336, 339, 342-47, 370, 379-85, 393-95, 398, 437, 439, 454, 513-14, 517, 521, 524-25, 588-99, 598-99, 651
  aircraft for, 293, 298, 339-40, 342-44, 398
  air force, 297-98, 343-44, 381, 570
  and B-29s, 591
  plan for air operations, 233-34, 243-45, 380-83, 588
  supplies for, 336
  views, 233-34, 381
Chiang, Madame, 213, 215, 219, 228, 512, 514, 527

INDEX

Chiang Kai-shek, Generalissimo, 50-51, 72, 75-76, 78-79, 127, 199-201, 203, 206-224, 227-32, 237-41, 243, 245, 247-48, 281, 292-93, 297, 336, 338-47, 355, 379-80, 382-85, 387, 395, 398, 400-401, 434-40, 442, 444-45, 453, 458, 469, 497, 504, 511-12, 515, 520-28, 530, 535-37, 539-42, 569-71, 573, 584-85, 588-89, 598, 644-52, 662-64, 700, 712, 724
   relation to Stilwell, 200, 215-17, 220-21, 245-46, 511-12
   Roosevelt's view of, 521
   Three Demands, 221-24
Chile, 39
China, 19-22, 38-39, 43, 60, 71, 87-89, 93, 108-9, 157, 198-249, 256, 305, 522, 571-80, 588-90
   aid to, 386, 393, 434, 439, 443, 678
   air bases, 133, 368, 380, 384, 443, 456, 462, 589, 600
   aircraft for, 20, 202-9, 215, 223, 293, 297-98, 339-40, 342-47, 381, 394-95, 466, 570
   airfields in, 213, 216, 231, 233-34, 448, 460, 494-97, 500, 503, 591
   air force in, 290, 297, 306, 339, 394, 454
   air forces for, 301
   air lift to, 435-37, 516-17, 538-41
   air operations from, 40, 248, 298, 336, 342, 346, 372, 373, 381, 387, 395, 402, 409, 428, 434, 449, 456, 462-63, 465, 470-71, 491, 493, 496-97, 499-500, 505, 514, 577-78, 589-90, 592, 596, 599, 601-2, 660
   air operations in, 371-72, 379, 387, 402, 409, 503-4, 576
   air strength, 127, 342, 432
   air supplies for, 432, 453-55
   air supply, 450, 466, 471, 515
   air support of, 438
   air transport for, 202, 204-5, 213, 234, 242, 293, 295, 298, 306, 337, 343, 368-69, 380, 393-94, 442, 450, 452, 517, 540, 569, 575
   air transport route to, 202-3, 216, 399, 432, 434, 437, 439, 450, 454, 461, 468, 471, 509, 512, 575, 579-80
   air transports for, 213, 298, 513, 542
   allocation of resources for, 439
   as a base, 71, 109, 198, 211, 225, 368, 408, 549, 551, 555-56, 577
   B-29s in, 299, 485-86, 489, 491, 493-95, 497, 588-89
   bases in, 260, 293, 368, 382, 449, 459-60, 493, 703
   British divisions in, 681
   British Naval Commander in Chief, 58
   British view of, 72, 74, 199, 217-18, 227, 459, 515
   communications with, 216-17, 247, 398
   guerrillas in, 14
   importance of, 71, 109, 293-94, 449, 546
   Indian divisions for, 681
   Japanese attacks on, 5, 127, 234, 300, 353, 366
   Japanese in, 178

924   INDEX

China (Cont'd)
   King's views of, 393, 546
   land route to, 310, 353, 369, 462, 493, 512, 569-70, 641, 643,
       649, 652, 678
   lend-lease to, 112, 205, 210-12, 215-16, 220-21, 223-24, 226-27
   MacArthur predicts collapse, 160
   manpower in, 71, 530, 546, 549
   operations in, 552, 711-12
   operations in support of. *See* ANAKIM; RAVENOUS.
   port, 368, 449, 464, 500, 549
   Russian claims on, 521
   sea route to, 388, 428, 460, 545, 577
   supplies for, 79, 204-6, 208, 241, 359, 377, 391, 399, 455-56
   supply line, 200, 204, 259, 463, 631
   support for, 42, 226, 231, 408, 453
   tonnage for. *See* Hump tonnage.
China Air Force, 602
China Air Task Force, 339, 343, 345
China-Burma-India Theater (CBI) 89, 168, 199, 214, 227, 229-31, 234,
       240-43, 357, 432, 443-44, 512, 588, 591, 594, 679, 728
   U.S. troops in, 227-29, 232, 236, 238, 241, 436, 439, 498, 643
China coast, 8, 551-53, 555, 577-78, 581, 588-90, 603, 605, 608,
       613, 624, 627, 629, 656-57, 702
   attacks on, 608, 655, 690
   British use of air bases, 654
   landings on, 580, 658-59, 689-90, 711, 713
   sea route to, 579, 687
China Defense Supplies (CDS), 202, 211
China National Aviation Corporation (CNAC), 202-3, 207, 385
China Sea, 83, 623, 696
China Station, Commander in Chief, 11, 14, 18
China Theater, 50, 75-76, 79, 215-17, 220, 227-28, 438-39, 445, 511,
       516, 522, 577, 652, 678, 711
Chindwin River, 240, 247, 289, 337-38, 399, 572, 574, 585, 638, 640
Chindwin Valley, 277, 285, 295, 398
Chinese Air Force, 203, 223, 233-34, 339, 344-45, 381, 432, 525,
       593, 597-98
Chinese-American Task Force, 526-27
Chinese-American Wing, 589, 597, 600
Chinese Army, 80, 219, 343-44, 346, 395, 432, 503, 525, 569
   in India, 523
   psychology, 647
   Stilwell's command of, 80, 646-49
   training, 214, 522
Chinese Communists, 211, 232, 646, 648, 703
Chinese cooperation, 469
Chinese Eastern Railway, 682
Chinese military mission, 208
Chinese Nationalists, 646
Chinese troops in Burma, 79, 80, 279, 444, 449

925   INDEX

Chinese troops in India, 214. *See also* Ramgarh.
Chin Hills, 376, 573
Choiseul Bay, 306
Christmas Island, 39, 55, 57, 75, 111
Chuchow, 381
Chungking, 72-73, 75, 77-78, 203, 221, 233, 238, 336, 339, 342-44, 387
  military council, 73
  road to, 569
  security of, 645
Chungking Conference, 22-23 December 1941, 73-74, 79
Churchill, Winston, 14, 36, 40, 47, 61, 71, 86, 88, 93-95, 111-12, 115, 121, 125-26, 141, 164-66, 179, 186, 192, 214, 249-50, 278, 286, 288-90, 298, 301, 360, 386, 388, 393-96, 400, 403-4, 407-9, 433, 437-43, 445, 454-57, 469, 472, 497, 517, 520-23, 526, 528-29, 531, 534-40, 542, 571, 584, 630-31, 643-44, 662-63, 671, 680-81, 683, 700, 720, 722
  and allocation of aircraft, 156, 198
  and ANAKIM, 286, 294, 296, 354, 357, 394-95, 408
  and Arnold-Slessor-Towers agreement, 162
  and British participation, 282, 289-90, 473-76, 631, 636-38, 662
  and BUCCANEER, 529, 535-36, 539
  and command in CBI, 201
  and end of the war, 466-67
  and invasion of Europe, 104, 149-52, 386, 535
  and Middle East, 111, 166
  and naval support for the Burma campaign, 247
  and RAVENOUS, 294
  and SEAC, 437-43, 509-10
  and shipping, 93, 112
  and Singapore, 631, 662
  and Sumatra, 455-56
  and TORCH, 186
  requests U.S. forces for Australia and New Zealand, 93, 112
  views on the importance of China, 72, 398, 521-22
Chusan Archipelago, 658-59, 680, 590-91, 693, 702
Civil strife, 652
Clark-Kerr, Amb. Sir Archibald, 670
Coke industry, 497-98, 593, 660
Colclough, Capt. Oswald S., 484
Colombo, 86, 115, 130, 205, 473-74
Combat cargo groups, 639-42
Combat cargo squadrons, 666
Combined Chiefs of Staff, establishment of, 50, 60
Combined Intelligence Committee (CIC), 232, 713-14
Combined Liaison Committee, 445
Combined Military Transportation Committee (CMTC), 112, 166-67, 196, 349
Combined Munitions Assignments Board (CMAB), 159, 162, 217

926   INDEX

Combined Munitions Assignments Committee (Ground) (CMAC(G)), 217
Combined Shipping Adjustment Board (CSAB), 196
Combined Staff Planners (CPS), 67, 90, 93, 107, 112, 114, 155-57,
    165, 229, 232, 234-37, 239-40, 251-52, 254, 258, 276-77,
    283, 304, 348-49, 396-97, 402, 404-6, 408, 444, 459-60,
    462-63, 469-71, 475, 486, 492, 495, 499, 501-2, 504, 506,
    535, 540-41, 709
Combined Striking Force, 510
Command, 699-701. *See also* Unified command.
    in ABC-1, 11
    in joint operations, 143
    in the Pacific, 479-82, 565-66, 686-95
    in the South and Southwest Pacific, 116. *See also* Solomons-
        New Guinea-New Britain.
Commander in Chief, Japan Area (CINCJAPA), 690-92
Commander in Chief, Pacific Ocean Areas (CinCPOA), 100-103
Command force (air), 112
Commandos, 112, 338
Communications, Allies, line of
    British to Far East, 39
    Burma-China, 228, 299, 354-55, 468
    Hawaii-Australia, 118-19
    Hawaii-Samoa-Fiji, 137
    Hawaii-Southwest Pacific Area, 169
    in Burma, 640
    India-Assam, 451, 453, 516
    India-China, 206, 285
    in Southwest Pacific Area, 102
    Japanese attacks on, 380
    Mandalay-Rangoon, 451
    Netherlands East Indies-New Britain, 326
    sea and air, 41, 157-58, 391
    sea in the Far East, 13
    sea in the Pacific, 30, 181, 423
    to Alaska, 41, 157-58, 391
    to Assam, 515
    to Australasia, 37
    to Australia, 32, 40, 56, 89, 137, 180-81, 261, 299, 300, 372,
        423
    to China, 216-17, 247, 355, 368, 398, 468, 652
    to India, 215
    to New Zealand, 98, 261, 299, 300
    to Southwest Pacific Area, 102, 109, 111, 116, 118, 309-10
    West Coast-Hawaii, 56, 261
    with Australia, New Zealand, India, 14
    with Far East, 55
    with Luzon, 44, 52
    with Philippines, 558
    with Red Sea and Persian Gulf, 157
Communications, Japanese, line of, 45, 280, 406, 505, 525, 614, 713

attack on, 393, 402-3, 409
  in Burma, 398
  in China, 713
  Japan-Burma, 235, 380, 393, 400, 434, 455, 464, 468, 525, 711
  Japan-China, 203, 460, 657
  Japan, Shanghai, 381
  through Formosa, 234
  with mainland, 657, 672-73
  with Manchuria, 658
  with Rangoon, 239
Congress Party, 227
Conolly, Rear Adm. R.L., 181
Convoys, 55-59, 63, 69-70, 82, 740n11
Cooke, R.Adm. Charles M., 133-34, 143, 148-49, 180, 185, 252, 266, 278, 286, 294, 296, 314-17, 324-26, 329-31, 356, 389, 396, 416, 419, 425, 430, 441, 443, 455-56, 460, 462, 465, 475, 477, 483, 489, 491, 504, 614, 706
  re aircraft, 185
  views on strategy, 180
Cooper, Duff, 45
Coral Sea, Battle of, 127-28, 140, 270, 331
Coral Sea-Solomons Area, 329
CORONET, 703, 707, 709
  and SEAC operations, 711
  British participation in, 714-16
  support in China, 712
Corps, British
  IV, 295, 514, 523, 574
  XV, 523, 582
Corps, Chinese, 514
Corps, Indian, 3rd, 62
Corps, U.S. XXIV, 621
Corregidor, 34, 62, 91, 93, 127, 139
CPS 28/3, 160
CPS 83, 459, 465
CPS 86/2, 502
Crimea, 113
Cross-Channel invasion, 251-58
CULVERIN, 524, 573
  U.S. naval support for, 519
Cunningham, Adm. Sir Andrew B., 192, 440, 524, 632, 637
Currie, Lauchlin, 20, 74, 76, 217, 221-23, 232, 342
Curtin, John, Prime Minister of Australia, 84, 99, 121, 123-26, 164-66, 179, 192
  and MacArthur, 125-26
  return of 9th Division, 165-66
Cyprus, 263

Dairen, 682-83
Dakar, 40

928 INDEX

Damodar River, 447
Darwin, 18, 42, 67, 69, 82
   B-29 attacks from, 595
Davao, 608
Davis, Maj. R.W., 179
DC-4, 213
Deane, Brig. Gen. John R., 194, 532, 668-71, 675, 682, 684
Deployment
   of aircraft. *See* Aircraft, deployment of.
   of air forces, 158, 162, 314
   of Australian forces, 314
   of ground forces, 111-12, 158, 162, 314
   of U.S. and British forces
      1942, 157-59
      1943, 182
      1944, 258, 404
      1945, 708
      of U.S. forces, Pacific 1943, 314
      of U.S. forces worldwide, 110
      of U.S. naval forces, 158, 320
DeWitt, Lt. Gen, John L., 273, 345, 483
Dibrugarh, 452, 579-80
Dill, Field Marshal Sir John, 83, 114, 150, 155, 205, 207, 237-38, 240, 252, 255, 336-41, 346, 349, 440-41, 537, 572, 582
Dilly, Portuguese Timor, 68
Dimapur, 585
Dinjan, 203
Divisions, Australian
   6th, 83
   7th, 141, 189
   9th, 165-67
Divisions, British
   7th, 582-83
Divisions, Chinese
   14th, 664
Divisions, Indian
   7th, 585
Divisions, Japanese, 126
   56th, 584-85
Divisions, New Zealand
   2nd, 166-67
   3rd, 567
Divisions, US
   Americal, 140
   7th, 417, 483
   25th, 165-66, 190, 192, 266
   28th, 418
   32nd, 141
   37th, 140
   41st, 112, 141
   43rd, 177, 181
   1st Marine, 140, 174-75, 266-67, 417-18, 420, 422, 425
   2nd Marine, 266-67, 412, 420, 425-26

INDEX

3rd Marine, 268, 418, 559
4th Marine, 416
Dominion forces, 467, 626
Douglas, Air Chief Marshal Sir Sholto, 437-38, 440-41
Douglas, Lewis, 194-96, 355
Doyle, Capt. Austin K., 497-501
Duncan, Capt. Donald B., 127, 594-95, 616, 626, 629, 656, 691-92, 704
Duncan, Capt. J.H., 134
Dutch
    aircraft, 122-23
    forces, 635-36
    in ABDA, 48-50, 66, 68-70
    in the Far East, 13, 50
    participation, 634, 716-17
    shipping, 85
Dutch East Indies. *See* Netherlands East Indies.
Dutch Harbor, 133, 272, 331
DRACULA, 640-41, 643, 661-62, 666
Drake Plan, 505
DRAGOON, 629
Drum, Lt Gen. Hugh A., 76-79

Eaker, Lt. Gen. Ira C., 707
Eastern Archipelago, 82
Eastern Solomons, Battle of, 178, 182
Eastern Theater, 14
East Indies barrier, 42
East Indies Fleet, 714
East New Guinea Area, 261
Economic pressure, 102, 113, 158, 714
Economic warfare, 108, 284
Eden, Foreign Secretary Anthony, 520, 671
Efate, 111, 117, 119, 128, 139, 187
Eichelberger, Lt. Gen. Robert L., 266
Eisenhower, Brig. Gen. Dwight D., 48, 173, 185, 282
Eisenhower pattern of command, 439, 442, 444, 481
El Alamein, 150, 165-66, 192
ELKTON, 312-16, 320-23, 326-27, 351
Ellice Islands, 138, 300, 310, 424, 476
Embargoes, 22
Embick, Lt. Gen. Stanley D., 557, 668-69
Emergency Air Transport Program, 213
Emirau Island, 545, 564, 566
Emmons, Lt. Gen. D.C., 147
Empress Augusta Bay, 487
End of the war, planning date, 431, 463, 466-67, 492-93, 499, 501, 642-43, 678, 714
Engineers, 513-15
Eniwetok, 416-17, 423, 476-77, 490, 545, 547-48, 551, 554, 558
Enterprise, 178, 190, 197

Espiritu Santo, 187, 190, 558
Estimate of the situation, 112, 126-27
EUREKA Conference agreements. See Teheran
Evatt, Dr. H.V., 96, 121-25
Evill, Air Marshal D.C.S., 155, 162-63, 218

Faisi, 197, 313, 327, 430, 487
Fantan, 176
Far East, defense of, 10
Far East Air Force, 694
Far Eastern Forces, Russian, 673
Fast carrier task forces, 620
Fauro Island, 306
Federal Communications Board (FCB), 442
Ferris, Brig. Gen. Benjamin G., 514-15, 574-75
Ferry Group, 1st, 207, 798n39
Fighter coverage, MacArthur's view, 308
Fiji Islands, 32, 55-58, 96, 107, 137-38, 300, 424
    aircraft for, 106, 111, 128-29
    antiaircraft regiment for, 129
    defenses, 56-57, 117
    garrison for, 140
    threat to, 128
Filipino forces, 91-92
Finschhafen, 308, 329, 332, 418, 487
FIRST CULVERIN, 499, 500, 518-19
Fleet Marine Force, 617
Fleets. See countries.
Fleets, U.S.
    Asiatic, 33, 45, 69
    Third, 544, 568
    Seventh, 544, 567, 622-23
Fletcher, R. Adm. F.J., 128
Flores Sea, 90
Flying Tigers, 79
Force "H", 10, 28
Forearm, 559
Formosa. See also Luzon vs. Formosa. 370, 381, 461-62, 500, 502-4, 550-53, 555-60, 574, 577-78, 588-90, 596-97, 602-24, 629, 656
    air bases on, 460, 463, 613, 622
    amphibious operations, 589
    and Stilwell, 581
    attack on, 579-80, 626-27, 655
    B-29 bases on, 556, 596, 615, 660
    bombing of, 522
    British use of air bases on, 654
    bypassing, 502, 605-6, 611, 613-14, 621-22
    D-Day for, 602
    Japanese line of communications through, 234

        neutralization of, 619
        occupation, 687-88
        or Luzon. *See* Luzon or Formosa.
        SEAC support, 597
        sea route to, 460
        seizure of, 499, 501, 556
        strategic bombing force, 461
Formosa Channel, Japanese shipping, 381
Formosa-Luzon-China, 552-53, 559, 577-78, 581
Formosa Strait, 299, 522, 603, 613
Forrestal, SecNav James, 707
Fort Hertz, 452
Fort Mills, 93
Free French, 57, 95
Fremantle, 85
French participation, 634, 716-17
Friendship, 203-4. *See also* Sino-American Cooperative Association.
Funafuti, 138, 310, 424

G-2, Army, 183
Gandhi, 208
Gasmata, 308
Gasoline, 397, 452, 454, 456, 575, 597-98
Gauss, Amb. Clarence E., 222
Gavutu, 174
Geelvink Bay, 488, 548, 555
Generalissimo's Plan, 232-33, 235-37
Germany
    air bombardment of. *See* Air offensive.
    major attack on, 158
Ghormley, Vice Adm. Robert L., 145-49, 168, 171, 175, 177, 179, 183,
        190, 308, 330
Gibraltar, 10
Gilbert Islands, 82, 137, 285, 300, 310, 327, 409, 416-17, 421-26,
        428-30, 458, 461, 475-79, 501, 505, 520, 543
Giles, Lt. Gen. Barney M., 600, 613, 689
Glassford, Rear Adm. William A., 18, 33-34, 65
Gliders for SEAC, 641
Gona, 174, 418
GRANITE, 545, 551
GRANITE II, 613, 615
Great Britain. *See* United Kingdom.
Greenwich, 555-56
Gruber, Brig. Gen. W.R., 215, 223, 228-30
Guadalcanal, 102-3, 162, 174, 177, 183, 188-91, 196-97, 265, 304,
        309, 311, 487, 558. *See also* Solomon Islands.
    airfield on, 187
    completion of campaign, 418
    critical situation in, 183, 193
    Japanese airfield on, 148, 174

Guadalcanal (Cont'd)
   Japanese in, 168
   Japanese reenforcements for, 178
   Japanese resistance in, 264, 266
   reenforcements for, 179, 253
Guam, 7, 12, 26, 42, 152, 306, 430-31, 490, 503, 542, 545-46, 557-58, 615
Guerrilla operation, Wingate's, 451
Guerrillas in China, 14, 203
Gwa, 338, 378
Gymkhana, 554
Gymnast, 79, 105, 112, 150

Habbakuks, 466
Hainan, 228, 370, 381, 461, 696
Haiphong, 232
Halmahera, 82, 373, 546, 549, 555-56, 560, 604-5, 608
Halsey, Vice Adm. William F., 82, 137, 190, 270, 308-11, 487, 543-45, 566, 568, 620-21
   directives to, 334, 563
Halverson Detachment (HALPRO), 214
Hammann, 140
Handy, Maj. Gen. Thomas T., 214, 269-70, 323, 329-31, 352, 482, 486, 504, 516-17, 553, 614, 617, 624
Hankow, 381, 387, 598-99, 601, 604, 646
Hanoi, 228, 232, 601
Hansa Bay, 490, 554
Hansell, Brig. Gen. Haywood S., 501, 557, 594
Harmon, Maj. Gen. M.F., 163, 175-77, 183, 190, 316, 320
Harriman, Amb. W. Averell, 532, 669-71, 682-83
Harrison, Maj. Gen. D., 577-78
Hart, Adm. Thomas C., 18, 34, 42, 51, 63, 69-71
Hawaii, 12, 27-29, 42, 55, 89, 107, 109, 129, 157, 180, 187, 260, 300, 314-15
   aircraft for, 111
   aircraft in, 128, 187
   defense of, 27, 39, 111, 138, 158
   Japanese raids, 37
   Marine air units, 268
   mobile air force, 117, 119, 170
   reenforcement of, 27-29, 39
   security of, 259
Hawaii-Midway line, 56
Hawaiian Air Force, 147
Hawaiian Coastal Frontier, 30
Hawaii-Samoa line, 56, 137
Helfrich, Vice Adm. Conrad, 70-71, 83
Henderson Field, 177, 182, 190
Hengyang, 381, 598-99, 601
Henzada, 338, 376
Hiroshima, 724
Hokkaido, 482, 486, 489, 500, 502-3, 655-57, 690, 723

carrier raid on, 421
invasion of, 499, 501
Hollandia, 430, 490, 492, 554-59, 560, 562, 566, 604, 695
Homalin, 232
Hong Kong, 12, 26, 42, 62, 368, 381, 446, 456, 460-62, 464, 522, 635, 711
Hong Kong-Formosa area, 462
Honshu, 500, 608-9, 687, 690, 594, 712, 723. *See also* CORONET.
   air attack, 657
   British participation, 715-16
   invasion of, 489, 502, 655-66, 658, 680-81, 703, 707
Hopkins, Harry, 47-48, 75, 88, 93, 125, 132, 171, 349, 384, 386, 400, 539
   and Chennault, 245, 347, 514
   and shipments to Russia, 55
   and shipping for ANAKIM, 355-56
   and T.V. Soong, 211, 214, 379
   trip to London, 1942, 152, 171
Hornet, 127, 190
Ho Ying-chen, Gen., 73, 341, 585, 590
Hsiung Shih-Fei, Gen., 208-10
Hukawng Valley, 238, 240, 277, 281, 523, 582
Hull, Maj. Gen. John E., 288, 612-14, 706
Hull, SecState Cordell, 22, 520
Humboldt Bay, 490, 555
Hump, 203, 227, 246, 340, 663
   air bases, 385
   aircraft for, 223, 231, 236, 242-43, 343, 526
   air route, 202, 494
   air transport, 210, 231, 242, 337, 382, 515-16, 540
   C-36s for, 527
   diversion from, 527, 582-86, 598
Hump tonnage, 210-14, 216-17, 233-34, 243, 339-40, 343-45, 347, 369-70, 379, 382-84, 395, 399, 434-37, 453-54, 493, 513-18, 523, 525-27, 539, 541, 573-74, 578-79, 581-83, 589, 599, 645, 660
   allocation of, 203, 347, 385, 434, 513, 526-27, 541-42, 589-90, 596-602, 660-61
Huon Peninsula, 312, 327
Hurley, Brig. Gen. Patrick J., 648-51, 660
HUSKY, 296, 348-49, 351, 357, 359, 366, 377, 413

Iberian Peninsula, 142, 149
ICEBERG, 658
Ie Island, 658
Illustrious, 280
Imphal, 202, 204, 235, 240, 277, 400, 454, 465, 469, 584, 586
   advance from, 338, 376, 398, 436-37, 447, 449-50, 569, 572
   attack from, 452, 576
   British forces, 543, 569, 575, 638

Imphal (Cont'd)
  forces in, 575
  Japanese concentration in, 583
  offensive from, 513-14, 523, 640
  operations in, 396, 453, 518
Imphal-Kalewa Road, 210
Imphal Plain, 583
Indaw, 523, 641
India, 14, 37, 40, 42-43, 71, 83, 85, 86, 89, 93, 99, 109-11, 115-16, 126, 198-249, 256, 298, 468, 509
  air bases in, 77, 298, 353, 383-84, 465, 493, 504-5
  airfields in, 77, 282, 497-98
  allocation of resources to, 443
  B-29 bases in, 497-98, 588, 596, 660-61
  British forces in, 282, 295, 383
  Chinese force in, 227. *See also* Imphal; Ramgarh.
  command arrangements, 437
  defense of, 158
  Japanese attack on, 300
  landing craft for, 529-30
  lend-lease for, 205
  operations from, 253, 392-93
  shipping for, 195-96, 228
  supply routes to, 394, 451
  threat to, 152, 205-6
  transportation in, 204-5, 449
  troops for, 194
  US troops in, 216, 227-29, 678-80
India-China Ferry Command, 203
India-China route. *See* Hump, Burma Road, Ledo Road.
Indian Army, 437
Indian Command, 50-51
Indian forces, 714
Indian Ocean, 85, 90, 93, 110, 112, 115, 117-18, 129-30, 196, 206, 278, 374, 457, 499, 630
  British fleet in, 18, 69-70, 115, 164, 192, 247, 473, 475, 501, 504-5, 523, 635
  communications, 37
  control of, 304
  defense, 158
  naval activity, 369
  troop shipping, 348
Indian Ocean Area, 90
Indian Theater, 102
Indochina, 22, 50, 75, 203, 232-34, 285, 438, 442, 445, 508-9, 601, 627, 697, 699-701
  British operations, 368, 627
  Japanese control of, 225, 601
  supply line to, 380
Ingersoll, Adm. Royal E., 634
Inner Mongolia, 721

Intelligence
    Pacific Fleet, 129
    sought from Soviets, 532
Intelligence, radio, in China, 203-4
Intelligence facilities
    Andaman Islands, 519
Intelligence reports, 42, 127, 130, 132-33, 140, 171, 174, 189, 545, 702, 724
International War Council, China, 80, 200, 221
Invasion of Japan. *See* Japan, invasion of.
Iowa, 520
Irrawaddy River, 378, 399, 451
Irrawaddy Valley, 202
Ismay, Gen. Sir Hastings, 288, 475
Italian Fleet, 473
Italy, surrender, 472
Iwo Jima, 680, 686

Jaluit, 300, 306, 310, 416, 423-24, 476
Japan
    air offensive against, 299, 368, 432, 434, 437, 456, 459-60, 495-97, 499, 504
    B-29 targets, 593
    bombing of, 336, 370, 432, 434, 456, 459-61, 470-71, 493-94, 500-501, 503-5, 522, 620, 627, 702-3, 718, 724
    British air support, 655
    carrier-based air attacks on, 84, 421
    coke industry, 497-98, 593
    incendiary bombing of, 713
    invasion of, 136, 272-73, 368-69, 428, 431-32, 459, 461, 489, 499-500, 503-4, 551, 605, 624-25, 627-29, 643, 653, 655-56, 658-59, 686-94, 702, 709, 713, 718
    isolation of, 488, 503-4. *See also* Blockade.
    occupation of, 493, 724
    pressure on, 102, 113, 169-70, 175, 260, 262-63, 281, 283-84, 290, 321-22, 353, 358-60, 403, 406-7, 418, 426-27, 503, 628, 725
    shipping centers, 593
    Soviet air operations against, 673
    strategy, 300, 366
    surrender, 724
Japan area (JAPA), 690
Japanese airfields, 143, 148, 174
Japanese Air Force, 370, 460
    deployment of, 183
Japanese Fleet, 328, 460, 499, 505, 545, 622-23, 631, 657, 702
Japanese shipping, 500-501, 503
    losses, 69, 165, 387
Japan first strategy, 150, 254, 256
Japan Sea, 713, 721

Japen, 430
Java, 6, 12, 17, 43, 62-63, 67, 69, 81, 83-86, 97, 110, 121, 393, 680, 717
  air attacks, 82
  Japanese occupation, 139
  troops in, 84-85, 758n104
Java Sea, 90, 474-75
JCS 23, 112-13, 118, 158
JCS 48, 130, 158
JCS 93, 258
JCS 112, 266
JCS 167, 259-60
JCS 238/1, 325-26
JCS 272, 364
JCS 283, 374
JCS 287, 372
JCS 287/1, 401
JCS 290, 371-72
JCS 297, 376
JCS 303, 376-78
JCS 304, 373-74, 402
JCS 311, 418
JCS 446, 428-31
JCS 521/6, 708
JCS 713, 551-53
JCS 713/4, 562
JCS 713/9, 616
JCS 742, 592-93
JCS 924, 627
JCS 1176, 672-73, 675
Johnson, Louis, 205
Johnston Island, 12, 30, 39, 62
Joint Action of the Army and the Navy, 29
Joint Administrative Committee (JAdC), 452
Joint Aircraft Committee, 20
Joint Board, 4-9, 15-17, 20-21, 28-30, 32, 36, 39, 60, 65, 146, 244
Joint Chiefs of Staff
  establishment of, 60
Joint Deputy Chiefs of Staff, 269, 277, 602
Joint Intelligence Committee (JIC), 459
Joint Logistics Committee (JLC), 491-92, 520, 566, 578, 597, 620, 633, 660-61, 698, 712
Joint Military Transportation Committee (JMTC), 478, 561, 563
Joint Planning Committee (American-British), 43-44, 47-48, 50, 56-58, 77
Joint Planning Committee (JPC), 4, 6-7, 20-21, 29, 33-34
Joint Planning Staff, British, 155, 285, 287, 294
Joint Plans Section, British, 228
Joint Staff, Chinese, 81
Joint Staff Planners (JPS), 103, 109-10, 112, 117-18, 134-35, 138,

155, 159-60, 179-81, 189, 262-64, 273, 283-84, 312, 314-17,
322-25, 328, 363-65, 369, 371-72, 378, 416, 418, 420-22,
425-28, 447-48, 457, 478-79, 486, 489, 492, 494-97, 501-52,
520-21, 552-57, 559, 562, 565-66, 571, 592-95, 599-600,
602, 605, 607-10, 612-17, 626-27, 629, 635-36, 639-41,
655-60, 665-66, 670-75, 677-78, 681, 684, 687-88, 691-92,
696-98, 700, 702-4, 707-12, 715, 718
  Aleutians, 415, 484
  allocation of aircraft, 106, 117-18, 155, 159-60, 162, 179-81,
183-84, 187-88, 264, 269, 494-95
  and ABDA, 89
  assistance to Russia, 134-35
  British in the Pacific, 501-2
  Burma operations, 242, 284, 296, 519, 571-80
  CBI, 443-44
  China, 522, 571-80, 588-90
  collaboration with the USSR, 132, 673
  ELKTON, 316-17
  Gilberts and Marshalls, 420-22, 425-26, 476-77
  Kuriles, 486
  SEAC, 508-10, 571-80, 640-41
  shipping, 195, 478, 483, 562, 639
  strategic concept 251-52, 254, 304-5, 322, 367, 371-72, 390, 401,
459-63, 492, 529
  troops for Australia, 165, 167
Joint Strategic Survey Committee (JSSC), 242, 258-59, 261-63, 292,
304, 312, 314-15, 350-51, 358-59, 364-67, 372, 374-76, 378,
387-88, 390, 423, 425, 446-47, 485-86, 489, 503, 505-6,
519-20, 551, 553-54, 557, 559, 565, 595-96, 604-5, 619-20,
634-35, 641, 668, 687, 700
Joint Supply Committee, 40
Joint U.S. Strategic Committee (JUSSC), 89, 107-8, 110-13, 132,
134-35, 160-61, 182-83, 188, 254, 257-58, 304-7, 363,
367-68
Joint War Plans Committee (JWPC), 327, 363-74, 377-78, 405, 409,
416-19, 423-25, 427-29, 451, 456, 458-59, 479, 483-84,
486-99, 494, 496-98, 502, 508, 510-11, 555-56, 566, 580,
589, 592, 596-97, 599, 604-10, 612-13, 616, 626-29, 634-35,
640, 654-57, 669, 672, 677, 680-81, 687, 697, 701, 709,
711, 715, 718
  Pink Team, 427, 459
  Rainbow Team, 416, 422, 427
  Red Team, 458-59
  Senior Team, 501
JPS 67/4, 367
JPS 205, 416, 418
JPS 205/1, 421-22, 426
JPS 205/2, 421-22, 426
JPS 205/3, 426

938 INDEX

Jungle fighting, 451, 466, 633
JWPC 9/1, 377
JWPC 15, 368

Kabaw Valley, 572
Kai Islands, 546
Kaladan Valley, 570, 572
Kalemyo, 338, 569
Kalewa, 204, 232, 338, 399, 569, 578, 641, 662
Kamaing, 523, 527
Kamchatka Peninsula, 131, 272-73, 371, 670, 672, 676, 685
  observers in, 673
  occupation of, 673-74
  operations in, 675
  strategic air bases in, 673
  survey of, 685
  US bases in, 669
  US Strategic Air Force, 671, 681-82
Karachi, 34, 203, 209
Katha, 399, 578-79, 641
Kavieng, 308, 312-13, 425, 427-28, 430, 487, 490, 544-55, 547-48, 554-56, 559, 564
  Japanese airfield, 148
  neutralization, 567
  US air base, 558
KEELBLOCKS II, 673
Kenney, Lt. Gen. George C., 315, 547
Kerch Peninsula, 131
Khabarovsk, weather station, 721
Khartoum, 215
Khudyakov, Marshal of Aviation 685
Kienow, 381
Kieta, 267, 308, 425, 430, 477
Kikai, 658
Kilindini, 293
King, Admiral Ernest J., 4, 36, 49-50, 58-59, 71, 83, 92-93, 101, 116-17, 120, 128-30, 133, 136-39, 141, 143-45, 147, 149, 151-52, 158-59, 174, 176, 179, 181-87, 189, 193-94, 206, 230, 232, 242, 254-55, 257, 260-62, 264-65, 268-71, 278-82, 286-88, 290, 296, 299-300, 308-12, 317, 322-24, 332-34, 348-51, 353-54, 356-57, 360-61, 363, 379, 389-92, 399-400, 402-3, 406, 414, 418-20, 423, 426, 430-32, 441, 443, 445, 448, 456, 463-65, 473-75, 477-83, 489, 491, 503-4, 506, 520, 524-25, 529-30, 532, 535-40, 545-47, 549-50, 551, 553-54, 558-61, 564-65, 568, 572, 590, 594-95, 605, 607-8, 610, 613-17, 620-24, 628, 630-34, 637-38, 651, 656-57, 660, 670, 673, 680, 687, 689-94, 697, 702-5, 709, 721, 725-26
  and aid to Russia, 133
  and air reenforcements, 176, 182, 184-87, 269

          and the Aleutians, 483, 485-86
          and allocation of aircraft, 155, 158-59, 324
          and ANZAC area, 58-59, 89, 96
          and the British, 260, 287, 430, 473-74
          and British participation, 430, 473-75, 630-34, 637-38, 697-98
          and BUCCANEER, 520, 529-30, 536-37, 539-40
          and a Burma operation, 232, 293-94, 296, 353-54, 356-57, 379,
             399-400, 441, 448, 451, 465, 572, 640
          and casualty rates, 703
          and command in 1945, 687, 689, 694
          and command in the Pacific, 96-99, 101-3, 480-83
          and command of the Solomons operation, 143-46, 264-65, 269-70,
             308, 311-12, 332-34
          and command of VLR bombers, 594-96, 694
          and importance of Formosa, 603, 614
          and intelligence, 130
          and Kiska, 415
          and New Caledonia, 57
          and New Guinea campaign, 175
          and a northern route to Japan, 273
          and occupation of British territory, 139
          and RENO V, 608, 613
          and a sea route to Siberia, 628, 670, 673
          and shipping, 323, 390, 400, 456, 477
          and Sumatra, 456, 463-65
          and a switch to the Pacific, 151-52
          and Tulagi, 143-45, 149, 183-84
          and unified command, 268-70
          Commander in Chief, U.S. Fleet, 55-56
          discusses operations for 1943-44, 418-20, 426, 430-32
          opposes U.S. naval forces in the Indian Ocean, 206
          proposes command areas, 89, 96, 98-99
          seeks proportionate division of resources, 262-63, 279-81
          selection of Luzon or Formosa, 610, 614-17, 622-24
          states objective in the Pacific, 55-56
          views on ABDA, 49, 89
          views on China, 198, 293-94, 298, 373-74, 393, 448, 465
          views on strategy, 138, 169-70, 260-61, 280, 290, 299-300, 389-92,
             402-3, 406, 549-50, 725-26
Kinkaid, Rear Adm. Thomas C., 414, 484, 547, 634
Kirby, Brit. Maj. Gen. S.W., 339
Kiriwina Island, 306-7, 309, 326, 329, 332, 373, 413, 418
Kirk, Amb. Alexander, 523
Kiska, 133, 140, 272-73, 284, 414-15, 430, 482-83
Kittyhawks, 123
Knox, Frank, SecNav, 16, 47
Koepang, 67-69, 82
Kokoda, 174-75
Kokoda trail, 178, 189-90
Kolombangara, 487

Komsomolsk, 684
Korea, 298, 381, 549, 551, 593, 658, 703, 713
Korolenko, General, 275
Kra Isthmus, 13, 393, 400, 468, 662
Kra Peninsula, 370, 464
Kume, 658
Kung, Madame, 512
Kunming, 71, 96, 202-3, 382, 451-52, 468, 494, 569, 576, 580, 648, 660, 662, 664, 678
  air bases, 599
  Japanese threat, 662-63
  security of, 397
Kuomintang, 211
Kurile Islands, 415, 474, 482-84, 486, 489, 500, 503, 656-57, 669, 674, 697
  attack on, 532, 655
  B-29 bases, 486
  operations, 675, 720
  passage through, 673
  Russian claim, 682
Kurusu, Saburo, 22
Kusaie, 416, 423, 428, 476-77, 490, 545
Kuter, Brig. Gen. Laurence S., 495, 590, 685
Kwajalein, 416, 421, 423-24, 476, 483, 545, 547-48, 553
Kwanchowwan, 381
Kwantung Army, 627, 668, 672, 703
Kweilin, 381, 500, 580, 599, 601, 648
  air bases, 505, 599, 653
Kyaukpyu, 338
Kyushu, 504, 608-9, 614-15, 618-20, 622, 627-29, 656-57, 687, 690-91, 695, 702, 706-7, 712, 714, 723-24. *See also* OLYMPIC.
  invasion of, 655, 658-59, 672, 680, 703-5

Lae, 146, 177, 284, 306, 308, 327, 329, 332, 418, 430, 487
  Japanese bases, 142, 148, 175
Lancaster bombers, 654
Land, Vice Adm. Emory S., 195-96, 356
Landing craft, 240, 261, 287, 295-97, 389, 418, 448, 463, 470, 504, 529-30, 535-42, 633
  availability of, 287, 404, 542
  for ANAKIM, 289, 293-94, 307, 357, 393-94
  for ANVIL, 539-40, 569
  for BUCCANEER, 531, 534-41, 569
  for Burma, 236, 240
  for ELKTON, 320
  for India, 441, 447-48
  for OVERLORD, 540
  for SHINGLE, 571
  for PIGSTICK, 571
  production, 405, 542
  withdrawal from BUCCANEER, 538-40

Laokai, 232
La Perouse Strait, 685, 690, 693
Lashio, 71, 202, 232, 239, 353, 396, 398-99, 500, 578, 641, 662
LCTs, 448
League of Nations, 5
Leahy, Adm. William D., 189, 193-96, 230, 232, 244, 246-47, 253,
    255, 257, 259, 263, 267, 278, 322, 324, 332, 345, 349,
    353, 378, 387, 389, 391-94, 399, 406, 420, 441, 443,
    445, 456, 463, 468-69, 479, 485, 491, 504, 510, 521,
    532-33, 535-37, 558, 561, 572, 605, 610, 614, 616,
    618-19, 633, 635-36, 638, 681, 684, 694, 702, 710, 726
  and British participation, 474, 636-38, 681
  and BUCCANEER, 531, 535
  and China, 230, 236, 394, 521, 525, 681
  and command of VLR bombers, 694
  and deployment of air forces 186-87, 257, 322
  and invasion of Japan, 504, 702
  and SEAC, 445
  and shipping for ANAKIM, 353-54
  appointment, 170-71
  strategy, 230, 259, 263, 324, 349, 391, 401-2, 406, 618-19, 726
Leary, Rear Adm. H.F., 59
Ledo, 204, 240, 277, 337-38, 353, 378, 398, 400, 436, 454, 465,
    469, 500, 526, 584
  advance from, 247, 338, 449-50, 569
  Chinese force at, 525, 543, 574
  operations, 453
  Stilwell's base, 585
Ledo Force, 572, 575, 579, 584, 638, 640, 647
Ledo-Kunming Road, 581
Ledo-Myitkyina Road, 210
Ledo Road, 226, 238, 246, 285, 292, 337, 353, 393, 396-97, 450-52,
    456, 464, 469, 498, 500, 514, 573, 575-76, 578, 846n59
  British view, 292, 295
  capacity, 456
  Chinese forces, 438
  responsibility for, 238
  supplies for, 513
  support operations, 450
Legaspi, 607
Lembang, 61
Lend-lease, 21-22, 55, 76, 106, 155, 241, 349, 648, 650-52, 698,
    719-20
  equipment in Rangoon, 31, 74
  for Burma, 231
  for China, 72, 77, 200, 202-3, 205, 210-11, 215-16, 219-21,
    226-27, 443-44, 511, 651
  for India, 205
  for Indian Army, 369
  for Russia, 55, 194
  shipping for, 112, 194, 241
Lend-Lease Act, 15, 20

942 INDEX

Lesser Sunda Islands, 699
Lexington, 128
Leyte, 607, 610, 613, 615-17, 620-21, 629
   airfield construction, 657
   campaign, 621
   invasion, 653
   occupation, 688
   operations after 618
   XX Bomber Command bases, 660
Leyte Gulf, Battle of, 653
Libya, 93
Limited offensive, 138-39, 140, 143, 158, 251, 256, 260
Lincoln, Brig. Gen. G.A., 679, 692, 704
Lincoln, Col. L.J., 257
Lindsay, Col, Richard C. 599, 656
Lingayen, 613, 621, 623
Lingayen Gulf, 608, 614-15, 622, 657-58
Lingayen Straits, 607
Lishui, 381
Little, Adm. Sir Charles, 59
Little Kiska, 414
Litvinov, Amb. Maxim, 132-33
Liuchow, 711
Loiwing, 203, 641
Lombok, 82
London Committee, 49
London Naval Conference, 1930, 5
Long range penetration brigade (LRPB), 396, 447, 572, 582, 585-86
Long range penetration group (LRPG), 397, 451, 457, 469, 523, 575, 583-85
Lorengau, 308
Low, Capt. F.S., 127
Loyalty Islands, 13
Loyang, 646
Lunga Ridge, 190
Lungling, 235, 285, 295, 585
Lushai Hills, 338
Luzon, 8, 17, 26, 32, 34-35, 44, 423, 460-61, 504, 549-53, 555-56, 559-60, 577-78, 581, 603-24, 629-30, 696
   airfields, 654
   air transport to China, 711
   B-29s, 660
   bypassing, 556, 560, 596-97, 610-13
   campaign, 657
   invasion of, 500, 653
   occupation of, 687-88, 690-93
   or Formosa, 596, 603-24, 614-20
Luzon-Formosa-China coast, 551-53, 555, 558-59, 604

MacArthur, Gen. Douglas, 16-17, 33-35, 42, 45, 48, 61, 85, 96-99, 101, 103, 119, 121, 129, 131, 141-43, 148-49, 163-64, 168,

INDEX

>   177, 191, 232, 268, 271-72, 304, 308-9, 330, 419, 427-28,
>   467, 487-88, 503, 505-6, 542-47, 550, 552-55, 560-61,
>   563-68, 595, 602-3, 605-8, 610-13, 617, 621-24, 632-37,
>   653, 657-58, 687-89, 691, 694-99, 701, 704-5, 715-16, 726
>   and aircraft, 159, 345
>   and air support for New Caledonia, 119
>   and allocation of forces, 124
>   and B-29s, 592
>   and British Fleet support, 502
>   and British participation, 632-35
>   and Chiang Kai-shek, 232
>   and command in Solomons-New Guinea-New Britain campaign, 264-66
>   and Eastern Fleet, 192
>   and Russian participation, 131
>   arrival in Australia, 99, 121
>   as a political figure, 272
>   chiding of, 125
>   Commanding General, U.S. Army Forces, Far East, 17
>   directives to, 99-103, 121, 146-47, 329-34, 545, 557, 559-60,
>   563, 565-67, 620, 624, 688, 690-94, 706, 724
>   estimate of the situation, 125-27
>   leaves the Philippines, 91-92
>   makes requests of Churchill, 125
>   on bypassing Luzon, 611-12
>   pattern of command, 439-40, 442-44
>   plans, 141, 175, 189, 308, 312-13, 422-23, 488, 506, 548-49,
>   554-55, 608, 621
>   political problems, 266, 272
>   strategic views, 144-46, 174-75, 191, 422-23, 548, 557
>   Supreme Commander, Southwest Pacific Area, 96-103, 121
>   views on Japanese strategy, 178-79

Macassar Straits, 63, 69-70
Macready, Lt. Gen. G.N., 349, 357
Madang, 142, 308, 326, 329, 332, 418, 425, 430
Maddocks, Col. Ray T., 305
Magruder, Brig. Gen. John, 21, 73-75, 79, 210
Majuro, 547
Makin Island, 424-25, 428, 478, 520
Malacca, Straits of, 294, 368, 370-71, 428, 430-31, 455, 460, 463,
      468, 524, 699, 717
Malaya, 12-14, 17, 26-27, 37, 42-43, 45, 50, 54, 62-63, 65-66, 69,
      71, 81, 86, 240, 423, 438, 442, 462-63, 468, 475, 500,
      573, 611, 631-32
  amphibious operations in, 450
  attack on, 449
  capture of, 461
  Japanese in, 71, 225
  liberation of, 678, 717
  supply line from Japan, 380
Malay Barrier, 10-11, 15, 18, 30-31, 35, 43-44, 52, 62-63, 70, 89,
      90, 109, 136, 152, 192, 299-301, 306, 575, 627, 654, 697

Malay Peninsula, 392, 627, 630, 697, 710
Malaysia, 10, 39
  Eastern 102
Maloelap, 416, 421, 423-24, 476
Malta Conference, 677-82
Manchuria, 5, 380, 521, 549, 551, 627, 658
  air attacks on, 592
  coke ovens, 593
  Japanese aircraft in, 183
  Japanese army in, 670
  Japanese invasion, 1931, 5
  railroads, 682-83
  Russian designs on, 521
  Soviet offensive, 668-69, 673, 713, 724
Mandalay, 232, 235, 239, 295, 297, 337-38, 378, 397, 399, 451, 500, 524, 575, 641
Mandalay Plain, 640, 666
Mandalay Plan, 526, 640
Mandated Islands, 127, 164, 422-23, 431, 460, 500, 502-3, 567
Mandell, Brig. Gen. H.C., 614
Manila, 18, 34, 69, 608, 621
Manila Bay, 4, 6, 18
Manokwari, 430, 492
Manpower, 279
  Australian, 165
Manus Island, 308, 370-71, 425-26, 429-30, 490, 544-45, 547-48, 554-55, 549, 558-59, 563-66, 697, 699
  base at, 563-66, 699
Marianas, 8, 280, 403, 409, 423, 430-31, 433, 461, 476, 490, 492, 496, 500-501, 542, 545, 549-52, 555-56, 558-60, 562, 588, 604-5, 607, 609, 615, 617
  air support from, 597
  as bases, 546
  B-29s in, 493, 496, 542, 547, 562, 592-93, 595-96, 660-61
  seizure of, 556-57
  shipping for, 562
Marianas-Carolines-Palau-Mindanao, 556
Marines
  amphibious troops, 138. *See also* Divisions.
Maritime Commission, 204
Maritime Provinces, 493, 496, 669, 673
  Japanese attack on, 134, 300
  sea route to, 628, 670
  Soviet forces, 713
  US bases, 299, 684, 720
  US forces in, 671, 675
Markham Valley, 329
Marshall, Gen. George C., 9, 17, 28, 35-36, 43, 45-50, 54-55, 61, 66, 76, 91-94, 97, 99-101, 104, 117, 119-20, 122, 126, 129-31, 133, 138, 141, 144-52, 158-59, 164, 173-77,

183-87, 189, 191, 193, 205-6, 210, 219, 222-23, 227-28,
230-32, 241-43, 254-55, 260, 262-66, 268, 271, 273, 275-76,
278-79, 281-82, 287-88, 292-94, 298, 308, 322-24, 326,
328-29, 332-34, 341-42, 345-47, 352-57, 372-73, 383, 389,
394, 398, 400-401, 406, 420, 422, 427, 431, 439, 443-44,
454, 456, 464-66, 469, 472, 474, 477, 479-83, 485, 491,
504, 507, 514, 516-17, 522, 524-25, 527, 529-33, 535,
537-39, 545, 550-54, 558, 561, 563-65, 568, 572, 581-82,
585, 589-90, 594, 598-600, 605, 608, 611, 617-22, 624,
633-36, 639, 643, 645-51, 657, 660, 663-65, 670, 679-81,
687-89, 691-92, 695-96, 701, 704-7, 709, 715, 721-22, 724,
726
  and allocation of aircraft, 66, 176-77, 183-87
  and BUCCANEER, 530-31, 537-39
  and Burma, 231, 237-38, 241-43, 293-94, 353-55, 398, 454, 456,
    464-66, 679, 715
  and China, 199, 228, 242, 246, 346, 448
  and command, joint, 99-101, 480-82
  and command, unified, 265-66, 687-89, 691-92
  and command in ABDA, 43, 45-50, 51
  and command in the Solomons, 144-46, 264-66, 268-71, 308, 329,
    332-34
  and command of OLYMPIC, 704-7
  and deployment of forces, 119-20, 129, 158, 173, 177, 184, 406,
    480
  and shipping, 55, 138, 158, 177, 228, 242, 353-54, 561
  and Siberian bases, 275, 670
  and Soviet participation, 131, 133, 721
  and Stilwell, 222, 342, 347, 439, 582, 645-51
  and strategy, 169-70, 260, 262-64, 268, 287-88, 372-73, 551-54
    726
  MacArthur's departure from Corregidor, 92-93
  trip to London, 114-15, 117, 152, 171, 229, 252
  Wingate and jungle warfare, 451
Marshall, Maj. Gen. Richard J., 562
Marshall Islands, 6, 8, 11, 24, 30-31, 82, 136-37, 139, 280, 285,
  289-90, 300, 310, 327, 370-74, 403, 409, 414-26, 428-31,
  458, 461, 474-79, 496, 501, 505, 543, 545-49, 554, 604,
  617
Martaban, Gulf of, 235, 239
Matsuwa, 690
MATTERHORN, 573, 592-93, 595, 600
Mayu Peninsula, 570
McCain, Rear Adm. J.S., 147, 187
McCloy, John J., 204, 212, 214
McCream, Capt, J.L., 119
McFarland, Brig. Gen. A.J., 679
McHugh, Lt. Col. James M., 243-44
McMorris, Rear Adm. Charles J., 546-47
McNair, Lt. Gen. Leslie J., 265

McNarney, Maj. Gen. Joseph T., 117, 172, 265-66, 312, 366, 378-79,
    386, 394, 399, 460, 602, 605, 619, 633, 635
Mediterranean, 93, 166, 255-56, 261-62, 280, 283, 286-88, 295,
    302, 318, 354, 365, 375, 528-29
  transfer of aircraft to SEAC, 586, 639
  vs. ANAKIM, 262
  vs. BUCCANEER, 529-30
Melbourne, 59
Merrill, Brig. Gen. Frank D., 527
Merrill's Marauders, 102
Michela, Col. Joseph A., 134
Middle East, 37, 55, 108, 111, 113, 150, 154, 185, 214
  aircraft for, 113, 122, 182, 185, 214
  Australian troops in, 165
  security of, 153, 158
Mid-Pacific islands, 111
Midway, Battle of, 331
Midway-Hawaii line, 299, 300, 310
Midway Island, 8, 12, 30, 37, 39, 55-56, 128-29, 133, 140, 169,
    271, 300, 422
Miles, Brig. Gen. Sherman, 68
Miles, Com. Milton E., 198, 203, 303-4, 651
Military Joint Planning Committee, 40
Military Representatives of the Associated Pacific Powers (MRP),
    164, 209
Mille, 416, 423-24, 476
Milne Bay, 175, 178, 191, 558
Minahasa, 62
Minbu, 396
Mindanao, 34, 92-93, 422, 488, 506, 546, 548-49, 551-52, 555-60,
    562, 589, 605, 607, 610, 613, 621
  air support from, 597
  bypassing, 607, 609
  occupation, 604, 696
  support from China, 589-90
Mindoro, 607, 653, 657, 688
Mindoro Strait, 550
Mining, 660
Misamis, 617
Miyako, 658
Miyako Jima, 655
Mobile air force, 111, 116-19, 128, 147-48, 170, 179-81, 187, 315
Mobile divisions, 118
Mogaung, 337, 572, 579, 586, 645
Mogaung Valley, 585
Mogok, 641, 662
Molotov, V.M., 132, 134, 520, 683
Moluccas, 62, 699
Molucca Sea, 63, 70
Mongolian Plateau, 675-76

Monsoon, 213, 228, 231, 237, 240, 247, 289, 292, 295, 341, 536, 539,
    572, 581, 638, 642
Montgomery, Gen. Sir Bernard L., 165
Monywa, 574, 576
Moore, Capt, C.J., 421
Morotai Island, 607-8, 617, 620-21, 653, 695, 715
Mortlock, 545, 554-57
Moscow, 73
Moulmein, 236, 239, 295, 464-65, 468
Mountbatten, Vice Adm. Lord Louis, 296, 446, 469, 506-12, 515-17,
    519, 521-28, 535, 538-41, 569-72, 574, 576, 579-86, 591,
    594, 602, 639-42, 645, 649, 661-66, 679, 701, 710-11,
    717-18
  directive, 518, 582, 678, 680, 717
Mow, Maj. Gen. P.T., 19
Munda, New Georgia, 267, 306-9, 322, 487
Munitions allocations, 229, 279
Munitions Assignments Board (MAB), 107, 122-23, 204, 207-8, 210-12,
    214, 220, 511
Munitions Assignments Board (London) (MAB(L)), 123
Munitions Assignments Committee (Air) (MAC(A)), 122, 206-7
Munitions Assignments Committee (Ground) (MAC(G)), 211-14
Mussolini, 413
Mutual cooperation, 329
Mutual coordination, 331, 333
Myitkyina, 203-4, 240, 285, 295, 353, 378, 396, 398-99, 451, 500,
    523, 569, 572-74, 576, 578-81, 586, 601, 638, 645, 648,
    664

Nadzab, 487
Nagasaki, 724
Naiden, Brig. Gen. Earl L., 203
Nanchang, 299, 381
Nanking, 381
Nanning, 601, 711
Nanpo Shoto, 623. *See also* Bonins.
Nansei Shoto, 623. *See also* Ryukyus.
Natal, 34
Nauru, 421, 424-26, 428, 476, 478
Navy Air Transport Services, 445
Navy Group, China, 651
Nelson, Donald, 648
Netherlands, 73, 100
Netherlands Air Force in Australia, 122-23
Netherlands East Indies, 12, 14-15, 18, 24, 26, 32, 34-35, 37, 39,
    40, 43-45, 50, 54, 60, 62-64, 66-67, 69, 73, 82, 86, 88,
    90, 93, 98, 110, 122, 139, 260, 280, 299, 300, 326, 380,
    423, 489-90, 491, 504, 548, 558, 575, 592-93, 604, 611,
    622, 627, 630, 632-33, 687, 695-97, 699, 712, 716
  air attacks on, 592, 595, 654

948   INDEX

Netherlands East Indies (Cont'd)
   aircraft for, 68-69, 107
   allocations to, 123
   bypassing, 695
   Japanese communications to, 550
   Japanese in, 139-40
   oil refineries, bombing, 491, 593, 595
   strategic bombing, 555
Netherlands Purchasing Commission, 122
New Britain, 58, 82, 102, 143, 168, 189, 232, 250, 264, 284-85,
      308-9, 326-27, 329, 332, 370, 422, 425, 430, 477, 487,
      490, 543, 558
   Army plan, 142
   British naval support for, 475
   command of invasion, 145, 264
   Japanese in, 137, 139-40
   MacArthur's plans, 141
New Caledonia, 8, 13, 55, 57-58, 67-68, 76, 96, 107, 128, 140, 300
   airfield in, 56, 187
   air support for, 119
   allocation of aircraft, 68, 111, 129
   defenses of, 57, 117
   reenforcements for Solomons, 172
New Delhi, 200, 227, 336-38, 515
New Delhi Plan, 376
New Georgia, 309-11, 313, 327, 413, 418, 487
New Guinea, 8, 58, 65, 89, 97-98, 107, 116, 127, 129, 141, 143, 164,
      168, 189-91, 232, 250, 264, 268, 271, 284-85, 289, 305-9,
      329, 366, 370-74, 403, 409, 413-14, 418, 422, 425-28, 430,
      432, 461, 463, 467, 478-79, 487-88, 499-501, 504, 542-46,
      548-49, 551-52, 554, 556, 560, 566-67, 607, 615, 617, 634
   aircraft for, 186
   Army plan, 142, 146
   British naval support, 475
   command, 145
   Japanese airfield, 174
   Japanese attacks, 127, 366
   Japanese in, 127, 139-40, 174-75, 178
   MacArthur's plans, 141, 175
   rate of advance, 550
   US airfields, 148
New Guinea-Mindanao axis, 549, 551-52
New Hanover, 428
New Hebrides, 98, 138, 148, 475
New Ireland, 65, 82, 140-41, 145-46, 284, 308, 312, 329, 370, 428-29,
      478, 544, 558
Newport News, supplies for China, 204-5, 210-12
Newton, Vice Adm John H., 568
New Zealand, 14, 18, 36, 39, 42, 45, 53, 56-58, 60, 67, 88-90, 93,
      95, 97, 100, 102-3, 107, 109-10, 126, 256

949   INDEX

    aircraft for, 67, 106-7, 123-24, 160
    and China, 73
    British obligation to, 473
    defense of, 11, 58-59, 111, 158, 161, 163-67
    forces, 139, 634-36
    line of communications to, 180, 259-60, 299-300
    troops in Middle East, 112, 166-67
Ngakyedauk Pass, 582
Nickel, 56-57
Nicobar, 192, 662
Nikolaevsk, 684
Nimitz, Adm. Chester, 102-3, 128, 137, 140-41, 143, 146, 148, 177, 179, 266-68, 273, 304, 308-12, 331, 414, 419-20, 423-24, 479-82, 544-49, 552-55, 557-59, 561, 563-68, 595, 602, 605, 607-10, 613, 617, 620-23, 632, 637, 658-59, 673, 686-87, 689, 690-91, 693-94, 701, 704-5, 716
    and MacArthur, 141
    command set-up, 479-82
    directives to, 99-103, 146-47, 188, 273, 329-34, 426-27, 477-78, 545, 555-67, 620, 624, 688, 690-94, 702, 706, 724
    dual staff, 479-82
    establishment of Pacific Ocean Areas, 96-103
    plans, 267-68, 309, 423-24, 478-79, 607, 613, 658
    troops and aircraft for the Southwest Pacific Area, 186
Nine Power Treaty, 1922, 5
Ningpo Peninsula, 658-59, 680, 690, 693, 702
Noble, Adm. Sir Percy, 360, 448, 630
Noemfoor, 615
Nome, 132-33
Nomura, Kichisaburo, 22
North Africa, 142, 149-50, 153, 282, 316-19. *See also* TORCH.
Northern Combat Area Command, 662
Northern Pacific Area, 96
North Pacific Area, 98, 127-29, 272, 328, 482-87, 552
North Pacific Sub-Area, 98
Norway, 142, 149
Noumea, 266, 558
Nukufetau, 424

Oahu, 476
Objective, long term, 136, 139
OCTAGON, 620, 697, 708
   agreements, 625-44, 677, 701-2
Office of Economic Warfare (OWE), 442
Office of Strategic Services (OSS), 442
Office of War Information (OWI), 442
Oil, 45, 115, 278, 373, 504, 595, 695
Oil fields, Dutch, 463
Oil refineries, 491, 593, 595
Okhotsk, Sea of, 675, 721

Okinawa, 615, 654, 658, 680, 686, 702, 713
Okino Daito, 658
OLYMPIC, 703-7, 709, 711-12
Onslow, Australia, 65, 438
Operations Division (OPD), 158-59, 162, 177, 212, 217, 223, 230-31, 236, 244, 256, 265, 268, 276, 352-53, 426, 478, 510, 544, 592, 617, 631, 649. *See also* War Plans Division, Army
Orange Plans, 3-6, 136, 280, 372, 423
Outer Mongolia, 521, 682
OVERLORD, 431, 448, 541, 629-30
Owen Stanley Mountains, 174-75, 178, 189

P-38s, 184
P-40s, 66, 99, 106, 122, 184, 234
PAC-AID, 601
Pacific Area, 93-95
Pacific Fleet, 15-16, 23, 28, 30-31, 55-59, 82, 88-89, 98, 107-8, 134, 136-37, 139-40, 150, 169, 267, 269-70, 475, 480, 545, 550, 563, 621-23
   commander's staff, 479-82
Pacific Fleet Intelligence, 129
Pacific Military Conference, 312-34, 415
Pacific Mobile Air Force, 147
Pacific Ocean, 88, 93
Pacific Ocean Area, 98-99
Pacific Ocean Areas, 99, 137, 765n59
   air bases in, 431
   communications, security of, 259
   defense of, 116
Pacific Shipping Conference, 562-63
Pacific War Council, 50, 60, 83-84, 93, 95-98, 103, 119, 123, 150, 164, 207, 247, 440
   London, 164
Padjoe oil refineries, 593
Pakkoku, 378, 500
Palau, 430-31, 545-46, 551-52, 555-56, 558-60, 562, 565, 597, 607, 620-21
Palau-Guam line, 557
Palaus, 409, 428, 433, 490-92, 549, 555-56, 558, 560, 563, 615, 621, 653. *See also* Pelews.
Palembang, 82-83, 593
Palmyra Island, 12, 30, 37, 39, 55, 57, 480
Panama Canal, 27, 29, 37
Paoshan, 435, 500
Papua, 189
Paramushiru Island, 133, 274, 430, 482-86, 496, 673
Paratroops, 142, 523
Paris Peace Pact, 5
Park, Air Marshal Sir Keith, 437
Patch, Maj. Gen. Alexander M., 140

Patton, General George, 185
Pearl Harbor, 8, 16, 26, 38, 55
   ship losses, 739n4
Pegu, 235, 239, 640
Peirse, Air Marshal Sir Richard E.C., 51, 61, 218, 347, 357, 393, 591
Peleliu, 607, 620
Pelews, 8, 461, 550, 553. *See also* Palaus.
Penang, 387, 393, 400
Percival, Lt. Gen. A.E., 81
Persia, 442
Persian Gulf, 93, 109, 157, 366
Pescadores, 624
Petroleum products, 452. *See also* Oil.
Petropavlovsk, 132, 274, 484, 671
   naval forces at, 673
   weather station, 721
Philippine Army, 17
Philippine Coastal Frontier, 17
Philippines, 6-8, 10-13, 15-19, 26-27, 31-37, 39-45, 50, 52, 54-55,
      61-62, 65, 86, 90-92, 98-99, 102, 121, 126, 136, 139, 152,
      260, 299, 380, 403, 461, 488, 499-501, 503-6, 522, 542,
      545-53, 558, 560, 567, 603-4, 609, 632, 653, 660, 689-90,
      693, 695-97, 699, 714
   air attacks on, 36, 621
   air support from China, 590
   and ABDA, 36, 61-62
   as long range objective, 136, 139, 151-53, 280, 372, 428, 431,
      488, 553
   British base, 697
   bypassing, 596-97, 606-7, 610-13
   command in, 61-62, 86, 98-99, 689-90
   end of campaign, 695
   evacuation of MacArthur, 91-93
   evacuation of Quezon, 91-92
   in Southwest Pacific Area, 99
   Japanese invasion of, 32, 45
   Orange Plan, 6
   or Formosa, 603-24
   recapture of, 31, 368, 403
   reenforcements to, 16-19, 27, 32-36, 39, 43-44, 54-55, 65, 91,
      736n43
   relief of, 33, 35-36, 62, 742n36
   return to, 653
Phillips, Adm. Tom, 18, 69-70
Photographic reconnaissance, 423, 478, 519
Phuket, 710-11
PIGSTICK, 570-73
Pinlebo, 399
Pipeline, Burma, 397, 456, 498, 513, 575, 577-82, 589
   Assam to Kunming, 4-inch, 468-69

952   INDEX

Pipeline, Burma (Cont'd)
    Calcutta to Assam, 6-inch, 468-69
    Calcutta to Kunming, 452
Plan "Y", 640-41
Plan "Z", 640-41
POL, 581. *See also* Oil, Petroleum
Political control over military strategy, 49, 95
Political issues and considerations, 78, 82, 103, 124, 166-67, 199, 217, 266, 272, 289, 353, 423, 515, 521, 529, 537-38, 612, 647
Political vs. military, 365, 719, 603
Ponape, 373, 417, 428, 430, 478, 490-91, 545
POPPY, 176
Portal, Air Chief Marshal Sir Charles, 47, 281-82, 287, 299, 399, 401, 406, 432, 444, 466-67, 530, 533, 535-36, 642, 679, 716
Port Arthur, 682
Port Darwin, 32-34, 65
Port Dickson, 710-11
Porter, 190
Port Moresby, 66, 127-29, 140, 142, 174-75, 189, 191
Port Swettenham, 710-11
Port Teller, 274
Portuguese participation, 68, 634, 716-17
POST-ELKTON, 351
Postwar planning, 686
Potsdam Declaration, 722-24
Pound, Adm. Sir Dudley, 44, 59, 280, 282, 294, 322, 406
Pownall, Lt. Gen. Sir Henry, 61
PRE-PAC-AID, 601-2
Prince of Wales, 18, 26, 42
Production, 40-41, 155, 158-59, 258
Prome, 202, 338, 396-97
Propaganda, 108
Psychological warfare, 722

QUADRANT agreements, 445, 471, 483, 487, 492, 499, 507, 509, 512-20, 522, 575, 577
Quebec, 457, 620
Queen Elizabeth, 405
Queen Mary, 405
Quezon, Pres. Manuel, 16, 91-93

Rabaul, 65, 128, 144, 146, 148, 168, 175, 197, 266-68, 270, 280, 284-85, 288-90, 299, 300, 304, 306-9, 312-13, 323, 326-29, 350, 370, 374, 422, 425-30, 473, 477, 487-88, 536, 547, 559
    command for, 270-71
    Japanese airfield, 148
    Japanese in, 171, 177, 189

MacArthur's view, 144
neutralization, 370, 427, 429, 477, 490, 543, 567
plans for, 142-43, 146
Rabaul-Kavieng area, 559
Radio silence, 144
Radio stations in Siberia, 721
Railroads
Bangkok-Burma, 541
Burma-China, 231
Dimapur-Ledo, 585
in Assam, 517
in Burma, 355
India, 205, 450
India-Assam, 436
Manchuria, 682-83
Mandalay-Myitkyina, 451
to Bangkok, 540
Trans-Siberian, 670-72, 682
Railway Commission, 517
Rainbow Plans, 8
Rainbow No. 5, 8, 12, 17, 27, 30, 55, 136
Ramgarh, 227, 231, 240
Chinese forces at, 277, 338, 438, 448, 511, 569, 662
training project, 224, 232, 238-39, 382
Ramree Island, 338, 378, 393, 396, 398, 400, 404, 430, 455-58, 464-65, 468, 470, 537, 541, 652
Rangoon, 34, 42, 73-74, 77, 79, 81, 88, 200, 202, 223, 232, 337-38, 340, 370, 376, 384, 394, 396-97, 400, 435, 451, 456, 458, 461, 463-65, 468, 578, 640-42, 666, 710-11. *See also* DRACULA.
airborne attack, 338, 524, 640
air offensive, 239
amphibious operation, 230, 295-96, 354, 640
attack on, 369, 518
British plan for, 234-36
Japanese communications with, 239
loss of, 226
port closing, 204
roads from, 355
US participation, 643
Rangoon River, 396
Rangoon Road, 338
RASHNESS, 712
RAVENOUS, 279-81, 289, 292-94, 298, 350, 356
Reconaissance
B-29s, 601
photographic, 423, 478, 519
Redeployment from Europe, 431, 446, 466-67, 520, 625-26, 642-43, 655, 657, 680, 686, 707-10, 712
Red Sea, 93, 109, 112, 157, 195-96

Reenforcements, 39, 42-44, 50-57, 63, 65, 68, 88-89, 105, 112-13, 181, 189, 193
  aircraft, 115, 149, 176, 180, 269
  for ABDA, 54, 83-86
  for Burma, 74
  for Burma and Malaya, 81
  for South Pacific, 175-77, 180, 184, 189
  for Southwest Pacific Area, 149, 189
  for the Philippines. *See* Philippines, reenforcements.
  for the Solomons, 176-78
  for Timor, 82
  ground, 176-81
  naval, 69-70, 84, 149
Reeves, Rear Adm. John W., 483-84
Rekata Bay, 306-7
RENO, 548, 551-52, 554-55
RENO III, 487-88, 506, 548
RENO V, 608-9, 613
Repair facilities, Soviet, 721
Replacements, 30, 172
Repulse, 18, 26, 42
Riddell-Webster, Gen. Sir Thomas, 451-52
Ritchie, Col. William L. 613
ROADMAKER, 554
Roberts, Col. Frank N., 419, 422, 425, 478, 508, 544, 557-58, 580, 599, 609, 616, 626, 656
ROGER, 711
Rogers, Maj. Elmer J., Jr., 46
Rommel, Gen. Erwin, 141, 150
ROMULUS, 662-63
Roosevelt, Pres. Franklin D., 40, 44, 61, 71, 84, 91-96, 99, 100, 103-4, 111-12, 115, 117, 119-21, 124-26, 138-39, 156, 164-66, 173, 179, 186, 191, 193-96, 201-2, 215-16, 232, 238, 241-42, 244-46, 282, 288, 290, 292, 297-98, 301, 336, 340, 342, 349, 363-64, 376, 379, 382-84, 386-87, 393-96, 399, 400, 433-36, 457-58, 467, 469, 473-74, 497, 511, 514-17, 520-23, 527-28, 531-40, 542, 569-71, 584, 589, 610-11, 631-32, 637, 643-51, 663, 681, 683-84
  and aircraft and troops for Australia, 119-20
  and areas of strategic responsibility, 88-89, 93-94, 103
  and Arnold-Slessor-Towers Agreement, 162
  and BOLERO vs. ANAKIM, 352
  and British participation, 290
  and Chennault, 246, 293, 297, 342, 346-47, 352, 384, 394, 517
  and Chiang Kai-shek, 201, 208, 213, 215-16, 220-23, 238, 248-49, 340, 342, 345, 347, 379-80, 384, 469, 511, 514-15, 523-24, 527-28, 540-41, 569-70, 584, 589, 598, 645-51, 663, 700
  and Churchill, 40-44, 47-49, 52-53, 55, 84, 88-89, 93-94, 111-12, 125, 150, 152, 201, 250, 278, 282, 290, 363-64, 386-87, 393-94, 400, 403-4, 407, 409, 433, 438-46, 457-58, 467,

469, 474, 497, 517, 521, 523, 528, 531, 571, 584, 631, 637, 643-44, 663, 681, 683-84, 700
 and command in China, 438-46
 and command organization, 88-89, 93-96, 266
 and dissolution of ABDA, 86
 and evacuation of MacArthur, 92-93
 and prewar measures, 9, 14-15
 and Russian participation, 131, 133-34, 275-76, 290, 531-34, 683-84
 and SEAC, 438-46
 and Stalin, 275-76
 and Stilwell, 220-22, 379, 384-85, 645-46, 649-51
 cables MacArthur, 126
 considers transfer to the Pacific, 151-52, 173
 views on strategy, 152
 views on the importance of China, 72, 207, 394
Rostov, 113
ROUNDUP, 116, 149-50, 173, 229, 261, 292, 386-88
 vs. ANAKIM, 262-63, 292
Royal Australian Air Force (RAAF), 66, 107, 122, 159, 163
Royal New Zealand Air Force (RNZAF), 163, 567
Rubber, 45
Russell Islands, 306, 310-11, 558
Russia, 37-38, 40-41, 55, 76, 108, 152, 259, 521
 aid to, 112, 131, 275, 349-51
 air bases, 294. *See also* Siberia.
 British views on, 255-56, 287
 cooperation with, 305
 declaration of war, 724
 developing a strategic air force, 681-82
 lend-lease, 55, 211
 participation, 40-41, 130-35, 273-75, 290, 371, 407, 431, 484, 489, 493, 496, 501, 503-5, 521, 531-33, 552, 626-27, 657, 668, 681-85, 720-21
 ports in, 532
 possible collapse of, 152, 229, 254-56, 367
 postwar demands of, 682-83
 route to China, 157
 supplying, 262, 275, 283, 391, 684
 support of, 108, 110, 150-51, 158, 287, 289, 300, 387
Russian Far Eastern Forces 673
Ryukyus, 461, 590, 608, 614, 622-24, 627, 629, 653-54, 656-58, 680, 688, 702, 705
 air bases in, 660
 B-29s in, 660
 command of campaign for, 692-93
 occupation of, 690

Sabang, 662
Sadiya, 202, 204, 212

956   INDEX

St. Lawrence Island, 133
St. Matthias Islands, 428
Saipan, 152, 545-46, 604, 615
   Japanese base on, 129
   strategic bombers in, 503
Sakhalin, 669, 682, 685
Salamaua, 306, 308, 327, 329, 332, 413, 418, 487
   Japanese bases in, 142, 148, 175
   plan to capture, 146, 177
Salamaua peninsula, 284
Salween River, 81, 569, 585, 589-90, 638, 648-49
Samar, 617
Samoa, 8, 12, 30, 32, 37, 39, 56, 57, 96, 98, 137-38, 140, 300, 306, 310
   air bases on, 424
   aircraft for, 128
   amphibious division in, 118
   defenses of, 117
   Marine air units for, 268
Sandoway, 338, 378, 396-98
Santa Cruz Island, 143, 146, 148-49, 190, 331
Santa Isabel Island, 306, 418
Sarangani Bay, 607-8, 617, 629
Sardinia, 242, 262, 279, 375. *See also* Brimstone.
Sarmi, 604
SAUCY, 435
Savo Island, 174, 253
Schouten Islands, 604
Schuirmann, Rear Adm. R.E., 427
Services of Supply, U.S. Army, 177, 213
   India, 212
Sevastopol, 112, 150
SEXTANT decisions, 550, 573, 575, 625, 628, 630, 708
Shanghai, 370, 381, 522, 713
Shangri-la, 127
Shan Kai Kwan, 381
Shemya Island, 274, 328
Shantung, 549, 551, 555
Shantung Peninsula, 658, 690
Sherman, Capt. Forrest P., 315, 550-51, 556-57, 614-15, 617
Shikoku, 690, 723
Shimushu Island, 274
Shingbwiyang, 295
SHINGLE, 571
Shipping, 32, 54-55, 57, 102, 104-5, 110, 112, 138, 158, 173, 176-77, 188-98, 242, 261-62, 268, 278, 287, 316, 323-24, 351-56, 357-58, 364, 381, 388-89, 392, 457, 463, 488, 497-98, 560-62, 660, 695
   allocation of, 112, 158, 359, 404, 456, 460, 698-99
   assault, 357. *See also* Landing craft.

availability of, 104-5, 242, 287, 321, 323-25, 335, 339, 405, 470, 477-78
cargo, 112, 405, 452, 561
for ANAKIM, 292, 339, 348-50, 352, 358, 393-94
for Australia, 124-25
for Burma, 112, 242, 292
for China, 210, 216, 712
for ELKTON, 320-21
for HUSKY, 348-49
for lend-lease, 112, 204-5, 210-12
for redeployment, 708-9
for the Army, 1943, 241
for the Pacific, 153
for the South and Southwest Pacific, 148-49, 194-95, 293
for the Southwest Pacific Area, 110
for TORCH, 192
from Atlantic projects, 105
Japanese, 165, 233, 260, 285, 298, 310, 380-81, 387, 457-58, 465
Japanese, attacks on, 109, 285, 298-99, 336, 486, 601
Japanese, on the Yangtze River, 370
Japanese, Soviet attacks on, 669
Japanese attacks on, 366
Japanese losses of, 165
priorities for, 119, 182-83, 195, 348-50, 562
routing of in Southwest Pacific Area, 102, 124
shortage of, 105, 112, 154, 182, 194, 241, 251, 268, 295-97, 316, 321, 348-50, 354, 391-92, 400, 414
to India, 228, 293, 494
transport, 148
troops, 54-55, 93, 112, 119, 166, 177, 228, 236, 268, 405, 452, 474, 478, 491, 561, 709-10
use of, 324-26
Shortland Islands, 191, 306
Shwebo, 574, 576, 578, 641, 662
Siam, 392, 715, 717. See also Thailand.
Siberia, 42, 493
air and sea routes to, 672-73, 675
air bases, 274-75, 627
air forces in, 39
air operations from, 628
air route from Alaska, 134-35, 275
assistance to, 279
bases in, 131, 272-76
basing of US air units, 505, 669, 675, 685
bomber bases, 496
heavy bombers in, 670
Japanese attack on, 160, 272-76, 366
Japanese invasion of, 305, 367
Japanese threat to, 157, 160, 178
Soviet forces in, 668, 671

Siberia (Cont'd)
  stockpiles, 685
  supply route to, 275, 674-75, 684
  survey of, 274
  threat to, 134
  visit to, 132
  weather stations, 675-76
Siberian Air Ferry Service, 274-75
Sicily, 289, 291, 301, 363, 375, 387, 409, 413
SICKLE, 335, 348-51, 355, 359, 366, 374
Singapore, 10, 12-13, 15, 18, 28, 31, 34-36, 39-40, 42-46, 54,
    62-64, 66, 69, 70, 73, 82, 88-90, 93, 370, 438, 446,
    455-56, 462-64, 499, 503, 518, 578, 631, 662, 698-99,
    710, 715
Singapore Conference, 44-46
Singapore-Hong Kong, 462-64
Sino-American Cooperative Organization (SACO), 203-4
Sittang River, 81, 235, 239, 572
SLEDGEHAMMER, 116, 141-42, 149, 152, 173, 214, 386-87
Slessor, Air Vice Marshal, 156
Slim, Lt. Gen. William J., 527, 645
Slocum, Capt. H.B., 462
Smith, Rear Adm. W.W., 356
Society Islands, 57
Soembawa, 82
Soerabaya, 18, 33-34, 42, 65, 69, 82-83
Solomon Islands, 24, 98, 102, 107, 116, 137, 171, 188-91, 250,
    260-61, 284-85, 305-12, 328-31, 333, 403, 409, 414, 418,
    424, 426, 461, 463, 474, 487-88, 543, 564
  British naval support for, 475
  campaign for, 164, 168-72, 300, 371
  command of, 143-45, 264
  crisis, 188
  Japanese attacks on, 366
  Japanese in, 127, 139-40, 149
  landings in, 174
  naval support for, 424
  operations, 140-49, 154, 165, 230, 268, 305, 327, 329, 372
  plans, 139, 141-44, 147
  U.S. air attacks, 142
Solomons-New Britain-New Guinea region, 102, 168, 189, 261, 309
  campaign, command of, 143-47, 264-72, 308-9, 311-12
  project, 285, 475
Solomons-New Guinea campaign, 164
Solomons Sea, 267
Somervell, Lt. Gen. Brehon, 242, 278, 336-37, 339, 351-53, 356-57,
    482, 489, 511-12, 517-18, 521, 525, 527, 538-39, 580-81, 643
Somerville, Vice Adm. Sir J.F., 247, 338, 347, 357, 393, 437
Soong, T.V., 19, 20, 77, 79-80, 200, 202, 204, 208, 211, 214, 220,
    222, 238, 341, 379, 384-85, 398, 434-35, 469, 511, 648

South America, 106, 110
South China Sea, 299, 368, 428, 430, 456, 460, 463, 499, 522, 628, 697, 699
Southeast Asia Command (SEAC), 437-46, 506, 508-12, 518, 523-24, 538, 634-35, 639-40, 661-66, 678-80, 699-700, 710-11, 717-18
Southeast Pacific Area, 765n59
Southeast Pacific Sub-Area, 98
Southern Shan States, 202
South Japan Sea, 460
South Manchurian Railroad, 682
South Pacific Sub-Area, 98
Southwestern Pacific Council, 49
Soviet. *See* Russia.
Spaatz, Gen. Carl, 185, 694
Spain, 185
Spruance, Rear Adm. Raymond A., 315, 326-27, 610
Stalin, Premier Joseph, 133-34, 275-76, 520-21, 533, 539-40, 644, 668-69, 675, 682-84, 721
Standley, Amb. William H., 132, 134
Stark, Adm. Harold R., 8, 9, 16, 18, 28-29, 36, 50, 54, 71, 92, 131, 136, 138
State-War-Navy Coordinating Committee (SWNCC), 722
Stettinius, SecState Edward R., 683
Stilwell, Lt. Gen. Joseph W., 198-208, 210-32, 234, 248, 292, 337, 340, 342, 345-47, 382-84, 387, 393-97, 399, 435, 437-39, 448, 494-95, 509-12, 514-17, 521-25, 527, 543, 569, 573-76, 580-82, 588-93, 592-94, 596, 598, 600, 602
  and Chiang Kai-shek, 215-17, 219-21, 245-46, 511-12
  and command of B-29s, 593, 596
  and command of Tenth Air Force, 237
  and deployment of Tenth Air Force, 206
  command status, 200-201, 220-22, 444-45, 511-12, 645-51
  directives to, 592-94, 596
  in SEAC, 441-45, 512
  mission of, 72, 79
  recall of, 645-52
  training project, 226-27, 231, 238, 382, 448
  vs. Chennault, 234, 243, 245-46, 342, 346-48, 379-85, 395
Stimson, SecWar Henry L., 76, 79, 92, 200, 222, 648, 650, 707, 722
Stopford, Lt. Gen. J., 540
Strafford, Air Commodore S.C., 252
Strategic bombing, 257, 593, 659-60, 693, 714. *See also* air offensive; B-29s; VLR bombers, Twentieth Air Force; Japan, air offensive against.
Strategic commitments, 351, 359
Strategic concept, 108-110, 116, 136, 139, 151-53, 157, 186, 250-52, 254, 258-59, 261, 280, 299-301, 304-5, 322, 366-68, 371-72, 390-91, 401, 407, 428, 459-63, 492, 529, 627-30, 718
Strategic defensive, 108, 154, 157-58, 186, 251, 254, 259, 261

Strategic defensive (Cont'd)
    in Burma, 229-30
    in Europe, 180
Strategic deployment of forces, 108, 164, 594
Strategic hypothesis, 251-53
Strategic policy, 157-59, 305
Strategic reserve, 188, 257
Strategic responsibility, 88-90, 100, 156, 161, 199, 218, 234, 276
Strategic undertakings, 351, 359, 380-81
Stratemeyer, Maj. Gen. George E., 259, 323-25, 495, 521, 524, 527, 591, 597
Streett, Brig. Gen. St. Clair, 265
Submarines, British, 90, 475
Submarine operations, 36, 500
Submarines, Soviet, 669
Submarines, U.S., 63-64, 84, 294, 298, 501
Subversive activities, Japan, 14
Suichwan, 381
Suifu, 202
Sultan, Maj. Gen. Daniel I., 597, 600, 639, 645, 651-52, 663-64, 666
Sulu Sea, 368, 460, 500
Sumatra, 43, 62, 69, 82, 83, 86, 89, 192, 240, 370, 378, 387, 393-94, 400, 438, 442, 449, 455-57, 461, 463-64, 468, 493, 499, 500, 518-19, 573-76, 578-79, 631-32, 634, 662, 680, 717
Sunda Strait, 438, 627
SUPER-GYMNAST, 53-54
Supreme Commander, SWPA, 100-103, 145-46
Supreme War Council, 40, 73, 207, 209
Surigao, 616, 620, 629
Surprise, 523
Sutherland, Maj. Gen. R.K., 315-16, 326-28, 491, 505-6, 546, 550-51, 553-54, 557-58
Suva, 558
Swatow, 656
Switch to Pacific, 150-52, 254, 256

Tactical air force, British, 715-16
Tai Shan, 658
Takoradi, 205
Talasea, 308
Talaud, 617, 621, 629
TALON, 662
Tamu, 204, 232, 338, 572
Tanaga Island, 273
Tanambogo, 174
Tanimbars, 546
Taongi, 417
Tarakan, 62, 696
Tarawa, 310, 421, 423-25, 428, 478, 520

TARZAN, 523, 526, 528, 536-42, 570
Task Force 5, 33
Task Force 8, 129
Taungup, 337-38, 396-98
Tedder, Air Marshal Sir Arthur, 440
Teheran, 472
Teheran agreements, 533
Tengchung, 585
Ter Poorten, Lt. Gen. H., 51, 61, 83
Thailand, 13, 26, 42, 50, 75, 228, 232-33, 239, 295, 298, 380, 438, 442, 445, 699
   Japanese control of, 225
   Japanese line of communications to, 463
Theobald, Rear Adm. Robert A., 129
Thirty-division plan for China, 202, 204, 223-24, 226, 232, 238, 342, 382
Three Demands, 214-17, 221-24, 228-29, 238
Tibet, 157
Tiddim, 338, 572
Timberman, Col. Thomas S., 240, 245-46
Timor, Dutch, 67, 69
Timor, Portuguese, 13, 62, 67-68, 82, 90, 97, 232, 306, 373, 717
Timor Sea, 65
Tinian, 503, 545-46, 615
Tobruk, 141, 214
Tokyo, 305, 609, 627, 629-30, 643
   Doolittle raid, 127, 133, 170
Tokyo Plain, 707
Tonga Islands, 138
Tongatabu, 119, 139
   aircraft allocations, 111
   antiaircraft regiments at, 172
   defenses, 117
   garrison, 138
Tonkin, Gulf of, 438
Tonolei, 308
TORCH, 153-54, 163, 165, 170, 181-82, 184-86, 192-93, 252, 254-56, 352, 457
   follow-up, 261
   shipping, 349, 359
Torres Strait, 66, 87
Toungoo, 202
Towers, Rear Adm. J.H., 122, 129, 155, 162, 547
Townsville, 66
Transport aircraft, 236
   diversion from the Hump, 598
   from China, 202-7, 297, 542, 597-98
   for SEAC, 642, 664, 666
Transportation
   India, 206-7, 449

Transportation (Cont'd)
   India to Assam, 451-53
Trans-Siberian Railroad, 670-71, 682
   Japanese attack, 672
Treasury Islands, 487
TRIDENT agreements, 403-9, 413-15, 418, 429-30, 432, 434, 436, 446-49, 454, 513
Trincomalee, 115, 205
Trobriand Islands 309
Troop lift, 463
Troubridge, Rear Adm. T., 540
Truk, 31, 136, 141-42, 152, 280, 285-86, 288-89, 300-301, 373, 403, 417, 428, 430-31, 458, 490-91, 501, 542, 546, 553-55
   attack on, 547, 557
   bombing, 558
   bypassing, 546, 553-54, 556-58, 560
   carrier attack on, 545
   neutralization of, 560
Truk-Guam-Saipan, 152
Truman, President Harry S., 700, 706-7, 720-24
Tsushima Straits, 713
Tulagi, 128, 141, 143, 168, 267, 310-11
   air attack on, 128
   critical situation in, 183
   Japanese in, 140
   Japanese naval base, 137
   occupation of, 145-46, 174
   plans for, 143-45, 147, 149
Tulsa, 74
Turkey, 115, 259, 261, 357, 409
Turner, Rear Adm. Richmond Kelly, 16, 29, 32, 58, 98-99, 109, 112, 116-17, 122, 132, 610, 771n24
Tushan, 580
Tutuila, Samoa, 141, 480
TWILIGHT, 495-96
Tydings-McDuffie Act, 16

U-boats, 158
Ukhrul, 232
Ulithi, 555, 558, 607, 621
Unalaska, 485
Unconditional surrender, 358, 371, 388, 390, 407, 413, 460, 488-89, 498, 627-28, 681, 702-3, 718, 722-23
Unified command, 29, 43-44, 46, 48, 61-71, 89, 96, 164, 194, 265-66, 270-72, 311, 331-34, 439, 686-89, 728
   in ABDA, 43-44, 46, 48, 52-53
   in CBI, 201
   in China, 75
   in the South and Southwest Pacific, 265-72
   in the Southwest Pacific area, 164

King's views on, 270
Marshall's views on, 194, 268, 271
Navy view of, 269-70
United Kingdom, 100
air offensive from, 324-25, 391, 431
allocations to, 123, 316-20, 323
U.S. Army Strategic Air Force (USASTAF), 693-95
U.S. Planning Team, 402
Unity of command, 144
in Southeast Asia, 437-38
in the South and Southwest Pacific, 144, 329-30
Unlimited emergency, state of, 15
Upolu, 480
Upper Sittang Valley, 202
USSR, 72. *See also* Russia.
aircraft for, 106
collaboration, 131-32, 669
participation, 672

Vandegrift, Maj. Gen. A.A., 196, 617
Van Mook, Gov. Gen., 85-86
Vella Lavella, 413, 487
Victory Program, 40
Vitiaz Strait, 313, 488
Vittrup, Lt. Col. R.L., 179
Vladivostok, 132, 669, 673-74
Vladivostok Peninsula, 670
VLR bombers, 470, 491, 522, 590-91. *See also* B-29s.
command of, 593-94
from Marianas, 492
Vogelkop, 373, 428-29, 433, 487-88, 492, 542, 548, 554-55, 605, 608,
Voroshilov, Marshal, 533

Wakde, 31, 37, 39, 42, 55, 300, 373, 416-17, 421, 424, 428, 430,
476-77, 545, 604-5
Wallace, Vice Pres. Henry A., 647
Wallis Island, 480
War Cabinet, British, 150
War criminals, 723
War Plans Division, Army, 27, 35, 46, 48, 68, 75-78, 98, 112, 114,
138, 141-42. *See also* Operations Division.
War Plans Division, Navy, 30, 58, 68, 90, 99, 133, 137, 139, 141-43,
269, 309-10, 415-16, 608, 689
War Production Board (WPB), 648
War Shipping Administration (WSA), 194-96, 241
Washington Naval Conference, 1922, 5
Wau, 175
Wavell, Gen. Sir Archibald, 47, 50-51, 53, 61-71, 79, 81-84, 86-87,
90, 110, 131, 200, 205-6, 218, 226-27, 237-38, 240, 243-44,
247, 292, 295, 336-37, 341, 347, 355, 357, 383, 393-94,
398, 437

Weather information network, 203
Weather stations, 685, 721
    Mongolian Plateau, 675-76
    Siberia, 675-76
Wedemeyer, Gen. Albert C., 173, 179, 180, 254, 258, 265, 278, 294, 315, 318-23, 326, 329, 337, 444, 464, 521, 540, 575-76, 578, 641, 660-61, 663-66, 677-78, 711-12
    named Commander, US Forces, China Theater, 651-52
Welles, Sumner, 92
West coast, US, 12, 27, 38, 56
Western Defense Command, 172
Wewak, 426, 428, 430, 479
Wheeler, Lt. Gen. Raymond A., 578
Wheeler, Maj. Gen. R.A., 212-13, 233, 355, 514, 521, 527
Williamson, Col. Adrian, 419, 495
Willkie, Wendell, 243
Willson, Vice Adm. Russell, 172, 184-85, 242, 263, 503, 557
    views on invasion of Japan, 503
Wingate, Brig. Orde C., 451, 455, 475
Woleai, 428, 555-57
Woodlark Island, 309, 326, 329, 332, 373, 413, 418
Wotje, 416, 421, 423-24, 476
Wrangel Island, 131
Wuchang, 599
Wyman, Col. W.G., 75

Yalta Conference, 682-86
Yap, 8, 428, 555, 558, 607
    bypassing, 621-22
Yangtze, River, 233, 242, 246, 370, 387, 713
    Japanese shipping, 381
Yellow Sea, 500, 703
Yeu, 641
Y-Force, 238, 584-85
Yorktown, 128, 140
Yunnan, 20, 172, 224, 240, 382, 284-85, 398, 400, 449, 469, 584
    advance from, 234, 239, 337-38, 378, 451, 518
    airfields in, 353
    Chinese attack from, 246-47, 337-38, 454, 523, 569
    Chinese Expeditionary Troops, 511
    Chinese forces in, 277, 295, 297, 342, 355, 438-39, 448, 451, 515-17, 524, 539, 569, 573, 589-90
    Japanese threat to, 232
Yunnan forces, 575, 579, 584-85, 638, 640, 648, 650
    command of, 247
    withdrawal of, 649
Yunnan Province, 232
Yushan, 381